# The New Testament and Wycliffe Bible Commentary

# The New Testament and Wycliffe Bible Commentary

Moody Press

Chicago

First Edition     1971
Second Edition    1972
Third Edition     1972
Fourth Edition    1973

THE IVERSEN-NORMAN ASSOCIATES
NEW YORK

Library of Congress Catalog Card Number: 72–183345

Printed in the United States of America

ISBN: 0-8024-5920-X

# The New Testament

## CONTENTS

# Foreword

Myriads of commentaries on the Word, along with scores of Bible dictionaries, encyclopedias, concordances and other study helps line the library shelves. Contemporary versions and revisions of earlier translations of the Bible are rapidly multiplying. The result is a kaleidoscope of choices when one desires a resource book to help ascertain the meaning of difficult or obscure Bible passages.

The basic aim of "The New Testament and Wycliffe Bible Commentary" is to provide, in a single volume, God's Word and helpful commentary on its meaning. To do this, verses of Scripture along with explanatory comments on these verses, have been arranged in parallel columns on the same page. Pastors, Sunday School teachers, and every student of Scripture will find this unique volume ideal for private study, family devotions, or for use in the classroom and pew.

The King James Version of the New Testament was selected because of its unexcelled literary beauty. Although one of the oldest, it remains the basic English translation. The Wycliffe Bible Commentary was selected because it presents the best insights of contemporary scholarship.

THE IVERSEN ASSOCIATES

# THE
# NEW TESTAMENT

## OF OUR LORD AND SAVIOUR
## JESUS CHRIST

Translated out of the original Greek and with the former
translations diligently compared and revised

Set forth in 1611
And commonly known as the

## KING JAMES VERSION

# THE EPISTLE DEDICATORY

Great and manifold were the blessings, most dread Sovereign, which
Almighty God, the Father of all mercies, bestowed upon us the people
of England, when first he sent Your Majesty's Royal Person to rule and
reign over us. For whereas it was the expectation of many, who
wished not well unto our Sion, that upon the setting of that bright
Occidental Star, Queen Elizabeth of most happy memory, some thick
and palpable clouds of darkness would so have overshadowed this
Land, that men should have been in doubt which way they were to
walk; and that it should hardly be known, who was to direct the unsettled State; the appearance of Your Majesty, as of the Sun in his
strength, instantly dispelled those supposed and surmised mists, and
gave unto all that were well affected exceeding cause of comfort; especially when we beheld the Government established in Your Highness,
and Your hopeful Seed, by an undoubted Title, and this also accompanied with peace and tranquillity at home and abroad.

But among all our joys, there was no one that more filled our
hearts, than the blessed continuance of the preaching of God's sacred
Word among us; which is that inestimable treasure, which excelleth
all the riches of the earth; because the fruit thereof extendeth itself,
not only to the time spent in this transitory world, but directeth and
disposeth men unto that eternal happiness which is above in heaven.

Then not to suffer this to fall to the ground, but rather to take it up,
and to continue it in that state, wherein the famous Predecessor of
Your Highness did leave it: nay, to go forward with the confidence and
resolution of a Man in maintaining the truth of Christ, and propagating
it far and near, is that which hath so bound and firmly knit the hearts
of all Your Majesty's loyal and religious people unto You, that Your
very name is precious among them: their eye doth behold You with
comfort, and they bless You in their hearts, as that sanctified Person,
who, under God, is the immediate Author of their true happiness.
And this their contentment doth not diminish or decay, but every day
increaseth and taketh strength, when they observe, that the zeal of
Your Majesty toward the house of God doth not slack or go backward, but is more and more kindled, manifesting itself abroad in the

farthest parts of Christendom, by writing in defence of the Truth, (which hath given such a blow unto that man of sin, as will not be healed,) and every day at home, by religious and learned discourse, by frequenting the house of God, by hearing the Word preached, by cherishing the Teachers thereof, by caring for the Church, as a most tender and loving nursing Father.

There are infinite arguments of this right Christian and religious affection in Your Majesty; but none is more forcible to declare it to others than the vehement and perpetuated desire of accomplishing and publishing of this work, which now with all humility we present unto Your Majesty. For when Your Highness had once out of deep judgment apprehended how convenient it was, that out of the Original Sacred Tongues, together with comparing of the labours, both in our own, and other foreign Languages, of many worthy men who went before us, there should be one more exact Translation of the Holy Scriptures into the English Tongue; Your Majesty did never desist to urge and to excite those to whom it was commended, that the work might be hastened, and that the business might be expedited in so decent a manner, as a matter of such importance might justly require.

And now at last, by the mercy of God, and the continuance of our labours, it being brought unto such a conclusion, as that we have great hopes that the Church of England shall reap good fruit thereby; we hold it our duty to offer it to Your Majesty, not only as to our King and Sovereign, but as to the principal Mover and Author of the work: humbly craving of Your most Sacred Majesty, that since things of this quality have ever been subject to the censures of illmeaning and discontented persons, it may receive approbation and patronage from so learned and judicious a Prince as Your Highness is, whose allowance and acceptance of our labours shall more honour and encourage us, than all the calumniations and hard interpretations of other men shall dismay us. So that if, on the one side, we shall be traduced by Popish Persons at home or abroad, who therefore will malign us, because we are poor instruments to make God's holy Truth to be yet more and more known unto the people, whom they desire still to keep in ignorance and darkness; or if, on the other side, we shall be maligned by selfconceited Brethren, who run their own ways, and give liking unto nothing, but what is framed by themselves, and hammered on their anvil; we may rest secure, supported within by the truth and innocency of a good conscience, having walked the ways of simplicity and integrity, as before the Lord; and sustained without by the powerful protection of Your Majesty's grace and favour, which will ever give countenance to honest and Christian endeavours against bitter censures and uncharitable imputations.

The Lord of heaven and earth bless Your Majesty with many and happy days, that, as his heavenly hand hath enriched Your Highness with many singular and extraordinary graces, so You may be the wonder of the world in this latter age for happiness and true felicity, to the honour of that great GOD, and the good of his Church, through Jesus Christ our Lord and only Saviour.

# THE
# WYCLIFFE
# BIBLE
# COMMENTARY

Edited by

CHARLES F. PFEIFFER
OLD TESTAMENT

EVERETT F. HARRISON
NEW TESTAMENT

MOODY PRESS . CHICAGO

# The Wycliffe Bible Commentary

# PUBLISHER'S PREFACE

### (HOW TO USE THIS BOOK)

#### The Approach

THE *Wycliffe Bible Commentary* is an entirely new commentary on the whole Bible written and edited by a number of scholars representing a wide cross section of American Protestant Christianity. Within the limits of its more than a million and one-quarter words, it attempts to treat the entire text of the Old and New Testaments on a phrase by phrase basis. In addition, summaries of the major sections of each Biblical book generally appear in the text in connection with the main headings in the outline. Thus, the reader is permitted an overview and a detailed discussion of a passage of Scripture at the same time.

In the commentaries on the various books the writers present the results of their own careful, personal Bible study. But also they have preserved some of the best work of the older commentators and have utilized the insights of contemporary scholarship. While they infuse the whole with a fresh spirit, at the same time they manifest their unflinching belief in the divine inspiration of Holy Scripture.

Although the Biblical text used in the preparation of this commentary is that of the King James Version, several of the writers made their own translations of the books on which they worked. Occasionally they use phrases from their own translations in the text of the commentaries. For the convenience of the reader, all Biblical phraseology appears in bold face type, as do all the Biblical verse numbers. In this way numbers of verses are clearly distinguished from points in the outline. In cases in which the writer prefers to employ a reading from some version other than the King James, the source of such phraseology is identified. While the commentaries on the various books emphasize the interpretation of the actual words of Scripture, each is accompanied by a brief introductory discussion of authorship, date of composition, historical background, and the like. To provide the reader with further background information, a brief review of the inter-testamental period has been included.

To improve appearance of the printed page, pronouns referring to deity (which appear in large numbers) are not capitalized, except when capitalization is necessary for clarity of meaning. Also in the interest of typographical appearance, *Lord* and *God*, when they are translations of the Hebrew *YHWH*, are not printed in capitals as in the King James Version. Often the Hebrew *YHWH* is represented by the English *Jehovah*. But in some instances the contributors preferred the spelling of *Yahweh*, which is gaining favor among Biblical scholars.

The basic aim of this volume is to determine the meaning of the text of Scripture. It is therefore, strictly speaking, neither a devotional nor a technical exegetical treatment. It seeks to present the Biblical message in such a way that the serious Bible student will find extensive help within its pages.

The contributors to this commentary represent a total of more than fifteen denominational backgrounds. Among the forty-eight writers are professors in twenty-five schools of Christian higher education. With such a variety of backgrounds, it is to be expected that contributors will differ among themselves in some matters of interpretation. No editorial effort has been made to bring these differences into absolute conformity; writers have been given freedom of expression in such cases. The reader will discover, therefore, some differences in outlook in such instances as parallel passages in the Gospels and in the books of Kings and Chronicles.

## Bibliography

Each of the books in this commentary is accompanied by a bibliography. Occasionally, when an author has treated related books (e.g., I, II Peter; I, II Thessalonians; Ezra, Nehemiah, Esther), he has chosen to place all of his bibliographies in one list. In such cases, the reader is directed to the full bibliographical listing.

The fact that a writer has included a given title does not mean that he recommends it as thoroughly conservative or thoroughly ac-curate. Writers have listed both works which they have referred to and those which will be of use to the reader. In the interests of standard-ization and economy of space, all annotations which might have classified books according to theological position and usefulness have been omitted.

Because many readers will be interested in knowing about conservative commentaries on the whole Bible or large sections of it, a few of the larger works are listed here. Old favorites are John Peter Lange's *Commentary on the Holy Scriptures* (24 vols.); C. J. Ellicott's *Commentary on the Whole Bible* (8 or 4 vols.); Matthew Henry's *Commentary on the Whole Bible* (6 vols. or 1 vol. abridgement); Jamieson, Fausset, and Brown's *A Commentary Critical, Experimental, and Practical on the Old and New Testaments* (6 vols. or 1 vol. abridgement); Matthew Henry, Thomas Scott, and others, *A Devotional Commentary on the Entire Bible;* and Alexander Maclaren's *Expositions of Holy Scripture* (25 vols.). A newer one-volume commentary that has enjoyed wide usefulness is *The New Bible Commentary,* edited by F. Davidson, A. M. Stibbs, and E. F. Kevan. While no attempt is made here to mention works on individual books of either Testament, it would be too bad to ignore C. H. Spurgeon's great classic on the Psalms, *The Treasury of David* (6 vols.).

More specialized commentaries on one or the other of the Testaments — commentaries which are not too heavily loaded with Hebrew and Greek for the serious student of the English Bible to find them of some use — include the following: C. F. Keil and F. Delitzsch, *Biblical Commentary on the Old Testament* (25 vols.); Marvin H. Vincent, *Word Studies in the New Testament* (4 vols.); A. T. Robertson, *Word Pictures in the New Testament* (6 vols.); and Henry Alford, *The Greek Testament* (4 vols.) or the one-volume *New Testament for English Readers.*

The student who is interested in questions of Biblical introduction, such as authorship, date, occasion for writing, and the like, will find the following four books helpful: Merrill F. Unger's *Introductory Guide to the Old Testament;* Henry C. Thiessen's *New Testament Introduction;* and D. Edmond Hiebert's *Introduction to the Pauline Epistles* and *Introduction to the Non-Pauline Epistles.* An especially useful conservative Bible atlas is *Baker's Bible Atlas,* prepared by Charles F. Pfeiffer; *Unger's Bible Dictionary* and the *New Bible Dictionary* provide information on special problems related to interpretation of Scripture.

## Contributors

Genesis: Kyle M. Yates, Sr., Th.D., Ph.D., Professor of Old Testament, Baylor University, Waco, Tex.

Exodus: Philip C. Johnson, Th.D., Professor of Bible, Gordon College, Beverly Farms, Mass.

Leviticus: Robert O. Coleman, Th.D., Assistant Professor of Biblical Introduction, Southwestern Baptist Theological Seminary, Fort Worth, Tex.

Numbers: Elmer Smick, S.T.M., Ph.D., Professor of Ancient Languages, Covenant College and Theological Seminary, St. Louis, Mo.

Deuteronomy: Meredith G. Kline, Th.M., Ph.D., Associate Professor of Old Testament, Westminster Theological Seminary, Philadelphia, Pa.

Joshua: John Rea, A.M., Th.D., Professor of Old Testament, Moody Bible Institute, Chicago, Ill.

Judges: Charles F. Pfeiffer, Th.M., Ph.D., Professor of Old Testament, Gordon Divinity School, Beverly Farms, Mass.

Ruth: Charles F. Pfeiffer (see under Judges).

I and II Samuel: Fred E. Young, B.D., Ph.D., Professor of Old Testament, Central Baptist Theological Seminary, Kansas City, Kan.

I Kings: John T. Gates, S.T.D., Professor of Bible and Philosophy, St. Paul Bible College, St. Paul, Minn.

II Kings: Harold Stigers, Ph.D., Instructor in Ancient Languages, Covenant College and Theological Seminary, St. Louis, Mo.

I and II Chronicles: J. Barton Payne, A.M., Th.D., Associate Professor of Old Testament, Wheaton College Graduate School, Wheaton, Ill.

Ezra, Nehemiah, and Esther: John C. Whitcomb, Jr., Th.D., Professor of Old Testament and Director of Post-Graduate Studies, Grace Theological Seminary, Winona Lake, Ind.

Job: Meredith G. Kline (see under Deuteronomy).

Psalms: Kyle M. Yates, Jr., Th.D., Associate Professor of Old Testament and Biblical Archaeology, Golden Gate Baptist Theological Seminary, Mill Valley, Calif.

Proverbs: R. Laird Harris, Th.M., Ph.D., Professor of Old Testament, Covenant College and Theological Seminary, St. Louis, Mo.

Ecclesiastes: Robert Laurin, Th.M., Ph.D., Professor of Old Testament and Hebrew, California Baptist Theological Seminary, Covina, Calif.

Song of Solomon: Sierd Woudstra, Th.D. candidate, pastor, Calvin Christian Reformed Church, Ottawa, Ont., Canada.

Isaiah: Gleason L. Archer, Jr., B.D., Ph.D., Professor of Biblical Languages, Fuller Theological Seminary, Pasadena, Calif.

Jeremiah: John F. Graybill, B.D., Ph.D., Director, Department of Bible and Theology, Barrington College, Barrington, R. I.

Lamentations: Ross Price, M.Th., D.D., Professor of Theology, Pasadena College, Pasadena, Calif.

Ezekiel: Anton T. Pearson, Th.D., Professor of Old Testament Language and Literature, Bethel College and Seminary, St. Paul, Minn.

Daniel: Robert D. Culver, Th.D., Professor of Bible, Northwestern College, Minneapolis, Minn.

Hosea: Charles F. Pfeiffer (see under Judges).

Joel: Derward Deere, Th.D., Professor of Old Testament Interpretation, Golden Gate Baptist Theological Seminary, Mill Valley, Calif.

Amos: Arnold C. Schultz, M.A., Th.D., Professor of Old Testament and Archaeology, Northern Baptist Theological Seminary, Chicago, Ill.

Obadiah and Jonah: G. Herbert Livingston, B.D., Ph.D., Professor of Old Testament, Asbury Theological Seminary, Wilmore, Ky.

Micah: E. Leslie Carlson, A.M., Th.D., Professor of Biblical Introduction and Semitic Languages, Southwestern Baptist Theological Seminary, Fort Worth, Tex.

Nahum: Charles L. Feinberg, Th.D., Ph.D., Dean and Professor of Semitics and Old Testament, Talbot Theological Seminary, La Mirada, Calif.

Habakkuk: David W. Kerr, Th.D., Dean and Professor of Old Testament Interpretation, Gordon Divinity School, Beverly Farms, Mass.

Zephaniah: H. A. Hanke, Th.D., Professor of Bible, Asbury College, Wilmore, Ky.

Haggai: Charles L. Feinberg (see under Nahum).

Zechariah: Charles L. Feinberg (see under Nahum).

Malachi: Burton L. Goddard, Th.D., Director of Library and Professor of Biblical Languages and Exegesis, Gordon Divinity School, Beverly Farms, Mass.

From Malachi to Matthew: Charles F. Pfeiffer (see under Judges).

Matthew: Homer A. Kent, Jr., Th.D., Professor of New Testament and Greek, Grace Theological Seminary, Winona Lake, Ind.

Mark: Donald W. Burdick, Th.D., Professor of New Testament, Conservative Baptist Theological Seminary, Denver, Colo.

Luke: Merrill C. Tenney, Ph.D., Dean of the Graduate School, Wheaton College, Wheaton, Ill.

John: Everett F. Harrison, Th.D., Ph.D., Professor of New Testament, Fuller Theological Seminary, Pasadena, Calif.

Acts: George E. Ladd, B.D., Ph.D., Professor of Biblical Theology, Fuller Theological Seminary, Pasadena, Calif.

Romans: A. Berkeley Mickelsen, B.D., Ph.D., Professor of Bible and Theology, Graduate School, Wheaton College, Wheaton, Ill.

I Corinthians: S. Lewis Johnson, Jr., Th.D., Professor of New Testament Literature and Exegesis, Dallas Theological Seminary, Dallas, Tex.

II Corinthians: Wick Broomall, Th.M., Pastor, Westminster Presbyterian Church, Augusta, Georgia.

Galatians: Everett F. Harrison (see under John).

Ephesians: Alfred Martin, Th.D., Dean of Faculty, Professor of Old Testament Synthesis, Moody Bible Institute, Chicago, Ill.

Philippians: Robert H. Mounce, Th.M., Ph.D., Associate Professor of Biblical Literature and Greek, Bethel College and Seminary, St. Paul, Minn.

Colossians: E. Earle Ellis, B.D., Ph.D., lecturer and writer on the New Testament, currently engaged in research and writing in Germany.

I and II Thessalonians: David A. Hubbard, Th.M., Ph.D., Chairman of the Division of Biblical Studies and Philosophy, Westmont College, Santa Barbara, Calif.

I and II Timothy, Titus: Wilbur B. Wallis, S.T.M., Ph.D., Professor of New Testament Language and Literature, Covenant College and Theological Seminary.

Philemon: E. Earle Ellis (see under Colossians).

Hebrews: Robert W. Ross, Ph.D. candidate, Acting Head, Department of History, Northwestern College, Minneapolis, Minn.

James: Walter W. Wessel, Ph.D., Associate Professor of Biblical Literature, Bethel College and Theological Seminary, St. Paul, Minn.

I and II Peter: Stephen W. Paine, Ph.D., President and Professor of Greek, Houghton College, Houghton, N. Y.

I, II, III John: Charles C. Ryrie, Th.D., Ph.D., Chairman of the Department of Systematic Theology, Dean of the Graduate School, Dallas Theological Seminary, Dallas, Tex.

Jude: David H. Wallace, Th.M., Ph.D., Professor of Biblical Theology, California Baptist Theological Seminary, Covina, Calif.

Revelation: Wilbur M. Smith, D.D., Professor of English Bible, Fuller Theological Seminary, Pasadena, Calif.

## Abbreviations

a. Books of the Bible.

1. OT Gen Ex Lev Num Deut Josh Jud Ruth I Sam II Sam I Kgs II Kgs I Chr II Chr Ezr Neh Est Job Ps Prov Eccl Song Isa Jer Lam Ezk Dan Hos Joel Amos Ob Jon Mic Nah Hab Zeph Hag Zech Mal

2. NT Mt Mk Lk Jn Acts Rom I Cor II Cor Gal Eph Phil Col I Thess II Thess I Tim II Tim Tit Phm Heb Jas I Pet II Pet I Jn II Jn III Jn Jude Rev

b. Apocrypha.

I Esd (I Esdras); II Esd (II Esdras); Tob (Tobit); Wisd Wisdom of Solomon); Sir (The Wisdom of Jesus the son of Sirach, or Ecclesiasticus); Bel (Bel and the Dragon); I Macc (I Maccabees); II Macc (II Maccabees)

c. Periodicals, reference works, dictionaries, and versions.

| | |
|---|---|
| A-S | Abbott-Smith, *Manual Greek Lexicon of the NT* |
| Alf | Alford's *Greek Testament* |
| ANET | *Ancient Near Eastern Texts,* ed. by Pritchard |
| Arndt | Arndt-Gingrich, *Greek-English Lexicon* |
| ASV | American Standard Version |
| AV | Authorized Version |
| BA | *Biblical Archaeologist* |
| BASOR | *Bulletin,* American Schools of Oriental Research |
| BDB | Brown, Driver, Briggs, *Hebrew-English Lexicon of the OT* |
| Beng | Bengel's *Gnomon* |
| BS | *Bibliotheca Sacra* |
| BTh | *Biblical Theology* |
| BV | Berkeley Version |
| CBSC | Cambridge Bible for Schools and Colleges |
| Crem | Cremer's *Biblico-Theological Lexicon of NT Greek* |
| DeissBS | Deissmann, *Bible Studies* |
| Deiss LAE | Deissmann, *Light from the Ancient East* |
| EQ | *Evangelical Quarterly* |

| | |
|---|---|
| ERV | English Revised Version (1881) |
| Exp | *The Expositor* |
| ExpB | *The Expositor's Bible* |
| ExpGT | *The Expositor's Greek Testament* |
| ExpT | *The Expository Times* |
| HDAC | *Hastings' Dictionary of the Apostolic Church* |
| HDB | *Hastings' Dictionary of the Bible* |
| HDCG | *Hastings' Dictionary of Christ and the Gospels* |
| HERE | *Hastings' Encyclopedia of Religion and Ethics* |
| HR | Hatch and Redpath, *Concordance to the LXX* |
| HZNT | *Handbuch zum Neuen Testament* (Lietzmann) |
| IB | *Interpreter's Bible* |
| ICC | *International Critical Commentary* |
| Interp | *Interpretation* |
| ISBE | *International Standard Bible Encyclopaedia* |
| JewEnc | *Jewish Encyclopaedia* |
| JBL | *Journal of Biblical Literature* |
| JBR | *Journal of Bible and Religion* |
| JFB | Jamieson, Fausset, and Brown, *A Commentary Critical, Experimental and Practical on the Old and New Testaments* |
| JNES | *Journal of Near Eastern Studies* |
| Jos | Josephus' *Antiquities of the Jews, et al.* |
| JPS | Jewish Publication Society Version of the Old Testament |
| JQR | *Jewish Quarterly Review* |
| JTS | *Journal of Theological Studies* |
| KB | Koehler and Baumgartner, *Lexicon in Veteris* |
| KD | Keil and Delitzsch, *Commentary on the OT* |
| LSJ | Liddell, Scott, Jones, *Greek-English Lexicon* |
| LXX | Septuagint |
| MM | Moulton and Milligan, *The Vocabulary of the Gr. Test.* |
| MNT | *Moffatt's New Testament Commentary* |
| MSt | McClintock and Strong, *Cyclopaedia of Biblical, Theological, and Ecclesiastical Literature* |
| MT | Masoretic Text |
| Nestle | Nestle (ed.) *Novum Testamentum Graece* |
| NovTest | *Novum Testamentum* |
| NTS | *New Testament Studies* |
| Pesh | Peshitta (Syriac) |
| PTR | Princeton Theological Review |
| RB | *Revue Biblique* |
| RSV | Revised Standard Version |
| RTWB | *Richardson's Theological Word Book* |

| | |
|---|---|
| SBK | *Kommentar zum Neuen Testament aus Talmud und Midrasch* (Strack and Billerbeck) |
| SHERK | *The New Schaff-Herzog Encyclopedia of Religious Knowledge* |
| ThT | *Theology Today* |
| Trench | *Trench's Synonyms of the New Testament* |
| TWNT | *Theologisches Wörterbuch zum Neuen Testament* (Kittel) |
| VT | *Vetus Testamentum* |
| Vulg | Vulgate Version |
| Wett | Wettstein's *Novum Testamentum Graecum* |
| WC | Westminster Commentaries |
| WH | Westcott and Hort, *Text of the Greek NT* |
| WTJ | Westminster Theological Journal |
| ZAW | *Zeitschrift für die alttestamentliche Wissenschaft* |
| ZNW | *Zeitschrift für die neutestamentliche Wissenschaft* |

d. Others.

| | |
|---|---|
| A. D. | *anno domini* (in the year of our Lord) |
| art. | article |
| B. C. | Before Christ |
| c. | circa (about) |
| cen. | century |
| cf. | *confer* (compare) |
| ch. | chapter |
| *Com.* | *Commentary* |
| e. g. | *exempli gratia* (for example) |
| *et al.* | and others |
| f., ff. | following |
| Gr. | Greek |
| Heb. | Hebrew |
| i. e. | *id est* (that is) |
| marg. | margin, marginal reading |
| MS., MSS. | manuscript, manuscripts |
| p., pp. | page, pages |
| pl. | plural |
| sing. | singular |

## Transliteration

Hebrew and Greek words have been transliterated according to the following form:

| Greek | | Hebrew | | | |
|---|---|---|---|---|---|
| | | **Consonants**[1] | | **Vocalization**[2] | |
| α – a | | א – ' | מ ם – m | בָה – bâ | בֹ – bo [3] |
| ą – â | | ב בּ – b | ן נ – n | בוֹ – bô | בֻ – bu [3] |
| ε – e | | ג ג – ḡ | ס – s | בוּ – bû | בְ – be |
| η – ē | | ד ד – d | ע – ' | בֵּי – bê | בִ – bi [3] |
| η – ê | | ה – h | ף פ – p | בֶּי – bè | בֲ – bă |
| o – o | | ו – w | ץ צ – ṣ | בִי – bî | בֳ – bŏ |
| ω – ō | | ז – z | ק – q | בָ – bā | בֱ – bĕ |
| ῳ – ô | | ח – ḥ | ר – r | בֹ – bŏ | בְ – b° |
| ζ – z | | ט – ṭ | שׁ – sh | בֻ – bū | בָה – bāh |
| θ – th | | י – y | שׂ – ś | בֵ – bē | בָא – bā' |
| ξ – x | | ך כ – k | ת ת – t | בִ – bī | בֵה – bēh |
| υ – y | | ל – l | | בַ – ba | בֶה – beh |
| φ – ph | | | | | |
| χ – ch | | | | | |
| ψ – ps | | | | | |
| ' – h | | | | | |

[1]*Dagesh lene* is not indicated. *Dagesh forte* is represented by doubling the letter.

[2]This is an *orthographic equation* and not a scientific representation.

[3]In closed syllables.

## Acknowledgments

The Publishers are greatly indebted to the editors of this volume, Dr. Charles F. Pfeiffer and Dr. Everett F. Harrison, and to the contributors, who have given their services so heartily. Especially appreciated is their outstanding co-operation in fulfilling the exacting requirements of a one-volume commentary of this kind. The Publishers also wish to acknowledge the splendid assistance of Dr. John Rea and Mr. Walter Dunnett, of the Moody Bible Institute Faculty, for their editorial help; of Mr. Herbert Klingbeil, director of Moody Correspondence School, for co-ordinating various aspects of the work; and of Dr. Howard F. Vos, textbook editor of Moody Press, for his detailed supervision of the work from its inception to its publication.

# THE NEW TESTAMENT

# THE GOSPEL ACCORDING TO MATTHEW

## INTRODUCTION

*Author.* Abundant early historical testimony ascribes this Gospel to Matthew the publican, also called Levi by Mark and Luke. Modern doubts of Matthaean authorship are the product of hypotheses developed to explain the Synoptic Problem. But these hypotheses cannot alter the testimony of the early church, whose writers quoted this Gospel more frequently than any other. Since Matthew was not particularly prominent among the Twelve, and there was no special tendency to demand apostolic authorship for the Synoptics (e.g., Mk, Lk), no a priori reason exists for ascribing the Gospel to him unless he actually wrote it.

As a former taxgatherer Matthew was well qualified to produce such a Gospel. His business knowledge of shorthand enabled him to record fully the discourses of Jesus. His acquaintance with figures is reflected in his frequent mention of money, his interest in large sums (Mt 18:24; 25:15), and his general interest in statistics (e.g., 1:17).

*Composition and Date.* The great frequency of citations and allusions to Matthew found in the Didache, Epistle of Barnabas, Ignatius, Justin Martyr, and others attests its early composition and widespread use. The literary connections of this Gospel must be considered in its relations to the other Synoptics, and also to the statement of Papias that "Matthew wrote the words in the Hebrew dialect, and each one interpreted as he could" (Eusebius *Ecclesiastical History* 3.39). Many have explained Papias' statement as referring to an Aramaic original from which our Greek Gospel is a translation. Yet our Greek text does not bear the marks of a translation, and the absence of any trace of an Aramaic original casts grave doubts upon this hypothesis. Goodspeed argues at length that it would be contrary to Greek practice to name a Greek translation after the author of an Aramaic original, for Greeks were concerned only with the one who put a work into Greek. As examples he cites the Gospel of Mark (it was not called the Gospel of Peter) and the Greek Old Testament, which was called the Septuagint

(*Seventy*) after its translators, not after its Hebrew authors (E. J. Goodspeed, *Matthew, Apostle and Evangelist*, pp. 105, 106). Thus Papias is understood to mean that Matthew recorded (by shorthand?) the discourses of Jesus in Aramaic, and later drew upon these when he composed his Greek Gospel. Though it is surely possible that Mark was written first, and may have been available to Matthew, there was no slavish use of this shorter Gospel by Matthew, and many have argued for the complete independence of the two books.

The date of Matthew's Gospel must be prior to A.D. 70, for there is no hint in it that Jerusalem was in ruins (all predictions of its destruction being clearly prophetic). Such passages as 27:8 ("unto this day") and 28:15 ("until this day") argue for an interval of some length, but fifteen or twenty years following the Resurrection would be sufficient.

*Special Emphases.* The testimony of Irenaeus and Origen that Matthew was written for converts from Judaism is corroborated by a study of its content. There is more frequent use of the Old Testament (Robertson's *Harmony of the Gospels* lists 93 quotations in Mt, 49 in Mk, 80 in Lk, and 33 in Jn). Much attention is given to demonstrating that Jesus fulfilled Messianic prophecy and thus was Israel's Messiah, who would establish the promised kingdom. The discourses that Matthew records at length distinguish this Gospel, and emphasize the principles, scope, and movements of the Messianic kingdom (Mt 5–7; 13; 24–25). Thus Jewish Christians (who numbered in the thousands in the early church; Acts 2:41, 47; 4:4; 5:14, 28; 6:1, 7) were given an authoritative explanation that faith in Jesus involved no repudiation of the Old Testament, but was the very goal toward which Old Testament revelation pointed. Of course, these same questions face Gentile converts in proportion to their understanding of the Old Testament. And therefore Matthew's Gospel occupies a place of prominence in Christian thinking which quite justifies its position as the first Gospel in our New Testament.

1

# OUTLINE

# ST. MATTHEW

### CHAPTER 1

THE book of the generation of Jesus Christ, the son of David, the son of Abraham.

2. Abraham begat Isaac; and Isaac begat Jacob; and Jacob begat Judas and his brethren;

3. And Judas begat Phares and Zara of Thamar; and Phares begat Esrom; and Esrom begat Aram;

4. And Aram begat Aminadab; and Aminadab begat Naasson; and Naasson begat Salmon;

5. And Salmon begat Booz of Rachab; and Booz begat Obed of Ruth; and Obed begat Jesse;

6. And Jesse begat David the king; and David the king begat Solomon of her *that had been the wife* of Urias;

7. And Solomon begat Roboam; and Roboam begat Abia; and Abia begat Asa;

8. And Asa begat Josaphat; and Josaphat begat Joram; and Joram begat Ozias;

9. And Ozias begat Joatham; and Joatham begat Achaz; and Achaz begat Ezekias;

10. And Ezekias begat Manasses; and Manasses begat Amon; and Amon begat Josias;

11. And Josias begat Jechonias and his brethren, about the time they were carried away to Babylon:

# COMMENTARY

## I. The Birth and Childhood of Jesus Christ. 1:1–2:23.

**A. Genealogy of Christ. 1:1-17.** This family line from Abraham to Jesus, proceeding through the kings of the Davidic house, is clearly intended to present the claim of Jesus to the throne of David. Although the throne had been vacant for nearly six centuries, no one could expect serious consideration by the Jews as the Messiah unless he could prove his royal descent. (Lk 3:23-38 presents another genealogy, apparently Mary's, to show the actual blood descent of Jesus, which was also from the Davidic family.)

**1. The book of the generation.** A Hebrew expression variously understood as the title of the whole Gospel of Matthew, the first two chapters, or the first seventeen verses. A similar expression in Gen 5:1 is broad enough to include both genealogy and the narrative that is interwoven (Gen 5:1–6:8). **Jesus** is the historical name; **Christ** (the equivalent of the Heb. Messiah, "anointed one") is the title of his office. The two names were not generally used together as a proper name until after the Ascension. **Son of David** and **son of Abraham** relate Jesus to the Messianic promises (Gen 12:3; 13:15; 22:18; II Sam 7:12,13; 22:51).

**2.** The list begins with **Abraham**, the father of the race to which Matthew was particularly writing, and the first one to whom the Messianic promise was given. **Judah and his brethren.** Although the line of descent came through Judah (Gen 49:10), all the patriarchs were heirs of the Messianic promise.

**3-6. Tamar** (see Gen 38). It was unusual for women to be listed in Jewish genealogies. Yet four women are listed here (though the descent was through the man in each case). Two were Gentiles (Rahab, Ruth); three bore moral blots (Tamar, Rahab, Bath-sheba). Is there not here another evidence of the grace of God in his plan to save sinners? The repetition of the title **David the king** emphasizes the royal character of this genealogy.

**7-11.** These verses name kings, all of whom are also listed in I Chr 3:10-16. After **Joram** Matthew omits the names of Ahaziah, Joash, and Amaziah, and after **Josiah** he omits Jehoiakim. The omissions are doubtless due to his arbitrary shortening of the list to give three groups of fourteen, perhaps as an aid to the memory. **Son** and **begat** indicate direct de-

3

12. And after they were brought to Babylon, Jechonias begat Salathiel; and Salathiel begat Zorobabel;

13. And Zorobabel begat Abiud; and Abiud begat Eliakim; and Eliakim begat Azor;

14. And Azor begat Sadoc; and Sadoc begat Achim; and Achim begat Eliud;

15. And Eliud begat Eleazar; and Eleazar begat Matthan; and Matthan begat Jacob;

16. And Jacob begat Joseph the husband of Mary, of whom was born Jesus, who is called Christ.

17. So all the generations from Abraham to David *are* fourteen generations; and from David until the carrying away into Babylon *are* fourteen generations; and from the carrying away into Babylon unto Christ *are* fourteen generations.

scent, but not necessarily immediate descent. **Jechonias**, son of Jehoiakim and grandson of Josiah, was regarded by the Jews in exile as their last legitimate king; and Ezekiel's prophecies are dated from him, although Zedekiah, his uncle, followed him as king.

**12-16. Salathiel** (or Shealtiel) is named as the son of Jechonias (cf. I Chr 3:17). This does not contradict Jer 22:28-30, for the predicted childlessness referred to reigning children. (The naming of Salathiel as the son of Neri in Lk 3:27 is better understood of different persons, rather than the result of levirate marriage.) From this point the names, which do not appear in the OT, must have been derived from Joseph's family records. One would expect descendants of royalty to preserve their lineage. Of **Joseph** it is not said that he "begat" Jesus, a marked change from the preceding expressions, and an obvious indication of the virgin birth, which Matthew subsequently explains. The feminine form of the pronoun **whom** also omits Joseph from involvement in the birth of Jesus. This genealogy makes him Christ's legal father because he was Mary's husband, but nothing more. The remarkable reading of the Sinaitic Syriac Version, "Joseph to whom was betrothed Mary the virgin begat Jesus," cannot be correct, and if intended to deny the virgin birth, contradicts itself in the succeeding verses.

**17. Fourteen generations.** This threefold grouping, arbitrarily constructed (as indicated by omissions), must have been intended as an arrangement for convenience. The three periods of national history are covered — theocracy, monarchy, hierarchy. Matthew's computation presents a problem because he lists only forty-one names. Some would solve it by counting David twice, as the end of the first group and the first name in the second (Matthew himself seems to do this; v. 17). Others count the Captivity as one item in the list. The problem is of no importance per se.

B. Birth of Christ. 1:18-25. The circumstances of the birth are related from Joseph's standpoint, and some of the details had to be derived from him (e.g., vv. 19,20). If he had already died before Jesus' ministry began, as many infer from the absence of further mention, Matthew's information may have come from the brothers of Jesus.

4

18. Now the birth of Jesus Christ was on this wise: When as his mother Mary was espoused to Joseph, before they came together, she was found with child of the Holy Ghost.

19. Then Joseph her husband, being a just *man*, and not willing to make her a public example, was minded to put her away privily.

20. But while he thought on these things, behold, the angel of the Lord appeared unto him in a dream, saying, Joseph, thou son of David, fear not to take unto thee Mary thy wife: for that which is conceived in her is of the Holy Ghost.

21. And she shall bring forth a son, and thou shalt call his name JESUS: for he shall save his people from their sins.

22. Now all this was done, that it might be fulfilled which was spoken of the Lord by the prophet, saying,

23. Behold, a virgin shall be with child, and shall bring forth a son, and they shall call his name Emmanuel, which being interpreted is, God with us.

24. Then Joseph being raised from sleep did as the angel of the Lord had bidden him, and took unto him his wife:

25. And knew her not till she had brought forth her firstborn son: and he called his name JESUS.

18. **Betrothed.** Among the Jews, marriage vows were said at the betrothal, and required divorce to end them. Custom decreed an interval, usually a year, before the bride should take residence in her husband's house and physical union be consummated. During this interval Mary was found with child, a circumstance usually punishable by death (Deut 22:23, 24). Apparently Mary did not explain her situation to Joseph but chose to leave this delicate matter in the hands of God. She could hardly have expected Joseph to accept her story without some divine authentication.

19. **Public example.** Rather than make a public accusation of fornication, with perhaps a demand for the full penalty, Joseph resolved to use the lax divorce laws and give Mary the writing of divorcement privately, with the accusation stated in a veiled way. **To put her away** means to divorce, not to break an engagement. How he must have loved her!

20. **Thou son of David.** This address by the angel (Gabriel? Lk 1:26) is a princely title. Though Joseph was in humble circumstances, he was heir to the vacant Davidic throne. The naming of the **Holy Ghost** as the agent in Mary's conception points clearly to the distinct personality of this Divine Being, and to the full awareness by ordinary Jews of this Person without further explanation.

21. **Jesus** is from the Hebrew for *Jehovah saves*, and points to the purpose of his coming. **His people** relates Jesus to the Messianic promises made to Israel, although the cross would extend this salvation from sins to Gentiles as well.

22,23. The miraculous conception is stated to be the fulfillment of Isa 7:14. Whether there was an earlier fulfillment in Isaiah's day is neither discussed nor suggested. Possibly these words were spoken by the angel and thus were an aid to Joseph's faith. **Emmanuel** was not used as a proper name of Jesus, but describes his person as the Son of God.

24,25. Joseph ended the period of betrothal by taking Mary to live in his home so that Jesus at His birth would be his legitimate son and heir to the throne. However, he **knew her not** sexually prior to the birth. Neither **till** nor **firstborn** necessarily indicates what happened afterward. However, one would naturally infer that the normal relationship of marriage would follow, unless one is committed to defend the perpetual virginity of Mary. Matthew betrays no such inclination.

### CHAPTER 2

NOW when Jesus was born in Bethlehem of Judea in the days of Herod the king, behold, there came wise men from the east to Jerusalem,

2. Saying, Where is he that is born King of the Jews? for we have seen his star in the east, and are come to worship him.

3. When Herod the king had heard *these things*, he was troubled, and all Jerusalem with him.

4. And when he had gathered all the chief priests and scribes of the people together, he demanded of them where Christ should be born.

5. And they said unto him, In Bethlehem of Judea: for thus it is written by the prophet,

6. And thou Bethlehem, *in* the land of Juda, art not the least among the princes of Juda: for out of thee shall come a Governor, that shall rule my people Israel.

7. Then Herod, when he had privily called the wise men, inquired of them diligently what time the star appeared.

8. And he sent them to Bethlehem, and said, Go and search diligently for the young child; and when ye have found *him*, bring me word again, that I may come and worship him also.

9. When they had heard the king, they departed; and, lo, the star, which they saw in the east, went before them, till it came and stood over where the young child was.

10. When they saw the star, they rejoiced with exceeding great joy.

C. Visit of the Magi. 2:1-12. Matthew, who alone records this incident, shows the contrast in attitudes between the non-Jewish wise men who journeyed far to see Jesus and the Jewish authorities who would not go five miles.

1. Bethlehem of Judea was also called Ephrath (Gen 35:16,19). One must read Lk 2:1-7 to learn how it was that the birth occurred in Bethlehem instead of in Nazareth. Herod the king, known as Herod the Great, was the son of Antipater, an Edomite, and was made king by the Romans in 43 B.C. His death occurring in 4 B.C. (our calendars err by at least four years) gives us the latest possible date for the birth of Christ. Wise men *(magoi)* originally denoted the priestly caste among the Persians and Babylonians (cf. Dan 2:2,48; 4:6,7; 5:7). Later the name was applied by the Greeks to any sorcerer or charlatan (Acts 8:9; 13:8). Matthew uses the term in the better sense to designate honorable men from an Eastern religion. It is entirely conceivable that these men had made contact with Jewish exiles, or with the prophecies and influence of Daniel, and thus were in possession of OT prophecies regarding Messiah.

2. His star. All attempts to explain the star as a natural phenomenon are inadequate to account for its leading the Magi from Jerusalem to Bethlehem and then standing over the house. Rather, it was a special manifestation used of God both when it first appeared to indicate the fact of Christ's birth, and when it reappeared over Jerusalem to guide the Magi to the place. Since a direct revelation to the Magi is recorded (v. 12), there is nothing improbable in assuming a direct revelation at the beginning to impart the significance of the star.

3-6. When word reached Herod that the Magi were making search in Jerusalem for the King of the Jews, the king consulted the chief priests and scribes, two of the groups comprising the Sanhedrin. He was given the prediction in Mic 5:2 which clearly names Bethlehem as the birthplace of Messiah.

7,8. Herod summoned the wise men, under pretense of sincere interest, and requested exact information of the star's first appearance (it was apparently not as yet seen in Jerusalem). His motive, however, was to help him fix the precise date of Jesus' birth, that he might more easily locate and destroy Him.

9,10. The star which they saw in the east now reappeared to act as guide from Jerusalem to Bethlehem.

11. And when they were come into the house, they saw the young child with Mary his mother, and fell down, and worshipped him: and when they had opened their treasures, they presented unto him gifts; gold, and frankincense, and myrrh.

12. And being warned of God in a dream that they should not return to Herod, they departed into their own country another way.

13. And when they were departed, behold, the angel of the Lord appeareth to Joseph in a dream, saying, Arise, and take the young child and his mother, and flee into Egypt, and be thou there until I bring thee word: for Herod will seek the young child to destroy him.

14. When he arose, he took the young child and his mother by night, and departed into Egypt:

15. And was there until the death of Herod: that it might be fulfilled which was spoken of the Lord by the prophet, saying, Out of Egypt have I called my son.

16. Then Herod, when he saw that he was mocked of the wise men, was exceeding wroth, and sent forth, and slew all the children that were in Bethlehem, and in all the coasts thereof, from two years old and under, according to the time which he had diligently inquired of the wise men.

17. Then was fulfilled that which was spoken by Jeremy the prophet, saying,

18. In Rama was there a voice heard, lamentation, and weeping, and great mourning, Rachel weeping for her children, and would not be comforted, because they are not.

11. **The house** (not the manger) in which the Magi found the infant Jesus points to the fact that this visit followed Jesus' birth by a considerable interval, perhaps of months (cf. v. 16). The three gifts have given rise to the tradition of three wise men. Tradition even names them: Caspar, Melchior, and Balthasar. But tradition is not necessarily fact. **Gold, frankincense, and myrrh** were thought by ancient commentators to show recognition of Jesus as King, Son of God, and one destined to die, respectively.

12. **Warned of God.** A special divine revelation directed the Magi to avoid Herod on their return.

D. Flight into Egypt and Massacre of the Infants. 2:13-18. Again we are indebted to Matthew alone for this material. Both incidents are related to OT passages. Such correlation of OT and NT passages is characteristic of this Gospel.

13,14. Joseph a second time received angelic instruction (cf. 1:20), and took Jesus and Mary to **Egypt.** The hurried trip seems to have begun the same night the Magi departed. In Egypt, where there was a large Jewish population, the family would have been welcome without undue notice. The apocryphal Gospel of the Infancy relates fanciful miracles occurring there (ch. IV).

15. **The death of Herod** after a revolting illness is recorded in detail by Josephus (*Antiq.* xvii. 6.5). **That is might be fulfilled** relates this experience to Hos 11:1, a passage referring historically to the deliverance of the Israelites from Egypt. Matthew sees Israel in this prophecy as a type of Jesus Christ, God's unique **son.**

16. **Slew all the children.** That Herod's murderous act (which included no more than a few dozen infants, because of the smallness of Bethlehem) should have gone unrecorded in other histories is not surprising, because of the king's frequent outrages. He was the murderer of his wife and three sons. Josephus calls him "a man of great barbarity towards all men equally" (*Antiq.* xvii. 8.1). **Two years old and under** shows that Herod was taking no chances of missing his victim. Jesus was not necessarily two years old.

17,18. **Rachel weeping for her children.** A quotation of Jer 31:15, which depicts the wailing at the time of Israel's exile. That calamity, caused by Israel's sin, eventually brought Herod to the throne, and now this new atrocity. Matthew views both calamities as part of the same picture.

19. But when Herod was dead, behold, an angel of the Lord appeareth in a dream to Joseph in Egypt,

20. Saying, Arise, and take the young child and his mother, and go into the land of Israel: for they are dead which sought the young child's life.

21. And he arose, and took the young child and his mother, and came into the land of Israel.

22. But when he heard that Archelaus did reign in Judea in the room of his father Herod, he was afraid to go thither: notwithstanding, being warned of God in a dream, he turned aside into the parts of Galilee:

23. And he came and dwelt in a city called Nazareth: that it might be fulfilled which was spoken by the prophets, He shall be called a Nazarene.

## CHAPTER 3

IN those days came John the Baptist, preaching in the wilderness of Judea,

2. And saying, Repent ye: for the kingdom of heaven is at hand.

E. Residence at Nazareth. 2:19-23. From Matthew one would suppose that Bethlehem was the original residence. Luke supplements by showing Nazareth to be the former home. Joseph apparently intended to dwell permanently in Bethlehem until his plans were divinely altered.

19-22. They are dead. A reference to Herod, and thus an idiom reminiscent of Ex 4:19. Archelaus, son of Herod the Great and his Samaritan wife, Malthace, was as brutal as his father. Thus Joseph needed to be warned (or instructed) of God as to the next step.

23. Nazareth seems to have been chosen by Joseph himself, within the providence of God. Why Matthew regarded this as a fulfillment of prophecy is difficult to understand. By the prophets prevents our seeking only one OT passage, thus making doubtful any play on words based on *nēser*, "branch," in Isa 11:1, although this is the common view. It seems better to understand Matthew as seeing in this residence at little Nazareth, a most unlikely place for Messiah (Jn 1:46), a fulfillment of all those OT prophecies which indicate that Messiah would be despised (e.g., Isa 53:3; Ps 22:6; Dan 9:26).

II. The Beginnings of the Ministry of Jesus Christ. 3:1–4:11.

A. The Forerunner of Christ. 3:1-12. All four Gospels describe John's preparatory ministry, and Luke gives a full description of his remarkable birth (Lk 1:5-25, 57-80).

1. In those days relates to the previous verse, which speaks of Jesus as residing at Nazareth. Precise data are given in Lk 3:1,2. John the Baptist, called by this name even by Josephus (*Antiq. xviii.* 5.2), did his preaching near the Jordan River in the northern part of the wilderness of Judea, a barren wasteland extending along the west shore of the Dead Sea.

2. Repent means "to change the mind," but implies more than mere change of opinion. As a religious term in Scripture, it involves a complete change of attitude regarding sin and God, accompanied by a sense of sorrow and a corresponding change in conduct. The kingdom of heaven is at hand (or *has come near*), the reason John called on men to repent. This title, peculiar to Matthew in the NT, is based on Dan 2:44; 7:13,14,27. It refers to the Messianic kingdom promised in the OT, of which Jesus was about to be presented as king. (The term, "kingdom of

3. For this is he that was spoken of by the prophet Esaias, saying, The voice of one crying in the wilderness, Prepare ye the way of the Lord, make his paths straight.

4. And the same John had his raiment of camel's hair, and a leathern girdle about his loins; and his meat was locusts and wild honey.

5. Then went out to him Jerusalem, and all Judea, and all the region round about Jordan,

6. And were baptized of him in Jordan, confessing their sins.

7. But when he saw many of the Pharisees and Sadducees come to his baptism, he said unto them, O generation of vipers, who hath warned you to flee from the wrath to come?

8. Bring forth therefore fruits meet for repentance:

9. And think not to say within yourselves, We have Abraham to our father: for I say unto you, that God is able of these stones to raise up children unto Abraham.

10. And now also the axe is laid unto the root of the trees: therefore every tree which bringeth not forth good fruit is hewn down, and cast into the fire.

11. I indeed baptize you with water unto repentance: but he that cometh after me is mightier than I, whose shoes I am not worthy to bear: he shall baptize you with the Holy Ghost, and with fire:

God," often has a wider connotation, but usually in the Gospels the two are used interchangeably.) This Messianic kingdom of heaven, although promised as a literal earthly kingdom, nevertheless would be based on spiritual principles, and would demand a right relationship with God for entrance; hence the call to repent.

3,4. This is he that was spoken of by the prophet Isaiah (Isa 40:3-5) definitely relates the prophecy to John, a fact noted in each Gospel (Mk 1:2,3; Lk 3:4-6; Jn 1:23). Camel's hair and a leathern girdle is probably intentionally similar to Elijah's clothing (II Kgs 1:8; cf. Lk 1:17; Mt 17:10-13), and was the usual dress of prophets (Zech 13:4). Locusts. An allowable and not uncommon food (Lev 11:22).

5,6. John's preaching accorded with the mood of expectancy that had gripped many hearts, and caused a general enthusiasm to hear him, as indicated by all. As they came, they were being baptized to indicate acceptance of his message. Baptism was practiced by Jews when making proselytes, and for remedial and purifying purposes; and thus the outward form was no innovation by John, although the significance was new. Even the Qumran community observed a ritualistic baptism, though certainly not for the same reason that John baptized (W. S. LaSor, Amazing Dead Sea Scrolls, pp. 205,206).

7-10. Pharisees. Members of a prominent religious party. They claimed to be guardians of the Mosaic law and adhered rigidly to the traditions of the fathers. Christ characterized them as hypocrites (Lk 11:44; 12:1). Sadducees. A party of religious rationalists, who denied the future life. They were politically powerful, including the priestly aristocracy in their number. John realized that their coming was mere display, not indicative of spiritual change, and likened them to vipers fleeing before the onrushing brush fire. Having Abraham as their national father would not insure them against divine judgment. God was not obligated to them individually to fulfill his promises. Of these stones. Perhaps an allusion to Isa 51:1,2, but more likely a reference to the pebbles at John's feet, which could be made to respond to the creative touch of God, as Adam was formed from the dust. By the dramatic figure of the ax . . . lying at the root of the trees, John shows that time is running out for his hearers. The woodsman is about to appear.

11,12. John's baptism, a public testimony that the participant had repented, is to be followed by Messiah's, which is with

12. Whose fan *is* in his hand, and he will thoroughly purge his floor, and gather his wheat into the garner; but he will burn up the chaff with unquenchable fire.

13. Then cometh Jesus from Galilee to Jordan unto John, to be baptized of him.

14. But John forbade him, saying, I have need to be baptized of thee, and comest thou to me?

15. And Jesus answering said unto him, Suffer *it to be so* now: for thus it becometh us to fulfil all righteousness. Then he suffered him.

16. And Jesus, when he was baptized, went up straightway out of the water: and, lo, the heavens were opened unto him, and he saw the Spirit of God descending like a dove, and lighting upon him:

17. And lo a voice from heaven, saying, This is my beloved Son, in whom I am well pleased.

the **Holy Ghost** and with **fire**. Some relegate both terms to Pentecost; others, to the Judgment. In view of verse 12, it seems clear that the baptism with the Holy Ghost refers to Christ's saving believers (**wheat**), and the fire describes judgment upon the wicked (**burn up the chaff**). Compare Mal 4:1 (a chapter which in the NT is applied to John; see Lk 1:17). Thus John looks at Messiah's work from the usual OT standpoint, without regarding the interval between the first and second comings, an interval of which he may have been unaware. **Fan.** A wooden shovel for tossing grain against the wind after threshing. The lighter chaff would be blown away, leaving the grain to settle in a pile.

B. Baptism of Christ. 3:12-17. The coming of Jesus to be baptized by John is set in quiet contrast to the hypocritical coming of · the Pharisees and Sadducees (v. 7). All three Synoptists record this baptism, and John's Gospel includes the Baptist's later testimony to it (Jn 1:29-34).

**13,14. But John was hindering him.** The Greek verb emphasizes the continuing remonstrance. In the light of Jn 1:31-33, it may be asked how John recognized the superiority of Jesus so as to speak thus. We need not infer, however, that these kinsmen were total strangers, but rather that John did not yet know him as the official Messiah until the sign of the descending Spirit should occur (Jn 1:33).

**15. Thus it becometh us.** Although it was true that the positions of John and Jesus would shortly be reversed, in the present instance (**now**) it was the fitting thing to do. Certainly Jesus was not repenting of any personal sin. Yet, as the Substitute who would provide **righteousness** for sinful humanity, he here identifies himself with those whom he came to redeem, and thus publicly begins his work. Jesus, while on earth, always carried on the religious duties of the righteous Jew, such as synagogue worship, attendance at feasts, and payment of the temple tax.

**16,17.** The descending ·**Spirit of God** fulfilled the predicted sign to John that Jesus was the Messiah (Jn 1:33; cf. Isa 11:2; 42:1; 59:21; 61:1). As the Spirit came upon OT prophets for special guidance at the start of their ministries, so now He came upon Jesus without measure. Of course, this relates to Jesus in his humanity. **Dove.** An ancient symbol of purity, innocence, and gentleness (see Mt 10:16). The **voice from heaven** occurred at three key points in Christ's ministry: at his baptism, at his transfiguration (17:5), and

## CHAPTER 4

THEN was Jesus led up of the Spirit into the wilderness to be tempted of the devil.

2. And when he had fasted forty days and forty nights, he was afterward ahungered.

3. And when the tempter came to him, he said, If thou be the Son of God, command that these stones be made bread.

4. But he answered and said, It is written, Man shall not live by bread alone, but by every word that proceedeth out of the mouth of God.

5. Then the devil taketh him up into the holy city, and setteth him on a pinnacle of the temple,

6. And saith unto him, If thou be the Son of God, cast thyself down: for it is written, He shall give his angels charge concerning thee: and in *their* hands they shall bear thee up, lest at any time thou dash thy foot against a stone.

7. Jesus said unto him, It is written again, Thou shalt not tempt the Lord thy God.

8. Again, the devil taketh him up into an exceeding high mountain, and showeth him all the kingdoms of the world, and the glory of them;

9. And saith unto him, All these things will I give thee, if thou wilt fall down and worship me.

10. Then saith Jesus unto him, Get thee hence, Satan: for it is written, Thou shalt worship the Lord thy God, and him only shalt thou serve.

11. Then the devil leaveth him, and, behold, angels came and ministered unto him.

just prior to the cross (Jn 12:28).

**C. Temptation of Christ. 4:1-11.** The most obvious sense of this passage, with its parallels, is that an actual historical experience took place. Viewpoints that deny this do not lessen the difficulties of interpretation. The various tests were directed against the human nature of Jesus, and he resisted in that realm. However, the perfect union of the divine and human natures in his person made the outcome certain, for God can never sin. But this in no way lessened the force of the attack.

**1. Led up of the Spirit.** An indication of the submission (voluntary) of Christ to the Spirit during his earthly ministry. **To be tempted.** A word meaning *to try* or *test,* sometimes, as here; *an enticement to evil.* The Spirit was leading Jesus in order to bring about this test. **The devil.** The name means *slanderer,* and denotes one of the characteristics of Satan, great opposer of God and God's people. **2. Forty days and forty nights.** The three tests recorded here followed this time period, but other temptations had occurred throughout the period (Lk 4:2).

**3,4. If thou be the Son of God** does not imply doubt on the part of Satan, but rather forms the basis for his suggestion. The subtlety of the test is evident, for neither bread nor hunger is sinful per se. **Man shall not live by bread alone** (Deut 8:3) was Christ's Scriptural answer. Even wandering Israel was made to see that the source of bread (i.e., God) was more important than the bread itself. Jesus refused to work a miracle to avoid personal suffering when such suffering was part of God's will for him.

**5-7.** The second temptation occurred on **the pinnacle,** or *wing* of the Temple in Jerusalem, perhaps the porch towering above the Kidron valley. Satan employed Scripture (Ps 91:11,12) to make Christ prove His claim that He abode by every word that came from the mouth of God. **It is written again** pointed to the totality of Scripture as the guide for conduct and basis for faith. **Thou shalt not tempt the Lord** (Deut 6:16; cf. Ex 17:1-7). Such presumptuous action in putting God to the test is not faith but doubt, as Israel's experience had proved.

**8-11.** The **exceeding high mountain** is literal, but its location is unknown. By some supernatural act Satan showed Christ **all the kingdoms of the world. I will give thee** indicates that Satan had something to bestow; otherwise the test would have had no validity. As the god of

11

**12.** Now when Jesus had heard that John was cast into prison, he departed into Galilee;

**13.** And leaving Nazareth, he came and dwelt in Capernaum, which is upon the seacoast, in the borders of Zabulon and Nephthalim:

**14.** That it might be fulfilled which was spoken by Esaias the prophet, saying,

**15.** The land of Zabulon, and the land of Nephthalim, *by* the way of the sea, beyond Jordan, Galilee of the Gentiles;

**16.** The people which sat in darkness saw great light; and to them which sat in the region and shadow of death light is sprung up.

this world (II Cor 4:4) and prince of the power of the air (Eph 2:2), Satan does exercise sway over earthly kingdoms although as a usurper and within limits. He offered this control to Jesus in exchange for worship, and thus was offering to Christ that which eventually will be His in a far more glorious fashion (Rev 11:15). The coupling of **worship** and **serve** in Jesus' reply (from Deut 6:13) is significant, for the one involves the other. For Christ to bow before Satan would have been to acknowledge the devil's lordship. Such an offer deserved Christ's direct rebuke. Matthew's statement, **then** Satan **leaveth him,** shows that his order of temptations is the chronological one (contrast Lk 4:1-13). Jesus repulsed the mightiest blows of Satan not by a thunderbolt from heaven, but by the written Word of God employed in the wisdom of the Holy Spirit, a means available to every Christian.

### III. The Ministry of Jesus Christ. 4:12–25:46.

Matthew's analysis of Christ's ministry is built upon four clearly noted geographical areas: Galilee (4:12), Perea (19:1), Judea (20:17), and Jerusalem (21:1). With the other Synoptists he omits the early Judean ministry, which occurs chronologically between 4:11 and 4:12 (cf. Jn 1-4). Perhaps Matthew starts with Capernaum in Galilee because that is where his own association with Christ began (9:9).

A. In Galilee. 4:12–18:35.

1) Residence Established at Capernaum. 4:12-17.
**12. When Jesus had heard.** The imprisonment of John, with its accompanying publicity, made Christ's retirement a practical necessity in the best interests of his work. **13. Leaving Nazareth.** Luke 4:16-31 shows that the reason for the removal to Capernaum was the attempted murder of Christ after a synagogue service. Capernaum became the home of Jesus for the rest of his ministry.
**14-16. That it might be fulfilled** refers to Isa 9:1,2, from which the geographical terms are rather loosely quoted. **Beyond Jordan,** a somewhat puzzling phrase here, but still best understood as Perea, which, along with Galilee, formed the border area of Israel. This region, more exposed to foreign influences than Judea, had a mixed population, and the spiritual state of the people was usually low. The coming of the **light** of Christ into such an area of spiritual **darkness** had been foretold by

17. From that time Jesus began to preach, and to say, Repent: for the kingdom of heaven is at hand.

18. And Jesus, walking by the sea of Galilee, saw two brethren, Simon called Peter, and Andrew his brother, casting a net into the sea: for they were fishers.

19. And he saith unto them, Follow me, and I will make you fishers of men.

20. And they straightway left *their* nets, and followed him.

21. And going on from thence, he saw other two brethren, James *the son* of Zebedee, and John his brother, in a ship with Zebedee their father, mending their nets; and he called them.

22. And they immediately left the ship and their father, and followed him.

23. And Jesus went about all Galilee, teaching in their synagogues, and preaching the gospel of the kingdom, and healing all manner of sickness and all manner of disease among the people.

24. And his fame went throughout all Syria: and they brought unto him all sick people that were taken with divers diseases and torments, and those which were possessed with devils, and those which were lunatic, and those that had the palsy; and he healed them.

the prophet, and his prediction was now fulfilled.

**17. Repent.** The same message John had preached in Judea was now proclaimed by Jesus in Galilee (cf. 3:2).

2) Call of Four Disciples. 4:18-22. Jesus had previously met some if not all of these men in Judea when John the Baptist was still active (Jn 1:35-42). Now in Galilee that association was renewed and made permanent (cf. Mk 1:16-20; Lk 5:1-11).

**18-20. Sea of Galilee.** A lake in the Jordan valley 680 feet below sea level, 7 miles wide, 14 miles long, abounding in fish, and subject to sudden storms. **Simon** was casting the net with his brother **Andrew,** who had introduced him to Jesus some months earlier (Jn 1:40,41). The invitation, **Follow me,** called these believers to constant companionship with Jesus. Christ's plans for them called for training that would fit them to reclaim lost men. **Straightway.** The immediate response reveals the great impact of their earlier meeting.

**21,22. James** and **John,** another pair of brothers, were partners with Simon and Andrew (Lk 5:10). **Mending their nets.** Matthew and Mark agree on this fact, but Luke seems to differ. Rather than assume two incidents, it seems more reasonable to harmonize the accounts in some manner, as S. J. Andrews does (*The Life of Our Lord upon the Earth*, pp. 247,248). Most likely the men were engaged in casting and mending when Christ first approached. Our Lord then made use of Simon's boat, produced the miraculous catch, and called Simon and Andrew to follow him. Upon returning to shore, James and John began to repair the broken net, and Jesus then called them also to follow him.

3) General Survey of the Galilean Ministry. 4:23-25. These verses summarize the events unfolded in the succeeding chapters. Christ's ministry during these days involved **teaching** (*didaskōn*), **proclaiming** (*kērussōn*), and **healing** (*therapeuōn*).

**23,24. Synagogues.** Local places of worship and religious instruction. For a sample of Jesus' synagogue preaching, see Lk 4:16-30. **Gospel of the kingdom** was the good news Jesus proclaimed that the Messianic king had arrived to set up the promised kingdom. Accompanying this announcement were miracles of **healing,** predicted of the kingdom and thus credentials of the king (Isa 35:4-6; Mt 11:2-6). **Syria.** Here a reference to the

25. And there followed him great multitudes of people from Galilee, and *from* Decapolis, and *from* Jerusalem, and *from* Judea, and *from* beyond Jordan.

### CHAPTER 5

AND seeing the multitudes, he went up into a mountain: and when he was set, his disciples came unto him:

2. And he opened his mouth, and taught them, saying,

3. Blessed *are* the poor in spirit: for theirs is the kingdom of heaven.

region northward. **Possessed with demons.** Scripture here clearly distinguishes demon possession from ordinary physical disease.

**25.** In addition to those who came to be healed, others from far and wide followed without this motivation. **Decapolis.** A federation of ten independent Greek cities under the protection of Syria, lying east of Galilee. **Beyond Jordan.** The region to the east known as Perea. Thus all of Palestine, and the adjacent areas, came under the influence of this ministry.

4) Sermon on the Mount. 5:1—7:29. This is the same discourse as that recorded in Lk 6:20-49, for the differences can be harmonized or accounted for, and the similarity of the beginnings, endings, and subject matter makes the identification most probable. Furthermore, both accounts record the healing of the centurion's servant as the next event. The objection that Matthew places this discourse before his own call (9:9; contrast Lk 5:27 ff.) is explained by his lack of strict chronological order elsewhere. Here, since Matthew had described Christ's activity in proclaiming the arrival of the Kingdom (4:17,23), it was proper for him to include for his readers a full discussion by Jesus of this subject. Hence the Sermon on the Mount is not primarily a statement of principles for the Christian church (which was yet unrevealed), nor an evangelistic message for the unsaved, but a delineation of the principles that would characterize the Messianic kingdom Christ was announcing. Later, Israel's rejection of her King delayed the coming of his kingdom, but even now Christians, having given their allegiance to the King and having been made spiritually to anticipate some of the blessings of his kingdom (Col 1:13), may see God's ideal in this sublime discourse and will assent to its high standard.

**1. Multitudes.** A reference to the crowds of the previous verse, and an indication that this discourse was not given till the Galilean ministry was in full swing. Further proof is the advanced level of instruction herein contained. **The mountain.** The unnamed elevation, apparently near Capernaum, on which Jesus found a level place to speak (Lk 6:17). **His disciples.** Luke shows that the Twelve had just been chosen (Lk 6:12-16), and the sermon was directed primarily to them (cf. Lk 6:20). However, some of it was heard by the multitudes (Mt 7:28; Lk 6:17).

a) Characteristics of Kingdom Citizens. 5:3-12.

**3. Blessed.** *Happy.* A description of a

4. Blessed *are* they that mourn: for they shall be comforted.

5. Blessed *are* the meek: for they shall inherit the earth.

6. Blessed *are* they which do hunger and thirst after righteousness: for they shall be filled.

7. Blessed *are* the merciful: for they shall obtain mercy.

8. Blessed *are* the pure in heart: for they shall see God.

9. Blessed *are* the peacemakers: for they shall be called the children of God.

10. Blessed *are* they which are persecuted for righteousness' sake: for theirs is the kingdom of heaven.

11. Blessed are ye, when *men* shall revile you, and persecute *you*, and shall say all manner of evil against you falsely, for my sake.

12. Rejoice, and be exceeding glad: for great *is* your reward in heaven: for so persecuted they the prophets which were before you.

13. Ye are the salt of the earth: but if the salt have lost his savor, wherewith shall it be salted? it is thenceforth good for nothing, but to be cast out, and to be trodden under foot of men.

14. Ye· are the light of the world. A city that is set on a hill cannot be hid.

15. Neither do men light a candle, and put it under a bushel, but on a candlestick; and it giveth light unto all that are in the house.

16. Let your light so shine before men, that they may see your good works, and glorify your Father which is in heaven.

believer's inner condition. When describing a person in God's will, it is virtually equivalent to "saved." Psalm 1 gives an OT picture of the blessed man, who evidences his nature by the things he does. The Beatitudes, also, are not primarily promises to the individual but a description of him. They do not show a man how to be saved, but describe the characteristics manifested by one who is born again. **Poor in spirit.** Opposite of proud in spirit. Those who have recognized their poverty in spiritual things and have allowed Christ to meet their need have become heirs of the **kingdom of heaven.**

**4,5. Mourn** (cf. Isa 61:3). A sense of anguish for sin characterizes the blessed man. But genuine repentance will bring comfort to the believer. Since Christ bore the sins of every man, the comfort of full forgiveness is readily available (I Jn 1:9). **Meek.** Mentioned only by Matthew. An obvious allusion to Ps 37:11. The source of this meekness is Christ (Mt 11:28,29), who bestows it when men submit their wills to his. **Inherit the earth.** The earthly Messianic kingdom.

**6-9. Hunger and thirst after righteousness.** A deep passion for personal righteousness. Such desire is evidence of dissatisfaction with present spiritual attainment (contrast Pharisee, Lk 18:9 ff.). **Merciful** (cf. Ps 18:25). Those who put pity into action can expect similar mercy both from men and God. **Pure in heart.** Those whose moral being is free from contamination with sin, without divided interests or loyalties. To them, as possessors of God's pure nature, belongs the unclouded vision of God, which will reach consummation when Christ returns (I Cor 13:12; I Jn 3:2). **Peacemakers.** As God is "the God of peace" (Heb 13:20) and Christ is "Prince of Peace" (Isa 9:6), so peacemakers in the Kingdom will be recognized as partaking of God's nature, and will be properly honored.

**10-12. Persecuted for righteousness' sake.** At the establishment of the Messianic kingdom, such wrongs will be set right. And even within that kingdom the presence of men with sinful natures will make evil a possibility, although it will be judged at once. **The prophets.** The OT seers who foretold the kingdom and proclaimed its righteous character met the same opposition (Jeremiah, Jer 20:2; Zechariah, II Chr 24:21).

b) Function of Kingdom Citizens. 5:13-16. **Salt.** A common food preservative, often used symbolically. Believers are a restraint upon the world's corruption. Un-

15

17. Think not that I am come to destroy the law, or the prophets: I am not come to destroy, but to fulfil.

18. For verily I say unto you, Till heaven and earth pass, one jot or one tittle shall in no wise pass from the law, till all be fulfilled.

19. Whosoever therefore shall break one of these least commandments, and shall teach men so, he shall be called the least in the kingdom of heaven: but whosoever shall do and teach *them*, the same shall be called great in the kingdom of heaven.

20. For I say unto you, That except your righteousness shall exceed *the righteousness* of the scribes and Pharisees, ye shall in no case enter into the kingdom of heaven.

21. Ye have heard that it was said by them of old time, Thou shalt not kill; and whosoever shall kill shall be in danger of the judgment:

believers are often kept from evil deeds because of a moral consciousness traceable to Christian influence. **Lost its savor** (ASV). Whether this can happen chemically is disputed. Thomson avows that the impure salt of Palestine may become insipid (*The Land and the Book,* p. 381). However, Christ's illustration may be hypothetical to show the anomaly of a useless believer. **Ye are the light.** Believers function positively to illuminate a world in darkness because they possess Christ, who is the Light (Jn 8:12). Christ's light should shine forth publicly, like the cluster of white stone houses in a Palestinian **city.** It should also be displayed in our individual, private relationships (**candle, lampstand, house**).

c) Standards of the Kingdom Compared to Mosaic Law. 5:17-48.

**17-20. Not to destroy.** Christ answers the objection that he was flouting the OT by denying any effort to annul or abrogate the Law. **But to fulfill.** Christ fulfilled the OT by obeying the Law perfectly, by fulfilling its types and prophecies, and by paying the full penalty of the Law as the Substitute for sinners. (Consequently, believers, by justification, have Christ's righteousness imputed to them; Rom 3:20-26; 10:4.) **Verily I say.** The first use of this impressive formula by Jesus, indicating a statement of utmost importance. **Till heaven and earth pass.** Though regarded by some as idiomatic for *never,* it is probably an eschatological reference (Mt 24:35; Rev 21:1). **Jot.** Smallest letter of the Hebrew alphabet (*yodh*). **Tittle.** Tiny projection on certain Hebrew letters. Those who are not opposed in principle to God's law but have avoided its lesser requirements will not be cast out of the Kingdom but will have a lesser reward **in the kingdom. Your righteousness.** Distinguished from the righteousness of **scribes** and **Pharisees,** which consisted in mere outward, unspiritual conformity to the Mosaic code, even though scrupulously observed. The believer's righteousness is based upon that imputed righteousness of Christ obtained by faith (Rom 3:21,22), which enables him to live righteously (Rom 8:2-5). Only such may **enter into the kingdom** Christ proclaimed.

**21-26. First illustration: murder.** Jesus shows how his fulfillment of the Law went far deeper than mere outward conformity. **Whosover shall kill** marks a traditional enlargement of Ex 20:13, but it still deals only with the act of murder. **The judgment.** The Jewish civil court, as

22. But I say unto you, That whosoever is angry with his brother without a cause shall be in danger of the judgment: and whosoever shall say to his brother, Raca, shall be in danger of the council: but whosoever shall say, Thou fool, shall be in danger of hell fire.

23. Therefore if thou bring thy gift to the altar, and there rememberest that thy brother hath aught against thee;

24. Leave there thy gift before the altar, and go thy way; first be reconciled to thy brother, and then come and offer thy gift.

25. Agree with thine adversary quickly, while thou art in the way with him; lest at any time the adversary deliver thee to the judge, and the judge deliver thee to the officer, and thou be cast into prison.

26. Verily I say unto thee, Thou shalt by no means come out thence, till thou hast paid the uttermost farthing.

27. Ye have heard that it was said by them of old time, Thou shalt not commit adultery:

28. But I say unto you, That whosoever looketh on a woman to lust after her hath committed adultery with her already in his heart.

29. And if thy right eye offend thee, pluck it out, and cast it from thee: for it is profitable for thee that one of thy members should perish, and not that thy whole body should be cast into hell.

30. And if thy right hand offend thee, cut it off, and cast it from thee: for it is profitable for thee that one of thy members should perish, and not that thy whole body should be cast into hell.

31. It hath been said, Whosoever shall put away his wife, let him give her a writing of divorcement:

32. But I say unto you, That whosoever shall put away his wife, saving for the cause of fornication, causeth her to commit adultery: and whosoever shall marry her that is divorced committeth adultery.

based on Deut 16:18 (see also Josephus *Antiq.* iv. 8.14). **Angry.** The best manuscripts omit "without a cause," although Eph 4:26 indicates that some restriction may properly be inferred. **Raca.** Probably "empty head" (from an Aramaic word meaning "empty one"). **Thou fool.** Since this series calls for epithets progressively more severe, Bruce sees **Raca** as contempt for a man's head, and **fool** as contempt for his character (ExpGT, I, 107). **Gehenna of fire.** Literally a reference to the valley of Hinnom outside Jerusalem, where rubbish, offal, and carcasses were burned, and thus a graphic metaphor for the place of eternal torment. (For its gruesome history, see Jer 7:31,32; II Chr 28:3; 33:6; II Kgs 23:10.) Christ locates the root of murder in the heart of the angry man, and promises that in His kingdom swift judgment will be dealt out before murder can result. **At the altar.** Indication of the Jewish coloring of this address. **Hath something against thee,** i.e., if you have wronged your brother. **First be reconciled** obligates the would-be worshiper to make amends with the offended beforehand to make his gift acceptable (cf. Ps 66:18). **Adversary.** An opponent at law (cf. Lk 12:58,59). Since judgment is on the way, offenders should hasten to square accounts. **Till thou hast paid.** Probably a literal situation in the kingdom. If, however, the **prison** is symbolic of hell, the implied possibility of payment and release applies only to the parable, not to its interpretation. Scripture is clear that those in hell are there forever (Mt 25:41, 46), because their debt is unpayable.

27-30. Second illustration: adultery. Jesus indicated that the sin described in Ex 20:14 lies deeper than the overt act. **Every one that looketh** characterizes the man whose glance is not checked by holy restraint, and who forms the impure purpose of lusting after her. The act will follow when opportunity occurs. **Right eye.** To the man who blames the sin on his eye, Jesus shows the logical procedure to follow. As we amputate diseased organs to save lives, so an **eye** (or a **hand**) so hopelessly affected needs drastic treatment. Of course, Jesus wanted his hearers to see that the real source of sin lies not in the physical organ but in the **heart.** A man's evil heart must be changed if he would escape final ruin in **hell** (Gehenna; see comment on 5:22).

31,32. Third illustration: divorce. Mosaic regulation (Deut 24:1) protected woman from man's caprice by insisting on the **certificate of divorce.** Divorce was, however, a concession to human sin (Mt

33. Again, ye have heard that it hath been said by them of old time, Thou shalt not forswear thyself, but shalt perform unto the Lord thine oaths:

34. But I say unto you, Swear not at all; neither by heaven; for it is God's throne:

35. Nor by the earth; for it is his footstool: neither by Jerusalem; for it is the city of the great King.

36. Neither shalt thou swear by thy head, because thou canst not make one hair white or black.

37. But let your communication be, Yea, yea; Nay, nay: for whatsoever is more than these cometh of evil.

38. Ye have heard that it hath been said, An eye for an eye, and a tooth for a tooth:

39. But I say unto you, That ye resist not evil: but whosoever shall smite thee on thy right cheek, turn to him the other also.

19:8). The Mosaic grounds of "uncleanness" had been variously explained, from adultery (Shammai) to the most trivial dislike by the husband (Hillel). In Jewish custom only men could obtain divorces. **Fornication.** Some restrict this term to Jewish custom, as describing unfaithfulness during the betrothal period (cf. Joseph's problem, 1:18,19), and thus find no cause whatever for divorce today. Others see "fornication" as equivalent to "adultery" in this passage, and thus the one cause for divorce allowed by Christ. Certainly there are no grounds beyond this possible exception. **Maketh her an adulteress** (ASV). Understood usually as potential, since she may be forced into another marriage. Since this may not necessarily occur, Lenski treats the difficult passive as *brings about that she is stigmatized as adulterous* (*Interpretation of St. Matthew's Gospel,* pp. 230-235), and regards the sin as an unjust suspicion brought upon the injured party.

**33-37.** Fourth illustration: oaths. The OT basis is Lev 19:12 and Deut 23:21 (cf. Ex 20:7). **Forswear.** Swear falsely, perjure oneself. Jewish abuse of oath-taking caused Jesus to say, **Swear not at all.** It is difficult to find any loopholes in this directive (see also Jas 5:12). Thus no believer should employ an oath to authenticate his statements. Even the state will usually allow an affirmation instead of an oath if requested. **By heaven.** Jews used their ingenuity to classify various oaths, and generally discounted those that did not mention God specifically. Jesus showed that such deceptively subtle reasoning was false, for God is still implicated when men invoke **heaven, earth,** or **Jerusalem;** and even swearing by one's own head implicates the One who holds the power over it. **Let your speech be, Yea, yea** (ASV). A solemn affirmation or denial is sufficient for a believer. **Whatsoever is more than these.** By adding oaths to our statements, we either admit that our usual speech cannot be trusted, or else we lower ourselves to the level of a lying world, that follows **the evil one** (ASV). Cf. Jn 8:44.

**38-42.** Fifth illustration: retaliation. **An eye for an eye** (Ex 21:24). A judicial principle that made the punishment fit the crime. However, it was not intended to permit men to take vengeance into their own hands (Lev 19:18). **Resist not evil.** Probably, "the evil man." Jesus shows the Kingdom citizens how they should respond to personal injury. (He is not discussing government's obligation to maintain order.) A child of God should

40. And if any man will sue thee at the law, and take away thy coat, let him have *thy* cloak also.

41. And whosoever shall compel thee to go a mile, go with him twain.

42. Give to him that asketh thee, and from him that would borrow of thee turn not thou away.

43. Ye have heard that it hath been said, Thou shalt love thy neighbor, and hate thine enemy.

44. But I say unto you, Love your enemies, bless them that curse you, do good to them that hate you, and pray for them which despitefully use you, and persecute you;

45. That ye may be the children of your Father which is in heaven: for he maketh his sun to rise on the evil and on the good, and sendeth rain on the just and on the unjust.

46. For if ye love them which love you, what reward have ye? do not even the publicans the same?

47. And if ye salute your brethren only, what do ye more *than others?* do not even the publicans so?

48. Be ye therefore perfect, even as your Father which is in heaven is perfect.

## CHAPTER 6

TAKE heed that ye do not your alms before men, to be seen of them: otherwise ye have no reward of your Father which is in heaven.

2. Therefore when thou doest *thine* alms, do not sound a trumpet before thee, as the hypocrites do in the synagogues and in the streets, that they may have glory of men. Verily I say unto you, They have their reward.

3. But when thou doest alms, let not thy left hand know what thy right hand doeth:

4. That thine alms may be in secret: and thy Father which seeth in secret himself shall reward thee openly.

willingly suffer loss by assault (v. 39), lawsuits (v. 40), compulsory regulations (v. 41), begging (v. 42 a), and loans (v. 42 b). **Coat.** Undergarment or tunic. **Cloak.** More expensive outer garment, sometimes used as a bed covering (see Ex 22:26,27), and thus could not be held overnight as security for debt (Deut 24:12,13). **Compel thee.** A word of Persian origin, depicting the custom of postal couriers having authority to press persons into service whenever needed (cf. Simon of Cyrene, Mt 27:32). This high standard of conduct should cause all believers to endeavor in so far as possible to live as befits their calling and to long for the day when Christ's righteous rule will make this ideal fully workable in every phase of life.

**43-48.** Sixth illustration: love of enemies. **Thou shalt love thy neighbor** (Lev 19:18,34) summarizes the entire second table of the Law (cf. Mt 22:39). **Hate thine enemy.** This unscriptural addition missed the heart of the law of love; yet it must have been a popular interpretation. The Manual of Discipline from Qumran contains the following rule: ". . . to love all that He has chosen and hate all that He has rejected" (1 QS I. 4). **Love your enemies.** The love (*agapaō*) enjoined is that intelligent love which comprehends the difficulty and extends itself to rescue the enemy from his hate. Such love is akin to God's loving action toward rebellious men (Jn 3:16), and thus is a demonstration that those who so love are true **sons** of their **Father. Publicans.** Jewish collectors of the Roman taxes, hated by their countrymen because of their flagrant extortions and their association with the despised conquerors. The command **Be ye therefore perfect** is to be restricted to the matter of love in this context. As God's love is complete, not omitting any group, so must the child of God strive for maturity in this regard (cf. Eph 5:1,2). This cannot mean sinlessness, for Mt 5:6,7 shows that the blessed ones still hunger for righteousness and need mercy.

d) Attitudes of Kingdom Citizens. 6:1—7:12. Jesus now contrasts the righteous living he expects with the hypocrisy of the Pharisees and their followers (5:20).

**1-4.** First example: alms. **Alms.** Verse 1 has **righteousness** in the better texts, and is introductory to the entire discussion. Practical righteousness is in view here. **Before men.** Although we are commanded to let our light shine (5:16), deeds of righteousness must not be done for self-glorification (**to be seen of them**).

5. And when thou prayest, thou shalt not be as the hypocrites *are:* for they love to pray standing in the synagogues and in the corners of the streets, that they may be seen of men. Verily I say unto you, They have their reward.

6. But thou, when thou prayest, enter into thy closet, and when thou hast shut thy door, pray to thy Father which is in secret; and thy Father which seeth in secret shall reward thee openly.

7. But when ye pray, use not vain repetitions, as the heathen *do:* for they think that they shall be heard for their much speaking.

8. Be not ye therefore like unto them: for your Father knoweth what things ye have need of, before ye ask him.

9. After this manner therefore pray ye: Our Father which art in heaven, Hallowed be thy name.

10. Thy kingdom come. Thy will be done in earth, as *it is* in heaven.

11. Give us this day our daily bread.

Alms is proper in verse 2 and denotes charitable giving. **Sound a trumpet.** Metaphorical for "publicize." **Hypocrites.** From the Greek word for actors playing a part. **They have their reward in full.** Commercial use of this word indicates full payment with a receipt. Showy righteousness has received its full payment; God will add nothing to it. Those content to do their giving secretly shall be rewarded, not by man's applause, but by their heavenly **Father.** Omit openly.

**5-15.** Second example: prayer. **Standing in the synagogues.** This was the usual manner (Mk 11:25) and place for prayer and is not denounced. But the intent of one who claims that the hour of prayer caught him in a prominent place and who loves such display is condemned. **Enter into thy closet.** Public prayer is not pronounced wrong (Jesus himself prayed publicly, Lk 10:21,22; Jn 11:41,42), but vain display is. Private praying is the finest training ground for public prayer. Omit **openly. Vain repetitions** (i.e., *babbling speech*) are characteristic of pagan (heathen or **Gentile**) praying, as ostentation is of **hypocrites.** Such action regards prayer as an effort to overcome God's unwillingness to respond by wearying him with words. Yet it is not mere length nor repetition that Christ condemns (Jesus prayed all night, Lk 6:12, and repeated his petitions, Mt 26:44), but the unworthy motive that prompts such religious acts.

Jesus proceeds to give an example of a suitable prayer, which is a marvel of broad scope and brevity. Though it was certainly not intended to be recited superstitiously (the very action Christ was decrying, v. 7), and it does not embody all of his teaching about prayer (cf. Jn 16:23,24), yet it can be prayed (not just recited) with sincerity by all true believers. Christians, of course, will realize in view of later revelation that the prayer is possible on the basis of Christ's merits.

**Our Father.** A form of address not common in OT prayers, but precious to all NT believers. The first three petitions of the prayer concern God and his program; the last four, man and his needs. **Hallowed.** Here the meaning is, "be held in reverence, treated as holy." **Thy kingdom come.** The Messianic kingdom. Not only Jews but all believers in Christ should have a vital interest in its arrival.

**Our daily bread.** This first request for personal needs employs a term, **daily,** found only once in secular Greek (Arndt, p. 296). Opinions of its meaning vary among "daily," "necessary for existence," and "for the coming day." There is no strong

12. And forgive us our debts, as we forgive our debtors.

13. And lead us not into temptation, but deliver us from evil: For thine is the kingdom, and the power, and the glory, for ever. Amen.

14. For if ye forgive men their trespasses, your heavenly Father will also forgive you:

15. But if ye forgive not men their trespasses, neither will your Father forgive your trespasses.

16. Moreover when ye fast, be not, as the hypocrites, of a sad countenance: for they disfigure their faces, that they may appear unto men to fast. Verily I say unto you, They have their reward.

17. But thou, when thou fastest, anoint thine head, and wash thy face;

18. That thou appear not unto men to fast, but unto thy Father which is in secret: and thy Father which seeth in secret shall reward thee openly.

19. Lay not up for yourselves treasures upon earth, where moth and rust doth corrupt, and where thieves break through and steal:

20. But lay up for yourselves treasures in heaven, where neither moth nor rust doth corrupt, and where thieves do not break through nor steal:

21. For where your treasure is, there will your heart be also.

22. The light of the body is the eye: if therefore thine eye be single, thy whole body shall be full of light.

23. But if thine eye be evil, thy whole body shall be full of darkness. If therefore the light that is in thee be darkness, how great is that darkness!

24. No man can serve two masters: for either he will hate the one, and love the other; or else he will hold to the one, and despise the other. Ye cannot serve God and mammon.

reason to change the AV, ASV, or RSV, however. **Forgive us our debts.** Sins viewed as moral and spiritual debts to God's righteousness. These are not the sins of the unregenerate (only disciples are taught this prayer), but of believers, who need to confess them. **As we forgive.** Forgiveness of sin, whether under Mosaic law or in the Church, is always by God's grace and based on Christ's atonement. However, the case of a believer confessing his sin and asking God's forgiveness while withholding forgiveness from someone else is not only incongruous but hypocritical. A forgiving spirit is made easier for Christians when they consider how much God has already forgiven (Eph 4:32). An unforgiving spirit is sin, and should itself be confessed. **Lead us not into temptation.** Cf. Jas 1:13,14; Lk 22:40. A plea that God, in his providence, will spare the supplicant from needless temptations. The doxology in 6:13 b is a liturgical interpolation from I Chr 29:11.

**16-18.** Third example: fasting. **When ye fast.** Mosaic law (under which Christ's hearers lived) prescribed one fast annually, the Day of Atonement (Lev 16:29, "afflict your souls"). Phariseeism added two fasts weekly, on Mondays and Thursdays, and used them as occasions for public displays of piety. The true function of fasting, however, was to indicate deep contrition, and the temporary devoting of all one's energies to prayer and spiritual communion. But fasting that requires spectators is mere acting. Jesus instituted no fasts for his disciples, though voluntary fasting appears occasionally in the apostolic church (Acts 13:2.3).

**19-24.** Fourth example: wealth. A common error of Phariseeism and Judaism in general was the undue emphasis upon material wealth as evidence of God's approval. Jesus explained that **treasures upon earth** are fleeting, being subject to loss from **moth** (cf. raiment, v. 25), **eating** (a more likely translation of *brōsis*, cf. meat, v. 25), and **thieves.** The Kingdom citizen should rather store up **treasures in heaven** by concentration upon righteousness (see v. 33). **The lamp of the body,** that which receives and dispenses the light, **is the eye.** If the **eye,** used here figuratively for one's spiritual understanding, be **single** (opposite of "twofold"), not afflicted with double vision in this matter of treasures—an affliction which is **evil**—then the individual can regard riches in their proper perspective. The impossibility of serving two masters in a slave relationship is a graphic illustration. **Mammon.** Though its derivation is uncertain, it appears to

25. Therefore I say unto you, Take no thought for your life, what ye shall eat, or what ye shall drink; nor yet for your body, what ye shall put on. Is not the life more than meat, and the body than raiment?

26. Behold the fowls of the air: for they sow not, neither do they reap, nor gather into barns; yet your heavenly Father feedeth them. Are ye not much better than they?

27. Which of you by taking thought can add one cubit unto his stature?

28. And why take ye thought for raiment? Consider the lilies of the field, how they grow; they toil not, neither do they spin:

29. And yet I say unto you, That even Solomon in all his glory was not arrayed like one of these.

30. Wherefore, if God so clothe the grass of the field, which to-day is, and to-morrow is cast into the oven, *shall he* not much more *clothe* you, O ye of little faith?

31. Therefore take no thought, saying, What shall we eat? or, What shall we drink? or, Wherewithal shall we be clothed?

32. (For after all these things do the Gentiles seek:) for your heavenly Father knoweth that ye have need of all these things.

33. But seek ye first the kingdom of God, and his righteousness; and all these things shall be added unto you.

34. Take therefore no thought for the morrow: for the morrow shall take thought for the things of itself. Sufficient unto the day *is* the evil thereof.

## CHAPTER 7

JUDGE not, that ye be not judged.

be an Aramaic word for wealth, here personified. Note that Jesus condemns not wealth but enslavement to wealth.

**25-34. Fifth example: anxiety.** Those without wealth may fall victims to faithless worry. Hence the natural transition. **Take no thought.** Not a prohibition of foresight and planning (cf. I Tim 5:8; Prov 6:6-8; 30:25), but of anxiety over daily needs. **Is not the life more than meat?** Since life itself and the body were provided by God, shall we not trust him to provide that which is less important? Since God provides sustenance for birds that have not ability to sow, reap, and store, how much more can men, who have been provided with these abilities, trust their heavenly Father! **Add one cubit unto his stature.** Food is essential to growth. Yet even here God controls. As a child grows to maturity, God adds much more than **one cubit** (about eighteen inches), but anxiety can only hinder and not help. Some wish to translate **span of life** rather than **stature**, and attempt to find instances of **cubit** as a measure of time. However, the former interpretation fits the passage well. **Lilies.** What particular flowers are denoted by this word is uncertain, but they must have been in bloom on this occasion, since Jesus refers to **one of these. Solomon.** The most magnificent Hebrew king. **Grass of the field.** The lilies just mentioned, the beauty of which is short-lived, and which soon find themselves cut with the grasses and used for fuel for man's needs in the baking **oven** (Jas 1:11). **O ye of little faith.** An expression used four times in Matthew, once in Luke, as an encouragement to growth in faith as well as a gentle reproof. **The Gentiles seek.** A reference to the attention of Gentiles to material things because they know not God as a heavenly Father (cf. 6:7,8). **Seek ye first.** Christ's hearers, who had already given allegiance to the King, must continue seeking (durative verb) the Kingdom by concentrating upon spiritual values and resting their full confidence in God; and God who knew their temporal needs would supply what was necessary. **The morrow will be anxious for itself** (ASV). A striking personification. **Sufficient unto the day is the evil.** This evil is clearly physical, referring to the problems that may arise. It is senseless to add tomorrow's cares to those of today.

**7:1-12. Sixth example: judging others. Judge not.** The present imperative suggests that it is the habit of judging others that is condemned. Though the word **judge** is itself neutral as to the verdict, the sense here indicates an unfavorable

2. For with what judgment ye judge, ye shall be judged: and with what measure ye mete, it shall be measured to you again.

3. And why beholdest thou the mote that is in thy brother's eye, but considerest not the beam that is in thine own eye?

4. Or how wilt thou say to thy brother, Let me pull out the mote out of thine eye; and, behold, a beam *is* in thine own eye?

5. Thou hypocrite, first cast out the beam out of thine own eye; and then shalt thou see clearly to cast out the mote out of thy brother's eye.

6. Give not that which is holy unto the dogs, neither cast ye your pearls before swine, lest they trample them under their feet, and turn again and rend you.

7. Ask, and it shall be given you; seek, and ye shall find; knock, and it shall be opened unto you:

8. For every one that asketh receiveth; and he that seeketh findeth; and to him that knocketh it shall be opened.

9. Or what man is there of you, whom if his son ask bread, will he give him a stone?

10. Or if he ask a fish, will he give him a serpent?

11. If ye then, being evil, know how to give good gifts unto your children, how much more shall your Father which is in heaven give good things to them that ask him?

12. Therefore all things whatsoever ye would that men should do to you, do ye even so to them: for this is the law and the prophets.

judgment. Critics of others must stop short of final condemnation, for men cannot judge motives, as God can (cf. Jas 4:11,12). Believers are not to avoid all judging (cf. 7:6,16), for Christians need to judge themselves and offending members (I Cor 5:3-5,12,13). **That ye be not judged.** The aorist subjunctive form is better understood of God's judgment than of human judgment (cf. 6:14,15). **Mote.** A speck of straw or chaff, or a splinter of wood. **Beam.** A log or plank, used of the main beam of a roof or floor; here it represents a censorious spirit. The illustration is intentionally exaggerated to show the ludicrous position of one who sets himself up to judge others. Such a person is termed **hypocrite**, for he pretends to act as a physician, when he is really ailing himself. This command does not relieve believers from making moral distinctions, however. Those who have heard the Gospel and the invitation of Christ, and by their response have shown their nature to be unalterably vicious (**dogs** and **swine** were particularly repulsive to Jesus' audience), must not be allowed to treat these precious things as cheap (cf. 13:11-15).

The following verses on prayer (cf. Lk 11:9-13) answer the believer's problems arising from the instructions on judging. The need of discerning between dogs and swine while avoiding the beam in the eye demands wisdom from above. Hence Jesus encourages his followers to **ask, seek,** and **knock,** that their deficiencies may be met from the divine supply. The three imperatives are in climactic order, and their durative forms suggest not only perseverance but frequent prayer for any and all needs. There is a certain rough resemblance between a **loaf** (small round cake of bread) and a **stone,** and between a **fish** and a **serpent,** but no father would practice such deception upon a hungry child. **Being evil.** A reference to man's sinfulness (even disciples have this sinful nature). **Good things** is replaced in Lk 11:13 (another occasion) by the **Holy Spirit,** the Bestower of all good. **Therefore.** Verse 12 applies the foregoing instruction. Though evil by nature, we are still acknowledged by God as his children and promised answers to prayer. Hence, rather than judging others, we are to treat them as we would like to be treated. This summary of the OT (**the law and the prophets**) is restatement of the second table of the Law (Mt 22:36-40; Rom 13:8-10), and rests upon the first, for man's relation to God is always basic to his relation to his fellows.

13. Enter ye in at the strait gate: for wide *is* the gate, and broad *is* the way, that leadeth to destruction, and many there be which go in thereat:

14. Because strait *is* the gate, and narrow *is* the way, which leadeth unto life, and few there be that find it.

15. Beware of false prophets, which come to you in sheep's clothing, but inwardly they are ravening wolves.

16. Ye shall know them by their fruits. Do men gather grapes of thorns, or figs of thistles?

17. Even so every good tree bringeth forth good fruit; but a corrupt tree bringeth forth evil fruit.

18. A good tree cannot bring forth evil fruit, neither *can* a corrupt tree bring forth good fruit.

19. Every tree that bringeth not forth good fruit is hewn down, and cast into the fire.

20. Wherefore by their fruits ye shall know them.

21. Not every one that saith unto me, Lord, Lord, shall enter into the kingdom of heaven; but he that doeth the will of my Father which is in heaven.

22. Many will say to me in that day, Lord, Lord, have we not prophesied in thy name? and in thy name have cast out devils? and in thy name done many wonderful works?

23. And then will I profess unto them, I never knew you: depart from me, ye that work iniquity.

e) Concluding Exhortations to Kingdom Citizens. 7:13-27.

**13,14. Enter ye in by the narrow gate** (ASV). To those who had already entered by faith into relation with Christ (as well as others who were listening; v. 28), our Lord describes the comparative unpopularity of their new position. The order of **gate** and **way** suggests the gate as the entrance to the way, symbolic of a believer's initial experience with Christ, which introduces him to the life of godliness. The first Christians were called those of "the Way" (Acts 9:2; 19:9,23; 22:4; 24:14,22). Though the mass of mankind is upon the **broad way** that leads to **destruction** (eternal ruin), the other **gate** and **way** are so small as to need **finding**. Yet the same God who provided Christ, who is both gate and way (Jn 14:6), also causes men to find the portal (Jn 6:44). **Life.** Here a contrasting parallel to **destruction** and thus a reference to the blessed state in heaven, though this eternal life begins at regeneration.

**15-20.** Those who enter upon the narrow way must beware of **false prophets,** who claim to guide believers but really practice deception. **Sheep's clothing** is not to be regarded as prophets' garb, but is an evident contrast to vicious **wolves.** God's people in all ages have needed to beware of deceptive leaders (Deut 13:1; Acts 20:29; I Jn 4:1; Rev 13:11-14). **By their fruits.** The doctrines produced by these false prophets, rather than the works they perform, since outward appearances may not cause suspicion. The test of the prophet is his conformity to Scripture (I Cor 14:37; Deut 13:1-5). **Corrupt tree.** One that is decayed, worthless, unusable. The worthlessness of such a tree calls for its swift removal from the orchard lest it infect the others.

**21-23.** Jesus solemnly implies his divine Sonship (**my Father**) and his position as Judge (**will say to me in that day**), and warns that false leaders (those who have **prophesied** in Christ's name, **cast out demons,** and performed many **wonderful works**) will be fully unmasked and judged. The mere performance of spectacular deeds (even supernatural ones) is not necessarily divine authentication (Deut 13:1-5; II Thess 2:8-12; Mt 24:24). The judgment to occur **in that day** will determine who **shall enter into the kingdom of heaven** (Mt 25:31-46). Though the specific reference must be to those still living at the establishment of the Millennial kingdom (otherwise they would be among the wicked dead who are not raised until after the Millennium, Rev 20:5), the result is

24. Therefore whosoever heareth these sayings of mine, and doeth them, I will liken him unto a wise man, which built his house upon a rock:

25. And the rain descended, and the floods came, and the winds blew, and beat upon that house; and it fell not: for it was founded upon a rock.

26. And every one that heareth these sayings of mine, and doeth them not, shall be likened unto a foolish man, which built his house upon the sand:

27. And the rain descended, and the floods came, and the winds blew, and beat upon that house; and it fell: and great was the fall of it.

28. And it came to pass, when Jesus had ended these sayings, the people were astonished at his doctrine:

29. For he taught them as one having authority, and not as the scribes.

## CHAPTER 8

WHEN he was come down from the mountain, great multitudes followed him.

2. And, behold, there came a leper and worshipped him, saying, Lord, if thou wilt, thou canst make me clean.

3. And Jesus put forth his hand, and touched him, saying, I will; be thou clean. And immediately his leprosy was cleansed.

4. And Jesus saith unto him, See thou tell no man; but go thy way, show thyself to the priest, and offer the gift that Moses commanded, for a testimony unto them.

the same to both groups; and thus the warning is pertinent. **I never knew you.** In the intensive sense of *know with favor,* or *acknowledge* (cf. Ps 1:6; Amos 3:2).

**24-27.** The supreme importance of building upon the right foundation. The man whose house collapsed was at fault not because he failed to labor, but because he did not use the rock. Christ himself (I Cor 3:11) and his teaching. **These sayings of mine.** Chapters 5–7. **Doeth them.** Obedience to the teaching. The sermon is addressed to believers and presupposes faith in Jesus as Messiah. This is not legalism. No works founded upon mere human effort are of any spiritual value, but faith in Christ **the rock** brings about that regeneration which manifests itself in godly living.

**28,29. When Jesus had ended these sayings.** Lenski notes the correctness of Matthew's psychological observation. As Jesus spoke, the crowds were in rapt attention; but when he ceased, tension relaxed and amazement engulfed them (*Interpretation of St. Matthew's Gospel,* p. 314). **Not as the scribes** calls attention to the fact that the scribes, in lecturing, appealed repeatedly to the opinions of distinguished rabbis and to traditional interpretations. How tedious compared to Christ's authoritative, "I say unto you"! (5:18,20,22, *et al.)*

5) Ten Miracles and Related Events. 8:1–9:38. The narratives of these two chapters are topically arranged, and the order differs somewhat from that of Mark and Luke. However, Matthew's description of the cleansing of the leper as immediately following the Sermon on the Mount must be chronological (cf. 8:1), whereas neither Mark nor Luke is specific as to its time.

**8:1-4.** Cleansing of a leper. **Leper.** For a description of Biblical leprosy see Lev 13,14, and the Bible dictionaries. In the OT this loathsome disease was made symbolic of sin's effect upon man. (The laws were not primarily hygienic, for one completely covered with leprosy could be pronounced clean; Lev 13:12,13.) **Worshipped him.** The faith in Jesus' power demonstrated by the leper (**If thou wilt;** not "If thou canst") shows his prostrate worship to have been religious, not Eastern courtesy. **Touched him.** An act simultaneous with Jesus' healing statement, and thus not ceremonially defiling. **Tell no man.** Not to avoid publicity, since **great multitudes** witnessed the miracle, but to prevent premature notice from reaching the **priest,** lest he be prejudiced against the man. Christ wanted the cleans-

5. And when Jesus was entered into Capernaum, there came unto him a centurion, beseeching him,

6. And saying, Lord, my servant lieth at home sick of the palsy, grievously tormented.

7. And Jesus saith unto him, I will come and heal him.

8. The centurion answered and said, Lord, I am not worthy that thou shouldest come under my roof: but speak the word only, and my servant shall be healed.

9. For I am a man under authority, having soldiers under me: and I say to this *man*, Go, and he goeth; and to another, Come, and he cometh; and to my servant, Do this, and he doeth *it*.

10. When Jesus heard *it*, he marveled, and said to them that followed, Verily I say unto you, I have not found so great faith, no, not in Israel.

11. And I say unto you, That many shall come from the east and west, and shall sit down with Abraham, and Isaac, and Jacob, in the kingdom of heaven:

12. But the children of the kingdom shall be cast out into outer darkness: there shall be weeping and gnashing of teeth.

13. And Jesus said unto the centurion, Go thy way; and as thou hast believed, *so* be it done unto thee. And his servant was healed in the selfsame hour.

14. And when Jesus was come into Peter's house, he saw his wife's mother laid, and sick of a fever.

15. And he touched her hand, and the fever left her: and she arose, and ministered unto them.

16. When the even was come, they brought unto him many that were possessed with devils: and he cast out the spirits with *his* word, and healed all that were sick:

17. That it might be fulfilled which was spoken by Esaias the prophet, saying, Himself took our infirmities, and bare *our* sicknesses.

ing officially pronounced first, so that the explanation would be a testimony unto them (i.e., the antagonistic priests). Unfortunately, the man disregarded the caution and thereby caused Christ much inconvenience (Mk 1:45).

**5-13.** Healing of a centurion's servant. **Centurion.** Luke indicates that he made his appeal to Jesus through Jewish elders and other friends (Lk 7:1-10). Centurions are uniformly pictured in the NT as men of good character (Mt 27:54; Acts 10:22; 27:3,43; *et al.*). This man was probably a Gentile commander in the forces of Herod Antipas, who kept foreign troops (Jos *Antiq.* xvii. 8.3). **Sick of the palsy.** The Greek *paralytikos* denoted paralysis caused by a variety of diseases affecting muscles and organs of the body. **I am not worthy.** This Gentile, perhaps not even a proselyte (though he had built a Jewish synagogue, Lk 7:5) thought it presumptuous to ask Jesus to come to his house. **I am a man under authority.** The meaning is: If this minor officer could issue orders to his subordinates, how much more could Christ, who possesses all authority, give a command that His will be done. **He marvelled.** An indication that the omniscience of Christ's divine nature did not prevent normal human responses. In spite of Israel's wealth of revelation, it was a Gentile whose faith in Christ's authority glowed most brightly. Thus Jesus announces that his Messianic kingdom shall be enjoyed by many who are not Jews. **Shall sit down with Abraham.** The figure of a banquet is often used of the Kingdom (Isa 25:6; Lk 14:15-24). **The sons** (or *children*) **of the kingdom.** Jews, who were the recipients of the prophecies and thus the original heirs, are here told that without true faith mere race is not sufficient qualification for Christ's kingdom. **Outer darkness.** The darkness outside the lighted banquet hall (cf. 22:13). **As thou hast believed.** The man believed Jesus could heal at a distance, and so He did.

**14-17.** Healing of Peter's mother-in-law and others. **When Jesus was come.** From a synagogue service (Lk 4:38; Mk 1:29). **Sick of a fever.** With guests expected, this illness must have greatly distressed the household. **Ministered unto them.** The healing was complete, without gradual recuperation. The suggestion that Peter's wife was dead, since his mother-in-law did the serving, contradicts I Cor 9:5. **When the even was come.** At sundown, the Sabbath being past, many sick and demonpossessed were brought for healing. **Bare our diseases.** Matthew 9:6 shows that Christ's healing of disease (one of sin's ef-

18. Now when Jesus saw great multitudes about him, he gave commandment to depart unto the other side.

19. And a certain scribe came, and said unto him, Master, I will follow thee whithersoever thou goest.

20. And Jesus saith unto him, The foxes have holes, and the birds of the air *have* nests; but the Son of man hath not where to lay *his* head.

21. And another of his disciples said unto him, Lord, suffer me first to go and bury my father.

22. But Jesus said unto him, Follow me; and let the dead bury their dead.

23. And when he was entered into a ship, his disciples followed him.

24. And, behold, there arose a great tempest in the sea, insomuch that the ship was covered with the waves: but he was asleep.

25. And his disciples came to *him*, and awoke him, saying, Lord, save us: we perish.

26. And he saith unto them, Why are ye fearful, O ye of little faith? Then he arose, and rebuked the winds and the sea; and there was a great calm.

27. But the men marveled, saying, What manner of man is this, that even the winds and the sea obey him!

fects) indicated his competence to deal with its ultimate cause. Thus these healings were a partial fulfillment of Isa 53:4 (see ASV and RSV margins), which was completed at Calvary when the sin of man was borne by Christ.

**18-22. Interview with prospective followers.** The chronological connection of this passage is complicated by the Lukan parallel (9:57 ff.), which places it much later. Perhaps the first interview occurred as Jesus prepared to embark, and Matthew adds the later incident to the same paragraph, whereas Luke groups three similar incidents at the occasion of one of the others. **One, a scribe.** Though few of these religious scholars were favorably attracted to Christ (cf. Mk 12:28-34; contrast Lk 11:53,54), this man offered to become a permanent disciple. Jesus evidently saw in this proposal, however, a failure to estimate fully the rigors of true discipleship. **Son of man.** A title understood by the Jews of Messiah (Jn 12:34), and as equivalent to "Son of God" (Lk 22:69,70). It was Christ's usual designation of himself, apparently derived from Dan 7:13,14. **Suffer me first to go and bury my father.** This man, already a disciple, was asked by Jesus to follow him (Lk 9:59). Having just received word of his father's death, he requested a delay. The suggestion that the man's father was still alive (since Jewish burials occurred on the day of death, and the small delay would not warrant Christ's reply) does not lessen the difficulty, for among the Jews a man's responsibility to an aged parent was as great as his duty to the dead. Jesus saw in the man's hesitation a weakness of allegiance. **Leave the dead to bury their own dead** (ASV). When Christ calls a man for a specific task (Lk 9:60), the disciple must sometimes forego what otherwise he would perform. Those who are spiritually dead are capable of caring for the physically dead.

**23-27. Stilling of the storm. Great tempest.** The word usually used for "earthquake" is employed here, perhaps connoting the turbulence of the water, a violence causing terror even to experienced sailors. Violent storms are not unknown on Galilee (W.M. Thomson, *The Land and the Book*, p. 347). **Why are ye fearful** (*deiloi*) shows their fear to be cowardly, indicative of **little faith.** Had not Jesus commanded this trip to the other side (Lk 8:22)? Yet their turning to him in extremity shows a root of faith which could be developed. **Rebuked the winds and the sea.** Christ commanded not only the winds, but also the sea, which otherwise would have continued billowing for some time.

28. And when he was come to the other side into the country of the Gergesenes, there met him two possessed with devils, coming out of the tombs, exceeding fierce, so that no man might pass by that way.

29. And, behold, they cried out, saying, What have we to do with thee, Jesus, thou Son of God? art thou come hither to torment us before the time?

30. And there was a good way off from them a herd of many swine feeding.

31. So the devils besought him, saying, If thou cast us out, suffer us to go away into the herd of swine.

32. And he said unto them, Go. And when they were come out, they went into the herd of swine: and, behold, the whole herd of swine ran violently down a steep place into the sea, and perished in the waters.

33. And they that kept them fled, and went their ways into the city, and told every thing, and what was befallen to the possessed of the devils.

34. And, behold, the whole city came out to meet Jesus: and when they saw him, they besought him that he would depart out of their coasts.

## CHAPTER 9

AND he entered into a ship, and passed over, and came into his own city.

2. And, behold, they brought to him a man sick of the palsy, lying on a bed: and Jesus seeing their faith said unto the sick of the palsy; Son, be of good cheer; thy sins be forgiven thee.

3. And, behold, certain of the scribes said within themselves, This man blasphemeth.

4. And Jesus knowing their thoughts said, Wherefore think ye evil in your hearts?

5. For whether is easier, to say, Thy sins be forgiven thee; or to say, Arise, and walk?

**28-34.** Healing of two demon-possessed men (cf. Mk 5:1-20; Lk 8:26-39). **Country of the Gadarenes** (ASV). So called from the city of Gadara to the southeast. Mark and Luke have "Gerasenes" (ASV), from the village named Khersa (Gerasa)—now in ruins on the lake shore—which was perhaps in the district belonging to Gadara. **Two possessed with demons.** The other Synoptists mention only the more prominent one of the two. Demoniacs in the NT are pictured neither as gross sinners nor as victims of insanity (though demonism may produce such effects), but as persons whose minds have come under the control of an evil spirit or spirits. That such phenomena should be especially prominent during the days of Christ's earthly ministry is consistent with Satan's efforts to counteract God's program. Demons knew exactly who Jesus was (**thou Son of God**), were aware that their ultimate doom was sure (**the time,** v. 29), and always gave Christ absolute obedience. The owners of the **herd of swine** were probably Jews, who were thus violating Mosaic law—at least in spirit—in this Jewish territory (under Herod Philip). Hence they brought no legal action against Jesus for the loss. Why this strange request of the demons? Perhaps it was to grasp at one last chance to avoid confinement in the abyss (Lk 8:31; Rev 20:1-3). But the swine, by stampeding into the waters, thwarted whatever purpose the demons may have entertained. **They besought him that he would depart.** This request, arising from fear (Lk 8:37), came from the populace, not just from the owners. Awe-struck but unrepentant, they wanted no more of Christ.

**9:1-8.** Healing of a paralytic (cf. Mk 2:1-12; Lk 5:17-26). **His own city.** Capernaum (Mk 2:1; Mt 4:13). **Sick of the palsy.** This paralytic was lowered through the roof by four friends because of the density of the crowd (Mk 2:3,4). **Seeing their faith.** This includes the faith of the sick man, since forgiveness of sins is given only to those with faith (though healing was sometimes granted before faith was present). **Thy sins are forgiven** (ASV). In this case, the man's condition seems either to have been the direct result of sin or else to have caused him to reflect most seriously upon his sinfulness. **This man blasphemeth.** The charge by the **scribes** and Pharisees, here seen opposing Jesus in Galilee for the first time, condemned him for taking to himself the prerogatives of God (Lk 5:21). **Which is easier?** An unanswerable question. The statements are equally simple to pronounce; but to say either, with accompany-

28

6. But that ye may know that the Son of man hath power on earth to forgive sins, (then saith he to the sick of the palsy,) Arise, take up thy bed, and go unto thine house.

7. And he arose, and departed to his house.

8. But when the multitudes saw *it*, they marveled, and glorified God, which had given such power unto men.

9. And as Jesus passed forth from thence, he saw a man, named Matthew, sitting at the receipt of custom: and he saith unto him, Follow me. And he arose, and followed him.

10. And it came to pass, as Jesus sat at meat in the house, behold, many publicans and sinners came and sat down with him and his disciples.

11. And when the Pharisees saw *it*, they said unto his disciples, Why eateth your master with publicans and sinners?

12. But when Jesus heard *that*, he said unto them, They that be whole need not a physician, but they that are sick.

13. But go ye and learn what *that* meaneth, I will have mercy, and not sacrifice: for I am not come to call the righteous, but sinners to repentance.

14. Then came to him the disciples of John, saying, Why do we and the Pharisees fast oft, but thy disciples fast not?

15. And Jesus said unto them, Can the children of the bridechamber mourn, as long as the bridegroom is with them? but the days will come, when the bridegroom shall be taken from them, and then shall they fast.

16. No man putteth a piece of new cloth unto an old garment; for that which is put in to fill it up taketh from the garment, and the rent is made worse.

17. Neither do men put new wine into old bottles: else the bottles break, and the wine runneth out, and the bottles perish: but they put new wine into new bottles, and both are preserved.

ing performance, requires divine power. An imposter, of course, in seeking to avoid detection, would find the former easier. Jesus proceeded to heal the illness that men might know that he had authority to deal with its cause, thus foreshadowing the atonement. **Had given such power unto men.** Christ's authoritative forgiving and healing regarded as divine gifts to mankind.

**9-13.** Call of Matthew, and the feast in his house. All the Synoptics record this incident as following the healing of the paralytic. **Matthew.** Also called *Levi* (Mk 2:14; Lk 5:27). **Sitting at the place of toll** (ASV). Capernaum (9:1) was situated near the highway that led from Damascus to the coastal cities, and was thus a favorable spot for collecting duties on goods shipped by road or across the Sea of Galilee. Edersheim describes from rabbinic sources the vexatious taxes that were exacted, and the classifications of taxgatherers, of which Matthew, as a customhouse officer, was of the worst kind (*Life and Times of Jesus,* I, 515-518). **He arose and followed him.** This act marked a complete break with the past; there could be no turning back. His position would be filled by another, and to find new employment would be difficult for a publican. **As Jesus sat at meat in the house.** This feast in Matthew's house (Lk 5:29) was held perhaps some time after his call. To it he invited **publicans and sinners,** his former associates who were living contrary to God's will as revealed in the OT. Doubtless he invited them so that Jesus might win them to himself. To the **Pharisees,** who drew the most rigid distinctions and regarded themselves as righteous, Jesus responded that his ministry was needed by **sinners,** just as a physician['s] services are needed by the sick. **The righteous.** Jesus used the Pharisees' estimate of themselves to answer their objection. **I will have mercy and not sacrifice** (Hos 6:6). A merciful attitude toward the spiritually needy is far better than the mere formality of religious duties (**sacrifice**) without concern for others.

**14-17.** This interview with the **disciples of John** must also have occurred at Matthew's feast (note close connection in Lk 5:33). **Pharisees fast oft.** To the one annual Scriptural fast (Day of Atonement) had been added fasts each Monday and Thursday, observed by Pharisees and others, including John's disciples (Lk 5:33). Christ's reply recalled John's own statement (Jn 3:29), likening our Lord's ministry to a wedding feast. **Sons of the bridechamber.** The attendants of the bridegroom who assist him. When Christ

18. While he spake these things unto them, behold, there came a certain ruler, and worshipped him, saying, My daughter is even now dead: but come and lay thy hand upon her, and she shall live.

19. And Jesus arose, and followed him, and *so did* his disciples.

20. And, behold, a woman, which was diseased with an issue of blood twelve years, came behind *him*, and touched the hem of his garment:

21. For she said within herself, If I may but touch his garment, I shall be whole.

22. But Jesus turned him about, and when he saw her, he said, Daughter, be of good comfort; thy faith hath made thee whole. And the woman was made whole from that hour.

23. And when Jesus came into the ruler's house, and saw the minstrels and the people making a noise,

24. He said unto them, Give place: for the maid is not dead, but sleepeth. And they laughed him to scorn.

25. But when the people were put forth, he went in, and took her by the hand, and the maid arose.

26. And the fame hereof went abroad into all that land.

27. And when Jesus departed thence, two blind men followed him, crying, and saying, *Thou* Son of David, have mercy on us.

28. And when he was come into the house, the blind men came to him: and Jesus saith unto them, Believe ye that I am able to do this? They said unto him, Yea, Lord.

29. Then touched he their eyes, saying, According to your faith be it unto you.

30. And their eyes were opened; and Jesus straitly charged them, saying, See *that* no man know *it*.

31. But they, when they were departed, spread abroad his fame in all that country.

the Bridegroom shall be taken away by violent death, then shall they fast. True fasting results from sorrow (note **mourn**), not from ritual. **A piece of undressed cloth** (ASV). A patch of unsized or unshrunken material, when the whole garment was washed, would shrink and tear away the material to which it was sewed. **New wine,** having not yet fermented, would burst **old wineskins** which no longer had elasticity. Thus Christ and his message were much more than contemporary Judaism patched up or rejuvenated.

**18-26.** Healing of a woman with hemorrhage, and raising of a ruler's daughter. **Ruler.** One of the synagogue rulers, named Jairus, probably of Capernaum (Mk 5:21,22). **My daughter is even now dead.** Matthew has summarized several details. Mark and Luke record that Jairus first said she was dying, and later was informed by messengers that she had died. **She shall live.** Though his faith was less than the centurion's (8:8), it was nevertheless remarkable. En route to the house of Jairus, Jesus was approached from behind by a woman **suffering from hemorrhage** (or AV, *diseased with an issue of blood*) for twelve years. This ailment was ceremonially defiling (Lev 15:19-30), a fact that may explain her action. **The border of his garment** (ASV). Probably the tassel on each of the four corners of his outer garment, worn by Israelites in accordance with Num 15:38 and Deut 22:12. Again Matthew condenses the account but notes that Jesus made clear to the woman that **faith,** not the tassel, had obtained this cure. Jesus proceeded to the house where death had occurred. Already **the flute-players** (ASV) and other mourners had gathered for the ancient funeral pageantry (Jer 9:17; 48:36). **The maid is not dead but sleepeth.** Compare Jesus' similar statement regarding Lazarus (Jn 11:11,14). The statement is neither a mistaken opinion of Jesus, nor a literal truth that she was merely unconscious, nor an argument that death is soul sleep. Rather it was spoken in the light of what he was going to do. **This news** spread throughout the region, in spite of Christ's warning against publicity (Mk 5:43; Lk 8:56).

**27-31.** Healing of two blind men. This narrative and the next are peculiar to Matthew. **Thou Son of David.** A Messianic designation. Since at this time Jesus was avoiding public titles that would be regarded as political, he did not acknowledge these blind men until all had entered the house. **According to your faith be it done unto you** (ASV). Cf. 8:13. The recog-

32. As they went out, behold, they brought to him a dumb man possessed with a devil.

33. And when the devil was cast out, the dumb spake: and the multitudes marveled, saying, It was never so seen in Israel.

34. But the Pharisees said, He casteth out devils through the prince of the devils.

35. And Jesus went about all the cities and villages, teaching in their synagogues, and preaching the gospel of the kingdom, and healing every sickness and every disease among the people.

36. But when he saw the multitudes, he was moved with compassion on them, because they fainted, and were scattered abroad, as sheep having no shepherd.

37. Then saith he unto his disciples, The harvest truly *is* plenteous, but the laborers *are* few;

38. Pray ye therefore the Lord of the harvest, that he will send forth laborers into his harvest.

## CHAPTER 10

AND when he had called unto *him* his twelve disciples, he gave them power *against* unclean spirits, to cast them out, and to heal all manner of sickness and all manner of disease.

nition of Jesus as Messiah, with its blessed implications to such men as these (Isa 35:5,6), received the blessing asked for. **Spread abroad his fame.** Unable to contain their gratitude, they did not obey Christ's stern warning to be silent.

**32-34. Healing of a dumb demoniac.** Though demoniacs were often violent and vocal, this one was **dumb** and **was brought to him** by others. Matthew describes the event with a minimum of details, noting chiefly the reaction by the multitudes. **Never so seen in Israel.** This statement may be the impression gained over a period of time, culminating in this latest miracle. The **Pharisees'** accusation of Jesus' league with the **prince of the devils** must have reference to this particular miracle. The charge may not have been made to Jesus directly, since he does not deal with it until it is made again (Mt 12:24-29).

**35-38. Another Galilean tour.** Opinion divides over whether this paragraph describes a third Galilean circuit (cf. Mt 4:23; Lk 8:1; so A. T. Robertson, *Harmony of the Gospels*), or is a summarization of Christ's activities which began at 4:23 (Lenski; Alford). **Jesus was going about.** The Greek indicates continued action. **Teaching, preaching,** and **healing** reaffirm the activities named in 4:23. **Moved with compassion.** This deep sympathy of Jesus is often named as prompting his miracles (14:14; 15:32; 20:34). Two illustrations picture Christ's concept of the multitudes: shepherdless sheep, and a ripened harvest. **Distressed** (ASV). Wearied, harassed. **Scattered,** or lying down, prostrated from exhaustion and neglect. But Jesus saw the people also as a rich spiritual **harvest,** in need of **laborers** to gather it. The disciples are commanded to **pray** for the **Lord of the harvest** (Jesus himself; cf. 3:12, where John applies the same figure to Christ) to **send forth** the workers. As so often occurs, those who prayed were themselves sent (ch. 10).

6) Mission of the Twelve. 10:1-42. After an explanatory statement and a listing of the Twelve, Matthew gives Christ's charge to them for their first mission. The message is in three sections, marked by the recurring phrase, "Verily, I say unto you" (vv. 15,23, and 42). a) Instructions for the immediate journey (vv. 5-15). b) Warning of future persecutions, culminated by the Second Advent (vv. 16-23). c) General encouragement for all believers (vv. 24-42).

**1. His twelve disciples.** This group had been formed some time previously, and now after a time of instruction (Mk 3:14)

2. Now the names of the twelve apostles are these; The first, Simon, who is called Peter, and Andrew his brother; James *the son* of Zebedee, and John his brother;

3. Philip, and Bartholomew; Thomas, and Matthew. the publican; James *the son* of Alpheus, and Lebbeus, whose surname was Thaddeus;

4. Simon the Canaanite, and Judas Iscariot, who also betrayed him.

5. These twelve Jesus sent forth, and commanded them, saying, Go not into the way of the Gentiles, and into *any* city of the Samaritans enter ye not:

6. But go rather to the lost sheep of the house of Israel.

7. And as ye go, preach, saying, The kingdom of heaven is at hand.

8. Heal the sick, cleanse the lepers, raise the dead, cast out devils: freely ye have received, freely give.

9. Provide neither gold, nor silver, nor brass in your purses;

10. Nor scrip for *your* journey, neither two coats, neither shoes, nor yet staves: for the workman is worthy of his meat.

they were sent on a mission. **He gave them authority.** The right and the ability. Included in these delegated powers was the ability to cast out **unclean spirits** and to heal all kinds of **disease** (note that Jesus clearly differentiated between demon possession and disease). **2. The names of the twelve apostles** are listed three other places (Mk 3:16 ff.; Lk 6:14 ff.; Acts 1:13). Comparison shows that each list has three groups containing the same four names, though not always in the same order. However, Peter is always the first name in group one, Philip is always first in group two, and James of Alphaeus first in group three. Judas Iscariot when included is always last. Matthew lists them in pairs, probably because they were sent out that way (Mk 6:7). **Apostles.** Papyri discoveries confirm the meaning of "a duly-empowered representative of a higher official." **The first, Simon.** Not the first chosen, nor merely the first one in the list, but probably a reference to Peter's prominence in the apostolic circle (cf. 26:40; Pentecost; Cornelius' house; and others). But he was first among equals. The NT knows nothing of a Petrine supremacy over all apostles (cf. Gal 2:11; I Pet 5:1). **3. Bartholomew** is a patronymic of Nathanael (Jn 1:46). **Matthew the publican.** A self-effacing epithet employed only in the author's Gospel. **Thaddaeus** (ASV), also called Lebbaeus (in some ancient texts), is apparently the same as Judas the brother of James (Lk 6:16; Acts 1:13). **4. Simon,** called here by the Aramaic **Cananaean,** meaning "zealot" (cf. Lk; Acts). He apparently had belonged to the fanatical political group of the Zealots. **Iscariot.** Probably meaning "man of Kerioth," Kerioth being a town in Judea.

5. Jesus' order prohibiting any mission to the **Gentiles** or to **any city of the Samaritans** (racial half-breeds who maintained a rival worship and were despised by Jews; Jn 4:9,20) was not due to prejudice (Jn 4) nor was it permanent (Acts 1:8). **6,7.** At present, however, their message announced the Messianic **kingdom of heaven** (see 3:2; 4:23), to which **the house of Israel** was heir. **8.** Included among the miraculous powers given to them was authority to **raise the dead,** although there is no record that such power was employed on this mission. These ministrations were to be performed **freely,** without charge, for their authority had been received in this manner. **9. Provide neither gold.** These instructions apply only to this specific mission of limited duration (cf. Lk 22:35,36). Money was not to be carried in their **purses** (belts, girdles). **10. Scrip.** Knapsack, trav-

11. And into whatsoever city or town ye shall enter, inquire who in it is worthy; and there abide till ye go thence.

12. And when ye come into a house, salute it.

13. And if the house be worthy, let your peace come upon it: but if it be not worthy, let your peace return to you.

14. And whosoever shall not receive you, nor hear your words, when ye depart out of that house or city, shake off the dust of your feet.

15. Verily I say unto you, It shall be more tolerable for the land of Sodom and Gomorrah in the day of judgment, than for that city.

16. Behold, I send you forth as sheep in the midst of wolves: be ye therefore wise as serpents, and harmless as doves.

17. But beware of men: for they will deliver you up to the councils, and they will scourge you in their synagogues;

18. And ye shall be brought before governors and kings for my sake, for a testimony against them and the Gentiles.

19. But when they deliver you up, take no thought how or what ye shall speak: for it shall be given you in that same hour what ye shall speak.

20. For it is not ye that speak, but the Spirit of your Father which speaketh in you.

21. And the brother shall deliver up the brother to death, and the father the child: and the children shall rise up against *their* parents, and cause them to be put to death.

22. And ye shall be hated of all *men* for my name's sake: but he that endureth to the end shall be saved.

23. But when they persecute you in this city, flee ye into another: for verily I say unto you, Ye shall not have gone over the cities of Israel, till the Son of man be come.

eler's bag. They were not to procure extra coats, extra sandals, nor a staff (though they might use the sandals and staff they already had, Mk 6:8,9). Support would come from grateful hearers. **11. Search out who in it is worthy** (ASV). As they proclaimed their message (v. 7), the response would reveal who was spiritually disposed toward them. When hospitality was offered, the disciples were to accept it for the duration of their visit. **12.** They were to give the customary greeting (salute, which consisted of the rich *shalom*, "peace"). **13.** If the disciples should discover that their host was **not** worthy but really antagonistic to their purpose and message, their pronouncement of peace would not be wasted but would **return** for use somewhere else. **14.** If antagonism forced the abandonment of such a house or even of a whole city, the symbolism of shaking off the dust from their feet would vividly and yet solemnly portray the disciples' freedom from involvement in their opponents' guilt and coming judgment. **15. Sodom and Gomorrah.** Two oft-used examples of doomed cities (Isa 1:9; cf. Gen 18:20; 19:24-28). **Verily I say unto you.** This formula closes each section of this instruction (cf. vv. 23,42).

**16.** This second portion of the instruction looks beyond the specific mission to future dangers, and even gives a glimpse of eschatological times. **Wolves.** Vicious opponents (7:15; Lk 10:3; Jn 10:12; Acts 20:29). **Wise as serpents and harmless as doves.** "Alone, the wisdom of the serpent is mere cunning, and the harmlessness of the dove little better than weakness; but in combination, the wisdom of the serpent would save them from unnecessary exposure to danger; the harmlessness of the dove, from sinful expedients to escape it" (JFB, III, 81). **17. Councils.** The local courts found in every city (Deut 16:18). **18. Governors and kings.** There is no suggestion that this happened on their first mission; thus with typical prophetic method, Jesus uses the present occasion for treating matters some distance away in time. Agrippa I, Felix, Festus, Agrippa II, Sergius Paulus, and Gallio were some who heard testimony regarding Christ and the apostles. **19,20. Be not anxious.** The Spirit would provide the apostles with their oral testimony (as well as inspire their writings). **21,22.** Persecution of the most heartbreaking kind, even within families, must be expected. Yet there must be no yielding to despair, for deliverance is promised (cf. 24:13). **23. Flee ye into another.** Martyrdom was not to be sought; reasonable care for life was to be taken. Before all the

24. The disciple is not above *his* master, nor the servant above his lord.

25. It is enough for the disciple that he be as his master, and the servant as his lord. If they have called the master of the house Beelzebub, how much more *shall they call* them of his household?

26. Fear them not therefore: for there is nothing covered, that shall not be revealed; and hid, that shall not be known.

27. What I tell you in darkness, *that* speak ye in light: and what ye hear in the ear, *that* preach ye upon the housetops.

28. And fear not them which kill the body, but are not able to kill the soul: but rather fear him which is able to destroy both soul and body in hell.

29. Are not two sparrows sold for a farthing? and one of them shall not fall on the ground without your Father.

30. But the very hairs of your head are all numbered.

31. Fear ye not therefore, ye are of more value than many sparrows.

32. Whosoever therefore shall confess me before men, him will I confess also before my Father which is in heaven.

cities of Israel should be visited in this way, the **Son of man** would **come.** In the similar context of Mt 24:8-31 the Great Tribulation and the Second Advent are in view. Hence, the "coming of the Son of man" is probably eschatological here also. This would have been more readily understood by the disciples, who would hardly have thought to equate this "coming" with the destruction of Jerusalem in A.D. 70. Here then is a promise of deliverance from the greatest persecution of all.

The concluding portion gives general encouragement for all believers (vv. 24-42). **24,25.** Christ's relation to believers is presented by three figures: **disciple** and **teacher, servant** and **lord, master of the house** and **members of the household.** If Jesus himself received ill-treatment, his subordinates could hardly expect to fare better. **Beelzebub** (better, *Beelzebul* or *Beezebul*) was regarded as "prince of the demons" (Mt 12:24; Lk 11:15), apparently identical with Satan. This spelling occurs nowhere else in Jewish literature outside the NT. Exact explanation is uncertain, though it seems related to "Baalzebub," the god of Ekron (II Kgs 1:16). **26,27. Fear them not.** This encouragement is based on the knowledge that God's ultimate judgment will vindicate believers and deal with persecutors. Thus, in accord with this oft-used maxim of Jesus, that which the Twelve had received privately (**in darkness, in the ear**) must be fearlessly publicized (**in light, upon the housetops**). **28.** To answer the objection that such action would endanger their lives, Jesus reminds them that it is more important to fear him who has authority over the **soul** as well as over the **body,** and can bring both to eternal ruin in **hell** (Gehenna). This clearly is speaking of God, not Satan, for believers are never commanded to fear Satan (but to resist him); nor does Satan destoy men in hell (he himself is punished there). **29-31.** God's providence, which extends even to the smallest details of this world, provides an additional antidote for fear. **Two sparrows.** Familiar birds in Palestine, used occasionally for food. **A farthing** (*assarion*). The Roman *as* or *assarion* was a copper coin, worth about one-sixteenth of a denarius (Arndt). Luke says two of these coins would buy five sparrows (12:6). **Without your Father.** Not only without his knowledge; the thought contextually is that without his providential direction not even such insignificant events can occur. This providence applies even to the minutest parts of our being (**all the hairs of your head**). **32,33.** The prospect of divine judgment may also serve as a deterrent to yield-

33. But whosoever shall deny me before men, him will I also deny before my Father which is in heaven.

34. Think not that I am come to send peace on earth: I came not to send peace, but a sword.

35. For I am come to set a man at variance against his father, and the daughter against her mother, and the daughter-in-law against her mother-in-law.

36. And a man's foes *shall be* they of his own household.

37. He that loveth father or mother more than me is not worthy of me: and he that loveth son or daughter more than me is not worthy of me.

38. And he that taketh not his cross, and followeth after me, is not worthy of me.

39. He that findeth his life shall lose it: and he that loseth his life for my sake shall find it.

40. He that receiveth you receiveth me; and he that receiveth me receiveth him that sent me.

41. He that receiveth a prophet in the name of a prophet shall receive a prophet's reward; and he that receiveth a righteous man in the name of a righteous man shall receive a righteous man's reward.

42. And whosoever shall give to drink unto one of these little ones a cup of cold *water* only in the name of a disciple, verily I say unto you, he shall in no wise lose his reward.

ing before persecution. **Whosoever shall confess me** refers to genuine acknowledgment of Jesus as Lord and Saviour, with all that those terms imply. **Before men.** Indicative of a public confession before human interrogators, as contrasted with Christ's acknowledgment of believers before the **Father in heaven. Whosoever shall deny me** (cf. II Tim 2:12). The Greek tense (aorist, constative) refers not to one moment of denial (e.g., Peter's), but to the life in its entirety, which Christ is capable of assessing precisely.

**34-39.** The foregoing warnings of danger ahead might cause one to wonder why there should be such hazard. Jesus explains that his message, delivered in a rebellious and wicked world, would be met with hostility. **Sword.** A symbol of sharp conflict and division, as shown by examples in verses 35,36. **To set at variance** means literally *to divide in two.* Christ's Gospel has often brought cleavage even within family circles, not through any fault of the Gospel, but because of the rebellious attitude of sinful, unrepentant hearts. The illustration shows such a divided family of five: **father** and **mother,** unmarried **daughter,** married son (**man**), and his **bride,** who lived in the father's home, after Oriental custom. **37.** Heartbreaking as these divisions are, a disciple must not let his natural affections cause any weakening of his attachment to Christ. A time may come when he will be forced to make a choice. **38. His cross.** Though Jesus had not yet mentioned his coming crucifixion, this first reference to a **cross** by our Lord needed no explanation. The Jews had seen thousands of their countrymen crucified by the Romans (Jos *Antiq.* xvii. 10.10). Hence allegiance even to death, if necessary, is demanded if we would be **worthy** or fit to be called Christ's followers. **39. He that findeth his life.** *Psychē* denotes that which animates the body and in which the consciousness and spirit reside. "Life" and "soul" are two English attempts to translate this many-sided word. The sense is: He who in persecution saves his life by denying Christ will lose it eventually forever (particularly the soul aspect); but he who loses his life because of devotion to Christ will save his soul eternally.

**40-42.** To conclude this charge Jesus shows that those who risk persecution shall be appropriately rewarded. **He that receiveth you.** Not as a mere house guest but as a messenger of Christ. Our Lord regards this welcome as if done to himself. **He that receiveth a prophet in the name of a prophet,** i.e., because he is a prophet (God's commissioned spokesman). Those

## CHAPTER 11

AND it came to pass, when Jesus had made an end of commanding his twelve disciples, he departed thence to teach and to preach in their cities.

2. Now when John had heard in the prison the works of Christ, he sent two of his disciples,

3. And said unto him, Art thou he that should come, or do we look for another?

4. Jesus answered and said unto them, Go and show John again those things which ye do hear and see:

5. The blind receive their sight, and the lame walk, the lepers are cleansed, and the deaf hear, the dead are raised up, and the poor have the gospel preached to them.

6. And blessed is *he*, whosoever shall not be offended in me.

7. And as they departed, Jesus began to say unto the multitudes concerning John, What went ye out into the wilderness to see? A reed shaken with the wind?

8. But what went ye out for to see? A man clothed in soft raiment? behold, they that wear soft *clothing* are in kings' houses.

9. But what went ye out for to see? A prophet? yea, I say unto you, and more than a prophet.

10. For this is *he*, of whom it is written, Behold, I send my messenger before thy face, which shall prepare thy way before thee.

11. Verily I say unto you, Among them that are born of women there hath not risen a greater than John the Baptist: notwithstanding, he that is least in the kingdom of heaven is greater than he.

who are not prophets themselves may share their labors and also their reward. One of these little ones. The smallest service performed to aid the most insignificant of Christ's servants (cf. Mt 25:40) shall not go unnoticed by our Lord.

7) Christ's Answer to John, and Related Discourse. 11:1-30. Here Jesus answers John's keen question, gives to the crowds a tribute to his imprisoned forerunner, and castigates the cities that rejected Him.

2. On John's imprisonment by Herod at Machaerus, east of the Dead Sea (Jos *Antiq.* xviii. 5.2), see 4:12; 14:1-12. He sent by his disciples (ASV). Men who had remained loyal to John, and at this stage felt no reason to leave him. 3. Art thou the Coming One? A common designation for Messiah (Mk 11:9; Lk 13:35). In view of John's prior pronouncements and supernatural revelation (Jn 1:29-34), to accuse him of doubts concerning Jesus' Messiahship seems most unfair. Rather, since the character of Jesus' ministry semed to lack the judgment aspect that John had predicted (Mt 3:10-12), he may have wondered whether an additional Messianic figure needed to appear, such as Elijah (cf. Mal 4:5; Jn 1:19-21). 4,5. Jesus' kindly reply called attention to his works, which John would recognize as Messianic credentials (Isa 29:18,19; 35:5,6; 61:1). The dead are raised up. Luke describes one such miracle just prior to this interview (Lk 7:11-17). 6. Whosoever shall find none occasion of stumbling in me (ASV). This encouraging stimulus to John's faith reminded him and all believers that recognition of Jesus as Messiah is characteristic of the spiritually blessed man (Jn 20:31).

7-19. Tribute to John. 7. Reed shaken with the wind. A wavering person. Christ's obvious intent denied that John was such, and hence one must not ascribe faithlessness to John's previous inquiry. 8. Soft raiment. Though a rich wardrobe might be expected of a politician's emissary, John's well-known prophetic garb (3:4) bespoke his spiritual mission. 9,10. Much more than a prophet (ASV). John was not only the last of the OT line of inspired spokesmen, but was also the predicted forerunner of Messiah (Mal 3:1), especially chosen to introduce Messiah to Israel. 11. Consequently, no human being is greater than John. Jesus here destroys any suspicions of friction between himself and John. He that is least in the kingdom of heaven is greater than he. In this statement John seems to be regarded as outside the kingdom. Hence the kingdom of heaven must still be regarded as the Messianic

12. And from the days of John the Baptist until now the kingdom of heaven suffereth violence, and the violent take it by force.

13. For all the prophets and the law prophesied until John.

14. And if ye will receive *it*, this is Elias, which was for to come.

15. He that hath ears to hear, let him hear.

16. But whereunto shall I liken this generation? It is like unto children sitting in the markets, and calling unto their fellows,

17. And saying, We have piped unto you, and ye have not danced; we have mourned unto you, and ye have not lamented.

18. For John came neither eating nor drinking, and they say, He hath a devil.

19. The Son of man came eating and drinking, and they say, Behold a man gluttonous, and a winebibber, a friend of publicans and sinners. But wisdom is justified of her children.

kingdom announced by both John and Jesus (3:2; 4:17). John, whose ministry was one of preparation, was now imprisoned and soon to die. But those who had responded to the announcement and were now in the circle of Jesus' followers were the nucleus of His kingdom. They were being given new truths and privileges, and after national rejection of Jesus, would be baptized into a new spiritual body, the Church (a part of the Messianic kingdom, Col 1:13; Rev 20:6). John was the friend of the bridegroom, but the disciples became the bride (Jn 3:29). When Jesus spoke these words (before Pentecost, Acts 2), kingdom of heaven was the most intelligible term he could have used. **12. The kingdom of heaven suffereth violence.** This verb may be regarded either as middle — *violently forces its way* (cf. Lk 16:16), or as passive — *is violently treated.* The latter is more consistent with the next clause. From John's initial announcement of the coming of the Kingdom, the response had been a violent one, whether by vicious opponents (cf. vv. 18,19; 14:3,4) or by enthusiastic supporters. **The violent take it by force** (or, *seize it*). Compare Lk 16:16. Among the most prominent of Christ's adherents were the publicans, harlots, and other open sinners, who flocked to our Lord in great numbers. **13-15.** John was the last of the prophets of the OT dispensation who foretold the coming of Messiah. Included in these OT predictions was the coming of **Elijah** to usher in the great Day of the Lord (Mal 4:5). Though John himself denied that he was the resurrected Elijah (Jn 1:21), Jesus states that if the Jews had fully received Him and His Kingdom, John would have fulfilled the OT prediction (Mt 17:10-13; cf. Lk 1:17). Since this did not occur, John did not fulfill all that was predicted of Elijah; and hence the complete fulfillment is still future. This passage clearly shows the contingent nature of the kingdom offer.

**16-19.** In marked contrast to this glowing estimate of John was the prevailing sentiment of the crowds toward John and Jesus. **This generation.** The contemporaries of John and Jesus (v. 12). **Like unto children.** This homely parable portrays a scene in the public concourse, where a group of peevish children cannot decide what game to play (cf. Lk 7:31-35). Suggestions that they play wedding (**piped, danced**) and funeral (**mourned, lamented**) prove unappealing; so they play nothing. Similarly, John's ascetic ministry brought the charge that he was **demon**-possessed. But Jesus' habit of contacting sinners and sharing their social customs elicited the

37

20. Then began he to upbraid the cities wherein most of his mighty works were done, because they repented not:

21. Woe unto thee, Chorazin! woe unto thee, Bethsaida! for if the mighty works, which were done in you, had been done in Tyre and Sidon, they would have repented long ago in sackcloth and ashes.

22. But I say unto you, It shall be more tolerable for Tyre and Sidon at the day of judgment, than for you.

23. And thou, Capernaum, which art exalted unto heaven, shalt be brought down to hell: for if the mighty works, which have been done in thee, had been done in Sodom, it would have remained until this day.

24. But I say unto you, That it shall be more tolerable for the land of Sodom in the day of judgment, than for thee.

25. At that time Jesus answered and said, I thank thee, O Father, Lord of heaven and earth, because thou hast hid these things from the wise and prudent, and hast revealed them unto babes.

26. Even so, Father; for so it seemed good in thy sight.

27. All things are delivered unto me of my Father: and no man knoweth the Son, but the Father; neither knoweth any man the Father, save the Son, and he to whomsoever the Son will reveal him.

vicious and untrue claims that he was **gluttonous**, a **winebibber**, as evil as his companions. However, the **wisdom** of the courses of action of both men was proved (**justified**) by the results.

**20-24. Upbraiding of the cities. Wherein most of his mighty works were done.** No miracles are recorded in the Gospels as having occurred in **Chorazin** or **Bethsaida** (not Bethsaida Julias). Probably these two villages were so close to the larger **Capernaum** that many of the miracles performed at Capernaum were witnessed by inhabitants of all three communities. **Tyre and Sidon.** Prominent Phoenician coastal cities, the objects of divine judgment under Nebuchadnezzar and Alexander (cf. Ezk 26 – 28). **Sackcloth and ashes** (cf. Jon 3:5-8). The common Eastern way of demonstrating grief. Had they been granted the opportunities of these Jewish cities, Jesus says, they **would have repented.** Why such opportunities were not granted must be left with the sovereign purposes of God, who sent Christ first to the house of Israel. Yet the greater spiritual privileges granted Chorazin and Bethsaida made their unbelief more culpable. As for **Capernaum,** which, as Jesus' home, had the greatest opportunity of all, the rhetorical question, **Shalt thou be exalted unto heaven?** (ASV), implies a negative answer. **Thou shalt go down unto Hades.** The state of its inhabitants at the **judgment** will be worse than that of **Sodom,** a city proverbial for wickedness.

**25-30.** Jesus concludes the discourse with an explanation of men's unbelief, and a gracious invitation. **25. Jesus answered.** The following verses are an answer to the problems raised by the previous discussion. **I thank thee, O Father.** The verb *exomologoumai* describes a confession or full acknowledgment, coupled with praise. **Wise and understanding** (ASV). Spiritual awareness of Christ and his Kingdom is not arrived at through intellect or common sense. **Babes.** Those who, in response to Christ's message, recognize their spiritual helplessness are able to receive his teaching (18:3). The glory of the Gospel is that both the learned and the ignorant may become babes. **26.** The final explanation of human response, however, lies in the **good pleasure** of God (cf. Eph 1:5; Phil 2:13). **27. All things are delivered unto me of my Father.** Jesus claims an authority which distinguishes him from all other persons (cf. Mt 28:18; Jn 13:3). Here that authority is stated as involving the revelation of God to men. **Neither knoweth any man the Father, save the Son.**

28. Come unto me, all *ye* that labor and are heavy laden, and I will give you rest.

29. Take my yoke upon you, and learn of me; for I am meek and lowly in heart: and ye shall find rest unto your souls.

30. For my yoke *is* easy, and my burden is light.

### CHAPTER 12

AT that time Jesus went on the sabbath day through the corn; and his disciples were ahungered, and began to pluck the ears of corn, and to eat.

2. But when the Pharisees saw *it*, they said unto him, Behold, thy disciples do that which is not lawful to do upon the sabbath day.

3. But he said unto them, Have ye not read what David did, when he was ahungered, and they that were with him;

4. How he entered into the house of God, and did eat the showbread, which was not lawful for him to eat, neither for them which were with him, but only for the priests?

5. Or have ye not read in the law, how that on the sabbath days the priests in the temple profane the sabbath, and are blameless?

6. But I say unto you, That in this place is *one* greater than the temple.

7. But if ye had known what *this* meaneth, I will have mercy, and not sacrifice, ye would not have condemned the guiltless.

8. For the Son of man is Lord even of the sabbath day.

The mutual knowledge of the Father and the Son is perfect, but it is limited to them unless revelation is imparted to mankind. **To whomsoever the Son will reveal. The** Son as the image of God is the revealer of the invisible God (Col 1:15); he is the Logos, the expression of the unseen God (Jn 1:1,18). Hence Matthew is in agreement with thoughts more frequently expressed by John and Paul. This shows that the Biblical writers were essentially of one mind regarding the truth that man is dependent upon God's grace in Christ for all spiritual knowledge. **28. Come unto me.** In view of the authority vested in Christ (v. 27), this invitation vibrates with opportunity. **All ye that labor.** Men whose wearisome efforts to achieve spiritual rest have not eased the burden of man-made obligations (23:4). **29,30. Take my yoke.** A Jewish metaphor for discipline and discipleship. "Put your neck under the yoke, and let your soul receive instruction" (Sir 51:26). Christ alone is the Teacher who by his person and work can instruct men regarding the Father, and bring them the **rest** of soul which is the very essence of true spiritual experience, a rest involving removal of sin's guilt and the possession of eternal life. **My burden is light.** The obligations involved in the Gospel are blessed ones, and strength to bear them is supplied with the yoke.

8) Opposition from the Pharisees. 12:1-50. Matthew records a series of incidents showing the nature of Pharisaic hostility.

1-8. Pharisees oppose plucking grain on the Sabbath. **1.** As the group journeyed through the **grainfields,** the disciples exercised their legal privilege of plucking and eating the grain (Deut 23:25). **2.** To the **Pharisees,** who must have been taking a walk through the same fields, the act appeared **not lawful** because it involved a breaking of the **sabbath day.** Rabbinically interpreted, plucking grain was reaping, and thus was work (Ex 20:10). **3,4.** Christ's first reply recalls **David** and the **shewbread** (I Sam 21:1-6). Though divine Law restricted the shewbread to the priests (Lev 24:9), extreme human need overruled this regulation, and the rabbis so understood it. **5,6.** A second illustration shows that the law of Sabbath rest was not absolute, for the priests were required by that very law to work on the Sabbath (Num 28:9,10). The argument is, if priests can be guiltless in working on the Sabbath for furthering temple worship, how much more are the disciples guiltless in using the Sabbath for the work of Christ, who is the reality to which the Temple pointed.

9. And when he was departed thence, he went into their synagogue:

10. And, behold, there was a man which had *his* hand withered. And they asked him, saying, Is it lawful to heal on the sabbath days? that they might accuse him.

11. And he said unto them, What man shall there be among you, that shall have one sheep, and if it fall into a pit on the sabbath day, will he not lay hold on it, and lift *it* out?

12. How much then is a man better than a sheep? Wherefore it is lawful to do well on the sabbath days.

13. Then saith he to the man, Stretch forth thine hand. And he stretched *it* forth; and it was restored whole, like as the other.

14. Then the Pharisees went out, and held a council against him, how they might destroy him.

15. But when Jesus knew *it*, he withdrew himself from thence: and great multitudes followed him, and he healed them all;

16. And charged them that they should not make him known:

17. That it might be fulfilled which was spoken by Esaias the prophet, saying,

18. Behold my servant, whom I have chosen; my beloved, in whom my soul is well pleased: I will put my Spirit upon him, and he shall show judgment to the Gentiles.

19. He shall not strive, nor cry; neither shall any man hear his voice in the streets.

20. A bruised reed shall he not break, and smoking flax shall he not quench, till he send forth judgment unto victory.

21. And in his name shall the Gentiles trust.

22. Then was brought unto him one possessed with a devil, blind, and dumb: and he healed him, insomuch that the blind and dumb both spake and saw.

23. And all the people were amazed, and said, Is not this the Son of David?

7. Christ's third argument points to Pharisaic misunderstanding of Hos 6:6, **mercy and not sacrifice** (cf. Mt 9:13). God desires proper hearts far more than externals which have become mere formalities. A spiritual understanding of Christ and the disciples by the Pharisees would have prevented their judging these **innocent ones. 8. Lord of the sabbath.** Since Jesus as Son of man is master of the Sabbath day, the disciples who had used the Sabbath in the course of following him were employing it in a proper way.

**9-21.** Pharisees oppose healing on the Sabbath. (Cf. Mk 3:1-6; Lk 6:6-11.) **9. Into their synagogue.** Luke shows that it occurred on a different Sabbath. **10,11. Is it lawful to heal on the sabbath day?** The OT made no prohibition, but some rabbis regarded it as work. Jesus, however, by pointing to what any individual would have done for an unfortunate **sheep**, makes his own obligation clear. **12.** Since man is incomparably **of more value** (ASV) than a sheep, He must come to his aid. To avoid doing good when such is within one's power is really to do harm (see Mk and Lk accounts). **13,14.** The miracle only enraged the **Pharisees**, who immediately plotted (along with the Herodians, Mk 3:6) **to destroy him.** Thus in Galilee, as recently in Jerusalem (Jn 5:18), murderous hatred was taking definite form. Men who called healing a Sabbath violation felt no qualms about plotting murder. **15. He withdrew himself.** Knowledge of the plot prompted Jesus to avoid open conflict at this time, for his hour was not yet come. He thus transferred his ministrations to other areas (Mk 3:7), and **he healed them all. 16.** However, he cautioned those healed (especially the demoniacs, Mk 3:11,12) not to use the miracles to publicize him as Messiah and so excite the crowds and the opposition. **17-21. That it might be fulfilled.** This gracious, non-provocative ministry of Jesus is shown by Matthew to be consistent with Messianic prophecy (Isa 42:1-4). For as Jesus emphasized the righteous and spiritual aspects of his Kingdom, he did not engage in public haranguing, nor political demagoguery. Neither did he trample on the weak in order to gain his ends. **Smoking flax.** The wick of a lamp in which the oil is about gone — symbolic of those who are feeble.

**22-37.** Pharisees oppose Christ's demon expulsion. **22. One possessed with a demon.** The demon possession had caused two side effects — blindness and dumbness. The healing removed all three afflictions. **23. Can this be the Son of David?** The

**24.** But when the Pharisees heard *it,* they said, This *fellow* doth not cast out devils, but by Beelzebub the prince of the devils.

**25.** And Jesus knew their thoughts, and said unto them, Every kingdom divided against itself is brought to desolation; and every city or house divided against itself shall not stand:

**26.** And if Satan cast out Satan, he is divided against himself; how shall then his kingdom stand?

**27.** And if I by Beelzebub cast out devils, by whom do your children cast *them* out? therefore they shall be your judges.

**28.** But if I cast out devils by the Spirit of God, then the kingdom of God is come unto you.

**29.** Or else, how can one enter into a strong man's house, and spoil his goods, except he first bind the strong man? and then he will spoil his house.

**30.** He that is not with me is against me; and he that gathereth not with me scattereth abroad.

**31.** Wherefore I say unto you, All manner of sin and blasphemy shall be forgiven unto men: but the blasphemy *against* the Holy Ghost shall not be forgiven unto men.

**32.** And whosoever speaketh a word against the Son of man, it shall be forgiven him: but whosoever speaketh against the Holy Ghost, it shall not be forgiven him, neither in this world, neither in the *world* to come.

negative answer implied by the question reveals that even though the miracle had raised the possibility of his Messiahship (**Son of David,** cf. 1:20; 9:27), the people were predisposed to unbelief. **24.** The vicious charge that Christ's power over demons was derived from a league with **Beelzebul** (see comment on 10:25) was fully known by Jesus and refuted publicly in unanswerable fashion. **25,26.** The simple analogy of a **divided kingdom, city,** or **house** as tending to self-destruction refutes the charge. For in expelling demons, Jesus was assuredly frustrating the works of Satan, and we must credit Satan with a reasonable amount of shrewdness. (Nor can it be allowed that Satan might permit one such expulsion to confuse the issue, for this expulsion was no isolated case.) **27. By whom do your sons cast them out?** Since some of these Pharisees' associates (compare the OT expression "sons of the prophets") claimed the power of exorcism, how illogical to attribute similar effects to different causes. Whether or not the Jews did perform valid exorcisms is not necessary to the argument *(ad hominem).* The fact that the Pharisees claimed it made the argument effective. If, however, Jesus implies that at least some of the Pharisaic exorcisms were genuine, then it must be assumed that the power came from God (otherwise Christ's argument is greatly weakened). **28,29.** Christ's final argument calls attention to his own ministry, particularly to his expulsion of demons, which was evidence enough that the **kingdom of God has come.** The description of Christ's ministry as an entry into a **strong man's house** (Satan's domain) and a spoiling of **his goods** (Christ's power over demons), provides clear proof that the **strong man** (Satan) has **first** been bound. Jesus' victory over Satan at the temptation (4:1-11) demonstrated our Lord's superiority. **30. He that is not with me is against me.** In the conflict with Satan, neutrality is impossible.

**31,32. Every sin and blasphemy shall be forgiven unto men.** The general principle. Atonement by Christ at Calvary would be sufficient to remit the guilt of all sins, even the most aggravated forms of slander against God (**blasphemy**). One sin, however, is declared unpardonable: **whosoever shall speak against the Holy Spirit.** In view of Jesus' previously stated principle, this unpardonableness cannot be due to inadequacy of the atonement, nor may we infer any peculiar sacredness of the Third Person of the Trinity. Many ex-

**33.** Either make the tree good, and his fruit good; or else make the tree corrupt, and his fruit corrupt: for the tree is known by *his* fruit.

**34.** O generation of vipers, how can ye, being evil, speak good things? for out of the abundance of the heart the mouth speaketh.

**35.** A good man out of the good treasure of the heart bringeth forth good things: and an evil man out of the evil treasure bringeth forth evil things.

**36.** But I say unto you, That every idle word that men shall speak, they shall give account thereof in the day of judgment.

**37.** For by thy words thou shalt be justified, and by thy words thou shalt be condemned.

**38.** Then certain of the scribes and of the Pharisees answered, saying, Master, we would see a sign from thee.

**39.** But he answered and said unto them, An evil and adulterous generation seeketh after a sign; and there shall no sign be given to it, but the sign of the prophet Jonas:

**40.** For as Jonas was three days and three nights in the whale's belly; so shall the Son of man be three days and three nights in the heart of the earth.

plain this sin as the attributing of the miraculous works of the Spirit to Satanic power (cf. Mk 3:29,30), and see no possibility of its being committed today (so Chafer, Broadus, Gaebelein). Others, however, regard the accusation of the Pharisees as being symptomatic, and not the sin itself. The following verses point to the corrupt heart as the cause of the sin. The particular function of the Spirit is to bring conviction and repentance, and make men receptive to the invitation of Christ. Hence hearts that hate God and blaspheme Christ (I Tim 1:13) may yet be convicted and brought to repentance by the Spirit. But he who rejects every overture of the Spirit removes himself from the only force that can lead him to forgiveness (Jn 3:36). That such a settled state can be reached in this life is clearly implied by the passage. The OT describes these as sinning "with a high hand" (Num 15:30, ASV); for them no atonement was possible. Men cannot read hearts, and thus cannot judge when others have reached such a state. The real possibility of this sin does not weaken the gospel invitation, "Whosoever will," for by its very nature such will have no willingness to accept. As for the Pharisees of Jesus' audience, it is not stated whether or not they had fully committed this sin, but the warning is clear. Their considerable instruction made their responsibility great; their previous hostility showed their determined unbelief.

**33-35. Make the tree good.** A passage, similar to 7:16-20, where the speech of men is shown to be indicative of the state of the human **heart. 36,37.** On the **day of judgment** the Lord will consider every man's life in its entirety, even **every idle word** (not necessarily evil) coming from the overflow of his heart. Only the divine Judge is capable of recording, evaluating, and rendering a verdict on such matters.

**38-45.** Pharisees and scribes demand a sign. **38. We wish to see a sign from you.** They discounted previous miracles. What they wanted was some sensational deed in keeping with their ideas of Messiah (cf. Mt 16:1), a sign that would require no faith, only sight. **39. Adulterous generation.** A description of the nation as spiritually unfaithful in its vows to Jehovah (cf. Jer 3:14,20). To such a nation, the one great sign of the Resurrection is here foretold (and had been suggested even earlier, Jn 2:19-21). **40.** The experience of **Jonah,** who was released from the **belly of the sea-monster,** was typical of the coming interment and resurrection of Jesus after **three days and three nights in the**

41. The men of Nineveh shall rise in judgment with this generation, and shall condemn it: because they repented at the preaching of Jonas; and, behold, a greater than Jonas is here.

42. The queen of the south shall rise up in the judgment with this generation, and shall condemn it: for she came from the uttermost parts of the earth to hear the wisdom of Solomon; and, behold, a greater than Solomon is here.

43. When the unclean spirit is gone out of a man, he walketh through dry places, seeking rest, and findeth none.

44. Then he saith, I will return into my house from whence I came out; and when he is come, he findeth it empty, swept, and garnished.

45. Then goeth he, and taketh with himself seven other spirits more wicked than himself, and they enter in and dwell there: and the last state of that man is worse than the first. Even so shall it be also unto this wicked generation.

46. While he yet talked to the people, behold, his mother and his brethren stood without, desiring to speak with him.

47. Then one said unto him, Behold, thy mother and thy brethren stand without, desiring to speak with thee.

48. But he answered and said unto him that told him, Who is my mother? and who are my brethren?

heart of the earth. Those holding to the traditional Friday crucifixion explain the time here as idiomatic for parts of three days (Friday, Saturday, Sunday). Those holding to Wednesday crucifixion explain the reference literally as denoting seventy-two hours, from sundown Wednesday to sundown Saturday (e.g., W. G. Scroggie, *Guide to the Gospels*, pp. 569-577). **41.** The Ninevites, having received Jonah and his message after his miraculous deliverance, **repented.** Thus their action places Israel in a much worse light, for nationally she has remained unrepentant, both before and after the Resurrection, even though there was **more than** (AV, *a greater than*) **Jonah here.** **42.** Likewise the interest in Solomon's **wisdom** (divinely bestowed) by the **queen** of Sheba (I Kgs 10:1-13) will put into sad contrast at the judgment the unbelief of current Judaism. **43-45.** A striking parable, suggested naturally by the occasion (12:22 ff.), pictures Israel's (and the Pharisees') precarious situation. The expelled demon, finding no resting place in the **dry places** (indicated elsewhere as abodes of demons: Isa 13:21; Baruch 4:35; Rev 18:2), returns to his former habitation, which is now more attractive (**swept, garnished**) but **unoccupied.** He re-enters with seven other spirits, and the result is greater degeneration. **So shall it be.** Israel (nationally and individually) had been morally cleansed by the ministries of John and Jesus. Since the Exile, the evils of open idolatry had been removed. Yet, in most cases, the reformation which was meant to be preparatory had stopped short. Israel's house was "empty." Christ was not invited to occupy it. Hence **this wicked generation** will reach an even worse state. A few years later these same Jews faced the horrors of A.D. 66–70. End-time members of this race (*genea*) will especially be victimized by demons (Rev 9:1-11).

**46-50.** Christ's mother and brethren. **46,47. His mother and brethren.** These brethren are presumably the children of Joseph and Mary, born after Jesus. **Seeking to speak to him** indicates effort was being made, but the crowds were too great (Lk 8:19). Reasons for their concern are obvious. Previously, Jesus' preaching at Nazareth had forced the family to move to Capernaum (4:13; Lk 4:16-31; Jn 2:12). Now he had brought the Pharisees into open and blasphemous opposition. In addition, friends had reported that the strain of this ministry was affecting his health (Mk 3:21). Verse 47 adds little new information, and many ancient manuscripts omit it. **48. Who is my moth-**

49. And he stretched forth his hand toward his disciples, and said, Behold my mother and my brethren!

50. For whosoever shall do the will of my Father which is in heaven, the same is my brother, and sister, and mother.

## CHAPTER 13

THE same day went Jesus out of the house, and sat by the sea side.

2. And great multitudes were gathered together unto him, so that he went into a ship, and sat; and the whole multitude stood on the shore.

3. And he spake many things unto them in parables, saying, Behold, a sower went forth to sow;

4. And when he sowed, some *seeds* fell by the wayside, and the fowls came and devoured them up:

5. Some fell upon stony places, where they had not much earth: and forthwith they sprung up, because they had no deepness of earth:

6. And when the sun was up, they were scorched; and because they had no root, they withered away.

7. And some fell among thorns; and the thorns sprung up, and choked them:

8. But other fell into good ground, and brought forth fruit, some a hundredfold, some sixtyfold, some thirtyfold.

9. Who hath ears to hear, let him hear.

er? By this intriguing question Jesus startles the crowd to prepare them for a precious truth. **50. Whosoever shall do the will of my Father.** This "doing" is not some form of work-righteousness, but is man's response to Christ's invitation. "This is the work of God, that ye believe on him whom he hath sent" (Jn 6:29). The spiritual relationship between Christ and believers is closer than the closest of blood ties. This saying offered no disrespect to Mary, nor to his brothers, for at a later time we find them sharing this spiritual relation (Acts 1:14). Yet neither is there any suggestion that the mother of Jesus had special access to his presence.

9) A Series of Parables on the Kingdom. 13:1-58. This first extended series of parables was given on one of the busiest days recorded of Jesus' ministry. Matthew's account lists seven parables, and a concluding one of application. Mark records four, including one not in Matthew. Luke records three, not all together. Two of the parables were interpreted by Jesus (The Sower, The Tares), and a third one partially (The Net); this provides a scheme for understanding the others. **1. The same day.** Matthew alone relates this event to the previous discussion. The crowds being so great (as to prevent even his family from reaching him; 12:46), **Jesus went out of the house** to the sea side. **2.** Using a **boat** as a platform, he **sat** in the usual manner of teachers and addressed those on the **shore. 3a. Parables.** Plausible narratives used by Jesus to convey spiritual truth through comparisons. Though Jesus was not the inventor of parabolic teaching, his use of the method far surpassed that of all other teachers in effectiveness and depth of truth portrayed.

**3b-23. The Sower. 3b. The sower.** The definite article is probably generic. All sowers performed in similar fashion. **4.** As the sower scattered his seed, **some** fell on the parched earth of the path that ran through the field. Such seed lying on the surface would quickly attract the **birds. 5,6. Stony places.** Not ground covered with rocks, but a rock ledge covered with a thin layer of soil. Seed sown here would sprout quickly, for the sun would soon warm the thin crust; but for lack of sufficient **root** and moisture, the plant would shortly become **scorched** and **withered. 7. Among thorns.** Ground infested with thorn roots that plowing had not removed. **8. Good ground.** The fertile soil of Galilee was capable of producing harvests of the magnitude mentioned here (W. M. Thomson, *Land and Book*, p. 83). **9. Who hath**

10. And the disciples came, and said unto him, Why speakest thou unto them in parables?

11. He answered and said unto them, Because it is given unto you to know the mysteries of the kingdom of heaven, but to them it is not given.

12. For whosoever hath, to him shall be given, and he shall have more abundance: but whosoever hath not, from him shall be taken away even that he hath.

13. Therefore speak I to them in parables: because they seeing see not; and hearing they hear not, neither do they understand.

14. And in them is fulfilled the prophecy of Esaias, which saith, By hearing ye shall hear, and shall not understand; and seeing ye shall see, and shall not perceive:

15. For this people's heart is waxed gross, and *their* ears are dull of hearing, and their eyes they have closed; lest at any time they should see with *their* eyes, and hear with *their* ears, and should understand with *their* heart, and should be converted, and I should heal them.

16. But blessed *are* your eyes, for they see: and your ears, for they hear.

17. For verily I say unto you, That many prophets and righteous *men* have desired to see *those things* which ye see, and have not seen *them*; and to hear *those things* which ye hear, and have not heard *them*.

18. Hear ye therefore the parable of the sower.

ears to hear, let him hear. A declaration that this simple story, without preface or explanation, had a deeper meaning.

10-17. In response to the disciples' question, Jesus states his reason for speaking in parables. 10. Why? Previously he had used parables, but this occasion was obviously different. Now the parables themselves formed the basis of the teaching; they were not mere illustrations. 11. The mysteries of the kingdom of heaven identifies the content of these parables as being revelation previously hidden pertaining to the Kingdom. The interpretation relates them to the present day. The glories of the Messianic reign were clearly sketched in the OT. But the rejection of Messiah and the interval between his first and second comings was not understood. These parables describe the strange form of the Kingdom while the King is absent, during which time the Gospel is preached and a spiritual nucleus is developed for the establishment of the Messianic reign (Col 1:13; Mt 25:34). The revelation of these mysteries in parabolic form was due to the existence of two distinct groups: to you it is given; to them it is not given. 12. Whosoever hath. The disciples, having responded in faith to Jesus, already possessed much truth regarding Messiah and his program. Careful reflection upon these parables would enlighten them further. Whosoever hath not. The determined unbelievers who had refused the previous teaching of Jesus (cf. chs. 10; 11) were not being given the bare truths to trample under foot (cf. 7:6). Yet there is grace even here, for they were spared the greater guilt of rejecting the plainest teaching, and there remained the possibility that the intriguing parable might arouse curiosity and bring about a change of heart. 13-15. The settled state of spiritual insensibility among the people is viewed as a partial fulfillment (is being fulfilled) of Isa 6:9,10. Matthew's quotation follows the LXX, and emphasizes the obstinate unbelief of the people. (The Hebrew, *make the heart of this people fat*, presents the condition as a judgment from God upon their spiritual hardness.) 16,17. The disciples, who had responded to Messiah, were beneficiaries of privileges longed for by prophets and righteous men in the OT economy (cf. I Pet 1:10-12).

18-23. Jesus' interpretation of the parable explains the fate of the Word in this age as due, humanly speaking, to the condition of human hearts. 18. The sower. Not identified, but in conformity with the next parable, it is clearly Christ himself,

45

**19.** When any one heareth the word of the kingdom, and understandeth *it* not, then cometh the wicked one, and catcheth away that which was sown in his heart. This is he which received seed by the wayside.

**20.** But he that received the seed into stony places, the same is he that heareth the word, and anon with joy receiveth it;

**21.** Yet hath he not root in himself, but dureth for a while: for when tribulation or persecution ariseth because of the word, by and by he is offended.

**22.** He also that received seed among the thorns is he that heareth the word; and the care of this world, and the deceitfulness of riches, choke the word, and he becometh unfruitful.

**23.** But he that received seed into the good ground is he that heareth the word, and understandeth *it;* which also beareth fruit, and bringeth forth, some a hundredfold, some sixty, some thirty.

**24.** Another parable put he forth unto them, saying, The kingdom of heaven is likened unto a man which sowed good seed in his field:

**25.** But while men slept, his enemy came and sowed tares among the wheat, and went his way.

**26.** But when the blade was sprung up, and brought forth fruit, then appeared the tares also.

**27.** So the servants of the householder came and said unto him, Sir, didst not thou sow good seed in thy field? from whence then hath it tares?

**28.** He said unto them, An enemy hath done this. The servants said unto him, Wilt thou then that we go and gather them up?

**29.** But he said, Nay; lest while ye gather up the tares, ye root up also the wheat with them.

**30.** Let both grow together until the harvest: and in the time of harvest I will say to the reapers, Gather ye together first the tares, and bind them in bundles to burn them: but gather the wheat into my barn.

and those who represent him (13:37). **19.** The word of the kingdom (*word of God,* Lk 8:11), symbolized by the seed, is the message Jesus proclaimed concerning himself and his kingdom. **He that was sown by the way side** (ASV). This is not a mixing of figures, but a viewing of the seed in the soil as culminating in the plant, and thus representative of the individual case. The wayside hearer is the completely unresponsive one, from whom Satan (**the wicked one**), either personally or through his agents (**birds,** v. 4, are often symbolic of evil: Jer 5:26,27; Rev 18:2), soon removes all spiritual impressions. **20,21.** The seed on the rocky ledge describes the case of the shallow, emotional hearer (**immediately with joy**) whose initial enthusiasm is completely withered by the invigorating and necessary sun of **tribulation** or **persecution. 22.** The seed sprouting **among the thorns** depicts the preoccupied hearer whose heart is already full of **care** and worldly interests (the thorns were already in the soil, but not visible at the planting). A divided allegiance prevents the maturing of spiritual values. **23.** The only hearers who are approved are those of the **good ground.** Only here is **fruit** produced (Gal 5:22,23), and fruitfulness is the test of life (Jn 15:1-6). The explanation of how the hearts arrived at these conditions is outside the scope of this parable.

**24-30. The Tares.** For the interpretation see 13:36-43. **24. The kingdom of heaven is likened unto a man.** Christ characterizes the interregnum by the case of a man who had the following experience. **25,26. While men slept.** At night; the most probable time for this wicked work. Neither here nor in the interpretation is this detail regarded as negligence. **Tares.** *Zizania,* it is generally agreed, denotes darnel *(lolium temulentum),* a noxious plant, practically indistinguishable from wheat until the ear has developed. **27. Whence then hath it tares?** The extent of the useless growth could not be accounted for by chance (e.g., wind-blown seed), but only by deliberate planting. Yet, was it not obvious that the householder had planted good seed? (An affirmative answer is implied.) **28. An enemy hath done this.** Instances of such forthright malice are on record (Alford, *New Testament for Eng. Readers,* pp. 98,99). **29,30. The season of the harvest.** When the differences between the wheat and the darnel were most pronounced, and separation could be done economically by the **reapers.** Hence the tares were first bundled **for burning,** and then the wheat was gathered.

31. Another parable put he forth unto them, saying, The kingdom of heaven is like to a grain of mustard seed, which a man took, and sowed in his field:

32. Which indeed is the least of all seeds: but when it is grown, it is the greatest among herbs, and becometh a tree, so that the birds of the air come and lodge in the branches thereof.

33. Another parable spake he unto them; The kingdom of heaven is like unto leaven, which a woman took, and hid in three measures of meal, till the whole was leavened.

34. All these things spake Jesus unto the multitude in parables; and without a parable spake he not unto them:

35. That it might be fulfilled which was spoken by the prophet, saying, I will open my mouth in parables; I will utter things which have been kept secret from the foundation of the world.

**31,32.** The Mustard Seed. This parable resembles the first two in that all mention a man, a field, and seed. Consistently interpreted, in each the **man** symbolizes Christ, the **field** is the world, and the **seed** is the Word which tells of Christ and his kingdom. **Mustard seed.** Its smallness was proverbial (cf. Mt 17:20). Yet in this instance it grows until it is **greater than the herbs** (ASV), and it becomes a tree. Instances of unusual growth in Palestine have been noted by travelers, but rarely, if ever, to the extent described here (cf. Mk 4:32). That such growth is regarded as unfavorable is suggested by the **birds** that **lodge in the branches.** In this parable series, birds are agents of evil (13:4,19), as they are frequently in Scripture (Jer 5:26,27; Rev 18:2). History confirms the fact that from the smallest beginning, the church made astounding growth through the proclamation of Christ's message. Yet such unusual growth has provided roosting places for those who are enemies of God, who seek the shade and fruit of the tree for their own interests (even nations like to be called "Christian"). Disciples are warned that the mere bigness of what appears outwardly to be Christ's kingdom is not essentially a contradiction of the Lord's teaching that true believers are a little flock surrounded by wolves (Lk 12:32; Mt 10:16).

**33-35.** The Leaven. Though some interpret this parable and the preceding as depicting the spreading influence of the Gospel, such explanations violate Jesus' use of these symbols elsewhere, as well as the import of other parables (e.g., The Tares) which show evil existing till the end of the age. **33. Leaven.** A lump of old dough in a high state of fermentation. Leaven in the OT is generally symbolic of evil. In Christ's later uses of this symbol, it refers to evil doctrine of the Pharisees, Sadducees, and Herod (Mt 16:6-12; Mk 8:15). Paul's references (I Cor 5:6,7; Gal 5:9), which certainly regard leaven as evil, seem greatly influenced by Christ's parable. **Three measures of meal.** Apparently a common quantity employed in baking (Gen 18:6). The **woman** (in contrast to the **man** in the other parables) is the opponent of Christ and infuses the kingdom in this age with false doctrine. Elsewhere she is called "Wickedness" (Zech 5:7,8), "Jezebel" (Rev 2:20 ff.), and the "great harlot" (Rev. 17:1 ff.). By this characterization of leaven in the meal, believers are warned to beware of false doctrine which would infiltrate all parts of the kingdom in its interregnal aspect.

**34,35.** On this occasion Christ spoke

36. Then Jesus sent the multitude away, and went into the house: and his disciples came unto him, saying, Declare unto us the parable of the tares of the field.

37. He answered and said unto them, He that soweth the good seed is the Son of man;

38. The field is the world; the good seed are the children of the kingdom; but the tares are the children of the wicked one;

39. The enemy that sowed them is the devil; the harvest is the end of the world; and the reapers are the angels.

40. As therefore the tares are gathered and burned in the fire; so shall it be in the end of this world.

41. The Son of man shall send forth his angels, and they shall gather out of his kingdom all things that offend, and them which do iniquity;

42. And shall cast them into a furnace of fire: there shall be wailing and gnashing of teeth.

43. Then shall the righteous shine forth as the sun in the kingdom of their Father. Who hath ears to hear, let him hear.

44. Again, the kingdom of heaven is like unto treasure hid in a field; the which when a man hath found, he hideth, and for joy thereof goeth and selleth all that he hath, and buyeth that field.

publicly (to the multitude) in symbolic language alone, without interpretation. Only to the disciples did he explain the symbolism (13:10 ff.; 13:36 ff.). Matthew regarded this as reminiscent of Ps 78:2, and saw in Jesus the most perfect fulfillment of the prophet's function.

**36-43. Christ's interpretation of The Tares.** For the parable itself see 13:24-30. **36. Declare unto us the parable.** This parable was more involved than The Mustard Seed and The Leaven, and its implication of persisting evil may have conflicted with the disciples' notions. Our Lord's explanation of the symbols shows that major details are important, but some features are merely to give form to the story and are not symbolic (e.g., the men who slept, servants of the householder, binding of the bundles). **38,39. The field is the world.** Not the Church. **Children of the kingdom.** As in the explanation of The Sower, the seed is here regarded as having produced plants (13:19). The springing up of Christ's true followers in this world is counterfeited by the **devil,** whose **children** often masquerade as believers (II Cor 11:13-15). **40-43.** Though efficient removal in the early stages is shown to be impossible (v. 29), at the end angels will be delegated to **gather** the tares out of his **kingdom.** Thus the tares in the world are also regarded as being in the Kingdom in some sense. It must be, therefore, in the peculiar form of the Kingdom during the interregnum. Final removal will be done by angels at the **consummation of the age** — the end of Daniel's seventieth week, and the time of the second coming of Christ, when He will establish his glorious reign (Mt 25:31-46; Dan 12:3). It must be observed again that the Church and the Kingdom are not co-extensive, though prior to the Rapture, subjects of the Kingdom are also members of the Church. After the Church is removed at the Rapture, there will be Kingdom subjects on earth during the Tribulation. The statement that the tares will be gathered "first" (vv. 30, 41-43) clearly shows this to occur not at the Rapture (at which time the saints are gathered) but at the end of the Tribulation. For a similar statement, see comment on Mt 24:40-42, where those taken away are judged, and those left enter into blessing.

**44. The Hid Treasure.** Though the treasure is usually explained as Christ, the Gospel, salvation, or the Church, which a sinner should be willing to sacrifice all to obtain, the consistent use of the **man** in this series as referring to Christ, and the action of hiding again after finding make

**45.** Again, the kingdom of heaven is like unto a merchantman, seeking goodly pearls:

**46.** Who, when he had found one pearl of great price, went and sold all that he had, and bought it.

**47.** Again, the kingdom of heaven is like unto a net, that was cast into the sea, and gathered of every kind:

**48.** Which, when it was full, they drew to shore, and sat down, and gathered the good into vessels, but cast the bad away.

**49.** So shall it be at the end of the world: the angels shall come forth, and sever the wicked from among the just,

**50.** And shall cast them into the furnace of fire: there shall be wailing and gnashing of teeth.

**51.** Jesus saith unto them, Have ye understood all these things? They say unto him, Yea, Lord.

**52.** Then said he unto them, Therefore every scribe *which is* instructed unto the kingdom of heaven, is like unto a man *that is* a householder, which bringeth forth out of his treasure *things* new and old.

**53.** And it came to pass, *that* when Jesus had finished these parables, he departed thence.

such views unlikely. Rather, the **treasure hidden in the field** depicts the place of national Israel during the interregnum (Ex 19:5; Ps 135:4). To this obscure nation came Christ. The nation, however, rejected him, and so, by the divine purpose, she was removed from her momentary prominence; even today she remains obscured to outward view as to her relation to the Messianic kingdom (Mt 21:43). Yet Christ gave his very life (**all that he hath**) to purchase the whole field (the world, II Cor 5:19; I Jn 2:2), and thus obtained full ownership by right of discovery and redemption. When he comes again, the treasure will be unearthed and fully displayed (Zech 12,13).

**45,46.** The Pearl. This parable, similar in its movement to that of the Hid Treasure, is often explained in the same way; but such explanations are vulnerable to some of the same objections. It is consistent, however, to regard the **merchant man** as Christ, who came seeking men and women (**goodly pearls**) who would respond to him and his message. Eventually he gave his life (**all that he had**) to purchase **one pearl of great price** (I Cor 6:20). The **one pearl** depicts that other great company in the Kingdom, the Church, composed of men and women who are made one in the Church (I Cor 10:17; 12:12,13).

**47-50.** The Net. A parable similar to The Tares, but with a different emphasis. This **net** is the large seine, often left in the water for some time. It depicts the Gospel, which was sent out into the world (**sea** in Scripture often symbolizes the restless nations, Lk 21:25; Dan 7:3,17) by Christ and his apostles. Among the various kinds of **fish** enveloped by the net are some **unusable** ones, which Jesus interpreted as **wicked** men, and which in The Tares are shown to have been put there by Satan (cf. also birds in the branches, v. 32). Not all who seem responsive to the Gospel are genuinely converted.

**51-53.** Conclusion to the parables. The disciples, who had been given not only the parables but also principles of interpretation (cf. Mk 4:34), indicated their comprehension of this teaching. Jesus then compared their status as informed **scribe**[s] (i.e., teachers and interpreters of God's truth) to that of an efficient head of a household who has a rich storehouse with which to perform his duties. **Things new and old.** Old truths long possessed in the OT and new truths such as those revealed in these parables.

**54-58.** A visit to Nazareth. Matthew appends this incident to illustrate most poignantly the spread of opposition that

54. And when he was come into his own country, he taught them in their synagogue, insomuch that they were astonished, and said, Whence hath this *man* this wisdom, and *these* mighty works?

55. Is not this the carpenter's son? is not his mother called Mary? and his brethren, James, and Joses, and Simon, and Judas?

56. And his sisters, are they not all with us? Whence then hath this *man* all these things?

57. And they were offended in him. But Jesus said unto them, A prophet is not without honor, save in his own country, and in his own house.

58. And he did not many mighty works there because of their unbelief.

## CHAPTER 14

AT that time Herod the tetrarch heard of the fame of Jesus,

2. And said unto his servants, This is John the Baptist; he is risen from the dead; and therefore mighty works do show forth themselves in him.

3. For Herod had laid hold on John, and bound him, and put *him* in prison for Herodias' sake, his brother Philip's wife.

had necessitated the parabolic method (13:11-15). This visit, recorded also in Mk 6:1-6, is distinct from an earlier one recounted in Lk 4:16-30 (occurring prior to Mt 4:13). **54. His own country.** Nazareth and its environs. **55. The carpenter's son.** Mark's account (6:3) indicates that some called Jesus "the carpenter," showing that our Lord had learned Joseph's trade. **His brethren.** (For a detailed discussion of whether these are uterine brothers, half brothers, or cousins, see J. A. Broadus, *Commentary on the Gospel of Matthew,* pp. 310-312, or P. S. Schaff in *Lange's Commentary on Matthew,* pp. 255-260.) In the absence of any intimation that these **brethren** are to be regarded in an unusual sense, the common understanding of them as children of Joseph and Mary should be inferred. It seems strongly probable that two of them, **James** and **Judas** (Jude), became writers of NT epistles. **56,57.** Though Christ's mother and brothers had moved to Capernaum (4:13), his sisters had evidently married and remained at Nazareth **(with us).** Since Christ's boyhood and early manhood had been undistinguished by any miracles (cf. Jn 2:11), his fellow townsmen were unable to account for or to accept this new development. Thus Jesus employs the same proverb as before to explain their response (Lk 4:24). **58. Not many mighty works there.** Only a few healings (Mk 6:5). **Because of their unbelief.** Christ's power did not depend on men's faith (cf. Jn 9:6, 36; Lk 7:11-15). However, unbelief prevented many opportunities for miracles inasmuch as not many people came to him.

10) Withdrawal of Jesus Following John's Beheading. 14:1-36. The interest of Herod in the reports regarding Jesus was viewed by our Lord as the signal to withdraw. Matthew's order, which previously has been often topical, now becomes chronological throughout.

14:1-12. Herod's guilty interest. **1. Herod the tetrarch.** Herod Antipas, son of Herod the Great, and ruler of Galilee and Perea. His ignorance of Jesus prior to this time may have been due to his absence from the country or to his luxurious habits, which hindered his taking interest in religious movements. **2. This is John the Baptist.** This explanation, first suggested by others (Lk 9:7), eventually was adopted by Herod, who attributed the miracles to a **risen** John, though John had performed no miracles when living. **3,4. Herodias.** Daughter of Aristobolus, a half brother of Antipas. She had been married to her uncle, Herod Philip, and had borne him

4. For John said unto him, It is not lawful for thee to have her.

5. And when he would have put him to death, he feared the multitude, because they counted him as a prophet.

6. But when Herod's birthday was kept, the daughter of Herodias danced before them, and pleased Herod.

7. Whereupon he promised with an oath to give her whatsoever she would ask.

8. And she, being before instructed of her mother, said, Give me here John Baptist's head in a charger.

9. And the king was sorry: nevertheless for the oath's sake, and them which sat with him at meat, he commanded it to be given her.

10. And he sent, and beheaded John in the prison.

11. And his head was brought in a charger, and given to the damsel: and she brought it to her mother.

12. And his disciples came, and took up the body, and buried it, and went and told Jesus.

13. When Jesus heard of it, he departed thence by ship into a desert place apart: and when the people had heard thereof, they followed him on foot out of the cities.

14. And Jesus went forth, and saw a great multitude, and was moved with compassion toward them, and he healed their sick.

15. And when it was evening, his disciples came to him, saying, This is a desert place, and the time is now past; send the multitude away, that they may go into the villages, and buy themselves victuals.

a daughter, Salome. Antipas, however, persuaded her to leave her husband and marry him, though he was already married to the daughter of King Aretas (who escaped to her father, and a war ensued). Such a marriage was adulterous and incestuous. **5. When he would have put him to death.** Herod was torn by mixed emotions (see also v. 9). Pressure from Herodias was balanced by political and even personal considerations (Mk 6:20), and thus final disposition of John had been delayed. **6,7.** The implacable Herodias had not relented, however, and the celebration of **Herod's birthday** provided her opportunity for revenge. Debasing her own daughter by sending her to perform a suggestive dance before Herod and his courtiers, she extracted from this puppet ruler a grandiose promise more fitting for a Persian monarch (Mk 6:23; cf. Est 5:3). **8-11. Being put forward by her mother** (ASV) locates the source of the conspiracy. **Give me here John the Baptist's head upon a platter.** Taking advantage of the opportunity, she made her gory request, which left no room for evasion or delay. This banquet must have been held at Machaerus, where John was imprisoned (Jos *Antiq*. xviii. 5. 2.). **12. His disciples came,** and after burying the headless body, they told Jesus. The problem of earlier days (11:2-6) had been satisfactorily resolved, and now John's followers turned logically to Jesus. In all probability they attached themselves to him.

**13-21. Feeding the five thousand.** The only miracle of Jesus recorded in all four Gospels. It occurred at Passover season (Jn 6:4), thus one year before Christ's death. **13,14. When Jesus heard of it, he departed.** Herod's murder of John and his subsequent notice of the activities of Jesus prompted this withdrawal. Another reason was the return of the Twelve from their mission (Mk 6:30; Lk 9:10), who needed a respite from the crowds and further instruction from Jesus. Soon, however, Jesus surrendered his privacy to minister to the multitude, who had followed **on foot. 15. When it was evening.** The Jews distinguished two evenings, the first beginning about three o'clock, and the second at sundown (cf. Ex 12:6, ASV marg.). The first evening is meant in verse 15; the second in verse 23. Harmonization demands that Jn 6:5-7 be understood as occurring previously. But though Jesus had confronted Philip with the problem earlier in the day, no solution had been reached by the **disciples** except **to send the multitudes away.** And already the **time was past** for locating food and lodging (Lk 9:12)

16. But Jesus said unto them, They need not depart; give ye them to eat.

17. And they say unto him, We have here but five loaves, and two fishes.

18. He said, Bring them hither to me.

19. And he commanded the multitude to sit down on the grass, and took the five loaves, and the two fishes, and looking up to heaven, he blessed, and brake, and gave the loaves to *his* disciples, and the disciples to the multitude.

20. And they did all eat, and were filled: and they took up of the fragments that remained twelve baskets full.

21. And they that had eaten were about five thousand men, beside women and children.

22. And straightway Jesus constrained his disciples to get into a ship, and to go before him unto the other side, while he sent the multitudes away.

23. And when he had sent the multitudes away, he went up into a mountain apart to pray: and when the evening was come, he was there alone.

24. But the ship was now in the midst of the sea, tossed with waves: for the wind was contrary.

25. And in the fourth watch of the night Jesus went unto them, walking on the sea.

26. And when the disciples saw him walking on the sea, they were troubled, saying, It is a spirit; and they cried out for fear.

in this sparsely inhabited region. **16-18. Give ye them to eat.** By laying this responsibility upon the disciples, Christ intended to awaken in them an awareness that association with him included provision for every need. Andrew mentioned the lad with **five** barley **loaves** and **two fishes,** but he seemed totally unaware of the divine possibilities (Jn 6:8,9). **19.** Jesus, however, called for an orderly reclining of the multitude upon the **grass,** and after he had **blessed** the loaves and fishes (equivalent to "giving thanks," Jn 6:11), he distributed by the **disciples** to the **multitude. 20. Fragments.** Broken pieces that had not been eaten (not merely crumbs here). **Twelve baskets full.** Small wicker baskets (different from the large hamper-like baskets mentioned in 15:37), used for carrying articles while traveling. They may have belonged to the apostles, and the fragments collected in them may have supplied the apostles' need. **21. Five thousand men, beside women and children.** The nearness of Passover suggests that these may have been gathering in Galilee for the trip to Jerusalem.

**22-36. Christ's walking on the water. 22. Straightway he constrained the disciples.** The urgency of this action was due to the attempt by the people to make Jesus king by force (Jn 6:15). **23. Mountain.** A secluded place for prayer, apart from the distractions of the unspiritual crowd. The significance of this situation, similar to that of Satan's third temptation (4:8,9), drove Jesus to prayer, that his purpose might be unswerving. From this **mountain** Christ could also observe the disciples in their boat (Mk 6:48). **Evening.** Cf. comment on verse 15. **24.** Ancient manuscripts vary between **in the midst of the sea** and **many furlongs distant from the land** (ASV marg.). John 6:19 shows the distance from shore to have been from three to three and one-half miles. **25. Fourth watch of the night.** That is, from 3 to 6 A.M. The men had been rowing since some time after sundown and were nearing exhaustion. Rough sea and head winds prevented progress. Though the disciples had witnessed Jesus' power over a storm (Mt 8:23-27), this time he was not with them. The new lesson for them was that Christ's power would sustain them in every appointed task, regardless of whether he was present bodily. **Walking on the sea.** To do this required mastery over gravity, wind, and wave. **26. An apparition.** A spectre or ghost. The frantic disciples gave way to current superstition. Perhaps they felt it was a harbinger of death to them. **27. It is I.** On such a dark, stormy night, the

27. But straightway Jesus spake unto them, saying, Be of good cheer; it is I; be not afraid.

28. And Peter answered him and said, Lord, if it be thou, bid me come unto thee on the water.

29. And he said, Come. And when Peter was come down out of the ship, he walked on the water, to go to Jesus.

30. But when he saw the wind boisterous, he was afraid; and beginning to sink, he cried, saying, Lord, save me.

31. And immediately Jesus stretched forth *his* hand, and caught him, and said unto him, O thou of little faith, wherefore didst thou doubt?

32. And when they were come into the ship, the wind ceased.

33. Then they that were in the ship came and worshipped him, saying, Of a truth thou art the Son of God.

34. And when they were gone over, they came into the land of Gennesaret.

35. And when the men of that place had knowledge of him, they sent out into all that country round about, and brought unto him all that were diseased;

36. And besought him that they might only touch the hem of his garment: and as many as touched were made perfectly whole.

### CHAPTER 15

THEN came to Jesus scribes and Pharisees, which were of Jerusalem, saying,

2. Why do thy disciples transgress the tradition of the elders? for they wash not their hands when they eat bread.

sound of the familiar voice brought reassurance where sight was insufficient.

28-33. Peter's walking on the water is given by Matthew only. **28,29. Lord, if it be thou.** With characteristic impulsiveness he desired to be given a command to come to Jesus **on the water.** But to accuse Peter of ostentation is to find more fault than Jesus did. **30. When he saw the wind,** i.e., its effects. Though formerly the wind had been just as strong, Peter's full attention had been centered in faith on Jesus, and the Lord had honored his faith by granting him supernatural power. When the concentration of faith was broken, Peter reverted to the control of natural powers. **31. Jesus stretched forth his hand.** A new display of supernatural power, not just physical rescue by human strength. **Thou of little faith.** The miracle had been granted to show, first, that complete faith in Jesus as the divine Messiah is sufficient for every appointed task, and second, that Jesus' refusal to accept the political proposals of the crowd (Jn 6:15) should not disillusion them. **32,33. Thou art the Son of God.** Equivalent to the Divine Deliverer, the Messiah or Christ. Though such identification had been made earlier by the disciples (Jn 1:41,49), there was an ever increasing realization by the Twelve of what these terms meant.

34-36. **They came to the land, unto Gennesaret.** A fertile plain several miles south of Capernaum. Since the discourse in the synagogue at Capernaum seems to have taken place on the day following the miraculous feeding (Jn 6:22,59), this paragraph may be a general description of events that covered several days or weeks, before and after the visit to Capernaum. The desire of the sick to **touch the hem of his garment** was probably motivated by reports of the cure of hemorrhage that had previously occurred in this region (9:20).

11) Conflict with the Pharisees over Tradition. 15:1-20. Local opposition from Galilean Pharisees (ch. 12) was now reinforced by a delegation from Jerusalem. Such opposition would increase in frequency and intensity during this final year. **1. From Jerusalem, Pharisees and scribes.** Probably sent from headquarters to check on Jesus and harass him. **2. Why do thy disciples transgress.** Though the charge is oblique, the insinuation is clear that Jesus' teaching is responsible for the breach. **They wash not their hands.** The rabbinic custom (not Mosaic) was not hygienic but ceremonial. Its binding force was popularly considered greater than that of the Law it-

3. But he answered and said unto them, Why do ye also transgress the commandment of God by your tradition?

4. For God commanded, saying, Honor thy father and mother: and, He that curseth father or mother, let him die the death.

5. But ye say, Whosoever shall say to *his* father or *his* mother, *It is* a gift, by whatsoever thou mightest be profited by me;

6. And honor not his father or his mother, *he shall be free.* Thus have ye made the commandment of God of none effect by your tradition.

7. *Ye* hypocrites, well did Esaias prophesy of you, saying,

8. This people draweth nigh unto me with their mouth, and honoreth me with *their* lips; but their heart is far from me.

9. But in vain they do worship me, teaching *for* doctrines the commandments of men.

10. And he called the multitude, and said unto them, Hear, and understand:

11. Not that which goeth into the mouth defileth a man; but that which cometh out of the mouth, this defileth a man.

12. Then came his disciples, and said unto him, Knowest thou that the Pharisees were offended, after they heard this saying?

13. But he answered and said, Every plant, which my heavenly Father hath not planted, shall be rooted up.

14. Let them alone: they be blind leaders of the blind. And if the blind lead the blind, both shall fall into the ditch.

self, and some rabbis went to absurd lengths to observe it (see Mk 7:4). **3. Why do you also transgress the commandment of God.** An admission that Christ's disciples transgressed the elders' tradition, but the contrast to the **commandment of God** showed the logic of such action. **4-6.** Some traditions actually violated the Law itself. The fifth commandment (Ex 20:12; 21:17) was violated by the callous strategem of calling whatever might have been used for assisting one's parents a gift (to God), and thus beyond the claim of the parents. As if God wants from a man what belongs to his parents! Whether the property eventually was given to God is not discussed, though there are evidences of abuses. **7-9.** To summarize, Jesus cites Isa 29:13, in which **this people** may be regarded not merely as contemporaries of the prophet, but as the nation of Israel throughout her history; or else the denunciation of Isaiah's contemporaries was a typical prophecy of Messiah's contemporaries. **10. And he called the multitude.** The preceding exchange had been somewhat private between Christ and the Pharisees and scribes. **11. Not that which goeth into the mouth defileth a man. Defileth** is literally *makes common*, derived from the Levitical distinction between foods allowed by God and all others, viewed as common, profane, "unclean." By this statement, Jesus is not abrogating the Levitical code (nor should Mk 7:19 be so interpreted), an abrogation not announced till after Pentecost (Acts 10–11), but was stating the principle that moral defilement is spiritual, not physical. Food is amoral (I Tim 4:3-5). Sin lies in the heart of the man who disobeys God and perverts its use. Even the defilement arising to a Jew from eating meat Levitically unclean was caused not by the food itself, but by the rebellious heart that acted in disobedience to God. **12-14.** The **disciples** were apparently disturbed over Christ's offending these influential **Pharisees**, and 15:15 indicates they did not understand fully the import of Jesus' statement. **Every plant.** Doctrine of mere human tradition, such as these Pharisees were demanding. **Shall be rooted up.** A prediction of ultimate destruction of all false doctrine, the symbolism perhaps including the persons holding these teachings (cf. 13:19,38 for similar combining). **Let them alone.** As teachers of spiritual truth, the traditionalists were to be abandoned. They were as **blind** spiritually as those who depended on them. **Pit.** Not a *ditch* (AV) beside the road, but an open cistern in the field.

**15. Declare unto us this parable.** Peter

15. Then answered Peter and said unto him, Declare unto us this parable.

16. And Jesus said, Are ye also yet without understanding?

17. Do not ye yet understand, that whatsoever entereth in at the mouth goeth into the belly, and is cast out into the draught?

18. But those things which proceed out of the mouth come forth from the heart; and they defile the man.

19. For out of the heart proceed evil thoughts, murders, adulteries, fornications, thefts, false witness, blasphemies:

20. These are *the things* which defile a man: but to eat with unwashen hands defileth not a man.

21. Then Jesus went thence, and departed into the coasts of Tyre and Sidon.

22. And, behold, a woman of Canaan came out of the same coasts, and cried unto him, saying, Have mercy on me, O Lord, *thou* Son of David; my daughter is grievously vexed with a devil.

23. But he answered her not a word. And his disciples came and besought him, saying, Send her away; for she crieth after us.

24. But he answered and said, I am not sent but unto the lost sheep of the house of Israel.

25. Then came she and worshipped him, saying, Lord, help me.

referred to the statement of 15:11 (as comparison with Mk 7:15-17 indicates). **Parable** is used here in the sense of "difficult saying." The difficulty lay not in the use of symbols but in the departure from tradition, which had confused moral and ceremonial defilement. **16. Are ye also even yet without understanding?** Christ's amazement, though he had not dealt with this specific subject before (but compare 9:14-17; chs. 5—7), suggests that spiritually enlightened persons should have understood this principle, for it has always been true. **17.** Whatever defilement is attached to foods entering the **mouth** is physical and is removed from the body at the **draught**, i.e., the latrine, or privy. **18,19.** But things proceeding **out of the mouth** are spiritually defiling, for all sinful words and deeds find their source in **evil thoughts**, arising in an evil **heart** (cf. 5:21-48). After **evil thoughts**, violations of the Commandments, from the sixth through the ninth, are listed, concluding with **blasphemies**—abusive speech against God or man. **20. To eat with unwashen hands defileth not.** Thus Jesus summarizes by returning to the original question.

12) Withdrawal to Phoenicia, and Healing of a Canaanitish Woman's Daughter. 15:21-28. The forthright attack by the Pharisees (vv. 1,2), emboldened by the recent execution of John and the opposition of Herod, prompted this second withdrawal. The interview with the woman pictures clearly the historical setting of Christ's ministry, together with the wider aspects of his grace. **21. Withdrew into the parts of Tyre and Sidon** (ASV). Though some dispute the point, it seems clear that Jesus actually left the land of Israel and Herod's jurisdiction (cf. also Mk 7:31, ASV), to stay secluded for a time in Phoenicia. **22. A Canaanitish woman.** By race. Inhabitants of this region are called Canaanites in Num 13:29; Jud 1:30,32,33. Mark 7:26 designates her as Syrophoenician in citizenship. **Son of David.** This Messianic designation by the woman implies some awareness of Jewish religion; yet the passage does not suggest that she was a proselyte. **23. He answered her not a word.** Partly to be explained by Jesus' attempt to remain secluded (Mk 7:24). However, the discussion that follows indicates the focus of Christ's mission, and this procedure of Jesus made the instruction most effective. The fact that Mark omits mention of Christ's silence may indicate that this action was not so startling as one might suppose. **Send her away.** This statement by the impatient disciples may

26. But he answered and said, It is not meet to take the children's bread, and to cast *it* to dogs.

27. And she said, Truth, Lord: yet the dogs eat of the crumbs which fall from their masters' table.

28. Then Jesus answered and said unto her, O woman, great *is* thy faith: be it unto thee even as thou wilt. And her daughter was made whole from that very hour.

29. And Jesus departed from thence, and came nigh unto the sea of Galilee; and went up into a mountain, and sat down there.

30. And great multitudes came unto him, having with them *those that were* lame, blind, dumb, maimed, and many others, and cast them down at Jesus' feet; and he healed them:

31. Insomuch that the multitude wondered, when they saw the dumb to speak, the maimed to be whole, the lame to walk, and the blind to see: and they glorified the God of Israel.

32. Then Jesus called his disciples *unto him*, and said, I have compassion on the multitude, because they continue with me now three days, and have nothing to eat: and I will not send them away fasting, lest they faint in the way.

33. And his disciples say unto him, Whence should we have so much bread in the wilderness, as to fill so great a multitude?

imply that Christ should grant her request and thus dismiss the case, for his reply reveals that an appeal had been made. **26. To take the children's bread and cast it to dogs.** This Gentile woman was acquainted with the Jews' custom of referring to Gentiles as dogs and to themselves as God's children. The seeming harshness of Christ's expression is softened by the fact that the term denotes not the vicious, wild scavengers that roamed the streets, but **little dogs** (*kunaria*) that lived as pets in people's houses. Jesus told this Gentile what he told a Samaritan woman, that at this time all were dependent on Israel for Messiah and his blessings (Jn 4:21-23). Jesus had healed Gentiles on other occasions, but here in Phoenicia he had to be careful not to give the impression that he was abandoning Israel (cf. Mt 4:24; 8:5). **27,28. Even the little dogs eat of the crumbs.** The woman accepted fully the divine order, and her faith grasped the truth that applied to her. It was this faith that Christ praised. **Great is thy faith.** The second Gentile to be praised for faith (8:10), and the third instance of Christ's healing at a distance (Mt 8:13; Jn 4:50).

13) Return to the Sea of Galilee (Decapolis, Mk 7:31), and Performing of Miracles. 15:29-38. Mark shows that Jesus proceeded northward in Phoenicia through Sidon, then eastward across the Jordan, and finally southward through Decapolis till he reached the Sea of Galilee. This route suggests that he deliberately avoided the domain of Herod Antipas.

**29-31. Healing the multitudes. 29. Sea of Galilee.** Apparently the southeast shore. **30. Multitudes** came. Of the many who were healed, Mark has described the case of a deaf and dumb man (Mk 7:32-37). **31. They glorified the God of Israel.** An indication that these were Gentile environs in which Jesus imparted the knowledge of the true God and the Messianic promises.

**32-38. Feeding the four thousand.** To claim that this narrative relates the same incident as the feeding of the five thousand is to make this Gospel and Mark mere collections of traditions that have become confused, and to treat the words of Jesus in Mt 16:9,10 as mere invention. The differences in details are numerous, and there is nothing essentially improbable about two miraculous feedings. **32. They continue with me now three days.** What food had been brought was now exhausted. **33. Whence should we have so much bread?** To insist that the Twelve had forgotten the previous feeding is unwarranted. They merely state their personal inability to sup-

34. And Jesus saith unto them, How many loaves have ye? And they said, Seven, and a few little fishes.

35. And he commanded the multitude to sit down on the ground.

36. And he took the seven loaves and the fishes, and gave thanks, and brake *them,* and gave to his disciples, and the disciples to the multitude.

37. And they did all eat, and were filled: and they took up of the broken *meat* that was left seven baskets full.

38. And they that did eat were four thousand men, beside women and children.

39. And he sent away the multitude, and took ship, and came into the coasts of Magdala.

## CHAPTER 16

THE Pharisees also with the Sadducees came, and tempting desired him that he would show them a sign from heaven.

2. He answered and said unto them, When it is evening, ye say, *It will be* fair weather: for the sky is red.

3. And in the morning, *It will be* foul weather to-day: for the sky is red and lowering. O *ye* hypocrites, ye can discern the face of the sky; but can ye not *discern* the signs of the times?

4. A wicked and adulterous generation seeketh after a sign; and there shall no sign be given unto it, but the sign of the prophet Jonas. And he left them, and departed.

ply, and refrain from presuming to ask Jesus for another miracle (in view of Jn 6:26). **34-38.** From **seven** loaves and a few **fishes** Christ fed the **multitude of four thousand men** and their families in much the same way as he had fed the five thousand. The uneaten pieces amounted to **seven baskets full.** Here the **baskets** are the larger *spurides,* or hampers, which the disciples may have been using on their recent journey, as compared to the smaller *kophinoi* of 14:20, a distinction maintained in 16:9,10. The seven baskets may have contained more than the twelve on the previous occasion.

14) Renewed Conflict with the Pharisees and Sadducees. 15:39—16:4.

**39. Magdala.** Better, *Magadan.* The location is unknown. Mark 8:10 has *Dalmanutha,* the location of which is similarly uncertain. The place was apparently on the west shore of Galilee. **16:1. Pharisees and Sadducees came.** Traditional foes, joined by a common hatred of Jesus. Sadducees appear only two other times in the Gospel record: at John's baptism (3:7), and during Christ's last week (22:23). **A sign from heaven.** This request, similar to that in 12:38, minimizes all previous miracles of Jesus, and demands a spectacular display that is unmistakably of heavenly origin. This they asked with the ulterior design of **tempting him,** by making him do what he had formerly refused to do (12:39) or else discrediting him by showing his inability. The part of Christ's reply recorded in 16:2,3 is missing in many ancient manuscripts, but contained by some. The figure is similar to that in Lk 12:54-56. It calls attention to men's ability to forecast the weather from available data, but the complete inability of Christ's contemporaries to read the spiritual **signs of the times.** John's preaching, Jesus' teaching and works, Daniel's prophecy of the seventy weeks—all should have been significant factors to the discerning. **4. The sign of the prophet Jonah.** (Cf. comment on 12:38-40.) A reference to Christ's bodily resurrection. This was the great sign to which he always pointed when pressed (Jn 2:18-22; Mt 12:38-40), to believers a precious proof of their redemption but to unbelievers a portent of coming judgment by the risen Christ.

15) Withdrawal to the Region of Caesarea Philippi. 16:5—17:23. This fourth retirement takes Jesus again to Gentile surroundings, away from the tensions of constant opposition (cf. Bethsaida Julias, 14:13; Phoenicia, 15:21; Decapolis, 15:29;

5. And when his disciples were come to the other side, they had forgotten to take bread.

6. Then Jesus said unto them, Take heed and beware of the leaven of the Pharisees and of the Sadducees.

7. And they reasoned among themselves, saying, It is because we have taken no bread.

8. Which when Jesus perceived, he said unto them, O ye of little faith, why reason ye among yourselves, because ye have brought no bread?

9. Do ye not yet understand, neither remember the five loaves of the five thousand, and how many baskets ye took up?

10. Neither the seven loaves of the four thousand, and how many baskets ye took up?

11. How is it that ye do not understand that I spake it not to you concerning bread, that ye should beware of the leaven of the Pharisees and of the Sadducees?

12. Then understood they how that he bade them not beware of the leaven of bread, but of the doctrine of the Pharisees and of the Sadducees.

13. When Jesus came into the coasts of Caesarea Philippi, he asked his disciples, saying, Whom do men say that I, the Son of man, am?

14. And they said, Some say that thou art John the Baptist; some, Elias; and others, Jeremias, or one of the prophets.

15. He saith unto them, But whom say ye that I am?

16. And Simon Peter answered and said, Thou art the Christ, the Son of the living God.

Mk 7:31). During this period, perhaps of several months' duration, occurred the momentous confession of Peter, Christ's detailed prediction of His coming passion, and the Transfiguration.

**5-12. Conversation en route. 5. To the other side,** i.e., to the northeast part (Bethsaida Julias, Mk 8:22), en route to Caesarea Philippi (Mt 16:13). **Forgot to take bread.** Rapid departure from Magadan may have caused this oversight, so that only one old loaf could be found in the boat (Mk 8:14). **6. Leaven of the Pharisees and Sadducees.** (On leaven, see 13: 33.) The permeating evil influence of these determined opponents of Christ is the point involved. **7-11.** Yet the disciples, embarrassed at their oversight, failed to grasp the symbolism. **O ye of little faith.** Jesus knew that their failure to understand was due to their anxiety over provisions, and reminded them of the lessons of trust they should have learned. **12. The teaching of the Pharisees and Sadducees.** Pharisees were legalists and traditionalists, whose emphasis upon ritual was hypocritical and spiritually deadening (Lk 12:1). Sadducees were rationalists, who did not believe in resurrection nor in the existence of spirit beings that cannot be explained naturally (Acts 23:8). They numbered among themselves the priestly hierarchy of Israel. Warning against such subtle rationalistic teachings is still pertinent.

**13-20. Peter's confession. 13. The parts of Caesarea Philippi** (ASV). The outlying villages (Mk 8:27). Jesus is not said to have entered the city. **Caesarea Philippi.** About twenty-five miles north of the Sea of Galilee. **14.** The variety of opinions which men held concerning Jesus showed that although many connected him with Messianic prophecy, none regarded him properly. **John the Baptist** was the predicted forerunner (3:1-3; 14:1,2). **Elijah** was to precede the "day of the Lord" (Mal 4:5,6). **Jeremiah** was expected by some to appear and restore the ark he had supposedly hidden (II Macc 2:1-8). **15,16.** After causing the Twelve to dispose of erroneous ideas, Jesus asked their personal opinion. **Thou art the Christ, the Son of the living God.** All doubtless concurred, but Peter rose to the occasion with the unequivocal response. Similar statements had been uttered before, some much earlier (Jn 1:41, 49), but many false notions about the character and purpose of Messiah needed to be removed. Thus the statement by Peter here is not the product of early enthusiasm but of studied reflection and solemn faith. The popular notion of a mere political leader is superseded by the concept of the Messiah

17. And Jesus answered and said unto him, Blessed art thou, Simon Bar–jona: for flesh and blood hath not revealed *it* unto thee, but my Father which is in heaven.

18. And I say also unto thee, That thou art Peter, and upon this rock I will build my church; and the gates of hell shall not prevail against it.

19. And I will give unto thee the keys of the kingdom of heaven: and whatsoever thou shalt bind on earth shall be bound in heaven; and whatsoever thou shalt loose on earth shall be loosed in heaven.

as the Son of God, the definite article the marking him out as unique. **17.** Such spiritual knowledge was not the product of unaided humanity (**flesh and blood;** compare this expression in Gal 1:16; Eph 6:12; Heb 2:14), but of divine revelation. Spiritual truth can be comprehended only by those whose spiritual faculties have been made alive by God (I Cor 2:11-14). Such spiritual discernment was an evidence of Peter's **blessed** spiritual state.

**18. Upon this rock I will build my church.** There is an obvious play upon the words **Peter** (*Petros*, proper name denoting a piece of rock) and **rock** (*petra*, a rocky mass). The spiritual body, the **church**, mentioned here for the first time, is built upon the divinely revealed fact about Christ confessed by Peter (I Cor 3:11; I Pet 2:4) as men are made aware of and acknowledge His person and work (so Chrysostom, Augustine). Another view common among some Protestants (Alford, Broadus, Vincent) is that Peter (along with the other apostles; Eph 2:20; Rev 21:14) is the **rock,** but without the papal supremacy ascribed to him by unscriptural Romish notions. **The gates of Hades shall not prevail against it. Hades** (equivalent to **Sheol**), the realm of the dead. **Gates.** The entrance to Hades, which is usually death. Christ's Church, which would be inaugurated at Pentecost, would not be at the mercy of physical death, for the Lord's resurrection would insure the resurrection of all believers. More specifically, believers who die before the resurrection go immediately to be with Christ, not to Hades (Eph 4:8, RSV; Phil 1:23; II Cor 5:8). **19. The keys of the kingdom of heaven. Keys** symbolize authority to open. **To thee** relates this promise to Peter alone. It refers to the choice of Peter, as first among equals, for officially opening the **kingdom** (since Pentecost, including the whole sphere of Christian profession; cf. 13:3-52) to Jews (Acts 2:14 ff.) and Gentiles (Acts 10:1–11:18; 15:7,14). Some, however, explain the passage eschatologically, as applying to the reign of the saints over the earth in the Millennium (A. J. McClain, *The Greatness of the Kingdom*, p. 329 f.). **Whatsoever thou shalt bind on earth.** This part of the responsibility was later given to all the disciples (18:18), who were eventually empowered for the task (Jn 20:22,23). If Jn 20:23 be an explanation of the binding and loosing, as meaning remitting and retaining sins, then Acts 10:43 is an instance of its exercise. By the proclamation of the Gospel, announcement is made that acceptance brings loosing from sin's guilt and penalty, and

20. Then charged he his disciples that they should tell no man that he was Jesus the Christ.

21. From that time forth began Jesus to show unto his disciples, how that he must go unto Jerusalem, and suffer many things of the elders and chief priests and scribes, and be killed, and be raised again the third day.

22. Then Peter took him, and began to rebuke him, saying, Be it far from thee, Lord: this shall not be unto thee.

23. But he turned, and said unto Peter, Get thee behind me, Satan: thou art an offense unto me: for thou savorest not the things that be of God, but those that be of men.

24. Then said Jesus unto his disciples, If any *man* will come after me, let him deny himself, and take up his cross, and follow me.

25. For whosoever will save his life shall lose it: and whosoever will lose his life for my sake shall find it.

26. For what is a man profited, if he shall gain the whole world, and lose his own soul? or what shall a man give in exchange for his soul?

rejection leaves the sinner bound for judgment. **20. Tell no man that he was Christ.** The populace as yet would only be politically aroused by such disclosure. **21-27.** Jesus' prediction of his death and resurrection. **21. From that time forth began Jesus.** Now that Jesus had a nucleus of followers who truly believed in him as Messiah (16:16), he entered upon a period of plain teaching regarding his redemptive work. **Elders, chief priests,** and **scribes** formed the Sanhedrin. **Be killed and be raised again.** Though Christ clearly predicted his resurrection following his death, this consequence failed to register with the Twelve. **Third day.** Equivalent to "after three days," Mk 8:31. **22.** Peter's remonstrance, **Be it far from thee, Lord** (an idiom meaning, "God have mercy on thee and spare thee"), showed his complete failure to recognize in the Jewish Messiah the aspect of suffering (Isa 53). **23. Get thee behind me, Satan.** Similar to Jesus' words to Satan in 4:10, uttered here in a comparable situation. Satan, using Peter as his tool, was again trying to turn Jesus aside from the suffering that was His lot. **Thou mindest not the things of God** (ASV). Peter's divinely revealed avowal (v.16) had briefly displayed the appropriateness of his Christ-given name, but here he shows the presence of carnal weakness. Before Pentecost the Twelve often vacillated between keen spiritual discernment and the grossest carnality. And such is often tragically the case among believers today.

**24.** At this point Jesus and the Twelve were joined by a multitude (Mk 8:34), even though the Lord had been in relative seclusion. **Let him deny himself,** i.e., renounce or disown himself, as far as being able to merit eternal life is concerned. **Take up his cross and follow me.** A well-known figure of suffering and death (cf. comment on 10:38,39). Here it pictures the conversion of a sinner who must recognize his own spiritual poverty, and then accept Christ (His person and teaching), even though it will mean assuming, in some sense, suffering that would otherwise not occur. **25. Whosoever will save his life shall lose it** (cf. on 10:39). He who is unwilling to assume the hazards involved in being a disciple of Christ will ultimately lose his life eternally. But the converse is also true. **26. If he shall gain the whole world and forfeit his life** (ASV). **Life** is *psychē*, the Greek term covering both English concepts of "life" and "soul." Luke 9:25 uses the word "self." The figure pictures a business transaction in which a man exchanges his very life (including the

27. For the Son of man shall come in the glory of his Father with his angels; and then he shall reward every man according to his works.

28. Verily I say unto you, There be some standing here, which shall not taste of death, till they see the Son of man coming in his kingdom.

### CHAPTER 17

AND after six days Jesus taketh Peter, James, and John his brother, and bringeth them up into a high mountain apart,

2. And was transfigured before them: and his face did shine as the sun, and his raiment was white as the light.

3. And, behold, there appeared unto them Moses and Elias talking with him.

soul) for this world's attractions. What would such a man use to buy back his *psychē?* 27. The Son of man shall come. At Christ's second coming, he will settle all accounts. Thus, suffering for Christ, even unto death, will receive its proper reward. 28. To stress the reality of his coming and kingdom as an incentive to men to follow him, even in suffering, Christ gave the promise of verse 28. This coming of the Son of man in his kingdom is explained by some as the destruction of Jerusalem and by others as the beginning of the Church. But referring it to the Transfiguration meets the requirements of the context (all Synoptists follow this statement with the Transfiguration, Mk 9:1; Lk 9:27). Furthermore, Peter, who was one of those standing here, referred to the Transfiguration in the same words (II Pet 1:16-18). Chafer calls the Transfiguration a "preview of the coming kingdom on earth" (L. S. Chafer, *Systematic Theology,* V, 85).

17:1-13. The Transfiguration. At this strategic moment in the ministry of Jesus, when he had evoked from Peter the true designation of himself (16:16), and had announced his coming death and resurrection, there was granted to three disciples this most remarkable experience.

1. After six days. So also Mk 9:2. Luke's "about eight days" (9:28) counts the termini as well as the interval. Peter, James, and John. These former business associates (Lk 5:10) were granted special privileges on two other occasions (Lk 8:51; Mt 26:37). Can it be that they had more spiritual perception at this time than the others? High mountain. The traditional Mount Tabor is contextually unlikely. More probable is a location near Caesarea Philippi (16:13), perhaps one of the spurs of Hermon. 2. He was transfigured before them. The verb *(metamorphoō)* denotes a transformation of the essential form, proceeding from within, and is used in Rom 12:2 and II Cor 3:18 of the spiritual transformation that characterizes Christians as the new nature is manifested in them. Though for believers this transformation is a gradual experience, to be completed when Christ is seen (II Cor 3:18; I Jn 3:2), in the case of Jesus, the glorious form that was usually veiled was briefly displayed. 3. Moses and Elijah, the outstanding representatives, in Jewish thinking, of the Law and the Prophets, appeared talking with him about the coming events at Jerusalem (Lk 9:31). Such conversation showed the disciples that the death of Messiah was not incompatible with the OT. Viewing the Transfiguration as a preview of the

**4.** Then answered Peter, and said unto Jesus, Lord, it is good for us to be here: if thou wilt, let us make here three tabernacles; one for thee, and one for Moses, and one for Elias.

**5.** While he yet spake, behold, a bright cloud overshadowed them: and behold a voice out of the cloud, which said, This is my beloved Son, in whom I am well pleased; hear ye him.

**6.** And when the disciples heard *it*, they fell on their face, and were sore afraid.

**7.** And Jesus came and touched them, and said, Arise, and be not afraid.

**8.** And when they had lifted up their eyes, they saw no man, save Jesus only.

**9.** And as they came down from the mountain, Jesus charged them, saying, Tell the vision to no man, until the Son of man be risen again from the dead.

**10.** And his disciples asked him, saying, Why then say the scribes that Elias must first come?

**11.** And Jesus answered and said unto them, Elias truly shall first come, and restore all things.

**12.** But I say unto you, That Elias is come already, and they knew him not, but have done unto him whatsoever they listed. Likewise shall also the Son of man suffer of them.

**13.** Then the disciples understood that he spake unto them of John the Baptist.

**14.** And when they were come to the multitude, there came to him a *certain* man, kneeling down to him, and saying,

Messianic kingdom (16:28), some have seen in Moses (who had died) and Elijah (who had passed from this life without dying) representatives of the two groups that Christ will bring with him to establish his kingdom: dead saints who are resurrected and living saints who have been translated. Likewise the three disciples are seen as representing men living on earth at the time of the Second Advent (L. S. Chafer, *Systematic Theology*, V, 85-94; G. N. H. Peters, *Theocratic Kingdom*, II, 559-561). **4,5. Peter answered,** i.e., responded to the situation. A desire to prolong this experience prompted Peter to offer to erect (**I will make**) three brush **tabernacles,** such as worshipers built for the Feast of Tabernacles. In response, the Divine **voice came out of the cloud** acknowledging Jesus as God's **beloved Son,** and commanding the disciples, **Hear ye him.** Moses and Elijah had nothing new to impart (Heb 1:1,2). **6-9.** Frightened by the voice, the disciples were reassured but cautioned at the conclusion of these events. **Tell the vision to no man.** Apparently not even the other apostles were to be informed at this time. The things they had witnessed would only confuse and politically arouse the less perceptive. **10. Why then say the scribes that Elijah must first come?** The presence of Elijah on the mount and the subsequent command to silence prompted the question. If this was the predicted coming of Elijah (Mal 4:5), then surely it was time for public announcement. If not, how could Jesus be Messiah, for that personage was to be preceded by Elijah? **11. Elijah indeed cometh** (ASV). Futuristic present form. Jesus here claims that Mal 4:5 will be fulfilled. **12,13. Elijah is come already.** To the unspiritual Jews who were merely hunting for signs, John himself had said, "I am not Elijah" (i.e., the resurrected OT prophet, Jn 1:21). Yet to those who were spiritually sensitive, John had come "in the spirit and power of Elijah" (Lk 1:17), and men had been directed to Christ by him. Thus Jesus' offer of the kingdom was a valid offer, contingent upon national acceptance, and Israel could not blame the absence of Elijah for her failure to recognize Jesus. God in his foreknowledge knew that Israel, at the first coming of Christ, would not be ready for the final Elijah's ministry, and so he sent John "in the spirit and power of Elijah" instead.

**14-20.** Healing of a demon-possessed epileptic. Each Synoptist follows the Transfiguration with this account, but the narrative in Mark (9:14-29) is the fullest. **15. Lord, have mercy on my son, for he is**

15. Lord, have mercy on my son; for he is lunatic, and sore vexed: for ofttimes he falleth into the fire, and oft into the water.

16. And I brought him to thy disciples, and they could not cure him.

17. Then Jesus answered and said, O faithless and perverse generation, how long shall I be with you? how long shall I suffer you? bring him hither to me.

18. And Jesus rebuked the devil; and he departed out of him: and the child was cured from that very hour.

19. Then came the disciples to Jesus apart, and said, Why could not we cast him out?

20. And Jesus said unto them, Because of your unbelief: for verily I say unto you, If ye have faith as a grain of mustard seed, ye shall say unto this mountain, Remove hence to yonder place; and it shall remove: and nothing shall be impossible unto you.

21. Howbeit this kind goeth not out but by prayer and fasting.

22. And while they abode in Galilee, Jesus said unto them, The Son of man shall be betrayed into the hands of men:

23. And they shall kill him, and the third day he shall be raised again. And they were exceeding sorry.

24. And when they were come to Capernaum, they that received tribute *money* came to Peter, and said, Doth not your master pay tribute?

25. He saith, Yes. And when he was come into the house, Jesus prevented him, saying, What thinkest thou, Simon? of whom do the kings of the earth take custom or tribute? of their own children, or of strangers?

26. Peter saith unto him, Of strangers. Jesus saith unto him, Then are the children free.

epileptic (ASV). Literally, *moonstruck* (cf. Latin etymology of "lunatic"). The symptoms are generally regarded as describing epilepsy, produced here by demon possession. 17. O faithless and perverse generation. In words similar to those of Deut 32:5, Jesus cites the faithlessness of the nine apostles as characteristic of their generation. Their faithlessness consisted in their failure to appropriate fully the power granted them in 10:8. 18. Jesus by removing the demon (the cause) brought about the cure of the illness (the effect). 19. Why could not we cast him out? This was doubtless their first failure after they had received Christ's authorization (10:8). 20. Because of your unbelief. Not unbelief in Jesus as Messiah, but doubts as to his words given to them formerly (10:8). As a grain of mustard seed. Its smallness was proverbial. The power of faith is illustrated by its ability to remove this mountain. (Did Jesus point to the Mount of Transfiguration?) Rather than soften the expression by making "mountain" symbolic of any difficulty, it is best to treat it literally. However, it must be borne in mind that Scriptural faith is a trust in God's revealed Word and will. Hence faith to move a mountain can be exercised only when God reveals that to be his will. Verse 21 is omitted by the best manuscripts, being an interpolation from Mk 9:29.

22,23. Renewed prediction of death and resurrection. While they were gathering themselves together in Galilee (ASV marg.). Though manuscript evidence is conflicting, this reading seems best attested and agrees well with Mk 9:30. Because of Jesus' desire for secrecy, the Twelve may have returned by separate routes, and upon meeting again, received this disclosure. The Son of man shall be delivered up. Delivered up is less interpretative than *betrayed* (AV), though it may suggest betrayal.

16) Instruction of the Twelve at Capernaum. 17:24—18:35.

24-27. Payment of the temple tax. 24. Capernaum. The final visit of Jesus to this city of his residence. Does not your master pay the half-shekel *(didrachma)?* This ecclesiastical assessment, based on Ex 30:11-16, was originally for the support of the Tabernacle, and was reinstituted after the Exile (Neh 10:32, one-third shekel). Apparently in Jesus' time the Jews followed Nehemiah's annual plan, but charged at Moses' rate. The payment, usually made in the spring, was some months overdue. 25,26. Jesus spake first to him (ASV), i.e.,

27. Notwithstanding, lest we should offend them, go thou to the sea, and cast a hook, and take up the fish that first cometh up; and when thou hast opened his mouth, thou shalt find a piece of money: that take, and give unto them for me and thee.

## CHAPTER 18

AT the same time came the disciples unto Jesus, saying, Who is the greatest in the kingdom of heaven?

2. And Jesus called a little child unto him, and set him in the midst of them,

3. And said, Verily I say unto you, Except ye be converted, and become as little children, ye shall not enter into the kingdom of heaven.

4. Whosoever therefore shall humble himself as this little child, the same is greatest in the kingdom of heaven.

5. And whoso shall receive one such little child in my name receiveth me.

6. But whoso shall offend one of these little ones which believe in me, it were better for him that a millstone were hanged about his neck, and *that* he were drowned in the depth of the sea.

7. Woe unto the world because of offenses! for it must needs be that offenses come; but woe to that man by whom the offense cometh!

anticipated him. Recognizing Peter's confusion, arising from loyalty to Jesus' integrity and perhaps anxiety over lack of funds, our Lord shows by illustration that the **children** of **kings** are exempt from **toll.** Thus Jesus, the Son of God, is not personally obligated to pay tribute for the support of God's house. **27. Lest we cause them to stumble.** For Jesus to have claimed his privilege would very possibly have created wrong impressions among the people, including perhaps disrespect for God's house. The miracle, demonstrating Jesus' omniscience in knowing which fish had the **shekel,** and his omnipotence in causing it to be the first one caught, emphasized the fact of his deity (and thus his right of exemption from the tax), which might have been obscured by the payment he intended to make. **Shekel.** A *statēr,* equal to four drachmas or two half-shekels, and thus sufficient for Jesus and Peter.

**18:1-14.** Instruction on greatness. **1. Who is the greatest?** The background of this question lay in a dispute among the disciples as they journeyed (Mk 9:33; Lk 9:46). Perhaps it had been kindled by the prominence given to the three at Caesarea Philippi (17:1) or to Peter in the temple tax incident (17:27). **2-4.** Calling to himself a **little child,** he warned the disciples that unless they turned from exalted opinions of themselves, their problem would not be one of relative greatness but of entrance into the **kingdom of heaven** (the Messianic kingdom they looked for him to establish). The absence of pride in position is the aspect of childhood referred to here. To enter Christ's kingdom, a man must realize his personal inadequacy, and his complete dependence on the Lord. He must experience a new birth (Jn 3:3 ff.).

**5. One such little child,** i.e., a person who, by believing, has become as a little child (cf. v. 6). Verses 5-14 no longer discuss the actual child of the illustration (1-4), but a childlike believer. **In my name.** On the basis of Christ. Welcoming other believers because of Christ (not because of prestige, wealth, etc.) is regarded as done to Christ himself (10:42). **6. Cause one of these little ones which believe on me to stumble. Little ones** also refers to believers. The awful judgment awaiting those who would harm the faith of believers is made dramatic by a comparison. **Millstone.** Literally, *ass stone,* the larger upper stone turned by an ass. **7.** Though it is inevitable that **occasions of stumbling** (ASV) occur, for these are among God's means of disciplining as well as molding the character of believers, the human offender is morally responsible for his guilt. **8,9.** Thus, if nec-

8. Wherefore if thy hand or thy foot offend thee, cut them off, and cast *them* from thee: it is better for thee to enter into life halt or maimed, rather than having two hands or two feet to be cast into everlasting fire.

9. And if thine eye offend thee, pluck it out, and cast *it* from thee: it is better for thee to enter into life with one eye, rather than having two eyes to be cast into hell fire.

10. Take heed that ye despise not one of these little ones; for I say unto you, That in heaven their angels do always behold the face of my Father which is in heaven.

11. For the Son of man is come to save that which was lost.

12. How think ye? if a man have a hundred sheep, and one of them be gone astray, doth he not leave the ninety and nine, and goeth into the mountains, and seeketh that which is gone astray?

13. And if so be that he find it, verily I say unto you, he rejoiceth more of that *sheep,* than of the ninety and nine which went not astray.

14. Even so it is not the will of your Father which is in heaven, that one of these little ones should perish.

15. Moreover if thy brother shall trespass against thee, go and tell him his fault between thee and him alone: if he shall hear thee, thou hast gained thy brother.

16. But if he will not hear *thee, then* take with thee one or two more, that in the mouth of two or three witnesses every word may be established.

17. And if he shall neglect to hear them, tell *it* unto the church: but if he neglect to hear the church, let him be unto thee as a heathen man and a publican.

18. Verily I say unto you, Whatsoever ye shall bind on earth shall be bound in heaven; and whatsoever ye shall loose on earth shall be loosed in heaven.

19. Again I say unto you, That if two of you shall agree on earth as touching any thing that they shall ask, it shall be done for them of my Father which is in heaven.

20. For where two or three are gathered together in my name, there am I in the midst of them.

essary, one should take the most drastic measures to avoid offending. (See on 5: 29,30.) **10. These little ones.** Childlike believers (not actual children, except as they may be believers). **Their angels.** Angels who are charged with the care of believers as a group (Heb 1:14). There is not sufficient warrant here for the idea that each individual believer has a particular angel assigned to him. (Acts 12:15 reflects a current opinion of angels, but is not necessarily a truth.) Verse 11 was probably interpolated from Lk 19:10.

**12-14.** The importance of even the lowliest believer is illustrated by the parable of The Lost Sheep. Since the shepherd is greatly concerned over a single straying sheep, how important is our obligation not to minimize such unfortunate ones. This parable was used on another occasion (Lk 15:4-7) to illustrate the salvation of sinners.

**15-20.** Instruction on procedure toward offenders. **15.** In spite of the severest warnings, offenses will be committed. Procedures are outlined to show the injured party how to respond. His first responsibility is to go privately to the offender, without waiting for an apology. Such procedure makes it easier for him to obtain a confession. If he is successful, he will gain the offending brother as a friend and restore him to the fellowship of the Lord and the congregation. **16.** If a second overture is necessary, several witnesses should be present at the interview (see Deut 19: 15). **17. Tell it unto the church.** When the offender remains impenitent (and the sin is sufficiently grave as to affect the congregation), the church must consider the matter. The **church** here cannot mean the synagogue, in view of the prerogatives mentioned in 18:18,19. A Christian church is in prospect, as indicated by the implied absence of Jesus (v. 20). Failure to heed the counsel of the **church** must cause the offender to be treated as an outsider (**Gentile, publican**). Of course, such treatment should involve efforts to reach him with the Gospel. **18: Whatsoever ye shall bind on earth** (cf. 16:19). The decision of the congregation in such matters, reached through prayer, the Word, and the Spirit, will be ratified in heaven. See also Jn 20: 23. **19,20.** The promise that prayer will be answered if even **two agree** provides additional proof that the prayerful decisions of the congregation in disciplinary actions will be divinely honored. This promise pertaining to united prayer must be considered in the light of Christ's other teaching on the subject (cf. I Jn 5:14). **There am I in the midst.** A promise of Christ's special presence in the smallest

21. Then came Peter to him, and said, Lord, how oft shall my brother sin against me, and I forgive him? till seven times?

22. Jesus saith unto him, I say not unto thee, Until seven times: but, Until seventy times seven.

23. Therefore is the kingdom of heaven likened unto a certain king, which would take account of his servants.

24. And when he had begun to reckon, one was brought unto him, which owed him ten thousand talents.

25. But forasmuch as he had not to pay, his lord commanded him to be sold, and his wife, and children, and all that he had, and payment to be made.

26. The servant therefore fell down, and worshipped him, saying, Lord, have patience with me, and I will pay thee all.

27. Then the lord of that servant was moved with compassion, and loosed him, and forgave him the debt.

28. But the same servant went out, and found one of his fellow servants, which owed him a hundred pence: and he laid hands on him, and took *him* by the throat, saying, Pay me that thou owest.

29. And his fellow servant fell down at his feet, and besought him, saying, Have patience with me, and I will pay thee all.

30. And he would not: but went and cast him into prison, till he should pay the debt.

31. So when his fellow servants saw what was done, they were very sorry, and came and told their lord all that was done.

32. Then his lord, after that he had called him, said unto him, O thou wicked servant, I forgave thee all that debt, because thou desiredst me:

33. Shouldest not thou also have had compassion on thy fellow servant, even as I had pity on thee?

34. And his lord was wroth, and delivered him to the tormentors, till he should pay all that was due unto him.

35. So likewise shall my heavenly Father do also unto you, if ye from your hearts forgive not every one his brother their trespasses.

conceivable congregation.

**21-35. Instruction on forgiveness. 21 Lord, how oft?** The preceding explanation regarding offenders implied a willingness by the offended to forgive. Peter wondered how far forgiveness should be extended for repeated offenses. **Seven times?** Rabbinic teaching (based on Amos 1:3; Job 33:29,30, ASV) demanded only three. **22.** Jesus, however, lifted the matter beyond the realm of practical computation by requiring **seventy times seven.** Rather than seek a numerical standard, the believer must follow the example of his Lord (Col 3:13).

**23.** The parable of the unmerciful servant teaches that men who have experienced God's forgiveness are accountable to display forgiveness toward others. This is the standard of the **kingdom of heaven** (see comment on 13:11). The Oriental **king** (interpreted as the heavenly Father; v. 35) is depicted as making a reckoning with his slaves. **24. One,** apparently a satrap with access to vast sums of the king's revenue, was found to owe **ten thousand talents.** (The value of a talent differed at various times, according to the metal involved, but was always comparatively high). **25-27.** However, by prostrating himself before the king, he secured a complete cancellation of the **debt** (Greek, *loan;* viewed graciously instead of as embezzlement). **28-30.** Leaving the king's presence, the forgiven servant proceeded to demand settlement from a **fellow servant** owing him a **hundred pence** (one penny, *denarius,* equaled a day's wages, 20:2), a most insignificant amount compared to the talents. **31-33. Shouldest not thou also have had mercy.** Certainly sinners who have experienced God's forgiveness ought to display a kindred spirit toward others, especially since offenses that men commit against one another are infinitesimal when compared with the enormity of man's debt to God. **34,35. Delivered him to the tormentors.** Herein is the crux of the interpretation. It cannot refer to the eternal ruin of one truly saved, for that would conflict with the clearest teaching elsewhere. Neither can it refer to some nonscriptural purgatory. Yet the fact that the servant had been forgiven the debt makes it unlikely that he was a mere professed believer. However, if we view the torments as temporal evils visited upon unforgiving believers by their **heavenly Father,** the previous difficulties are avoided. **Tormentors** (*basanistai*) is derived from the verb *basanizō,* which is used to describe sickness (Mt 4:24; 8:6), and adverse circumstances (Mt 14:24). Lot "tormented his

## CHAPTER 19

AND it came to pass, *that* when Jesus had finished these sayings, he departed from Galilee, and came into the coasts of Judea beyond Jordan;

2. And great multitudes followed him; and he healed them there.

3. The Pharisees also came unto him, tempting him, and saying unto him, Is it lawful for a man to put away his wife for every cause?

4. And he answered and said unto them, Have ye not read, that he which made *them* at the beginning made them male and female,

5. And said, For this cause shall a man leave father and mother, and shall cleave to his wife: and they twain shall be one flesh?

6. Wherefore they are no more twain, but one flesh. What therefore God hath joined together, let not man put asunder.

7. They say unto him, Why did Moses then command to give a writing of divorcement, and to put her away?

8. He saith unto them, Moses because of the hardness of your hearts suffered you to put away your wives: but from the beginning it was not so.

9. And I say unto you, Whosoever shall put away his wife, except *it be* for fornication, and shall marry another, committeth adultery: and whoso marrieth her which is put away doth commit adultery.

soul" by contact with evil men (II Pet 2:8). Such torments God may use to chasten and produce a proper spirit among his children (I Cor 11:30-32). Thus the divine forgiveness here is that which we must experience daily in order to enjoy perfect fellowship with our heavenly Father, and it fits well this context in which relations among believers are discussed (vv. 15-20).

B. In Perea. 19:1 — 20:16. Matthew notes the departure of Jesus from Galilee and describes the final journey to Jerusalem. Comparison with Lk 9:51–18:14 indicates another trip to Jerusalem and a ministry lasting some months. Thus a gap of perhaps six months must be inferred in 19:1 between **departed from Galilee** and **came into the borders of Judea beyond Jordan.**

1) Teaching on Divorce. 19:1-12. **1. Beyond Jordan.** From the Greek *peran* (beyond) came the name "Perea" for the district on the east side of the Jordan River. **3. Is it lawful for a man to put away his wife for every cause?** The strict school of Shammai held that divorce was lawful only for a wife's shameful conduct. Hillel, however, interpreted Deut 24:1 in the widest possible way, and allowed divorce for every conceivable cause. Thus Jesus was being asked, "Do you agree with the most prevalent interpretation (Hillel's)?" **4-6.** Rather than align himself with either position, Jesus cites the purpose of God in creation (Gen 1:27; 2:24). Since God's purpose called for man and wife to be **one flesh,** any disruption of marriage violates God's will. **7,8. Why then did Moses command?** Their citing Moses (Deut 24:1) and the **bill of divorcement** in opposition to Jesus showed their misunderstanding of that regulation. For the provision was a protection of wives from men's caprice, not an authorization for husbands to divorce at will. **9,10. Except it be for fornication** (cf. on 5:31). If **fornication** be regarded as a general term including adultery (an identification most uncertain in the NT), then our Lord allowed divorce only for the cause of infidelity by the wife. (Among Jews, only husbands could divorce. Mark, in writing for Gentile readers, states the converse also, Mk 10:12.) However, if **fornication** be viewed in its usual meaning, and referred here to unchastity by the bride during betrothal (cf. Joseph's suspicions, Mt 1:18,19), then Christ allowed no grounds whatever for divorce of married persons. Thus he agreed neither with Shammai nor Hillel. Such a high and restricted view of marriage would

10. His disciples say unto him, If the case of the man be so with *his* wife, it is not good to marry.

11. But he said unto them, All *men* cannot receive this saying, save *they* to whom it is given.

12. For there are some eunuchs, which were so born from *their* mother's womb: and there are some eunuchs, which were made eunuchs of men: and there be eunuchs, which have made themselves eunuchs for the kingdom of heaven's sake. He that is able to receive *it*, let him receive *it*.

13. Then were there brought unto him little children, that he should put *his* hands on them, and pray: and the disciples rebuked them.

14. But Jesus said, Suffer little children, and forbid them not, to come unto me; for of such is the kingdom of heaven.

15. And he laid *his* hands on them, and departed thence.

16. And, behold, one came and said unto him, Good Master, what good thing shall I do, that I may have eternal life?

17. And he said unto him, Why callest thou me good? *there is* none good but one, *that is,* God: but if thou wilt enter into life, keep the commandments.

18. He saith unto him, Which? Jesus said, Thou shalt do no murder, Thou shalt not commit adultery, Thou shalt not steal, Thou shalt not bear false witness,

19. Honor thy father and *thy* mother: and, Thou shalt love thy neighbor as thyself.

20. The young man saith unto him, All these things have I kept from my youth up: what lack I yet?

account for the disciples' remonstrance, It is not good to marry. It seems unlikely that the disciples, after having imbibed the ideals of Jesus, would have felt the limiting of divorce to cases of adultery an intolerable burden. 11. All men cannot receive this saying, i.e., the statement of the disciples. Though at times marriage may not be expedient, not all men are so constituted as to abstain. 12. Some are incapable of marriage because of congenital defects; others because of injury or restrictions imposed by men. Still others may forego the privilege of marriage in order to devote themselves more completely to the service of God (e.g., Paul, I Cor 7:7,8,26,32-35). This statement certainly casts no reflection upon marriage; rather it concludes a discussion in which marriage was exalted to its original pure state.

2) Blessing of the Children. 19:13-15. The little children must have been very small, some perhaps being infants (Mk 10:16). The disciples resented the intrusion and rebuked the parents who had brought them (cf. Mk 10:13; Lk 18:15). Yet Jesus was always interested in the young and the weak. During this delightful moment, he reminded the disciples of a forgotten lesson (18:3). Of such is the kingdom of heaven. Since entrance to this Kingdom requires that men become childlike in faith, the disciples would do well to be more gracious to actual children.

3) Interview with the Rich Young Man. 19:16-30. The reader should follow the ASV in this passage, since much assimilation from parallel accounts appears in the AV. 16. What good thing shall I do? This young questioner (called a "ruler" by Luke) felt sure that eternal life was gained by the performance of deeds. 17. Why asketh thou me concerning that which is good? One there is who is good. Mark and Luke indicate that Jesus had been addressed as "Good Master." Our Lord probed his questioner by making him review how he really estimated Jesus, and then sent him to what God had already revealed in His Law. 18,19. Jesus cited the sixth, seventh, eighth, ninth, and fifth commandments of the Decalogue, and a summarization of the second table — love thy neighbor as thyself. These were not stated as the means of salvation (this was never the purpose of the Law), but were intended to indicate the young man's need. 20. All these things have I kept. Not the words of one brazenly self-righteous, but of one who thought that conformity in externals constituted keeping of the Law. 21. Perfect. Com-

21. Jesus said unto him, If thou wilt be perfect, go *and* sell that thou hast, and give to the poor, and thou shalt have treasure in heaven: and come *and* follow me.

22. But when the young man heard that saying, he went away sorrowful: for he had great possessions.

23. Then said Jesus unto his disciples, Verily I say unto you, That a rich man shall hardly enter into the kingdom of heaven.

24. And \gain I say unto you, It is easier for a camel to go through the eye of a needle, than for a rich man to enter into the kingdom of God.

25. When his disciples heard *it*, they were exceedingly amazed, saying, Who then can be saved?

26. But Jesus beheld *them*, and said unto them, With men this is impossible; but with God all things are possible.

27. Then answered Peter and said unto him, Behold, we have forsaken all, and followed thee; what shall we have therefore?

28. And Jesus said unto them, Verily I say unto you, That ye which have followed me, in the regeneration when the Son of man shall sit in the throne of his glory, ye also shall sit upon twelve thrones, judging the twelve tribes of Israel.

29. And every one that hath forsaken houses, or brethren, or sisters, or father, or mother, or wife, or children, or lands, for my name's sake, shall receive a hundredfold, and shall inherit everlasting life.

30. But many *that are* first shall be last; and the last *shall be* first.

### CHAPTER 20

FOR the kingdom of heaven is like unto a man *that is* a householder, which went out early in the morning to hire laborers into his vineyard.

plete, mature, without the lack which he sorely felt. **Go, sell, give.** Jesus unmasked the young man's problem by demonstrating one of its effects. The exhortation to dispense his belongings quickly revealed how far short he had come in grasping the spirit of God's commandments. **Come, follow me.** Here is the positive invitation to put faith in Christ. **22. He went away sorrowful.** The prospect of abandoning his great possessions was so distressing that he failed to find the goal he sought.

**23. It is hard for a rich man to enter** (ASV). The difficulty with wealth lies not in its possession (many righteous men in Scripture had wealth — Abraham, Job, Joseph of Arimathaea) but in the false trust it inspires (I Tim 6:17; Mk 10:24). **24. Camel** and **needle's eye** are meant literally, as attested by a similar Talmudic proverb using an elephant. The simile was meant to show an impossibility by naming the largest beast known in Palestine and the smallest of apertures. **25. Who then can be saved?** The disciples apparently subscribed in some measure to the prevailing view that riches indicated divine favor. Hence if rich men were excluded, how could others possibly be saved? Perhaps there was latent the thought that all men are afflicted to some degree with the desire for worldly wealth. **26.** Jesus succinctly avowed that salvation is the work of God. Only God can overrule this false trust in human riches and provide true righteousness.

**27. We have left all.** What the young man had refused to do (cf. Mt 4:20,22; 9:9). **What then shall we have?** Not necessarily a reflection of a mercenary spirit, but a forthright question that drew an appropriate answer. **28. Regeneration.** The word appears elsewhere in the NT only in Tit 3:5 (of spiritual rebirth of the individual). Here it denotes the rebirth that will occur in society and creation when Messiah establishes his reign (cf. Acts 3:21; Rom 8:19). **Twelve thrones.** Specifically for the Twelve in the Millennium. **29,30.** Any sacrifice made for Christ will be amply rewarded. However, a caution must be observed. **Many** (not all) **that are first shall be last.** This axiom, repeated in 20:16 after an explanatory parable, is true in many senses. Here the context suggests its application to those who had first (in time) established their relation to Christ and might develop an attitude of presumption.

4) Parable of the Laborers in the Vineyard. 20:1-16. This parable illustrates Christ's previous teaching, and enlarges

2. And when he had agreed with the laborers for a penny a day, he sent them into his vineyard.

3. And he went out about the third hour, and saw others standing idle in the market place,

4. And said unto them; Go ye also into the vineyard, and whatsoever is right I will give you. And they went their way.

5. Again he went out about the sixth and ninth hour, and did likewise.

6. And about the eleventh hour he went out, and found others standing idle, and saith unto them, Why stand ye here all the day idle?

7. They say unto him, Because no man hath hired us. He saith unto them, Go ye also into the vineyard; and whatsoever is right, *that* shall ye receive.

8. So when even was come, the lord of the vineyard saith unto his steward, Call the laborers, and give them *their* hire, beginning from the last unto the first.

9. And when they came that *were hired* about the eleventh hour, they received every man a penny.

10. But when the first came, they supposed that they should have received more; and they likewise received every man a penny.

11. And when they had received *it*, they murmured against the goodman of the house,

12. Saying, These last have wrought *but* one hour, and thou hast made them equal unto us, which have borne the burden and heat of the day.

13. But he answered one of them, and said, Friend, I do thee no wrong: didst not thou agree with me for a penny?

14. Take *that* thine *is*, and go thy way: I will give unto this last, even as unto thee.

15. Is it not lawful for me to do what I will with mine own? Is thine eye evil, because I am good?

16. So the last shall be first, and the first last: for many be called, but few chosen.

17. And Jesus going up to Jerusalem took the twelve disciples apart in the way, and said unto them,

18. Behold, we go up to Jerusalem; and the Son of man shall be betrayed unto the chief priests and unto the scribes, and they shall condemn him to death,

19. And shall deliver him to the Gentiles to mock, and to scourge, and to crucify *him:* and the third day he shall rise again.

20. Then came to him the mother of Zebedee's children with her sons, worshipping *him*, and desiring a certain thing of him.

19:30 (cf. 20:16). **1. Householder.** The master of a **vineyard** needed an increase of workers at harvest time. **Early in the morning.** The first workers were hired at dawn. **2. A penny** *(denarius)* **a day.** The usual wage for a laborer or soldier. **3-7. Others standing idle.** Not working because no man had hired them. No hint is given that they were lazy. From this group of unemployed in the marketplace, the householder hired additional workers at 9 A.M., 12 noon, 3 P.M., and 5 P.M. Each responded immediately to the opportunity. **8. When even was come.** Cf. Deut 24:15. **9-12.** That those hired first might see what was done, payment was begun with those most recently hired. Each worker received one denarius, regardless of the duration of his service. **13,14.** To one of the murmuring group which had labored longest, the householder explained that the contract had been fully performed. As to the others, the employer's obligation to them was his own affair. **15. Is thine eye evil because I am good?** The sense is, Are you envious (Prov 28:22) because I am generous? **16. The last shall be first.** This statement, repeated from 19:30, shows that the parable continued the previous instruction of the Twelve (19:27-30). The parable teaches that service for Christ will be faithfully rewarded, and that equal faithfulness to one's opportunity will be equally rewarded. However, only God can adequately assess faithfulness and opportunities, and thus human judgments may be reversed. The ASV omits the final clause of verse 16 on textual grounds.

C. In Judea. 20:17-34. Matthew is particularly conscious of geographical movements (4:12; 16:13; 17:24; 19:1; 21:1). Having been east of Jordan in Perea, Jesus and his band now moved directly toward Jerusalem. This section describes events on the journey from Perea to Jerusalem, in the vicinity of Jericho in Judea (v. 29).

1) Another Prediction of Christ's Death and Resurrection. 20:17-19. The third direct and detailed prediction of Christ's passion (cf. 16:21; 17:22,23, plus the bare statement of 17:12). It enlarges upon some of the previous information. For the first time Jesus indicated that his death would be at the hands of the **Gentiles**, who would mock, scourge, and crucify him.

2) Ambitious Request of Zebedee's Sons. 20:20-28. Mark presents the request as coming from the sons. Matthew shows that they at first asked through their mother, but that later they personally joined

21. And he said unto her, What wilt thou? She saith unto him, Grant that these my two sons may sit, the one on thy right hand, and the other on the left, in thy kingdom.

22. But Jesus answered and said, Ye know not what ye ask. Are ye able to drink of the cup that I shall drink of, and to be baptized with the baptism that I am baptized with? They say unto him, We are able.

23. And he saith unto them, Ye shall drink indeed of my cup, and be baptized with the baptism that I am baptized with: but to sit on my right hand, and on my left, is not mine to give, but *it shall be given to them* for whom it is prepared of my Father.

24. And when the ten heard *it,* they were moved with indignation against the two brethren.

25. But Jesus called them *unto him,* and said, Ye know that the princes of the Gentiles exercise dominion over them, and they that are great exercise authority upon them.

26. But it shall not be so among you: but whosoever will be great among you, let him be your minister;

27. And whosoever will be chief among you, let him be your servant:

28. Even as the Son of man came not to be ministered unto, but to minister, and to give his life a ransom for many.

29. And as they departed from Jericho, a great multitude followed him.

the conversation. **20. Mother of Zebedee's children.** Salome, apparently the sister of the Virgin Mary, as shown by comparing Mt 27:56 with Mk 15:40 and Jn 19:25. **21.** The request for seats of highest honor in Christ's kingdom may have been prompted by his previous revelation about the twelve thrones (19:28). Though it arose from the idea that the kingdom would very shortly be established (Lk 19:11), and betrayed a spirit not altogether humble, it should be noted that it was based on a firm faith that Jesus was the Messiah and his kingdom a reality. Such faith Jesus was willing to purge and nourish. **22,23. Cup.** Here a symbol of Christ's sufferings (cf. 26:39,42). **To be baptized with the baptism.** Broadus explains, "to be plunged in the same sufferings" *(Comm. on Matt.,* p. 417). The assent of these two to the stern demands of Jesus was doubtless sincere. James was the first disciple to die for Christ (Acts 12:2); John suffered variously over the longest period of time. Yet assignment of the positions requested is the prerogative of the Father. **24. Moved with indignation.** A response of the **ten** which may have been aggravated by the procedure of the two in pleading their case through a kinswoman of Jesus. **25-27.** Our Lord's answer showed that though human governments maintain greatness by the authority of various officials forced upon their inferiors, his kingdom would be different. Willingness to serve is the mark of spiritual greatness. **28.** The greatest examplar of this principle is the **Son of man.** The supreme display occurred at Calvary, where he gave **his life** as a **ransom** to God, against whom men have sinned and were subject to penalty. **For many.** Christ's death here is clearly substitutionary, "in the stead of" *(anti)* **many.** (See A. T. Robertson, *Grammar of the Greek New Testament,* pp. 572-574.) **Many** does not seem intended to be restrictive here, but is in contrast to the *one* who died. However, the choice was a happy one in view of the clear teaching elsewhere that not all would avail themselves of the proffered salvation.

**3) Healing of Two Blind Men. 20:29-34.** Parallel accounts (Mk 10:46-52; Lk 18:35-43) pose problems of harmonization, but this fact prohibits any suggestion of collusion. **29. As they departed from Jericho.** Mark agrees, but Luke places the incident on the approach to the city. The main city of Roman Jericho, occupied by poorer Jews, lay about a mile east of Herod's winter headquarters (also called

71

30. And, behold, two blind men sitting by the wayside, when they heard that Jesus passed by, cried out, saying, Have mercy on us, O Lord, *thou* Son of David.

31. And the multitude rebuked them, because they should hold their peace: but they cried the more, saying, Have mercy on us, O Lord, *thou* Son of David.

32. And Jesus stood still, and called them, and said, What will ye that I shall do unto you?

33. They say unto him, Lord, that our eyes may be opened.

34. So Jesus had compassion *on them*, and touched their eyes: and immediately their eyes received sight, and they followed him.

## CHAPTER 21

AND when they drew nigh unto Jerusalem, and were come to Bethphage, unto the mount of Olives, then sent Jesus two disciples,

2. Saying unto them, Go into the village over against you, and straightway ye shall find an ass tied, and a colt with her: loose *them*, and bring *them* unto me.

3. And if any *man* say aught unto you, ye shall say, The Lord hath need of them; and straightway he will send them.

4. All this was done, that it might be fulfilled which was spoken by the prophet, saying,

5. Tell ye the daughter of Sion, Behold, thy King cometh unto thee, meek, and sitting upon an ass, and a colt the foal of an ass.

6. And the disciples went, and did as Jesus commanded them,

7. And brought the ass, and the colt, and put on them their clothes, and they set *him* thereon.

8. And a very great multitude spread their garments in the way; others cut down branches from the trees, and strewed *them* in the way.

9. And the multitudes that went before, and that followed, cried, saying, Hosanna to the Son of David: Blessed *is* he that cometh in the name of the Lord; Hosanna in the highest.

Jericho), which contained the palace, fortress, and houses of Herod's wealthy friends. (See Lucetta Mowry, BA, XV, 2, p. 34). Thus the miracle could have occurred between the two Jerichos, with Luke understandably thinking in terms of the Herodian city, where his next incident (Zacchaeus) most probably occurred. **30-34. Two blind men.** The other evangelists mention only the more prominent Bartimaeus (cf. the two demoniacs, Mt 8:28). **Thou son of David.** By this title they meant the Messiah. Previously Jesus had prohibited its public use, but now as he approaches Jerusalem, he is ready to claim it (cf. 21:16; Lk 19:40).

D. In Jerusalem. 21:1–25:46. In tracing the movements of Jesus to Jerusalem, Matthew omits the trip from Jericho to Bethany six days before Passover (Jn 12:1), which preceded the Triumphal Entry by one day (Jn 12:12).

1) Triumphal Entry. 21:1-11. The first of a series of visits to Jerusalem during this final week (cf. 21:18; Mk 11:19). **1. Bethphage.** A village apparently between Bethany and Jerusalem, since Jesus had lodged in Bethany the previous night (Jn 12:1,12). Certain location is yet unknown. **Mount of Olives.** The hill east of Jerusalem that offered travelers their first glimpse of the city. **2,3.** The explicit instructions of Jesus regarding the ass and colt indicate the significance of the event. On other occasions Jesus had usually walked, and here the distance was not more than two miles. **4,5.** Fulfillment of Zech 9:9 was the motivation for this act, although the disciples were unaware of it before the Resurrection (Jn 12:16). Jews generally regarded the passage as Messianic (Edersheim, *Life and Times of Jesus*, II, 736). **6-8.** Both animals were brought (the ass being needed to quiet the previously unridden colt), but all the Evangelists testify that Jesus rode the colt. Some from the multitude spread their garments on the path as a mark of homage to him whom they now acclaimed as King (II Kgs 9:13). Others strewed palm fronds in the way (Jn 12:13). The ass was a lowly beast, and no Jewish king since Solomon had ridden upon one officially. But meekness and lowliness were earmarks of Messiah predicted by Zechariah, and now fulfilled. **9. Hosanna.** A Hebrew expression meaning *Save now*. The shouts of the crowd, employing the phrases of Ps 118:25,26, clearly proclaimed their hopes for Jesus as Messiah, **Son of David.** Previously Christ had shunned all such public displays (although confessing his Messiah-

10. And when he was come into Jerusalem, all the city was moved, saying, Who is this?

11. And the multitude said, This is Jesus the prophet of Nazareth of Galilee.

12. And Jesus went into the temple of God, and cast out all them that sold and bought in the temple, and overthrew the tables of the money changers, and the seats of them that sold doves,

13. And said unto them, It is written, My house shall be called the house of prayer; but ye have made it a den of thieves.

14. And the blind and the lame came to him in the temple; and he healed them.

15. And when the chief priests and scribes saw the wonderful things that he did, and the children crying in the temple, and saying, Hosanna to the Son of David; they were sore displeased,

16. And said unto him, Hearest thou what these say? And Jesus saith unto them, Yea; have ye never read, Out of the mouth of babes and sucklings thou hast perfected praise?

17. And he left them, and went out of the city into Bethany; and he lodged there.

18. Now in the morning, as he returned into the city, he hungered.

19. And when he saw a fig tree in the way, he came to it, and found nothing thereon, but leaves only, and said unto it, Let no fruit grow on thee henceforward for ever. And presently the fig tree withered away.

20. And when the disciples saw it, they marveled, saying, How soon is the fig tree withered away!

ship to individuals; Jn 4:26; Mt 16:16-20); but now he had made careful preparations for an unmistakable presentation of himself to the nation. 10,11. Who is this? The Messianic acclamation prompted this question from those who perhaps did not know Jesus (he had been avoiding Jerusalem during much of his ministry).

2) Cleansing of the Temple. 21:12-17. A similar cleansing of the Temple is recorded at the beginning of Jesus' ministry (Jn 2:13-22), but there is no reason to doubt that there were two such instances. Jesus often repeated his words and deeds. These evil men soon reverted to their wicked ways, for the financial inducements were most attractive. 12. Jesus went into the temple. This was the day following the Triumphal Entry (Mk 11:11,12). Matthew records events here without the time. Them that sold and bought in the temple. The outer Court of the Gentiles contained the stalls where sacrificial animals might be purchased and tables where foreign coinage might be exchanged for shekels of the sanctuary. This mart, a rich source of extortion, was controlled by the family of the high priest Annas. Shortly before the war of the Jews with Rome, popular indignation against these Bazaars of Annas caused their removal (see Edersheim, Life and Times of Jesus, I, 367-372). 13. It is written. Isa 56:7 and Jer 7:11. Den of robbers. A refuge for robbers, whose foul practices were protected by the sacred precincts. 14-16. Matthew alone records the healings that brought renewed Hosannas from the children (masculine, boys) in the Temple. In responding to the disapproving priests, Jesus employed Ps 8:2 to show that God will get praise to himself, even from those whom men regard as insignificant. 17. To Bethany and lodged there. The village at the foot of the Mount of Olives (cf. Lk 21:37). Whether he spent the night in a house in town or in the open air is uncertain (cf. Lk 24:50 with Acts 1:12 for interchanging of these names).

3) Cursing of the Barren Fig Tree. 21:18-22. Again Mark (11:12-14,19-25) must be consulted for the chronology. Matthew telescopes both phases of the incident into one. 18. Now in the morning. According to Mark, this was the morning of the day in which he cleansed the Temple. 19,20. Fig tree. This common tree of Palestine often symbolized the nation of Israel (Hos 9:10; Joel 1:7). A peculiarity of the tree is that the fruit and leaves usually appear at the same time, with the fruit sometimes coming first. The next crop would be ex-

21. Jesus answered and said unto them, Verily I say unto you, If ye have faith, and doubt not, ye shall not only do this *which is done* to the fig tree, but also if ye shall say unto this mountain, Be thou removed, and be thou cast into the sea; it shall be done.

22. And all things, whatsoever ye shall ask in prayer, believing, ye shall receive.

23. And when he was come into the temple, the chief priests and the elders of the people came unto him as he was teaching, and said, By what authority doest thou these things? and who gave thee this authority?

24. And Jesus answered and said unto them, I also will ask you one thing, which if ye tell me, I in like wise will tell you by what authority I do these things.

25. The baptism of John, whence was it? from heaven, or of men? And they reasoned with themselves, saying, If we shall say, From heaven; he will say unto us, Why did ye not then believe him?

26. But if we shall say, Of men; we fear the people; for all hold John as a prophet.

27. And they answered Jesus, and said, We cannot tell. And he said unto them, Neither tell I you by what authority I do these things.

pected in June. This particular tree had put forth foliage in April to such an extent that one would expect it to have produced fruit as well. Here seems to be an instance in which, because of Christ's self-emptying (Phil 2:7), he refrained from using his omniscience in order that his human response might be entirely genuine. **Let no fruit grow on thee.** Spoken with the solemnity of doom. Although there is no statement that the situation should be regarded as parabolic, that seems to be the only reasonable explanation of the incident (for trees have no moral responsibility). It provided a graphic sequel to the earlier parable of Lk 13:6-9 regarding the Jewish nation, unfruitful despite every advantage. **Immediately the fig tree withered away.** Immediately can surely be broad enough to allow for several hours. It was first noticed by the disciples on the next morning, at which time it had withered to the roots (Mk 11:20). **21,22.** To the amazed disciples Jesus explained that such power (for even greater deeds) was available to them through believing prayer. This kind of faith, however, will only ask those things that it knows to be God's will (cf. on 17:20).

4) Questioning of Jesus' Authority, and His Parabolic Answer. 21:23—22:14. **23.** During this third visit to the **temple** on successive days, Jesus was approached by officials from the Sanhedrin (**chief priests, elders,** and scribes, Mk 11:27). **By what authority?** Authorization was usually granted by the Sanhedrin or some eminent rabbi, who bore testimony to the validity of the teaching as being duly received from proper traditional sources (see Edersheim, *Life and Times of Jesus,* II, 381-383). **These things.** A reference to Christ's deeds (cleansing the Temple, miracles) as well as his teaching and his acceptance of the homage due to Messiah. **25-27. The baptism of John.** Representative of the ministry of John. Christ's counterquestion was not an evasion of the Sanhedrin's demand, but served the dual purpose of implying the answer (cf. Jn 5:33-35) and exposing the dishonesty of the Sanhedrin. John the Baptist, whose ministry was popularly recognized as genuinely prophetic, had publicly proclaimed Jesus as Messiah and taught that men should trust Him (Jn 3:26-30; Jn 1:29-37; Acts 19:4). Thus the officials saw clearly the dilemma Christ's question posed for them. If they acknowledged John's divine authorization, they would be obligated to acknowledge what he had taught about Jesus — that He was Mes-

28. But what think ye? A *certain* man had two sons; and he came to the first, and said, Son, go work to-day in my vineyard.

29. He answered and said, I will not; but afterward he repented, and went.

30. And he came to the second, and said likewise. And he answered and said, I *go*, sir; and went not.

31. Whether of them twain did the will of *his* father? They say unto him, The first. Jesus saith unto them, Verily I say unto you, That the publicans and the harlots go into the kingdom of God before you.

32. For John came unto you in the way of righteousness, and ye believed him not; but the publicans and the harlots believed him: and ye, when ye had seen *it*, repented not afterward, that ye might believe him.

33. Hear another parable: There was a certain householder, which planted a vineyard, and hedged it round about, and digged a winepress in it, and built a tower, and let it out to husbandmen, and went into a far country:

34. And when the time of the fruit drew near, he sent his servants to the husbandmen, that they might receive the fruits of it.

35. And the husbandmen took his servants, and beat one, and killed another, and stoned another.

36. Again, he sent other servants more than the first: and they did unto them likewise.

37. But last of all he sent unto them his son, saying, They will reverence my son.

38. But when the husbandmen saw the son, they said among themselves, This is the heir; come, let us kill him, and let us seize on his inheritance.

siah. Yet a denial of John would bring public wrath upon them. Such cowardly and dishonest men deserved no further answer.

28-32. Parable of the Two Sons. Matthew alone records the three parables (cf. Mk 12:1, "parables") spoken at this time, evoked by the Sanhedrists' opposition to Jesus' authority. The parable of The Two Sons is interpreted by Jesus as depicting the conflicting responses of the religious outcasts and their leaders toward the ministry of John, which was preparatory to His own. The son (actually, *child*) who first said I will not but later *repented* and went pictures the publicans and harlots, religious outcasts who eventually accepted John's message. Many of them became followers of Jesus (Lk 15:1,2). The son who said I go but went not describes the religious leaders who first gave an aloof sort of approval to John (Jn 5:35) but never followed through (Lk 7:29,30). Thus the publicans and harlots, by responding to John, demonstrated their readiness for the Messianic kingdom of God. The way of righteousness (II Pet 2:21) describes John's preaching (cf. 22:16, "way of God") in terms suggestive of Noah (II Pet 2:5), and probably denotes the content of his message rather than his personal behavior.

33-46. Parable of the Wicked Husbandmen. This parable further answers the question of Jesus' authority by showing him as the divine Son sent by the Father. Though the main lines of the parable are so clear that the Sanhedrists could not escape their import, one must not attempt to press all the details. The householder certainly represents God the Father; yet his mistaken optimism (v. 37) cannot be predicated of God. Perhaps we should see in the actions of the householder the way God appears to man to act. 33. A vineyard. Symbol of the theocracy of Israel, familiar to every Jew. Cf. Isa 5:1-7; Ps 80:8-16. Verse 43 equates the vineyard with the kingdom of God, clearly pointing to the kingdom as mediated to Israel through divinely chosen kings. In the parable the householder is depicted as making every provision for the welfare of the vineyard. 35. Beat one, killed another, stoned another. For records of the shameful treatment accorded God's emissaries to Israel, see Jer 20:1,2; 37:15; 38:6; I Kgs 19:10; 22:24; II Chr 24:21. 37. Last of all he sent his son. The extraordinary patience of the householder reveals the utter depravity of the husbandmen. 38. Let us kill him and seize on his inheritance. Exactly this sentiment had been uttered recently by Jewish leaders (Jn 11:47-53).

**39.** And they caught him, and cast *him* out of the vineyard, and slew *him*.

**40.** When the lord therefore of the vineyard cometh, what will he do unto those husbandmen?

**41.** They say unto him, He will miserably destroy those wicked men, and will let out *his* vineyard unto other husbandmen, which shall render him the fruits in their seasons.

**42.** Jesus saith unto them, Did ye never read in the Scriptures, The stone which the builders rejected, the same is become the head of the corner: this is the Lord's doing, and it is marvelous in our eyes?

**43.** Therefore say I unto you, The kingdom of God shall be taken from you, and given to a nation bringing forth the fruits thereof.

**44.** And whosoever shall fall on this stone shall be broken: but on whomsoever it shall fall, it will grind him to powder.

**45.** And when the chief priests and Pharisees had heard his parables, they perceived that he spake of them.

**46.** But when they sought to lay hands on him, they feared the multitude, because they took him for a prophet.

### CHAPTER 22

AND Jesus answered and spake unto them again by parables, and said,

**2.** The kingdom of heaven is like unto a certain king, which made a marriage for his son,

**3.** And sent forth his servants to call them that were bidden to the wedding: and they would not come.

From this point on, the scope of the parable passes from history to prophecy. **39. Slew him.** A prediction of Jesus' death at the hands of these very men. **40,41.** At this point the Jewish leaders apparently did not grasp the full import of the parable (though they did shortly, v. 45), and so readily answered Jesus' question, pronouncing their own judgment. **42-44.** Jesus' use of Ps 118:22,23 pointed to his ultimate triumph following rejection. The same passage is also quoted in Acts 4:11 and I Pet 2:6,7. As a result of this triumph, the kingdom of God will be taken away from the possession of these leaders (and the contemporary nation of Israel, as shown by the mention of another **nation**). **A nation bringing forth the fruits thereof.** A reference to the Church (called by Peter a "holy nation" in a context where the same OT passage is used; I Pet 2:7-9). With Pentecost came the formation of a new body, the Church, which would be the spiritual nucleus of the Messianic (mediatorial) kingdom. Though these individual Jewish leaders were thus permanently removed from the Kingdom, Rom 9-11 explains that the nation of Israel will once again be brought to the blessings of salvation at the close of the present age of Gentile prominence (Rom 11:25). Today the Church enjoys certain spiritual aspects of the Kingdom in that she has acknowledged Christ as King (Col 1:13), and is being prepared for a share in the coming reign. This aspect of the mediatorial kingdom is described in the parables of Mt 13. **45,46. They feared.** The Jewish leaders were hindered in their plans for Jesus' death (Jn 11:53) by their fear of his popularity with the crowds. The same fear prevented their defamation of John's memory (Mt 21:26).

**22:1-14. Parable of the Marriage Feast.** Though this parable is similar to that in Lk 14:16-24, the differences in certain details and in the occasion render unnecessary any attempt at making the two identical. Any teacher has the privilege of repeating illustrations and changing details to suit a new situation. **1. In parables,** i.e., parabolically. **2. Kingdom of heaven.** The mediatorial kingdom as depicted in Mt 13:11ff., viewed during the period from Jesus' first coming until the full establishment of the Messianic reign. The **king, his son,** and the **marriage feast** are representative of the Father, Christ (Jn 3:29), and the Messianic kingdom (Isa 25:6; 55:1). If the scene describes a marriage that involved the recognition of the son as heir, then refusal to attend showed disloyalty as well as discourtesy. This ac-

4. Again, he sent forth other servants, saying, Tell them which are bidden, Behold, I have prepared my dinner: my oxen and *my* fatlings *are* killed, and all things *are* ready: come unto the marriage.

5. But they made light of *it*, and went their ways, one to his farm, another to his merchandise:

6. And the remnant took his servants, and entreated *them* spitefully, and slew *them*.

7. But when the king heard *thereof*, he was wroth: and he sent forth his armies, and destroyed those murderers, and burned up their city.

8. Then saith he to his servants, The wedding is ready, but they which were bidden were not worthy.

9. Go ye therefore into the highways, and as many as ye shall find, bid to the marriage.

10. So those servants went out into the highways, and gathered together all as many as they found, both bad and good: and the wedding was furnished with guests.

11. And when the king came in to see the guests, he saw there a man which had not on a wedding garment:

12. And he saith unto him, Friend, how camest thou in hither not having a wedding garment? And he was speechless.

13. Then said the king to the servants, Bind him hand and foot, and take him away, and cast *him* into outer darkness; there shall be weeping and gnashing of teeth.

14. For many are called, but few *are* chosen.

counts for the violent destruction brought upon the rebels by the king's forces. **3-6. To call them that were bidden.** Oriental custom included an initial invitation and a second call at the stated hour. The invited ones, here certainly Israel, refused this call, and when further explanatory entreaties were made, became either brazenly rude or positively murderous. Compare Jewish treatment of John (Mt 21:25), Stephen (Acts 7:59), and James (Acts 12:2). **7. Burned their city.** A prediction of the destruction of Jerusalem in A.D. 70. The Roman army under Titus is regarded in the parable as God's instrument (**his armies**). **8,9. Go ye therefore into the highways** (ASV, *partings of the highways;* RSV, *thoroughfares*). This is usually referred to evangelization of Gentiles (which seems clearly to be intended in Lk 14:23). Here, however, the marriage feast naturally implies a bride as distinct from the guests; yet evangelization of the Gentiles in the church age provides the bride, not the guests. Inasmuch as Christ was explaining to unbelieving Jews about their relation to the Messianic kingdom, perhaps these guests who later responded represent Jews who will respond during the Tribulation. **10. Both bad and good.** Open sinners and morally upright. Both are objects of God's gracious invitation, and many of both groups respond. **11. Wedding garment.** Because absence of this garment excluded the man from the feast, we conclude that the garment represents an absolute requirement for entrance to the Kingdom. Thus it represents the robe of imputed righteousness that God graciously provides to man through faith (Isa 61:10). The custom of kings in providing suitable garments when granting interviews appears to be assumed here, since the culprit is held responsible for his lack, and persons gathered from the highways may not have had proper raiment even if they had had time to clothe themselves. **12. Friend.** Fellow, comrade. A form of address to someone whose name is not known. The man without the wedding garment depicts the person who claims to be ready for Christ's kingdom, but is not. Other parables have depicted him as a tare, and an unusable fish. **13. Outer darkness.** In the parable, this is descriptive of the blackness of night outside the brightly lighted palace (the dinner [*ariston*, v. 4] which began at midday had now run into the night); the darkness and the **weeping and gnashing of teeth** are clearly indicative of the torments of Gehenna (13:42; 25:30,46). **14. Many are called, but few are chosen.** There is a general call of God

15. Then went the Pharisees, and took counsel how they might entangle him in *his* talk.

16. And they sent out unto him their disciples with the Herodians, saying, Master, we know that thou art true, and teachest the way of God in truth, neither carest thou for any *man:* for thou regardest not the person of men.

17. Tell us therefore, What thinkest thou? Is it lawful to give tribute unto Caesar, or not?

18. But Jesus perceived their wickedness, and said, Why tempt ye me, *ye* hypocrites?

19. Show me the tribute money. And they brought unto him a penny.

20. And he saith unto them, Whose *is* this image and superscription?

21. They say unto him, Caesar's. Then saith he unto them, Render therefore unto Caesar the things which are Caesar's; and unto God the things that are God's.

22. When they had heard *these words*, they marveled, and left him, and went their way.

23. The same day came to him the Sadducees, which say that there is no resurrection, and asked him,

to sinners which invites them to the joys of salvation (11:28), but which may be resisted and rejected. Comparatively **few** are actually selected for this privilege. Scripture clearly indicates a divine election that brings sinners to God. Yet Scripture also indicates that man is responsible for his indifference (v. 5), rebellion (v. 6), and self-righteousness (v. 12).

5) Questioning of Jesus by Various Groups. 22:15-46. These discussions took place on the same day as the previous parables, one of the busiest days of Jesus' ministry. **15-22.** Pharisees' and Herodians' question about tribute. **15. Entangle him.** Entrap, ensnare. **16. Their disciples.** Rabbinical students, sent by their Pharisaic masters. **Herodians.** A group of Jews whose characteristics are not fully known. They apparently advocated the return to rule of the Herodian family (whose rule had ended in Judea and Samaria A.D. 6 with the appointment of Roman procurators). These two groups united in their common hatred of Jesus as a possible Messiah. **17.** After an elaborate introduction (which was certainly not believed by the speakers), their carefully planned question was propounded. **Is it lawful to give tribute unto Caesar?** *Kēnsos* is a Latin loanword, referring to the Roman poll tax imposed upon every Jew. The question presupposed a dilemma: Jesus must either acknowledge servitude to Rome (and thus compromise any claim of Messiahship), or risk being charged with disloyalty to Rome. Our Lord's enemies were so sure of the inflammatory nature of the latter charge that they used it against him a few days later, in spite of his clear denial (Lk 23:2). **19. Show me the poll tax coin** (AV, *the tribute money*). The tax was paid with the *denarius*, equal to a soldier's or a laborer's day-wage. **20,21.** By causing his questioners to acknowledge **Caesar's** image and inscription on the coin, Christ elicited from them the principle of his answer. **Render . . . unto Caesar the things that are Caesar's.** Broadus paraphrases, "You got this from Caesar, pay it back to him" (*Comm. on Matt.*, p. 453). Caesar's coinage represented Caesar's government, with its attendant benefits. For these the subject was obligated to pay (cf. Rom 13:1-7). **The things that are God's.** Here spiritual obligations are regarded as separate, though they are not devoid of relationship. Proper subjection to civil power is part of one's spiritual obligation (I Pet 2:13-15), but a believer must always be finally subject to the will of God (Acts 4:19,20).

24. Saying, Master, Moses said, If a man die, having no children, his brother shall marry his wife, and raise up seed unto his brother.

25. Now there were with us seven brethren: and the first, when he had married a wife, deceased, and, having no issue, left his wife unto his brother:

26. Likewise the second also, and the third, unto the seventh.

27. And last of all the woman died also.

28. Therefore in the resurrection, whose wife shall she be of the seven? for they all had her.

29. Jesus answered and said unto them, Ye do err, not knowing the Scriptures, nor the power of God.

30. For in the resurrection they neither marry, nor are given in marriage, but are as the angels of God in heaven.

31. But as touching the resurrection of · the dead, have ye not read that which was spoken unto you by God, saying,

32. I am the God of Abraham, and the God of Isaac, and the God of Jacob? God is not the God of the dead, but of the living.

33. And when the multitude heard *this*, they were astonished at his doctrine.

23-33. Sadducees' question about the resurrection. 23. Sadducees, which say. Absence of an article in the better manuscripts suggests the true rendering to be *Sadducees came saying*. Their denial of the resurrection was bolstered by an illustration to prove its supposed absurdity. (Cf. Acts 23:8 for Sadducean tenets.) 24-27. Moses said. A reference to Deut 25:5 ff. The illustration adduced could conceivably occur among the Jews through the custom of levirate marriage (from the Latin word *levir* meaning "brother-in-law"). Such practice, followed by other ancient peoples as well, had largely fallen into disuse. Hence the case supposed by the Sadducees was no burning issue but a theological conundrum. 28. In the resurrection, the reality of which the Sadducees derided, whose wife shall she be? All seven were equally married to her, and no offspring from any of the unions could cause priority. 29. Not knowing the scriptures nor the power of God. The error of the Sadducees was their failure to understand the Scriptural teaching regarding the resurrection and the ability God can bring to the situation. Their illustration presupposed that resurrection will restore men to the same form of existence they had before (a view commonly held by the Pharisees), though Scripture nowhere affirms this. They did not credit God with the power to raise the dead to a more glorious state (cf. I Cor 15:40-50). 30. But are as the angels, i.e., in the matter of marriage. Jesus did not state that the resurrected dead would become angels. Nor does this passage imply that the dearest of earthly relationships will be forgotten in the life to come. Just how these relationships will be affected by the possession of glorified bodies is not explained, but all Scripture supports the view that the resurrected state is one of blessedness and perfect fellowship. 31-33. Spoken unto you by God. Jesus took his questioners to a direct statement of God himself (not mediated through Moses, as in v. 24). I am the God of Abraham (Ex 3:6). Instead of employing some of the more specific passages in the Prophets or the Writings (concerning which Sadducean opinion was doubtful), Jesus cited from the Torah a statement to which he gave the profoundest interpretation. By using the revered covenant name of God, Jesus implied the immortality of these patriarchs. As Plummer observed, "What is dead can have a Creator or a Controller; but only living beings can have a God" (*Gosp. According to St. Matt.*, p. 307).

34-40. A Pharisaic lawyer's question

**34.** But when the Pharisees had heard that he had put the Sadducees to silence, they were gathered together.

**35.** Then one of them, *which was* a lawyer, asked *him a question*, tempting him, and saying,

**36.** Master, which *is* the great commandment in the law?

**37.** Jesus said unto him, Thou shalt love the Lord thy God with all thy heart, and with all thy soul, and with all thy mind.

**38.** This is the first and great commandment.

**39.** And the second *is* like unto it, Thou shalt love thy neighbor as thyself.

**40.** On these two commandments hang all the law and the prophets.

**41.** While the Pharisees were gathered together, Jesus asked them,

**42.** Saying, What think ye of Christ? whose son is he? They say unto him, *The son* of David.

**43.** He saith unto them, How then doth David in spirit call him Lord, saying,

**44.** The Lord said unto my Lord, Sit thou on my right hand, till I make thine enemies thy footstool?

**45.** If David then call him Lord, how is he his son?

**46.** And no man was able to answer him a word, neither durst any *man* from that day forth ask him any more *questions.*

about the great commandment. Consult Mark's account (12:28-34) for additional details, including the interesting aftermath. **34. When the Pharisees had heard.** The discomfiture of the Sadducees produced by Jesus' masterful reply to the resurrection question would have suited the Pharisees. However, a clear-cut victory of Jesus would not have been welcome even to them, inasmuch as they shared the Sadducees' hatred of him. **35. A lawyer.** An expert expounder of Mosaic law. **36. Which is the great commandment in the law?** The ulterior purpose of the lawyer is not fully evident, and it must be noticed that Jesus treated the question forthrightly and then commended the astuteness of the lawyer's response (Mk 12:34). It is often suggested that he wanted to draw Jesus into argument regarding the rabbis' computation of 613 commandments. **37-40.** Our Lord summarized the two tables of the Law in the words of Deut 6:5 and Lev 19:18. Proper regard for God and one's neighbor is the essence of man's duty. All the OT interprets and applies these principles (Rom 13:8). **All thy heart.** In Hebrew thought, heart symbolized the whole self, in which the soul and mind, the animating and reasoning elements, are contained. All-encompassing love for God will cause one to perform every moral duty. But such an unattainable standard merely shows the corruption of man's heart.

**41-46.** Jesus' counterquestion about Messiah. **42. What think ye of the Christ?** Virtually the same question he had asked earlier of the Twelve (16:15). **The son of David.** The Davidic lineage of Messiah was taught by the scribes (Mk 12:35). **43-45.** By pointing his hearers to Ps 110, which was interpreted by the Jews as Messianic (see Edersheim, *Life and Times of Jesus,* App. IX), Jesus showed their inadequate understanding of that Scripture. This psalm of David (the authorship of which Jesus clearly affirms), presents the **Lord** (Jehovah) as speaking to Messiah; and David calls Messiah **my Lord** *(Adonai)*. Thus the Jews, who acknowledged Messiah as David's descendant, were confronted by this psalm, where David calls this descendant his "Lord" and superior. The prevailing idea of Messiah as a king who would be merely a political ruler was shown to be inadequate. Furthermore, this psalm was given **in the Spirit** (Holy Spirit, Mk 12:36), the product of supernatural revelation. **46. Neither durst any man . . . ask him any more questions.** Though Mark and Luke comment similarly at slightly different places (Mk 12:34; Lk 20:40),

## CHAPTER 23

THEN spake Jesus to the multitude, and to his disciples,

2. Saying, The scribes and the Pharisees sit in Moses' seat:

3. All therefore whatsoever they bid you observe, *that* observe and do; but do not ye after their works: for they say, and do not.

4. For they bind heavy burdens and grievous to be borne, and lay *them* on men's shoulders; but they *themselves* will not move them with one of their fingers.

5. But all their works they do for to be seen of men: they make broad their phylacteries, and enlarge the borders of their garments,

6. And love the uppermost rooms at feasts, and the chief seats in the synagogues,

7. And greetings in the markets, and to be called of men, Rabbi, Rabbi.

8. But be not ye called Rabbi: for one is your Master, *even* Christ; and all ye are brethren.

9. And call no *man* your father upon the earth: for one is your Father, which is in heaven.

10. Neither be ye called masters: for one is your Master, *even* Christ.

11. But he that is greatest among you shall be your servant.

12. And whosoever shall exalt himself shall be abased; and he that shall humble himself shall be exalted.

examination shows that each Synoptist placed the comment appropriately for his material. From that day forth there were no more interruptions by such questioners.

6) Jesus' Public Denunciation of the Pharisees. 23:1-39. Some of the material in this discourse the Lord had used previously (Lk 11:39 ff.), but now he makes his denunciation at the Temple in Jerusalem, in the stronghold of his enemies. 1-12. Warning against the Pharisees. This portion is directed particularly to the disciples, although in the presence of the multitude. 2. Sit on Moses' seat. That is, they occupy Moses' position among you as expounders of the Law. 3,4. Wherefore whatsoever they say to you, do. In so far as their teaching presented what Moses gave, the people were obligated to observe. Do not ye after their works. Their works included their strained interpretations and perversions of the Law, which enabled them to flout the spiritual import of the OT. Their multitudinous additions to the Law, here designated as heavy burdens, grievous to be borne, were part of their works. They themselves will not move them. Though rabbinic casuistry could doubtless find loopholes for evading what was unpleasant, this statement probably means that they never lifted a finger to remove any of the burdens (move is in contrasting parallel to lay on). 5. Phylacteries. Small cases containing strips of parchment on which were written Ex 13:2-10,11-17; Deut 6:4-9; 11:13-22. The cases were bound with straps to the forehead and to the left arm. The practice arose after the Captivity from an extremely literal understanding of Ex 13:16. Pharisees wore them for ostentation. Enlarge the borders of their garments. Tassels worn on the four corners of the outer garment, in accordance with Num 15:38 and Deut 22:12. Jesus wore such tassels (Mt 9:20; 14:36), but the Pharisees enlarged theirs for show. 6,7. Seats of honor at feasts and synagogues were objects of Pharisaic desire, along with effusive greetings in public places, which drew attention to their high position. Rabbi. A title equivalent to *teacher* or *doctor,* and applied by Jews to their spiritual instructors. 8-12. The next words are addressed specifically to the disciples. Christ's followers should not seek to be called by these titles of Rabbi, Father, or Master, as did the Pharisees. However, this is not an absolute prohibiting of officials nor the use of appropriate titles, for Paul calls himself "father" of the Corinthians and Timothy his "child" (I Cor 4:15,17). He that is greatest clearly shows

13. But woe unto you, scribes and Pharisees, hypocrites! for ye shut up the kingdom of heaven against men: for ye neither go in *yourselves*, neither suffer ye them that are entering to go in.

14. Woe unto you, scribes and Pharisees, hypocrites! for ye devour widows' houses, and for a pretense make long prayer: therefore ye shall receive the greater damnation.

15. Woe unto you, scribes and Pharisees, hypocrites! for ye compass sea and land to make one proselyte; and when he is made, ye make him twofold more the child of hell than yourselves.

16. Woe unto you, *ye* blind guides, which say, Whosoever shall swear by the temple, it is nothing; but whosoever shall swear by the gold of the temple, he is a debtor!

17. Ye fools and blind: for whether is greater, the gold, or the temple that sanctifieth the gold?

18. And, Whosoever shall swear by the altar, it is nothing; but whosoever sweareth by the gift that is upon it, he is guilty.

19. *Ye* fools and blind: for whether *is* greater, the gift, or the altar that sanctifieth the gift?

20. Whoso therefore shall swear by the altar, sweareth by it, and by all things thereon.

21. And whoso shall swear by the temple, sweareth by it, and by him that dwelleth therein.

22. And he that shall swear by heaven, sweareth by the throne of God, and by him that sitteth thereon.

23. Woe unto you, scribes and Pharisees, hypocrites! for ye pay tithe of mint and anise and cummin, and have omitted the weightier *matters* of the law, judgment, mercy, and faith: these ought ye to have done, and not to leave the other undone.

24. Ye blind guides, which strain at a gnat, and swallow a camel.

the validity of differing rank. But a spirit of humility should govern believers, not the self-seeking ambition of the Pharisees, which usurped for itself authority that belongs to God.

**13-36.** Seven woes upon the Pharisees. Here attention is turned from the disciples to the Pharisees, who formed part of the crowd. **13. Hypocrites!** An epithet stressing the sham of the Pharisees and their scribes. **Ye shut the kingdom of heaven.** As religious leaders and recognized interpreters of Scripture, they should have been the first to respond to Jesus and should have influenced others to follow. Yet those **attempting to enter** (present tense is tendential or perhaps futuristic [Dana and Mantey, *Manual Grammar of the Greek New Testament*, pp. 185,186]) they were preventing by their false leadership. Verse 14 is an interpolation from Mk 12:40 and Lk 20:47. **15. Ye compass sea and land.** A zealous search. **Proselyte.** Not the God-fearing Gentile who stopped short of circumcision (i.e., proselyte of the gate), but the Gentile who had been persuaded to adopt Judaism *in toto*, including all the traditions taught by such Pharisees. **Twofold more a son of Gehenna than yourselves.** Proselytes made by these unspiritual Pharisees (and doubtless added to their sect) would merely add rabbinic traditions to their pagan notions. .**16-22.** The third **woe** castigates the Pharisees as **blind guides** and **fools** because of their perversions of truth in oath-taking. It is bad enough that a man's word cannot be trusted apart from an oath. But the Pharisees had taught that there are distinctions in the binding force of various oaths. Oaths that used general references to the **temple** or the **altar** did not obligate the user to perform them, but mention of the more specific **gold of the temple** or the **gift** on the altar were binding. Jesus showed the absurdity of such reasoning by pointing out that the greater (**temple, altar, God**) includes the smaller (**gold, gift, heaven**). In view of such perversity, Christ taught, "Swear not at all" (Mt 5:33-37).

**23,24.** The fourth **woe** pictures the Pharisees' scrupulous care in minor matters and their neglect of more important duties. The tithing of various herbs was based on Lev 27:30. **Mint, dill,** and **cummin** were garden plants used for seasoning foods. **Judgment, mercy,** and **faith.** These ethical and spiritual obligations (cf. Mic 6:8) are **weightier matters of the law** and thus are of primary importance, although the **other** matters (tithing) were also expected of God's people. By such practice, the Pharisees had scrupulously strained

25. Woe unto you, scribes and Pharisees, hypocrites! for ye make clean the outside of the cup and of the platter, but within they are full of extortion and excess.

26. *Thou* blind Pharisee, cleanse first that *which is* within the cup and platter, that the outside of them may be clean also.

27. Woe unto you, scribes and Pharisees, hypocrites! for ye are like unto whited sepulchres, which indeed appear beautiful outward, but are within full of dead *men's* bones, and of all uncleanness.

28. Even so ye also outwardly appear righteous unto men, but within ye are full of hypocrisy and iniquity.

29. Woe unto you, scribes and Pharisees, hypocrites! because ye build the tombs of the prophets, and garnish the sepulchres of the righteous,

30. And say, If we had been in the days of our fathers, we would not have been partakers with them in the blood of the prophets.

31. Wherefore ye be witnesses unto yourselves, that ye are the children of them which killed the prophets.

32. Fill ye up then the measure of your fathers.

33. *Ye* serpents, *ye* generation of vipers, how can ye escape the damnation of hell?

34. Wherefore, behold, I send unto you prophets, and wise men, and scribes: and *some* of them ye shall kill and crucify; and *some* of them shall ye scourge in your synagogues, and persecute *them* from city to city:

35. That upon you may come all the righteous blood shed upon the earth, from the blood of righteous Abel unto the blood of Zacharias son of Barachias, whom ye slew between the temple and the altar.

36. Verily I say unto you, All these things shall come upon this generation.

out the gnat (the Levitically unclean insect that might fall into the cup), but proceeded to swallow the camel (the largest unclean animal in Palestine; Lev 11:4). **25,26.** The fifth **woe** portrays the Pharisees' misplaced emphasis on externals. **Ye cleanse the outside of the cup.** The figure points to the Pharisees' concern for ritualistic purification (rabbinic, not Mosaic) and neglect of the contents of the cup. **Within they are full from extortion and excess** (ASV). The Pharisees supported their mode of living by preying upon others. Conformity to rabbinic ritual could not alter this inner corruption. **27,28.** The sixth **woe** describes the hidden influence of the Pharisees. **Whited sepulchres.** Each spring, following the rainy season, graves were whitewashed lest the unwary defile themselves ceremonially by touching them (Num 19:16; cf. Ezk 39:15). This recently performed custom provided a timely illustration of the Pharisees' outward attractiveness but inward defilement. Luke 11:44 uses graves in a slightly different illustration. **29-31.** The seventh **woe** describes the Lord's hearers as partaking of the same nature as their wicked ancestors. By their acts of building and beautifying the tombs of murdered prophets, they supposed they were disavowing those murders. But Jesus stated that their acts proved the very opposite. For by building the tombs, they merely completed what their fathers (spiritual as well as racial) had begun. Their own plotting to murder Jesus (21:46; 22:15; Jn 11:47-53) proved them to be true sons of them that slew the prophets. **32. Fill ye up then the measure of your fathers.** Compare the similar command to Judas, Jn 13:27. **33. Generation of vipers.** Cf. John's denunciation in 3:7. **34-36. I send unto you prophets.** A similar statement in Lk 11:49 attributes this sending to the "wisdom of God." Thus Jesus, as the very personification of God's wisdom, claims for himself this title (I Cor 1:24). **Prophets, wisemen, scribes.** Terms particularly adapted to his audience. The terms would include also the early Christian witnesses, such as Peter, James, Stephen, and Paul. These persecutions here foretold would fill up the measure of the Jews' guilt, so that divine destruction would come upon that **generation** of the nation. **Abel to Zacharias** includes all the murders recorded in the OT, from the first book (Gen 4:8) to the last in the Hebrew canon (II Chr 24:20-22). The failure of these Pharisees to learn the lessons of history and repent of their wickedness, the same that had characterized their fathers,

**37.** O Jerusalem, Jerusalem, *thou* that killest the prophets, and stonest them which are sent unto thee, how often would I have gathered thy children together, even as a hen gathereth her chickens under *her* wings, and ye would not!

**38.** Behold, your house is left unto you desolate.

**39.** For I say unto you, Ye shall not see me henceforth, till ye shall say, Blessed *is* he that cometh in the name of the Lord.

meant that in God's sight they shared the guilt. Further persecutions would make this indisputably clear. **Zacharias, son of Barachias.** In II Chr 24:20 he is called, "son of Jehoiada the priest," perhaps after an illustrious grandfather who had recently died at the age of one hundred and thirty (II Chr 24:15). Matthew may have had documents that named his father. (For an evaluation of all views, see Broadus, *Comm. on Matt.*, pp. 476,477).

**37-39.** Lament over Jerusalem. Jesus had expressed similar feelings earlier (Lk 13:34,35; 19:41-44). **37. Thou that killest the prophets.** This link with verse 34 provides an easy transition to Christ's public lament over the rebellious city. **How often would I.** An inadvertent testimony to the authenticity of John's Gospel, which alone records numerous visits of Jesus to Jerusalem. **38. Your house is left unto you desolate.** Cf. I Kgs 9:7; Jer 22:5; 12:7. **House** is variously interpreted as the nation, the city, and the Temple. Inasmuch as Jesus uttered these words as he left the Temple for the last time (24:1), the Temple identification is very attractive. A temple abandoned by Messiah becomes **your house,** not God's. **39. Ye shall not see me henceforth.** The Lord's public ministry was finished. Following the Resurrection, Jesus made appearances only to chosen witnesses (Acts 10:41). **Till ye shall say.** At Christ's second coming the Jews as a nation will recognize their rejected Messiah, and will welcome his return (Rom 11; Zech 12:10).

7) Olivet Discourse. 24:1—25:46. This discussion contains some of the most difficult of Jesus' utterances. The apocalyptic nature of the material resembles some of the prophetic discourses of the OT, where the mingling of historical and typical elements makes interpretation difficult. Some see the fulfillment of most of these predictions in the destruction of Jerusalem, A.D. 70. Others regard the sermon as descriptive of the church age, and of a tribulation through which the Church must pass before Christ returns. The view that sees here our Lord's description of Daniel's seventieth week relies heavily on parallels found in Daniel and Revelation, and accords well with the question of the disciples that called forth the discourse. By this interpretation, Matthew's account deals entirely with events still future. Luke alone (21:12-24) records the intervening church age, introducing after his parallel discussion of eschatological events a section beginning, "But before all these things."

## CHAPTER 24

AND Jesus went out, and departed from the temple: and his disciples came to *him* for to show him the buildings of the temple.

2. And Jesus said unto them, See ye not all these things? verily I say unto you, There shall not be left here one stone upon another, that shall not be thrown down.

3. And as he sat upon the mount of Olives, the disciples came unto him privately, saying, Tell us, when shall these things be? and what *shall be* the sign of thy coming, and of the end of the world?

4. And Jesus answered and said unto them, Take heed that no man deceive you.

5. For many shall come in my name, saying, I am Christ; and shall deceive many.

6. And ye shall hear of wars and rumors of wars: see that ye be not troubled: for all *these things* must come to pass, but the end is not yet.

7. For nation shall rise against nation, and kingdom against kingdom: and there shall be famines, and pestilences, and earthquakes, in divers places.

**1. The buildings of the temple.** The magnificence of Herod's temple was known far and wide. The massive limestone blocks adorned with golden ornamentation made a dazzling sight (Jos *Wars* v. 5.6). **2. Not be left here one stone upon another.** Jesus responded in a mood far different from their nationalistic pride. He predicted the most severe destruction, which occurred A.D. 70 (Jos *Wars* vii. 1.1). **3. Mount of Olives.** The hill overlooking the city and the Temple from the east. **The disciples came to him privately.** With the temple crowds now left behind, the disciples could question him in seclusion. **When shall these things be?** That is, the destruction of the Temple. **The sign of thy coming and of the consummation of the age?** Jewish interpreters of the OT had clearly seen that the coming of Messiah would usher in the "age to come," accompanied by destruction of the wicked. It must be remembered that the Twelve asked in the light of their traditional understanding, and Jesus' answer in this discourse surely assumed this. Thus the **consummation of the age** (ASV marg.) refers to the age of which they were a part and had knowledge. That such an age formed a great part of their thinking appears in Acts 1:6. The age in question was described in Dan 9:25-27 as a period of "seventy weeks," of which only sixty-nine had passed when Messiah was "cut off." Jesus directly implies that this particular time period is involved when he describes in 24:15 an event that Daniel places in the middle of the seventieth week. Hence the Olivet Discourse is primarily concerned with the tribulation of Israel, a period known in Daniel as the "seventieth week" and described also in Rev 6—19, which will culminate in Christ's return.

a) First Half of the Tribulation. 24:4-14. Daniel's seventieth week has two clearly marked halves (Dan 9:27). There is an amazing correspondence between the order of the seals in Rev 6 and the order of events in Mt 24:4-14. Thus these verses must be placed in the first three and one-half years of the Tribulation, after the Church has been raptured. **5. Saying, I am Christ** (cf. Rev 6:1,2; first seal: Antichrist). Though such tendencies may develop during the church age (I Jn 4:3), the specific reference is to the final Antichrist and his associates. There is no record of any person's claiming to be Christ between A.D. 30 and 70. **6. Wars and rumors of wars** (cf. Rev 6:3,4; second seal: warfare). **7. Famines** (cf. Rev 6:5,6; third seal:

8. All these *are* the beginning of sorrows.

9. Then shall they deliver you up to be afflicted, and shall kill you: and ye shall be hated of all nations for my name's sake.

10. And then shall many be offended, and shall betray one another, and shall hate one another.

11. And many false prophets shall rise, and shall deceive many.

12. And because iniquity shall abound, the love of many shall wax cold.

13. But he that shall endure unto the end, the same shall be saved.

14. And this gospel of the kingdom shall be preached in all the world for a witness unto all nations; and then shall the end come.

15. When ye therefore shall see the abomination of desolation, spoken of by Daniel the prophet, stand in the holy place, (whoso readeth, let him understand,)

16. Then let them which be in Judea flee into the mountains:

17. Let him which is on the housetop not come down to take any thing out of his house:

18. Neither let him which is in the field return back to take his clothes.

19. And woe unto them that are with child, and to them that give suck in those days!

20. But pray ye that your flight be not in the winter, neither on the sabbath day:

famine). **Pestilences and earthquakes** (cf. Rev 6:7,8; fourth seal: death for one-fourth of the earth). **8. Beginning of sorrows.** Literally, *of birthpains*, suggesting the travail shortly to be followed by a happier day. **9. Shall kill you** (cf. Rev 6:9-11; fifth seal: martyrs). **11. Many false prophets . . . shall deceive many.** Cf. II Thess 2:8-12. **12. The love of many shall wax cold.** The severity of these calamities will cause the majority of Israel to abandon any pretense of piety. **13.** But the distinguishing mark of the **saved** Jewish remnant will be their enduring in faith **to the end. 14. Gospel of the kingdom.** The good news of salvation in the Messiah, with the emphasis that the Messianic kingdom is about to be established. This message will go into **all the world** during the Tribulation through the efforts of the two witnesses (Rev 11:3-12) and the sealed remnant of Israel (Rev 7).

b) Last Half of the Tribulation. 24:15-28. **15. When ye therefore shall see the abomination of desolation spoken by Daniel the prophet.** The abomination of desolation reproduces the LXX rendering of Dan 9:27; 12:11; 11:31, of which the first two are certainly eschatological, while the last predicts the profanation of worship by Antiochus, whose act foreshadowed the final abomination. This event occurs in the middle of the seventieth week (Dan 9:27), and its length is variously described as "42 months" (Rev 11:2; 13:5), "1,260 days" (Rev 12:6), or "time, times, and half a time" (Dan 7:25; 12:7; Rev 12:14). **The holy place.** The Temple, to be restored. This enigmatic **abomination** is connected with worship, and other passages would suggest it to be the idolatrous homage that the Antichrist will demand for himself. See Rev 13:5-8; II Thess 2:1-4. It was clearly future in Jesus' day, thus canceling those views of Daniel that find all the fulfillments in the days of Antiochus. Nor can the reference be limited to the catastrophe of A.D. 70, for Mt 24:21 limits the reference to the greatest of all tribulations (cf. Dan 12:1). **16-20. Then.** The use of this temporal particle here and in 24:21 and 23 puts all the events of this section within the framework of the final three and one-half years. The terrors of persecution under Antichrist will make immediate flight necessary (Rev 12:6,14). No time will be available for preparation. Inevitable hardships are foretold. **Neither on the sabbath day.** A reference to the difficulty of travel (securing lodging, meals, services) on the Sabbath in an area where Jews will be

21. For then shall be great tribulation, such as was not since the beginning of the world to this time, no, nor ever shall be.

22. And except those days should be shortened, there should no flesh be saved: but for the elect's sake those days shall be shortened.

23. Then if any man shall say unto you, Lo, here is Christ, or there; believe it not.

24. For there shall arise false Christs, and false prophets, and shall show great signs and wonders; insomuch that, if it were possible, they shall deceive the very elect.

25. Behold, I have told you before.

26. Wherefore if they shall say unto you, Behold, he is in the desert; go not forth: behold, he is in the secret chambers; believe it not.

27. For as the lightning cometh out of the east, and shineth even unto the west; so shall also the coming of the Son of man be.

28. For wheresoever the carcass is, there will the eagles be gathered together.

29. Immediately after the tribulation of those days shall the sun be darkened, and the moon shall not give her light, and the stars shall fall from heaven, and the powers of the heavens shall be shaken:

30. And then shall appear the sign of the Son of man in heaven: and then shall all the tribes of the earth mourn, and they shall see the Son of man coming in the clouds of heaven with power and great glory.

31. And he shall send his angels with a great sound of a trumpet, and they shall gather together his elect from the four winds, from one end of heaven to the other.

32. Now learn a parable of the fig tree; When his branch is yet tender, and putteth forth leaves, ye know that summer is nigh:

33. So likewise ye, when ye shall see all these things, know that it is near, even at the doors.

observing such restrictions. This does not necessarily imply that Christian Jews will observe Sabbath worship. Jesus was employing concepts familiar to his hearers, none of whom as yet could know of the change to Sunday.

**21. Then shall be great tribulation.** The additional description, **not since the beginning of the world,** makes Christ's reference to Dan 12:1 unmistakable. The further notice, **nor ever shall be,** prevents our identification of this with anything less than the final tribulation under Antichrist just prior to the resurrection (Dan 12:2). **22. Except those days should be shortened.** Antichrist's violent measures will be cut short by the sudden appearing of Christ, who will destroy the wicked one (II Thess 2:8). **23-26.** During this intense persecution of Israel, many would-be deliverers will arise, as the Maccabean heroes did in the inter-Testament period. But the **elect** are here warned that the deliverance will not be in any partial or gradual manner. **27.** Rather, with the suddenness and universality of **lightning** (language of appearance, **east . . . unto west**), so shall the **Son** of man come to judge the oppressors. **28. Carcase.** The spiritually dead and decaying mass of the wicked. **Eagles.** The term included birds that feed on carrion; hence, *vultures,* the agents of divine judgment. Cf. Rev 19:17,18.

c) The Coming of the Son of Man. 24: 29-31. **29. Immediately after the tribulation of those days.** Cf. on 24:21. No reference is made here to the Rapture of the Church (cf. I Thess 4:16,17). Rather, the words describe the actual return of Christ to end the Tribulation and establish the Messianic reign. **The sun be darkened.** These accompanying astral phenomena are foretold also in Joel 3:15 and Isa 13:9,10. **30. The sign of the Son of man.** Interpreters are not agreed on the identification of this **sign.** Lange's explanation of it as the Shekinah or glory of Christ is followed by many scholars. Whatever its exact form, its appearance will cause the Jews (**all the tribes**) to **mourn** as they recognize their Messiah (cf. Zech 12:10-12). **Clouds of heaven, power,** and **great glory** describe the same scene in Dan 7:13,14; II Thess 1:7,9. **31.** The **angels** who gather **his elect** are the same who are described in 13:30, 41-43 as removing the tares from the wheat, that the wheat might then be gathered into the barn.

d) Illustrations to promote watchfulness. 24:32—25:30.

**32-36. The fig tree.** A frequent Biblical symbol of the nation of Israel (Jer 24; Joel

34. Verily I say unto you, This generation shall not pass, till all these things be fulfilled.

35. Heaven and earth shall pass away, but my words shall not pass away.

36. But of that day and hour knoweth no *man*, no, not the angels of heaven, but my Father only.

37. But as the days of Noe *were*, so shall also the coming of the Son of man be.

38. For as in the days that were before the flood they were eating and drinking, marrying and giving in marriage, until the day that Noe entered into the ark,

39. And knew not until the flood came, and took them all away; so shall also the coming of the Son of man be.

40. Then shall two be in the field; the one shall be taken, and the other left.

1:6,7; Hos 9:10). Jesus also had used this figure previously (Lk 13:6). The peculiar trait of the tree mentioned earlier (21:19, 20) is that fruit and leaves appear at about the same time; when leaves are present, summer is near. Jesus thus associated a revitalized nation with the approach of these eschatological events. **34. This generation shall not pass away.** To explain generation (*genea*) here as the lifetime of the disciples obligates one to seek the fulfillment of all these events by A.D. 70. But that is manifestly impossible unless one spiritualizes the second coming of Christ. However, *genea* also can mean "race" or "family," and this yields good sense here. In spite of terrible persecution, the Jewish nation will not be exterminated, but will exist to share the blessings of the Millennial reign. In support of this view, Alford points out that Christians of ancient times continued to expect the Lord's coming even after the apostles and their contemporaries had passed away (*New Testament for English Readers*, p. 169). **35. Heaven and earth shall pass away.** Cf. Rom 8:19-22; I Cor 7:31; Rev 21:1. The truth of these solemn predictions of Christ will not experience the slightest alteration. **36.** The exact moment of fulfillment, however, lies in the authority of the **Father** alone (cf. Acts 1:7). No scheme of date-setting by men is possible. The phrase, **neither the Son** (omitted by AV, but included in ASV and RSV on strong textual evidence), indicates that the perfect knowledge which all members of the Godhead share was part of that which Jesus voluntarily refrained from using during his earthly ministry, except in those instances when such knowledge was needed for his purpose.

**37-39.** The days of Noah. As the **days of Noah** closed an era with judgment, so shall Christ's return. In an age of great wickedness (Gen 6), men went about their daily living undisturbed by impending doom (**eating, drinking, marrying, giving in marriage**). But the **flood took away all** the wicked, so that only the righteous were left to inherit the earth. Likewise the **coming of the Son of man,** following the Great Tribulation (vv. 29-31) will remove the wicked, in order that the faithful remnant who have come out of the Tribulation may participate in the Millennial blessings (cf. 25:31-46; 13:30,41-43,49,50).

**40-42.** The two in the field, and the two at the mill. **Then** places this illustration in the same period as the preceding, precisely explained in verse 29 as "after the tribulation." Thus it does not refer to the Rapture of the Church. **Two in the field.** The Second Coming will be so sudden and dis-

41. Two *women shall be* grinding at the mill; the one shall be taken, and the other left.

42. Watch therefore; for ye know not what hour your Lord doth come.

43. But know this, that if the goodman of the house had known in what watch the thief would come, he would have watched, and would not have suffered his house to be broken up.

44. Therefore be ye also ready: for in such an hour as ye think not the Son of man cometh.

45. Who then is a faithful and wise servant, whom his lord hath made ruler over his household, to give them meat in due season?

46. Blessed *is* that servant, whom his lord when he cometh shall find so doing.

47. Verily I say unto you, That he shall make him ruler over all his goods.

48. But and if that evil servant shall say in his heart, My lord delayeth his coming;

49. And shall begin to smite *his* fellow servants, and to eat and drink with the drunken;

50. The lord of that servant shall come in a day when he looketh not for *him*, and in an hour that he is not aware of,

51. And shall cut him asunder, and appoint *him* his portion with the hypocrites: there shall be weeping and gnashing of teeth.

## CHAPTER 25

THEN shall the kingdom of heaven be likened unto ten virgins, which took their lamps, and went forth to meet the bridegroom.

criminatory that persons working together will be separated, **one** man (masculine numeral) snatched away to judgment, and **one** man left to enjoy blessing. **Two women grinding at the mill.** This task was regularly performed by women, either mother and daughter, sisters, or female slaves (see Thomson, *Land and Book*, pp. 526,527). **Watch therefore.** Although the emphasis here is upon the coming of the **Son of man** after the Tribulation, the warning is pertinent to all believers, for all are to be watchful and ready for his coming. The delineation of various phases of his coming is revealed later. This encouragement to watchfulness is repeated in 24:44 and 25:13.

**43,44.** The master of the house. If the household master had been watchful, he could have prevented damage and loss. **Broken up.** Literally, *dug through*, a reference to houses of sun-dried brick in Palestine, comparatively easy to enter. Believers have less excuse for carelessness than this **master**, who had not been forewarned that a thief was coming.

**45-51.** The faithful servant and the evil servant. **45-47.** The figure depicts a **trustworthy** and **prudent servant** who is placed by his master over the other **domestic servants.** Faithful performance of his duties will bring increased privilege and responsibility when his lord returns. **48,49.** In contrast, the **evil servant** is a servant in name only, for he flouts his lord's instructions and assumes the rights of authority for himself. His defection is both doctrinal (my lord delayeth his coming) and ethical (smite his fellowservants, eat and drink with the drunken). He mistakes the uncertainty of the time of coming for a certainty that it will not be soon. Every believer (whether church age or Tribulation saint) is a servant of God with a definite area of responsibility. **50,51.** The coming of Christ will be sudden and unexpected, and will unmask such hypocrites. **Shall cut him asunder.** The literal meaning, "to cut in two," describes the physical punishment (cf. II Sam 12:31; Heb 11:37), and the following words (with the hypocrites . . . weeping and gnashing of teeth) affirm the eternal result.

**25:1-13.** The Ten Virgins. A beautiful story lifted from contemporary marriage custom, but interpreted by evangelicals in widely varying fashion. Some explain the virgins as the professing members of the Church awaiting the return of Christ. Others apply the parable to the Jewish remnant in the Tribulation. Though the central theme of watchfulness is applicable to either group, this writer feels that the

2. And five of them were wise, and five *were* foolish.

3. They that *were* foolish took their lamps, and took no oil with them:

4. But the wise took oil in their vessels with their lamps.

5. While the bridegroom tarried, they all slumbered and slept.

6. And at midnight there was a cry made, Behold, the bridegroom cometh; go ye out to meet him.

7. Then all those virgins arose, and trimmed their lamps.

8. And the foolish said unto the wise, Give us of your oil; for our lamps are gone out.

9. But the wise answered, saying, *Not so;* lest there be not enough for us and you: but go ye rather to them that sell, and buy for yourselves.

10. And while they went to buy, the bridegroom came; and they that were ready went in with him to the marriage: and the door was shut.

11. Afterward came also the other virgins, saying, Lord, Lord, open to us.

12. But he answered and said, Verily I say unto you, I know you not.

latter interpretation meets the demands of content and context more precisely. **1. Then** places the parable within the framework mentioned in 24:29 and 24:40. **The kingdom of heaven.** Cf. on Mt 3:2; 13:11. **Ten virgins . . . went forth to meet the bridegroom.** Jewish weddings had two phases. The bridegroom went first to the bride's home to obtain his bride and observe religious ceremonies. Then he would take his bride to his own home for a resumption of the festivities. The parable gives no intimation that the virgins (plural) expect to marry the bridegroom. This is not a polygamous wedding. Rather, at the end of the Tribulation, Christ will be returning to earth (his domain) after taking to himself the Church as his bride in heaven (her home during the Tribulation). This understanding is reflected in the Western text of this passage, which says, "to meet the bridegroom and the bride." Cf. also Lk 12:35,36, "when he will return from the wedding." Hence the Church as such is not in view here. Interest centers upon the virgins who wish to participate in the wedding feast, representative of the professing Jewish remnant (Rev 14:1-4). **3. Foolish.** Stupid. **Lamps.** Torches, each having a wick and a space for oil. **No oil with them. Oil,** regularly symbolic in Scripture of the Holy Spirit (Zech 4; Isa 61:1). Here a reference to the possession of the Holy Spirit in regeneration (Rom 8:9). All ten appeared outwardly the same (virgins, lamps, similar activity), but five did not partake of the Holy Spirit, which at this time had been given to Israel that they might be ready for Messiah (Zech 12:10). **5. All slumbered and slept.** The parable attaches no blame to this detail. Hence it perhaps pictures the assurance of the remnant as they awaited the bridegroom, rather than their carelessness; but in the case of the foolish virgins, it was a false assurance. **6,7. Trimmed their lamps.** Cleaned the wicks, lighted them, and adjusted the flames. A person going about Oriental streets at night must carry a lighted torch. So the virgins prepared to join the procession as the bridegroom approached. **8. Our lamps are going out.** The foolish virgins, who had provided no oil, saw their dry wicks flicker for a few moments and then die. To insist that they had some oil but not enough contradicts 25:3. The failure to provide any oil at all displays their stupidity. **9. Buy for yourselves.** Language of the parable. The Holy Spirit is a free gift, but may be depicted by such metaphors (cf. Isa 55:1). Each person must obtain his own supply. **10-12.** While the foolish were gone, the bride-

13. Watch therefore; for ye know neither the day nor the hour wherein the Son of man cometh.

14. For *the kingdom of heaven is* as a man traveling into a far country, *who* called his own servants, and delivered unto them his goods.

15. And unto one he gave five talents, to another two, and to another one; to every man according to his several ability; and straightway took his journey.

16. Then he that had received the five talents went and traded with the same, and made *them* other five talents.

17. And likewise he that *had received* two, he also gained other two.

18. But he that had received one went and digged in the earth, and hid his lord's money.

19. After a long time the lord of those servants cometh, and reckoneth with them.

20. And so he that had received five talents came and brought other five talents, saying, Lord, thou deliveredst unto me five talents: behold, I have gained beside them five talents more.

21. His lord said unto him, Well done, *thou* good and faithful servant: thou hast been faithful over a few things, I will make thee ruler over many things: enter thou into the joy of thy lord.

22. He also that had received two talents came and said, Lord, thou deliveredst unto me two talents: behold, I have gained two other talents beside them.

23. His lord said unto him, Well done, good and faithful servant; thou hast been faithful over a few things, I will make thee ruler over many things: enter thou into the joy of thy lord.

24. Then he which had received the one talent came and said, Lord, I knew thee that thou art a hard man, reaping where thou hast not sown, and gathering where thou hast not strewed:

groom came, and the feast began. Later the foolish virgins returned, the implication being that no oil could be obtained at such an hour. I know you not. A statement similar in import to 7:23. Christ will reject all relationship with persons whose claim is profession only.

14-30. The Talents. A parable similar to that of The Pounds, which had been given a few days earlier at Jericho (Lk 19:11-27). The Pounds illustrated the truth that equal gifts, if used with unequal diligence, may be unequally rewarded. The Talents showed that unequal gifts, if used with equal faithfulness, will be equally rewarded. The preceding parable of The Virgins stressed the need for alert preparation for Christ's coming. The Talents emphasized the need for faithful service during his absence.

14. The elliptical nature of the sentence, which causes English translators to supply various words at the beginning, shows its close connection with the previous material. As a man going into another country. The man is clearly the Son of man (v. 13).
15. A talent was a unit of coinage of comparatively high value. Here the talents were silver (v. 18, *argurion*, "silver money"). Depending upon who issued them, talents ranged in value from $1,625 (Aegina) to $1,080 (Attic). A talent was worth much more than a pound *(mina)*. According to his several ability. The talents represent differing responsibilities to be exercised in accord with each man's capacity. 16,17. The first two servants, though possessing different amounts of money, were equally diligent and doubled their capital. 18. The servant who possessed only one talent displayed no diligence and was not challenged by his opportunity. Digged in the earth. A common hiding place (Mt 13:44). 19. After a long time. An indication that Christ's return would not be immediate, although the expression is indefinite. In the parable the return was yet within the lifetime of the servants. 20-23. At their lord's return the first two servants had different sums to present, but both offered increases of 100 per cent and received the same commendation and reward. Well done, good and faithful servant. Faithfulness is the virtue being examined. I will set thee over many things. Part of the reward consisted in gaining higher responsibilities and privileges with the lord. Enter thou into the joy of thy lord. Probably a reference to a believer's sharing Christ's joy, which is His by right of His perfect performance of the Father's will (Jn 15:10,11). 24,25. The unprofitable servant, however, reveals by

**25.** And I was afraid, and went and hid thy talent in the earth: lo, *there* thou hast *that is* thine.

**26.** His lord answered and said unto him, *Thou* wicked and slothful servant, thou knewest that I reap where I sowed not, and gather where I have not strewed:

**27.** Thou oughtest therefore to have put my money to the exchangers, and *then* at my coming I should have received mine own with usury.

**28.** Take therefore the talent from him, and give *it* unto him which hath ten talents.

**29.** For unto every one that hath shall be given, and he shall have abundance: but from him that hath not shall be taken away even that which he hath.

**30.** And cast ye the unprofitable servant into outer darkness: there shall be weeping and gnashing of teeth.

his explanation an utterly false view of his master. **A hard man.** Harsh, cruel, merciless. **Reaping where thou hast not sown,** i.e., profiting from the labor of others. **Gathering where thou didst not scatter.** It is not certain whether this clause is parallel in thought to the preceding, or whether it pictures the next stage of harvest, the winnowing. If the latter, then the servant accuses his lord of gathering into his barn that which another's labor had scattered with the winnowing shovel to separate the grain from the chaff. **I was afraid.** He pleads his fear of risk and the necessity of accounting for possible loss. This servant was blind to the fact that his master was a generous, loving man, who wanted him to participate in wonderful joys. **26. Thou knewest.** Perhaps this should be regarded as a question, "Did you know that . . . ?" Without acknowledging the truth of this opinion, the master judges the slave on the basis of his plea, to show the baseness of such an attitude. **27.** If the servant really feared the risk of business ventures, then he should have deposited the talent with the **bankers** so that it would have drawn **interest.** Although Israelites were forbidden to extract interest from each other, they could do so from Gentiles (Deut 23: 20). **28,29.** Therefore, the talent was taken from this lazy and rebellious servant and given to the one who was most able to use it profitably. **30. Cast ye the unprofitable servant into outer darkness.** The weeping and gnashing of teeth show clearly that this symbolizes eternal punishment (8:12; 13:42,50; 22:13; 24:51). Herein is the crux of the interpretation. If this reckoning is the judgment of the believer's works, then we apparently have a true believer suffering the loss of his soul because of the barrenness of his works. But that interpretation would contradict Jn 5:24. Or, if the unprofitable servant represents a mere professing Christian, whose real nature is thus unmasked, then it appears that the judgment of believers' works and the damnation of sinners occur together, although Rev 20 separates these judgments by 1,000 years. The best solution applies the parable to the Tribulation saints (whether Jew or Gentile) because of the clear association with the preceding verses. This explanation agrees with other Scriptures that at the time of Christ's return, the believing remnant will be gathered to enjoy Millennial blessings, but those then living who have no real belief in their Messiah will be removed (Ezk 20:37-42). Of course, the principle is true for men of all ages that God holds men responsible for their use of his gifts.

31. When the Son of man shall come in his glory, and all the holy angels with him, then shall he sit upon the throne of his glory:

32. And before him shall be gathered all nations: and he shall separate them one from another, as a shepherd divideth *his* sheep from the goats:

33. And he shall set the sheep on his right hand, but the goats on the left.

34. Then shall the King say unto them on his right hand, Come, ye blessed of my Father, inherit the kingdom prepared for you from the foundation of the world:

35. For I was ahungered, and ye gave me meat: I was thirsty, and ye gave me drink: I was a stranger, and ye took me in:

36. Naked, and ye clothed me: I was sick, and ye visited me: I was in prison, and ye came unto me.

37. Then shall the righteous answer him, saying, Lord, when saw we thee ahungered, and fed *thee?* or thirsty, and gave *thee* drink?

38. When saw we thee a stranger, and took *thee* in? or naked, and clothed *thee?*

39. Or when saw we thee sick, or in prison, and came unto thee?

40. And the King shall answer and say unto them, Verily I say unto you, Inasmuch as ye have done *it* unto one of the least of these my brethren, ye have done *it* unto me.

41. Then shall he say also unto them on the left hand, Depart from me, ye cursed, into everlasting fire, prepared for the devil and his angels:

e) Judgment of All the Nations. 25:31-46. **31.** Then shall he sit upon the throne of his glory. The same scene as 24:30,31, marking the coming of the Son of man to end the Great Tribulation and usher in the Millennium. **32,33.** Before him shall be gathered all the nations. This judgment scene must be distinguished from that of Revelation 20 (Great White Throne), for that follows the resurrection of the wicked at the close of the Millennium. Here the nations must mean the persons living on earth when Christ returns. They will be judged as individuals, not as groups (them, v. 32, is masculine gender, whereas nations is neuter). Such a judgment of living men at the time of Christ's glorious coming is foretold in Joel 3:1,2. It will result in a separation into two groups, with the group compared to sheep placed at Christ's right hand, the position of honor and blessing. **34.** To these who had been pronounced blessed by the Father, Christ as the King (only use of this title by Jesus) invites, Come . . . inherit the kingdom (Millennial). **35-40.** As evidence of the regenerated character of these sheep-like persons, Jesus cites their deeds of kindness done to "my brethren," which he treats as done to himself. It seems clear that the sheep and the goats are distinct from my brethren. Hence the interpretation of the nations as Gentiles and my brethren as the faithful Jewish remnant who will proclaim the gospel of the Kingdom in all the world (24:14; Rev 7:1-8) meets the exigencies of the passage. (That Jesus earlier called all believers his "brethren" does not change the demands of this context; 12:47-50.) These Jewish believers will bring about the conversion of an unnumbered multitude of Gentiles (Rev 7:9-14), who will evidence their faith by their deeds. Their visiting those in prison suggests that danger will be involved in a man's publicly acknowledging Christ and His emissaries during that period.

**41. Depart from me, ye cursed.** Many have noted the absence of the Greek article with cursed (as differing from its use in "ye blessed," v. 34). Thus the participle, being circumstantial rather than substantive, may indicate that the phrase means "Depart from me under a curse" (ASV marg.). Though the righteous have been pronounced blessed by the Father and enter a kingdom prepared for them before creation, the fate of the wicked is not stated in such specific terms of election. The everlasting fire was not prepared for them but for the devil and his angels (Rev 20:10). Neither do men inherit eternal fire (contrast the righteous, v. 34), but go

42. For I was ahungered, and ye gave me no meat: I was thirsty, and ye gave me no drink:

43. I was a stranger, and ye took me not in: naked, and ye clothed me not: sick, and in prison, and ye visited me not.

44. Then shall they also answer him, saying, Lord, when saw we thee ahungered, or athirst, or a stranger, or naked, or sick, or in prison, and did not minister unto thee?

45. Then shall he answer them, saying, Verily I say unto you, Inasmuch as ye did *it* not to one of the least of these, ye did *it* not to me.

46. And these shall go away into everlasting punishment: but the righteous into life eternal.

## CHAPTER 26

AND it came to pass, when Jesus had finished all these sayings, he said unto his disciples,

2. Ye know that after two days is *the feast of* the passover, and the Son of man is betrayed to be crucified.

3. Then assembled together the chief priests, and the scribes, and the elders of the people, unto the palace of the high priest, who was called Caiaphas,

4. And consulted that they might take Jesus by subtilty, and kill *him*.

5. But they said, Not on the feast *day*, lest there be an uproar among the people.

there by refusing God's grace. **42-45.** Jesus points to the goats' lack of the good characteristics displayed by the sheeplike ones. Sins of omission, not heinous deeds of violence, are chosen as indicative of spiritual state. **46. Eternal punishment** and **eternal life** both employ the same adjective *(aiōnios)*. Any attempt to reduce the punishment by restricting **eternal** reduces the bliss of the righteous by the same amount. While **eternal** may imply a qualitative as well as a quantitative concept, the aspect of unending duration cannot be dissociated from the word. It was the regular word for the concept of "eternal," as lexicons attest. Eternal punishment is mentioned in such passages as Mt 18:8; II Thess 1:9; Jude 13; *et al.* Thus at the beginning of the Millennium, a judgment is held, and the wicked are removed, so that only regenerated persons will enter the Millennial kingdom (cf. Jn 3:3).

## IV. The Passion of Jesus Christ. 26:1— 27:66.

This section, of incalculable importance to every Christian, is filled with dramatic human interest. Yet the details supplied by the Evangelists have caused problems, chiefly chronological, from earliest times. Nevertheless, the factual way in which each Gospel (written by men who were themselves emotionally involved) treats these highly emotional events makes these sublime treatises the more remarkable.

A. Plot Against Jesus. 26:1-16.

**1-5.** Final prediction of his death. **2. After two days.** Since the Passover was eaten on the evening of Nisan 14 (sundown actually began Nisan 15), this prediction was made on the evening of Nisan 12. **Passover.** The first great feast in the Jewish calendar, commemorating Israel's deliverance from Egypt and the "sparing" (meaning of Heb. root transliterated into Gr. as *pascha)* of their firstborn when God smote the Egyptians (cf. Ex 12). Passover was followed immediately by the seven days' Feast of Unleavened Bread (Nisan 15-21), and the entire festival was often called "Passover." **The Son of man is betrayed.** Cf. predictions in 16:21; 17:22; 20:18. Here Christ first foretells that his death will occur at Passover time. **3-5.** This prediction ran counter to the plans of the plotters, however. Fearful of the crowds in Jerusalem, many of whom were Galilean supporters of Jesus, they agreed not to make any move **during the feast.** They may well have expected to delay action for a full week. But Jesus fixed the time of his death in advance, contrary to

94

6. Now when Jesus was in Bethany, in the house of Simon the leper,

7. There came unto him a woman having an alabaster box of very precious ointment, and poured it on his head, as he sat at meat.

8. But when his disciples saw *it*, they had indignation, saying, To what purpose *is* this waste?

9. For this ointment might have been sold for much, and given to the poor.

10. When Jesus understood *it*, he said unto them, Why trouble ye the woman? for she hath wrought a good work upon me.

11. For ye have the poor always with you; but me ye have not always.

12. For in that she hath poured this ointment on my body, she did *it* for my burial.

13. Verily I say unto you, Wheresoever this gospel shall be preached in the whole world, *there* shall also this, that this woman hath done, be told for a memorial of her.

their scheming, and overruled so that he would die as the true Passover. Caiaphas had functioned as high priest since about A.D. 18. He had previously called for Jesus' death (Jn 11:49,50).

6-13. Anointing at Bethany. Interpreters are not agreed on the chronological connections of this event. In view of Jn 12:1, "six days before the Passover," either Matthew (and Mark) or John has followed topical rather than chronological order. Because neither Mark nor Matthew actually dates the event more precisely than "now when Jesus was in Bethany," it seems best to follow the clear chronology in Jn 12:1. Thus Matthew, having described the conspiracy, now reverts to an earlier event to show the circumstances that prompted Judas to the actual betrayal. Parallels are Mk 14:3-9; Jn 12:1-8 (Lk 7:36-50 relates a different incident).

6. Simon the leper. Doubtless a healed leper who felt much gratitude toward Jesus. 7. A woman. Mary, the sister of Martha and Lazarus (Jn 12:3; 11:1,2). Very precious ointment. Parallel accounts describe the ointment as nard, with a value in excess of 300 denarii. 8,9. When the disciples saw the lavish outpouring of this ointment on the body (v. 12) of Jesus (both head, v. 7, and feet, Jn 12:3), they grumbled with indignation, regarding such use as waste. Matthew singles out no one for particular blame (perhaps ashamed at his own participation). But John cites Judas as the instigator, and shows the hypocrisy of his avowed concern for the poor. 10-13. Jesus explained that one must be spiritually discerning so as not to miss an irrecoverable opportunity. Deeds of benevolence are good and are always in order (Mk 14:7). But there would never be another opportunity to do what Mary did. She did it to prepare me for burial (ASV). It is unwarranted to suggest that Jesus was inventing motives for Mary. He had previously announced his approaching death (Jn 10:11,17,18; Mt 16:21; 17:22; 20:18). Instead of closing her mind to the prediction, as the disciples seemed to do (cf. Mt 16:22), Mary believed it. She apparently realized that when the tragedy struck, there would be no time for customary courtesies. Only if Mary's act is seen as born of her spiritual comprehension can the tremendous praise from Jesus be properly understood. As it happened, this was the only anointing his body received. The women who later came to perform this task found only the empty tomb.

14-16. Conspiracy of Judas. How closely then is to be understood with the preceding paragraph cannot be ascertained

14. Then one of the twelve, called Judas Iscariot, went unto the chief priests,

15. And said *unto them,* What will ye give me, and I will deliver him unto you? And they covenanted with him for thirty pieces of silver.

16. And from that time he sought opportunity to betray him.

(Mk merely says "and"). If 26:6-13 be regarded as parenthetical, to explain one of the roots of the betrayal, then the plot of Judas may belong to the same time as verses 1-5. By such a view, the indignation at Simon's house six days before the Passover (Jn 12:1,2) developed into a matured conspiracy during the next four days. **Iscariot.** Man of Kerioth, a town in Judea. **They covenanted with him.** The preferred translation is, *they weighed unto him.* Matthew employs the same word as the LXX in Zech 11:12, to which he seems to be consciously alluding. The LXX uses *histēmi* to translate *shakal,* "to weigh out money" (another instance is I Kgs 20:39 [LXX, III Kgs 21:39]). Thus Judas was paid at this time, a fact which the other accounts neither note nor contradict. **Thirty pieces of silver.** Probably shekels. A comparatively small sum, the valuation of a slave (Ex 21:32).

B. The Final Meal. 26:17-30. Probably no harmonistic problem in the Gospels has been as perplexing as the one presented here. Was this final meal the Jewish Passover? The Synoptics imply that it was. Yet John seems equally clear that the Passover was yet future at the time of the feet-washing (Jn 13:1), meal (13:29), trials (18:28), and crucifixion (19:14,31). Some scholars are content to admit an irreconcilable conflict. Others insist that one account must be wrong. It has also been argued that Jesus ate an anticipatory Passover one day in advance of the legal observance. Reinforcement of this view has recently come to light at Qumran, where discoveries have shown that the Qumran sect always observed Passover on Tuesday night. Thus it is suggested that Jesus ate a Passover on Tuesday (as the Synoptics imply), while orthodox Judaism observed Passover on Friday. (See J. A. Walther, "Chronology of Passion Week," JBL, June, 1958, p. 116 ff.) Against this view stands the great improbability that such a remarkable deviation from orthodox Judaism would pass without some special notice in the Gospels, or that a Passover meal could be properly observed in Jerusalem prior to the traditional time (e.g., lambs were to be slain at the Temple shortly before the Passover meal; cf. I Cor 5:7). A more worthy proposal explains either John or the Synoptics in the light of the other. Both possibilities have been tried, although there are admitted difficulties with either method. The present writer prefers to explain the Synoptics by the clear statements of John, which perhaps were partially intended by him to clarify

17. Now the first *day* of the *feast of* unleavened bread the disciples came to Jesus, saying unto him, Where wilt thou that we prepare for thee to eat the passover?

18. And he said, Go into the city to such a man, and say unto him, The Master saith, My time is at hand; I will keep the passover at thy house with my disciples.

19. And the disciples did as Jesus had appointed them; and they made ready the passover.

20. Now when the even was come, he sat down with the twelve.

21. And as they did eat, he said, Verily I say unto you, that one of you shall betray me.

22. And they were exceeding sorrowful, and began every one of them to say unto him, Lord, is it I?

23. And he answered and said, He that dippeth *his* hand with me in the dish, the same shall betray me.

24. The Son of man goeth as it is written of him: but woe unto that man by whom the Son of man is betrayed! it had been good for that man if he had not been born.

25. Then Judas, which betrayed him, answered and said, Master, is it I? He said unto him, Thou hast said.

ambiguous points in the chronology. According to this view, the Last Supper was in no sense the Passover meal; rather, Jesus died at the very hour the Passover lambs were being slain at the Temple (cf. I Cor 5:7). Neverthless, Jesus gave directions to his disciples to make the usual arrangements for the feast, for two reasons: (1) the disciples would eat it; (2) Jesus did not wish to foretell at this time the exact moment of his death.

17-19. Preparation for the Passover. 17. First day of unleavened bread. The fourteenth of Nisan, on which leaven was removed from the houses in preparation for the feasts of Passover and Unleavened Bread (cf. Mk 14:12; Lk 22:7). This day began at sundown on the thirteenth, and it is to the opening hours of this day that reference is made. 18,19. In response to the disciples' question, Jesus sent them to a man at whose house the group would assemble. I will keep the Passover. To this statement of general purpose must be added the words of Lk 22:16, ASV, "I will not eat it," in which he later indicates that the general plan will be interrupted. Perhaps he did not wish Judas to know his plans so specifically this far in advance.

20-30. The Last Supper. 20. When even was come. Later that same evening (early hours of the fourteenth), Jesus joined the disciples at the supper hour (Lk 22:14). 21. One of you shall betray me. First announcement that the "delivering up" of the Son of man (17:22; 20:18; 26:2) was to be by one of the Twelve. What shock that statement must have caused! 22. The fact that eleven of the disciples innocently asked, Lord, is it I? shows that they realized their own weakness, although their questions were so phrased as to expect a negative answer—"*It is not I, is it?*" 23. He that dippeth his hand with me. Since the group probably ate from a common dish, this statement did not identify the traitor, except to emphasize the dastardly nature of the betrayal, as occurring among intimate companions. 24. As it is written. The death of Christ was unfolding as predicted in various OT passages. Yet God's sovereignty over all events never relieves man of responsibility or guilt. 25. When Judas saw that his silence was cause for suspicion, he also asked, Is it I, Rabbi? To him Jesus answered, Thou hast said. It does not appear that the others heard this answer amid the general hum of conversation. Whether Christ's explanation to John (and Peter) occurred before or after the indication to Judas cannot be ascertained (Jn 13:23-26). When Judas left shortly, none knew that Satan had ener-

26. And as they were eating, Jesus took bread, and blessed *it*, and brake *it*, and gave *it* to the disciples, and said, Take, eat; this is my body.

27. And he took the cup, and gave thanks, and gave *it* to them, saying, Drink ye all of it;

28. For this is my blood of the new testament, which is shed for many for the remission of sins.

29. But I say unto you, I will not drink henceforth of this fruit of the vine, until that day when I drink it new with you in my Father's kingdom.

30. And when they had sung a hymn, they went out into the mount of Olives.

31. Then saith Jesus unto them, All ye shall be offended because of me this night: for it is written, I will smite the shepherd, and the sheep of the flock shall be scattered abroad.

32. But after I am risen again, I will go before you into Galilee.

33. Peter answered and said unto him, Though all *men* shall be offended because of thee, *yet* will I never be offended.

34. Jesus said unto him, Verily I say unto thee, That this night, before the cock crow, thou shalt deny me thrice.

35. Peter said unto him, Though I should die with thee, yet will I not deny thee. Likewise also said all the disciples.

36. Then cometh Jesus with them unto a place called Gethsemane, and saith unto the disciples, Sit ye here, while I go and pray yonder.

gized him so that he would immediately put the plot into operation (Jn 13:27-30).

**26.** Matthew's account of the consecration of the bread and the wine is similar to Mark's; Luke's resembles that in I Cor 11:23-26. **This is my body.** For full discussion of the opposing views of Romanism, Luther, Calvin, and Zwingli, consult Bible dictionaries. The obvious meaning of the passage prevents our understanding the bread in any sense other than symbolic, for his actual body was also present. (Cf. similar metaphors: Jn 10:7; 15:1.) These symbols were to be reminders to the disciples (Lk 22:19) of their absent Lord, and memorials of the cost of their redemption. **27,28. Drink ye all of it,** i.e., all of you. **The new testament** or covenant was put in force by the death of Christ. The old covenant given by God to Israel required continual sacrifices for sin. But Christ's death provided a perfect sacrifice, and made possible both justification and regeneration (Heb 8:6-13). **Shed for many.** (Cf. 20:28.) Christ's death, while sufficient in itself to care for the **remission of sins** for every person, is here regarded as actually effective only for believers. **29. I will not drink henceforth.** This statement directed the gaze of the disciples ahead to the Father's kingdom (the Messianic kingdom of God, Mk 14:25) and to a time of joy and fellowship at the great Marriage Supper. **30. When they had sung an hymn, they went out.** Before this occurred, the discourse of John 14 must have been delivered.

C. Prediction of Peter's Denial. 26:31-35. Did this occur before they left the upper room (Jn 13:36-38; Lk 22:31-34) or after (Mk 14:27-31; Mt)? Since it seems impossible to harmonize these accounts without doing violence to two of them, it is more feasible to understand two separate warnings to Peter. **31. All ye shall be offended.** Though only Peter denied Jesus, all eleven forsook him and fled (v. 56). Jesus regarded this as fulfillment of Zech 13:7. **32. I will go before you into Galilee.** This was the great postresurrection meeting mentioned several times (28:7,10,16). It does not preclude other appearances, however, some of them earlier in Judea. **33-35.** Peter's boastfulness in rating his devotion superior to that of the others **(though all men shall be offended)** cast reflection upon them and thus drew forth their own avowals of loyalty. This experience was undoubtedly in Jesus' mind when he later asked Peter, "Lovest thou me more than these?" (Jn 21:15).

D. Events in Gethsemane. 26:36-56. **36-46.** The prayer. **36. Gethsemane.**

37. And he took with him Peter and the two sons of Zebedee, and began to be sorrowful and very heavy.

38. Then saith he unto them, My soul is exceeding sorrowful, even unto death: tarry ye here, and watch with me.

39. And he went a little further, and fell on his face, and prayed, saying, O my Father, if it be possible, let this cup pass from me: nevertheless, not as I will, but as thou *wilt*.

40. And he cometh unto the disciples, and findeth them asleep, and saith unto Peter, What, could ye not watch with me one hour?

41. Watch and pray, that ye enter not into temptation: the spirit indeed *is* willing, but the flesh *is* weak.

The name means "oil press," and here describes a garden frequented by Jesus and the disciples. It lay across the Kedron on the Mount of Olives (Lk 22:39; Jn 18:1,2), and doubtless contained olive trees and a press for extracting oil. The spot shown to travelers today must be near the place, although the ancient trees cannot be the originals (Jos *Wars* vi.1.1). **37,38.** Stationing eight disciples together, Jesus took Peter, James, and John farther into the garden. Finally he withdrew even from them to pray alone. The agony of soul he experienced is depicted by **sorrowful, sore troubled** (AV, *very heavy*), **exceedingly sorrowful, even unto death.** He gave commandment to the closest three (as well as, more generally, to all) to **watch,** i.e., to lend strength by their alert presence and sympathy. **39. If it be possible,** i.e., morally possible, consistent with the Father's will. **Let this cup pass from me.** The key to understanding Christ's agony lies in identifying **the cup.** Although any normal human being would shrink from the horrors of crucifixion, martyrs have often faced cruel death without such extreme distress (cf. Lk 22:44). Nor can we adopt the view that Christ feared premature death at the hands of Satan, for the cup came from the Father, not from Satan (Jn 18:11). Furthermore, Christ's life could only be given voluntarily (Jn 10:17,18). **Cup** is used figuratively in Scripture either of God's blessing (cf. Ps 23:5) or of his wrath (cf. Ps 75: 8). Hence, the most satisfying explanation of the cup refers it to the divine wrath which Christ would incur at the cross as he became man's sin-bearer. This experience during which God for a time was separated from his Son, gave rise to the awful cry of Mt 27:46. If one man's sin can cause him bitter grief when he feels the estrangement of God, how incomparable must have been the anguish of Jesus, who knew what it meant to assume the guilt of all men. **Not as I will, but as thou wilt.** From beginning to end, Christ's prayer was perfectly submissive to the Father. And the prayer was answered, not by removal of the cup, but by strength to drink (Lk 22:43), and ultimately by resurrection "out of death" (Heb 5:7). **40,41.** Finding the disciples sleeping from the draining effects of prolonged emotion and fatigue, Jesus singled out Peter for particular counsel (perhaps in view of his recent boasts), and urged him to continual alertness and prayer lest events surprise him into yielding to **temptation. The spirit is willing.** Man's spiritual nature illuminated by the Holy Spirit. **But the flesh is weak.** Some think that **flesh** here denotes a consti-

**42.** He went away again the second time, and prayed, saying, O my Father, if this cup may not pass away from me, except I drink it, thy will be done.

**43.** And he came and found them asleep again: for their eyes were heavy.

**44.** And he left them, and went away again, and prayed the third time, saying the same words.

**45.** Then cometh he to his disciples, and saith unto them, Sleep on now, and take *your* rest: behold, the hour is at hand, and the Son of man is betrayed into the hands of sinners.

**46.** Rise, let us be going: behold, he is at hand that doth betray me.

**47.** And while he yet spake, lo, Judas, one of the twelve, came, and with him a great multitude with swords and staves, from the chief priests and elders of the people.

**48.** Now he that betrayed him gave them a sign, saying, Whomsoever I shall kiss, that same is he; hold him fast.

**49.** And forthwith he came to Jesus, and said, Hail, Master; and kissed him.

**50.** And Jesus said unto him, Friend, wherefore art thou come? Then came they, and laid hands on Jesus, and took him.

**51.** And, behold, one of them which were with Jesus stretched out *his* hand, and drew his sword, and struck a servant of the high priest, and smote off his ear.

**52.** Then said Jesus unto him, Put up again thy sword into his place: for all they that take the sword shall perish with the sword.

**53.** Thinkest thou that I cannot now pray to my Father, and he shall presently give me more than twelve legions of angels?

tutional part of man's being which is not sinful if controlled by the spirit (and thus the proverb may be applied to Jesus also); others, that it denotes the sinful nature that all men possess (Jesus excepted). **42-45.** In substance, this prayer was uttered three times; and each time the submission of the Son was entire. Yet it is clear that Jesus knew what the outcome would be. **Sleep on now.** Probably not irony, but a simple statement that their opportunity to be useful in the crisis had passed. **46.** At this moment, however, Jesus noticed the approach of the enemy. **Let us be going.** Not in flight, but to meet them (Jn 18:4).

**47-56.** The arrest. **47. Great multitude.** A force of Roman soldiers, with their usual swords, under command of a chiliarch (Jn 18:12); Jewish temple police under orders from the **chief priests** and **elders**, armed with clubs (Jn 18:12); some of the chief priests and elders (Lk 22:52). **48. He . . . gave them a sign.** Most of the Roman soldiers would not have known Jesus. **49. Kissed him.** The compound form here *(katephilēsen)* suggests an intensive, warm embrace (in contrast to the simpler form mentioned in v. 48). **50. Friend.** Comrade, companion *(hetaire)*. The term recognizes their previous association, without the connotation of affection. **For what are you come?** Are these words of Jesus elliptical, to which we must add some verb, as "Do that for which you are come" (ASV)? Or a question, "Why are you come?" Or a sad exclamation, "For what a reason you are come!" Whatever the precise intent, Judas and the soldiers proceeded with their plan. **51. One of them.** Identified by John as Peter. **Drew his sword.** The disciples had two of these short swords (Lk 22:38). **Smote the servant.** John, well acquainted with the high-priestly family, records the servant's name as Malchus (Jn 18:10,15). **His ear.** Cf. Lk 22:51. Peter's rash act, while well-intentioned, seriously compromised our Lord's position, and necessitated a miraculous healing to undo the disastrous effects it might have had at the trial (cf. Jn 18:36). Yet so complete was the miracle that the issue of the mutilation was never raised by Christ's accusers. **52. They that take the sword shall perish with the sword.** Christ and his message were not to be defended nor advanced with carnal weapons. This general principle stated by Jesus is confirmed by human experience. "The sword is visited by the sword in war; the sword of retribution opposes the arbitrary sword of rebellious sedition; and the sword taken up unspiritually in a spiritual cause, is avenged by the certain, though perhaps

54. But how then shall the Scriptures be fulfilled, that thus it must be?

55. In that same hour said Jesus to the multitudes, Are ye come out as against a thief with swords and staves for to take me? I sat daily with you teaching in the temple, and ye laid no hold on me.

56. But all this was done, that the Scriptures of the prophets might be fulfilled. Then all the disciples forsook him, and fled.

57. And they that had laid hold on Jesus led *him* away to Caiaphas the high priest, where the scribes and the elders were assembled.

58. But Peter followed him afar off unto the high priest's palace, and went in, and sat with the servants, to see the end.

59. Now the chief priests, and elders, and all the council, sought false witness against Jesus, to put him to death;

60. But found none: yea, though many false witnesses came, *yet* found they none. At the last came two false witnesses,

61. And said, This *fellow* said, I am able to destroy the temple of God, and to build it in three days.

62. And the high priest arose, and said unto him, Answerest thou nothing? what *is it which* these witness against thee?

63. But Jesus held his peace. And the high priest answered and said unto him, I adjure thee by the living God, that thou tell us whether thou be the Christ, the Son of God.

long-delayed, sword of historical vengeance" (J. P. Lange, *Matthew*, p. 486). **53,54. Twelve legions of angels.** Each Roman legion at full strength contained 6,000 men. Christ refrained from invoking the incomparably superior forces at his command, that the Scriptures which foretold his suffering might be fulfilled. **55,56. As against a robber.** The presence of weapons suggests that they expected a violent defense, as of a bold robber (not the hasty flight of a "thief"). Yet all past experience with Jesus should have belied that notion. Can it be (as Plummer and others suggest) that this amazing reaction of Jesus in attributing these events to fulfilled prophecy marked the point of Judas' turning from devilish plotter to remorseful suicide?

E. Events at the Jewish Trials. 26:57– 27:2. Jesus was led first to Annas, the ex-high priest, who still retained much prestige (Jn 18:12-23). After the preliminary hearing, which allowed time for the Sanhedrin to gather for this highly irregular night session, Jesus was taken to the Sanhedrin. At dawn, a second Sanhedrin session formally condemned him (Mt 27:1).

**57-68.** First Sanhedrin trial. **57. Caiaphas the high priest.** Son-in-law of the deposed Annas. It appears probable that Caiaphas and Annas had residences in the same building, perhaps separated by a courtyard. By this time the **scribes, elders,** and **chief priests** had assembled in this extraordinary session. **58. Peter followed,** and gained entrance to the **courtyard** (not AV *palace*), with the aid of John (Jn 18:15,16). **59. Sought false witness.** These Jews knew they had no real case against Jesus; hence they had to use trumped up charges. **60,61.** Yet the charges were so vague and inconsistent that they could not find even two witnesses — the minimum specified by law (Deut 17:6) — who agreed with each other. Finally **two** were produced who misquoted and misapplied a statement of Jesus uttered three years previously (Jn 2:19). **I am able to destroy the temple of God.** The actual statement had attributed the destroying to the Jews; and the reference was to his body, not to the Herodian edifice (Jn 2:21). Perhaps some of Jesus' statements in the Olivet Discourse (24:2) had been crudely garbled by Judas and combined with this statement (Jn 2:19). **62. Answerest thou nothing?** Caiaphas hoped to force the captive into some unguarded statement. Yet the wild charges hurled at Jesus were best answered by this dignified silence (cf. Isa 53:7). **63. I adjure thee.** A formula which informed Jesus that his answer would be regarded

**64.** Jesus saith unto him, Thou hast said: nevertheless I say unto you, Hereafter shall ye see the Son of man sitting on the right hand of power, and coming in the clouds of heaven.

**65.** Then the high priest rent his clothes, saying, He hath spoken blasphemy; what further need have we of witnesses? behold, now ye have heard his blasphemy.

**66.** What think ye? They answered and said, He is guilty of death.

**67.** Then did they spit in his face, and buffeted him; and others smote *him* with the palms of their hands,

**68.** Saying, Prophesy unto us, thou Christ, Who is he that smote thee?

**69.** Now Peter sat without in the palace: and a damsel came unto him, saying, Thou also wast with Jesus of Galilee.

**70.** But he denied before *them* all, saying, I know not what thou sayest.

**71.** And when he was gone out into the porch, another *maid* saw him, and said unto them that were there, This *fellow* was also with Jesus of Nazareth.

**72.** And again he denied with an oath, I do not know the man.

as under oath. **The Christ, the Son of God.** Although some dispute the full import of Son of God, it seems clear that Caiaphas employed it in the unique sense of deity, since acknowledgment brought the charge of blasphemy. This was the real cause for Christ's condemnation (Jn 19:7), and had been the basis of earlier plots against him (Jn 5:18). Reports of other incidents that supported this claim must certainly have reached the high priest's ears (Jn 1:34,49; 9:35-37; 11:27; Mt 14:33; 8:29; *et al.*). **64. Thou hast said.** An unequivocal confession that he was the divine Messiah. (Jesus' statement under oath does not vitiate the teaching of 5:34, where he legislates for his followers. In his unique position as Son of God, the factors that make an oath objectionable for men are not relevant to him.) **The Son of man sitting on the right hand of power and coming in the clouds of heaven** (cf. Dan 7:13,14; Ps 110:1). A pronouncement that the positions of Jesus and his judges would eventually be reversed. **65,66. Rent his clothes.** An indication of righteous horror, doubtless performed sincerely (although mistakenly). Jewish tradition specified in some detail how such an act was to be done. **Blasphemy.** The charge of greatest religious outrage. Because Jesus openly acknowledged that of which he had long been accused (Jn 5:18), and applied Dan 7:13, 14 to himself, he was pronounced **guilty of death** (i.e., deserving to die), probably by acclamation at this night trial, rather than by formal ballot. **67,68.** The physical violence inflicted on Jesus by his captors (probably the subordinate officers, Lk 22:63) included spitting in his face, striking him with fists, striking him either with rods or with open hands (i.e., slapping), and blindfolding (Lk 22:64) in order to mock his prophetic office.

**69-75. Peter's denials.** The three denials occurred throughout the stages of the Jewish trials and are variously grouped by the Evangelists. The differences among the narratives argue strongly for independence of composition. Yet essential agreement can be found, and the details admit various ways of harmonization. (See tables in Alford, *NT for Eng. Readers,* p. 199; S. J. Andrews, *Life of Our Lord,* p. 518.) **69. The palace.** Rather, the courtyard. **One maid came.** Identified by John as the portress who had admitted Peter (Jn 18: 16,17). **71,72. Into the porch.** Probably the vestibule or passage leading to the street. **Another maid.** Mark's "the maid" would suggest the same one previously mentioned (though perhaps he means merely *the* one at the porch); Luke says

**73.** And after a while came unto *him* they that stood by, and said to Peter, Surely thou also art *one* of them; for thy speech bewrayeth thee.

**74.** Then began he to curse and to swear, *saying,* I know not the man. And immediately the cock crew.

**75.** And Peter remembered the word of Jesus, which said unto him, Before the cock crow, thou shalt deny me thrice. And he went out, and wept bitterly.

## CHAPTER 27

WHEN the morning was come, all the chief priests and elders of the people took counsel against Jesus to put him to death:

**2.** And when they had bound him, they led *him* away, and delivered him to Pontius Pilate the governor.

**3.** Then Judas, which had betrayed him, when he saw that he was condemned, repented himself, and brought again the thirty pieces of silver to the chief priests and elders,

**4.** Saying, I have sinned in that I have betrayed the innocent blood. And they said, What *is that* to us? see thou *to that.*

**5.** And he cast down the pieces of silver in the temple, and departed, and went and hanged himself.

**6.** And the chief priests took the silver pieces, and said, It is not lawful for to put them into the treasury, because it is the price of blood.

**7.** And they took counsel, and bought with them the potter's field, to bury strangers in.

**8.** Wherefore that field was called, The field of blood, unto this day.

the interrogator was a man. Thus it appears that the second denial was prompted by the scrutiny of several individuals. **With an oath.** Forgetful of the warning of Jesus against such swearing to establish one's truthfulness (5:34). **73. After a little while.** About an hour (Lk 22:59). **They that stood by.** Particularly, a kinsman of Malchus (Jn 18:26). **Your speech makes you evident** (AV, *bewrayeth thee*). Galilean accents and pronunciation. **74. Began to curse.** To call down a curse upon himself if he were lying. **And to swear.** To invoke heaven as a witness to his words (cf. 5:34-37). **A cock crew.** The second crowing that night (Mk 14:72). **75. Peter remembered** (cf. Mt 26:34). Though dependence upon the flesh had caused his memory of Christ's warnings to fail, the simple crowing of a rooster awakened Peter to the enormity of his sin as a flouting of Jesus' gracious attempts to forestall it. **Wept bitterly.** Contrast the remorseful but unrepentant Judas (27:5).

**27:1,2.** Second Sanhedrin trial. **When the morning was come.** Jewish law forbade night trials and specified that capital cases must have at least two trials, a day apart. This daybreak session was an effort to bring a semblance of legality to the whole sordid procedure. **Pontius Pilate.** Roman procurator of Judea, who was present in Jerusalem at the Passover festival. His official residence was Caesarea. Rome had reserved to herself the final decision in court cases involving capital punishment and the execution of death sentences.

F. Remorse of Judas. 27:3-10. **3. When he saw that he was condemned.** This would be evident from watching Jesus being taken to Pilate. **Repented himself** (*metamelētheis*). Not the usual NT word for repentance to salvation. Here it indicates remorse, without any apparent commitment of himself to God. His "change of mind" was chiefly toward the money, which he now loathed. Finding the **chief priests and elders** (perhaps still at Caiaphas' house, or en route to Pilate), he tried to return the **silver. 5.** Their refusal caused him (perhaps after an interval of continued reflection) to hurl it **into the sanctuary** (*naos*) of the Temple. **Hanged himself.** This detail and the ensuing ones do not contradict Acts 1:18,19. Several ways of harmonization are possible. **6. It is not lawful.** (Cf. Deut 23:18). This dishonorable money could not enter the temple **treasury** (*korbanas*), although these priests had felt no impropriety in paying it out (26:15). **7,8. The field of the potter.** Apparently some well-known plot of

9. Then was fulfilled that which was spoken by Jeremy the prophet, saying, And they took the thirty pieces of silver, the price of him that was valued, whom they of the children of Israel did value;

10. And gave them for the potter's field, as the Lord appointed me.

11. And Jesus stood before the governor: and the governor asked him, saying, Art thou the King of the Jews? And Jesus said unto him, Thou sayest.

12. And when he was accused of the chief priests and elders, he answered nothing.

13. Then said Pilate unto him, Hearest thou not how many things they witness against thee?

14. And he answered him to never a word; insomuch that the governor marveled greatly.

15. Now at *that* feast the governor was wont to release unto the people a prisoner, whom they would.

16. And they had then a notable prisoner, called Barabbas.

17. Therefore when they were gathered together, Pilate said unto them, Whom will ye that I release unto you? Barabbas, or Jesus which is called Christ?

ground. The use of this "blood money" gave its name to the field (cf. Acts 1:19 for another detail that made the name appropriate). **Until this day.** An indication that Matthew wrote quite some time after the event, although not after A.D. 70, when the Romans obliterated most such landmarks. **9,10. Jeremiah the prophet.** This reference by Matthew to a prophecy seemingly spoken by Zechariah (11:12,13) has evoked an array of explanations. Some hold that here **Jeremiah**, the name of the first book in the OT Prophets, is taken to stand for the whole section containing Zechariah (just as the name "Psalms" is applied to the whole section of the Writings because it is the first book; Lk 24:44). A passage in the Talmud (*Baba Bathra* 14 b) supports this order of Jeremiah as the first book, but it must be recognized that Isaiah is usually placed first. Another possibility is that Matthew amalgamated Zech 11:12,13 with Jer 18:2-12 and 19:1-15, and merely cited one of the sources.

G. Events at the Roman Trials. 27:11-31. Matthew selects certain aspects of the trial, but for their connections one must consult the parallel accounts. However, Matthew alone records the interesting details of 27:19,24.

**11. Before the governor.** Resumption of the narrative interrupted at 27:2. **Art thou the King of the Jews?** A question prompted by the formal charges given Pilate by the Jews (Lk 23:2; Jn 18:28-33). **Thou sayest.** To this answer, which surely indicated assent to the question, Jesus added an explanation of the nature of his kingdom (Jn 18:34-38). This interview occurred within the Praetorium, while the Jews remained outside. **12-14.** To the clamoring Jews, however, who **accused** him upon his reappearance before them, **he answered nothing.** Yet this silence was not taken by Pilate as admission of guilt, but as a most unusual composure, causing him to begin a series of attempts to release Jesus without antagonizing the Sanhedrin.

**15. The governor was wont to release unto the people one prisoner.** Origin of this custom, whether Roman or Jewish is unknown. **16. A notable prisoner called Barabbas.** One who was guilty of insurrection, robbery, and murder (Jn 18:40; Mk 15:7). Broadus suggests that since the two crucified with Jesus were robbers, they may have been Barabbas' followers, and thus Jesus literally took Barabbas' place (*Comm. on Matt.*, pp. 562,563). Exegesis that plays on the etymology of Barabbas ("son of a father"), or adopts the highly

18. For he knew that for envy they had delivered him.

19. When he was set down on the judgment seat, his wife sent unto him, saying, Have thou nothing to do with that just man: for I have suffered many things this day in a dream because of him.

20. But the chief priests and elders persuaded the multitude that they should ask Barabbas, and destroy Jesus.

21. The governor answered and said unto them, Whether of the twain will ye that I release unto you? They said, Barabbas.

22. Pilate saith unto them, What shall I do then with Jesus which is called Christ? They all say unto him, Let him be crucified.

23. And the governor said, Why, what evil hath he done? But they cried out the more, saying, Let him be crucified.

24. When Pilate saw that he could prevail nothing, but that rather a tumult was made, he took water, and washed his hands before the multitude, saying, I am innocent of the blood of this just person: see ye to it.

25. Then answered all the people, and said, His blood be on us, and on our children.

26. Then released he Barabbas unto them: and when he had scourged Jesus, he delivered him to be crucified.

inferior reading "Jesus Barabbas" for allegorizing or homiletical purposes is unwarranted. **18. He knew that for envy.** The ridiculous character of the accusations was evident to Pilate, and the passionate actions of the accusers showed him that personal grievance was involved. It was obvious that such a spiritually minded teacher (Jn 18:36,37) would be opposed by these unscrupulous and materialistic religionists.

**19. While he was sitting on the judgment seat.** While Pilate awaited the Jews' answer regarding Barabbas, his wife sent him a message that interrupted the proceedings. The portent of the **dream** mentioned in the message unsettled Pilate and caused him to delay judgment. We do not know whether the dream was sent directly from God, or is to be explained psychologically as the working of a mind troubled over the plot against Jesus. (Pilate must have known of the plot, for he allowed a chiliarch and Roman soldiers to participate, and his wife may have learned of it from him; Jn 18:12.) The apocryphal *Gospel of Nicodemus* quotes the Jews as responding: "Did we not say unto thee, he is a conjuror? Behold, he hath caused thy wife to dream" (2:3). **20,21.** During this interval the **chief priests** and **elders** influenced the multitude to demand the release of **Barabbas** instead of Jesus. The degree of moral and spiritual depravity evidenced by such a choice is almost incredible. **22,23. Let him be crucified.** That is, executed in the Roman fashion, ostensibly as the result of the charges laid against him, and thus as the substitute for Barabbas. **24. He took water.** A Jewish symbolic custom (Deut 21:6-9), the meaning of which is natural and obvious. Yet Pilate's use was mockery, for he had to bear the responsibility for ordering the execution. (Proper use of the symbol was to absolve innocent men from implication in a wrongful death.) **The blood of this righteous man** (AV, *just person*). Was Pilate reflecting the influence of his wife's message as he used her description of Jesus? **25. His blood be upon us and on our children.** The subsequent history of Israel reveals the awful consequences of that cry. These words, so quickly uttered, have not rested easily upon the heads of the original leaders (cf. Acts 5:28), nor upon those of their descendants. **26. When he had scourged Jesus.** This cruel torture was applied upon the bare body by means of a leather whip that had pieces of bone or metal imbedded in its thongs. The scourging preceded the delivery to the soldiers for crucifixion. John indicates that it was not performed as the

27. Then the soldiers of the governor took Jesus into the common hall, and gathered unto him the whole band *of soldiers.*

28. And they stripped him, and put on him a scarlet robe.

29. And when they had platted a crown of thorns, they put *it* upon his head, and a reed in his right hand: and they bowed the knee before him, and mocked him, saying, Hail, King of the Jews!

30. And they spit upon him, and took the reed, and smote him on the head.

31. And after that they had mocked him, they took the robe off from him, and put his own raiment on him, and led him away to crucify *him.*

32. And as they came out, they found a man of Cyrene, Simon by name: him they compelled to bear his cross.

33. And when they were come unto a place called Golgotha, that is to say, a place of a skull,

34. They gave him vinegar to drink mingled with gall: and when he had tasted *thereof,* he would not drink.

35. And they crucified him, and parted his garments, casting lots: that it might be fulfilled which was spoken by the prophet, They parted my garments among them, and upon my vesture did they cast lots.

36. And sitting down they watched him there;

37. And set up over his head his accusation written, THIS IS JESUS THE KING OF THE JEWS.

first stage of the execution, but was another attempt by Pilate to satiate the blood-thirsty crowd and cause them to abandon their demands for crucifixion (Jn 19:1-6). **Delivered him.** Officially ordered the soldiers to execute him. **27. Into the Praetorium.** This seems to locate the trial at the Castle of Antonia, since it explains more readily the presence of a whole cohort (600 men, one-tenth of a legion), which is known to have been stationed there. Others identify the Praetorium as Herod's palace. **28-31.** After receiving the order to prepare Jesus for execution, the callous soldiers enlivened their work by the crudest mockery. Stripping Jesus of his own garments, they arrayed him in a **scarlet robe,** perhaps a soldier's cloak, faded to resemble royal purple (Mk 15:17). Substituting **thorns** for a crown, a **reed** for a scepter, and spitting for the kiss of homage, they showed their cruel contempt for the Son of God.

H. The Crucifixion. 27:32-56. **32. Simon. Of Cyrene.** His sons were known to the readers of Mark's Gospel (Mk 15:21). **Him they compelled.** Commandeered for this service (see comment on 5:41). **33. Golgotha.** Aramaic word meaning "skull," equivalent to the Latin *calvaria.* Whether the name was derived from a skull-shaped mound, or from its reputation as an execution place, is unknown. Equally uncertain is its location. The traditional Church of the Holy Sepulchre, while within the present walls of Jerusalem, was outside the old north wall of Jesus' day and could well have been the place. Others argue the claims of Gordon's Calvary, farther to the north. **34. Wine mingled with gall** (cf. Ps 69:21). The intent of this drugged potion was to deaden pain and make prisoners easier to handle, but Jesus, after a taste, refused to drink. **35. They crucified him.** For the technical details of crucifixions, consult Bible dictionaries. It must be noted that the Evangelists sketch the scene in stark simplicity, all the more effective for its restraint. **Parted his garments, casting lots.** John 19:23,24 explains that the soldiers divided the items four ways and gambled for the seamless coat. The final clause beginning, **that it might be fulfilled,** is textually doubtful, probably being an interpolation from Jn 19:24. **36. They watched him.** Part of the soldiers' duty was to prevent premature removal. **37. Over his head his accusation.** During the procession to Golgotha, the placard prepared by Pilate (Jn 19:19) was probably paraded at the front or hung around Jesus' neck, according to the usual cus-

**38.** Then were there two thieves crucified with him; one on the right hand, and another on the left.

**39.** And they that passed be reviled him, wagging their heads,

**40.** And saying, Thou that destroyest the temple, and buildest *it* in three days, save thyself. If thou be the Son of God, come down from the cross.

**41.** Likewise also the chief priests mocking *him*, with the scribes and elders, said,

**42.** He saved others; himself he cannot save. If he be the King of Israel, let him now come down from the cross, and we will believe him.

**43.** He trusted in God; let him deliver him now, if he will have him: for he said, I am the Son of God.

**44.** The thieves also, which were crucified with him, cast the same in his teeth.

**45.** Now from the sixth hour there was darkness over all the land unto the ninth hour.

**46.** And about the ninth hour Jesus cried with a loud voice, saying, Eli, Eli, lama sabachthani? that is to say, My God, my God, why hast thou forsaken me?

tom. THIS IS JESUS THE KING OF THE JEWS. (Cf. Mk 15:26; Lk 23:38; Jn 19:19.) The varying accounts are in no way contradictory. John's record is fullest; the others pick out the essential elements. The fact that the title appeared in the three languages may account for some variations in the records (Jn 19:20). **38. Two robbers.** The same description as is applied to Barabbas (Jn 18:40), an indication that Jesus literally took Barabbas' place. **39. Wagging their heads** (Ps 22:17). A sneering, mocking gesture. **40.** The taunts hurled at Jesus for claiming that he could destroy the temple and that he was the Son of God were based on events at the Sanhedrin trial (26:61,63,64). **41-43.** The chief priests, scribes, and elders joined in the mocking, not by addressing Jesus directly, but by speaking derisively about him to the crowd. **He saved others.** A statement probably not meant as an acknowledgment of his miracles, but intended to cast strong suspicion upon such claims because of his present inability to **save himself.** Their words were far truer than they knew; for to save others in the spiritual sense for which he had come, he had to voluntarily lay down his own life. Smarting under Pilate's insult to their nationalism, the leaders challenged Jesus' title, **King of Israel,** by demanding a sign and promise. **We will believe him.** Yet previous attitudes and reactions of these men show the falsity of their promise (Jn 12:9,10). **44. The robbers also.** Later one of them changed his attitude toward Jesus (Lk 23:39-43).

**45.** Jesus was placed upon the cross at 9 A.M. ("third hour," Mk 15:25). After three hours had passed, a supernatural **darkness** enveloped **all the land** from the **sixth** to the **ninth** hour (noon to 3 P.M.). Since Passover occurred at full moon, this darkness could not have been a solar eclipse. It was clearly supernatural in its timing, although God may possibly have employed some providential means to bring it about. Whether **all the land** is restricted to a somewhat local area, or is to be understood as "all the earth" (global) is impossible to determine. **46. My God, my God, why hast thou forsaken me?** (Ps 22:1) The only utterance from the cross recorded by Matthew and Mark. The full import of this cry cannot be fathomed. But certainly its basis lay not in the physical suffering primarily, but in the fact that for a time Jesus was made *sin* for us (II Cor 5:21); and in paying the penalty as the sinner's substitute, he was accursed of God (Gal 3:13). God as Father did not forsake him (Lk 23:46); but God as Judge had to be separated from him if he was

**47.** Some of them that stood there, when they heard *that*, said, This *man* calleth for Elias.

**48.** And straightway one of them ran, and took a sponge, and filled *it* with vinegar, and put *it* on a reed, and gave him to drink.

**49.** The rest said, Let be, let us see whether Elias will come to save him.

**50.** Jesus, when he had cried again with a loud voice, yielded up the ghost.

**51.** And, behold, the veil of the temple was rent in twain from the top to the bottom; and the earth did quake, and the rocks rent;

**52.** And the graves were opened; and many bodies of the saints which slept arose,

**53.** And came out of the graves after his resurrection, and went into the holy city, and appeared unto many.

**54.** Now when the centurion, and they that were with him, watching Jesus, saw the earthquake, and those things that were done, they feared greatly, saying, Truly this was the Son of God.

**55.** And many women were there beholding afar off, which followed Jesus from Galilee, ministering unto him:

**56.** Among which was Mary Magdalene, and Mary the mother of James and Joses, and the mother of Zebedee's children.

to experience spiritual death in the place of sinful men. **47-49.** This outcry prompted the suggestion that Jesus was calling for Elijah, doubtless because of the similarity of sound between **Eli** (*my God*) and **Elias** (Elijah). Though some suggest that the darkness had now caused the more superstitious actually to fear that the predicted Messianic figure might come, succeeding attitudes make this doubtful. Rather, it was a further mocking jibe at his Messianic claims. **Let be.** This sentiment was uttered by the crowds, who wanted the soldier to desist from ministering to Jesus (Mt); and also by the soldier himself, after giving the drink, as telling the crowds to cease objecting to his act (Mk). **50.** Jesus, having his throat refreshed by the vinegar (not the drugged potion of 27:34), **cried again with a loud voice.** All the Synoptics indicate that the death of Christ was not the exhaustion of crucifixion, but a voluntary surrender of his life.

**51. Veil of the temple.** The curtain dividing the Holy Place from the Holy of Holies (Ex 26:31). This event, symbolic of the permanent opening of God's presence to man by the atoning death of Christ (cf. Heb 10:19-23), could have been reported by the priests who were later converted (Acts 6:7). **52,53.** At Christ's death many graves of OT saints were **opened**, and their bodies were resurrected **after his resurrection** (cf. Acts 26:23; I Cor 15:20) This amazing circumstance mentioned only by Matthew raises many questions but cannot properly be denied. The six previous resurrections in Scripture (I Kgs 17; II Kgs 4; 13; Mt 9; Lk 7; Jn 11) were all restorations to earthly existence. Such is not necessarily true of those in Matthew 27. The phenomenon is clearly symbolic of Christ's victory over death as it affects believers. Many see here a visible demonstration that Christ's death and resurrection effected the release from Sheol-Hades of the righteous dead (Eph 4:8,9). What happened to these resurrected saints subsequently is not stated. **54. Truly this man was the Son of God.** Though it is presently popular to explain the centurion's statement in terms of pagan concepts (cf. RSV), it must be noted that his comment was based upon his observation of some remarkable phenomena. And it must be regarded as possible that the man, having been in Jewish surroundings for a time, may now have come to faith. After all, pagans can become Christians. **55,56. Mary Magdalene.** First mention in Matthew. Traditions which give her a dishonorable past are without Scriptural basis. **Mary the mother of James and Joses.** Also

57. When the even was come, there came a rich man of Arimathea, named Joseph, who also himself was Jesus' disciple:

58. He went to Pilate, and begged the body of Jesus. Then Pilate commanded the body to be delivered.

59. And when Joseph had taken the body, he wrapped it in a clean linen cloth,

60. And laid it in his own new tomb, which he had hewn out in the rock: and he rolled a great stone to the door of the sepulchre, and departed.

61. And there was Mary Magdalene, and the other Mary, sitting over against the sepulchre.

62. Now the next day, that followed the day of the preparation, the chief priests and Pharisees came together unto Pilate,

63. Saying, Sir, we remember that that deceiver said, while he was yet alive, After three days I will rise again.

64. Command therefore that the sepulchre be made sure until the third day, lest his disciples come by night, and steal him away, and say unto the people, He is risen from the dead: so the last error shall be worse than the first.

65. Pilate said unto them, Ye have a watch: go your way, make it as sure as ye can.

66. So they went, and made the sepulchre sure, sealing the stone, and setting a watch.

called the wife of Cleopas (Jn 19:25). **Mother of Zebedee's children.** Same as Salome (Mk 15:40), and apparently a sister of the Virgin Mary (Jn 19:25).

I. Burial. 27:57-66. **57. When even was come.** Time from 3 P.M. to 6 P.M. (Ex 12:6, ASV marg.). **A rich man.** Cf. Isa 53:9. **Joseph of Arimathaea** was a Sanhedrist (Lk 23:50,51), whose wealth enabled him to own a tomb close to Jerusalem, though he lived elsewhere. **58. Asked for the body.** An act of no little courage, since, not being a relative, he would doubtless need to explain his reasons. **59,60.** Receiving permission, Joseph himself **took the body** from the cross and, assisted by Nicodemus, wrapped it in the usual linen cloth (Jn 19:39,40). **61.** Observing the scene were the two Marys mentioned in 27:56.

**62. The day after the preparation** (ASV). Usually explained as Saturday (cf. Mk 15:42), viewing the entombment as from Friday night till Sunday morning. However, this **preparation** day was the day before the Passover Feast day (Jn 19: 14,31), which feast may have occurred that year on Wednesday night. Perhaps this accounts for Matthew's not using the term "Sabbath" here, lest it be confused with Saturday. According to this view, the entombment lasted a full seventy-two hours, from sundown Wednesday to sundown Saturday. Such a view gives more reasonable treatment to Mt 12:40. It also explains **after three days** and **on the third day** in a way that does least violence to either. **63,64.** How the Sanhedrists learned of Christ's private prediction is not explained (from Judas, perhaps?). The disciples, by failing to grasp its meaning, had largely forgotten the prediction; but these enemies were taking no chances. They feared that the spreading of a report of a resurrection (**the last error**) would be more disastrous to them than the following Jesus had gained, for a time, as Messiah (**the first delusion**). **65,66.** Obtaining Pilate's order, **Take a guard** (ASV marg.), the Sanhedrists took the additional precaution of **sealing the stone,** probably by connecting it to the tomb by a cord and wax or clay, so that tampering could be detected.

**V. The Resurrection of Jesus Christ. 28: 1-20.**

Matthew's account of the Resurrection includes fewer details than the accounts of Luke and John. Yet to him alone we are indebted for the report of the soldiers (vv. 11-15) and for the full baptismal formula

### CHAPTER 28

IN the end of the sabbath, as it began to dawn toward the first *day* of the week, came Mary Magdalene and the other Mary to see the sepulchre.

2. And, behold, there was a great earthquake: for the angel of the Lord descended from heaven, and came and rolled back the stone from the door, and sat upon it.

3. His countenance was like lightning, and his raiment white as snow:

4. And for fear of him the keepers did shake, and became as dead *men*.

5. And the angel answered and said unto the women, Fear not ye: for I know that ye seek Jesus, which was crucified.

6. He is not here: for he is risen, as he said. Come, see the place where the Lord lay.

7. And go quickly, and tell his disciples that he is risen from the dead; and, behold, he goeth before you into Galilee; there shall ye see him: lo, I have told you.

8. And they departed quickly from the sepulchre with fear and great joy; and did run to bring his disciples word.

9. And as they went to tell his disciples, behold, Jesus met them, saying, All hail. And they came and held him by the feet, and worshipped him.

10. Then said Jesus unto them, Be not afraid: go tell my brethren that they go into Galilee, and there shall they see me.

11. Now when they were going, behold, some of the watch came into the city, and showed unto the chief priests all the things that were done.

12. And when they were assembled with the elders, and had taken counsel, they gave large money unto the soldiers,

13. Saying, Say ye, His disciples came by night, and stole him *away* while we slept.

14. And if this come to the governor's ears, we will persuade him, and secure you.

15. So they took the money, and did as they were taught: and this saying is commonly reported among the Jews until this day.

(v. 19). The substantial agreement of the four narratives, coupled with a wide variety of details and viewpoints, demonstrates their truthfulness and yet their independence of one another.

A. Discovery of the Empty Tomb. 28:1-8. 1. In the end of the sabbath. The use of *opse* as an improper preposition for "after" is now clearly recognized (Arndt, p. 606), so that the translation here should be after the sabbath, in conformity with Mk 16:1,2; Lk 24:1; Jn 20:1. Mary Magdalene, the ·other Mary (27:56,61), and certain other women came at the break of dawn on Sunday to do the anointing of Jesus' body. 2-4. As they approached, an earthquake occurred, and an angel rolled back the great stone from the entrance. This was not the moment of resurrection, but was rather intended to reveal the empty tomb to the witnesses. The resurrected Christ was not confined by natural barriers (cf. Jn 20:19,26), and must have arisen about sundown on Saturday night (see on 27:62). 5-8. It seems that Mary Magdalene immediately left to notify Peter and John (Jn 20:1,2), and did not hear the announcement, He is risen, which the angel made to the other women. He goeth before you into Galilee. The directions for the great public appearance in Galilee as previously predicted (26:32) do not exclude earlier personal appearances to individuals or small groups in Jerusalem.

B. Appearance of Jesus. 28:9,10. And behold, Jesus met them. The first clause in verse 9 (AV) must be omitted on textual grounds. This appearance of Jesus came after the women had reported the angel's message to the disciples (Lk 24:9-11). Meanwhile, Mary Magdalene, having informed Peter and John of the empty tomb, followed them to the site, and, remaining there, became the first to see the risen Christ (Mk 16:9; Jn 20:1-18). Now on this second appearance, Jesus gave the women essentially the same directions that the angel had delivered (v. 7).

C. Report of the Soldiers. 28:11-15. Recorded here only. These soldiers had been turned over to the Sanhedrin by Pilate, and so reported to them (27:65,66). Their report resulted in the calling of a Sanhedrin session, at which a large bribe was voted to insure the soldiers' continued cooperation in hiding the truth. The self-contradictory nature of the account they were to circulate (as if *sleeping* soldiers would know what had happened, or that *all* would have been sleeping at once, or that *Roman* soldiers would incriminate

16. Then the eleven disciples went away into Galilee, into a mountain where Jesus had appointed them.

17. And when they saw him, they worshipped him: but some doubted.

18. And Jesus came and spake unto them, saying, All power is given unto me in heaven and in earth.

19. Go ye therefore, and teach all nations, baptizing them in the name of the Father, and of the Son, and of the Holy Ghost:

20. Teaching them to observe all things whatsoever I have commanded you: and, lo, I am with you alway, *even* unto the end of the world. Amen.

themselves in this way) makes its acceptance most incredible. Yet the story was widely disseminated among Jews (no article). Matthew, writing particularly for the Jewish viewpoint, gives the sordid details that explain the tale. The promise of the Sanhedrin to **persuade** Pilate if he should take action may mean that a bribe would be offered, or that they would assure the governor that the Sanhedrin was satisfied with the soldiers' performance.

D. The Great Commission. 28:16-20. **16.** This appearance to the **eleven** in **Galilee,** fulfilling previous instruction (26: 32; 28:7,10), is doubtless the appearance to "above five hundred" mentioned by Paul (I Cor 15:6). Galilee was the home of most of Christ's followers, and the most likely place for such a crowd to be unmolested by the authorities. **17. They worshipped him, but some doubted.** True acknowledgment of his deity by most (cf. the prior case of Thomas, Jn 20:28); hesitation by a few. Difficulty in understanding these doubters as being among the Eleven after the appearances to them in Jerusalem has led many to identify them as among Paul's five hundred. Yet Matthew, while certainly not excluding the presence of others, can hardly have had such in view here. It is better to accept this as a surprising but honest commentary on the facts, and as further indication that the disciples were not a credulous group, but believed only on the basis of "many infallible proofs" (Acts 1:3). **18. All authority has been given unto me.** The ensuing commission is backed by the authority of him who is God's mediatorial King, with power extending to every realm. **19. Make disciples of all the nations** (ASV). The task of evangelizing, enlisting men under the lordship of Christ. **Baptizing them.** The symbolic rite by which one publicly acknowledges his personal commitment to the Christian message. **The name of the Father and of the Son and of the Holy Ghost.** The full formula to be employed, emphasizing the distinctively Christian character of this baptism as compared to earlier types of Jewish ablutions. **20. Teaching them.** Inculcating Christ's precepts as outlining the proper manner of life for his followers. **Lo, I am with you all the days.** A blessed promise that Christ's presence as well as his authority shall empower his servants to perform this commission.

# BIBLIOGRAPHY

ALFORD, HENRY. *New Testament for English Readers*. Chicago: Moody Press, reprinted 1956.

ANDREWS, SAMUEL J. *The Life of Our Lord*. Grand Rapids: Zondervan Publishing House, reprinted 1954.

ATKINSON, BASIL F. C. "The Gospel According to Matthew," *New Bible Commentary*. Edited by F. Davidson, A. M. Stibbs, and E. F. Kevan. Grand Rapids: Wm. B. Eerdmans Publishing Co., 1953.

BROADUS, JOHN A. *Commentary on the Gospel of Matthew*. Philadelphia: American Baptist Publishing Society, 1886.

BROWN, DAVID. "Matthew," *Commentary Critical, Experimental, and Practical of the Old and New Testaments*. Edited by Robert Jamieson, A. R. Fausset, and David Brown. Vol. V. Grand Rapids: Wm. B. Eerdmans Publishing Co., reprinted 1948.

BRUCE, A. B. "The Synoptic Gospels," *The Expositor's Greek Testament*. Edited by W. Robertson Nicoll. Vol. I. Grand Rapids: Wm. B. Eerdmans Publishing Co., n.d.

EDERSHEIM, ALFRED. *Life and Times of Jesus the Messiah*. Grand Rapids: Wm. B. Eerdmans Publishing Co., reprinted 1945.

GAEBELEIN, A. C. *Gospel of Matthew*. New York: Our Hope, 1910.

LANGE, J. P. *The Gospel According to Matthew*. Translated by Philip Schaff. *A Commentary on the Holy Scriptures*. Grand Rapids: Zondervan Publishing House, reprint edition, n.d.

LENSKI, R. C. H. *The Interpretation of St. Matthew's Gospel*. Columbus: Wartburg Press, 1943.

McCLAIN, A. J. *Greatness of the Kingdom*. Grand Rapids: Zondervan Publishing House, 1959.

PLUMMER, ALFRED. *Exegetical Commentary on the Gospel According to St. Matthew*. New York: Charles Scribner's Sons, 1910.

ROBERTSON, A. T. *A Harmony of the Gospels for Students of the Life of Christ*. New York: Harper & Brothers, 1922.

# THE GOSPEL
# ACCORDING TO MARK

## INTRODUCTION

*Author.* Although the Gospel of Mark in itself is anonymous, sufficient evidence is available to provide positive identification of the author. All available testimony from the early Church Fathers names Mark, the attendant of Peter, as the writer of the book. The tradition concerning the Marcan authorship goes back to Papias at the end of the first century or early in the second, and it is confirmed in the writings of such men as Irenaeus, Clement of Alexandria, Origen, and Jerome, as well as in the second century Anti-Marcionite Prologue. That Mark, the companion of Peter, was the John Mark of Acts 12:12,25; 15:37-39 is not specifically stated, but this has been the consensus of opinion among all but the more radical critics. Such identification is made by Vincent Taylor *(The Gospel According to Mark*, p. 26), Harvie Branscomb *(The Gospel of Mark*, p. xxxviii) and H. B. Swete *(The Gospel According to Mark*, p. xix).

The evidence from the Gospel itself is in agreement with the historical testimony of the early church. It is obvious that the author was familiar with Palestine, and with Jerusalem in particular. He makes geographical references which are correct in fine detail (11:1), thus revealing his personal knowledge of the area. He knows Aramaic, the language of Palestine, as is indicated by his use of Aramaic words (5:41; 7:34) as well as by the evidence of Aramaic influence on his Greek. That he was conversant with Jewish institutions and customs is to be seen in the familiarity with which he refers to such items (1:21; 2:14,16; 7:2-4). These characteristics all point toward a Palestinian Jew as author; and according to Acts 12:12, John Mark fits this description, since his home was in Jerusalem. Furthermore, there are indications in the New Testament that Mark and the Apostle Peter sustained a close relationship to one another. It has been noted that there is a striking similarity between the general outline of Mark's Gospel and the sermon of Peter in Caesarea (Acts 10:34-43), which may point toward Peter as the main source for Mark's material. To this may be added Peter's reference to Mark as his son (I Pet 5:13).

Upon the basis, therefore, of both external and internal evidence, it is possible to affirm confidently that John Mark, the son of Mary, and the attendant of Paul and Peter, was the author of the second Gospel. We first hear of the man Mark in Acts 12:12 in connection with a prayer meeting in his mother's house. As a young man he traveled with Paul and Barnabas as far as Perga on their first missionary tour (Acts 13:5,13). Because he did not continue with the party, but returned home, Paul refused to take him on his second journey (Acts 15:36-41). Instead, Mark accompanied his cousin Barnabas (Col 4:10, ASV) to the island of Cyprus. Much later, he appeared with Paul during his first Roman imprisonment (Col 4:10; Phm 23,24). He was with Peter in Babylon (I Pet 5:13); and Paul, during his second imprisonment, requested Timothy to bring Mark to Rome because he had shown himself to be useful in the work (II Tim 4:11).

*Date and Place of Writing.* There is no explicit statement in the Gospel itself, nor in the rest of the New Testament, from which we may ascertain a specific date for the origin of the book. In recent years the majority of scholars have placed it somewhere between A.D. 50 and 80, with the preponderance of opinion favoring A.D. 65—70. Our best basis for dating is the information from the Church Fathers. Irenaeus says, "Matthew also issued a written Gospel among the Hebrews in their own dialect, while Peter and Paul were preaching at Rome and laying the foundations of the church. After their departure, Mark, the disciple and interpreter of Peter, did also hand down to us in writing what had been preached by Peter" (Irenaeus *Against Heresies* III. i. 1). The word *exodon*, here translated "departure," is used in Lk 9:31, where it is rendered as "decease" (AV), referring to our Lord's death. The Apostle Peter, also, uses the word in alluding to his own approaching death (see II Pet 1:15). That Irenaeus was placing the writing of Mark after the death of Peter and Paul is corroborated by the Anti-Marcionite Prologue, which plainly asserts, "After the death of Peter himself, he wrote down this same gospel. . . ." Such evidence would seem to require a date after A.D. 67, the probable year of Paul's martyrdom. On the other hand, the fact that the prediction of Jerusalem's destruction (Mk 13) is not set forth as fulfilled may point to a date prior to A.D. 70. The most plausible dating, therefore, would seem to be 67–70.

Although Chrysostom placed the origin of the Gospel in Egypt, there is every reason to look for its birthplace in the city of Rome. That such is the case is explicitly stated by the Anti-Marcionite Prologue and Clement of Alexandria, as well as being implied by Irenaeus.

*Readers.* It has been an almost unanimous opinion that the second Gospel was directed to the Roman mind. The Marcan habit of explaining Jewish terms and customs points toward Gentile readers (5:41; 7:2-4,11,34). The statements of Clement of Alexandria to the effect that those in Rome who heard Peter preach insisted that Mark provide them with a written account are sufficient basis for believing that the Gospel was penned for Roman Christians. That the readers were Romans may be borne out by the presence of certain Latinisms occurring in the book. That they were Christians is further confirmed by the introduction to the Gospel, in which prior understanding on the part of the readers is assumed. John the Baptist is introduced without any attempt at identification; his imprisonment is referred to as though the readers were already familiar with the fact; the terms *baptize* (1:4) and *Holy Ghost* (1:8) are used without any explanation.

*Characteristics.* Several striking peculiarities of Mark's account make it unique among the Gospels. The manner of writing has been described as graphic, forceful, and dramatic. A vivid realism characterizes both Mark's style and his unvarnished reporting of the facts. Events are described without alteration or extensive interpretation, and their presentation is marked by an "on-the-spot" quality found in the reports of eyewitnesses. A marked vigor and a note òf urgency may be sensed in almost any portion of the writing. The characteristic word of this Gospel of action is *euthys*, which occurs some forty-one times and is translated *straightway, immediately, forthwith, anon.* Greek tenses are used effectively to augment the dramatic and graphic effect of a life story that is already dramatic by virtue of its intrinsic nature. In numerous places words of unusual forcefulness appear, such as "driveth" (1:12), compared with

"led," which appears in the other Synoptic Gospels (Mt 4:1; Lk 4:1).

In harmony with these peculiarities is the brevity of the book itself and the concise reports of individual events (cf. Mk 1:12,13; Mt 4:1-11).

*Content.* The Gospel begins with a brief record of events that opened the public ministry of our Lord, namely, his baptism and temptation. Mark has thus omitted, by design of course, any account of the birth and first thirty years of Christ's life. He also makes no reference to the early ministry in Judea, which is recorded in Jn 2:13—4:3. Without any explanation of the intervening events, the author moves from the temptation to the Galilean ministry. The first period of the work in northern Palestine was marked by tremendous success as crowds flocked to hear the new teacher, with the result that he found it necessary to restrict the gatherings to the country areas (Mk 1:45). People came from Judea and Idumea to the south, from Perea to the east, and from Tyre and Sidon to the north (3:7,8). Almost simultaneously, our Gospel records the beginnings of hostility to Christ on the part of the Jewish leaders. This opposition intensified until it became one of the chief characteristics of the second period of the work in Galilee. As a result of the enmity of these leaders and the superstitious suspicions of Herod Antipas, Jesus began a series of systematic retirements from the region of Galilee, always remaining in the general area and often returning to Capernaum for a brief stay. During these days his main occupation was the training of the disciples. The hour toward which he had been purposefully moving was fast approaching, and it was at this point that he began to prepare his own, by repeated explanations, for the consummation of his earthly work in his death and resurrection.

Following the withdrawals for disciple training, Mark traces Christ's last trip to Jerusalem by way of Perea. In so doing our author has again omitted a sizable block of material. He has passed by the entire later Judean ministry and the greater part of the work beyond Jordan in Perea. In keeping with the characteristic brevity of the Evangelist, he moves immediately into an account of the Passion Week. To this short period Mark devotes almost six of his sixteen chapters, a proportion which is fully justified when one realizes that this is the purposed consummation toward which the life of our Lord had been moving.

# OUTLINE

I. The title. 1:1.
II. The preparation for Christ's ministry. 1:2-13.
  A. His forerunner. 1:2-8.
  B. His baptism. 1:9-11.
  C. His temptation. 1:12,13.
III. Christ's ministry in Galilee. 1:14—6:30.
  A. Call of the first four disciples. 1:14-20.
  B. First Galilean preaching tour. 1:21-45.
  C. Development of official opposition. 2:1—3:12.
  D. Appointment of the Twelve. 3:13-19.
  E. Concern of Christ's friends, and accusations of his enemies. 3:20-35.
  F. Parables by the seaside. 4:1-34.
  G. Trip to Gadara. 4:35—5:20.
  H. The woman with a hemorrhage, and the daughter of Jairus. 5:21-43.
  I. Another Galilean preaching tour. 6:1-30.
IV. Christ's withdrawals from Galilee. 6:31—9:50.
  A. Withdrawal to the eastern shore of the lake. 6:31-56.
  B. Discussion of the unwarranted exaltation of tradition. 7:1-23.
  C. Withdrawal to the region of Tyre and Sidon. 7:24-30.
  D. Withdrawal to Decapolis. 7:31—8:9.
  E. Withdrawal to Caesarea Philippi. 8:10—9:50.
V. Christ's ministry in Perea. 10:1-52.
  A. Discussions of divorce, children, and wealth. 10:1-31.
  B. Conversation on the way to Jerusalem. 10:32-45.
  C. The healing of blind Bartimaeus. 10:46-52.
VI. Christ's concluding ministry in Jerusalem. 11:1—13:37.
  A. The entrance into Jerusalem and the Temple. 11:1-26.
  B. Final controversies with the Jewish leaders. 11:27—12:44.
  C. The Olivet apocalypse. 13:1-37.
VII. Christ's passion and resurrection. 14:1—16:20.
  A. Treachery and devotion. 14:1-11.
  B. The Lord's passion. 14:12—15:47.
  C. The Lord's resurrection. 16:1-20.

## ST. MARK

### CHAPTER 1

THE beginning of the gospel of Jesus Christ, the Son of God;

2. As it is written in the prophets, Behold, I send my messenger before thy face, which shall prepare thy way before thee.

3. The voice of one crying in the wilderness, Prepare ye the way of the Lord, make his paths straight.

4. John did baptize in the wilderness, and preach the baptism of repentance for the remission of sins.

## COMMENTARY

### I. The Title. 1:1.

These words stand as a title indicating the content of the book as a whole. The gospel here is not the book, but the message, the good news of salvation through Jesus Christ. The facts of the life and death of Christ make up the beginning of the gospel, which implies that the apostolic preaching was the continuation. The Son of God. To Mark, no less than to John, the deity of Christ is of prime importance, and thus he includes it in the title of his Gospel.

### II. The Preparation for Christ's Ministry. 1:2-13.

A. His Forerunner. 1:2-8. Passing by the birth and early years of Christ's life, Mark turns at once to the opening events of the Lord's public ministry. As predicted in the OT, Jesus was preceded by a herald sent to prepare men for his appearance. John the Baptist came as the last representative of the old order with the express purpose of introducing the key personality of the new.

2. As it is written. This clause is to be connected with verse 4. John's baptism and preaching were in accordance with the Scriptures. This was a formula used to designate "an unalterable contract" (Adolf Deissmann, *Paul, A Study in Social and Religious History*, p. 101). In the prophets. The citation here is probably a blending of Mal 3:1 and Ex 23:20.

3. This portion of the quotation is an almost exact reproduction of the LXX reading of Isa 40:3.

4. The word baptize means *to dip or submerge* and thus refers to an immersion. This was not an entirely new rite, since Jewish proselyte baptism was a form of self-immersion (G. F. Moore, *Judaism in the First Three Centuries of the Chris-*

5. And there went out unto him all the land of Judea, and they of Jerusalem, and were all baptized of him in the river of Jordan, confessing their sins.

6. And John was clothed with camel's hair, and with a girdle of a skin about his loins; and he did eat locusts and wild honey;

7. And preached, saying, There cometh one mightier than I after me, the latchet of whose shoes I am not worthy to stoop down and unloose.

8. I indeed have baptized you with water: but he shall baptize you with the Holy Ghost.

9. And it came to pass in those days, that Jesus came from Nazareth of Galilee, and was baptized of John in Jordan.

10. And straightway coming up out of the water, he saw the heavens opened, and the Spirit like a dove descending upon him:

*tian Era,* I, 331-335). John proclaimed the baptism of **repentance,** that is, a baptism characterized by, and signifying, repentance. In the NT repentance has a deeper connotation than its original sense of a change of mind. It has come to refer to an inner change of direction and purpose, a turning from sin to righteousness. Josephus makes it clear that this was the prerequisite for baptism by John (*Antiquities of the Jews* XVIII. v. 2). **For the remission of sins.** The Greek preposition *eis* at times was used with the meaning, "because of." Hence, the meaning may be that John baptized because of the forgiveness of sins.

5. Speaking in hyperbole, Mark depicts the throngs that streamed out from all parts of Judea. **There went out.** The imperfect tense portrays in motion picture fashion the continual procession of folk to be **baptized** (also imperfect tense). The rite was performed **in the river of Jordan,** an expression which is to be taken literally.

7. In verses 7,8 Mark records the core of the Baptist's message. He **preached,** or proclaimed as a herald (*kēryssō*), the fact of the coming One. **Latchet.** The leather strap used to fasten sandals. John did not consider himself worthy to attend the Messiah even 'as a slave.

8. The pouring out of **the Holy Ghost** was expected to be a feature of Messianic times (Joel 2:28,29; Acts 1:5; 2:4,16-21). The whole age between Christ's first and second advents is viewed as being Messianic, marked by the ministry of the Spirit.

B. His Baptism. 1:9-11. The high point in the ministry of the forerunner came when the "one mightier" than he arrived to submit to baptism. This act marked the official opening of Jesus' public ministry.

9. **In Jordan.** The Greek preposition *eis,* meaning, "in," "into," along with the words, "coming up out of the water" (v. 10), indicate an entrance into the river suggestive of immersion. In answer to the question as to why the sinless Christ was baptized with the baptism of repentance, it should be pointed out that this was a deliberate act of identification with sinners. Furthermore, he was in full sympathy with John's ministry, and to be baptized was the right thing to do (Mt 3:15).

10. Observe the first occurrence of Mark's characteristic **straightway** *(euthys);* see Introduction, *Characteristics.* Mark's word translated **opened** is much more forceful in the original, meaning *to tear*

11. And there came a voice from heaven, *saying,* Thou art my beloved Son, in whom I am well pleased.

12. And immediately the Spirit driveth him into the wilderness.

13. And he was there in the wilderness forty days tempted of Satan; and was with the wild beasts; and the angels ministered unto him.

14. Now after that John was put in prison, Jesus came into Galilee, preaching the gospel of the kingdom of God,

15. And saying, The time is fulfilled, and the kingdom of God is at hand: repent ye, and believe the gospel.

*apart, rend asunder.* **The Spirit.** Cf. Isa 61:1; Acts 10:38.

C. His Temptation. 1:12,13. Mark, in concise summary, records the temptation of Christ in two verses, whereas Matthew and Luke employ eleven and thirteen verses respectively. It is fitting that the ministry of the Saviour begin this way. He further evinces his solidarity with mankind by submitting to the temptations "common to man" (I Cor 10:13).

**12. Immediately.** Same word rendered "straightway" in 1:10. The word **spirit,** although not capitalized in the AV, refers to the Holy Spirit as in 1:8,10. The temptation of Jesus was no unavoidable accident. Mark's forceful style is to be observed in the word **driveth,** whereas the other Gospels use "led."

**13.** See sections on Mt 4:1-11 and Lk 4:1-13 for details of the temptations. That this was a genuine temptation which Christ found necessary to resist may be deduced from Heb 2:18; 4:15. It was a reality, not a farce, and by means of its awful reality Christ became qualified to be our High Priest and our Example in times of temptation. That he would not yield to the tempter's solicitations was assured by the omnipotence of his holy will.

### III. Christ's Ministry in Galilee. 1:14–6:30.

A. Call of the First Four Disciples. 1:14-20. Again Mark omits a portion of the life and work of Christ as he moves directly from the temptation to the beginning of the Galilean ministry. After an introductory statement (vv. 14,15), he relates the call of the four fishermen to discipleship.

**14. After that John was put in prison.** These words suggest that Mark consciously passes over a number of events. See Jn 1:35–4:42. **The gospel . . . of God.** Manuscript evidence is strongly in favor of the omission of the words **of the kingdom.** The message Christ kept proclaiming (*kēryssōn,* durative action) during the Galilean ministry was the good news that comes from God.

**15.** Mark adds an amplification of the message. **The time is fulfilled.** The season (*kairos*) of preparation, the OT period, had come to its consummation according to the plan of God (cf. Gal 4:4). **The kingdom of God** refers to the sovereignty, the royal reign, of God (Arndt, pp. 134, 135). This divine sovereignty is described as being **at hand,** or better, as having *drawn near.* It was not actually pres-

16. Now as he walked by the sea of Galilee, he saw Simon and Andrew his brother casting a net into the sea: for they were fishers.

17. And Jesus said unto them, Come ye after me, and I will make you to become fishers of men.

18. And straightway they forsook their nets, and followed him.

19. And when he had gone a little further thence, he saw James the *son* of Zebedee, and John his brother, who also were in the ship mending their nets.

20. And straightway he called them: and they left their father Zebedee in the ship with the hired servants, and went after him.

21. And they went into Capernaum; and straightway on the sabbath day he entered into the synagogue, and taught.

22. And they were astonished at his doctrine: for he taught them as one that had authority, and not as the scribes.

23. And there was in their synagogue a man with an unclean spirit; and he cried out,

24. Saying, Let *us* alone; what have we to do with thee, thou Jesus of Nazareth? art thou come to destroy us? I know thee who thou art, the Holy One of God.

25. And Jesus rebuked him, saying, Hold thy peace, and come out of him.

26. And when the unclean spirit had torn him, and cried with a loud voice, he came out of him.

27. And they were all amazed, insomuch that they questioned among themselves, saying, What thing is this? what new doctrine *is* this? for with authority commandeth he even the unclean spirits, and they do obey him.

28. And immediately his fame spread abroad throughout all the region round about Galilee.

29. And forthwith, when they were come out of the synagogue, they entered into the house of Simon and Andrew, with James and John.

ent, but potentially so. The terms of entrance are **repent . . . believe the gospel.** John's was a message of repentance, but here a new and positive note is added. The kingdom in these verses is spiritual and present (cf. Jn 3:3,5; Col 1:13). Elsewhere, Scripture describes the future, eschatological kingdom.

**16. Simon and Andrew** had previously become acquainted with Christ as Messiah (Jn 1:40-42). It is also probable that John (Mk 1:19) was one of those referred to in Jn 1:35-39 as following Jesus.

B. **First Galilean Preaching Tour. 1:21-45.** The Galilean ministry is marked by three preaching tours, in which Christ systematically carried his message to every part of Galilee. The first and third of these tours are reported by Mark. In this section the ministry in Capernaum and in the Galilean countryside is described, with greater emphasis being placed on the former. Verses 21-34 are descriptive of one day's activities in the seaside town.

**21. Capernaum** was an important town on the main road to Damascus, the location of a tax office, the town of the first five disciples whom Jesus called, as well as the headquarters for his Galilean ministry. **Taught.** It was the custom to invite qualified persons to teach in the synagogue.

**22. They were astonished.** A forceful word, meaning *to strike with intense amazement*. **Doctrine.** It was his manner of teaching, as well as the content, that amazed them, because of its difference from the teaching of the scribes. The latter were students and teachers of the written and oral law, whose manner of teaching was to quote the authoritative statements of the scribes who had gone before. Jesus spoke as one having direct authority from God.

**24. Let us alone.** Literally, *What to us and, to thee?* which means, "What have you to do with us?" The man speaks for himself and the demon within. **I know thee.** He was aware of Christ's true identity as **the Holy One of God,** indicating supernatural knowledge imparted by the demon.

**25. Hold thy peace.** A strong word meaning *to muzzle.* The force of the command is almost equal to our "shut up." **Come out.** Both imperatives in this verse are calls for instantaneous compliance.

**26. Had torn him.** The spirit convulsed the man as he left him.

**29.** Leaving the synagogue, they went to the house of Simon, with whom Andrew, his brother, apparently lived. **James and John** accompanied them, but it is not

30. But Simon's wife's mother lay sick of a fever; and anon they tell him of her.

31. And he came and took her by the hand, and lifted her up; and immediately the fever left her, and she ministered unto them.

32. And at even, when the sun did set, they brought unto him all that were diseased, and them that were possessed with devils.

33. And all the city was gathered together at the door.

34. And he healed many that were sick of divers diseases, and cast out many devils; and suffered not the devils to speak, because they knew him.

35. And in the morning, rising up a great while before day, he went out, and departed into a solitary place, and there prayed.

36. And Simon and they that were with him followed after him.

37. And when they had found him, they said unto him, All *men* seek for thee.

38. And he said unto them, Let us go into the next towns, that I may preach there also: for therefore came I forth.

39. And he preached in their synagogues throughout all Galilee, and cast out devils.

40. And there came a leper to him, beseeching him, and kneeling down to him, and saying unto him, If thou wilt, thou canst make me clean.

41. And Jesus, moved with compassion, put forth *his* hand, and touched him, and saith unto him, I will; be thou clean.

42. And as soon as he had spoken, immediately the leprosy departed from him, and he was cleansed.

43. And he straitly charged him, and forthwith sent him away;

44. And saith unto him, See thou say nothing to any man: but go thy way, show thyself to the priest, and offer for thy cleansing those things which Moses commanded, for a testimony unto them.

45. But he went out, and began to publish *it* much, and to blaze abroad the matter, insomuch that Jesus could no more openly enter into the city, but was without in desert places: and they came to him from every quarter.

to be understood that it was also their home. This is probably the house referred to on later occasions which served as Jesus' headquarters and to which he returned from his preaching tours.

30. **Lay sick of a fever.** Mark pictures Peter's mother-in-law as lying prostrate and burning up with fever.

32. This busy day in Capernaum was a Sabbath (v. 21), which is probably the reason for Mark's careful explanation that the diseased were brought **when the sun did set.** Healing was not to be done on the Sabbath, nor was any load to be carried. **They brought.** The Greek imperfect tense signifies continuing action, meaning that they kept on bringing them one after another. **Possessed with devils.** There is but one devil. The plural, **devils,** in the AV is to be understood as referring to demons. *Daimonizomenous* means "demon-possessed." Cf. 1:34,39.

34. **Suffered not the devils to speak.** The demons were identifying Jesus as **Christ the Son of God** (Lk 4:41), but he repeatedly refused (Gr., imperfect tense) to let them speak. This knowledge of his person is further evidence that these were not merely cases of mental illness.

35. **A great while before day** refers to the early part of the last watch of the night, perhaps between three and four o'clock in the morning. His purpose was to spend time in prayer in preparation for the preaching tour that was to take him into all Galilee.

39. No hyperbole is intended in the expression, **throughout all Galilee.** Instead the intent is to supply a brief summary of the first Galilean preaching tour.

40. No doubt the cleansing of the leper (vv. 40-45) occurred on the Galilean tour. **Make me clean.** Leprosy resulted in ceremonial uncleanness (Lev 13:1-3). Notice the leper's faith in Christ's ability.

43. Jesus **straitly charged** the man. Mark's verb carries strong emotion, and is used here in the sense of a very stern warning. It originally meant *to snort in anger.* **He sent him away,** or, more literally, *thrust him out (exebalen;* cf. 1:12).

44. **Say nothing . . . but go.** He was to go at once to the priest and fulfill the Law's requirements (Lev 14:1 ff.). Until pronounced clean by the authorities, he had no right to resume his normal social relationships. This was to be done **for a testimony.** No witness could have been more striking and authoritative than the priest's declaration of cleansing.

45. The man's failure to comply at once added to Jesus' tremendous popularity as

## CHAPTER 2

AND again he entered into Capernaum after *some* days; and it was noised that he was in the house.

2. And straightway many were gathered together, insomuch that there was no room to receive *them*, no, not so much as about the door: and he preached the word unto them.

3. And they come unto him, bringing one sick of the palsy, which was borne of four.

4. And when they could not come nigh unto him for the press, they uncovered the roof where he was: and when they had broken *it* up, they let down the bed wherein the sick of the palsy lay.

5. When Jesus saw their faith, he said unto the sick of the palsy, Son, thy sins be forgiven thee.

6. But there were certain of the scribes sitting there, and reasoning in their hearts,

7. Why doth his *man* thus speak blasphemies? who can forgive sins but God only?

8. And immediately, when Jesus perceived in his spirit that they so reasoned within themselves, he said unto them, Why reason ye these things in your hearts?

9. Whether is it easier to say to the sick of the palsy, *Thy* sins be forgiven thee; or to say, Arise, and take up thy bed, and walk?

10. But that ye may know that the Son of man hath power on earth to forgive sins, (he saith to the sick of the palsy,)

11. I say unto thee, Arise, and take up thy bed, and go thy way into thine house.

12. And immediately he arose, took up the bed, and went forth before them all; insomuch that they were all amazed, and glorified God, saying, We never saw it on this fashion.

a worker of miracles. Crowds were so large that he found it necessary to hold the gatherings **in desert places**, i.e., uninhabited or wilderness locations. And **they came to him** in streams (*ērchonto*, imperfect tense) from everywhere.

C. Development of Official Opposition. 2:1–3:12. The purpose of the author in this section is to show the development of conflict between Christ and the Jewish officials. The mushrooming popularity of the Lord would naturally arouse their disfavor, since his message, by its very nature, was contradictory to their beliefs and practices. Consequently, in each of the five incidents recorded here, the Pharisees are seen either complaining among themselves or openly raising questions or objections.

1. This return to Capernaum marked the completion of the first tour of Galilee. The expression **after some days** is best taken as referring to the report that he had returned. Hence, the verse should read, "And when he entered again into Capernaum, after some days it was reported that he was at home." The **house** was probably Peter's (1:29), and he may well have relayed to Mark the account which follows.

3. **Palsy** is better understood as paralysis. The man is called *paralytikon*.

4. **Press.** An old word for a crowd. An ancient flat-roofed house usually had a stairway to the roof, which would have enabled the bearers to carry the paralytic up without difficulty. **Uncovered the roof.** This was accomplished by digging through the composite of grass, plaster, tiles, and lath, as indicated by Mark's *exoryxantes*—**had broken it up** (AV). The **bed** was a mattress or pallet, such as was used by the poor.

7. If a person accepts the assumption of the scribes that Jesus was mere man, he must arrive likewise at their conclusion. He was speaking **blasphemies.** The basic conflict concerned the deity of Christ.

10. **That ye may know.** The healing of the paralytic became a proof of the Lord's power to forgive sins and thus of his deity. **Son of man.** This is the title that Jesus chose to use almost exclusively for himself. Its background is to be found in Daniel and in the extra-Biblical apocalyptic literature of the Jews, where it had become a designation of the Messiah (cf. Dan 7:13, 14). **Power.** The Greek word means *authority.*

12. That he arose **immediately** indicates another instantaneous healing, so complete that the man could carry his own pallet. The result was that **they were all amazed.** They were so greatly astonished

13. And he went forth again by the sea side; and all the multitude resorted unto him, and he taught them.

14. And as he passed by, he saw Levi the *son* of Alpheus sitting at the receipt of custom, and said unto him, Follow me. And he arose and followed him.

15. And it came to pass, that, as Jesus sat at meat in his house, many publicans and sinners sat also together with Jesus and his disciples; for there were many, and they followed him.

16. And when the scribes and Pharisees saw him eat with publicans and sinners, they said unto his disciples, How is it that he eateth and drinketh with publicans and sinners?

17. When Jesus heard *it*, he saith unto them, They that are whole have no need of the physician, but they that are sick: I came not to call the righteous, but sinners to repentance.

18. And the disciples of John and of the Pharisees used to fast: and they come and say unto him, Why do the disciples of John and of the Pharisees fast, but thy disciples fast not?

19. And Jesus said unto them, Can the children of the bridechamber fast, while the bridegroom is with them? as long as they have the bridegroom with them, they cannot fast.

that they were beside themselves. The verb *existēmi* means "to remove out of place," or "to drive one out of one's senses."

**13.** The first charge against the Lord in the series of conflicts recorded by Mark was the accusation of blasphemy (2:1-12). A second complaint now is raised in 2:13-17 to the effect that Christ associated with outcasts.

**14. Levi the son Alphaeus** is the same as Matthew (Mt 9:9; Mk 3:18). **Receipt of custom.** The tax office. Capernaum was located on the road leading from Mesopotamia to Egypt, as well as near the junction of the highway to Damascus. Its situation near the border of Herod Antipas' territory explains the presence there of a tollhouse.

**15. Sat at meat.** The verb means *to recline at a meal,* the customary manner of eating at that time. **His house.** Cf. Lk 5:29. **Publicans.** A designation for tax collectors. The privilege of collecting taxes was purchased by payment of the total tax fee required by the government. The collector was then free to extract as much as possible from the people through extortion. Usually the actual collection was made by lesser collectors, to which class Matthew probably belonged. These men were despised because of their service for a foreign overlord and their fraudulent practices.

**16. The scribes and Pharisees.** The Pharisees were a sect of laymen who followed rigorously the precepts of the written and oral law, being meticulous in their attempts to maintain ceremonial purity. They viewed with disdain those who were not as strict as they were in observing the commandments, referring to them as "the people of the land" (cf. Jn 7:49). The class designated as **sinners** here probably included all non-Pharisees.

**17. They that are whole.** Those who are strong and healthy. Jesus was answering the critics from their own point of view. They assumed that they themselves were righteous, and therefore not in need of help. Jesus speaks as the physician whose duty it is to help the sick.

**18.** The next incident recorded by Mark is the interrogation concerning fasting (2:18-22). **Used to fast.** The Greek says simply that they *were fasting.* Perhaps the very time of Levi's feast was a fast day, since it was the practice of the Pharisees to fast twice a week, on Mondays and Thursdays (Lk 18:12). The nature of John's ministry and message was in harmony with the observance of fasting.

**19. The children of the bridechamber.** Literally, *the sons of the bridechamber.*

20. But the days will come, when the bridegroom shall be taken away from them, and then shall they fast in those days.

21. No man also seweth a piece of new cloth on an old garment; else the new piece that filled it up taketh away from the old, and the rent is made worse.

22. And no man putteth new wine into old bottles; else the new wine doth burst the bottles, and the wine is spilled, and the bottles will be marred: but new wine must be put into new bottles.

23. And it came to pass, that he went through the corn fields on the sabbath day; and his disciples began, as they went, to pluck the ears of corn.

24. And the Pharisees said unto him, Behold, why do they on the sabbath day that which is not lawful?

25. And he said unto them, Have ye never read what David did, when he had need, and was ahungered, he, and they that were with him?

26. How he went into the house of God in the days of Abiathar the high priest, and did eat the showbread, which is not lawful to eat but for the priests, and gave also to them which were with him?

27. And he said unto them, The sabbath was made for man, and not man for the sabbath:

28. Therefore the Son of man is Lord also of the sabbath.

## CHAPTER 3

AND he entered again into the synagogue; and there was a man there which had a withered hand.

These were the close friends of the bridegroom who served as his attendants, a figure used here to refer to Jesus' disciples. Christ came to announce glad tidings (cf. 1:14,15); with such a message of joy, fasting was completely incongruous.

**21. New cloth.** This is cloth which has not been treated by the fuller, not shrunk or sized. **Else the new piece.** A close translation of the original would read *otherwise the filling* (that is, the patch) *takes* (tears) *away from it, the new from the old.* When the unshrunken patch becomes wet, it shrinks and tears away from the older, previously shrunk cloth. Thus it is not wise to attempt to patch the old system with the new.

**22. Old bottles.** Actually the word refers to wineskins, containers made from the skins of animals. The expansion caused by the fermenting of **new wine** would burst old wineskins because they had already been stretched as much as possible. Thus it is not possible to confine to the structure of the old legalism the vitality of the new experience produced by faith in Christ.

**23.** The next two occasions for opposition to Christ concern Sabbath practices (2:23–3:6). **The corn fields.** Corn, our maize, was not known to the translators of the AV. They used the term as we use the word "grain." The disciples were picking, not **ears of corn**, but heads of grain, such as barley or wheat.

**24. That which is not lawful.** It was not the appropriating of the grain to which they objected, for the Law allowed this (Deut 23:25); they were criticizing manual labor on the Sabbath. In their zeal to keep the letter of the Law to its last detail, they viewed the picking of the grain as harvesting and thus as a violation of Ex 20:10.

**25.** Jesus replied by citing **what David did** one time, as recorded in I Sam 21:1-6. His question expects an affirmative answer. The salient feature of the incident is found in the statement that **he had need.** Christ is declaring that human need supersedes all mere ritual and ceremony.

**27. The sabbath** was not intended to be a heartless despot that man must serve regardless of the cost to himself; rather it was given to meet man's need for rest.

**28. Lord also of the sabbath.** Christ was not asserting his freedom to violate the Sabbath law, but rather he was declaring his qualification to interpret that law.

**3:1.** The second Sabbath controversy recorded by Mark (3:1-6) occurred in **the synagogue,** probably in Capernaum, since

2. And they watched him, whether he would heal him on the sabbath day; that they might accuse him.

3. And he saith unto the man which had the withered hand, Stand forth.

4. And he saith unto them, Is it lawful to do good on the sabbath days, or to do evil? to save life, or to kill? But they held their peace.

5. And when he had looked round about on them with anger, being grieved for the hardness of their hearts, he saith unto the man, Stretch forth thine hand. And he stretched *it* out: And his hand was restored whole as the other.

6. And the Pharisees went forth, and straightway took counsel with the Herodians against him, how they might destroy him.

7. But Jesus withdrew himself with his disciples to the sea: and a great multitude from Galilee followed him, and from Judea,

8. And from Jerusalem, and from Idumea, and *from* beyond Jordan; and they about Tyre and Sidon, a great multitude, when they had heard what great things he did, came unto him.

9. And he spake to his disciples, that a small ship should wait on him because of the multitude, lest they should throng him.

10. For he had healed many; insomuch that they pressed upon him for to touch him, as many as had plagues.

11. And unclean spirits, when they saw him, fell down before him, and cried, saying, Thou art the Son of God.

3:7 speaks of a withdrawal **to the sea.**

2. The Lord's critics **watched him** persistently and closely. The verb indicates a malicious lying in wait to trap a person. Practicing medicine on the Sabbath was forbidden by rabbinic tradition unless the sick person was on the verge of death, which was not true in this case. Consequently, if Christ healed the man, the Jews were ready to **accuse Him** as a Sabbath violator.

4. **Is it lawful.** The question of Jesus harks back to the principle of need that had been set forth in the previous Sabbath encounter. To meet this man's need would be **to do good;** to fail to do so would be **to do evil. They held their peace.** The Greek imperfect tense pictures them as persisting in their silence. To reply would have been damaging. Obviously, it was not lawful to do evil, and to do good would be to heal the man.

6. The **Herodians** were not primarily a religious sect. Instead they were men who were politically devoted to the Herodian family. Consequently, they had no real affinity with the Pharisees, who zealously hated foreign domination; but a common opponent can bring enemies into strange coalitions.

7. The incident recorded in verses 7-12 provides another glimpse of the widespread fame of the Lord, which brought people from far and near to see and hear him. The crowd was composed of persons from every section except Samaria, even including some from areas outside Palestine, such as Tyre and Sidon (vv. 7,8). **The sea** to which **Jesus withdrew** was the Sea of Galilee.

9. **Small ship.** The more accurate translation today would be *small boat.* The crowd was so large that it was pressing *(thlibō)* upon Jesus, and he was in danger of being crushed. Therefore the boat was to **wait on him** in order that he might get into it if it became necessary to escape the pressure of the crowd.

10. This great popularity developed because **he had healed many.** The eager desire of the sick and afflicted to receive help is apparent in the words **they pressed upon him.** Literally, they *fell upon him,* Mark says, meaning that they approached the Lord eagerly, practically throwing themselves upon him. The verb is durative in force, describing continued action.

11. See comments on 1:24,34.

D. Appointment of the Twelve. 3:13-19. From the beginning of the work in Galilee (1:14) to the choice of the twelve

12. And he straitly charged them that they should not make him known.

13. And he goeth up into a mountain, and calleth *unto him* whom he would: and they came unto him.

14. And he ordained twelve, that they should be with him, and that he might send them forth to preach,

15. And to have power to heal sicknesses, and to cast out devils:

16. And Simon he surnamed Peter;

17. And James the *son* of Zebedee, and John the brother of James; and he surnamed them Boanerges, which is, The sons of thunder:

18. And Andrew, and Philip, and Bartholomew, and Matthew, and Thomas, and James the *son* of Alpheus, and Thaddeus, and Simon the Canaanite,

19. And Judas Iscariot, which also betrayed him: and they went into a house.

apostles, Jesus had been experiencing remarkable success in reaching the people with his message. He had access to the synagogues, and official opposition was only beginning to solidify. During these days he was gathering around him a group of followers from whom he would select a permanent band of disciples. In contrast, the second period of the Galilean ministry was marked by the presence of the twelve disciples as Christ's appointed assistants. The ministry to the multitudes went on, but there was also an attempt on Jesus' part to begin the instruction of his disciples. His popularity with the common people and the opposition from the leaders continued to develop until finally it became necessary for him to withdraw from Galilee.

13. The choice of the disciples occurred on **a mountain**, probably in the vicinity of Capernaum. It appears that Jesus asked a larger group to accompany him on the journey to the hill country.

14. Out of this larger group he selected **twelve** whom he appointed as his apostles (cf. Lk 6:13). **Ordained.** The Greek verb is better rendered as "appointed" (*epoiēsen;* literally, *he made*). The purpose of the appointment was twofold: that they should be with him (for companionship and training), and that they might go out to preach and to cast out demons (v. 15).

16. For the occasion when Simon was **surnamed Peter,** see Jn 1:42, where the Aramaic, *Cephas,* is used instead of the Greek, **Peter.**

17. **Boanerges.** This side of their personalities may be seen in Lk 9:54.

18. **Andrew.** The brother of Peter (Jn 1:40,41). **Bartholomew.** May be identical with Nathanael (Jn 1:45-51; 21:2). **James the son of Alphaeus** may be the same as James the less (Mk 15:40). **Thaddaeus** is also called Lebbaeus (Mt 10:3) and is the same as Judas the brother of James the less (Lk 6:16). **Simon the Canaanite** is more correctly designated Simon Zelotes (Acts 1:13), or Simon the Zealot. The word **Canaanite** is misleading, for the term found in the better Greek manuscripts is *Kananaion,* a transliteration of an Aramaic term meaning "zealot." Apparently Simon, before becoming a disciple of Christ, was a member of the fanatically patriotic party of Zealots, who were in favor of immediate revolt against Roman overlordship.

19. It is at this point that Matthew and Luke place the Sermon on the Mount. **Into an house.** An expression meaning "to come home." Christ probably returned to Peter's house in Capernaum.

**20.** And the multitude cometh together again, so that they could not so much as eat bread.

**21.** And when his friends heard *of it*, they went out to lay hold on him: for they said, He is beside himself.

**22.** And the scribes which came down from Jerusalem said, He hath Beelzebub, and by the prince of the devils casteth he out devils.

**23.** And he called them *unto him*, and said unto them in parables, How can Satan cast out Satan?

**24.** And if a kingdom be divided against itself, that kingdom cannot stand.

**25.** And if a house be divided against itself, that house cannot stand.

**26.** And if Satan rise up against himself, and be divided, he cannot stand, but hath an end.

**27.** No man can enter into a strong man's house, and spoil his goods, except he will first bind the strong man; and then he will spoil his house.

**28.** Verily I say unto you, All sins shall be forgiven unto the sons of men, and blasphemies wherewith soever they shall blaspheme:

**29.** But he that shall blaspheme against the Holy Ghost hath never forgiveness, but is in danger of eternal damnation:

**30.** Because they said, He hath an unclean spirit.

**E.** Concern of Christ's Friends, and Accusations of His Enemies. 3:20-35. These verses are indicative of the attitudes of friends and foes toward Jesus. Both groups misunderstood him, with the result that his friends became overly concerned for his welfare, while his enemies turned to vicious accusations against him.

**20. They could not . . . eat bread.** Again Mark provides a glimpse of the great crowds that continually came to hear and see Christ. **Bread** is to be understood as referring to food in general.

**21.** The **friends** who became concerned were actually members of Jesus' family, which is the normal connotation of the Greek phrase, *hoi par' autou*. It seems that word came to his mother and brothers in Nazareth concerning his ceaseless activity. Their purpose was **to lay hold on** Christ and take him with them by force, because they felt that he was overwrought and mentally disturbed.

**22.** When the family arrived at Capernaum, they found the Lord engaged in controversy with **the scribes . . . from** Jerusalem. The discussion was occasioned by the scribes' repeated accusations (Gr., imperfect tense, *elegon*) that Jesus was in league with satanic power. **Beelzebub.** The source and meaning of the word are not certain, but it is obviously used here to refer to the devil, **the prince** of demons (not **devils;** see on 1:32). The accusation was that Christ was empowered by Satan himself and that by this means he cast out demons.

**23.** Jesus took the initiative and **called** his accusers to come and meet him face to face. The logic he used against these accusers is unanswerable: If it is agreed that demons are Satan's servants, then it is illogical to assert that he is casting out his own servants. This argument the Lord reiterated in 3:24-27, supporting it by a series of illustrations.

**27.** The **strong man** is intended to represent Satan. To cast out demons is to enter his **house** and **spoil his goods.** Christ was asserting that instead of being in league with Satan, He was engaged in combat against him.

**29.** Blasphemy **against the Holy Ghost** is the act of slandering, reviling, speaking maliciously against the Spirit. For such a sin there is never any **forgiveness. In danger of.** A more correct translation would be *guilty,* or *bound by,* in the sense of being in its grasp. All of the better manuscripts read *eternal sin* rather than **eternal damnation.**

**30. Because they said.** The statements

31. There came then his brethren and his mother, and, standing without, sent unto him, calling him.

32. And the multitude sat about him, and they said unto him, Behold, thy mother and thy brethren without seek for thee.

33. And he answered them, saying, Who is my mother, or my brethren?

34. And he looked round about on them which sat about him, and said, Behold my mother and my brethren!

35. For whosoever shall do the will of God, the same is my brother, and my sister, and mother.

### CHAPTER 4

AND he began again to teach by the sea side: and there was gathered unto him a great multitude, so that he entered into a ship, and sat in the sea; and the whole multitude was by the sea on the land.

2. And he taught them many things by parables, and said unto them in his doctrine,

3. Hearken; Behold, there went out a sower to sow:

4. And it came to pass, as he sowed, some fell by the wayside, and the fowls of the air came and devoured it up.

5. And some fell on stony ground, where it had not much earth; and immediately it sprang up, because it had no depth of earth:

6. But when the sun was up, it was scorched; and because it had no root, it withered away.

of the scribes are to be taken as revealing the nature of this eternal offense. They explained Christ's miracles of exorcism as being accomplished by satanic power, when in reality they were wrought by the Holy Spirit. However, we are not to interpret this passage as teaching that the mere statement against the Spirit is the unpardonable sin, for this would be contrary to the general teaching of Scripture that any and all sins will be forgiven to the repentant soul. The essence of the "eternal sin" is the attitude of heart that underlies the act. In the light of Scripture as a whole, this attitude can only be a fixed, unrepentant state of mind that persists in defiant rejection of the overtures of the Holy Spirit.

31. While Jesus was engaged in this discussion with the scribes, **his brethren and his mother** came and were **calling him.** They apparently had journeyed from Nazareth to take him home with them for the rest and recuperation they assumed he needed (cf. 3:20,21). **Brethren.** See comments on 6:3.

33. Christ seized upon this occasion as an opportunity to point up the importance of being spiritually related to himself.

34. Entrance into God's family is gained by doing **the will of God,** and such obedience begins by hearing, believing, and following God's Son.

F. Parables by the Seaside. 4:1-34. Here a different method of teaching comes to the fore. While Christ had made use of parabolic teaching to a limited extent previously, it was not until this point in his ministry that he began to employ it as a major vehicle of expression. As crowds grew, as opposition intensified, and as superficial followers multiplied, Jesus adopted the parable as a means of instructing his own disciples, on the one hand, and of concealing the substance of his teaching from superficial and antagonistic hearers on the other. On this occasion he used the parables to illustrate certain characteristics of the Kingdom.

1. The setting for the presentation of the first of these parables was **by the seaside,** which presumably refers to the Sea of Galilee. Again the pressure of the crowd forced the Lord to address the people from a boat standing off the shore a short distance.

4. The soil **by the way side** had been compacted by the passage of many feet, so that the seed lay on the surface in plain view, and the birds **came and devoured it.**

5,6. The second area where seed fell was **stony ground,** which is not to be un-

7. And some fell among thorns, and the thorns grew up, and choked it, and it yielded no fruit.

8. And other fell on good ground, and did yield fruit that sprang up and increased, and brought forth, some thirty, and some sixty, and some a hundred.

9. And he said unto them, He that hath ears to hear, let him hear.

10. And when he was alone, they that were about him with the twelve asked of him the parable.

11. And he said unto them, Unto you it is given to know the mystery of the kingdom of God: but unto them that are without, all *these* things are done in parables:

12. That seeing they may see, and not perceive; and hearing they may hear, and not understand; lest at any time they should be converted, and *their* sins should be forgiven them.

13. And he said unto them, Know ye not this parable? and how then will ye know all parables?

14. The sower soweth the word.

15. And these are they by the wayside, where the word is sown; but when they have heard, Satan cometh immediately, and taketh away the word that was sown in their hearts.

16. And these are they likewise which are sown on stony ground; who, when they have heard the word, immediately receive it with gladness;

17. And have no root in themselves, and so endure but for a time: afterward, when affliction or persecution ariseth for the word's sake, immediately they are offended.

derstood as soil containing stones but as rock with a thin covering of soil. The heat from the sun made this ground first a hot-bed producing rapid germination and then a furnace that **scorched** and **withered** the tender plant.

8. And the remainder of the seed was sown **on good ground.** It is only reasonable to assume that the great bulk of the seed was sown on this kind of soil, and not a mere 25 per cent, as is sometimes asserted. **That sprang up and increased.** It was not the fruit that sprang up. These two participles refer to the word **other,** and hence it was the seed that was growing.

11. **The mystery.** In the pagan mystery religions, the initiate was instructed in the esoteric teaching of the cult, which was not revealed to outsiders. On the kingdom of God, see comments on 1:15. The **mystery of the kingdom** in its ultimate development is the full-orbed message of the Gospel (cf. Rom 16:25,26). The purpose of **parables** was to instruct the initiates without revealing the items of instruction to the ones who were **without.** This is in keeping with the Biblical principle that spiritual understanding is restricted to those who have become **spiritual** by properly relating themselves to Christ and his message (I Cor 2:6 ff.).

12. That such was the purpose of Christ's use of parables is further confirmed by a quotation from the OT. The citation is introduced with the Greek conjunction *hina* **(that),** which in this instance cannot have a resultant meaning but must indicate purpose (Alf, I, 333). This verse is a free rendering of Isa 6:9,10, giving the gist, but not reproducing the exact wording, of the prophetic passage.

14. **The sower** (v. 3) is not identified, but he obviously represents Christ himself and all others who proclaim the Gospel. The seed stands for **the word,** which is, as Luke explains, the word of God, or the message which comes from God.

15. The birds of 4:4 are representative of **Satan,** who comes to those who hear the message and prevents any germination of the seed. These folk merely hear the word, and that is all.

16. Cf. verses 5,6. Some hearers of the word **receive it** with alacrity. The appearance of sincerity and genuine joy is present.

17. The statement that they **have no root** indicates the superficiality of their reception of the word. They **endure but for a time,** or *are temporary,* which is a better translation of *proskairoi.* The heat

18. And these are they which are sown among thorns; such as hear the word,

19. And the cares of this world, and the deceitfulness of riches, and the lusts of other things entering in, choke the word, and it becometh unfruitful.

20. And these are they which are sown on good ground; such as hear the word, and receive *it*, and bring forth fruit, some thirty-fold, some sixty, and some a hundred.

21. And he said unto them, Is a candle brought to be put under a bushel, or under a bed? and not to be set on a candlestick?

22. For there is nothing hid, which shall not be manifested; neither was any thing kept secret, but that it should come abroad.

23. If any man have ears to hear, let him hear.

24. And he said unto them, Take heed what ye hear. With what measure ye mete, it shall be measured to you; and unto you that hear shall more be given.

25. For he that hath, to him shall be given; and he that hath not, from him shall be taken even that which he hath.

26. And he said, So is the kingdom of God, as if a man should cast seed into the ground;

27. And should sleep, and rise night and day, and the seed should spring and grow up, he knoweth not how.

of the sun (v. 6) illustrates the coming of **affliction or persecution**, which soon becomes a stumblingblock or a snare to them, and they fall away because their experience of the word was not genuine.

19. Cf. 4:7. The **cares** are anxieties and worries concerning the interests of this present evil age (**world** is an inaccurate translation of *aiōn,* which refers to a period of time). The **deceitfulness of riches** has reference to the deceptive nature of wealth, always promising to satisfy and yet never able to fulfill the promise. The third hindrance is the longing or craving for **other things,** a general category including anything else which would choke the word and cause it to become **unfruitful.**

20. Cf. 4:8. The good soil signifies the persons who **hear the word and receive it.** A commentary on the meaning of **receive** is supplied by Mt 13:23 and Lk 8:15. These are people who hear, who understand, who are sincere, and who appropriate the message of the Gospel permanently.

21. The sayings of 4:21-25 are general statements that Christ seems to have used at various times (on v. 21 cf. Mt 5:15; on v. 23 cf. Mt 11:15; 13:9,43; Lk 14:35; on v. 24b cf. Mt 7:2; on v. 25 cf. Mt 25:29). Christ's purpose on this occasion was to emphasize the responsibility incumbent upon the hearer of the parables. He who has been enlightened must in turn enlighten others (Mk 4:21-23). **Candle.** *Lamp* is a more accurate translation. **Bushel.** Not the same as the present-day bushel; comparable to our peck measure. The **candlestick** was in reality a lampstand for the open-bowl oil lamps used in that day.

25. **He that hath.** The principle set forth in this statement is to be applied specifically to the realm of truth and its appropriation. He who lays hold of truth and uses it will receive more enlightenment, but he who refuses to appropriate truth will lose even the understanding of truth which he once had.

26. The second parable of the Kingdom which Mark records is that of the soil producing spontaneously (vv. 26-29). In reality, it takes up where the Parable of the Soils left off, going on to describe the actual growth of the seed which bears fruit. The aspect of **the kingdom** in view here is the present, spiritual aspect, in its internal reality as well as its external manifestations. This kingdom is extended by the sowing of the **seed** of the word (cf. v. 14).

**28.** For the earth bringeth forth fruit of herself; first the blade, then the ear, after that the full corn in the ear.

**29.** But when the fruit is brought forth, immediately he putteth in the sickle, because the harvest is come.

**30.** And he said, Whereunto shall we liken the kingdom of God? or with what comparison shall we compare it?

**31.** *It is* like a grain of mustard seed, which, when it is sown in the earth, is less than all the seeds that be in the earth:

**32.** But when it is sown, it groweth up, and becometh greater than all herbs, and shooteth out great branches; so that the fowls of the air may lodge under the shadow of it.

**33.** And with many such parables spake he the word unto them, as they were able to hear *it.*

**34.** But without a parable spake he not unto them: and when they were alone, he expounded all things to his disciples.

**35.** And the same day, when the even was come, he saith unto them, Let us pass over unto the other side.

**36.** And when they had sent away the multitude, they took him even as he was in the ship. And there were also with him other little ships.

**37.** And there arose a great storm of wind, and the waves beat into the ship, so that it was now full.

**28.** The reason why the earth brings forth **fruit of herself** (*automatē*, "automatically") is that the seed contains life which, when placed in the proper environment, produces growth. The characteristic of the present, spiritual kingdom of grace, as set forth by this parable, is that the message of the Gospel, by its very nature, when sown in men's hearts produces growth and fruitfulness spontaneously.

**30.** Mark's third parable of the Kingdom concerns the mustard seed (vv. 30-32). The AV points up the true nature of a parable by translating *parabolē* as **comparison.**

**31.** Here the Kingdom is compared to a **grain of mustard seed.** Much has been written concerning the identification of this plant, but it seems best to take it to be the common black mustard, which has a seed about the size of the head of a pin (Harold N. and Alma L. Moldenke, *Plants of the Bible,* pp. 59-62). Its seed was one of the smallest known to the people of Galilee.

**32.** The remarkable phenomenon of this particular mustard plant is that, though it is really an herb, it may grow to be ten or twelve feet high, with a stem the size of a man's arm, and become a resting place for the smaller varieties of birds. This parable is a further development of the characteristics of the present, spiritual kingdom of God. The main point here is that the seed of the Gospel message will produce phenomenal growth. From small beginnings, the Kingdom, which had only drawn near in the person of Christ (1:14,15), will, by reason of its own inner and supernatural vitality, grow to tremendous proportions. This does not mean that it will result in world conversion, nor that man by his efforts will bring in the kingdom of God on earth as a Utopian development, nor that the Kingdom and the Church are identical. The parable does, however, picture the kingdom of grace as including multitudes of redeemed persons who through the years have come to swell its ranks to phenomenal size.

G. Trip to Gadara. 4:35–5:20. Probably for the sake of privacy and relaxation, Jesus proposed a trip across the lake of Galilee. With the vividness so characteristic of our author, Mark gives a graphic account of the stilling of the storm (4:35-41) and of the freeing of the demonized man whom Christ met on the other side (5:1-20).

**37.** The **great storm of wind** was typical of the Sea of Galilee, situated in a

38. And he was in the hinder part of the ship, asleep on a pillow: and they awake him, and say unto him, Master, carest thou not that we perish?

39. And he arose, and rebuked the wind, and said unto the sea, Peace, be still. And the wind ceased, and there was a great calm.

40. And he said unto them, Why are ye so fearful? how is it that ye have no faith?

41. And they feared exceedingly, and said one to another, What manner of man is this, that even the wind and the sea obey him?

## CHAPTER 5

AND they came over unto the other side of the sea, into the country of the Gadarenes.

2. And when he was come out of the ship, immediately there met him out of the tombs a man with an unclean spirit,

3. Who had *his* dwelling among the tombs; and no man could bind him, no, not with chains:

4. Because that he had been often bound with fetters and chains, and the chains had been plucked asunder by him, and the fetters broken in pieces: neither could any *man* tame him.

pocket, as it was, with hills on every side. The rising of the warm air of the day allowed the cooler air from the hills to rush down the ravines onto the lake with twisting, whirlwind action that churned the waters into an angry tempest. Mark's account paints a vivid picture, taking his readers to the very scene of action. **The waves** *kept beating* (Gr. imp. tense) into the boat and *it is already filling* (Gr. pres. tense) with water.

39. In contrast, Mark recounts the command of Christ to the storm. The Greek aorist tense is used to show that he **rebuked** it once (point action), and the **wind ceased** *at once* (Gr. aorist), and a **calm** came immediately (Gr. aorist). There was no necessity for the Lord to repeat his command, for it brought instantaneous obedience. **Peace, be still.** Literally, *Be silent. Be muzzled.* Lenski interestingly translates the perfect tense imperative of Christ's second command, "Put the muzzle on and keep it on" (R. C. H. Lenski, *The Interpretation of Mark's Gospel,* p. 201).

40. **Fearful.** Christ rebuked them for their cowardly fear, and turned the occasion into a stimulus for faith. He was suggesting that if their confidence had been in God, even though he himself was asleep, they would have had no reason to fear.

41. **Feared exceedingly.** Literally, *they feared with great fear.* The Greek term used here is not the same as in verse 40. This word can mean "reverential, respectful fear or awe." Notwithstanding all the mighty works the disciples had witnessed, so phenomenal was this miracle that they still wondered who their teacher really was. **What manner of man.** The Greek text has, *Who then is this?*

5:1. **The Gadarenes.** Greek manuscripts are divided among three names here – Gadarenes, Gerasenes, and Gergesenes. The best evidence favors Gerasenes, a term which some have taken to refer to the well-known Gerasa, twenty miles southeast of the Sea of Galilee. There is good reason, however, to believe that Mark refers to a small town of the same name on the eastern shore, the ruins of which are today called Kersa (cf. Harvie Branscomb, *Mark,* pp. 89,90).

3. This man had his habitual **dwelling** in or among the tombs, as the Greek imperfect tense shows. He had reached a stage so extreme that he could no longer be bound by anyone, even **with chains.**

4. The impossibility of restraining the man is emphasized dramatically by vivid terms and tenses. The **fetters** were used on

5. And always, night and day, he was in the mountains, and in the tombs, crying, and cutting himself with stones.

6. But when he saw Jesus afar off, he ran and worshipped him,

7. And cried with a loud voice, and said, What have I to do with thee, Jesus, *thou* Son of the most high God? I adjure thee by God, that thou torment me not.

8. For he said unto him, Come out of the man, *thou* unclean spirit.

9. And he asked him, What *is* thy name? And he answered, saying, My name *is* Legion: for we are many.

10. And he besought him much that he would not send them away out of the country.

11. Now there was there nigh unto the mountains a great herd of swine feeding.

12. And all the devils besought him, saying, Send us into the swine, that we may enter into them.

13. And forthwith Jesus gave them leave. And the unclean spirits went out, and entered into the swine; and the herd ran violently down a steep place into the sea, (they were about two thousand,) and were choked in the sea.

the feet. As often as he had been bound he had pulled the chains apart and crushed the fetters into pieces. No one could . . . tame him. The Greek text indicates that no one had strength enough to tame this wild beast of a man.

5. Throughout **night and day** he was continually (Gr. text) **crying** with screams and shrieks and **cutting himself** with stones. The latter verb is an intensive form, meaning that he was cutting himself up or slashing himself to pieces.

7. **Jesus, thou Son of the most high God.** A remarkable indication of supernatural knowledge. The afflicted man was aware both of the human name of Jesus and of his Deity, although this, as it appears, was his first encounter with Christ, Such knowledge is proof that the man was not merely insane; he was indwelt by demonic powers who knew the true identity of Christ. **Torment me not.** Matthew 8:29 reads, "Art thou come hither to torment us before the time?" And Lk 8:31 (ASV) provides further light by reporting that they asked him not to send them "into the abyss." The torment of which the demons spoke is the final punishment after the day of judgment; they asked not to be imprisoned in the abyss before that time.

9. The question, **What is thy name?** was addressed to the one unclean spirit (demon) mentioned in verse 8. This same spirit replies in 5:9,10. In contrast, all of the demons speak in verse 12. **Legion.** A unit in the Roman army consisting of more than 6,000 men. **We are many.** The one demon was spokesman for the many that had possessed the man.

10. The significance of the phrase, **out of the country,** is to be seen in Luke's reference to **the abyss** (8:31, ASV). They feared being returned to the place of detention to remain in a disembodied state until the judgment.

12,13. Rather than being disembodied, they begged to be sent **into the swine. Jesus gave them leave.** The question persistently provoked by this passage concerns the ethical propriety of Jesus' action, resulting as it did in the destruction of the property of others. A common answer has been that Jews had no right to own pigs, and that Christ thus rebuked their breaking Mosaic law. But since the region of Decapolis contained a mixed population of both Jews and Gentiles, we have no assurance that the owners were Jews or that this was the purpose of Christ's action. Notice that he did not command the demons to enter the swine; he permitted them. It was the demons, not

14. And they that fed the swine fled, and told *it* in the city, and in the country. And they went out to see what it was that was done.

15. And they come to Jesus, and see him that was possessed with the devil, and had the legion, sitting, and clothed, and in his right mind; and they were afraid.

16. And they that saw *it* told them how it befell to him that was possessed with the devil, and *also* concerning the swine.

17. And they began to pray him to depart out of their coasts.

18. And when he was come into the ship, he that had been possessed with the devil prayed him that he might be with him.

19. Howbeit Jesus suffered him not, but saith unto him, Go home to thy friends, and tell them how great things the Lord hath done for thee, and hath had compassion on thee.

20. And he departed, and began to publish in Decapolis how great things Jesus had done for him: and all *men* did marvel.

21. And when Jesus was passed over again by ship unto the other side, much people gathered unto him; and he was nigh unto the sea.

22. And, behold, there cometh one of the rulers of the synagogue, Jairus by name; and when he saw him, he fell at his feet,

23. And besought him greatly, saying, My little daughter lieth at the point of death: *I pray thee*, come and lay thy hands on her, that she may be healed; and she shall live.

the Lord, who caused the destruction. The fact that Christ permitted the act makes him no more responsible than God is responsible for evil of any kind because he permits it. The devil's affliction of Job is a case in point (Job 1:12; 2:6,7).

15. They **were afraid,** not of the cured man, but of the remarkable power that had cured him. They were aware of supernatural power in the person of Christ but unaware of his infinite love and mercy.

17. Unknowingly they begged the source of potential blessing and salvation **to depart** out of their country. **Coasts.** The Greek word means *boundary, border,* and in the plural it may refer to the territory surrounded by these boundaries.

18. While Jesus was getting into the boat, the cured demoniac kept begging to **be with him.** He alone, among all his countrymen, saw in Jesus not someone to fear but someone to love.

19. **Jesus suffered him not.** That is, he did not permit the man to go with him. Instead, he commanded him to go to his own people and report to them what **great things the Lord hath done.** A basic principle underlies Christ's command. Man is not delivered from bondage merely for his own enjoyment of God-given freedom, but also that he may give testimony to others concerning the divine Deliverer. In the country east of the Sea of Galilee there was no reason to fear any crisis caused by excessive popularity. Thus the cured demoniac was urged to broadcast his story. **Hath had compassion.** The Greek verb means *to have mercy or pity* on someone.

20. **In Decapolis.** This is the region southeast of the Sea of Galilee in which were located ten cities (*deka*, "ten"; *polis*, "city"), Grecian in organization and culture.

H. The Woman with a Hemorrhage, and the Daughter of Jairus. 5:21-43. Two remarkable miracles are described in the following verses. The healing of the woman with the hemorrhage occurred without any apparent conscious act on Christ's part. The raising of the daughter of Jairus was the second instance in Christ's ministry of the restoration of life to the dead (cf. Lk 7:11 ff.).

22. Jairus was **one of the rulers of the synagogue,** which identifies him as one of the elders who were in charge of the services in the synagogue attended by Jesus at Capernaum.

23. **He besought him greatly.** He kept begging, perhaps repeatedly and desperately. **Little daughter.** All commentators

24. And *Jesus* went with him; and much people followed him, and thronged him.

25. And a certain woman, which had an issue of blood twelve years,

26. And had suffered many things of many physicians, and had spent all that she had, and was nothing bettered, but rather grew worse,

27. When she had heard of Jesus, came in the press behind, and touched his garment.

28. For she said, If I may touch but his clothes, I shall be whole.

29. And straightway the fountain of her blood was dried up; and she felt in *her* body that she was healed of that plague.

30. And Jesus, immediately knowing in himself that virtue had gone out of him, turned him about in the press, and said, Who touched my clothes?

31. And his disciples said unto him, Thou seest the multitude thronging thee, and sayest thou, Who touched me?

32. And he looked round about to see her that had done this thing.

33. But the woman fearing and trembling, knowing what was done in her, came and fell down before him, and told him all the truth.

34. And he said unto her, Daughter, thy faith hath made thee whole; go in peace, and be whole of thy plague.

note the diminutive form as a term of endearment. **At the point of death.** A good paraphrase of the Greek text, which indicates that she was in the very last stage of her illness. **I pray thee.** These words were supplied by the translators of the AV. Mark's Greek vividly portrays the anguish of this poor father as he pleads with broken phrases: "My little daughter is lying at death's door — that you may come and . . ."

**24.** The multitude following Christ kept crowding against him on every side (Gr. imp. tense, *synethlibon*).

**25. An issue of blood.** None of the Gospels specifically describes the nature of this hemorrhage except to say that it was a chronic ailment.

**26.** Mark is very frank in his comments concerning the woman's experience with **many physicians.** She went to doctor after doctor to be healed. Instead, she suffered many things at their hands, she spent all that she had, and still she grew worse. Luke, the physician, is not so blunt in his description (Lk 8:43).

**27. The press.** The crowd that kept pressing in on Christ.

**28. She said.** "She kept saying" (Gr. imp. tense), probably to herself.

**29,30.** This healing was unique, not merely because it was instantaneous but because it occurred without any apparent conscious participation by Christ. However, **Jesus immediately** was aware of what had occurred. We are not to assume that touching the garment had a magical effect, but rather that Jesus in omniscience recognized the touch of faith and granted the woman's desire. Or it may be assumed that the healing was not a conscious act of Christ, and that it was God the Father who healed the woman. In that case Jesus, in the limitation of his humanity, was not aware of it until the miracle occurred. **Virtue.** It was "power" (Gr., *dynamin*) that was operative in the healing. The question **Who touched my clothes?** may have been asked in order to reveal the miracle to the crowd, if it be assumed that the healing was consciously done on Christ's part. If not, Christ may also have been asking for his own information.

**31.** As usual, Mark's graphic use of tenses is enlightening. He reports that **his disciples** kept saying, "You see the crowd continually thronging you . . . ."

**32.** Evidently the woman was not found with one glance, for Mark says that he kept looking **round about** himself (Gr. imp. tense, mid. voice).

**34. Thy faith.** We see this woman's

35. While he yet spake, there came from the ruler of the synagogue's *house certain* which said, Thy daughter is dead; why troublest thou the Master any further?

36. As soon as Jesus heard the word that was spoken, he saith unto the ruler of the synagogue, Be not afraid, only believe.

37. And he suffered no man to follow him, save Peter, and James, and John the brother of James.

38. And he cometh to the house of the ruler of the synagogue, and seeth the tumult, and them that wept and wailed greatly.

39. And when he was come in, he saith unto them, Why make ye this ado, and weep? the damsel is not dead, but sleepeth.

40. And they laughed him to scorn. But when he had put them all out, he taketh the father and the mother of the damsel, and them that were with him, and entereth in where the damsel was lying.

41. And he took the damsel by the hand, and said unto her, Talitha cumi; which is, being interpreted, Damsel, (I say unto thee,) arise.

42. And straightway the damsel arose, and walked; for she was *of the age* of twelve years. And they were astonished with a great astonishment.

43. And he charged them straitly that no man should know it; and commanded that something should be given her to eat.

faith in action in 5:27,28, a confidence so strong that she did not feel it necessary to arrest Jesus' attention. **Made thee whole . . . be whole.** The first expression literally means *has saved you*, referring to salvation from her physical affliction. The second expression means *to be well, healthy,* and is a present imperative, meaning that she was to continue in health.

35. The question of the messengers, **Why troublest thou . . . further?** indicates that they did not expect a restoration of life. **Master.** The Greek text has *didaskalon,* "teacher."

36. Jesus, ignoring the messengers' remarks, said to the ruler, "Stop fearing! Just keep on believing!" Both verbs are in the present tense in Greek. The report had struck fear into the man's heart, but Christ urged him not to forsake his previous faith.

38. **The tumult.** Among the Jews mourning for the dead was anything but subdued and respectful. Professional mourners were hired to provide a demonstration of sorrow. Matthew 9:23 (ASV) mentions the flute-players and the crowd which were also making a tumult.

39. The impropriety of the demonstration moved Christ to ask, **Why make ye this ado?** or, more literally, "Why are you making such an uproar?" Christ's statement that the girl was **not dead** but sleeping has been taken by some to mean that she was not really dead but only in a coma. However, Lk 8:55 says that **her spirit came again,** indicating that she had been dead. Christ's reference to death as sleep was intended to suggest that the condition was temporary and that the person would awaken again.

40. The mourners, taking Jesus' figure of speech literally, kept laughing (Gr. imp. tense) him **to scorn.** They knew that the girl was dead, and they were sure that death is permanent. **Put them all out.** Mark's verb is forceful, meaning, *to thrust out.* Christ drove the jeering crowd from the house.

41. **Talitha cumi.** Transliteration of the Aramaic for, "Little girl, arise." Mark inserts the words, **I say unto thee.**

42. **Straightway** the girl **arose** (point action) and was walking around (continuous action). **Twelve years.** She was old enough to walk. The parents and disciples were indescribably **astonished** at the miracle, so much so that they were beside themselves with amazement.

43. Jesus commanded **that no man should know** lest the parents should proclaim the news abroad and the widespread

## CHAPTER 6

AND he went out from thence, and came into his own country; and his disciples follow him.

2. And when the sabbath day was come, he began to teach in the synagogue: and many hearing *him* were astonished, saying, From whence hath this *man* these things? and what wisdom *is* this which is given unto him, that even such mighty works are wrought by his hands?

3. Is not this the carpenter, the son of Mary, the brother of James, and Joses, and of Juda, and Simon? and are not his sisters here with us? And they were offended at him.

4. But Jesus said unto them, A prophet is not without honor, but in his own country, and among his own kin, and in his own house.

5. And he could there do no mighty work, save that he laid his hands upon a few sick folk, and healed *them*.

6. And he marveled because of their unbelief. And he went round about the villages, teaching.

excitement should precipitate a crisis before the hour for the Saviour's death had arrived (Jn 12:23,27).

I. Another Galilean Preaching Tour. 6:1-30. Mark records but two of the Lord's three tours of Galilee, the first with the four fishermen (1:35-45), and the third at the conclusion of the Galilean ministry (6:1-30). The second tour occurred shortly after the choice of the Twelve (Lk 8:1-3). The third was different from the preceding two in that the disciples were sent out two by two (Mk 6:7), after which Christ went from town to town preaching and teaching by himself (Mt 11:1). The tour should be viewed as including the visit to Nazareth (Mk 6:1-6). It was also during this time that Herod became exercised concerning the great popularity of the Lord (6:14-16).

**1. From thence.** That is, from Capernaum. While the place to which Jesus went is not specifically named, it is obvious from the following verses that **his own country** refers to his home town, Nazareth.

**3.** Jesus is called **the brother of James** and the others, a designation which should be taken literally. There is no Biblical reason whatever for not understanding these four men and their **sisters** to be the children of Joseph and Mary, born some time after Jesus. **James** became the leader of the Jerusalem church (Acts 15:13 ff.) and the author of the epistle that bears his name. **Juda** is the same as Jude, the author of the general epistle of Jude. The townspeople **were offended.** This verb originally meant "to be caught in a trap or snare." They were caught in the snare of their own unbelief, and stumbled when they could have risen to their greatest opportunity.

**5.** Christ was unable to do any **mighty work** there. However, it was not that he tried to heal some and found himself incapable, but that so few people had faith enough to come to him for healing.

**6.** Where the Lord Jesus might have expected to find the greatest faith in himself, he found the most persistent **unbelief.** And even though he was the omniscient Son of God, **he marvelled** at his unbelieving acquaintances. **He went.** The Greek imperfect tense describes the action as in process. He was going from village to village, **teaching** in every town. This ministry in Nazareth and in the villages is the first stage of the third Galilean preaching tour.

7. And he called *unto him* the twelve, and began to send them forth by two and two; and gave them power over unclean spirits;

8. And commanded them that they should take nothing for *their* journey, save a staff only; no scrip, no bread, no money in *their* purse:

9. But *be* shod with sandals; and not put on two coats.

10. And he said unto them, In what place soever ye enter into a house, there abide till ye depart from that place.

11. And whosoever shall not receive you, nor hear you, when ye depart thence, shake off the dust under your feet for a testimony against them. Verily I say unto you, It shall be more tolerable for Sodom and Gomorrah in the day of judgment, than for that city.

12. And they went out, and preached that men should repent.

13. And they cast out many devils, and anointed with oil many that were sick, and healed *them.*

14. And king Herod heard *of him;* (for his name was spread abroad;) and he said, That John the Baptist was risen from the dead, and therefore mighty works do show forth themselves in him.

15. Others said, That it is Elias. And others said, That it is a prophet, or as one of the prophets.

16. But when Herod heard *thereof,* he said, It is John, whom I beheaded: he is risen from the dead.

17. For Herod himself had sent forth and laid hold upon John, and bound him in prison for Herodias' sake, his brother Philip's wife; for he had married her.

7. The second stage of the tour was introduced when Jesus called the Twelve and **began to send them forth.** This apparently was the first time they had gone out without Christ, and it therefore constituted an advanced step in their training. **Power.** *Authority.*

8. They were to **take nothing for their journey.** This was designed to train them in the practice of faith in preparation for the time when they would be on their own. **No scrip.** A traveling bag for carrying provisions. **Money.** This term refers to small copper coins. They were not even to take small change. **Purse.** A belt or girdle worn to hold the loose Oriental garments in place; it was also used to carry money.

9. The intention was that they should take no extra wearing apparel. **Coats.** The garment referred to is the undergarment worn next to the skin, rather than a coat.

11. They were to **shake off the dust** not in personal animosity but as **a testimony** to show the seriousness of rejecting the message of the Son of God. The statement concerning **Sodom and Gomorrha** was not in the earliest Greek manuscripts.

13. Anointing **with oil** was a common medical practice (cf. Lk 10:34; Jas 5:14). W. K. Hobart *(The Medical Language of St. Luke,* pp. 28,29) records numerous citations from ancient writers to this effect. Swete *(Mark,* p. 119) says that ritualistic anointing of the sick did not appear until the second century. Thus these healings were a combination of miracle and medicine.

14. The incident recorded in 6:14-29 occurred during the third tour of Galilee (cf. vv. 12,13,30). This **king Herod** was Herod Antipas, son of Herod the Great, and tetrarch of Galilee and Perea. The continuing ministry of Christ and his disciples in Galilee had spread his fame to every part of the region. Here, for the first time, we have evidence that the reputation of Christ had come to the attention of government officials.

15. A common rumor among the people was that he was Elijah returning in fulfillment of Mal 4:5 (cf. Mt 16:14; Jn 1:21), or that he was **a prophet** after the pattern of the OT prophets.

17. The **prison** where John was incarcerated was located at Machaerus, on the eastern shore of the Dead Sea (Jos *Antiquities* xviii. 5.2). The marital relationships of the Herods were scandalous. Herodias was the wife of her half-uncle, Herod Philip I, but she left him to marry another half-uncle his brother, Herod

18. For John had said unto Herod, It is not lawful for thee to have thy brother's wife.

19. Therefore Herodias had a quarrel against him, and would have killed him; but she could not:

20. For Herod feared John, knowing that he was a just man and a holy, and observed him; and when he heard him, he did many things, and heard him gladly.

21. And when a convenient day was come, that Herod on his birthday made a supper to his lords, high captains, and chief *estates* of Galilee;

22. And when the daughter of the said Herodias came in, and danced, and pleased Herod and them that sat with him, the king said unto the damsel, Ask of me whatsoever thou wilt, and I will give *it* thee.

23. And he sware unto her, Whatsoever thou shalt ask of me, I will give *it* thee, unto the half of my kingdom.

24. And she went forth, and said unto her mother, What shall I ask? And she said, The head of John the Baptist.

25. And she came in straightway with haste unto the king, and asked, saying, I will that thou give me by and by in a charger the head of John the Baptist.

26. And the king was exceeding sorry; *yet* for his oath's sake, and for their sakes which sat with him, he would not reject her.

27. And immediately the king sent an executioner, and commanded his head to be brought: and he went and beheaded him in the prison,

Antipas. Herod Antipas was already married to the daughter of Aretas, king of Arabia, but he sent this wife away.

**18. John had said.** He was saying it repeatedly (Gr. imp. tense).

**19. Herodias had a quarrel against him.** Literally, Mark says that she continually had it in for him. She, unlike Herod, felt no attraction to John and his preaching; on the contrary, she kept wanting to kill him.

**20.** With Herod it was different. In spite of his loose living, he was moved by John's life and message. **Observed him.** Better, he *protected him* and would not allow Herodias to kill him. **He did many things.** The most authentic reading says, *. . . he was perplexed.* The conflict between his admiration for John and the attraction of his sinful relationships kept him in a state of inner confusion. Nevertheless, he **heard** (Gr., *kept hearing*) him **gladly.**

**21.** Herodias had waited with cunning for **a convenient day** to penetrate Herod's defense of John. The elite of the governmental, military, and social circles were invited (**lords, high captains, chief estates,** respectively).

**22. The daughter** referred to was Salome, the child of Herodias by her previous marriage. It is estimated that the girl was no more than twenty years old at this time (Vincent Taylor, *Mark,* p. 314). For the daughter of a ruler to entertain nobility in this fashion was entirely out of place. It was the work of a slave, not of a princess. This, however, was Herodias' opportune moment (v. 21), and Herod, under the sway of liquor and sensuality, fell into her trap. **Sat with him.** Rather, *reclined with him* (see on 2:15).

**25.** The request of Herodias was marked by urgency. She wanted the deed accomplished before Herod could find a way to avoid it. Salome returned **straightway with haste** and asked that her request be granted, not **by and by** (AV), but *at once* (Gr.). **Charger.** An archaic word for a platter.

**26.** Although the request deeply grieved Herod, he found it impossible to go back on his oaths before such an august group. It was more important to save face than to preserve the life of God's prophet. It was no wonder that afterward his conscience troubled him (vv. 14,16).

**27.** Herod's palace at Machaerus was also a fortress and as such would have contained a **prison.** Thus the execution scene was not far removed from the banquet room.

28. And brought his head in a charger, and gave it to the damsel; and the damsel gave it to her mother.

29. And when his disciples heard *of it,* they came and took up his corpse, and laid it in a tomb.

30. And the apostles gathered themselves together unto Jesus, and told him all things, both what they had done, and what they had taught.

31. And he said unto them, Come ye yourselves apart into a desert place, and rest a while: for there were many coming and going, and they had no leisure so much as to eat.

32. And they departed into a desert place by ship privately.

33. And the people saw them departing, and many knew him, and ran afoot thither out of all cities, and outwent them, and came together unto him.

28. It appears that Salome remained in the dining hall until John had been executed and they **brought his head to her.** The apparent calmness with which she made the request and then carried the gory dish **to her mother** is indicative of the calloused nature of the girl.

30. Having completed the parenthetical explanation concerning the fate of John, Mark returns to the disciples and the preaching tour. He records nothing concerning the time consumed or the events that happened. He simply reports that the apostles came back together again. The designation, "apostle," is most appropriate here. The word speaks of one sent forth on a mission, and the disciples were returning from such an assignment.

### IV. Christ's Withdrawals from Galilee. 6:31—9:50.

The Lord had so thoroughly covered Galilee with his message that Galileans in every walk of life were aware of his ministry. Among many of the common people his popularity stood at such a peak that they were ready to set him up by force as their king. The antipathy of the Jewish religious leaders was dangerously near the boiling point. And Herod himself had now become exercised concerning the popularity of Christ. The situation was shaping up toward a premature crisis, while as yet the ministry of Christ had not been completed. The result was that Jesus made four systematic withdrawals from Galilee, one to the eastern shore of the sea (6:31-56), one to the region of Tyre and Sidon (7:24-30), one to Decapolis (7:31—8:9), and the fourth to Caesarea Philippi (8:10—9:50). During this time Christ was occupied with the training of the twelve disciples in preparation for the time of his death.

A. Withdrawal to the Eastern Shore of the Lake. 6:31-56. This section of the Gospel records the feeding of the five thousand (6:31-44), the miracle of walking on the water (6:45-52), and the healings on the plain of Gennesaret (6:53-56). Instead of being a period of rest and retirement from the crowds, it was a time of continued activity.

31. The **desert place** was probably on the northeast shore of the Sea of Galilee. It was not desert; the expression means "a deserted place, a wilderness." After the stress and strain of the preaching tour they needed to **rest a while.**

33. **Many knew him.** As people saw them leaving, they recognized (Gr. text)

34. And Jesus, when he came out, saw much people, and was moved with compassion toward them, because they were as sheep not having a shepherd: and he began to teach them many things.

35. And when the day was now far spent, his disciples came unto him, and said, This is a desert place, and now the time *is* far passed:

36. Send them away, that they may go into the country round about, and into the villages, and buy themselves bread: for they have nothing to eat.

37. He answered and said unto them, Give ye them to eat. And they say unto him, Shall we go and buy two hundred pennyworth of bread, and give them to eat?

38. He saith unto them, How many loaves have ye? go and see. And when they knew, they say, Five, and two fishes.

39. And he commanded them to make all sit down by companies upon the green grass.

40. And they sat down in ranks, by hundreds, and by fifties.

41. And when he had taken the five loaves and the two fishes, he looked up to heaven, and blessed, and brake the loaves, and gave *them* to his disciples to set before them; and the two fishes divided he among them all.

42. And they did all eat, and were filled.

43. And they took up twelve baskets full of the fragments, and of the fishes.

44. And they that did eat of the loaves were about five thousand men.

45. And straightway he constrained his disciples to get into the ship, and to go to the other side before unto Bethsaida, while he sent away the people.

46. And when he had sent them away, he departed into a mountain to pray.

47. And when even was come, the ship was in the midst of the sea, and he alone on the land.

them. That the crowds were able to anticipate where Christ was heading and to precede him there seems to confirm the view that the wilderness place (v. 31) was on the northeast shore of the lake.

**34.** When Jesus landed (AV, **came out**), it became apparent that he and his men would not be able to enjoy the planned period of rest. Nevertheless his reaction was not one of annoyance; instead he **was moved with compassion.** He saw the people in their need as shepherdless sheep, having no spiritual leader (cf. Num 27:17; I Kgs 22:17).

**36. Country.** Mark's word literally means *fields,* which probably refers to the farms of the countryside.

**37. Give ye.** The emphasis is on the subject, **ye.** The monetary term used here, **pennyworth,** is the word *dēnariōn,* the Roman denarius worth about eighteen cents at that time (Arndt, p. 178).

**40. In ranks.** The Greek term meant *a garden bed* (Arndt, p. 705). Mark's picture of the scene is that of groups of people scattered like beds of flowers on the green grass (v. 39). No doubt the variegated colors of the clothing served to create such an impression when seen at a distance.

**41.** The verbs **had taken, looked, blessed,** and **brake** are all in the aorist tense in Greek, signifying instantaneous action. But the verb **gave** is in the imperfect tense, showing, in contrast, that he kept giving to the disciples. It is at this point that the miracle of a multiplied supply occurred.

**43.** The astonishing fact was not that the people were merely filled, but that there was a superabundant supply. The **baskets** were large handbaskets used for carrying food. In general, however, they were smaller than the ones used at the feeding of the four thousand (see comments on 8:8).

**44.** The count of **five thousand** did not include women and children (cf. Mt 14:21).

**45.** Christ **constrained his disciples,** which is to say that he compelled them to enter the boat (not **ship**) and set sail **unto Bethsaida.** Evidently the place of the miracle was south of Bethsaida Julias (Lk 9:10), and Christ directed the disciples to sail to the town and meet him there. The reason for this abrupt dispersion of the people, as given by John (6:14,15), was the danger of a revolutionary attempt to make Jesus king.

**47. When even was come.** That is,

48. And he saw them toiling in rowing; for the wind was contrary unto them: and about the fourth watch of the night he cometh unto them, walking upon the sea, and would have passed by them.

49. But when they saw him walking upon the sea, they supposed it had been a spirit, and cried out:

50. For they all saw him, and were troubled. And immediately he talked with them, and saith unto them, Be of good cheer: it is I; be not afraid.

51. And he went up unto them into the ship; and the wind ceased: and they were sore amazed in themselves beyond measure, and wondered.

52. For they considered not *the miracle* of the loaves; for their heart was hardened.

53. And when they had passed over, they came into the land of Gennesaret, and drew to the shore.

54. And when they were come out of the ship, straightway they knew him,

55. And ran through that whole region round about, and began to carry about in beds those that were sick, where they heard he was.

56. And whithersoever he entered, into villages, or cities, or country, they laid the sick in the streets, and besought him that they might touch if it were but the border of his garment: and as many as touched him were made whole.

when six o'clock, the hour of sunset, had arrived.

**48.** Since it was not yet dark, he could still see them from the land **toiling in rowing. Toiling,** from a verb meaning *to torment* or *distress,* pictures the difficulty of the disciples as they attempted to row into the contrary wind. The **fourth watch of the night** lasted from three to six in the morning. Jesus delayed his coming to their aid from sunset until about 3:00 A.M. The statement that he **would have passed by them** should not pose any problem concerning Christ's sincerity. He was not walking directly toward the boat, so that to the disciples it appeared that he would have passed by if they had not cried out (v. 49). Rather than suddenly entering the boat, Jesus was, no doubt, giving them time to see him.

**49. A spirit.** This is not the Greek word for "spirit," but a term which means an *apparition.* They thought they were seeing a ghost.

**50. Be of good cheer.** This verb carries with it the idea of courage, which was probably the thought uppermost in the mind of Christ. The present tense prohibition, **be not afraid,** means *stop fearing.*

**51.** Without a word from Christ **the wind ceased** (Gr., *became weary*) its blowing. The astonishment that was gripping the disciples was the result of a double miracle. The Greek text omits the words, **and wondered.**

**52.** Not only had they forgotten that Christ had previously stilled the waves (4:39), but they did not understand (Gr. text) the miracle **of the loaves.** Because **their heart was hardened,** they did not grasp the truth concerning the deity of Christ which the miracles were continually demonstrating.

**53.** Jesus probably entered the boat somewhere off the shore from Bethsaida Julias, after which they **passed over** to the western shore of the lake again. **Gennesaret** was the name of a plain lying along the shore of the lake south of Capernaum. A small town of the same name was also located in the vicinity.

**55.** Mark provides a glimpse of the kind of scene that must have appeared many times when Jesus came to an area. The people hurried to bring their sick folk before Christ moved from their neighborhood.

**56. Besought him.** The repeated requests of person after person are depicted by this verb. This is the second reference in Mark to healings effected by touching Christ's garment (cf. 5:27-29).

141

## CHAPTER 7

THEN came together unto him the Pharisees, and certain of the scribes, which came from Jerusalem.

2. And when they saw some of his disciples eat bread with defiled, that is to say, with unwashen hands, they found fault.

3. For the Pharisees, and all the Jews, except they wash *their* hands oft, eat not, holding the tradition of the elders.

4. And *when they come* from the market, except they wash, they eat not. And many other things there be, which they have received to hold, *as* the washing of cups, and pots, brazen vessels, and of tables.

5. Then the Pharisees and scribes asked him, Why walk not thy disciples according to the tradition of the elders, but eat bread with unwashen hands?

6. He answered and said unto them, Well hath Esaias prophesied of you hypocrites, as it is written, This people honoreth me with *their* lips, but their heart is far from me.

7. Howbeit in vain do they worship me, teaching *for* doctrines the commandments of men.

8. For laying aside the commandment of God, ye hold the tradition of men, *as* the washing of pots and cups: and many other such like things ye do.

9. And he said unto them, Full well ye reject the commandment of God, that ye may keep your own tradition.

10. For Moses said, Honor thy father and thy mother; and, Whoso curseth father or mother, let him die the death:

11. But ye say, If a man shall say to his father or mother, *It is* Corban, that is to say, a gift, by whatsoever thou mightest be profited by me; *he shall be free.*

B. Discussion of the Unwarranted Exaltation of Tradition. 7:1-23. These verses record the clash between Christ and the Pharisees on the basic issue of the source of authority. Does tradition carry divine authority? Is it equal to, or superior to, the written Word of God? Also involved here is the discussion of the real nature of defilement and cleansing. The setting for this section apparently was the vicinity of Capernaum.

2. Mark's explanation of Jewish customs is noteworthy, indicating as it does that this Gospel was written for Gentile consumption. **Defiled . . . hands.** Hands ceremonially unclean. **They found fault** does not appear in the best manuscripts. The sentence is left incomplete as Mark breaks off to introduce the explanation of verses 3,4.

3. **The Pharisees** had so extended their influence that the washing of the hands had, in a general way, become the practice of **all the Jews.** The Greek text does not support the use of the word **oft.** Instead it reads *with a fist,* probably referring to the act of rubbing the fist of one hand in the palm of the other when washing. The **tradition of the elders** was the unwritten corpus of commands and teachings of the honored rabbis of the past, a body of 613 rules designed to regulate every aspect of life.

6. Jesus did not mean that Isaiah specifically predicted the practices of the first century Jews, but rather that Isaiah's words concerning the people of his own day were applicable also to the Jews of Christ's day. The quotation is from Isa 29:13, following the LXX with slight alteration. The term **hypocrites** is an epithet well chosen, for it referred originally to an actor who wore a mask and appeared to be what he really was not.

8. The main point of the quotation from Isaiah concerns the substitution of **the tradition of men** for **the commandment of God.** This is not an overstatement, for the Pharisees viewed oral tradition as being more authoritative than the written law of the OT.

10. In 7:9-13 this exaltation of tradition is given specific illustration. The law of **Moses** concerning honor to parents is quoted. The first citation is from Deut 5:16 and is identical with both the Hebrew and the LXX. The second, which is from Ex 21:17, follows the Hebrew text very closely.

11. In contrast Christ cites the rabbinical tradition that sets aside the God-given Mosaic commandment. **Corban** is the

12. And ye suffer him no more to do aught for his father or his mother;

13. Making the word of God of none effect through your tradition, which ye have delivered: and many such like things do ye.

14. And when he had called all the people *unto him*, he said unto them, Hearken unto me every one *of you*, and understand:

15. There is nothing from without a man, that entering into him can defile him: but the things which come out of him, those are they that defile the man.

16. If any man have ears to hear, let him hear.

17. And when he was entered into the house from the people, his disciples asked him concerning the parable.

18. And he saith unto them, Are ye so without understanding also? Do ye not perceive, that whatsoever thing from without entereth into the man, *it* cannot defile him;

19. Because it entereth not into his heart, but into the belly, and goeth out into the draught, purging all meats?

20. And he said, That which cometh out of the man, that defileth the man.

21. For from within, out of the heart of men, proceed evil thoughts, adulteries, fornications, murders,

22. Thefts, covetousness, wickedness, deceit, lasciviousness, an evil eye, blasphemy, pride, foolishness:

transliteration of a Hebrew word meaning a gift, as Mark explains for the benefit of his Gentile readers. The word was used to refer to something devoted to God by a vow which was inviolable. If a son declared that the amount needed to support his parents was **Corban**, that vow was unalterable, even setting aside the Mosaic command.

13. The **word of God** is placed in sharp contrast to tradition of men. Notice that Christ viewed the Mosaic law as having been spoken by God. To make **of none effect** is to make void or to nullify. The present tense, **do ye**, speaks of habitual practice.

14. In verses 14-16 the Lord returns to the subject of defilement and cleansing, but here he is speaking not only to the Pharisees and scribes but to the crowd whom **he had called** together. Subsequently Christ discusses the matter with his disciples (7:17-23).

15. **Nothing from without a man**—that is, nothing physical—can defile him morally or spiritually. In the case under discussion (v. 2), eating with unwashed hands cannot produce spiritual uncleanness. Such defilement is internal in origin. A man is defiled by thoughts that originate in the heart and come out in the forms of words or actions. Herein Jesus explained the spiritual significance of the laws of the clean and unclean (Lev 11). One of the reasons why they were given was to teach this very truth of spiritual defilement, but these Jewish leaders never got beyond the mere externals.

19. The **heart** in Biblical usage is not merely the seat of the emotions but also the place of mental and volitional activity. It refers to the inner, nonphysical man. **The belly** refers to the body cavity that contains the stomach and intestines. After the digestive process is complete, the remainder passes **out into the draught**, that is, into the drain. The AV does not make clear what is meant by the phrase, **purging all meats**. The best explanation is that it should be connected with **he saith** (v. 18). Jesus, by his explanation in 7:18,19, declared all food to be 'clean.' He set aside the Levitical distinction between the clean and unclean (cf. Acts 10:14,15).

20-22. These verses contain Jesus' explanation of what he meant by **that which cometh out of the man.** The **evil thoughts** are to be understood as being evil reasonings or designs, deliberate thoughts. The word for **deceit** carries the more potent connotation of treachery. **Lasciviousness** is uncontrolled and unconcealed immorality. The words, **evil eye,** in any other

23. All these evil things come from within, and defile the man.

24. And from thence he arose, and went into the borders of Tyre and Sidon, and entered into a house, and would have no man know *it:* but he could not be hid.

25. For a *certain* woman, whose young daughter had an unclean spirit, heard of him, and came and fell at his feet:

26. The woman was a Greek, a Syrophenician by nation; and she besought him that he would cast forth the devil out of her daughter.

27. But Jesus said unto her, Let the children first be filled: for it is not meet to take the children's bread, and to cast *it* unto the dogs.

28. And she answered and said unto him, Yes, Lord: yet the dogs under the table eat of the children's crumbs.

29. And he said unto her, For this saying go thy way; the devil is gone out of thy daughter.

30. And when she was come to her house, she found the devil gone out, and her daughter laid upon the bed.

culture than that of the Jews, could refer to the casting of a spell. Among the Jews, however, it is an expression for envy. In this context **foolishness** is more moral than intellectual.

C. Withdrawal to the Region of Tyre and Sidon. 7:24-30. In this brief section Mark reports a rather lengthy journey of Christ to the region of Phoenicia, where the incident with the Syrophoenician woman occurred.

**24. The borders of Tyre and Sidon.** An idiomatic expression for the region of Tyre and Sidon. This was the only time, so far as the record goes, when Christ went out of Palestine into strictly Gentile territory. His purpose on these tours outside Galilee was not primarily to minister to the multitudes, but to instruct his disciples, which is the reason why he **would have no man know** that he was there.

**26. A Greek.** This is the same as identifying the woman as a Gentile. By birth she was a Syrian of the region of Phoenicia. **She besought him.** Mark's use of the Greek imperfect tense pictures the repeated request of the woman. **Devil.** Should be translated *demon.*

**27.** Jesus used the term **children** to represent the Jews. His mission was first to the Jews in order that they might, in turn, fulfill their duty of becoming a blessing to all nations through the world-wide proclamation of the Gospel. **The dogs.** This was a common Jewish term of reproach applied to Gentiles. However, it is softened by the use of the diminutive form meaning "little dogs" or "puppies." These were the family pets, not the wild dogs of the street.

**28.** The woman's undaunted reply was the response of faith. **The dogs under the table.** Taking up Christ's diminutive term for dogs, she paints a touching scene of the puppies licking up the crumbs dropped by the children. All she asked was a crumb of the blessings available to the Jews.

**29.** Jesus recognized in **this saying** of the woman the evidence of genuine faith (cf. Mt 15:28). Already as He spoke the demon had left (Gr. perf. tense) her daughter. The unique feature of this miracle was that it was performed at a distance without any vocal command of Christ.

D. Withdrawal to Decapolis. 7:31—8:9. The return from the region of Tyre and Sidon did not take Christ back to Galilee; instead his route skirted the eastern shore of the lake, leading him into the Decapolis. There Jesus healed the deaf man who had

31. And again, departing from the coasts of Tyre and Sidon, he came unto the sea of Galilee, through the midst of the coasts of Decapolis.

32. And they bring unto him one that was deaf, and had an impediment in his speech; and they beseech him to put his hand upon him.

33. And he took him aside from the multitude, and put his fingers into his ears, and he spit, and touched his tongue;

34. And looking up to heaven, he sighed, and saith unto him, Ephphatha, that is, Be opened.

35. And straightway his ears were opened, and the string of his tongue was loosed, and he spake plain.

36. And he charged them that they should tell no man: but the more he charged them, so much the more a great deal they published it;

37. And were beyond measure astonished, saying, He hath done all things well: he maketh both the deaf to hear, and the dumb to speak.

## CHAPTER 8

IN those days the multitude being very great, and having nothing to eat, Jesus called his disciples unto him, and saith unto them,

2. I have compassion on the multitude, because they have now been with me three days, and have nothing to eat:

an impediment of speech (7:31-37), and he fed the crowd of 4,000.

31. Mark is the most explicit of the Gospel writers at this point. He tells us that Jesus left the region of Tyre and passed through Sidon (so the best Gr. MSS) approximately twenty-five miles to the north, going deep into Gentile territory. Then turning south he passed along the eastern shore of the Sea of Galilee into the region of Decapolis (see comments on 5:20).

32. The extent of the impediment of speech is debatable. Mogilalon may be used of one who is completely mute, but its literal meaning is speaking with difficulty. The statement of 7:35 that he spoke plainly seems to indicate that previously he had not been able to speak clearly. However, the exclamation of the people in 7:37 was that he made the speechless (Gr.) to speak.

33. That it was not necessary for the Lord to touch a person in order to heal him had been demonstrated previously (cf. 2:3-12; 3:5; 7:29,30). Here Jesus put his fingers into the deaf man's ears to indicate what He was going to do for him and thus to help him to believe. Two other symbolical acts followed. He spit and He touched his tongue. The text does not say that He applied the saliva to the tongue.

34. He sighed. The word may refer to a groan. Perhaps this was an expression of sympathy or of distress because of the suffering of mankind. Ephphatha. An Aramaic word that Mark translates for his Gentile readers.

35. The string of his tongue. The bond (Gr.) which held his tongue was released. Plain. He began to speak rightly or plainly.

36. Christ still needed to avoid excessive publicity (cf. on 5:43). However, the people would not be stilled. They kept proclaiming (Gr. imp. tense) the miracle all the more exceedingly.

37. Beyond measure. The astonishment of the people exceeded all bounds. Mark uses a very strong word here (hyperperissōs).

8:1. The feeding of the four thousand is not given a specific setting other than the general statement that it occurred in a wilderness place (v. 4). In those days. The Greek text adds the word "again," probably with reference to the recent feeding of the five thousand.

2. Jesus was moved with compassion toward these people just as he had been on the occasion of the feeding of the five thousand (6:34), but here his concern was

**3.** And if I send them away fasting to their own houses, they will faint by the way: for divers of them came from far.

**4.** And his disciples answered him, From whence can a man satisfy these *men* with bread here in the wilderness?

**5.** And he asked them, How many loaves have ye? And they said, Seven.

**6.** And he commanded the people to sit down on the ground: and he took the seven loaves, and gave thanks, and brake, and gave to his disciples to set before *them;* and they did set *them* before the people.

**7.** And they had a few small fishes: and he blessed, and commanded to set them also before *them.*

**8.** So they did eat, and were filled: and they took up of the broken *meat* that was left seven baskets.

**9.** And they that had eaten were about four thousand: and he sent them away.

**10.** And straightway he entered into a ship with his disciples, and came into the parts of Dalmanutha.

**11.** And the Pharisees came forth, and began to question with him, seeking of him a sign from heaven, tempting him.

caused by their physical need rather than by their spiritual condition.

**6.** Here, as in the feeding of the five thousand, the words **took, gave thanks,** and **brake** are all in the aorist tense in Greek, but the word **gave** is in the imperfect tense, showing that Christ kept giving the bread to the disciples for distribution (cf. 6:41).

**8.** The sufficiency of the miracle is seen in the statements that they **were filled** and that there was an abundance (Gr.) that **was left.** The word **meat,** inserted by the translators of the AV, refers to food in general. These **baskets** were a different type than those used after the feeding of the five thousand. This is indicated by the distinction made between two kinds in 8:19,20 (Gr. text). The kind of basket used this time was often quite large. It was the kind used to let Saul down over the wall at Damascus (Acts 9:25). Thus the seven hampers of 8:8 probably held more than the twelve provision baskets of 6:43.

E. Withdrawal to Caesarea Philippi. 8:10–9:50. The fourth and last withdrawal from Galilee was northward into the region of Caesarea Philippi. Coming from Decapolis, Jesus crossed to the west coast of the Sea of Galilee, where the Pharisees met him with a request for a sign (8:10-12). He then traveled by boat in a northeasterly direction to Bethsaida Julias (8:13-21), where he healed a blind man (8:22-26). From there his journey took him overland to the vicinity of Caesarea Philippi. Here again, Christ's main activity was that of instructing his disciples concerning such themes as his person, his death and resurrection, their discipleship, and his coming in glory as prefigured by the Transfiguration (8:27–9:13). Here also he cured another demoniac (9:14-29). Following this, Christ returned to Galilee, still continuing the instruction of the Twelve (9:30-50).

**10.** At the present time scholars cannot pinpoint the town of **Dalmanutha** with any degree of certainty. The context seems to assume a location across the sea from Bethsaida, probably on the western shore (cf. vv. 13,22). Matthew calls it Magadan (Mt 15:39; Gr. text), a place equally unknown to us today.

**11. The Pharisees** were asking for a sensational sign from God which would prove that Jesus was the Messiah. **Tempting him.** The Greek word *peirazō* means "to test." Rather than attempting to entice Jesus to sin, they were putting him to the test of their unbelieving minds.

**12.** And he sighed deeply in his spirit, and saith, Why doth this generation seek after a sign? verily I say unto you, There shall no sign be given unto this generation.

**13.** And he left them, and entering into the ship again departed to the other side.

**14.** Now *the disciples* had forgotten to take bread, neither had they in the ship with them more than one loaf.

**15.** And he charged them, saying, Take heed, beware of the leaven of the Pharisees, and *of* the leaven of Herod.

**16.** And they reasoned among themselves, saying, *It is* because we have no bread.

**17.** And when Jesus knew *it*, he saith unto them, Why reason ye, because ye have no bread? perceive ye not yet, neither understand? have ye your heart yet hardened?

**18.** Having eyes, see ye not? and having ears, hear ye not? and do ye not remember?

**19.** When I brake the five loaves among five thousand, how many baskets full of fragments took ye up? They say unto him, Twelve.

**20.** And when the seven among four thousand, how many baskets full of fragments took ye up? And they said, Seven.

**21.** And he said unto them, How is it that ye do not understand?

**22.** And he cometh to Bethsaida; and they bring a blind man unto him, and besought him to touch him.

**23.** And he took the blind man by the hand, and led him out of the town; and when he had spit on his eyes, and put his hands upon him, he asked him if he saw aught.

**24.** And he looked up, and said, I see men as trees, walking.

**25.** After that he put *his* hands again upon his eyes, and made him look up; and he was restored, and saw every man clearly.

**26.** And he sent him away to his house, saying, Neither go into the town, nor tell *it* to any in the town.

**27.** And Jesus went out, and his disciples, into the towns of Caesarea Philippi: and by the way he asked his disciples, saying unto them, Whom do men say that I am?

**12.** Such persistent refusal to believe caused Christ to sigh **deeply in his spirit.** The word, appearing here in its intensified form, probably means that he actually groaned as the sense of weariness and grief penetrated to the depths of his heart. The question of Christ is better translated, *Why is this generation continually seeking a sign?* (cf. Jn 2:18; Mt 12:38). Matthew adds an exception to the statement of Christ that **no sign** would be given (Mt 16:4). The sign of Jonah is explained in Mt 12:39,40 as referring to Christ's resurrection, the most significant miracle of all.

**15.** Jesus **charged them** repeatedly (Gr. imp. tense), showing the urgent need to be continually on guard (Gr. pres. tense, **Take heed, beware**). Leaven is here used to symbolize something with a dangerously pervasive influence. Luke 12:1 explains that **the leaven of the Pharisees** is hypocrisy. The **leaven of Herod** may be the influence of the Herodians, which was a spirit of worldliness, an infectious secularism.

**19,20.** The disciples had so soon forgotten the lessons inherent in the feedings of the **five thousand** and the **four thousand**. The Son of God does not need to worry about food for thirteen men on a short voyage across the lake. He had but recently demonstrated his power to supply food for more than nine thousand persons.

**22.** The healing of the **blind man** occurred when Jesus passed through **Bethsaida** Julias on his way to Caesarea Philippi.

**23.** Jesus **led him out of the town**, probably to avoid excessive publicity (cf. v. 26). Here, as in the case of the deaf man (7:33), saliva was used, not as a healing application, but as an aid to the sightless man's faith.

**24.** This healing was unique in that it consisted of two stages. After the first healing acts, the man saw people indistinctly as moving objects, like **trees walking.**

**25.** The second stage of healing was preceded by the touching of the eyes. The Greek text does not say that Jesus **made him look up,** but rather that the man *looked intently.* And when he did so, he began to see all things **clearly.**

**26.** Again in order to avoid the results of undue publicity, Christ sent the man **to his house.** That He told him not to **go into the town** indicates that he lived elsewhere, perhaps in the surrounding countryside.

**27.** Going north from Bethsaida, Christ came to **the towns of Caesarea Philippi.** Matthew (16:13) explains that he came into the *parts* (Gr.) or the region of Cae-

28. And they answered, John the Baptist: but some *say*, Elias; and others, One of the prophets.

29. And he saith unto them, But whom say ye that I am? And Peter answereth and saith unto him, Thou art the Christ.

30. And he charged them that they should tell no man of him.

31. And he began to teach them, that the Son of man must suffer many things, and be rejected of the elders, and *of* the chief priests, and scribes, and be killed, and after three days rise again.

32. And he spake that saying openly. And Peter took him, and began to rebuke him.

33. But when he had turned about and looked on his disciples, he rebuked Peter, saying, Get thee behind me, Satan: for thou savorest not the things that be of God, but the things that be of men.

34. And when he had called the people *unto him* with his disciples also, he said unto them, Whosoever will come after me, let him deny himself, and take up his cross, and follow me.

sarea. Mark has reference to the villages located in the country surrounding the larger city. This Caesarea, located in the northwest section of the tetrarchy of Philip, was designated Philippi to distinguish it from Caesarea on the Mediterranean coast.

**29. Whom say ye.** This was the point at which Christ was aiming. The emphasis is on the word "you." "But *you* (in contrast to others), who do *you* say that I am?" **Peter** acted as spokesman for the disciples. His confession of Jesus as **the Christ** is more fully given in Mt 16:16, which adds the words, "the Son of the living God." Jesus is both the promised Messiah and the unique Son of God.

**30.** Here again Christ commanded silence, probably because of the revolutionary ideas connected with the Messianic concept. Christ was not ready at that time to establish an earthly Messianic kingdom.

**31.** Instead, at his first coming Christ was to **suffer,** and **be killed,** and **rise again.** Particular attention should be given to the sharp contrast between the glowing confession of Peter and Christ's immediate declaration of suffering and death. Notice that the One who was to die was designated by the Messianic title, **Son of man.** The cross was a necessary aspect of Messiah's work. He **must suffer.**

**32. He spake . . . openly.** The Greek imperfect tense is used to show that Jesus began and continued to speak of his death. No longer did he refer to it in veiled fashion (cf. Jn 2:19), but from this time on he instructed his disciples **openly** and explicitly concerning the fact. This was the next stage in their training. **Peter took him** aside and rebuked him for speaking in such a manner. In Peter's mind violent death did not harmonize with Messianic dignity.

**33.** Peter's attempt to dissuade the Lord from going to the cross was similar to the temptation in the wilderness. In this instance, **Satan** with great subtilty, used one of Christ's closest disciples (cf. Lk 4:13, RSV). Notice the similar rebuke in Mt 4:10. **Savourest.** The Greek verb refers to the set of the mind, the direction of thought. Peter's mind was running contrary to the purposes of God.

**34.** The instruction recorded in 8:34-38 is the natural outgrowth of the fact of Christ's suffering. **Whosoever will come after** Christ must walk the path which he walked, the path of denial and cross-bearing. The **cross** is the symbol of suffering, and self-denial speaks of readiness to suffer for someone else. Christ is the pattern;

35. For whosoever will save his life shall lose it; but whosoever shall lose his life for my sake and the gospel's, the same shall save it.

36. For what shall it profit a man, if he shall gain the whole world, and lose his own soul?

37. Or what shall a man give in exchange for his soul?

38. Whosoever therefore shall be ashamed of me and of my words, in this adulterous and sinful generation, of him also shall the Son of man be ashamed, when he cometh in the glory of his Father with the holy angels.

## CHAPTER 9

AND he said unto them, Verily I say unto you, That there be some of them that stand here, which shall not taste of death, till they have seen the kingdom of God come with power.

2. And after six days Jesus taketh *with him* Peter, and James, and John, and leadeth them up into a high mountain apart by themselves: and he was transfigured before them.

the disciple is to keep following him (Gr. pres. imperative).

35. The paradox of these verses is resolved by understanding that the Lord used the term **life** in two different senses. The first expression, **save his life**, has reference to the preservation of physical life from death. The person who is completely devoted to the protection of this life will miss the life that is eternal. On the contrary, the person who is so devoted to Christ that he is willing to **lose his life** is the person who gains true life. He finds that **to die is gain** (Phil 1:21). This is not a description of the way of salvation for the lost, but rather of the philosophy of life for the disciple.

36. Here the contrast is between **world** and **soul**. The latter term is the same as **life** in verse 35. Both are translations of *psyche*. This principle applies on the physical level as well as on the spiritual. What is the value of obtaining all that the world has to offer if a person dies and cannot enjoy it? Or, what is the good of amassing a world of earthly possessions for a few short years if it means the loss of eternal life.

38. When Christ used the expression, **ashamed of me and of my words**, he was drawing a contrast with the attitude of willingness to lose one's life for his sake and the Gospel's (v. 35). To **be ashamed** is to deny Christ in the hour of trial rather than to own him at the risk of death. It is to take one's stand with this **sinful generation** instead of with Christ. **Adulterous.** Used spiritually to describe unfaithfulness to God. In like manner, when the Lord comes as Judge, he will **be ashamed** and will disown those who have disowned him.

9:1. The chapter division here is unfortunate, since this verse is clearly the conclusion of the discourse recorded in the last part of Mark 8. **Verily** is a term of solemn assurance. It is the Greek word *amen*, from which our "amen" is derived. **Shall not taste of death.** The original is much stronger—*shall by no means taste of death*. The coming of **the kingdom of God** in this statement has been variously interpreted. However, in the preceding verse Christ speaks of his advent in glory, and in the following verses Mark records the Transfiguration. The coming of the Kingdom may well be identical with the glorious coming of the King (8:38), of which Christ's transfiguration was a foretaste.

2. The **high mountain** was traditionally identified as Mount Tabor in Galilee, but this is too far from Caesarea Philippi.

3. And his raiment became shining, exceeding white as snow; so as no fuller on earth can white them.

4. And there appeared unto them Elias with Moses: and they were talking with Jesus.

5. And Peter answered and said to Jesus, Master, it is good for us to be here: and let us make three tabernacles; one for thee, and one for Moses, and one for Elias.

6. For he wist not what to say; for they were sore afraid.

7. And there was a cloud that overshadowed them: and a voice came out of the cloud, saying, This is my beloved Son: hear him.

8. And suddenly, when they had looked round about, they saw no man any more, save Jesus only with themselves.

9. And as they came down from the mountain, he charged them that they should tell no man what things they had seen, till the Son of man were risen from the dead.

10. And they kept that saying with themselves, questioning one with another what the rising from the dead should mean.

11. And they asked him, saying, Why say the scribes that Elias must first come?

12. And he answered and told them, Elias verily cometh first, and restoreth all things; and how it is written of the Son of man, that he must suffer many things, and be set at nought.

13. But I say unto you, That Elias is indeed come, and they have done unto him whatsoever they listed, as it is written of him.

Mount Hermon seems to fit the description more satisfactorily. **Transfigured.** From the Greek *metamorphoō* (source of our word "metamorphosis"), which refers to a change of essential form, not a superficial change of outward appearance. Our Lord's human body was glorified, and it is in this glorified body that he will some day come to establish his kingdom.

3. **As snow.** Not found in the best Greek manuscripts. A **fuller** is one who treats new cloth, shrinking and cleansing it.

4. **Elias** is a transliteration of the Greek word for *Elijah*. Why Moses and Elijah were the two chosen to appear is not stated. It is noteworthy that both left this life under unusual circumstances. Furthermore, Moses represented the Law, while Elijah was one of the prophets. Luke's Gospel (9:31) states that the subject of their conversation was the imminent death of Christ, a theme which runs through the OT, both in the Law and in the Prophets.

6. **Wist.** Old English word for "knew." **Sore afraid.** They were terrified.

9. The charge that they should tell no man was in keeping with Jesus' policy of restraint lest the current erroneous Messianic ideas be fanned into flames. After the Resurrection the danger of precipitating a popular uprising would no longer be present. Then the experience on the mount would have spiritual value for the disciples as a confirmation of their faith (cf. II Pet 1:16-18).

11. The question concerning Elijah arose because of the presence of the prophet at the Transfiguration. **The scribes,** in this instance, drew their teaching from Mal 4:5,6. It may have been that the disciples were wondering if the appearance on the mount was the fulfillment of the prediction.

12. This prophecy received confirmation by the Lord, and the tense used (futuristic present) indicates that it shall be fulfilled in the future. Elijah is going to come and restore all things (cf. Mal 4:6) before the Messiah comes. **How it is written.** Most students view the remainder of this verse as a question, "How is it written . . . ?" The coming of Elijah was predicted in the Scriptures. What about the predictions that the Messiah should suffer and be rejected? Christ was attempting to stir the thinking of his followers that they might understand that the Son of man must first suffer before the coming of Elijah and the glorious advent of Messiah.

13. But there was a sense in which Elijah had already come. Matthew 17:13 explains that He was speaking of John the

14. And when he came to *his* disciples, he saw a great multitude about them, and the scribes questioning with them.

15. And straightway all the people, when they beheld him, were greatly amazed, and running to *him* saluted him.

16. And he asked the scribes, What question ye with them?

17. And one of the multitude answered and said, Master, I have brought unto thee my son, which hath a dumb spirit;

18. And wheresoever he taketh him, he teareth him; and he foameth, and gnasheth with his teeth, and pineth away: and I spake to thy disciples that they should cast him out; and they could not.

19. He answereth him, and saith, O faithless generation, how long shall I be with you? how long shall I suffer you? bring him unto me.

20. And they brought him unto him: and when he saw him, straightway the spirit tare him; and he fell on the ground, and wallowed foaming.

21. And he asked his father, How long is it ago since this came unto him? And he said, Of a child.

22. And ofttimes it hath cast him into the fire, and into the waters, to destroy him: but if thou canst do any thing, have compassion on us, and help us.

23. Jesus said unto him, If thou canst believe, all things *are* possible to him that believeth.

24. And straightway the father of the child cried out, and said with tears, Lord, I believe; help thou mine unbelief.

25. When Jesus saw that the people came running together, he rebuked the foul spirit, saying unto him, *Thou* dumb and deaf spirit, I charge thee, come out of him, and enter no more into him.

26. And *the spirit* cried, and rent him sore, and came out of him: and he was as one dead; insomuch that many said, He is dead.

27. But Jesus took him by the hand, and lifted him up; and he arose.

28. And when he was come into the house, his disciples asked him privately, Why could not we cast him out?

29. And he said unto them, This kind can come forth by nothing, but by prayer and fasting.

Baptist. This was not to say that John was Elijah in person, but that he came in the likeness of Elijah (cf. Lk 1:17; Jn 1:21). **Whatsoever they listed.** That is, they did with him what they desired, referring to his death at the request of Herodias.

**15. Greatly amazed.** The explanations of this amazement can all be reduced to two possibilities. One, they were amazed because of the remaining glow of the Transfiguration on Jesus' face. Two, the amazement was caused by the opportune but unexpected appearance of Jesus at the moment of the embarrassing defeat of the nine disciples. The first view is rendered improbable by the absence of any statement concerning a continuing glow on Jesus' face.

**17.** The **dumb spirit** was a demon that afflicted the boy with dumbness and deafness (v. 25).

**18. Taketh him.** The father described the action of the demon in seizing or laying hold on the boy. His reaction appears to have been similar to that of an epileptic fit.

**19.** It is clear that the disciples were weak because of unbelief. The disappointment of our Lord seems almost to verge on impatience. Suffer. Literally, *How long shall I put up with you?*

**20. Tare.** This is a strong word meaning that he convulsed the boy with such violence that it seemed he would tear him in pieces. **Wallowed.** The Greek word means *to roll*. The imperfect tense should be translated, *He kept rolling.*

**23. If thou canst.** In the Greek text an article precedes this whole clause for the purpose of drawing attention to it. It is as though Jesus said, "Consider this clause— if thou canst." The word **believe** does not appear in the best manuscripts. Having called specific attention to the man's **if,** Jesus proceeded to show his need for faith.

**24.** The anguish that filled the father's heart is portrayed by his immediate response as he **cried out** in almost contradictory ejaculations. He did **believe,** and yet he was acutely conscious of the **unbelief** that struggled with his desire to trust implicitly. His unbelief was not an obstinate refusal to believe; it was a weakness with which the man himself could not deal. Hence his cry to Christ for help.

**29. This kind.** An indication that there are different types of demons. It seems that the one indwelling this boy was unusually vicious and powerful. From Jesus' previous remark about unbelief (v. 19) and from the statement in this verse concerning the need of **prayer,** it is apparent that the nine

30. And they departed thence, and passed through Galilee; and he would not that any man should know *it*.

31. For he taught his disciples, and said unto them, The Son of man is delivered into the hands of men, and they shall kill him; and after that he is killed, he shall rise the third day.

32. But they understood not that saying, and were afraid to ask him.

33. And he came to Capernaum: and being in the house he asked them, What was it that ye disputed among yourselves by the way?

34. But they held their peace: for by the way they had disputed among themselves, who *should be* the greatest.

35. And he sat down, and called the twelve, and saith unto them, If any man desire to be first, *the same* shall be last of all, and servant of all.

36. And he took a child, and set him in the midst of them: and when he had taken him in his arms, he said unto them,

37. Whosoever shall receive one of such children in my name, receiveth me; and whosoever shall receive me, receiveth not me, but him that sent me.

38. And John answered him, saying, Master, we saw one casting out devils in thy name, and he followeth not us; and we forbade him, because he followeth not us.

39. But Jesus said, Forbid him not: for there is no man which shall do a miracle in my name, that can lightly speak evil of me.

disciples had attempted to cast out the demon without relying upon God's power (cf. Mt 17:20). Unbelief and prayerlessness are sure to result in spiritual impotency. Many of the best Greek manuscripts omit the reference to **fasting,** as well as the parallel passage in Mt 17:21. It is to be noted that there would have been no opportunity for the disciples to meet this situation with fasting, but they surely could have trusted and prayed.

**31. He taught his disciples.** This had been the Lord's main occupation during the withdrawals, and still he continued instructing them (Gr. imp. tense), for they were slow to comprehend (v. 32). The heart of his teaching was his coming death and resurrection.

**33.** The return to **Capernaum** brought him again to **the house** of Peter, which had been the headquarters for his Galilean campaign. The verb, **asked,** is in the imperfect tense, probably to indicate that Jesus continued to question the disciples concerning their discussion on the road.

**34.** Instead of replying to Jesus' interrogation, **they held their peace.** Again the imperfect tense shows that they persisted in their silence. They were ashamed to reveal the unworthy subject of their discussion. He had tried to explain his coming death, but their minds were occupied with thoughts of personal greatness in the Messianic kingdom (cf. Mt 18:1).

**36,37.** The humble act of receiving one child in Christ's name is a deed of true greatness. It is this willingness to take the lowly position of service, even to a child in arms, which is the mark of genuine stature; for to do so is to render service to Christ and, through him, to the Father. This involves the humbling of one's self as a little child (see Mt 18:4).

**38.** Perhaps a desire to change the subject led **John** to speak. Apparently Jesus' remark concerning acts done in his name reminded John of the exorcist whom they had seen and who used the **name** of Jesus. **Master.** This is the word for "teacher." **We forbad him.** They kept on forbidding this unknown miracle worker (imp. tense). Their reason, **he followeth not us,** reveals a basically selfish attitude, an unwillingness to accept anyone except those of their own circle. Scofield calls this sectarianism.

**39. Forbid him not.** Literally, *Stop forbidding him.* Jesus did not quibble about details. If the man was using Christ's name in a sincere effort to help others, he was not to be hindered. A breadth of spirit that ought to characterize God's people is evidenced here. Our Lord's logic was two-

**40.** For he that is not against us is on our part.

**41.** For whosoever shall give you a cup of water to drink in my name, because ye belong to Christ, verily I say unto you, he shall not lose his reward.

**42.** And whosoever shall offend one of *these* little ones that believe in me, it is better for him that a millstone were hanged about his neck, and he were cast into the sea.

**43.** And if thy hand offend thee, cut it off: it is better for thee to enter into life maimed, than having two hands to go into hell, into the fire that never shall be quenched:

**44.** Where their worm dieth not, and the fire is not quenched.

**45.** And if thy foot offend thee, cut it off: it is better for thee to enter halt into life, than having two feet to be cast into hell, into the fire that never shall be quenched:

**46.** Where their worm dieth not, and the fire is not quenched.

**47.** And if thine eye offend thee, pluck it out: it is better for thee to enter into the kingdom of God with one eye, than having two eyes to be cast into hell fire:

fold. First, such a man would not soon turn against Christ after working miracles in His name.

**40.** The second reason for Christ's prohibition was that since the man was not against Christ and the disciples, then to some extent he was on their side.

**41.** This verse further emphasizes the breadth of attitude displayed in 9:39,40. No one who is seeking to serve the Lord, no matter how seemingly unimportant his service may be, is excluded from Christ's circle. The importance of this principle is seen in the use of the word **verily** *(amēn)*, and in the strong double negative which may be translated, . . . **will by no means lose his reward** (RSV).

**42.** The thought of this verse is linked to that of 9:37 by the term **little ones.** Likewise, verses 42-48 are related, being centered around the idea of offenses. It is possible that the action of the disciples in rebuking the anonymous exorcist (v. 38) may have offended him. This would explain why Christ discussed offenses at this point. The undeveloped faith of the exorcist was not to be hindered but encouraged. Harsh criticism of spiritual immaturity may only serve to drive persons away from the Lord. **Offend.** The Greek word *skandalizō* means to place a snare or trap in a person's way, causing him to stumble. The **little ones** may be taken literally as referring to children that believe, or they may be those who are little in faith or spiritually undeveloped. Probably the latter is the intention of Jesus. The **millstone** was the large flat stone turned by a donkey in grinding grain.

**43.** Jesus turned from the offense of others to the offense of one's self. It is possible for a person to place a stumbling block in his own way. Undoubtedly the command to **cut . . . off** the offending **hand** is figurative and hyperbolic. The sense of the verse is that anything which causes a person to fall into sin should be removed immediately. These verses are not to be taken literally as commanding an extreme asceticism. It must be remembered that the seat of sin is the soul, not any organ of the physical body. **Enter into life.** The parallel expression in 9:47 is **enter into the kingdom of God.** These terms are the opposites of **hell** and are to be understood as referring to the life of the saved in the eternal kingdom. **Hell** is the translation of the Greek *geenna,* which in turn is a transliteration of the Hebrew *gê hinnōm,* meaning "valley of Hinnom." This was a valley southwest of Jerusalem which was accursed because it had been the scene of

**48.** Where their worm dieth not, and the fire is not quenched.

**49.** For every one shall be salted with fire, and every sacrifice shall be salted with salt.

**50.** Salt *is* good: but if the salt have lost his saltness, wherewith will ye· season it? Have salt in yourselves, and have peace one with another.

Moloch worship. Later it became the site of the city dump, where continual fires burned, reducing the rubbish to ashes. The garbage and refuse deposited there would also have been infested with many worms. In Jewish thought this valley became a symbol of the place of eternal punishment.

**48.** The language of this verse is taken from the LXX of Isa 66:24. The **worm** that **dieth not** is a figure of speech drawn from the actual valley of Hinnom, where worms were continually at work. It is a picture of the unending torture and destruction of hell.

**49.** This verse and the following are among the most difficult in the Gospels. First, it should be noted that the second clause of 9:49 was probably a later addition, since it has poor manuscript support. It may have been a marginal attempt to explain this difficult passage. The introductory word **for** *(gar)* would normally tie this statement to the preceding one, in which case it serves to support or explain the former assertion. It may then mean that everyone who enters hell shall be preserved, as salt preserves, through an eternity of torment.

**50.** Taking up the word **salt,** used in 9:49 in connection with hell, Jesus goes on to say that Christ's followers are to be as salt, letting their influence be felt in the world (cf. Mt 5:13). **Have salt in yourselves.** He commanded the disciples to be permeated with this purifying influence. In order to be a wholesome influence, they must themselves be the possessors of this wholesomeness. **Have peace.** Christ concludes with one last reference to the dispute over greatness recorded in 9:34. Both commands are in the present tense, calling for an enduring practice.

## V. Christ's Ministry in Perea. 10:1-52.

With one statement Mark summarizes about six months of Christ's ministry (v. 1). His mention of Judea covers the later Judean period, recorded largely in Jn 7:10– 10:39 and Lk 10:1–13:21; the reference to **the farther side of Jordan** has to do with the Perean ministry, the greater part of which is reported in Lk 13:22–19:28. The events of Mk 10:2-52 are in reality the closing events of this Perean period (cf. Lk 18:15–19:28).

A. Discussions of Divorce, Children, and Wealth. 10:1-31. These conversations probably occurred somewhere in Perea. No exact location is given. In 10:2-12 Christ answered the Pharisees' interroga-

## CHAPTER 10

AND he arose from thence, and cometh into the coasts of Judea by the farther side of Jordan: and the people resort unto him again; and, as he was wont, he taught them again.

2. And the Pharisees came to him, and asked him, Is it lawful for a man to put away *his* wife? tempting him.

3. And he answered and said unto them, What did Moses command you?

4. And they said, Moses suffered to write a bill of divorcement, and to put *her* away.

5. And Jesus answered and said unto them, For the hardness of your heart he wrote you this precept.

6. But from the beginning of the creation God made them male and female.

7. For this cause shall a man leave his father and mother, and cleave to his wife;

8. And they twain shall be one flesh: so then they are no more twain, but one flesh.

9. What therefore God hath joined together, let not man put asunder.

10. And in the house his disciples asked him again of the same *matter.*

11. And he saith unto them, Whosoever shall put away his wife, and marry another, committeth adultery against her.

12. And if a woman shall put away her husband, and be married to another, she committeth adultery.

tion concerning the legality of divorce; 10:13-16 indicates Jesus' attitude toward children; and 10:17-31 records the coming of the rich young ruler and the resultant discussion of wealth.

**1. From thence.** Jesus left Capernaum, where he had stopped briefly at Peter's home (9:33). The word **coasts** is better translated *regions.* There is an important textual problem here concerning the expression **Judaea by the farther side of Jordan.** The manuscript evidence favors the reading *Judea and the farther side of Jordan.* At first this appears to be an impossible text, since it seems to have reversed the natural order of Perea and Judea. Coming from Galilee, Jesus would have gone through Perea first, and then through Judea. However, this difficulty is removed by viewing 10:1 as a summary of the later Judean and the Perean periods of Christ's ministry. Following the period of withdrawals, Jesus went first to Judea for three months; then he went to Perea for approximately the same length of time. Thus, the order in Mark's summary—Judea first and then Perea—is correct. **As he was wont.** That is, as was his custom. The verb **taught** (Gr. imp. tense) signifies a continuing occurrence. For examples of this teaching, see such passages as Lk 13:22—18:14.

**2.** The question put by **the Pharisees** concerned one of the debated subjects of that day. The scribes who followed Hillel held that a man could divorce his wife for almost any cause. The followers of Shammai, on the other hand, insisted that divorce was lawful only in case of adultery. **Tempting.** The same Greek word may mean either "to tempt" or "to test." Their question was put with an ulterior motive in order to test Christ.

**4. Suffered.** That is, Moses permitted divorce. The Mosaic regulation is found in Deut 24:1. It is to be noted that the Pharisees did not state the condition under which Moses permitted divorce.

**5. For the hardness of your heart.** The stipulation of Moses was not in reality a command, but a concession because of man's unsatisfactory spiritual condition. It was an attempt to regulate and control divorce rather than to encourage it.

**6-8.** The statement beginning **God made them** (v. 6) and ending **shall be one flesh** (v. 8) is taken verbatim from Gen 1:27; 2:24 (LXX). The condition which existed in **the beginning** is indicative of God's ideal. He meant marriage to be a lifelong union in all cases.

**11.** The man, in this case, commits **adultery against her,** not because of the

13. And they brought young children to him, that he should touch them; and *his* disciples rebuked those that brought *them*.

14. But when Jesus saw *it*, he was much displeased, and said unto them, Suffer the little children to come unto me, and forbid them not; for of such is the kingdom of God.

15. Verily I say unto you, Whosoever shall not receive the kingdom of God as a little child, he shall not enter therein.

16. And he took them up in his arms, put *his* hands upon them, and blessed them.

17. And when he was gone forth into the way, there came one running, and kneeled to him, and asked him, Good Master, what shall I do that I may inherit eternal life?

18. And Jesus said unto him, Why callest thou me good? *there is* none good but one, *that is*, God.

19. Thou knowest the commandments, Do not commit adultery, Do not kill, Do not steal, Do not bear false witness, Defraud not, Honor thy father and mother.

20. And he answered and said unto him, Master, all these have I observed from my youth.

divorce, but because of the remarriage. Although he has gone through the legal divorce procedure, in God's sight he is still married to his first wife. Matthew adds the exception of fornication (Mt 19:9).

13. The events recorded in this verse probably took place in the house (cf. v. 10). **Brought.** They *kept bringing* (Gr. text) the children. The attitude of the disciples seems to have been based on the conception that the Lord's time was too valuable to be wasted on children.

14. The translation, **was much displeased,** is not forceful enough to represent the Greek verb, which means *to be indignant.* Mark's Gospel is unique in its description of the emotions of Christ. **Suffer.** Used in the sense of "permit." Jesus' prohibition literally means, *Stop forbidding them.* The reason he offers for his action is that the kingdom of God is made up of such persons. It is clear that he had the present, spiritual kingdom in mind.

16. The age of these children is suggested by the fact that Jesus **took them up in his arms.** He **blessed them** is a compound verb describing the heart-felt fervor with which Christ uttered the words of blessing (cf. Gen 14:19,20; 27:26-29; 48:15-20).

17. The conversation with the rich young ruler took place as Jesus was leaving the house where he had lodged, probably somewhere in Perea (cf. v. 10). Mark simply states that **there came one running,** but he does not mention that the man was a young synagogue ruler. These facts are provided by Matthew and Luke. **Master.** This is the word for "teacher" *(didaskale)*. He conceived of **eternal life** as something to be earned by doing good (Mt 19:16).

18. The question, **Why callest thou me good?** was aimed at leading the young man to consider the true identity of Jesus. It was an indirect assertion of His deity, since goodness or sinlessness is a quality of God alone.

19. Christ cited some of **the commandments** without regard for their order in Ex 20. The command, **Defraud not,** may be intended to represent the tenth commandment, which concerns covetousness. The purpose of calling attention to the Law was to show the young man his inability to gain eternal life by good works.

20. **All these have I observed.** The young man could truthfully make such a claim, but his righteousness was an external obedience. It was as the righteousness of the scribes and Pharisees (Mt 5:20; cf. Phil 3:6).

21. Then Jesus beholding him loved him, and said unto him, One thing thou lackest: go thy way, sell whatsoever thou hast, and give to the poor, and thou shalt have treasure in heaven: and come, take up the cross, and follow me.

22. And he was sad at that saying, and went away grieved: for he had great possessions.

23. And Jesus looked round about, and saith unto his disciples, How hardly shall they that have riches enter into the kingdom of God!

24. And the disciples were astonished at his words. But Jesus answereth again, and saith unto them, Children, how hard is it for them that trust in riches to enter into the kingdom of God!

25. It is easier for a camel to go through the eye of a needle, than for a rich man to enter into the kingdom of God.

26. And they were astonished out of measure, saying among themselves, Who then can be saved?

27. And Jesus looking upon them saith, With men *it is* impossible, but not with God: for with God all things are possible.

28. Then Peter began to say unto him, Lo, we have left all, and have followed thee.

29. And Jesus answered and said, Verily I say unto you, There is no man that hath left house, or brethren, or sisters, or father, or mother, or wife, or children, or lands, for my sake, and the gospel's,

30. But he shall receive a hundredfold now in this time, houses, and brethren, and sisters, and mothers, and children, and lands, with persecutions; and in the world to come eternal life.

31. But many *that are* first shall be last; and the last first.

32. And they were in the way going up to Jerusalem; and Jesus went before them: and they were amazed; and as they followed, they were afraid. And he took again the twelve, and began to tell them what things should happen unto him,

21. **Beholding him.** Jesus looked intently and searchingly at him, and He **loved him.** No doubt He recognized the sincerity of the man's search for something to meet his spiritual need; He saw the potential represented in this upright young leader. Then He went to the heart of the man's problem, his devotion to his wealth rather than to God. Therein lay the **one thing** he lacked. In order to **follow** Jesus, he must remove the obstacle, his love of money. It was not works of charity that would gain for him eternal life; it was becoming identified with Christ.

23. The Lord did not deny the possibility that a rich person can be saved; he merely said that it is difficult. **The kingdom of God** is the present, spiritual kingdom, composed of the regenerated people of God (Jn 3:3,5).

25. The idea that **the eye of a needle,** referred to here, was a small gate through which a camel could enter only on his knees is without warrant. The word for **needle** refers specifically to a sewing needle. Furthermore, Jesus was not talking about what man considers possible, but about what seems to be impossible (cf. v. 27). With man it is impossible for **a camel to go through the eye** of a sewing needle.

29,30. **Verily** introduces a statement of solemn assurance. The word **wife** is omitted in the better Greek texts. **An hundredfold.** The items enumerated here may be taken literally to refer to such things as the many homes which will be opened to God's servants and the many new relationships in the household of God. Or they may be taken as figuratively describing the manifold spiritual blessings which the Lord heaps upon those who follow him sacrificially. The **world to come,** in the original language, is *the coming age.* It has reference to the eternal state to be ushered in by Messiah's second advent and the events connected with it, such as the Day of the Lord, cataclysmic judgments, the Millennium, and the final assize.

B. Conversation on the Way to Jerusalem. 10:32-45. The discussion recorded in these verses took place somewhere in Perea as Jesus was on his way, for the last time, to Jerusalem. Again he repeated the assertions concerning his death and resurrection (vv. 32-34), attempting by repetition to impress the facts upon his disciples. And again the temptation to seek self-advancement plagued the disciples (vv. 35-45).

32. This journey **to Jerusalem** was, as Jesus knew, the one that would take him

33. *Saying,* Behold, we go up to Jerusalem; and the Son of man shall be delivered unto the chief priests, and unto the scribes; and they shall condemn him to death, and shall deliver him to the Gentiles:

34. And they shall mock him, and shall scourge him, and shall spit upon him, and shall kill him; and the third day he shall rise again.

35. And James and John, the sons of Zebedee, come unto him, saying, Master, we would that thou shouldest do for us whatsoever we shall desire.

36. And he said unto them, What would ye that I should do for you?

37. They said unto him, Grant unto us that we may sit, one on thy right hand, and the other on thy left hand, in thy glory.

38. But Jesus said unto them, Ye know not what ye ask: can ye drink of the cup that I drink of? and be baptized with the baptism that I am baptized with?

39. And they said unto him, We can. And Jesus said unto them, Ye shall indeed drink of the cup that I drink of; and with the baptism that I am baptized withal shall ye be baptized:

40. But to sit on my right hand and on my left hand is not mine to give; but *it shall be given to them* for whom it is prepared.

41. And when the ten heard *it,* they began to be much displeased with James and John.

42. But Jesus called them *to him,* and saith unto them, Ye know that they which are accounted to rule over the Gentiles exercise lordship over them; and their great ones exercise authority upon them.

43. But so shall it not be among you: but whosoever will be great among you, shall be your minister:

44. And whosoever of you will be the chiefest, shall be servant of all.

to his death. The fact that Jesus went before them, walking alone, was a surprising departure from his usual practice of companionship with his disciples. No doubt there was something about his strange aloofness that amazed them and made them afraid. The tenses used here indicate that this was a continuing situation that went on for some time.

33,34. An advance beyond previous predictions is apparent in the number of details given (cf. 8:31; 9:31). Notice the statement, we go up to Jerusalem, which indicates that the fulfillment of these predictions would come during this visit to the city. Yet the disciples still did not understand what Christ was attempting to explain to them (Lk 18:34). Their concept of the Messiah led them to think only in terms of glory and kingship (cf. Mk 10:35-37).

35. Matthew states that James and John came with their mother and made their request through her (20:20). Matthew also says, Then came . . . , which may indicate that this self-seeking request of the two disciples followed immediately on the Saviour's teaching concerning his death.

37. The right hand of a king was the place of honor, and the left hand was next in importance. In thy glory. Or, in thy kingdom (Mt 20:21), which explains that the disciples had in mind the glory of the Messianic kingdom.

38. The Lord, recognizing that they asked in ignorance, began to show them that such rewards must be earned. The cup and the baptism speak of Christ's suffering, into which the disciple must be able and willing to enter. In Gethsemane he spoke of his death as a "cup" (14:36); in Lk 12:50 the term "baptism" is a figure for suffering and death.

40. The honors of the right hand and the left hand are not to be passed out to friends as favors. Such reward must go to them for whom it is prepared, that is, to the ones who earn it by faithfulness in life and service.

42. This sorry spectacle of selfish ambition became an occasion for the Lord to re-emphasize the nature of true greatness (cf. 9:35). First, he reminded the Twelve of the world's standard of greatness. It is customary for rulers and dignitaries to exercise lordship and authority over the people.

43. But this must not be the custom among the followers of Christ. In contrast, the one who would be great must be a minister to his fellows.

**45.** For even the Son of man came not to be ministered unto, but to minister, and to give his life a ransom for many.

**46.** And they came to Jericho: and as he went out of Jericho with his disciples and a great number of people, blind Bartimeus, the son of Timeus, sat by the highway side begging.

**47.** And when he heard that it was Jesus of Nazareth, he began to cry out, and say, Jesus, *thou* Son of David, have mercy on me.

**48.** And many charged him that he should hold his peace: but he cried the more a great deal, *Thou* Son of David, have mercy on me.

**45.** Jesus himself was the supreme example of one who manifested true greatness. He who was God's Messiah (Son of man; see on 2:10) might well have asserted his right to be ministered unto by men. Instead he came to serve and to give his life for mankind. **A ransom.** This significant word was common in the Greek world of Jesus' day, where it was used to refer to the price paid to free a slave (Adolf Deissmann, *Light from the Ancient East,* trans. L. R. M. Strachan, p. 327 ff.). This was the price demanded by a holy God in order that justice might be satisfied in the forgiveness of sins. As a result of this payment, the believer is freed from sin and Satan. **For many.** The Greek preposition *anti* is more accurately translated *in the place of,* as overwhelming evidence from Greek sources demonstrates (cf. J. H. Moulton and George Milligan, *The Vocabulary of the Greek Testament,* pp. 46,47; Arndt, pp. 72,73; Vincent Taylor, pp. 444,445).

C. The Healing of Blind Bartimaeus. 10:46-52. This section tells how Jesus, with his disciples, came from Perea across the Jordan to Jericho in Judea, where he restored the sight of Bartimaeus, the last healing miracle of his public ministry.

**46.** The **Jericho** of Jesus' day was located about five miles west of Jordan and fifteen miles northeast of Jerusalem. The site of the Canaanite city of Joshua's day lay one mile to the north. There is a difficulty in harmonization here. Matthew and Mark say that the miracle occurred as Jesus **went out of Jericho;** Luke places it as **he was come nigh unto Jericho** (18:35). Perhaps the most plausible solution is that the healing occurred as Jesus left the site of old Jericho and entered the new city of Jericho. The difficulty with this explanation is that there is no evidence that the old Jericho was inhabited in Jesus' time. This problem arises, no doubt, from our lack of complete historical and geographical information. We may be assured that no discrepancy would exist if all the facts were known. Meanwhile, the divergence is a testimony to the independent character of the two accounts.

**47.** The blind beggar, by calling Jesus the **son of David,** was recognizing Him as Messiah. The belief that the Messiah would be a descendant of David was common among the Jews of that day.

**48. Charged him.** Many kept commanding (Gr. text) him to be silent. He, however, kept crying (imp. tense) all the more. He refused to be silenced.

49. And Jesus stood still, and commanded him to be called. And they call the blind man, saying unto him, Be of good comfort, rise; he calleth thee.

50. And he, casting away his garment, rose, and came to Jesus.

51. And Jesus answered and said unto him, What wilt thou that I should do unto thee? The blind man said unto him, Lord, that I might receive my sight.

52. And Jesus said unto him, Go thy way; thy faith hath made thee whole. And immediately he received his sight, and followed Jesus in the way.

## CHAPTER 11

AND when they came nigh to Jerusalem, unto Bethphage and Bethany, at the mount of Olives, he sendeth forth two of his disciples,

**49. Be of good comfort.** The verb means *to be of good cheer, to be courageous.* It was as though they said, "Cheer up!"

**50.** The verbs of this verse suggest with what haste Bartimaeus responded to the call. He threw off his cloak, jumped up (**rose,** AV), and **came to Jesus.** This was the opportunity of a lifetime, and it must not be allowed to slip away.

**51. Lord.** The Aramaic word *rabbouni* used by Mary Magdalene at the Resurrection (Jn 20:16). It was a term of high respect, a strengthened form of "rabbi," combining, in some measure, the meanings of teacher and of Lord.

**52.** The healing was in response to the man's **faith,** demonstrated, as it was, by his persistent eagerness, by his recognition of Jesus as Messiah, and by the term *rabbouni.* The verb *anablepō* (**receive . . . sight**) means to have sight restored, indicating that the man had not always been blind. **Made thee whole.** The Greek word is *sōzō,* meaning "to save," a term often used in the Gospels to refer to physical healing. It may be paraphrased, "Your faith has healed you."

### VI. Christ's Concluding Ministry in Jerusalem. 11:1–13:37.

In this section Mark has recorded the last acts and teachings of the Saviour prior to his passion. All of these events took place in and around Jerusalem. Here occurred the 'Triumphal Entry' and the cleansing of the Temple (11:1-26), the numerous controversies with Jewish leaders (11:27–12:44), and the extended apocalyptic discourse on the Mount of Olives (13:1-37).

A. The Entrance into Jerusalem and the Temple. 11:1-26. From this point on, Christ abandoned the cautious attitude that had caused him to withdraw from areas of tension and possible crisis. Now he challenged the Jewish leaders. In the entry into Jerusalem he openly provoked disapproval and opposition. This 'Triumphal Entry' should be viewed not as the coming of a glorious king, but as the presentation of a Saviour who was soon to suffer.

**1.** Comparison with Jn 12:1 reveals that Jesus came first to **Bethany,** where he spent the night. Then on the day after the Sabbath he made his entrance into **Jerusalem.** Bethany lay a little less than two miles to the southeast of Jerusalem, not far from the eastern slope of **the mount of Olives.** The location of Bethphage is

2. And saith unto them, Go your way into the village over against you: and as soon as ye be entered into it, ye shall find a colt tied, whereon never man sat; loose him, and bring *him.*

3. And if any man say unto you, Why do ye this? say ye that the Lord hath need of him; and straightway he will send him hither.

4. And they went their way, and found the colt tied by the door without in a place where two ways met; and they loose him.

5. And certain of them that stood there said unto them, What do ye, loosing the colt?

6. And they said unto them even as Jesus had commanded: and they let them go.

7. And they brought the colt to Jesus, and cast their garments on him; and he sat upon him.

8. And many spread their garments in the way; and others cut down branches off the trees, and strewed *them* in the way.

9. And they that went before, and they that followed, cried, saying, Hosanna; Blessed *is* he that cometh in the name of the Lord:

10. Blessed *be* the kingdom of our father David, that cometh in the name of the Lord: Hosanna in the highest.

11. And Jesus entered into Jerusalem, and into the temple: and when he had looked round about upon all things, and now the eventide was come, he went out unto Bethany with the twelve.

more difficult, but the best evidence seems to point toward a place at the foot of the eastern slope. Mark's order is the reverse of the direction taken by Jesus, but he is viewing the locations of the towns from the standpoint of Jerusalem, which is mentioned first. John gives reason for believing that Jesus arrived in Bethany on Friday (12:1). Since the journey to Jerusalem was more than a Sabbath day's journey, it is assumed that Christ spent Saturday in Bethany and that the 'Triumphal Entry' occurred on Sunday.

**2.** The **village** was Bethphage, as Mt 21:1 makes clear. **Over against you.** That is, "opposite you." Whether Jesus knew of the colt by previous observation or by supernatural perception is not made clear.

**3.** It appears that he expected that the owner of the colt would know who **the Lord** was and would be willing to lend the animal to him. The preferred Greek texts read, *and immediately he will send it here again,* a promise on the part of Jesus to return the animal. Matthew states that there were two animals, an ass and a colt (21:2).

**7.** The **garments** placed on the colt were outer cloaks or robes, the bright colors of which would give the colt the appearance of bearing the accouterments of royalty.

**8.** Others spread their robes **in the way,** making a royal carpet for the procession. Still others brought leaves, which they scattered on the path. John describes them as palm branches (12:13).

**9.** The crowd surrounded the Lord; some **went before** him; others **followed.** And they kept crying (Gr. imp. tense), **Hosanna.** This is a transliteration of a Hebrew expression meaning, *Save, I pray,* coming from Ps 118:25. It had become a term of praise and acclamation, as well as a plea for help. **Blessed be he that cometh . . .** is an exact quotation from the LXX of Ps 118:26. This was one of the Hallel Psalms sung in connection with the Passover festival, and was thus particularly appropriate at this time. That the crowd used the words in a Messianic sense is made clear by the next verse.

**10.** The people felt that the Messianic **kingdom of . . . David** was about to be established. **Hosanna in the highest** undoubtedly means, "Save, now, thou who art in the highest heavens." It is a cry addressed to God himself.

**11. Jesus entered . . . into the temple.** The word *hieron* refers to the whole temple complex, including the courts and porches. When he **looked round about,** his eyes would surely take in the booths

12. And on the morrow, when they were come from Bethany, he was hungry:

13. And seeing a fig tree afar off having leaves, he came, if haply he might find any thing thereon: and when he came to it, he found nothing but leaves; for the time of figs was not *yet*.

14. And Jesus answered and said unto it, No man eat fruit of thee hereafter for ever. And his disciples heard *it*.

15. And they come to Jerusalem: and Jesus went into the temple, and began to cast out them that sold and bought in the temple, and overthrew the tables of the money changers, and the seats of them that sold doves;

16. And would not suffer that any man should carry *any* vessel through the temple.

17. And he taught, saying unto them, Is it not written, My house shall be called of all nations the house of prayer? but ye have made it a den of thieves.

18. And the scribes and chief priests heard *it*, and sought how they might destroy him: for they feared him, because all the people was astonished at his doctrine.

19. And when even was come, he went out of the city.

20. And in the morning, as they passed by, they saw the fig tree dried up from the roots.

21. And Peter calling to remembrance saith unto him, Master, behold, the fig tree which thou cursedst is withered away.

22. And Jesus answering saith unto them, Have faith in God.

23. For verily I say unto you, That whosoever shall say unto this mountain, Be thou removed, and be thou cast into the sea; and shall not doubt in his heart, but shall believe that those things which he saith shall come to pass; he shall have whatsoever he saith.

24. Therefore I say unto you, What things soever ye desire, when ye pray, believe that ye receive *them*, and ye shall have *them*.

25. And when ye stand praying, forgive, if ye have aught against any; that your Father also which is in heaven may forgive you your trespasses.

of the money-changers and of the sellers of doves, which were to be the objects of his displeasure on the following day.

**12. On the morrow.** That is, on Monday. After spending the night in Bethany, the Lord set out again for Jerusalem.

**13.** It was normal for the fig tree in the vicinity of Jerusalem to begin to put forth new leaves in the latter part of March or early April, the time of the Passover. This tree was apparently fully leaved out, in which case it should have had ripened figs on it ,although the time of ripe figs was in June. That it was the leaves which caused Jesus to expect fruit is made clear by the Greek word translated **haply** (AV). This is the inferential conjunction *ara*, meaning "therefore." Jesus saw the leaves at a distance and came to see "if therefore he might find fruit."

**15.** This is the second purging of the Temple, not in any sense to be identified with the first, which occurred at the very beginning of Christ's ministry (Jn 2:13-17). Those who **sold and bought, the money-changers,** and those **that sold doves** were in the employ of Annas and the high priestly family. The animals were sold for sacrificial purposes, and the money-changers exchanged the common currency for the half-shekel necessary to pay the temple tax. Exorbitant rates, however, were charged.

**17.** Jesus' quotation comes from Isa 56:7, where the prophet declares God's house to be a **house of prayer,** a place set apart for sacred use. Not only did the Lord accuse them of desecrating the Temple by using it for business, but he pointed out that they made dishonest gain from the grossly unfair prices they charged. **Den of thieves.** Taken from Jer 7:11.

**20. In the morning.** This was Tuesday morning, and Christ was returning to Jerusalem again for the day.

**22.** The only significance of the cursing of the fig tree which the Gospels state is to be found in these verses. Jesus used it as an example of **faith in God.** Any further symbolical meaning is without Scriptural justification.

**24. Believe.** A present tense imperative, calling for persistent, continuing faith. **Receive.** Superior manuscript evidence favors the aorist tense—*you did receive.* In other words, we are to keep on believing that God has already given us our request.

**25. Forgive . . . that your Father . . . may forgive you.** Statements such as these, which make God's forgiveness dependent on our forgiveness have been misunderstood as being legal in nature. However,

26. But if ye do not forgive, neither will your Father which is in heaven forgive your trespasses.

27. And they come again to Jerusalem: and as he was walking in the temple, there come to him the chief priests, and the scribes, and the elders,

28. And say unto him, By what authority doest thou these things? and who gave thee this authority to do these things?

29. And Jesus answered and said unto them, I will also ask of you one question, and answer me, and I will tell you by what authority I do these things.

30. The baptism of John, was *it* from heaven, or of men? answer me.

31. And they reasoned with themselves, saying, If we shall say, From heaven; he will say, Why then did ye not believe him?

32. But if we shall say, Of men; they feared the people: for all *men* counted John, that he was a prophet indeed.

33. And they answered and said unto Jesus, We cannot tell. And Jesus answering saith unto them, Neither do I tell you by what authority I do these things.

## CHAPTER 12

AND he began to speak unto them by parables. A *certain* man planted a vineyard, and set a hedge about *it*, and digged *a place for* the winevat, and built a tower, and let it out to husbandmen, and went into a far country.

Christ does not here address himself to the unsaved but to his disciples, those who have already entered into a saving relationship with himself. The forgiveness of which he speaks is not the initial forensic act of forgiveness which abolishes the guilt of sin. It is rather the forgiveness of a father which restores fellowship. The point here is that a disciple cannot pray effectively if an unforgiving spirit has broken his fellowship with God.

B. Final Controversies with the Jewish Leaders. 11:27–12:44. The debates recorded in this section all took place on one busy day — Tuesday of the passion week. They concerned the following subjects: the source of our Lord's authority (11:27-33); the parable of the vineyard and the husbandmen (12:1-12); a question about taxation (12:13-17); the resurrection (12:18-27); the greatest commandment (12:28-34); the Messiah's relationship to David (12:35-40). The section closes with an account of the widow's gift of two mites (12:41-44).

27. **Come again to Jerusalem.** This was Tuesday morning. The comments on the withered fig tree (vv. 20-25) were spoken on the way to Jerusalem. **The chief priests.** Technically there was but one high priest, but the term had come to include all the living ex-high priests. In this case, at least Annas, the father-in-law of the high priest, Caiaphas, would have been included.

28. Their questions were two in number: What kind (*poiâ*) of **authority** do you possess? What is the source of **this authority?** By **these things,** the officials referred to Christ's purging of the Temple (cf. Jn 2:18). It was said that the Temple could be cleansed only by the Sanhedrin, by a prophet, or by the Messiah.

30. **From heaven.** In an attempt to avoid the use of the Divine name, the Jews often employed the term "heaven" when speaking of God.

31,32. By this question Jesus placed these religious leaders on the horns of a dilemma. If John's ministry was of divine origin, then they, as spiritual leaders, should have been the first to **believe him.** If, however, they stated that his ministry was of human origin, they would have reduced John to an imposter, and this would have invoked the displeasure of **the people** against them.

**12:1. Parables.** That Jesus gave more than one parable on this occasion is seen by a comparison with Mt 21:28-32, where the story of the wicked husbandmen is

2. And at the season he sent to the husbandmen a servant, that he might receive from the husbandmen of the fruit of the vineyard.

3. And they caught *him*, and beat him, and sent *him* away empty.

4. And again he sent unto them another servant; and at him they cast stones, and wounded *him* in the head, and sent *him* away shamefully handled.

5. And again he sent another; and him they killed, and many others; beating some, and killing some.

6. Having yet therefore one son, his wellbeloved, he sent him also last unto them, saying, They will reverence my son.

7. But those husbandmen said among themselves, This is the heir; come, let us kill him, and the inheritance shall be ours.

8. And they took him, and killed *him*, and cast *him* out of the vineyard.

9. What shall therefore the lord of the vineyard do? he will come and destroy the husbandmen, and will give the vineyard unto others.

10. And have ye not read this Scripture; The stone which the builders rejected is become the head of the corner:

11. This was the Lord's doing, and it is marvelous in our eyes?

12. And they sought to lay hold on him, but feared the people; for they knew that he had spoken the parable against them: and they left him, and went their way.

13. And they send unto him certain of the Pharisees and of the Herodians, to catch him in *his* words.

preceded by that of the two sons. The introduction to the parable, as found in Mk 12:1 is unmistakably drawn from Isa 5:1,2. The fact that the vineyard there was representative of Israel (Isa 5:7) gave the Jewish leaders the clue for interpreting the parable of Jesus. **Hedge.** *The word* used by Mark means *fence;* it may have been a stone fence or wall. The **place for the winefat** was a pit or trough beneath the winepress for the purpose of catching the juice. The **tower** was a combination watchtower and storage place. The husbandmen were farmers, in this case vine growers, used here to represent the religious leaders of Israel, such as those being addressed by Jesus (cf. 11:27; 12:12).

2. The **servant,** as in 12:4,5, represents a prophet whom God sent to Israel.

3. The fact that they **caught** and **beat** him is indicative of the persecution of the prophets of the OT (cf. Mt 23:34,37).

6. **One son, his wellbeloved.** These words are an obvious description of Christ himself (cf. 1:11; 9:7). The term **reverence** is too strong. *Respect* or *give heed to* is more accurate.

7,8. The plot to **kill him** was a description of the scheming in which the Jewish leaders were engaged at that very time in order to put Jesus to death.

9. The prediction that the owner would **destroy the husbandmen** was fulfilled in A.D. 70, when the Romans under Titus destroyed Jerusalem and put an end to any semblance of self-rule which the Jews had previously enjoyed. The **others** unto whom the vineyard was to be given are further described in Mt 21:43, where Jesus is quoted as saying, **The kingdom of God shall be taken from you, and given to a nation bringing forth the fruits thereof.** This is an obvious reference to the Gentiles and the Church.

10. The question, **have ye not read,** is phrased to expect a positive answer. The quotation in this verse and the next is cited verbatim from the LXX of Ps 118:22,23. **The stone** is Christ, who was rejected by **the builders,** the religious leaders of the Jews.

13. In 12:13-17 **the Pharisees** and the Herodians question Jesus concerning payment of tribute to Caesar. This combination is unusual, for the Pharisees had little in common with the Herodians. The former were unalterably opposed to any foreign overlordship, while the latter were supporters of the foreign government of the Herods. The one group

14. And when they were come, they say unto him, Master, we know that thou art true, and carest for no man; for thou regardest not the person of men, but teachest the way of God in truth: Is it lawful to give tribute to Caesar, or not?

15. Shall we give, or shall we not give? But he, knowing their hypocrisy, said unto them, Why tempt ye me? bring me a penny, that I may see it.

16. And they brought it. And he saith unto them, Whose is this image and superscription? And they said unto him, Caesar's.

17. And Jesus answering said unto them, Render to Caesar the things that are Caesar's, and to God the things that are God's. And they marveled at him.

18. Then come unto him the Sadducees, which say there is no resurrection; and they asked him, saying,

19. Master, Moses wrote unto us, If a man's brother die, and leave his wife behind him, and leave no children, that his brother should take his wife, and raise up seed unto his brother.

20. Now there were seven brethren: and the first took a wife, and dying left no seed.

21. And the second took her, and died, neither left he any seed: and the third likewise.

22. And the seven had her, and left no seed: last of all the woman died also.

23. In the resurrection therefore, when they shall rise, whose wife shall she be of them? for the seven had her to wife.

would have objected to the Roman tax; the other would have favored it. The motive of these incongruous conspirators was ulterior. They sought to catch him in his words as a hunter catches his prey.

14. Carest for no man. This was intended to be taken in a complimentary sense, meaning that his teaching was not influenced by what friends or foes thought. The tribute in question was a poll tax which had to be paid personally into the Roman treasury. Is it lawful? They wanted him to answer concerning the rightness or wrongness of the tax in the eyes of God.

15. Why tempt ye me? The Lord perceived the dilemma into which they sought to draw him. They thought that if he answered in the affirmative, the Jewish people, who hated the poll tax, would rise up and reject him and his claims; but if he replied in the negative, he could be charged with opposition to Rome. A penny. This coin was the denarius, with which the tax had to be paid.

17. Render. The verb means to pay back in full. It assumes an obligation to Caesar. For the privileges provided by the Roman government, the people were indebted to help support that government (cf. Rom 13:1-7). By the same token they were also to pay their obligations to God. And there is no incongruity in paying the two debts, for both payments are for the accomplishment of God's will. Such an answer completely dissolved the anticipated dilemma, with the result that the questioners were completely amazed (marvelled, exethaumazon, an intensified word for great astonishment).

18. The question of the Sadducees (vv. 18-27) quite naturally concerned the resurrection, which Jesus taught and they denied. For the Sadducees there was no such thing as existence after death. They also denied the reality of angels and spirits (Acts 23:8).

19. Moses wrote. A free statement of the levirate law of marriage is found in Deut 25:5-10. If a man died without children, his brother was to marry his wife, and the first son of that union was then considered the child of the dead husband.

23. The problem which is raised seems unanswerable. In the resurrection . . . whose wife shall she be . . . ? The possibility of a resurrection is only assumed by the Sadducees as a basis for their argument. The purpose of the question was to attempt to prove the impossibility of a resurrection by reducing it to an absurdity.

24. And Jesus answering said unto them, Do ye not therefore err, because ye know not the Scriptures, neither the power of God?

25. For when they shall rise from the dead, they neither marry, nor are given in marriage; but are as the angels which are in heaven.

26. And as touching the dead, that they rise; have ye not read in the book of Moses, how in the bush God spake unto him, saying, I *am* the God of Abraham, and the God of Isaac, and the God of Jacob?

27. He is not the God of the dead, but the God of the living: ye therefore do greatly err.

28. And one of the scribes came, and having heard them reasoning together, and perceiving that he had answered them well, asked him, Which is the first commandment of all?

29. And Jesus answered him, The first of all the commandments *is*, Hear, O Israel; The Lord our God is one Lord:

30. And thou shalt love the Lord thy God with all thy heart, and with all thy soul, and with all thy mind, and with all thy strength: this *is* the first commandment.

24. **Err.** The Greek verb means *to lead astray.* They were being led astray (or, they were leading themselves astray) for two reasons. One, they did not understand what the OT Scriptures taught concerning resurrection (cf. vv. 26,27). Two, they underestimated **the power of God** to raise the dead and to resolve all seeming difficulties connected with the idea of a resurrection.

25. With this one statement of fact Jesus swept away their apparent problem. They had erroneously assumed the continuation of marriage relationships after the resurrection. Instead, Christ explained, people will have the same relations as **the angels.** There will be no need for conjugal union nor the reproduction of children.

26. The question, **have ye not read,** expects an affirmative answer, for Christ knew well that these Sadducees were thoroughly familiar with the Pentateuch. He referred specifically to Ex 3:6, quoting the LXX.

27. The truth demonstrated here is the fact of immortality. To be the God of Abraham is to be in fellowship with Abraham. It is therefore not possible to be **the God of the dead,** but only **of the living.** Thus when God spoke out of the burning bush, though the patriarchs had been dead for years, he was still in fellowship with them. The argument of Christ then assumes that since there is life after death, this is sufficient to prove that resurrection will follow. Perfect human existence demands the union of soul with body.

28. The question concerning the chief commandment (vv. 28-34) came from **one of the scribes.** He, no doubt, was a Pharisee, for he approved of Jesus' answer to the Sadducees. There seems to be no ulterior motive in this inquiry (cf. vv. 28,32-34).

29,30. Jesus does not go to the traditions of the scribes for his reply, but to the written Law, to Deut 6:4,5. The quotation is taken from the LXX, with the addition of the words **and with all thy mind.** The **mind** and the **heart** are really one and the same in Hebrew thought. The words, **Hear O Israel; The Lord our God is one Lord,** from the creed known as the "Shema" and recited daily by devout Jews. It asserts the distinctive principle of Hebrew faith, that **God is one.** The meaning of this command to **love the Lord** is that he is to be loved with all man's powers and capacities. This is the

31. And the second *is* like, *namely* this, Thou shalt love thy neighbor as thyself. There is none other commandment greater than these.

32. And the scribe said unto him, Well, Master, thou hast said the truth: for there is one God; and there is none other but he:

33. And to love him with all the heart, and with all the understanding, and with all the soul, and with all the strength, and to love *his* neighbor as himself, is more than all whole burnt offerings and sacrifices.

34. And when Jesus saw that he answered discreetly, he said unto him, Thou art not far from the kingdom of God. And no man after that durst ask him *any question.*

35. And Jesus answered and said, while he taught in the temple, How say the scribes that Christ is the son of David?

36. For David himself said by the Holy Ghost, The LORD said to my Lord, Sit thou on my right hand, till I make thine enemies thy footstool.

37. David therefore himself calleth him Lord; and whence is he *then* his son? And the common people heard him gladly.

38. And he said unto them in his doctrine, Beware of the scribes, which love to go in long clothing, and *love* salutations in the market places,

39. And the chief seats in the synagogues, and the uppermost rooms at feasts:

40. Which devour widows' houses, and for a pretense make long prayers: these shall receive greater damnation.

foundation and the summary of man's total duty to God.

**31. The second** commandment is quoted verbatim from Lev 19:18 (LXX). Here, likewise, is the basis and the sum of man's obligation to man. These two commandments are foundational to the teachings of all the Law and the Prophets (Mt 22:40).

**34. Discreetly.** That is, with intelligence. Christ declared the man to have the kind of spiritual understanding which, if persisted in, would lead him into **the kingdom of God.** The present, spiritual kingdom, which is entered by faith and new birth, is in mind here (cf. Jn 3:3,5). Mark closes his account of this discussion with a strong statement showing how completely Christ had silenced his opponents. **No man** was daring to question him any longer. Never again did they attempt to trap Christ with a theological or legal conundrum.

**35.** However, Christ had not yet finished with his opponents. He had a question for them concerning the relationship of David to the Messiah (vv. 35-40). The citation of the teaching of the scribes represents the standard Jewish view that the Messiah would be a descendant of David.

**36.** The quotation is taken from Ps 110:1 (LXX), a passage which the Jews had long recognized as Messianic. By his introduction to the passage, Christ affirmed the Davidic authorship as well as the divine inspiration of the psalm. His purpose in using David's words was to press home from the Scripture itself the truth of the deity of the Messiah.

**37.** The fact Jesus pointed up was that David called **him Lord.** How, then, can the Messiah be both David's exalted Lord and **his son?** Matthew states that no one was able to answer this question (22:46). Yet, standing before them, the incarnate Son of God, Israel's Messiah, was himself the answer personified. He was a descendant of David "according to the flesh" and the Son of God "according to the spirit of holiness" (Rom 1:3,4).

**38. Doctrine.** Our word "teaching" represents Mark's meaning more accurately. The **long clothing** was the long flowing robe of a wealthy person or a dignitary. The **salutations** are explained in Mt 23:7.

**39.** The **uppermost rooms** are better described as the seats (couches) of honor at banquets.

**40.** In spite of their recognition as honorable community leaders, the scribes

41. And Jesus sat over against the treasury, and beheld how the people cast money into the treasury: and many that were rich cast in much.

42. And there came a certain poor widow, and she threw in two mites, which make a farthing.

43. And he called *unto him* his disciples, and saith unto them, Verily I say unto you, That this poor widow hath cast more in, than all they which have cast into the treasury:

44. For all *they* did cast in of their abundance; but she of her want did cast in all that she had, *even* all her living.

## CHAPTER 13

AND as he went out of the temple, one of his disciples saith unto him, Master, see what manner of stones and what buildings *are here!*

were actually guilty of the most despicable kind of dishonesty. They made **long prayers** in the homes of widows to cover up the fact that they were engaged in crooked schemes to deprive them of their very **houses.**

**41.** Located in the temple area known as the Court of the Women, **the treasury** contained thirteen trumpet-shaped chests for the deposit of gifts and the temple tax. It appears that Jesus continued watching the giving for some time and that he observed a number of wealthy persons making gifts (cf. Gr. imp. tense used with the verbs **beheld** and **cast,** second occurrence).

**42.** Of the Greek synonyms for poverty, Mark chose a word descriptive of the beggarly condition of a pauper in order to characterize this **poor widow.** She gave an amount equal to **two mites** or a **farthing.** A mite *(lepton)* was the smallest of copper coins, normally equal to one-eighth of a cent (Arndt, p. 473). The farthing *(kodrantēs)* was a Roman coin valued at one-quarter of a cent (Arndt, p. 438).

**44.** The principle enunciated by our Lord on this occasion is that a gift is to be evaluated not by its size, but by a comparison of the gift with the total amount possessed by the giver. A large donation out of abundance may be less significant than a small donation out of poverty. This woman gave the smallest possible gift, but it was more significant than the others, for it was **all that she had.**

C. The Olivet Apocalypse. 13:1-37. The Olivet Discourse occurred on Tuesday after the conclusion of the controversies in the temple courts with the Jewish leaders. It may be broken down into the following divisions: the questions of the disciples (13:1-4); the conditions characteristic of this present age (13:5-13); the coming crisis (13:14-23); the second advent of Christ (13:24-27); instruction concerning watchfulness (13:28-37).

**1.** In the light of Josephus' descriptions of the Temple, it is not surprising to find one of the disciples exclaiming concerning the **manner of stones** and the **buildings.** Josephus depicts the stones as being thirty-seven by twelve by eighteen feet in size. He further states that the ". . . front was all of polished stone, insomuch that its fitness, to such as had not seen it, was incredible, and to such as had seen it, was greatly amazing" *(Antiq* XV. xi. 3-5).

2. And Jesus answering said unto him, Seest thou these great buildings? there shall not be left one stone upon another, that shall not be thrown down.

3. And as he sat upon the mount of Olives, over against the temple, Peter and James and John and Andrew asked him privately,

4. Tell us, when shall these things be? and what *shall be* the sign when all these things shall be fulfilled?

5. And Jesus answering them began to say, Take heed lest any *man* deceive you:

6. For many shall come in my name, saying, I am *Christ;* and shall deceive many.

7. And when ye shall hear of wars and rumors of wars, be ye not troubled: for *such things* must needs be; but the end *shall* not *be* yet.

8. For nation shall rise against nation, and kingdom against kingdom: and there shall be earthquakes in divers places, and there shall be famines and troubles: these *are* the beginnings of sorrows.

9. But take heed to yourselves: for they shall deliver you up to councils; and in the synagogues ye shall be beaten: and ye shall be brought before rulers and kings for my sake, for a testimony against them.

10. And the gospel must first be published among all nations.

2. Jesus used the strong Greek double negative construction *(ou mē)* twice in this verse in order to deny that one stone would be left upon another. It was positively certain that the Temple would be completely destroyed, a fact confirmed by history when in A.D. 70 under Titus the Temple, along with the city, was laid in ruins.

4. These things. An obvious reference to the prediction stated in 13:2. There is reason to believe, however, that the disciples also had in mind the sequence of end-time events. Their second question amplified the first in that it asked for the sign which would indicate that fulfillment was about *(mellê)* to take place. From Matthew we learn that the disciples also asked concerning the sign of Christ's coming and of the end of the age (24:3).

5. Jesus began his answer by picturing the conditions characteristic of this present age (vv. 5-13). The first is the presence of deceivers, against whom the disciple must take heed constantly (Gr., pres. imper.).

6. In my name. These words refer to the coming of false messiahs, who will claim the position and authority that belong to Christ alone. The prediction has been fulfilled on numerous occasions. Perhaps the most outstanding personage making such a claim was Bar Cochba (A.D. 132).

8. Wars are characteristic of the entire age, as are earthquakes and famines. The word troubles is omitted by the better Greek manuscripts. All of these conditions are described as the beginnings of sorrows. Thus, they are set in direct contrast to the end (v. 7). The word sorrows actually means *birth-pains*, a term used by the Jews to describe the afflictions and woes that are to usher in the coming of the Messiah.

9. The disciple is commanded to take heed, that is, to be constantly on the alert (Gr., pres. imper.). Councils. Literally *sanhedrins*. The arrests and beatings foretold here begin to find their fulfillment in the book of Acts (cf. 4:5 ff.; 5:27 ff.), as do also the appearances before rulers and kings (cf. 12:1 ff.; 24:1 ff.; 25:1 ff.). These appearances were to be for a testimony to them *(autois)*, not against them, as in the AV. Consider Paul's witness to Felix (Acts 24:24,25) and Agrippa (Acts 26).

10. Another feature of the age is the world-wide preaching of the gospel. The end (v. 7) cannot come until the evangel-

11. But when they shall lead *you*, and deliver you up, take no thought beforehand what ye shall speak, neither do ye premeditate: but whatsoever shall be given you in that hour, that speak ye: for it is not ye that speak, but the Holy Ghost.

12. Now the brother shall betray the brother to death, and the father the son; and children shall rise up against *their* parents, and shall cause them to be put to death.

13. And ye shall be hated of all *men* for my name's sake: but he that shall endure unto the end, the same shall be saved.

14. But when ye shall see the abomination of desolation, spoken of by Daniel the prophet, standing where it ought not, (let him that readeth understand,) then let them that be in Judea flee to the mountains:

istic task has first been accomplished. Matthew 24:14 concludes the saying with the statement, then shall the end come, referring to the end of the age.

13. In the midst of all the disturbances, the moral declension, and the persecutions, endurance becomes the mark of spiritual genuineness. **The end.** Since the conditions described in 13:5-13 are age-long, "the end" does not here refer to the end of the age, but rather to the end of life or of the trial. **Be saved.** In this context physical deliverance cannot be meant. The promise is that the one who endures shall be saved spiritually. The endurance, however, is not the basis of the salvation. In keeping with the general teaching of the NT, endurance is to be viewed as the result of the new birth (cf. Rom 8:29-39; I Jn 2:19). A person who has been regenerated, and thus endures, will most surely experience the consummation of the salvation experience.

14. Having pointed out some of the salient features of this age, Christ went on to describe the coming crisis (vv. 14-23). The **abomination of desolation** is an expression taken verbatim from Dan 12:11 (LXX). It is also found with slight variations in Dan 9:27; 11:31. Among the Jews the term **abomination** was used to describe idolatry or sacrilege (cf. Ezk 8:9,10,15,16). It seems, therefore, that both Daniel and Christ were speaking of an appalling profanation of the Temple. The first fulfillment of Daniel's prophetic use of the term, some writers claim, was the erection of an altar to Zeus on the altar of burnt offering at the command of Antiochus Epiphanes in 168 B.C. (I Macc 1:54,59). Christ's use of the words had immediate reference to the profanation of the Temple by the Romans (A.D. 70). It must be remembered that the disciples had asked concerning the destruction of the Temple (Mk 13:2,4). Furthermore, the instructions given in 13:14b-18 seem to fit that occasion best. However, the close relation of these conditions to Christ's second advent (vv. 24-27) demands an additional application to the time of the end. The conditions of the days of Antiochus Epiphanes and of the Roman destruction of the Temple were foreshadowings of the days of the Antichrist immediately prior to Christ's return (cf. II Thess 2:3,4; Rev 13:14,15). **Standing where it ought not.** In the holy place (Mt 24:15). The appearance of the appalling profanation would be a sign for dwellers in Judea to **flee to the mountains** in order to avoid

15. And let him that is on the housetop not go down into the house, neither enter *therein*, to take any thing out of his house:

16. And let him that is in the field not turn back again for to take up his garment.

17. But woe to them that are with child, and to them that give suck in those days!

18. And pray ye that your flight be not in the winter.

19. For *in* those days shall be affliction, such as was not from the beginning of the creation which God created unto this time, neither shall be.

20. And except that the Lord had shortened those days, no flesh should be saved: but for the elect's sake, whom he hath chosen, he hath shortened the days.

21. And then if any man shall say to you, Lo, here *is* Christ; or, lo, *he is* there; believe *him* not:

22. For false Christs and false prophets shall rise, and shall show signs and wonders, to seduce, if *it were* possible, even the elect.

23. But take ye heed: behold, I have foretold you all things.

24. But in those days, after that tribulation, the sun shall be darkened, and the moon shall not give her light,

25. And the stars of heaven shall fall, and the powers that are in heaven shall be shaken.

the coming siege. The specific reference of this command, as well as of those in verses 15-18, was to the soon-coming destruction of Jerusalem (A.D. 70).

**15,16.** The need for haste would be so urgent that there would be no time to tarry **to take anything** for the flight.

**17,18.** It would be a very difficult time for expectant mothers and those with babes in arms. A flight **in the winter** would add to the difficulties of an already difficult situation.

**19.** This summary description of the tribulations of **those days** certainly applied to the horrors of A.D. 70, as a comparison with Josephus' *Wars of the Jews* (Preface, 4; V, VI) will show. However, there is reason to believe that Christ looked beyond Roman days to the great final tribulation which will precede his second coming. This is suggested by the words **neither shall be,** which are a translation of a strong Greek denial (*ou mē*).

**20.** It is not possible to limit this verse to the situation in A.D. 70. None of the suggested explanations based on such a limitation is satisfactory. There are elements here that go beyond that time and are more correctly associated with the end of the age. The reference to 'the elect' seems to point to the saved during the days of the Great Tribulation just prior to Christ's return. For their sake God has **shortened the days** of that period of terrible affliction.

**22.** So bold will these deceivers be that they will aim to lead astray **even the elect.** However, the clause, **if it were possible,** shows that it is unthinkable that they should succeed. On the identification of **the elect,** see Lk 18:7; Rom 8:33; Col 3:12; I Pet 1:2.

**24,25.** The prophecy now moves on to the Second Advent (vv. 24-27). Christ specifically placed this great event **in those days after that tribulation,** obviously referring to the time described in 13:14-23. This necessitates one of two explanations. Either Christ was to come shortly after A.D. 70 or the afflictions of verses 14-23 have a double reference, both to the destruction of Jerusalem by Titus and to the Great Tribulation at the end of the age. Since the former explanation is impossible, the latter interpretation is viewed as the key to the understanding of the chapter as a whole. The language used to describe the disturbances in the heavens is largely taken from the OT (cf. Isa 13:10; 34:4; Joel 2:10,30,31). While it is best to avoid an extreme literalism here, there is no reason

26. And then shall they see the Son of man coming in the clouds with great power and glory.

27. And then shall he send his angels, and shall gather together his elect from the four winds, from the uttermost part of the earth to the uttermost part of heaven.

28. Now learn a parable of the fig tree: When her branch is yet tender, and putteth forth leaves, ye know that summer is near:

29. So ye in like manner, when ye shall see these things come to pass, know that it is nigh, *even* at the doors.

30. Verily I say unto you, that this generation shall not pass, till all these things be done.

31. Heaven and earth shall pass away: but my words shall not pass away.

32. But of that day and *that* hour knoweth no man, no, not the angels which are in heaven, neither the Son, but the Father.

for not understanding these expressions to refer to actual celestial changes that will immediately precede Christ's coming. It is not at all strange that so momentous an event should be introduced in this manner.

**26.** This is the personal, bodily return of Christ to the earth **with great power and glory,** which is described in such passages as Acts 1:11; II Thess 1:7-10; 2:8; Rev 1:7; 19:11-16. "Against the background of a darkened heaven, the Son of Man is revealed in the Shekinah glory of God . . ." (G. R. Beasley-Murray, *A Commentary on Mark Thirteen,* p. 89). The language used here is drawn from Dan 7:13. **They shall see.** His coming will be visible to all men.

**27.** At this point the resurrection of the righteous dead and the transformation of the living saints will occur (cf. I Cor 15:51-53; I Thess 4:13-18). Then he **shall gather together his elect,** the redeemed of all ages, past and present. Concerning the word **elect,** see on 13:22. The word *episynaxei,* **gather together,** is the verb form of the noun *episynagōgē,* "gathering together," in II Thess 2:1. They will be gathered to the descending Lord from every part of the earth (**the four winds**), even from the farthest extremities (**uttermost part of the earth** and of **heaven**).

**28,29.** Having finished the delineation of future events, the Lord turned to a discussion of the need for watchfulness (vv. 28-37). There is no indication that Israel is symbolized here by the fig tree. Instead, the parable is a simple demonstration of the truth that coming events cast their shadows before them. When these things begin to come to pass, we will know that the consummation is very near. The **things** to which Christ refers are the events described in verses 14-25.

**30.** The most natural explanation of the expression, **this generation,** is that it refers to the generation of people alive when Christ was speaking. During their lifetime all these things were to come to pass in the destruction of Jerusalem in A.D. 70. This event is employed by Christ as a preliminary picture prefiguring, in all its essential characteristics, the end of the age (cf. Mk 9:1).

**32.** The exact **day** and **hour** of Christ's return are not humanly discernible. In fact, the time is known only by God the Father. The statement that **the Son** did not know the time of the consummation is to be understood in the light of his self-limitation during the days of his hu-

33. Take ye heed, watch and pray: for ye know not when the time is.

34. *For the Son of man is* as a man taking a far journey, who left his house, and gave authority to his servants, and to every man his work, and commanded the porter to watch.

35. Watch ye therefore: for ye know not when the master of the house cometh, at even, or at midnight, or at the cockcrowing, or in the morning:

36. Lest coming suddenly he find you sleeping.

37. And what I say unto you I say unto all, Watch.

## CHAPTER 14

AFTER two days was *the feast of* the passover, and of unleavened bread: and the chief priests and the scribes sought how they might take him by craft, and put *him* to death.

2. But they said, Not on the feast *day*, lest there be an uproar of the people.

3. And being in Bethany, in the house of Simon the leper, as he sat at meat, there came a woman having an alabaster box of ointment of spikenard very precious; and she brake the box, and poured *it* on his head.

miliation (cf. Phil 2:5-8). He had assumed a position of complete subjection to the Father, exercising his divine attributes only at the Father's bidding (cf. Jn 8:26, 28,29).

**33. Take ye heed.** This present tense imperative calls for constant alertness. The same is true of the verb **watch,** which means *to keep oneself awake* (Arndt, pp. 13,14). Such watchfulness is necessary because we do not know when these end-time events may break upon us.

**35.** The disciple is to **watch** continually (Gr. pres. tense). This verb, as well as that in verse 33, means *to be or keep awake.* It calls for constant alertness as over against sleep or drowsiness (Arndt, p. 166; cf. v. 36). **At even . . . midnight . . . cockcrowing . . . morning.** These are the four watches of the night according to the Roman reckoning.

**36.** Such watchfulness is necessary lest the Lord come when we do not expect him. This is what he means by finding us **sleeping.** To a person who is not watching, Christ's coming will be sudden. One who is on the alert will see the signs of the Lord's return (vv. 28,29) and will not be taken by surprise.

## VII. Christ's Passion and Resurrection. 14:1–16:20.

Mark's narrative moves now into the final scenes of Christ's life on earth. These were the events that surrounded his death and resurrection. They were the acts that would accomplish eternal redemption for all people everywhere who would receive it.

**A. Treachery and Devotion. 14:1-11.** These verses begin with a description of the treachery with which the priests and scribes plotted Jesus' death (vv. 1,2). In contrast, this is followed by a moving account of the devotion of Mary (vv. 3-9). Then, in even sharper contrast, the Evangelist relates the traitorous plot of Judas to betray the Lord (vv. 10,11).

**1. After two days.** The point from which these two days were figured was probably late Tuesday afternoon, at which time the Jewish leaders were seeking **how they might take him by craft.** This would place the Passover meal on Thursday evening.

**3.** The time was Tuesday evening; Christ had returned to **Bethany** to spend the night. We know nothing of **Simon the leper** beyond what is given in these verses, although some have mistakenly

4. And there were some that had indignation within themselves, and said, Why was this waste of the ointment made?

5. For it might have been sold for more than three hundred pence, and have been given to the poor. And they murmured against her.

6. And Jesus said, Let her alone; why trouble ye her? she hath wrought a good work on me.

7. For ye have the poor with you always, and whensoever ye will ye may do them good: but me ye have not always.

8. She hath done what she could: she is come aforehand to anoint my body to the burying.

9. Verily I say unto you, Wheresoever this gospel shall be preached throughout the whole world, *this* also that she hath done shall be spoken of for a memorial of her.

10. And Judas Iscariot, one of the twelve, went unto the chief priests, to betray him unto them.

11. And when they heard *it*, they were glad, and promised to give him money. And he sought how he might conveniently betray him.

identified him with Simon the Pharisee in Lk 7:36-50. **Sat at meat.** That is, reclined on a couch at the table. The woman of the story was Mary, the sister of Martha (cf. Jn 12:2,3). The **alabaster box** was a flask with a long neck that was broken off in order to use the contents (Arndt, pp. 33,34). **Ointment of spikenard.** The Greek text is best translated *ointment of genuine nard.* The nard plant was used to make perfume. **Very precious.** The cost was approximately fifty-five dollars for a pound (cf. v. 5).

**5. Three hundred pence.** That is, three hundred denarii. This was a Roman silver coin worth about eighteen cents. **They murmured.** The verb used here expresses strong emotion, originally meaning *to snort.* A more expressive translation would be, *they began to scold her severely.*

**8.** He explained the true reason for Mary's action. The deed was not merely an act of devotion, but a conscious intention **to anoint** Christ in anticipation of his approaching death and burial. Because Mary had sat at the feet of Jesus and listened intently to his teaching, she had come to understand, even better than the disciples, the truth of his coming death.

**10.** Judas' reaction to the rebuke of Jesus was traitorous. A complete analysis of the man's motives for going **unto the chief priests** is not possible with our limited knowledge. Luke explains it by saying that **Satan entered** into him (22:3). We know that his love of money was a partial reason for the betrayal (cf. Mt 26:14,15). It is also possible that he had been disillusioned by Christ's failure to rise up against Rome and establish a free Jewish kingdom.

**11.** The amount of money they **promised to give him** was thirty pieces of silver (Mt 26:15), which would be worth between twenty and twenty-five dollars. **He sought.** Continuing action (Gr. imp. tense). From this time on Judas was constantly looking for the right moment to **betray him.**

**B. The Lord's Passion. 14:12—15:47.** Mark's account of Christ's suffering and death may be outlined as follows: the events surrounding the last supper (14:12-25); the journey to Gethsemane (14:26-42); the arrest (14:43-52); the trials (14:53—15:15); the crucifixion (15:16-41); the burial (15:42-47). The usual chronology assumes that Wednesday was spent as a day of rest in Bethany and

12. And the first day of unleavened bread, when they killed the passover, his disciples said unto him, Where wilt thou that we go and prepare that thou mayest eat the passover?

13. And he sendeth forth two of his disciples, and saith unto them, Go ye into the city, and there shall meet you a man bearing a pitcher of water: follow him.

14. And wheresoever he shall go in, say ye to the goodman of the house, The Master saith, Where is the guest chamber, where I shall eat the passover with my disciples?

15. And he will show you a large upper room furnished *and* prepared: there make ready for us.

16. And his disciples went forth, and came into the city, and found as he had said unto them: and they made ready the passover.

17. And in the evening he cometh with the twelve.

18. And as they sat and did eat, Jesus said, Verily I say unto you, One of you which eateth with me shall betray me.

19. And they began to be sorrowful, and to say unto him one by one, *Is* it I? and another *said, Is* it I?

20. And he answered and said unto them, *It is* one of the twelve, that dippeth with me in the dish.

that the events of the section under consideration occurred on Thursday and Friday. It is not explicitly stated that such a day of rest intervened, but a comparison of the Gospel records makes it necessary to assume that it did.

12. The first day of unleavened bread may, at first thought, be taken to be the day after the Passover, or Nisan 15 (cf. Lev 23:5,6). However, Mark makes it plain that he is referring to Nisan 14; he says it was when they killed the passover (cf. Ex 12:6). It is known that the Feast of Unleavened Bread was regarded as beginning on the day of the Passover (cf. Jos *Antiq.* II. xv. 1). This was Thursday. The Passover lambs would have been killed in the afternoon, and the Passover meal would have been eaten after sundown on the beginning of Nisan 15.

14. Having followed the servant to the house, the disciples were to make their request of the goodman of the house (Gr., *master of the house, householder*). Who the owner was is not known. Some have suggested that the home was that of Mark, but this is speculation. The Greek text also reads, *Where is my guest-chamber?* It seems from the use of the pronoun, that the Lord had previously made arrangements for use of the room. Eat the passover. Some, on the basis of certain statements in John's Gospel, suppose that the meal was not the Passover, but one prior to the Passover (cf. Jn 13:1,29; 18:28; 19:14,31). However, it is clear that Mark represents Christ as intending to eat the Passover. Furthermore, the statements in John do not necessarily demand the view that the Last Supper preceded the time of the Passover (A. T. Robertson, *A Harmony of the Gospels,* pp. 279-284).

16. Not only did Christ intend to eat the Passover, but Mark specifically states that the disciples made ready the Passover. This would include the killing and roasting of the lamb and provision of the other prescribed items.

17. In the evening. The Passover was eaten after sunset on the beginning of the fifteenth of Nisan.

19. The question, Is it I? expected an answer in the negative, and may be translated, *It is not I, is it?* So monstrous a crime seemed incredible to the eleven. Matthew says (26:25) that Judas also asked the question, but this was obviously an attempt to hide his treachery.

20. In the dish. To eat together, and especially to partake of the contents of the common bowl, was a sign of warm

21. The Son of man indeed goeth, as it is written of him: but woe to that man by whom the Son of man is betrayed! good were it for that man if he had never been born.

22. And as they did eat, Jesus took bread, and blessed, and brake *it*, and gave to them, and said, Take, eat; this is my body.

23. And he took the cup, and when he had given thanks, he gave *it* to them: and they all drank of it.

24. And he said unto them, This is my blood of the new testament, which is shed for many.

25. Verily I say unto you, I will drink no more of the fruit of the vine, until that day that I drink it new in the kingdom of God.

26. And when they had sung a hymn, they went out into the mount of Olives.

friendship. In the light of this custom, Judas' planned betrayal is revealed as still more heinous.

21. As it is written. See on 1:2. The OT passage to which Jesus had reference would seem to be one that describes his betrayal, perhaps Ps 41:9. Notice that God's sovereign purpose, expressed in the words, it is written, did not at all free Judas of moral responsibility for his act.

22. At the Passover meal the bread which Jesus used would have been the unleavened cakes prescribed for the feast. When Jesus said, This is my body, he obviously meant, "This symbolizes my body." His physical body was still present with them. This is similar to the symbolical usage which occurs in Jn 6:35; 8:12; 10:9. The same is true of his statement concerning his blood (Mk 14:24).

23. The cup. We have no way of knowing which of the four Passover cups Jesus used. In any case, however, the contents would have been wine mixed with two-thirds water.

24. The new testament. In both Matthew and Mark the best Greek texts omit the word for new. However, see Lk 22:20; I Cor 11:25. While the Greek word *diathēkē* may refer to a testament or will, the OT background of Christ's remark demands the translation, *covenant* (cf. Ex 24:8). This is not the term used to express an agreement between equal parties *(synthēkē)*. God alone initiated the terms of the covenant, and man could only accept or reject. The blood of Christ is the blood of the new covenant promised in Jer 31:31-34 (cf. Heb 8:6-13). For many. While the Greek preposition, *hyper,* may mean "in behalf of," it is used many times to mean "instead of." Taylor says that this is one of the clearest evidences that Jesus viewed his death as vicarious (Vincent Taylor, *Mark,* p. 548).

25. No more. A strong denial meaning that Jesus would by no means any more drink with them during this present age. The kingdom of God in this remark is eschatological, probably referring to association in the Millennial kingdom to be established when Christ returns (Rev 20:4-6).

26. The hymn, according to Passover usage, would have been a portion of the Hallel Psalms (Ps 115—118). The journey to the Garden of Gethsemane on the mount of Olives and Christ's three sessions of prayer are recorded in 14:26-42.

27. And Jesus saith unto them, All ye shall be offended because of me this night: for it is written, I will smite the shepherd, and the sheep shall be scattered.

28. But after that I am risen, I will go before you into Galilee.

29. But Peter said unto him, Although all shall be offended, yet *will* not I.

30. And Jesus saith unto him, Verily I say unto thee, That this day, *even* in this night, before the cock crow twice, thou shalt deny me thrice.

31. But he spake the more vehemently, If I should die with thee, I will not deny thee in any wise. Likewise also said they all.

32. And they came to a place which was named Gethsemane: and he saith to his disciples, Sit ye here, while I shall pray.

33. And he taketh with him Peter and James and John, and began to be sore amazed, and to be very heavy;

34. And saith unto them, My soul is exceeding sorrowful unto death: tarry ye here, and watch.

35. And he went forward a little, and fell on the ground, and prayed that, if it were possible, the hour might pass from him.

36. And he said, Abba, Father, all things *are* possible unto thee; take away this cup from me: nevertheless, not what I will, but what thou wilt.

37. And he cometh, and findeth them sleeping, and saith unto Peter, Simon, sleepest thou? couldest not thou watch one hour?

**27. Be offended.** The word originally meant *to catch in a trap or snare.* It came to refer, also, to the act of causing someone to stumble. Jesus said, therefore, that the events of that night would take all of them unawares and prove to be a snare or a stumblingblock. **Because of me this night.** Omitted by a number of the most significant Greek manuscripts. **It is written.** See on 1:2. The quotation is taken from Zech 13:7, being freely translated from the Hebrew text.

**30.** Christ stressed the immediacy of the occurrence — **this day . . . this night.** Also he addressed Peter with the emphatic personal pronoun, **thou.** Of all the disciples, Peter, though he insisted on his loyalty, would **deny the Lord.** No contradiction is to be imagined with the other Gospels concerning the number of times the **cock** was to **crow.** The others merely state the fact that the denial would come before cock-crowing (the third watch of the night; see on 13:35). Mark gives added detail by mentioning the specific number of times that the cock would crow.

**31. He spake.** Peter repeatedly affirmed his boast (Gr. imp. tense), and he did so emphatically (**vehemently**). **In any wise.** An excellent translation of the Greek double negative, *ou mē,* which expresses strong denial. With this, all of the disciples kept agreeing (Gr. imp., *elegon*).

**33. Sore amazed.** A strong word, expressing deep emotional upset and distress. It has been translated in various ways *(to be completely upset, to be terrified, appalled, deeply agitated).* Mark adds to this the expression, **very heavy** *(adēmonein),* which speaks of bewilderment and distress (MM, p. 9).

**34.** Jesus was distressed and grieved to the very point of **death.** Hence, he asked them to **watch** (Gr., "to remain awake, alert, and watchful").

**35. The hour** concerning which Jesus prayed was the time when, in the plan of God, he was to suffer and die as an atonement for sin (cf. Jn 12:23,27; 13:1).

**36. Abba** is the Aramaic word for "father." **This cup** refers to the same things as **the hour** (v. 35). It was the cup of a suffering and death which were more than physical. The agony from which the Lord shrank was the agony of soul resulting from bearing the guilt of a lost world. The suffering was to be spiritual suffering, a separation from God the Father (cf. Mk 15:34). And it was concerning this that Christ prayed

38. Watch ye and pray, lest ye enter into temptation. The spirit truly *is* ready, but the flesh *is* weak.

39. And again he went away, and prayed, and spake the same words.

40. And when he returned, he found them asleep again, (for their eyes were heavy,) neither wist they what to answer him.

41. And he cometh the third time, and saith unto them, Sleep on now, and take *your* rest: it is enough, the hour is come; behold, the Son of man is betrayed into the hands of sinners.

42. Rise up, let us go; lo, he that betrayeth me is at hand.

43. And immediately, while he yet spake, cometh Judas, one of the twelve, and with him a great multitude with swords and staves, from the chief priests and the scribes and the elders.

44. And he that betrayed him had given them a token, saying, Whomsoever I shall kiss, that same is he; take him, and lead *him* away safely.

45. And as soon as he was come, he goeth straightway to him, and saith, Master, Master; and kissed him.

46. And they laid their hands on him, and took him.

47. And one of them that stood by drew a sword, and smote a servant of the high priest, and cut off his ear.

48. And Jesus answered and said unto them, Are ye come out, as against a thief, with swords and *with* staves to take me?

49. I was daily with you in the temple teaching, and ye took me not: but the Scriptures must be fulfilled.

asking that the cup might be removed if it was possible for God to accomplish his redemptive purpose by some other means. Nevertheless he was in perfect submission to the Father, desiring his will alone.

**38.** Here the Lord adds the command to **pray** (Gr., *keep praying*) in order that they might not **enter into temptation**. This danger must be interpreted as specifically referring to the coming testings associated with the Lord's arrest and death.

**40. Heavy.** Literally, their eyes were *weighted down* with sleep. The old English word **wist** meant *knew*. They had no excuse.

**41.** He came to them **the third time** after praying once more (Mt 26:44). It is difficult to know in what sense Jesus meant the remark concerning sleeping and resting. Some take it as a question (RSV); others see in it a "kind of sad bitterness" (Ezra P. Gould, *Mark*, pp. 271,272). Now that he had emerged from the darkness of the hour, he no longer needed the assurance that they were in some sense facing the trial with him. This seems to be the thought behind the words, **It is enough. Is betrayed.** The present tense which should be translated *is being betrayed*, signifies that the betrayal was taking place at that very moment.

**43.** The following verses (43-52) recount the arrest of Christ. The mob was led by **Judas**, who knew that Jesus often retired to the seclusion of Gethsemane (Jn 18:2). The **multitude** included some of the Roman cohort garrisoned in Jerusalem as well as the temple police (Jn 18:3). No doubt the soldiers were armed **with swords** and the temple police with **staves** (clubs). The **chief priests, the scribes,** and **the elders** were the three groups of which the Sanhedrin was composed, indicating that the arresting party had been officially dispatched by that body.

**45. Judas,** in mock respect, played the part of a loyal disciple, greeting his teacher as **Master** (Gr., *rabbi*) and then kissing him fervently. The Greek verb for the latter act is a strengthened form of the word translated "kiss" in verse 44. By this intensified act of mock devotion Judas only added to his guilt.

**48.** Christ rebuked them for treating him as though he were an armed robber or highwayman (**thief**, AV).

**49.** This arrest in an out-of-the-way place under cover of darkness was entirely unnecessary, since he had been in

50. And they all forsook him, and fled.

51. And there followed him a certain young man, having a linen cloth cast about *his* naked *body;* and the young men laid hold on him:

52. And he left the linen cloth, and fled from them naked.

53. And they led Jesus away to the high priest: and with him were assembled all the chief priests and the elders and the scribes.

54. And Peter followed him afar off, even into the palace of the high priest: and he sat with the servants, and warmed himself at the fire.

55. And the chief priests and all the council sought for witness against Jesus to put him to death; and found none.

56. For many bare false witness against him, but their witness agreed not together.

57. And there arose certain, and bare false witness against him, saying,

58. We heard him say, I will destroy this temple that is made with hands, and within three days I will build another made without hands.

59. But neither so did their witness agree together.

60. And the high priest stood up in the midst, and asked Jesus, saying, Answerest thou nothing? what *is it which* these witness against thee?

the temple teaching every day. By this protest Christ pointed out the absurdity of their procedures, thus undercutting their reasons for arrest and trial. Yet God had foreseen their actions and predicted the course of events in **the scriptures** (for example, cf. Isa 53:8,9,12). Therefore, regardless of the logic of Christ's protests, the arrest would issue in trial and the trial in execution.

**51. A certain young man.** The Greek word *neaniskos* was used of men between twenty-four and forty years of age (Arndt, p. 536). No other Gospel records this incident. Consequently we have no further information concerning the person's identity. It has often been suggested, perhaps correctly, that Mark was making a veiled reference to himself. There seems to be no other reason why this insignificant event was included.

**52. Naked.** The word *gymnos* does not necessarily mean naked; it was also used to describe a person clothed only in an undergarment.

**53.** Here the account turns to the Jewish and Roman trials of Christ (14:53—15:15). Mark moves immediately to the account of the night trial before the Sanhedrin (vv. 53-65). That the examining body was the Sanhedrin is shown by the presence of **all the chief priests and the elders and the scribes.** The high priest at this time was Caiaphas.

**54.** Perhaps because he was determined to fulfill his boast of loyalty, **Peter followed** Jesus. However, fear held him at a distance, and as a result he was not able to slip into the house of the high priest with the crowd. Mark's word translated **palace** is *aulēn* and actually refers to a courtyard. John explains (18:15, 16) that another disciple secured an entrance for Peter. **The servants** with whom he sat were probably temple police and attendants of the high priest.

**55.** The word translated **council** is *synedrion,* from which the word "sanhedrin" comes. They carried on a prolonged search (*ezētoun,* imp. tense) for witnesses against Jesus. These members of the Jewish court were acting as prosecutors.

**58,59.** These persons were speaking of Christ's remark during his early Judean ministry on the occasion of the first cleansing of the Temple (Jn 2:19). The falsity of their witness was evidenced by their misuse of the statement and by their failure to agree.

**60.** Embarrassed by the disagreement of the witnesses, **the high priest** at-

**61.** But he held his peace, and answered nothing. Again the high priest asked him, and said unto him, Art thou the Christ, the Son of the Blessed?

**62.** And Jesus said, I am: and ye shall see the Son of man sitting on the right hand of power, and coming in the clouds of heaven.

**63.** Then the high priest rent his clothes, and saith, What need we any further witnesses?

**64.** Ye have heard the blasphemy: what think ye? And they all condemned him to be guilty of death.

**65.** And some began to spit on him, and to cover his face, and to buffet him, and to say unto him, Prophesy: and the servants did strike him with the palms of their hands.

**66.** And as Peter was beneath in the palace, there cometh one of the maids of the high priest:

**67.** And when she saw Peter warming himself, she looked upon him, and said, And thou also wast with Jesus of Nazareth.

tempted to involve Christ in the discussion, apparently hoping that his answer would prove his guilt.

**61.** The question, **Art thou the Christ?** places the personal pronoun in the emphatic position; it may be rendered, *You, are you the Messiah?* It was common for the Jews to use some such term as **the Blessed** when referring to God, in order that they might not become guilty of taking the divine name in vain. Matthew makes it clear (26:63) that the high priest placed Jesus under solemn oath, which made it obligatory for him to answer. He had no way out but to bear witness which would be turned against him.

**62.** With a forthright assertion, Jesus answered, **I am.** The remainder of his reply is couched in terms taken from Dan 7:13 and Ps 110:1. The **right hand of power** is the right hand of God. Christ assured his judges that the day would come when they would see him as Messiah, exercising the power of deity and coming in judgment (see on 13:26).

**63.** This was the kind of reply desired by the high priest. He promptly **rent his clothes,** as he was required to do at the sound of blasphemy (cf. H. B. Swete, *Mark,* pp. 359,360). No **further witnesses** were needed, since Jesus had been forced to bear witness against himself, an illegal procedure under Jewish law.

**64.** The declaration of Christ was interpreted as **blasphemy** because the officials viewed Jesus as a mere man (cf. Jn 10:33). The question of his guilt was put to the whole council, and they unanimously **condemned him to be guilty.** The established penalty for blasphemy was **death** (Lev 24:16).

**65.** Apparently it was **some** of the members of the Sanhedrin who began to treat Jesus in the shameful manner described. For such highly placed, respected religious leaders of Judaism, the acts of these dignitaries were most degrading. They covered **his face** with a blindfold when they struck him in order to make a mockery of his supernatural knowledge (cf. Lk 22:64). When he was turned over to **the servants** (the temple police), these followed the example of the officials and began to **strike** him. The word *rapisma* refers either to a blow with a rod or to a slap with the palm of the hand.

**67. Looked upon him.** The word indicates that she fixed her gaze on him. Because of John's intercession for Peter Jn 18:15,16), the maid no doubt was sure that Peter was a follower of Jesus.

68. But he denied, saying, I know not, neither understand I what thou sayest. And he went out into the porch; and the cock crew.

69. And a maid saw him again, and began to say to them that stood by, This is one of them.

70. And he denied it again. And a little after, they that stood by said again to Peter, Surely thou art one of them: for thou art a Galilean, and thy speech agreeth thereto.

71. But he began to curse and to swear, saying, I know not this man of whom ye speak.

72. And the second time the cock crew. And Peter called to mind the word that Jesus said unto him, Before the cock crow twice, thou shalt deny me thrice. And when he thought thereon, he wept.

## CHAPTER 15

AND straightway in the morning the chief priests held a consultation with the elders and scribes and the whole council, and bound Jesus, and carried him away, and delivered him to Pilate.

68. Peter's denial was strengthened by repetition (know not, neither understand). Caught by the unexpected identification, he forgot his boast of loyalty. The porch to which Peter withdrew was the forecourt or vestibule leading from the street into the courtyard. Many ancient texts omit the words, and the cock crew.

69. The Greek text indicates that this was the same maid who had previously accused Peter. However, Mt 26:71 speaks of another maid, while Lk 22:58 states that another person (masculine) addressed Peter directly. It is not necessary to find contradictions among the accounts here. There were evidently two maids, the doorkeeper and another, who pointed Peter out to the bystanders. In addition, a man said to Peter, "You also are one of them."

70. The third accusation came from several persons who stood by. There were probably a number of statements made, as the imperfect tense *elegon* may well show. John 18:26 reveals that one of those making accusations was a relative of the person whose ear Peter had cut off.

71. To curse and to swear. These verbs do not mean that Peter used profanity as the term is understood today. Instead, he called down a curse probably upon himself (RSV), if he was not telling the truth, and he placed himself under oath in making his denial.

72. Here the manuscript evidence justifies the inclusion of the words, the second time (see on v. 68). The best texts also contain the word "immediately" (*euthys*). The sound of the cock followed hard on the third denial, striking deep into the consciousness of the fallen disciple. At the same time Peter saw Jesus looking down upon him (Lk 22:61) from a room above the courtyard. He thought thereon. The word *epibalōn* has long been a problem of translation here. Probably the RSV rendering, *he broke down*, is best (MM, p. 235; Taylor, *Mark*, p. 576). Whereas *epibalōn* describes the onset of the weeping, the imperfect tense *eklaien*, he wept, depicts the continuation of it.

15:1. This verse describes a second meeting of the Sanhedrin very early in the morning. Luke 22:66-71 gives a fuller record of this phase of the Jewish trial. It appears to have been an attempt to make the condemnation legal, since it was illegal to hold a trial at night. At this time the Romans did not permit the Jews

2. And Pilate asked him, Art thou the King of the Jews? And he answering said unto him, Thou sayest *it*.

3. And the chief priests accused him of many things; but he answered nothing.

4. And Pilate asked him again, saying, Answerest thou nothing? behold how many things they witness against thee.

5. But Jesus yet answered nothing; so that Pilate marveled.

6. Now at *that* feast he released unto them one prisoner, whomsoever they desired.

7. And there was *one* named Barabbas, *which lay* bound with them that had made insurrection with him, who had committed murder in the insurrection.

8. And the multitude crying aloud began to desire *him to do* as he had ever done unto them.

9. But Pilate answered them, saying, Will ye that I release unto you the King of the Jews?

10. For he knew that the chief priests had delivered him for envy.

11. But the chief priests moved the people, that he should rather release Barabbas unto them.

12. And Pilate answered and said again unto them, What will ye then that I shall do *unto him* whom ye call the King of the Jews?

13. And they cried out again, Crucify him.

14. Then Pilate said unto them, Why, what evil hath he done? And they cried out the more exceedingly, Crucify him.

15. And *so* Pilate, willing to content the people, released Barabbas unto them, and delivered Jesus, when he had scourged *him*, to be crucified.

to inflict the sentence of capital punishment. Consequently it was necessary to take Jesus **to Pilate,** who was the Roman procurator over Judea.

**2.** The Roman trial is described in 15:2-15. For a more complete account of the Roman trial see Jn 18:28—19:16. One of the charges was that Jesus claimed to be a **king,** and it was out of this allegation that Pilate's question grew. A claim to kingship was ground for trial for treason. Jesus' reply, **Thou sayest,** is capable of being variously interpreted. However, in the light of Jn 18:34-38 it seems best to understand it as an affirmative answer, which, as John shows, was accompanied by an explanation as to what kind of a king Jesus claimed to be.

**3,4.** These verses picture **the chief priests** as they threw a barrage of accusations against Jesus. So vicious was the attack that **Pilate** could not understand the calm demeanor of the prisoner (cf. v. 5).

**6.** The governor had established a practice of releasing **one prisoner** each year at the Passover, perhaps as an attempt to maintain the good will of the Jews. The verbs **he released** and **they desired** (Gr., *asked*) are both in the imperfect tense, showing that these were customary acts; i.e., "He used to release . . . ."

**7.** The prisoner **Barabbas** was no mere petty thief. He was a robber (Jn 18:40), as well as an insurrectionist and a murderer. It appears that the man was a Jew who had participated in an uprising against Rome, a very similar crime to that of which the Jews were accusing Jesus (Ezra P. Gould, *Mark,* p. 285).

**8. Crying aloud.** The better ancient manuscripts read *anabas,* "went up" (ASV). The crowd asked Pilate to perform his customary act (**had ever done;** Gr. imp. tense) of releasing a prisoner. It seems that the crowd was requesting the release of Barabbas, since he may well have been a kind of hero to them because of his part in the rebellion against Rome.

**11.** At this point the crowd might have been tempted to request the release of Jesus, but the priests **moved the people** to ask for Barabbas. The word *anaseiō* means "to incite, to stir up," or more literally, *to shake up,* showing their excited agitation of the mob.

**15. Willing to content the people.** The Greek expression *(to hikanon poiēsai)* implies that he was willing to satisfy the Jews, even if he had to sacrifice an inno-

16. And the soldiers led him away into the hall, called Pretorium; and they call together the whole band.

17. And they clothed him with purple, and platted a crown of thorns, and put it about his *head,*

18. And began to salute him, Hail, King of the Jews!

19. And they smote him on the head with a reed, and did spit upon him, and bowing *their* knees worshipped him.

20. And when they had mocked him, they took off the purple from him, and put his own clothes on him, and led him out to crucify him.

21. And they compel one Simon a Cyrenian, who passed by, coming out of the country, the father of Alexander and Rufus, to bear his cross.

22. And they bring him unto the place Golgotha, which is, being interpreted, The place of a skull.

23. And they gave him to drink wine mingled with myrrh: but he received *it* not.

cent man to do it. **Scourged.** This act was accomplished with a whip made of strips of leather having rough pieces of metal tied at the ends of the strips. The victim was bent forward over a short post, and the punishment was administered to his naked back. Often the resultant deep gashes opened the flesh to the very bone.

**16.** It was not yet 9:00 A.M. The trial before Pilate was followed very shortly by the crucifixion (15:16-41). **The soldiers** to whom Jesus was committed were Roman military personnel under the jurisdiction of Pilate. **The hall.** The Greek word is *aulē,* "courtyard," the same as in 14:54, where it is translated "palace" (AV). Mark explains that it was **called Praetorium,** a term which could well refer either to the palace of Herod or to the fortress of Antonia, where the Roman troops were quartered (cf. Arndt, p. 704). At any rate, it seems to refer to the soldiers' barracks. The **band** was a Roman cohort containing approximately six hundred men. However, the figure varied with the situation, and in this instance could have been much less.

**19.** The three verbs, **smote, spit,** and **worshipped,** are all in the imperfect tense, depicting the repetition of these acts. Soldier after soldier made bitter mockery of Jesus' misunderstood claim to be a king.

**21.** John 19:17 explains that as the procession set out for the execution, Jesus was bearing his own cross. Shortly, however, the soldiers came upon **Simon** and forced him to carry the instrument of execution. This man's identity was evidently known by Mark's Roman readers, for Mark mentions his sons, **Alexander and Rufus,** as familiar persons. There was a Rufus in Rome when Paul wrote the Epistle to the Romans (16:13).

**22. Golgotha** is an Aramaic word meaning *a skull.* The place was probably so named by reason of its shape. The traditional site, still favored by many, is at the Church of the Holy Sepulcher. Others insist on the hill known as Gordon's Calvary. In the interests of objectivity we must admit that, at the present time, sure identification of the spot is impossible.

**23. Gave.** The imperfect tense, *edidoun,* is better translated *they were going to give.* Jesus refused the drink after tasting it and discovering what it was (Mt 27:34). **Myrrh** served as a drug administered to deaden the torture of the horrible death of crucifixion. Jesus, however, refused to allow such a stupifying potion to cloud his senses.

24. And when they had crucified him, they parted his garments, casting lots upon them, what every man should take.

25. And it was the third hour, and they crucified him.

26. And the superscription of his accusation was written over, THE KING OF THE JEWS.

27. And with him they crucify two thieves; the one on his right hand, and the other on his left.

28. And the Scripture was fulfilled, which saith, And he was numbered with the transgressors.

29. And they that passed by railed on him, wagging their heads, and saying, Ah, thou that destroyest the temple, and buildest it in three days,

30. Save thyself, and come down from the cross.

31. Likewise also the chief priests mocking said among themselves with the scribes, He saved others; himself he cannot save.

32. Let Christ the King of Israel descend now from the cross, that we may see and believe. And they that were crucified with him reviled him.

33. And when the sixth hour was come, there was darkness over the whole land until the ninth hour.

34. And at the ninth hour Jesus cried with a loud voice, saying, Eloi, Eloi, lama sabachthani? which is, being interpreted, My God, my God, why hast thou forsaken me?

24. The details of the crucifixion are absent from all of the Gospels. It is known from Jn 20:25 that nails were used to fasten the hands to the cross. Crucifixion was recognized as being one of the most cruel forms of execution employed in the ancient world. Often the victim was left on the cross for several days before death relieved his intense suffering. The garments of the condemned man were left to the executioners.

25. The time of the crucifixion is placed at the third hour, which was the Jewish designation for 9:00 A.M. The trial before Pilate occurred about the sixth hour, according to Roman time, which would be 6:00 A.M. (cf. Jn 19:14).

26. It was customary to use a placard of some kind indicating the name and the accusation of the condemned man. Mark gives only the crime of which Jesus was accused. John indicates that the superscription also contained the identification, Jesus of Nazareth (19:19). There is no contradiction; Mark is merely more concise.

27. The two criminals crucified with Jesus were more than mere petty thieves. As in 14:48, lēstēs means "robber, highwayman."

29,30. Railed on him. The passers-by kept blaspheming (eblasphēmoun, imp. tense) Jesus. Wagging their heads. They shook their heads in scornful disapproval. The logic behind their sarcasm was an argument from the greater to the lesser. If he could rebuild the Temple in three days, certainly he could easily come down from the cross.

31. The chief priests and the scribes likewise participated in the mockery, but among themselves. Their oft-repeated sarcasm concerning Christ's inability to save himself was in reality a denial that he could help anybody. If he could not deliver himself from suffering and death, how could he deliver anyone else?

33. Three hours had passed; it was now noon, the sixth hour. At the hour of the sun's brightest light, darkness came (egeneto) over the whole land. This could not have been a total eclipse so that the whole earth was darkened, as Lenski argues (Lenski, Interpret. of Mark, pp. 713-714), for the Passover occurred at the time of the full moon, when no such eclipse is possible. What caused the darkness is not stated. Certainly the timing of the phenomenon was supernatural. The ninth hour was 3:00 P.M. (see on v. 25).

34. Jesus had been on the cross for six hours. His cry was a quotation from Ps 22:1. Eloi, Eloi, lama sabachthani is a

35. And some of them that stood by, when they heard *it*, said, Behold, he calleth Elias.

36. And one ran and filled a sponge full of vinegar, and put *it* on a reed, and gave him to drink, saying, Let alone; let us see whether Elias will come to take him down.

37. And Jesus cried with a loud voice, and gave up the ghost.

38. And the veil of the temple was rent in twain from the top to the bottom.

39. And when the centurion, which stood over against him, saw that he so cried out, and gave up the ghost, he said, Truly this man was the Son of God.

transliteration from Aramaic, the native tongue of Christ. Mark, as his custom was, gave the meaning of the Aramaic for his Roman readers. This cry of abandonment provides a glimpse into the inner sufferings of Christ on the cross. His greatest agony was not physical; it was rather agony of soul as he bore the guilt of the world's sin. The sense in which God had **forsaken** Christ was that the Father withdrew from communion with the Son. No longer did he evidence his love toward his Son. Instead, Christ had become the object of the Father's displeasure, for he was the sinner's Substitute. Christ became "sin for us" (II Cor 5:21), and a holy God cannot look with favor upon sin.

36. The **vinegar** was a sour wine that quenched thirst more readily than water (Arndt, pp. 577,578). Since this was not a drugged mixture as in verse 23, Jesus received it without protest (cf. Jn 19:29,30). **Whether Elias will come.** There is no reason for assuming that the speakers were sincere in their words. This was no doubt a continuation of the mockery that is so evident in 15:29-32.

37. **Gave up the ghost.** The Greek word is *exepneusen,* which literally means that he *breathed out* or *expired.* It was not a prolonged struggle, such as the imperfect tense would describe. Instead, the aorist tense depicts a brief, momentary occurrence. He breathed out his spirit and was gone.

38. **The veil** was the heavy curtain that separated the Holy Place from the Holy of Holies in **the temple** *(naos,* "sanctuary"). For a description see Josephus *Wars of the Jews* V. v. 4. The rent moved **from the top to the bottom,** perhaps pointing to the divine origin of the occurrence. Its timing was significant. Since this was the hour of the evening sacrifice, the rending of the veil could not have happened unnoticed. The significance of the opening of the Holy of Holies is set forth in Heb 9:7,8; 10:19-22.

39. **A centurion** normally had one hundred men under his command. In this instance the officer was in charge of the smaller detachment assigned to the crucifixion. **Over against him.** That is, he stood facing the cross. The centurion's declaration that Jesus **was the Son of God** ought not to be taken in the full Christian sense. In the first place, the article does not appear in the Greek text. It should, therefore, read "a son of God" or, at the most, "God's Son." The pagan background of the Roman officer must not be overlooked. He may well have viewed Jesus as a super-

40. There were also women looking on afar off: among whom was Mary Magdalene, and Mary the mother of James the less and of Joses, and Salome;

41. Who also, when he was in Galilee, followed him, and ministered unto him; and many other women which came up with him unto Jerusalem.

42. And now when the even was come, because it was the preparation, that is, the day before the sabbath,

43. Joseph of Arimathea, an honorable counselor, which also waited for the kingdom of God, came, and went in boldly unto Pilate, and craved the body of Jesus.

44. And Pilate marveled if he were already dead: and calling *unto him* the centurion, he asked him whether he had been any while dead.

45. And when he knew *it* of the centurion, he gave the body to Joseph.

46. And he bought fine linen, and took him down, and wrapped him in the linen, and laid him in a sepulchre which was hewn out of a rock, and rolled a stone unto the door of the sepulchre.

47. And Mary Magdalene and Mary *the mother* of Joses beheld where he was laid.

### CHAPTER 16

AND when the sabbath was past, Mary Magdalene, and Mary the *mother* of James, and Salome, had bought sweet spices, that they might come and anoint him.

human being, but that he possessed the full Christian concept of the deity of Christ is unlikely. Furthermore, Luke records that he declared Jesus to be a righteous man (23:47). For a forceful presentation of the opposite view, see Lenski, *Interpretation of Mark*, pp. 725-727.

40. **Mary Magdalene** is not to be confused with Mary of Bethany (Jn 12:1 ff.) nor with the sinful woman of Lk 7:37. She came from Magdala in Galilee, and she had experienced deliverance from demon possession at the command of Jesus (Lk 8:2). The second **Mary** seems to have been the mother of James the son of Alphaeus, one of the disciples (Mk 3:18). **Salome** is described as the mother of James and John, the sons of Zebedee (Mt 27:56).

42. The account of the Passion closes with a description of the burial of Jesus (vv. 42-47). **The even was come.** The evening referred to here must of necessity have been the early evening, between the hour of the evening sacrifice (3:00 P.M.) and sunset (about 6:00 P.M.). The arrangements for burial had to be made before the beginning of the sabbath at sundown (cf. Jn 19:31-37). Notice Mark's explanation of the Jewish term, **the preparation,** for his Gentile readers.

43. We know nothing about **Joseph of Arimathaea** except what the Gospels present in connection with this event (cf. Mt 27:57; Lk 23:51; Jn 19:38). **Craved.** That is, he requested (*aiteō*) the body.

46. The **fine linen** was wound around the body of Jesus in strips (cf. Jn 19:40, Gr. text). The **sepulchre** had been **hewn out** of the rock by a stonecutter, a common practice in that vicinity. Matthew states that the tomb belonged to Joseph and that it was new (27:60). The **stone** which was **rolled** before the door was probably a flat, circular slab which rolled in a channel carved out of the rock for that purpose.

C. The Lord's Resurrection. 16:1-20. The last chapter of the Gospel falls into two clearly distinguished sections. The visit of the three women to the tomb occupies 16:1-8. The remainder of the chapter, 16:9-20, forms a summary of the resurrection appearances of Christ, concluding with his ascension.

1. Since **the sabbath** ended at sundown, it appears that the three women mentioned in 15:40 went to one of the shops that had been opened again for the evening and purchased the desired materials. The **sweet spices** (*arōmata*) were in a liquid form, such as perfumed oil, for the women planned to anoint the body of Jesus.

2. And very early in the morning, the first *day* of the week, they came unto the sepulchre at the rising of the sun.

3. And they said among themselves, Who shall roll us away the stone from the door of the sepulchre?

4. And when they looked, they saw that the stone was rolled away: for it was very great.

5. And entering into the sepulchre, they saw a young man sitting on the right side, clothed in a long white garment; and they were affrighted.

6. And he saith unto them, Be not affrighted: ye seek Jesus of Nazareth, which was crucified: he is risen; he is not here: behold the place where they laid him.

7. But go your way, tell his disciples and Peter that he goeth before you into Galilee: there shall ye see him, as he said unto you.

8. And they went out quickly, and fled from the sepulchre; for they trembled and were amazed: neither said they any thing to any *man;* for they were afraid.

**2. Very early.** John says that it was still dark (20:1), whereas Mark states that it was **at the rising of the sun.** The apparent conflict is easily resolved if we assume that the women began their journey while it was yet dark and arrived at the tomb just after the sun had risen.

**4. When they looked.** The word is *anablepō*, meaning "to look up." Perhaps as they approached they were walking with bowed heads.

**5.** Mark reports that **they saw a young man.** Matthew describes the person as an angel who had removed the stone (28:2-4). And Luke says there were two men in dazzling clothes (24:4). The variety is evidence that these are the reports of several eyewitnesses, each of whom described what impressed her most. The full story would include the appearance of two angels, one of whom rolled the stone away and spoke to the women. **Affrighted.** The word is more accurately translated as *utterly amazed.* Lenski uses the word "dumbfounded" *(Interpret. of Mark,* p. 742).

**6. Be not affrighted.** It should be rendered, *Stop being utterly amazed.* The angel assured them that Jesus had **risen** and left, in proof of which he called their attention to **the place where they laid him.** John 20:6,7 informs us that the grave cloths (ASV) were still there in their place.

**7.** Notice how **Peter** is singled out in the arrangement for a meeting in **Galilee.** By this means the fallen disciple was assured that Christ had not rejected him as a result of his denials (14:66-72). Comparison with the other Gospels shows that the disciples did not leave at once for Galilee and that Christ first appeared to Peter (Lk 24:34) and then to the disciples that evening (Lk 24:36). The meeting in Galilee is recorded in Mt 28:16-20.

**8. They trembled and were amazed.** Mark's original is much stronger. He says, ". . . trembling and astonishment were gripping them." It is no wonder that they **fled from the sepulchre.** The statement that they said nothing **to any man** must be understood in the light of the other Gospels. They said nothing to anyone along the way, for they were afraid and in a hurry to take the news to the disciples (cf. Mt 28:8; Lk 24:9,10).

**Textual note, 16:9-20.** In the two most trustworthy manuscripts of the Greek NT (the Vaticanus and Sinaiticus) the Gospel ends with 16:8, as it does also in several early versions. Both Eusebius and Jerome state that the ending was missing from

9. Now when *Jesus* was risen early the first *day* of the week, he appeared first to Mary Magdalene, out of whom he had cast seven devils.

10. *And* she went and told them that had been with him, as they mourned and wept.

11. And they, when they had heard that he was alive, and had been seen of her, believed not.

12. After that he appeared in another form unto two of them, as they walked, and went into the country.

13. And they went and told *it* unto the residue: neither believed they them.

14. Afterward he appeared unto the eleven as they sat at meat, and upbraided them with their unbelief and hardness of heart, because they believed not them which had seen him after he was risen.

15. And he said unto them, Go ye into all the world, and preach the gospel to every creature.

16. He that believeth and is baptized shall be saved; but he that believeth not shall be damned.

most of the manuscripts of their day. In addition, several texts and versions offer a shorter substitute in the place of 16:9-20. By far the greater number of manuscripts have the longer conclusion, but many of them are of a late date and an inferior quality. By the recognized standards of textual evaluation, both the longer and shorter endings must be rejected, and this is the judgment of almost all textual scholars. Lenski is one of the few commentators who argue for the longer ending (*Interpret. of Mark,* pp. 750-755). In addition, an examination of verses 9-20 cannot fail to impress the careful student with the fact that these verses differ markedly in style from the rest of the Gospel. Perhaps the most acceptable explanation is that the end of the original Gospel may have been torn off and lost before additional copies could be made. Perhaps others attempted to supply a substitute ending, the most successful of which was that which now appears in 16:9-20.

**9-11.** The original account, which is here summarized, is to be found in Jn 20:11-18. Notice the author's emphasis on the unbelief of the disciples (Mk 16:11, 13,14).

**12,13.** For a more complete record of this event, see Lk 24:13-35. **In another form.** Luke 24:16 says that their eyes were somehow affected so that they did not recognize Christ. Whether Christ had actually changed his appearance we do not know. The **residue** were the eleven disciples in Jerusalem (Lk 24:33).

**14-18.** This appearence to **the eleven** followed immediately upon the report of the Emmaus travelers (Lk 24:36-49; Jn 20:19-25). Luke and John do not create the impression that Jesus scolded them for **their unbelief and hardness of heart,** but that he recognized how hard it was for them to believe, and he sought to remove their difficulty by offering proofs of his resurrection. **He that believeth and is baptized.** This verse has been used by some to attempt to prove that baptism is necessary for salvation. In the first place, the fact that the statement appears only in this questionable conclusion to the book of Mark should indicate the need for caution in the use of the verse as a prooftext. And then, it should be noted that in the second half of the verse the only basis for condemnation is a refusal to believe. It may therefore be concluded that the only basis of salvation is belief. Such an interpretation is in full harmony with the teaching of the NT as a whole on the subject (cf. Rom 3:28; Eph 2:8,9). The statement concerning casting out

17. And these signs shall follow them that believe; In my name shall they cast out devils; they shall speak with new tongues;

18. They shall take up serpents; and if they drink any deadly thing, it shall not hurt them; they shall lay hands on the sick, and they shall recover.

19. So then, after the Lord had spoken unto them, he was received up into heaven, and sat on the right hand of God.

20. And they went forth, and preached every where, the Lord working with *them*, and confirming the word with signs following. Amen.

demons (**devils**) and speaking with **new tongues** (v. 17) could well have reference to occurrences in the early church as recorded in Acts. Even the words about taking up **serpents** may be an allusion to Paul's experience in Acts 28:1-6. The NT contains no other passage dealing with drinking poison (**any deadly thing**). Even if this passage were unquestionably genuine, it could not reasonably be used as a basis for the deliberate and presumptuous handling of snakes and drinking of poison which are practiced by certain extreme religious sects.

**19,20.** This final summary is concerned with the ascension of Christ and the continuing ministry of his followers. The phrase, **after the Lord had spoken,** may seem to imply that Christ's ascension occurred immediately after his appearance to the eleven on the evening of the day of his resurrection (vv. 14-18). However, a comparison with Lk 24:50-53 and Acts 1:1-11 shows that forty days had elapsed since his death. The closing verse of the Gospel could well serve as a very brief summary of the book of Acts. **The Lord ... confirming the word.** Note the striking resemblance to Heb 2:4.

# BIBLIOGRAPHY

ALFORD, HENRY. *The Greek Testament.* Revised by Everett F. Harrison. Vol. I. Chicago: Moody Press, 1958.

BEASLEY-MURRAY, G. R. *A Commentary on Mark Thirteen.* London: Macmillan and Co. Ltd., 1957.

BRANSCOMB, HARVIE. *The Gospel of Mark (The Moffatt New Testament Commentary).* London: Hodder and Stoughton Ltd., 1952.

BRUCE, ALEXANDER B. "The Synoptic Gospels," *The Expositor's Greek Testament.* Edited by W. Robertson Nicoll. Vol. I. Grand Rapids: Wm. B. Eerdmans Publishing Co., n.d.

EARLE, RALPH. *The Gospel According to Mark (The Evangelical Commentary on the Bible).* Grand Rapids: Zondervan Publishing House, 1957.

GOULD, EZRA P. *The Gospel According to St. Mark (The International Critical Commentary).* Edinburgh: T. & T. Clark, 1948.

GRANT, FREDERICK C. and LUCCOCK, H. E. "The Gospel According to St. Mark," *The Interpreter's Bible.* Vol. 7. New York: Abingdon-Cokesbury Press, 1951.

LENSKI, R. C. H. *The Interpretation of St. Mark's Gospel.* Columbus: The Wartburg Press, 1951.

ROBERTSON, A. T. *Word Pictures in the New Testament.* Vol. I. New York: Harper & Brothers, 1930.

SWETE, HENRY B. *The Gospel According to St. Mark.* London: Macmillan and Co. Ltd., 1953.

TAYLOR, VINCENT. *The Gospel According to St. Mark.* London: Macmillan and Co. Ltd., 1953.

VINCENT, MARVIN R. *Word Studies in the New Testament.* Vol. I. Grand Rapids: Wm. B. Eerdmans Publishing Co., 1946.

WUEST, KENNETH S. *Mark in the Greek New Testament.* Grand Rapids: Wm. B. Eerdmans Publishing Co., 1950.

# THE GOSPEL
# ACCORDING TO LUKE

## INTRODUCTION

The Gospel according to Luke is the most complete account of the life of Jesus that has survived from the apostolic age. It was designed to be a full presentation of the career of the Saviour from his birth to his ascension, and was part of a larger work including the book of Acts, which carried the history forward into the missionary activity of the church as far as the establishment of the Christian community in Rome.

*Author.* According to the uniform testimony of the church, Luke, a Gentile physician and companion of Paul, was the author of the Third Gospel. His name is not mentioned in its pages, but the consensus of available evidence tends to confirm the tradition.

The close relation of the Gospel to the Acts shows that the two works had a common author, and that whatever clues to his identity can be furnished by the one will apply to the interpretation of the other. Both works were addressed to the same man, Theophilus (Lk 1:3; Acts 1:1). The content of Luke fits perfectly the description of "the former treatise" mentioned in the introduction of Acts (Acts 1:1). The continuity of style and of teaching on the person of Christ, the dominant emphasis on the work of the Holy Spirit, the pervasive interest in ministry to the Gentiles, and the writer's constant awareness of contemporary historical events point to a designed unity.

On this basis, the facts supplied by Acts concerning its author will apply also to the Gospel. The author was a Gentile convert, possibly of the church at Antioch, where Paul served with Barnabas at the beginning of his ministry (Acts 11:25, 26). The writer joined him later at Troas, as his use of the pronoun "we" indicates (Acts 16:10), accompanied him to Philippi, and presumably remained there while Paul visited Jerusalem. When Paul returned to Philippi, Luke went back with him to Jerusalem (Acts 20:5–21:15), where Paul was arrested and placed in protective custody. At the close of Paul's detention in Caesarea, Luke accompanied him to Rome (Acts 27:1–28:15).

Paul speaks of Luke three times in his epistles, calling him "the beloved physician" (Col 4:14; Phm 24), and indicating later that he was the last friend to remain with him in his second imprisonment (II Tim 4:11).

Paul's statement that Luke was a physician is corroborated by the language Luke uses and by the interest he shows in disease and in healing. An outstanding example of his bent of mind appears in the difference between his account and that of Mark regarding the woman with an issue of blood (Lk 8:43; Mk 5:26). He diagnoses the woman's case as incurable, whereas Mark emphasizes the helplessness of the physicians.

Luke's ministry was broad. Doctor, pastor, traveling evangelist, historian, and writer, he was tremendously versatile and active. He had a wide acquaintance with the Christian leaders of the first century, and he seems to have had important special connections also with Roman officials.

Tradition has preserved a few interesting legends about him, though they may not be authentic. According to these stories, Luke was an artist, who painted a picture of the Virgin Mary. He never married, and in his later years retired to Bithynia, where he died. Other legends say that he was martyred in Greece.

*Sources.* The content of Luke bears a general resemblance to that of Matthew and of Mark because all three of the Synoptic Gospels deal with the common occurrences of the life of Jesus. Probably a large portion of Luke's narrative which coincides with the content of Matthew and Mark may be derived from the narrative preaching of the apostolic missionaries. One widely accepted theory adds that Luke used Mark's Gospel and a special discourse source in much the same fashion as Matthew did. According to his own testimony he knew of other accounts (Lk 1:1,2), but how much he used them is uncertain. A great deal of Luke's material, however, is unique. His story of the events relating to the birth of Christ differs from that of Matthew in viewpoint and in some details. He selects more of Jesus' story parables than do Matthew and Mark, and he puts greater stress on individual characters in his narrative. In the discussion of the Resurrection he introduces the walk to Emmaus, which none of the other Gospels contains in full.

These unique features he must have obtained from eyewitnesses, for he was not personally present at the events he describes. In his introduction he states that he did so (Lk 1:2), and later in the Gospel he mentions persons from whom he could have derived his information. Mary, the mother of Jesus, may have supplied the content of the first two chapters; Mary Magdalene, Joanna the wife of Chuza (Herod's steward), and other women (8:3) could have given him many personal reminiscences. If Luke traveled in Palestine during Paul's imprisonment at Caesarea, he could have interviewed countless people who would have remembered hearing Jesus preach and teach. From the preaching of Paul and of other apostles whom he heard, he could have drawn much of the doctrinal application that appears both in the Gospel and in Acts.

*Date.* Because of the abrupt ending of the book of Acts, it seems likely that Luke concluded his writing at the end of Paul's two years' imprisonment at Rome. If the Gospel was written previously, as the introduction to Acts indicates (Acts 1:1), it must have been composed, at the latest, prior to A.D. 62, when the Roman imprisonment ended. Perhaps Luke gathered the material for it during his ten years of service with Paul, and then, before leaving Palestine with Paul on the journey to Rome, he sent it from Caesarea to his friend Theophilus. If so, the Gospel could have been written as early as A.D. 58. The allusion to a siege and capture of Jerusalem (Lk 21:20-24) has been interpreted by some to mean that the Gospel must have been written after the fall of the city in A.D. 70. Such a conclusion is not necessary if one considers that the content of the chapter is a prophecy, and that Luke is merely recording the words of Jesus about the future.

The affinity in language between Luke's account of the Last Supper (22:14-23) and Paul's summary (I Cor 11:23-26) may indicate that Luke was repeating the words which Paul himself used on numerous occasions. If so, the composition and publication of the Gospel would be related more closely to the time of Paul than to a period of thirty or more years later.

*Place.* No clue to the place of publication is given to us. One tradition connects the Gospel with Greece, possibly Athens. Another suggestion would place it in Antioch of Syria, where Luke's friends may have lived. Caesarea seems to be the most likely place of composition, but the Gospel might have been completed and sent to Theophilus from Rome, if not from Caesarea itself.

*Destination.* Theophilus, to whom the Gospel was addressed, was probably a Gentile of high social standing. Luke salutes him with the title, "most excellent," which he reserves elsewhere in his writings for Roman officials (Acts 24:3; 26:25; AV, *most noble*). Nothing is known of him directly beyond the two allusions in Luke 1:3 and Acts 1:1. He was a Christian convert, interested in knowing more about his new faith than he could learn from mere routine instruction. Luke's two treatises were designed to make him an intelligent believer.

*The Development of the Thought.* The Gospel of Luke unfolds the career of Jesus as one would present its high lights to an audience through a moving picture. It begins with his ancestry and birth, continues through his earthly ministry to the Passion, and comes to a climax in the Resurrection. Acts continues his work in the church through the Holy Spirit down to Paul's arrival at Rome. The Gospel, then, is devoted to the first half of this progressive presentation of the person of Christ.

The structure of Luke follows the same general order as that of Matthew and Mark, since that is determined by the life of Christ itself. The presentation of the facts is fuller in some respects, but is less topical than Matthew's and is more flowing than Mark's.

*Summary of Message.* The message of Luke's Gospel can be summarized in Jesus' words to Zacchaeus as Luke records them: "For the Son of man is come to seek and to save that which was lost" (19:10). The character and purpose of Jesus as Saviour are the main theme of this book. The activity and teaching of Jesus in Luke are focused on lifting men out of their sins and bringing them back to life and hope. The miracles, the

parables, the teachings, and the acts of
Jesus exemplify his redemptive power and
will.

The concept of Jesus as Son of man
emphasizes his humanity and his compassionate feeling for all men. He was to be
"a light to lighten the Gentiles, and the

glory of . . . Israel" (2:32). Luke writes as a
Gentile Christian, with deep appreciation
of God's revelation through the Hebrew
people, and yet with a warm sympathy
for those who are not included in the
first covenant of the Law. His Gospel is
truly universal in scope.

# OUTLINE

I. Introduction. 1:1-4.
II. The announcement of the Saviour. 1:5—2:52.
    A. The annunciation to Zacharias. 1:5-25.
    B. The annunciation to Mary. 1:26-56.
    C. The birth of John. 1:57-80.
    D. The birth of Jesus. 2:1-20.
    E. The presentation in the Temple. 2:21-40.
    F. The visit to Jerusalem. 2:41-52.
III. The appearance of the Saviour. 3:1—4:15.
    A. The introduction of John the Baptist. 3:1-20.
    B. The baptism of Jesus. 3:21,22.
    C. The genealogy. 3:23-38.
    D. The temptation. 4:1-13.
    E. The entrance into Galilee. 4:14,15.
IV. The active ministry of the Saviour. 4:16—9:50.
    A. The definition of his ministry. 4:16-44.
    B. The proofs of his power. 5:1—6:11.
    C. The choice of the apostles. 6:12-19.
    D. A digest of his teaching. 6:20-49.
    E. A cross section of his ministry. 7:1—9:17.
    F. The climax of his ministry. 9:18-50.
V. The road to the cross. 9:51—18:30.
    A. The perspective of the cross. 9:51-62.
    B. The ministry of the Seventy. 10:1-24.
    C. Popular teaching. 10:25—13:21.
    D. The beginning of public debate. 13:22—16:31.
    E. Instruction of the disciples. 17:1—18:30.
VI. The suffering of the Saviour. 18:31—23:56.
    A. The progress to Jerusalem. 18:31—19:27.
    B. The entry into Jerusalem. 19:28-44.
    C. The teaching in Jerusalem. 19:45—21:4.
    D. The Olivet Discourse. 21:5-38.
    E. The last supper. 22:1-38.
    F. The betrayal. 22:39-53.
    G. The arrest and trial. 22:54—23:25.
    H. The crucifixion. 23:26-49.
    I. The burial. 23:50-56.
VII. The resurrection. 24:1-53.
    A. The empty tomb. 24:1-12.
    B. The walk to Emmaus. 24:13-35.
    C. The appearance to the disciples. 24:36-43.
    D. The last commission. 24:44-49.
    E. The ascension. 24:50-53.

# COMMENTARY

**I. Introduction. 1:1-4.**

Luke's Gospel is the only one that tells
what method the author used in composing it. The content of the introduction is
intended to strengthen the reader's confidence in what the Gospel will tell about
Christ.

# ST. LUKE

## CHAPTER 1

FORASMUCH as many have taken in hand to set forth in order a declaration of those things which are most surely believed among us,

2. Even as they delivered them unto us, which from the beginning were eyewitnesses, and ministers of the word;

3. It seemed good to me also, having had perfect understanding of all things from the very first, to write unto thee in order, most excellent Theophilus,

4. That thou mightest know the certainty of those things, wherein thou hast been instructed.

5. THERE was in the days of Herod, the king of Judea, a certain priest named Zacharias, of the course of Abia: and his wife *was* of the daughters of Aaron, and her name *was* Elisabeth.

6. And they were both righteous before God, walking in all the commandments and ordinances of the Lord blameless.

7. And they had no child, because that Elisabeth was barren; and they both were *now* well stricken in years.

8. And it came to pass, that, while he executed the priest's office before God in the order of his course,

9. According to the custom of the priest's office, his lot was to burn incense when he went into the temple of the Lord.

# COMMENTARY

1. **Taken in hand.** A literal translation of the Greek verb, which means "to attempt," or "to undertake." **Declaration.** The word implies a formal narrative which is a concise summary of facts. **Things . . . most surely believed.** The phrase may mean "things fulfilled," but has the sense of "things that are taken for granted as true," or "the acknowledged facts of the case." 2. **Delivered.** Paul uses this same word concerning the oral transmission of the content of the Gospel (I Cor 11:23; 15:3). **Eyewitnesses, and ministers of the word.** Eyewitnesses implies that the informants of Luke had seen Jesus in person and because of commitment to him had become **ministers of the word. Ministers** does not have a professional meaning in the modern sense; it was used of synagogue attendants (Lk 4:20). 3. **To me also.** Luke was as well qualified to write a Gospel as any others. **Perfect understanding.** Paul uses the same expression to say that Timothy had "fully known" the experiences of his career (II Tim 3:10). This knowledge is the familiarity which a man has with contemporary facts. **From the very first** (Gr. *anothen*). In the one other place where Luke uses the word (Acts 26:5), it means "from the beginning." Luke claims complete familiarity with the life of Jesus. **Most excellent.** A title elsewhere used by Luke only of officials or of the nobility (Acts 23:26; 24:3; 26:25). 4. **Know.** The Greek word means *to have full knowledge.* **Instructed** may imply either general oral information, or formal instruction. Luke was writing to confirm what Theophilus had learned by word of mouth.

## II. The Announcement of the Saviour. 1:5—2:52.

The first two chapters of the Gospel are concerned with the circumstances of Jesus' birth and indicate clearly that the coming of the Saviour was a direct intervention of God in human affairs.

## A. The Annunciation to Zacharias. 1:5-25.

5. **Herod, the king.** Herod the Great, an Edomite by blood and Jewish by religion, was king over Judea from 37 B.C. to 4 B.C. He was an able ruler, but ruthless and corrupt. **Course of Abia.** There were twenty-four "courses" or divisions of the priesthood, based on the families of the descendants of Aaron, of which the family of Abia (or Abijah) was one (I Chr

10. And the whole multitude of the people were praying without at the time of incense.

11. And there appeared unto him an angel of the Lord standing on the right side of the altar of incense.

12. And when Zacharias saw *him*, he was troubled, and fear fell upon him.

13. But the angel said unto him, Fear not, Zacharias: for thy prayer is heard; and thy wife Elisabeth shall bear thee a son, and thou shalt call his name John.

14. And thou shalt have joy and gladness; and many shall rejoice at his birth.

15. For he shall be great in the sight of the Lord, and shall drink neither wine nor strong drink; and he shall be filled with the Holy Ghost, even from his mother's womb.

16. And many of the children of Israel shall he turn to the Lord their God.

17. And he shall go before him in the spirit and power of Elias, to turn the hearts of the fathers to the children, and the disobedient to the wisdom of the just; to make ready a people prepared for the Lord.

18. And Zacharias said unto the angel, Whereby shall I know this? for I am an old man, and my wife well stricken in years.

19. And the angel answering said unto him, I am Gabriel, that stand in the presence of God; and am sent to speak unto thee, and to show thee these glad tidings.

20. And, behold, thou shalt be dumb, and not able to speak, until the day that these things shall be performed, because thou believest not my words, which shall be fulfilled in their season.

21. And the people waited for Zacharias, and marveled that he tarried so long in the temple.

22. And when he came out, he could not speak unto them: and they perceived that he had seen a vision in the temple; for he beckoned unto them, and remained speechless.

23. And it came to pass, that, as soon as the days of his ministration were accomplished, he departed to his own house.

24. And after those days his wife Elisabeth conceived, and hid herself five months, saying,

25. Thus hath the Lord dealt with me in the days wherein he looked on *me*, to take away my reproach among men.

26. And in the sixth month the angel Gabriel was sent from God unto a city of Galilee, named Nazareth,

27. To a virgin espoused to a man whose name was Joseph, of the house of David; and the virgin's name *was* Mary.

24:10). 7. **They had no child.** A calamity to a Jewish family.

8. **The priest's office.** Each member of the course took his turn in serving at the altar of the Temple for a specified period of the year. 9. **His lot.** The opportunity to minister at the altar was determined by drawing lots, and usually came only once in a lifetime. 10. **The whole multitude of the people were praying.** As the smoke of the incense rose from the altar, the people joined in silent prayer. 11. **An angel of the Lord.** No description of angels is given in the NT, but they must have had some distinctive features to differentiate them from men. Their appearance is usually connected with some special divine communication. 12. **Zacharias . . . was troubled** by the unexpected appearance of another person in the Holy Place and was apprehensive of what he might announce.

13. **The angel said.** Note the parallel between the announcement of the birth of John and the announcement of the birth of Samson (Jud 13:3-5). In both cases the parents had despaired of having children, and the promised child was empowered from birth for a special task. 15. **Filled with the Holy Ghost.** Ghost is an archaic English word for "spirit." 17. **In the spirit and power of Elias.** Elijah was the stern prophet of repentance who rebuked Ahab, the idolatrous king of Israel (I Kgs 21:17-24). John's calling was to arouse the nation, and to make the people ready for the coming of Christ (Mal 4:5,6). 19. **I am Gabriel.** The angel's name means *man of God.* He appears to men in order to make special announcements of the purpose of God (cf. Dan 8:16; 9:21; Lk 1:26).

21. **Marvelled that he tarried.** Since the rite of offering incense usually took a short time, Zacharias' delay may have caused alarm. The people may have thought that the priest had died. 23. **The days of his ministration.** The priests served in their course for a limited time, and then were free to return to their homes. Zacharias' home was in the hill country, probably not far from Jerusalem (1:39).

B. The Annunciation to Mary. 1:26-56.

27. **To a virgin espoused to a man whose name was Joseph.** The Jewish law held espousal or engagement to be as binding as marriage. An engagement was completed after negotiations had been carried on by the groom's representative

**28.** And the angel came in unto her, and said, Hail, *thou that art* highly favored, the Lord *is* with thee: blessed *art* thou among women.

**29.** And when she saw *him*, she was troubled at his saying, and cast in her mind what manner of salutation this should be.

**30.** And the angel said unto her, Fear not, Mary: for thou hast found favor with God.

**31.** And, behold, thou shalt conceive in thy womb, and bring forth a son, and shalt call his name JESUS.

**32.** He shall be great, and shall be called the Son of the Highest; and the Lord God shall give unto him the throne of his father David:

**33.** And he shall reign over the house of Jacob for ever; and of his kingdom there shall be no end.

**34.** Then said Mary unto the angel, How shall this be, seeing I know not a man?

**35.** And the angel answered and said unto her, The Holy Ghost shall come upon thee, and the power of the Highest shall overshadow thee: therefore also that holy thing which shall be born of thee shall be called the Son of God.

**36.** And, behold, thy cousin Elisabeth, she hath also conceived a son in her old age; and this is the sixth month with her, who was called barren.

**37.** For with God nothing shall be impossible.

**38.** And Mary said, Behold the handmaid of the Lord; be it unto me according to thy word. And the angel departed from her.

**39.** And Mary arose in those days, and went into the hill country with haste, into a city of Juda;

**40.** And entered into the house of Zacharias, and saluted Elisabeth.

**41.** And it came to pass, that, when Elisabeth heard the salutation of Mary, the babe leaped in her womb; and Elisabeth was filled with the Holy Ghost:

**42.** And she spake out with a loud voice, and said, Blessed *art* thou among women, and blessed *is* the fruit of thy womb.

**43.** And whence *is* this to me, that the mother of my Lord should come to me?

**44.** For, lo, as soon as the voice of thy salutation sounded in mine ears, the babe leaped in my womb for joy.

**45.** And blessed *is* she that believed: for there shall be a performance of those things which were told her from the Lord.

**46.** And Mary said, My soul doth magnify the Lord,

**47.** And my spirit hath rejoiced in God my Saviour.

and the dowry money had been paid to the girl's father. After the betrothal, the groom could claim the bride at any time. The legal aspect of marriage was included in the betrothal; the wedding was merely a recognition of the agreement that had already been established. Joseph had a perfect right to travel with Mary to Bethlehem. **Of the house of David.** By adoptive right as the reputed son of Joseph, Jesus could claim the kingly heritage of the house of David.

**28. Highly favoured.** The word may be translated, *full of grace,* but it refers to one who is a recipient of favor rather than to the source of grace. **29. What manner of salutation this should be.** To be singled out from all other women for a blessing was disturbing. Mary could not understand why she had been selected for this honor.

**31. Thou shalt . . . call his name Jesus.** Jesus is the Greek form of the Hebrew *Joshua,* which means, *Jehovah is salvation.* Compare Matthew's account of the annunciation to Joseph (Mt 1:21). **32. The throne of his father David.** David's descendants had reigned over Judah from the United Kingdom to the Exile in one unbroken dynasty. The angel predicted that Jesus would complete this succession. **33. And he shall reign over the house of Jacob for ever.** This reign can be both temporal and spiritual.

**34. How shall this be, seeing I know not a man?** Mary's question confirms the statement of her virginity in verse 27. Joseph had not yet taken her as his wife. **35. The Holy Ghost shall come upon thee.** In contrast to the pagan legends of antiquity concerning the reputed offspring of gods and men, there was no physical intervention. The Holy Spirit's creative act in the body of Mary provided the physical means for the Incarnation. **36. Thy cousin Elizabeth.** If Mary and Elizabeth were first cousins, Jesus and John the Baptist were second cousins. **38. Behold the handmaid of the Lord.** Mary's unhesitating acceptance showed her devout and obedient character. She was willing to risk disgrace and divorce to comply with God's command.

**43. The mother of my Lord.** Elizabeth's salutation shows that she was ready to acknowledge Mary's Son as her Lord.

**46. My soul doth magnify the Lord.** Verses 46 to 56 are called the *Magnificat,* from the first word in the Latin translation. Compare the prayer of Hannah (I Sam 2:1-10). **47. God my Saviour.** Mary

**48.** For he hath regarded the low estate of his handmaiden: for, behold, from henceforth all generations shall call me blessed.

**49.** For he that is mighty hath done to me great things; and holy *is* his name.

**50.** And his mercy *is* on them that fear him from generation to generation.

**51.** He hath showed strength with his arm; he hath scattered the proud in the imagination of their hearts.

**52.** He hath put down the mighty from *their* seats, and exalted them of low degree.

**53.** He hath filled the hungry with good things; and the rich he hath sent empty away.

**54.** He hath holpen his servant Israel, in remembrance of *his* mercy;

**55.** As he spake to our fathers, to Abraham, and to his seed for ever.

**56.** And Mary abode with her about three months, and returned to her own house.

**57.** Now Elisabeth's full time came that she should be delivered; and she brought forth a son.

**58.** And her neighbors and her cousins heard how the Lord had showed great mercy upon her; and they rejoiced with her.

**59.** And it came to pass, that on the eighth day they came to circumcise the child; and they called him Zacharias, after the name of his father.

**60.** And his mother answered and said, Not *so*; but he shall be called John.

**61.** And they said unto her, There is none of thy kindred that is called by this name.

**62.** And they made signs to his father, how he would have him called.

**63.** And he asked for a writing table, and wrote, saying, His name is John. And they marveled all.

**64.** And his mouth was opened immediately, and his tongue *loosed*, and he spake, and praised God.

**65.** And fear came on all that dwelt round about them: and all these sayings were noised abroad throughout all the hill country of Judea.

**66.** And all they that heard *them* laid *them* up in their hearts, saying, What manner of child shall this be? And the hand of the Lord was with him.

**67.** And his father Zacharias was filled with the Holy Ghost, and prophesied, saying,

**68.** Blessed *be* the Lord God of Israel; for he hath visited and redeemed his people,

**69.** And hath raised up a horn of salvation for us in the house of his servant David;

**70.** As he spake by the mouth of his holy

was not sinless; she acknowledged her need of a Saviour. **48. Handmaiden** (Gr. *doulē*). Literally, *a female slave*. **49. Hath done to me great things.** Better: *hath done great things for me.* **51. The imagination of their hearts.** Imagination (cf. I Chr 29:18) carries the meaning of "conceit," or the boastful expectations of which they were proud. **54. Holpen.** Old English for "helped."

### C. The Birth of John. 1:57-80.

**59. To circumcise the child.** A Jewish boy was circumcised eight days after birth, at which time a name was usually given him. **60. Called John.** John from the Hebrew *Yohanan*, means "God is gracious." **61. There is none of thy kindred that is called by this name.** Children usually carried family names. In this case the choice of a different name was significant of special expectation for the child. **63. He asked for a writing table.** Wax tablets were used in ancient times for temporary notes.

**65. These sayings were noised abroad.** Perhaps Luke learned of these facts through talking with some of the people who lived in the hill country.

**67. Filled with the Holy Ghost.** This phrase is used eight times in the Lukan writings, including two previous occurrences in this chapter (1:15,41). In all eight instances it is connected with equipment for speech or preaching. It implies a special control and preparation by the Spirit for delivering a message from God. **Prophesied.** This word does not apply exclusively to prediction, but may refer to the declaration of God's message for men, whether it relates to the past, the present, or the future.

**68. Blessed be the Lord God of Israel.** Luke, although a Gentile, connects the heart of the message with the God of the OT. **Visited and redeemed his people.** Zacharias recognized in the birth of John the beginnings of the fulfillment of the coming of the Messiah. **69. An horn of salvation.** The horns of an ox were a symbol of power. Many passages in the OT use this figure of speech, especially in the Psalms (cf. Ps 18:2; 89:24; 132:17; 148:14). **70. His holy prophets.** God has had his representatives in all ages and in all places. Enoch, who was God's messenger before the Flood, was called a prophet (Jude 14). **73. The oath.** The Lord had sworn to Abraham that his descendants would be preserved through the bondage of Egypt, and that they should possess

prophets, which have been since the world began:

71. That we should be saved from our enemies, and from the hand of all that hate us;

72. To perform the mercy *promised* to our fathers, and to remember his holy covenant;

73. The oath which he sware to our father Abraham,

74. That he would grant unto us, that we, being delivered out of the hand of our enemies, might serve him without fear,

75. In holiness and righteousness before him, all the days of our life.

76. And thou, child, shalt be called the prophet of the Highest: for thou shalt go before the face of the Lord to prepare his ways;

77. To give knowledge of salvation unto his people by the remission of their sins,

78. Through the tender mercy of our God; whereby the dayspring from on high hath visited us,

79. To give light to them that sit in darkness and *in* the shadow of death, to guide our feet into the way of peace.

80. And the child grew, and waxed strong in spirit, and was in the deserts till the day of his showing unto Israel.

### CHAPTER 2

AND it came to pass in those days, that there went out a decree from Caesar Augustus, that all the world should be taxed.

2. (*And* this taxing was first made when Cyrenius was governor of Syria.)

3. And all went to be taxed, every one into his own city.

4. And Joseph also went up from Galilee, out of the city of Nazareth, into Judea, unto the city of David, which is called Bethlehem, (because he was of the house and lineage of David,)

5. To be taxed with Mary his espoused wife, being great with child.

6. And so it was, that, while they were there, the days were accomplished that she should be delivered.

7. And she brought forth her firstborn son, and wrapped him in swaddling clothes, and laid him in a manger; because there was no room for them in the inn.

8. And there were in the same country shepherds abiding in the field, keeping watch over their flock by night.

the promised land (Gen 15:13,18). **78. Dayspring from on high. Dayspring,** an old term for sunrise, refers to the rising of the "Sun of righteousness" (see Mal 4:2). The entire passage contains echoes of the last chapter of Malachi's prophecy.

D. The Birth of Jesus. 2:1-20.

**1. A decree. from Caesar Augustus.** Luke is the only one of the Gospel writers who dates his material by the reigning emperor (see also 3:1). **Decree** (Gr. *dogma*). An imperial order. **Caesar Augustus.** The first emperor of Rome, who reigned from 27 B.C. to A.D. 14. **All the world.** This means all the empire, not the entire known world. **Taxed.** Augustus had ordered a census of the empire which would serve as a basis for taxation. The decree was issued about 8 B.C., but probably did not actually go into effect until a few years later. **2. Cyrenius was governor of Syria.** P. Sulpicius Quirinius was made governor of Syria in A.D. 6, and took a census of Judea at that time. There is good evidence that he was twice governor of Syria, and that his first governorship was from 4 B.C. to A.D. 1. The preceding census may have been closing when he first took office. **3. Into his own city.** In Judea each man went back to the city of his ancestors, where his family records were kept. **4. Galilee** was the region around the Lake of Gennesaret, or Lake of Galilee. It had a large Gentile population, and from the days of the prophets had been known as "Galilee of the Gentiles" (Isa 9:1). **Nazareth.** A city in the hills of Galilee, located on the trade route that ran from the coastal plain across to Damascus and the East. **Judea.** The province south of Samaria and north of Edom and the desert, bounded on the west by the Mediterranean Sea and on the east by the Jordan River and the Dead Sea. **Bethlehem.** The original home of David's family. **5. Espoused wife.** See on 1:27.

**7. Firstborn son.** This may imply that Mary had other children later (cf Mk 6: 3). **Manger.** A feeding trough for cattle. Joseph and Mary may have taken shelter in the stable. Tradition says that it was a cave in the side of the hill behind the inn. **8. Keeping watch over their flock by night.** The exact date of Jesus' birth is unknown; the legendary date of December 25 cannot be traced back farther than the fourth century. **9. The heavenly visitation was attended with the radiance

9. And, lo, the angel of the Lord came upon them, and the glory of the Lord shone round about them; and they were sore afraid.

10. And the angel said unto them, Fear not: for, behold, I bring you good tidings of great joy, which shall be to all people.

11. For unto you is born this day in the city of David a Saviour, which is Christ the Lord.

12. And this *shall be* a sign unto you; Ye shall find the babe wrapped in swaddling clothes, lying in a manger.

13. And suddenly there was with the angel a multitude of the heavenly host praising God, and saying,

14. Glory to God in the highest, and on earth peace, good will toward men.

15. And it came to pass, as the angels were gone away from them into heaven, the shepherds said one to another, Let us now go even unto Bethlehem, and see this thing which is come to pass, which the Lord hath made known unto us.

16. And they came with haste, and found Mary and Joseph, and the babe lying in a manger.

17. And when they had seen *it*, they made known abroad the saying which was told them concerning this child.

18. And all they that heard *it* wondered at those things which were told them by the shepherds.

19. But Mary kept all these things, and pondered *them* in her heart.

20. And the shepherds returned, glorifying and praising God for all the things that they had heard and seen, as it was told unto them.

21. And when eight days were accomplished for the circumcising of the child, his name was called JESUS, which was so named of the angel before he was conceived in the womb.

22. And when the days of her purification according to the law of Moses were accomplished, they brought him to Jerusalem, to present *him* to the Lord;

23. (As it is written in the law of the Lord, Every male that openeth the womb shall be called holy to the Lord;)

24. And to offer a sacrifice according to that which is said in the law of the Lord, A pair of turtledoves, or two young pigeons.

25. And, behold, there was a man in Jerusalem, whose name *was* Simeon; and the same man *was* just and devout, waiting for the consolation of Israel: and the Holy Ghost was upon him.

of the divine glory that was present when God manifested himself (Ex 16:10; 20: 18; 40:34; II Chr 7:1; Ezk 1:27,28). **10. Fear not.** The angel's word was the usual greeting for men to whom such an apparition would be terrifying (cf. 1:13,30). **All people.** The ASV translates more accurately, *all the people,* meaning Israel. **11. Saviour.** In the OT God was the Saviour of his people (Isa 25:9; 33: 22). While the prophets thought of him chiefly as a saviour from political oppression, Luke broadens the concept to make Jesus a Saviour from sin. **Christ the Lord.** Christ means *anointed,* the Messiah of Israel, who was the promised Deliverer. **Lord.** A title that the Greek pagans applied to their kings, whom they hailed as gods. A Christian can apply the title only to Christ (I Cor 8:6). **12. And this shall be a sign.** Literally, *the sign.* **14. Peace, good will toward men.** The ASV follows a different manuscript reading—*among men of his good pleasure.* The peace is not given to men who possess good will toward God, but to men whom he is inclined to favor.

**15. This thing which is come to pass.** The shepherds did not doubt the reality of the angel's proclamation, but accepted it at face value. **19. Mary kept . . . and pondered them in her heart.** The appearance of the heavenly visitors to the shepherds confirmed the mysterious secret of the Annunciation.

E. The Presentation in the Temple. 2:21-40.

**21. And when eight days were accomplished.** Jesus, like John, was named according to the message of Gabriel (1:13, 59-63). The circumcision may have taken place in Bethlehem. **22. The days of her purification.** According to the law of Moses, a woman who had a male child was reckoned unclean for seven days. On the eighth day the child was circumcised, and she remained unclean for thirty-three days afterwards. At the end of that time she presented a sacrifice at the Temple and was ceremonially cleansed (Lev 12:2-6). The sacrifice offered was in proportion to the financial ability of the family. **24. A pair of turtledoves.** The offering of the birds indicates that Joseph and Mary were poor (Lev 12:8). For the presentation of the offering they traveled to Jerusalem, which was only a few miles from Bethlehem.

**25. Simeon.** Simeon may have been one of the Hasidim, sincere and earnest

26. And it was revealed unto him by the Holy Ghost, that he should not see death, before he had seen the Lord's Christ.

27. And he came by the Spirit into the temple: and when the parents brought in the child Jesus, to do for him after the custom of the law,

28. Then took he him up in his arms, and blessed God, and said,

29. Lord, now lettest thou thy servant depart in peace, according to thy word:

30. For mine eyes have seen thy salvation,

31. Which thou hast prepared before the face of all people;

32. A light to lighten the Gentiles, and the glory of thy people Israel.

33. And Joseph and his mother marveled at those things which were spoken of him.

34. And Simeon blessed them, and said unto Mary his mother, Behold, this *child* is set for the fall and rising again of many in Israel; and for a sign which shall be spoken against;

35. (Yea, a sword shall pierce through thy own soul also;) that the thoughts of many hearts may be revealed.

36. And there was one Anna, a prophetess, the daughter of Phanuel, of the tribe of Aser: she was of a great age, and had lived with a husband seven years from her virginity;

37. And she *was* a widow of about fourscore and four years, which departed not from the temple, but served *God* with fastings and prayers night and day.

38. And she coming in that instant gave thanks likewise unto the Lord, and spake of him to all them that looked for redemption in Jerusalem.

39. And when they had performed all things according to the law of the Lord, they returned into Galilee, to their own city Nazareth.

40. And the child grew, and waxed strong in spirit, filled with wisdom; and the grace of God was upon him.

41. Now his parents went to Jerusalem every year at the feast of the passover.

42. And when he was twelve years old, they went up to Jerusalem after the custom of the feast.

43. And when they had fulfilled the days, as they returned, the child Jesus tarried behind in Jerusalem; and Joseph and his mother knew not *of it.*

worshipers of God, who kept the Law in spirit as well as in letter. **Just** expresses his attitude toward men; **devout,** his attitude to God. **Consolation of Israel.** The expected Messiah, who would deliver the Jews from their oppressors. **26. And it was revealed unto him.** A special individual prediction was given to Simeon as a reward for his devotion. **28. Blessed God, and said.** The words of Simeon, like the Psalms of David, were spoken in Hebrew poetry.

**32. A light to lighten the Gentiles.** Simeon perceived the true purpose of God to reach out to the Gentiles as well as to Israel. Luke, a Gentile, must have been specially interested in his prophecy. **34. This child.** Jesus was not just one more Jewish child, but was pivotal for faith. Those who believed in him rose to new heights; those who rejected him fell into darker despair. **35. Yea, a sword.** Simeon hinted that Mary would suffer deep sorrow because of Him. **36. Anna, a prophetess.** In both Old and New Testament times, women were gifted with prophetic powers. Deborah (Jud 4:4) was one of the earliest leaders of Israel, and the daughters of Philip the evangelist prophesied (Acts 21:9). **37. She was a widow of about fourscore and four years.** Anna had lived with a husband seven years before his death. If she was married at the age of twelve, she must now have been over one hundred years of age, unless Luke intended eighty-four years to comprise her total age. Like Simeon, she belonged to the pious remnant of Judaism. **38. Redemption in Jerusalem.** The greatness of Anna's faith is shown by her confidence that this infant was the promised means of national redemption.

**40. And the child grew, and waxed strong in spirit.** Luke is the sole source of information about Jesus' childhood. All sorts of fanciful legends about our Lord's youth were written and published in the apocryphal Gospels, but none of them appear in the Scriptures.

F. The Visit to Jerusalem. 2:41-52.

**42. They went up to Jerusalem.** Devout Jews customarily attended the Passover at Jerusalem. Jesus, being twelve years old, was approaching the normal age for being received into Judaism as a "son of the law," which would make him a full member of the religious community. **43. Jesus tarried behind.** Like any normal boy, he may have been intrigued by the sights of the city; it is

**44. But they, supposing him to have been in the company, went a day's journey; and they sought him among *their* kinsfolk and acquaintance.**

**45. And when they found him not, they turned back again to Jerusalem, seeking him.**

**46. And it came to pass, that after three days they found him in the temple, sitting in the midst of the doctors, both hearing them, and asking them questions.**

**47. And all that heard him were astonished at his understanding and answers.**

**48. And when they saw him, they were amazed: and his mother said unto him, Son, why hast thou thus dealt with us? behold, thy father and I have sought thee sorrowing.**

**49. And he said unto them, How is it that ye sought me? wist ye not that I must be about my Father's business?**

**50. And they understood not the saying which he spake unto them.**

**51. And he went down with them, and came to Nazareth, and was subject unto them: but his mother kept all these sayings in her heart.**

**52. And Jesus increased in wisdom and stature, and in favor with God and man.**

more likely that he was particularly interested in the teaching of the rabbis.

**46. They found him in the temple.** His interest shows that he had awakened to the need of understanding the Law. He was listening closely to the leading teachers, who were astounded by the clarity and insight of his replies to their questions. **48. Son, why hast thou thus dealt with us?** Like any true mother, Mary had missed him when the caravan had stopped at the end of the day. She was obviously worried. **49. About my Father's business.** The ASV translates: *Knew ye not that I must be in my Father's house?* Both renderings imply that the youth had a keen realization of his relation to God. He was astounded that Mary and Joseph had not understood that relation, and he reminded them that since God was his true Father, he belonged in God's house.

**50. And they understood not.** Joseph and Mary did not comprehend the full import of Jesus' words, which were the first recorded sign of his growing independence (cf. Jn 2:4). **51. And was subject unto them.** Jesus' independence was not rebellion. He returned to Nazareth and remained with the family until the beginning of his public ministry. **Kept all these sayings in her heart.** Though she did not understand what he meant, Mary did not forget his words. Perhaps Luke learned of them directly from her.

**52. And Jesus increased in wisdom and stature, and in favour with God and man.** He was not a prodigy in the sense that he was abnormal. **Increased** (Gr. "increase" is lit., *cut one's way forward*) means that there was growth in his size, consciousness, and comprehension of events. He was perfect in every stage as he attained it. He was free from the flaws that disfigure the rest of men at each stage of growth.

### III. The Appearance of the Saviour. 3:1 –4:15.

The account of the ministry of John the Baptist, the genealogy, and the temptation of Jesus are intended to give a background for the Saviour whom Luke is presenting. The baptism relates him to contemporary spiritual life; the genealogy affirms his relation to the human race; and the temptation proves his competence to meet the moral problems that confront humanity.

A. The Introduction of John the Baptist. 3:1-20.

## CHAPTER 3

NOW in the fifteenth year of the reign of Tiberius Caesar, Pontius Pilate being governor of Judea, and Herod being tetrarch of Galilee, and his brother Philip tetrarch of Iturea and of the region of Trachonitis, and Lysanias the tetrarch of Abilene,

2. Annas and Caiaphas being the high priests, the word of God came unto John the son of Zacharias in the wilderness.

3. And he came into all the country about Jordan, preaching the baptism of repentance for the remission of sins;

4. As it is written in the book of the words of Esaias the prophet, saying, The voice of one crying in the wilderness, Prepare ye the way of the Lord, make his paths straight.

5. Every valley shall be filled, and every mountain and hill shall be brought low; and the crooked shall be made straight, and the rough ways *shall be* made smooth;

6. And all flesh shall see the salvation of God.

7. Then said he to the multitude that came forth to be baptized of him, O generation of vipers, who hath warned you to flee from the wrath to come?

1. **Now in the fifteenth year of the reign of Tiberius Caesar.** Luke, being a careful historian, dates the beginning of the Saviour's career by the year of the reigning emperor. Tiberius was the adopted son of Augustus (2:1). Since he succeeded to the throne in A.D. 14, his fifteenth year would be about A.D. 28 or 29. The other personages named here were ruling in Palestine at the same time. **Governor.** Pontius Pilate, who is mentioned again in connection with the trial of Jesus (23:1-25), was procurator (imperial governor) of Judea from A.D. 26 to 36. He was responsible to the emperor for the welfare of the province. **Tetrarch of Galilee.** A tetrarch was strictly the ruler of one quarter of a given territory. **Herod** was Antipas, a son of Herod the Great, who ruled over Galilee and the territory east of the Jordan River. **Ituraea,** the realm of Philip, another son of Herod the Great, lay to the northeast of Galilee, and east of Mount Hermon. Of **Lysanias** little is known, except that he was monarch of the little kingdom of Abilene on the eastern slope of the Lebanon mountains, northeast of Damascus. 2. **Annas and Caiaphas.** Caiaphas was the ruling high priest; Annas, his father-in-law, was high priest emeritus, and wielded a strong influence (Jn 18:13). **The word of God.** The divine call came to John as it did to OT prophets (Hos 1:1; Joel 1:1; Jon 1:1; Mic 1:1).

3. **The baptism of repentance.** Plummer (ICC, p. 86) says that "repentance baptism" is baptism connected with repentance, an external symbol of the inward change. Repentance means a change of mind or attitude that is not solely emotional, but that involves a reversal of previous thinking and conduct. **For the remission of sins.** The purpose of John's preaching was to bring men into the experience of forgiveness. 4. **Make his paths straight.** See Isa 40:3-5. In ancient times there were few paved roads. When a king traveled, his subjects built highways for him so that his chariot would not be mired in mud or in sand. Similarly, John was preparing the way for Jesus by his preaching so that all flesh might see God's salvation. By equating the prophet's words (Isa 40:3), "Prepare ye the way of the Lord [Jehovah]" with John's mission, Luke shows that he ascribes deity to Christ. 6. **And all flesh shall see the salvation of God.** The writer makes plain at the outset of Jesus' ministry that He had a universal message. 7. **O generation of vipers.** Like his

8. Bring forth therefore fruits worthy of repentance, and begin not to say within yourselves, We have Abraham to *our* father: for I say unto you, That God is able of these stones to raise up children unto Abraham.

9. And now also the axe is laid unto the root of the trees: every tree therefore which bringeth not forth good fruit is hewn down, and cast into the fire.

10. And the people asked him, saying, What shall we do then?

11. He answereth and saith unto them, He that hath two coats, let him impart to him that hath none; and he that hath meat, let him do likewise.

12. Then came also publicans to be baptized, and said unto him, Master, what shall we do?

13. And he said unto them, Exact no more than that which is appointed you.

14. And the soldiers likewise demanded of him, saying, And what shall we do? And he said unto them, Do violence to no man, neither accuse *any* falsely; and be content with your wages.

15. And as the people were in expectation, and all men mused in their hearts of John, whether he were the Christ, or not;

16. John answered, saying unto *them* all, I indeed baptize you with water; but one mightier than I cometh, the latchet of whose shoes I am not worthy to unloose: he shall baptize you with the Holy Ghost and with fire:

17. Whose fan *is* in his hand, and he will thoroughly purge his floor, and will gather the wheat into his garner; but the chaff he will burn with fire unquenchable.

18. And many other things in his exhortation preached he unto the people.

19. But Herod the tetrarch, being reproved by him for Herodias his brother Philip's wife, and for all the evils which Herod had done,

20. Added yet this above all, that he shut up John in prison.

21. Now when all the people were baptized, it came to pass, that Jesus also being baptized, and praying, the heaven was opened,

22. And the Holy Ghost descended in a bodily shape like a dove upon him, and a voice came from heaven, which said, Thou art my beloved Son; in thee I am well pleased.

23. And Jesus himself began to be about thirty years of age, being (as was supposed) the son of Joseph, which was *the son* of Heli,

24. Which was *the son* of Matthat, which

prophetic forebears, John denounced the sins of the people in vigorous language. **8. We have Abraham to our father.** To is equivalent to the modern "as." Jews were singularly proud of Abraham as the head of their race, with whom God had made his covenant. Believing that they inherited the blessing of God through Abraham, they trusted in their descent from him to bring them salvation (Jn 8:33). John the Baptist warned them that God would make the very stones to become descendants of Abraham. **9. The axe is laid unto the root of the trees.** Unproductive trees were cut down for firewood. The nation had not brought forth fruits that God expected, and judgment was imminent.

**11. Meat** in the AV does not mean flesh alone, as it does today in our vocabulary, but is a general word for food. **12. Publicans** were tax collectors, noted for their rapacity. A certain part of men's earnings was demanded for taxes, but the publicans usually asked more, and enriched themselves by the difference. They were hated by the people, who considered them traitors because they worked for Rome. **14. And the soldiers likewise.** Soldiers were often brutal to civilians, and practiced extortion upon them. **Do violence to no man.** The Greek word for do violence (*diaseisete*) means "to shake down," an ancient counterpart of modern slang. **15. Whether he were the Christ or not.** Christ is a general term meaning "Messiah." It is a title, not a proper name. **16. Latchet.** A shoelace. **He shall baptize you with the Holy Ghost and with fire.** As baptism with water signifies repentance, so the coming of the Holy Spirit is proof of the presence of God. Fire is a symbol of purification and power. **17. Whose fan is in his hand.** The "fan" was the winnowing shovel, used to throw grain into the air so that the chaff would blow away, while the clean kernels fell back to the threshing floor.

**19. Herod the tetrarch.** Herod had married Herodias, the wife of his brother Philip. When John reproved him publicly, Herodias was enraged, and demanded that John be imprisoned. Herod arrested him, and finally, at his wife's request, ordered the Baptist's execution.

B. The Baptism of Jesus. 3:21,22.

**21. Jesus . . . being baptized.** By submitting to the baptism of John, he classed himself with sinners, though sinless him-was *the son* of Levi, which was *the son* of Melchi, which was *the son* of Janna, which was *the son* of Joseph,

25. Which was *the son* of Mattathias, which was *the son* of Amos, which was *the son* of Naum, which was *the son* of Esli, which was *the son* of Nagge,

26. Which was *the son* of Maath, which was *the son* of Mattathias, which was *the son* of Semei, which was *the son* of Joseph, which was *the son* of Juda,

27. Which was *the son* of Joanna, which was *the son* of Rhesa, which was *the son* of Zorobabel, which was *the son* of Salathiel, which was *the son* of Neri,

28. Which was *the son* of Melchi, which was *the son* of Addi, which was *the son* of Cosam, which was *the son* of ,Elmodam, which was *the son* of Er,

29. Which was *the son* of Jose, which was *the son* of Eliezer, which was *the son* of Jorim, which was *the son* of Matthat, which was *the son* of Levi,

30. Which was *the son* of Simeon, which was *the son* of Juda, which was *the son* of Joseph, which was *the son* of Jonan, which was *the son* of Eliakim,

31. Which was *the son* of Melea, which was *the son* of Menan, which was *the son* of Mattatha, which was *the son* of Nathan, which was *the son* of David,

32. Which was *the son* of Jesse, which was *the son* of Obed, which was *the son* of Booz, which was *the son* of Salmon, which was *the son* of Naasson,

33. Which was *the son* of Aminadab, which was *the son* of Aram, which was *the son* of Esrom, which was *the son* of Phares, which was *the son* of Juda,

34. Which was *the son* of Jacob, which was *the son* of Isaac, which was *the son* of Abraham, which was *the son* of Thara, which was *the* son of Nachor,

35. Which was *the son* of Saruch, which was *the son* of Ragau, which was *the son* of Phalec, which was *the son* of Heber, which was *the son* of Sala,

36. Which was *the son* of Cainan, which was *the son* of Arphaxad, which was *the son* of Sem, which was *the son* of Noe, which was *the son* of Lamech,

37. Which was *the son* of Mathusala, which was *the son* of Enoch, which was *the son* of Jared, which was *the son* of Maleleel, which was *the son* of Cainan,

38. Which was *the son* of Enos, which was *the son* of Seth, which was *the son* of Adam, which was *the son* of God.

self, and began his redemptive mission. The opening of heaven was the divine acknowledgment of Jesus' sonship. **22. And the Holy Ghost descended**. The dove was a symbol of innocence and harmlessness, a messenger of peace (cf. Gen 8:8,9). **A voice came from heaven**. Compare Luke 9:35; John 12:28.

C. The Genealogy. 3:23-28.

**23. And Jesus began to be about thirty years of age, being (as was supposed) the son of Joseph**. The genealogy of Jesus disagrees with that of Matthew, which gives the legal line of royal descent. Luke's gives the human line, possibly through Mary, if Joseph is reckoned as her father's son through marriage. Luke carries the line back to Adam to emphasize Jesus' descent from the first father of the human race, while Matthew begins with the covenant heads: Abraham, to whom God promised the land (Gen 12:7), and David, to whom He pledged an everlasting kingdom (II Sam 7:12,13,16). The names in the genealogy differ from the spelling in the OT because they are given in Greek form.

D. The Temptation. 4:1-13.

The account of the temptation of our Lord is given in both Luke and Matthew. Jesus, like Adam (Gen 3:6), was tested in the three areas of physical appetite, worldly ambition, and spiritual attainment, in order that he might be proved competent for his mission. Where the first man failed, he triumphed.

**1. Led by the Spirit**. The first recorded directive of the Holy Spirit led to testing. **The wilderness**. The traditional scene of the Temptation is a barren territory northwest of the Dead Sea, completely devoid of vegetation or shelter of any kind. **2. Forty days**. A common period for trial (Gen 7:4; Ex 24:18; I Kgs 19:8; Jon 3:4). **3. If thou be the Son of God**. The Greek condition used implies that the devil did not doubt that Jesus was the Son of God, but rather assumed that Jesus did possess the right to create. **Bread**. Bread in Palestine was not in the form of oblong loaves, but in flat round cakes. The stones on the ground looked like cakes of bread. **4. It is written**. Jesus did not compose his own answer for the tempter, but drew his reply from the revelation of Scripture. **Man shall not live by bread alone** (Deut 8:3). Man needs bread, but bread is not all he needs. Material gratification of the appetites can never sat-

## CHAPTER 4

AND Jesus being full of the Holy Ghost returned from Jordan, and was led by the Spirit into the wilderness,

2. Being forty days tempted of the devil. And in those days he did eat nothing: and when they were ended, he afterward hungered.

3. And the devil said unto him, If thou be the Son of God, command this stone that it be made bread.

4. And Jesus answered him, saying, It is written, That man shall not live by bread alone, but by every word of God.

5. And the devil, taking him up into a high mountain, showed unto him all the kingdoms of the world in a moment of time.

6. And the devil said unto him, All this power will I give thee, and the glory of them: for that is delivered unto me; and to whomsoever I will, I give it.

7. If thou therefore wilt worship me, all shall be thine.

8. And Jesus answered and said unto him, Get thee behind me, Satan: for it is written, Thou shalt worship the Lord thy God, and him only shalt thou serve.

9. And he brought him to Jerusalem, and set him on a pinnacle of the temple, and said unto him, If thou be the Son of God, cast thyself down from hence:

10. For it is written, He shall give his angels charge over thee, to keep thee:

11. And in *their* hands they shall bear thee up, lest at any time thou dash thy foot against a stone.

12. And Jesus answering said unto him, It is said, Thou shalt not tempt the Lord thy God.

13. And when the devil had ended all the temptation, he departed from him for a season.

14. And Jesus returned in the power of the Spirit into Galilee: and there went out a fame of him through all the region round about.

15. And he taught in their synagogues, being glorified of all.

isfy the deepest longings of the human spirit.

5. All the kingdoms of the world. From the heights of the mountain range one could see the territories formerly occupied by the empires of Egypt, Assyria, Babylon, Persia, Greece, and now Rome. 6. All this power will I give thee. Christ had come to claim the world as his kingdom, and the devil was offering it to him on "easy" terms. 7. If thou therefore wilt worship me. By worshiping, Jesus would trade his independence for the kingdoms of the world. If he accepted these terms, he would not actually be the sovereign, because he would be compelled to acknowledge the overlordship of Satan. 8. Thou shalt worship the Lord thy God (Deut 6:13). He would admit only the authority of God as supreme. He could not compromise.

9. A pinnacle of the temple. One of the battlements or towers (Gr. *pterygion*, "a little wing"), that overlooked the courtyard or perhaps the Kidron Valley. If Jesus had leaped from the battlement and had landed unharmed among the crowds below, they would have hailed him as the Messiah from heaven, and his reputation would have been made instantly. 10. It is written. In the third temptation the devil omitted part of the verse, which reads, "to keep thee in all thy ways." God had not promised to keep his servant in an act of foolish presumption, but only when he was walking in God's ways (see Ps 91:11,12).

13. For a season. The words imply that the temptation or attack was renewed later. The Saviour lived constantly under the pressure of evil. The devil is a real personality, though not necessarily visible.

E. The Entrance into Galilee. 4:14,15.

Matthew, Mark, and Luke begin Jesus' ministry with Galilee; John records an earlier ministry in Judea (Jn 2:13—4:3). Luke stresses the place of the Holy Spirit in the career of Jesus (cf. Lk 1:35; 3:21, 22; 4:1).

IV. The Active Ministry of the Saviour. 4:16—9:50.

The first part of our Lord's ministry occupied about two and one-half years. It covers the choice of the apostles, the larger amount of his teaching and healing, and comes to its climax in the Transfiguration. Luke was endeavoring to show Theophilus the divine character of Jesus,

16. And he came to Nazareth, where he had been brought up: and, as his custom was, he went into the synagogue on the sabbath day, and stood up for to read.

17. And there was delivered unto him the book of the prophet Esaias. And when he had opened the book, he found the place where it was written,

18. The Spirit of the Lord is upon me, because he hath anointed me to preach the gospel to the poor; he hath sent me to heal the broken-hearted, to preach deliverance to the captives, and recovering of sight to the blind, to set at liberty them that are bruised,

19. To preach the acceptable year of the Lord.

20. And he closed the book, and he gave it again to the minister, and sat down. And the eyes of all them that were in the synagogue were fastened on him.

21. And he began to say unto them, This day is this Scripture fulfilled in your ears.

22. And all bare him witness, and wondered at the gracious words which proceeded out of his mouth. And they said, Is not this Joseph's son?

23. And he said unto them, Ye will surely say unto me this proverb, Physician, heal thyself: whatsoever we have heard done in Capernaum, do also here in thy country.

24. And he said, Verily I say unto you, No prophet is accepted in his own country.

25. But I tell you of a truth, many widows were in Israel in the days of Elias, when the heaven was shut up three years and six months, when great famine was throughout all the land;

26. But unto none of them was Elias sent, save unto Sarepta, a city of Sidon, unto a woman that was a widow.

27. And many lepers were in Israel in the time of Eliseus the prophet; and none of them was cleansed, saving Naaman the Syrian.

28. And all they in the synagogue, when they heard these things, were filled with wrath,

and the prophetic nature of his mission.

A. The Definition of His Ministry. 4:16-44.

16. Nazareth. Jesus began his ministry in his home town. Into the synagogue. During the Babylonian captivity after the destruction of the Temple, the Jewish people instituted synagogues as local centers of worship. Even when the Temple was restored, synagogue worship persisted. Luke notes that Jesus had been accustomed to attend synagogue services regularly on the Sabbath. Members participated in the service, and were frequently asked to read the Scripture and make appropriate remarks. Paul did most of his preaching in synagogues (cf. Acts 13:14,15). 17. The book of the prophet Esaias. The synagogue followed a regular order of readings. Jesus probably took the passage that was usually read on that day. 18. He hath anointed me. The passage was taken from Isa 61:1,2, which was a prophecy of the Messianic Age. 20. Book. The writings of the OT were scrolls mounted on handles, which were read by rolling up one side while unrolling the other. Minister. After Jesus had read, he rolled up the scroll and handed it back to the assistant who had charge of the Scriptures. Scrolls were costly to make, and were very carefully preserved. 21. This day is this scripture fulfilled. The reader's opening words of comment must have been a shock to his hearers. They had known him from boyhood and had taken him for granted. When he claimed to be the fulfillment of this Messianic prophecy, they were astounded. 22. The gracious words. Luke does not give a verbatim report of all that Jesus said. He must have expounded the first part of the text, applying it to himself. Is not this Joseph's son? The question of the villagers shows that they knew nothing of Jesus' origin, but assumed that he was the son of Joseph and Mary by natural birth. As he strengthened his claims, they wondered what right he had to do so. 23. Physician, heal thyself. The Lord often taught by proverbs or parables. On this occasion he was anticipating the demand of the people that he perform in Nazareth the miracles that he had done in Capernaum. 24. No prophet is accepted in his own country. In the following verses Jesus pointed out not only that he expected rejection by his own village, but that his greatest ministry might be to the Gentile world. 28. They . . . were filled with wrath.

29. And rose up, and thrust him out of the city, and led him unto the brow of the hill whereon their city was built, that they might cast him down headlong.

30. But he, passing through the midst of them, went his way,

31. And came down to Capernaum, a city of Galilee, and taught them on the sabbath days.

32. And they were astonished at his doctrine: for his word was with power.

33. And in the synagogue there was a man, which had a spirit of an unclean devil, and cried out with a loud voice,

34. Saying, Let *us* alone; what have we to do with thee, *thou* Jesus of Nazareth? art thou come to destroy us? I know thee who thou art; the Holy One of God.

35. And Jesus rebuked him, saying, Hold thy peace, and come out of him. And when the devil had thrown him in the midst, he came out of him, and hurt him not.

36. And they were all amazed, and spake among themselves, saying, What a word *is* this! for with authority and power he commandeth the unclean spirits, and they come out.

37. And the fame of him went out into every place of the country round about.

38. And he arose out of the synagogue, and entered into Simon's house. And Simon's wife's mother was taken with a great fever; and they besought him for her.

39. And he stood over her, and rebuked the fever; and it left her: and immediately she arose and ministered unto them.

40. Now when the sun was setting, all they that had any sick with divers diseases brought them unto him; and he laid his hands on every one of them, and healed them.

41. And devils also came out of many, crying out, and saying, Thou art Christ the Son of God. And he rebuking *them* suffered them not to speak: for they knew that he was Christ.

42. And when it was day, he departed and went into a desert place: and the people sought him, and came unto him, and stayed him, that he should not depart from them.

43. And he said unto them, I must preach the kingdom of God to other cities also: for therefore am I sent.

44. And he preached in the synagogues of Galilee.

The announcement that he had no ministry for the people of Nazareth because they would not accept him aroused their anger, and they tried to kill him by mob action. **29. The brow of the hill.** Nazareth was built on hills, some of which were quite steep. **30. Passing through the midst of them.** His commanding presence and divine protection took him unharmed through the angry mob.

**31. Capernaum.** A small city on the shore of Galilee, about twenty-five miles northeast of Nazareth. Jesus carried on an extensive ministry in the synagogue. Luke gives a sample day out of Jesus' career, filled with teaching and healing.

**33. A spirit of an unclean devil.** *Demon* is a better translation. **Devil** is properly used only of Satan. Demon possession was common in Jesus' day, and was distinguished from insanity (see Mt 4: 24). In places where the powers of evil are recognized and worshiped, it is still current. Demons are evil intelligences who seek to gain control of human beings as media of expression. **34. Let us alone.** The evil spirits recognized him and expressed fear and hatred of him. **35. Hold thy peace, and come out of him.** Our Lord never allowed the demons to advertise him. His authority over them was a proof of the validity of the Messianic claims that he had made at Nazareth.

**38. Simon's house.** The call of Simon was recorded by John (Jn 1:41,42). Luke has not mentioned him before, but takes for granted the reader's knowledge that Simon was already a disciple. His summons to service is given later. **A great fever.** Only Luke uses the adjective great, reflecting his medical interest. **40. When the sun was setting.** Sunset marked the end of the Jewish day. With the closing of the Sabbath, it was lawful to carry the sick. So many were brought to the Lord that he must have spent a large part of the night in ministering to them.

**42. He departed.** Often after a busy day Jesus retired from the crowds in order to pray (see 5:16; 6:12). **43. The kingdom of God.** The realm and rule of God through the Messiah was the subject of the Saviour's preaching. His ethics, his deeds, his redemptive work, and his promise to return all belong within the scope of this subject. The Jewish people of his time expected that the kingdom would mean chiefly a restoration of the independence of Israel. Jesus gave it a much fuller content.

B. The Proofs of His Power. 5:1—6:11.

## CHAPTER 5

AND it came to pass, that, as the people pressed upon him to hear the word of God, he stood by the lake of Gennesaret,

2. And saw two ships standing by the lake: but the fishermen were gone out of them, and were washing *their* nets.

3. And he entered into one of the ships, which was Simon's, and prayed him that he would thrust out a little from the land. And he sat down, and taught the people out of the ship.

4. Now when he had left speaking, he said unto Simon, Launch out into the deep, and let down your nets for a draught.

5. And Simon answering said unto him, Master, we have toiled all the night, and have taken nothing: nevertheless at thy word I will let down the net.

6. And when they had this done, they inclosed a great multitude of fishes: and their net brake.

7. And they beckoned unto *their* partners, which were in the other ship, that they should come and help them. And they came, and filled both the ships, so that they began to sink.

8. When Simon Peter saw *it*, he fell down at Jesus' knees, saying, Depart from me; for I am a sinful man, O Lord.

9. For he was astonished, and all that were with him, at the draught of the fishes which they had taken:

10. And so *was* also James, and John, the sons of Zebedee, which were partners with Simon. And Jesus said unto Simon, Fear not; from henceforth thou shalt catch men.

11. And when they had brought their ships to land, they forsook all, and followed him.

12. And it came to pass, when he was in a certain city, behold a man full of leprosy; who seeing Jesus fell on *his* face, and besought him, saying, Lord, if thou wilt, thou canst make me clean.

13. And he put forth *his* hand, and touched him, saying, I will: be thou clean. And immediately the leprosy departed from him.

This next division of Luke continues the proofs of Jesus' power, preparatory to a greater emphasis on public teaching.

**1. Lake of Gennesaret.** Another name for the lake of Galilee. It is a large body of water, about thirteen miles long and eight miles wide, surrounded by hills. In our Lord's day the region around it was heavily populated, and there were numerous cities on its shores. Capernaum and Bethsaida (to the north) were centers of the fishing industry. **2. Washing their nets.** Cleaning the nets was the regular morning's work after a night of fishing. **3. He entered into one of the ships.** The lake front provided an auditorium, for there was gently rising land along the shore, and the acoustics were good. In order that he might not be crowded, Jesus borrowed Simon Peter's boat for a pulpit. **4. Let down your nets for a draught.** The fish came nearer the surface at night to feed; in the daytime they went down to the cooler waters deep in the lake. **5. Nevertheless at thy word.** Though Peter's experience as a fisherman made him quite sure that they would catch nothing, his words show faith in Jesus. He was ready to believe the Master's word even in matters in which Jesus would not naturally be considered an expert. **6. Their net brake.** Literally, *their nets began to break.* The catch of fish was so large that neither the nets nor the boats could hold it.

**8. Depart from me; for I am a sinful man, O Lord.** This proof that Jesus knew even more about fishing than Peter did, and the gift of fish, which more than compensated for the futile work of the preceding night, made the disciple see himself in a new light. In contrast with Jesus, whose deity was indicated by this miracle, Peter realized that he was sinful, and felt unworthy to have Jesus with him. **10. Fear not; from henceforth thou shalt catch men.** Simon and his partners, James and John, had already become disciples of Jesus, but had continued with their business. Now Jesus called them to special service, and they left all to follow him.

**12. Full of leprosy.** The language implies an advanced case. Leprosy was a common disease in the Orient. In its final stages it causes disfigurement of the body, as the various members decay. The Law required the segregation of lepers outside the towns (Lev 13:45,46). **If thou wilt.** The leper did not doubt Jesus' competence to heal; he was uncertain of His attitude. **13. I will.** Since the disease was

14. And he charged him to tell no man: but go, and show thyself to the priest, and offer for thy cleansing, according as Moses commanded, for a testimony unto them.

15. But so much the more went there a fame abroad of him: and great multitudes came together to hear, and to be healed by him of their infirmities.

16. And he withdrew himself into the wilderness, and prayed.

17. And it came to pass on a certain day, as he was teaching, that there were Pharisees and doctors of the law sitting by, which were come out of every town of Galilee, and Judea, and Jerusalem: and the power of the Lord was *present* to heal them.

18. And, behold, men brought in a bed a man which was taken with a palsy: and they sought *means* to bring him in, and to lay *him* before him.

19. And when they could not find by what *way* they might bring him in because of the multitude, they went upon the housetop, and let him down through the tiling with *his* couch into the midst before Jesus.

20. And when he saw their faith, he said unto him, Man, thy sins are forgiven thee.

21. And the scribes and the Pharisees began to reason, saying, Who is this which speaketh blasphemies? Who can forgive sins, but God alone?

22. But when Jesus perceived their thoughts, he answering said unto them, What reason ye in your hearts?

23. Whether is easier, to say, Thy sins be forgiven thee; or to say, Rise up and walk?

24. But that ye may know that the Son of man hath power upon earth to forgive sins, (he said unto the sick of the palsy,) I say unto thee, Arise, and take up thy couch, and go into thine house.

25. And immediately he rose up before them, and took up that whereon he lay, and departed to his own house, glorifying God.

26. And they were all amazed, and they glorified God, and were filled with fear, saying, We have seen strange things to-day.

27. And after these things he went forth, and saw a publican, named Levi, sitting at the receipt of custom: and he said unto him, Follow me.

28. And he left all, rose up, and followed him.

29. And Levi made him a great feast in his own house: and there was a great company of publicans and of others that sat down with them.

usually considered incurable, the sudden healing may have been a surprise to the man and to all who knew him. **14. Go, and shew thyself to the priest.** The Law provided that cases of leprosy must be inspected by the priests, who acted as a board of health in the Jewish commonwealth (Lev 14:1-32). Jesus wanted the man to go through the proper channels, so that he could be reinstated in the community.

**17. Pharisees and doctors of the law.** The fame of the Teacher had brought to Galilee religious leaders from all parts of the land. They were listening critically to his teaching.

**18. A man which was taken with a palsy.** The case was difficult, and healing would be all the more convincing. **19. Let him down through the tiling.** Luke describes the house as a Roman dwelling with a tile roof, such as would have been found in the cities familiar to his readers. **20. Man, thy sins are forgiven thee.** Our Lord began with the man's spiritual need, which was greater than his physical need.

**21. Blasphemies.** Jesus' critics were shocked at his assuming a right that belongs to God alone—the right to forgive sins. The Lord did not say that since he was the Son of God with authority, they were wrong in their assumption. Instead, he proposed a test of that authority. **23. Whether is easier.** It would be easier to say, "Thy sins be forgiven," because if they were not, there would be no outward evidence. If Jesus had commanded healing, and the man had not been healed, everybody would have known that the healer was fraudulent.

**24. Arise, and take up thy couch.** Jesus made his power to cure a test of his power to forgive. By accomplishing what his critics acknowledged as the more difficult, he showed that he could do what they thought to be easier. **Couch** is a bedroll, not a piece of furniture. **25. And immediately he rose up.** The cure was complete, and the Lord's critics were silenced. The miracle demonstrated that Jesus could remove the paralysis of both spirit and body.

**27. Levi** is identical with Matthew (Mt 9:9). **Receipt of custom.** Taxes on goods transported along the caravan road were levied by Herod's agents, of whom Matthew may have been one. **29. Levi made him a great feast.** Matthew, a man of wealth, gave a special dinner for his associates that they might meet Jesus. The Pharisees had rejected the publicans ut-

30. But their scribes and Pharisees murmured against his disciples, saying, Why do ye eat and drink with publicans and sinners?

31. And Jesus answering said unto them, They that are whole need not a physician; but they that are sick.

32. I came not to call the righteous, but sinners to repentance.

33. And they said unto him, Why do the disciples of John fast often, and make prayers, and likewise *the disciples* of the Pharisees; but thine eat and drink?

34. And he said unto them, Can ye make the children of the bridechamber fast, while the bridegroom is with them?

35. But the days will come, when the bridegroom shall be taken away from them, and then shall they fast in those days.

36. And he spake also a parable unto them; No man putteth a piece of a new garment upon an old; if otherwise, then both the new maketh a rent, and the piece that was *taken* out of the new agreeth not with the old.

37. And no man putteth new wine into old bottles; else the new wine will burst the bottles, and be spilled, and the bottles shall perish.

38. But new wine must be put into new bottles; and both are preserved.

39. No man also having drunk old *wine* straightway desireth new; for he saith, The old is better.

## CHAPTER 6

AND it came to pass on the second sabbath after the first, that he went through the corn fields; and his disciples plucked the ears of corn, and did eat, rubbing *them* in *their* hands.

terly and would have nothing to do with them, but Jesus reached out to them. Forgiveness was for publicans as well as for others. **30. Publicans and sinners** were classed together. The publicans had a reputation for avarice and graft. **32. I came not to call the righteous.** Jesus implied that he could do nothing for the "righteous" Pharisees, who were sure of their own perfection. He wanted to reach those who recognized and acknowledged their need.

**33. Why do the disciples of John fast often.** The people were puzzled, since Jesus' ethical standards were no lower than those of John and the Pharisees. They wondered why his disciples were not as strict as John's. **34. The children of the bridechamber.** The phrase is a Hebrew idiom, meaning the friends of the bridegroom. While Jesus was with the disciples, there was no reason for mourning. But he intimated (v. 35) that some day he would be taken away from them, and that then fasting would be in order. The figure of the friend of the bridegroom was used by John the Baptist himself in speaking of his relation to the Lord (Jn 3:29). **36. And he spake also a parable.** The Lord's parables were illustrations or incidents taken from daily life by which he conveyed spiritual teaching. They revealed truth to those who could discern it, and concealed mysteries from those who were not ready for them. Patched garments were common in Palestine, because the people were poor. New cloth, sewed on an old garment, will shrink when washed, and so will pull apart the older and weaker cloth. **37. Bottles** were not glass containers, but skins of animals used as sacks for liquid. The old wineskins had lost their elasticity, and would not hold the new wine, which might still be in partial process of fermentation. Likewise the new teaching of the kingdom of God could not be contained within the forms of the Law, but must be expressed in new ways. A fresh revelation had come in Christ, which demanded a different form of worship. **6:1. The second sabbath after the first.** The phrase is a reference to the usage of the Jewish calendar. It may mean the second Sabbath that came in the sequence after the opening of the religious year at the Passover. Some manuscripts of Luke omit the term entirely. **Corn** in the AV is a general word for grain. **Plucked the ears.** Travelers were allowed to pick grains or fruits for immediate

2. And certain of the Pharisees said unto them, Why do ye that which is not lawful to do on the sabbath days?

3. And Jesus answering them said, Have ye not read so much as this, what David did, when himself was ahungered, and they which were with him;

4. How he went into the house of God, and did take and eat the showbread, and gave also to them that were with him; which it is not lawful to eat but for the priests alone?

5. And he said unto them, That the Son of man is Lord also of the sabbath.

6. And it came to pass also on another sabbath, that he entered into the synagogue and taught: and there was a man whose right hand was withered.

7. And the scribes and Pharisees watched him, whether he would heal on the sabbath day; that they might find an accusation against him.

8. But he knew their thoughts, and said to the man which had the withered hand, Rise up, and stand forth in the midst. And he arose and stood forth.

9. Then said Jesus unto them, I will ask you one thing; Is it lawful on the sabbath days to do good, or to do evil? to save life, or to destroy it?

10. And looking round about upon them all, he said unto the man, Stretch forth thy hand. And he did so: and his hand was restored whole as the other.

11. And they were filled with madness; and communed one with another what they might do to Jesus.

12. And it came to pass in those days, that he went out into a mountain to pray, and continued all night in prayer to God.

13. And when it was day, he called *unto him* his disciples: and of them he chose twelve, whom also he named apostles;

14. Simon, (whom he also named Peter,) and Andrew his brother, James and John, Philip and Bartholomew,

15. Matthew and Thomas, James the *son* of Alpheus, and Simon called Zelotes,

16. And Judas *the brother* of James, and Judas Iscariot, which also was the traitor.

17. And he came down with them, and stood in the plain, and the company of his disciples, and a great multitude of people out of all Judea and Jerusalem, and from the seacoast of Tyre and Sidon, which came to hear him, and to be healed of their diseases;

18. And they that were vexed with unclean spirits: and they were healed.

19. And the whole multitude sought to touch him: for there went virtue out of him, and healed *them* all.

consumption, but not to harvest freely on another man's land (Deut 23:24,25).

**2. That which is not lawful to do.** The strict interpretation of the Law regarded picking and rubbing out grain as work, which was not allowed on the Sabbath. **3. Have ye not read.** Jesus referred to the Scripture for a different illustration from the life of David (I Sam 21:1-6). If David could do in an emergency that which was unlawful, why could not He? **5. Lord . . . of the sabbath.** In addition to the authority to forgive sins, Jesus claimed sovereignty over the Sabbath law.

**7. And the scribes and Pharisees watched him.** Angered by their defeat in argument regarding Sabbath observance and by the claims which they regarded as presumptuous, the scribes and Pharisees were now eager to trap Jesus. **9. Is it lawful on the sabbath days to do good, or to do evil?** Since it was lawful to do good on the Sabbath, and since healing was a good deed, the healing was above criticism. **11. They were filled with madness.** Beaten in argument and discredited before the people, Jesus' opponents were driven to desperation. This verse marks the beginning of Christ's controversy with the Jewish leaders that lasted all during the rest of his career.

C. The Choice of the Apostles. 6:12-19.

**12. Continued all night in prayer.** The rise of opposition and the problem of choosing the right men as his close associates called for protracted counsel with the Father. **13. Disciples . . . apostles.** A disciple is a learner; an apostle is *one sent*, commissioned to deliver a message. **14-16.** The following list agrees with those in Matthew and Mark (Mt 10:2-4; Mk 3:16-19), except for the name of Judas the brother of James, who may be the same as Thaddaeus in the other two Gospels.

**17. And he came down with them, and stood in the plain.** Bible students have questioned whether the following text is parallel to the Sermon on the Mount of Matthew 5–7, since the latter was spoken on a mountain. **Plain** really means "a level place," which could have been on the side of the mountain. Or, it is possible that Jesus repeated his teaching on more than one occasion. **19. Virtue.** An archaic translation for a word meaning *power*.

20. And he lifted up his eyes on his disciples, and said, Blessed *be ye* poor: for yours is the kingdom of God.

21. Blessed *are ye* that hunger now: for ye shall be filled. Blessed *are ye* that weep now: for ye shall laugh.

22. Blessed are ye, when men shall hate you, and when they shall separate you *from their company*, and shall reproach *you*, and cast out your name as evil, for the Son of man's sake.

23. Rejoice ye in that day, and leap for joy: for, behold, your reward *is* great in heaven: for in the like manner did their fathers unto the prophets.

24. But woe unto you that are rich! for ye have received your consolation.

25. Woe unto you that are full! for ye shall hunger. Woe unto you that laugh now! for ye shall mourn and weep.

26. Woe unto you, when all men shall speak well of you! for so did their fathers to the false prophets.

27. But I say unto you which hear, Love your enemies, do good to them which hate you,

28. Bless them that curse you, and pray for them which despitefully use you.

29. And unto him that smiteth thee on the *one* cheek offer also the other; and him that taketh away thy cloak forbid not *to take thy* coat also.

30. Give to every man that asketh of thee; and of him that taketh away thy goods ask *them* not again.

31. And as ye would that men should do to you, do ye also to them likewise.

32. For if ye love them which love you, what thank have ye? for sinners also love those that love them.

33. And if ye do good to them which do good to you, what thank have ye? for sinners also do even the same.

34. And if ye lend *to them* of whom ye hope to receive, what thank have ye? for sinners also lend to sinners, to receive as much again.

35. But love ye your enemies, and do good, and lend, hoping for nothing again; and your reward shall be great, and ye shall be the children of the Highest: for he is kind unto the unthankful and *to* the evil.

36. Be ye therefore merciful, as your Father also is merciful.

37. Judge not, and ye shall not be judged: condemn not, and ye shall not be condemned: forgive, and ye shall be forgiven:

## D. A Digest of His Teaching. 6:20-49.

Luke's report of the sermon differs from that of Matthew in several respects. He balances four beatitudes with four woes, instead of giving nine beatitudes. He omits the discussion of the application of the Law, and some of the teaching on prayer. A few parables in this sermon are paralleled elsewhere in Luke. There are no contradictions in the accounts, but only different arrangements of material. The address was gauged particularly for the disciples, although the multitude listened to it.

20. **Blessed be ye poor.** While traveling with Jesus, the apostles had no visible means of support, and were dependent on gifts. 21. **Blessed are ye that hunger now.** Satisfaction comes only to those who have a real desire. Matthew implies that the hunger is spiritual. **Blessed are ye that weep.** Jesus knew that those who were faithful to him would have to share in his sorrows, but he promised them also a share in his triumph (cf. Jn 16:20). 22. **Blessed . . . when men shall hate you.** The conflict which had already begun between Jesus and the leaders of the nation involved his followers also (cf. Jn 15:18-25).

27. **Love your enemies.** Love was the heart of the Saviour's teaching, because it is the essence of the character of God. 29. **Unto him that smiteth thee on the one cheek offer also the other.** The Lord was trying to teach his disciples love instead of revenge. They were to follow his example in returning good for evil. 35. **Love ye your enemies.** The principle that Jesus inculcated was the one that brought him to earth (cf. Rom 5:8; I Jn 4:10).

38. Give, and it shall be given unto you; good measure, pressed down, and shaken together, and running over, shall men give into your bosom. For with the same measure that ye mete withal it shall be measured to you again.

39. And he spake a parable unto them; Can the blind lead the blind? shall they not both fall into the ditch?

40. The disciple is not above his master: but every one that is perfect shall be as his master.

41. And why beholdest thou the mote that is in thy brother's eye, but perceivest not the beam that is in thine own eye?

42. Either how canst thou say to thy brother, Brother, let me pull out the mote that is in thine eye, when thou thyself beholdest not the beam that is in thine own eye? Thou hypocrite, cast out first the beam out of thine own eye, and then shalt thou see clearly to pull out the mote that is in thy brother's eye.

43. For a good tree bringeth not forth corrupt fruit; neither doth a corrupt tree bring forth good fruit.

44. For every tree is known by his own fruit. For of thorns men do not gather figs, nor of a bramble bush gather they grapes.

45. A good man out of the good treasure of his heart bringeth forth that which is good; and an evil man out of the evil treasure of his heart bringeth forth that which is evil: for of the abundance of the heart his mouth speaketh.

46. And why call ye me, Lord, Lord, and do not the things which I say?

47. Whosoever cometh to me, and heareth my sayings, and doeth them, I will show you to whom he is like:

48. He is like a man which built a house, and digged deep, and laid the foundation on a rock: and when the flood arose, the stream beat vehemently upon that house, and could not shake it; for it was founded upon a rock.

49. But he that heareth, and doeth not, is like a man that without a foundation built a house upon the earth; against which the stream did beat vehemently, and immediately it fell; and the ruin of that house was great.

38. Good measure, pressed down, and shaken together, and running over. The figure of speech is taken from the practice of the Oriental grain merchant, who fills the basket of his customer as full as possible until the grain runs over the edge.

41. The mote . . . the beam. Perhaps Jesus had had the unpleasant experience of getting a piece of sawdust in his eye when he worked in Joseph's carpenter shop. As a bit of sawdust is to a plank, so is the small offense in the brother's life as compared with the greater offense in one's own life.

48. When the flood arose. Because the hills in Palestine had little vegetation on them, the winter rains produced violent floods that swept away any building in their path. Sand would wash away quickly; the buildings founded on rock would remain. Christ taught that the only secure foundation for enduring life could be found in his teachings and truth. By this exclusive claim he made himself the arbiter of human destiny and the object of all true faith.

## CHAPTER 7

NOW when he had ended all his sayings in the audience of the people, he entered into Capernaum.

2. And a certain centurion's servant, who was dear unto him, was sick, and ready to die.

3. And when he heard of Jesus, he sent unto him the elders of the Jews, beseeching him that he would come and heal his servant.

4. And when they came to Jesus, they besought him instantly, saying, That he was worthy for whom he should do this:

5. For he loveth our nation, and he hath built us a synagogue.

6. Then Jesus went with them. And when he was now not far from the house, the centurion sent friends to him, saying unto him, Lord, trouble not thyself; for I am not worthy that thou shouldest enter under my roof:

7. Wherefore neither thought I myself worthy to come unto thee: but say in a word, and my servant shall be healed.

8. For I also am a man set under authority, having under me soldiers, and I say unto one, Go, and he goeth; and to another, Come, and he cometh; and to my servant, Do this, and he doeth it.

9. When Jesus heard these things, he marveled at him, and turned him about, and said unto the people that followed him, I say unto you, I have not found so great faith, no, not in Israel.

10. And they that were sent, returning to the house, found the servant whole that had been sick.

11. And it came to pass the day after, that he went into a city called Nain; and many of his disciples went with him, and much people.

**E. A Cross Section of His Ministry. 7:1—9:17.**

In the section between the appointment of the apostles and the climax of Jesus' ministry at the Transfiguration, Luke gives a series of our Lord's acts and teachings which do not make a connected narrative, but which illustrate the character of his ministry. Miracles of healing and parables that contained a story seem to have interested Luke particularly.

**1. Capernaum.** After teaching the disciples, Jesus returned to the city. Perhaps his disciples visited their homes while he ministered in the locality. **2. A certain centurion's servant.** The centurions were the backbone of the Roman army. Usually they came up through the ranks to posts of command because of their character. This officer seems to have been different from the usual hard type of Roman military man. He had a genuine affection for his servant, and he loved the Jewish nation, which most of the Romans despised. **3. The elders of the Jews.** His relation with the elders must have been good, else they would not have pled his cause. Perhaps the centurion felt that no Jewish rabbi would do a favor for a Gentile Roman. **5. A synagogue.** The ruins of the synagogue now standing in Capernaum show Roman architecture with Jewish motifs carved on the stones. The synagogue to which Luke alludes was earlier, but this later one may have preserved something of its style.

**6. Lord, trouble not thyself.** Literally, *Do not skin yourself*. This may be a piece of slang that Luke has preserved. **8. For I also am a man set under authority.** The centurion recognized that just as he had authority vested in him by Rome, so Jesus had authority from God that enabled him to exercise power over disease. **9. Not in Israel.** The insight and faith of the pagan made a refreshing contrast to the unbelief of Jesus' own people, from whom he had a right to expect more.

**11. Nain** was about ten miles southeast of Nazareth. Near the eastern gate of

12. Now when he came nigh to the gate of the city, behold, there was a dead man carried out, the only son of his mother, and she was a widow: and much people of the city was with her.

13. And when the Lord saw her, he had compassion on her, and said unto her, Weep not.

14. And he came and touched the bier: and they that bare *him* stood still. And he said, Young man, I say unto thee, Arise.

15. And he that was dead sat up, and began to speak. And he delivered him to his mother.

16. And there came a fear on all: and they glorified God, saying, That a great prophet is risen up among us; and, That God hath visited his people.

17. And this rumor of him went forth throughout all Judea, and throughout all the region round about.

18. And the disciples of John showed him of all these things.

19. And John calling *unto him* two of his disciples sent *them* to Jesus, saying, Art thou he that should come? or look we for another?

20. When the men were come unto him, they said, John Baptist hath sent us unto thee, saying, Art thou he that should come? or look we for another?

21. And in that same hour he cured many of *their* infirmities and plagues, and of evil spirits; and unto many *that were* blind he gave sight.

22. Then Jesus answering said unto them, Go your way, and tell John what things ye have seen and heard; how that the blind see, the lame walk, the lepers are cleansed, the deaf hear, the dead are raised, to the poor the gospel is preached.

23. And blessed is *he*, whosoever shall not be offended in me.

24. And when the messengers of John were departed, he began to speak unto the people concerning John, What went ye out into the wilderness for to see? A reed shaken with the wind?

25. But what went ye out for to see? A man clothed in soft raiment? Behold, they which are gorgeously appareled, and live delicately, are in kings' courts.

Nain, along the road to Capernaum, are rock tombs. Jesus, approaching from Capernaum, may have met the funeral procession coming out of the city on the way to these tombs. **12. A widow.** The lot of a widow in the East was hard, since she could not easily find gainful employment, and so was dependent on her nearest male relatives. **Much people.** There were many witnesses of the miracle who could testify to its genuiness. **13. Weep not.** Loud wailing was conventional at Eastern funerals; in fact, mourners were often hired to supply it. The command to stop weeping, spoken by an utter stranger, may have seemed rude. **14. Bier.** The Greek word denotes either a stretcher on which a corpse was carried, or the coffin itself.

**16. And there came a fear.** The sudden resuscitation of the corpse must have been terrifying for those in the funeral procession, even though they rejoiced over it. **God hath visited his people.** For many years there had been no prophetic testimony in Israel. The magnitude of this miracle compelled the people to believe that Jesus must be a prophet. **18. The disciples of John.** The ministry of John the Baptist was slowly being eclipsed by that of Jesus. The rumor of this miracle at Nain must have been widely discussed if it penetrated the fortress of Machaerus (see Jos *Wars of the Jews* VII. vi. 2) in the wilderness east of the Dead Sea, where John was a captive. **20. Art thou he that should come? or look we for another?** The long imprisonment discouraged John, and made him wonder whether Jesus was the Messiah after all. **22. Then Jesus answering.** Jesus answered by challenging the messengers of John to observe demonstrations of his power. And he appealed to John not to be **offended** (v. 23) by the way he conducted his ministry. "Offend" (Gr. *skandalizo*) has the meaning of "cause to go astray," or "cause to err," rather than "to displease."

**24.** The Lord paid his tribute to John by asking three questions of the people. **A reed shaken with the wind?** The reeds in the marshes bend with the wind; they do not maintain any one position. Jesus said that John was a man of convictions, who did not change with every fad. **25. A man clothed in soft raiment?** Ordinary clothing was made of coarse hand-woven materials; only the very wealthy wore imported silks and linens. John was rugged, a man who could endure hardships and who belonged to the common peo-

26. But what went ye out for to see? A prophet? Yea, I say unto you, and much more than a prophet.

27. This is *he*, of whom it is written, Behold, I send my messenger before thy face, which shall prepare thy way before thee.

28. For I say unto you, Among those that are born of women there is not a greater prophet than John the Baptist: but he that is least in the kingdom of God is greater than he.

29. And all the people that heard *him*, and the publicans, justified God, being baptized with the baptism of John.

30. But the Pharisees and lawyers rejected the counsel of God against themselves, being not baptized of him.

31. And the Lord said, Whereunto then shall I liken the men of this generation? and to what are they like?

32. They are like unto children sitting in the market place, and calling one to another, and saying, We have piped unto you, and ye have not danced; we have mourned to you, and ye have not wept.

33. For John the Baptist came neither eating bread nor drinking wine; and ye say, He hath a devil.

34. The Son of man is come eating and drinking; and ye say, Behold a gluttonous man, and a winebibber, a friend of publicans and sinners!

35. But wisdom is justified of all her children.

36. And one of the Pharisees desired him that he would eat with him. And he went into the Pharisee's house, and sat down to meat.

37. And, behold, a woman in the city, which was a sinner, when she knew that *Jesus* sat at meat in the Pharisee's house, brought an alabaster box of ointment,

ple. **26. A prophet?** Among the Hebrews the prophet was the highest type of leader, since he was commissioned and inspired by God. The people of Nain had called Jesus a prophet, and the same title was applied to him on other occasions (Jn 4:19; 7:40; 9:17). **27. This is he of whom it is written.** The quotation from Mal 3:1 is doubly significant. It establishes John as the forerunner of the Messiah, which places him above all the other prophets. **Thee** in the original of the quoted text reads "me," and refers to God, who speaks these words, adding, "and the Lord, whom ye seek, shall suddenly come to his temple, even the messenger of the covenant, whom ye delight in." By implication, then, Jesus is identified with **the Lord** of Malachi, and his deity is affirmed. **28. Not a greater prophet than John the Baptist.** John was the greatest and last of the prophets, and the herald of a new dispensation. **He that is least in the kingdom of God.** John knew only that redemption and the work of the Holy Spirit would be introduced by Jesus (Jn 1:29-34); he did not live to see the work of Christ perfected. Those who live in the era of the kingdom of God have greater privileges and powers than John.

**29. Justified God.** This word is used by Luke more than by the other Gospel writers. The ordinary people acknowledged the righteousness of God by accepting the condemnation of their sins through John's message, and they expressed repentance by submitting to baptism.

**31. Whereunto then shall I liken the men of this generation?** Jesus illustrated the behavior of the Pharisees from the games of children which he had probably played as a boy. If someone proposed that they "play wedding," the others would not dance; if one suggested that they "play funeral," the others would not mourn. No matter what was suggested, they would not be pleased. They called John crazy because he abstained from luxuries; they accused Jesus of being a glutton and a reveler because he attended feasts.

**36. And one of the Pharisees desired him that he would eat with him.** *Invited* would be a better rendering than **desired.** The Pharisee's motives may not have been wholly good; he probably wanted to catch Jesus in some act or utterance. **37. A woman . . . which was a sinner.** The intrusion of this woman was intolerable to the respectable Pharisee be-

38. And stood at his feet behind *him* weeping, and began to wash his feet with tears, and did wipe *them* with the hairs of her head, and kissed his feet, and anointed *them* with the ointment.

39. Now when the Pharisee which had bidden him saw *it*, he spake within himself, saying, This man, if he were a prophet, would have known who and what manner of woman *this is* that toucheth him; for she is a sinner.

40. And Jesus answering said unto him, Simon, I have somewhat to say unto thee. And he saith, Master, say on.

41. There was a certain creditor which had two debtors: the one owed five hundred pence, and the other fifty.

42. And when they had nothing to pay, he frankly forgave them both. Tell me therefore, which of them will love him most?

43. Simon answered and said, I suppose that *he*, to whom he forgave most. And he said unto him, Thou hast rightly judged.

44. And he turned to the woman, and said unto Simon, Seest thou this woman? I entered into thine house, thou gavest me no water for my feet: but she hath washed my feet with tears, and wiped *them* with the hairs of her head.

45. Thou gavest me no kiss: but this woman, since the time I came in, hath not ceased to kiss my feet.

46. My head with oil thou didst not anoint: but this woman hath anointed my feet with ointment.

cause of her evil reputation and because she was not an invited guest. **An alabaster box.** Alabaster was a fine translucent stone, used only to make decorative pieces. The box of ointment must have been exceedingly valuable, and was possibly the proceeds of her sin. **38. Stood at his feet behind him.** Guests at dinner did not sit at tables, but reclined on couches with their heads toward the table. It would have been easy for this woman to kneel at the end of the couch on which Jesus lay.

**39. This man, if he were a prophet, would have known.** The Pharisee expected Jesus, as a wise rabbi and a religious leader, to reject the woman's attention as insulting. The rabbis of that time never talked with a woman in public if they could help it, and if they did, their conduct was exceptional (Jn 4:27). Simon concluded that Jesus was either stupid or lax. **40. And Jesus answering said.** Simon had not said a word audibly, but Jesus read his thoughts, and answered by the parable that follows. The story must have held the attention of the guests at dinner and at the same time made the point unmistakably plain.

**41. A certain creditor.** As a wealthy man, Simon must have been a creditor himself on numerous occasions. Perhaps Jesus knew he was generous, and used this story to appeal to him personally. **Five hundred pence . . . fifty. Penny** represents the Roman *denarius*, worth about seventeen cents. The first creditor owed about $85.00; the second, $8.50.

**42. Which . . . will love him the most?** Simon may have taken the story to be simply a conundrum proposed as part of the dinner conversation. **43. I suppose** may indicate that he was a bit hesitant to commit himself, because he felt that Jesus had an ulterior motive in telling the story. There was, however, only one logical answer, and he gave it.

**44. Thou gavest me no water.** Omission of washing a guest's feet was a serious breach of etiquette, and Jesus could have regarded it as a direct insult. His presence at the dinner, however, was a mark of his willingness to overlook Simon's neglect. **45. Thou gavest me no kiss.** In the East today men frequently greet each other by a kiss on the cheek. It was a common polite greeting of friends in Jesus' time (cf. Rom 16:16; I Cor 16:20; I Thess 5:26). **46. My head with oil.** A touch of perfumed oil would have been a part of the preliminaries to the feast, but Simon had omitted even

47. Wherefore I say unto thee, Her sins, which are many, are forgiven; for she loved much: but to whom little is forgiven, *the same* loveth little.

48. And he said unto her, Thy sins are forgiven.

49. And they that sat at meat with him began to say within themselves, Who is this that forgiveth sins also?

50. And he said to the woman, Thy faith hath saved thee; go in peace.

## CHAPTER 8

AND it came to pass afterward, that he went throughout every city and village, preaching and showing the glad tidings of the kingdom of God: and the twelve *were* with him,

2. And certain women, which had been healed of evil spirits and infirmities, Mary called Magdalene, out of whom went seven devils,

3. And Joanna the wife of Chuza Herod's steward, and Susanna, and many others, which ministered unto him of their substance.

4. And when much people were gathered together, and were come to him out of every city, he spake by a parable:

5. A sower went out to sow his seed: and as he sowed, some fell by the wayside; and it was trodden down, and the fowls of the air devoured it.

6. And some fell upon a rock; and as soon as it was sprung up, it withered away, because it lacked moisture.

this inexpensive favor. The woman had used costly ointment. **47. To whom little is forgiven.** Jesus contrasted Simon's lack of courtesy with the devotion of this woman, and implied that Simon had not experienced a deep forgiveness.

**48. And he said unto her.** Jesus had already said (v. 47) that the woman's sins, which he did not deny, had been forgiven; but to clear her before the public he made a direct declaration. **49.** The same question was asked at the healing of the paralytic (5:21). **50. Saved** can mean "made whole" either in a physical or in a spiritual sense. The latter meaning is intended. This woman cannot be identified with Mary Magdalene, nor with Mary of Bethany, despite the similarity of the latter's act recorded in the account of the dinner at Bethany (Mt 26:6-13; Mk 14:3-9; Jn 12:1-9). The differences between these episodes are greater than the resemblances.

**8:1. He went throughout every city and village.** Jesus made a systematic tour of Galilee, reaching the masses of the people in preparation for his final appeal to them. **The twelve were with him.** Does this statement imply that previously they had not always traveled with him? Perhaps they spent part of their time in self-support. **2. And certain women.** Luke seems to have been personally acquainted with them. Joanna (v. 3) is not mentioned outside of this Gospel. **3. Which ministered unto him.** Their gratitude to Jesus for healing prompted the gifts that helped to support him and the disciples on the preaching tours.

**4. He spake by a parable.** This parable is narrated and interpreted by all three of the Synoptic Gospels (Mt 13:3-23; Mk 4:3-25). It is an outstanding sample of the Lord's method of teaching. Usually known as the Parable of the Sower, it could better be called the Parable of the Soils.

**5. A sower went out to sow.** Mechanized farming was unknown in Palestine. One of the most familiar sights in the rural communities was the farmer scattering seed over the plowed soil. **The way side.** Except for a few main highways there were no paved roads, only tracks through the fields. Wayfarers would beat the ground hard as they walked between villages. **6. A rock** (Gr. *tēn petran*, the rock). Palestine is a very stony country. The seed did not fall on bare rock, but on thin soil covering a ledge of rock. The warmth of the rock would cause the seed to sprout quickly,

7. And some fell among thorns; and the thorns sprang up with it, and choked it.

8. And other fell on good ground, and sprang up, and bare fruit a hundredfold. And when he had said these things, he cried, He that hath ears to hear, let him hear.

9. And his disciples asked him, saying, What might this parable be?

10. And he said, Unto you it is given to know the mysteries of the kingdom of God: but to others in parables; that seeing they might not see, and hearing they might not understand.

11. Now the parable is this: The seed is the word of God.

12. Those by the wayside are they that hear; then cometh the devil, and taketh away the word out of their hearts, lest they should believe and be saved.

13. They on the rock *are they*, which, when they hear, receive the word with joy; and these have no root, which for a while believe, and in time of temptation fall away.

14. And that which fell among thorns are they, which, when they have heard, go forth, and are choked with cares and riches and pleasures of *this* life, and bring no fruit to perfection.

15. But that on the good ground are they, which in an honest and good heart, having heard the word, keep *it*, and bring forth fruit with patience.

16. No man, when he hath lighted a candle, covereth it with a vessel, or putteth *it* under a bed; but setteth *it* on a candlestick, that they which enter in may see the light.

17. For nothing is secret, that shall not be made manifest; neither *any thing* hid, that shall not be known and come abroad.

18. Take heed therefore how ye hear: for whosoever hath, to him shall be given; and whosoever hath not, from him shall be taken even that which he seemeth to have.

19. Then came to him *his* mother and his brethren, and could not come at him for the press.

20. And it was told him *by certain* which said, Thy mother and thy brethren stand without, desiring to see thee.

21. And he answered and said unto them, My mother and my brethren are these which hear the word of God, and do it.

but the soil would dry out rapidly, and the young shoots would wither. **7. Thorns.** Thorn bushes grew in clumps, and were hard to eradicate. Even if the tops of the bushes were cut away, the roots would remain in the ground. **8. Good ground.** The soil of Palestine is rich, and when properly irrigated will produce large crops.

**9. What might this parable be?** The problem for the disciples was to discover the application of the facts stated; the facts themselves were simple and familiar. **10. The mysteries of the kingdom of God.** "Mystery" (Gr. *mysterion*) is a fact or truth revealed only to the initiated. The truth of God cannot be understood by those who have no spiritual discernment (I Cor 2:14). The disciples would see new truth through the parables; the others would think of them only as entertaining stories.

**11. Now the parable is this:** The Parable of the Soils is one of the few that Jesus interpreted. It gives a key both to his methods of teaching and to the mental processes that lay behind them. **The word of God** is the truth of God, whether written or spoken. In this parable the Lord was thinking of his own teaching as given to the crowds. **14. Bring no fruit to perfection.** There may be fruit, but the ears of grain will be scanty and stunted. **15. Honest and good heart.** Two Greek words (*kalos* and *agathos*), both meaning "good," are used. The former connotes beauty; the latter, nobility or uprightness.

**16. Candle** is properly a lamp (Gr. *lychnon*), a little clay dish in which olive oil and a wick were placed. It gave a very feeble light. Placed under a pot or a piece of furniture, it would give no illumination. It was usually set on a lampstand (**candlestick**) so that its light would radiate in every direction. **17. For nothing is secret, that shall not be made manifest.** Truth is like a light; it cannot be kept secret if it is to be useful. **18. Take heed therefore how ye hear.** The listener has as much to do with the effectiveness of the message as the speaker does.

**19. His mother and his brethren.** Little is said in the Gospels about Jesus' family. His brothers did not believe in his claims (Jn 7:5). The nature of their errand is not revealed. Possibly they felt that Jesus was making extravagant claims and was embarrassing them by his assertions of authority. **21. My mother and my brethren are these.** He declared

**22.** Now it came to pass on a certain day, that he went into a ship with his disciples: and he said unto them, Let us go over unto the other side of the lake. And they launched forth.

**23.** But as they sailed, he fell asleep: and there came down a storm of wind on the lake; and they were filled *with water*, and were in jeopardy.

**24.** And they came to him, and awoke him, saying, Master, Master, we perish. Then he arose, and rebuked the wind and the raging of the water: and they ceased, and there was a calm.

**25.** And he said unto them, Where is your faith? And they being afraid wondered, saying one to another, What manner of man is this! for he commandeth even the winds and water, and they obey him.

**26.** And they arrived at the country of the Gadarenes, which is over against Galilee.

**27.** And when he went forth to land, there met him out of the city a certain man, which had devils long time, and ware no clothes, neither abode in *any* house, but in the tombs.

**28.** When he saw Jesus, he cried out, and fell down before him, and with a loud voice said, What have I to do with thee, Jesus, *thou* Son of God most high? I beseech thee, torment me not.

**29.** (For he had commanded the unclean spirit to come out of the man. For oftentimes it had caught him: and he was kept bound with chains and in fetters; and he brake the bands, and was driven of the devil into the wilderness.)

**30.** And Jesus asked him, saying, What is thy name? And he said, Legion: because many devils were entered into him.

**31.** And they besought him that he would not command them to go out into the deep.

that kinship with him is spiritual, not primarily physical.

**22. Let us go over unto the other side of the lake.** The east side of the lake was largely uninhabited. Jesus wanted to get away from the crowds in order to rest and to talk with his disciples. **23. He fell asleep.** The Saviour was subject to human limitations, and the fatigue of his ministry had worn him out. **A storm of wind** was not unusual on Galilee. The lake lies 680 feet below sea level and is surrounded by hills. As the air on the heights cools toward the end of the day, it flows down through the defiles of the hills to the lake surface and churns it into foam. **They were filled with water, and were in jeopardy.** The high waves dashed into the open vessel, so that it was in danger of sinking. **24. We perish.** The storm must have been unusually violent to frighten experienced fishermen who knew every mood of the lake. **Then he arose, and rebuked the wind.** Jesus had authority over the powers of nature. In the natural course of the passing of a storm, complete calm would not have followed instantly.

**26. The country of the Gadarenes.** The miracle could hardly have taken place at Gadara, which was seven miles from the lake. A well-attested reading in a number of older manuscripts is *Gergesa* or *Gerasa*. There was a village by the lake opposite Capernaum, the site of which is marked today by ruins called *Khersa*, near which were precipitous rocky slopes and abandoned tombs. The territory belonged to Gadara, and thus could be called "the country of the Gadarenes." The variation in manuscript readings may reflect the confusion of early scribes over the identity of the place, or even differing viewpoints on the part of the Evangelists. The territory along the lake was wilderness. **27. A certain man, which had devils a long time.** The demoniac was so dangerous that he had been driven from civilization, and had found refuge in the deserted tombs. **28. What have I to do with thee.** Recognizing Jesus as the Son of God, the demon was overcome by fear of the judgment that Christ might pronounce upon him. **29. He was kept bound with chains and in fetters.** The demon-possessed man required forcible restraint. With supernatural strength he broke his bonds, and escaped.

**30. A** Roman **legion** comprised about 6,000 men. The expression here may mean only a great number. **31. The deep**

32. And there was there a herd of many swine feeding on the mountain: and they besought him that he would suffer them to enter into them. And he suffered them.

33. Then went the devils out of the man, and entered into the swine: and the herd ran violently down a steep place into the lake, and were choked.

34. When they that fed *them* saw what was done, they fled, and went and told *it* in the city and in the country.

35. Then they went out to see what was done; and came to Jesus, and found the man, out of whom the devils were departed, sitting at the feet of Jesus, clothed, and in his right mind: and they were afraid.

36. They also which saw *it* told them by what means he that was possessed of the devils was healed.

37. Then the whole multitude of the country of the Gadarenes round about besought him to depart from them; for they were taken with great fear: and he went up into the ship, and returned back again.

38. Now the man, out of whom the devils were departed, besought him that he might be with him: but Jesus sent him away, saying,

39. Return to thine own house, and show how great things God hath done unto thee. And he went his way, and published throughout the whole city how great things Jesus had done unto him.

40. And it came to pass, that, when Jesus was returned, the people *gladly* received him: for they were all waiting for him.

41. And, behold, there came a man named Jairus, and he was a ruler of the synagogue; and he fell down at Jesus' feet, and besought him that he would come into his house:

42. For he had one only daughter, about twelve years of age, and she lay a dying. But as he went the people thronged him.

43. And a woman having an issue of blood twelve years, which had spent all her living upon physicians, neither could be healed of any,

44. Came behind *him*, and touched the border of his garment: and immediately her issue of blood stanched.

45. And Jesus said, Who touched me? When all denied, Peter and they that were with him said, Master, the multitude throng thee and press *thee*, and sayest thou, Who touched me?

means the abyss of destruction to which all evil spirits are doomed (Rev 9:1; 11:7; 20:1,3). **32. Many swine.** The pigs were raised for sale in the Gentile markets of the Decapolis. Jews would not have purchased or used them. **33. The herd ran violently . . . into the lake, and were choked.** The eastern shore of the lake is so precipitous that if the animals started to run, they would have been unable to stop. Pigs cannot swim well, and so the whole herd was lost.

**35. Clothed, and in his right mind.** Some have questioned the right of Jesus to permit the destruction of another's property. A choice of values was involved. Which was worth more—the man, or the pigs? **37. Besought him to depart from them.** The people evidently valued their pigs more than they did the man, for they feared further trouble, and urged Jesus to leave. **38. Now the man . . . besought him that he might be with him.** The attitude of the healed demoniac was the exact opposite of that of his former neighbors. **Jesus sent him away.** The Lord did not repudiate him, but gave him a commission to discharge. He became an effective witness to the Saviour's power.

**41. And, behold, there came a man named Jairus.** No place is named as the setting for the raising of Jairus' daughter, but Capernaum is the most likely location. Verse 40 says that Jesus had **returned**, which implies going back to a place originally left. Jairus may have been one of the elders who came to Jesus to intercede for the centurion's servant (7:3).

**43. And a woman having an issue of blood twelve years.** Luke makes clear that hers was an incurable case, which defied the skill of all the physicians. **44. Touched the border of his garment.** The **border** was really a tassel (Gr. *kraspedon*) which a rabbi wore on his garment. The outer robe was a large square of heavy woolen cloth, draped over the wearer's back in such a way that the tassel of one corner hung between his shoulder blades. In the throng the woman crept up behind Jesus and touched the tassel. **45. Who touched me?** Jesus felt a flow of power going out from him, and knew that someone had touched him. The question seemed silly to the disciples, since he was being jostled on all sides by the crowd. But the Lord could discern the difference between the casual accidental bodily contacts, and the out-

46. And Jesus said, Somebody hath touched me: for I perceive that virtue is gone out of me.

47. And when the woman saw that she was not hid, she came trembling, and falling down before him, she declared unto him before all the people for what cause she had touched him, and how she was healed immediately.

48. And he said unto her, Daughter, be of good comfort: thy faith hath made thee whole; go in peace.

49. While he yet spake, there cometh one from the ruler of the synagogue's *house*, saying to him, Thy daughter is dead; trouble not the Master.

50. But when Jesus heard *it*, he answered him, saying, Fear not: believe only, and she shall be made whole.

51. And when he came into the house, he suffered no man to go in, save Peter, and James, and John, and the father and the mother of the maiden.

52. And all wept, and bewailed her: but he said, Weep not; she is not dead, but sleepeth.

53. And they laughed him to scorn, knowing that she was dead.

54. And he put them all out, and took her by the hand, and called, saying, Maid, arise.

55. And her spirit came again, and she arose straightway: and he commanded to give her meat.

56. And her parents were astonished: but he charged them that they should tell no man what was done.

### CHAPTER 9

THEN he called his twelve disciples together, and gave them power and authority over all devils, and to cure diseases.

2. And he sent them to preach the kingdom of God, and to heal the sick.

3. And he said unto them, Take nothing for *your* journey, neither staves, nor scrip, neither bread, neither money; neither have two coats apiece.

4. And whatsoever house ye enter into, there abide, and thence depart.

5. And whosoever will not receive you, when ye go out of that city, shake off the very dust from your feet for a testimony against them.

6. And they departed, and went through the towns, preaching the gospel, and healing every where.

7. Now Herod the tetrarch heard of all that was done by him: and he was perplexed, because that it was said of some, that John was risen from the dead;

reach of faith. **46. Virtue.** See comment on 6:19.

**47. And when the woman saw that she was not hid.** She had sought secrecy to avoid any possible embarrassment, but when her act was discovered, she was frightened. **48. Daughter, be of good comfort.** Jesus' tact and kindliness gave her reassurance. He confirmed the healing, and sent her away relieved.

**49. While he yet spake.** The delay had been fatal. The news must have disheartened Jairus, and perhaps aroused in him resentment against the woman who had interrupted the Master's plans. **50. Fear not: believe only.** Christ's power and compassion were unlimited. **51. He suffered no man to go in.** After the notable healing of the woman, Jesus wanted no further publicity. **52. She is not dead, but sleepeth.** He spoke of death as sleep because he was thinking of it as a state from which one will awake. The mourners looked upon it as the end of life (cf. Jn 11:11-14).

**55. He commanded to give her meat.** He was aware of ordinary practical needs as well as of emergencies. **56. He charged them that they should tell no man what was done.** He did not want the populace to use his miracles as a reason for making him a political figure. He intended that his power should be used to relieve suffering and to help the needy; he wanted to avoid mere showmanship.

**9:1. Power and authority. Power** is inherent ability; **authority** is the right to exercise it. **2. To preach . . . and to heal.** Their ministry was to be an extension of his. **3. Take nothing for your journey.** Jesus wanted to test their faith by making no elaborate preparations for the journey. Deissmann suggests that the **scrip** (Gr. *pēra*) was the wallet which a beggar carried (LAE, pp. 108-110). Jesus forbade the disciples to beg as representatives of other religions did. **4. There abide.** They were not to go from house to house in search of the most comfortable lodgings, but were to accept whatever was offered. **5. Shake off the very dust.** If their word was refused, they were to indicate their rejection of the city by this emphatic gesture. **6. Every where.** Galilee was thoroughly covered.

**7. Herod the tetrarch** was the ruler of Galilee who had imprisoned and executed John the Baptist. He had feared John's influence, and he thought that Jesus might be the Baptist's successor. **8.**

8. And of some, that Elias had appeared; and of others, that one of the old prophets was risen again.

9. And Herod said, John have I beheaded; but who is this, of whom I hear such things? And he desired to see him.

10. And the apostles, when they were returned, told him all that they had done. And he took them, and went aside privately into a desert place belonging to the city called Bethsaida.

11. And the people, when they knew *it*, followed him: and he received them, and spake unto them of the kingdom of God, and healed them that had need of healing.

12. And when the day began to wear away, then came the twelve, and said unto him, Send the multitude away, that they may go into the towns and country round about, and lodge, and get victuals: for we are here in a desert place.

13. But he said unto them, Give ye them to eat. And they said, We have no more but five loaves and two fishes; except we should go and buy meat for all this people.

14. For they were about five thousand men. And he said to his disciples, Make them sit down by fifties in a company.

15. And they did so, and made them all sit down.

16. Then he took the five loaves and the two fishes, and looking up to heaven, he blessed them, and brake, and gave to the disciples to set before the multitude.

17. And they did eat, and were all filled: and there was taken up of fragments that remained to them twelve baskets.

18. And it came to pass, as he was alone praying, his disciples were with him; and he asked them, saying, Whom say the people that I am?

Elias. Elijah, the most spectacular of the Hebrew prophets, had ascended alive into heaven, and the prophet Malachi (4:5) had predicted that he would return to prepare the way for the Messiah. 9. Herod. . . . desired to see him. Herod's conscience and his curiosity made him want to see Jesus, probably with evil intent (cf. 13:32). 10. Desert place. Not a barren waste, but uninhabited country. Bethsaida was a small town on the north shore of the lake, east of the inlet of the Jordan River, a moderate distance from the larger cities on the west side of the lake. 12. And when the day began to wear away. The disciples realized that the crowds were hungry, and that they should be fed before they became faint. 13. Give ye them to eat. Jesus commanded the disciples to estimate their own resources, and to use what they had. Five loaves and two fishes. The loaves were round cakes, like biscuits; the fish were small pickled fish, used as relish. 14. Five thousand men. If women and children were present, as Matthew hints (Mt 14:21), the crowd may have been as large as ten thousand. Make them sit down by fifties. Jesus knew how to organize a crowd. Seating the groups would prevent confusion, and would make serving easier. 16. Then he took . . . and . . . blessed . . . and brake, and gave. As Jesus broke the bread and fish, he multiplied them, so that he gave the disciples a constant supply of food to transmit to the crowd. 17. Twelve baskets provided a generous share for each of the disciples. The basket (Gr. *kophinos*) was a large container, perhaps the size of a modern bushel.

F. The Climax of His Ministry. 9:18-50.

With this section of the Gospel, Luke brings the ministry of the Saviour to a turning point. In the Galilean ministry, which ended with the feeding of the five thousand, Jesus had come to the peak of his popularity, and with his refusal to become a king (Jn 6:15), he began to lose public support. The confession of Peter and the revelation of the Transfiguration to the inner circle of disciples began the progress toward the cross, which dominates the latter part of this Gospel. 18. He was alone praying. Luke notes that Jesus prayed at every great crisis of his life (3:21; 5:16; 6:12; 11:1;

19. They answering said, John the Baptist; but some *say*, Elias; and others *say*, that one of the old prophets is risen again.

20. He said unto them, But whom say ye that I am? Peter answering said, The Christ of God.

21. And he straitly charged them, and commanded *them* to tell no man that thing;

22. Saying, The Son of man must suffer many things, and be rejected of the elders and chief priests and scribes, and be slain, and be raised the third day.

23. And he said to *them* all, If any *man* will come after me, let him deny himself, and take up his cross daily, and follow me.

24. For whosoever will save his life shall lose it: but whosoever will lose his life for my sake, the same shall save it.

25. For what is a man advantaged, if he gain the whole world, and lose himself, or be cast away?

26. For whosoever shall be ashamed of me and of my words, of him shall the Son of man be ashamed, when he shall come in his own glory, and *in his* Father's, and of the holy angels.

27. But I tell you of a truth, there be some standing here, which shall not taste of death, till they see the kingdom of God.

22:44). Whom say the people that I am? The Lord changed the focus of the disciples' attention from his deeds and teachings to himself. 20. But whom say ye that I am? Having nurtured their faith and having given them ample opportunity to observe him, Jesus wanted a confession of their personal faith, not a random opinion. Peter answering said, The Christ of God. Peter's affirmation of faith in Jesus as the Messiah promised in the OT was not based on political pretensions on the part of the Master, nor upon any extravagant claims. Jesus' power and authority were self-authenticating.

21. And he straitly charged them. The Lord did not want to be publicized as the leader of a revolutionary movement. The work of the cross must precede any deliverance of the nation from political oppressors. 22. The Son of man must suffer . . . and be raised the third day. Must (Gr. *dei*) denotes logical necessity. Christ was obligated to fulfill the purpose of God as revealed in the Scriptures. This concept appears in the preaching of the early church (Acts 2:23,24; 13:17-34; 17:3; 26:22,23). The death of Jesus was a tragedy, but it was not an accident; for he was fulfilling the purpose of God in redemption.

23. If any man will come after me. The disciples followed the Master at his initial call to them (5:11), but at that time they had no idea his career would end at the cross. They were still thinking in terms of conquest and of power (22:24). This appeal was a solemn warning to re-evaluate the cost of being his disciples. Deny means exactly what Peter did at the trial of Jesus: he refused to recognize him. Take up his cross daily. A voluntary acceptance of the responsibilities and sufferings incidental to being a disciple of Christ. Follow (Gr. *akoloutheite*). An imperative involving persistent action: "Let him keep on following me." 24. For whosoever will save his life. Life (Gr. *psychēn*) is *soul*, or *personality*. Jesus demanded the consecration of the whole man to his cause. For my sake. He claimed to be the final criterion of all human values.

26. When he shall come in his own glory. In the same discourse, Jesus predicted both the cross and the triumphal establishment of the Kingdom at his second coming. 27. There be some standing here. These words seemingly require the return of Christ within the lifetime of the apostles, but he did not come. The most logical explanation is that Je-

28. And it came to pass about an eight days after these sayings, he took Peter and John and James, and went up into a mountain to pray.

29. And as he prayed, the fashion of his countenance was altered, and his raiment *was* white *and* glistering.

30. And, behold, there talked with him two men, which were Moses and Elias:

31. Who appeared in glory, and spake of his decease which he should accomplish at Jerusalem:

32. But Peter and they that were with him were heavy with sleep: and when they were awake, they saw his glory, and the two men that stood with him.

33. And it came to pass, as they departed from him, Peter said unto Jesus, Master, it is good for us to be here: and let us make three tabernacles; one for thee, and one for Moses, and one for Elias: not knowing what he said.

34. While he thus spake, there came a cloud, and overshadowed them: and they feared as they entered into the cloud.

35. And there came a voice out of the cloud, saying, This is my beloved Son: hear him.

36. And when the voice was past, Jesus was found alone. And they kept *it* close, and told no man in those days any of those things which they had seen.

37. And it came to pass, that on the next day, when they were come down from the hill, much people met him.

38. And, behold, a man of the company cried out, saying, Master, I beseech thee, look upon my son; for he is mine only child.

39. And, lo, a spirit taketh him, and he suddenly crieth out; and it teareth him that he foameth again, and bruising him, hardly departeth from him.

40. And I besought thy disciples to cast him out; and they could not.

41. And Jesus answering said, O faithless and perverse generation, how long shall I be with you, and suffer you? Bring thy son hither.

42. And as he was yet a coming, the devil threw him down, and tare *him*. And Jesus rebuked the unclean spirit, and healed the child, and delivered him again to his father.

43. And they were all amazed at the mighty power of God. But while they wondered every one at all things which Jesus did, he said unto his disciples,

44. Let these sayings sink down into your ears: for the Son of man shall be delivered into the hands of men.

sus was speaking of the Transfiguration as a sample of the coming of the Kingdom, given to some of the disciples as a pledge of the future (cf. II Pet 1:11,16-19).

**29. The fashion of his countenance was altered.** For a short time Jesus resumed the glory which he had left to come to earth. His body and clothing became incandescent with the glow of deity. **30. Two men, which were Moses and Elias.** Both of these men had left the world under unusual circumstances: Moses had been buried by the hand of God (Deut 34:5,6), and Elijah had been taken up in a whirlwind (II Kgs 2:11). They represented the Law and the prophets, subordinate to Jesus, but important witnesses to his work. **31. Spake of his decease.** The work of the cross was of supreme importance to the heavenly counsels. **Decease** is literally *exodus*. Jesus' death was a withdrawal from one sphere and the beginning of a new life in another.

**32. Heavy with sleep.** The event took place at night. **They saw his glory.** Compare the testimony of John (Jn 1:14). **33. Let us make three tabernacles.** Literally, *huts*. Peter was thinking of a temporary shelter, for he wanted to enjoy the company of the celestial visitors for a time. **34. A cloud.** Not a rain cloud, but the Shekinah which marked the presence of God (Ex 13:21,22; 40:38; Num 9:15; Ps 99:7; Isa 4:5; II Chr 7:1). **35. A voice.** The Father repeated his approval of Jesus at the close of his Son's popular ministry (see 3:22).

**37. On the next day.** Christ returned from the glory of the Transfiguration to continue his ministry and to die. The first step on the road of humiliation was the embarrassment over his disciples' impotence. **41. O faithless and perverse generation.** The Lord was speaking to the disciples, not to the father. In spite of their privileges and previous experience in ministry for him, they were still powerless.

**44. Let these sayings sink down into your ears.** Jesus was making a supreme effort to acquaint the disciples with the change in his outlook. **46. Which of them should be greatest.** This is the complement of verse 45. They had not learned to evaluate life in terms of the cross (9:23-26). **47. Jesus . . . took a child.** He used the child as an illustration of unpretentious humility. The child had not attained any place of importance in society, and was typical of the least (v. 48) of whom

**45.** But they understood not this saying, and it was hid from them, that they perceived it not: and they feared to ask him of that saying.

**46.** Then there arose a reasoning among them, which of them should be greatest.

**47.** And Jesus, perceiving the thought of their heart, took a child, and set him by him,

**48.** And said unto them, Whosoever shall receive this child in my name receiveth me; and whosoever shall receive me, receiveth him that sent me: for he that is least among you all, the same shall be great.

**49.** And John answered and said, Master, we saw one casting out devils in thy name; and we forbade him, because he followeth not with us.

**50.** And Jesus said unto him, Forbid *him* not: for he that is not against us is for us.

**51.** And it came to pass, when the time was come that he should be received up, he steadfastly set his face to go to Jerusalem,

**52.** And sent messengers before his face: and they went, and entered into a village of the Samaritans, to make ready for him.

**53.** And they did not receive him, because his face was as though he would go to Jerusalem.

**54.** And when his disciples James and John saw *this*, they said, Lord, wilt thou that we command fire to come down from heaven, and consume them, even as Elias did?

**55.** But he turned, and rebuked them, and said, Ye know not what manner of spirit ye are of.

**56.** For the Son of man is not come to destroy men's lives, but to save *them*. And they went to another village.

**57.** And it came to pass, that, as they went in the way, a certain *man* said unto him, Lord, I will follow thee whithersoever thou goest.

**58.** And Jesus said unto him, Foxes have holes, and birds of the air *have* nests; but the Son of man hath not where to lay *his* head.

**59.** And he said unto another, Follow me. But he said, Lord, suffer me first to go and bury my father.

**60.** Jesus said unto him, Let the dead bury their dead: but go thou and preach the kingdom of God.

our Lord was speaking.

**49. He followeth not with us.** The disciples were bigoted. Because this man was not of their company, they were ready to discount his work completely.

## V. The Road to the Cross. 9:51–18:30.

This section of Luke's Gospel, which is largely peculiar to him, contains many episodes and parables which are not found elsewhere, and which may have been the results of his personal research. The chronology is difficult; the section seems to be a collection of stories rather than a complete narrative. It does, however, represent the teaching of Jesus in the last year of his ministry, and reflects a period of rejection and tension.

A. The Perspective of the Cross. 9:51-62.

**51. That he should be received up.** There are two possible interpretations: either Luke used the word **received up** (cf. Acts 1:2) in the broad sense of the entire Passion ministry (including the Ascension); or else he implied that Jesus, instead of returning to the Father immediately at the height of his public career, deliberately chose the way of humiliation that led to the cross. The second alternative has some support in the teaching of Heb 12:2, which says that "in exchange for the joy set before him he endured the cross" (original translation). **52. A village of the Samaritans.** The Samaritans were descendants of colonists whom the Assyrian kings had planted in Palestine after the fall of the northern kingdom in 721 B.C. Because of their mixed blood and different religious customs, the Jews hated them. Pilgrims to Jerusalem ordinarily did not go through Samaria. **54. Wilt thou that we command fire to come down.** James and John resented the slight to Jesus, and wanted revenge. **56. For the Son of man is not come to destroy men's lives, but to save them.** Luke's quotation exemplifies the purpose of Jesus to save men, which is repeated at intervals in his Gospel. **58. The Son of man hath not where to lay his head.** The rejection at Samaria gave point to this utterance. The Lord of the earth had less that he could call his own than the beasts and the birds. **59. Suffer me first to go and bury my father.** The speaker did not mean that his father had died, but that he was obligated to care for him until he died. **60. Let the dead bury their dead.** The spiritually in-

61. And another also said, Lord, I will follow thee; but let me first go bid them farewell, which are at home at my house.

62. And Jesus said unto him, No man, having put his hand to the plow, and looking back, is fit for the kingdom of God.

## CHAPTER 10

AFTER these things the Lord appointed other seventy also, and sent them two and two before his face into every city and place, whither he himself would come.

2. Therefore said he unto them, The harvest truly *is* great, but the laborers *are* few: pray ye therefore the Lord of the harvest, that he would send forth laborers into his harvest.

3. Go your ways: behold, I send you forth as lambs among wolves.

4. Carry neither purse, nor scrip, nor shoes: and salute no man by the way.

5. And into whatsoever house ye enter, first say, Peace *be* to this house.

6. And if the son of peace be there, your peace shall rest upon it: if not, it shall turn to you again.

7. And in the same house remain, eating and drinking such things as they give: for the laborer is worthy of his hire. Go not from house to house.

8. And into whatsoever city ye enter, and they receive you, eat such things as are set before you:

9. And heal the sick that are therein, and say unto them, The kingdom of God is come nigh unto you.

10. But into whatsoever city ye enter, and they receive you not, go your ways out into the streets of the same, and say,

11. Even the very dust of your city, which cleaveth on us, we do wipe off against you: notwithstanding, be ye sure of this, that the kingdom of God is come nigh unto you.

ert can wait for death; Jesus summoned the spiritually alive to follow him. **62. No man . . . looking back, is fit for the kingdom of God.** Looking back is continued action. A farmer who is plowing must always look forward if he is to plow a straight furrow.

**B. The Ministry of the Seventy. 10:1-24.**

Only Luke records the mission of the Seventy. Jesus must have had a large following if he could command the services of seventy men for a preaching mission in the cities of Galilee and Judea. Edersheim (Alfred Edersheim, *The Life and Times of Jesus the Messiah*, Vol. II, p. 135) suggests that Jesus sent them out at some point before the Feast of Tabernacles preceding his death. It might be deduced from his language that he had been rejected by the crowds in the Galilean cities (10:13,15), and that he was anticipating leaving the district permanently.

**1. After these things.** Luke's chronology is indefinite; but he locates these events after the crisis of the Transfiguration. **Two and two.** Jesus had sent out the Twelve in the same way on a previous mission (Mk 6:7). Sending them in pairs strengthened their witness, and made the traveling more pleasant. **Whither he himself would come.** The Seventy were to prepare the people for his last appeal to them. **2. The harvest.** Jesus used this figure often in speaking of the ingathering of believers (Jn 4:35,36; Mt 13:30,39).

**4. Carry neither purse, nor scrip, nor shoes.** The trip was to be brief, and its urgency demanded haste. They were forbidden to encumber themselves with needless baggage. **Salute no man.** The Lord did not want them to be unfriendly, but the Eastern salutations were so elaborate that they might have wasted a great deal of time in ceremony. **6. The son of peace.** A Hebrew idiom, meaning *a peaceful man.* Son of was frequently employed with a noun to emphasize a characteristic. John and James were called "sons of thunder" (Mk 3:17) because of their violent disposition. **7. Go not from house to house.** Jesus wanted his disciples to be messengers, not beggars. They were not to wander about, looking for the most comfortable quarters and the most congenial company.

**9. Heal the sick.** Christ imparted to the disciples the power to heal as an extension of his ministry. There is no indication

12. But I say unto you, that it shall be more tolerable in that day for Sodom, than for that city.

13. Woe unto thee, Chorazin! woe unto thee, Bethsaida! for if the mighty works had been done in Tyre and Sidon, which have been done in you, they had a great while ago repented, sitting in sackcloth and ashes.

14. But it shall be more tolerable for Tyre and Sidon at the judgment, than for you.

15. And thou, Capernaum, which art exalted to heaven, shalt be thrust down to hell.

16. He that heareth you heareth me; and he that despiseth you despiseth me; and he that despiseth me despiseth him that sent me.

17. And the seventy returned again with joy, saying, Lord, even the devils are subject unto us through thy name.

18. And he said unto them, I beheld Satan as lightning fall from heaven.

19. Behold, I give unto you power to tread on serpents and scorpions, and over all the power of the enemy; and nothing shall by any means hurt you.

20. Notwithstanding, in this rejoice not, that the spirits are subject unto you; but rather rejoice, because your names are written in heaven.

21. In that hour Jesus rejoiced in spirit, and said, I thank thee, O Father, Lord of heaven and earth, that thou hast hid these things from the wise and prudent, and hast revealed them unto babes: even so, Father; for so it seemed good in thy sight.

22. All things are delivered to me of my Father: and no man knoweth who the Son is, but the Father; and who the Father is, but the Son, and *he* to whom the Son will reveal *him*.

23. And he turned him unto *his* disciples, and said privately, Blessed *are* the eyes which see the things that ye see:

24. For I tell you, that many prophets and kings have desired to see those things which ye see, and have not seen *them;* and to hear those things which ye hear, and have not heard *them.*

25. And, behold, a certain lawyer stood up, and tempted him, saying, Master, what shall I do to inherit eternal life?

26. He said unto him, What is written in the law? how readest thou?

that all of them retained this power permanently. **12. In that day.** This phrase was used frequently in the prophetic books of the OT to denote the final day of judgment (Amos 8:9; 9:11; Zeph 1:14; Zech 12:8,11; 13:1; 14:4). **Sodom.** A city of Abraham's time, which was so vile that God destroyed it by an exceptional judgment (Gen 19:13,24). **13. Tyre and Sidon** were Phoenician cities noted for their luxury and debauchery. **Sackcloth.** A rough cloth worn by mourners as a sign of grief.

**17. And the seventy returned.** Their mission seems to have been successful. The Twelve failed to cure the demoniac boy (9:40); but the Seventy reported that even the demons fled at the mention of Jesus' name. **18. I beheld Satan as lightning fall.** *In the act of falling* would be a fair translation. Jesus implied that the power of Satan was broken, and that the success of these disciples was an evidence of the victory. **19. Power** is authority, the right to command. **20. Rejoice, because your names are written in heaven.** The greatest cause for rejoicing is not the momentary victory over supernatural forces, but the eternal triumph of being enrolled among the citizens of heaven. **Written** may mean inscribed on a public register (cf. Heb 12:23; Rev 3:5; 22:19).

**21. Jesus rejoiced.** The successful tour of the Seventy encouraged Jesus, for the power of Satan had not been sufficient to keep the revelation of God from these men. **22. No man knoweth who the Son is, but the Father.** This verse has a strong resemblance to the phraseology of Jesus as recorded in the Gospel of John (cf. Jn 5:22,23). Since it was spoken in private, it may indicate that the Johannine discourses were private in nature. Our Lord's public discourses seem to have been given in a different style.

C. Popular Teaching. 10:25—13:21.

**25. A certain lawyer.** In the Jewish community the 'lawyer' was an expert in the religious teachings of the Mosaic law rather than an advocate in court. **Tempted.** The lawyer was testing Jesus to see what he would say in answering a catch question. **Eternal life** was a current topic of religious debate (18:18). **26. What is written in the law?** The Saviour accepted the authority of the OT as the revelation of God. His question implies that the lawyer could have found the answer to his query in the Scriptures

27. And he answering said, Thou shalt love the Lord thy God with all thy heart, and with all thy soul, and with all thy strength, and with all thy mind; and thy neighbor as thyself.

28. And he said unto him, Thou hast answered right: this do, and thou shalt live.

29. But he, willing to justify himself, said unto Jesus, And who is my neighbor?

30. And Jesus answering said, A certain *man* went down from Jerusalem to Jericho, and fell among thieves, which stripped him of his raiment, and wounded *him*, and departed, leaving *him* half dead.

31. And by chance there came down a certain priest that way; and when he saw him, he passed by on the other side.

32. And likewise a Levite, when he was at the place, came and looked *on him*, and passed by on the other side.

33. But a certain Samaritan, as he journeyed, came where he was; and when he saw him, he had compassion *on him*,

34. And went to *him*, and bound up his wounds, pouring in oil and wine, and set him on his own beast, and brought him to an inn, and took care of him.

35. And on the morrow when he departed, he took out two pence, and gave *them* to the host, and said unto him, Take care of him: and whatsoever thou spendest more, when I come again, I will repay thee.

36. Which now of these three, thinkest thou, was neighbor unto him that fell among the thieves?

37. And he said, He that showed mercy on him. Then said Jesus unto him, Go, and do thou likewise.

38. Now it came to pass, as they went, that he entered into a certain village: and a certain woman named Martha received him into her house.

39. And she had a sister called Mary, which also sat at Jesus' feet, and heard his word.

had he really searched them. **27. And he answering said.** The lawyer's answer was a composite of two texts—Deut 6:5 and Lev 19:18. The former was a part of the Jewish *Shema*, or creed, which was customarily recited in the synagogue worship. **Heart** (Gr. *kardia*) is the inner life, not necessarily only emotion. **Soul** (Gr. *psychē*) is personality, the conscious being. **Strength** (Gr. *ischui*) is physical strength. **Mind** (Gr. *dianoia*) is the capacity to think. **29. Willing to justify himself.** Realizing that he had been caught by his own words, since he had not kept the Law, the lawyer began to quibble over a definition. Strict Jews would not acknowledge that any non-Jew was a neighbor.

**30. A certain man.** Although Jesus' story is called a parable, it may well have been a report of an actual occurrence. **Went down from Jerusalem.** Literally true, for Jerusalem is 2,600 feet above sea level, and Jericho is nearly 1,300 feet below sea level. The road is crooked and narrow, winding down through rocky defiles, where robbers could easily hide. **32. A Levite.** Levites served in the Temple. Neither the priest nor the Levite attempted to aid the man. They may have thought that he was dead, and did not wish to defile themselves by contact with a corpse. **33. But a certain Samaritan.** The Samaritans were scorned by Jews because they were descended from Gentile ancestry and because their kind of worship was different from that of orthodox Judaism. They worshiped in Mount Gerizim rather than in Jerusalem, and maintained a priesthood of their own. A small group still survives in the village of Nablus, near the site of ancient Shechem. **34. And went to him.** If the robbers were still lurking in the vicinity, the Samaritan was risking his life. Jesus showed that the Samaritan had the attitude of love which the Law commanded. **35. Two pence.** The equivalent of two days' wages. He was paying the expenses of a perfect stranger, simply because of good will. **36. Which . . . was neighbour.** This question shamed the lawyer into admitting that the true neighbor was not either of the priestly officials of Judaism, but the Samaritan.

**38. A certain village.** John (12:1) says that the village was Bethany, about two miles from Jerusalem on the road that led to Jericho and Trans-Jordan. Jesus must have visited there frequently as he traveled between Galilee and Jerusalem. **Martha** seems to have been the older sister, who took the responsibility for the household. **39. Heard his word.** The

40. But Martha was cumbered about much serving, and came to him, and said, Lord, dost thou not care that my sister hath left me to serve alone? bid her therefore that she help me.

41. And Jesus answered and said unto her, Martha, Martha, thou art careful and troubled about many things:

42. But one thing is needful; and Mary hath chosen that good part, which shall not be taken away from her.

### CHAPTER 11

AND it came to pass, that, as he was praying in a certain place, when he ceased, one of his disciples said unto him, Lord, teach us to pray, as John also taught his disciples.

2. And he said unto them, When ye pray, say, Our Father which art in heaven, Hallowed be thy name. Thy kingdom come. Thy will be done, as in heaven, so in earth.

3. Give us day by day our daily bread.

4. And forgive us our sins; for we also forgive every one that is indebted to us. And lead us not into temptation; but deliver us from evil.

Greek word (ēkouen) means that she was continually listening to the Master, or that it was her custom to do so. "Who always used to listen to his teaching" would be a good paraphrase. **40. Cumbered.** The Greek word (periespato) means *to be pulled away* or *to be pulled apart*, hence "distracted," "overburdened." **41. Martha, Martha.** On several occasions, according to Luke's account, Jesus repeated a name when he wanted to make some unusually impressive statement (see 22:31; cf. Acts 9:4). **42. But one thing is needful.** Martha thought "many things" were necessary for the Lord's comfort, and was wearing herself out to prepare them. Her company meant more to him than her cooking.

**11:1. As he was praying.** Neither Luke nor Matthew locates exactly the occasion on which Jesus gave his disciples this model prayer. Matthew includes it in the Sermon on the Mount (Mt 6:9-13). **2. When ye pray, say.** He did not intend them to repeat this prayer in parrot-like fashion. Rather, its several petitions were to serve as a guide to right attitude and content. **Our Father.** Jesus used a child's word for **father**, which appears also in Rom 8:15. It is used by modern Hebrews within the family circle, and implies familiarity based on love. God is the Father of all who receive Christ (Jn 1:12). **Hallowed be thy name.** The first petition concerns the honor of God, not the needs of the suppliant. The holiness of God must not be marred by the act of the one praying. **Thy kingdom come.** The rule of God must become universally acknowledged. Jesus would not have told his disciples to pray for the coming of the Kingdom if it had been present. **Thy will be done.** God's will is done in heaven by the angels without hesitation or dissent. The prayer calls for the same kind of obedience from the worshiper. **3. Give us day by day.** The Greek is concise and graphic: *Keep giving to us our daily allotment.* **4. Forgive us our sins** is both a plea and a confession. It is an acknowledgment of need, because man is a sinner; and it is a plea for divine grace. **Indebted to us.** Sin is a debt owed to God which man himself can never pay. "In whom (Christ) we have redemption through his blood, the forgiveness of sins, according to the riches of his grace" (Eph 1:7). **Lead us not into temptation.** Temptation does not necessarily mean solicitation to evil, for God never tempts in that sense (Jas 1:13). The prayer asks that the believer may be spared from

5. And he said unto them, Which of you shall have a friend, and shall go unto him at midnight, and say unto him, Friend, lend me three loaves;

6. For a friend of mine in his journey is come to me, and I have nothing to set before him?

7. And he from within shall answer and say, Trouble me not: the door is now shut, and my children are with me in bed; I cannot rise and give thee.

8. I say unto you, Though he will not rise and give him, because he is his friend, yet because of his importunity he will rise and give him as many as he needeth.

9. And I say unto you, Ask, and it shall be given you; seek, and ye shall find; knock, and it shall be opened unto you.

10. For every one that asketh receiveth; and he that seeketh findeth; and to him that knocketh it shall be opened.

11. If a son shall ask bread of any of you that is a father, will he give him a stone? or if *he ask* a fish, will he for a fish give him a serpent?

12. Or if he shall ask an egg, will he offer him a scorpion?

13. If ye then, being evil, know how to give good gifts unto your children; how much more shall *your* heavenly Father give the Holy Spirit to them that ask him?

14. And he was casting out a devil, and it was dumb. And it came to pass, when the devil was gone out, the dumb spake; and the people wondered.

15. But some of them said, He casteth out devils through Beelzebub the chief of the devils.

16. And others, tempting *him,* sought of him a sign from heaven.

17. But he, knowing their thoughts, said unto them, Every kingdom divided against itself is brought to desolation; and a house *divided* against a house falleth.

18. If Satan also be divided against himself, how shall his kingdom stand? because ye say that I cast out devils through Beelzebub.

testing which might force him into evil. **5. Which of you shall have a friend,** The following parable was given by Jesus to illustrate the certainty of answer to prayer. In it he placed prayer on the basis of personal friendship with God. **Midnight.** The most dangerous and inconvenient hour for a call. People in our Lord's day seldom ventured out at night for fear of bandits. **6. A friend . . . in his journey is come.** If the friend traveled on foot all day, and did not arrive until midnight, he must have been desperately hungry. Hospitality demanded that he be fed.

**7. The door is now shut, and my children are with me in bed.** Eastern homes did not have a separate bedroom. Usually the father of the family bolted the door, then unrolled mats on the floor for the children. He and his wife occupied the bed or space nearest the wall. It would have been impossible to reach the outer door without disturbing the children. **8. Because of his importunity.** The persistent knocking of the midnight caller was more troublesome than opening the door and handing out the bread.

**9. Ask** for what you do not possess; **seek** for what is not apparent; **knock** that obstacles may be removed. These three words epitomize the content of persistent prayer. **10. For every one.** Our Lord promised a complete answer; he made no exceptions. **11. A father.** Jesus indicated a stronger tie between God and man than between friend and friend. God is a father, and bestows His gifts not just because man is persistent, but because He loves His children. He will do no less for them than any earthly father would do for his family. **13. If ye then.** If human beings who are evil can act in a gracious and loving manner, how much more will God do so? **The Holy Spirit.** Matthew, in a parallel passage, says "good things" (Mt 7:11). Luke places special emphasis on the gift of the Holy Spirit.

**15. Beelzebub.** The Greek text of the better manuscripts reads *Beelzebul,* a rendering of the Hebrew *Baalzebul,* "lord of flies," or "lord of the dwelling." It was the title given to one of the gods of the Philistines, and had been brought over into Judaism as a title of Satan. Since Jesus' enemies would not admit that he came from God, they attributed his power over demons to a superdemonic source. **16. A sign from heaven.** The utter unreasonableness of his enemies is demonstrated by their demand for a sign when they had just witnessed one. **18. If Satan also be**

19. And if I by Beelzebub cast out devils, by whom do your sons cast *them* out? therefore shall they be your judges.

20. But if I with the finger of God cast out devils, no doubt the kingdom of God is come upon you.

21. When a strong man armed keepeth his palace, his goods are in peace:

22. But when a stronger than he shall come upon him, and overcome him, he taketh from him all his armor wherein he trusted, and divideth his spoils.

23. He that is not with me is against me; and he that gathereth not with me scattereth.

24. When the unclean spirit is gone out of a man, he walketh through dry places, seeking rest; and finding none, he saith, I will return unto my house whence I came out.

25. And when he cometh, he findeth *it* swept and garnished.

26. Then goeth he, and taketh *to him* seven other spirits more wicked than himself; and they enter in, and dwell there: and the last *state* of that man is worse than the first.

27. And it came to pass, as he spake these things, a certain woman of the company lifted up her voice, and said unto him, Blessed *is* the womb that bare thee, and the paps which thou hast sucked.

28. But he said, Yea, rather, blessed *are* they that hear the word of God, and keep it.

29. And when the people were gathered thick together, he began to say, This is an evil generation: they seek a sign; and there shall no sign be given it, but the sign of Jonas the prophet.

30. For as Jonas was a sign unto the Ninevites, so shall also the Son of man be to this generation.

31. The queen of the south shall rise up in the judgment with the men of this generation, and condemn them: for she came from the utmost parts of the earth to hear the wisdom of Solomon; and, behold, a greater than Solomon *is* here.

32. The men of Nineveh shall rise up in the judgment with this generation, and shall condemn it: for they repented at the preaching of Jonas; and, behold, a greater than Jonas *is* here.

divided against himself. The Lord pointed out that it would be foolish to think that Satan would be undoing his own work. **19. By whom do your sons cast them out?** If his works should be attributed to the power of the devil, could the Jews make a better claim for their own children who exorcised demons? **20. With the finger of God.** A figure of speech for the power of God. Jesus' exercise of God's power proved that he had brought the rule of God among men.

**21. A strong man armed.** Satan is the strong man who keeps his possessions in his grasp. **22. A stronger than he.** Jesus asserted his superiority over Satan, and his ability to release men from the devil's power. **23. He that is not with me.** Compare this with its opposite in 9:50. In the former instance he was speaking of a man who was unconsciously co-operative with him, while in this instance he was speaking of those who were consciously opposed to him.

**24. When the unclean spirit is gone out of a man.** Christ used the miracle that he had just performed as an illustration of a spiritual truth. The vacuum left by the banishment of evil must be filled with that which is good, or else the evil will become worse. **Through dry places.** The deserts were supposedly inhabited by evil spirits (see Isa 13:19-22).

**27. Blessed is the womb.** By pronouncing a blessing on Jesus' mother, this woman was complimenting the Saviour himself. **28. Blessed are they that hear the word of God, and keep it.** The Lord intimated that he desired not compliments but obedience.

**29. The sign of Jonas the prophet.** The miraculous restoration of Jonah from threatened death, to fulfill his commission to the Ninevites, was typical of the Resurrection. Christ's return from death was as great a proof of His ministry as Jonah's rescue was of his. **31. The queen of the south** was the ruler of Sheba, a country in the southern tip of Arabia. **She came from the utmost parts of the earth.** Since travel was slow and difficult, the long journey of the queen was a proof of her eagerness to meet Solomon (I Kgs 10:1-10). **The wisdom of Solomon.** Solomon would be classed today as a writer, a scientist, a connoisseur of art, a patron of industry, and a statesman. Our Lord claimed that he was **greater** than Solomon. **32. The preaching of Jonas** brought repentance to the pagan inhabitants of the populous and wicked city of Nineveh (Jon 3:5-9; 4:11). Jesus claimed that he

33. No man, when he hath lighted a candle, putteth *it* in a secret place, neither under a bushel, but on a candlestick, that they which come in may see the light.

34. The light of the body is the eye: therefore when thine eye is single, thy whole body also is full of light; but when *thine eye* is evil, thy body also *is* full of darkness.

35. Take heed therefore, that the light which is in thee be not darkness.

36. If thy whole body therefore *be* full of light, having no part dark, the whole shall be full of light, as when the bright shining of a candle doth give thee light.

37. And as he spake, a certain Pharisee besought him to dine with him: and he went in, and sat down to meat.

38. And when the Pharisee saw *it*, he marveled that he had not first washed before dinner.

39. And the Lord said unto him, Now do ye Pharisees make clean the outside of the cup and the platter; but your inward part is full of ravening and wickedness.

40. *Ye* fools, did not he, that made that which is without, make that which is within also?

41. But rather give alms of such things as ye have; and, behold, all things are clean unto you.

42. But woe unto you, Pharisees! for ye tithe mint and rue and all manner of herbs, and pass over judgment and the love of God: these ought ye to have done, and not to leave the other undone.

43. Woe unto you, Pharisees! for ye love the uppermost seats in the synagogues, and greetings in the markets.

44. Woe unto you, scribes and Pharisees, hypocrites! for ye are as graves which appear not, and the men that walk over *them* are not aware *of them*.

45. Then answered one of the lawyers, and said unto him, Master, thus saying thou reproachest us also.

46. And he said, Woe unto you also, *ye* lawyers! for ye lade men with burdens grievous to be borne, and ye yourselves touch not the burdens with one of your fingers.

47. Woe unto you! for ye build the sepulchres of the prophets, and your fathers killed them.

48. Truly ye bear witness that ye allow the deeds of your fathers: for they indeed killed them, and ye build their sepulchres.

49. Therefore also said the wisdom of God, I will send them prophets and apostles, and *some* of them they shall slay and persecute:

was a greater preacher than Jonah. The world did not recognize his greatness of wisdom or of person.

**33. A candle.** Literally, *a lamp*. **A secret place.** The word (Gr. *kryptēn*) may be translated *cellar* (see Arndt *in loco*). **A bushel** (Gr. *modios*, a word borrowed from Latin). A measure holding about a peck. **Candlestick.** A Lamp Stand. **34. Single.** Unclouded, properly focused, or healthy. **Evil** refers to physical defectiveness.

**37. A certain Pharisee besought him to dine with him.** Luke records numerous occasions on which the Lord was invited to dinner (5:29; 7:36; 14:1; 19:5; cf. Jn 2:1-11; 12:1,2). He utilized these opportunities to reach men who would not otherwise have listened to him. **38. He marvelled that he had not first washed.** The Pharisees washed regularly before meals as a ceremonial observance. Jesus' neglect to do so seemed to be a direct refusal to keep the Law, and an insult to his host. The Pharisee's reaction may have been spoken, or the Lord may have read his thoughts.

**39. Ye Pharisees make clean the outside.** The Pharisees were the Puritans of Judaism, who were exceedingly strict about the external observance of the Law. Jesus criticized them drastically for their hypocrisy, for they harbored all kinds of covetousness and cruelty in their hearts. **40. Ye fools.** A term that Christ used seldom, and only of those who were morally perverted, not just mentally obtuse. **41. Give alms of such things as ye have.** If the Pharisees would give generously to the poor, they would not have to worry about ceremonial cleansings. **42. Ye tithe mint and rue and all manner of herbs.** They tithed even the vegetables that grew in their gardens, but failed to meet the larger obligation of love to their fellow men. **43. The uppermost seats in the synagogues.** The front seats in the synagogues were usually reserved for the most important members. **44. Graves which appear not.** Any contact with a corpse or with a grave was a defilement. Even to step on a grave without knowing it they held to be a breach of the Law. Usually graves were painted white so that they would be visible by night as well as by day. Jesus said that the Pharisees, by their example, unconsciously caused other men to break the Law and defile themselves.

**47. Ye build the sepulchres of the prophets.** The martyrs of one generation become the heroes of the next. It was easier for the children to build monuments

50. That the blood of all the prophets, which was shed from the foundation of the world, may be required of this generation;

51. From the blood of Abel unto the blood of Zacharias, which perished between the altar and the temple: verily I say unto you, It shall be required of this generation.

52. Woe unto you, lawyers! for ye have taken away the key of knowledge: ye entered not in yourselves, and them that were entering in ye hindered.

53. And as he said these things unto them, the scribes and the Pharisees began to urge *him* vehemently, and to provoke him to speak of many things:

54. Laying wait for him, and seeking to catch something out of his mouth, that they might accuse him.

## CHAPTER 12

IN the mean time, when there were gathered together an innumerable multitude of people, insomuch that they trode one upon another, he began to say unto his disciples first of all, Beware ye of the leaven of the Pharisees, which is hypocrisy.

2. For there is nothing covered, that shall not be revealed; neither hid, that shall not be known.

3. Therefore, whatsoever ye have spoken in darkness shall be heard in the light; and that which ye have spoken in the ear in closets shall be proclaimed upon the housetops.

4. And I say unto you my friends, Be not afraid of them that kill the body, and after that have no more that they can do.

5. But I will forewarn you whom ye shall fear: Fear him, which after he hath killed hath power to cast into hell; yea, I say unto you, Fear him.

6. Are not five sparrows sold for two farthings, and not one of them is forgotten before God?

7. But even the very hairs of your head are all numbered. Fear not therefore: ye are of more value than many sparrows.

8. Also I say unto you, Whosoever shall confess me before men, him shall the Son of man also confess before the angels of God:

9. But he that denieth me before men shall be denied before the angels of God.

to the prophets than for their fathers to obey them. **50. Of this generation.** The rejection of God's messengers culminated in the crime of Jesus' generation, because they refused him. **51. From the blood of Abel unto the blood of Zacharias. Abel** was the first martyr of OT history (Gen 4:8). **Zacharias** was the last (II Chr 24:20-22), according to the order of books in the Hebrew Bible, which, unlike the English Bible, ends with Chronicles. **52. Ye have taken away the key of knowledge.** Jesus accused the experts in the Law of not fulfilling their tasks. They were supposed to enlighten the people by explaining the Law; instead, they had kept them in ignorance.

**12:1. The leaven of the Pharisees.** Leaven is generally figurative of evil. The effect of fermentation and consequent decay was typical of the insidious operation of sin in the human heart. **3. Closets.** The inner rooms or storechambers of an Eastern house, to which only the privileged few had access. Words spoken in them would not normally be heard by anybody else. **Upon the house tops.** An allusion to the public announcement of news by shouting gossip from one housetop to another.

**5. Fear him.** This refers to God and not to Satan, for Satan cannot determine the destiny of a human soul. **Fear** implies not cringing dread but healthy respect. **Hell.** a translation of *Gehenna*, a Greek form of the Hebrew *Ge-hinnom*, or "Valley of Hinnom," which lay on the southwestern side of old Jerusalem. In the days of the kings it had been the center of idol worship, and in later reforms it was converted into the city dump. Fires were kept burning constantly there to consume the combustible rubbish. The place was used as a picture of the fate of the lost.

**6. Are not five sparrows sold for two farthings.** On another occasion Jesus quoted the price of sparrows as two for a farthing (Mt 10:29). They were so cheap that an extra one was thrown in for the price of four, yet Jesus said that the infinite God is concerned with the death of each sparrow. **7. Ye are of more value.** Since God's tremendous compassion for man is parallel with his authority over man's destiny, His concern should evoke love rather than fear.

**8. Confess.** Jesus was appealing to the disciples to make a public avowal of loyalty to him. **9. He that denieth me.** Here, to deny is not to deprive, as in some uses, but to disown. Jesus claimed the right to commend or to condemn any man in the

10. And whosoever shall speak a word against the Son of man, it shall be forgiven him: but unto him that blasphemeth against the Holy Ghost it shall not be forgiven.

11. And when they bring you unto the synagogues, and *unto* magistrates, and powers, take ye no thought how or what thing ye shall answer, or what ye shall say:

12. For the Holy Ghost shall teach you in the same hour what ye ought to say.

13. And one of the company said unto him, Master, speak to my brother, that he divide the inheritance with me.

14. And he said unto him, Man, who made me a judge or a divider over you?

15. And he said unto them, Take heed, and beware of covetousness: for a man's life consisteth not in the abundance of the things which he possesseth.

16. And he spake a parable unto them, saying, The ground of a certain rich man brought forth plentifully:

17. And he thought within himself, saying, What shall I do, because I have no room where to bestow my fruits?

18. And he said, This will I do: I will pull down my barns, and build greater; and there will I bestow all my fruits and my goods.

19. And I will say to my soul, Soul, thou hast much goods laid up for many years; take thine ease, eat, drink, *and* be merry.

20. But God said unto him, *Thou* fool, this night thy soul shall be required of thee: then whose shall those things be, which thou hast provided?

21. So *is* he that layeth up treasure for himself, and is not rich toward God.

22. And he said unto his disciples, Therefore I say unto you, Take no thought for your life, what ye shall eat; neither for the body, what ye shall put on.

23. The life is more than meat, and the body *is more* than raiment.

24. Consider the ravens: for they neither sow nor reap; which neither have storehouse nor barn; and God feedeth them: how much more are ye better than the fowls?

25. And which of you with taking thought can add to his stature one cubit?

26. If ye then be not able to do that thing which is least, why take ye thought for the rest?

27. Consider the lilies how they grow: they toil not, they spin not; and yet I say unto you, that Solomon in all his glory was not arrayed like one of these.

28. If then God so clothe the grass, which is to-day in the field, and to-morrow is cast into the oven; how much more *will he clothe* you, O ye of little faith?

presence of God. **10. Him that blasphemeth against the Holy Ghost.** The slander against the Holy Spirit is irremediable because it cuts a man off from the only power that can change his inner life. The Holy Spirit is God's messenger to men, on whom believers are dependent for their knowledge of the reality of God's truth. **11. Take ye no thought.** An instruction for martyrs, not for preachers or teachers.

**13. Master, speak to my brother.** Not justice, but possession was what this man desired. He wanted Jesus to exercise his authority, but did not ask him to inquire into the merits of the case. **14. Who made me a judge.** The Lord refused to make a decision for the personal convenience of one man.

**16. The ground of a certain rich man.** Again Jesus may have been citing an actual example (cf. 11:30 ff.) to illustrate the principle stated in verse 15. **17. What shall I do.** The landowner was embarrassed by riches, but he did not consider the possibility of utilizing his bumper crops for the benefit of others. **18. Barns.** Greek *apothēkē*, a granary or storehouse.

**19. Soul, thou hast much goods laid up for many years.** On the assurance of a large crop, the gentleman-farmer was ready to retire. He made several false assumptions: that the soul could be satisfied with goods; that the goods would last for many years; and that he would live to enjoy them. **20. This night thy soul shall be required of thee.** The rich man had not counted on the abrupt summons that called him to face God and to leave the property he had so carefully amassed. **21. Rich toward God.** Jesus implied that wealth could be invested for eternal values (cf. 16:9). **22. Take no thought for your life.** Christ did not commend negligence, but taught that food and clothing are neither man's sole nor primary concern. What man *is* is more important than what he *has*. **25. Stature** (Gr. *hēlikia*) may mean "age" (Jn 9:21) rather than "size." The problem of the rich man was not his height, but the time he had to enjoy the goods.

**27. Consider the lilies.** These flowers were probably anemones, or windflowers. They grew profusely in the fields of Galilee, coloring them brilliantly with reds and purples, the royal colors. **Solomon in all his glory**, i.e., when dressed in his court costume, was not so splendid as these humble flowers. **28. Tomorrow is cast into the oven.** Wood for fuel is almost unobtainable in Palestine; consequently, dry grass and weeds are used for cooking.

**29.** And seek not ye what ye shall eat, or what ye shall drink, neither be ye of doubtful mind.

**30.** For all these things do the nations of the world seek after: and your Father knoweth that ye have need of these things.

**31.** But rather seek ye the kingdom of God; and all these things shall be added unto you.

**32.** Fear not, little flock; for it is your Father's good pleasure to give you the kingdom.

**33.** Sell that ye have, and give alms; provide yourselves bags which wax not old, a treasure in the heavens that faileth not, where no thief approacheth, neither moth corrupteth.

**34.** For where your treasure is, there will your heart be also.

**35.** Let your loins be girded about, and *your* lights burning;

**36.** And ye yourselves like unto men that wait for their lord, when he will return from the wedding; that, when he cometh and knocketh, they may open unto him immediately.

**37.** Blessed *are* those servants, whom the lord when he cometh shall find watching: verily I say unto you, that he shall gird himself, and make them to sit down to meat, and will come forth and serve them.

**38.** And if he shall come in the second watch, or come in the third watch, and find *them* so, blessed are those servants.

**39.** And this know, that if the goodman of the house had known what hour the thief would come, he would have watched, and not have suffered his house to be broken through.

**40.** Be ye therefore ready also: for the Son of man cometh at an hour when ye think not.

**41.** Then Peter said unto him, Lord, speakest thou this parable unto us, or even to all?

**42.** And the Lord said, Who then is that faithful and wise steward, whom *his* lord shall make ruler over his household, to give *them their* portion of meat in due season?

**43.** Blessed *is* that servant, whom his lord when he cometh shall find so doing.

**44.** Of a truth I say unto you, that he will make him ruler over all that he hath.

**45.** But and if that servant say in his heart, My lord delayeth his coming; and shall begin to beat the menservants and maidens, and to eat and drink, and to be drunken;

The grass has a short life; but if God is willing to clothe it with gorgeous colors, how much more care will he expend on man, whose spirit lives forever!

**30. For all these things do the nations of the world seek after.** Material possessions are the chief quest of the Gentiles, who (from the Jewish standpoint) know not God. Jesus said that for his disciples these material possessions should have secondary value. **31. But rather seek ye the kingdom of God.** The Master gave his disciples a new objective in life — to work for the kingdom of God.

**35. Let your loins be girded about, and your lights** (*lamps*) **burning.** Because the Eastern garb was long and flowing, the wearer had to tuck the skirts of his robe into his belt to allow freedom of motion. Lamps were kindled by live coals, for matches were unknown.

**36. When he will return from the wedding.** The Oriental groom, after a supper with his friends, went to the house of the bride to claim her. Since the return procession took place late at night, the groom expected his servants to be dressed for work and to have their lamps lighted. The traditional wedding preparation was a symbol of readiness for his return. **39. What hour the thief would come.** The change of figure from the bridegroom to the thief emphasizes the element of unexpected appearance. Paul applied the same figure of speech to the Second Coming (I Thess 5:2).

**41. Lord, speakest thou this parable unto us, or even to all?** In order to make clear whether he was addressing the disciples exclusively or the entire crowd around him, Jesus spoke the next parable.

**43. That servant** (Gr. *doulos*, "slave"). A steward was often a slave who was charged with managing his master's household. **45. My lord delayeth his coming.** The parable teaches that skepticism about the Lord's return produces misuse of authority and laxity of conduct. **46. The Lord of that servant will come.** The coming of the Lord will bring rewards to the faithful and judgment to the unfaithful. **Cut him in sunder.** Probably this should be taken literally, for the Roman masters had power of life and death over their slaves. To mismanage an estate would have brought the death penalty. **48. For unto whomsoever much is given, of him shall be much required.** The language suggests degrees of punishment.

**49. I am come to send fire on the earth; and how I wish it were already kindled!** (original translation) Our Lord

**46.** The lord of that servant will come in a day when he looketh not for *him*, and at an hour when he is not aware, and will cut him in sunder, and will appoint him his portion with the unbelievers.

**47.** And that servant, which knew his lord's will, and prepared not *himself*, neither did according to his will, shall be beaten with many *stripes*.

**48.** But he that knew not, and did commit things worthy of stripes, shall be beaten with few *stripes*. For unto whomsoever much is given, of him shall be much required; and to whom men have committed much, of him they will ask the more.

**49.** I am come to send fire on the earth; and what will I, if it be already kindled?

**50.** But I have a baptism to be baptized with; and how am I straitened till it be accomplished!

**51.** Suppose ye that I am come to give peace on earth? I tell you, Nay; but rather division:

**52.** For from henceforth there shall be five in one house divided, three against two, and two against three.

**53.** The father shall be divided against the son, and the son against the father; the mother against the daughter, and the daughter against the mother; the mother-in-law against her daughter-in-law, and the daughter-in-law against her mother-in-law.

**54.** And he said also to the people, When ye see a cloud rise out of the west, straightway ye say, There cometh a shower; and so it is.

**55.** And when *ye see* the south wind blow, ye say, There will be heat; and it cometh to pass.

**56.** *Ye* hypocrites, ye can discern the face of the sky and of the earth; but how is it that ye do not discern this time?

**57.** Yea, and why even of yourselves judge ye not what is right?

**58.** When thou goest with thine adversary to the magistrate, *as thou art* in the way, give diligence that thou mayest be delivered from him; lest he hale thee to the judge, and the judge deliver thee to the officer, and the officer cast thee into prison.

**59.** I tell thee, thou shalt not depart thence, till thou hast paid the very last mite.

## CHAPTER 13

THERE were present at that season some that told him of the Galileans, whose blood Pilate had mingled with their sacrifices.

**2.** And Jesus answering said unto them, Suppose ye that these Galileans were sinners above all the Galileans, because they suffered such things?

realized that his mission was divisive and disturbing. He saw clearly that the cross would be a point of controversy and argument, and wished that his lifting up (Jn 12:32) had already been accomplished. **50. I have a baptism to be baptized with.** Christ was referring to his death (cf. Mk 10:38). He felt that his power would be restricted until the work of the cross could be finished. **51. Nay; but rather division.** Judaism was a family religion, in which the people worshiped by households rather than as individuals. Jesus foresaw that his claims would cut across family life, and would necessitate individual decisions.

**56. How is it that ye do not discern this time?** Jesus' contemporaries did not realize the importance of his coming, nor the seriousness of rejecting him. **58. The officer.** The local constable or sheriff (Gr. *praktori*), who carried out the orders of the court.

**13:1. Whose blood Pilate had mingled with their sacrifices.** Probably the Galileans, who were fanatical nationalists, had created a disturbance in Jerusalem. Pilate, who was there during the feast, had sent soldiers to intervene. The result was a bloody clash in the temple courts. Such action was entirely in keeping with Pilate's known character. **2. Sinners above all the Galileans.** Any unusual calamity is often interpreted as a special judgment on those affected. **3. I tell you, Nay.** Jesus did not assent to the idea that the victims of Pilate were exceptionally sinful, but said that a similar doom awaited all who were unrepentant. He may have had in mind the imminent fate of the city in the Roman siege of A.D. 70 (cf. 19:41-44; 21:20-24). **4. Or those eighteen.** He alluded to another recent happening that had been the talk of the town, and he drew a similar application. **6. He spake also this parable.** The fruitless fig tree was symbolic of the Jewish nation. Isaiah (5:2) used a similar parable based on a vine. The owner of the fig tree had every right to expect fruit, and was justly disappointed when there was none. **7. Cut it down; why cumbereth it the ground?** Judgment was the only answer to fruitlessness. **8. Lord, let it alone this year also.** The farmer of the landlord's estate interceded for the tree, that it might have one more chance. Jesus implied that his nation was having its last opportunity to make good before the judgment of God would fall because of its rebellion and unproductiveness.

**10. And he was teaching in one of the synagogues on the sabbath.** The episode

3. I tell you, Nay: but, except ye repent, ye shall all likewise perish.

4. Or those eighteen, upon whom the tower in Siloam fell, and slew them, think ye that they were sinners above all men that dwelt in Jerusalem?

5. I tell you, Nay: but, except ye repent, ye shall all likewise perish.

6. He spake also this parable; A certain *man* had a fig tree planted in his vineyard; and he came and sought fruit thereon, and found none.

7. Then said he unto the dresser of his vineyard, Behold, these three years I come seeking fruit on this fig tree, and find none: cut it down; why cumbereth it the ground?

8. And he answering said unto him, Lord, let it alone this year also, till I shall dig about it, and dung *it:*

9. And if it bear fruit, *well:* and if not, *then* after that thou shalt cut it down.

10. And he was teaching in one of the synagogues on the sabbath.

11. And, behold, there was a woman which had a spirit of infirmity eighteen years, and was bowed together, and could in no wise lift up *herself.*

12. And when Jesus saw her, he called *her to him,* and said unto her, Woman, thou art loosed from thine infirmity.

13. And he laid *his* hands on her: and immediately she was made straight, and glorified God.

14. And the ruler of the synagogue answered with indignation, because that Jesus had healed on the sabbath day, and said unto the people, There are six days in which men ought to work: in them therefore come and be healed, and not on the sabbath day.

15. The Lord then answered him, and said, *Thou* hypocrite, doth not each one of you on the sabbath loose his ox or *his* ass from the stall, and lead *him* away to watering?

16. And ought not this woman, being a daughter of Abraham, whom Satan hath bound, lo, these eighteen years, be loosed from this bond on the sabbath day?

17. And when he had said these things, all his adversaries were ashamed: and all the people rejoiced for all the glorious things that were done by him.

18. Then said he, Unto what is the kingdom of God like? and whereunto shall I resemble it?

19. It is like a grain of mustard seed, which a man took, and cast into his garden; and it grew, and waxed a great tree; and the fowls of the air lodged in the branches of it.

that follows was one of a number recounted in the Gospels concerning our Lord's healing on the Sabbath, which was a recurrent source of contention between himself and the Pharisees. **11. A woman which had a spirit of infirmity.** The woman was a victim of demon possession. Demoniac power sometimes was manifested in violent behavior (8:29) and sometimes by the crippling of a bodily member (11:14). Jesus spoke of the woman as one whom Satan had bound (13:16). **12. He called her.** His action was unsolicited; he took the initiative.

**14. The ruler of the synagogue** represented the standards of Judaism by his stringent interpretation of the Law. He did not speak directly, but by his pronouncement he condemned Jesus' action. **15. The Lord then answered.** The ruler of the synagogue knew the statute; the Lord knew how to apply the exception. Why should not this woman have relief from suffering on the Sabbath, if the Law provided for the prevention of thirst for animals? **16. Ought not this woman.** Jesus went further than to suggest that the healing was allowable; he asserted that it was obligatory.

**18. Unto what is the kingdom of God like?** The two parables that follow next parallel Mt 13:31-33, which cites them as part of a series describing the kingdom of God. The interpretations of these have been varied, and there has been considerable controversy over them. It is well to remember that usually each parable was spoken to make only one point, and that details not necessary for the point should not be overstressed. **19. It is like a grain of mustard seed.** The mustard plant was the largest that grew in Palestine. Its tremendous growth in one season from the smallest of the seeds to a shrub the size of a small tree illustrated prophetically the growth of the kingdom from the insignificant beginnings of Jesus' company of disciples into the spiritual realm which became universally recognized. **21. It is like leaven.** The figure here concerns the silent and yet powerful growth of the kingdom among men (cf. 12:1). Jesus did not assert that the world would be converted; he did imply that it would be affected by the kingdom.

**D. The Beginning of Public Debate. 13:22—16:31.**

**22. Journeying toward Jerusalem.** With this phrase Luke returns to the theme

20. And again he said, Whereunto shall I liken the kingdom of God?

21. It is like leaven, which a woman took and hid in three measures of meal, till the whole was leavened.

22. And he went through the cities and villages, teaching, and journeying toward Jerusalem.

23. Then said one unto him, Lord, are there few that be saved? And he said unto them,

24. Strive to enter in at the strait gate: for many, I say unto you, will seek to enter in, and shall not be able.

25. When once the master of the house is risen up, and hath shut to the door, and ye begin to stand without, and to knock at the door, saying, Lord, Lord, open unto us; and he shall answer and say unto you, I know you not whence ye are:

26. Then shall ye begin to say, We have eaten and drunk in thy presence, and thou hast taught in our streets.

27. But he shall say, I tell you, I know you not whence ye are; depart from me, all *ye* workers of iniquity.

28. There shall be weeping and gnashing of teeth, when ye shall see Abraham, and Isaac, and Jacob, and all the prophets, in the kingdom of God, and you *yourselves* thrust out.

29. And they shall come from the east, and *from* the west, and from the north, and *from* the south, and shall sit down in the kingdom of God.

30. And, behold, there are last which shall be first; and there are first which shall be last.

31. The same day there came certain of the Pharisees, saying unto him, Get thee out, and depart hence; for Herod will kill thee.

32. And he said unto them, Go ye, and tell that fox, Behold, I cast out devils, and I do cures to-day and to-morrow, and the third *day* I shall be perfected.

33. Nevertheless I must walk to-day, and to-morrow, and the *day* following: for it cannot be that a prophet perish out of Jerusalem.

34. O Jerusalem, Jerusalem, which killest the prophets, and stonest them that are sent unto thee; how often would I have gathered thy children together, as a hen *doth gather* her brood under *her* wings, and ye would not!

35. Behold, your house is left unto you desolate: and verily I say unto you, Ye shall not see me, until *the time* come when ye shall say, Blessed *is* he that cometh in the name of the Lord.

of 9:51. He built this section of the Gospel on the Saviour's last journey. **23. Are there few that be saved?** So stringent was the Lord's ethical teaching that his hearers were sure that only a few could be saved. **24. The strait gate.** Strait is an old English word meaning *narrow*.

**25. When once the master of the house is risen up, and hath shut to the door.** The door of an Oriental house was locked at night to keep out marauders, and was not opened again until morning. If any man knocked late at night, he was regarded with suspicion, and was usually turned away. **26. We have eaten and drunk in thy presence.** In the Orient, to eat and drink with a man was a mark of permanent friendship. **27. I know you not whence ye are.** Salvation depends on personal acquaintance with him, not upon knowledge of his reputation. **28. There shall be weeping and gnashing of teeth. There** means "in that place." **30. There are last which shall be first.** The implication is that the hour of judgment will bring many surprises.

**31. Herod will kill thee.** The Pharisees may only have been trying to scare Jesus out of the country. On the other hand, Herod did have an uneasy conscience, and thought that Jesus might have been John the Baptist risen from the dead (cf. 9:7). **32. That fox.** One of the few contemptuous terms our Lord used. It connotes both slyness and cowardice. **The third day I shall be perfected.** He indicated that he had a definite plan for his life, and that he did not fear Herod's threat. **33. It cannot be that a prophet perish out of Jerusalem.** His reply to the Pharisees meant that he was endangered not by Herod's threats, but by the hostility of their own city.

**34. O Jerusalem, Jerusalem.** Christ's lamentation over the city was prompted by his love and by his foresight. He was well aware of the fate that awaited it. **35. Behold, your house is left unto you desolate.** The destruction of the temple in A.D. 70 and the later expulsion of the Jews under Hadrian (A.D. 135) overthrew completely the Jewish commonwealth. **Blessed is he that cometh.** A quotation from Ps 118:26 which was applied to the Messiah. Jesus identified himself with the nation's hope.

**14:1. He went into the house of one of the chief Pharisees to eat bread** (cf. 11:37). **They watched him.** The Pharisees observed (Gr. *paretērounto*) Jesus closely (cf. 6:7) with the motive of

## CHAPTER 14

AND it came to pass, as he went into the house of one of the chief Pharisees to eat bread on the sabbath day, that they watched him.

2. And, behold, there was a certain man before him which had the dropsy.

3. And Jesus answering spake unto the lawyers and Pharisees, saying, Is it lawful to heal on the sabbath day?

4. And they held their peace. And he took *him*, and healed him, and let him go;

5. And answered them, saying, Which of you shall have an ass or an ox fallen into a pit, and will not straightway pull him out on the sabbath day?

6. And they could not answer him again to these things.

7. And he put forth a parable to those which were bidden, when he marked how they chose out the chief rooms; saying unto them,

8. When thou art bidden of any *man* to a wedding, sit not down in the highest room; lest a more honorable man than thou be bidden of him;

9. And he that bade thee and him come and say to thee, Give this man place; and thou begin with shame to take the lowest room.

10. But when thou art bidden, go and sit down in the lowest room; that when he that bade thee cometh, he may say unto thee, Friend, go up higher: then shalt thou have worship in the presence of them that sit at meat with thee.

11. For whosoever exalteth himself shall be abased; and he that humbleth himself shall be exalted.

12. Then said he also to him that bade him, When thou makest a dinner or a supper, call not thy friends, nor thy brethren, neither thy kinsmen, nor *thy* rich neighbors; lest they also bid thee again, and a recompense be made thee.

13. But when thou makest a feast, call the poor, the maimed, the lame, the blind:

14. And thou shalt be blessed; for they cannot recompense thee: for thou shalt be recompensed at the resurrection of the just.

trapping him if possible. **2. And, behold, there was a certain man before him.** The presence of this man was unexpected. Perhaps he had come to the feast in hope of healing. **Dropsy.** A swelling of the body caused by the retention of excessive liquid in the tissues. The man's pitiful condition would have been obvious to all. **3. Jesus . . . spake unto the lawyers and Pharisees.** He repeated his question of the previous occasion (6:9). **4. They held their peace.** His critics did not know how to answer. If they had said that healing on the Sabbath was not permissible, they would have condemned themselves; if they had said that it was, they could not have criticized him. **5. Which of you shall have an ass or an ox fallen into a pit.** He had used the same argument on two previous occasions (6:9; 13:15).

**7. And he put forth a parable.** At this dinner our Lord spoke three parables. The first two (14:7-11,12-14) were evoked by the behavior of the guests and the host; the third (vv. 15-24) was a reply to a comment. **They chose out the chief rooms.** Social position was important in the society of that day, and each guest wanted to occupy as high a place of honor as he could. **Rooms.** A better translation would be *places*. The word refers to the location of the seat, not to the dining hall. **9. The lowest room.** By the time that the guest found the best place and discovered that it was reserved for someone else, the intermediate places would have been filled, and only the lowest would be left. **10. Friend, go up higher.** If the host found an honored guest in a lower place, he would invite him to a reserved seat at the head table. **11. He that humbleth himself shall be exalted.** Christ used the immediate situation to illustrate a general spiritual principle. Plummer says: "Humility is the passport to promotion in the kingdom of God" (ICC, p. 358).

**12. Then said he also to him that bade him.** Jesus had a word for the host as well as for the guest. **Call not thy friends, nor thy brethren, neither thy kinsmen, nor thy rich neighbours.** The kingdom of God is not a closed society of the wealthy nor an exclusive club for friends. **13. Call the poor, the maimed, the lame, the blind.** Our Lord rebuked the selfish practice of entertaining only those who can return the favor. He wanted his host to see that his wealth gave him an opportunity to aid the indigent and helpless. **14. The resurrec-**

15. And when one of them that sat at meat with him heard these things, he said unto him, Blessed *is* he that shall eat bread in the kingdom of God.

16. Then said he unto him, A certain man made a great supper, and bade many:

17. And sent his servant at supper time to say to them that were bidden, Come; for all things are now ready.

18. And they all with one *consent* began to make excuse. The first said unto him, I have bought a piece of ground, and I must needs go and see it: I pray thee have me excused.

19. And another said, I have bought five yoke of oxen, and I go to prove them: I pray thee have me excused.

20. And another said, I have married a wife, and therefore I cannot come.

21. So that servant came, and showed his lord these things. Then the master of the house being angry said to his servant, Go out quickly into the streets and lanes of the city, and bring in hither the poor, and the maimed, and the halt, and the blind.

22. And the servant said, Lord, it is done as thou hast commanded, and yet there is room.

23. And the lord said unto the servant, Go out into the highways and hedges, and compel *them* to come in, that my house may be filled.

tion of the just. The language used here supports the idea of a double resurrection, one of the righteous, and one of the wicked (cf. Jn 5:29; I Cor 15:23; Phil 3:11; I Thess 4:16; Heb 11:35; Rev 20:5,6), separated by an interval of time.

15. Blessed is he. The guest who made this observation was trying to commend himself to the Master by a pious remark. Jesus used the following parable to show him that the kingdom of God demands real purpose, not casual approval.

16. A certain man made a great supper. The parable would have had interest for all of the guests present, because it dealt with an occasion like their own. 17. And sent his servant at supper time. According to custom, the invitation was issued some days or weeks in advance, but courtesy required that when the time came, a personal invitation should be extended by the call of a messenger. 18. And they all with one consent began to make excuse. To refuse an invitation at the last moment was an unpardonable breach of etiquette. I have bought a piece of ground, and I must needs go and see it. The excuse was hollow, for no sane businessman would buy land that he had not seen. Or, if he had seen it once, the second viewing could wait, since the transaction had evidently been completed. 19. I have bought five yoke of oxen. The second excuse was worse than the first. Land would be a permanent possession, and might appreciate in value; but the oxen would be worthless if they were not satisfactory at purchase. The new owner was eager to ascertain how the oxen would work. But since he had already acquired them, another day's delay in the test would not have changed their condition. 20. I have married a wife. The prospective guest evidently thought this excuse was valid, since it involved the most important event of a lifetime.

21. The master of the house being angry. The refusal of the invited guests was a direct insult. Go out quickly. The feast was ready, and there was no time to spare. The host would not wait for the guests who had treated him rudely, but ordered his servants to bring the beggars. 22. And yet there is room. Since beggars abound in any Eastern city, there would have been no difficulty in gathering a large company of them. 23. Compel them to come in. Oriental etiquette required that the feast should not begin

24. For I say unto you, That none of those men which were bidden shall taste of my supper.

25. And there went great multitudes with him: and he turned, and said unto them,

26. If any *man* come to me, and hate not his father, and mother, and wife, and children, and brethren, and sisters, yea, and his own life also, he cannot be my disciple.

27. And whosoever doth not bear his cross, and come after me, cannot be my disciple.

28. For which of you, intending to build a tower, sitteth not down first, and counteth the cost, whether he have *sufficient* to finish *it?*

29. Lest haply, after he hath laid the foundation, and is not able to finish *it*, all that behold *it* begin to mock him,

30. Saying, This man began to build, and was not able to finish.

31. Or what king, going to make war against another king, sitteth not down first, and consulteth whether he be able with ten thousand to meet him that cometh against him with twenty thousand?

32. Or else, while the other is yet a great way off, he sendeth an ambassage, and desireth conditions of peace.

33. So likewise, whosoever he be of you that forsaketh not all that he hath, he cannot be my disciple.

34. Salt *is* good: but if the salt have lost his savor, wherewith shall it be seasoned?

35. It is neither fit for the land, nor yet for the dunghill; *but* men cast it out. He that hath ears to hear, let him hear.

## CHAPTER 15

THEN drew near unto him all the publicans and sinners for to hear him.

2. And the Pharisees and scribes murmured, saying, This man receiveth sinners, and eateth with them.

3. And he spake this parable unto them, saying,

4. What man of you, having a hundred sheep, if he lose one of them, doth not leave the ninety and nine in the wilderness, and go after that which is lost, until he find it?

until all places were filled. The servants were commanded to invite even the travelers in the bypaths of the surrounding country. **24. None of those men which were bidden shall taste of my supper.** Once having refused, they were forever excluded. The application of this parable centers on the rejection of Jesus by his nation. When the chosen guests for the kingdom of God refused to heed the call of the Messiah, he turned to others who normally would not have been invited.

**25. And there went great multitudes with him.** The next few verses do not relate directly to the feast, but to our Lord's outdoor preaching; yet they are used by Luke as a sequel to the story. This appeal of Jesus explained the nature of the call which he gave to those in "the highways and the hedges." **26. And hate not.** Christ certainly was not commanding men to hate their own families in the sense of bearing them ill will or malice. This is strong language to indicate that devotion to one's family must take second place to devotion to Christ. **27. And whosoever doth not bear his cross.** The cross of the disciple is that particular humiliation or hardship that he would incur by becoming a follower of Jesus. Publicly carrying a cross was the brand of a criminal doomed to execution (cf. 9:23,24). **33. So likewise, whosoever . . . of you.** The Lord asked for intelligent appraisal of the cost of discipleship and for complete renunciation of all claims to one's own life.

**34. Salt is good.** A similar teaching appears in the Sermon on the Mount (Mt 5:13). The ordinary salt of that time was of poor quality, and quickly lost its flavor when exposed to air.

**15:1. Sinners** designates the people of the street whom the Pharisees looked upon with contempt because they did not know the Law (Jn 7:49). The three parables in this chapter were spoken particularly for this audience, and illustrate God's interest in them. **2. Murmured.** The Pharisees grumbled because they had no appreciation of Jesus' real motive in wishing to reclaim abandoned persons.

**4. Wilderness** was simply open pasture. **That which is lost.** A shepherd counted his sheep at the close of each day to make sure that none had strayed. If one was missing, he searched for it immediately. **After.** The preposition (Gr. *epi*) means not only that the shepherd tracked down the sheep, but also that he made

5. And when he hath found *it*, he layeth *it* on his shoulders, rejoicing.

6. And when he cometh home, he calleth together *his* friends and neighbors, saying unto them, Rejoice with me; for I have found my sheep which was lost.

7. I say unto you, that likewise joy shall be in heaven over one sinner that repenteth, more than over ninety and nine just persons, which need no repentance.

8. Either what woman having ten pieces of silver, if she lose one piece, doth not light a candle, and sweep the house, and seek diligently till she find *it?*

9. And when she hath found *it*, she calleth *her* friends and *her* neighbors together, saying, Rejoice with me; for I have found the piece which I had lost.

10. Likewise, I say unto you, there is joy in the presence of the angels of God over one sinner that repenteth.

11. And he said, A certain man had two sons:

12. And the younger of them said to *his* father, Father, give me the portion of goods that falleth *to me*. And he divided unto them *his* living.

13. And not many days after the younger son gathered all together, and took his journey into a far country, and there wasted his substance with riotous living.

14. And when he had spent all, there arose a mighty famine in that land; and he began to be in want.

15. And he went and joined himself to a citizen of that country; and he sent him into his fields to feed swine.

contact with it. The word connotes persistence and success. **5. Layeth it on his shoulders.** Unlike most animals, a sheep cannot find its own way back to the fold. The shepherd had to bring it. **6. Lost.** The expression is strong, emphasizing possessiveness—"my sheep, my lost one" (Gr. *to probaton mou, to apolōlos*). **7, Just persons, which need no repentance.** A semi-ironical reference to the Pharisees, who regarded themselves as infinitely better than the publicans and sinners.

**8. Either what woman.** The second parable would have appealed to the woman who lived most of her life indoors, as the first parable would have appealed to the man who lived outdoors. **Having ten pieces of silver.** Coins were scarcer in Palestine than they are in modern civilization, for much commerce was carried on by barter. These coins were *drachmas*, each worth about fifteen to seventeen cents of American money. They represented the savings of many years. **Light a candle.** Since the poorer Oriental houses did not have windows, a lamp was needed even in daytime in order to inspect the dark corners. **Sweep the house.** The coin could easily have been lost in the dirt of the mud floor. **9. Friends and neighbours.** These words in Greek are feminine, indicating that the woman called together her women friends for a party.

**11. A certain man had two sons.** This parable has been called the Parable of the Prodigal Son. It could better be called the Parable of the Lost Sons, or The Wonderful Father. **12. The portion of goods that falleth to me.** An heir was entitled to claim his share of an estate during his father's lifetime if he wished to do so. The eldest son could claim two thirds; the other children would divide the rest (Deut 21:17). **His living.** Literally, *his life* (Gr. *ton bion*), since his property was the source of his sustenance.

**13. A far country.** Many of the wealthier young men of Jesus' time went abroad to Rome or to Antioch for the gay life of the city. **Wasted.** The same word is used of sowing or scattering seed (Gr. *dieskorpisen*). **Riotous** (Gr. *asōtōs*). That is, wasteful. **14. In that land.** The Greek preposition *kata*, translated **in**, implies that the famine was widespread and included the whole territory where the boy was living. **Began to be in want**, or, *began to fall behind.*

**15. Joined himself.** The expression is strong; literally, *he glued himself* (Gr. *ekollēthē*). Desperation forced him to at-

16. And he would fain have filled his belly with the husks that the swine did eat: and no man gave unto him.

17. And when he came to himself, he said, How many hired servants of my father's have bread enough and to spare, and I perish with hunger!

18. I will arise and go to my father, and will say unto him, Father, I have sinned against heaven, and before thee,

19. And am no more worthy to be called thy son: make me as one of thy hired servants.

20. And he arose, and came to his father. But when he was yet a great way off, his father saw him, and had compassion, and ran, and fell on his neck, and kissed him.

21. And the son said unto him, Father, I have sinned against heaven, and in thy sight, and am no more worthy to be called thy son.

22. But the father said to his servants, Bring forth the best robe, and put *it* on him; and put a ring on his hand, and shoes on *his* feet:

23. And bring hither the fatted calf, and kill *it*; and let us eat, and be merry:

24. For this my son was dead, and is alive again; he was lost, and is found. And they began to be merry.

25. Now his elder son was in the field: and as he came and drew nigh to the house, he heard music and dancing.

26. And he called one of the servants, and asked what these things meant.

27. And he said unto him, Thy brother is come; and thy father hath killed the fatted calf, because he hath received him safe and sound.

28. And he was angry, and would not go in: therefore came his father out, and entreated him.

29. And he answering said to *his* father, Lo, these many years do I serve thee, neither transgressed I at any time thy commandment; and yet thou never gavest me a kid, that I might make merry with my friends:

30. But as soon as this thy son was come, which hath devoured thy living with harlots, thou hast killed for him the fatted calf.

31. And he said unto him, Son, thou art ever with me, and all that I have is thine.

tach himself to some prominent person for the sake of support. **To feed swine.** The lowest possible humiliation for a Jew. **16. Husks.** The pods of the carob tree, or locust tree, which John the Baptist ate (Mt 3:4). They were long beans, sweet to the taste, and were often part of the diet of poor people. **Gave.** The verb implies a custom or process: "Nobody used to give him anything."

**17. Hired servants.** Hired servants in Bible times had a harder lot than slaves, because their employment was more uncertain, whereas slaves could be sure of food and shelter. **18. Against heaven.** In obedience to the third commandment, "Thou shalt not take the name of thy God in vain," the Jews substituted other terms for God lest they accidentally blaspheme (cf. Mt 5:34; 26:64,65). **19. Make me.** This petition indicates a complete change in his attitude. When he left home, he said, "Give me . . . . " He left with a selfish demand; he returned with a humble prayer.

**20. When he was yet a great way off, his father saw him.** The father was eagerly watching for the return of the wayward boy. **21. Father, I have sinned.** The boy never finished the speech he had prepared (cf. vv. 18,19). All the father wanted was the confession.

**22. The best robe.** The best robe was reserved for an honored guest. **A ring** marked the position of sonship which he had forfeited when he deserted the family circle. **23. The fatted calf.** One animal was usually held in readiness for a special occasion, that honored guests might be served quickly (cf. Gen 18:7). **Be merry** has the connotation of a party. **25. Musick and dancing** were probably supplied by hired entertainers. The return of the younger son was cause for a major celebration.

**28. He was angry.** The reaction of the older son was jealousy and disgust. He was bitter over what he regarded as an injustice. **29. Lo, these many years do I serve thee.** A modern translation would be: "See here! I have been slaving for you all these years, and . . . . " The language implies self-righteousness, self-pity, and an inward alienation from his father's feeling comparable to the younger son's outer alienation from the family. **A kid** would have been of small value compared to the fattened calf. The son was accusing his father of cheating him out of a small gift, while lavishing extravagant favors on the prodigal. **30. This thy son.** "This son of yours." The

32. It was meet that we should make merry, and be glad: for this thy brother was dead, and is alive again; and was lost, and is found.

## CHAPTER 16

AND he said also unto his disciples, There was a certain rich man, which had a steward; and the same was accused unto him that he had wasted his goods.

2. And he called him, and said unto him, How is it that I hear this of thee? give an account of thy stewardship; for thou mayest be no longer steward.

3. Then the steward said within himself, What shall I do? for my lord taketh away from me the stewardship: I cannot dig; to beg I am ashamed.

4. I am resolved what to do, that, when I am put out of the stewardship, they may receive me into their houses.

5. So he called every one of his lord's debtors *unto him*, and said unto the first, How much owest thou unto my lord?

6. And he said, A hundred measures of oil. And he said unto him, Take thy bill, and sit down quickly, and write fifty.

7. Then said he to another, And how much owest thou? And he said, A hundred measures of wheat. And he said unto him, Take thy bill, and write fourscore.

8. And the lord commended the unjust steward, because he had done wisely: for the children of this world are in their generation wiser than the children of light.

9. And I say unto you, Make to yourselves friends of the mammon of unrighteousness; that, when ye fail, they may receive you into everlasting habitations.

10. He that is faithful in that which is least is faithful also in much: and he that is unjust in the least is unjust also in much.

11. If therefore ye have not been faithful in the unrighteous mammon, who will commit to your trust the true *riches*?

12. And if ye have not been faithful in that which is another man's, who shall give you that which is your own?

13. No servant can serve two masters: for either he will hate the one, and love the other; or else he will hold to the one, and despise the other. Ye cannot serve God and mammon.

14. And the Pharisees also, who were covetous, heard all these things: and they derided him.

15. And he said unto them, Ye are they which justify yourselves before men; but God knoweth your hearts: for that which is highly esteemed among men is abomination

older brother was contemptuous, and ready to think the worst of the younger brother.

**32. It was meet.** By this parable, as well as by the two preceding, Jesus showed God's attitude toward sinners. He did not approve of their rebellious attitude nor of their evil deeds, but he welcomed them back and restored them to favor when they were penitent.

**16:1. A certain rich man.** This parable, and the one following it, may well have been taken from life. The **steward** was the manager of the household and of the estate. **Wasted his goods.** The same word that was used of the prodigal son (15:13). **4. I am resolved what to do.** Literally, *I know* (Gr. *egnōn*). In Luke's graphic style, "I have it!" He had a sudden clever idea. **They** has no expressed antecedent, but it refers to his master's debtors. The steward's device, while strictly dishonest, was effective.

**5. So he called every one of his lord's debtors.** As long as he was officially steward, he had the power to set the amount of rental payments; and until he was discharged, his decisions must stand. Even if the owner dismissed him, he could not alter the decisions which the steward had made previously. **6. An hundred measures of oil.** Olive oil was one of the common products of Palestine. A liquid measure was about nine gallons. **7. A measure** (Gr. *korous*, taken from the Heb. *cor*) was a little more than ten bushels. **8. And the lord commended the unjust steward.** While the steward's employer did not approve of his action, he could not help admiring his resourcefulness. **Wisely** means *shrewdly, cleverly*.

**9. Make to yourselves friends of the mammon of unrighteousness. Of** should be translated *by means of*. **Mammon** is an Aramaic word meaning money or property. The dishonest steward knew that he would have a claim on those whose bills he had arbitrarily reduced. They would appreciate the financial relief, and would be glad to aid him. The Lord implied that earthly property can be used to help others, whose gratitude will ensure a welcome in eternity. **11. If therefore ye have not been faithful.** The use of material wealth is a test of character. Those who cannot use it wisely do not deserve to have spiritual responsibilities entrusted to them.

**16. The law and the prophets were until John.** Jesus declared that John the Baptist marked the end of an era. The

in the sight of God.

16. The law and the prophets *were* until John: since that time the kingdom of God is preached, and every man presseth into it.

17. And it is easier for heaven and earth to pass, than one tittle of the law to fail.

18. Whosoever putteth away his wife, and marrieth another, committeth adultery: and whosoever marrieth her that is put away from *her* husband committeth adultery.

19. There was a certain rich man, which was clothed in purple and fine linen, and fared sumptuously every day:

20. And there was a certain beggar named Lazarus, which was laid at his gate, full of sores,

21. And desiring to be fed with the crumbs which fell from the rich man's table: moreover the dogs came and licked his sores.

22. And it came to pass, that the beggar died, and was carried by the angels into Abraham's bosom: the rich man also died, and was buried;

23. And in hell he lifted up his eyes, being in torments, and seeth Abraham afar off, and Lazarus in his bosom.

24. And he cried and said, Father Abraham, have mercy on me, and send Lazarus, that he may dip the tip of his finger in water, and cool my tongue; for I am tormented in this flame.

25. But Abraham said, Son, remember that thou in thy lifetime receivedst thy good things, and likewise Lazarus evil things: but now he is comforted, and thou art tormented.

old dispensation of the Law was in force until he began proclaiming the coming of the Messiah and introducing the kingdom of God. **Every man presseth into it.** Presseth involves the idea of violence. Expositors differ as to whether Luke meant that men are crowding to enter the kingdom, or that they are bringing hostile pressure to bear against it (cf. Mt 11:12; see Arndt *in loco*). The former idea is preferable on grammatical grounds. **17. One tittle.** The tittle (Gr. *keraian*, "little horn") was a small projection or "hook" that distinguished one Hebrew letter from another similar to it. Jesus was saying that, even down to its smallest point, the Law would maintain its authority and certainty.

**18. Whosoever putteth away his wife, and marrieth another, committeth adultery.** The Law stipulated that a man could set aside his wife if he "found some uncleanness in her" (Deut 24:1). While the original provision undoubtedly alluded to moral defects, it had been interpreted with shocking laxity. Rabbi Hillel is said to have taught that a man might divorce his wife for spoiling his dinner (Plummer, in ICC, p. 390). Our Lord's words make permanent monogamous marriage the ideal for believers.

**19. There was a certain rich man, which was clothed in purple and fine linen, and fared sumptuously every day.** Wool, dyed **purple**, was costly and could be worn only by the wealthy. **Linen**, used for undergarments, was equally expensive. **Fared sumptuously.** Lived gaily. Life for him was one continual party, free from hardship and drudgery. **20. Lazarus.** This is the only parable of Jesus in which a proper name is given. **At his gate.** Lazarus' friends laid him at the rich man's gate as an appeal to his sympathy. **21. Desiring to be fed with the crumbs.** The fragments of food and the "left-overs" were flung to the dogs or given to beggars (cf. Mk 7:28). **The dogs . . . licked his sores.** Dogs were the scavengers of the Oriental streets, and were usually vicious. The beggar was too helpless to drive them away, and so was at their mercy. He may have feared the fate of Jezebel (II Kgs 9:35, 36).

**22. The beggar died.** No mention of burial occurs, not because the corpse was left exposed, but because he was probably buried in a pauper's grave with no ceremony. **Abraham's bosom.** The guest reclined on Abraham's right side, the place of honor. **The rich man . . . was**

26. And beside all this, between us and you there is a great gulf fixed: so that they which would pass from hence to you cannot; neither can they pass to us, that *would come* from thence.

27. Then he said, I pray thee therefore, father, that thou wouldest send him to my father's house:

28. For I have five brethren; that he may testify unto them, lest they also come into this place of torment.

29. Abraham saith unto him, They have Moses and the prophets; let them hear them.

30. And he said, Nay, father Abraham: but if one went unto them from the dead, they will repent.

31. And he said unto him, If they hear not Moses and the prophets, neither will they be persuaded, though one rose from the dead.

## CHAPTER 17

THEN said he unto the disciples, It is impossible but that offenses will come: but woe *unto him*, through whom they come!

2. It were better for him that a millstone were hanged about his neck, and he cast into the sea, than that he should offend one of these little ones.

3. Take heed to yourselves: If thy brother trespass against thee, rebuke him; and if he repent, forgive him.

4. And if he trespass against thee seven times in a day, and seven times in a day turn again to thee, saying, I repent; thou shalt forgive him.

5. And the apostles said unto the Lord, Increase our faith.

6. And the Lord said, If ye had faith as a grain of mustard seed, ye might say unto this sycamine tree, Be thou plucked up by the root, and be thou planted in the sea; and it should obey you.

7. But which of you, having a servant plowing or feeding cattle, will say unto him by and by, when he is come from the field, Go and sit down to meat?

8. And will not rather say unto him, Make ready wherewith I may sup, and gird thyself, and serve me, till I have eaten and drunken; and afterward thou shalt eat and drink?

9. Doth he thank that servant because he did the things that were commanded him? I trow not.

10. So likewise ye, when ye shall have done all those things which are commanded you, say, We are unprofitable servants: we have done that which was our duty to do.

buried. The parable emphasizes that the beggar was carried by angels into paradise; the best that could be said for the rich man was that he was buried. **23. And in hell** (Gr. *hades*). This word, equivalent to the Hebrew *sheol*, may mean the unseen world in general, or the place of punishment. Hades contained both Gehenna and paradise. **26. A great gulf fixed.** The gap between hell and heaven is unbridgeable and permanent. **29. They have Moses and the prophets.** The Law contained the revelation of God sufficient for their instruction. **31. If they hear not Moses and the prophets.** Miracles do not in themselves produce faith. Jesus' words were prophetic, for when he rose from the dead, his enemies were no more inclined to accept him than they had been before.

E. Instruction of the Disciples. 17:1– 18:30.

**17:1. Offences.** Those acts that cause others to deviate from the path of right as well as shocking their moral sensibilities. **2. A millstone.** The parallel in Mk 9:42 calls it a millstone turned by a donkey (Gr. *mylos onikos*), which indicates a mill larger than the ordinary domestic one. The Lord's words are unusually severe. **4. Seven times in a day.** Seven offenses in one day would bring the person affected to the point of exasperation.

**5. Increase our faith.** The apostles could not believe that a habitual offender could be forgiven. **6. Faith as a grain of mustard seed.** The mustard seed was the smallest of all the seeds known to the farmers of Palestine (cf. 13:19). Christ emphasized the vitality of faith rather than its quantity. **This sycamine tree.** Most scholars identify it with the black mulberry tree, though the same word (Gr. *sycaminos*) in the LXX and elsewhere denotes the sycamore. The mulberry tree, cultivated in Palestine for its fruit, could be found almost everywhere. The transplanting of such a tree into the sea seems fanciful; but Jesus was endeavoring to show his disciples that faith knows no impossibilities.

**7. By and by.** In modern English this phrase means, "in the remote future"; in the English of 1611, i.e., of the AV, it means "immediately," which is the true rendering of the Greek text. **9. Doth he thank that servant.** A slave's work was taken as a matter of course; only that which was done beyond the line of duty

11. And it came to pass, as he went to Jerusalem, that he passed through the midst of Samaria and Galilee.

12. And as he entered into a certain village, there met him ten men that were lepers, which stood afar off:

13. And they lifted up *their* voices, and said, Jesus, Master, have mercy on us.

14. And when he saw *them*, he said unto them, Go show yourselves unto the priests. And it came to pass, that, as they went, they were cleansed.

15. And one of them, when he saw that he was healed, turned back, and with a loud voice glorified God,

16. And fell down on *his* face at his feet, giving him thanks: and he was a Samaritan.

17. And Jesus answering said, Were there not ten cleansed? but where *are* the nine?

18. There are not found that returned to give glory to God, save this stranger.

19. And he said unto him, Arise, go thy way: thy faith hath made thee whole.

20. And when he was demanded of the Pharisees, when the kingdom of God should come, he answered them and said, The kingdom of God cometh not with observation:

21. Neither shall they say, Lo here! or, lo there! for, behold, the kingdom of God is within you.

22. And he said unto the disciples, The days will come, when ye shall desire to see one of the days of the Son of man, and ye shall not see *it*.

23. And they shall say to you, See here; or, see there: go not after *them*, nor follow *them*.

24. For as the lightning, that lighteneth out of the one *part* under heaven, shineth unto the other *part* under heaven; so shall also the Son of man be in his day.

called for special commendation.

**11. As he went to Jerusalem.** Luke resumes the narrative of the last journey (cf. 13:22) on which this section (9:51—18:30) is built. **Through the midst of Samaria and Galilee.** Perhaps *between* would be a better rendering (Gr. *diameson*). He followed the border between the two provinces across the Jordan, and down the east side of the river; for the next place mentioned is Jericho (19:1), the point at which pilgrims usually returned to the west side.

**12. Ten . . . lepers, which stood afar off.** Hebrew law forbade lepers to approach close to anybody else. They were at such a distance from Jesus that he had not noticed them until they called to him. **14. Go shew yourselves unto the priests.** Compare the parallel case in 5:12-14. **As they went, they were cleansed.** All of the ten had faith to obey the Master in spite of appearances. They accepted the healing as accomplished, though they had not experienced it. **15. And one of them . . . turned back.** Gratitude was even rarer than faith. **16. And he was a Samaritan.** The only man of the ten who expressed thanks was a despised Samaritan, from whom the pious Jews expected nothing.

**20. When the kingdom of God should come.** Both John the Baptist and Jesus had preached that the kingdom of God was at hand. The Pharisees expected that if Jesus was the Messiah, he would introduce his rule with a sudden assertion of power and an outward conquest of the land. He had a different program in mind, and his answer covered the two main points of that program. **The kingdom of God cometh not with observation.** Its initial advent would not be a political coup or the result of some visible movement. **21. The kingdom of God is within you.** Within, Greek *entos*, may mean *among*. A kingdom is not just a territory, nor a system of governmental machinery. Its basic existence is in the unity and loyalty of a people. Jesus asserted that the kingdom of God was already present and needed only to be recognized. He had brought the kingdom with him and was living among them.

**22. The days of the Son of man.** The Jews used this phrase to denote the Messianic age. **Son of man** was a title of the Messiah employed in Dan 7:13,14. **And ye shall not see it.** The coming of the Messiah would be long delayed. **24. For as the lightning . . . shineth.** As a flash of lightning is immediately apparent

25. But first must he suffer many things, and be rejected of this generation.

26. And as it was in the days of Noe, so shall it be also in the days of the Son of man.

27. They did eat, they drank, they married wives, they were given in marriage, until the day that Noe entered into the ark, and the flood came, and destroyed them all.

28. Likewise also as it was in the days of Lot; they did eat, they drank, they bought, they sold, they planted, they builded;

29. But the same day that Lot went out of Sodom it rained fire and brimstone from heaven, and destroyed *them* all.

30. Even thus shall it be in the day when the Son of man is revealed.

31. In that day, he which shall be upon the housetop, and his stuff in the house, let him not come down to take it away: and he that is in the field, let him likewise not return back.

32. Remember Lot's wife.

33. Whosoever shall seek to save his life shall lose it; and whosoever shall lose his life shall preserve it.

34. I tell you, in that night there shall be two *men* in one bed; the one shall be taken, and the other shall be left.

35. Two *women* shall be grinding together; the one shall be taken, and the other left.

36. Two *men* shall be in the field; the one shall be taken, and the other left.

from one end of the horizon to the other, so the true Messiah will be evident to all men when he comes to set up his kingdom. He will not arise in obscurity, nor be confined to one locality. **25. But first must he suffer many things.** This verse established beyond doubt that Jesus was speaking of himself, for he elaborated upon the same theme in 18:31-34. His interrogators had no concept of a suffering Messiah, but the must in this verse refers to the prophetic Scriptures, as 24:44 indicates. He looked upon his coming death in Jerusalem as a part of his Messianic mission, to be followed later by the revelation of power "in his day" (v. 24).

**26. And as it was in the days of Noe.** The verse implies an interim of delay between the offenses and the ultimate moment of judgment. **The days of the Son of man.** Retribution would not be immediate, but it would be inevitable. **27. They did eat, they drank, they married.** These things were not in themselves wrong, but the preoccupation of the people with them showed that they were living on a wholly materialistic plane, with no thought of God. The judgment of the flood caught them unprepared. **Until the day that Noe entered into the ark.** The moment of the judgment is coincident with or immediately subsequent to the removal of God's servant. Both in the case of Noah and in the case of Lot (see v. 29), God's people were taken away from the scene of judgment before it occurred.

**30. Even thus.** Material prosperity and apparent security will prevail at the time of Christ's return. **31. Upon the house top.** The flat roof of the Oriental house, accessible by an outside stairway, was used as a porch, and sometimes for sleeping in the hot season. The man on the rooftop would not have time to enter his house to get his valuables; he should flee immediately. A parallel to this prediction occurred in the siege of Jerusalem. According to Eusebius, the Christians in the city abandoned it during a temporary withdrawal of the Roman invaders, and fled to a village called Pella, where they survived the fall of the city (*Ecclesiastical History* III. v).

**34. One shall be taken, and the other shall be left.** Verses 34, 35, and 36 are alike in meaning; but each refers to a different time. Men are in bed at night; women grind corn in the early morning just before daylight; and workers are in the field during the daylight hours. Instan-

37. And they answered and said unto him, Where, Lord? And he said unto them, Wheresoever the body *is*, thither will the eagles be gathered together.

## CHAPTER 18

AND he spake a parable unto them *to this end*, that men ought always to pray, and not to faint;

2. Saying, There was in a city a judge, which feared not God, neither regarded man:

3. And there was a widow in that city; and she came unto him, saying, Avenge me of mine adversary.

4. And he would not for a while: but afterward he said within himself, Though I fear not God, nor regard man;

5. Yet because this widow troubleth me, I will avenge her, lest by her continual coming she weary me.

6. And the Lord said, Hear what the unjust judge saith.

7. And shall not God avenge his own elect, which cry day and night unto him, though he bear long with them?

8. I tell you that he will avenge them speedily. Nevertheless, when the Son of man cometh, shall he find faith on the earth?

9. And he spake this parable unto certain which trusted in themselves that they were righteous, and despised others:

taneous action is implied; for the coming of the Lord at one moment would occur at different times of day at different points on the globe. **Taken** is often applied to the saints, but it may refer to the gathering out of offenders to judgment. Compare the allusions to the tares (Mt 13:41,42) and to the vine of the earth (Rev 14:18,19).

**37. Wheresoever the body is, thither will the eagles be gathered together.** When the disciples wished to know where the persons removed would be taken, Jesus answered by a proverb. **Body** may be translated *corpse* (cf. Mt 24:28, *carcase*), and **eagles** are really *vultures,* for the true eagle does not eat carrion. The interpretation that the birds represent the saints gathering around Christ is foreign to the meaning of the proverb. It refers rather to the sudden descent of judgments upon a decadent and evil culture.

**18:1. And he spake a parable unto them.** Much of the preceding discourse is paralleled in Matthew 24, but this parable is unique to Luke. It shows that he was making an immediate application of Jesus' prophecy. Readiness for his return will be conditioned by prayer.

**2. A judge.** Perhaps the judge was a Roman magistrate, who would have had no personal interest in the needs of Jewish people. **3. Came** (Gr. *ērcheto*) is in the imperfect tense, which implies that she kept appearing frequently in the courtroom of the judge. **Avenge me** (Gr. *ekdikēson*) of is not a request for punishment of her adversary, but for a decree that would give protection from his injustices. **4. And he would not.** The verb expresses his state of mind rather than a single act. The widow's persistence wore down the judge's obduracy. **5. She weary me.** Literally, *lest she give me a black eye.* Greek *hypōpiazē* may mean either "to annoy," or "to damage reputation."

**7. Elect.** Luke uses this word only twice: once of the Messiah (23:35), and once of the people whom he has chosen and called. **8. Shall he find faith on the earth?** The rhetorical question implies that faith will be scarce. Our Lord's words do not predict a general improvement in the spiritual condition of the world before his coming.

**9. And he spake this parable.** The second parable in this chapter may not have been spoken on the same occasion as the first. If it was, it doubtless bears a special relation to the coming of the Kingdom. The setting of future life per-

10. Two men went up into the temple to pray; the one a Pharisee, and the other a publican.

11. The Pharisee stood and prayed thus with himself, God, I thank thee, that I am not as other men *are*, extortioners, unjust, adulterers, or even as this publican.

12. I fast twice in the week, I give tithes of all that I possess.

13. And the publican, standing afar off, would not lift up so much as *his* eyes unto heaven, but smote upon his breast, saying, God be merciful to me a sinner.

14. I tell you, this man went down to his house justified *rather* than the other: for every one that exalteth himself shall be abased; and he that humbleth himself shall be exalted.

15. And they brought unto him also infants, that he would touch them: but when *his* disciples saw *it*, they rebuked them.

16. But Jesus called them *unto him*, and said, Suffer little children to come unto me, and forbid them not: for of such is the kingdom of God.

17. Verily I say unto you, Whosoever shall not receive the kingdom of God as a little child shall in no wise enter therein.

vades the whole chapter (18:16,24,30).

10. Two men went up into the temple to pray; the one a Pharisee, and the other a publican. Jesus used this contrast to illustrate the difference between false worship and true penitence. 11. The Pharisee stood and prayed. Standing was a common posture for prayer (Mt 6:5; Mk 11:25). But in the case of the Pharisee, it may mean that he sought to be noticed. With himself refers to his attitude rather than to his position. He was praying *to* himself or *for* himself, rather than *by* himself. I am not as other men are. Undoubtedly his conduct was as good as he said it was. The problem was not with his action, but with his self-righteous attitude. 12. I fast twice in the week. Fasting was part of the Jewish ritual, but it did not require two days' fasting per week. The Pharisee was exceeding the requirements of the Law. All that I possess. A better translation would be, *I give tithes of all that I gain.*

13. Standing afar off. The Pharisee stood in the center of the temple area, where he would be noticed; the publican crept into a corner. God be merciful to me, the sinner. The verb "propitiate" (Gr. *hilasthēti*), occurs in Heb 2:17, where it is rendered *make reconciliation.* It implies the offering of a sacrifice that makes a satisfactory basis for forgiving the guilt of the offending person. The publican did not plead his good works, but the sacrifice that had been offered. The sinner. The definite article is employed to show that the publican was thinking only of his own sins. He was the greatest of sinners in his own eyes. 14. Justified. This is the one passage in the Third Gospel where this word has a theological meaning. Luke may have drawn it from the Pauline theology (Acts 13:39; Rom 3:23-26), with which he was quite familiar. It means to reckon as righteous rather than to be righteous. Because of his trust in the sacrifice and his confession of sin, the publican was accepted as right in the sight of God.

15. And they brought unto him also infants. Parents often brought small children to a rabbi to be blessed. The disciples thought that the people were imposing on their Master's time and strength. 16. Jesus called them. Christ's attitude was contrary to that of the average Jewish adult, who felt that children were unimportant. 17. As a little child. The children came to Jesus without pretense and without fear. They had complete

18. And a certain ruler asked him, saying, Good Master, what shall I do to inherit eternal life?

19. And Jesus said unto him, Why callest thou me good? none *is* good, save one, *that is,* God.

20. Thou knowest the commandments, Do not commit adultery, Do not kill, Do not steal, Do not bear false witness, Honor thy father and thy mother.

21. And he said, All these have I kept from my youth up.

22. Now when Jesus heard these things, he said unto him, Yet lackest thou one thing: sell all that thou hast, and distribute unto the poor, and thou shalt have treasure in heaven: and come, follow me.

23. And when he heard this, he was very sorrowful: for he was very rich.

24. And when Jesus saw that he was very sorrowful, he said, How hardly shall they that have riches enter into the kingdom of God!

25. For it is easier for a camel to go through a needle's eye, than for a rich man to enter into the kingdom of God.

faith that he would receive them and treat them kindly. Eagerness and expectancy characterize those who receive the kingdom.

**18. And a certain ruler.** Matthew (19:16-30) and Mark (10:17-31) narrate this same story. Only Luke calls the inquirer a ruler. If he was young, he was probably too young to occupy a place in the Sanhedrin, but he may have belonged to the aristocracy. **Good Master.** The adjective (Gr. *agathos*) connotes moral goodness, nobility of character. **What shall I do.** The question shows that the ruler was dissatisfied with himself and with his moral attainments. He had not found the life of which the Law spoke (Lev 18:5), and was sure that he had overlooked some commandment. **19. Why callest thou me good?** Jesus wanted to know whether the title was an idle compliment, or whether the young man had carefully thought through who He was. **20. Thou knowest the commandments.** Jesus did not quote the first four commandments, which deal with man's relation to God, nor the last commandment, which deals with an internal feeling. He cited only those commandments that are concerned with outward human relations. **21. All these have I kept.** The young man told the truth as far as he knew it. He had observed the code scrupulously, and he felt that he had nothing to regret. Paul said of himself that as "touching the righteousness which was in the law," he was "blameless" (Phil 3:6).

**22. Yet lackest thou one thing.** The righteousness of the Law was negative. Jesus demanded a complete positive devotion. **Sell all that thou hast.** Jesus always fitted his instructions to the need of the individual. Avarice was this man's peculiar sin, and Jesus demanded action from him that would run exactly counter to his weakness. **23. He was very sorrowful.** Had he not been sincerely interested in Jesus, he would not have been sorrowful, but would have dismissed Him with contempt. He wanted what Jesus had to offer, but not enough to meet His terms. The measure of his sorrow was the measure of his wealth.

**24. How hardly.** Hardly does not mean "scarcely," as in modern English, but "with what difficulty." **25. It is easier for a camel to go through a needle's eye.** Luke uses the word for a surgical needle (Gr. *belonēs*). Attempts to explain this saying by a confusion between *camel* (Gr. *kamēlos*) and *cable (kamilos)*, or by a figurative use of the phrase to mean the

26. And they that heard *it* said, Who then can be saved?

27. And he said, The things which are impossible with men are possible with God.

28. Then Peter said, Lo, we have left all, and followed thee.

29. And he said unto them, Verily I say unto you, There is no man that hath left house, or parents, or brethren, or wife, or children, for the kingdom of God's sake,

30. Who shall not receive manifold more in this present time, and in the world to come life everlasting.

31. Then he took *unto him* the twelve, and said unto them, Behold, we go up to Jerusalem, and all things that are written by the prophets concerning the Son of man shall be accomplished.

32. For he shall be delivered unto the Gentiles, and shall be mocked, and spitefully entreated, and spitted on:

33. And they shall scourge *him*, and put him to death; and the third day he shall rise again.

34. And they understood none of these things: and this saying was hid from them, neither knew they the things which were spoken.

35. And it came to pass, that as he was come nigh unto Jericho, a certain blind man sat by the wayside begging:

small gate in a city wall have not been convincing. Jesus was using a current hyperbolic expression to show how difficult it would be for a man of wealth to accept discipleship with him and to enter the kingdom of God. **26. Who then can be saved?** According to Jewish thinking, prosperity was a sign of the favor of God for those who kept the Law (Deut 28: 1-8). If a man was rich, he must therefore be a good man. Christ's utterance was a shock to his disciples, because they were sure that a wealthy man must be righteous.

## VI. The Suffering of the Saviour. 18:31 —23:56.

At this point Luke resumes the parallel with the other two Synoptic Gospels, and begins his account of the last days of Jesus' life. The whole section should be viewed in the light of Christ's death, though not all of the content is directly concerned with it. The Passion is the undertone of these parables, miracles, and debates.

A. The Progress to Jerusalem. 18:31— 19:27.

**31. Behold, we go up to Jerusalem.** With this third announcement of his coming death (cf. 9:22,44) Jesus began the last stage of the journey to Jerusalem. **All things that are written.** Luke, as well as the writers of the other Gospels, asserts emphatically that Jesus was living in accordance with the Messianic predictions of the OT. **33. They shall scourge him.** In the hand of a strong man the Roman scourge was a deadly weapon. It consisted of a number of leather thongs set in a wooden handle, each of which was usually loaded with small pieces of lead tied into it at intervals. In a few strokes it could cut a man's back to ribbons. **The third day he shall rise again.** The four Gospels agree that Jesus predicted he would rise on the third day (Mt 20:19; Mk 10:34; Jn 2:19). **35. He was come nigh unto Jericho.** The differences between Luke's narrative and those of Matthew (20:29-34) and Mark (10:46-52) have caused considerable argument. Luke says that the miracle took place as Jesus approached Jericho; Matthew and Mark say that it occurred as he left. Mark and Luke assert that one man was healed; Matthew mentions two men. Luke was probably speaking of the Gentile city of Jericho, built by Herod and situated some little distance from the

36. And hearing the multitude pass by, he asked what it meant.

37. And they told him, that Jesus of Nazareth passeth by.

38. And he cried, saying, Jesus, *thou* Son of David, have mercy on me.

39. And they which went before rebuked him, that he should hold his peace: but he cried so much the more, *Thou* Son of David, have mercy on me.

40. And Jesus stood, and commanded him to be brought unto him: and when he was come near, he asked him,

41. Saying, What wilt thou that I shall do unto thee? And he said, Lord, that I may receive my sight.

42. And Jesus said unto him, Receive thy sight: thy faith hath saved thee.

43. And immediately he received his sight, and followed him, glorifying God: and all the people, when they saw *it*, gave praise unto God.

### CHAPTER 19

AND *Jesus* entered and passed through Jericho.

2. And, behold, *there was* a man named Zaccheus, which was the chief among the publicans, and he was rich.

3. And he sought to see Jesus who he was; and could not for the press, because he was little of stature.

4. And he ran before, and climbed up into a sycamore tree to see him; for he was to pass that *way*.

5. And when Jesus came to the place, he looked up, and saw him, and said unto him, Zaccheus, make haste, and come down; for to-day I must abide at thy house.

6. And he made haste, and came down, and received him joyfully.

7. And when they saw *it*, they all murmured, saying, That he was gone to be guest with a man that is a sinner.

8. And Zaccheus stood, and said unto the Lord; Behold, Lord, the half of my goods I give to the poor; and if I have taken any thing from any man by false accusation, I restore *him* fourfold.

site of the old Jericho that had been the Jewish city. Matthew and Mark had the old city in mind. In other words, the miracle took place between the Old and New Testament Jerichos. A writer could view the event as occurring after Jesus left the one town or before he reached the other. (See J. P. Free, *Archaeology and Bible History*, pp. 294,295.) **36. The multitude.** Plummer (ICC, p. 430) thinks that the crowd consisted of a delegation of pilgrims from Galilee going up to Jerusalem for the Passover.

**38. And he cried.** The word (Gr. *eboēsen)* means *to cry for help.* **Jesus, thou son of David.** He applied to Jesus a royal title, which involved belief in His Messiahship. **39. They . . . rebuked him.** He was creating a disturbance, and interrupting the Master, who may have been teaching as he was walking along. **He cried.** A different term from the word in verse 38. This one means to utter a loud cry. **40. And Jesus stood.** He halted that he might locate the man and answer his petition.

**19:1. And Jesus entered and passed through Jericho.** Because of its warm climate, it was a favorite winter resort of the aristocracy. **2. A man named Zacchaeus, which was the chief among the publicans.** Plummer suggests that he was "Commissioner of Taxes" (ICC, p. 433). Since Jericho was a city of much commerce, there was ample opportunity to collect import duty. **4. A sycamore tree.** The word is different from the one in 17:6, and denotes the mulberry fig, a tree quite common in Palestine. It grew to large size, with low spreading branches that could easily be climbed. **5. Jesus . . . looked up.** Ordinarily men are not likely to see what is above eye level when there are interests or distractions around them. Jesus was already aware of the presence of Zacchaeus, and was interested in him. **Come down; for to day I must abide at thy house.** Zacchaeus must have been pleased with Jesus' unprecedented concession in eating dinner with a tax collector, but embarrassed to be found in such an undignified position.

**8. And Zacchaeus stood, and said.** There is no indication as to *when* Zacchaeus spoke these words. It seems most likely that he did so after the dinner, when he had observed the Lord's demeanor and had heard his words. He was convicted of his sins, and had to act on the conviction. **The half of my goods I give to the poor.** Giving was a new experience for Zacchaeus. Like most tax

9. And Jesus said unto him, This day is salvation come to this house, forasmuch as he also is a son of Abraham.

10. For the Son of man is come to seek and to save that which was lost.

11. And as they heard these things, he added and spake a parable, because he was nigh to Jerusalem, and because they thought that the kingdom of God should immediately appear.

12. He said therefore, A certain nobleman went into a far country to receive for himself a kingdom, and to return.

13. And he called his ten servants, and delivered them ten pounds, and said unto them, Occupy till I come.

collectors, he had previously been interested only in taking. **If I have taken any thing.** The type of conditional sentence used here (Gr. *ei . . . esykophantēsa*) implies that he knew well that he had extorted money from others. It could be translated, "Since . . . " The **if** implies an actuality, not a hypothetical case. **Fourfold.** The Law required only the restoration of the principal, with 20 per cent interest (Lev 6:5; Num 5:7), but Zacchaeus imposed upon himself a much severer penalty, comparable to that exacted for robbery (Ex 22:1).

**9. This day is salvation come to this house.** In this context salvation refers to inner wholeness, the salvation of the soul. **Forsomuch as he also is a son of Abraham.** The covenant of God's blessing had been given to Abraham, and those who claimed it were called "children of Abraham" (Gal 3:7). Salvation had come to Zacchaeus not because of his blood descent, but because of his faith, which was like Abraham's. **10. For the Son of man is come to seek and to save that which was lost.** This text is a summary of the entire message of the Gospel of Luke, which stresses the seeking and saving work of the heavenly Messiah.

**11. He added and spake a parable.** An awkwardly literal translation, which may go back to Jesus' Aramaic idiom. He added a parable to what he had already been saying. **Because they thought that the kingdom of God should immediately appear.** In spite of Jesus' repeated predictions of the cross, the disciples were still expecting his triumph in the immediate restoration of the kingdom of David. The parable was intended to give them the proper perspective of his plans.

**12. A certain nobleman.** The parable may have been modeled on the well-known episode of Herod's son, Archelaus, who went to Rome to obtain title to the kingdom which his father, Herod the Great, had left to him. His brother, Antipas, supported by many of the leaders among the Jews, protested the claim, and rejected his rulership. Since the event took place about the time of Christ's birth, it was a well-known story thirty years later (cf. Jos *Antiquities* xvii. 9.3; 11.1). **13. Ten pounds.** This parable is different from the parable of the talents given in Matthew (25:14-30), though there is a close resemblance between the two. In this instance the servants were treated equally, and only ten out of a possibly larger number were tested. A pound was worth 100 drachmas, about $16.50 in

14. But his citizens hated him, and sent a message after him, saying, We will not have this *man* to reign over us.

15. And it came to pass, that when he was returned, having received the kingdom, then he commanded these servants to be called unto him, to whom he had given the money, that he might know how much every man had gained by trading.

16. Then came the first, saying, Lord, thy pound hath gained ten pounds.

17. And he said unto him, Well, thou good servant: because thou hast been faithful in a very little, have thou authority over ten cities.

18. And the second came, saying, Lord, thy pound hath gained five pounds.

19. And he said likewise to him, Be thou also over five cities.

20. And another came, saying, Lord, behold, *here is* thy pound, which I have kept laid up in a napkin:

21. For I feared thee, because thou art an austere man: thou takest up that thou layedst not down, and reapest that thou didst not sow.

22. And he saith unto him, Out of thine own mouth will I judge thee, *thou* wicked servant. Thou knewest that I was an austere man, taking up that I laid not down, and reaping that I did not sow:

23. Wherefore then gavest not thou my money into the bank, that at my coming I might have required mine own with usury?

24. And he said unto them that stood by, Take from him the pound, and give *it* to him that hath ten pounds.

25. (And they said unto him, Lord, he hath ten pounds.)

26. For I say unto you, That unto every one which hath shall be given; and from him that hath not, even that he hath shall be taken away from him.

27. But those mine enemies, which would not that I should reign over them, bring hither, and slay *them* before me.

28. And when he had thus spoken, he went before, ascending up to Jerusalem.

29. And it came to pass, when he was come nigh to Bethphage and Bethany, at the mount called *the mount* of Olives, he sent two of his disciples,

30. Saying, Go ye into the village over against *you;* in the which at your entering ye shall find a colt tied, whereon yet never man sat: loose him, and bring *him hither.*

American money. **Occupy** (Gr. *pragma-teusasthe)* means to engage in business. The servants were expected to invest their funds, and to give an account when their master returned. **14. His citizens hated him.** See comment on verse 12.

**15. When he was returned, having received the kingdom.** The parallelism of this parable implies that the return brought the right to possess and to develop the kingdom. **17. Have thou authority over ten cities.** The awarding of responsibility over territories implies that the master was parceling out governmental posts, and strengthens the idea that this parable was based on the accession of Archelaus. **18. And the second came.** The man who gained less was not reproved for his smaller profit. He was commended, and was given responsibility equal to his ability.

**22. Thou wicked servant.** The servant considered himself honest because he returned the pound with no loss; the master called him wicked because he returned it with no gain. **23. Usury** in the Elizabethan English of the AV did not have the connotation of excessive interest. **24. Give it to him that hath ten pounds.** From the standpoint of the servants, the giving of the extra pound to the one who had the most seemed unjust. From the standpoint of the master, he had already lost interest on the pound, and he wanted to invest it where the returns had the prospect of being largest. **27. But those mine enemies.** A distinction is drawn between the reproof of a servant and the execution of an enemy. The judgment of believers for reward and that of the opposing world for condemnation seem to be distinguished here.

B. The Entry into Jerusalem. 19:28-44.

**28. He went before, ascending up to Jerusalem.** He walked ahead of the disciples, who may have followed reluctantly. They knew very well that their Master was already under sentence by the Jewish leaders (Jn 11:16).

**29. When he was come nigh to Bethphage and Bethany.** Bethany lay on the southeastern side of the Mount of Olives, halfway up the rocky slope, a bit west of the modern village of *el 'Azariyeh.* Bethphage, of which there is no trace remaining, was a short distance farther up the slope, near the top (see Emil G. Kraeling, *Bible Atlas,* pp. 395-398).

**30. The village over against you.** Perhaps the road did not pass directly

31. And if any man ask you, Why do ye loose *him*? thus shall ye say unto him, Because the Lord hath need of him.

32. And they that were sent went their way, and found even as he had said unto them.

33. And as they were loosing the colt, the owners thereof said unto them, Why loose ye the colt?

34. And they said, The Lord hath need of him.

35. And they brought him to Jesus: and they cast their garments upon the colt, and they set Jesus thereon.

36. And as he went, they spread their clothes in the way.

37. And when he was come nigh, even now at the descent of the mount of Olives, the whole multitude of the disciples began to rejoice and praise God with a loud voice for all the mighty works that they had seen;

38. Saying, Blessed *be* the King that cometh in the name of the Lord: peace in heaven, and glory in the highest.

39. And some of the Pharisees from among the multitude said unto him, Master, rebuke thy disciples.

40. And he answered and said unto them, I tell you that, if these should hold their peace, the stones would immediately cry out.

41. And when he was come near, he beheld the city, and wept over it,

42. Saying, If thou hadst known, even thou, at least in this thy day, the things *which belong* unto thy peace! but now they are hid from thine eyes.

43. For the days shall come upon thee, that thine enemies shall cast a trench about thee, and compass thee round, and keep thee in on every side,

44. And shall lay thee even with the ground, and thy children within thee; and they shall not leave in thee one stone upon another; because thou knewest not the time of thy visitation.

45. And he went into the temple, and began to cast out them that sold therein, and them that bought;

46. Saying unto them, It is written, My house is the house of prayer; but ye have made it a den of thieves.

47. And he taught daily in the temple. But the chief priests and the scribes and the chief of the people sought to destroy him,

48. And could not find what they might do: for all the people were very attentive to hear him.

through the village. **A colt tied.** Matthew (21:2) informs us that the animal was a donkey, the common beast of burden for the poorer people of Palestine. Horses were used chiefly by the wealthy, or for purposes of war. Christ's entry into Jerusalem on a donkey was symbolic of his humility and of his peaceful intentions. **31. Because the Lord hath need of him.** Jesus must have had an understanding with the owner that he could use the donkey whenever he wished. **33. The owners . . . said . . . Why loose ye the colt?** They did not recognize the disciples, but they knew Jesus. **35. And they cast their garments upon the colt.** Our Lord had been traveling with a crowd of pilgrims (18:36), who had witnessed the miracle of the healing of Bartimaeus. They were sure that Jesus would claim his Messianic throne in Jerusalem at the Passover season, and so they made a public demonstration of acclaim.

**37. The whole multitude of the disciples.** The language suggests that more than the Twelve are included here. Jesus had many friends in Galilee, a large number of whom may have been among the pilgrims. Their excitement increased as the city of Jerusalem came in sight. **38. Blessed be the King.** This quotation from Psalm 118 (vv. 25,26) was sung by pilgrims as they ascended the road to the Holy City. The psalm was Messianic, so that the very use of its words indicated the popular estimate of Jesus.

**40. The stones would immediately cry out.** Christ asserted that his sovereignty must be acknowledged. This firm avowal of his claims made the subsequent action of the leaders of the nation all the more culpable. They could not say that they had rejected him unknowingly.

**41. He beheld the city.** From the summit of the Mount of Olives it is possible to see the entire city in panorama. Jesus was not excited by the applause of the crowd, because he saw prophetically the miseries that would overtake Jerusalem after his rejection. **43. For the days shall come.** He foresaw the siege and final capture of Jerusalem by the Romans under Vespasian and Titus in A.D. 70. **44. They shall not leave in thee one stone upon another.** With the exception of a few half-buried foundations, there is scarcely a vestige of the Jerusalem of that day now standing.

C. The Teaching in Jerusalem. 19:45—21:4.

**45. And [he] began to cast out them**

## CHAPTER 20

AND it came to pass, *that* on one of those days, as he taught the people in the temple, and preached the gospel, the chief priests and the scribes came upon *him* with the elders,

2. And spake unto him, saying, Tell us, by what authority doest thou these things? or who is he that gave thee this authority?

3. And he answered and said unto them, I will also ask you one thing; and answer me:

4. The baptism of John, was it from heaven, or of men?

5. And they reasoned with themselves, saying, If we shall say, From heaven; he will say, Why then believed ye him not?

6. But and if we say, Of men; all the people will stone us: for they be persuaded that John was a prophet.

7. And they answered, that they could not tell whence *it was.*

8. And Jesus said unto them, Neither tell I you by what authority I do these things.

9. Then began he to speak to the people this parable; A certain man planted a vineyard, and let it forth to husbandmen, and went into a far country for a long time.

10. And at the season he sent a servant to the husbandmen, that they should give him of the fruit of the vineyard: but the husbandmen beat him, and sent *him* away empty.

11. And again he sent another servant: and they beat him also, and entreated *him* shamefully, and sent *him* away empty.

12. And again he sent a third: and they wounded him also, and cast *him* out.

that sold. Because pilgrims could not bring with them sacrificial animals or the proper coins for the Temple tax, the priests had provided concessions where these might be purchased. The business had become a source of graft and had introduced an atmosphere of commercialism into the temple worship. Jesus asserted his right over his Father's house by expelling the merchants.

**20:1. The chief priests and the scribes.** The religious leaders were desperate because Jesus was successfully bidding against them for popular favor. **2. By what authority doest thou these things?** Where did this Galilean prophet obtain either the right or the power to change the administration of the Temple and to perform miracles? If they forced him to make an extravagant claim, they could discredit him with the multitude.

**3. I will also ask you one thing.** Whenever our Lord's opponents tried to corner him with a dilemma, he by a counterquestion put them in a worse position (cf. Jn 7:53 — 8:11; Lk 20:19-40). **4. The baptism of John.** Did John come on divine authority, or on human authority? **5. They reasoned with themselves.** Jesus had forced the Pharisees either to acknowledge that they had refused to heed a messenger of God, or to expose themselves to popular disfavor. **8. Neither tell I you.** Why should he explain the truth concerning himself when they would not believe the truth about John, who was his forerunner?

**9. Then began he to speak to the people this parable.** From the Pharisees, whom he had silenced, Christ turned to the multitude, and told a parable similar to one used by Isaiah (5:1-7), to explain God's dealing with the nation. **A certain man planted a vineyard.** The culture of grapes was one of the chief occupations in Palestine, and involved a large investment of time and money. **And let it forth to husbandmen.** By the sharecropping system the landlord usually collected about one third of the crop as rent. **10. He sent a servant.** Rent was collected by an agent. Jesus indicated that God's servants, the prophets, had come to enforce his rightful claims on the people who had used his property. **The husbandmen beat him.** Many of the prophets were mistreated by the people, or even died violent deaths. Elijah was forced to hide (I Kgs 17:1-7), Jeremiah was thrown into a dungeon (Jer 38:6), and legend says that Isaiah was placed in a hollow tree and sawed in two.

13. Then said the lord of the vineyard, What shall I do? I will send my beloved son: it may be they will reverence *him* when they see him.

14. But when the husbandmen saw him, they reasoned among themselves, saying, This is the heir: come, let us kill him, that the inheritance may be ours.

15. So they cast him out of the vineyard, and killed *him*. What therefore shall the lord of the vineyard do unto them?

16. He shall come and destroy these husbandmen, and shall give the vineyard to others. And when they heard *it*, they said, God forbid.

17. And he beheld them, and said, What is this then that is written, The stone which the builders rejected, the same is become the head of the corner?

18. Whosoever shall fall upon that stone shall be broken; but on whomsoever it shall fall, it will grind him to powder.

19. And the chief priests and the scribes the same hour sought to lay hands on him; and they feared the people: for they perceived that he had spoken this parable against them.

20. And they watched *him*, and sent forth spies, which should feign themselves just men, that they might take hold of his words, that so they might deliver him unto the power and authority of the governor.

21. And they asked him, saying, Master, we know that thou sayest and teachest rightly, neither acceptest thou the person *of any*, but teachest the way of God truly:

22. Is it lawful for us to give tribute unto Caesar, or no?

23. But he perceived their craftiness, and said unto them, Why tempt ye me?

24. Show me a penny. Whose image and superscription hath it? They answered and said, Caesar's.

25. And he said unto them, Render therefore unto Caesar the things which be Caesar's, and unto God the things which be God's.

13. **My beloved son.** The last appeal of the owner was to send his son. He expected that the renters would respect the person and authority of his heir. Jesus by this metaphor placed himself far above the prophets, who were only servants. 14. **Let us kill him, that the inheritance may be ours.** The Pharisees rejected Jesus' claims, thinking that they were the true heirs of God. 15. **They cast him out of the vineyard, and killed him.** Christ's prophecy of the outcome of his last week in Jerusalem was a clear contrast to the expectations of the multitude. 16. **And shall give the vineyard to others.** A prediction of the removal of God's favor from Israel to the Gentiles. 17. **The stone which the builders rejected.** This citation from Ps 118:22, the same psalm from which the multitude took their greeting at the entry into Jerusalem, our Lord applied to himself. The early preachers of the NT interpreted it (Acts 4:11; I Pet 2:7) as a clear prediction of Messiah's rejection and subsequent exaltation. 18. **Shall be broken.** Those who stumble over Christ injure themselves. **Will grind him to powder.** Those who are judged by him will suffer irreparable loss. The verb means "to winnow grain," or "to tread under foot." 19. **The same hour.** The priests took action immediately, because they feared that Jesus might incite a popular uprising. 20. **And they . . . sent forth spies.** Realizing that they could not legally condemn him to death, they tried to trap him so that they could turn him over to the Roman governor with an incriminating charge. 21. **We know that thou sayest and teachest rightly.** Their words were pure flattery, though literally true. 22. **Is it lawful . . . to give tribute unto Caesar, or no?** The question posed a deadly dilemma. If Jesus said, "No," he could be accused of revolutionary tendencies; if he said, "Yes," he would be regarded as a collaborator with Rome and would lose favor with the public. 24. **Show me a penny.** The penny (Gr. *denarius*) was a silver coin issued by Rome, and was the chief monetary unit. The bronze coins of lower denomination did not carry the emperor's image. **Image and superscription.** The image was the likeness of the emperor's face; the superscription was the imperial title. 25. **Render therefore unto Caesar.** The very fact that the Jews used the coin showed that they acknowledged his rule, for a king's domain was considered to extend as far

26. And they could not take hold of his words before the people: and they marveled at his answer, and held their peace.

27. Then came to *him* certain of the Sadducees, which deny that there is any resurrection; and they asked him,

28. Saying, Master, Moses wrote unto us, If any man's brother die, having a wife, and he die without children, that his brother should take his wife, and raise up seed unto his brother.

29. There were therefore seven brethren: and the first took a wife, and died without children.

30. And the second took her to wife, and he died childless.

31. And the third took her; and in like manner the seven also: and they left no children, and died.

32. Last of all the woman died also.

33. Therefore in the resurrection whose wife of them is she? for seven had her to wife.

34. And Jesus answering said unto them, The children of this world marry, and are given in marriage:

35. But they which shall be accounted worthy to obtain that world, and the resurrection from the dead, neither marry, nor are given in marriage:

36. Neither can they die any more: for they are equal unto the angels; and are the children of God, being the children of the resurrection.

37. Now that the dead are raised, even Moses showed at the bush, when he calleth the Lord the God of Abraham, and the God of Isaac, and the God of Jacob.

38. For he is not a God of the dead, but of the living: for all live unto him.

39. Then certain of the scribes answering said, Master, thou hast well said.

40. And after that they durst not ask him any *question at all.*

41. And he said unto them, How say they that Christ is David's son?

42. And David himself saith in the book of Psalms, The LORD said unto my Lord, Sit thou on my right hand,

43. Till I make thine enemies thy footstool.

44. David therefore calleth him Lord, how is he then his son?

45. Then in the audience of all the people he said unto his disciples,

46. Beware of the scribes, which desire to walk in long robes, and love greetings in the markets, and the highest seats in the synagogues, and the chief rooms at feasts;

as his coins were accepted. (See SBK, *Das Evangelium nach Matthaus,* p. 884.) If the Jews thus admitted Caesar as their lord, they could not criticize Jesus. **26. And they could not take hold of his words before the people.** His reply was a marvel of exactness, compactness, and directness. There was nothing in it by which he could be incriminated, yet he had answered their question, and had in addition reminded them of their obligation to God.

**27. The Sadducees, which deny that there is any resurrection.** The Sadducees, fewer in number than the Pharisees, were the priestly party, more interested in politics than in religion. They adhered strictly to the written law of the first five books of Moses, rejecting traditional elaborations of interpretation. They did not believe in angels, nor in spirits, nor in life after death (cf. Acts 23:8).

**28. Moses wrote unto us, If any man's brother die.** The case that they cited was built on the Mosaic Law, which they held to be of final authority (Deut 25:5-10). It provided that if a man died childless, his brother should marry the widow and raise a son to succeed to the property of the deceased. The purpose of this law was to preserve families from extinction. In this instance, the case was purely hypothetical. **33. Therefore in the resurrection whose wife of them is she?** The Sadducees had used this as a stock passage for disproving the afterlife. If all seven, one after the other, had the woman to wife in this world, she would, of course, be the wife of all seven simultaneously in the next world. In that case the Law would be promoting in the future life what it condemned in the present life. Such a conclusion would be absurd; therefore, according to their logic, there could be no future life.

**34. And Jesus answering said unto them.** The Sadducees had the right logic but the wrong premise. They were assuming wrongly that the conditions in the future life would be identical with those here. Jesus asserted that in the age to come there would be neither marriage nor death. **37. Now that the dead are raised.** Having met their negative argument, the Lord presented a positive argument of his own, using the same inferential method. **41. How say they that Christ (*Messiah*) is David's son?** The Messiah was commonly called the son (or descendant) of David (cf. 18:38). **44. David therefore calleth him Lord, how is he then his son?** In Hebrew custom, a son was

47. Which devour widows' houses, and for a show make long prayers: the same shall receive greater damnation.

## CHAPTER 21

AND he looked up, and saw the rich men casting their gifts into the treasury.

2. And he saw also a certain poor widow casting in thither two mites.

3. And he said, Of a truth I say unto you, that this poor widow hath cast in more than they all:

4. For all these have of their abundance cast in unto the offerings of God: but she of her penury hath cast in all the living that she had.

5. And as some spake of the temple, how it was adorned with goodly stones and gifts, he said,

6. As for these things which ye behold, the days will come, in the which there shall not be left one stone upon another, that shall not be thrown down.

7. And they asked him, saying, Master, but when shall these things be? and what sign will there be when these things shall come to pass?

8. And he said, Take heed that ye be not deceived: for many shall come in my name, saying, I am Christ; and the time draweth near: go ye not therefore after them.

9. But when ye shall hear of wars and commotions, be not terrified: for these things must first come to pass; but the end is not by and by.

10. Then said he unto them, Nation shall rise against nation, and kingdom against kingdom:

11. And great earthquakes shall be in divers places, and famines, and pestilences; and fearful sights and great signs shall there be from heaven.

12. But before all these, they shall lay their hands on you, and persecute you, delivering you up to the synagogues, and into prisons, being brought before kings and rulers for my name's sake.

13. And it shall turn to you for a testimony.

14. Settle it therefore in your hearts, not to meditate before what ye shall answer:

15. For I will give you a mouth and wisdom, which all your adversaries shall not be able to gainsay nor resist.

16. And ye shall be betrayed both by parents, and brethren, and kinsfolk, and friends; and some of you shall they cause to be put to death.

17. And ye shall be hated of all men for my name's sake.

always in subjection to his father. For David to speak of his son as "Lord" violated proper usage.

**21:1. He ... saw the rich men casting their gifts into the treasury.** There were chests in the court of the Temple, where gifts could be deposited. **2. Two mites. A mite** (Gr. *lepton*) was half a farthing, and worth about one-fifth of a cent. Two mites made the smallest offering that was acceptable. **4. All the living that she had.** Jesus commended the widow not for the size of her gift, but for the sacrifice involved.

D. The Olivet Discourse. 21:5-38.

**7. When shall these things be?** There is a double perspective in this discourse: the destruction of the Temple and the establishment of the kingdom at Christ's return. **8. Take heed that ye be not deceived.** Many false Messiahs came in the generation immediately following Jesus. **9. The end is not by and by.** He gave fair warning that there would be wars and disturbances of various kinds, but that the end would not be immediate. He expected a period of considerable length to elapse between his removal from earth and his return. **11. And great earthquakes shall be in divers places, and famines, and pestilences.** These predictions may be taken literally as signs of the end. **12. They shall lay their hands on you, and persecute you . . . for my name's sake.** He was speaking prophetically of the Christian community; the persecution would be for his name's sake. The succeeding verses find their counterpart in the narrative of the persecutions in Acts.

**20. And when ye shall see Jerusalem compassed with armies.** It is possible that some of our Lord's hearers lived to see the siege and capture of Jerusalem in A.D. 70. **21. Then let them which are in Judea flee to the mountains.** Only the flight of the Christians from the beleaguered city delivered them from the fate of the Jewish inhabitants who stayed. During a lull in the attack, the Christians left and went to Pella. Those who remained either died of starvation, or were sold as slaves. **24. Jerusalem shall be trodden down of the Gentiles.** From A.D. 70 until the reconstruction of the nation of Israel, Jerusalem was in the hands of Gentiles. **Until the times of the Gentiles be fulfilled.** Compare with "the fullness of the Gentiles" in Rom 11:25. The phrase implies that God has scheduled

18. But there shall not a hair of your head perish.

19. In your patience possess ye your souls.

20. And when ye shall see Jerusalem compassed with armies, then know that the desolation thereof is nigh.

21. Then let them which are in Judea flee to the mountains; and let them which are in the midst of it depart out; and let not them that are in the countries enter thereinto.

22. For these be the days of vengeance, that all things which are written may be fulfilled.

23. But woe unto them that are with child, and to them that give suck, in those days! for there shall be great distress in the land, and wrath upon this people.

24. And they shall fall by the edge of the sword, and shall be led away captive into all nations: and Jerusalem shall be trodden down of the Gentiles, until the times of the Gentiles be fulfilled.

25. And there shall be signs in the sun, and in the moon, and in the stars; and upon the earth distress of nations, with perplexity; the sea and the waves roaring;

26. Men's hearts failing them for fear, and for looking after those things which are coming on the earth: for the powers of heaven shall be shaken.

27. And then shall they see the Son of man coming in a cloud with power and great glory.

28. And when these things begin to come to pass, then look up, and lift up your heads; for your redemption draweth nigh.

29. And he spake to them a parable; Behold the fig tree, and all the trees;

30. When they now shoot forth, ye see and know of your own selves that summer is now nigh at hand.

31. So likewise ye, when ye see these things come to pass, know ye that the kingdom of God is nigh at hand.

32. Verily I say unto you, This generation shall not pass away, till all be fulfilled.

33. Heaven and earth shall pass away; but my words shall not pass away.

34. And take heed to yourselves, lest at any time your hearts be overcharged with surfeiting, and drunkenness, and cares of this life, and so that day come upon you unawares.

35. For as a snare shall it come on all them that dwell on the face of the whole earth.

36. Watch ye therefore, and pray always, that ye may be accounted worthy to escape all these things that shall come to pass, and to stand before the Son of man.

a day of opportunity for Gentiles, which will close with Israel's future restoration to favor.

**25. And there shall be signs in the sun, and in the moon.** If the preceding verses predict the fall of Jerusalem and the final destruction of the Jewish commonwealth, the following verses must deal with the time of the end, and with the signs of Christ's appearing (cf. v. 11). **26. Men's hearts failing them for fear.** The political and social crises, together with the physical disturbances in the world, will be more than men can endure. **The powers of heaven shall be shaken.** The final judgments of God will be attended by a change in the whole physical universe (cf. II Pet 3:10,11).

**27. Coming in a cloud.** A cloud of luminous glory will bring Christ back to earth, making an unmistakable "sign" of his reality (cf. 9:31,32,34; Mt 17:5; Acts 1:9,11; Rev 1:7). **28. And when these things begin to come to pass.** The language implies a process that will extend over a period of time, giving warning to those who are able to interpret the signs. **Redemption** is deliverance, the completion of the salvation of God (cf. Rom 13:11).

**29. Behold the fig tree.** A common tree in Palestine, which put out fruit buds very early in the spring. **31. The kingdom of God is nigh at hand.** Jesus showed by these words that the kingdom of God had not been fully realized, and that it would come in the future. These words are complementary to 17:21: "The kingdom of God is within you." **32. This generation.** Matthew (24:34), Mark (13:30), and Luke quote this utterance in substantially the same words. If it means the generation of those living when the words were spoken, then the entire chapter up to verse 25 will have to be interpreted as referring to the overthrow of Jerusalem and the collapse of the Jewish commonwealth. If, however, **generation** means the race of Israel, Jesus was predicting only that the people would survive until his return. Either interpretation is in harmony with Luke's usage of the term.

**34. And so that day come upon you unawares.** A better translation would be, *come upon you suddenly* (Gr. *aiphnidios*). The Lord did not say that the end would be wholly unannounced; he had already described certain warning signs. He did intimate that it would come more suddenly than might be expected. **36. That ye may be accounted worthy.** An alternate manuscript reading, *that ye might be*

37. And in the daytime he was teaching in the temple; and at night he went out, and abode in the mount that is called *the mount* of Olives.

38. And all the people came early in the morning to him in the temple, for to hear him.

## CHAPTER 22

NOW the feast of unleavened bread drew nigh, which is called the passover.

2. And the chief priests and scribes sought how they might kill him; for they feared the people.

3. Then entered Satan into Judas surnamed Iscariot, being of the number of the twelve.

4. And he went his way, and communed with the chief priests and captains, how he might betray him unto them.

5. And they were glad, and covenanted to give him money.

6. And he promised, and sought opportunity to betray him unto them in the absence of the multitude.

7. Then came the day of unleavened bread, when the passover must be killed.

8. And he sent Peter and John, saying, Go and prepare us the passover, that we may eat.

9. And they said unto him, Where wilt thou that we prepare?

10. And he said unto them, Behold, when ye are entered into the city, there shall a man meet you, bearing a pitcher of water; follow him into the house where he entereth in.

11. And ye shall say unto the goodman of the house, The Master saith unto thee, Where is the guest chamber, where I shall eat the passover with my disciples?

12. And he shall show you a large upper room furnished: there make ready.

13. And they went, and found as he had said unto them: and they made ready the passover.

14. And when the hour was come, he sat down, and the twelve apostles with him.

15. And he said unto them, With desire I have desired to eat this passover with you before I suffer:

16. For I say unto you, I will not any more eat thereof, until it be fulfilled in the kingdom of God.

17. And he took the cup, and gave thanks, and said, Take this, and divide *it* among yourselves:

18. For I say unto you, I will not drink of the fruit of the vine, until the kingdom of God shall come.

*strong enough to,* is slightly preferable. The testing of the last days will require exceptional fortitude.

**37. At night he . . . abode in the mount . . . of Olives.** During the Passover week the city of Jerusalem was always crowded with pilgrims from all parts of the empire. Christ and his disciples may have slept on the grass among the olive trees in the Garden of Gethsemane.

**38. The people came early in the morning.** Jesus maintained a regular teaching schedule in the court of the Temple.

E. The Last Supper. 22:1-38.

1. **The Passover** was the greatest and most sacred feast of the Jewish religious year, celebrating the redemption of the nation from the bondage in Egypt. The passover lamb, whose blood was originally sprinkled on the doorposts to avert the judgment of death (Ex 12:7), was typical of Christ (I Cor 5:7). 3. **Then entered Satan into Judas surnamed Iscariot.** The treachery of Judas was the result of a trend in his life. He had never taken an unselfish interest in Jesus. When the Lord made clear that he was not going to claim the throne of Israel but that he expected to die, Judas was disappointed, and resolved to save himself if possible. His attitude gave an opening for Satanic suggestion and control (cf. Jn 13:2,27).

7. **The day of unleavened bread.** All leaven was rigidly excluded from the Jewish household at the Passover season. 10. **There shall a man meet you, bearing a pitcher of water.** It was unusual for a man to carry water, for such work was relegated to the women of the household, or to slaves. Our Lord's charge to Peter and John reads as if he had made previous arrangements for a contact by means of a secret signal. He wanted the place of meeting to remain unknown, so that he might eat with his disciples without being arrested. 12. **A large upper room furnished.** The room was already prepared for a feast.

15. **With desire I have desired.** A Hebrew idiom which intensifies the meaning of the verb (cf. Gen 22:17). **Before I suffer.** He indicated that the entire supper should be interpreted in the light of his death. 16. **Until it be fulfilled in the kingdom of God.** There is a connection between the Passover and the kingdom of God. The latter is the fulfillment of God's purpose of redemption, as the former was one of its first manifestations.

19. **This is my body.** He identified him-

19. And he took bread, and gave thanks, and brake *it*, and gave unto them, saying, This is my body which is given for you: this do in remembrance of me.

20. Likewise also the cup after supper, saying, This cup *is* the new testament in my blood, which is shed for you.

21. But, behold, the hand of him that betrayeth me *is* with me on the table.

22. And truly the Son of man goeth, as it was determined: but woe unto that man by whom he is betrayed!

23. And they began to inquire among themselves, which of them it was that should do this thing.

24. And there was also a strife among them, which of them should be accounted the greatest.

25. And he said unto them, The kings of the Gentiles exercise lordship over them; and they that exercise authority upon them are called benefactors.

26. But ye *shall* not *be* so: but he that is greatest among you, let him be as the younger; and he that is chief, as he that doth serve.

27. For whether *is* greater, he that sitteth at meat, or he that serveth? *is* not he that sitteth at meat? but I am among you as he that serveth.

28. Ye are they which have continued with me in my temptations.

29. And I appoint unto you a kingdom, as my Father hath appointed unto me;

30. That ye may eat and drink at my table in my kingdom, and sit on thrones judging the twelve tribes of Israel.

31. And the Lord said, Simon, Simon, behold, Satan hath desired *to have* you, that he may sift *you* as wheat:

32. But I have prayed for thee, that thy faith fail not: and when thou art converted, strengthen thy brethren.

33. And he said unto him, Lord, I am ready to go with thee, both into prison, and to death.

34. And he said, I tell thee, Peter, the cock shall not crow this day, before that thou shalt thrice deny that thou knowest me.

35. And he said unto them, When I sent you without purse, and scrip, and shoes, lacked ye any thing? And they said, Nothing.

self with the passover emblems. As the body and blood of the lamb had been the sacrifice that was instrumental in accomplishing the redemption from Egypt, so he would be the sacrifice that would effect redemption under the new covenant. There is no indication in his language that the bread and wine were to be physically transformed into his body and blood. **Which is given for you.** This phrase and the entire succeeding text through verse 20 are omitted in the Western text, which usually amplifies rather than omits. It is possible that these lines did not belong in the original text of Luke (see WH, II, Appendix, p. 64), though there is a close parallel to them in I Cor 11:23-26.

**22. And truly the Son of man goeth, as it was determined.** The death of the Saviour was part of the divine plan for the redemption of men. **24. And there was also a strife among them, which of them should be accounted the greatest.** The disciples had never lost the desire for a high post in the anticipated kingdom. Their attitude of rivalry toward each other created the situation that caused Jesus to wash their feet, as recorded in John 13. **25. Benefactor** (Gr. *euergetēs*) was a title carried by the Greek kings of Egypt and Syria. **27. He that serveth** (Gr. *diakonos*) was not used of slaves, but of those who performed tasks for the aid of others. **29. I appoint unto you a kingdom.** Jesus did not deny that there would be a kingdom in which his disciples would rule. His affirmation revealed his confidence that his death would not end their hopes, but that ultimately he would see the reward of his sufferings and share it with the disciples. **30. The twelve tribes of Israel.** A similar promise is quoted in Mt 19:28. The disciples would have understood this to mean a literal rule over Israel, restored to national status.

**31. And the Lord said, Simon, Simon.** Jesus spoke to Simon Peter as the representative of the Twelve. **You.** A plural pronoun. **Sift you as wheat.** Wheat was sifted to remove the dirt and chaff, and to eliminate the broken and withered grains. The temptations of the devil often serve the purpose of revealing strength as well as weakness in believers. **32. But I have prayed for thee.** The singular pronoun indicates that the Lord had a special concern for Peter. He knew the failure impending because of Peter's overconfidence; yet he would not relinquish him, nor depose him from his position of leadership.

36. Then said he unto them, But now, he that hath a purse, let him take *it*, and likewise *his* scrip: and he that hath no sword, let him sell his garment, and buy one.

37. For I say unto you, that this that is written must yet be accomplished in me, And he was reckoned among the transgressors: for the things concerning me have an end.

38. And they said, Lord, behold, here *are* two swords. And he said unto them, It is enough.

39. And he came out, and went, as he was wont, to the mount of Olives; and his disciples also followed him.

40. And when he was at the place, he said unto them, Pray that ye enter not into temptation.

41. And he was withdrawn from them about a stone's cast, and kneeled down, and prayed,

42. Saying, Father, if thou be willing, remove this cup from me: nevertheless, not my will, but thine, be done.

43. And there appeared an angel unto him from heaven, strengthening him.

44. And being in an agony he prayed more earnestly: and his sweat was as it were great drops of blood falling down to the ground.

36. He that hath no sword, let him . . . buy one. This strange command occurs only in Luke. Jesus said that two swords would be enough (v. 38), though these would hardly have been adequate to defend the entire group against an arresting party. Did he mean that the possession of the weapons would technically place him among transgressors, and thus fulfill the letter of the prophecy quoted from Isa 53:12?

F. The Betrayal. 22:39-53.

There is a change of scene between verses 38 and 39. Jesus and the disciples had left the upper room, and had resorted to the Mount of Olives.

40. Temptation. Severe trial rather than solicitation to evil.

42. Father, if thou be willing, remove this cup. All four Gospels refer to the "cup" (Mt 26:39; Mk 14:36; Jn 18:11), though John does not reproduce this prayer. Various interpretations of its meaning have been given: the fear of death, the suffering of death, the possibility of death before he could complete the work of the cross, or the burden of the world's sin. In Revelation 14:10 and 16:19 the "cup" is symbolic of the wrath of God. No one of these interpretations may be final, but the cup must stand for the suffering which confronted him. He had done nothing to deserve it, but he had to endure it if he was to finish his work. Nevertheless not my will. These words do not express a grudging concession or resignation to fate, but the ready acceptance of the will of the Father as the highest good and the supreme desire of his heart.

43. And there appeared an angel unto him from heaven. Verses 43 and 44 do not appear in the Western text, and may not have been a part of the original writing of Luke. On the other hand, they are well attested by other manuscript tradition, and are not the kind of statement that would have been invented by scribes (cf. note on v. 19). Strengthening him. The answer to his prayer was not removal of the cup, but strengthening to bear it. 44. As it were great drops of blood. Luke does not say that the perspiration was blood; he says that it was like blood. There are a few cases recorded in medical history in which intense mental suffering has been accompanied by the oozing of blood from the skin because of a breakdown of the blood vessels. 45.

45. And when he rose up from prayer, and was come to his disciples, he found them sleeping for sorrow,

46. And said unto them, Why sleep ye? rise and pray, lest ye enter into temptation.

47. And while he yet spake, behold a multitude, and he that was called Judas, one of the twelve, went before them, and drew near unto Jesus to kiss him.

48. But Jesus said unto him, Judas, betrayest thou the Son of man with a kiss?

49. When they which were about him saw what would follow, they said unto him, Lord, shall we smite with the sword?

50. And one of them smote the servant of the high priest, and cut off his right ear.

51. And Jesus answered and said, Suffer ye thus far. And he touched his ear, and healed him.

52. Then Jesus said unto the chief priests, and captains of the temple, and the elders, which were come to him, Be ye come out, as against a thief, with swords and staves?

53. When I was daily with you in the temple, ye stretched forth no hands against me: but this is your hour, and the power of darkness.

54. Then took they him, and led *him*, and brought him into the high priest's house. And Peter followed afar off.

55. And when they had kindled a fire in the midst of the hall, and were set down together, Peter sat down among them.

56. But a certain maid beheld him as he sat by the fire, and earnestly looked upon him, and said, This man was also with him.

57. And he denied him, saying, Woman, I know him not.

58. And after a little while another saw him, and said, Thou art also of them. And Peter said, Man, I am not.

59. And about the space of one hour after another confidently affirmed, saying, Of a truth this *fellow* also was with him; for he is a Galilean.

60. And Peter said, Man, I know not what thou sayest. And immediately, while he yet spake, the cock crew.

61. And the Lord turned, and looked upon Peter. And Peter remembered the word of the Lord, how he had said unto him, Before the cock crow, thou shalt deny me thrice.

62. And Peter went out, and wept bitterly.

63. And the men that held Jesus mocked him, and smote *him*.

Sleeping for sorrow. The disciples were not insensitive to their Master's agony, but were worn out by the physical and emotional tension.

47. While he yet spake. Had Jesus chosen to escape to Perea, he could have been safely out of reach of his enemies by the time Judas had completed his negotiations. His surrender was voluntary. 48. Betrayest thou the Son of man with a kiss? Judas used the customary Eastern gesture of friendship to mark Jesus as the one to be arrested. 50. Cut off his right ear. The four Evangelists note that the servant of the high priest was wounded in the scuffle, but only John and Luke mention his right ear. Luke must have obtained his information from an eyewitness.

52. The chief priests, and captains of the temple, and the elders. The band that came to arrest Jesus was probably composed of the temple guard, though the language of John (Jn 18:3,12) can be interpreted to mean a Roman cohort. 53. Your hour, and the power of darkness. Darkness was symbolic of the power of Satan (cf. Eph 6:12). Jesus acknowledged the devil's temporary triumph, but anticipated his own victory.

G. The Arrest and Trial. 22:54—23:25.

54. The high priest's house. Joseph Caiaphas was the legally appointed high priest, but his father-in-law, Annas, being high priest emeritus, was still a powerful figure, and was frequently consulted on affairs of state. John says that Jesus was conducted first to Annas (Jn 18:13). They probably lived in the same palace, so that no long transit was involved between the interviews. Peter followed afar off. Luke does not narrate the substance of the interview with Annas; he is chiefly interested in presenting the action of Peter.

55. A fire. Since Jerusalem is 2,600 feet above sea level, in the spring the nights are cold. 59. He is a Galilean. The Galileans spoke Aramaic with a heavy guttural accent. Peter could not hide his origin. 60. The cock crew. "Cockcrow" was a Roman division of time, marking the close of the third watch, about three o'clock in the morning. 61. The Lord . . . looked upon Peter. Just a glance, as he passed by on the way to Pilate's hall, was sufficient to remind Peter of the enormity of his act.

63. And the men that held Jesus mocked him. The treatment of Jesus by

64. And when they had blindfolded him, they struck him on the face, and asked him, saying, Prophesy, who is it that smote thee?

65. And many other things blasphemously spake they against him.

66. And as soon as it was day, the elders of the people and the chief priests and the scribes came together, and led him into their council, saying,

67. Art thou the Christ? tell us. And he said unto them, If I tell you, ye will not believe:

68. And if I also ask *you*, ye will not answer me, nor let *me* go.

69. Hereafter shall the Son of man sit on the right hand of the power of God.

70. Then said they all, Art thou then the Son of God? And he said unto them, Ye say that I am.

71. And they said, What need we any further witness? for we ourselves have heard of his own mouth.

### CHAPTER 23

AND the whole multitude of them arose, and led him unto Pilate.

2. And they began to accuse him, saying, We found this *fellow* perverting the nation, and forbidding to give tribute to Caesar, saying that he himself is Christ a king.

3. And Pilate asked him, saying, Art thou the King of the Jews? And he answered him and said, Thou sayest *it*.

the henchmen of the Sanhedrin was wholly illegal. A prisoner was supposed to be held inviolate until he was condemned officially. But our Lord was left to the mercy of an irresponsible guard between the close of the hearing before the priests and his appearance before Pilate.

**66. As soon as it was day.** According to Jewish law, the Sanhedrin (council) could not convene at night. Matthew (26:57,58) and Mark (14:53,55) say that there was a preliminary hearing at the house of the high priest, and that formal sentence was passed early in the morning (Mt 27:1; Mk 15:1). Luke mentions only the latter. The *assembly*, or Sanhedrin, consisted of seventy or seventy-two of the elders and teachers of the nation. It was allowed by Rome to pass judgment on religious and civil issues, but could not inflict capital punishment without the concurrence of the Roman governor.

**67. Art thou the Christ?** Luke reports two questions asked by the Sanhedrin. This one, if answered in the affirmative, could have been interpreted as a confession of treason, for every messiah was regarded as a potential rebel against the Roman government. **69. Hereafter shall the Son of man sit on the right hand of the power of God.** Jesus claimed Messiahship by asserting that subsequently he would be elevated to the right hand of God. **70. Art thou then the Son of God?** The second question was intended to incriminate Jesus with the people. If he claimed to be the Son of God, he could be charged with blasphemy. **Ye say that I am.** The expression is equivalent to "Yes."

**23:1. And the whole multitude ... led him unto Pilate.** Pontius Pilate was the Roman governor of Palestine from A.D. 26 to 36. His official residence was in Caesarea, but he usually visited Jerusalem during the Passover season in order to keep a watchful eye on the crowds there. It seems probable that he had been forewarned of the arrest of Jesus in order that he might be on hand early in the morning for the trial. **2. And they began to accuse him.** The charges the priests brought were calculated to incriminate the prisoner in a Roman court, since violations of the Mosaic law would have carried no weight with Pilate. Their falsity has already been shown by the total presentation of Christ's life and words in this Gospel.

**3. Art thou the King of the Jews?**

4. Then said Pilate to the chief priests and *to* the people, I find no fault in this man.

5. And they were the more fierce, saying, He stirreth up the people, teaching throughout all Jewry, beginning from Galilee to this place.

6. When Pilate heard of Galilee, he asked whether the man were a Galilean.

7. And as soon as he knew that he belonged unto Herod's jurisdiction, he sent him to Herod, who himself also was at Jerusalem at that time.

8. And when Herod saw Jesus, he was exceeding glad: for he was desirous to see him of a long *season*, because he had heard many things of him; and he hoped to have seen some miracle done by him.

9. Then he questioned with him in many words; but he answered him nothing.

10. And the chief priests and scribes stood and vehemently accused him.

11. And Herod with his men of war set him at nought, and mocked *him*, and arrayed him in a gorgeous robe, and sent him again to Pilate.

12. And the same day Pilate and Herod were made friends together; for before they were at enmity between themselves.

13. And Pilate, when he had called together the chief priests and the rulers and the people,

14. Said unto them, Ye have brought this man unto me, as one that perverteth the people; and, behold, I, having examined *him* before you, have found no fault in this man touching those things whereof ye accuse him:

15. No, nor yet Herod: for I sent you to him; and, lo, nothing worthy of death is done unto him.

16. I will therefore chastise him, and release *him*.

17. (For of necessity he must release one unto them at the feast.)

18. And they cried out all at once, saying, Away with this *man*, and release unto us Barabbas:

19. (Who for a certain sedition made in the city, and for murder, was cast into prison.)

20. Pilate therefore, willing to release Jesus, spake again to them.

21. But they cried, saying, Crucify *him*, crucify him.

22. And he said unto them the third time, Why, what evil hath he done? I have found no cause of death in him: I will therefore chastise him, and let *him* go.

23. And they were instant with loud voices, requiring that he might be crucified:

The English translation does not give the full force of the Greek sentence: "YOU are the king of the Jews?!" Pilate was astonished that so ordinary-looking a person should claim to be a king. Luke does not give the examination of Jesus in full detail, but only the verdict. **4. I find no fault in this man.** Pilate was not pronouncing on the prisoner's sinlessness, but was simply saying that he had committed no crime that demanded legal action.

**5. Galilee** was a center of constant turbulence and revolt. **7. He belonged unto Herod's jurisdiction.** Pilate had no direct jurisdiction over Galilee, since it had been made part of the puppet kingdom of Herod. He welcomed an opportunity to send this embarrassing prisoner to another judge. **Who himself also was at Jerusalem.** Herod, as a nominal Jew, was under obligation to attend the Passover feast.

**8. And when Herod saw Jesus, he was exceeding glad.** The fame of Jesus had come to Herod's ears, and had excited his fears (9:9) and his curiosity. **9. He answered him nothing.** Jesus did not fear Herod, and refused to waste his time on a trifler. To Herod the whole affair was one vast joke. **11.** The **gorgeous robe** was probably one of Herod's cast-off robes, which he put on Jesus to mock his royal claims. **12. Pilate and Herod were made friends.** Pilate's gesture of recognizing Herod's rulership relieved any tension of jealousy between the two officials.

**15. Nothing worthy of death is done unto him.** Better, *done by him.* Pilate was ready to acquit Jesus on the merits of the case. **16. Chastise him.** Pilate suggested a token scourging to "teach him a lesson." **17. He must release one unto them.** It was the custom of the Roman governor to release one political prisoner at the Passover as a conciliatory gift to the people (see Jn 18:39). **18. Release unto us Barabbas.** Bar-abbas in Aramaic means *son of the father.* **19. Who for a certain sedition . . . was cast into prison.** Barabbas was an outlaw, perhaps a Galilean Zealot who had been caught in an uprising (cf. Jn 18:40).

H. The Crucifixion. 23:26-49.

**26. Simon, a Cyrenian.** The Jews of Cyrene had a synagogue of their own in Jerusalem (Acts 6:9). Simon had lodged outside the city over night, and was coming in for the day's worship at the Temple. The guard, seizing him, im-

and the voices of them and of the chief priests prevailed.

24. And Pilate gave sentence that it should be as they required.

25. And he released unto them him that for sedition and murder was cast into prison, whom they had desired; but he delivered Jesus to their will.

26. And as they led him away, they laid hold upon one Simon, a Cyrenian, coming out of the country, and on him they laid the cross, that he might bear *it* after Jesus.

27. And there followed him a great company of people, and of women, which also bewailed and lamented him.

28. But Jesus turning unto them said, Daughters of Jerusalem, weep not for me, but weep for yourselves, and for your children.

29. For, behold, the days are coming, in the which they shall say, Blessed *are* the barren, and the wombs that never bare, and the paps which never gave suck.

30. Then shall they begin to say to the mountains, Fall on us; and to the hills, Cover us.

31. For if they do these things in a green tree, what shall be done in the dry?

32. And there were also two others, malefactors, led with him to be put to death.

33. And when they were come to the place, which is called Calvary, there they crucified him, and the malefactors, one on the right hand, and the other on the left.

34. Then said Jesus, Father, forgive them; for they know not what they do. And they parted his raiment, and cast lots.

35. And the people stood beholding. And the rulers also with them derided *him*, saying, He saved others; let him save himself, if he be Christ, the chosen of God.

36. And the soldiers also mocked him, coming to him, and offering him vinegar,

37. And saying, If thou be the King of the Jews, save thyself.

38. And a superscription also was written over him in letters of Greek, and Latin, and Hebrew, THIS IS THE KING OF THE JEWS.

pressed him to carry the cross of Jesus. Usually the prisoner carried his own, but our Lord, worn out by the tensions of the preceding hours, was unable to do so.

**27. A great company . . . which also bewailed and lamented him.** Only Luke mentions this episode. The action of the trial had taken place before Christ's friends realized what was happening and could organize a protest. **28. Weep for yourselves, and for your children.** The Lord foresaw the destruction of the city and the miseries that would fall upon its inhabitants. **31. For if they do these things in a green tree.** He quoted a current proverb. The application means that if such injustice can be perpetrated against an innocent man in the time of peace, what will befall the people of the city in time of war?

**32. Malefactors.** Matthew calls them "brigands" (Mt 27:44). **33. The place, which is called Calvary.** The exact site is not known. All landmarks were destroyed in the siege of Jerusalem, and so identification is uncertain. The place of execution was outside the wall of the city, near a main-traveled highway. Opinion is divided today between placing it at the Church of the Holy Sepulcher, or at Gordon's Calvary, just north of the Damascus Gate. Calvary (Lat.) or Golgotha (Aram.) means "skull." Evidently the hill was so named either from the configuration of the land, which looked like a skull, or because bones were strewn about the execution ground. The latter alternative is less likely because of Jewish scruples against unburied bodies.

**34.** This verse, like one or two others preceding (22:19,43) is absent from some of the best manuscripts. Like several other such disputed texts, it is undoubtedly a genuine utterance of Jesus. It is harder to account for its omission than for its inclusion. **And they parted his raiment, and cast lots.** The clothing of condemned prisoners became the property of the execution squad. Turban, sandals, girdle, cloak, and tunic would have made five items. The fifth, in this instance, the tunic, would either have had to be divided into four parts for equal distribution, which would have rendered it useless, or else assigned by lot.

**36. Offering him vinegar.** The soldiers drank a cheap sour wine, which was much like grape vinegar. **38. And a superscription.** The crimes of the con-

39. And one of the malefactors which were hanged railed on him, saying, If thou be Christ, save thyself and us.

40. But the other answering rebuked him, saying, Dost not thou fear God, seeing thou art in the same condemnation?

41. And we indeed justly; for we receive the due reward of our deeds: but this man hath done nothing amiss.

42. And he said unto Jesus, Lord, remember me when thou comest into thy kingdom.

43. And Jesus said unto him, Verily I say unto thee, To-day shalt thou be with me in paradise.

44. And it was about the sixth hour, and there was a darkness over all the earth until the ninth hour.

45. And the sun was darkened, and the veil of the temple was rent in the midst.

46. And when Jesus had cried with a loud voice, he said, Father, into thy hands I commend my spirit: and having said thus, he gave up the ghost.

47. Now when the centurion saw what was done, he glorified God, saying, Certainly this was a righteous man.

48. And all the people that came together to that sight, beholding the things which were done, smote their breasts, and returned.

49. And all his acquaintance, and the women that followed him from Galilee, stood afar off, beholding these things.

50. And, behold, *there was* a man named Joseph, a counselor; *and he was* a good man, and a just:

51. (The same had not consented to the counsel and deed of them:) *he was* of Arimathea, a city of the Jews; who also himself waited for the kingdom of God.

52. This *man* went unto Pilate, and begged the body of Jesus.

demned were listed on a placard, which was hung around his neck or nailed above his head on the cross. The Gospel records of the inscriptions differ (cf. Mt 27:37; Mk 15:26; Jn 19:19), and there may have been slight differences in the wording as it appeared in the different languages. The full inscription was probably, This is *Jesus of Nazareth*, the King of the Jews.

**39. If thou be Christ.** The better Greek text does not contain a condition. "You are the Messiah, aren't you? [Well, then,] save yourself and us!" The first thief was really sarcastic. **42. Lord, remember me when thou comest into thy kingdom.** The tone of this request is utterly different from the cynical fling of the other brigand. This man showed amazing confidence in Jesus; for he saw him dying on a cross, and yet believed that he would come in a kingdom. **Said** (Gr. *elegen*) is in the imperfect tense, which means that the request was repeated. **43. Paradise** is an old Persian term for a park or a garden, a beauty spot. It became a name for the abode of God (cf. II Cor 12:4).

**44. The sixth hour.** Time was reckoned from daybreak, about six o'clock in the morning. The sixth hour was noon. **A darkness.** The failure of the sun's light cannot be attributed to an eclipse, which would have been impossible during the full Passover moon. **45. The veil of the temple was rent in the midst.** The veil hung within the Temple, separating the Holy Place, where the priests ministered, from the presence of God in the Holy of Holies. It was made of thick woven material, which a man could not have torn with his own strength. The rending of the veil from the top to the bottom was distinctly supernatural.

**46. I commend my spirit.** He dismissed his spirit to the Father. His death was conscious and voluntary. **47. The centurion.** See comment on 7:2. This man, a Gentile, accustomed to seeing all kinds and conditions of men, confessed that Jesus was a **righteous man.**

I. The Burial. 23:50-56.

**50. Joseph, a counsellor.** Joseph of Arimathea was a member of the Sanhedrin, who had not consented to the verdict of death for Jesus. He was a disciple, and may not have been present when the council convened; if he was present, he registered a dissenting vote (v. 51 a). **52. This man went unto Pilate.**

53. And he took it down, and wrapped it in linen, and laid it in a sepulchre that was hewn in stone, wherein never man before was laid.

54. And that day was the preparation, and the sabbath drew on.

55. And the women also, which came with him from Galilee, followed after, and beheld the sepulchre, and how his body was laid.

56. And they returned, and prepared spices and ointments; and rested the sabbath day according to the commandment.

## CHAPTER 24

NOW upon the first *day* of the week, very early in the morning, they came unto the sepulchre, bringing the spices which they had prepared, and certain *others* with them.

2. And they found the stone rolled away from the sepulchre.

To make a request for the body of a condemned criminal would immediately have put Joseph in a suspicious light. He showed courage to make the request. **53. Wrapped it in linen.** The verb means *to roll tightly, to wrap by winding.* It occurs only here, in Mt 27:59, and in Jn 20:7. The implication is that the body was not just carelessly wrapped in a sheet, but that Joseph, with his assistants, carefully wound it in bandage-like swathes, and deposited it in his own tomb. **54. That day was the preparation.** According to general tradition, Jesus died on Friday afternoon, the "preparation" for the Sabbath that began at sunset. The body was, therefore, hastily placed in the tomb, in expectation of completing the burial after the Sabbath had passed. **55. The women . . . beheld the sepulchre.** The women witnessed the burial and noted how the body was laid. They could not have been mistaken later about the location of the tomb nor about the reality of the burial. **56. They . . . prepared spices and ointments.** Spices and unguents of various kinds were used to preserve the body, and were also a tribute of love and of respect to the dead.

### VII. The Resurrection. 24:1-53.

Luke's account of the Resurrection differs from the other narratives in content, though it agrees with them in the essential facts. Each of the Gospel writers mentions the visit of the women to the tomb; but the appearance of the Lord to the disciples en route to Emmaus is reported only by Luke. He gives three main episodes of the Resurrection: the announcement to the women, the walk to Emmaus, and the appearance in the upper room. He concludes the Gospel with the ascension from Bethany.

### A. The Empty Tomb. 24:1-12.

**1. Upon the first day of the week, very early in the morning.** The first day commenced on Saturday afternoon. Mark seems to imply (16:1,2) that the women finished the purchase of spices on the preceding evening, and came to the tomb at an hour when they would not be disturbed by others. **2. They found the stone rolled away from the sepulchre.** The tomb was a cave cut into the solid rock, across the entrance of which a circular stone could be rolled to keep out intruders. The women were

3. And they entered in, and found not the body of the Lord Jesus.

4. And it came to pass, as they were much perplexed thereabout, behold, two men stood by them in shining garments:

5. And as they were afraid, and bowed down *their* faces to the earth, they said unto them, Why seek ye the living among the dead?

6. He is not here, but is risen: remember how he spake unto you when he was yet in Galilee,

7. Saying, The Son of man must be delivered into the hands of sinful men, and be crucified, and the third day rise again.

8. And they remembered his words,

9. And returned from the sepulchre, and told all these things unto the eleven, and to all the rest.

10. It was Mary Magdalene, and Joanna, and Mary *the mother* of James, and other *women that were* with them, which told these things unto the apostles.

11. And their words seemed to them as idle tales, and they believed them not.

12. Then arose Peter, and ran unto the sepulchre; and stooping down, he beheld the linen clothes laid by themselves, and departed, wondering in himself at that which was come to pass.

surprised to find the tomb open. **3. Found not the body.** They knew exactly where to look for it, but it had vanished. All the accounts agree that the tomb was empty on the morning of the first day. **4. They were much perplexed.** The women had no inkling of what had happened. Obviously there was no plot on the part of the disciples to remove the body (as the Jewish leaders charged) or these women would have had some hint of it. Perhaps they thought that Joseph and his assistants had moved the body to a safer place. **Two men stood by them.** Matthew (28:2-6) and Mark (16:5) say that an angel within the tomb gave them the news that Jesus had risen. There is no essential conflict; one may have been the spokesman for both. Two witnesses attended Jesus at the Transfiguration (Lk 9:30) and at his ascension (Acts 1:10). Luke may be suggesting that the same two appeared at the Resurrection. **In shining garments.** Shining (Gr. *astraptousē*) means flashing like lightning. **6. Remember how he spake . . . in Galilee.** The discussion at the Transfiguration was "his decease which he should accomplish at Jerusalem" (9:31). And before leaving Galilee, Jesus had given his disciples explicit instructions about the necessity of his coming death (18:31-34). **8. And they remembered his words.** When he had first spoken about these things, the minds of the disciples had been preoccupied with other concepts; but the Resurrection put all of his teaching in a new perspective. **9. And to all the rest.** Jesus had with him in Jerusalem a larger group of followers than just the eleven disciples. Joseph of Arimathea, Nicodemus, the women, and many others were undoubtedly included in the group. **10. Mary Magdalene, and Joanna, and Mary the mother of James.** Mary Magdalene was probably so named from the town of Magdala in Galilee, where she had lived. Joanna was the wife of Chuza, Herod's steward (see 8:3). Mary the mother of James is mentioned by Matthew (27:56) and Mark (15:40). **11. Idle tales.** The Greek word (*lēros*) means literally, *nonsense*. The disciples were not ready to believe the first story they heard, but began a critical investigation. **12. Then arose Peter.** The entire twelfth verse does not appear in the Western text of Luke, but is included in other manuscripts, and accords with the account given in Jn 20:2-10 (cf. 22: 19; 24:34). **The linen clothes** were wide

13. And, behold, two of them went that same day to a village called Emmaus, which was from Jerusalem *about* threescore furlongs.

14. And they talked together of all these things which had happened.

15. And it came to pass, that, while they communed *together* and reasoned, Jesus himself drew near, and went with them.

16. But their eyes were holden that they should not know him.

17. And he said unto them, What manner of communications *are* these that ye have one to another, as ye walk, and are sad?

18. And the one of them, whose name was Cleopas, answering said unto him, Art thou only a stranger in Jerusalem, and hast not known the things which are come to pass there in these days?

19. And he said unto them, What things? And they said unto him, Concerning Jesus of Nazareth, which was a prophet mighty in deed and word before God and all the people:

20. And how the chief priests and our rulers delivered him to be condemned to death, and have crucified him.

21. But we trusted that it had been he which should have redeemed Israel: and beside all this, to-day is the third day since these things were done.

22. Yea, and certain women also of our company made us astonished, which were early at the sepulchre;

23. And when they found not his body, they came, saying, that they had also seen a vision of angels, which said that he was alive.

24. And certain of them which were with us went to the sepulchre, and found *it* even so as the women had said: but him they saw not.

25. Then he said unto them, O fools, and slow of heart to believe all that the prophets have spoken:

26. Ought not Christ to have suffered these things, and to enter into his glory?

bandage-like strips that were wound around the body. **Laid by themselves.** There was no body in them, but they kept the same position they had when it was there. **Wondering in himself.** Peter could not understand why the cloths should have been left, and how the body could have been extracted from the wrappings.

B. The Walk to Emmaus. 24:13-35.

13. **A village called Emmaus.** Probably the same as the modern 'Amwas, nineteen miles west and slightly north of Jerusalem. **About threescore furlongs.** The distance given by the conventional text is about eight miles, but two of the older manuscripts say 160 furlongs, which would be about 20 miles. 16. **Their eyes were holden.** In several instances Jesus was not readily recognized after the Resurrection.

18. **Cleopas** was the husband of one of the Marys (Jn 19:25), and was possibly the father of James the Less (Lk 24:10). He may have been Luke's informant. **Art thou only a stranger in Jerusalem.** The event of the death of Jesus was so well known that these two men could not understand how even a casual visitor in the city would not have heard of it. 19. **Jesus of Nazareth, which was a prophet.** The words of Cleopas reveal the disciples' estimate of Jesus. They had not come into the full realization of his deity.

21. **But we trusted.** They were disillusioned. They had expected that Jesus would usher in the Messianic kingdom, and nothing of the sort had happened. **The third day.** The situation was hopeless, for with the arrival of the third day after death, there could be no hope of natural restoration. 22. **And certain women.** The bewilderment of the disciples was increased by the report of the women. They could not very well deny the truth of the report; yet there was no positive evidence of resuscitation. 24. **And certain of them.** They referred to Peter and John, mentioned above. These confirmed the fact that the tomb was empty. **But him they saw not.** For these men, only the verifiable appearance of Jesus himself would have been convincing.

25. **All that the prophets have spoken.** A clear testimony to the fact that Christ's coming was predicted in the OT. 26. **Ought not Christ to have suffered these things?** Jesus intimated that the events

27. And beginning at Moses and all the prophets, he expounded unto them in all the Scriptures the things concerning himself.

28. And they drew nigh unto the village, whither they went: and he made as though he would have gone further.

29. But they constrained him, saying, Abide with us; for it is toward evening, and the day is far spent. And he went in to tarry with them.

30. And it came to pass, as he sat at meat with them, he took bread, and blessed *it*, and brake, and gave to them.

31. And their eyes were opened, and they knew him; and he vanished out of their sight.

32. And they said one to another, Did not our heart burn within us, while he talked with us by the way, and while he opened to us the Scriptures?

33. And they rose up the same hour, and returned to Jerusalem, and found the eleven gathered together, and them that were with them,

34. Saying, The Lord is risen indeed, and hath appeared to Simon.

35. And they told what things *were done* in the way, and how he was known of them in breaking of bread.

36. And as they thus spake, Jesus himself stood in the midst of them, and saith unto them, Peace *be* unto you.

37. But they were terrified and affrighted, and supposed that they had seen a spirit.

38. And he said unto them, Why are ye troubled? and why do thoughts arise in your hearts?

39. Behold my hands and my feet, that it is I myself: handle me, and see; for a spirit hath not flesh and bones, as ye see me have.

40. And when he had thus spoken, he showed them *his* hands and *his* feet.

41. And while they yet believed not for joy, and wondered, he said unto them, Have ye here any meat?

42. And they gave him a piece of a broiled fish, and of a honeycomb.

43. And he took *it*, and did eat before them.

of the past week should have been no surprise to them. The Messiah would logically be expected to suffer and to enter into glory, because the OT had foreshadowed it. **27. And beginning at Moses.** From the first of Genesis to the last of Zechariah there were scattered prophecies of the coming Messiah. Our Lord's exposition of these passages has not been preserved as a discourse, but probably his explanations formed the basis of apostolic interpretations of the OT in the sermons in Acts and in the Epistles.

**29. Abide with us.** They were extending common courtesy to a stranger who had a longer journey before him, but had no shelter for the night. Because of the dangers of the road, people did not usually travel by night. **31. And their eyes were opened.** Their guest's assumption of the place of the host, and perhaps something in his gestures as he broke the bread revealed his identity.

**33. They rose up the same hour.** The discovery was so great that they could not wait until morning, but returned to Jerusalem immediately to inform the others of their experience. Their journey to Emmaus may have been a sample of the dispersion that would have taken place had not the disciples been held together in Jerusalem by the hope of further appearances of Christ. **34. The Lord . . . hath appeared to Simon.** No record of this interview with Peter has been preserved, except one allusion in I Cor 15:5. The effect on Peter is mentioned in I Pet 1:3 ff.

C. The Appearance to the Disciples. 24:36-43.

**36. Jesus himself stood in the midst.** The risen Christ seemed to have the ability to appear and disappear at will. His resurrected body possessed powers that transcended the laws of ordinary matter. **37. They were terrified and affrighted.** Obviously they were not expecting him, nor was this simply a hallucination. **39. Behold my hands and my feet.** The scars that he carried indicated his identity with the man whom they had seen crucified. **Handle me.** A ghost would not have been tangible. **41. While they yet believed not for joy.** Their attitude changed, but still the miracle was too great to be comprehended. **43. And he . . . did eat before them.** Ghosts do not consume food. Peter mentioned this convincing evidence when he

44. And he said unto them, These *are* the words which I spake unto you, while I was yet with you, that all things must be fulfilled, which were written in the law of Moses, and *in* the prophets, and *in* the psalms, concerning me.

45. Then opened he their understanding, that they might understand the Scriptures,

46. And said unto them, Thus it is written, and thus it behooved Christ to suffer, and to rise from the dead the third day:

47. And that repentance and remission of sins should be preached in his name among all nations, beginning at Jerusalem.

48. And ye are witnesses of these things.

49. And, behold, I send the promise of my Father upon you: but tarry ye in the city of Jerusalem, until he be endued with power from on high.

50. And he led them out as far as to Bethany, and he lifted up his hands, and blessed them.

51. And it came to pass, while he blessed them, he was parted from them, and carried up into heaven.

52. And they worshipped him, and returned to Jerusalem with great joy:

53. And were continually in the temple, praising and blessing God. Amen.

presented the Gospel to Gentiles (Acts 10:41).

**D. The Last Commission. 24:44-49.**

**44. And he said unto them.** This appearance was not his last, but it is the last Luke records before the Ascension. He has utilized it to bring out the message that Jesus expected his disciples to deliver to the world. **In the law of Moses, and in the prophets, and in the psalms.** These were the three main divisions of the Jewish canon of Scripture. The Prophets included some of the historical books, and the Psalms included other poetical books. **46. It behoved Christ to suffer, and to rise.** These two facts became the heart of apostolic preaching (cf. I Cor 15:3). **47. Repentance and remission of sins** were the doctrines stressed in the preaching at Pentecost (Acts 2:38). **Among all nations, beginning at Jerusalem.** The program outlined by Jesus accords exactly with the theme developed in Luke's second volume, The Acts of the Apostles (Acts 1:8).

**49. The promise of my Father.** The Lord referred to the Holy Spirit, whose coming had been promised in Joel 2:28, the passage that Peter used at Pentecost. **Tarry ye in the city.** Had the disciples dispersed immediately to their own homes, the movement would have been dissipated, and there would have been no united impact by the Spirit upon the world.

E. The Ascension. 24:50-53.

**51. While he blessed them, he was parted from them, and carried up into heaven.** The Western text omits "and was carried up into heaven," but comparison with Acts 1:9 confirms the genuineness of the accepted text.

# BIBLIOGRAPHY

### HISTORICAL BACKGROUND

HAYES, DOREMUS A. *The Synoptic Gospels and the Book of Acts.* New York: The Methodist Book Concern, n.d.

MACLACHLAN, H. *St. Luke, the Man and His Work.* London: Longmans, Green, & Co., 1920.

ROBERTSON, A. T. *Luke the Historian in the Light of Research.* New York: Charles Scribner's Sons, 1923.

### COMMENTARIES

GELDENHUYS, NORVAL. *Commentary on the Gospel of Luke (The New International Commentary on the New Testament).* Grand Rapids: Wm. B. Eerdmans Publishing Co., 1951.

GODET, FREDERIC. *A Commentary on the Gospel of Luke.* Translated from the second French edition by E. W. Shalders and M. D. Cusin. Third edition. New York: Funk & Wagnalls, Publishers, 1887.

MORGAN, G. CAMPBELL. *The Gospel According to St. Luke.* New York: Fleming H. Revell Co., 1931.

PLUMMER, ALFRED. *A Critical and Exegetical Commentary on the Gospel According to St. Luke (The International Critical Commentary).* Fifth Edition. Edinburgh: T. & T. Clark, 1922.

THOMAS, W. H. GRIFFITH. *Outline Studies in the Gospel of Luke.* Grand Rapids: Wm. B. Eerdmans Publishing Co., 1950.

# THE GOSPEL ACCORDING TO JOHN

## INTRODUCTION

*Character of the Book.* Simple in language and structure, this writing is nevertheless a profound exposition of the person of Christ in a historical setting. It has a message for the humble disciple of the Lord and for the most advanced theologian.

Certain similarities between it and the Synoptic Gospels are readily discernible. It presents the same person as its central figure. We read of him as Son of God, Son of man, Messiah, Lord, Saviour, etc. Not many years ago it was the fashion in some circles to conclude that the Jesus of John was the result of a theological process in the early church whereby the man of Nazareth had been elevated to the position of deity. This view is no longer tenable, for further study has brought the conviction that the Christology of the Synoptics and the Christology of John are fundamentally one and the same. A merely human Jesus is as much a stranger to the Synoptics as to John.

As the historical pattern unfolds in the Fourth Gospel, it is seen to resemble in its broad outline the course of events as portrayed in the Synoptics — the preparatory ministry of John the Baptist, the call of certain disciples to learn and serve, the twofold ministry of word and deed (miracle), the same tension between popular enthusiasm for the Lord and opposition from official Judaism, the crucial importance of the person and the authority of Jesus. Likewise, in respect to the closing events of Christ's life on earth, there is the same pattern of betrayal, arrest and trial, death by crucifixion, and resurrection.

To be sure, considerable diversity from the Synoptics is apparent also. Whereas the Synoptics mention only one Passover, and therefore seem to limit the ministry of Christ to one year, John mentions at least three Passovers (2:23; 6:4; 13:1), which suggests that the ministry was spread over three years. In the Synoptics the ministry is located almost in its entirety in Galilee, while John emphasizes the activity of Jesus in Judea and has little to say about the Galilean campaign. In the Synoptics the public teaching of our Lord revolves around "the kingdom of God." The expression is almost absent from the Fourth Gospel, where the discourses are centered largely in Jesus himself, his relation to the Father, and his indispensability to man in his spiritual need (cf. the *I am's*). Certain historical details raise problems. An example is the cleansing of the Temple, placed by John early in the ministry (chapter 2), but put at the close of the ministry by the Synoptic writers. The simplest explanation here is probably the true one — that there were two cleansings. Another example pertains to the call of the disciples, which according to the Synoptists occurred in Galilee. John narrates the call of several men in a Judean setting, at the very inception of the ministry (chapter 1). The problem is eased when one reflects that the very readiness of the Galilean fishermen to leave their nets and follow Jesus is most easily explained on the basis of prior acquaintance and tentative discipleship, such as the Fourth Gospel reveals. It is somewhat disturbing to find Jesus regarded as the Messiah in this Gospel at the very inception of his work (John 1), when the knowledge of the Messiahship seems to come at a much later time in the other Gospels. The two representations are not incompatible, however, for Peter's announcement at Caesarea-Philippi (Mt 16: 16) need not be understood as a conviction arrived at then for the first time (cf. Mt 14:33). Truth known before has now deepened through personal experience of the Son of God.

*Author.* Although the book does not name the writer, he is indicated as 'the beloved disciple' (21:20,23,24) and the close companion of Peter. The testimony of the ancient church is to the effect that this is John, the son of Zebedee (cf. 21: 2). Irenaeus is the chief witness. Some scholars have questioned whether one who was unschooled and inexperienced (Acts 4:13) could have written such a work. Time, motivation, and the enablement of the Spirit ought not to be underestimated in evaluating the ability of John and the overcoming of handicaps.

Many moderns prefer to hold that an unknown disciple is the actual author of this Gospel, even though most of the material may well go back to John as its source. But this is a needless exchange of a known for an unknown.

*Date and Place of Composition.* According to Christian tradition, John spent the latter years of his life at Ephesus, where he carried on a ministry of preaching and teaching, as well as writing. From this point he was exiled to Patmos in the reign of the Emperor Domitian. His Gospel seems to presuppose a knowledge of the Synoptic tradition and for this reason should be placed last in the series, possibly somewhere between 80 and 90. Some have put it even later. The discovery in Egypt of fragments of the Gospel, which have been dated from the first half of the second century, requires the writing of the Gospel within the limits of the first century.

*Purpose.* On the positive side this is stated in John 20:30,31 as the hope that conviction will be created in the readers that Jesus is the Christ, the Son of God, so that life will come through faith in him. The choice of material is calculated to lead to exactly this conclusion. Subordinate objectives may be allowed, such as the refutation of Docetism, a point of view that denied the true humanity of Jesus (cf. 1:14), and the exposure of Judaism as an inadequate system of religion that crowned its other sins by refusing its promised Messiah (1:11, etc.).

## OUTLINE

I. Prologue. 1:1-18.
II. Christ's ministry in the world. 1:19—12:50.
    A. The testimony of John the Baptist. 1:19-36.
    B. The gathering of disciples. 1:37-51.
    C. The wedding at Cana. 2:1-11.
    D. The first visit to Jerusalem and Judea. 2:12—3:36.
        1. The cleansing of the Temple. 2:12-22.
        2. The signs. 2:23-25.
        3. The Nicodemus incident. 3:1-15.
        4. The issues latent in the Gospel message. 3:16-21.
        5. Further witness from John the Baptist. 3:22-30.
        6. The credentials of Christ. 3:31-36.
    E. The mission to Samaria. 4:1-42.
    F. The healing of the nobleman's son. 4:43-54.
    G. The healing of the lame man in Jerusalem. 5:1-16.
    H. Jesus' self-defense. 5:17-47.
    I. The feeding of the five thousand and the discourse on the Bread of Life. 6:1-71.
    J. Jesus at the Feast of Tabernacles. 7:1-53.
    K. The woman taken in adultery. 8:1-11.
    L. The self-disclosure of Jesus. 8:12-59.
    M. The restoration of the man born blind. 9:1-41.
    N. Christ, the Good Shepherd. 10:1-42.
    O. The raising of Lazarus. 11:1-57.
    P. Jesus in Bethany and Jerusalem. 12:1-50.
III. Christ's ministry to his own. 13:1—17:26.
    A. The foot washing. 13:1-17.
    B. The announcement of the betrayal. 13:18-30.
    C. The upper room discourse. 13:31—16:33.
    D. The great prayer. 17:1-26.
IV. The sufferings and the glory. 18:1—20:31.
    A. The betrayal. 18:1-14.
    B. Jesus on trial before the Jews. 18:15-27.
    C. The ordeal before Pilate. 18:28—19:16.
    D. The crucifixion and burial. 19:17-42.
    E. The resurrection appearances. 20:1-29.
    F. The purpose of this Gospel. 20:30,31.
V. Epilogue. 21:1-25.

## ST. JOHN

### CHAPTER 1

IN the beginning was the Word, and the Word was with God, and the Word was God.

2. The same was in the beginning with God.

3. All things were made by him; and without him was not any thing made that was made.

4. In him was life; and the life was the light of men.

5. And the light shineth in darkness; and the darkness comprehended it not.

6. There was a man sent from God, whose name was John.

7. The same came for a witness, to bear witness of the Light, that all men through him might believe.

8. He was not that Light, but was sent to bear witness of that Light.

## COMMENTARY

### I. Prologue. 1:1-18.

Without delay the writer presents the central figure of the Gospel, but does not call him Jesus or Christ. At this point he is the Logos (Word). This term has OT roots, suggesting there the concepts of wisdom, power, and a special relation to God. It was widely used, too, by philosophers to express such ideas as reason and mediation between God and the world. In John's day all classes of readers would have understood its suitability here, where revelation is the keynote. But the unique feature is that the Logos is also the Son of the Father, who became incarnate in order to reveal God fully (1:14,18).

A. The Pre-existent Logos. 1:1,2. The **beginning** of the Gospel (cf. Mk 1:1) is tied in with the beginning of the creation (Gen 1:1) and reaches beyond it to a glimpse of the Godhead "before the world was" (cf. Jn 17:5). The Word did not become; he **was**. **With God** suggests equality as well as association. **The Word was God** (deity) without confusion of the persons.

B. The Cosmic Logos. 1:3-5. He was the agent in creation. **By him.** Through him.

3. **All things** embrace the totality of matter and existence, but viewed here in their individual status rather than as universe. 4. **Life** is **in him,** not simply through him. As the life, the Word communicated **light** (the knowledge of God) to **men.** 5. The **darkness** is primarily moral. Not everyone profits by the light (cf. 3:19). Probably the thought is not identical with 1:9,10; so **the darkness comprehended it not** is a less likely translation than *the darkness has not overcome it* (RSV).

C. The Incarnate Logos. 1:6-18. Included here is a summary of the mission of John the forerunner.

6. **Was.** Better, *came.* This is John's emergence in history, as **sent** from **God.** The phrase summarizes the material of Lk 1:5-80; 3:1-6. 7. John came for **witness** or testimony, which is a leading emphasis of this Gospel (1:15,34; 5:33, 36,37; 15:26,27; 19:35; 21:24). His commission was to witness to **the Light,** which had been shining ever since the Creation and was about to enlighten

9. *That* was the true Light, which lighteth every man that cometh into the world.

10. He was in the world, and the world was made by him, and the world knew him not.

11. He came unto his own, and his own received him not.

12. But as many as received him, to them gave he power to become the sons of God, *even* to them that believe on his name:

13. Which were born, not of blood, nor of the will of the flesh, nor of the will of man, but of God.

14. And the Word was made flesh, and dwelt among us, (and we beheld his glory, the glory as of the only begotten of the Father,) full of grace and truth.

men with his presence. The witness was designed to cause men to **believe** (the noun "faith" does not occur in this Gospel, but the verb is almost a refrain; cf. 20:31). **9. The true Light** does not make John a false light. It denotes light in the antitypical, ultimate sense— the sun, not a candle. Hence, to revere John unduly after the Light has dawned is wrong (3:30; Acts 19:1-7). The syntax of the verse in the Greek is difficult. *The true light that enlightens every man was coming into the world* (RSV) is the most probable rendering. By his presence among men the Logos would bring an illumination surpassing that which he had been affording men before his coming.

**10,11.** The Light was real and glowing, but the response was disappointing. Beyond this similarity in the two verses lie studied differences: **was, came; the world, his own; knew not, received not.** Failure to discern the preincarnate Logos is more understandable than the tragic refusal of his own people to receive him when he came among them.

**12,13.** Not all refused the Light. Those who received him gained **power** (authority, right) to **become** (then and there) **sons** (children) of God. Those who **received** are described as those who **believe on his name** (person). See 20:31. These are two ways of saying the same thing. Believers are further described in terms of what God does for them. They are **born . . . of God.** This is not a natural process such as brings people into the world—not of **blood** (literally, *bloods*), suggesting the mingling of paternal and maternal strains in procreation. **The will of the flesh** suggests the natural, human desire for children, as **the will of man** (the word for husband) suggests the special desire for progeny to carry on a family name. So the new birth, something supernatural, is carefully guarded from confusion with natural birth.

**14.** Before faith could bring about the new birth, it had to have an object on which to rest, even the incarnation of **the Word,** the Son of God. God, having expressed himself in creation and history, where the activity of the Logos was evident but his person veiled, now revealed himself through the Son in human form, which was no mere semblance, but flesh. John could have used "man" but he chose to state the truth of the incarnation emphatically so as to contradict

15. John bare witness of him, and cried, saying, This was he of whom I spake, He that cometh after me is preferred before me; for he was before me.

16. And of his fulness have all we received, and grace for grace.

17. For the law was given by Moses, *but* grace and truth came by Jesus Christ.

18. No man hath seen God at any time; the only begotten Son, which is in the bosom of the Father, he hath declared *him.*

19. And this is the record of John, when the Jews sent priests and Levites from Jerusalem to ask him, Who art thou?

those with Gnostic tendencies. This false view of Christ refused to acknowledge that pure deity could take a material body, since matter was regarded as something evil (cf. I Jn 4:2,3; II Jn 7). **Dwelt.** *Tabernacled.* In combination with **glory** it suggests the personalizing of the bright cloud that rested on the tabernacle in the wilderness (Ex 40:34). The Word incarnate is also the answer to Moses' prayer (Ex 33:18). John has no account of the Transfiguration, for he presents the whole ministry as a tranfiguration, except that the light he speaks of is moral and spiritual (full of grace and truth-rather than something visual (cf. Jn 1:17).

**15.** Further notice (cf. 1:7) is taken of the testimony of the Baptist in the light of Jesus' public appearance. Jesus came **after** John in time but went **before** him in importance, even as He was before him as the Eternal One (cf. 1:1). **16.** The Evangelist confirms the uniqueness of Christ. Not only John the Baptist but **all** believers have partaken of his **fulness** —the completeness of deity (cf. **full** in 1: 14). **Grace for grace** pictures one manifestation of grace as piled on another— a fullness indeed. **17.** As Jesus Christ surpassed John (1:15), so does He excel Moses. Both brought something from God, but the one brought **the law** which condemns; the other **grace** which redeems from law. **Truth** suggests the reality of Christ's revelation of God.

**18.** God is invisible, being Spirit (cf. 4:24; I Tim 6:16). Theophanies do not reveal his essence. But God's only **Son** (here the leading manuscripts have **God** rather than **Son**; cf. Jn 1:1) does. **In the bosom of the Father** recalls **with God** (1:1). The Son's mission was to **declare** (the Greek word gives us our "exegete") the Father. Christ interpreted God to man. Nothing is lost (cf. Heb 1:2,3; Gal 1:15).

## II. Christ's Ministry in the World. 1: 19—12:50.

A. The Testimony of John the Baptist. 1:19-36. In his burning desire to magnify Christ, John turned an inquiry about himself into a strong witness to the greater One about to manifest himself. Jesus' baptism at the hands of John, not narrated in this Gospel, had already occurred (see 1:26).

**19. The Jews.** As usual in John, this means leaders of the nation. These **priests** were of the Pharisees (v. 24). Two things

20. And he confessed, and denied not; but confessed, I am not the Christ.

21. And they asked him, What then? Art thou Elias? And he saith, I am not. Art thou that Prophet? And he answered, No.

22. Then said they unto him, Who art thou? that we may give an answer to them that sent us. What sayest thou of thyself?

23. He said, I *am* the voice of one crying in the wilderness, Make straight the way of the Lord, as said the prophet Esaias.

24. And they which were sent were of the Pharisees.

25. And they asked him, and said unto him, Why baptizest thou then, if thou be not that Christ, nor Elias, neither that Prophet?

26. John answered them, saying, I baptize with water: but there standeth one among you, whom ye know not;

27. He it is, who coming after me is preferred before me, whose shoe-latchet I am not worthy to unloose.

28. These things were done in Bethabara beyond Jordan, where John was baptizing.

29. The next day John seeth Jesus coming unto him, and saith, Behold the Lamb of God, which taketh away the sin of the world!

30. This is he of whom I said, After me cometh a man which is preferred before me; for he was before me.

31. And I knew him not: but that he should be made manifest to Israel, therefore am I come baptizing with water.

32. And John bare record, saying, I saw the Spirit descending from heaven like a dove, and it abode upon him.

prompted the deputation: the strong preaching of John, which captivated the multitudes (Mt 3:5), and his baptizing activity (Jn 1:26). Such a person excited so much concern in these leaders that they asked, **Who art thou?** 20. John read their thoughts. They, like the multitudes (Lk 3:15), were wondering if he could be the promised **Christ. 21.** His denial led to a second question. Elias (Elijah) was expected before the coming of the Messiah (Mal 4:5). Though John was not Elijah in person, he was that one in function (Mt 17:10-13). By **that prophet** we are probably to understand the prophet of Deut 18:15,18. By some he was taken to be distinct from the Messiah (Jn 7:40).

**22-24.** The deputation could not be satisfied with negations. Pressed to reveal his role, John replied in the language of prophecy (Isa 40:3). It was a true identification. John had lived in **the wilderness** and there had lifted up his **voice** to announce the near approach of the kingdom (Lk 1:80; 3:2,3). **25-28.** Such a minor role did not seem sufficient justification for John's administration of baptism. But he defended himself—it was merely **with water.** It proclaimed the presence of sin and the need of a purification which he himself could not effect. The ultimate work of purification (so he hinted) rested with a greater than he, One who was still an unknown to the authorities (1:26). John counted himself unworthy to be His servant. This conversation was held at **Bethabara,** east of Jordan. Leading manuscripts have *Bethany*, not to be confused with the Bethany of 11:1,18.

**29. The next day** introduces a new situation. The deputation had departed and Jesus appeared on the scene. Yet there was no conversation between him and John. Content with affirming to the Pharisees the greatness of Christ, John now became specific about His person and work. His own ministry was grounded on the fact of sin; that of Christ was concerned with sin's removal. Christ was God's **Lamb.** History (Ex 12:3) and prophecy (Isa 53:7) unite in providing the background for this title. The daily temple sacrifices may be in mind also.

**31-34.** When Jesus came to John's baptism, the Baptist did not recognize Him (cf. Lk 1:80), but he had received a sign of identification from God—**the Spirit descending from heaven like a dove** and remaining on Him. Along with the sign was given a word concerning

33. And I knew him not: but he that sent me to baptize with water, the same said unto me, Upon whom thou shalt see the Spirit descending, and remaining on him, the same is he which baptizeth with the Holy Ghost.

34. And I saw, and bare record that this is the Son of God.

35. Again the next day after, John stood, and two of his disciples;

36. And looking upon Jesus as he walked, he saith, Behold the Lamb of God!

37. And the two disciples heard him speak, and they followed Jesus.

38. Then Jesus turned, and saw them following, and saith unto them, What seek ye? They said unto him, Rabbi, (which is to say, being interpreted, Master,) where dwellest thou?

39. He saith unto them, Come and see. They came and saw where he dwelt, and abode with him that day: for it was about the tenth hour.

40. One of the two which heard John *speak*, and followed him, was Andrew, Simon Peter's brother.

41. He first findeth his own brother Simon, and saith unto him, We have found the Messias, which is, being interpreted, the Christ.

42. And he brought him to Jesus. And when Jesus beheld him, he said, Thou art Simon the son of Jona: thou shalt be called Cephas, which is by interpretation, A stone.

the work He should perform with the heavenly equipment thus given—He would baptize with the Spirit. Such a one, John knew, could be no less than **the Son of God.** No one of lesser stature could make such authoritative use of the divine Spirit. John gave three sterling testimonies to Christ s person and work. As the Lamb, His mission was to be one of redemption. As baptizer with the Spirit, He would found tne Church. As Son of God, He would be worthy of adoration and obedience.

35,36. These verses are transitional. They inform us that John had **disciples** and also that he desired to transfer them to Jesus. This was an important part of his work as forerunner, as the remainder of the chapter attests.

B. The Gathering of Disciples. 1:37-51. John's unselfish desire to glorify Christ bore fruit among his own followers. Without any command or suggestion from him in addition to his testimony, **two disciples** followed Jesus. One is identified as **Andrew.** Silence regarding the name of the other points to the writer of the Gospel, who withholds his name out of modesty.

37-42. **They followed Jesus.** The physical act expressed the intent to follow in a spiritual sense. **What seek ye?** Such a question could be a rebuff, but not when spoken kindly. The counterquestion, **Where dwellest thou?** like their following him, could suggest a deeper sense —What is the secret of your spiritual life and power? His abode could not have enticed them, but the lofty converse that followed lingered as a fragrant memory. Years later John remembered the **hour** of day—four in the afternoon.

41. The meaning of **first** is unclear. No further activity by Andrew is stated. Possibly **first** is intended to suggest that the other disciple (John) likewise sought out his brother James, who appears early in the Synoptic narratives as a follower of Jesus (Mk 1:16-20). **Findeth . . . found.** The narrative is alive with the joy of discovery (cf. Jn 1:43,45). **Messias,** the Hebrew term for "anointed one," has its counterpart in the Greek word **Christ.** Did Andrew dare to call Jesus the Christ because the Baptist had so identified Him to his followers, or because of the hours spent in Jesus' company? 42. Andrew's personal work began early and with his own kin. The change of name from **Simon** to **Cephas,** the Aramaic for Peter, meaning *stone,* probably

43. The day following Jesus would go forth into Galilee, and findeth Philip, and saith unto him, Follow me.

44. Now Philip was of Bethsaida, the city of Andrew and Peter.

45. Philip findeth Nathanael, and saith unto him, We have found him, of whom Moses in the law, and the prophets, did write, Jesus of Nazareth, the son of Joseph.

46. And Nathanael said unto him, Can there any good thing come out of Nazareth? Philip saith unto him, Come and see.

47. Jesus saw Nathanael coming to him, and saith of him, Behold an Israelite indeed, in whom is no guile!

48. Nathanael saith unto him, Whence knowest thou me? Jesus answered and said unto him, Before that Philip called thee, when thou wast under the fig tree, I saw thee.

49. Nathanael answered and saith unto him, Rabbi, thou art the Son of God; thou art the King of Israel.

50. Jesus answered and said unto him, Because I said unto thee, I saw thee under the fig tree, believest thou? thou shalt see greater things than these.

51. And he saith unto him, Verily, verily, I say unto you, Hereafter ye shall see heaven open, and the angels of God ascending and descending upon the Son of man.

denotes a promised change from weakness to stability and strength (Lk 22:31, 32).

43. Again the change of day is noted (cf. 1:29,35, in contrast to the absence of such features in the Prologue). This time Jesus does the finding (cf. Lk 19:10), and gives a command to Philip to follow (contrast Jn 1:37).

45-51. Philip vindicated Jesus' confidence in him as a disciple by finding Nathanael and breathing to him his conviction that Jesus of Nazareth was the long-awaited One who fulfilled the predictions of Moses and the prophets. One may witness to the Lord even if his understanding is incomplete or even faulty. Jesus of Nazareth revealed himself shortly as the heavenly Son of man (v. 51). Even Nathanael came quickly to perceive that the son of Joseph was the Son of God (v. 49). Nathanael's first impulse was to doubt that Nazareth was capable of producing any good thing, much less the Messiah (v. 46). This does not necessarily imply that the town had a bad reputation, but rather suggests the inconsequential character of the place. Come and see. Experience is better than argument. An Israelite without guile suggests a contrast to Jacob, who became Israel only by a conversion experience. The same penetration that read the heart of Simon (v. 42) like an open book and pierced to the inner life of Nathanael (vv. 47,48) was now cordially acknowledged in the latter's confession—Son of God...King of Israel. The shade of the fig tree, a quiet retreat for a reverent soul, had been silently shared by the discerning Christ. Philip realized that the teacher must be more than he saw in Him. And the end was not yet, for the Saviour promised greater things. Jacob was still in the background (v. 51). His vision of angels at Bethel would be surpassed as the disciples (ye) came to see in the Son of man the one to whom heaven was open (cf. Mt 3:16) and the one who, as Mediator, links heaven and earth. Son of man. A title denoting a supernatural, heavenly figure in Dan 7:13 and in the Jewish apocalypses, was Jesus' preferred method of designating himself, according to the Gospels. This name was preferable to "Messiah" because it did not suggest political aspirations along lines of a temporal kingdom such as most Jews were looking for. The glory of the Son (Jn 1:14), seen in part by these early followers (vv. 39, (46), was to unfold more hereafter.

## CHAPTER 2

AND the third day there was a marriage in Cana of Galilee; and the mother of Jesus was there:

2. And both Jesus was called, and his disciples, to the marriage.

3. And when they wanted wine, the mother of Jesus saith unto him, They have no wine.

4. Jesus saith unto her, Woman, what have I to do with thee? mine hour is not yet come.

5. His mother saith unto the servants, Whatsoever he saith unto you, do *it*.

6. And there were set there six waterpots of stone, after the manner of the purifying of the Jews, containing two or three firkins apiece.

7. Jesus saith unto them, Fill the waterpots with water. And they filled them up to the brim.

8. And he saith unto them, Draw out now, and bear unto the governor of the feast. And they bare *it*.

C. The Wedding at Cana. 2:1-11. This brief return to Galilee was not marked by public ministry, but involved an incident that bears on the deepening of the disciples' confidence in Jesus, continuing the emphasis of John 1. Some light is thrown on our Lord's relation to his mother and also on his attitude toward social life (cf. Mt 11:19). The turning of the water into wine is noted as his first miracle.

1. The third day seems to relate to 1:43. Two days or more would have been required for the journey to Cana, which was located about seven and a half miles north of Nazareth. John notes the presence of the mother of Jesus at the marriage. His avoidance of the name *Mary* here and in 19:26 may be due to a restraint similar to that which hides his own name. He had a special relation to Mary (19:27).

2. It is uncertain whether Jesus timed the journey in order to be present for the marriage or whether the invitation to him and his disciples came after their arrival in Galilee. If the latter is the correct alternative, the depletion of the supply of wine may be readily explained. Other guests may have arrived unexpectedly also. Nathanael, whose home was in Cana, possibly had something to do with the arrangements.

3-5. Mary came to Jesus with the tidings that the wine supply had been exhausted. In his reply, the use of Woman does not involve disrespect (cf. 19:26). What have I to do with thee? The words indicate division of interest and seem to suggest a measure of rebuke. Mary may have expected Jesus to use the situation to call attention to himself in a way that would have furthered his Messianic program. But his hour had not yet come. Later references point to the cross as the focal point of the hour (7:30; 8:20; 12:23; 13:1; 17:1). Jesus wanted his mother to understand that the former relationship between the two of them (Lk 2:51) was at an end. She was not to interfere in his mission. Mary wisely did not dispute the matter. If she could not command him, she could instruct the servants to obey his directions. Thus she showed her confidence in him.

6-8. In meeting the emergency, Jesus made use of six waterpots of stone, such as the Jews used for purifying—the washing of the hands before and after meals, and various ceremonial washings. Each would have held about twenty gallons.

9. When the ruler of the feast had tasted the water that was made wine, and knew not whence it was, (but the servants which drew the water knew,) the governor of the feast called the bridegroom,

10. And saith unto him, Every man at the beginning doth set forth good wine; and when men have well drunk, then that which is worse: *but* thou hast kept the good wine until now.

11. This beginning of miracles did Jesus in Cana of Galilee, and manifested forth his glory; and his disciples believed on him.

When these had been filled, Jesus instructed the servants to draw out. This seems to refer to the act of taking water out of the large containers by dipping from them and putting into smaller receptacles. What was drawn was then carried to the governor of the feast. Some consider that the governor was little more than a butler; others see in him a friend of the bridegroom who was requested to act as a master of ceremonies (cf. Ecclesiasticus 32:1ff.).

9,10. A taste of the wine assured this functionary that it was of superior quality, so much superior that he felt constrained to compliment the bridegroom for treating his guests with unusual consideration, giving them good wine at the end of the feast, when many would be so filled as not to be able to discern whether the wine was good or inferior. The shortage of wine was relieved by Jesus' intervention. The deeper truth is that, symbolically, Judaism is here revealed as deficient (in its stress upon ceremonial washings to the neglect of spiritual matters, and in its depletion, indicated by the empty water jars), whereas Christ brings fullness of blessing of the highest sort (cf. 7:37-39). Moreover, he does it without calling attention to himself, a refreshing example.

11. Beginning of miracles. This statement refutes the apocryphal Gospels which report boyhood miracles by Jesus. The word for miracle, which John uses throughout, means *sign*, indicating that the outward act is intended to reveal the purpose behind it, throwing light on the person of Christ or his work. Glory in this case is a term calling attention to the potency of Jesus to accomplish a spiritual transformation, as suggested by the changing of water into wine (cf. 11:40). His disciples believed on him. In contrast to the ruler of the feast, who was characterized by ignorance (v. 9) and to the servants, who had *knowledge* of the miracle (v. 9), the disciples were moved to *faith*. They alone truly profited by the sign.

D. The First Visit to Jerusalem and Judea. 2:12–3:36.

1) The Cleansing of the Temple. 2:12-22. Even though this is not called a sign, it was a more momentous event than the miracle at Cana, for it bore directly on the mission of Jesus, being a Messianic act of a public nature. Once again Judaism was shown to be deficient, and

12. After this he went down to Capernaum, he, and his mother, and his brethren, and his disciples; and they continued there not many days.

13. And the Jews' passover was at hand, and Jesus went up to Jerusalem,

14. And found in the temple those that sold oxen and sheep and doves, and the changers of money sitting:

15. And when he had made a scourge of small cords, he drove them all out of the temple, and the sheep, and the oxen; and poured out the changers' money, and overthrew the tables;

16. And said unto them that sold doves, Take these things hence; make not my Father's house a house of merchandise.

even corrupt, for the Father's house was being defiled. Jesus related the incident to his resurrection (vv. 19-21). It revealed the unbelief of the Jews (vv. 18-20) and the faith of the disciples (v. 22). As an event, it should be distinguished from a later cleansing prior to Jesus' death (Mk 11:15-19).

**12.** This verse is transitional. The importance of Capernaum for Jesus' ministry is stressed in the Synoptic Gospels. He made it his Galilean headquarters—"his own city" (Mt 9:1). The rift with his **Brethren** (brothers) had not yet developed (Jn 7:3-5).

**13.** The Jews' passover (cf. 2:6). Once again John is intent on exposing the deficiencies of Judaism. The sacred memorial of the deliverance from Egypt was being abused. Since it was Jesus' habit to observe the national festivals, as it had been the habit of Joseph and Mary (Lk 2:41), he went up to Jerusalem.

**14-16.** Jesus the worshiper now became a reformer. The Sanhedrin was permitting, and probably controlling for its own financial interest, a traffic in sacrificial animals and money changing. This traffic, carried on in the large area known as the Court of the Gentiles, was to the advantage of the pilgrim, since he could acquire his sacrifice here rather than bring it with him. Presumably there was a guarantee that the animal was "without blemish." Various kinds of coinage could be changed at the tables for the Palestinian half shekel required for the annual temple tax. This traffic turned the Temple into a mart of trade. Incensed at the sacrilege, Jesus went into action. Quickly he fashioned a **scourge** out of the ropes lying about the place. With this whip he drove the men **(them)** and the animals out of the temple area and upset the tables of the money changers, sending their coins ringing here and there on the pavement. The doves could not well be driven. It was necessary only that their owners take them out. Such strenuous measures needed justification, and it was found in this, that the **Father's house** had been perverted into a **house of merchandise**. The Lord had come suddenly to his Temple and had purified the sons of Levi (Mal 3:1-3). A deeper lesson than the removal of corruption may have been intended by this expulsion of sacrificial animals, even the anticipation of the day when the Temple and its sacrifices would be gone and the final sacrifice of the Lamb of God be achieved (cf. 2:21; 1:29).

17. And his disciples remembered that it was written, The zeal of thine house hath eaten me up.

18. Then answered the Jews and said unto him, What sign showest thou unto us, seeing that thou doest these things?

19. Jesus answered and said unto them, Destroy this temple, and in three days I will raise it up.

20. Then said the Jews, Forty and six years was this temple in building, and wilt thou rear it up in three days?

21. But he spake of the temple of his body.

22. When therefore he was risen from the dead, his disciples remembered that he had said this unto them; and they believed the Scripture, and the word which Jesus had said.

23. Now when he was in Jerusalem at the passover, in the feast *day*, many believed in his name, when they saw the miracles which he did.

24. But Jesus did not commit himself unto them, because he knew all *men*,

25. And needed not that any should testify of man; for he knew what was in man.

### CHAPTER 3

THERE was a man of the Pharisees, named Nicodemus, a ruler of the Jews:

17. The incident recalled to the disciples a passage in a Messianic psalm (69:9)—"Zeal for thy house will consume me" (RSV). A hint may be found here that this zeal, which cost him opposition at the moment, would eventually cost him his life (cf. Jn 2:19).

18-22. Such drastic action quickly brought a demand from the Jews (leaders) that Jesus produce an incontestable sign to show that he had authority for his conduct. He always resisted such a demand (6:30; Mt 16:1). This time he was content to point to the future. Destroy this temple. The figurative character of the utterance is evident, not only from Jn 2:21, but from the utter unlikelihood that the Jews would destroy their own Temple. These words are not to be taken as a command or invitation, but are in the nature of a hypothesis—"If you destroy, I will raise up." In three days is equivalent to "on the third day." Taking him literally, the Jews felt that his statement was ridiculous, since the Temple had required forty-six years to build. Herod had begun its reconstruction in 20 B.C. Some work still remained to be done, but the structure was sufficiently complete to be spoken of as built. (For the use of the figure temple for the body, see I Cor 6:19.) This prophecy helped to promote faith on the part of the disciples, but not until after the resurrection of their Lord from the dead (cf. Jn 12:16).

2) The Signs. 2:23-25. This section is transitional, having specially close connection with the following incident. It is summary in nature, picturing Jesus as performing various signs in Jerusalem that are left undescribed. The important thing is the response, which in this case was not rank unbelief, nor the full confidence in Christ attributed to the disciples, but something that may be called miracle-faith. Its unsatisfactory character is certified by the fact that Jesus did not commit himself unto these people, because he knew the human heart and discerned the lack of genuine trust. For somewhat similar instances, note 8:30-59; 12:42, 43.

3) The Nicodemus Incident. 3:1-15. In contrast to the many in Jerusalem who "believed" but to whom Jesus refused to commit himself, Nicodemus looms as one to whom the Lord opened his heart, one who became a true disciple. At the same time the passage em-

2. The same came to Jesus by night, and said unto him, Rabbi, we know that thou art a teacher come from God: for no man can do these miracles that thou doest, except God be with him.

3. Jesus answered and said unto him, Verily, verily, I say unto thee, Except a man be born again, he cannot see the kingdom of God.

4. Nicodemus saith unto him, How can a man be born when he is old? can he enter the second time into his mother's womb, and be born?

5. Jesus answered, Verily, verily, I say unto thee, Except a man be born of water and *of* the Spirit, he cannot enter into the kingdom of God.

6. That which is born of the flesh is flesh; and that which is born of the Spirit is spirit.

7. Marvel not that I said unto thee, Ye must be born again.

8. The wind bloweth where it listeth, and thou hearest the sound thereof, but canst not tell whence it cometh, and whither it goeth: so is every one that is born of the Spirit.

phasizes an earlier theme—the limitations of current Judaism—by showing the inability of this leader to comprehend the spiritual truth enunciated by Jesus.

**1,2.** The **Pharisees** were the religious leaders of the nation. Nicodemus not only belonged to this group, but was a **ruler of the Jews,** a member of the Sanhedrin. He came to see Jesus **by night,** probably out of expediency. The official attitude toward the Nazarene, after the cleansing of the Temple, must have been one of strong opposition. John may be suggesting also the blindness of this man concerning divine things. Nicodemus was ready to concede that Jesus was a **teacher** sent of God, the miracles being witness. This could mean that he was a prophet of greater power than John, who did no miracle. **We know** suggests that others were thinking along similar lines. Whether there is any intended hint that Jesus might be the Messiah is not clear. **3,4.** In the mind of Nicodemus the miracles may well have been indications of the speedy coming of the kingdom of God in a political sense. But Jesus introduced an entirely different concept of the kingdom, with the signs pointing to a spiritual reign of God. To be **born again** is to be born anew, from above. Nicodemus was nonplused. He knew that a man can not be born over again in a physical sense. Perhaps Jesus meant that it is just as impossible for one who is **old** to change his outlook and his ways.

**5-8.** Jesus now described the new birth in terms of **water** and **Spirit.** Of these two, Spirit is the more crucial (see v. 6). Water may well refer to the emphasis of John the Baptist on repentance and cleansing from sin as the necessary background for, even the negative side of, the new birth. Less natural is any allusion to the Word (I Pet 1:23). The positive ingredient is the injection of new creation life by the regenerating power of the Spirit (cf. Tit 3:5). **Ye must be born again.** This is not merely a personal but a universal demand. The necessity lies in the inadequacy of **the flesh.** This includes what is merely natural and what is sinful—man as he is born into this world and lives his life apart from God's grace. Flesh can only reproduce itself as flesh, and this cannot pass muster with God (cf. Rom 8:8). The law of reproduction is "after its kind." So likewise the Spirit produces spirit, a life born, nurtured, and matured by the Spirit of God. If this spells mystery, let it be recognized that there is mystery in nature also. **Wind**

9. Nicodemus answered and said unto him, How can these things be?

10. Jesus answered and said unto him, Art thou a master of Israel, and knowest not these things?

11. Verily, verily, I say unto thee, We speak that we do know, and testify that we have seen; and ye receive not our witness.

12. If I have told you earthly things, and ye believe not, how shall ye believe, if I tell you *of* heavenly things?

13. And no man hath ascended up to heaven, but he that came down from heaven, *even* the Son of man which is in heaven.

14. And as Moses lifted up the serpent in the wilderness, even so must the Son of man be lifted up:

15. That whosoever believeth in him should not perish, but have eternal life.

(*pneuma*, the same word as for "Spirit") produces observable effects as it blows, but its source and future movements remain hidden. So the redeemed life shows itself as something effective, though defying analysis by the natural man (cf. I Cor 2:15).

**9,10.** The perplexity of Nicodemus drew a gentle rebuke from Jesus. Could it be that **a master** (lit., *the teacher*) **of Israel** did not know these things? They were not new (Ezk 11:19). A spiritual kingdom and a spiritual life to match it are not foreign to the teaching of the OT.

**11-13.** Furthermore, others could testify to the reality of these things—**we speak.** Jesus was pleased to associate his followers with himself. **Ye** (you and others like you) receive not the witness. **Earthly things** are the things already discussed, such as the nature of the kingdom and of spiritual birth and life. **Heavenly things** are matters which the Son of man, by his coming down from heaven, had to reveal as new and distinctive (cf. Mt 11:25-27). The last four words of 3:13 are not contained in the leading manuscripts.

**14,15.** There is another **must** answering to the imperative of the new birth (cf. 3:7). The lifting up of the Son of man cannot well refer to the Ascension, in view of the elevation of the brazen **serpent** on a pole (Num 21:8), with which it is here compared. The allusion is to the cross (Jn 12:32,33). As men afflicted with the bite of the deadly serpent looked with expectancy and hope toward that which resembled the reptile that had set the virus of death flowing in their veins, so sinners must look in faith to Christ their substitute, who came in the likeness of sinful flesh and for sin (Rom 8:3). The issue of such faith is **eternal life.** Apart from this faith one must **perish.** This is not annihilation but the tragedy of being cut off eternally from God. Apparently Nicodemus took to heart the warning and the challenge (Jn 7:50,51; 19:39,40). At this point, it seems, the words of Jesus cease and those of John resume, judging from the phraseology, which has several analogies to other portions of the Gospel where John is unquestionably responsible for the material.

4) The Issues Latent in the Gospel Message. 3:16-21. Love for sin prompts men to reject the light of Christ, whereas those who welcome the light are ready to put their trust in him.

16. For God so loved the world, that he gave his only begotten Son, that whosoever believeth in him should not perish, but have everlasting life.

17. For God sent not his Son into the world to condemn the world; but that the world through him might be saved.

18. He that believeth on him is not condemned: but he that believeth not is condemned already, because he hath not believed in the name of the only begotten Son of God.

19. And this is the condemnation, that light is come into the world, and men loved darkness rather than light, because their deeds were evil.

20. For every one that doeth evil hateth the light, neither cometh to the light, lest his deeds should be reproved.

21. But he that doeth truth cometh to the light, that his deeds may be made manifest, that they are wrought in God.

22. After these things came Jesus and his disciples into the land of Judea; and there he tarried with them, and baptized.

23. And John also was baptizing in Aenon near to Salim, because there was much water there: and they came, and were baptized.

24. For John was not yet cast into prison.

**16,17.** John enlarges on the statement of Jesus (3:15), retaining **whosoever, perish, believeth, eternal** (*everlasting* also translates the same Greek word) **life.** The added elements are the love of God and the consequent giving of his Son, who is described as the **only begotten.** This means unique, one of a kind. Sons by adoption do not become members of the Godhead. The breadth of the divine love is emphasized in that its object is the (whole) **world.** Though the coming of Christ involved judgment, as the rest of this section attests, the direct purpose of that coming, resting on the divine love, was not condemnation but salvation (3:17).

**18-21.** The believer in Christ does not come into judgment for his sins either now or in the future (the verb form is flexible enough to cover both aspects). On the other hand, the one who refuses to believe stands judged by virtue of that refusal. He has decided his own fate. The essential idea in judgment is a distinction, a separation (the root meaning of the word); and the coming of Christ as the light proved a great dividing influence. Instead of responding to the love of God by loving his Son, most men loved the darkness in preference to the light because they were attached to their pattern of life, which was **evil** (wicked). In 3:20 evil is a different word, denoting what is morally worthless. The offender knows he is enmeshed in wrong, but refuses to advance into the light of Christ lest his deeds, which he loves, be exposed. On the other hand, the one who comes to the light is described as one who **doeth truth.** He acts in accordance with what he knows to be right (cf. 18:37). This conformity to what he knows to be the truth prepares him to advance into the full light of Christ and be saved. All his works are **wrought in God,** who has been leading him to this climax of faith (cf. 1:47).

5) Further Witness from John the Baptist. 3:22-30. The fact that Jesus and his disciples carried on a work of preaching and baptizing in Judea while John and his followers conducted a similar work in another area led to the suspicion that the two were in competition. John denied this emphatically, gladly taking a role of subordination to Jesus.

**22-24. After these things.** The Nicodemus episode is ended. **The land of Judea** is named in distinction from Jerusalem, where Jesus had been laboring (2:13—3:21). Jesus' baptizing activity presupposes

**25.** Then there arose a question between *some* of John's disciples and the Jews about purifying.

**26.** And they came unto John, and said unto him, Rabbi, he that was with thee beyond Jordan, to whom thou bearest witness, behold, the same baptizeth, and all *men* come to him.

**27.** John answered and said, A man can receive nothing, except it be given him from heaven.

**28.** Ye yourselves bear me witness, that I said, I am not the Christ, but that I am sent before him.

**29.** He that hath the bride is the bridegroom: but the friend of the bridegroom, which standeth and heareth him, rejoiceth greatly because of the bridegroom's voice: this my joy therefore is fulfilled.

**30.** He must increase, but I *must* decrease.

**31.** He that cometh from above is above all: he that is of the earth is earthly, and speaketh of the earth: he that cometh from heaven is above all.

preaching. His relation to baptism seems to have been only supervisory (cf. 4:2; I Cor 1:14). Aenon and Salim have not been positively identified but are now thought to have been a few miles east of Mount Gerizim, rather than south of Bethshan in the upper Jordan Valley. **They came.** People generally, who were interested in John's message. John's imprisonment is noted here as something familiar to the readers, since it is reported in all the Synoptic Gospels.

**25,26.** John's disciples were drawn into an altercation with some Jews (there is good basis for reading *a Jew* here) over the issue of purifying. The writer does not tell us whether this means purification in general as practiced by the Jews, or the baptism practiced by John and Jesus over against those purifyings, or the baptisms of John and Jesus in contrast to each other. Perhaps the last is the most likely, in view of the sequel. **They came.** Probably John's disciples. **He.** Failure to mention Jesus more definitely seems like studied depreciation. John's disciples were concerned over the waning position of their leader. The crowds were now thronging Jesus.

**27-30.** The Baptist deplored any thought of rivalry between himself and Jesus. His own place, given by God (**from heaven**), was not that of the Christ but that of the forerunner (v. 28). His position was not that of the Bridegroom, who should take the people of God to himself. This was reserved for Another. Rather, he was the friend of the Bridegroom. It was the function of such a man to act as go-between in making the marriage arrangements. His **joy** was vicarious—participation in the happiness of the groom as a new family was formed. John's work was done in launching the work of Jesus. He could baptize only with water, not with the Spirit. He could announce the coming of the kingdom but not enter into it himself. His cause had to fade, in the nature of the case, as that of Jesus increased (v. 30). This was God's plan. And so Jesus, in addition to being superior to Judaism, was superior to the movement that centered about John (cf. Acts 19:1-3).

6) The Credentials of Christ. 3:31-36. Here the Evangelist reflects on the distinctives of Jesus, especially as these set him apart from the Baptist. He has a heavenly origin, which puts him above earthlings and earthly things (cf. 3:13). He bears his testimony to what he sees and hears, a testimony to heavenly things (cf. 16:13). Only regenerate men, those born

32. And what he hath seen and heard, that he testifieth; and no man receiveth his testimony.

33. He that hath received his testimony hath set to his seal that God is true.

34. For he whom God hath sent speaketh the words of God: for God giveth not the Spirit by measure *unto him*.

35. The Father loveth the Son, and hath given all things into his hand.

36. He that believeth on the Son hath everlasting life: and he that believeth not the Son shall not see life; but the wrath of God abideth on him.

## CHAPTER 4

WHEN therefore the Lord knew how the Pharisees had heard that Jesus made and baptized more disciples than John.

2. (Though Jesus himself baptized not, but his disciples,)

3. He left Judea, and departed again into Galilee.

4. And he must needs go through Samaria.

5. Then cometh he to a city of Samaria, which is called Sychar, near to the parcel of ground that Jacob gave to his son Joseph.

6. Now Jacob's well was there. Jesus therefore, being wearied with *his* journey, sat thus on the well: *and* it was about the sixth hour.

7. There cometh a woman of Samaria to draw water: Jesus saith unto her, Give me to drink.

8. (For his disciples were gone away unto the city to buy meat.)

9. Then saith the woman of Samaria unto him, How is it that thou, being a Jew, askest drink of me, which am a woman of Samaria? for the Jews have no dealings with the Samaritans.

10. Jesus answered and said unto her, If thou knewest the gift of God, and who it is that saith to thee, Give me to drink; thou wouldest have asked of him, and he would have given thee living water.

of the Spirit, can appreciate his testimony (Nicodemus was in the background of John's thought here). Those who do receive his testimony need no other authentication (cf. I Jn 5:10). Christ declares the words of God (Jn 3:34) as a faithful witness. The fullness of those words, as well as their accuracy, is guaranteed by the unmeasured gift of the Spirit granted to him. The original suggests that through him the same Spirit is given to others without measure (cf. 1:33). Further, the Christ is the special object of God's love and is the custodian of divine riches (cf. 16:15; Mt 11:27). He is the touchstone of eternal life or abiding wrath (Jn 3:36).

### E. The Mission to Samaria. 4:1-42.

Samaria, a territory to be avoided if possible by Jews, became the scene of a spiritual triumph: a well, a woman, a witness, the winning of a harvest of Samaritans to faith. Samaritanism as well as Judaism needed the corrective of Christ; it needed to be replaced by new creation life.

1-4. The growing popularity of Jesus, exceeding that of John, began to come to the ears of the Pharisees. To avoid trouble with them at this time, Jesus determined to leave the area and go into Galilee. This is where most of his work was done, according to the Synoptic records. He must go through Samaria. Ordinarily in John this word points to a divine necessity, and it may do so here, indicating the need of dealing with the Samaritans and opening to them the gateway to life. Along with this may be the more evident need of reaching Galilee by the most direct route.

5,6. Sychar (very likely Sychem, i.e., Shechem) was a few miles southeast of the city of Samaria and fairly close to Mount Gerizim as well as to the ground given by Jacob to Joseph (Gen 48:22). Jacob left also a well as a legacy (Jn 4:6). This is reported to be about eighty-five feet in depth. Here Jesus, wearied with the journey and the midday (sixth hour) heat, paused to rest.

7-10. A woman of Samaria. Not a reference to the city of Samaria, which was too far away, but to the territory of the Samaritans. She came equipped to draw water. Since the village of Sychar had water, it is possible that the woman's solitary journey to Jacob's well from day to day indicates a species of ostracism by the other women of the community (cf. 4:18). Jesus broke the silence with a request for a drink. It was a natural request in view of

11. The woman saith unto him, Sir, thou hast nothing to draw with, and the well is deep: from whence then hast thou that living water?

12. Art thou greater than our father Jacob, which gave us the well, and drank thereof himself, and his children, and his cattle?

13. Jesus answered and said unto her, Whosoever drinketh of this water shall thirst again:

14. But whosoever drinketh of the water that I shall give him shall never thirst; but the water that I shall give him shall be in him a well of water springing up into everlasting life.

15. The woman saith unto him, Sir, give me this water, that I thirst not, neither come hither to draw.

16. Jesus saith unto her, Go, call thy husband, and come hither.

17. The woman answered and said, I have no husband. Jesus said unto her, Thou hast well said, I have no husband:

18. For thou hast had five husbands; and he whom thou now hast is not thy husband: in that saidst thou truly.

his weariness. It is a poignant reminder of our Lord's humanity. Whether the request was fulfilled or not (the latter seems more probable), it led to conversation. The departure of the disciples was providential, for the woman would not have entered into discussion with Jesus in their presence. Two things amazed the woman: that Jesus would make such a request of a woman, for a rabbi avoided contact with women in public; and particularly that he would speak thus to one who was a Samaritan. In explanation of her amazement, the writer adds the observation that Jews had no dealings with Samaritans. This cannot be taken in an absolute sense, for it is refuted by verse 8. It may point to the bad feeling between the two people. The Jews despised the Samaritans because they were a mixed people in blood and in religion, who nevertheless possessed the Pentateuch and professed to worship the God of Israel. A narrower meaning has been proposed for the woman's saying — "Jews do not make common use (of vessels) with Samaritans." This fits the situation well (D. Daube, *The New Testament and Rabbinic Judaism,* pp. 375-382). In his reply Jesus moved away from his own need to suggest that the woman had one which was deeper, one he was able to supply through **the gift of God.** Some explain this in personal terms as referring to Christ himself (3:16), but it is probably better to make it equivalent to **living water.** John 7:37-39 is the best commentary (cf. Rev 21:6).

11,12. Thinking in terms of the well beneath them, the woman was puzzled. Jesus had no utensil for drawing and the well was deep. At the bottom was the **living** (running) **water** fed by a spring. Could this rabbi hope to conjure up what Jacob secured only by hard toil? He would indeed be **greater** if he could do this.

13-15. Water from the well had to be consumed again and again, but the water Christ dispenses will so satisfy that one **shall never thirst.** Such is the refreshment of **everlasting life.** A parallel may be drawn with the repeated sacrifices of the old covenant and the one-for-all sacrifice of the Lamb of God. Still misunderstanding, but now receptive, the woman asked for such water, that her lot might be easier (4:15).

16-18. Before the woman could receive the gift of living water, she had to be made to realize how desperately she needed it. This gift was for the inner life, which in her case was empty indeed. **Thy husband ....no husband... five husbands ... not thy husband.** The dreary history of her

19. The woman saith unto him, Sir, I perceive that thou art a prophet.

20. Our fathers worshipped in this mountain; and ye say, that in Jerusalem is the place where men ought to worship.

21. Jesus saith unto her, Woman, believe me, the hour cometh, when ye shall neither in this mountain, nor yet at Jerusalem, worship the Father.

22. Ye worship ye know not what: we know what we worship; for salvation is of the Jews.

23. But the hour cometh, and now is, when the true worshippers shall worship the Father in spirit and in truth: for the Father seeketh such to worship him.

24. God *is* a Spirit: and they that worship him must worship *him* in spirit and in truth.

25. The woman saith unto him, I know that Messias cometh, which is called Christ: when he is come, he will tell us all things.

26. Jesus saith unto her, I that speak unto thee am *he.*

27. And upon this came his disciples, and marveled that he talked with the woman: yet no man said, What seekest thou? or, Why talkest thou with her?

28. The woman then left her waterpot, and went her way into the city, and saith to the men,

29. Come, see a man, which told me all things that ever I did: is not this the Christ?

30. Then they went out of the city, and came unto him.

marital life was unfolded by Jesus' penetration and by her own admission. It is probable that divorce entered into at least some of the five relationships which preceded the final illegitimate status. Morally, the woman had been going downhill for some time.

**19,20.** To the woman, Jesus was first a Jew, then one entitled to be called **Sir,** and now a **prophet.** He had looked into her soul. The reference to worship on nearby Mount Gerizim, established in competition to that of the Jews at Jerusalem, may have been a diversionary tactic, but more likely it was an indication of a heart hunger to know the way to God.

**21-24. The hour cometh.** In the new order that Christ has come to inaugurate, the place of worship is subordinated to the Person. The important thing is that men **worship the Father,** whom the Son has come to declare. By using **ye,** Jesus may be anticipating the conversion of the Samaritan men. The Samaritan worship was a confused thing (cf. II Kgs 17: 33). **Salvation is of the Jews** in the sense that special revelation came to them concerning the right approach to God; and Jesus himself, as the Saviour, came from this people (Rom 9:5). **The hour . . . now is.** Even before the new dispensation is inaugurated in its universalistic character, true worshipers are privileged to worship God as Father **in spirit and in truth. Spirit** seems to glance back at Jerusalem and its worship in terms of letter (the Law), whereas **truth** is in contrast to the inadequate and false worship of the Samaritans. The new kind of worship is imperative because God is **Spirit** (not *a* Spirit).

**25,26.** The woman's allusion to the Messiah was probably based on Deut 18: 15-18, which was accepted by the Samaritans as Scripture. As the prophet par excellence, the Messiah would be able to **tell . . . all things.** This wistful projection into the future was unnecessary. **I that speak unto thee am he.** It would have been dangerous for Jesus to announce himself in this fashion among the Jews, where ideas of Messiahship were politically colored. Here, apparently, he judged it to be safe. The seed was planted, and just in time, for the conversation was ended by the arrival of the disciples.

**27-30.** The disciples marveled that Jesus would break convention by talking with the woman (see on v. 9). But reverence for their teacher kept them from open questioning. Unimpeded by her **waterpot,** the woman retired with all

31. In the mean while his disciples prayed him, saying, Master, eat.

32. But he said unto them, I have meat to eat that ye know not of.

33. Therefore said the disciples one to another, Hath any man brought him *aught* to eat?

34. Jesus saith unto them, My meat is to do the will of him that sent me, and to finish his work.

35. Say not ye, There are yet four months, and *then* cometh harvest? behold, I say unto you, Lift up your eyes, and look on the fields; for they are white already to harvest.

36. And he that reapeth receiveth wages, and gathereth fruit unto life eternal: that both he that soweth and he that reapeth may rejoice together.

37. And herein is that saying true, One soweth, and another reapeth.

38. I sent you to reap that whereon ye bestowed no labor: other men labored, and ye are entered into their labors.

39. And many of the Samaritans of that city believed on him for the saying of the woman, which testified, He told me all that ever I did.

40. So when the Samaritans were come unto him, they besought him that he would tarry with them: and he abode there two days.

41. And many more believed because of his own word;

42. And said unto the woman, Now we believe, not because of thy saying: for we have heard *him* ourselves, and know that this is indeed the Christ, the Saviour of the world.

speed to the town, her act pledging her purpose to return and proclaiming her determination to have the living water henceforth. She did more than Jesus asked, going not to one man, but to **the men** of the place with the news of her exciting experience. She did not presume to teach them, but put a thought in their minds, phrased tentatively: Is this, perchance, the Christ? The men were sufficiently impressed to go along with her to the well.

**31-38.** Meanwhile the disciples pressed Jesus to take food, but he declined on the ground that he had nourishment of which they were ignorant. This, he explained, was the doing of God's **will** (v. 34). He had been doing this in their absence, and he had done it in the light of the cross, where he would **finish** God's appointed work (cf. 17:4; 19:30). His ministry was one of both sowing and reaping. **Four months** till **harvest** would be a normal expectation in the natural realm, but by lifting up their eyes the disciples could see a harvest already **white** (the approaching Samaritans), the result of his sowing (4:35). In spiritual work, **sower** and **reaper** are ordinarily different persons, who rejoice together in what their combined efforts have accomplished (vv. 36,37). Here in Samaria and in many other situations the disciples, although not the sowers of the seed, might reap. **Others** may include Jesus and the woman of Samaria. In a sense even Moses may belong here, as being humanly responsible for implanting the seed of Messianic expectation in the heart of the woman.

**39-42.** Here we learn of the fruit which Christ and the woman were able to gather as sower and reaper. **Many** believed on the Lord because of the woman's testimony. This led to an invitation to stay in their midst, which Christ consented to do for **two days.** During those days, others who had heard the woman's testimony and had been inclined to believe in Jesus became full-fledged believers because of what they received through **his own word,** i.e., from Jesus' own lips (v. 42). **Saviour of the world** — a grateful confession, since it meant that Samaritans as well as Jews could be saved.

**F. The Healing of the Nobleman's Son. 4:43-54.**

This incident is the only item of ministry reported by John in connection with this visit of Jesus to Galilee. The boy, lying sick at Capernaum, was healed by

43. Now after two days he departed thence, and went into Galilee.

44. For Jesus himself testified, that a prophet hath no honor in his own country.

45. Then when he was come into Galilee, the Galileans received him, having seen all the things that he did at Jerusalem at the feast: for they also went unto the feast.

46. So Jesus came again into Cana of Galilee, where he made the water wine. And there was a certain nobleman, whose son was sick at Capernaum.

47. When he heard that Jesus was come out of Judea into Galilee, he went unto him, and besought him that he would come down, and heal his son: for he was at the point of death.

48. Then said Jesus unto him, Except ye see signs and wonders, ye will not believe.

49. The nobleman saith unto him, Sir, come down ere my child die.

50. Jesus saith unto him, Go thy way; thy son liveth. And the man believed the word that Jesus had spoken unto him, and he went his way.

51. And as he was now going down, his servants met him, and told him, saying, Thy son liveth.

52. Then inquired he of them the hour when he began to amend. And they said unto him, Yesterday at the seventh hour the fever left him.

53. So the father knew that it was at the same hour, in the which Jesus said unto him, Thy son liveth: and himself believed, and his whole house.

54. This is again the second miracle that Jesus did, when he was come out of Judea into Galilee.

## CHAPTER 5

AFTER this there was a feast of the Jews; and Jesus went up to Jerusalem.

Jesus' word when He was at Cana, miles away.

**43-45.** The meaning of Jesus' **own country** has been much discussed. Possibly the easiest solution is that Galilee as a whole is meant. A lack of honor was to be expected there in contrast to the growing popularity accorded him in Judea (3:26; 4:1). The fact that Galileans who had been at Jerusalem and had seen his miracles there were ready to welcome him does not put them in the class of true and permanent believers (cf. 2:23-25; 4:48). Eventually the Galileans would desert him (6:66).

While at Cana, Jesus had a visit from a certain nobleman (*basilikos*, indicating a royal figure or one in royal service). The father's hope of getting healing from Jesus for his son seems to have been based on contact with Galileans who had seen our Lord's miracles at Jerusalem (4:47; cf. v. 45). Having journeyed from Capernaum to Cana, the father made repeated and urgent request (*ērōta*) that Jesus would come down and heal the boy. Jesus expressed fear that the father, like so many others, was so preoccupied with the report of wonders performed that he would not **believe.** More important than the boy's health was the father's faith. The father's reply breathes the desperation of need (cf. Mk 9:22-24). Jesus proved himself worthy of faith and also sympathetic to the suppliant's feelings — Go thy way; thy son liveth. His faith developing fast, the man believed **the word** of Christ apart from any visible sign, and went his way satisfied.

**51-54.** The servants of the nobleman, anxiously watching their master's son in his absence, noted the drastic change in his condition and started out to meet the father with the good news. The nobleman himself, already restful in his faith, was interested now in learning the time of the change. When he compared the time of the departure of the fever with the time of his interview with Jesus, he knew the healing was no accident. He himself believed. His faith was confirmed by experience. Faith spread to the entire household (v. 53). At the first Cana miracle the disciples had believed. The **second** miracle from the same spot resulted in a wider circle of faith.

G. The Healing of the Lame Man in Jerusalem. 5:1-16.

Both the time and the place of this miracle have been much disputed. If this feast of the Jews was the Passover, then

2. Now there is at Jerusalem by the sheep *market* a pool, which is called in the Hebrew tongue Bethesda, having five porches.

3. In these lay a great multitude of impotent folk, of blind, halt, withered, waiting for the moving of the water.

4. For an angel went down at a certain season into the pool, and troubled the water: whosoever then first after the troubling of the water stepped in was made whole of whatsoever disease he had.

5. And a certain man was there, which had an infirmity thirty and eight years.

6. When Jesus saw him lie, and knew that he had been now a long time *in that case*, he saith unto him, Wilt thou be made whole?

7. The impotent man answered him, Sir, I have no man, when the water is troubled, to put me into the pool: but while I am coming, another steppeth down before me.

four such feasts are mentioned in John, making the ministry extend to approximately three and a half to four years, provided John lists them all (the others are 2:23; 6:4; 11:55). Since the best manuscript authorities lack the definite article, some feast other than the Passover is probably intended. The place of the miracle may now be identified with some confidence, following the excavation in 1888 of such a pool as John describes, located in the northeastern part of Jerusalem, near the Church of St. Anne. The various readings in the manuscripts for the name of the pool are bewildering. Beth-zatha (RSV) is well attested. It probably means "House of Olives."

**2-4.** The five porches or porticoes, now uncovered, sheltered a great company of sick, some **blind,** others **lame,** others **withered,** i.e., paralyzed. They were there in hope of being healed when the water was troubled. While our manuscript tradition is such that the end of verse 3 and all of verse 4 cannot be regarded as part of the original text of John, this portion is an early tradition. J. Rendel Harris found evidence in several places throughout the East of a superstition to the effect that at the New Year an angel was expected to stir the water in certain localities, enabling one person to obtain healing by being the first to get into the water after the disturbance. On this basis he judged the feast of this chapter to have been Trumpets, announcing the New Year (so Westcott. See J. Rendel Harris, *Side Lights on New Testament Research,* pp. 36-69). The remains of the Church of St. Anne include the figure of an angel, testifying to this belief and the custom of seeking healing under these special circumstances.

**5-7.** There is nothing to indicate the precise nature of the ailment that had gripped this sick man for so many years, except that he could not move without help. It is not at all likely that he remained there all this time. Rather, he was brought when the moving of the water was expected. Jesus **knew.** Since nothing is said of the impartation of knowledge by others, we are to conclude that here, as with Nathanael and the woman of Samaria, Jesus discerned the true state of affairs by his own power of perception. **Wilt thou be made whole?** In this case Jesus took the initiative. The question was not needless, for many who are chronic invalids have no hope of cure. Others use their sickness as a means of eliciting sympathy, hence do not really

8. Jesus saith unto him, Rise, take up thy bed, and walk.

9. And immediately the man was made whole, and took up his bed, and walked: and on the same day was the sabbath.

10. The Jews therefore said unto him that was cured, It is the sabbath day: it is not lawful for thee to carry *thy* bed.

11. He answered them, He that made me whole, the same said unto me, Take up thy bed, and walk.

12. Then asked they him, What man is that which said unto thee, Take up thy bed, and walk?

13. And he that was healed wist not who it was: for Jesus had conveyed himself away, a multitude being in *that* place.

14. Afterward Jesus findeth him in the temple, and said unto him, Behold, thou art made whole: sin no more, lest a worse thing come unto thee.

15. The man departed, and told the Jews that it was Jesus, which had made him whole.

16. And therefore did the Jews persecute Jesus, and sought to slay him, because he had done these things on the sabbath day.

17. But Jesus answered them, My Father worketh hitherto, and I work.

18. Therefore the Jews sought the more to kill him, because he not only had broken the sabbath, but said also that God was his Father, making himself equal with God.

want to be healed. The sick man had the desire for healing, but lacked the means (v. 7). **8,9.** Three commands by Jesus imply the impartation of strength. The healing was instantaneous. **Bed.** Mattress or pallet.

**10-13.** Quickly the healing became the subject of dispute, because it had been performed on **the sabbath day. The Jews.** In this case not the common people, but their rulers (cf. 1:19). Apparently they observed the man walking through the streets toward his home, carrying his pallet. This violated the Sabbath rest (Jer 17:21). In his confusion, the healed man could only explain that his benefactor had commanded him to do this very thing (Jn 5:11). He could not identify the healer, for he had not learned his name, and now it seemed impossible to find out, for Jesus had left the scene.

**14-16.** Because he was not guilty of intentional violation of the Law, the healed man was permitted to go his way. Later on he proceeded to the Temple to give thanks for his healing. There Jesus found him and gave him a message of warning. **Sin no more, lest a worse thing come unto thee.** Physical healing at Jesus' hands may be supposed to include forgiveness of sins (cf. Mk 2:9-12). This forgiveness must not be lightly accepted. The **worse thing** is left undefined, and the warning is the more effective for this reason. Returning to the Jews, the man identified Jesus as the healer, probably not because he had taken offense at Jesus' warning, but because he felt an obligation, as a member of the community, to supply information sought by the authorities. This led the rulers to **persecute** Jesus. To them his guilt as a lawbreaker was plain. He had violated the Sabbath. **These things** are not defined. The verb is "he was doing," as though to suggest there were other similar grievances. The words **and sought to slay him** lack sufficient manuscript authority.

H. Jesus' Self-defense. 5:17-47.

The following discourse deals with the authority of Jesus, which he grounds in his special relation to the Father.

**17,18.** Since working was the basis for contention, Jesus points to God as a continuing worker. Although the Father rested from his creative activity (Gen 2:2), he must work to sustain the universe. He must work also to bring in the new creation. The meaning seems to be that all the while the Father had been working, the Son had been working too. This

19. Then answered Jesus and said unto them, Verily, verily, I say unto you, The Son can do nothing of himself, but what he seeth the Father do: for what things soever he doeth, these also doeth the Son likewise.

20. For the Father loveth the Son, and showeth him all things that himself doeth: and he will show him greater works than these, that ye may marvel.

21. For as the Father raiseth up the dead, and quickeneth *them*; even so the Son quickeneth whom he will.

22. For the Father judgeth no man, but hath committed all judgment unto the Son:

23. That all *men* should honor the Son, even as they honor the Father. He that honoreth not the Son honoreth not the Father which hath sent him.

24. Verily, verily, I say unto you, He that heareth my word, and believeth on him that sent me, hath everlasting life, and shall not come into condemnation; but is passed from death unto life.

25. Verily, verily, I say unto you, The hour is coming, and now is, when the dead shall hear the voice of the Son of God: and they that hear shall live.

26. For as the Father hath life in himself; so hath he given to the Son to have life in himself;

27. And hath given him authority to execute judgment also, because he is the Son of man.

was a greater claim than to assert that the Father had been working and now the Son was assuming the burden. The Jews caught the implication: Jesus was asserting that God was his own Father, thus claiming equality with God. This was worse than working on the Sabbath. Such blasphemy called for death (cf. Jn 7:30).

**19,20.** This discourse continued without apparent interruption from the Jews. No arrogance marked Jesus' claim, which was balanced by complete dependence on and subordination to the Father. This is true sonship, Jesus points out, to learn from the Father and reproduce what is seen (v. 19). The Son's perception is aided by the Father's revelation to him concerning the meaning of **all things** that are done by the Father. To demonstrate the reality of the relationship between the two, **greater works** than **these** (the healing of the impotent man and similar signs) will be forthcoming.

**21-24.** One of these greater works is the raising of the dead (v. 21). Clearly this is as much a creative act as the original impartation of life. If the Son has power to quicken whom he will, he partakes of the Father's power. **Judgment** is a second sphere in which the divine authority is manifest. This function has been given over to the Son. Note that resurrection and judgment are closely related eschatological functions, of which there were foregleams during Christ's ministry, such as the resurrection of Lazarus and the judgment upon Satan (16:11). Behind this sharing of authority is the design that the Son shall receive honor equally with the Father. To refuse it is to dishonor the Father (5:23). The two themes of (1) life out of death and (2) judgment are now brought together (v. 24); but the resurrection here is spiritual, not physical, namely, participation in **everlasting life.** One must believe on the One who sent the Son, not in the sense of by-passing the Son, but as perceiving that faith in the Father and in the Son are indivisible.

**25-30.** Jesus enlarges on his power to give spiritual quickening (vv. 25,26). This work belongs to the future, he says, but is also **now** going on (note contrast with v. 28). **The dead** in this case are not in the graves, as in verse 28, but are dead in sin. Their quickening comes through hearing **the voice of the Son of God** (cf. v. 24 — he that heareth my word; 6:60; 18:37). In nothing is the Son independent of the Father, even in the fundamental matter of life itself (5:26).

28. Marvel not at this: for the hour is coming, in the which all that are in the graves shall hear his voice,

29. And shall come forth; they that have done good, unto the resurrection of life; and they that have done evil, unto the resurrection of damnation.

30. I can of mine own self do nothing: as I hear, I judge: and my judgment is just; because I seek not mine own will, but the will of the Father which hath sent me.

31. If I bear witness of myself, my witness is not true.

32. There is another that beareth witness of me; and I know that the witness which he witnesseth of me is true.

33. Ye sent unto John, and he bare witness unto the truth.

34. But I receive not testimony from man: but these things I say, that ye might be saved.

35. He was a burning and a shining light: and ye were willing for a season to rejoice in his light.

36. But I have greater witness than *that* of John: for the works which the Father hath given me to finish, the same works that I do, bear witness of me, that the Father hath sent me.

37. And the Father himself, which hath sent me, hath borne witness of me. Ye have neither heard his voice at any time, nor seen his shape.

38. And ye have not his word abiding in you: for whom he hath sent, him ye believe not.

39. Search the Scriptures; for in them ye think ye have eternal life: and they are they which testify of me.

40. And ye will not come to me, that ye might have life.

Once again Christ sets forth his authority in judgment (v. 27). **Son of man** is used here, as it is in Dan 7:13, in connection with judgment and dominion. It is a technical eschatological term, denoting more than humanity but including it. As Lord of resurrection, Jesus will summon all from their graves (cf. Acts 24:15). In view of Rev 20:4,5, we are to think of a time interval between these two phases of resurrection. The doing of **good** includes having faith in the Son of God, even as doing **evil** includes the rejection of the Son and his claims. **Damnation.** Literally *judgment.* The next verse (Jn 5:30) is transitional, retaining the mention of **judgment** from the recent context and anticipating by its use of the first person of the pronoun the material that follows. The Son alone has this unique relation to the Father.

**31-40.** In this passage the theme of witness is uppermost. If Jesus were to bear witness to himself, he says, in isolation from the Father's witness, it would be untrue because incomplete and unsupported. He could not expect the Jews to receive it. But his witness is actually not of this sort (cf. 8:18). **Another** bears witness, even the Father. Unfortunately the Jews do not recognize the Father's witness (cf. 7:28; 8:19), and so are incapacitated for recognizing the support it brings to Jesus' claims (5:32). A second witness was John the Baptist, who was sought out by the Jews themselves for his testimony (1:26; 3:26). This witness was in accord with **the truth,** as the descent of the Spirit upon Jesus proved. However helpful such witness may have been in leading others to a right evaluation of himself, Jesus did not rely upon it as necessary to his own awareness of person and mission (5:34). Yet John's word, acknowledged by Jesus, was intended to help these people to **be saved.** Jesus here characterizes John as the **burning** and **shining** lamp. As burning, he gradually faded (3:30), but as shining, he enabled men to see their need of the greater Light (cf. 1:8). As such, his testimony outlived him. **For a season.** John's popularity did not last long. A third witness to Jesus is found in his **works,** which were given to him by the Father to perform, in order to attest his divine mission (v. 36). **Finish.** Nothing tentative or incomplete. The works prepared the way for the work, which we now know was finished on Calvary and which needs no revision.

As a part of the greater witness, our

41. I receive not honor from men.

42. But I know you, that ye have not the love of God in you.

43. I am come in my Father's name, and ye receive me not: if another shall come in his own name, him ye will receive.

44. How can ye believe, which receive honor one of another, and seek not the honor that *cometh* from God only?

45. Do not think that I will accuse you to the Father: there is *one* that accuseth you, *even* Moses, in whom ye trust.

46. For had ye believed Moses, ye would have believed me: for he wrote of me.

47. But if ye believe not his writings, how shall ye believe my words?

Lord includes the testimony of the Father contained in the Scriptures (5:37-40). This he clearly distinguishes from the Father's immediate testimony to him (v. 32). The inaccessibility of God, due to his spirituality (v. 37) is overcome to a considerable degree through the revelation of himself in the Scriptures of the OT. But that **word** had not taken root in Jesus' hearers. The proof lies in the fact that they had not received him of whom the Word speaks (5:38). **Search** may be either indicative or imperative in this instance, but the sense of the passage favors the indicative. The Jews were in the habit of searching **the Scriptures** because they recognized that these contain the secret of **eternal life.** Acquaintance with the Law was the goal of Jewish piety; so the written Word tended to become an end in itself. But the Scriptures testify of a *person!* The tragedy was that that very Person was now present, and religious men would not come to him for the life they vainly sought in the letter of the Word (v. 40).

**41-47.** Jesus did not want men to believe in him simply that he might have **honour** from them (v. 41). The Greek word is *doxa,* often rendered *glory.* The basic reason for the lack of response to him and his claims was lack of response to God. They lacked **the love of God,** i.e., love for God. Since Jesus had come in the Father's name, this lack of love for God made it impossible for them to see that he was one with the Father, and receive him. In the event that one should come **in his own name,** not resting, as Jesus did, on the authority of the Father, he would have a ready response (v. 43). This was probably not intended as a prophecy of the coming of any one figure, but was spoken to point up a principle involving sinful human nature. The Jews were guilty of seeking honor and glory from one another (cf. 12:43) rather than from the only God, who is the only source of true and abiding recognition. Jesus' mission was not one of accusation and judgment. This was unnecessary anyway in the case of his hearers, because an accuser existed in Moses. The Jews put unbounded confidence in what Moses wrote (v. 45), but at the crucial point they did not believe at all, for they failed to receive Moses' prophetic announcements regarding the Christ. Here we are to think not simply of individual passages, such as Deut 18:15-18, but of the very incompleteness of revelation apart from One to come, and of the con-

## CHAPTER 6

AFTER these things Jesus went over the sea of Galilee, which is *the sea* of Tiberias.

2. And a great multitude followed him, because they saw his miracles which he did on them that were diseased.

3. And Jesus went up into a mountain, and there he sat with his disciples.

4. And the passover, a feast of the Jews, was nigh.

5. When Jesus then lifted up *his* eyes, and saw a great company come unto him, he saith unto Philip, Whence shall we buy bread, that these may eat?

6. And this he said to prove him: for he himself knew what he would do.

7. Philip answered him, Two hundred pennyworth of bread is not sufficient for them, that every one of them may take a little.

demnation of the Law, which called for a Saviour. The written revelation and the personal revelation are basically one (v. 47).

I. The Feeding of The Five Thousand and The Discourse on The Bread of Life. 6:1-71.

Some scholars, advocating the view that chapters 5 and 6 have become transposed, have pointed out certain advantages in reversing them. But lack of manuscript evidence for it is a formidable barrier to acceptance of the view.

The miracle before us is the only "sign" recorded in all four Gospels. Mark and Luke speak of Jesus as teaching the multitude prior to the miracle, but John alone records the discourse which Jesus gave on the following day.

**1-4.** The other side of the sea, in this case, is the eastern shore. Another name for this body of water is the Lake of Gennesaret (Lk 5:1). Attracted by Jesus' miracles, a great crowd followed him around the north shore. This presupposes a ministry of some duration, perhaps several months, in the Galilean area, after the events of chapter 5 located in Jerusalem. **A mountain.** The highlands. Mention of the nearness of the Passover is significant. Since John does not record the institution of the Lord's Supper as a part of his recital of the events of Passion Week, he is probably drawing the attention of the reader to the bearing of the miracle and the discourse on the central sacrament of the Christian faith.

**5-7.** The nearest town was Bethsaida. It would have been difficult for the people to get bread, due to the distance and the lateness of the hour. Jesus assumed that he and his company would make provision (v. 5). He counseled with Philip about ways and means, knowing in himself what he would do, but desiring to **prove** (test) the faith of his disciples. Philip was a native of Bethsaida (1: 44). Two hundred denarii worth of bread, the apostle estimated, would hardly be enough. A denarius equaled about twenty cents and was the usual daily wage of a laborer. A laborer with an average-size family of five probably spent half his daily income for food. Assuming that the family ate three meals a day, we can conclude that a half denarius would have furnished them a day's food or fifteen meals. A whole denarius would have provided two days' rations or thirty meals. Two hundred denarii would have provided one meal for some 6,000 people.

8. One of his disciples, Andrew, Simon Peter's brother, saith unto him,

9. There is a lad here, which hath five barley loaves, and two small fishes: but what are they among so many?

10. And Jesus said, Make the men sit down. Now there was much grass in the place. So the men sat down, in number about five thousand.

11. And Jesus took the loaves; and when he had given thanks, he distributed to the disciples, and the disciples to them that were set down; and likewise of the fishes as much as they would.

12. When they were filled, he said unto his disciples, Gather up the fragments that remain, that nothing be lost.

13. Therefore they gathered *them* together, and filled twelve baskets with the fragments of the five barley loaves, which remained over and above unto them that had eaten.

14. Then those men, when they had seen the miracle that Jesus did, said, This is of a truth that Prophet that should come into the world.

15. When Jesus therefore perceived that they would come and take him by force, to make him a king, he departed again into a mountain himself alone.

16. And when even was *now* come, his disciples went down unto the sea,

17. And entered into a ship, and went over the sea toward Capernaum. And it was now dark, and Jesus was not come to them.

In this crowd the men alone numbered about 5,000 (6:10). **8,9.** It proved unnecessary to drain the treasury and cause troublesome delay by seeking to purchase food. Andrew stepped forward with information about a **lad.** The Greek word is used for a wide range of ages. It may indicate a slave also, but this is improbable here. **Barley loaves.** The cheap food of the common people. The loaves were scarcely more than buns. The supply seemed pitifully small for the need. **10,11.** Order was necessary for the large operation in view. At Jesus' command, given through the disciples, the people were seated. Mention of grass indicates the spring of the year (cf. v. 4). It helped to make the crowd comfortable. Jesus then gave thanks for the provision (Did he include thanks for the boy's generosity?), then distributed to the disciples, and they to the multitude. In the process of distribution the miracle occurred. The people had **as much as they would** (wished for) both of bread and fish, in contrast to Philip's estimate— "a little." **12,13.** The prodigality of the giving was matched by the stringency of the measures for conserving what was left over. God's gifts are not to be wasted. **Twelve baskets** were needed to hold **the fragments,** and so all of the disciples were kept busy.

**14,15.** There was no doubt that a miracle had been performed. The people saw it and were impressed by it. All had been benefited. They saw that their benefactor was no ordinary person, and concluded that he must be the expected **prophet** (Deut 18:18). Here, as in John 4, the **prophet** seems to be identified with the Messiah, whereas in John 1:20,21 the two are differentiated. In the public mind there was probably no hard and fast line between the two representations. The prophet would become **king** at any rate, if this crowd could have its way. Such a move would at once express their gratitude for the miracle and also insure the harnessing of Jesus' wonder-working power to the nation's needs, both economic and military. The popular expectation of Messiah was about to express itself in dramatic fashion. But he whose kingdom was not of this world (18:36), perceiving the intention, foiled it by withdrawal.

**16-21.** The Lord who had met the need of the throng now met the need of his disciples, who were caught in a storm at night on the lake. Without Jesus, but apparently expecting him to come to

18. And the sea arose by reason of a great wind that blew.

19. So when they had rowed about five and twenty or thirty furlongs, they see Jesus walking on the sea, and drawing nigh unto the ship: and they were afraid.

20. But he saith unto them, It is I; be not afraid.

21. Then they willingly received him into the ship: and immediately the ship was at the land whither they went.

22. The day following, when the people, which stood on the other side of the sea, saw that there was none other boat there, save that one whereinto his disciples were entered, and that Jesus went not with his disciples into the boat, but *that* his disciples were gone away alone;

23. (Howbeit there came other boats from Tiberias nigh unto the place where they did eat bread, after that the Lord had given thanks:)

24. When the people therefore saw that Jesus was not there, neither his disciples, they also took shipping, and came to Capernaum, seeking for Jesus.

25. And when they had found him on the other side of the sea, they said unto him, Rabbi, when camest thou hither?

26. Jesus answered them and said, Verily, verily, I say unto you, Ye seek me, not because ye saw the miracles, but because ye did eat of the loaves, and were filled.

27. Labor not for the meat which perisheth, but for that meat which endureth unto everlasting life, which the Son of man shall give unto you: for him hath God the Father sealed.

them (v. 17), the disciples headed for Capernaum. To the handicap of the dark was now added the distress of high wind and wave. Forward progress had brought them about twenty-five or thirty furlongs from the shore (each such measure—*stadios*—was about six hundred feet). As the situation grew desperate, Jesus drew near. To the fear of the storm was now added the fear of the apparition. But the voice of Jesus, saying, It is I; be not afraid, banished their fears. They welcomed him into the ship and found themselves immediately at the land. The Synoptists tell us that on this occasion Jesus walked on the water. His miraculous power manifested itself also in removing the barrier of distance. Gravity and space alike are under his control. John adds no interpretation to his account. The passage is useful as teaching that despite opposing forces, Jesus will enable his people to achieve the goals he has set for them, including heaven itself.

**22-25.** The setting for the discourse is given in these verses. Perhaps it was the storm that kept the people from leaving the area of the miracle of the multiplication of the loaves, plus the impression that Jesus was still nearby. The desire to have him as their leader and provider was still strong. Seeing that he had not departed with his disciples, they were perplexed as to his movements. When a search of the area failed to reveal him, and boats arrived from Capernaum, the crowd determined to take shipping and cross the lake in the hope of finding him on the other side. When . . . ? (6:25) Jesus was a man of mystery to them.

**26-34.** Rebuked by the Lord, the people demanded a sign as the basis for faith in him. Even though they had seen the miracle (cf. 6:14), Jesus charged them with not seeing, i.e., not looking beyond the external aspect. They saw only the provision of material sustenance and felt its satisfaction (v. 26). **Meat** (v. 27). A general word for food or eating. Jesus' teaching here had a double edge, for he contrasted food that perishes with food that endures unto **everlasting life,** and also pitted **labor** over against **give** (cf. Isa 55:1,2). Even the food Jesus had provided across the lake was perishable. But he had that to give which would be significant for eternal life. His power to do this rested in the authority which God the Father had vested in him (**sealed** by the divine voice at the baptism and by the bestowal of the Spirit). The warning about labor did not fully "register,"

28. Then said they unto him, What shall we do, that we might work the works of God?

29. Jesus answered and said unto them, This is the work of God, that ye believe on him whom he hath sent.

30. They said therefore unto him, What sign showest thou then, that we may see, and believe thee? what dost thou work?

31. Our fathers did eat manna in the desert; as it is written, He gave them bread from heaven to eat.

32. Then Jesus said unto them, Verily, verily, I say unto you, Moses gave you not that bread from heaven; but my Father giveth you the true bread from heaven.

33. For the bread of God is he which cometh down from heaven, and giveth life unto the world.

34. Then said they unto him, Lord, evermore give us this bread.

35. And Jesus said unto them, I am the bread of life: he that cometh to me shall never hunger; and he that believeth on me shall never thirst.

36. But I said unto you, That ye also have seen me, and believe not.

37. All that the Father giveth me shall come to me; and him that cometh to me I will in no wise cast out.

38. For I came down from heaven, not to do mine own will, but the will of him that sent me.

39. And this is the Father's will which hath sent me, that of all which he hath given me I should lose nothing, but should raise it up again at the last day.

40. And this is the will of him that sent me, that every one which seeth the Son, and believeth on him, may have everlasting life: and I will raise him up at the last day.

for the people demanded to know what they must **do** to work the works of God (v. 28), that is, to perform works acceptable to him. In answer, the Lord pointed to faith as the greatest, the indispensable work (v. 29). This seemed to be an unusual requirement. After all, many had spoken for God in the past and had not called for faith in themselves but only in the One who sent them. So the crowd felt justified in requesting a special sign to support this special claim. To believe him they must have something akin to the bringing down of **bread from heaven** (6:31), in contrast to the miracle across the lake.

In order to avoid misunderstanding, Jesus reminded his hearers that it was not Moses but God who gave the bread in the desert, who also was granting the true bread from heaven. By **true** we are to understand the perfect, that which answers to men's deepest need. Christ identified the bread as **he** (v. 33), one who had actually come down from heaven to give **life** to the world. But the explicit identification with himself was not yet made. The people wanted **this bread**, but apparently still thought of it in material terms, much as the woman of Samaria thought of living water (v. 34).

**35-65.** This section comprises the discourse proper, interrupted three times by questions and discussion.

**35.** Jesus now finally identified himself as **the bread of life.** Not only does he have life in himself, but he is able to impart it to others. But this bread is not something external, something apart from himself. One must **come** to him, which is the equivalent of believing on him. For those who come, spiritual hunger will be forever banished. Eating and drinking occur together here, perhaps in anticipation of verse 53. One need never turn from Christ to another for satisfaction.

**36.** Seeing had not resulted in believing (cf. 6:30). "He Himself was the sign which the Jews could not read. No other more convincing could be given" (B. F. Westcott, *The Gospel According to St. John*). **37.** Even so, the Son was not discouraged, for **all** who were the gift of the Father to him would come, and in coming would find in him no spirit of rejection but rather glad welcome. **38.** This reception was inevitable, for the will of the Father was the delight of the Son. **39,40.** This will was not confined to the call but extended also to the preservation of those who were given to Christ (cf. 17:12). The reunion of the

41. The Jews then murmured at him, because he said, I am the bread which came down from heaven.

42. And they said, Is not this Jesus, the son of Joseph, whose father and mother we know? how is it then that he saith, I came down from heaven?

43. Jesus therefore answered and said unto them, Murmur not among yourselves.

44. No man can come to me, except the Father which hath sent me draw him: and I will raise him up at the last day.

45. It is written in the prophets, And they shall be all taught of God. Every man therefore that hath heard, and hath learned of the Father, cometh unto me.

46. Not that any man hath seen the Father, save he which is of God, he hath seen the Father.

47. Verily, verily, I say unto you, He that believeth on me hath everlasting life.

48. I am that bread of life.

49. Your fathers did eat manna in the wilderness, and are dead.

50. This is the bread which cometh down from heaven, that a man may eat thereof, and not die.

51. I am the living bread which came down from heaven: if any man eat of this bread, he shall live for ever: and the bread that I will give is my flesh, which I will give for the life of the world.

52. The Jews therefore strove among themselves, saying, How can this man give us *his* flesh to eat?

53. Then Jesus said unto them, Verily, verily, I say unto you, Except ye eat the flesh of the Son of man, and drink his blood, ye have no life in you.

54. Whoso eateth my flesh, and drinketh my blood, hath eternal life; and I will raise him up at the last day.

55. For my flesh is meat indeed, and my blood is drink indeed.

56. He that eateth my flesh, and drinketh my blood, dwelleth in me, and I in him.

57. As the living Father hath sent me, and I live by the Father; so he that eateth me, even he shall live by me.

58. This is that bread which came down from heaven: not as your fathers did eat manna, and are dead: he that eateth of this bread shall live for ever.

last day will defy the power of death.

**41,42.** The offense of the humanity of the Nazarene blinded the hearers. They knew too much about him, including his supposed parentage, to accept the conclusion that he **came down from heaven** (cf. Mk 6:2,3). **43,44.** Those who murmured (as did their fathers in the desert) at the high claim of the Son of man showed that they did not know what it was to have the Father **draw** them. Without such a drawing, an inclination of the heart induced by God, one cannot **come** to Christ. One cannot lean to his own understanding. **45.** The drawing comes through teaching rather than through some mystical process. Here Christ quoted Isa 54:13. If the **all** be emphasized, it removes any element of restriction that may seem to lurk in the idea of drawing as stated in Jn 6:44. **46.** But immediate knowledge of God can come only through the One who has **seen** the Father. This is a leading claim of the Gospel (cf. 1:18). **47,48.** Truths given earlier are emphasized again.

**49-51.** The Jews had demanded that Jesus bring down bread from heaven. What permanent profit would result? The fathers who ate the manna were **dead**, but those who partook of the bread which is the Son of God would not die (spiritually), for the very life of God was theirs. The **flesh** of Jesus, his actual corporeal existence, was to be given for the life of the world. This pointed to the cross. **52-54.** Still thinking in material terms, the Jews argued with one another over the possibility of Jesus' giving them his flesh to eat (v. 52). Making the matter still more difficult, our Lord indicated that his blood as well as his flesh had to be received if one would have life (v. 53). In view of the OT prohibition against consuming blood (Lev 7:26,27), the offense at Jesus' words must have been heightened. Those words seem to anticipate the significance of the Lord's Supper.

**55-58.** The following quotation will best summarize the thought: "The Eucharistic food and drink are physically bread and wine, spiritually the Flesh and Blood of the Son of man: the true food and drink because they effect the sacred union of the Son of God with those who believe on Him, and thus communicate eternal life and guarantee immortality. The union of the Father and the Son is thereby extended to embrace the believers also. As the Father communicates life to the Son, so the Son com-

59. These things said he in the synagogue, as he taught in Capernaum.

60. Many therefore of his disciples, when they had heard *this*, said, This is a hard saying; who can hear it?

61. When Jesus knew in himself that his disciples murmured at it, he said unto them, Doth this offend you?

62. *What* and if ye shall see the Son of man ascend up where he was before?

63. It is the Spirit that quickeneth; the flesh profiteth nothing: the words that I speak unto you, *they* are spirit, and *they* are life.

64. But there are some of you that believe not. For Jesus knew from the beginning who they were that believed not, and who should betray him.

65. And he said, Therefore said I unto you, that no man can come unto me, except it were given unto him of my Father.

66. From that *time* many of his disciples went back, and walked no more with him.

67. Then said Jesus unto the twelve, Will ye also go away?

68. Then Simon Peter answered him, Lord, to whom shall we go? thou hast the words of eternal life.

69. And we believe and are sure that thou art that Christ, the Son of the living God.

70. Jesus answered them, Have not I chosen you twelve, and one of you is a devil?

71. He spake of Judas Iscariot *the son* of Simon: for he it was that should betray him, being one of the twelve.

municates life to those who feed on Him, and will bestow on them immortality" (Hoskyns). The feeding need not be confined to Eucharistic celebration.

**59.** A fine synagogue has been excavated at Capernaum, which has a pot of manna as one of its decorative motifs. Though this structure comes from a period later than the time of Jesus, a synagogue probably stood on the same spot in Jesus' day.

**60-65.** This section concerns especially the reaction of **disciples** to Jesus' words. These are to be distinguished alike from "the Jews" of the foregoing context and the Twelve in the following verses. These disciples had been followers, but felt, in view of the teaching, that they could not continue. The **hard saying** refers to the necessity of eating Christ's flesh and drinking his blood. His ascension, which for true believers would confirm his claims, would only add to the offense for those who could not receive his humanity offered for them in death on the cross (v. 62). Even Christ's **flesh**, declared to be so indispensable, would profit nothing except as the Spirit vivified it to the believer. His own **words**, however, partook of the character of spirit, that is, were life-giving. They could save, not in independence of the historic work of the cross, but as pointing to that work and interpreting it. The very resistance encountered by his words among would-be disciples demonstrated that their faith was superficial. Jesus discerned not only the presence of pseudo-faith, but the potential of betrayal on the part of one of his followers.

**66-71.** The effect of the discourse on the Twelve is now unfolded. This was the parting of the ways for many who had been disciples (6:66). Their departure prompted the question of Jesus to the Twelve as to their intentions (v. 67). Peter, as the rock, stood his ground. His confession is similar to that recorded by the Synoptists in connection with the Caesarea-Philippi incident (Mt 16:16), but in keeping with the discourse it emphasizes that Jesus has **the words of eternal life** (cf. Jn 6:63). Others saw in them only words. Peter saw a fruition unto life eternal, even though he did not yet understand the cross. Another in that company could not so speak, for he was a devil (*diabolos*). The meaning is not that he was an instrument of Satan when Christ chose him, but that he had become such. Judas belonged with the departing throng, but he stayed on. Of-

## CHAPTER 7

AFTER these things Jesus walked in Galilee: for he would not walk in Jewry, because the Jews sought to kill him.

2. Now the Jews' feast of tabernacles was at hand.

3. His brethren therefore said unto him, Depart hence, and go into Judea, that thy disciples also may see the works that thou doest.

4. For *there is* no man *that* doeth any thing in secret, and he himself seeketh to be known openly. If thou do these things, show thyself to the world.

5. For neither did his brethren believe in him.

6. Then Jesus said unto them, My time is not yet come: but your time is always ready.

7. The world cannot hate you; but me it hateth, because I testify of it, that the works thereof are evil.

8. Go ye up unto this feast: I go not up yet unto this feast; for my time is not yet full come.

9. When he had said these words unto them, he abode *still* in Galilee.

fended that Jesus refused to be made king, as we gather from closely studying his career, he would one day betray Him in spite for having betrayed the confidence of those who trusted Him to lead them to Messianic victory.

J. Jesus at the Feast of Tabernacles. 7:1-53.

This chapter is thoroughly Christ-centered in the sense that Christ is the subject of much discussion and diverse reaction as well as the theme of Jesus' self-disclosure.

**1. After these things.** The reference seems to be to the events of the last chapter. Despite the breach with so many former disciples, Jesus found it safer to abide in Galilee than to return to Judea, where there was open hostility. **2.** The period spent in Galilee is bounded by the Passover and the Feast of Tabernacles, an interval of slightly more than six months. Judging from the Synoptics, Jesus spent most of this time in out-of-the-way places, teaching his disciples.

**3-9.** With the approach of this autumn feast, which drew Jews from far and wide for the joyful festivities, Jesus' brothers professed to see in the occasion a capital opportunity for him to extend his influence. His **disciples** in Judea, perhaps including many Galileans who had been offended or had grown cold in their attitude, could be won over by seeing his **works.** The brothers were a miniature of the great bulk of the nation, not questioning the reality of the works, but failing to **believe** in him. Their counsel was that, whereas Jesus was remaining **in secret,** he needed to be known **openly.** This is substantially what Satan sought to suggest to our Lord in the second temptation. Jesus' season had not arrived (elsewhere often called "my hour"—the time of his manifestation in death). The brethren had no such spiritual regulation of their movements. They did not know the hatred of the world, for they were a part of it. On the other hand, Jesus, as the Truth, had to testify against the **evil** in the world. He could not go to Jerusalem simply to gain popularity. If he went, it would be to expose sin. **I go not up yet.** The word **yet** is lacking in many good authorities, and was probably a scribal addition to avoid contradiction with verse 10. Jesus meant by this refusal that he was not going up on the terms suggested by his brothers. He would go in his own time and way, but would remain in Galilee for the time being.

10. But when his brethren were gone up, then went he also up unto the feast, not openly, but as it were in secret.

11. Then the Jews sought him at the feast, and said, Where is he?

12. And there was much murmuring among the people concerning him: for some said, He is a good man: others said, Nay; but he deceiveth the people.

13. Howbeit no man spake openly of him for fear of the Jews.

14. Now about the midst of the feast Jesus went up into the temple, and taught.

15. And the Jews marveled, saying, How knoweth this man letters, having never learned?

16. Jesus answered them, and said, My doctrine is not mine, but his that sent me.

17. If any man will do his will, he shall know of the doctrine, whether it be of God, or *whether* I speak of myself.

18. He that speaketh of himself seeketh his own glory: but he that seeketh his glory that sent him, the same is true, and no unrighteousness is in him.

19. Did not Moses give you the law, and *yet* none of you keepeth the law? Why go ye about to kill me?

20. The people answered and said, Thou hast a devil: who goeth about to kill thee?

21. Jesus answered and said unto them, I have done one work, and ye all marvel.

22. Moses therefore gave unto you circumcision; (not because it is of Moses, but of the fathers;) and ye on the sabbath day circumcise a man.

23. If a man on the sabbath day receive circumcision, that the law of Moses should not be broken; are ye angry at me, because I have made a man every whit whole on the sabbath day?

24. Judge not according to the appearance, but judge righteous judgment.

**10-13.** When he did go up to the feast, he went unobtrusively, **in secret**, as it were, without any fanfare. Meanwhile **the Jews** (the leaders) kept looking for him among the crowds and asking, "Where is that man?" The people were discussing him also, with some difference of opinion, the judgments wavering between the verdict of **good man** and **deceiver.** Fear of the Jews kept the discussion in hushed tones (7:13; cf. 9:22).

**14,15.** About the midst of the feast, i.e., in the middle of the week of festivities, which ended with an eighth day convocation (Lev 23:36). Entering the Temple, Jesus began to teach. The leaders were astonished at his expositions, especially in view of the fact that he had not been trained in the rabbinic schools (contrast Paul, Acts 22:3).

**16-18.** Apparently it was the content of Jesus' teaching rather than his manner or diction that caused astonishment. Instead of boasting in his ability, Jesus explained that the teaching belonged to the One who had sent him, tracing it directly to God instead of acknowledging his debt to some human teacher as the scribes were accustomed to do. Anyone who had the moral aim of pleasing God (doing His will) would be able to determine whether Jesus' teaching was independent or was a faithful reproduction of the divine. He would detect that Jesus was not seeking his own **glory** but that of the One who sent him. Such a person would be sympathetically attracted to Jesus.

**19-24.** Jesus charged the Jews with failure to keep the Law. In this respect they were not doing the will of God. How, then, could they receive him whom God had sent? Their murderous intent toward him was in itself a breaking of the sixth commandment. The crowd, taking their stand with the rulers but not knowing their designs, thought Jesus must be mad, tormented by a demon, to imagine that his life was in danger (v. 20). It was in order for the Lord to get at the roots of the animosity of the leaders. The **one work** he had done in Jerusalem that made all men **marvel** but that turned the rulers against him was the healing of the impotent man on the Sabbath (ch. 5). Moses himself, so carefully honored by the Jews, commanded circumcision (although the practice originated with **the fathers** and not with Moses), so that it had to be carried out on the eighth day (Lev 12:3) even if that day was **the sabbath. Therefore** (Jn 7:22)

25. Then said some of them of Jerusalem, Is not this he, whom they seek to kill?

26. But, lo, he speaketh boldly, and they say nothing unto him. Do the rulers know indeed that this is the very Christ?

27. Howbeit we know this man whence he is: but when Christ cometh, no man knoweth whence he is.

28. Then cried Jesus in the temple as he taught, saying, Ye both know me, and ye know whence I am: and I am not come of myself, but he that sent me is true, whom ye know not.

29. But I know him; for I am from him, and he hath sent me.

30. Then they sought to take him: but no man laid hands on him, because his hour was not yet come.

31. And many of the people believed on him, and said, When Christ cometh, will he do more miracles than these which this *man* hath done?

32. The Pharisees heard that the people murmured such things concerning him; and the Pharisees and the chief priests sent officers to take him.

33. Then said Jesus unto them, Yet a little while am I with you, and *then* I go unto him that sent me.

34. Ye shall seek me, and shall not find *me*: and where I am, *thither* ye cannot come.

35. Then said the Jews among themselves, Whither will he go, that we shall not find him? will he go unto the dispersed among the Gentiles, and teach the Gentiles?

36. What *manner of* saying is this that he said, Ye shall seek me, and shall not find *me*: and where I am, *thither* ye cannot come?

is not entirely clear as to its bearing on the matter. It possibly points to this line of thought—that circumcision on the Sabbath was agreeable to and actually pointed to such a work as Jesus had wrought, since the restoration of a man both physically and spiritually was even more significant than the administering of the sign of the covenant.

**25-27.** Here we encounter the reflections concerning Jesus of a group which must be distinguished from "the people" of verse 20. These were inhabitants of Jerusalem who knew that the intention of the rulers was to kill Jesus. Yet the fact that Jesus was able to speak **boldly** in public made them speculate as to whether the rulers had reversed themselves and were now concluding that this man was the Christ (v. 26). Further meditation on the problem led them to dismiss this possibility, for Jesus' origin excluded him from consideration (cf. 6:42). The Messiah was to be a man of mystery—no man knoweth whence he is (cf. Mt 24:24-26).

**28-31.** Jesus granted, as a starting point, that his hearers both knew him and whence he was (v. 28). Yet even on the earthly level, they were not properly informed, being ignorant of his birthplace and presumably also of the circumstances behind his birth (cf. v. 52). They were ignorant of him in his divine being, and thereby revealed their ignorance of God who sent him. This rebuke brought a show of displeasure. The men of Jerusalem were ready to lay hands on Jesus, but were providentially prevented from carrying out their design (v. 30). Christ's **hour** is a reference to the time appointed by God for his death. Some in the crowd were not ready to dismiss the possibility that Jesus might be the Christ. But apparently they believed in him only on the basis of the **miracles** and therefore were no different from earlier believers who were such only in name (cf. 2:23-25).

**32-36.** Always alert to what the man in the street was saying, the **Pharisees** and **chief priests** (Sadducees) sent **officers** to capture Jesus. Such appeared again at the arrest in the garden (18:3,12). They constituted a Jewish police force for the temple area. In the light of this development, Jesus insisted that his **little while** (cf. 16:16) was not dictated by human plots against him but by the consummation of his work and his return to the Father (v. 33). The search of the people for him then would be fruitless. Time was running out for them to seek him aright. **Dispersed among the Gentiles.** Literally,

37. In the last day, that great *day* of the feast, Jesus stood and cried, saying, If any man thirst, let him come unto me, and drink.

38. He that believeth on me, as the Scripture hath said, out of his belly shall flow rivers of living water.

39. (But this spake he of the Spirit, which they that believe on him should receive: for the Holy Ghost was not yet *given*; because that Jesus was not yet glorified.)

40. Many of the people therefore, when they heard this saying, said, Of a truth this is the Prophet.

41. Others said, This is the Christ. But some said, Shall Christ come out of Galilee?

42. Hath not the Scripture said, That Christ cometh of the seed of David, and out of the town of Bethlehem, where David was?

43. So there was a division among the people because of him.

44. And some of them would have taken him; but no man laid hands on him.

45. Then came the officers to the chief priests and Pharisees; and they said unto them, Why have ye not brought him?

46. The officers answered, Never man spake like this man.

*the dispersion of the Greeks*. It probably means the dispersion of the Jews among the Greeks, making possible a reaching of Greeks themselves in the Jewish synagogues. This is exactly what Jesus did through his Church in later times; so the statement is unconsciously prophetic (cf. 11:52).

37-39. On the last day . . . of the feast. This could have been the seventh day or the eighth. The latter was a kind of adjunct to the feast and also a conclusion to the year's cycle of feasts. If Jesus' reference to thirst is consciously connected with the priests' practice of bringing water in a golden pitcher each day from the pool of Siloam and pouring it out at the altar, then Jesus' cry of invitation would have special point on the eighth day, when, it seems, this ceremony was omitted. The thirst of the wilderness journey had its divinely supplied satisfaction, but it recurred. Jesus offered lasting spiritual satisfaction (cf. 4:14). Again Judaism was exposed as inadequate. The thought progresses; for the believer in Jesus, who finds this satisfaction, becomes in turn a means of blessing to others as a conductor of rivers of living water (7:38). Any allusion to Christ himself (cf. 19:34) is doubtful. The scripture cannot be identified. Some possible passages are Ex 17:6; Isa 44:3,4; 58:11; Ezk 47:1-9; Zech 14:8. An alternative is that John has reference to no Scripture passage but to the consensus of several. The promise of new life in abundance is attributed here to the Spirit, who is given to all who believe. But at this time the Spirit had not come in the epochal sense of Pentecost (cf. 14:26; 15:26; 16:7). Glorified, i.e., reached the goal of his mission in death, resurrection and ascension. It is the glorified Christ whom the Spirit mediates to men.

40-44. The loud cry and the nature of the words of Jesus led many of his hearers to identify him with the prophet who should come (Deut 18:15; Jn 1:21; 6:14). Others were prepared to think of him as the Messiah. This raised the problem of his origin. To meet the requirement of Scripture, Messiah had to come from David's seed and from David's town, Bethlehem. The people, in their ignorance, thought of Jesus as simply a Galilean. Those who looked on him as a pretender and deceiver were in favor of laying hands on him, but were providentially restrained (7:44).

45-49. The officers who had previously been sent to take Jesus (v. 32) now re-

47. Then answered them the Pharisees, Are ye also deceived?

48. Have any of the rulers or of the Pharisees believed on him?

49. But this people who knoweth not the law are cursed.

50. Nicodemus saith unto them, (he that came to Jesus by night, being one of them,)

51. Doth our law judge *any* man, before it hear him, and know what he doeth?

52. They answered and said unto him, Art thou also of Galilee? Search, and look: for out of Galilee ariseth no prophet.

53. And every man went unto his own house.

## CHAPTER 8

JESUS went unto the mount of Olives.

2. And early in the morning he came again into the temple, and all the people came unto him; and he sat down, and taught them.

3. And the scribes and Pharisees brought unto him a woman taken in adultery; and when they had set her in the midst,

ported back empty-handed. They, like others (vv. 30,44), were restrained from laying hands on the Son of God, and they could explain their failure only on the ground that no man ever spoke as he did. They sensed something supernatural in him and were powerless to carry out their commission. The answer of the Pharisees is that such men ought to get their guidance from their superiors. So far the rulers (members of the Sanhedrin) and the Pharisees (the teachers of the people) had maintained a solid front against Jesus. **Have any of the rulers . . . believed?** This remained true, but not for long, since one of the rulers was about to declare for Jesus, or at least defend him. The Pharisees sought to explain popular interest in Jesus on the ground that the people were ignorant of the Law and were therefore cursed (cf. Deut 28:15). Jewish sources indicate that there was often bad feeling between the Pharisees and the *am ha-areṣ* or people of the land.

**50,51.** However well the Pharisees knew the Law, they were not abiding by it themselves, as Nicodemus had the courage to point out. They had sought to arrest a man in violation of the Law, which required that a man be heard before he could be apprehended in this fashion (Deut 1:16). So the Jews were unfaithful to their own Law, on which they prided themselves (cf. v. 19). Ignoring the exposure by Nicodemus, the Pharisees appealed to sectionalism even as they had just appealed to class. Nicodemus had ventured to talk in defense of a Galilean, as though he were one himself. What had Galilee to offer? It had produced no prophet. In thus excluding Jesus from the ranks of the prophets, the Pharisees revealed their own ignorance, for Jonah at least had come from this section (II Kgs 14:25; cf. Josh 19:13).

K. The Woman Taken in Adultery. 8:1-11.

Manuscript authority is strongly against the genuineness of this paragraph (including 7:53), and the language is hardly Johannine. Yet the story is clearly a true one, which early found a place in the text of the Fourth Gospel.

**1.** When in Jerusalem Jesus usually bivouacked on the Mount of Olives.

**2.** As a lad he had visited the Temple to be taught (Lk 2:46). Now he was there to teach, with people crowding around him. **3.** The teaching session was interrupted by the arrival of scribes and Pharisees, who were leading a woman ap-

4. They say unto him, Master, this woman was taken in adultery, in the very act.

5. Now Moses in the law commanded us, that such should be stoned: but what sayest thou?

6. This they said, tempting him, that they might have to accuse him. But Jesus stooped down, and with *his* finger wrote on the ground, *as though he heard them not.*

7. So when they continued asking him, he lifted up himself, and said unto them, He that is without sin among you, let him first cast a stone at her.

8. And again he stooped down, and wrote on the ground.

9. And they which heard *it*, being convicted by *their own* conscience, went out one by one, beginning at the eldest, *even* unto the last: and Jesus was left alone, and the woman standing in the midst.

10. When Jesus had lifted up himself, and saw none but the woman, he said unto her, Woman, where are those thine accusers? hath no man condemned thee?

11. She said, No man, Lord. And Jesus said unto her, Neither do I condemn thee: go, and sin no more.

12. Then spake Jesus again unto them, saying, I am the light of the world: he that followeth me shall not walk in darkness, but shall have the light of life.

prehended in adultery. Angered at Jesus' success and frustrated by their inability to get rid of him, these leaders now seized on an opportunity to embarrass him before the people. They embarrassed the woman, too, by placing her in the midst.

5. Reminding Jesus of the requirement of stoning for this offense (Deut 22:23, 24), these leaders sought his verdict on the matter. They were tempting him by putting him in a dilemma. If he upheld the Law, which was apparently not being applied rigorously in such cases, he could be made to appear heartless. If he advocated mercy, he could be heralded as having too lenient a view of the application of the Law. If the Pharisees had been truly concerned for the maintenance of the Law, they would have brought the male offender also.

6. It is useless to speculate as to what Jesus wrote. Nothing is made of the writing in the narrative. Only what the group heard from him (v. 9) is crucial. 7. Without sin. Not necessarily the sin in question, but sin in general. 9. Jesus' words had the effect of shifting attention from himself and the woman to the accusers. Conscience began to do its work. Beginning at the eldest. Their age made them leaders, and their longer experience of sin gave them greater cause for self-accusation. Only two remained — the sinner and the Friend of sinners. Jesus could have cast the stone, for he was sinless; but he was more concerned with the rehabilitation of the sinner than with seeing that the Law was meticulously satisfied. If his word, Neither do I condemn thee, sounds too lenient, it is balanced by the sequel, Go, and sin no more. The Searcher of Hearts saw that there was penitence in the heart of the woman. All that was needed was a warning for the future.

L. Jesus' Self-disclosure. 8:12-59.

On the side of Jesus' opponents there was the question, "Who are you?" (v. 25), which is the perennial question. From Christ's own standpoint he was the light of the world, yet One who was not of this world, the One who had come to set men free from their sins, the eternal "I AM." At every point he stood in sharp contrast to his objectors. The physical setting was still the Temple (v. 20).

12. I am the light of the world. The background for this statement may reside in the practice of lighting the candelabra in the Court of the Women (where the treasury was located, v. 20) during the

13. The Pharisees therefore said unto him, Thou bearest record of thyself; thy record is not true.

14. Jesus answered and said unto them, Though I bear record of myself, *yet* my record is true: for I know whence I came, and whither I go; but ye cannot tell whence I come, and whither I go.

15. Ye judge after the flesh; I judge no man.

16. And yet if I judge, my judgment is true: for I am not alone, but I and the Father that sent me.

17. It is also written in your law, that the testimony of two men is true.

18. I am one that bear witness of myself, and the Father that sent me beareth witness of me.

19. Then said they unto him, Where is thy Father? Jesus answered, Ye neither know me, nor my Father: if ye had known me, ye should have known my Father also.

20. These words spake Jesus in the treasury, as he taught in the temple: and no man laid hands on him; for his hour was not yet come.

21. Then said Jesus again unto them, I go my way, and ye shall seek me, and shall die in your sins: whither I go, ye cannot come.

22. Then said the Jews, Will he kill himself? because he saith, Whither I go, ye cannot come.

23. And he said unto them, Ye are from beneath; I am from above: ye are of this world; I am not of this world.

Feast of Tabernacles, and in the glory cloud of the wilderness wanderings which those lights were intended to represent, and also in the creation light (1:4, 9), now conceived in spiritual terms. He is the light of life.

**13-18.** Ready to find fault, the Pharisees objected to such self-testimony and labeled it untrue (v. 13). Self-testimony is often untrue and therefore needs support from others; but in Jesus' case, his witness to himself was true, for he had absolute knowledge of his own origin and destiny. Naturally there was no human witness who could corroborate such matters (v. 14). The Pharisees *judged* (i.e., came to an opinion) on mere fleshly considerations. They were blinded to spiritual truth (cf. I Cor 2:14). On the other hand, when Jesus judges (though he did not come for that purpose primarily — cf. Jn 3:17), it is properly a verdict, and so can stand eternally, for it is true. The Father endorses it and shares in it (v. 16). If the testimony of two men is true (the Law required at least two witnesses as a safeguard of justice; Deut 17:6), how much more valid is the witness of Christ, who has the Father as witness along with himself (Jn 7:18). The witness of the Father at Christ's baptism and transfiguration are well-known features of the Synoptic record.

**19,20. Where is thy Father?** In other words, If he is an absentee, we cannot profit from his witness. This is "a supreme formulation of Jewish misunderstanding and unbelief" (E. C. Hoskyns, *The Fourth Gospel*). Actually, failure to perceive the true nature of Christ was a confession of ignorance of his Father (cf. 14:7,9). Friction flared again, but once more Jesus was untouched, because his course had not been completed (v. 20).

**21,22.** The coming of his hour would mean for Jesus that he could go his way (back to the Father), but not until he should have dealt with the sin problem. Because the Pharisees would not accept him, they would have to die in their sins. Their separation would be deepened and sealed. They could not come where he would be at that day. As Jesus' prediction of his departure had previously caused perplexity (7:35), so this time it led to the surmise that he was contemplating suicide (v. 22). His death, however, would not be self-inflicted; these men would help to bring it about.

**23.** The prospect of ultimate separation focused attention on present contrasts: beneath . . . above; of this world

24. I said therefore unto you, that ye shall die in your sins: for if ye believe not that I am *he*, ye shall die in your sins.

25. Then said they unto him, Who art thou? And Jesus saith unto them, Even *the same* that I said unto you from the beginning.

26. I have many things to say and to judge of you: but he that sent me is true; and I speak to the world those things which I have heard of him.

27. They understood not that he spake to them of the Father.

28. Then said Jesus unto them, When ye have lifted up the Son of man, then shall ye know that I am *he*, and *that* I do nothing of myself; but as my Father hath taught me, I speak these things.

29. And he that sent me is with me: the Father hath not left me alone; for I do always those things that please him.

30. As he spake these words, many believed on him.

31. Then said Jesus to those Jews which believed on him, If ye continue in my word, *then* are ye my disciples indeed;

32. And ye shall know the truth, and the truth shall make you free.

33. They answered him, We be Abraham's seed, and were never in bondage to any man: how sayest thou, Ye shall be made free?

34. Jesus answered them, Verily, verily, I say unto you, Whosoever committeth sin is the servant of sin.

35. And the servant abideth not in the house for ever: *but* the Son abideth ever.

36. If the Son therefore shall make you free, ye shall be free indeed.

. . . not of this world. Jesus declined to speak of heaven as "that world," for the term world here emphasizes man in revolt and distance from God. 24. The sin which accounted for their ignorance and hostility would lead them to a hopeless death unless — they believed in him as the I am (cf. Ex 3:14).

25. This was worse, from the Jews' point of view, than the claim of verse 12, for it was the absolute claim of deity. Christ's hearers demanded that he furnish a predicate. Who art thou? Since he had made himself sufficiently known, he was content to rest on his previous affirmations. The Greek may possibly mean that from the beginning he was all that he had been affirming (cf. 1:1). 26. The many things he might have said further would all have been true, but they would only have added to the condemnation of their hearers (cf. the many things which Jesus could say to the disciples, which would only add to their perplexity; 16:12). Yet opposition would not shut the mouth of Jesus. He would continue to speak to the world.

28. The death of the Son of man, his lifting up on the cross (cf. 3:14; 12:32) would vindicate him in the sense that it would lead to resurrection and exaltation, which in turn would bring the convicting ministry of the Spirit. Some, at least, would come to know that his claim that he was the Eternal had not been idly spoken (Acts 2:41; 4:4; 6:7).

30-32. The claims of Jesus, so simple and so lofty, impressed some of those who were present. Many believed. Yet before long they were picking up stones to cast at him (8:59). It is the old story of *pseudo* faith. In this case, they did not abide in his word — which is necessary for true discipleship, and which opens the way to knowing the truth more fully — to the point of being set free through it (v. 32). These compact statements are amplified in what follows.

33. The Jews resented the implication that they were not free. As Abraham's seed they had a standing superior to that of any other people (cf. Gal 4:22). They were sons of the heavenly King. They ignored, in this case, their political bondage to Rome, as being irrelevant. 34. Their bondage lay deeper than the external relations of life. The committing of sin puts one in the position of being the servant of sin. 35. The Son (Christ) abides in the house of the Father for ever as the true Isaac. Ishmael, though he be Abraham's seed, must go out. So with the

37. I know that ye are Abraham's seed; but ye seek to kill me, because my word hath no place in you.

38. I speak that which I have seen with my Father: and ye do that which ye have seen with your father.

39. They answered and said unto him, Abraham is our father. Jesus saith unto them, If ye were Abraham's children, ye would do the works of Abraham.

40. But now ye seek to kill me, a man that hath told you the truth, which I have heard of God: this did not Abraham.

41. Ye do the deeds of your father. Then said they to him, We be not born of fornication; we have one Father, *even* God.

42. Jesus said unto them, If God were your Father, ye would love me: for I proceeded forth and came from God; neither came I of myself, but he sent me.

43. Why do ye not understand my speech? *even* because ye cannot hear my word.

44. Ye are of *your* father the devil, and the lusts of your father ye will do: he was a murderer from the beginning, and abode not in the truth, because there is no truth in him. When he speaketh a lie, he speaketh of his own: for he is a liar, and the father of it.

45. And because I tell *you* the truth, ye believe me not.

46. Which of you convinceth me of sin? And if I say the truth, why do ye not believe me?

47. He that is of God heareth God's words: ye therefore hear *them* not, because ye are not of God.

48. Then answered the Jews, and said unto him, Say we not well that thou art a Samaritan, and hast a devil?

arrogant Jews. **36.** The truth which makes free (8:32) is now seen to be personal. The Son, who is the truth (14:6), makes men free (cf. Gal 4:4-7).

**37.** The Lord was willing to concede that his hearers were the seed of Abraham in the ordinary sense. But their antagonism to him showed that they were not spiritually akin to Abraham, who was a man of faith and obedience. **38.** Their inspiration came from a father other than Abraham, one whose sinister identity Christ soon declared. **39.** Abraham's children should be able to produce Abraham's works. He acted on revelation from God. **40.** Christ had spoken the truth (not simply truth as distinct from error, but the truth about his relation to the Father and the truth about his mission). Instead of receiving it, as Abraham would have done, these Jews sought to kill the Son of man.

**41.** They did have a father, whom they imitated, whose works they reproduced, but it was not Abraham. The Jews retaliated by a slur: "We be not born of fornication." The we is emphatic. Underlying this is apparently the charge of illegitimacy leveled at Jesus (this same charge colors Matthew's report of the birth of Jesus). We, the Jews were saying, are those who truly have God for our Father, whatever your claims may be. We go back of Abraham to God himself. **42.** Jesus refuted the claim by the simple fact that their attitude toward him was not one of love, of family affection. He knew he had come from God, no matter what they might think.

**43,44.** The true reason for their failure to receive him was their kinship with the devil. He was their father. No wonder they acted as he does (cf. Mt 23:15). His special sins are lying (seen in connection with the temptation in the garden) and murder (in the incitement of Cain to slay his brother — I Jn 3:12). **45,46.** Because they were of the devil, the liar, they would not accept the truth from Christ. Yet they could not convict him of sin. That being so, they should have accepted his testimony. **47.** The very failure to accept his word sealed the fact that they were not of God.

**48.** Smarting under a series of rebukes, the Jews struck back by calling Jesus a Samaritan, i.e., one not worthy of being called a member of the people of God even though he lived on Israelitish territory. A deeper note may be struck here if the intent is to repeat the slur about the birth of Jesus. The Samaritans were

**49.** Jesus answered, I have not a devil; but I honor my Father, and ye do dishonor me.

**50.** And I seek not mine own glory: there is one that seeketh and judgeth.

**51.** Verily, verily, I say unto you, If a man keep my saying, he shall never see death.

**52.** Then said the Jews unto him, Now we know that thou hast a devil. Abraham is dead, and the prophets; and thou sayest, If a man keep my saying, he shall never taste of death.

**53.** Art thou greater than our father Abraham, which is dead? and the prophets are dead: whom makest thou thyself?

**54.** Jesus answered, If I honor myself, my honor is nothing: it is my Father that honoreth me; of whom ye say, that he is your God:

**55.** Yet ye have not known him; but I know him: and if I should say, I know him not, I shall be a liar like unto you: but I know him, and keep his saying.

**56.** Your father Abraham rejoiced to see my day: and he saw *it*, and was glad.

**57.** Then said the Jews unto him, Thou art not yet fifty years old, and hast thou seen Abraham?

**58.** Jesus said unto them, Verily, verily, I say unto you, Before Abraham was, I am.

**59.** Then took they up stones to cast at him: but Jesus hid himself, and went out of the temple, going through the midst of them, and so passed by.

## CHAPTER 9

AND as *Jesus* passed by, he saw a man which was blind from *his* birth.

**2.** And his disciples asked him, saying, Master, who did sin, this man, or his parents, that he was born blind?

**3.** Jesus answered, Neither hath this man sinned, nor his parents: but that the works of God should be made manifest in him.

**4.** I must work the works of him that sent me, while it is day: the night cometh, when no man can work.

**5.** As long as I am in the world, I am the light of the world.

**6.** When he had thus spoken, he spat on the ground, and made clay of the spittle, and he anointed the eyes of the blind man with the clay,

**7.** And said unto him, Go, wash in the pool of Siloam, (which is by interpretation, Sent.) He went his way therefore, and washed, and came seeing.

mixed stock, born of the commingling of Israelites and foreigners. Seeking to account for Jesus' strong outbursts against them (cf. v. 52), the Jews charged him with having a devil (demon).

**49,50.** Jesus denied the allegation. To say such a thing as this about him was sheer contempt, a dishonoring of him which would be brought into judgment by the Father. **51,52.** Turning to another claim, Jesus promised deathlessness for those who would keep his word. This led to ridicule from the Jews, who interpreted his word physically. They knew that death had claimed the people of God, even Abraham.

**53-58.** Did Jesus imagine that he was greater than Abraham and the prophets? The answer is twofold. Abraham knew that Another greater than himself was to come. He saw Christ's day (was this insight not given most clearly at the offering of Isaac? See Rom 8:32). Did this mean that Jesus had seen Abraham? The Jews rejected this as ridiculous, for Jesus was a man in middle life, at the most (Jn 8:57). This led to the second great claim of Jesus respecting his relation to Abraham. **Before Abraham was, I am** (cf. v. 24). Abraham was not in the beginning with God. **59.** Such assertions sounded blasphemous. Once again stones were poised to end such claims, but again the Lord eluded his opponents and went his way.

M. The Restoration of the Man Born Blind. 9:1-41.

This section has affinity with 8:12, for now Christ's claim that he was the light of the world received demonstration. It also has close connection with the following chapter, for 10:21 indicates something of the impression made by this miracle.

**1-7.** The performing of the sign. Jesus saw the man; then the disciples asked about him. The interest of Jesus quickened theirs, but from a different standpoint. To the disciples the blind man was the occasion for theological speculation; to Jesus he was a human being to be pitied and helped. The question of the disciples (v. 2) was grounded in the belief that bodily infirmity or suffering was due to sin, whether of parents (Ex 20:5) or of the man himself, presumably on the basis of the soul's pre-existence, which some Jews held. Jesus dismissed the thought of any special sin on the part of the man or his parents and invited consideration of an entirely different approach. God had

8. The neighbors therefore, and they which before had seen him that he was blind, said, Is not this he that sat and begged?

9. Some said, This is he: others *said*, He is like him: *but* he said, I am *he*.

10. Therefore said they unto him, How were thine eyes opened?

11. He answered and said, A man that is called Jesus made clay, and anointed mine eyes, and said unto me, Go to the pool of Siloam, and wash: and I went and washed, and I received sight.

12. Then said they unto him, Where is he? He said, I know not.

13. They brought to the Pharisees him that aforetime was blind.

14. And it was the sabbath day when Jesus made the clay, and opened his eyes.

15. Then again the Pharisees also asked him how he had received his sight. He said unto them, He put clay upon mine eyes, and I washed, and do see.

16. Therefore said some of the Pharisees, This man is not of God, because he keepeth not the sabbath day. Others said, How can a man that is a sinner do such miracles? And there was a division among them.

17. They say unto the blind man again, What sayest thou of him, that he hath opened thine eyes? He said, He is a prophet.

permitted this condition to demonstrate His glory, as His power would become operative in this case (v. 3). Jesus called the disciples from idle speculation to action. The time for labor (day) was all too short. In the better manuscripts the text reads, We must work. The Master was linking the disciples with himself. It was their work as well as his, even though he did it unaided (v. 4). The thought anticipates 14:12. Jesus now repeated the majestic claim of 8:12, as though to apply this truth to the miracle about to be performed (v. 5). Anointing the eyes of the blind man with clay was not necessary for the cure, but it served to put the man's faith to a severe test. Would he obey? (cf. Naaman's healing) John suggests a symbolic significance in the name of the pool — Siloam (*sent*). Presumably the name originated because of the "sending" or issuing of the waters from the spring into the pool. In the present circumstance this name bears a higher sense, pointing to Christ as the one sent of the Father, a truth repeatedly set forth in this Gospel. Obedience issued in the gift of sight (v. 7).

**8-12.** Neighbors and passers-by gathered around the restored man. The one who sat and **begged** — a natural occupation for one so afflicted — now looked so different that he created a problem of identification. Who was he? His own affirmation of identity settled the discussion (v. 9). The next question, quite naturally, concerned the manner of the cure. Resisting any temptation to enlarge on the story, the erstwhile blind man repeated the steps faithfully. The third question was equally inevitable. Who had anointed the eyes and given the command to wash? Here no answer could be given (cf. 5:13). More light was to come in this matter (vv. 35-38).

**13-17.** The group just mentioned decided it had a duty to perform, namely, to take the man to the Pharisees, because of the extraordinary nature of what had occurred. Besides, the cure had taken place on the sabbath day (v. 14). Once more the man was obliged to give an account of the miracle. His report was briefer this time, perhaps indicating that he was losing patience at being interrogated so much (9:15). The report created division (*schisma*) among these religious leaders, who were doubtless meeting informally. This element is prominent in John, especially that deeper cleavage, noted so often, between faith and unbelief (1:11,12; 3:36, etc.). One group could see nothing beyond the fact that

18. But the Jews did not believe concerning him, that he had been blind, and received his sight, until they called the parents of him that had received his sight.

19. And they asked them, saying, Is this your son, who ye say was born blind? how then doth he now see?

20. His parents answered them and said, We know that this is our son, and that he was born blind:

21. But by what means he now seeth, we know not; or who hath opened his eyes, we know not: he is of age; ask him: he shall speak for himself.

22. These *words* spake his parents, because they feared the Jews: for the Jews had agreed already, that if any man did confess that he was Christ, he should be put out of the synagogue.

23. Therefore said his parents, He is of age; ask him.

24. Then again called they the man that was blind, and said unto him, Give God the praise: we know that this man is a sinner.

25. He answered and said, Whether he be a sinner *or no*, I know not: one thing I know, that, whereas I was blind, now I see.

26. Then said they to him again, What did he to thee? how opened he thine eyes?

the Sabbath had been broken. Others among them had difficulty in concluding that a sinner could accomplish such things. But their voices did not prevail. Still, to divert attention from their own perplexity, the Pharisees began questioning the man himself. What did he think of his benefactor? He showed more discernment than the leaders. Surely his friend could be no less than a **prophet** (v. 17). Indeed he was that, a prophet mighty in deed (here) and also in word (4:19; cf. Lk 24:19).

18-23. Instead of Pharisees, Jews are mentioned here, probably not as denoting a different body, but as emphasizing their official position and their hostility to Jesus (as often in this Gospel). These men reckoned that God would not have permitted a miracle on the Sabbath, so there must have been something amiss with the man's account. They thought it would be wise to check with his **parents** (9:18). The parents were positive on two matters: this was their son; he had been born blind. They could venture to agree also that he was now able to see, since the Jews had said this themselves. But beyond this they refused to go, even though they may have known the **means** if not the who of the miracle (v. 21). Fear caused them to rest all responsibility with their son to state the case. It was apparently common knowledge that the Jews (rulers) had decided before this time to excommunicate any person who acknowledged Jesus as the Christ, i.e., the promised Messiah.

24-34. The man who had gained his sight was recalled for further questioning. **Give God the praise** (glory). That is, give us the truth. See Josh 7:19. But their opening words revealed that they were not conducting an investigation. Their minds were sealed. They hoped to break the man's testimony. Unable to gainsay the miracle, they persisted in regarding Jesus as a **sinner**. Instead of entering into debate — before, he had countered the charge of sinner with his own estimate that Jesus was a prophet — the cured man turned to safe ground, his own experience. Here he could say, **I know**. Once blind, he was now able to **see**. Others could testify of him the same things — parents, neighbors, friends — but the statement was far more meaningful coming from his lips. The Jews' affirmation of knowledge was bombast, an ex cathedra utterance; this man's confession had the weight of simple truth behind it. Weakly the Jews went back over the same ground about the means by which the

27. He answered them, I have told you already, and ye did not hear: wherefore would ye hear *it* again? will ye also be his disciples?

28. Then they reviled him, and said, Thou art his disciple; but we are Moses' disciples.

29. We know that God spake unto Moses: *as for* this *fellow*, we know not from whence he is.

30. The man answered and said unto them, Why herein is a marvelous thing, that ye know not from whence he is, and *yet* he hath opened mine eyes.

31. Now we know that God heareth not sinners: but if any man be a worshipper of God, and doeth his will, him he heareth.

32. Since the world began was it not heard that any man opened the eyes of one that was born blind.

33. If this man were not of God, he could do nothing.

34. They answered and said unto him, Thou wast altogether born in sins, and dost thou teach us? And they cast him out.

35. Jesus heard that they had cast him out; and when he had found him, he said unto him, Dost thou believe on the Son of God?

36. He answered and said, Who is he, Lord, that I might believe on him?

37. And Jesus said unto him, Thou hast both seen him, and it is he that talketh with thee.

38. And he said, Lord, I believe. And he worshipped him.

39. And Jesus said, For judgment I am come into this world, that they which see not might see; and that they which see might be made blind.

40. And *some* of the Pharisees which were with him heard these words, and said unto him, Are we blind also?

41. Jesus said unto them, If ye were blind, ye should have no sin: but now ye say, We see; therefore your sin remaineth.

miracle was performed (v. 26).

Sensing that the purpose of the questioning was not to learn the facts, the man became impatient. Why did they want a second statement when they did not accept the first (v. 27)? Thoroughly disgusted, he began to do some needling of his own. Will ye also be his disciples? Now the Jews began to resort to verbal abuse, accusing the man of being Jesus' disciple, something he had not affirmed at all. Moses had given the Sabbath law, and they were standing under his banner. Jesus was an interloper, a disturber of the religious peace. The real issue was the observance of the Law versus the freedom of Christ's regime. If the Jews had read all of Moses and read him aright, they would not have rejected Jesus (cf. 5:45). As it was, they steadfastly refused to believe that God had spoken through him (9:29). He was an upstart. This attitude seemed unreasonable to the man born blind. It was **marvelous** (remarkable, amazing) that such men, who a few moments before were so confidently saying, **we know,** did not know whence Jesus was—a man who had done something notable. Where, then, was their infallibility in religious matters? From the Jews themselves, doubtless, he had heard the point which now he threw back at them, that God would not hear sinners. The argument was sound. Trapped as a result of their own interrogations, the Jews resorted to vilification. The man's former state of blindness proved that he had been **born in sins** (cf. 9:2) and was unfit to **teach** them. When they **cast him out,** they did not formally excommunicate him, but rather expelled him from their presence, which might have led to expulsion from the synagogue later. The man had not confessed Jesus as the Christ, but simply that he was of God.

35-41. Jesus, who first saw the man in his blind condition, then healed him, now **found** him (cf. 5:14). The outcasts met — Jesus, the one cast out long before, and the man who had been so disillusioned by his experience with the leaders of his people. But the meeting was not for the purpose of mutual condolence. **Dost thou believe on the Son of God?** This was both a challenge to faith and an assertion of deity. Some of the best manuscripts read *Son of man* here, which does not materially change the sense, since this denotes the man from heaven (cf. 3:13). The question found the heart of the man open and ready to believe. He simply asked for identification of the One sent from God.

## CHAPTER 10

VERILY, verily, I say unto you, He that entereth not by the door into the sheepfold, but climbeth up some other way, the same is a thief and a robber.

2. But he that entereth in by the door is the shepherd of the sheep.

3. To him the porter openeth; and the sheep hear his voice: and he calleth his own sheep by name, and leadeth them out.

4. And when he putteth forth his own sheep, he goeth before them, and the sheep follow him: for they know his voice.

5. And a stranger will they not follow, but will flee from him; for they know not the voice of strangers.

6. This parable spake Jesus unto them; but they understood not what things they were which he spake unto them.

It was time for the self-disclosure, much as in the case of the woman of Samaria (4:26). This time the man's use of **Lord** was certainly more meaningful (the RSV has rendered the occurrence in 9:36 by "Sir"). He had thought of his benefactor as a worshiper of God (v. 31); now he was prepared to worship Him (v. 38). This was far more than deference to a great man; it was religious worship. The episode does not close without accenting the division made by Jesus. One saw the light of day and passed on to see the light of life. Others, with supposedly greater knowledge of spiritual things, were nevertheless blind, and their contact with Christ sealed that blindness (v. 39). The boast, **we see,** since it assumed a wisdom that did not include faith in the Son of God, amounted to a confession of blindness due to the sin of closing their eyes to him who was the light of the world.

N. Christ the Good Shepherd. 10:1-42.
The setting is still Jerusalem. A connection between the presentation of Christ as the Good Shepherd and the events of the preceding chapter is readily perceived. The Pharisees, acting like hirelings, had no real concern for the sheep, as evidenced by their attitude toward the blind man. When this one had been cast out, Jesus came and welcomed him into His fold.

**1-6.** The teaching here is called a **parable** (v. 6), but the word differs from the usual term. It denotes a figure of speech. Here Jesus was laying the groundwork for the application of the figure to himself in the section which follows.

**1. Sheepfold.** An enclosure where the sheep were sheltered for the night, usually adjoining the house. It had a single door. One bent on robbery would try to climb the wall. **2,3.** The one who guarded the door was the **porter,** in contrast to the shepherd, who gained admittance from the porter. There is only one shepherd here. Christ has no rival, though there are undershepherds in his Church. His personal interest in the sheep is attested by his calling them **by name** (cf. 1:43). The presence of other sheep is suggested. Not all those who were numbered among the people of God in that time could be called the Lord's sheep. **Leadeth them out**—in contrast to the act of the Pharisees in expelling the man born blind. Confidence in the shepherd is based on the **voice,** which reveals the person (cf. Gen 27:22). No stranger can get the flock to follow him,

7. Then said Jesus unto them again, Verily, verily, I say unto you, I am the door of the sheep.

8. All that ever came before me are thieves and robbers: but the sheep did not hear them.

9. I am the door: by me if any man enter in, he shall be saved, and shall go in and out, and find pasture.

10. The thief cometh not, but for to steal, and to kill, and to destroy: I am come that they might have life, and that they might have *it* more abundantly.

11. I am the good shepherd: the good shepherd giveth his life for the sheep.

12. But he that is a hireling, and not the shepherd, whose own the sheep are not, seeth the wolf coming, and leaveth the sheep, and fleeth; and the wolf catcheth them, and scattereth the sheep.

13. The hireling fleeth, because he is a hireling, and careth not for the sheep.

14. I am the good shepherd, and know my *sheep*, and am known of mine.

even if he succeeds in climbing up into the fold. **6.** Jesus' audience did not catch the import of his teaching (cf. 9:41).

**7-18.** The Lord explained the figure in terms of his own person and mission.

**7.** The truth is greater than the forms through which it is conveyed. In real life the shepherd could not be identified with **the door.** But the thought is too valuable to let slip (cf. 14:6). **8. All that ever came before me.** This is not a reference to holy men of the old covenant, but to the Jewish leaders who had gained a hold on the nation before he raised his voice. **Thieves** are those who simply steal. **Robbers** are those who also commit violence (cf. Mt 23:25). **The sheep did not hear them.** A case in point was the blind man, who had turned away from these leaders in disgust.

**9.** Did Jesus refer to undershepherds of the flock or to all believers? Favorable to the former viewpoint is the fact that entering in has already been used of the shepherd (vv. 1,2). Further, to **go in and out** is a familiar OT expression for the activity of a leader (I Sam 18:16; II Sam 3:25). Nevertheless, the breadth of the language — any man — and the words **shall be saved** favor an inclusive reference. In a redemptive sense the word **save** occurs infrequently in John (3:17; 5:34; 12:47). The freedom of the believer, in contrast to his situation in Judaism, seems hinted at in the going **in and out,** and his new satisfaction (**shall find pasture**) was a welcome change from the aridity of the teaching to which he had been subjected. **10.** The work of the Good Shepherd is constructive. **Life** answers to being saved (v. 9), and abundance answers to finding pasture. Nothing in the original warrants the addition of **more** in the translation.

**11.** Here the central revelation in this whole pattern of thought is given. **As the good shepherd,** Jesus fulfilled the OT representation of Jehovah (Ps 23:1; Isa 40:11), and also set himself over against the leaders who injured the flock because they were evil in heart. Instead of taking life, this Shepherd was prepared to give his life for the sheep. It is a prophecy as well as an attitude (cf. 9:17). **12.** Of a different sort is **the hireling,** who cares not for the sheep and deserts them in a crisis. To some extent this picture reflects the unfaithful shepherds (leaders) of OT days as they are rebuked in the prophets (see Ezk 34 especially).

**14.** The care of the Shepherd is bound up with the mutuality of knowledge and affection that characterizes the relation

15. As the Father knoweth me, even so know I the Father: and I lay down my life for the sheep.

16. And other sheep I have, which are not of this fold: them also I must bring, and they shall hear my voice; and there shall be one fold, *and* one shepherd.

17. Therefore doth my Father love me, because I lay down my life, that I might take it again.

18. No man taketh it from me, but I lay it down of myself. I have power to lay it down, and I have power to take it again. This commandment have I received of my Father.

19. There was a division therefore again among the Jews for these sayings.

20. And many of them said, He hath a devil, and is mad; why hear ye him?

21. Others said, These are not the words of him that hath a devil. Can a devil open the eyes of the blind?

22. And it was at Jerusalem the feast of the dedication, and it was winter.

23. And Jesus walked in the temple in Solomon's porch.

24. Then came the Jews round about him, and said unto him, How long dost thou make us to doubt? If thou be the Christ, tell us plainly.

between him and the sheep. **15.** A bond of knowledge exists also between the Shepherd and the Father who sent him. The Son knows the will of the Father (which includes the laying down of the life of the Son for the sheep), and the Father knows the Son, and consequently knows that he can count on his obedience in carrying out this costly mission. **16. Fold.** The same word is rendered sheepfold in 9:1. **Other sheep I have.** The language is sovereign and prophetic (cf. Acts 18:10). **Not of this fold.** Is the reference to the Jews of the Dispersion? Hardly, for they were basically one with the Palestinian Jews. Jesus envisioned the Gentiles who would respond to the Gospel. **One fold.** This is not the same word as used above, and is properly rendered *flock* (cf. one Lord, one body in Eph 4:4, 5).

**17,18.** The Father loves the Son always (17:24), but he has a special reason for loving him because of his obedience unto death. The death was a commandment of the Father (cf. the must of 3:14; Mt 16:21). No man could touch the Son until his hour had come (19:11). He would deliver up his spirit to God (19:30). But death could not be the end. With an equal sovereignty of command, the Son would reverse the sentence of death and take up his life again. He could confidently predict his resurrection.

**19-21.** For the third time in this Gospel we read of division *(schisma)* created by Jesus among his hearers (cf. 7:43; 9:16). **Many** wanted to dismiss the Lord as demonized and unworthy of being listened to. Others were impressed by the **words** he spoke (doubtless his devotion for the sheep) combined with the recollection of the miracle performed on the **blind** man.

**22-30.** *Further Discussion over the Identity of Jesus.* Probably an interval of about two months separated this occasion from the preceding. The Feast of Tabernacles belonged to the fall of the year, and the Feast of the Dedication came in the **winter.** This celebration memorialized the cleansing and rededication of the Temple by Judas Maccabaeus after the sacrilege committed by Antiochus Epiphanes. The year was 165 B.C. Jesus was accosted by some of the Jews as he walked in Solomon's porch, located in the eastern portion of the Court of the Gentiles, the largest court in the Temple area, which surrounded the inner courts and the temple proper. Their probing was very direct. **Make us to doubt.** Literally,

25. Jesus answered them, I told you, and ye believed not: the works that I do in my Father's name, they bear witness of me.

26. But ye believe not, because ye are not of my sheep, as I said unto you.

27. My sheep hear my voice, and I know them, and they follow me:

28. And I give unto them eternal life; and they shall never perish, neither shall any *man* pluck them out of my hand.

29. My Father, which gave *them* me, is greater than all; and no *man* is able to pluck *them* out of my Father's hand.

30. I and *my* Father are one.

31. Then the Jews took up stones again to stone him.

32. Jesus answered them, Many good works have I showed you from my Father; for which of those works do ye stone me?

33. The Jews answered him, saying, For a good work we stone thee not; but for blasphemy; and because that thou, being a man, makest thyself God.

*lift up our soul.* In other words, Jesus was keeping them in suspense. They wanted a straight answer. Was he the Christ or not?

Our Lord put his finger on the difficulty. It was not lack of information but lack of willingness to believe. His own testimony should have been sufficient; if not, in their case, then his works had a witness to bear for him (cf. 14:11). There was no lack of clarity in his case; the trouble lay with them. Evidently they did not belong to him, since they had not been willing to follow him. They perceived that his shepherd teaching meant a new order, and they were not prepared to leave the Judaism they knew, to which they clung. Yet the new order offered blessing and security which they could not have known in their Pharisaism. Christ offered **eternal life** as a gift (10:28; cf. v. 10). In saying that they should **never perish** if they belonged to his sheep, Jesus used the strongest form of statement known to the language. This certainty was possible because the life offered was grounded in his gift (Rom 11: 29) rather than in human achievement. His own sheep are safe also from alien influences — **neither shall any man pluck them out of my hand.** The sheep belong to Christ because they are the Father's gift to him (10:29). Naturally the Father has a stake in their preservation. Since he is supreme — **greater than all** — it is unthinkable that any power will be able to snatch them away from his protective hand (cf. Rom 8:38,39). The conclusion of the matter is that no separation can be made between the Father and the Son. They are more than collaborators; they are one in essence (the word **one** is not masculine — one person — but neuter, oneness of being).

**31-33.** For the second time Jesus was menaced with stoning by his opponents (cf. 8:59). The provocation here was his claim of oneness with the Father, amounting to blasphemy in the eyes of the Jews, who denied Jesus' heavenly origin. In meeting their opposition, the Lord did not depend on repetition of his claim or enlargement on it, but turned from his words to his works. They were the easier to understand and appreciate. **Many good works.** Attention had been focused mainly on a few, but these were representative of others which are not reported (20:30). They were good works, as was to be expected if they emanated from the **Father.** Could the Jews seriously mean to stone a man because of **good** works? In an-

34. Jesus answered them, Is it not written in your law, I said, Ye are gods?

35. If he called them gods, unto whom the word of God came, and the Scripture cannot be broken;

36. Say ye of him, whom the Father hath sanctified, and sent into the world, Thou blasphemest; because I said, I am the Son of God?

37. If I do not the works of my Father, believe me not.

38. But if I do, though ye believe not me, believe the works; that ye may know, and believe, that the Father is in me, and I in him.

39. Therefore they sought again to take him; but he escaped out of their hand,

40. And went away again beyond Jordan into the place where John at first baptized; and there he abode.

41. And many resorted unto him, and said, John did no miracle: but all things that John spake of this man were true.

42. And many believed on him there.

swer, the Jews brushed aside all reference to works, which they could not deny, and returned to the issue of Jesus' words, which they felt bound to deny on the ground of blasphemy. To them Jesus was a man who had dared to make himself out to be God. On this ground they sought his death now, and on this ground they would seek it later (19:7).

34-38. In this impasse the one hope of finding a basis for further discussion lay in appeal to the law (there are strong manuscript witnesses favorable to the omission of your), since the Jews accepted that. Law is used here in the broad sense as referring to the OT Scriptures. The words in question, Ye are gods, occur in Ps 82:6, in reference to Hebrew judges. God's word had invested them with a certain divinity of status as his representatives. Since the Scripture (with special reference to the passage in question) could not be broken so as to enable men to reject the teaching, how could objection be raised against him whom the Father had specially set apart and sent into the world? For Christ to have said less than to affirm that he was the Son of God would have been to speak an untruth. To affirm his sonship was not blasphemy (Jn 10:36). If the Jews could not test his verbal claims, they could at least judge on the basis of the works (vv. 37,38; cf. vv. 25,32). It should be possible to progress through the works to a faith in the person. This is the thrust also in 20: 30,31.

39-42. The repeated assertion of oneness with the Father caused a threat of violence once more. It was time for the Lord to depart from the city. He found refuge at Bethany, beyond Jordan, where John had formerly baptized (v. 40). Even in retirement he could not be hid. People remembered what John had said about him, and they were able to note the difference between John's ministry, as devoid of miracle, and that of Jesus, which was marked by signs. Clearly the greater one had come, as John had stated. Unbelief was no longer reasonable. Many put their trust in Jesus there. Their faith throws into dark relief the stubborn unbelief of the leaders at Jerusalem.

O. The Raising of Lazarus. 11:1-57.

This account includes the narrative of the sickness, death, and resurrection of Jesus' friend and the reaction of official Judaism to the miracle. It concludes with a notice of the heightened popular interest in this man who was stirring the na-

## CHAPTER 11

NOW a certain *man* was sick, *named* Lazarus, of Bethany, the town of Mary and her sister Martha.

2. (It was *that* Mary which anointed the Lord with ointment, and wiped his feet with her hair, whose brother Lazarus was sick.)

3. Therefore his sisters sent unto him, saying, Lord, behold, he whom thou lovest is sick.

4. When Jesus heard *that*, he said, This sickness is not unto death, but for the glory of God, that the Son of God might be glorified thereby.

5. Now Jesus loved Martha, and her sister, and Lazarus.

6. When he had heard therefore that he was sick, he abode two days still in the same place where he was.

7. Then after that saith he to *his* disciples, Let us go into Judea again.

8. *His* disciples say unto him, Master, the Jews of late sought to stone thee; and goest thou thither again?

tion. The One who had proved himself the Light of the world by giving sight to the blind man now showed himself as the Life of men, the Overcomer of death.

**1-4.** John gives the setting for the miracle — the illness of Lazarus and the communication of this fact to Jesus. Mary and Martha are mentioned as though they were already familiar to the reader (cf. Lk 10:38-42), but Lazarus needs introduction because his name does not appear in the Lucan account. It is of interest that all three of these names occur on ossuary inscriptions of Judea excavated in recent years, showing that such names were common in this period (W. F. Albright, *The Archaeology of Palestine*, p. 244). The writer anticipates his own narrative of 12:1-9 in identifying Lazarus as the brother of that Mary who anointed the Lord (11:2). In conveying the information about Lazarus' illness to Jesus, the sisters showed remarkable restraint, being content simply to state the fact, without making request (v. 3). Yet the mention of Jesus' love for Lazarus was a species of appeal in itself, delicate indeed. **This sickness is not unto death.** Even as he spoke, Lazarus was probably already dead (cf. v. 39). The words belong to a higher plane of meaning, associated with the glory of God, which is also that of the Son. A resurrection would demonstrate that glory (a revelation of divine power) more fully than restoration from a sick bed.

**5,6.** Jesus' love for the entire family is noted, only to be challenged, in appearance at least, by his own inaction in remaining where he was for two days, with no move to return to Bethany. The latter part of the chapter helps to unravel this mystery. By waiting, then coming and raising Lazarus from the dead, Jesus stirred up such opposition as to make his own death certain. This was the measure of his love for the family at Bethany.

**7-16.** *Discussion between the Lord and his disciples over the Lazarus crisis.* Jesus proposed a return to Judea—not Bethany, as though they might visit the family, then return—but Judea, the center of opposition to himself. The disciples caught at this immediately. It seemed foolhardy, like walking into a trap. Jesus had barely escaped a stoning not long before (11:8; cf. 10:31,39). The Master's reply may have gained point by being spoken shortly after dawn. It applied both to himself and to his followers. He could safely go back to Judea as long

9. Jesus answered, Are there not twelve hours in the day? If any man walk in the day, he stumbleth not, because he seeth the light of this world.

10. But if a man walk in the night, he stumbleth, because there is no light in him.

11. These things said he: and after that he saith unto them, Our friend Lazarus sleepeth; but I go, that I may awake him out of sleep.

12. Then said his disciples, Lord, if he sleep, he shall do well.

13. Howbeit Jesus spake of his death: but they thought that he had spoken of taking of rest in sleep.

14. Then said Jesus unto them plainly, Lazarus is dead.

15. And I am glad for your sakes that I was not there, to the intent ye may believe; nevertheless let us go unto him.

16. Then said Thomas, which is called Didymus, unto his fellow disciples, Let us also go, that we may die with him.

17. Then when Jesus came, he found that he had *lain* in the grave four days already.

18. Now Bethany was nigh unto Jerusalem, about fifteen furlongs off:

19. And many of the Jews came to Martha and Mary, to comfort them concerning their brother.

20. Then Martha, as soon as she heard that Jesus was coming, went and met him: but Mary sat *still* in the house.

21. Then said Martha unto Jesus, Lord, if thou hadst been here, my brother had not died.

22. But I know, that even now, whatsoever thou wilt ask of God, God will give *it* thee.

as he was walking in the light of the Father's will. His enemies could not touch him until his hour had come. Then for a brief time the darkness of spiritual opposition would be permitted to close in upon him (v. 9). As for the disciples, it behooved them not to walk in the darkness of self-will and separation from him. Lacking his light, they would indeed stumble (cf. 9:4,5). **Our friend Lazarus sleepeth.** Not knowing of his death, the disciples interpreted this saying of the Lord literally and found in it ground of hope for his recovery. But Jesus had used "sleep" in a special sense as referring to believers' death (cf. Acts 7:60; I Thess 4:13). He followed this with the blunt announcement that Lazarus was dead (Jn 11:14). Another paradox is the Saviour's saying that he was glad he had not been there. The reason is clear. Had he been there, Lazarus would not have died (no one ever did in His presence); and in that case one of the greatest lessons of faith about to be impressed on the disciples through Lazarus' resurrection would have been impossible (v. 15). The disciples were never so advanced as not to need confirmation and development of their faith. Thomas, called Didymus *(twin),* was the first to respond to Jesus' second proposal to go into Judea (11:15,16; cf. v. 7).

**17-19. Four days.** Likely Lazarus died shortly after the messenger was sent. Allowing a day for his travel, two days of tarrying by Jesus, and one day for the return, we arrive at this total. The distance from Bethany beyond Jordan to Bethany near Jerusalem was about twenty miles. Since the home was only two miles from the city Jerusalem (v. 18), **many of the Jews** found it possible to come and offer condolences. **Jews** here does not refer to rulers. Their presence was two-edged, however. Having come to Bethany as mourners, some of them returned to Jerusalem as informers (11:46).

**20-27.** *The meeting between Jesus and Martha.* Both sisters appear in this account in characteristic roles. Martha, ready for action, was the one to welcome Jesus. Mary, absorbed in her grief, sat still. Martha had one regret—Jesus had not been there. What a difference his presence would have made! Yet she voiced no criticism. As already noted, Lazarus was dead when the news of his illness came to Jesus. Martha felt in Jesus a tower of strength. Her words (v. 22) almost defy analysis, however. They

328

23. Jesus saith unto her, Thy brother shall rise again.

24. Martha saith unto him, I know that he shall rise again in the resurrection at the last day.

25. Jesus said unto her, I am the resurrection, and the life: he that believeth in me, though he were dead, yet shall he live:

26. And whosoever liveth and believeth in me shall never die. Believest thou this?

27. She saith unto him, Yea, Lord: I believe that thou art the Christ, the Son of God, which should come into the world.

28. And when she had so said, she went her way, and called Mary her sister secretly, saying, The Master is come, and calleth for thee.

29. As soon as she heard that, she arose quickly, and came unto him.

30. Now Jesus was not yet come into the town, but was in that place where Martha met him.

31. The Jews then which were with her in the house, and comforted her, when they saw Mary, that she rose up hastily and went out, followed her, saying, She goeth unto the grave to weep there.

32. Then when Mary was come where Jesus was, and saw him, she fell down at his feet, saying unto him, Lord, if thou hadst been here, my brother had not died.

33. When Jesus therefore saw her weeping, and the Jews also weeping which came with her, he groaned in the spirit, and was troubled,

34. And said, Where have ye laid him? They say unto him, Lord, come and see.

35. Jesus wept.

36. Then said the Jews, Behold how he loved him!

are an expression of confidence in him as being in close touch with God and able to get a boon from him; yet immediate resurrection does not seem to have been in her mind (cf. v. 24). In affirming the resurrection of Lazarus, Jesus did not name any time (v. 23). Martha supplied this—at the last day; but she said it without enthusiasm, for meanwhile her brother lay in the embrace of death. The Lord now moved to correct Martha's imperfect faith (cf. v. 22) by drawing her attention to his lordship over death. **I am the resurrection and the life.** In this case the revelation of word preceded the revelation of deed. The teaching goes beyond the case of Lazarus and includes all who believe. Two truths are stated here. The believer may die, as Lazarus had done, but by Christ's power will **live**, i.e., experience resurrection. But even more important is the possession of eternal life gained through faith in Christ. Those who have this life can never die in the sense of being separated from the source of life (vv. 25,26). Challenged to believe this, Martha made the very confession for which this book was written (11:27; 20:31), but she did not understand the implications of her own statement. To her, Christ was not yet the absolute Lord of life and death, a complete Saviour (cf. vv. 39,40).

**28-32. Jesus and Mary.** Martha passed on to Mary quietly (**secretly**) the news that the Master (teacher) had come, probably hoping to make possible a private meeting with Jesus for her sister. But the Jews who were present followed Mary to the place outside the village where Jesus and Martha had met, for they thought at first that she was leaving the house to go to the grave. As token alike of reverence and of her own helplessness, Mary fell **at his feet.** Her opening words were the same as those of Martha. Probably this sentiment had been expressed over and over by the two after the death of their brother.

**33-37. The grief of Jesus.** He **groaned in the spirit.** The Greek word for **groaned**, repeated in verse 38, seems regularly to convey the thought of anger over something. Since Christ could hardly have felt anger toward Mary and the mourning friends, it is probable that his deep emotion was due to his inwardly protesting the havoc sin has brought into the world, with sickness and death and sorrow as its terrible entail. On the way to the tomb, Jesus **wept**, breaking

37. And some of them said, Could not this man, which opened the eyes of the blind, have caused that even this man should not have died?

38. Jesus therefore again groaning in himself cometh to the grave. It was a cave, and a stone lay upon it.

39. Jesus said, Take ye away the stone. Martha, the sister of him that was dead, saith unto him, Lord, by this time he stinketh: for he hath been *dead* four days.

40. Jesus saith unto her, Said I not unto thee, that, if thou wouldest believe, thou shouldest see the glory of God?

41. Then they took away the stone *from the place* where the dead was laid. And Jesus lifted up *his* eyes, and said, Father, I thank thee that thou hast heard *me*.

42. And I knew that thou hearest me always: but because of the people which stand by I said *it*, that they may believe that thou hast sent me.

43. And when he thus had spoken, he cried with a loud voice, Lazarus, come forth.

44. And he that was dead came forth, bound hand and foot with graveclothes; and his face was bound about with a napkin. Jesus saith unto them, Loose him, and let him go.

45. Then many of the Jews which came to Mary, and had seen the things which Jesus did, believed on him.

46. But some of them went their ways to the Pharisees, and told them what things Jesus had done.

47. Then gathered the chief priests and the Pharisees a council, and said, What do we? for this man doeth many miracles.

out into tears. This was silent weeping in contrast to Christ's audible weeping over Jerusalem (Lk 19:41). The Jews who were present saw in the weeping a proof of Jesus' great affection for Lazarus, but they saw in it also evidence of his limitation. He had given sight to the blind (Jn 11:9), but death was too great for his powers (v. 37). Perhaps in the second **groaning** there was a mingling of indignation at this shortsighted view of his power.

**38-44.** *The miracle itself.* This **cave** at Bethany has been described by one who inspected it in modern times as of the deep rock-cut type. **Take ye away the stone.** Only Christ could raise the dead, but others could participate according to their ability. Martha, shocked at such an order from Jesus, tried to interpose an objection; she thought the body had surely begun to decompose. **Four days** had elapsed since death. Without saying what he proposed to do, Jesus summoned Martha to faith, reminding her of his previous words, apparently harking back to verse 23. But this time he stated the coming event in terms of **the glory of God** (cf. 11:4). The glory here was the power of God in operation, declaring his sovereignty (cf. 2:11). There could be no turning back now; the stone was removed (v. 41). One thing more remained to be done. For the sake of the people (literally, *the multitude*) it had to be made clear that what was about to be done would be done through the community of life and power enjoyed by the Son with the Father—that they might **believe**. This was not a request to be heard but a prayer of thanksgiving for a constant bond of communion and understanding. The hold of death was broken by the voice of authority calling, **Lazarus, come forth.** Christ had declared that the time was coming when all the righteous dead would similarly obey that same authority (cf. 5: 28,29). The Lord left untouched the work of loving hands that had prepared the body for burial, that they might have the thrill of undoing that work and setting Lazarus free. (Recall human participation in removing the stone.)

**45,46.** The miracle resulted in a characteristically varying response. Many of the Jews . . . believed; others went to the Pharisees to report what had taken place.

**47-50.** *The effect upon the Sanhedrin.* This was one of **many** miracles. The rulers felt completely frustrated. What

48. If we let him thus alone, all *men* will believe on him; and the Romans shall come and take away both our place and nation.

49. And one of them, *named* Caiaphas, being the high priest that same year, said unto them, Ye know nothing at all,

50. Nor consider that it is expedient for us, that one man should die for the people, and that the whole nation perish not.

51. And this spake he not of himself: but being high priest that year, he prophesied that Jesus should die for that nation;

52. And not for that nation only, but that also he should gather together in one the children of God that were scattered abroad.

53. Then from that day forth they took counsel together for to put him to death.

54. Jesus therefore walked no more openly among the Jews; but went thence unto a country near to the wilderness, into a city called Ephraim, and there continued with his disciples.

55. And the Jews' passover was nigh at hand: and many went out of the country up to Jerusalem before the passover, to purify themselves.

56. Then sought they for Jesus, and spake among themselves, as they stood in the temple, What think ye, that he will not come to the feast?

57. Now both the chief priests and the Pharisees had given a commandment, that, if any man knew where he were, he should show *it*, that they might take him.

were they to do? They expressed the fear that all the people would **believe** on him—in the sense of giving him their support and following him as their Messiah. This would certainly bring the Romans down on the Jews with force, as they would interpret such a thing as a political revolution. Then the Jews would lose their **place** (Temple) and **nation.** Under the Romans, since the time of Julius Caesar, they had enjoyed certain privileges as "the nation of the Jews." Exactly the situation they feared did develop as a result of the war of the Jews against Rome, A.D. 66–70. Shaming the group into silence with his censure, "Ye know nothing at all," Caiaphas laid out a course of action that was ruthless but simple: Get rid of the offender. Make him die for the people, so that the whole nation would not perish. **That year.** Not a reference to tenure of office, but to the importance of that year for Israel and the world.

51,52. John wanted his readers to sense the fact that this utterance of the high priest was prophetic. The words, so to speak, were put into his mouth. **He prophesied.** Here is a Balaam who would curse Jesus, but out of the prophecy comes the realization of the purpose of God that Christ should die for the nation in a redemptive, vicarious sense, and even for a larger group, that all the dispersed children of God (in a prospective sense) would be brought together (cf. 10:16). How fitting it was that one who filled the office of high priest should unwittingly set forth the work of Christ as the Lamb who takes away sin!

53,54. The counsel of the high priest solidified the purpose of the council so that, from that time forth, it was fully determined on Jesus' death. On this account Jesus found it wise to retire from the area and go to a place called Ephraim, in a near-desert section. This has been tentatively identified as a place twelve miles or so north of Bethany, near where the high plateau breaks away in rugged terrain leading down to the Jordan valley.

55-57. With the Passover at hand, Jesus could not be absent from the city for long. Since the time was not yet ripe, Ephraim was no substitute for the upper room. Jesus' next doings are cloaked in silence. John shifts our attention to the pilgrims who began to wend their way to Jerusalem. For the most part they were friendly to Jesus, in contrast to the authorities, and exchanged opinions

## CHAPTER 12

THEN Jesus six days before the passover came to Bethany, where Lazarus was which had been dead, whom he raised from the dead.

2. There they made him a supper; and Martha served: but Lazarus was one of them that sat at the table with him.

3. Then took Mary a pound of ointment of spikenard, very costly, and anointed the feet of Jesus, and wiped his feet with her hair: and the house was filled with the odor of the ointment.

4. Then saith one of his disciples, Judas Iscariot, Simon's *son*, which should betray him,

5. Why was not this ointment sold for three hundred pence, and given to the poor?

6. This he said, not that he cared for the poor; but because he was a thief, and had the bag, and bare what was put therein.

7. Then said Jesus, Let her alone: against the day of my burying hath she kept this.

8. For the poor always ye have with you; but me ye have not always.

with one another as to whether their hero would dare to brave the opposition of the council by coming to the feast. There must have been many informers if the rulers had any hold at all upon the people (v. 57).

**P. Jesus in Bethany and Jerusalem. 12:1-50.**

The events included here are: the anointing of Jesus by Mary of Bethany (vv. 1-11); the Triumphal Entry (vv. 12-19); the coming of the Greeks (vv. 20-26); Jesus' consciousness of the approaching Passion (vv. 27-36); the unbelief of the people and their rulers (vv. 37-43); Jesus' final public plea for faith (vv. 44-50).

The supper at Bethany is narrated with certain variations from the accounts in Matthew and Mark. 1. **Six days before the passover,** i.e., Saturday. The other accounts give the location as the house of Simon the leper. John alone mentions the presence of Lazarus. 2. **They made him a supper.** Simon would have felt gratitude for his healing, and the sisters of Lazarus for the raising of their brother from the dead. 3. **A pound** *(litra)*, a measure of twelve ounces. **Spikenard.** Oil from a plant grown in northern India, very costly as an import into Palestine. Mary is always associated with **the feet of Jesus** (Lk 10:39; Jn 11:32). **The house was filled with the odour of the ointment.** This answers in its own way to the reported words of Jesus in the Synoptics that in the world-wide preaching of the Gospel this act would be told as a memorial of the woman. The fragrance of the act would have a wide distribution and a lasting effect.

5. Judas estimated the value of the nard at **three hundred pence,** or nearly sixty dollars. 6. His apparent concern for the poor was a cloak for his own covetousness. He had just missed a chance for theft on a larger scale than usual. Evidently he did not make a regular treasurer's report. 7. Jesus shielded Mary by cutting short the criticism. **Let her alone.** It appears from the Synoptics that Judas, stung by this rebuke, slipped out and bargained with the chief priests to betray the Master. Jesus saw in Mary's act a deep significance — **against the day of my burying hath she kept this.** However much Mary may have wished to help the poor ordinarily, she had reserved this precious portion for Christ. She anticipated his death. In contrast to the rulers, Mary believed in Jesus' person; in con-

9. Much people of the Jews therefore knew that he was there: and they came not for Jesus' sake only, but that they might see Lazarus also, whom he had raised from the dead.

10. But the chief priests consulted that they might put Lazarus also to death;

11. Because that by reason of him many of the Jews went away, and believed on Jesus.

12. On the next day much people that were come to the feast, when they heard that Jesus was coming to Jerusalem,

13. Took branches of palm trees, and went forth to meet him, and cried, Hosanna: Blessed is the King of Israel that cometh in the name of the Lord.

14. And Jesus, when he had found a young ass, sat thereon; as it is written,

15. Fear not, daughter of Sion: behold, thy King cometh, sitting on an ass's colt.

16. These things understood not his disciples at the first: but when Jesus was glorified, then remembered they that these things were written of him, and that they had done these things unto him.

17. The people therefore that was with him when he called Lazarus out of his grave, and raised him from the dead, bare record.

18. For this cause the people also met him, for that they heard that he had done this miracle.

19. The Pharisees therefore said among themselves, Perceive ye how ye prevail nothing? behold, the world is gone after him.

trast to many who believed in a general way, her faith included the work of the Saviour—his death.

**9.** Lazarus proved an attraction to many of the people, who came to see him as well as Jesus. These were curious but sympathetic. **10,11.** In contrast, the chief priests found in the situation reason to include Lazarus in their dark plotting as one who was enhancing the cause of Jesus. A second murder would not have disturbed their hardened consciences.

The next incident has become traditionally known as the Triumphal Entry, although such a title better fits Jesus' future coming. **12.** It is clear that those who sought to honor the Lord were pilgrims, not residents of Jerusalem. They had come for the feast of Passover. **13.** John alone mentions the use of palm branches. They are cited by the writer of II Maccabees (10:7) in connection with the rededication of the Temple by Judas Maccabaeus after its desecration by the Syrians. Hosanna. A Hebrew term meaning, *Save, I pray* (cf. Ps 118:25). In the NT its use is confined to this incident. At times it was not so much a prayer as an ascription of praise, and such is its use here. Jesus was being saluted as King of Israel, who had come with the authority of the Lord (Jehovah). These people were looking to him to establish David's kingdom with power (cf. Mk 11:10). The crowd was filled with Messianic expectation (cf. Jn 6:15).

**14,15. Jesus . . . found.** The story is given in Mk 11:1-6. John is the only Evangelist who describes the animal as a young ass (*onarion*). Jesus' act fulfilled the prophetic word (Zech 9:9). The ass, better than the horse, symbolized the meek and peaceful character of the King of Israel. This in itself declared that Jesus' understanding of the event differed from that of the throng. **16.** Only when Jesus was glorified, only when the Spirit had come to instruct and bring the things of Christ to their remembrance (7:39; 14:26), did the disciples view this whole scene in the light of Scripture and the plan of God.

**17,18.** John informs his readers that no small part of the enthusiasm displayed during the march on Jerusalem was due to the raising of Lazarus. The people who were with Jesus on that occasion bare record (*kept bearing witness*). Another group, pilgrims to the feast who had only heard of the miracle, advanced to meet Jesus and hail him as their national hero. **19.** This wave of popularity

20. And there were certain Greeks among them that came up to worship at the feast:

21. The same came therefore to Philip, which was of Bethsaida of Galilee, and desired him, saying, Sir, we would see Jesus.

22. Philip cometh and telleth Andrew: and again Andrew and Philip tell Jesus.

23. And Jesus answered them, saying, The hour is come, that the Son of man should be glorified.

24. Verily, verily, I say unto you, Except a corn of wheat fall into the ground and die, it abideth alone: but if it die, it bringeth forth much fruit.

25. He that loveth his life shall lose it; and he that hateth his life in this world shall keep it unto life eternal.

26. If any man serve me, let him follow me; and where I am, there shall also my servant be: if any man serve me, him will *my* Father honor.

27. Now is my soul troubled; and what shall I say? Father, save me from this hour: but for this cause came I unto this hour.

cast gloom in the camp of the Pharisees. In their pessimism they declared that the **world** (everybody concerned) had gone after Jesus. **20.** The movement toward Jesus continued in the incident of the Greeks who expressed a desire to see Jesus. They were representatives of the world in a larger sense than that suggested by the Pharisees. It was fitting that the **Greeks** should appear now, on the eve of the Passion. They would profit from the Saviour's death, as would the great host of Gentiles whom they represented. **Worship.** Jewish custom restricted them to the Court of the Gentiles. Soon, in Christ, the middle wall of partition would be broken down. It appears that these men resembled Cornelius of a later time. They could be called God-fearers, but were not proselytes who had joined the congregation of Israel. **21.** Philip is a Greek name. This disciple was a natural point of contact with Jesus. **See Jesus,** i.e., have an interview with him. **22.** Andrew also is a Greek name. This disciple seemed to specialize in bringing people to Christ (1:41; 6:8,9).

**23.** Without addressing the Greeks directly, Jesus met their need. They would not have to wait long to profit from his mission — **the hour is come. Glorified.** This is explained in the following verse. In John's Gospel glorification begins with death and includes resurrection. **24. Corn.** Grain or seed. Nature provides a parable of Jesus' career. Apart from death his life stands in isolation, with no power of increase. Death is the key to spiritual fruitfulness. **25. He that loveth his life.** The same principle obtains for the disciple. "He who seeks to gather round himself that which is perishable, so far perishes with it: he who divests himself of all that is of this world only, so far prepares himself for the higher life" (Westcott, *op. cit.)* **26. Let him follow.** Serving Christ involves following him, even unto death. This will be rewarded by sharing the glorious future with him, including recognition by the Father. This prospect is open to **any man** (Greek as well as Jew). **27.** By speaking of these things, Jesus was made more acutely conscious of the price he would soon be paying for the fulfillment of his office as Redeemer. **Save me.** This is a touch of Gethsemane distress. Jesus' natural inclination was to be saved from the **hour** that was drawing near. Such a prayer bears eloquent testimony to the awfulness of the hour. But Jesus' commitment was so complete that

28. Father, glorify thy name. Then came there a voice from heaven, *saying*, I have both glorified *it*, and will glorify *it* again.

29. The people therefore that stood by, and heard *it*, said that it thundered: others said, An angel spake to him.

30. Jesus answered and said, This voice came not because of me, but for your sakes.

31. Now is the judgment of this world: now shall the prince of this world be cast out.

32. And I, if I be lifted up from the earth, will draw all *men* unto me.

33. This he said, signifying what death he should die.

34. The people answered him, We have heard out of the law that Christ abideth for ever; and how sayest thou, The Son of man must be lifted up? who is this Son of man?

35. Then Jesus said unto them, Yet a little while is the light with you. Walk while ye have the light, lest darkness come upon you: for he that walketh in darkness knoweth not whither he goeth.

36. While ye have light, believe in the light, that ye may be the children of light. These things spake Jesus, and departed, and did hide himself from them.

37. But though he had done so many miracles before them, yet they believed not on him:

38. That the saying of Esaias the prophet might be fulfilled, which he spake, Lord, who hath believed our report? and to whom hath the arm of the Lord been revealed?

39. Therefore they could not believe, because that Esaias said again,

40. He hath blinded their eyes, and hardened their heart; that they should not see with *their* eyes, nor understand with *their* heart, and be converted, and I should heal them.

he had to face it. That was why he came. So the prayer was not prolonged.

28. Another prayer took its place. **Glorify thy name.** The Father would do this as he enabled the Son to face his hour and accomplish his mission. **I have . . . glorified.** The glory of the Son, manifested in life and work thus far, reflected glory on the name of the Father. **Again,** namely, in the Passion, which would issue in resurrection and exaltation. 29. **The people,** limited in their understanding, misinterpreted the Father's witness.

31. Jesus' hour would bring not only suffering for him but judgment upon the sinful world that would put him on the cross, and ruin for Satan, who heads up the world system. The expelled Christ would expel the one who drives men to reject Him (cf. Col 2:15). 32. Christ himself, when in apparent defeat, would actually be in position to draw men to himself by the power of his sacrifice. Glory would triumph over shame. Victory would shine through dark tragedy. **All men,** the Greeks included, would come to know the pull of his redeeming love. **Unto me.** Salvation is unto Christ as well as through him. 33. **What** (sort of) **death.** The lifting up answers to crucifixion. Jesus knew he would not die by stoning.

34. The **Christ** (*Messiah*) whom the people had learned to expect from the law (OT in general) **abideth for ever.** How, then, could Jesus as the Son of man fulfill this expectation by being lifted up to die? Such a Son of man did not agree with their Messianic expectations. The hopes they had entertained at Christ's entry into Jerusalem were now dashed. 35,36. Before the contact with the people was broken, Jesus warned them that the light was going to shine only for a limited time. If they did not receive it, darkness would cover them.

The warning apparently went unheeded. John summarizes the resistance to the light that continued to the end (vv. 37-43). 37. The miracles had not brought the multitudes to faith in the Lord. Only samples of the miracles out of **many** are found in John. 38. This lack of faith was in agreement with the prophetic announcement of Isaiah (53:1). Significantly, this is the chapter in Isaiah that gives prominence to the death of Messiah. 39,40. **They could not believe.** Their hardness of heart made this inevitable. **Blinded . . . hardened.** This activity of God cannot be viewed as deliberately planned to make faith impossible for

41. These things said Esaias, when he saw his glory, and spake of him.

42. Nevertheless among the chief rulers also many believed on him; but because of the Pharisees they did not confess *him*, lest they should be put out of the synagogue:

43. For they loved the praise of men more than the praise of God.

44. Jesus cried and said, He that believeth on me, believeth not on me, but on him that sent me.

45. And he that seeth me seeth him that sent me.

46. I am come a light into the world, that whosoever believeth on me should not abide in darkness.

47. And if any man hear my words, and believe not, I judge him not: for I came not to judge the world, but to save the world.

48. He that rejecteth me, and receiveth not my words, hath one that judgeth him: the word that I have spoken, the same shall judge him in the last day.

49. For I have not spoken of myself; but the Father which sent me, he gave me a commandment, what I should say, and what I should speak.

50. And I know that his commandment is life everlasting: whatsoever I speak therefore, even as the Father said unto me, so I speak.

## CHAPTER 13

NOW before the feast of the passover, when Jesus knew that his hour was come that he should depart out of this world unto the Father, having loved his own which were in the world, he loved them unto the end.

those who desire to believe. Rather, this is the answer of God to unbelief. The Lord would have to **heal** them if they **converted** (turned to him), so his faithfulness is not impugned. Judicial hardening is a phase of divine judgment. The quotation is from Isa 6:10. **I should heal.** Christ becomes the subject here. **41. His glory,** i.e., Christ's. Even as Isaiah foresaw His sufferings (cf. v. 38), so he saw His glory (Isa 6).

**42,43. Nevertheless** prepares the reader for an exception to the generally hardened condition of Israel. The "identity of these rulers who "believed" is unknown. Unwillingness to confess Christ, however, throws doubt on the complete genuineness of the faith of these men (cf. 2:23-25). They proved themselves unworthy of divine commendation.

At this point John introduces Jesus' final presentation of himself to the nation. **44,45. Cried,** emphasizing the public character of the teaching and its urgency. Jesus reaffirmed his commission from the Father (12:44) and his oneness with him (v. 45). **46. A light.** Cf. 1:7-9; 3:19; 8: 12; 9:5; 12:35. **47,48.** If the words of Christ were rejected now, they would act as judge in the last day. His words would never pass away. **49.** Jesus had said only what the Father had given him to speak. How then could he be guilty of blasphemy or untruth? **50. Life everlasting.** This is found in the spoken word of Jesus, even as it is present in himself as the Word (6:63; 1:1,4,18).

**III. Christ's Ministry to His Own. 13:1 –17:26.**

A. The Foot Washing. 13:1-17.

From the Synoptics we learn how Jesus sent two of his disciples to prepare the upper room for the feast and the fellowship he had planned to have with his disciples (Lk 22:7-13).

**1. Now before the feast of the passover.** This raises questions. Was the meal in the upper room a fellowship meal, or was it truly the Passover? In two other passages John seems to say that the Passover had not yet come (13:29; 18:28). It is clear from the Synoptics that Jesus and the disciples did eat the Passover. This dating in John may represent a protest against the official Jewish observance of the day, on the ground of following a different calendar, in line with the practice of the Qumran sect (Matthew Black, "The Arrest and Trial of Jesus and the Date of the Last Supper," in *New Testa-*

2. And supper being ended, the devil having now put into the heart of Judas Iscariot, Simon's *son*, to betray him;

3. Jesus knowing that the Father had given all things into his hands, and that he was come from God, and went to God;

4. He riseth from supper, and laid aside his garments; and took a towel, and girded himself.

5. After that he poureth water into a basin, and began to wash the disciples' feet, and to wipe *them* with the towel wherewith he was girded.

6. Then cometh he to Simon Peter: and Peter saith unto him, Lord, dost thou wash my feet?

7. Jesus answered and said unto him, What I do thou knowest not now; but thou shalt know hereafter.

8. Peter saith unto him, Thou shalt never wash my feet. Jesus answered him, If I wash thee not, thou hast no part with me.

*ment Essays: Studies in Memory of T. W. Manson,* ed. by A. J. B. Higgins, pp. 19-33). Another possibility is that the references in Jn 13:29 and 18:28 to the Passover as still future are to be explained as references to the Feast of Unleavened Bread, which was sometimes called the Passover (Lk 22:1). This began immediately after Passover and continued for a week. Even so, the meal referred to here seems to have been held before the Passover, whether it be regarded as a proper observance of the annual feast or not. **Hour.** Viewed here not from the standpoint of suffering but of vindication and return to the Father (cf. 19:30; Lk 23:46). **Loved them unto the end.** Or, at the end (at the conclusion of days of preparation and anticipation). This expression *(eis telos)* may also mean "unto the utmost" (cf. I Thess 2:16).

**2. Supper being ended.** Another reading, widely adopted in modern translations, yields the meaning, *while supper was going on.* The action taken by Jesus to wash the disciples' feet would have been more appropriate then than later. The love of Jesus stands in sharp contrast to the hatred of Satan and Judas. **3.** Possessed of the knowledge of his authority, of his divine origin, and of his certain return to the Father, Jesus did not disdain to humble himself to perform a menial service. This is the genius of the spirit of the Incarnation. **4,5.** The materials for washing the feet were present (cf. Lk 22:10), but there was no servant (Jesus had requested complete privacy). One of the disciples might have volunteered, but all were too proud. About this time they were disputing as to which of them should be regarded as the greatest (Lk 22:24).

**6.** It cannot be determined whether or not Christ came to Peter first of all. What is clear is Peter's sense of the unfitness of having the Lord perform this service on him. The pronouns **thou** and **my** are emphatic. Boldly the disciple said what he was thinking. **7.** In Jesus' reply there is a similar emphasis on **I** and **thou. Now . . . hereafter.** Not a reference to heaven or to the events of the evening, but to the enlightenment of the Spirit later on. **8.** More impressed with the inequity of the situation than with its hidden meaning, Peter insisted that Jesus should **never wash** his feet. But the rejoinder of the Lord lifted the act from one of menial service to one of spiritual significance. To be unwashed

9. Simon Peter saith unto him, Lord, not my feet only, but also *my* hands and *my* head.

10. Jesus saith to him, He that is washed needeth not save to wash *his* feet, but is clean every whit: and ye are clean, but not all.

11. For he knew who should betray him; therefore said he, Ye are not all clean.

12. So after he had washed their feet, and had taken his garments, and was set down again, he said unto them, Know ye what I have done to you?

13. Ye call me Master and Lord: and ye say well; for *so* I am.

14. If I then, *your* Lord and Master, have washed your feet; ye also ought to wash one another's feet.

15. For I have given you an example, that ye should do as I have done to you.

16. Verily, verily, I say unto you, The servant is not greater than his lord; neither he that is sent greater than he that sent him.

17. If ye know these things, happy are ye if ye do them.

18. I speak not of you all: I know whom I have chosen: but that the Scripture may be fulfilled, He that eateth bread with me hath lifted up his heel against me.

by Christ is to be unclean, to have **no** part with him. 9. The alternative of being sundered from Christ was far worse to Peter than the shame of being ministered unto in this way by his superior. Hence the impulsive inclusion of **hands** and **head**. All other parts were, of course, covered. Peter wanted nothing excluded that could be washed.

**10,11.** Peter needed to know that the virtue in the washing was not quantitative, for the act was symbolic of inward cleansing. **Washed** (from *louō*) denotes a complete body bath. **Wash . . . feet.** Here the word is *niptō*, appropriate for the washing of individual portions of the body, as in the previous narrative. The washing of regeneration makes one clean in God's sight. This is symbolized in Christian baptism, which is administered only once. Further cleansing of the spots of defilement is not a substitute for the initial cleansing but has meaning only in the light of it (cf. I Jn 1:9). **Ye are clean, but not all.** The reference is to Judas. Jesus **knew** his heart and his plan (cf. 6:70,71). For **clean,** see 15:3. Judas was an unregenerated man.

**12. Know ye what I have done to you?** The divine side of the act had already been explained in terms of cleansing, but the human side needed to be set forth—the act as symbolic of what disciples ought to do for one another. **13,14.** If their superior, the one who was Lord and Master (teacher), was willing to perform this service for them, surely they ought to do it for one another. Humility is not essentially self-abnegation but losing oneself in service to others. **15. An example.** This rules out any thought of foot-washing as a sacrament. Scripture is silent about the practice save as a loving ministration exercised as a matter of hospitality (I Tim 5:10).

B. The Announcement of the Betrayal. 13:18-30. Judas had been on the Lord's mind even during the foot-washing (vv. 10, 11). Now it was impossible to keep back any longer the disclosure that a betrayal would occur. In great wisdom Jesus succeeded in letting Judas know that He was aware of his intentions and in detaching him from the company. He thus provided the right kind of atmosphere in which to proceed with His teaching.

**18. I speak not of you all.** Judas could

19. Now I tell you before it come, that, when it is come to pass, ye may believe that I am *he.*

20. Verily, verily, I say unto you, He that receiveth whomsoever I send receiveth me; and he that receiveth me receiveth him that sent me.

21. When Jesus had thus said, he was troubled in spirit, and testified, and said, Verily, verily, I say unto you, that one of you shall betray me.

22. Then the disciples looked one on another, doubting of whom he spake.

23. Now there was leaning on Jesus' bosom one of his disciples, whom Jesus loved.

24. Simon Peter therefore beckoned to him, that he should ask who it should be of whom he spake.

25. He then lying on Jesus' breast saith unto him, Lord, who is it?

26. Jesus answered, He it is, to whom I shall give a sop, when I have dipped *it.* And when he had dipped the sop, he gave *it* to Judas Iscariot, *the son* of Simon.

27. And after the sop Satan entered into him. Then said Jesus unto him, That thou doest, do quickly.

28. Now no man at the table knew for what intent he spake this unto him.

29. For some *of them* thought, because Judas had the bag, that Jesus had said unto him, Buy *those things* that we have need of against the feast; or, that he should give something to the poor.

30. He then, having received the sop, went immediately out; and it was night.

not be expected to profit by the example given in the foot-washing. **I know whom I have chosen** — Judas included. The Scripture had pre-written the treachery of this man (Ps 41:9). Not all the verse is quoted, for the first half is not applicable. **19.** Any temptation on the part of the other disciples to question the wisdom of Jesus in the choice of Judas was thus precluded, for Christ was not being taken by surprise. When the Passion was over, these men would be able to look back and **believe** in their Lord more firmly than ever. **20.** Judas would not go forth as representative of Christ, but these men would. They bore the Saviour's name and authority. Those who responded would be responding to Christ. This principle is grounded in Jesus' own relation to the Father. **21.** Jesus now revealed the cause of the troubled state of his heart. A betrayer was in the midst— one of you.

**22.** Perplexity about the identity of the betrayer gripped the apostolic circle. Judas had played his part well. He was unsuspected by his fellows. **23.** The 'beloved disciple' occupied a place immediately next to Jesus at the table. He could lean on the Saviour's bosom because of the reclining position customarily used. **24.** Anxious to learn who the betrayer was, Peter, too far away to ask Jesus in person, beckoned John to inquire of the Lord. **25,26.** In response to the whispered question of John, Jesus identified the betrayer, not by name but by indicating that he was the one to whom He would hand the **sop,** a morsel given in token of special favor and friendship. He handed it to Judas. Iscariot probably means "man of Kerioth," a town in Judea.

**27.** Acceptance of the sop without acceptance of the pleading love that went with it meant that Judas was steeling his heart to do what he had contracted to do—betray the Lord. He had been discovered and resented it. From this hour Satan was fully in control. **Do quickly.** Further efforts to dissuade Judas were useless. **28. No man . . . knew.** Apparently Judas was seated next to Jesus, on the opposite side from John. The word of command that dismissed Judas was unconnected with the betrayal in the minds of the others. **29.** Knowing that Judas was their treasurer, they assumed that he was being sent out to make purchases for further feasting or else to share something with **the poor** (Neh 8:10). **30. It was night.** In a writing so sensitive to

**31.** Therefore, when he was gone out, Jesus said, Now is the Son of man glorified, and God is glorified in him.

**32.** If God be glorified in him, God shall also glorify him in himself, and shall straightway glorify him.

**33.** Little children, yet a little while I am with you. Ye shall seek me; and as I said unto the Jews, Whither I go, ye cannot come; so now I say to you.

**34.** A new commandment I give unto you, That ye love one another; as I have loved you, that ye also love one another.

symbolism and underlying meaning as this Gospel, these words must have special significance. They picture at once the benighted condition of Judas through surrender to hatred of Jesus and also the coming of the hour when the powers of darkness would engulf the Saviour.

C. The Upper Room Discourse. 13:31 —16:33. These precious words of Christ were spoken in the light of his impending departure to the Father and had in view conditions under which the Lord's followers would have to carry on without his personal presence (16:4). Three principal strands of teaching are discernible: (1) commands concerning the task set before the disciples, which was a fruit-bearing witness undergirded and permeated with love; (2) warnings about the opposition to be faced from the world and from Satan; and most of all (3) an exposition of the divine provisions by which the disciples would be sustained and made triumphant in the coming days. From time to time the Lord's teaching was interrupted by questions, showing that the disciples lacked understanding at many points.

**31-35.** *Announcement of the departure and command to love one another.* **31. Now is the Son of man glorified.** With the exit of Judas, the stage was rapidly being set for that series of events that would bring glory to the Son and to the Father. In death Christ would be glorified in the eyes of the Father (cf. I Cor 1:18,24). The Father would see in the death of the cross the fulfillment of his own purpose. Only after the Resurrection would the disciples sense the glorification. **32. God shall also glorify him in himself.** In the resurrection and exaltation of Jesus and in the pouring out of the Spirit upon the disciples, God would make it manifest that the One who was obedient unto death and was now honored for his fidelity, was one with himself, even as he had claimed.

**33. Little children.** Tender affection is sharpened by the poignancy of farewell. The Jews might **seek** him out of curiosity, and his own out of personal attachment; in either case, however, it would be vain for them to seek him in any physical sense. **34.** There was something, however, to which they could properly devote their energies. **A new commandment . . . love one another.** It was new in that the love was to be exercised toward others not be-

**35.** By this shall all *men* know that ye are my disciples, if ye have love one to another.

**36.** Simon Peter said unto him, Lord, whither goest thou? Jesus answered him, Whither I go, thou canst not follow me now; but thou shalt follow me afterward.

**37.** Peter said unto him, Lord, why cannot I follow thee now? I will lay down my life for thy sake.

**38.** Jesus answered him, Wilt thou lay down thy life for my sake? Verily, verily, I say unto thee, The cock shall not crow, till thou hast denied me thrice.

## CHAPTER 14

LET not your heart be troubled: ye believe in God, believe also in me.

**2.** In may Father's house are many mansions: if *it were* not *so*, I would have told you. I go to prepare a place for you.

cause they belonged to the same nation, but because they belonged to Christ. And it was new because it was to be the expression of the peerless love of Christ, which the disciples had seen in life and would see also in death. **As I have loved you** was at once the standard and the motive power of the love that was to be manifested. **35.** Such love would inevitably be a testimony to the world. It would perpetuate the remembrance of Christ and point to his continuing life, for this quality of love has been seen only in him. Men recognize the blessedness of such love even though they cannot of themselves produce it.

**36-38.** Peter refused to accept the prospect of separation. He was told that he could not follow Christ then, but he could **afterwards** (cf. Jn 21:19). Ready to follow **now**, Peter was prepared to give up his **life** for his Lord. Such self-assurance called for a sad rebuke. Peter's intended loyalty was to issue in base denial, thrice committed.

Chapter 14 deals largely with specific encouragements to counterbalance the departure of Jesus, the defection of Judas, and the predicted failure of Peter. These are: the ultimate provision of the Father's house; the return of Christ for his own; the prospect of doing greater works; unlimited prayer possibility; the gift of the Holy Spirit; and the provision of Christ's peace.

**1.** If Peter, the leader of the apostolic group, was going to fail, it is no wonder **hearts** were **troubled**. This word is used of Jesus himself in Jn 11:33; 12:27; 13:21. "He shared the experiences which in us He would comfort and control" (T. D. Bernard, *The Central Teaching of Jesus Christ*). **Believe** is probably an imperative in both cases. Everything seemed on the verge of collapse. A renewed faith in God was necessary. The cause of Jesus seemed faced with defeat; so faith in him was more needful than ever. Every fresh test as well as every new revelation is a summons to faith.

**2. My Father's house** (cf. 2:16). The Temple at Jerusalem, with its vast courts and numerous chambers, suggests the antitype in heaven. **Many mansions.** Places of *abode*. The same word as in 14:23. **I would have told you.** The disciple is warranted in assuming an adequate divine provision even when it is not stated. **I go to prepare.** As Peter and John had gone ahead to prepare the chamber for the supper, so Jesus was preceding the

341

3. And if I go and prepare a place for you, I will come again, and receive you unto myself; that where I am, *there* ye may be also.

4. And whither I go ye know, and the way ye know.

5. Thomas saith unto him, Lord, we know not whither thou goest; and how can we know the way?

6. Jesus saith unto him, I am the way, the truth, and the life: no man cometh unto the Father, but by me.

7. If ye had known me, ye should have known my Father also: and from henceforth ye know him, and have seen him.

8. Philip saith unto him, Lord, show us the Father, and it sufficeth us.

9. Jesus saith unto him, Have I been so long time with you, and yet hast thou not known me, Philip? he that hath seen me hath seen the Father; and how sayest thou *then*, Show us the Father?

10. Believest thou not that I am in the Father, and the Father in me? the words that I speak unto you I speak not of myself: but the Father that dwelleth in me, he doeth the works.

rest into glory to prepare "the upper room" for his own.

3. **I will come again.** Grammatically, this is a futuristic present, emphasizing both the certainty of the coming and the impending nature of the event. The coming does not emphasize heaven as such but rather the reunion of Christ and his people. **Where I am** — the most satisfying definition of heaven. This spatial language makes it difficult to interpret the verse as a provision for Christ's continuing presence with his people while they are on earth. The application of the words to the death of the believer is inadequate also, for in that experience the saints of God depart to be with Christ (Phil 1:23).

4. The best text yields the rendering, **And where I am going ye know the way.**

5. Thomas saw a double problem in Jesus' utterance. Since he, as well as others, did not understand the destination, how could he know the way? **6. The way.** This has special prominence because of the context. It had been somewhat anticipated in the teaching about the door (10:9). **The truth.** Christ as truth makes the way dependable and infallible (cf. 1:14; 8:32,36; Eph 4:20, 21). **The life** (cf. 1:4; 11:25). **No man cometh.** The verb puts Jesus on the side of God rather than on the side of man (he does not say, "goeth"). "No man can attain the Father except by perceiving the Truth and participating in the Life which is revealed to men in His Son. Thus, while being the guide, He does not guide to what is beyond Himself. Knowledge of the Son is the knowledge of God" (Hoskyns).

7. The wording suggests the disciples' failure to know Christ as he really was. In view of this last revelation, however, there could be no excuse for failure to know the Father as well as the Son. Some manuscripts have a different reading — "If ye have come to know me (as ye have), ye shall know my Father also."

8. Desire for objective experience is strong — **show us the Father** (cf. Ex 33:17). Philip felt he knew God, but not as Father in the intimate sense Jesus meant when He spoke of Him.

9. **So long time.** It was pathetically late for the request. The Son had been revealing the Father all along (10:30). That lay at the root of his mission (1:18).

10. Surely Philip must believe that there was community of life between Father and Son. Out of the union of the Son with the Father came **the words** that Jesus spoke. Out of the works which he performed came the demonstration that

11. Believe me that I *am* in the Father, and the Father in me: or else believe me for the very works' sake.

12. Verily, verily, I say unto you, He that believeth on me, the works that I do shall he do also; and greater *works* than these shall he do; because I go unto my Father.

13. And whatsoever ye shall ask in my name, that will I do, that the Father may be glorified in the Son.

14. If ye shall ask any thing in my name, I will do *it*.

15. If ye love me, keep my commandments.

16. And I will pray the Father, and he shall give you another Comforter, that he may abide with you for ever;

17. *Even* the Spirit of truth; whom the world cannot receive, because it seeth him not, neither knoweth him: but ye know him; for he dwelleth with you, and shall be in you.

the Father was dwelling in him and acting through him.

**11.** The appeal shifted from Philip to the Eleven. **Believe me.** That is, accept my testimony about my relation to the Father. A sufficiently high view of Christ makes his self-disclosure the final evidence. For those that need other evidence, the **works** are there to support the claim. **12. Greater works.** Not to be restricted to the signs such as Jesus wrought in the days of his flesh. The works could not be greater in quality than his, but greater in extent. **Because I go unto my Father.** This is the reason for the greater works. The restrictions imposed on Jesus by incarnation would be removed. His position with the Father would be related to the greater works in two ways: answering the prayers of his own, and sending the Paraclete as the unfailing source of wisdom and strength. The works, then, would not be done in independence of Christ. *He* would answer prayer; *he* would send the Spirit.

**13,14. Whatsoever.** The scope of prayer. **Ask.** The condition of prayer. **In my name.** The ground of prayer. This involves at least two things: praying in the authority Christ gives (cf. Mt 28:19; Acts 3:6) and praying in union with him, so that one does not pray outside His will. **That will I do.** The certainty of prayer. **That the Father may be glorified in the Son.** The purpose of prayer. **If ye shall ask.** The **if** is on the side of the one who prays, not on the side of Christ.

**15. If ye love me.** This is the atmosphere in which not only the command to pray but all other commands of the Lord will be honored by his servants. **Keep** is imperative in the AV, but very good manuscript authority calls for a future form — "ye will keep." Love is not primarily a sentimental attachment; it is the dynamic for obedience. **My commandments.** Ultimately, only God can command. Deity was speaking. **16.** These commandments can be kept only in the power of the Holy Spirit, called here **another Comforter.** A better translation at this point would be *helper*. At the time the AV was translated, **comforter** retained more of the original force of "strengthener" than it has today. The word **another** puts the Spirit in the same class with Jesus (cf. Phil 4:13). In the Spirit we have more than an occasional helper — **that he may abide with you for ever.**

**17. The Spirit of truth** (cf. 15:26; 16:13). He is illuminator as well as helper. His great theme is Christ the Truth (14:

18. I will not leave you comfortless: I will come to you.

19. Yet a little while, and the world seeth me no more; but ye see me: because I live, ye shall live also.

20. At that day ye shall know that I *am* in my Father, and ye in me, and I in you.

21. He that hath my commandments, and keepeth them, he it is that loveth me: and he that loveth me shall be loved of my Father, and I will love him, and will manifest myself to him.

6; 15:26). **Whom the world cannot receive.** The world is governed by the senses. Since the Spirit cannot be seen nor comprehended by reason, he remains outside the world's conscious experience (cf. I Cor 2:9-14). **Dwelleth with you.** A constant presence, compensating for the withdrawal of the Lord. **In you.** Not only with them as a presence permeating the corporate body, but dwelling in them individually. **18.** The same subject is continued. **Comfortless.** *Orphans.* The need of the disciples would be met when Christ came to them in resurrection blessing. This would bring with it the coming of the person of the Spirit (20: 22). As surely as the Spirit would be with them and in them, so would Christ. It would be impossible to differentiate the two, just as the Son and the Father are indivisible (cf. II Cor 3:17). Christ was not speaking here of his future coming, as in verse 3, but of a coming that would meet an immediate need.

**19.** For only a limited time would Christ be an object of sight to **the world.** Then would come death, and though it would be followed by resurrection, **this** would not restore him to the eyes of men (Mt 23:39). It was because these disciples were spiritually alive that they would be able to see him and become partakers of his risen life. **20. At that day** these men would be able to grasp what Jesus had been trying to tell them about his life with the Father, which was a life of interpenetration and communion, and also about their own life, which had now been likewise taken up into the divine and infused with it. **Ye shall know.** *Gnō-sesthe* speaks of discovery. Needless to say, this does not entitle the believer to say that he is God or the Son of God. Union is meaningless apart from the separate existence of those who compose it.

**21.** Jesus returned to the subject of love and the keeping of his commandments (cf. v. 15), but in view of the teaching in verse 20 now included mention of the Father. The keeping of Christ's commandments demonstrates love for Christ. This love invites the answering love of the Father, whose love for the Son is such that he must love all who have love for him. It brings also manifestation of the Son to the believer. What the disciples enjoyed by way of physical manifestation of the risen Lord to themselves following the Resurrection, they were to enjoy also in a spiritual sense throughout the rest of their earthly pilgrimage.

22. Judas saith unto him, not Iscariot, Lord, how is it that thou wilt manifest thyself unto us, and not unto the world?

23. Jesus answered and said unto him, If a man love me, he will keep my words: and my Father will love him, and we will come unto him, and make our abode with him.

24. He that loveth me not keepeth not my sayings: and the word which ye hear is not mine, but the Father's which sent me.

25. These things have I spoken unto you, being *yet* present with you.

26. But the Comforter, *which is* the Holy Ghost, whom the Father will send in my name, he shall teach you all things, and bring all things to your remembrance, whatsoever I have said unto you.

27. Peace I leave with you, my peace I give unto you: not as the world giveth, give I unto you. Let not your heart be troubled, neither let it be afraid.

28. Ye have heard how I said unto you, I go away, and come *again* unto you. If ye loved me, ye would rejoice, because I said, I go unto the Father: for my Father is greater than I.

**22. Judas . . . not Iscariot.** The reputation of the betrayer was so bad that John takes care not to permit any confusion of identification, despite the fact that the other Judas had left the room. This Judas could not understand a manifestation restricted to the chosen few, not that it was impossible (that very thing was occurring at the moment) but that it did not seem to accord with the glory of the Messianic office. If Christ was to come again, why not to the world? He was perplexed by Jesus' statement in verse 19. **23.** "The answer to Judas is, that the manifestation referred to must be limited, because it can only be made where there is that communion of love which proves itself by the spirit of self-denial and submission to the charge of Jesus" (William Milligan and W. F. Moulton, *Commentary on the Gospel of St. John*). This manifestation is not only very personal but it leads to a permanent relation — **make our abode with him.** Observe that the Son feels free to commit the Father to a certain course of action, another clear indication of deity. **24.** Here is the corollary on the negative side to the truth of the last verse. Once more Christ affirmed the unity of the Son's word with that of the Father.

**25,26. These things....all things.** The teaching of Christ touching the new conditions of the coming age was suggestive rather than complete (cf. 16:12). This deficiency was to be overcome by the coming of the Holy Spirit. His ministry to believers would be, in the main, to **teach** them (one of the great offices of Christ as well; the two are combined, by implication, in Acts 1:1). **All things** (cf. I Cor 2:13-15). These matters presumably would be based on the person and work of Christ, thus affording a continuation of Jesus' teaching. A part of the Spirit's work, in fact, would be that of recalling what Christ had spoken (cf. 2:22; 12:16).

**27. Peace.** A frequent word in connection with farewells (cf. Eph 6:23; I Pet 5:14). But this is a legacy rather than merely a conventional touch. **Leave** (*aphiēmi*) is rarely used in this sense. Another example occurs in the LXX of Ps 17:14. **My peace.** A distinctive brand of peace, different from that of **the world,** which would be panic-stricken at such an hour as this, with death so near. The gift of his peace would make his followers unafraid, as he was (cf. 16:33).

**28.** The Lord had no intention of hiding the fact of his departure, but he reminded them that the sadness of de-

29. And now I have told you before it come to pass, that, when it is come to pass, ye might believe.

30. Hereafter I will not talk much with you: for the prince of this world cometh, and hath nothing in me.

31. But that the world may know that I love the Father; and as the Father gave me commandment, even so I do. Arise, let us go hence.

## CHAPTER 15

I AM the true vine, and my Father is the husbandman.

2. Every branch in me that beareth not fruit he taketh away: and every *branch* that beareth fruit, he purgeth it, that it may bring forth more fruit.

parture was relieved by his promise to come again. **If ye loved me.** Their love was yet incomplete. Love desires the best for the one who is loved. The disciples should have rejoiced in his return to the Father. **My Father is greater than I.** This has nothing to do with essential being, and so does not contradict John 10:30 and other passages. The Father was in position to reward the Son for obedience unto death. There is a hint here that blessings would come from Christ's return to the Father that would benefit his followers; so their joy would not be entirely disinterested. **29.** All the outpoured blessings of the future would corroborate the word of Christ and would increase the confidence and faith of the disciples in him.

**30. The prince of this world** (cf. 12: 31). A reference to Satan. Here the immediate significance seems to be the betrayal by Judas, the tool of Satan, and the arrest of Jesus (cf. Lk 22:53). **Hath nothing in me.** No share in Christ's person or cause (cf. 13:8). There may be a suggestion here of the truth that Satan has nothing in Christ which is rightfully his own, which he can claim or lay hold of for his own interest. Christ is sinless and victorious over evil. **31.** The very thing that Satan was about to effect, namely, the death of Christ on the cross, was the thing which the Saviour was pressing forward to **do.** But he did it not as the helpless victim of Satan but out of love for the Father, knowing it was the Father's commandment (his expressed will). **Arise, let us go hence.** It is by no means certain that the command was carried out immediately. There is difficulty in supposing that the rest of the discourse could have been spoken in a public place, even in the Temple.

In chapter 15 the following strands of thought are discernible: fruit-bearing through abiding in Christ (vv. 1-11); love as the supreme fruit (vv. 12-17); the hatred of the world for the disciple, as for Christ (vv. 18-25); the divine and human witness to Christ (vv. 25-27).

**1. I am the true vine.** A contrast is probably intended with Israel, a vine of God's planting which proved unfruitful (Isa 5:1-7). **True.** Real, all that a vine should be in a spiritual sense. Christ is not merely the root or stock, but the whole plant. Included in him are his people. **Husbandman.** Both owner and caretaker. **2. Every branch in me.** To be in Christ is a spiritual fact of incalculable importance. **Beareth not fruit.** This is no would-

3. Now ye are clean through the word which I have spoken unto you.

4. Abide in me, and I in you. As the branch cannot bear fruit of itself, except it abide in the vine; no more can ye, except ye abide in me.

5. I am the vine, ye *are* the branches. He that abideth in me, and I in him, the same bringeth forth much fruit; for without me ye can do nothing.

6. If a man abide not in me, he is cast forth as a branch, and is withered; and men gather them, and cast *them* into the fire, and they are burned.

7. If ye abide in me, and my words abide in you, ye shall ask what ye will, and it shall be done unto you.

8. Herein is my Father glorified, that ye bear much fruit; so shall ye be my disciples.

9. As the Father hath loved me, so have I loved you: continue ye in my love.

be follower. As there are suckers that grow out from the plant but add nothing to its usefulness and must be cut away, so an unproductive child of God who persists in his own will may expect to be set aside. God's chastening hand may even remove such a person through death. **He purgeth it.** This applies to the fruitful branch. It is kept clean of any tendency to deadness or to mere growth of the branch as distinct from production of fruit. The object is **more fruit.**

3. **Clean through** (literally, *because of*) **the word.** Set apart from others by having received God's revelation in Christ. 4. **Abide in me, and I in you.** This recalls 14:20. But there the thought relates to position; here it relates to volition, the decision to depend consciously upon Christ as the condition of fruitfulness. Christ's answer is an inward manifestation — **I in you.** A branch detached from the vine is necessarily unfruitful. A vital union is in view. 5. The vine and the branches are distinguished. From the vine comes the life; from the branches, as a result, comes the fruit. The order is the same here as in 14:20 and 15:4. Our abiding in Christ connects us with the source of life. His abiding in us brings a steady supply of fruit — **much fruit. Without me.** Apart from me, severed from me.

6. It is a known fact that apart from producing grapes the vine has no use except to be burned for fuel (cf. Ezk 15: 6). **Men . . . they.** "The indefiniteness of the subject corresponds with the mysteriousness of the act symbolized" (Westcott). Since the subject is the bearing of fruit and not eternal life, the burning is a judgment upon fruitlessness, not an abandonment to eternal destruction. The branch is the potential of possible fruit-bearing, not the person himself. It speaks here of unfruitful works (cf. I Cor 3:15).

7. The **words** of Christ, as well as the person of Christ, may abide in the believer. It is the teaching of Christ that gives rise to the proper kind of praying. When the word of Christ dwells richly within (Col 3:16), one may safely ask what he **will,** and it **shall be done.** The teaching is similar to that in Jn 14: 13,14. 8. Discipleship is a growing, dynamic thing. The more fruit we bear, the more truly are we fulfilling the pattern of **disciples,** those who learn of Christ in order to be like him. God is **glorified** thereby. He is vindicated and rewarded for his investment in the vineyard.

9. The mention of **love** in this connection suggests that this is the chief item

10. If ye keep my commandments, ye shall abide in my love; even as I have kept my Father's commandments, and abide in his love.

11. These things have I spoken unto you, that my joy might remain in you, and *that* your joy might be full.

12. This is my commandment, That ye love one another, as I have loved you.

13. Greater love hath no man than this, that a man lay down his life for his friends.

14. Ye are my friends, if ye do whatsoever I command you.

15. Henceforth I call you not servants; for the servant knoweth not what his lord doeth: but I have called you friends; for all things that I have heard of my Father I have made known unto you.

16. Ye have not chosen me, but I have chosen you, and ordained you, that ye should go and bring forth fruit, and *that* your fruit should remain; that whatsoever ye shall ask of the Father in my name, he may give it you.

in the fruit which the Father is concerned to find in his children (cf. Gal 5:22). But this is not love in a general sense — rather, **my love**, the love of Christ. When he comes in to abide, he brings his love with him, which in turn is the very love enjoyed by Christ from the Father. Christian love becomes thereby divine in character. **Continue ye in my love.** Accept no substitutes. **10.** The enjoyment of the Saviour's love is conditioned on keeping his **commandments.** This is no arbitrary requirement, for Christ has operated under this rule himself in his relation to the Father. The disciple is not above his Lord. **11.** The life of love produces **joy.** Christ had it first, as the result of doing perfectly the Father's will and enjoying his love. This is imparted to his own, and in the process becomes personalized so as to become their joy. Possession may be partial at first, but the goal is to **be full,** leaving no room for fear or dissatisfaction.

The next section begins and ends with the command to love one another. **12,13.** Here is an epitomizing of the Christian's obligation. It is no longer an admonition to keep Christ's commandments in order to abide in his love (v. 10). It is rather an injunction to concentrate on the one commandment to have love for one another. **As I have loved you.** The measure of Christ's love for his own is his self-sacrifice, in which they benefit (cf. I Jn 3:16). Such a standard can be met only as Christ's own love is permitted to flow through the life of his people. The Synoptic announcements of the cross by Jesus emphasize its divine necessity; here the motivation is love. The cross is not something imposed but something embraced — **lay down his life.** Immediate proof of love is the willingness to give advance indication of the purpose to die for those who are **friends.** Death for them in no wise contradicts the purpose to die for a larger circle, even the world itself.

**14.** Friendship with Jesus does not eliminate the necessity for obedience. **15.** If this necessity seems to make **servants** out of friends, there is a difference. The servant is not taken into the confidence of his lord. Proof of the status of friends, in the case of the disciples, was their admission to the counsels of Christ, including all that the Father had disclosed to the Son. Nothing had been withheld. This does not mean that all had been understood by Jesus' followers.

**16.** Lest the disciples get the impression that they alone were in the plans of

17. These things I command you, that ye love one another.

18. If the world hate you, ye know that it hated me before *it hated* you.

19. If ye were of the world, the world would love his own; but because ye are not of the world, but I have chosen you out of the world, therefore the world hateth you.

20. Remember the word that I said unto you, The servant is not greater than his lord. If they have persecuted me, they will also persecute you; if they have kept my saying, they will keep yours also.

21. But all these things will they do unto you for my name's sake, because they know not him that sent me.

God, Christ now made clear that they had been granted their privileged position with a view to their declaring the message to others. They had been **chosen,** not with a view to their own pleasure or pride. Rather, Christ **ordained** (appointed) them with service in mind. **Go . . . bring forth fruit.** Previously the fruit meant love. Now it was to mean love in action, the heralding of the message of salvation and the winning of souls. There is a close connection in thought with John 12:24. **Remain.** The same word has been translated *abide* earlier in the chapter. That there would be abiding fruit was a gracious promise in view of the disappointing results during Jesus' own ministry, with many professing an interest in him, only to leave him after a time.

**17.** This verse is transitional. The disciples had to share love among themselves, for they would not get it from the world. At this point the word "love" all but disappears from the passage, being replaced by "hate" or "hatred" (eight times in as many verses).

**18. The world.** Unredeemed society, estranged from God, held in the grip of sin and the evil one, blind to spiritual truth and hostile to those who have the life of God in them. Hatred would not be visited upon the disciples in a spirit of anti-Semitism, but as a continuation of the hostility and hatred visited upon Christ. The attack would move from the Shepherd to the sheep. As surely as their lives would reflect Christ, so surely would they attract the hatred of sinful men (cf. Gal 4:29). **19.** Hostility is rooted in spiritual dissimilarity. The world is comfortable in the presence of its **own.** It is capable of a certain affection for such. The exclusiveness of the Christian society, a redeemed community within an unredeemed, excites displeasure. Rebuked by the holiness of those who are Christ's (cf. v. 22), the world shows its resentment.

**20.** The proof of genuineness in discipleship is the correspondence between the reaction of men to the ministry of Jesus' followers and the reaction of men to Christ in the days of his flesh. Some men would **persecute** them; others would keep their word. **Remember the word.** The reference is to Jn 13:16. Acts 4:13 is a powerful illustration of Jesus' teaching here. Having rid themselves of Jesus, as they thought, the rulers were dismayed to find themselves faced by disciples who acted as he did. **21. For my name's sake.** Christ suffered rejection because men did

22. If I had not come and spoken unto them, they had not had sin; but now they have no cloak for their sin.

23. He that hateth me hateth my Father also.

24. If I had not done among them the works which none other man did, they had not had sin: but now have they both seen and hated both me and my Father.

25. But *this cometh to pass*, that the word might be fulfilled that is written in their law, They hated me without a cause.

26. But when the Comforter is come, whom I will send unto you from the Father, *even* the Spirit of truth, which proceedeth from the Father, he shall testify of me:

27. And ye also shall bear witness, because ye have been with me from the beginning.

not really know the One who sent him. The disciples were being inducted into the circle of the misunderstood, sharing this distinction with their Lord.

22. This ignorance of Christ's identity and mission was grounded in the sin of men. Though Christ had not come to judge but rather to save, yet his very presence and witness stirred up manifestations of sin that otherwise would have remained dormant. Exposed by the Saviour, his enemies had no hiding place. Their one resort was to banish Christ from before their eyes. They had not had sin. The culminating sin of unbelief and rejection of the Saviour. 23. The cost of hating Christ is the condemnation of hating the Father as well. Men cannot treat the Father in one way and the Son in another.

24. The works (complementing the word of Christ in v. 22) were of such a character that men had to come to a verdict for or against him. In rejecting him, they had sin. It was sin accompanied by hatred which logically involved the Father in whose name the Son had come. 25. Their law. The very Scriptures which the Jews gloried in rose up to condemn them (Ps 69:4). Without a cause (*dōrean*). Such hatred is indefensible. It lacks all ground in the one who is hated. The same word occurs, with the same meaning, in Rom 3:24, where the ground of salvation is presented as being God himself and not the worthiness of man.

Such hatred demands a strong and fearless testimony to the world. John now describes the nature of this witness. 26, 27. The disciples would not face the world alone. They would have a divine helper, the Spirit of truth. He would press home the truth about men's sinful condition and the truth about Christ, the remedy for that sin. The Spirit was to come under a double commission, so to speak, being sent of the Son from the Father, in order to testify of Christ (cf. 16:7-13). Ye also bear witness. Probably indicative rather than imperative. From the standpoint of association with Jesus, which had given them the knowledge necessary for a valid witness, they were qualified now, since they had been with him from the beginning – from the early days of the ministry. Yet, to be effective, their witness had to be joined to that of the Spirit working in them and through them (cf. Acts 5:32).

In chapter 16 the dominant note remains the same – the departure of Christ and the anticipation of what this would

## CHAPTER 16

THESE things have I spoken unto you, that ye should not be offended.

2. They shall put you out of the synagogues: yea, the time cometh, that whosoever killeth you will think that he doeth God service.

3. And these things will they do unto you, because they have not known the Father, nor me.

4. But these things have I told you, that when the time shall come, ye may remember that I told you of them. And these things I said not unto you at the beginning, because I was with you.

5. But now I go my way to him that sent me; and none of you asketh me, Whither goest thou?

mean. The thought moves along the following lines: Christ's warning of coming persecution (16:1-4 a); his departure explained in the light of the coming of the Spirit and his ministry to the world (16: 4 b-11); the Spirit's ministry to believers (16:12-15); comforts to offset the pain of separation (16:16-28); the victory of the Son of God (16:29-33). The theme of persecution had been anticipated by the previous teaching (ch. 15) on the hatred of the world for Christ and his own.

1. **These things have I spoken unto you.** Primarily the information about the hatred of the world, so that the disciples might be forearmed, but also the reminder that they were witnesses to that very world which would despise them (cf. 15:27). Responsibility stiffens character. **That ye should not be offended.** The word "offended" presents the idea of stumbling because of an obstacle in the path rather than because of an inner tendency to defection. On this account the RSV rendering, *to keep you from falling away*, is not wholly satisfactory. Jesus' usual phrase is, "offended in me" (Lk 7: 23; Mt 26:31).

2. **Out of the synagogues** (cf. 9:22). A most painful experience to a Jew, whose tie with the nation was strong. Jewish believers in Jerusalem continued to mingle with their countrymen in the Temple after Pentecost, showing their sense of kinship with their people. **Will think that he doeth God service.** The best commentary is the confession of Saul of Tarsus concerning his persecuting days (Acts 26:9-11). He measured his zeal for his own religion by the terrors and ravages he inflicted on the church (Gal 1:13; Phil 3: 6).

3. Ignorance of Christ and his true relation to the Father helps to account for persecution. Such ignorance does not make the persecutor excusable. Paul labeled himself chief of sinners on this very account! (I Tim 1:13-15)

4. When persecution would strike, the memory of Christ's faithfulness in warning of these things would serve to strengthen his servants. To meet such things unprepared would bring dismay. **I was with you.** Christ was their shield against opposition. In the light of his soon going away, the present teaching took on a significance it could not have had before.

It was now in order to think more directly about this departure and about what it would mean for those who remained. 5. For Christ the going meant

6. But because I have said these things unto you, sorrow hath filled your heart.

7. Nevertheless I tell you the truth; It is expedient for you that I go away: for if I go not away, the Comforter will not come unto you; but if I depart, I will send him unto you.

8. And when he is come, he will reprove the world of sin, and of righteousness, and of judgment:

9. Of sin, because they believe not on me;

10. Of righteousness, because I go to my Father, and ye see me no more;

11. Of judgment, because the prince of this world is judged.

a return to the One who had sent him. This aspect of it had not laid hold of the minds of the disciples to any extent. They had not asked, Whither goest thou? 6. Instead, they had been preoccupied with their sense of loss. They were in the grip of sorrow.

7. It is expedient for you that I go away. The disadvantage in terms of separation and sorrow was to be outweighed by the gain occasioned by the coming of the Comforter (helper). One has only to compare the disciples at the end of Jesus' ministry with these same men after the coming of the Spirit to see how greatly they had advanced in understanding and in the effectiveness of their service. If I go not . . . the Comforter will not come (cf. 7:37-39). This is not a sign of hostility or jealousy between the Son and the Spirit. Indeed, the Spirit had come upon Christ to empower him for his work; and soon he would come upon Christ's followers, as though to compensate for the loss of the personal presence of the Lord.

8. He will reprove the world. Reprove may equally well be rendered *convict* or *convince*. The Spirit was to come first to the disciples (see end of v. 7), and through them he would undertake his mission of convicting men. In a sense this ministry correlates with the world's activity of persecution. The world may appear to make inroads on the Church, but there is a counterattack in the work of the Spirit, designed not to harm but to convert, or at least to convict. The Spirit, working through the apostles, produced conviction of sin in the very city where Jesus had been put to death (Acts 2:37).

9. Of sin. For the reason that the sin of the world came to sharp focus in the rejection of Jesus when there should have been acceptance of him, the Spirit makes this the important issue. In their blindness men were calling Jesus a sinner at the very time their own sin was leading them to put him to death. 10. Of righteousness. The very fact that Christ could solve the sin problem of mankind by his redeeming death revealed his perfect righteousness. Otherwise he would have required a Saviour for himself. The Father is the true judge of righteousness. His readiness to receive the Son back into glory is the proof that he found in him no deficiency (Rom 1:4; 4:25; I Tim 3:16). 11. Of judgment. When those who crucified Jesus saw that God did not interfere, they imagined that the judgment of God was being pronounced on him. Actually, another was being judged

12. I have yet many things to say unto you, but ye cannot bear them now.

13. Howbeit when he, the Spirit of truth, is come, he will guide you into all truth: for he shall not speak of himself; but whatsoever he shall hear, *that* shall he speak: and he will show you things to come.

14. He shall glorify me: for he shall receive of mine, and shall show *it* unto you.

15. All things that the Father hath are mine: therefore said I, that he shall take of mine, and shall show *it* unto you.

there, even Satan, the prince of this world. Satan rules by means of sin and death. Christ's triumph over sin at the cross and over death at the Resurrection heralded the fact that Satan had been judged. The execution of final judgment is only a matter of time.

At this point the thought moves away from the world. The Spirit's work on behalf of believers comes into view.

12. The discourse was not a complete exposition of the thoughts of Jesus toward his own. Held in reserve were **many things**. It was useless to venture upon them, for the disciples could not **bear them**. They were too immature. These truths would become more real to them as their experience grew. 13. The communication of these things could be safely deferred until **the Spirit of truth** came, who is a teacher as truly as the Lord himself. **All truth.** Not truth in every realm of knowledge, but truth in the things of God in the narrower sense, which we speak of as spiritual things (cf. I Cor 2:10). **He shall not speak of** (from) **himself.** He would not attempt to initiate the things he would teach, but like the Son (15:15), would pass on to men what was given to him from God the Father. One common source guarantees unity in the teaching. Ultimately believers are taught of God (I Thess 4:9). **Things to come.** The return of Christ and attendant events may be in view, but more immediately the **things to come** were the death and resurrection of Jesus and their effects, the very things over which the disciples had stumbled when Jesus had talked about them.

14. **Glorify.** Even as Christ was glorifying the Father by his obedience unto death, so the Spirit would glorify Christ by making clear the significance of his person and work. The Spirit's teaching mission would be first to **receive** the deposit of Christ-centered truth, then show it to believers. It follows that a ministry, to be Spirit-directed, must be one that magnifies Christ. 15. Since the things of Christ include the truths concerning the Father and his counsels, when the Spirit communicates the things of Christ, he communicates the whole truth.

Next the Lord dealt with the compensations that should ease the pain occasioned by his departure. These included the promise that the disciples would see him again (v. 16); their joy at seeing him (v. 22); the privilege of prayer (vv. 23,24); increased knowledge (v. 25);

16. A little while, and ye shall not see me: and again, a little while, and ye shall see me, because I go to the Father.

17. Then said *some* of his disciples among themselves, What is this that he saith unto us, A little while, and ye shall not see me: and again, a little while, and ye shall see me: and, Because I go to the Father?

18. They said therefore, What is this that he saith, A little while? we cannot tell what he saith.

19. Now Jesus knew that they were desirous to ask him, and said unto them, Do ye inquire among yourselves of that I said, A little while, and ye shall not see me: and again, a little while, and ye shall see me?

20. Verily, verily, I say unto you, That ye shall weep and lament, but the world shall rejoice; and ye shall be sorrowful, but your sorrow shall be turned into joy.

21. A woman when she is in travail hath sorrow, because her hour is come: but as soon as she is delivered of the child, she remembereth no more the anguish, for joy that a man is born into the world.

22. And ye now therefore have sorrow: but I will see you again, and your heart shall rejoice, and your joy no man taketh from you.

and the sustaining love of the Father for them (v. 27).

16. A little while. The phrase occurs seven times in four verses. This refers to the short interval that remained before his burial, when the disciples would no longer see him with the eyes of physical sight. The second little while designates the interval between his burial and his resurrection, after which they would see him again. Here the word see is not the same as in the first occurrence. It conveys here the thought of perception as well as of observation. Something of the meaning of this drama of redemption, which was now so mysterious, would dawn upon these men. The last clause, because I go to the Father, does not have sufficient manuscript authority to be retained in the text.

17. The words of Jesus were beyond the grasp of the disciples. Individuals among them had asked questions before this. These men (some of his disciples), too timid to voice their perplexity openly, conferred with one another instead of addressing the Lord. In this verse the words, because I go to the Father, are genuine. They are easily explained on the basis of Jesus' use of them in verse 10. This fact of his departure is the all-absorbing concern. 19,20. Recognizing their burning desire to have an answer to the problem of the little while in its twofold application, Jesus offered to supply an answer, yet not the precise answer they were hoping for. But he did indicate what the little while would mean for them in each instance. In the former, they would weep while the world rejoiced, for the death of the Saviour would bring utterly different reactions from believers than from the people of the world (cf. Rev 11:10). But the very thing that would bring sorrow would be turned into an occasion of joy when the disciples were able to see the cross in the light of the Resurrection, when the second "little while" would break upon them.

21. Jesus drew an analogy from human life for the supplanting of sorrow with joy. A woman's travail pains bring sorrow, but she forgets her pain in the joy of the birth. It may be significant that a man is said to be born (rather than a child). Christ in resurrection as the first-born from the dead (Col 1:18) joins with himself the new man, his Church, to which he imparts his risen life. 22. The joy of reunion would be an abiding experience; the second separation, occasioned by the Lord's ascension, would not affect that joy (Lk 24:51-53).

23. And in that day ye shall ask me nothing. Verily, verily, I say unto you, Whatsoever ye shall ask the Father in my name, he will give it you.

24. Hitherto have ye asked nothing in my name: ask, and ye shall receive, that your joy may be full.

25. These things have I spoken unto you in proverbs: but the time cometh, when I shall no more speak unto you in proverbs, but I shall show you plainly of the Father.

26. At that day ye shall ask in my name: and I say not unto you, that I will pray the Father for you:

27. For the Father himself loveth you, because ye have loved me, and have believed that I came out from God.

28. I came forth from the Father, and am come into the world: again, I leave the world, and go to the Father.

29. His disciples said unto him, Lo, now speakest thou plainly, and speakest no proverb.

30. Now are we sure that thou knowest all things, and needest not that any man should ask thee: by this we believe that thou camest forth from God.

23. In that day. The Lord was thinking of the conditions that would prevail after his return to the Father. In the intermediate period of the forty days after the Resurrection, the disciples did ask something (Acts 1:6). But when he was taken up, all opportunity for questions such as were now being asked would be gone. This does not mean there would be total lack of communication. The door of prayer would be open. If they would but ask, the Father would give the answers to their perplexities and would meet their needs. In my name (see the comment on 14:13,14). 24. Asked nothing. Here the word "asked" is used in the sense of making petition rather than framing a question. Due to the presence of Jesus in their midst, asking in his name had been unnecessary. But in the new day that was coming, their joy at seeing Jesus again would be maintained by this intercourse of prayer.

25. Proverbs. Not maxims, but obscure sayings. His teaching was often enigmatical to his followers. But a change was coming. "The return of Jesus to the Father inaugurated a new era, in which the Lord speaks to His disciples no longer obscurely but clearly and openly; it is presumed that the readers of the Gospel understand that He speaks to them through the Spirit which they have received" (Hoskyns, The Fourth Gospel). 26,27. In the future, prayer would indeed be in the name of Christ, but not in the sense that the Son would be the means of overcoming some sort of hesitancy or resistance in the Father which otherwise believers would encounter. On the contrary, the Father loveth them, and is ready to receive them because of their attitude toward his beloved Son. In contrast to the world, they have loved and trusted the Son as the one sent of God.

28. What the faith of the disciples should encompass is now set forth in its simplest and boldest outline. The first half of the statement had been affirmed more than once by one or more of the group; the second part deals with the burden of this discourse, the going away of their leader. Now he put this departure sharply and clearly — I leave the world, and go to the Father.

At this point the discourse was almost concluded. It ended on a double note — the pathetic failure of those Jesus had tried to instruct, and his own triumph, aided by the presence of the Father. 29, 30. Encouraged alike by the commenda-

31. Jesus answered them, Do ye now believe?

32. Behold, the hour cometh, yea, is now come, that ye shall be scattered, every man to his own, and shall leave me alone: and yet I am not alone, because the Father is with me.

33. These things I have spoken unto you, that in me ye might have peace. In the world ye shall have tribulation: but be of good cheer; I have overcome the world.

## CHAPTER 17

THESE words spake Jesus, and lifted up his eyes to heaven, and said, Father, the hour is come; glorify thy Son, that thy Son also may glorify thee:

2. As thou hast given him power over all flesh, that he should give eternal life to as many as thou hast given him.

3. And this is life eternal, that they might know thee the only true God, and Jesus Christ, whom thou hast sent.

tion of their faith and by the plain speaking of Jesus concerning his career, the disciples imagined that they were basking in the superior knowledge of the Son of God. **31,32.** A rude awakening was in store for them. They would be **scattered** (at the time of the arrest of Jesus) and he would be left **alone,** yet he would have the help of the Father. **33.** For their protection he provided his **peace** (cf. 14:27), which they would need as they faced the **tribulation** in store for them in the world. This is not only peace amid conflict, but peace which rests in the assurance of a victory now won by their champion over the world. Christ's victory is the objective reality which makes valid the inward gift of his peace.

D. The Great Prayer. 17:1-26. Jesus included himself in this prayer (vv. 1-5), but his chief concern was for his own. In both sections the element of dedication is strongly mingled with petition.

**1. Father.** Used regularly in Jesus' prayers, six times here. **The hour is come.** The time is undefined, as something well known between Father and Son. It was at once the time for suffering and for glorification. **Glorify thy Son.** Enable him to fulfill his course, accomplishing the salvation for which he came. Plainly Christ did not seek some honor here for his own sake, for in his own glorification through death, resurrection, and exaltation, he sought only to **glorify** the Father.

**2.** This glorification of the Father includes in it the elevation of the Son to glory and power, where he is head over all things (cf. Mt 28:18). **Power** means authority. Here it has especially in view the granting of **eternal life,** on the basis of Christ's finished work. The beneficiaries are described as those whom the Father has given to the Son. This is the description of the disciples which recurs most often throughout the prayer (vv. 2,6,9,11, 12,24).

**3.** Eternal life is set forth in terms of knowing God (cf. I Jn 5:20). The Jews did not know God, though they knew much about him. It is the claim of this verse and this whole Gospel that the knowledge of God which brings eternal life comes only through the knowledge of the Son. Since the Father and the Son are one, the knowledge is one. The knowledge of God implies the knowledge of his ways as well as of his person, and so includes the perception of his plan of salvation from sin. **Jesus Christ** (cf. 1:17).

4. I have glorified thee on the earth: I have finished the work which thou gavest me to do.

5. And now, O Father, glorify thou me with thine own self with the glory which I had with thee before the world was.

6. I have manifested thy name unto the men which thou gavest me out of the world: thine they were, and thou gavest them me; and they have kept thy word.

7. Now they have known that all things whatsoever thou hast given me are of thee.

8. For I have given unto them the words which thou gavest me; and they have received *them*, and have known surely that I came out from thee, and have believed that thou didst send me.

9. I pray for them: I pray not for the world, but for them which thou hast given me; for they are thine.

10. And all mine are thine, and thine are mine; and I am glorified in them.

Rare in the Gospels but common in the Epistles.

4. I have glorified thee on the earth. This our Lord explained in terms of finishing the work the Father gave him to do — the revelation of the Father, the exposure of sin, the choice and training of the Twelve, and most of all the death on the cross, which was so certain that it could be regarded as already completed. **Finished** means perfected as well as accomplished.

5. Having spoken of his work on the earth (v. 4), the Son now sought glorification with the Father in the heavenly realm. So the contrast is double, consisting of place and person. With thine own self . . . with thee. In thy presence. Before the world was. Cf. 1:1,2.

Verses 6-8 are transitional, still dealing with the work of Christ on earth but leading up to the petitions for the disciples.

6. A large part of the work of the Son on the earth had been to make the Father known to the disciples (cf. 1:14; 14:7-9). The success of this process is implied in the fact that these men were God's gift to the Son. Their understanding was not perfect, but it was sure and growing. **They have kept thy word.** Not a reference primarily to their obedience to individual commands or teachings, but to their readiness to receive the Son, his message and mission, in so far as they were able.

7,8. The disciples had advanced to the point of understanding that the character and gifts and labors of Christ must be traced to the invisible God, in whose name he had come. In particular the disciples had laid hold of the revelation of truth in Christ, recognizing it as truly of God. They had thus reached a point of development where it was safe to leave them. In their future work they would be representing one who himself had represented the living God. **Thou didst send me.** This expression reverberates through the prayer (vv. 3,8,18,21,23,25). It was a frequent claim of Christ in his discourses.

Having named the qualifications of the disciples as his representatives in the world, the Lord now interceded for them.

9. I pray not for the world. This does not mean that Christ never prayed for the world (cf. Lk 23:34). But he prayed for the disciples because they were the chosen medium of reaching the world after he himself had left it (vv. 21,23). 10. All mine are thine. Therefore the concern of the Son to pray for these men and the concern of the Father to hear and answer

11. And now I am no more in the world, but these are in the world, and I come to thee. Holy Father, keep through thine own name those whom thou hast given me, that they may be one, as we are.

12. While I was with them in the world, I kept them in thy name: those that thou gavest me I have kept, and none of them is lost, but the son of perdition; that the Scripture might be fulfilled.

13. And now come I to thee; and these things I speak in the world, that they might have my joy fulfilled in themselves.

14. I have given them thy word; and the world hath hated them, because they are not of the world, even as I am not of the world.

are alike understandable. The proprietary interest is mutual. **I am glorified in them.** The antecedent of **them** may be the things held in common by Father and Son, or better, the disciples who have been mentioned in the previous verse. It was to the glory of Christ that amid general unbelief and rejection, these men dared to trust and serve him. The word **glorified** is in the perfect tense, suggesting the continuance of their testimony to Christ.

The first specific petition was for the preservation of the disciples from the evil that is in the world (vv. 11-15). This in turn was to serve another purpose, one which is heavily emphasized in the rest of the prayer, namely, that they might be one.

**11. Keep.** Used in the sense of protective oversight, as in I Jn 5:18. The character of God as entirely dissimilar from evil and therefore interested in preserving his children, is emphasized in the address, **Holy Father.** On the positive side, this preservation would make the disciples **one,** reflecting the oneness between Father and Son. The bond is the holy love of God. This unity is seen in the early church (Acts 1:14; 2:1,44,46). **12.** The best attested Greek text reads, *I was keeping them in thy name which thou gavest to me.* Not only did Jesus keep his own disciples by the authority of the Father, but he kept them by the truth and power of the nature of God, which he himself revealed. **The son of perdition.** The word **perdition** is from the same root as the word **lost.** Jesus was saying that the loss was not a reflection on His keeping power as the shepherd of the flock. Rather, Judas had never really belonged to him except in a nominal, external sense (cf. 13:10,11). The idea in *perdition* is exactly the opposite of *preservation.* **The scripture.** Psa 41:9. **13. And now come I to thee.** Herein lay the occasion for the whole prayer and all the requests contained in it. The disciples' need for **joy** was particularly acute in the light of Judas' defection. The disciples needed to realize that such a case did not reflect on the Lord or on themselves. It was not to mar their joy in the possession of true faith and life. If Christ could rejoice even in the midst of such things (my joy), they should do so also. **14.** The reception of the word of Christ identified these men with him and set them apart from **the world,** which rejected and hated him and therefore had the same attitude toward them. **15.** De-

15. I pray not that thou shouldest take them out of the world, but that thou shouldest keep them from the evil.

16. They are not of the world, even as I am not of the world.

17. Sanctify them through thy truth: thy word is truth.

18. As thou hast sent me into the world, even so have I also sent them into the world.

19. And for their sakes I sanctify myself, that they also might be sanctified through the truth.

20. Neither pray I for these alone, but for them also which shall believe on me through their word;

21. That they all may be one; as thou, Father, *art* in me, and I in thee, that they also may be one in us: that the world may believe that thou hast sent me.

22. And the glory which thou gavest me I have given them; that they may be one, even as we are one:

23. I in them, and thou in me, that they may be made perfect in one; and that the world may know that thou hast sent me, and hast loved them, as thou hast loved me.

24. Father, I will that they also, whom thou hast given me, be with me where I am; that they may behold my glory, which thou hast given me: for thou lovedst me before the foundation of the world.

spite the unity between Christ and his own, he could not pray that the Father would take them out of the world. To do so would have frustrated the purpose of their call and training. As they labored and witnessed, they needed to be kept from **the evil**; otherwise their witness would have ceased to be pure. The reference may well be to the evil one himself (cf. Mt 6:13; I Pet 5:8). **16.** As regenerated men, the disciples no longer belonged to the world as a realm of spiritual evil, even though they resided in the world as a physical entity.

**17. Sanctify them through thy truth.** This is the second petition on behalf of the disciples. **Sanctify** means to set apart for God and holy purposes. That which reveals the holy will of God in his **truth,** and specifically that truth as enshrined in the **word** of Scripture. There one learns what God requires and how he enables one to fulfill the requirement. **18.** To be sent into the world by Christ as he was sent by the Father is the highest dignity that can be bestowed on men. **19.** Christ did not need to make himself holy, for he was that. But he did need to devote (sanctify) himself to his calling, that the disciples might have not only his example but his message to proclaim, and the power derived from his sacrifice whereby to proclaim it effectively.

**20,21.** The prayer reaches out to include those who will believe because of the testimony of these men (cf. 10:16; Acts 18:10). Faith is the necessary condition for enjoying the life of God and therefore of coming into that unity which is found first of all in the Godhead and then in the body of Christ, the Church. The unity is basically personal—**in us.** Its effect will be to elicit faith on the part of those in the world (cf. 13:35). **22. The glory.** Doubtless this points to the ultimate heavenly position of the Church, but it includes the privilege of serving and suffering, just as the Father bestowed this commission on the Son. This privilege helps to unify the saints as it is exercised in the light of Christ our forerunner within the veil. **23. Made perfect in one.** To be accomplished not by human effort, but by the gracious extension of the unity of the Godhead to those who belong to Christ. This is not a mechanical unity. Its cement is the love of God bestowed on men, that same love (marvelous to relate) which the Father has for the Son.

**24.** *The final petition.* **I will.** The spirit of the Incarnation was, Not my will but

25. O righteous Father, the world hath not known thee: but I have known thee, and these have known that thou hast sent me.

26. And I have declared unto them thy name, and will declare it; that the love wherewith thou hast loved me may be in them, and I in them.

## CHAPTER 18

WHEN Jesus had spoken these words, he went forth with his disciples over the brook Cedron, where was a garden, into the which he entered, and his disciples.

2. And Judas also, which betrayed him, knew the place: for Jesus ofttimes resorted thither with his disciples.

3. Judas then, having received a band of men and officers from the chief priests and Pharisees, cometh thither with lanterns and torches and weapons.

thine be done. It must be that Jesus was praying in the light of his finished work, which entitled him to express himself in this fashion. His will, to be sure, is not to be thought of as something really independent of the will of God. This petition builds on the last. To participate in the love of God in Christ can only result eventually in sharing the presence of Christ — with me where I am. Union leads to communion, a communion of love displayed in a setting of glory (cf. v. 5).
25. **Righteous Father.** He is righteous (1) in excluding the world from that glory, because it has not known him and therefore does not love him, and so can have no place in that final unity, and (2) in including those who have come to know him through the knowledge that Christ has and imparts. 26. Imparting the knowledge of God means imparting love, for God is love. This is not merely a label or a cold attribute. Christ knew the reality and power of the love of the Father for him and asked that this might brighten and warm the lives of those who were his, with whom his life was now so closely bound up.

## IV. The Sufferings and the Glory. 18: 1–20:31.

A. The Betrayal. 18:1-14. John's account emphasizes the poise of Jesus and his readiness to be taken, making needless the treachery of Judas on the one hand and the attempted display of loyalty by Peter on the other. Included here is the account of the arrest and the transfer of Jesus to the high priest's house.
1. Following the prayer, Jesus led his disciples across **the brook Kidron.** The word **brook** denotes a stream that flows in the winter. A garden on the eastern side was the destination. Matthew and Mark give the name as Gethsemane. John says nothing about the agony in the garden, though he shows awareness of the prayer struggle that took place there (cf. v. 11). We do not know why he omitted this incident. Perhaps he was seeking to give prominence to the element of confidence in the attitude of Jesus, which had already been expressed in prayer (17:4) and was now seen in his bearing and action. 2. **Ofttimes** (cf. Lk 22:39). It may have been the usual thing for Jesus and his company to spend the night there (Lk 21:37). Judas therefore knew where to look for the Lord on this night.
3. Judas, too, had a following when

4. Jesus therefore, knowing all things that should come upon him, went forth, and said unto them, Whom seek ye?

5. They answered him, Jesus of Nazareth. Jesus saith unto them, I am *he*. And Judas also, which betrayed him, stood with them.

6. As soon then as he had said unto them, I am *he*, they went backward, and fell to the ground.

7. Then asked he them again, Whom seek ye? And they said, Jesus of Nazareth.

8. Jesus answered, I have told you that I am *he*: if therefore ye seek me, let these go their way:

9. That the saying might be fulfilled, which he spake, Of them which thou gavest me have I lost none.

he entered the garden, but what a contrasting array! The **band** of soldiers (Gr. *speira*) denotes a Roman cohort, normally six hundred men, but not necessarily at full strength on this occasion. They were quartered in the Castle of Antonia, at the northern edge of the temple area (cf. Acts 21:31ff.). Apparently the Jewish authorities were able to call upon these forces for help in any emergency that threatened the public interest. The city was filled with pilgrims attending the feast, many of whom were sympathetic to Jesus and might have given trouble if they had been nearby when he was being apprehended. **Officers.** These were the temple police who were in the service of the Jewish rulers (cf. Acts 5:22). They bore lights for searching out their quarry and carried weapons for putting down any resistance that might be offered.

**4. Knowing all things.** This is a strongly marked feature of the Johannine presentation of the Christ, and has special prominence in relation to the events of the Passion (cf. 13:1,3). Nothing took our Lord by surprise. **Went forth.** Cf. 18:1 and the oft-repeated emphasis upon the more epochal going forth of the Son from the Father into the world, e.g., 16:28. **Whom seek ye?** The question served to put the oncoming host momentarily on the defensive and obliged them to state that their single objective was Jesus. This made it easier for him to ask that the disciples be permitted to go their way.

**5.** By answering, **Jesus of Nazareth,** the crowd indicated that they did not recognize him, due to the semidarkness and their distance from him. **I am he.** Literally, *I am.* This assertion can indicate merely identification, as in 9:9, or it can suggest the mysterious and majestic name of God himself (8:58). Perhaps both elements are fused together in this case. **Judas . . . stood with them.** At last he was in his own element, mingling with the enemies of Jesus. **6.** Nothing miraculous is implied here. The bearing of Jesus, plus the fact that he advanced toward them rather than sought flight, unnerved his captors. Remember that some of these same men had found themselves unable to lay hands on him previously (7:45,46). No doubt the majesty of his last utterance had something to do with their reaction also.

**7-9.** When the crowd confessed again that their objective was Jesus of Nazareth, he could the more readily ask that the disciples be permitted to leave. Their physical safety on this occasion may be

10. Then Simon Peter having a sword drew it, and smote the high priest's servant, and cut off his right ear. The servant's name was Malchus.

11. Then said Jesus unto Peter, Put up thy sword into the sheath: the cup which my Father hath given me, shall I not drink it?

12. Then the band and the captain and officers of the Jews took Jesus, and bound him,

13. And led him away to Annas first; for he was father-in-law to Caiaphas, which was the high priest that same year.

14. Now Caiaphas was he, which gave counsel to the Jews, that it was expedient that one man should die for the people.

15. And Simon Peter followed Jesus, and *so did* another disciple: that disciple was known unto the high priest, and went in with Jesus into the palace of the high priest.

16. But Peter stood at the door without. Then went out that other disciple, which was known unto the high priest, and spake unto her that kept the door, and brought in Peter.

17. Then saith the damsel that kept the door unto Peter, Art not thou also *one* of this man's disciples? He saith, I am not.

18. And the servants and officers stood there, who had made a fire of coals, for it was cold; and they warmed themselves: and Peter stood with them, and warmed himself.

regarded as a token that their spiritual preservation was assured (cf. 6:39; 17: 12). **10,11.** Peter's action in resorting to use of the sword is understandable in view of his declaration of loyalty in Jn 13:37. His possession of a sword is explained by Christ's counsel in Lk 22:35-38. The sword was symbolic of days of stress lying ahead, but was not intended for literal use. Hence Jesus' rebuke. John's mention of the name of the servant and his ear is an eyewitness touch. Malchus was not one of the officers but a personal slave of the high priest.

**12-14.** *The Arrest.* With Jesus himself calling for nonresistance, the band of soldiers, led by their **captain** and assisted by the Jewish officers, took (captured) Jesus and **bound** him. They did not want to risk any slip in their plans. The Synoptists tell about Jesus' appearance before Caiaphas, but say nothing about Annas in this connection. **First** calls attention of the reader to material now being supplied supplementary to the Synoptic accounts. Though Annas' son-in-law, Caiaphas, was the actual high priest at this time, Annas himself was far from inactive. In addition to Caiaphas, Annas had several sons who succeeded him in this office, giving this one family a monopoly on the high priesthood for over half a century. Luke is the only other writer who mentions Annas (Lk 3:2; Acts 4:6). Jewish sources label the regime of Annas as corrupt. The counsel of Caiaphas about Jesus had already been delivered to the Sanhedrin (11:49,50).

**B. Jesus on Trial Before the Jews.** 18:15-27.

**15.** Spurred by his declaration of loyalty to the Master in the presence of the disciples, Peter **followed** Jesus. **Another disciple.** This figure, unnamed, may be assumed to be John himself. **Known unto the high priest.** The word known is found again in Lk 2:44; 23:49. This connection, to be traced, very likely, through his mother and her family, enabled John to secure admission for Peter to the inner court. **Palace.** Courtyard. **17.** The girl who acted as doorkeeper, probably assuming Peter's connection with Jesus because she knew of John's, challenged him to declare himself, and got a denial. **18.** Presently Peter found himself with the captors of Jesus, warming himself by a fire in the courtyard. John interrupts the story of Peter's denial in order to report on the proceedings within, where Jesus was being examined.

19. The high priest then asked Jesus of his disciples, and of his doctrine.

20. Jesus answered him, I spake openly to the world; I ever taught in the synagogue, and in the temple, whither the Jews always resort; and in secret have I said nothing.

21. Why askest thou me? ask them which heard me, what I have said unto them: behold, they know what I said.

22. And when he had thus spoken, one of the officers which stood by struck Jesus with the palm of his hand, saying, Answerest thou the high priest so?

23. Jesus answered him, If I have spoken evil, bear witness of the evil: but if well, why smitest thou me?

24. Now Annas had sent him bound unto Caiaphas the high priest.

25. And Simon Peter stood and warmed himself. They said therefore unto him, Art not thou also *one* of his disciples? He denied *it*, and said, I am not.

26. One of the servants of the high priest, being *his* kinsman whose ear Peter cut off, saith, Did not I see thee in the garden with him?

27. Peter then denied again; and immediately the cock crew.

28. Then led they Jesus from Caiaphas unto the hall of judgment: and it was early; and they themselves went not into the judgment hall, lest they should be defiled; but that they might eat the passover.

**19,20. The high priest . . . asked Jesus.** Annas is apparently meant. This was not a trial, for the Sanhedrin had not been assembled; rather it was a hearing to get evidence to submit to that body when it was convened a few hours later. The inquiry touched Jesus' **disciples** and **doctrine.** It is not clear that Annas had in mind to prosecute the disciples. More likely he hoped to get a confession that these men were being prepared for revolutionary activity. Jesus ignored the matter. So far as his teaching was concerned, he denied having given secret instruction that might be construed as plotting against the authorities. He had taught **openly,** in public places such as the **synagogue** and **temple.** His teaching was not subversive.

**21. Why askest thou me?** Jesus implied that the procedure was illegal. There were no witnesses. He was being made to implicate himself by his testimony. **22.** One of the attending **officers** (others were in the courtyard) thought the answer impudent and struck Jesus to make him more docile in his attitude toward the high priest. **23,24.** When Christ pointed out the injustice involved, neither the officer nor Annas could make a defense of the procedure. There was nothing to do but to send the captive to Caiaphas (the AV incorrectly suggests that he had been previously sent).

**25-27.** The narrative returns to Peter. While Christ was denying the insinuations leveled against him — and justly so, Peter was denying his Lord sinfully. The two questions addressed to Peter were quite different. The first was tentative, as though expecting him to deny that he had a relation to Jesus; whereas the second pinned him down, the very form of the question assuming his guilt. He was now recognized as the one who had wielded the sword in the garden. The crowing of the cock reminded Peter of the Lord's prediction (13:38) and brought home to him his sin of denial. 'Cockcrowing' was the name of the third of the four watches into which the night was divided.

C. The Ordeal Before Pilate. 18:28—19:16.

**28.** Nothing is said about what took place in the house of Caiaphas. The assumption is that the readers are acquainted with the Synoptic tradition of the nighttime deliberations and the formal decree of the council arrived at in the early morning. **The hall of judgment** (Gr. *praitōrion,* a rendering of Lat. *praetorium,*

29. Pilate then went out unto them, and said, What accusation bring ye against this man?

30. They answered and said unto him, If he were not a malefactor, we would not have delivered him up unto thee.

31. Then said Pilate unto them, Take ye him, and judge him according to your law. The Jews therefore said unto him, It is not lawful for us to put any man to death:

32. That the saying of Jesus might be fulfilled, which he spake, signifying what death he should die.

33. Then Pilate entered into the judgment hall again, and called Jesus, and said unto him, Art thou the King of the Jews?

34. Jesus answered him, Sayest thou this thing of thyself, or did others tell it thee of me?

35. Pilate answered, Am I a Jew? Thine own nation and the chief priests have delivered thee unto me: what hast thou done?

the headquarters of the governor). See the discussion on 19:13. That they might eat the passover. The Jewish leaders, to be ceremonially clean, could not enter a pagan's quarters. They were more concerned with ritual cleanness than with the execution of justice. They were out for blood!

29,30. The Sanhedrin had not prepared a formal indictment against Jesus to submit to Pilate. They expected the governor to take their word for it that this man was a malefactor, i.e., a doer of evil. The answer was flippant. Pilate was disliked by the Jews.

31. Judge him according to your law. Pilate was satisfied that the very vagueness of the statement by the Jewish leaders indicated that the case was not one he needed to hear (cf. Acts 18:14). It is not lawful for us to put any man to death. All the Jews wanted was a verdict of death, the authority of the governor to cover their own decision against Jesus. The taking away of the right to inflict the death penalty made the Jews realize they were a subject people. This had exceptions, as in the case of a person, even a Roman, who transgressed the barrier that separated the Court of the Gentiles from the inner portion of the temple area. Stephen's death seems to violate John's statement, but it may have been based on the knowledge of the Jews that the governor would not interfere in that case. 32. Jesus had predicted that he would die by crucifixion, a Roman method of punishment, whereas the Jews used stoning (cf. Mt 20:19).

33. Pilate then took matters into his own hands, questioning Jesus within the Praetorium. John seems to suppose that his readers knew the Synoptic account, which included a charge leveled by the Jews against Jesus to the effect that he had declared himself king of the nation. Pilate was obliged to examine this matter on the grounds of possible revolutionary intent. Art thou the King of the Jews? The word thou is emphatic, as though Pilate were surprised that the appearance and attitude of Jesus so little fitted the claim of kingship. The prisoner seemed harmless.

34. Before he could answer the question, Jesus needed to know whether it came from Pilate himself as a Roman official or whether it was merely passed on as a bit of hearsay. Perhaps the high priest had discussed the case with Pilate when he asked for Roman soldiers to aid in capturing Jesus. 35. Pilate, unwilling

36. Jesus answered, My kingdom is not of this world: if my kingdom were of this world, then would my servants fight, that I should not be delivered to the Jews: but now is my kingdom not from hence.

37. Pilate therefore said unto him, Art thou a king then? Jesus answered, Thou sayest that I am a king. To this end was I born, and for this cause came I into the world, that I should bear witness unto the truth. Every one that is of the truth heareth my voice.

38. Pilate saith unto him, What is truth? And when he had said this, he went out again unto the Jews, and saith unto them, I find in him no fault *at all*.

39. But ye have a custom, that I should release unto you one at the passover: will ye therefore that I release unto you the King of the Jews?

40. Then cried they all again, saying, Not this man, but Barabbas. Now Barabbas was a robber.

## CHAPTER 19

THEN Pilate therefore took Jesus, and scourged *him*.

to be trapped into an admission that he had had anything to do with the situation, put the responsibility on the Jews. **Thine own nation.** Pilate could hardly have felt the pathos suggested by his words (cf. 1:11).

**36. My kingdom is not of this world.** "He does not say that this world is not the sphere of His authority, but that His authority is not of human origin" (Hoskyns). He was not a menace to the Roman authority. There was no place for the use of force in his kingdom. **37.** Pilate was nonplused. Here was a man who had spoken of his kingdom three times in rapid succession, yet he had none of the outward marks of kingship. **Art thou a king then?** Pilate could hardly believe that anyone would mistake the figure before him for a king. **Thou sayest that I am a king.** Jesus was hesitant to affirm that he was a king, lest Pilate misunderstand the nature of his kingship, which he now explained in terms of **truth.** Christ had come to bear witness to it. **Heareth my voice** (cf. 10:3,16).

**38.** Pilate saw that Jesus had no concern for politics or affairs of state and was far removed from a warlike spirit, and so he terminated the interview, saying rather disdainfully, it seems, **What is truth?** He was no philosopher nor religionist, but a man of action. Satisfied that the prisoner was not dangerous to Rome, he announced this to the Jews outside. **No fault.** This does not refer to sinlessness in this context, but to innocence of any wrongdoing the Jews had charged against him.

**39.** Sensing the tenacity of the rulers in their desire to get a conviction, Pilate thought he saw a way to get around them and uphold justice by releasing the prisoner. It was a yearly **custom** at Passover time for the governor to please the crowd by releasing one prisoner whom they requested. Pilate thought that, because Jesus was very popular, the people who had gathered by this time for their annual request would seek his release. **40.** Again John presupposes a knowledge of the Synoptic narrative by his reference to Barabbas. **Robber.** Brigand (cf. Acts 3:14).

**19:1-3.** At Pilate's order the prisoner was scourged. This was the governor's second expedient, the earlier attempt to secure release having failed because of the preference for Barabbas. Pilate thought the Jews might be satisfied if Jesus were humiliated and made to suffer in this fashion. The Lord had pre-

2. And the soldiers platted a crown of thorns, and put *it* on his head, and they put on him a purple robe,

3. And said, Hail, King of the Jews! and they smote him with their hands.

4. Pilate therefore went forth again, and saith unto them, Behold, I bring him forth to you, that ye may know that I find no fault in him.

5. Then came Jesus forth, wearing the crown of thorns, and the purple robe. And *Pilate* saith unto them, Behold the man!

6. When the chief priests therefore and officers saw him, they cried out, saying, Crucify *him*, crucify *him*. Pilate saith unto them, Take ye him, and crucify *him:* for I find no fault in him.

7. The Jews answered him, We have a law, and by our law he ought to die, because he made himself the Son of God.

dicted this treatment (Mt 20:19). See also Isa 53:5. **A crown of thorns.** This was mockery on the part of the soldiers, in view of Jesus' alleged kingship. Some have thought that this crown was fashioned from the sharp prongs of the date palm, thus connecting it with the nationalist hopes of the Jews expressed by the waving of palms when Jesus entered Jerusalem. Since the palm was an expression of Jewish hopes for independence even in Maccabean days, this action by the soldiers would have been the harsh answer of Rome to the Jews as a whole. From the Biblical standpoint the thorns may be said to express the curse of sin (Gen 3:17,18), which Christ was bearing for the race. **A purple robe.** Often associated with royalty. Clothed thus, Jesus became an object of sport and abuse by the soldiers.

**4,5. Pilate . . . went forth again.** He proposed to prepare the way for the showing of Jesus by a grandiose announcement. **Behold, I bring him forth to you.** This was in the spirit of the mockery of the soldiers. He, the Roman governor, would present the one who was reputed to be a king but now certainly could not be confused with a king. **Behold the man!** It is uncertain what Pilate meant to imply here. Some see in the situation a desire to create pity in the hearts of the Jews. But the setting suggests more the thought of scorn. **Man** may mean nothing more than "miserable creature." In any event, Pilate's words, **I find no fault in him,** have a strange ring. If the prisoner was innocent, why was flogging administered?

**6.** The answer of **the chief priests** was a resounding refusal to be satisfied with punishment of this character, however painful and humiliating. **Crucify, Crucify!** Pilate's reply, **Take ye him,** puts emphasis on the **ye.** In other words, "If there is any crucifying to be done here, you will have to do it." Pilate was dissociating himself from the Jews' desire, but not seriously giving permission to them to put Jesus to death. This was the third time the governor declared himself unable to find any **fault** (*aitia*) in Jesus. The word is used here in the legal sense of a proper ground of complaint.

**7.** Pilate was standing on Roman law. The Jews put something else over against it. **We have a law.** Emphasis falls on the **we.** Our law requires the death of the prisoner, **because he made himself the Son of God.** The individual passage in the background is Lev 24:16. Jesus had

8. When Pilate therefore heard that saying, he was the more afraid;

9. And went again into the judgment hall, and saith unto Jesus, Whence art thou? But Jesus gave him no answer.

10. Then saith Pilate unto him, Speakest thou not unto me? knowest thou not that I have power to crucify thee, and have power to release thee?

11. Jesus answered, Thou couldest have no power *at all* against me, except it were given thee from above: therefore he that delivered me unto thee hath the greater sin.

12. And from thenceforth Pilate sought to release him: but the Jews cried out, saying, If thou let this man go, thou art not Caesar's friend: whosoever maketh himself a king speaketh against Caesar.

been accused of blasphemy during his ministry (Jn 5:18) and at its close (Mk 14:62-64). **8. The more afraid.** Pilate's previous fear had been due to the angry persistence of Jesus' accusers, who would not be denied. Perhaps John is presupposing his readers' knowledge of the dream of Pilate's wife (Mt 27:19). The governor's new fear was that he was dealing with one who in some sense was supernatural — a son of a god. **9.** It began to appear to Pilate that this case had more to it than he had thought at first. So he took the prisoner within the Praetorium for another conference. **Whence art thou?** Not residence but origin and nature were in view. **No answer.** Pilate's spiritual incapacity (cf. 18:38) made reply useless.

**10.** The silence of the prisoner annoyed the governor. Perhaps he thought that by asserting his authority and advancing the reminder that life or death hung on his verdict, he could make Jesus talk. **11.** The device was only partially successful. Jesus talked, but only to state to Pilate his limitations. **Power.** Authority. Christ may have been affirming the broad truth of the divine control over the state (Rom 13:1 ff.), but the stress falls on the immediate situation. Pilate was powerless to do other than carry out the will of God in this case. **He that delivered me.** Any reference to Judas is hardly natural here. **The greater sin,** i.e., greater than that of Pilate. "The sin of Caiaphas is greater because Pilate's authority is from God; and it was the duty of Caiaphas to know and teach as well as do the will of God. But he, the official representative of Israel, the People of God, has had recourse to this heathen, who holds certain authority from God, in order that power conferred by God for the execution of justice may be employed for the perpetration of injustice" (William Temple, *Readings in St. John's Gospel*).

**12.** As a result of this verbal exchange, Pilate made renewed efforts to release his prisoner, driven alike by fear of this strange person before him and by the conviction that he was not worthy of death. The Jews, sensing fresh resolution in the governor, used their culminating argument. **Thou are not Caesar's friend.** The reigning emperor was Tiberius, to whom Pilate was responsible. Here was a threat to take the case to the imperial court. Caesar would not have looked lightly upon a situation in which one was known as a **king** without Roman consent. He would have viewed this as treason

13. When Pilate therefore heard that saying, he brought Jesus forth, and sat down in the judgment seat in a place that is called the Pavement, but in the Hebrew Gabbatha.

14. And it was the preparation of the passover, and about the sixth hour: and he saith unto the Jews, Behold your King!

15. But they cried out, Away with *him*, away with *him*, crucify him. Pilate saith unto them, Shall I crucify your King? The chief priests answered, We have no king but Caesar.

16. Then delivered he him therefore unto them to be crucified. And they took Jesus, and led *him* away.

17. And he bearing his cross went forth into a place called *the place* of a skull, which is called in the Hebrew Golgotha:

18. Where they crucified him, and two others with him, on either side one, and Jesus in the midst.

19. And Pilate wrote a title, and put *it* on the cross. And the writing was, JESUS OF NAZARETH THE KING OF THE JEWS.

20. This title then read many of the Jews; for the place where Jesus was crucified was nigh to the city: and it was written in Hebrew, *and* Greek, *and* Latin.

21. Then said the chief priests of the Jews to Pilate, Write not, The King of the Jews; but that he said, I am King of the Jews.

22. Pilate answered, What I have written I have written.

and might well have charged Pilate with inattention to duty. No doubt the governor feared that if a complaint were made regarding his handling of this case, other irregularities in his administration would come to light.

**13.** The time for decision had come. **Pilate . . . sat down in the judgment seat.** He had now to render his verdict. Due to the excavations of Père Vincent, **the Pavement** (*Lithostrōton*) is now almost certainly identified as the large paved area that was a part of the Castle of Antonia, at the northwest corner of the temple area. **Gabbatha** probably means "elevated ground." **14. It was the preparation of the passover.** "The hour of the double sacrifice is drawing near. It is midday. The Passover lambs are being prepared for sacrifice, and the Lamb of God is likewise sentenced to death" (Hoskyns). **Behold your King!** Whatever moved Pilate to make this final presentation (probably scorn for the Jews — such a king for such a people!), it was providentially used to draw from the lips of the Jews a complete repudiation of their Messianic hope — **We have no king but Caesar.** If language means anything, the very sovereignty of God over the nation was repudiated. Who was guilty of blasphemy now? **16. Delivered.** The verb is the same as that in verse 11. The Jews were now able to see their will accomplished. Jesus was to be crucified.

D. The Crucifixion and Burial. 19:17-42.

**17. Bearing his cross.** All the Synoptics state that Simon of Cyrene was compelled to bear the cross. John alone states that Jesus carried it. Luke's account makes room for both. Jesus started, but could not carry it all the way. **Golgotha.** Probably named from its appearance; hence a rounded hill. Its Latin equivalent is Calvary (Lk 23:33). It must have been outside the city (Heb 13:12). **18. Jesus in the midst.** His was the place of central importance, even in death.

**19.** His position is explained by the title affixed over the head of the crucified. Matthew and Mark use the word *aitia*, which John employs three times, in his account of the trial, in the sense of "charge." Pilate found no *aitia* in Jesus that warranted his death, but now he let the world know that here hung Israel's king, as though thereby involving the nation in defiance of Rome and deserving of this harsh rebuke. **20-22.** The very publicity given the title (three languages)

**23.** Then the soldiers, when they had crucified Jesus, took his garments, and made four parts, to every soldier a part; and also *his* coat: now the coat was without seam, woven from the top throughout.
**24.** They said therefore among themselves, Let us not rend it, but cast lots for it, whose it shall be: that the Scripture might be fulfilled, which saith, They parted my raiment among them, and for my vesture they did cast lots. These things therefore the soldiers did.
**25.** Now there stood by the cross of Jesus his mother, and his mother's sister, Mary the *wife* of Cleophas, and Mary Magdalene.
**26.** When Jesus therefore saw his mother, and the disciple standing by, whom he loved, he saith unto his mother, Woman, behold thy son!
**27.** Then saith he to the disciple, Behold thy mother! And from that hour that disciple took her unto his own *home.*
**28.** After this, Jesus knowing that all things were now accomplished, that the Scripture might be fulfilled, saith, I thirst.
**29.** Now there was set a vessel full of vinegar: and they filled a sponge with vinegar, and put *it* upon hyssop, and put *it* to his mouth.
**30.** When Jesus therefore had received the vinegar, he said, It is finished: and he bowed his head, and gave up the ghost.
**31.** The Jews therefore, because it was the preparation, that the bodies should not remain upon the cross on the sabbath day, (for that sabbath day was a high day,) besought Pilate that their legs might be broken, and *that* they might be taken away.

as well as the implication behind it, incensed the Jews, so that the chief priests requested that the wording be changed from a fact to a claim. This Pilate refused to do, showing an unyieldingness which sharply contrasts with his weakness during the trial.

**23,24.** Four soldiers took part in the crucifixion (cf. Acts 12:4). These took as personal spoil the garments of Jesus, dividing them among themselves. Sandals, headdress, outer garment *(himation),* and girdle were likely distributed, leaving the more valuable coat or tunic *(chitōn)* for the casting of lots. Josephus describes the high priest's robe in language similar to that used here *(Ant* III. 161). It has been suggested that in John's eyes this seamless robe may have symbolized the unifying power of the death of Christ as securing the one flock. The soldiers unconsciously fulfilled Scripture by their actions (Ps 22: 18).

**25-27.** Three women, all named Mary, took their station near the cross, sorrowfully contemplating the one who was so dear to them. The Greek text, however, is rather favorable to the mention of four, the mother's sister (Salome, the mother of John) being noted but left unnamed. If so, these four may be intended to present a sort of contrast to the Roman soldiers. Solicitous for his mother, Jesus gave her into the care of the 'beloved disciple.' His own brethren were not believers at this time. The unity of the Church, which the Lord was bringing into being, was to be spiritual rather than natural (cf. Mt 12: 50). **His own** (home). If John had a residence in Jerusalem, his acquaintance with the high priest is more readily explained (18:16).

**28. I thirst.** The physical need of the sufferer asserted itself, the only outward indication he permitted to escape his lips. Even so, he stated a fact rather than voicing an appeal. **30.** The **vinegar** was sour wine. It revived Jesus' strength, enabling him to say (with a loud cry, according to the other Gospels), **It is finished.** The same word *(tetelestai)* has already occurred in verse 28, rendered "accomplished." Emphasis here is not on the ending of the sufferings but on the completion of the mission of redemption. **Gave up the ghost.** Delivered over his spirit (to God).

**31. The sabbath day.** Only a short time remained before sunset and the coming of another day. No matter what the day, the Law required the removal of victims from the cross on the day of death (Deut

32. Then came the soldiers, and brake the legs of the first, and of the other which was crucified with him.

33. But when they came to Jesus, and saw that he was dead already, they brake not his legs:

34. But one of the soldiers with a spear pierced his side, and forthwith came there out blood and water.

35. And he that saw it bare record, and his record is true; and he knoweth that he saith true, that ye might believe.

36. For these things were done, that the Scripture should be fulfilled, A bone of him shall not be broken.

37. And again another Scripture saith, They shall look on him whom they pierced.

38. And after this Joseph of Arimathea, being a disciple of Jesus, but secretly for fear of the Jews, besought Pilate that he might take away the body of Jesus: and Pilate gave him leave. He came therefore, and took the body of Jesus.

39. And there came also Nicodemus, which at the first came to Jesus by night, and brought a mixture of myrrh and aloes, about a hundred pound weight.

40. Then took they the body of Jesus, and wound it in linen clothes with the spices, as the manner of the Jews is to bury.

41. Now in the place where he was crucified there was a garden; and in the garden a new sepulchre, wherein was never man yet laid.

42. There laid they Jesus therefore because of the Jews' preparation day; for the sepulchre was nigh at hand.

## CHAPTER 20

THE first day of the week cometh Mary Magdalene early, when it was yet dark, unto the sepulchre, and seeth the stone taken away from the sepulchre.

21:22,23). To have disregarded this law at Passover time would have been an especially heinous violation of the Sabbath. The breaking of the legs was designed to hasten death. **33,34.** The soldier, finding that death had cheated him of the pleasure of breaking the legs of Jesus, drove his spear into the side of the Saviour. **Blood and water.** This is quite a credible occurrence in the period immediately after death. **35.** John attaches singular importance to this incident, for he solemnly bears record to it. The death of the Saviour means a life-giving flow: blood for the cleansing from sin and water for the representation of the new life in the Spirit (cf. I Jn 5:6-8). **36,37.** These features of the death of Christ also served to fulfill Scripture (Ps 34:20; Zech 12:10).

**38-40.** In the hour of Jesus' death two secret disciples found a courage they had not possessed before. Joseph gained from Pilate permission to take down the body from the cross; then Nicodemus came forward to provide the **spices** and **linen** for preparing the body for burial. For more information on Joseph, see Mk 15:43.

**41.** The sepulcher belonged to Joseph (Mt 27:60). **42.** Burial preparations were hurried because the day was coming to a close. Fortunately, the spot was near to the place of crucifixion. More complete preparation of the body could be made after the Sabbath.

E. The Resurrection Appearances. 20: 1-29. The Sabbath rest in Jerusalem is passed by in silence. The body of Christ lay amid the stillness of the tomb. But the "must" of Mt 16:21 includes resurrection as well as suffering and death. The supreme test of the claims of Jesus of Nazareth was at hand.

**1. The first day of the week.** The day after the Sabbath, or the third day from Christ's crucifixion, according to the usual Jewish method of inclusive reckoning. Jesus' resurrection on this day determined the Christian day of worship (Acts 20:7). **Mary Magdalene.** It was well known that several women came early to the tomb, but John concentrates his narrative on Mary alone. The presence of others is assumed in the "we know not" of verse 2. It was the purpose of the women to anoint the body of Jesus more permanently (Mk 16:1). **The stone taken away.** With the stone in place, Mary would have had the problem of gaining access to the tomb; with the stone removed, she had a prob-

2. Then she runneth, and cometh to Simon Peter, and to the other disciple, whom Jesus loved, and saith unto them, They have taken away the Lord out of the sepulchre, and we know not where they have laid him.

3. Peter therefore went forth, and that other disciple, and came to the sepulchre.

4. So they ran both together: and the other disciple did outrun Peter, and came first to the sepulchre.

5. And he stooping down, *and looking in,* saw the linen clothes lying; yet went he not in.

6. Then cometh Simon Peter following him, and went into the sepulchre, and seeth the linen clothes lie,

7. And the napkin, that was about his head, not lying with the linen clothes, but wrapped together in a place by itself.

8. Then went in also that other disciple, which came first to the sepulchre, and he saw, and believed.

9. For as yet they knew not the Scripture, that he must rise again from the dead.

10. Then the disciples went away again unto their own home.

11. But Mary stood without at the sepulchre weeping: and as she wept, she stooped down, *and looked* into the sepulchre,

lem of another kind. To her mind, the situation had worsened.

2. Mary thought of the leading disciples—Simon Peter and the 'beloved disciple'—and ran to take the word to them. It is of interest that in Mary's eyes Peter, despite his denial, was still the acknowledged leader of the group. John, to a degree responsible for Peter's failure (18:16), had been seeking to comfort him. Mary's report of the opened tomb suggested to the two disciples the same fear that had gripped her heart — someone had taken the body.

3,4. Concern caused the two disciples to break into a run, leaving Mary to come at her own gait. The same concern led John to sprint ahead of Peter, though the two had started together. John may have been the more youthful. 5. Stooping down. The thought is best represented by our word "peer." Restrained by awe and timidity, John took in the interior of the tomb, but did not enter.

6,7. With his characteristic boldness, Peter did not pause at the entrance to look, but went in, and was thus able to see more clearly than John the disposition of the grave clothes. He noticed that they were not all in a heap, but that the headpiece was neatly wrapped and deposited in a place by itself. If the body had been removed, it was strange that the linen cloths were left behind, and even more strange that the napkin was so carefully arranged. Wrapped together. This verb is used of the act of winding graveclothes about the body of Jesus before the burial (Mt 27:59; Lk 23:53). It may signify that the head passed through the napkin, leaving it in its circular shape, or that Jesus deliberately folded it up before leaving the tomb.

8. Emboldened by Peter's entrance, John joined him within, took in the scene, and believed that the Lord had risen. This is not said of Peter. 9. The disciples had not received instruction from Christ relating his resurrection to the OT Scriptures (Lk 24:46). They had Jesus' prediction of resurrection, but did not understand this literally (Mk 9:10). 10. Their own home. The expression is literally, *to themselves,* meaning that they returned to their own quarters and to their own people. Mary (cf. 19:27) would thus have learned of the empty tomb very soon.

11. Mary Magdalene remained at the spot, hoping for some clue to the whereabouts of Jesus, struggling with her double grief over his death and the disap-

12. And seeth two angels in white sitting, the one at the head, and the other at the feet, where the body of Jesus had lain.

13. And they say unto her, Woman, why weepest thou? She saith unto them, Because they have taken away my Lord, and I know not where they have laid him.

14. And when she had thus said, she turned herself back, and saw Jesus standing, and knew not that it was Jesus.

15. Jesus saith unto her, Woman, why weepest thou? whom seekest thou? She, supposing him to be the gardener, saith unto him, Sir, if thou have borne him hence, tell me where thou hast laid him, and I will take him away.

16. Jesus saith unto her, Mary. She turned herself, and saith unto him, Rabboni; which is to say, Master.

17. Jesus saith unto her, Touch me not; for I am not yet ascended to my Father: but go to my brethren, and say unto them, I ascend unto my Father, and your Father; and *to* my God, and your God.

18. Mary Magdalene came and told the disciples that she had seen the Lord, and *that* he had spoken these things unto her.

pearance of his sacred form. **She stooped down** (cf. v. 5). **12.** She saw something the two disciples had not seen — two angels. Such was the experience of the other women also (Lk 24:22,23). **13.** Ordinarily a vision of angels would have brought a thrill, but Mary was too overborne with grief to feel any other emotion. She turned away before receiving any intimation from them that Jesus was risen (cf. Mk 16:6).

**14,15.** She was equally uninterested in another form that loomed up before her as she turned away into the garden. Her only concern was to press her search for the body, and there was a chance that this man was the gardener and might have removed it. **16.** Electrified at hearing her name spoken in the familiar voice of Jesus, she burst out, **Rabboni** (Master or Lord). Originally the form meant *my great one*, but the word had come to be used without possessive force. It is not unduly surprising that Mary recognized the voice of Jesus when he spoke her name but not when he first questioned her. Even the familiar can seem strange to us when we encounter it unexpectedly.

**17. Touch me not.** The Greek calls for a different rendering: *Stop clinging to me.* Apparently Mary's first impulse, in her frenzy of joy, was to grasp the sacred form. Jesus did not rebuke the other women for holding his feet (Mt 28:9), for this was an act of worship; nor did he shrink from inviting Thomas to touch him (Jn 20:27). But Mary needed to be taught that the Lord was not with her on the basis of the old relationship. He was already glorified. He belonged now to the heavenly realm, even though he was willing to tarry for a time to meet with his friends. **I am not yet ascended.** The implication was that Mary would be able to touch Jesus in some sense after the Ascension, i.e., she would touch him by faith in the blessed life of the Spirit. The closeness of that new relationship is attested by the fact that he spoke of his followers as **brethren** (cf. the anticipation of this in Mt 12:49). Even in the intimacy of the new order, however, Christ retained his own special relationship to God the Father. **My Father** is the language of deity; **my God** is the language of humanity.

**18.** The sense of being useful, of fulfilling Jesus' command to go to the disciples, relieved any feeling of hurt Mary may have experienced at the rebuff she had received. Her task is a miniature of

19. Then the same day at evening, being the first *day* of the week, when the doors were shut where the disciples were assembled for fear of the Jews, came Jesus and stood in the midst, and saith unto them, Peace *be* unto you.

20. And when he had so said, he showed unto them *his* hands and his side. Then were the disciples glad, when they saw the Lord.

21. Then said Jesus to them again, Peace *be* unto you: as *my* Father hath sent me, even so send I you.

22. And when he had said this, he breathed on *them*, and saith unto them, Receive ye the Holy Ghost:

23. Whosesoever sins ye remit, they are remitted unto them; *and* whosesoever *sins* ye retain, they are retained.

that given to the whole Church — to go and tell that Jesus has risen.

**19.** The disciples, having received the message from Mary, now had their first opportunity, as a group, to see Jesus in his risen state. It was the evening of the resurrection day. **For fear of the Jews.** This was natural in view of their flight from the garden, Annas' inquiry about them (18:19), and the expectation created by Jesus' teaching that if he suffered, they should expect to do so also (Mt 16: 24; Jn 15:20). The implication is plain that Jesus passed through the closed doors. He had power to dematerialize his body. **Peace be unto you** (cf. 14:27; 16:33). **20.** The word of peace had relieved fear. Now it was in order to establish identity. **He showed unto them his hands and his side.** According to Luke, even more graphic demonstration was needed in order to bring conviction (Lk 24:37-43). **Then were the disciples glad** (cf. 16:22).

**21.** The first **peace** (v. 19) was to quiet their hearts; the second was to prepare them for a fresh statement of their commission (cf. 17:18). Nothing had been changed in the plan of the Master for them. **22. He breathed on them.** This recalls the creation of man (Gen 2:7), as though to announce the new creation, resulting not so much from the infusion of the breath of God as from the reception of the Holy Spirit (cf. 7:39). This need not rule out any relation to the Spirit in the days of earlier discipleship any more than it rules out the Spirit's coming upon them at Pentecost. Here the Spirit was the necessary equipment for the task that lay ahead, which is stated next.

**23.** Christ gave authority to the apostles and possibly to others (cf. Lk 24:33 ff.) to forgive and to retain the sins of men. "Either . . . the disciples must possess unfailing insight into man's heart (such as in certain cases was granted to an apostle, cf. Acts 5:3), or the remission which they proclaim must be *conditionally* proclaimed. No one can maintain the former alternative. It follows, then, that what our Lord here commits to His disciples, to His Church, is the right authoritatively to declare, in His name, that there is forgiveness for man's sin, and on what conditions the sin will be forgiven" (Milligan and Moulton, *Commentary on John*) This scene involves the death of Christ (his wounds presented), his resurrection (declared by his living presence), the resultant commission to go and bear witness to him, the equipment for this

24. But Thomas, one of the twelve, called Didymus, was not with them when Jesus came.

25. The other disciples therefore said unto him, We have seen the Lord. But he said unto them, Except I shall see in his hands the print of the nails, and put my finger into the print of the nails, and thrust my hand into his side, I will not believe.

26. And after eight days again his disciples were within, and Thomas with them: *then* came Jesus, the doors being shut, and stood in the midst, and said, Peace *be* unto you.

27. Then saith he to Thomas, Reach hither thy finger, and behold my hands; and reach hither thy hand, and thrust *it* into my side; and be not faithless, but believing.

28. And Thomas answered and said unto him, My Lord and my God.

29. Jesus saith unto him, Thomas, because thou hast seen me, thou hast believed: blessed *are* they that have not seen, and *yet* have believed.

30. And many other signs truly did Jesus in the presence of his disciples, which are not written in this book:

31. But these are written, that ye might believe that Jesus is the Christ, the Son of God; and that believing ye might have life through his name.

task, and the message itself, centering in forgiveness of sins.

**24 25.** John notes Thomas' absence but does not explain it. Since Jesus did not rebuke Thomas on the score of his losing interest in his discipleship, it is precarious for us to do so. He may have preferred to be alone in his grief over the Saviour's death. The report of the others concerning their meeting with Jesus emphasized that they had seen the wounded hands and side of the Lord. Thomas demanded not only the sight of these, but the actual touching of them as the condition of believing that Jesus was alive from the dead.

**26.** A week later, with conditions the same as before, including the shut doors, Jesus came a second time and with the same greeting of **Peace. 27.** By his very language the Lord revealed that he knew what Thomas had asserted. Therefore he must have been alive when the doubting apostle spoke those words about the **hands** and the **side. 28.** His misgivings completely removed, Thomas rose to a mighty declaration of faith in response to Jesus' challenge. **My Lord and my God.** He knew he was in the presence of deity. **29. Because thou hast seen me.** There is nothing to demonstrate that Thomas touched the Saviour. The sight of him had been enough. But what about the multitudes who would not have this opportunity of sight? A blessing is pronounced on such, who dare to make the venture of faith (cf. I Pet 1:8).

F. The Purpose of This Gospel. 20:30, 31. The **signs** which dot the narrative of John have climaxed in the greatest of them all, the Resurrection. Lest the reader think otherwise, the writer hastens to note that the signs were **many.** Only a select few are included in this book. Yet it is the writer's expectation that these will enable the reader to believe that Jesus is the Christ (the object of Jewish expectation, based on OT prophecy, when that expectation is not perverted by false views of Messiahship) and the Son of God, revealing the Father by word and deed, culminating in obedience to the Father's will even unto death. **Believe** includes the ideas of faith's initial act and of progressing in faith as well. **Life through** (more literally, *in*) his name, i.e., in union with his own person.

Because this seems a natural conclusion to the Gospel, some scholars have concluded that the next chapter was

## CHAPTER 21

AFTER these things Jesus showed himself again to the disciples at the sea of Tiberias; and on this wise showed he *himself*.

2. There were together Simon Peter, and Thomas called Didymus, and Nathanael of Cana in Galilee, and the *sons* of Zebedee, and two other of his disciples.

3. Simon Peter saith unto them, I go a fishing. They say unto him, We also go with thee. They went forth, and entered into a ship immediately; and that night they caught nothing.

4. But when the morning was now come, Jesus stood on the shore; but the disciples knew not that it was Jesus.

5. Then Jesus saith unto them, Children, have ye any meat? They answered him, No.

6. And he said unto them, Cast the net on the right side of the ship, and ye shall find. They cast therefore, and now they were not able to draw it for the multitude of fishes.

7. Therefore that disciple whom Jesus loved saith unto Peter, It is the Lord. Now when Simon Peter heard that it was the Lord, he girt *his* fisher's coat *unto him,* (for he was naked,) and did cast himself into the sea.

added later, either by John himself or by another. But there is nothing to demand such a view of the closing chapter. It is full of suggestiveness as to how the Lord's continuing presence and power enable the Church to fulfill its ministry in the world.

## VI. Epilogue. 21:1-25.

1. The scene of the post-resurrection appearances shifts from Jerusalem to Galilee. **The sea of Tiberias** — another term for the Sea of Galilee (cf. 6:1). **2. Together.** This is accounted for, not on the basis of a common occupation, but on that of their discipleship and of their experience in seeing Jesus risen from the dead. Peter and John were to figure prominently in the incident about to be related. **3. I go a fishing.** Peter could not stand inactivity. The sight of his boat and the waters of his beloved Galilee, and perhaps the necessity of keeping body and soul together, dictated his sudden announcement. It is hazardous to conclude that Peter was going back to fishing as a permanent occupation. To be sure, the infinitive of the verb "to fish" is present tense, which may suggest sustained action. But this is offset by the fact that the verb **I go** suggests an expedition rather than a career. Further, the concurrence of the other disciples makes it clear that they understood Peter's purpose to be temporary. In view of the appearances of the Lord to them (cf. 20: 21-23), it is unthinkable that they were reverting to fishing as an occupation. **They caught nothing.** This was providential, preparing the way for Christ's intervention.

**4,5.** Standing on the shore, Jesus spoke but was not recognized. **Children** may be rendered *lads* without doing violence to the meaning. **Have ye any meat?** The form of the question carries the suspicion that they did not have any. **Meat.** Relish eaten with bread, but also used in the sense of fish. **No.** It hurts a fisherman to admit that he has caught nothing. **6. Cast the net on the right side.** The position of the boat remained the same, the fishing gear was the same, the men were the same, with the same skill; but now their empty nets became full, all because of the word of Christ (see Jn 15:5).

**7.** The miracle brought quick awareness to the 'beloved disciple' that the stranger must be Jesus. **It is the Lord.** Peter's mind must have flashed back to

8. And the other disciples came in a little ship, (for they were not far from land, but as it were two hundred cubits,) dragging the net with fishes.

9. As soon then as they were come to land, they saw a fire of coals there, and fish laid thereon, and bread.

10. Jesus saith unto them, Bring of the fish which ye have now caught.

11. Simon Peter went up, and drew the net to land full of great fishes, a hundred and fifty and three: and for all there were so many, yet was not the net broken.

12. Jesus saith unto them, Come *and* dine. And none of the disciples durst ask him, Who art thou? knowing that it was the Lord.

13. Jesus then cometh, and taketh bread, and giveth them, and fish likewise.

14. This is now the third time that Jesus showed himself to his disciples, after that he was risen from the dead.

15. So when they had dined, Jesus saith to Simon Peter, Simon, *son* of Jonas, lovest thou me more than these? He saith unto him, Yea, Lord; thou knowest that I love thee. He saith unto him, Feed my lambs.

another time on this same lake when at Jesus' word he let down the net and garnered a great catch of fish (Lk 5:1-11). Peter's eagerness to see Jesus in person suggests that he was not conscious of being out of the will of God in going fishing. **Coat.** It would have been improper to greet the Lord without being fully attired. **8.** The other disciples followed in the dinghy. **Two hundred cubits.** About one hundred yards.

**9.** Jesus' followers were about to be reminded that the one who grants success in Christian work is also sufficient for the daily needs of his own. **Fish.** A single fish. **Bread.** A single loaf. Jesus would make them suffice, as he had done with the loaves and fishes for the multitude.

**10. Bring of the fish which ye have now caught.** The purpose was not to augment what was already provided. There is no indication that the fish were prepared and cooked and eaten. Christ wanted the men to get the full thrill of their catch. Generously he said, "which ye have now caught," despite their impotence apart from himself. **11.** The fish were counted, which is customary. Their number simply indicates the greatness of the catch. If there is any symbolism connected with the unbroken net, it is to the effect that those who are won through Christ-directed service will not be lost, but will be preserved to reach the heavenly strand.

**12. Dine.** The word is especially suitable for breakfast, though used sometimes of other meals. It was a solemn occasion, with the disciples feeling a fresh sense of awe in the presence of the Lord. **14. The third time.** Two other appearances to the disciples as a group are recounted in the previous chapter. The remainder of this appearance concerns almost exclusively Peter and John, though the others profited from the teaching.

**15.** This scene has sometimes been called 'The Restoration of Peter,' but this may be misleading. Peter had already been restored in the sense of receiving forgiveness (Lk 24:34). But the leadership of an erring disciple could hardly have been accepted for the days ahead, either by Peter or his brethren, apart from Christ's explicit indication. **Lovest thou me?** More important than love for men is love for Christ. **More than these.** Some understand **these** to refer to the paraphernalia of fishing. If this were so, Peter could have answered without any evasion and without the use of a differ-

16. He saith to him again the second time, Simon, *son* of Jonas, lovest thou me? He saith unto him, Yea, Lord; thou knowest that I love thee. He saith unto him, Feed my sheep.

17. He saith unto him the third time, Simon, *son* of Jonas, lovest thou me? Peter was grieved because he said unto him the third time, Lovest thou me? And he said unto him, Lord, thou knowest all things; thou knowest that I love thee. Jesus saith unto him, Feed my sheep.

18. Verily, verily, I say unto thee, When thou wast young, thou girdedst thyself, and walkedst whither thou wouldest: but when thou shalt be old, thou shalt stretch forth thy hands, and another shall gird thee, and carry *thee* whither thou wouldest not.

19. This spake he, signifying by what death he should glorify God. And when he had spoken this, he saith unto him, Follow me.

20. Then Peter, turning about, seeth the disciple whom Jesus loved following; which also leaned on his breast at supper, and said, Lord, which is he that betrayeth thee?

21. Peter seeing him saith to Jesus, Lord, and what *shall* this man *do?*

22. Jesus saith unto him, If I will that he tarry till I come, what *is that* to thee? follow thou me.

23. Then went this saying abroad among the brethren, that that disciple should not die: yet Jesus said not unto him, He shall not die; but, If I will that he tarry till I come, what *is that* to thee?

ent word for **love** than Jesus used. The very fact that Jesus probed Peter's love in the presence of his brethren suggests that the others were involved. Peter had boasted that he would remain loyal even if the others did not (Mk 14:29). **Feed my lambs.** Christ is unwilling to entrust his little ones to one who does not love him.

**16.** The second round of question and answer brings a somewhat different commission, at least verbally. **Feed my sheep** is literally, *Shepherd* (or *tend) my sheep.*

**17.** Peter's grief here may be traced to two things. First, the threefold questioning may well have suggested his threefold denial. Second, Jesus abandoned his word for love (*agapaō*) and used the one Peter employed (*phileō*), a word indicative of warm affection but perhaps considered inferior to the other. This distinction is blunted, however, by the fact that elsewhere in John the second word is used in a very high sense (e.g., 5:20). **My sheep** (cf. 10:14,27). They are precious to the Lord; he gave his life for them. Peter needed love to assume the pastoral office.

**18.** The acceptance of this commission was to prove costly. Early days in Peter's life were times of freedom. One day this freedom would be withdrawn, but only when Peter was **old.** The prophecy assured him of years of service. **Stretch forth thy hands.** Suitable language for crucifixion. Early church tradition supports this manner of death for Peter. **19.** **By what** (sort of) **death.** He would be honored by suffering death in the same manner as his Lord. The word **glorify** has been used of the death of Jesus also (12: 23). **Follow me.** This led to a physical movement, but much more is implied (cf. 13:36). Peter was being summoned to an undeviating, faithful walk, to set his face like flint, even as Jesus had done in view of the approaching cross.

**20.** John followed also, without an invitation. Peter noticed it and commented on it. **21.** Being a friend of John, Peter was curious as to what future the Lord had in view for **this man. 22.** The answer of Jesus had one purpose, to rebuke Peter for being distracted over John's future. It was enough for him to be concerned about doing God's will in his own life. This rebuke is suggested by the emphatic **thou,** which is absent from verse 19. **23.** Jesus' words, however, were readily misconstrued as an assurance that John would live on until the Lord's return. The **if** was easily forgotten. John himself corrects this false impression.

24. This is the disciple which testifieth of these things, and wrote these things: and we know that his testimony is true.

25. And there are also many other things which Jesus did, the which, if they should be written every one, I suppose that even the world itself could not contain the books that should be written. Amen.

**24. This.** A reference to that disciple in verse 23, i.e., John. **Testifieth.** This may point to John's oral testimony of the things contained in the Gospel, in distinction from the fact that he also **wrote** them. **We know.** The identity of these persons who here add their witness to the veracity of John is unknown. Likely they were men associated with John in Ephesus, possibly elders of the church.

**25.** The thought is an extension of what has already been stated in 20:30. **I suppose.** This is awkward after the plural **we know** of the previous verse. Some think John's secretary permitted himself this closing word. Again we are reminded that our Gospel records are not intended to be full accounts of the activity of our Lord in the days of his flesh.

# BIBLIOGRAPHY

BARRET, C. K. *The Gospel According to St. John.* London: S.P.C.K., 1955.

DODD, C. H. *The Interpretation of the Fourth Gospel.* Cambridge: The University Press, 1953.

BERNARD, T. D. *The Central Teaching of Jesus Christ.* New York: Macmillan and Co., 1892.

HOSKYNS, E. C. *The Fourth Gospel.* Edited by F. N. Davey. London: Faber and Faber, Ltd., 1940.

MILLIGAN, WILLIAM and MOULTON, W. F. *Commentary on the Gospel of St. John.* Edinburgh: T. and T. Clark, 1898.

RIGG, W. H. *The Fourth Gospel and Its Message for Today.* London: Lutterworth Press, 1952.

TEMPLE, WILLIAM. *Readings in St. John's Gospel.* London: Macmillan and Co., Ltd., 1950.

WESTCOTT, B. F. *The Gospel According to St. John.* London: John Murray, 1896.

# THE ACTS OF THE APOSTLES

## INTRODUCTION

*Title.* The title as we know it was not attached to the original book but belongs to the second century A.D. The Gospel of Luke and The Acts are two volumes of a single work (see Commentary *in loc.*), and whatever title was originally prefixed to the Gospel served for both books. When the second volume began to circulate independently, this title was used to designate its contents.

*Author* Neither the Gospel nor The Acts names their author, but he was most probably Luke, a friend and companion of Paul. The clue to authorship is provided by the three "we" sections, where the narrative is in the first person plural (Acts 16:10-17; 20:5−21:18; 27:1−28:16), suggesting that the author was Paul's companion on these three occasions, and is using his travel diary as his source. Some have suggested that this travel document was written by an unknown companion of Paul and incorporated into Acts by a later unknown author. But the uniformity of style between this travel narrative and the rest of Acts and the retention of the first person plural make this most unlikely. Church tradition uniformly identifies Luke as Paul's companion, and the data of The Acts support this tradition.

*Date.* The date of Acts is linked with the problem of its abrupt ending (see Commentary *in loc.*). We do not know when it was written, but a date shortly after the conclusion of the narrative is likely. If so, Acts was written about A.D. 62.

*Sources.* Aside from his own travel diary, Luke may have used written sources, especially for the earlier chapters of his work. As a companion of Paul, he was in a position to gather firsthand information from the apostle. Furthermore, since Luke was in Palestine during Paul's Caesarean imprisonment (21:18; 27:1), he had ample opportunity to gather information about the early days of the church from eyewitnesses.

*Purpose.* Luke wrote to assure Theophilus as to "the certainty of those things, wherein thou hast been instructed" (Lk 1:4). Theophilus was probably a Gentile convert to Christianity, and Luke wrote to give him a greater knowledge of Christian origins than he already possessed. This included the story of the life, death, and resurrection of Jesus (the "Gospel"), and the establishment and extension of the church.

Strictly speaking, Luke did not write a *history* of the early church. This is not to suggest that his narration is unhistorical or inaccurate. However, the task of a "historian" is to give a comprehensive narrative of all of the important facts. This, obviously, Luke did not attempt. He tells us nothing about the churches in Galilee (Acts 9:31) or about the evangelization of Egypt or Rome. His story is not The Acts of the Apostles, for only three of the original twelve appear in his narrative—Peter, James, John; and the latter two are only mentioned. The book of Acts is The Acts of Peter and Paul. Furthermore, Peter is practically dropped from the story after the conversion of Cornelius, and we are left wondering what became of him. Again, Luke gives no explanation of the rise of elders in the church (11:30), of how James came to a place of leadership in the Jerusalem church (15:13), of what Paul did in Tarsus after his conversion (9:30; see 11:25), and of many other important historical matters. Furthermore, he passes over some events with a few words (18:19-23) but relates other events in great detail (21:17−26:32). In other words, Luke is telling a story, not writing a "history." His story is that of the main outlines of the extension of the church from Jerusalem to Rome via Samaria, Antioch, Asia, and Europe; and in this story, only Peter and Paul played outstanding roles. The ministry of the other apostles elsewhere in the eastern world was not important to Luke.

Two themes underlie the story of this expansion: the rejection of the Gospel by the Jews and its reception by the Gentiles; and the treatment of the early church by local and Roman officials. Luke's main purpose, therefore, in his two-volume work (Luke-Acts) is to explain to Theophilus how it came about that the Gospel which began with the promise of the restoration of the kingdom to Israel (Lk 1:32,33) ended with the Gentile church in Rome, distinct from Judaism.

Furthermore, Judaism was a religion recognized by Rome. The new religious fellowship that arose within Judaism and yet was not simply a sect in the older religion received the same recognition from Rome as did Judaism. Thus the Christian church became established in the Roman world as a legitimate religion distinct from Judaism.

*Acts and the Epistles.* The greatest problem in the history of the study of Acts has concerned its trustworthiness in comparison with the epistles of Paul. Luke does not refer to the epistles of Paul, and it is not always easy to correlate Paul's movements, as reflected in his epistles, with Luke's record. The greatest problem is: How can the events of Gal 1:16–2:10 be correlated with the Lukan narrative? Equally good scholars have felt that the visit of Gal 2:1-10 refers to (a) the famine visit of Acts 11:27-30 and (b) the council visit in Acts 15. Many scholars have felt that the narrative of Acts suffers in comparison with the epistles.

A second aspect of the problem is posed by the contrast between the portrait of Paul in Acts and that reflected in the missionary's own epistles. The Paul of Acts appears to be a flexible, reasonable person who was willing to compromise his principles for the sake of expediency (see 16:3; 21:26); while the Paul of the epistles is an inflexible person of unbending convictions (Gal 1:8; 2:3). The older Tübingen school of criticism built its theory of the history of the primitive church around a supposed conflict between Pauline and Judaistic Christianity, and held that The Acts reflects a late stage in the history of the conflict, when a synthesis was being achieved between the two contradictory viewpoints.

It is obviously impossible to deal in any detail with these problems, but they stand in the background of the study and often enter directly into the commentary.

## THE ESTABLISHMENT AND GROWTH OF THE CHURCH

I. Beginnings of the church. 1:1—2:47.
   A. Preparation: The post-resurrection ministry and ascension of Jesus. 1:1-14.
   B. Choice of Matthias. 1:15-26.
   C. Coming of the Holy Spirit. 2:1-41.
   D. Life of the primitive church. 2:42-47.
II. The church in Jerusalem. 3:1—5:42.
   A. A typical miracle and sermon. 3:1-26.
   B. First opposition from Jewish leaders. 4:1-37.
   C. Death of Ananias and Sapphira. 5:1-16.
   D. Second opposition from Jewish leaders. 7:17-42.
III. Extension of the church in Palestine through dispersion. 6:1—12:25.
   A. Choice of the seven. 6:1-7.
   B. Occasion of the dispersion: Ministry and matyrdom of Stephen. 6:8—8:3.
   C. The Gospel in Samaria. 8:4-25.
   D. Conversion of the Ethiopian eunuch. 8:26-40.
   E. Conversion of Saul. 9:1-31.
   F. Peter's ministry in Palestine and the first Gentile converts. 9:32—11:18.
   G. Establishment of a Gentile church at Antioch. 11:19-30.
   H. Persecution by Herod Agrippa I. 12:1-25.
IV. Extension of the church in Asia Minor and Europe. 13:1—21:17.
   A. First mission, Galatia. 13:1—14:28.
   B. Problem of the Gentile church, and council in Jerusalem. 15:1-35.
   C. Second mission, Asia Minor and Europe. 15:36—18:22.
   D. Third mission, Asia Minor and Europe. 18:23—21:17.
V. Extension of the church to Rome. 21:18—28:31.
   A. Rejection of the Gospel by Jerusalem. 21:18—26:32.
   B. Reception of the Gospel in Rome. 27:1—28:31.

# THE ACTS OF
# THE APOSTLES

## CHAPTER 1

.THE former treatise have I made, O Theophilus, of all that Jesus began both to do and teach,

2. Until the day in which he was taken up, after that he through the Holy Ghost had given commandments unto the apostles whom he had chosen:

3. To whom also he showed himself alive after his passion by many infallible proofs, being seen of them forty days, and speaking of the things pertaining to the kingdom of God:

4. And, being assembled together with *them*, commanded them that they should not depart from Jerusalem, but wait for the promise of the Father, which, *saith he*, ye have heard of me.

5. For John truly baptized with water; but ye shall be baptized with the Holy Ghost not many days hence.

6. When they therefore were come together, they asked of him, saying, Lord, wilt thou at this time restore again the kingdom to Israel?

# COMMENTARY

## I. Beginnings of the Church. 1:1—2:47.

A. Preparation. The Post-resurrection Ministry and Ascension of Jesus. 1:1-14.

**1,2.** The first two verses constitute a brief introduction that ties Acts to the Gospel of Luke. The introductory verses of the Gospel (Lk 1:1-4) are meant to serve both for the Gospel and for Acts; Acts 1:1,2 is a kind of secondary introduction that looks back to Lk 1:1-4. **The former treatise.** The Gospel of Luke. Acts is the second part of a two-volume work, Luke-Acts. The Gospel contains all that Jesus **began both to do and teach;** Acts traces the continued ministry of the ascended Christ through the Holy Spirit working in the apostles. We do not know who **Theophilus** was, whether a Christian who needed further instruction or an interested pagan (see Lk 1:3).

**2.** This reference to the Holy Spirit sounds the chief theological note of The Acts—the work of the Holy Spirit.

**3.** Our Lord's post-resurrection ministry of forty days had a twofold objective: to provide a positive demonstration of the reality of his resurrection, and to give further explanation of his teaching about the **kingdom of God.** We may therefore expect this theme to reappear in the apostles' ministry. The good news about the kingdom of God was the content of Philip's message in Samaria (8:12), of Paul's preaching and teaching in Ephesus (20:25), and of Paul's message to both Jews and Gentiles in Rome when he finally reached that city (28:23,31).

**4.** The command of Lk 24:49 is here repeated. Since the ministry of the apostles was to be the work of the Holy Spirit, they were to wait in Jerusalem until the promise of the coming of the Holy Spirit—given by the Father in the OT (Joel 2:28; Ezk 36:27) and confirmed through the Son—should be fulfilled. The word translated **assembled together** is of uncertain meaning and may also be rendered "eating with" or "lodging with."

**5.** The ministry of John the Baptist, baptizing men **with water,** was preparatory for the coming of Messiah. The greater reality, the baptism of **the Holy Spirit,** would shortly take place.

**6.** This verse expands the last words of verse 3. To the Jews of the first century, the **kingdom** of God meant an earthly, political kingdom for Israel. At one point in our Lord's ministry, the

7. And he said unto them, It is not for you to know the times or the seasons, which the Father hath put in his own power.

8. But ye shall receive power, after that the Holy Ghost is come upon you: and ye shall be witnesses unto me both in Jerusalem, and in all Judea, and in Samaria, and unto the uttermost part of the earth.

9. And when he had spoken these things, while they beheld, he was taken up; and a cloud received him out of their sight.

10. And while they looked steadfastly toward heaven as he went up, behold, two men stood by them in white apparel;

11. Which also said, Ye men of Galilee, why stand ye gazing up into heaven? this same Jesus, which is taken up from you into heaven, shall so come in like manner as ye have seen him go into heaven.

people were prepared to take Jesus by force and compel him to become their king (Jn 6:15). However, Christ's mission was not to bring the kingdom in earthly splendor but to bring it in spiritual power. This was a difficult lesson for the disciples to learn. During the forty days, one of their main questions was whether Jesus would soon establish this earthly kingdom through Israel.

7. Jesus replied that the answer to this question was no present concern of theirs. Times and seasons probably refer to the time which must elapse before the final establishment of God's kingdom, and to the character of the events that will accompany its establishment. The Father has determined these events by his own authority (RSV). This does not mean that God is through with Israel; Romans 11:26 says that all Israel shall be saved. The NT tells us almost nothing about the time and manner of the future salvation of Israel.

8. Rather than devoting themselves to questions about the final establishment of the Jewish kingdom, the apostles were to have a different concern. The Holy Spirit was to come upon them and to give them supernatural power, in the strength of which they would be witnesses of Christ throughout all the world. This verse is a table of contents of the book of Acts: in Jerusalem covers chapters 1—7; in all Judea, and in Samaria covers chapters 8:1—11:18; and unto the uttermost part of the earth covers 11:19 to the end of the book.

9. The cloud that received Christ upon his ascension was not merely a cloud of condensed vapor but was a symbol of the Shekinah glory which represents the glorious presence of God (Ex 33:7-11; 40:34; Mk 9:7). The ascension of Christ meant that he had broken off visible fellowship with his disciples on earth, and, still bearing his resurrected body, had entered into the invisible world of God's dwelling.

10. White is the color of angels' garb (Mt 28:3; Jn 20:12).

11. The angels informed the apostles that this experience was no repetition of the Transfiguration (Lk 9:27-36): Jesus had left them, but one day he would return to the earth in the same visible, glorious way in which he had departed. The expectation of the bodily return of Christ is central in Christian faith.

12. Then returned they unto Jerusalem from the mount called Olivet, which is from Jerusalem a sabbath day's journey.

13. And when they were come in, they went up into an upper room, where abode both Peter, and James, and John, and Andrew, Philip, and Thomas, Bartholomew, and Matthew, James *the son* of Alpheus, and Simon Zelotes, and Judas *the brother* of James.

14. These all continued with one accord in prayer and supplication, with the women, and Mary the mother of Jesus, and with his brethren.

15. And in those days Peter stood up in the midst of the disciples, and said, (the number of names together were about a hundred and twenty,)

16. Men *and* brethren, this Scripture must needs have been fulfilled, which the Holy Ghost by the mouth of David spake before concerning Judas, which was guide to them that took Jesus.

17. For he was numbered with us, and had obtained part of this ministry.

18. Now this man purchased a field with the reward of iniquity; and falling headlong, he burst asunder in the midst, and all his bowels gushed out.

19. And it was known unto all the dwellers at Jerusalem; insomuch as that field is called, in their proper tongue, Aceldama, that is to say, The field of blood.

20. For it is written in the book of Psalms, Let his habitation be desolate, and let no man dwell therein: and, His bishopric let another take.

21. Wherefore of these men which have companied with us all the time that the Lord Jesus went in and out among us,

22. Beginning from the baptism of John, unto that same day that he was taken up from us, must one be ordained to be a witness with us of his resurrection.

12. The Ascension had taken place from the **Mount of Olives,** which stands directly east of Jerusalem, about three thousand feet away. This was the distance permitted to a Jew to walk on the Sabbath day without breaking the Sabbath rest.

13. This upper room may have been the scene of the Last Supper (Lk 22:12) and was possibly located in the house of Mary, the mother of Mark (Acts 12:12). For other lists of the Twelve, see Mt 10:2 ff.; Mk 3:16 ff.; Lk 6:14 ff. **Simon Zelotes.** Simon the Cananaean. **Zelotes** *(the zealot)* may refer to the fervent character of Simon, but it more likely indicates that he belonged to a nationalistic party among the Jews that advocated open rebellion against Rome.

14. **His brethren.** Jesus' half-brothers (Mt 13:55), who did not believe in him before his death (Jn 7:5) but who were brought to faith by his resurrection. A resurrection appearance to James is recorded in I Cor 15:7. **The women** may designate either the wives of the disciples or the women mentioned in Lk 8:2; 24:10.

B. Choice of Matthias. 1:15-26. The apostolic college had been broken by the defection of Judas, and the apostles felt the need of choosing a man to take his place.

15. Peter now emerged as the natural leader among the 120 believers, who are called **brethren** *(disciples,* AV, is the reading of an inferior text). **Names** (AV) is a Semitic expression meaning persons (RSV) or individuals. 16. Peter reminded the company that Judas' betrayal of Jesus was not an unforeseen tragedy but was in the providential purposes of God and therefore foretold in the OT (see v. 20).

18,19. These verses are a note inserted by Luke into his record of Peter's remarks to explain to his readers Judas' fate. According to Mt 27:7, the high priests bought this field; but apparently they did so in the name of Judas, since the money was legally his. **Falling headlong** should possibly be translated *swelling up,* and refers to a fatal rupture. Augustine interprets this passage to mean, "he fastened a rope around his neck and, falling on his face, burst asunder in the midst." **Aceldama.** An Aramaic word meaning *field of blood.*

20. Peter quoted freely from Ps 69:25; 109:8. **Bishopric** means *office of overseer,* in a nontechnical sense.

21,22. The qualifications for Judas'

23. And they appointed two, Joseph called Barsabas, who was surnamed Justus, and Matthias.

24. And they prayed, and said, Thou, Lord, which knowest the hearts of all *men*, show whether of these two thou hast chosen,

25. That he may take part of this ministry and apostleship, from which Judas by transgression fell, that he might go to his own place.

26. And they gave forth their lots; and the lot fell upon Matthias; and he was numbered with the eleven apostles.

## CHAPTER 2

AND when the day of Pentecost was fully come, they were all with one accord in one place.

2. And suddenly there came a sound from heaven as of a rushing mighty wind, and it filled all the house where they were sitting.

3. And there appeared unto them cloven tongues like as of fire, and it sat upon each of them.

4. And they were all filled with the Holy Ghost, and began to speak with other tongues, as the Spirit gave them utterance.

successor in the apostolic college were two: he must have been a companion of Jesus, and he must have been a witness of Jesus' resurrection. There is no reference to ordination in these verses. **23.** We have no other information about these two equally qualified candidates. **24-26.** Such a choice by the casting of lots had an OT precedent (Prov 16:33), but it occurs nowhere else in the NT and is not normative for Christian practice. **That he might go to his own place.** Judas experienced the fate he deserved for his incredible treachery. Judas' place was filled not because he had died but because he had defected. When James, the brother of John, was executed (Acts 12:2), his place was not filled. The **Lord** to whom prayer was addressed (1:24) was probably the ascended Jesus, for he who had chosen the original twelve (v. 2) was now asked to choose another. **Lord** is the usual word in the Greek OT to designate God; it was used from the earliest days of the Church to designate the ascended Jesus.

C. Coming of the Holy Spirit. 2:1-41. There is a real sense in which the Church had its birthday on the day of Pentecost, when the Holy Spirit was given to men in a new way to bring believers in Jesus together into a new relationship.

**1. Pentecost,** meaning *fiftieth,* is the Greek word for the Feast of (seven) Weeks described in Lev 23:15-22, which celebrated the conclusion of the harvest. **2.** All the 120 disciples were gathered together in one body and **in one place**— probably the upper room (1:13). **With one accord** is the reading of an inferior text. The **sound from heaven** was **like** [that of] a **rushing mighty wind.** It was not a wind; it sounded **like** a wind. *Pneuma* can mean both wind and spirit; and wind is a symbol of the Spirit's power and also of his invisibility (Jn 3:8). What was seen was not actually tongues of fire but **tongues like fire. 3.** The visible sign was something that could only be likened to a flame of fire that **divided** into separate tongues which rested upon the individual disciples. Many understand this to be the fulfillment of John's promise of baptism with fire (Lk 3:16). However, no fire was present at Pentecost but something **like** fire; and the context in the Gospel suggests that the baptism of fire is the judgment of those who reject Messiah—the burning of the chaff with unquenchable fire. **4.** As the Holy Spirit was given to men, the disciples were baptized (1:5)

5. And there were dwelling at Jerusalem Jews, devout men, out of every nation under heaven.

6. Now when this was noised abroad, the multitude came together, and were confounded, because that every man heard them speak in his own language.

7. And they were all amazed and marveled, saying one to another, Behold, are not all these which speak Galileans?

8. And how hear we every man in our own tongue, wherein we were born?

9. Parthians, and Medes, and Elamites, and the dwellers in Mesopotamia, and in Judea, and Cappadocia, in Pontus, and Asia,

10. Phrygia, and Pamphylia, in Egypt, and in the parts of Libya about Cyrene, and strangers of Rome, Jews and proselytes,

11. Cretes and Arabians, we do hear them speak in our tongues the wonderful works of God.

12. And they were all amazed, and were in doubt, saying one to another, What meaneth this?

13. Others mocking said, These men are full of new wine.

14. But Peter, standing up with the eleven, lifted up his voice, and said unto them, Ye men of Judea, and all *ye* that dwell at Jerusalem, be this known unto you, and hearken to my words:

and at the same time **filled with the Holy Spirit.** The baptism of the Spirit is described in I Cor 12:13. It is the work of the Holy Spirit to join people of diverse racial and social backgrounds into one body—the body of Jesus Christ, which is his Church. In the strict sense of the word, Pentecost was the birthday of the Church. This baptism of the Spirit was never repeated. It was later extended to believers in Samaria (Acts 8), to the Gentiles (chs. 10; 11), and to the disciples of John the Baptist (19:1-6). The filling of the Spirit was often repeated, but not the baptism with the Spirit.

5. The disciples had now apparently moved down from the upper room to an open place in the city, possibly within the temple area, where a crowd assembled. The **devout men** were Diaspora Jews, who had been scattered throughout the Mediterranean world but who had returned to the Holy City to live.

6. The **other tongues** (v. 4). Not the language of religious ecstasy. By a miracle the language of the apostles was translated by the Holy Spirit into many diverse languages without a human translator. This phenomenon is not the same as the *glossolalia* or gift of tongues in I Cor 12; 14, which were unintelligible until interpreted. Possibly the Holy Spirit acted as interpreter at Pentecost, so that various language groups heard their own tongue without the mediation of a human interpreter. 7. It was an amazing thing that these men whose accent showed them to be Galilean Jews appeared capable of speaking many foreign languages. 9-11. These countries formed a circuit around the entire Mediterranean Sea. Most of these peoples could speak the popular Greek of the Hellenistic world, but they also spoke their native tongues (cf. 14:11). **Strangers of Rome. Jews** and Gentile converts (**proselytes**) from Rome, who were only temporarily residing in Jerusalem.

12,13. All of the hearers were at a loss (*in doubt*, AV) to understand what was happening. The accusation of drunkenness suggests that an ecstatic element as well as foreign languages was present in this first gift of tongues. 14. A large crowd had assembled because of this commotion (v. 6), probably in the outer court of the temple area. Peter offered an explanation of what had occurred before their eyes and then moved on to a proclamation of the Gospel, which was

15. For these are not drunken, as ye suppose, seeing it is *but* the third hour of the day.

16. But this is that which was spoken by the prophet Joel;

17. And it shall come to pass in the last days, saith God, I will pour out of my Spirit upon all flesh: and your sons and your daughters shall prophesy, and your young men shall see visions, and your old men shall dream dreams:

18. And on my servants and on my handmaidens I will pour out in those days of my Spirit; and they shall prophesy:

19. And I will show wonders in heaven above, and signs in the earth beneath; blood, and fire, and vapor of smoke:

20. The sun shall be turned into darkness, and the moon into blood, before that great and notable day of the Lord come:

embodied essentially in the announcement of the Messiahship of Jesus.

**15.** Peter first disposed of the suggestion that the disciples were drunk by pointing out that it was only nine o'clock in the morning and therefore too early for people to have become drunken. **16.** It was not spirits but the Holy Spirit that had taken possession of them. Peter quoted Joel 2:28-31, which foretells the outpouring of the Holy Spirit upon Israel in the Messianic era. It is important to note that a prophecy which in Joel was addressed to the nation Israel now had its fulfillment in the Christian church. However, in God's redemptive purpose, Israel is also to be included in the fulfillment of this prophecy (Rom 11:26).

**17. The last days** is not found in the prophecy of Joel but was added by Peter under divine inspiration. In the OT this phrase designates the Messianic era of the kingdom of God (Isa 2:2; Hos 3:5). The age of the Gospel is therefore one stage in the realization of the blessings of the Messianic age. In the OT era, the Holy Spirit was given primarily to people who occupied official positions in the theocracy of Israel—kings, priests, and prophets. The new mission of the Holy Spirit was to rest upon **all flesh**, that is, upon all of God's people and not only upon the official leaders. The promise that this new outpouring of the Spirit would result in a new manifestation of **prophecy,** of **visions,** and of **dreams,** was fulfilled in the experience of the apostles and prophets of the NT era. It was the Jewish belief that the Holy Spirit, who had inspired the OT prophets with their message, had been silent during the Inter-Testamental Period. Peter asserted that the Holy Spirit had now become active again in a new manifestation of God's redemptive purpose. This is seen in the last words of Acts 2:18, where Peter added to the prophecy of Joel the statement, **and they shall prophesy.** This new manifestation of prophecy was not so much foretelling the future as forth-telling the meaning of God's redemptive work through Jesus the Messiah.

**19,20.** The last half of this prophecy from Joel was not fulfilled in Peter's day as was the outpouring of the Spirit. The **day of the Lord.** The day of Christ's coming in glory to establish his kingdom in the world with power and glory. This final consummation will be attended by a judgment that will fall upon the earthly order, and out of the cosmic catastrophe will emerge a new redeemed order of nature and the world (Rom 8:21). The last days

21. And it shall come to pass, *that* whosoever shall call on the name of the Lord shall be saved.

22. Ye men of Israel, hear these words; Jesus of Nazareth, a man approved of God among you by miracles and wonders and signs, which God did by him in the midst of you, as ye yourselves also know:

23. Him, being delivered by the determinate counsel and foreknowledge of God, ye have taken, and by wicked hands have crucified and slain:

24. Whom God hath raised up, having loosed the pains of death: because it was not possible that he should be holden of it.

25. For David speaketh concerning him, I foresaw the Lord always before my face; for he is on my right hand, that I should not be moved:

26. Therefore did my heart rejoice, and my tongue was glad; moreover also my flesh shall rest in hope:

27. Because thou wilt not leave my soul in hell, neither wilt thou suffer thine Holy One to see corruption.

28. Thou hast made known to me the ways of life; thou shalt make me full of joy with thy countenance.

29. Men *and* brethren, let me freely speak unto you of the patriarch David, that he is both dead and buried, and his sepulchre is with us unto this day.

30. Therefore being a prophet, and knowing that God had sworn with an oath to him, that of the fruit of his loins, according to the flesh, he would raise up Christ to sit on his throne;

31. He, seeing this before, spake of the resurrection of Christ, that his soul was not left in hell, neither his flesh did see corruption.

32. This Jesus hath God raised up, whereof we all are witnesses.

are thus distinguished from the Day of the Lord.

21. This outpouring of the Holy Spirit will bring about a great day of salvation, and whoever calls on the name of the Lord shall be saved. Lord in Joel refers to God, but Peter and the early church applied this to the exalted Jesus.

22,23. Peter reviewed the life and death of Jesus to show that it was no mere accident but occurred within the redemptive plan of God. In spite of the fact that God had attested Christ by miracles and wonders and signs . . . in the midst of the Jews, they had turned him over to the hands of lawless men (RSV), the Romans, who ignored God's law, to have him crucified and slain. While neither the Romans nor the Jews were absolved from guilt, the death of Jesus had taken place in accordance with the definite plan (RSV) and foreknowledge of God.

24. Although human judges had put Jesus to death, a higher court had raised him from the dead, since it was impossible that the Messiah should remain under the power of death. 25-28. Peter next proved that the death of the Christ was a part of God's redemptive plan by showing that it was foreseen in the OT Scriptures. He quoted from Ps 16:8-11, a passage which in its own context refers to David and his hope of salvation from death. Even in death, David expected to behold the face of the Lord. He therefore could submit to the experience of death in hope that God would not abandon his soul to Hades (Sheol), the abode of the dead after death, nor permit him to see the corruption of the grave. Since God is the God of the living, in spite of the fact that the OT has no full revelation of life after death, David was confident that God would show him the ways of life and bring him into the fullness of joy in the Divine presence even after death.

29. The apostle made it clear that these verses could not refer to David, since David in fact died and experienced corruption. Indeed, his grave could be seen south of the city of Jerusalem. The psalmist, therefore, must have referred to David's greater son, the Messiah. 30,31. Hence the psalmist spoke prophetically of one of his descendants (RSV), the Christ, who would be seated on David's throne. In these words of David, Peter found a prophecy of the resurrection of Christ. 32. The resurrection of the Messiah, foreseen by the psalmist, could now be attested by the experience of the apostles.

33. Therefore being by the right hand of God exalted, and having received of the Father the promise of the Holy Ghost, he hath shed forth this, which ye now see and hear.

34. For David is not ascended into the heavens: but he saith himself, The LORD said unto my Lord, Sit thou on my right hand,

35. Until I make thy foes thy footstool.

36. Therefore let all the house of Israel know assuredly, that God hath made that same Jesus, whom ye have crucified, both Lord and Christ.

37. Now when they heard *this*, they were pricked in their heart, and said unto Peter and to the rest of the apostles, Men *and* brethren, what shall we do?

38. Then Peter said unto them, Repent, and be baptized every one of you in the name of Jesus Christ for the remission of sins, and ye shall receive the gift of the Holy Ghost.

39. For the promise is unto you, and to your children, and to all that are afar off, *even* as many as the Lord our God shall call.

33. Jesus had not only been raised from the dead; he had also been **exalted at the right hand of God** (RSV cf. v. 34) and had from this exalted position **poured out** upon his people the gift of the Holy Spirit foretold by Joel. **34,35.** Peter again quoted from the Psalms (110:1) to show that the exaltation of Christ was also in the prophetic Scriptures. The Lord God had said to David's Lord, the Messiah, that he should sit at God's right hand until all of his enemies were subdued. From these verses we must conclude that Christ is even now enthroned in the heavens and in a real sense is exercising his Messianic reign (Rev 3:21).

36. The heart of the Gospel is this: that Jesus, raised from the dead and exalted at the right hand of God, has been made both **Lord** and **Messiah**. His Messiahship means Lordship; he reigns at the right hand of God as Lord and King. The fulfillment of the Messianic office is realized in a new and unexpected way. The Lordship of Christ was the cardinal doctrine of primitive Christianity. Jesus entered into the exercise of his Lordship by virtue of his exaltation (Phil 2:9-11), and salvation is to be found in confessing Jesus as Lord (Rom 10:9).

37 Peter's hearers were both convinced and convicted. They were **cut to the heart** (RSV) by the realization that they had put to death God's Messiah, and they therefore asked what they might do to be delivered from this awful guilt.

38. Peter replied that God's mercy could forgive even this sin. A twofold response was required: **to repent** and **to be baptized in the name of Jesus the Christ.** To repent would mean to turn rightabout-face from their sinful ways and confess faith in Jesus as their Messiah. Baptism would be the public evidence of this repentant spirit. The result would be the **forgiveness** of their sins and the reception of the **gift of the Holy Spirit.** The reception of the Holy Spirit is not dependent upon baptism, but it follows baptism, which is the outward and visible sign of a penitent spirit. In the early church, converts were baptized without delay. So being baptized and receiving the Spirit were practically simultaneous.

39. This new age of Messianic blessing, Peter explained, would bestow the Holy Spirit not only upon such leaders as prophets, priests, and kings, but upon all who would repent, upon their descendants, and even upon those outside the family of Israel, even all whom God should call to salvation. **The gift of the Holy Spirit.** The

40. And with many other words did he testify and exhort, saying, Save yourselves from this untoward generation.

41. Then they that gladly received his word were baptized: and the same day there were added *unto them* about three thousand souls.

42. And they continued steadfastly in the apostles' doctrine and fellowship, and in breaking of bread, and in prayers.

43. And fear came upon every soul: and many wonders and signs were done by the apostles.

44. And all that believed were together, and had all things common;

45. And sold their possessions and goods, and parted them to all *men*, as every man had need.

46. And they, continuing daily with one accord in the temple, and breaking bread from house to house, did eat their meat with gladness and singleness of heart,

47. Praising God, and having favor with all the people. And the Lord added to the church daily such as should be saved.

gift of the Spirit himself, not some gift which the Spirit bestows.

**40,41.** The apostle thereupon exhorted his hearers to save themselves from **this crooked generation,** which had put Jesus to death, by accepting his plea to repent and his testimony that Jesus was their Messiah. The result was that some three thousand received his word and were baptized upon profession of their faith and were added to the fellowship of the little circle of believers. There is no indication that the apostles laid hands on these new converts in order that they might receive the Holy Spirit.

D. Life of the Primitive Church. 2:42-47. Luke now gives a brief sketch of the life and character of the early Christian community.

**42.** The apostles' doctrine or *teaching.* The teaching of the Lord, together with the proclamation of the life, death, and resurrection of Jesus and its meaning for man's salvation. This teaching was an authoritative tradition in the early church and later found embodiment in our New Testament. These early believers found delight in **fellowship** with one another, particularly in the **breaking of bread** (which probably consisted of a fellowship meal, together with the Lord's Supper) and in regular times of united prayer. **43.** The character of the early Christian community aroused in the people a sense of awe, that was reinforced by many miracles performed by the apostles.

**44,45.** So devoted to one another were those in the first Christian fellowship that wealthy believers sold their possessions to help care for the necessities of the poor members. Christian love manifested itself in a social program of material support for the poor. This Christian sharing seems to have been limited to the early years of the Jerusalem church and was not extended into new churches as the Gospel was carried beyond Judea.

**46.** The believers were still Jews continuing daily worship of God in the Temple in accordance with the Jewish practice. There was no thought of withdrawing from Judaism and establishing a separate movement. Their Christian fellowship manifested itself particularly in fellowship meals, conducted in various homes. Joyfulness and generosity of heart were two of the outstanding characteristics of the early Christians.

**47.** Not all the Jews received the witness to the Messiahship of the resurrected Jesus, but even those who rejected it looked upon the early Christian fellow-

## CHAPTER 3

NOW Peter and John went up together into the temple at the hour of prayer, *being* the ninth *hour.*

2. And a certain man lame from his mother's womb was carried, whom they laid daily at the gate of the temple which is called Beautiful, to ask alms of them that entered into the temple;

3. Who, seeing Peter and John about to go into the temple, asked an alms.

4. And Peter, fastening his eyes upon him with John, said, Look on us.

5. And he gave heed unto them, expecting to receive something of them.

6. Then Peter said, Silver and gold have I none; but such as I have give I thee: In the name of Jesus Christ of Nazareth rise up and walk.

7. And he took him by the right hand, and lifted *him* up: and immediately his feet and ankle bones received strength.

8. And he leaping up stood, and walked, and entered with them into the temple, walking, and leaping, and praising God.

9. And all the people saw him walking and praising God:

10. And they knew that it was he which sat for alms at the Beautiful gate of the temple: and they were filled with wonder and amazement at that which had happened unto him.

11. And as the lame man which was healed held Peter and John, all the people ran together unto them in the porch that is called Solomon's, greatly wondering.

12. And when Peter saw *it,* he answered unto the people, Ye men of Israel, why marvel ye at this? or why look ye so earnestly on us, as though by our own power or holiness we had made this man to walk?

ship with great favor. The result was that the Lord was daily adding to the new fellowship those who received the witness, and the Christian community received them as fellow believers.

## II. The Church in Jerusalem. 3:1–5:42.

The primitive church at first showed no inclination to embark upon a mission of world-wide evangelization. The first Christians were Jews living in Jerusalem as Jews who had found in Jesus the fulfillment of OT prophecy. Luke selects several episodes illustrating these early years.

A. A Typical Miracle and Sermon. 3:1-26. The healing of the lame man was one of many such miracles, but it was of singular importance because it provided the occasion for a typical sermon that illustrates the content of the apostolic preaching to the Jews. This in turn led to the first opposition from the Jewish leaders.

1. **Peter** and **John,** the brother of James, are frequently mentioned as the two leading apostles in the early church. The disciples continued to engage in Jewish worship of God in the **temple.** The **ninth hour,** or 3:00 P.M., was a time of prayer accompanying the evening sacrifice.

2. The apostles proceeded through the vast Court of the Gentiles to the gate called **Beautiful,** which led into the Court of the Women, where they found a lame man who was laid there day after day to beg. 6-8. Peter had no money to offer him, but he gave him something far better—strength for his crippled legs and feet. The healing was instantaneous; and the healed man accompanied the apostles into the Temple, leaping into the air in joy over his new-found strength, and shouting out praises to God. **9,10.** His shouts drew a crowd of people, who were amazed to behold the man whom they had daily seen at the Beautiful Gate now jumping up and down with joy.

11. Peter used this miracle as another occasion to bear witness to the saving power of Jesus. Apparently, after the service of prayer and sacrifice, Peter and John, together with the lame man, proceeded to the covered colonnade on the eastern side of the Court of the Gentiles, which was called **Solomon's porch** (AV) or *portico* (RSV). Here the crowd gathered and Peter addressed them.

12. Peter first disclaimed any credit for the miracle. It was not through the

ACTS 3:13-21

13. The God of Abraham, and of Isaac, and of Jacob, the God of our fathers, hath glorified his Son Jesus; whom ye delivered up, and denied him in the presence of Pilate, when he was determined to let *him* go.

14. But ye denied the Holy One and the Just, and desired a murderer to be granted unto you;

15. And killed the Prince of life, whom God hath raised from the dead; whereof we are witnesses.

16. And his name, through faith in his name, hath made this man strong, whom ye see and know: yea, the faith which is by him hath given him this perfect soundness in the presence of you all.

17. And now, brethren, I wot that through ignorance ye did *it*, as *did* also your rulers.

18. But those things, which God before had showed by the mouth of all his prophets, that Christ should suffer, he hath so fulfilled.

19. Repent ye therefore, and be converted, that your sins may be blotted out, when the times of refreshing shall come from the presence of the Lord;

20. And he shall send Jesus Christ, which before was preached unto you:

21. Whom the heaven must receive until the times of restitution of all things, which God hath spoken by the mouth of all his holy prophets since the world began.

apostles' **power** or **godliness** that the invalid had been healed.

**13.** It was the God of Israel, the God who had given the promises to the fathers, who had performed this miracle. The man had been healed because God had **glorified his servant Jesus** by his resurrection and ascension. **Son** (AV) is better translated *servant* (RSV), for the word refers to the servant of the Lord prophesied in Isa 52:13—53:12. Jesus could only be glorified after he had been **delivered up and denied** by the Jews before the Roman governor, **Pilate.**

**14. The Holy** One and the **Righteous One** were titles sometimes used to describe the Messiah. What an unthinkable crime that the Jews should demand the release of a murderer and criminal to put to death the Holy and Righteous One! **15. Prince of life.** Better, *Author of life.* Peter designated Jesus as the source and origin of life. Him the Jews tried to destroy, but God reversed their verdict by raising him from the dead. **16.** The structure of this verse is awkward both in English and in Greek, but its meaning is clear. The name of Jesus did not possess a magical power, but **faith in his name** brought healing.

**17.** The monstrous crime of murdering Jesus can be forgiven, for Peter admits that the Jews and their rulers did not realize that they were putting to death God's Messiah. **18.** The OT does not foretell a suffering Messiah, although it does predict a suffering servant of the Lord (Isa 53). After his resurrection, Jesus showed the disciples that these prophecies referred to his passion. **Christ.** Not a proper name here but the title meaning *Messiah.*

**19.** Peter now challenged the Jews to repent of their sins and to turn to God. **Be converted** (AV). *Turn around* from sin to God. This would mean reversing their verdict about Jesus and confessing him as God's Messiah. The result would be the **blotting out** of their sins and the enjoyment of the **times of refreshment** promised by the OT prophets.

**20.** The conversion of Israel will mean the return of the Messiah. It is the purpose of God to bring salvation to Israel before the coming of God's kingdom (Rom 11:26), and Peter pled with Israel to receive this salvation.

**21.** Jesus' death, resurrection, and ascension are not the end of his redemptive work. He is to come again in power and to establish a new order free from evil and sin. This restoration will include the redemption of nature (Rom 8:18-23) as well

394

**22.** For Moses truly said unto the fathers, A Prophet shall the Lord your God raise up unto you of your brethren, like unto me; him shall ye hear in all things whatsoever he shall say unto you.

**23.** And it shall come to pass, *that* every soul, which will not hear that Prophet, shall be destroyed from among the people.

**24.** Yea, and all the prophets from Samuel and those that follow after, as many as have spoken, have likewise foretold of these days.

**25.** Ye are the children of the prophets, and of the covenant which God made with our fathers, saying unto Abraham, And in thy seed shall all the kindreds of the earth be blessed.

**26.** Unto you first God, having raised up his Son Jesus, sent him to bless you, in turning away every one of you from his iniquities.

## CHAPTER 4

AND as they spake unto the people, the priests, and the captain of the temple, and the Sadducees, came upon them,

**2.** Being grieved that they taught the people, and preached through Jesus the resurrection from the dead.

as the perfecting of human society when God's will is done on earth as it is in heaven. **The times of refreshing** are a present blessing; the **establishing of all that God** spoke . . . **by his holy prophets** is a future blessing; but both are the result of the redeeming work of the Messiah.

**22,23.** These days of which Peter speaks were foretold as far back as **Moses,** who prophesied that God would raise up another prophet like himself (Deut 18:15-19), who would bring the word of God to his people with authority. The threat contained in verse 23 is combined from Deut 18:19 and Lev 23:29. **24,25.** These days of redemption that Peter was proclaiming were the constant theme of the prophets from the time of Samuel. The Jews were the sons of the prophets and of the covenant made with Abraham and were therefore the natural heirs of these Messianic promises.

**26.** While the promise of Abraham included the Gentile peoples, the blessings of the Messiah have been offered to the natural heirs of the covenant **first,** to turn them from their iniquities. **Son** (AV) is the word found in 3:13, meaning *servant* (RSV). **Raised up** refers to the historical appearance of Jesus rather than to his resurrection.

B. First Opposition from Jewish Leaders. 4:1-37. One of the main purposes of Acts is to show that the Jews who rejected and crucified Jesus continued their rebellion against God by rejecting the gospel of the resurrected and ascended Jesus proclaimed by the apostles. This chapter describes the beginning of this opposition, which culminated with the plots of the Jews to kill Paul on his last visit to Jerusalem (23:12-15; 25:1-3).

**1.** Such a large crowd gathered in Solomon's Porch that the temple police intervened. **The priests** belonged to a Jewish party called the **Sadducees.** They disagreed with the Pharisees over the interpretation of the Law and also denied the doctrine of resurrection and of the existence of angels and demons. The **captain of the temple** was a high officer next in authority to the high priest and had responsibility for the preservation of order in the Temple.

**2.** The Sadducees were **annoyed** (RSV) because Peter and John persistently proclaimed that Jesus had been raised from the dead and announced on the basis of his resurrection the hope of resurrection for men. The Pharisees believed in a future resurrection. The apostles declared

3. And they laid hands on them, and put *them* in hold unto the next day: for it was now eventide.

4. Howbeit many of them which heard the word believed; and the number of the men was about five thousand.

5. And it came to pass on the morrow, that their rulers, and elders, and scribes,

6. And Annas the high priest, and Caiaphas, and John, and Alexander, and as many as were of the kindred of the high priest, were gathered together at Jerusalem.

7. And when they had set them in the midst, they asked, By what power, or by what name, have ye done this?

8. Then Peter, filled with the Holy Ghost, said unto them, Ye rulers of the people, and elders of Israel,

9. If we this day be examined of the good deed done to the impotent man, by what means he is made whole;

10. Be it known unto you all, and to all the people of Israel, that by the name of Jesus Christ of Nazareth, whom ye crucified, whom God raised from the dead, *even* by him doth this man stand here before you whole.

11. This is the stone which was set at nought of your builders, which is become the head of the corner.

12. Neither is there salvation in any other: for there is none other name under heaven given among men, whereby we must be saved.

13. Now when they saw the boldness of Peter and John, and perceived that they were unlearned and ignorant men, they marveled; and they took knowledge of them, that they had been with Jesus.

that God had now provided a new ground for this hope.

3. Since it was late in the day, the temple police, under the direction of the priests, seized the two disciples and put them in prison for the night. 4. Luke inserts the comment that these events had great effect upon the people, and many believed, so that the number of believers reached five thousand.

5,6. The next morning the Sanhedrin assembled. This was the highest court of the Jews, and was composed of **rulers** or priests, **elders**, and **scribes. Scribes.** The professional students and teachers of the OT. Their disciples were called Pharisees. At this time **Caiaphas** was the presiding high priest and president of the Sanhedrin. His father, **Annas**, was the former high priest and a sort of elder statesman. The term **high priest**, or better *chief priest*, can be applied to various members of the families from which the high priests came. We know nothing about **John** or **Alexander**.

7. Peter and John were brought before the Sanhedrin and challenged to say by what authority laymen like themselves acted as they had. 8-10. Peter experienced a fresh enduement of the Spirit for his defense. He pointed out that he had done nothing but good to a crippled man. The former cripple was standing with Peter and John, and Peter declared his healing in the name of Jesus Christ of Nazareth, not by any **power** resident in the apostles themselves.

11,12. Peter was presumably defending himself, but he now turned from defense and began to proclaim the Gospel. He quoted from Ps 118:22, asserting that Christ was the **stone** which the **builders** of the Jewish nation **rejected** but which God had made the most important stone in the building. Furthermore, he said that there was salvation in Him alone; and that if the Jews rejected the saving power of His name, there would be no other way for them to find salvation. Destruction must fall on both them and the nation. **Head of the corner** may designate either the keystone in the foundation or the top corner at the juncture of two walls. **Salvation** here probably refers to life in the age to come.

13. Such speech amazed the Sanhedrin. **Unlearned and ignorant** does not refer to their intelligence or literacy but to the fact that they were not schooled in the tradition of the scribes but were, in fact, laymen. It was an uncommon thing for unschooled laymen to speak with such ef-

14. And beholding the man which was healed standing with them, they could say nothing against it.

15. But when they had commanded them to go aside out of the council, they conferred among themselves,

16. Saying, What shall we do to these men? for that indeed a notable miracle hath been done by them *is* manifest to all them that dwell in Jerusalem; and we cannot deny *it.*

17. But that it spread no further among the people, let us straitly threaten them, that they speak henceforth to no man in this name.

18. And they called them, and commanded them not to speak at all nor teach in the name of Jesus.

19. But Peter and John answered and said unto them, Whether it be right in the sight of God to hearken unto you more than unto God, judge ye.

20. For we cannot but speak the things which we have seen and heard.

21. So when they had further threatened them, they let them go, finding nothing how they might punish them, because of the people: for all *men* glorified God for that which was done.

22. For the man was above forty years old, on whom this miracle of healing was showed.

23. And being let go, they went to their own company, and reported all that the chief priests and elders had said unto them.

24. And when they heard that, they lifted up their voice to God with one accord, and said, Lord, thou *art* God, which hast made heaven, and earth, and the sea, and all that in them is;

25. Who by the mouth of thy servant David hast said, Why did the heathen rage, and the people imagine vain things?

26. The kings of the earth stood up, and the rulers were gathered together against the Lord, and against his Christ.

27. For of a truth against thy holy child Jesus, whom thou hast anointed, both Herod, and Pontius Pilate, with the Gentiles, and the people of Israel, were gathered together,

fectiveness and authority. The rulers already knew that Peter and John were disciples of Jesus, but they now recalled the fact that Jesus, too, although he was unlearned in the scribal traditions (Jn 7:15), had nevertheless amazed the people with the authority with which he spoke (Mk 1:22). Something of this same authority was now reflected in his disciples, and the miracle which had been performed upon the lame man made it difficult to deny the effectiveness of this authority.

15-17. The two disciples were now sent out while the members of the Sanhedrin deliberated. Though Peter and John had broken no law, they were gaining a dangerous popularity. The Sanhedrin decided that the only possible action was to threaten them and to command them to preach no more in the name of Jesus. The Sanhedrin took no steps whatsoever, as F. F. Bruce has pointed out *(Commentary on the Book of Acts)*, to disprove the central assertion of the apostles' preaching—that Jesus had been raised from the dead. The preaching of the apostles could easily have been frustrated had their proclamation of the Resurrection been proved false. The body of Jesus had vanished so completely that the Sanhedrin was utterly helpless to refute their message.

18. When Peter and John were recalled into the Sanhedrin, they were not punished but were commanded to break off all preaching in the name of Jesus. 19,20. The apostles answered that when they were required to choose between the will of God and the decree of men, they had no choice but to obey God.

21. The apostles had gained such popularity that the Sanhedrin dared not risk stirring up the anger of the people by punishing them. Furthermore, the Sadducees did not have the support of the people as did the Pharisees, and they had to be careful of public opinion.

22. The wonder of the miracle lay in the fact that this man was over forty years old.

24. A prayer meeting followed, in which the believers did not ask God to deliver them from future trouble and persecution but praised him because he is the ruler over all. They addressed him as **Sovereign Lord** (RSV), not simply *Lord* (AV). 25,26. The Christians experienced the persecution predicted in Ps 2:1-3. The rulers opposed both God and his **Anointed** One or *Messiah.* 27. The believers again referred to Jesus as the

28. For to do whatsoever thy hand and thy counsel determined before to be done.

29. And now, Lord, behold their threatenings: and grant unto thy servants, that with all boldness they may speak thy word,

30. By stretching forth thine hand to heal; and that signs and wonders may be done by the name of thy holy child Jesus.

31. And when they had prayed, the place was shaken where they were assembled together; and they were all filled with the Holy Ghost, and they spake the word of God with boldness.

32. And the multitude of them that believed were of one heart and of one soul: neither said any *of them* that aught of the things which he possessed was his own; but they had all things common.

33. And with great power gave the apostles witness of the resurrection of the Lord Jesus: and great grace was upon them all.

34. Neither was there any among them that lacked: for as many as were possessors of lands or houses sold them, and brought the prices of the things that were sold,

35. And laid *them* down at the apostles' feet: and distribution was made unto every man according as he had need.

36. And Joses, who by the apostles was surnamed Barnabas, (which is, being interpreted, The son of consolation,) a Levite, *and* of the country of Cyprus,

37. Having land, sold *it*, and brought the money, and laid *it* at the apostles' feet.

## CHAPTER 5

BUT a certain man named Ananias, with Sapphira his wife, sold a possession,

2. And kept back *part* of the price, his wife also being privy *to it*, and brought a certain part, and laid *it* at the apostles' feet.

3. But Peter said, Ananias, why hath Satan filled thine heart to lie to the Holy Ghost, and to keep back *part* of the price of the land?

holy **Servant** who was also the Anointed One. To them **Herod** Antipas, tetrarch over Galilee and Perea, represented the kings of the earth. **Pontius Pilate,** Roman governor of Judea, represented the rulers. The other opponents in the psalm they identified as the Romans **(Gentiles)** and the **people of Israel. 28.** Back of these evil acts of wicked men, they knew, lay the **predetermined** plan of God. **29,30.** The Christians did not pray for safety or protection but that, in the face of opposition, they might be faithful in proclaiming God's word.

**31.** The response to their prayer was a fresh infilling of the Holy Spirit, which was manifested in their fearless proclamation of the word of God. This was not, however, a fresh baptism of the Spirit.

**32.** Verses 32-37 contain another summary of the character of the early Christian fellowship similar to that in 2:42-47. One of the outstanding characteristics of this Spirit-filled church was unity, a sense of oneness that manifested itself in the sharing of material resources. **34.** To meet the needs of poor Christians, the more wealthy believers sold their lands or houses and brought the money to be used for the common welfare. **35.** The apostles supervised this ministry of love, which was carried out not on the basis of equality but on the basis of personal need. **36,37.** One Christian is singled out for special attention: **Joseph,** a Jewish Christian from the island of Cyprus, who had relatives in Jerusalem (cf. 12:12; Col 4:10). His surname, Barnabas may mean either *son of consolation* or *son of encouragement* or *exhortation.* Such surnames were often given to people to indicate their character.

C. Death of Ananias and 'Sapphira. 5:1-16. This incident shows us that the primitive church was not free from internal problems. Luke does not try to gloss over the situation but relates the event with black colors.

**1,2. Sapphira** in the Aramaic tongue means *beautiful.* Like Barnabas, she and her husband sold a **piece of property.** Ananias, with his wife's **knowledge** (RSV), determined upon the plan of bringing only part of the money to the apostles, but pretending that they were giving all. **3.** We are not told how Peter recognized this deception; it was probably by divine illumination. Peter charged Ananias not with deceiving him but with attempting to deceive the Holy Spirit. The Holy Spirit is obviously a person,

4. While it remained, was it not thine own? and after it was sold, was it not in thine own power? why hast thou conceived this thing in thine heart? thou hast not lied unto men, but unto God.

5. And Ananias hearing these words fell down, and gave up the ghost: and great fear came on all them that heard these things.

6. And the young men arose, wound him up, and carried *him* out, and buried *him*.

7. And it was about the space of three hours after, when his wife, not knowing what was done, came in.

8. And Peter answered unto her, Tell me whether ye sold the land for so much? And she said, Yea, for so much.

9. Then Peter said unto her, How is it that ye have agreed together to tempt the Spirit of the Lord? behold, the feet of them which have buried thy husband *are* at the door, and shall carry thee out.

10. Then fell she down straightway at his feet, and yielded up the ghost: and the young men came in, and found her dead, and, carrying *her* forth, buried *her* by her husband.

11. And great fear came upon all the church, and upon as many as heard these things.

and verse 4 shows that the Holy Spirit is also God.

4. The program of sharing wealth in the early church was a purely voluntary one and not compulsory. While the land remained in Ananias' possession, it was his alone to dispose of as he chose; and even after he had sold it, the money was his to do with as he pleased. Ananias' sin did not consist in his keeping back the money, but in his pretending a complete consecration to God while deliberately keeping back part of the money. This was the sin of an insincere consecration, for it meant lying to God.

5. When faced with the enormity of his sin, Ananias was completely overcome and immediately fell down and **breathed out** his life. We are not told what caused this stroke. Certainly Peter did not invoke his death. Whether or not Ananias expired from emotional shock, it was a judgment of God upon hypocritical consecration. 6. In ancient times in the Orient, since decomposition of dead bodies began almost immediately, burial followed death without delay.

7. Sapphira must have been removed from the scene by some distance, else the news of her husband's death would have reached her sooner. 9. Peter charged her with complicity in trifling with God. To tempt God (Ex 17:2; Deut 6:16), that is, to see how far one can go in presuming upon God's goodness, is a fearful sin. This was one of the temptations that our Lord faced (Mt 4:7). 10. The same fate that struck Ananias overtook Sapphira, and she fell down and expired. There is no reason to believe that Ananias and Sapphira were not saved persons. Their physical death was a divine judgment upon them which did not involve the question of their salvation. The very fact that they were believers determined the enormity of their sin. They were pretending to "surrender all" but were deliberately holding back from God. This is a sin that can be committed only by a Christian.

11. This event brought great awe and fear of God into the church and exercised a purifying influence. Here for the first time in Acts the word for church, *ekklēsia*, appears. It means, *called out*, and refers to the calling out of Greek citizens from their homes to the public assembly for civic purposes. The word is taken over by the Greek OT and used of Israel as the people of God. Its use in the NT therefore indicates that the

12. And by the hands of the apostles were many signs and wonders wrought among the people; (and they were all with one accord in Solomon's porch.

13. And of the rest durst no man join himself to them: but the people magnified them.

14. And believers were the more added to the Lord, multitudes both of men and women;)

15. Insomuch that they brought forth the sick into the streets, and laid *them* on beds and couches, that at the least the shadow of Peter passing by might overshadow some of them.

16. There came also a multitude *out* of the cities round about unto Jerusalem, bringing sick folks, and them which were vexed with unclean spirits: and they were healed every one.

17. Then the high priest rose up, and all they that were with him, (which is the sect of the Sadducees,) and were filled with indignation,

18. And laid their hands on the apostles, and put them in the common prison.

19. But the angel of the Lord by night opened the prison doors, and brought them forth, and said,

20. Go, stand and speak in the temple to the people all the words of this life.

21. And when they heard *that*, they entered into the temple early in the morning, and taught. But the high priest came, and they that were with him, and called the council together, and all the senate of the children of Israel, and sent to the prison to have them brought.

22. But when the officers came, and found them not in the prison, they returned, and told,

23. Saying, The prison truly found we shut with all safety, and the keepers standing without before the doors: but when we had opened, we found no man within.

24. Now when the high priest and the captain of the temple and the chief priests heard these things, they doubted of them whereunto this would grow.

25. Then came one and told them, saying, Behold, the men whom ye put in prison are standing in the temple, and teaching the people.

Church is the new people of God. The word is never used of a building. It designates both the church at large (5:11; 9:31; 20:28) and local congregations of believers (11:26; 13:1).

12. The early Christians did not have their own building for worship but met in Solomon's Porch, which bordered the east side of the vast temple area.

13,14. The death of Ananias and Sapphira had such a purifying influence that no one dared for purely human reasons to unite with the new fellowship. However, the church was held in high regard by the people. Only those who experienced a genuine, saving work of God dared to unite with the church; but there were great numbers of such believers.

D. Second Opposition from Jewish Leaders. 5:17-42. The popularity of the believers brought them again to the attention of the high priest and the Sadducees. One of the central motifs of Acts is the rejection of the Gospel by the Jewish nation. This section traces a further step in rejection and persecution by the Jewish officials.

17. Sect means simply *party* and carries no unfavorable connotations, as does the modern word. 18. This time all the apostles were seized and put into prison overnight to await a hearing before the Sanhedrin in the morning. 19,20. The apostles were supernaturally released during the night and were encouraged to continue witnessing to the people about the way of life and salvation. This Life. An unusual designation of the Christian message.

21. Early in the morning the Sanhedrin or council (which is also called the senate), consisting of both Sadducees and Pharisees, assembled and sent for the apostles to appear before them. 22,23. The guards went to the prison and found everything undisturbed, the doors locked and sentries alert; but the apostles had completely vanished. 24. The captain of the temple police was a member of the Sanhedrin. Chief priests. Heads of the several high priestly families and priests who had previously held the office of high priest and who continued to retain the title. These officials of the Sanhedrin apparently felt that the Christians had won converts within the circle of the temple guards, and it looked as though this new movement would grow out of hand.

25. In the midst of the deliberations, word came to the Sanhedrin that the

26. Then went the captain with the officers, and brought them without violence: for they feared the people, lest they should have been stoned.

27. And when they had brought them, they set *them* before the council: and the high priest asked them,

28. Saying, Did not we straitly command you that ye should not teach in this name? and, behold, ye have filled Jerusalem with your doctrine, and intend to bring this man's blood upon us.

29. Then Peter and the *other* apostles answered and said, We ought to obey God rather than men.

30. The God of our fathers raised up Jesus, whom ye slew and hanged on a tree.

31. Him hath God exalted with his right hand *to be* a Prince and a Saviour, for to give repentance to Israel, and forgiveness of sins.

32. And we are his witnesses of these things; and *so is* also the Holy Ghost, whom God hath given to them that obey him.

33. When they heard *that,* they were cut *to the heart,* and took counsel to slay them.

34. Then stood there up one in the council, a Pharisee, named Gamaliel, a doctor of the law, had in reputation among all the people, and commanded to put the apostles forth a little space;

apostles were again publicly **teaching the people** in the Temple. 26. The **captain** of the police, with his subordinates, persuaded the apostles to accompany the guard peaceably to the Sanhedrin. The captain dared not use violence in taking the apostles for fear of violent reaction from the people, who highly regarded these preachers and healers.

27,28. The apostles accompanied the police from the temple area to the meeting place of the Sanhedrin. The high priest charged them with two offenses: first, they had disobeyed the earlier injunction of the Sanhedrin to discontinue their teaching in the name of Jesus. Second, they were trying to bring against the Sanhedrin public blame for the crucifixion of Jesus. The apostles, of course, had no such intention, but their preaching of the cross gave this impression.

29. Peter replied that such an injunction from the Sanhedrin really confronted them with the choice of obeying men or obeying God. 30. In such a situation, only one choice was possible, especially since God had raised Jesus from the dead, whom the Jewish leaders had slain. By the expression, **God of our fathers,** Peter showed that he still regarded himself as a Jew. The early church did not break fellowship with the Jews but existed as a fellowship within Judaism. 31. While the Jews had inflicted upon Jesus the degradation of the cross (Deut 21:23), God had bestowed upon him the highest honor by making him a **Prince** (AV) or *Leader* (RSV) and **Saviour. Prince** is the same word translated "Author" in Acts 3:15.

32. The apostles' proclamation was grounded in the fact that they had witnessed the things of which they spoke. Furthermore, they did not speak merely as private individuals, but their witness was empowered by the Holy Spirit, who spoke through them. The Holy Spirit had been given not only to the apostles but to all who would obey him.

33. These words of Peter cut the priests to the quick and angered them. The word translated **cut** means *to saw in two.* The Sadducean wing of the Sanhedrin immediately laid plans to put the apostles to death. 34. Their evil purpose was frustrated by a scribe and **teacher of the law** *(doctor,* AV) named Gamaliel. Josephus, the Jewish historian, tells us that the party of the Pharisees was small in number but commanded such popularity and influence among the people that the Sadducees dared not take

35. And said unto them, Ye men of Israel, take heed to yourselves what ye intend to do as touching these men.

36. For before these days rose up Theudas, boasting himself to be somebody; to whom a number of men, about four hundred, joined themselves: who was slain; and all, as many as obeyed him, were scattered, and brought to nought.

37. After this man rose up Judas of Galilee in the days of the taxing, and drew away much people after him: he also perished; and all, *even* as many as obeyed him, were dispersed.

38. And now I say unto you, Refrain from these men, and let them alone: for if this counsel or this work be of men, it will come to nought:

39. But if it be of God, ye cannot overthrow it; lest haply ye be found even to fight against God.

40. And to him they agreed: and when they had called the apostles, and beaten *them*, they commanded that they should not speak in the name of Jesus, and let them go.

any action that the Pharisees opposed. The influence of Gamaliel's advice reflects this situation. Furthermore, Gamaliel was one of the most noted rabbis of the time. Saul of Tarsus had been his disciple (22:3), and he was widely known as the greatest teacher of the Law in his day.
35. Gamaliel warned the Sadducees, who were bent upon taking action without the support of the Pharisaic majority, against rash action.

36. He cited recent historical events to remind them that there had been other movements among the Jews that amounted to nothing, and that therefore they should have no fear of this new group who proclaimed Jesus to be Messiah. Josephus says that there were many such movements in those days of unrest. Gamaliel recalled one Theudas, who claimed to be a person of great importance and who persuaded some four hundred Jews to follow him. This movement was crushed and Theudas slain. We know nothing else about this man. About A.D. 45, a magician by the same name led a large number of Jews to the Jordan River, promising that he could separate the waters so that they could walk across the river on dry ground. The Roman governor, Crispus Fadus, sent horsemen and crushed the movement. This false messiah, however, was a different person from the one mentioned by Gamaliel.

37. Another insurrection was made by Judas of Galilee. When Herod Archelaus, one of the sons of Herod the Great (Mt 2:1,22), was deposed from the governorship of Judea, the country was placed under a Roman governor; and a census was held to determine the amount of tribute to be exacted from the people for Rome. This Judas stirred up a religious and nationalistic revolt on the grounds that God alone was Israel's king and He alone had the right to rule over the Jewish people. This movement was the beginning of what later became the Zealots; but the revolt under Judas was crushed by Rome.

38,39. Gamaliel counseled the Sanhedrin to trust God's providence. If God was in the movement, it would prosper; otherwise it would fail.

40. Gamaliel's influence was so great that he carried the decision of the Sanhedrin. A minor punishment of beating was inflicted, probably with thirty-nine blows (II Cor 11:24), for disobeying the Sanhedrin's earlier command.

**41.** And they departed from the presence of the council, rejoicing that they were counted worthy to suffer shame for his name.

**42.** And daily in the temple, and in every house, they ceased not to teach and preach Jesus Christ.

## CHAPTER 6

AND in those days, when the number of the disciples was multiplied, there arose a murmuring of the Grecians against the Hebrews, because their widows were neglected in the daily ministration.

**2.** Then the twelve called the multitude of the disciples *unto them*, and said, It is not reason that we should leave the word of God, and serve tables.

**41,42.** The apostles were by no means discouraged, for they considered it an honor to suffer for the name of Jesus. They continued their activities of **teaching and preaching of Jesus as the Messiah**, both publicly in the Court of the Gentiles **in the temple** and in their Christian gatherings in their private homes.

**III. Extension of the Church in Palestine Through Persecution and Dispersion. 6:1 – 12:25.**

Up to this point, the apostles had given no evidence of a purpose to carry the Gospel into all the world but had stayed in Jerusalem witnessing to the Jews. Luke now relates the beginnings of expansion of the church throughout Judea and Samaria, which was occasioned by the persecution that arose around Stephen. This expansion was accomplished not by the vision and purpose of the church but by the providential act of God in scattering the believers. To explain this persecution, Luke first relates how Stephen came into a position of prominence as one of the seven.

**A.** Choice of the Seven. 6:1-7. The church in its earliest days had no formal organization and no officials or leaders except the apostles. The numerical growth of the church and the rise of problems in its internal fellowship required the beginnings of organization and the choice of additional leaders or ministers.

**1.** Jews who were natives of Palestine spoke primarily Aramaic; but Jews who had lived in the Mediterranean world outside of Palestine spoke Greek and often did not know Aramaic. Many of these Diaspora Jews returned to Jerusalem to live, and some of them were converted and came into the church. A contention now arose between the Greek-speaking Christians (**Grecians**) and the Aramaic-speaking Christians (**Hebrews**) because it appeared that favoritism for the latter was being shown in the distribution of food to the **widows**. Widows were persons without any means of support, who were provided with the bare necessities of life by the Christian community.

**2.** The twelve apostles called together the entire church and pointed out that this responsibility for the care of the poor had become such a burden that they found themselves devoting most of their time to this material ministry and neglecting the ministry of the Word. Such neglect

3. Wherefore, brethren, look ye out among you seven men of honest report, full of the Holy Ghost and wisdom, whom we may appoint over this business.

4. But we will give ourselves continually to prayer, and to the ministry of the word.

5. And the saying pleased the whole multitude: and they chose Stephen, a man full of faith and of the Holy Ghost, and Philip, and Prochorus, and Nicanor, and Timon, and Parmenas, and Nicolas a proselyte of Antioch;

6. Whom they set before the apostles: and when they had prayed, they laid *their* hands on them.

7. And the word of God increased; and the number of the disciples multiplied in Jerusalem greatly; and a great company of the priests were obedient to the faith.

8. And Stephen, full of faith and power, did great wonders and miracles among the people.

9. Then there arose certain of the synagogue, which is called *the synagogue* of the Libertines, and Cyrenians, and Alexandrians, and of them of Cilicia and of Asia, disputing with Stephen.

10. And they were not able to resist the wisdom and the spirit by which he spake.

11. Then they suborned men, which said, We have heard him speak blasphemous words against Moses, and *against* God.

12. And they stirred up the people, and the elders, and the scribes, and came upon *him*, and caught him, and brought *him* to the council,

13. And set up false witnesses, which said, This man ceaseth not to speak blasphemous words against this holy place, and the law:

14. For we have heard him say, that this Jesus of Nazareth shall destroy this place, and shall change the customs which Moses delivered us.

15. And all that sat in the council, looking steadfastly on him, saw his face as it had been the face of an angel.

was not right. 3,4. They recommended that the distribution of food be placed under the direction of seven Spirit-filled men of good reputation. The apostles would then be free to devote themselves to the ministry of prayer and of preaching and teaching the Word.

5. Stephen was among the seven men chosen. All seven had Greek names and apparently were drawn from the Greek wing of the church. 6. The church at large selected these seven men, but the apostles approved the selection and appointed them to their office. The seven were then ordained to their office by the imposition of the apostles' hands. This laying on of hands was an OT custom (Gen 48:13 ff.; Lev 1:4; Num 27:23), which was also practiced by the Jews when men were admitted to the Sanhedrin. It was taken over by the early church for the ordination of these leaders. A preliminary qualification, however, was that the seven be filled with the Holy Spirit. Aside from the apostles, these seven were the first officials in the church. By tradition they have been designated deacons; but they are not so designated in the text.

7. The solution of this problem added to the effectiveness of the Christian testimony, and even many priests believed.

B. Occasion of the Dispersion: Ministry and Martyrdom of Stephen. 6:8—8:3.

8. Stephen was immediately marked out as a man of outstanding endowments and power.

9. He was bearing witness to the Messiahship of Jesus in the Jewish synagogues in Jerusalem, particularly in one that was attended by *Freedmen* (RSV; Libertines, AV) who had formerly lived in the four places named. A synagogue was composed of ten or more Jews who met together for the reading and interpretation of the Scriptures. An exaggerated tradition says there were 480 synagogues in Jerusalem. 10,11. This ministry of Stephen apparently led to a formal debate. When the Jews were unable to overcome the earnest leader in debate because of his wisdom and the power of the Spirit (RSV), they secretly instigated (RSV) witnesses who testified that he had spoken blasphemous words against the law of Moses and against God.

12. The faithful "deacon" was brought before the Sanhedrin to defend himself against these charges. 13-15. Stephen's alleged blasphemy against God was defined as blasphemy against the Temple. He had apparently been teaching that the

## CHAPTER 7

THEN said the high priest, Are these things so?

2. And he said, Men, brethren, and fathers, hearken; The God of glory appeared unto our father Abraham, when he was in Mesopotamia, before he dwelt in Charran,

3. And said unto him, Get thee out of thy country, and from thy kindred, and come into the land which I shall show thee.

4. Then came he out of the land of the Chaldeans, and dwelt in Charran: and from thence, when his father was dead, he removed him into this land, wherein ye now dwell.

5. And he gave him none inheritance in it, no, not *so much as* to set his foot on: yet he promised that he would give it to him for a possession, and to his seed after him, when *as yet* he had no child.

6. And God spake on this wise, That his seed should sojourn in a strange land; and that they should bring them into bondage, and entreat *them* evil four hundred years.

7. And the nation to whom they shall be in bondage will I judge, said God: and after that shall they come forth, and serve me in this place.

Jewish Temple was no longer necessary for the true worship of God. He was now charged with teaching that Jesus of Nazareth would destroy the Temple and pervert the practice of the law of Moses. This charge was not a pure fabrication, but a clever misrepresentation of what Stephen had actually taught.

7:1. The high priest and president of the Sanhedrin was still Caiaphas, who had presided at the trial and condemnation of Jesus.

2. The speech of Stephen that follows is not really a refutation of the charges leveled against him but rather a positive affirmation of his witness to Jesus Christ and to the Gospel. Stephen did not attempt to show that the charges against him were false. On the contrary, he set forth his conviction that the Temple and the land of Palestine were not necessary for the true worship of God. He outlined a brief sketch of Israel's history to show: (a) that God blessed their fathers even though those men did not live in the land of Palestine; (b) that during much of her history Israel did not worship God in the Temple; (c) and that even the possession of the Temple did not save Israel from being rebellious and disobedient against God. The purpose of this speech was to show from Israel's history that the possession of the Temple had been neither a necessity for nor a guarantee of the true worship of God. And this served to substantiate Stephen's main point that now that Messiah had come, the Jewish worship in the Temple in Jerusalem was superseded.

God's call to **Abraham** did not come in the Promised Land but when he was far away in **Mesopotamia**. Stephen related a divine visitation while Abraham was still in Mesopotamia, as a result of which he went first to **Haran**, where he lived for some time, and then later journeyed from Haran to Palestine. Genesis 11:31,32 does not record this earliest divine visitation; but Gen 15:7 and Neh 9:7 both indicate that God's call came originally to Abraham in Ur of the Chaldees in Mesopotamia.

5. Although Abraham dwelt in the land of Palestine, he did not actually possess the land, but held it only as a promise from God to him and to his descendants. Abraham's blessing, therefore, was not dependent upon possession of the land but upon the promise of God.

6,7. Abraham's descendants did not at once possess the land but spent four hundred years in captivity outside Pales-

8. And he gave him the covenant of circumcision: and so *Abraham* begat Isaac, and circumcised him the eighth day; and Isaac *begat* Jacob; and Jacob *begat* the twelve patriarchs.

9. And the patriarchs, moved with envy, sold Joseph into Egypt: but God was with him,

10. And delivered him out of all his afflictions, and gave him favor and wisdom in the sight of Pharaoh king of Egypt; and he made him governor over Egypt and all his house.

11. Now there came a dearth over all the land of Egypt and Chanaan, and great affliction: and our fathers found no sustenance.

12. But when Jacob heard that there was corn in Egypt, he sent out our fathers first.

13. And at the second *time* Joseph was made known to his brethren; and Joseph's kindred was made known unto Pharaoh.

14. Then sent Joseph, and called his father Jacob to *him*, and all his kindred, threescore and fifteen souls.

15. So Jacob went down into Egypt, and died, he, and our fathers,

16. And were carried over into Sychem, and laid in the sepulchre that Abraham bought for a sum of money of the sons of Emmor, *the father* of Sychem.

17. But when the time of the promise drew nigh, which God had sworn to Abraham, the people grew and multiplied in Egypt,

18. Till another king arose, which knew not Joseph.

19. The same dealt subtilely with our kindred, and evil entreated our fathers, so that they cast out their young children, to the end they might not live.

20. In which time Moses was born, and was exceeding fair, and nourished up in his father's house three months:

21. And when he was cast out, Pharaoh's daughter took him up, and nourished him for her own son.

22. And Moses was learned in all the wisdom of the Egyptians, and was mighty in words and in deeds.

23. And when he was full forty years old, it came into his heart to visit his brethren the children of Israel.

tine. **Four hundred** is a round number (cf. Gal 3:17, where the period is 430 years). **8.** God entered into covenant with Abraham and his descendants, giving the sign of circumcision as a seal of the agreement. This covenant blessing, Stephen implied, was not dependent upon the existence of the Temple but upon the promises and faithfulness of God.

**9,10.** Even when the patriarchs sold **Joseph into Egypt,** God did not forsake him because he was outside the land, but brought to him a wonderful deliverance, making him governor **over Egypt** and the **house** of Pharaoh.

**11-15.** When a great famine came to both Egypt and Palestine, God gave Joseph foresight to lay aside reserves of grain in Egypt as the means of preserving the patriarchs. Jacob and his family migrated to Egypt, where they were preserved by Joseph. The number **seventy-five** follows the account in the Septuagint or Greek translation of the OT; the number seventy in Gen 46:27 and Ex 1:5 is that of the Hebrew text. These two texts reflect two ways of numbering Jacob's family.

**16.** Although the patriarchs died in Egypt, their bodies were brought back to Palestine and were buried in the land God had promised to Abraham and his seed.

**17-43.** Stephen had been accused of blasphemy against Moses. By recounting the story of Moses and the giving of the Law, he showed that the possession of the Law did not preserve Israel from rebellion against God.

**17.** As the time approached when God had promised to bring the patriarchs out of Egypt to give them the land of Canaan, the people had no inclination to leave Egypt, where they were becoming numerous and prosperous. **18,19.** God thereupon raised up another **king** in Egypt who did not continue the practice of favoritism to Joseph and his family, but who treated the Israelites deceitfully, compelling them to destroy all of their infants by exposure.

**20,21.** Moses, who was born at this time, was **attractive** in the eyes of God. When after three months his parents had to cast him **out, Pharaoh's daughter adopted him** (RSV) and brought him up as her own son in the royal family. **22.** As the son of Pharaoh's daughter, Moses received the finest education available in Egypt, and he became a young man of eloquence and of vigorous action.

**23.** After coming to manhood, Moses

**24.** And seeing one *of them* suffer wrong, he defended *him*, and avenged him that was oppressed, and smote the Egyptian:

**25.** For he supposed his brethren would have understood how that God by his hand would deliver them; but they understood not.

**26.** And the next day he showed himself unto them as they strove, and would have set them at one again, saying, Sirs, ye are brethren; why do ye wrong one to another?

**27.** But he that did his neighbor wrong thrust him away, saying, Who made thee a ruler and a judge over us?

**28.** Wilt thou kill me, as thou didst the Egyptian yesterday?

**29.** Then fled Moses at this saying, and was a stranger in the land of Madian, where he begat two sons.

**30.** And when forty years were expired, there appeared to him in the wilderness of mount Sina an angel of the Lord in a flame of fire in a bush.

**31.** When Moses saw *it*, he wondered at the sight: and as he drew near to behold *it*, the voice of the Lord came unto him,

**32.** *Saying*, I *am* the God of thy fathers, the God of Abraham, and the God of Isaac, and the God of Jacob. Then Moses trembled, and durst not behold.

**33.** Then said the Lord to him, Put off thy shoes from thy feet: for the place where thou standest is holy ground.

**34.** I have seen, I have seen the affliction of my people which is in Egypt, and I have heard their groaning, and am come down to deliver them. And now come, I will send thee into Egypt.

**35.** This Moses whom they refused, saying, Who made thee a ruler and a judge? the same did God send *to be* a ruler and a deliverer by the hand of the angel which appeared to him in the bush.

**36.** He brought them out, after that he had showed wonders and signs in the land of Egypt, and in the Red sea, and in the wilderness forty years.

determined to leave the palace of Pharaoh to visit his people. Apparently, during these forty years he had had no contact with his people but had lived as an Egyptian in the house of Pharaoh.

**24,25.** When he saw one of his Israelite kinsmen being afflicted, he moved to his defense, and striking the Egyptian, killed him. Moses thought that his kinsmen would recognize him as one of their own sent by God to bring to them deliverance; but they did not recognize this fact.

**26.** The next day, when Moses found two of his kinsmen fighting with each other, he tried to reconcile them by pointing out that they were brothers and therefore should not fight together. **27,28.** The aggressor strongly rejected Moses' overture of peace. He accused him of meddling and of wishing to compound the murder that he had committed against the Egyptian on the preceding day.

**29.** When Moses realized that he was known as a murderer of an Egyptian in defense of the Israelites, he fled from Egypt and became an exile in Midian in northwest Arabia. Here he married and fathered two sons.

**30.** It was here in Mount Sinai, far from the Promised Land and without any temple, that God gave to Moses the wonderful revelation of Himself. **31,32.** At first Moses did not understand what the burning bush meant. Then God spoke to him, revealing Himself as the God of the patriarchs. The voice of the Lord filled Moses with a trembling fear, so that he dared not look upon the burning bush. **33.** This desolate spot in the wilderness was made a holy place because God appeared there. Accordingly He commanded Moses to remove his shoes as a token of reverence. Wherever God appears and speaks to men, there is holy ground.

**34.** God assured Moses that He had not forgotten His people even though they were in Egypt, and that He would soon fulfill His covenant promises and deliver them. **35.** God reversed the judgment of Moses' kinsmen. They scorned him because they thought he was trying to act as a ruler and a judge; God made Moses a ruler and deliverer of his people from Egypt. Deliverer carries the idea of redeemer.

**36.** This redemption was accomplished by a display of mighty power in Egypt and in the crossing of the Red Sea and in the forty years traveling from Egypt to the Promised Land.

37. This is that Moses, which said unto the children of Israel, A Prophet shall the Lord your God raise up unto you of your brethren, like unto me; him shall ye hear.

38. This is he, that was in the church in the wilderness with the angel which spake to him in the mount Sina, and *with* our fathers: who received the lively oracles to give unto us:

39. To whom our fathers would not obey, but thrust *him* from them, and in their hearts turned back again into Egypt,

40. Saying unto Aaron, Make us gods to go before us: for *as for* this Moses, which brought us out of the land of Egypt, we wot not what is become of him.

41. And they made a calf in those days, and offered sacrifice unto the idol, and rejoiced in the works of their own hands.

42. Then God turned, and gave them up to worship the host of heaven; as it is written in the book of the prophets, O ye house of Israel, have ye offered to me slain beasts and sacrifices *by the space of* forty years in the wilderness?

37. Moses' experience only foreshadowed that of a greater One who was to come after him. For Moses had predicted the coming of another prophet, to whom Israel should give heed (Deut 18:15, 18,19).

38. Israel under Moses' leadership was a type of the Church. The Greek word for church, *ekklēsia,* is used in Deut 18:16 to describe Israel as the congregation of God. The angel. The particular angel of the Lord who represents God and makes His presence real to men. Moses also received living oracles from God, that is, the OT Law (Ex 20). All of these blessings the people of Israel enjoyed from the hand of God while they were yet in the wilderness outside of the land and without a temple.

39. In spite of these blessings from the hand of God, the Israelites would not obey the Lord but rejected Moses and desired to turn back to Egypt. 40. When Moses was in the mountain, the people demanded that Aaron make idols for them to worship. Instead of worshiping God their Creator, they worshiped a golden calf which they themselves had fashioned (Ex 32:16,18). They gave as an excuse that Moses had disappeared and they did not know what had become of him.

41. Stephen was under accusation of blasphemy against Moses. His recital of history showed that the very ancestors of his accusers had themselves failed to keep the law of Moses and had rejected the divine order of worship for the worship of idols.

42. This tendency toward idolatry, reflected throughout the entire course of Israel's history, came to its climax with the Babylonian captivity, when Israel imitated her neighbors by worshiping the planets of the heavens as though they were deities (Deut 4:19; 17:3; II Kgs 21:3,5; 23:4,5; Jer 8:2; 19:13; Zeph 1:5). God abandoned Israel to this pagan idolatrous worship. Stephen quoted from Amos 5:25-27 to illustrate Israel's apostasy. The difference between the passage in Amos and that in Acts in our English versions is due to the fact that Stephen quoted from the Greek translation of the OT, which at this point deviates from its Hebrew original. Stephen indicated that the sacrifices offered to God were only external forms and possessed no spiritual reality (cf. Isa 1:10-14, where God rejects the sacrifices of his people because they do not come from obedient hearts).

43. Yea, ye took up the tabernacle of Moloch, and the star of your god Remphan, figures which ye made to worship them: and I will carry you away beyond Babylon.

44. Our fathers had the tabernacle of witness in the wilderness, as he had appointed, speaking unto Moses, that he should make it according to the fashion that he had seen.

45. Which also our fathers that came after brought in with Jesus into the possession of the Gentiles, whom God drave out before the face of our fathers, unto the days of David;

46. Who found favor before God, and desired to find a tabernacle for the God of Jacob.

47. But Solomon built him a house.

48. Howbeit the Most High dwelleth not in temples made with hands; as saith the prophet,

49. Heaven *is* my throne, and earth *is* my footstool: what house will ye build me? saith the Lord: or what *is* the place of my rest?

50. Hath not my hand made all these things?

51. Ye stiffnecked and uncircumcised in heart and ears, ye do always resist the Holy Ghost: as your fathers *did*, so *do* ye.

52. Which of the prophets have not your fathers persecuted? and they have slain them which showed before of the coming of the Just One; of whom ye have been now the betrayers and murderers:

53. Who have received the law by the disposition of angels, and have not kept *it*.

54. When they heard these things, they were cut to the heart, and they gnashed on him with *their* teeth.

**43.** Moloch and **Rephan** were two deities associated with the stars. The idolatry of the Jews' worship of the calf at Sinai and their formal, unspiritual worship of God through sacrifices in the wilderness led finally to their worship of pagan star deities. Because of this apostasy, God brought upon them the judgment of captivity beyond Babylon.

**44,45.** Israel's apostasy occurred in spite of the fact that God had given to them a clear witness. In the wilderness, God had commanded Moses to build a **tabernacle** or tent, which should be a witness to the presence of God in their midst (Ex 25:9, 40; 26:30; 27:8). The patriarchs brought this Tabernacle with them into the Promised Land under the leadership of Joshua. (The Gr. trans. of *Joshua* is Jesus). God drove out the nations from the land (the Gr. word means both **Gentiles** and nations), that Israel might possess it.

**46,47.** For many years after coming into the land, Israel had no temple but continued to worship God at the Tabernacle. **Tabernacle** in this verse is a different word from that in 6:44. David, a man after God's own heart, desired to provide a dwelling place for God; but this privilege was deferred until the time of Solomon. **48-50.** Stephen now declared emphatically that the **Most High** cannot be limited to structures made by man, because He fills all the world, and there is no sort of house which can contain Him.

**51,52.** If the Temple is not necessary for the worship of God, neither is it a guarantee that men will worship God rightly. Stephen accused those who worshiped in the Temple of being stiffnecked and **uncircumcised in heart and ears,** of resisting the Holy Spirit, and of betraying and murdering the **Righteous One,** thus following the example of their rebellious forefathers. Stephen had been accused of blaspheming the law of Moses. His answer was that it was not really he who was guilty of this sin but the Jewish people, who from the times of Moses had transgressed God's Word. He was accused of blaspheming God by setting aside the Temple. His answer was that Israel's history itself proved that the Temple was only a temporary institution and was not essential for the true worship of God.

**54.** When Stephen accused the Jews of blasphemy, they were filled with uncontrollable rage. **Gnashed with their**

**55.** But he, being full of the Holy Ghost, looked up steadfastly into heaven, and saw the glory of God, and Jesus standing on the right hand of God,

**56.** And said, Behold, I see the heavens opened, and the Son of man standing on the right hand of God.

**57.** Then they cried out with a loud voice, and stopped their ears, and ran upon him with one accord,

**58.** And cast *him* out of the city, and stoned *him:* and the witnesses laid down their clothes at a young man's feet, whose name was Saul.

**59.** And they stoned Stephen, calling upon *God,* and saying, Lord Jesus, receive my spirit.

**60.** And he kneeled down, and cried with a loud voice, Lord, lay not this sin to their charge. And when he had said this, he fell asleep.

## CHAPTER 8

AND Saul was consenting unto his death. And at that time there was a great persecution against the church which was at Jerusalem; and they were all scattered abroad throughout the regions of Judea and Samaria, except the apostles.

teeth. A sign of anger (Job 16:9; Ps 35:14).

**55,56.** Stephen was untroubled by the anger of the Sanhedrin. At this moment, God granted him a vision of the open heavens with the Son of man standing at His right hand. Stephen's words were, in effect, an assertion that the claim of Jesus recently made before this same judicial body to be the heavenly Son of man was not blasphemous, as the Sanhedrin had claimed, but was the very truth of God (Mk 14:62). Stephen claimed indeed that Jesus had now become the Son of man at the right hand of God.

Jesus is usually pictured seated at God's right hand (Ps 110:1; Heb 1:13). It is possible that he is here represented as rising from his throne to receive this martyr. The name the Son of man does not designate Jesus' humanity; it is a Messianic title, based upon Dan 7:13,14, and designates the Messiah as a heavenly, supernatural being. This is the only place outside the Gospels where the title is applied to Jesus.

**57-59.** It is not altogether clear whether Stephen's martyrdom was the result of a formal execution or of a lynching. A legal execution required the approval of the Roman governor, and since this was not secured, Stephen's death looks like a lynching. However, the mention of formal witnesses as required by the Law (Lev 24:14; Deut 17:7) suggests a legal execution. It is possible that the Sanhedrin executed Stephen without securing the official approval of Pilate. Stephen was led out of the city to the place of execution and stoned. The witnesses were the official executioners. Saul, who later became the Apostle Paul, was an observer of the execution and stood over the shed garments of the executioners. Saul is suddenly introduced into the narrative without explanation.

**59,60.** Dying, Stephen addressed the exalted Jesus as God Himself, praying Jesus to receive his spirit. His dying word was a prayer for forgiveness for his executioners. Sleep is a common Biblical metaphor for death.

**8:1.** Saul was consenting. Some have felt that these words indicate that Saul was a member of the Sanhedrin. This is not necessarily true. However, since he was from Cilicia, he was undoubtedly a member of the synagogue that debated with Stephen (6:9). Up to this time the church had shown no inclination to take the Gospel into all the world but had

410

2. And devout men carried Stephen *to his burial*, and made great lamentation over him.

3. As for Saul, he made havoc of the church, entering into every house, and haling men and women committed *them* to prison.

4. Therefore they that were scattered abroad went every where preaching the word.

5. Then Philip went down to the city of Samaria, and preached Christ unto them.

6. And the people with one accord gave heed unto those things which Philip spake, hearing and seeing the miracles which he did.

7. For unclean spirits, crying with loud voice, came out of many that were possessed *with them*: and many taken with palsies, and that were lame, were healed.

8. And there was great joy in that city.

9. But there was a certain man, called Simon, which beforetime in the same city used sorcery, and bewitched the people of Samaria, giving out that himself was some great one:

10. To whom they all gave heed, from the least to the greatest, saying, This man is the great power of God.

11. And to him they had regard, because that of long time he had bewitched them with sorceries.

12. But when they believed Philip preaching the things concerning the kingdom of God, and the name of Jesus Christ, they were baptized, both men and women.

13. Then Simon himself believed also: and when he was baptized, he continued with Philip, and wondered, beholding the miracles and signs which were done.

remained in Jerusalem. God used the persecution that followed the death of Stephen as the providential means of spreading the Gospel outside Jerusalem. The believers of the Jerusalem congregation were scattered everywhere, but the apostles were able to remain in the city to give stability to the church.

3. The moving spirit in this persecution was Saul (see Gal 1:13,23; I Cor 15:9; Phil 3:6). He was convinced that this new movement which proclaimed a crucified criminal to be the Messiah could not possibly be of God. For the OT pronounced a curse upon anyone who was hanged upon a tree. This was Scriptural proof, so far as Saul was concerned, that Jesus was a pretender and this new movement blasphemous.

C. The Gospel in Samaria. 8:4-25. Luke first records the extension of the Gospel to Samaria. The Samaritans were descendants from a mixture of the remnant of Israel with foreigners who were settled in Samaria by the conquering Assyrians when the upper classes were taken into exile (II Kings 17). The Samaritans had erected a rival temple upon Mount Gerizim (see Jn 4:20). Because the Jews regarded the Samaritans as both racial and religious half-breeds, violent racial prejudices had to be overcome before the church could become a truly universal people.

5. The city of Samaria. It is not clear whether Samaria is meant to designate a city or the country. Usually, the word in the NT designates the territory rather than the city. The city of Samaria had been rebuilt by Herod the Great as a Greek city and called Sebaste, in honor of the Roman emperor. Philip's message in Samaria was the Messiah (AV omits the definite article) that is, that Jesus was the Christ.

9-11. Before Philip came to Samaria, a magician by the name of Simon had practiced his magical arts, claiming "to be somebody." The people were deceived by his tricks and attributed to him the power of God which is called Great. Great was a word used by Greeks to designate the Jewish God.

12. The message of our Lord had been the gospel of the kingdom of God (Mt 4:23; 9:35). He had told his disciples to preach the gospel of the kingdom in all the world (Mt 24:14). Philip went to Samaria gospeling concerning the kingdom of God. The phrase is exactly the same except that the verb is used instead of the noun and the preposi-

14. Now when the apostles which were at Jerusalem heard that samaria had received the word of God, they sent unto them Peter and John:

15. Who, when they were come down, prayed for them, that they might receive the Holy Ghost:

16. (For as yet he was fallen upon none of them: only they were baptized in the name of the Lord Jesus.)

17. Then laid they *their* hands on them, and they received the Holy Ghost.

18. And when Simon saw that through laying on of the apostles' hands the Holy Ghost was given, he offered them money,

19. Saying, Give me also this power, that on whomsoever I lay hands, he may receive the Holy Ghost.

20. But Peter said unto him, Thy money perish with thee, because thou hast thought that the gift of God may be purchased with money.

21. Thou hast neither part nor lot in this matter: for thy heart is not right in the sight of God.

22. Repent therefore of this thy wickedness, and pray God, if perhaps the thought of thine heart may be forgiven thee.

23. For I perceive that thou art in the gall of bitterness, and *in* the bond of iniquity.

24. Then answered Simon, and said, Pray ye to the Lord for me, that none of these things which ye have spoken come upon me.

25. And they, when they had testified and preached the word of the Lord, returned to Jerusalem, and preached the gospel in many villages of the Samaritans.

tion is inserted. The gospel of the kingdom of God and the name of Jesus Christ are here interchangeable ideas.

**14-17.** The **apostles at Jerusalem** maintained a supervisory relationship over the entire church, and they therefore sent Peter and John to Samaria to investigate this new development. (John and his brother James had once asked Jesus whether they should not call down fire from heaven upon a certain Samaritan village; see Lk 9:52 ff.). It became evident to Peter and John that the gift of the Holy Spirit received at Pentecost had not been extended to the Samaritan converts. They had received the baptism of water but not the baptism of the Spirit. It was obvious to the two apostles that the faith of the people was genuine. They therefore laid their hands upon the converts, and the Holy Spirit came upon them. The meaning of this event has been a subject of controversy, but it must be pointed out that on the day of Pentecost and in the household of Cornelius (Acts 10), the Holy Spirit was given without the laying on of hands. Therefore it is arbitrary to select this one event and make it normative for Christian experience, and to insist that there is a special baptism of the Spirit that is bestowed subsequent to saving faith by the laying on of hands of those who have already received the experience. The significance of this event lies in the fact that these people were **Samaritans.** Here is the first step in which the church burst its Jewish bonds and moved toward a truly world-wide fellowship. The imposition of hands was not necessary for the Samaritans; but it was necessary for the apostles, that they might be fully convinced that God was indeed breaking the barriers of racial prejudice and including these half-breed people within the fellowship of the Church. This was not a new Pentecost but an extension of the one Pentecost to the Samaritan people.

**18-24.** Simon's desire to buy the gifts of God with money has given to us the word "simony." Peter's answer was, "To perdition with your money, and with you, too . . . unless you repent." It appears that Simon was really converted, but the habits of the old life and the **bond of iniquity** (v. 23) had not yet been broken. Simon was stricken with fear and pleaded with the apostles to intercede for him and seek God's forgiveness (v. 24).

**25.** Peter and John now engaged in a vigorous evangelistic program that carried them through many villages in Sa-

26. And the angel of the Lord spake unto Philip, saying, Arise, and go toward the south, unto the way that goeth down from Jerusalem unto Gaza, which is desert.

27. And he arose and went: and, behold, a man of Ethiopia, a eunuch of great authority under Candace queen of the Ethiopians, who had the charge of all her treasure, and had come to Jerusalem for to worship,

28. Was returning, and sitting in his chariot read Esaias the prophet.

29. Then the Spirit said unto Philip, Go near, and join thyself to this chariot.

30. And Philip ran thither to *him*, and heard him read the prophet Esaias, and said, Understandest thou what thou readest?

31. And he said, How can I, except some man should guide me? And he desired Philip that he would come up and sit with him.

32. The place of the Scripture which he read was this, He was led as a sheep to the slaughter; and like a lamb dumb before his shearer, so opened he not his mouth:

33. In his humiliation his judgment was taken away: and who shall declare his generation? for his life is taken from the earth.

34. And the eunuch answered Philip, and said, I pray thee, of whom speaketh the prophet this? of himself, or of some other man?

35. Then Philip opened his mouth, and began at the same Scripture, and preached unto him Jesus.

36. And as they went on *their* way, they came unto a certain water: and the eunuch said, See, *here is* water; what doth hinder me to be baptized?

maria. Then, having completed this tour, they returned to Jerusalem.

**D. Conversion of the Ethiopian Eunuch. 8:26-40.** Luke now records a further step in the expansion of the church beyond its initial Jewish setting by relating the conversion of the Ethiopian eunuch, who was probably a half-convert to Judaism, although he may possibly have been a Jew.

26. **Gaza**, formerly one of the five cities of the Philistines, was situated about two and a half miles from the sea. The city was destroyed in 93 B.C. but was rebuilt some thirty-six years later on a new site nearer the sea. **Which is desert** may refer either to the road (RSV) or, more likely, to the site of the older city.

27. Eunuchs were used in Oriental courts to fill positions of high authority. **Candace.** Not a proper name but the title of the royal office. The king of Ethiopia was thought to be the child of the sun and therefore too sacred to exercise the actual functions of governing. The queen mother, who was called **Candace**, exercised the rule. This eunuch was probably a God-fearing Gentile or half-convert to Judaism, who had gone to Jerusalem on a pilgrimage. As a eunuch, he could never have belonged to the OT people of God (Deut 23:1), but such persons are to receive the Gospel.

28. Riding in a covered chariot, probably drawn by oxen, he was reading from the Greek translation of the prophet Isaiah. 30. The ancients commonly read aloud, and Stephen heard the eunuch reading from Isaiah. 32,33. The passage of Scripture was Isa 53:7,8. It describes one who suffered in silence, to whom justice was denied, and who was slain.

34. Before the coming of Christ, the Jews did understand that this was a Messianic passage and that the sufferings of the servant were a prophecy of the sufferings of their Messiah. Later some interpreted the suffering servant to refer to the prophet and others to the people of Israel. 35. Philip showed the eunuch that this was a prophecy of Jesus. This goes back to our Lord's own teaching that he had come to serve and to give his life a ransom for many (Mk 10:45).

36. Northeast of Gaza is a wadi or valley where there is running water. Philip's explanation had apparently included a challenge to believe on Jesus and to be baptized, for the eunuch asked

37. And Philip said, If thou believest with all thine heart, thou mayest. And he answered and said, I believe that Jesus Christ is the Son of God.

38. And he commanded the chariot to stand still: and they went down both into the water, both Philip and the eunuch; and he baptized him.

39. And when they were come up out of the water, the Spirit of the Lord caught away Philip, that the eunuch saw him no more: and he went on his way rejoicing.

40. But Philip was found at Azotus: and passing through he preached in all the cities, till he came to Caesarea.

## CHAPTER 9

AND Saul, yet breathing out threatenings and slaughter against the disciples of the Lord, went unto the high priest,

2. And desired of him letters to Damascus to the synagogues, that if he found any of this way, whether they were men or women, he might bring them bound unto Jerusalem.

that Philip baptize him. **37.** This verse in our English versions is not found in the oldest Greek texts. It was added to our text at an early time and reflects the primitive Christian practice of baptizing men immediately upon confession of faith in Jesus Christ. **38.** One of our earliest post-Biblical Christian writings, the Didache (c. A.D. 125), says that baptism should be performed in running water if it is possible.

**39,40.** We do not know what became of the eunuch, but tradition says that he became a missionary among his own people. Philip visited **Azotus**, the old city of Ashdod, some twenty miles north of Gaza, and then journeyed north along the coast, preaching the Gospel in the various cities, probably including Lydda and Joppa (9:32 ff.). He then came to **Caesarea**, where he apparently settled down, for he was living there at a later date (21:8). Caesarea was a Gentile city and the official residence of the Roman procurators of Judea.

E. Conversion of Saul. 9:1-31. The account of Saul's conversion is inserted into the narrative of the extension of the Gospel in Palestine. The record of the ministry of Peter, who had gone through Samaria preaching the Gospel (8:25), is resumed at 9:32. As the Gospel moved out toward the Gentile world, God prepared a chosen vessel to be the main instrument in this mission. Therefore Luke breaks his narrative to relate Saul's conversion, and also to explain the end of the persecution of the church.

**1.** Saul's conversion is also related in 22:4-16 and 26:12-18. Although Saul was born and reared in the Gentile city of Tarsus in Cilicia (22:3), he had studied in Jerusalem at the feet of Gamaliel, one of the outstanding Jewish rabbis of the day (5:34 ff.). He was known as a brilliant student (Gal 1:14) and a zealous Pharisee (Phil 3:5). Now Saul played the role of the most zealous representative of the Jews in persecuting the church. The violence of his persecution is described in Acts 26:10,11. His aim was to compel Christians to deny their faith on penalty of imprisonment and even death. We do not know how common martyrdom was in this persecution.

**2.** The **high priest**, president of the Sanhedrin, had jurisdiction over Jews throughout Palestine. Saul secured from the priest letters of extradition to the **synagogues at Damascus** to bring any Christians who had fled there back to Jerusalem in bonds. There was a Jewish

3. And as he journeyed, he came near Damascus: and suddenly there shined round about him a light from heaven:

4. And he fell to the earth, and heard a voice saying unto him, Saul, Saul, why persecutest thou me?

5. And he said, Who art thou, Lord? And the Lord said, I am Jesus whom thou persecutest: *it is* hard for thee to kick against the pricks.

6. And he trembling and astonished said, Lord, what wilt thou have me to do? And the Lord *said* unto him, Arise, and go into the city, and it shall be told thee what thou must do.

7. And the men which journeyed with him stood speechless, hearing a voice, but seeing no man.

8. And Saul arose from the earth; and when his eyes were opened, he saw no man: but they led him by the hand, and brought *him* into Damascus.

9. And he was three days without sight, and neither did eat nor drink.

10. And there was a certain disciple at Damascus, named Ananias; and to him said the Lord in a vision, Ananias. And he said, Behold, I *am here*, Lord.

11. And the Lord *said* unto him, Arise, and go into the street which is called Straight, and inquire in the house of Judas for *one* called Saul, of Tarsus: for, behold, he prayeth,

12. And hath seen in a vision a man named Ananias coming in, and putting *his* hand on him, that he might receive his sight.

13. Then Ananias answered, Lord, I have heard by many of this man, how much evil he hath done to thy saints at Jerusalem:

community in Damascus of some ten to eighteen thousand people. **The Way.** A phrase used to describe the Christian faith (19:9, 23; 22:4; 24:14, 22).

**3,4.** The flash of light appeared to Saul near midday (22:6; 26:13), but the light was brighter than the sun. The voice from the midst of the light spoke to Saul in the Hebrew, or Aramaic, dialect (26:14). Although most Jews who lived in the Dispersion spoke Greek, Saul's parents spoke Aramaic and taught him this language (Phil 3:5). This was the language of instruction in the rabbinic schools in Jerusalem. The voice informed Saul that in persecuting the Christians, he had been persecuting Christ.

**5.** At first Saul did not understand the meaning of this experience. He asked the identity of the voice. **Lord** in Greek idiom often means "sir" (16:30; 25:26); but here it indicates a reverent and awe-struck response. The voice identified itself as that of the glorified Jesus. The words in the AV, **It is hard for thee to kick against the pricks,** are not found in this passage in the oldest Greek texts, but have been introduced here from 26:14.

**7.** Saul was accompanied by a caravan. The statement in this verse that the men heard a voice but saw no one appears to contradict 22:9 and 26:14, where it is said that they did not hear the voice. There are two possible solutions to this problem. The Greek construction in 9:7 is different from that in 22:9. The former statement may mean that they heard a sound and the latter verse that they did not understand its content. A second possibility is that 9:7 refers to Saul's voice speaking to the light; the men heard Saul's voice but they did not hear the voice speaking from the light to Saul (22:9).

**9.** The experience was so unsettling that for three days Saul could neither eat nor drink.

**10,11.** We know nothing about **Ananias** except what this passage tells us. Verse 13 indicates that he was apparently a resident of Damascus and not a refugee from Jerusalem. We do not know how the Gospel came to Damascus nor how Ananias was converted. The book of Acts does not give us a complete history of the early church, but relates only the most important events of its growth. The **street called Straight** ran through the heart of Damascus and may still be seen today.

**13.** A report of the ravages wrought

14. And here he hath authority from the chief priests to bind all that call on thy name.

15. But the Lord said unto him, Go thy way: for he is a chosen vessel unto me, to bear my name before the Gentiles, and kings, and the children of Israel:

16. For I will show him how great things he must suffer for my name's sake.

17. And Ananias went his way, and entered into the house; and putting his hands on him said, Brother Saul, the Lord, *even* Jesus, that appeared unto thee in the way as thou camest, hath sent me, that thou mightest receive thy sight, and be filled with the Holy Ghost.

18. And immediately there fell from his eyes as it had been scales: and he received sight forthwith, and arose, and was baptized.

19. And when he had received meat, he was strengthened. Then was Saul certain days with the disciples which were at Damascus.

20. And straightway he preached Christ in the synagogues, that he is the Son of God.

21. But all that heard *him* were amazed, and said; Is not this he that destroyed them which called on this name in Jerusalem, and came hither for that intent, that he might bring them bound unto the chief priests?

22. But Saul increased the more in strength, and confounded the Jews which dwelt at Damascus, proving that this is very Christ.

23. And after that many days were fulfilled, the Jews took counsel to kill him:

24. But their laying wait was known of Saul. And they watched the gates day and night to kill him.

by Saul against the Christians in Jerusalem had come to Damascus. **Saints.** A common NT word for believers. **15,16.** Suffering is to be looked upon not as the exception in the service of Christ, but as the normal thing.

17. Ananias' obedience was immediate and complete. The reception of the Holy Spirit through the laying on of Ananias' hands was an exceptional experience and not the normal thing (cf. 8:17). With the word **brother,** Ananias welcomed Saul into Christian fellowship. **18.** A flaky substance like **scales** fell from Saul's eyes, and he immediately regained his sight and was baptized.

19,20. The **certain days** that Saul spent in Damascus is a very indefinite note of time. Immediately after the vision of Christ, Saul went away to Arabia for some two or three years (Gal 1:15 ff.). The short ministry in Damascus may have taken place either before or after Saul's sojourn in Arabia. There were numerous synagogues in Damascus, and in them Saul proclaimed **Jesus** (RSV) as the **Son of God.** This is the first time this phrase occurs in Acts. It can designate the Messianic king as the object of God's favor (II Sam 7:14; Ps 2:7). This Messianic use of the **Son of God** is illustrated by the question of the high priest to Jesus (Mk 14:61). Probably the term here has the Messianic significance, for Acts 9:22 says that Saul's preaching proved that **Jesus was the Messiah.**

21,22. The transformation in Saul completely amazed his hearers. **Proving.** Literally, *putting together;* that is, putting together the OT prophecies with their fulfillment to show that Jesus was **the Messiah.** Saul's training in the OT as a rabbi now stood him in good stead.

23,24. The **many days** include between two and three years after Saul's conversion (Gal 1:18). "Three years" in Jewish reckoning may refer to a period of more than two full years. Comparison of this verse with II Cor 11:32 tells us that the Jews made a plot with the representative of King Aretas of Arabia. It is possible that the Nabataean kingdom of Aretas extended at this time so far as to include Damascus; but it is more likely that Aretas had a representative in the person of an ethnarch who ruled over the many Nabataeans living in Damascus. When Saul's ministry in Damascus incurred the animosity of both the Jews and the Nabataean authorities, they joined forces to watch the gates in an effort to capture him as he left the city.

25. Then the disciples took him by night, and let *him* down by the wall in a basket.

26. And when Saul was come to Jerusalem, he assayed to join himself to the disciples: but they were all afraid of him, and believed not that he was a disciple.

27. But Barnabas took him, and brought *him* to the apostles, and declared unto them how he had seen the Lord in the way, and that he had spoken to him, and how he had preached boldly at Damascus in the name of Jesus.

28. And he was with them coming in and going out at Jerusalem.

29. And he spake boldly in the name of the Lord Jesus, and disputed against the Grecians: but they went about to slay him.

30. *Which* when the brethren knew, they brought him down to Caesarea, and sent him forth to Tarsus.

31. Then had the churches rest throughout all Judea and Galilee and Samaria, and were edified; and walking in the fear of the Lord, and in the comfort of the Holy Ghost, were multiplied.

32. And it came to pass, as Peter passed throughout all *quarters*, he came down also to the saints which dwelt at Lydda.

33. And there he found a certain man named Eneas, which had kept his bed eight years, and was sick of the palsy.

34. And Peter said unto him, Eneas, Jesus Christ maketh thee whole: arise, and make thy bed. And he arose immediately.

25. One of the Christians owned a house built into the wall of Damascus. Saul was lowered through a window in the wall in a large woven basket, and thus escaped the plot.

26. When Saul returned to Jerusalem, he could not rejoin his former Jewish associates; and the few Christians who remained in the city (8:1) suspected that his profession of faith might be merely a front to further his persecution of the church. 27. Barnabas had either known Saul previously or he was a man of great discernment, for he recognized Saul's sincerity and introduced him to the apostles. The only apostles in Jerusalem at this time were Peter and James, the Lord's brother (Gal 1:18,19). James had been included in the apostolic circle.

28. Saul now busied himself with a Gospel ministry in Jerusalem. His ministry did not yet extend beyond the capital city into Judea (Gal 1:22-24). He addressed himself primarily to the Greek-speaking Jews or Hellenists—the same group to whom Stephen had previously witnessed (Acts 6:9). The Hellenists attempted to kill Saul as they had earlier brought about the death of Stephen.

30. Saul escaped with his life only through the help of his Christian brethren, who took him down to the seaport city of Caesarea, whence he sailed to his home city of Tarsus, in Cilicia. We now lose sight of Saul until 11:25; but he was unquestionably busy in Tarsus preaching the Gospel, although there is no record of this ministry.

31. Luke next describes the growth, both numerical and spiritual, of the church in all Judea and Galilee and Samaria. The plural churches (AV) is incorrect. The Church is one even though there are many local churches. Here is the first reference to churches in Galilee. We do not know when or how they were founded.

F. Peter's Ministry in Palestine and the First Gentile Converts. 9:32—11:18. Luke's narrative at this point reverts to the story of the extension of the Gospel throughout Judea through the ministry of Peter. Peter was last mentioned in 8:25, when he, with John, returned from Samaria to Jerusalem. Now we are told that Peter had engaged in a traveling ministry throughout Judea, preaching to the Christians who had been scattered in the various towns. It would be of great interest to have a complete record of Peter's ministry. In Lydda, he found a group of Christians who had probably

35. And all that dwelt at Lydda and Saron saw him, and turned to the Lord.

36. Now there was at Joppa a certain disciple named Tabitha, which by interpretation is called Dorcas: this woman was full of good works and almsdeeds which she did.

37. And it came to pass in those days, that she was sick, and died: whom when they had washed, they laid *her* in an upper chamber.

38. And forasmuch as Lydda was nigh to Joppa, and the disciples had heard that Peter was there, they sent unto him two men, desiring *him* that he would not delay to come to them.

39. Then Peter arose and went with them. When he was come, they brought him into the upper chamber: and all the widows stood by him weeping, and showing the coats and garments which Dorcas made, while she was with them.

40. But Peter put them all forth, and kneeled down, and prayed; and turning *him* to the body said, Tabitha, arise. And she opened her eyes: and when she saw Peter, she sat up.

41. And he gave her *his* hand, and lifted her up; and when he had called the saints and widows, he presented her alive.

42. And it was known throughout all Joppa; and many believed in the Lord.

43. And it came to pass, that he tarried many days in Joppa with one Simon a tanner.

## CHAPTER 10

THERE was a certain man in Caesarea called Cornelius, a centurion of the band called the Italian *band*,

2. A devout *man*, and one that feared God with all his house, which gave much alms to the people, and prayed to God always.

3. He saw in a vision evidently, about the ninth hour of the day, an angel of God coming in to him, and saying unto him, Cornelius.

4. And when he looked on him, he was afraid, and said, What is it, Lord? And he said unto him, Thy prayers and thine alms are come up for a memorial before God.

5. And now send men to Joppa, and call for *one* Simon, whose surname is Peter:

6. He lodgeth with one Simon a tanner, whose house is by the sea side: he shall tell thee what thou oughtest to do.

fled there in the dispersion caused by the persecution in Jerusalem. Philip had already evangelized this region (8:40). Here Peter healed the paralytic Aeneas.

35. The story of Aeneas' healing spread throughout the city of **Lydda** and throughout the plain of **Sharon**, which bordered the seacoast, and resulted in the conversion of many people. This area was populated in part by Gentiles; Luke is tracing the extension of the church from the Jewish Jerusalem community to the Gentile converts.

36. **Joppa.** A city on the seacoast, some ten miles northwest of Lydda. **Tabitha.** An Aramaic word meaning *gazelle*. **Dorcas.** Greek for the same. She was greatly beloved by the Christians for her good works and acts of charity. 37. The Jewish ceremonial laws of purification required the washing of a dead body. It was placed in an upper room in anticipation of burial. 39. **Widows,** who were among the most needy persons in the ancient world, were the particular objects of Tabitha's charity. They were probably wearing garments Dorcas had made for them.

43. Jews considered the business of tanning skins an unclean trade, since it involved handling dead bodies. It is significant that Peter, good Jew that he was, stayed with a man engaged in such a business.

10:1. Luke now records a very important final step in the extension of the Gospel to the Gentiles. Its importance is indicated by Luke's twice recording Peter's visit to Cornelius. This step raised some difficult problems as to the terms of social intercourse between the Jewish and the Gentile Christians and the terms of the admission of the Gentiles into the church. This question became the theme of the conference in Jerusalem in Acts 15.

A **centurion** was an officer in the Roman army who commanded a hundred men and was similar in rank and function to our noncommissioned officers. **Cornelius** commanded the **Italian cohort.** A Latin inscription has been preserved which indicates the presence in Syria of the "second Italian cohort of Roman citizens" in A.D. 69.

2. A few Gentiles became converts to Judaism and accepted all Jewish practices, including circumcision. A larger number stopped short of circumcision but accepted the Jewish belief in God, synagogue worship, the ethical teachings of the OT, and some of the Jewish religious practices. These people, who were called

7. And when the angel which spake unto Cornelius was departed, he called two of his household servants, and a devout soldier of them that waited on him continually;

8. And when he had declared all *these* things unto them, he sent them to Joppa.

9. On the morrow, as they went on their journey, and drew nigh unto the city, Peter went up upon the housetop to pray about the sixth hour:

10. And he became very hungry, and would have eaten: but while they made ready, he fell into a trance,

11. And saw heaven opened, and a certain vessel descending unto him, as it had been a great sheet knit at the four corners, and let down to the earth:

12. Wherein were all manner of four-footed beasts of the earth, and wild beasts, and creeping things, and fowls of the air.

13. And there came a voice to him, Rise, Peter; kill, and eat.

14. But Peter said, Not so, Lord; for I have never eaten any thing that is common or unclean.

15. And the voice *spake* unto him again the second time, What God hath cleansed, *that* call not thou common.

16. This was done thrice: and the vessel was received up again into heaven.

17. Now while Peter doubted in himself what this vision which he had seen should mean, behold, the men which were sent from Cornelius had made inquiry for Simon's house, and stood before the gate,

18. And called, and asked whether Simon, which was surnamed Peter, were lodged there.

19. While Peter thought on the vision, the Spirit said unto him, Behold, three men seek thee.

20. Arise therefore, and get thee down, and go with them, doubting nothing: for I have sent them.

21. Then Peter went down to the men which were sent unto him from Cornelius; and said, Behold, I am he whom ye seek: what *is* the cause wherefore ye are come?

22. And they said, Cornelius the centurion, a just man, and one that feareth God, and of good report among all the nation of the Jews, was warned from God by a holy angel to send for thee into his house, and to hear words of thee.

23. Then called he them in, and lodged *them*. And on the morrow Peter went away with them, and certain brethren from Joppa accompanied him.

God-fearers, were familiar with the OT in the Greek version as it was read in the synagogues. Devout God-fearers provided the most fertile soil in which the Gospel took root. Cornelius was such a "semi-proselyte." His **devout** character was manifested by his liberal **alms** to the people and his regular **prayers** to God.

7. Cornelius chose two trusted servants and a soldier who was a God-fearer like himself to go to Joppa to bring Peter.

9. Joppa is some thirty miles from Caesarea. The three messengers left Caesarea early in the morning and arrived in Joppa about noon.

Meanwhile, God was preparing Peter to receive them. About twelve o'clock Peter went up to the flat housetop to seek a quiet place **to pray. 10.** Since it was mealtime, he desired to eat and probably called downstairs to the house below to have food prepared. As he continued to pray, he fell into a state of ecstasy and saw a vision. **11.** In the vision he saw some kind of object, like a **great sheet,** lowered by the four corners from the opened heavens to the earth. **Vessel.** A Greek word that can designate almost any kind of useful material object.

12. In the sheet he beheld the three kinds of creatures described in Gen 6:20 —four-footed **animals, reptiles, and birds.** Wild beasts (AV) is not in the best texts. **13,14.** When commanded to **kill** some of these animals and **eat,** Peter replied that to do so would mean violating the Jewish ritual law against eating **unclean** foods. Leviticus 11 contains these laws. Animals that did not chew the cud and did not have cloven hooves were designated as unclean and were not to be used for food. Furthermore, clean animals had to be prepared in such a way that the blood did not remain within the carcass. Although Peter was a Christian, he was also a good Jew, who did not violate Jewish dietary rules.

15. The voice from heaven told him that God had now abolished these regulations about clean and unclean foods. Jesus had in effect taught the same thing (Mk 7:14-23) by teaching that foods which enter a man's body from without cannot defile his heart. The expression in Mk 7:19 b, "This he said, making all meats clean," is probably a word that Mark received from Peter. The apostle was learning for himself the true meaning of Jesus' teachings.

23,24. The next day Peter set out for Caesarea accompanied by the three mes-

24. And the morrow after they entered into Caesarea. And Cornelius waited for them, and had called together his kinsmen and near friends.

25. And as Peter was coming in, Cornelius met him, and fell down at his feet, and worshipped *him*.

26. But Peter took him up, saying, Stand up; I myself also am a man.

27. And as he talked with him, he went in, and found many that were come together.

28. And he said unto them, Ye know how that it is an unlawful thing for a man that is a Jew to keep company, or come unto one of another nation; but God hath showed me that I should not call any man common or unclean.

29. Therefore came I *unto you* without gainsaying, as soon as I was sent for: I ask therefore for what intent ye have sent for me?

30. And Cornelius said, Four days ago I was fasting until this hour; and at the ninth hour I prayed in my house, and, behold, a man stood before me in bright clothing,

31. And said, Cornelius, thy prayer is heard, and thine alms are had in remembrance in the sight of God.

32. Send therefore to Joppa, and call hither Simon, whose surname is Peter; he is lodged in the house of *one* Simon a tanner by the sea side: who, when he cometh, shall speak unto thee.

33. Immediately therefore I sent to thee; and thou hast well done that thou art come. Now therefore are we all here present before God, to hear all things that are commanded thee of God.

34. Then Peter opened *his* mouth, and said, Of a truth I perceive that God is no respecter of persons:

35. But in every nation he that feareth him, and worketh righteousness, is accepted with him.

36. The word which *God* sent unto the children of Israel, preaching peace by Jesus Christ: (he is Lord of all:)

37. That word, *I say*, ye know, which was published throughout all Judea, and began from Galilee, after the baptism which John preached;

38. How God anointed Jesus of Nazareth with the Holy Ghost and with power: who went about doing good, and healing all that were oppressed of the devil; for God was with him.

39. And we are witnesses of all things which he did both in the land of the Jews, and in Jerusalem; whom they slew and hanged on a tree:

sengers and six Jewish Christians from Joppa (11:12). At the house of Cornelius Peter found that the centurion was expecting him, and had gathered together his relatives and close friends.

27-29. Peter explained to Cornelius and his company that Jewish law made it "taboo" for a Jew to associate with or visit people of another nation. However, God had now so lifted Peter out of his Jewish scruples that he could no longer look upon any man as ceremonially common or unclean and therefore unfit for social fellowship. God had made his will so clear to Peter that he had accompanied the servants of Cornelius without any objection, a thing he would not have done as a Jew.

34. The apostle understood the significance of the vision given to him on the rooftop. He realized that the distinction between clean and unclean foods had an application to human beings, and that, contrary to Jewish belief, no people were to be thought of as unclean in the sight of God. God shows no partiality to any one people. A person who fears God and does what is right, whether he be Jew or Gentile, is accepted by God. This was a great lesson for a Jew to learn, and it marks a definite step in the extension of the church from a Jewish fellowship to a universal basis.

36. Peter preached the Gospel to Cornelius, pointing out that although God sent his Word first to Israel, Jesus is indeed Lord of all men. 37,38. Peter's proclamation of the Gospel included a brief summary of Jesus' ministry in Judea and Galilee, his anointing as Messiah at the time of his baptism, his good works, healings, and exorcism of demons. 39-41. It is notable that Peter says little about the meaning of Christ's death, and that he proclaims no doctrine of the atonement. The Gospel consists of the facts of Jesus' death and resurrection. Jesus' resurrection was not a publicly attested fact but was witnessed by chosen men and is confirmed particularly by the fact that these witnesses ate and drank with Jesus after his resurrection from the dead. 42,43. The Gospel includes an announcement of the coming judgment of both the living and the dead by the resurrected Jesus, and the offer of the forgiveness of sins to all who will believe in him.

Peter's sermon is our first example of preaching to the Gentiles. It contains very little reflection upon the meaning of the person of Christ, no emphasis upon

40. Him God raised up the third day, and showed him openly;

41. Not to all the people, but unto witnesses chosen before of God, *even* to us, who did eat and drink with him after he rose from the dead.

42. And he commanded us to preach unto the people, and to testify that it is he which was ordained of God *to be* the Judge of quick and dead.

43. To him give all the prophets witness, that through his name whosoever believeth in him shall receive remission of sins.

44. While Peter yet spake these words, the Holy Ghost fell on all them which heard the word.

45. And they of the circumcision which believed were astonished, as many as came with Peter, because that on the Gentiles also was poured out the gift of the Holy Ghost.

46. For they heard them speak with tongues, and magnify God. Then answered Peter,

47. Can any man forbid water, that these should not be baptized, which have received the Holy Ghost as well as we?

48. And he commanded them to be baptized in the name of the Lord. Then prayed they him to tarry certain days.

## CHAPTER 11

AND the apostles and brethren that were in Judea heard that the Gentiles had also received the word of God.

2. And when Peter was come up to Jerusalem, they that were of the circumcision contended with him,

3. Saying, Thou wentest in to men uncircumcised, and didst eat with them.

his pre-existence, incarnation, and deity, nor on the atoning character of his death. It is indeed a "primitive Christology," and consists primarily of the proclamation of the facts of Jesus' death, life, and resurrection, and the appeal to believe on him for the forgiveness of sins.

44. On the day of Pentecost, Peter had exhorted his hearers to repent, to be baptized for the forgiveness of sins, and to receive the Holy Spirit (2:38). At Caesarea, this order of events was changed, and the Holy Spirit fell upon Cornelius and his family before they were baptized. This was not a new Pentecost but an extension of Pentecost to include the Gentiles.

45. The believers of the circumcision refers to the Jewish Christians who had accompanied Peter from Joppa. Their astonishment was due to the fact that they had not understood that the Gospel was to be extended to the Gentiles. Although they were Christians, they were still Jews, and their Jewish prejudices had to be broken down.

46. The gift of tongues was given on this occasion that there might be no doubt whatsoever that God had given to the Gentiles the same gift he had bestowed upon Jewish believers. 47,48. Peter at once recognized that the Gentiles should be brought into the fellowship of the church, and he therefore commanded that Cornelius and his family be baptized in the name of Jesus Christ. Baptism in water followed baptism in the Spirit. Peter did not immediately return to Jerusalem but remained with Cornelius for some time, probably instructing him in the things of the Lord.

Chapter 11. It is surprising that in a short book Luke would devote so much space to a second recital of the conversion of Cornelius. This indicates that Luke considered this event one of the most important in the life of the early church.

1-3. News of the reception of the Gospel by the Gentiles reached the apostles and the Jewish Christians in Judea. Peter was apparently called to Jerusalem, and some of the Jewish Christians there disputed with him over the propriety of entering into such fellowship with Gentiles as to eat with them. It is likely that the expression, those of the circumcision, has a somewhat different connotation than the same phrase in 10:45. While the Jewish Christians in Jerusalem were discussing the significance of the salvation of the Gentiles, there emerged one party

4. But Peter rehearsed *the matter* from the beginning, and expounded *it* by order unto them, saying,

5. I was in the city of Joppa praying: and in a trance I saw a vision, A certain vessel descend, as it had been a great sheet, let down from heaven by four corners; and it came even to me:

6. Upon the which when I had fastened mine eyes, I considered, and saw four-footed beasts of the earth, and wild beasts, and creeping things, and fowls of the air.

7. And I heard a voice saying unto me, Arise, Peter; slay and eat.

8. But I said, Not so, Lord: for nothing common or unclean hath at any time entered into my mouth.

9. But the voice answered me again from heaven, What God hath cleansed, *that* call not thou common.

10. And this was done three times: and all were drawn up again into heaven.

11. And, behold, immediately there were three men already come unto the house where I was, sent from Caesarea unto me.

12. And the Spirit bade me go with them, nothing doubting. Moreover these six brethren accompanied me, and we entered into the man's house:

13. And he showed us how he had seen an angel in his house, which stood and said unto him, Send men to Joppa, and call for Simon, whose surname is Peter;

14. Who shall tell thee words, whereby thou and all thy house shall be saved.

15. And as I began to speak, the Holy Ghost fell on them, as on us at the beginning.

16. Then remembered I the word of the Lord, how that he said, John indeed baptized with water; but ye shall be baptized with the Holy Ghost.

17. Forasmuch then as God gave them the like gift as *he did* unto us, who believed on the Lord Jesus Christ, what was I, that I could withstand God?

18. When they heard these things, they held their peace, and glorified God, saying, Then hath God also to the Gentiles granted repentance unto life.

19. Now they which were scattered abroad upon the persecution that arose about Stephen traveled as far as Phenice, and Cyprus, and Antioch, preaching the word to none but unto the Jews only.

who later took the position that Gentiles must keep the Jewish law in order to be saved (15:1). This conservative party criticized Peter, for they recognized that a Jew who had table fellowship with Gentiles was in effect setting aside Jewish practices, and thereby ceased to be a Jew. They were not prepared to approve such a course of action; they believed that Jewish believers should not give up their Jewish practices.

4-15. By way of reply Peter related to the Jerusalem church the story of his vision of the sheet from heaven, his visit to Caesarea, and the coming of the Holy Spirit upon the Gentiles as upon the Jews on the day of Pentecost (v. 15).

16. This was the third gift of the Holy Spirit. The first was to the Jewish church in Jerusalem on the day of Pentecost (ch. 2); the second was to Samaritan believers (8:17); and now the third was to Gentiles. Undoubtedly Peter's experience in Samaria prepared him for this ministry to the Gentiles. 17. The gift of tongues made it clear that God had given the same gift to the Gentile believers as he had to Jewish believers when they believed on the Lord Jesus Christ. To refuse Gentiles baptism would have been to refuse to accept God's work and would in effect have been to withstand God.

18. Peter's recital satisfied the circumcision party for the time. But the question of the status of the Gentile Christians in the church was destined shortly to arise again and to create a serious problem.

G. Establishment of a Gentile Church at Antioch. 11:19-30. This section marks a new stage in the extension of the church from a Jewish fellowship in Jerusalem to a universal community. Previously, Luke related the inclusion of the Samaritans in the church and the conversion of the single Gentile family of Cornelius. Now he describes the beginnings of the first independent Gentile congregation in Antioch, which was to become the "mother church" of the Gentile mission in Asia and Europe. The narrative resumes the events of 8:4 and the persecution of Saul.

19. Phoenicia is the narrow strip of land bordering the Mediterranean. It extends north of Caesarea some 120 miles and includes Tyre and Sidon. The preaching of the Gospel was still limited to Jews, for the early church was very slow in realizing the universal character of the Gospel mission.

20. And some of them were men of Cyprus and Cyrene, which, when they were come to Antioch, spake unto the Grecians, preaching the Lord Jesus.

21. And the hand of the Lord was with them: and a great number believed, and turned unto the Lord.

22. Then tidings of these things came unto the ears of the church which was in Jerusalem: and they sent forth Barnabas, that he should go as far as Antioch.

23. Who, when he came, and had seen the grace of God, was glad, and exhorted them all, that with purpose of heart they would cleave unto the Lord.

24. For he was a good man, and full of the Holy Ghost and of faith: and much people was added unto the Lord.

25. Then departed Barnabas to Tarsus, for to seek Saul:

26. And when he had found him, he brought him unto Antioch. And it came to pass, that a whole year they assembled themselves with the church, and taught much people. And the disciples were called Christians first in Antioch.

27. And in these days came prophets from Jerusalem unto Antioch.

20. Some of the believers who had come from the island of **Cyprus** and **Cyrene** in North Africa (cf. 13:1) came to Antioch and launched the Gospel in a new direction. Antioch was the third largest city of the Roman Empire and the residence of the Roman governor of the province of Syria. While a large Jewish colony existed in Antioch, the city was primarily Gentile and Greek. The cult of the pagan deities, Apollo and Artemis, whose worship included ritual prostitution, had headquarters near by. Antioch was notorious for its moral degradation.

**Grecians** or **Greeks** (RSV) in this context refers to pure Greeks rather than to Greek-speaking Jews. The Gospel preached to the Gentiles proclaimed not primarily the Messiahship of Jesus but his Lordship. Messiahship was a Jewish concept that would not have been meaningful to Gentiles who had no Jewish background.

22. This new venture was immediately successful, and the mother **church in Jerusalem** sent **Barnabas** to supervise and confirm the new church as Peter and John had superintended the new work in Samaria (8:14-17). Barnabas, as his name suggests, was gifted in providing encouragement to new Christians, and he exhorted the new converts that **with purpose of heart** they would be faithful and would persevere.

25,26. Barnabas soon realized that the growing church needed additional guidance, and his mind turned to **Saul** of Tarsus, who had undoubtedly been engaged in missionary work in the vicinity of his home city (9:30; Gal 1:21). After some difficulty, he found Saul and brought him to Antioch, where they spent a **whole year** working in the church. The word **Christians** occurs in the NT only here, in 26:28, and in I Pet 4:16. The word is formed with the Latin suffix which designates "follower or partisan of" (cf. "Herodians" in Mk 3:6). There is no adequate reason to think that the term was used in derision. It simply means people who follow Christ.

27. The growing importance of the church in Antioch is illustrated by the ministry rendered to the mother church in Jerusalem at a time of famine. **Prophets** are mentioned in 13:1; 15:32; 21:9,10. They were not ordained official leaders but laymen who declared the will of God or future events under direct inspiration of the Holy Spirit. See I Cor 14:29-39. Prophets ranked next to apostles in the early church (I Cor 12:28; Eph 2:20; 3:5; 4:11; Rev 22:9).

28. And there stood up one of them named Agabus, and signified by the Spirit that there should be great dearth throughout all the world: which came to pass in the days of Claudius Caesar.

29. Then the disciples, every man according to his ability, determined to send relief unto the brethren which dwelt in Judea:

30. Which also they did, and sent it to the elders by the hands of Barnabas and Saul.

## CHAPTER 12

NOW about that time Herod the king stretched forth *his* hands to vex certain of the church.

2. And he killed James the brother of John with the sword.

28. **Agabus** appears again in 21:10. **The days of Claudius.** Roman historians refer to several famines during the reign of Claudius (A.D. 41—54), while Josephus, the Jewish historian, mentions a severe famine in Judea in A.D. 46.

30. **Elders.** Here is the first mention in Acts of these Christian officials. Luke gives no hint as to how the office of elder came into existence or by what means elders were chosen. A group of elders ruled over each Jewish synagogue, and it is probable that the Christian church adopted the Jewish pattern. Probably the believers constituted a number of house congregations in several homes, and the elders may have been the leaders of these several congregations (see Acts 15:6,23). Many scholars think that this famine visit was the journey mentioned in Gal 2:1-10. The "revelation" of Gal 2:2 may refer to the prophecy of Agabus. If this is so, fourteen years (Gal 2:1) had intervened since Saul's first visit to Jerusalem, and he was already a mature Christian and an experienced leader. The problem of whether the visit referred to in Gal 2:1-10 is the famine visit of Acts 11 or the council visit of Acts 15 is one of the most difficult problems in NT history.

H. Persecution by Herod Agrippa I. 12:1-25. Luke interrupts the flow of his narrative to record an event that had occurred a few years earlier. Since Herod died in A.D. 44, the famine mission must have occurred about A.D. 46. The Jerusalem community had met early opposition by the Jewish religious leaders, but the Christians were popular with the people. Violent persecution had arisen against Stephen and the Hellenistic wing under the leadership of Saul. Now for the first time, Luke records persecution from the ruling authorities in Palestine. It came not from Roman rulers but from a Jewish king.

1. **Herod the King** was Agrippa I, grandson of Herod the Great, who was king of all Palestine when Jesus was born. During our Lord's ministry, Herod Antipas, son of Herod the Great, was ruler over Galilee, while Judea was governed by Roman procurators. Between 41 and 44 A.D. Herod Agrippa was king over both Judea and Galilee. After his death in A.D. 44, the whole of Palestine again became a Roman province under Roman procurators.

2. **The death of James** was the first martyrdom of an apostle and marked a new attitude of hostility on the part of

3. And because he saw it pleased the Jews, he proceeded further to take Peter also. (Then were the days of unleavened bread.)

4. And when he had apprehended him, he put *him* in prison, and delivered *him* to four quaternions of soldiers to keep him; intending after Easter to bring him forth to the people.

5. Peter therefore was kept in prison: but prayer was made without ceasing of the church unto God for him.

6. And when Herod would have brought him forth, the same night Peter was sleeping between two soldiers, bound with two chains: and the keepers before the door kept the prison.

7. And, behold, the angel of the Lord came upon *him*, and a light shined in the prison: and he smote Peter on the side, and raised him up, saying, Arise up quickly. And his chains fell off from *his* hands.

8. And the angel said unto him, Gird thyself, and bind on thy sandals. And so he did. And he saith unto him, Cast thy garment about thee, and follow me.

9. And he went out, and followed him; and wist not that it was true which was done by the angel; but thought he saw a vision.

10. When they were past the first and the second ward, they came unto the iron gate that leadeth unto the city; which opened to them of his own accord: and they went out, and passed on through one street; and forthwith the angel departed from him.

11. And when Peter was come to himself, he said, Now I know of a surety, that the Lord hath sent his angel, and hath delivered me out of the hand of Herod, and *from* all the expectation of the people of the Jews.

12. And when he had considered *the thing*, he came to the house of Mary the mother of John, whose surname was Mark; where many were gathered together praying.

13. And as Peter knocked at the door of the gate, a damsel came to hearken, named Rhoda.

14. And when she knew Peter's voice, she opened not the gate for gladness, but ran in, and told how Peter stood before the gate.

the Jewish people toward the church. At first, the Jews held the Christians in high honor (5:13). Persecution by the Sanhedrin had been spearheaded by Saul. Now the king of the Jews, with popular support, directed persecution against the apostles. James thus fulfilled the prophecy of Jesus in Mk 10:39.

3. Herod is known to have followed a policy of catering to Jewish desires, and the popular response at his execution of James led him to seize **Peter** also. The **days of unleavened bread**, the seven days following the Passover, were holy days, when an execution would not be fitting. 4. Properly speaking, the **Passover** (AV *Easter* is incorrect) introduced the days of unleavened bread, but Luke uses the two terms interchangeably (Lk 22:1). Peter was guarded by four relays of four soldiers, one squad for each three-hour watch of the night. 5. **Prayer . . . without ceasing.** The Greek word may mean either *continuing* prayer or *earnest* prayer. The same word is used in Lk 22:44 of Jesus' prayer in Gethsemane.

6. Peter was chained to two soldiers, and two others stood at the doors. Although the apostle expected to be executed on the next day, he was able to sleep soundly. 7,8. The **garment.** The mantle or cloak worn over the ordinary clothing. 9. Peter thought that he was experiencing a vision or a dream and could not believe that it was real. 10. Peter and the angel passed two gates, each guarded by a soldier. The third gate, which led from the prison to the city, opened automatically. Possibly Peter was imprisoned in the Tower of Antonia, a military installation at the northwest corner of the temple area. One text refers to seven steps leading down to the city.

11. Peter now **came to himself,** for he had been walking as though in a trance. For the first time, the true significance of what had occurred came home to him. 12. He first hurried to the place where the Christians were gathered in prayer. This **house of Mary** was one of the chief meeting places of the church. "Churches," or buildings erected for Christian worship, are not known in the NT. **John Mark** (12:25; 12:5,13; 15:37-39; Col 4:10; Phil 2:1; II Tim 4:11) is here introduced for the first time. Good tradition relates that he later became Peter's interpreter in Rome and that his Gospel is based on Peter's preaching. He was probably one of the sources of Luke's information.

**14-16.** Although the believers had

15. And they said unto her, Thou art mad. But she constantly affirmed that it was even so. Then said they, It is his angel.

16. But Peter continued knocking: and when they had opened *the door*, and saw him, they were astonished.

17. But he, beckoning unto them with the hand to hold their peace, declared unto them how the Lord had brought him out of the prison. And he said, Go show these things unto James, and to the brethren. And he departed, and went into another place.

18. Now as soon as it was day, there was no small stir among the soldiers, what was become of Peter.

19. And when Herod had sought for him, and found him not, he examined the keepers, and commanded that *they* should be put to death. And he went down from Judea to Caesarea, and *there* abode.

20. And Herod was highly displeased with them of Tyre and Sidon: but they came with one accord to him, and, having made Blastus the king's chamberlain their friend, desired peace; because their country was nourished by the king's *country*.

21. And upon a set day Herod, arrayed in royal apparel, sat upon his throne, and made an oration unto them.

22. And the people gave a shout, *saying*, It *is* the voice of a god, and not of a man.

23. And immediately the angel of the Lord smote him, because he gave not God the glory: and he was eaten of worms, and gave up the ghost.

24. But the word of God grew and multiplied.

25. And Barnabas and Saul returned from Jerusalem, when they had fulfilled *their* ministry, and took with them John, whose surname was Mark.

been praying fervently for Peter's release, they were amazed when their prayers were answered. When the maid who answered Peter's knock, recognized the apostle's voice, she rushed back to the assembled church, leaving Peter standing at the locked gate. The believers thought that **Rhoda** was imagining things or that she had seen Peter's guardian **angel** (Mt 18:10; Heb 1:14). When Peter was admitted, his friends broke into excited questions, and he had to motion them to be silent.

17. **James**, the brother of Jesus, had become the acting head of the Jerusalem church, but he was not with the assembled church at this time. The **brethren** may be the elders of 11:30 who shared the rule of the church with James. After reporting his escape to the church, Peter "went underground," and Luke no longer traces his activities. However, the tradition that he went to Rome is refuted by Acts 15:2, for Peter was present at the council in Jerusalem.

19. The words translated **put to death** may mean "led off to prison"; but Roman law prescribed that if a prisoner escaped, the penalty due him should be inflicted on his guard. **Caesarea** was the Roman capital of the province of Judea; but **Judea** is used here not of the Roman province but of the dwelling place of the Jews.

20. Although **Tyre** and **Sidon** were free cities, they were dependent for their food upon the grain of Galilee in Herod's kingdom. For some unknown reason Herod was angry with these two cities. And so, to make peace with him, they presumably bribed Blastus to intercede with the king and gain a hearing for them. **21.** The **set day**, according to Josephus, was a feast in honor of the Emperor. To receive the delegates from Tyre and Sidon in state, Herod arrayed himself in robes made entirely of silver. **22,23.** Pagans commonly attributed divine attributes to their rulers. Josephus relates that after delivering this oration, Herod was struck down with a violent pain in the stomach and was carried to the palace, where, after five days of suffering, he died. His death occurred in A.D. 44, and Judea was then placed under Roman governors, two of whom (Felix and Festus) appear in the later narrative of Acts.

**24,25.** Luke now resumes his story of the church in Antioch (see 11:30).

IV. Extension of the Church in Asia
    Minor and Europe. 13:1—21:17.

## CHAPTER 13

NOW there were in the church that was at Antioch certain prophets and teachers; as Barnabas, and Simeon that was called Niger, and Lucius of Cyrene, and Manaen, which had been brought up with Herod the tetrarch, and Saul.

2. As they ministered to the Lord, and fasted, the Holy Ghost said, Separate me Barnabas and Saul for the work whereunto I have called them.

3. And when they had fasted and prayed, and laid *their* hands on them, they sent *them* away.

4. So they, being sent forth by the Holy Ghost, departed unto Seleucia; and from thence they sailed to Cyprus.

5. And when they were at Salamis, they preached the word of God in the synagogues of the Jews: and they had also John to *their* minister.

Chapter 13 brings us to the second half of Acts. In the first half, Jerusalem is the center of the narrative, and the main theme is the extension of the church from Jerusalem throughout Palestine. Now Jerusalem drops into the background, and Antioch becomes the center of the narrative because it sponsored the extension of the church in Asia and Europe. This extension was accomplished by three missions by Paul, each beginning and ending in Antioch.

A. First Mission: Galatia. 13:1–14:28. The first mission carried the Gospel from Antioch to Cyprus and to the cities in the southern part of the Roman province of Galatia.

1. The church in Antioch was characterized by many outstanding Christians. Niger. A Latin word meaning *black*, here used as a nickname. It apparently describes the dark complexion of Simeon and suggests that he was of African origin. He may have been the Simon of Cyrene mentioned in Mk 15:21, who carried Jesus' cross. The adjective describing Manaen means *foster brother* and was applied to boys of the same age as royal children who were brought up in the court. The title was retained after the boys reached adulthood. Herod, whose playmate was Manaen, was Herod Antipas, who ruled over Galilee and Perea between 4 B.C. and A.D. 39. Prophets were enabled to give new revelations of God's will by direct inspiration of the Holy Spirit. Teachers were gifted in the interpretation of (OT) Scripture.

2. The utterance of the Holy Spirit came probably through a prophet. 3. The call to this mission came from the Holy Spirit; the church recognized and confirmed the divine call. The laying on of hands does not constitute ordination but separation to a special task and approval of the mission.

4. Seleucia. The port of Antioch. Here Barnabas and Saul took ship for Cyprus, a large and important island. Possibly the evangelistic mission was begun in Cyprus because the island was Barnabas' home.

5. Salamis. The eastern port of Cyprus and its largest city. Jews were so numerous that there were several synagogues. It was Paul's custom to preach the Gospel "to the Jew first" (Rom 1:16); but the Gospel usually took root among the Gentiles who attended the Jewish synagogues. John Mark accompanied the apostles. Minister or *attendant*

6. And when they had gone through the isle unto Paphos, they found a certain sorcerer, a false prophet, a Jew, whose name *was* Bar-jesus:

7. Which was with the deputy of the country, Sergius Paulus, a prudent man; who called for Barnabas and Saul, and desired to hear the word of God.

8. But Elymas the sorcerer (for so is his name by interpretation) withstood them, seeking to turn away the deputy from the faith.

9. Then Saul, (who also *is called* Paul,) filled with the Holy Ghost, set his eyes on him,

10. And said, O full of all subtilty and all mischief, *thou* child of the devil, *thou* enemy of all righteousness, wilt thou not cease to pervert the right ways of the Lord?

11. And now, behold, the hand of the Lord *is* upon thee, and thou shalt be blind, not seeing the sun for a season. And immediately there fell on him a mist and a darkness; and he went about seeking some to lead him by the hand.

12. Then the deputy, when he saw what was done, believed, being astonished at the doctrine of the Lord.

13. Now when Paul and his company loosed from Paphos, they came to Perga in Pamphylia: and John departing from them returned to Jerusalem.

has been thought by some scholars to designate one whose function was to instruct the converts in the Gospel and in the Christian life.

**6. Paphos.** The official capital of the province. Bar-Jesus means *son of salvation*. He was a false prophet not because he gave false predictions but because he falsely claimed to be a prophet. It was a common practice for rulers to have magicians and astrologers in their retinue. **7. Sergius Paulus** was the proconsul of the province. Rome had two types of provinces—those under the emperor and those under the senate. The former, like Judea, were governed by procurators appointed by the emperors, while the latter were governed by proconsuls. In 22 B.C., the status of Cyprus was changed from imperial to senatorial province, as Luke correctly indicates.

**8. Elymas.** Another name for Bar-Jesus, probably a Semitic word bearing a meaning similar to the Greek *magos*, which means "sorcerer" or "magician." Elymas sensed that if the proconsul accepted the message of Barnabas and Saul, his own position would be impaired, and he therefore attempted to turn the proconsul from his faith.

**9. Saul** is the Semitic form, **Paul** the Greek. Of the several reasons suggested for the introduction of the Greek name, the most likely is that as Paul now assumed the position of leadership in the Gentile mission, the Greek form of his name was more appropriate, and Luke so designates him. **10.** Instead of "son of salvation," Elymas was a son of the devil. **11.** The word translated mist is used by medical writers to describe an inflammation of the eye that gives it a cloudy appearance.

**13.** The missionaries turned from Barnabas' native land of Cyprus to the country bordering Paul's native land. **Pamphylia.** A district on the coast of Asia Minor. **Perga.** A city situated about twelve miles inland. For some unexplained reason, John Mark forsook Paul and Barnabas and returned to Jerusalem. Paul considered this desertion inexcusable, for later when Barnabas wished Mark to accompany them on another trip, Paul refused to take him (15:37,38), and separated from Barnabas over this issue. Mark's desertion may have been due to some change in their missionary plans of which he did not approve. Others have suggested that he was jealous because Paul was outshining his cousin Barnabas. There is no reason to think

14. But when they departed from Perga, they came to Antioch in Pisidia, and went into the synagogue on the sabbath day, and sat down.

15. And after the reading of the law and the prophets, the rulers of the synagogue sent unto them, saying, Ye men *and* brethren, if ye have any word of exhortation for the people, say on.

16. Then Paul stood up, and beckoning with *his* hand said, Men of Israel, and ye that fear God, give audience.

that the basis of the difference was doctrinal.

14. Paul and Barnabas headed inland over the Taurus mountains and entered the southern part of the Roman province of Galatia. **Antioch.** The most important city of that part of Galatia. It was not situated in **Pisidia,** as the AV translates, but was near the region of Pisidia and had come to be designated **Pisidian Antioch.**

Many scholars, following the researches of William M. Ramsay, conclude that these cities of southern Galatia were those to which Paul wrote the letter to the Galatians. Other scholars have felt that **Galatia** designates the northern part of the province of Galatia, where the Galatian people of Gallic extraction lived. However, this "North Galatian" theory is beset by more problems than the "South Galatian" theory. It is probable that the Galatian epistle was addressed to the churches of Antioch, Iconium, Lystra, and Derbe. Sir William Ramsay speculated that Paul had been seized with malaria on the low-lying seacoast of Perga and was ill when he arrived in Antioch. Although this cannot be proved, it is an interesting possibility. As his custom was, Paul first went to the synagogue of the Jewish colony in Antioch on the Sabbath day.

15. A Jewish synagogue service consisted largely of prayers, a reading from the law and one from the **prophets,** and an exposition of the reading, which might be given by anyone in the congregation. The **rulers of the synagogue** were not "clergymen" but persons charged with the superintendence of the synagogue and its worship. Their office gave them authority to invite some one person to deliver the sermon. In accordance with this procedure, the two visitors were invited to give a word of exhortation. The main truths of Paul's sermon are as follows: 1. Jesus is the fulfillment of the history of God's dealings with Israel. 2. The Jews in Jerusalem rejected him, but in crucifying him they fulfilled God's purpose. 3. God fulfilled his promise to the fathers by raising Jesus from the dead. 4. The blessings of forgiveness and justification, which the Law could not provide, are now offered in Jesus' name to the Jews of the dispersion.

16. The synagogue congregation was composed of two groups: **men of Israel,** i.e., Jews; and **God-fearers**—Gentiles who worshiped God and attended the syna-

17. The God of this people of Israel chose our fathers, and exalted the people when they dwelt as strangers in the land of Egypt, and with a high arm brought he them out of it.

18. And about the time of forty years suffered he their manners in the wilderness.

19. And when he had destroyed seven nations in the land of Chanaan, he divided their land to them by lot.

20. And after that he gave *unto them* judges about the space of four hundred and fifty years, until Samuel the prophet.

21. And afterward they desired a king: and God gave unto them Saul the son of Cis, a man of the tribe of Benjamin, by the space of forty years.

22. And when he had removed him, he raised up unto them David to be their king; to whom also he gave testimony, and said, I have found David the *son* of Jesse, a man after mine own heart, which shall fulfil all my will.

23. Of this man's seed hath God, according to *his* promise, raised unto Israel a Saviour, Jesus:

24. When John had first preached before his coming the baptism of repentance to all the people of Israel.

25. And as John fulfilled his course, he said, Whom think ye that I am? I am not *he*. But, behold, there cometh one after me, whose shoes of *his* feet I am not worthy to loose.

26. Men *and* brethren, children of the stock of Abraham, and whosoever among you feareth God, to you is the word of this salvation sent.

27. For they that dwell at Jerusalem, and their rulers, because they knew him not, nor yet the voices of the prophets which are read every sabbath day, they have fulfilled *them* in condemning *him*.

28. And though they found no cause of death *in him*, yet desired they Pilate that he should be slain.

29. And when they had fulfilled all that was written of him, they took *him* down from the tree, and laid *him* in a sepulchre.

30. But God raised him from the dead:

31. And he was seen many days of them which came up with him from Galilee to Jerusalem, who are his witnesses unto the people.

32. And we declare unto you glad tidings, how that the promise which was made unto the fathers,

gogue without accepting all of the demands of the Jewish law (cf. 10:2).

17. Paul first cited some of the highlights in the history of Israel to show that the God who had led Israel through the centuries had now sent Jesus to be the Son of David of prophecy. The heart of the Biblical faith is that God has acted redemptively in history, first in Israel and then in Jesus Christ. The birth of Israel as a nation began with the deliverance from Egypt. With a high arm means with a display of power. 18. Suffered their manners may mean either that he put up with their conduct or that he nourished them like a father. 19. The seven nations are mentioned in Deut 7:1. The 450 years can hardly be intended to designate the period of the Judges, as the AV suggests, but probably includes the period of the sojourn, the wandering, and the distribution of the land during the period of the Judges.

21,22. The OT does not mention these forty years, but Josephus refers to them. David was the man after God's own heart and was obedient to his will, but God promised through the prophets to raise up a greater successor to David (Ezk 34:23; 37:24; Jer 23:5,39). The expectation of a Davidic king was a live hope among the Jews of the first century (see the pseudepigraphical Psalms of Solomon 17:23 ff.).

23. However, the promised Son of David had appeared as a Saviour rather than as a king; the word Jesus means Saviour (Mt 1:21). Raised does not refer to the Resurrection but to the historical appearance of Jesus the Saviour. 26,27. The promised salvation was fulfilled in the death of Jesus. The Jews in Jerusalem unknowingly fulfilled the Scripture because they failed to understand its true meaning and condemned Jesus to death. When the Sanhedrin had wanted Jesus' body removed from the cross before the beginning of the Sabbath (Jn 19:31), he had been buried by Joseph of Arimathea and Nicodemus (Lk 23:50 ff.; Jn 19:38 ff.).

30,31. The resurrection of Jesus, the central theme in the early proclamation and foundation of the Church, was attested by many witnesses whose witness still could be heard (RSV).

32,33. Jesus, Paul declared, was the fulfillment of the OT promise; the Messianic hope given to the fathers was fulfilled in him. He hath raised up Jesus probably designates Christ's appearance in history rather than his resurrection

33. God hath fulfilled the same unto us their children, in that he hath raised up Jesus again; as it is also written in the second psalm, Thou art my Son, this day have I begotten thee.

34. And as concerning that he raised him up from the dead, *now* no more to return to corruption, he said on this wise, I will give you the sure mercies of David.

35. Wherefore he saith also in another *psalm*, Thou shalt not suffer thine Holy One to see corruption.

36. For David, after he had served his own generation by the will of God, fell on sleep, and was laid unto his fathers, and saw corruption:

37. But he, whom God raised again, saw no corruption.

38. Be it known unto you therefore, men *and* brethren, that through this man is preached unto you the forgiveness of sins:

39. And by him all that believe are justified from all things, from which ye could not be justified by the law of Moses.

40. Beware therefore, lest that come upon you, which is spoken of in the prophets;

41. Behold, ye despisers, and wonder, and perish: for I work a work in your days, a work which ye shall in no wise believe, though a man declare it unto you.

42. And when the Jews were gone out of the synagogue, the Gentiles besought that these words might be preached to them the next sabbath.

43. Now when the congregation was broken up, many of the Jews and religious proselytes followed Paul and Barnabas; who, speaking to them, persuaded them to continue in the grace of God.

44. And the next sabbath day came almost the whole city together to hear the word of God.

45. But when the Jews saw the multitudes, they were filled with envy, and spake against those things which were spoken by Paul, contradicting and blaspheming.

from the dead. **Again** is not in the text. However, the historical appearance of Jesus included his resurrection from the dead, as the following verses indicate. **Thou art my Son** (Ps 2:7) does not refer to Jesus' deity so much as to his Messiahship. Part of this quotation was heard at Jesus' baptism (Mk 1:11) and indicated the entrance of Jesus into his Messianic mission. "Sonship" in Biblical thought is a many-sided concept and can designate Messiahship without in any way minimizing the reality of Christ's deity.

**34,35.** Prediction of the resurrection of Christ is found in Isa 55:3 and in Ps 16:10. Because David died, the promise of Ps 16:10 could not refer to him but must refer to his promised descendant. **36,37. David served his own generation by the will of God** can also be translated, *David served the will of God in his own generation.* David's career was limited to his own generation, for he died and saw corruption; the career of Jesus cannot be limited to any one time but belongs to all ages.

**38,39.** From Jesus' death and resurrection two blessings result—**forgiveness** and **justification.** Two interpretations of 13:39 are possible: while the Law justifies from some things, Christ justifies from all things; or, though the Law justifies from nothing, Christ justifies from everything. The latter rendition is the more natural, although many scholars have preferred the former and have found here a teaching differing from Paul's doctrine of justification. **40,41.** Paul concluded with a warning from Hab 1:5. If God's people did not repent, a great tragedy would befall them.

**42.** This new and thrilling message created great excitement. After the synagogue service, many of Paul's hearers showed themselves ready to accept his message. The proper text has no reference to **Jews** and **Gentiles** (AV) but only to the people (RSV). **43. Religious** or *devout* proselytes. An unusual expression that ought to indicate full converts to Judaism. However, from the context, it seems to refer to the "God-fearers" or Gentile half-converts to Judaism who accepted the Gospel.

**44,45.** During the week, the report of Paul's sermon spread throughout the city, and on the next Sabbath the synagogue was filled with Gentiles to hear Paul's word. Such a crowd of Gentiles in the synagogue provoked the Jews to envy, and they refuted his message and

46. Then Paul and Barnabas waxed bold, and said, It was necessary that the word of God should first have been spoken to you: but seeing ye put it from you, and judge yourselves unworthy of everlasting life, lo, we turn to the Gentiles.

47. For so hath the Lord commanded us, *saying*, I have set thee to be a light of the Gentiles, that thou shouldest be for salvation unto the ends of the earth.

48. And when the Gentiles heard this, they were glad, and glorified the word of the Lord: and as many as were ordained to eternal life believed.

49. And the word of the Lord was published throughout all the region.

50. But the Jews stirred up the devout and honorable women, and the chief men of the city, and raised persecution against Paul and Barnabas, and expelled them out of their coasts.

51. But they shook off the dust of their feet against them, and came unto Iconium.

52. And the disciples were filled with joy, and with the Holy Ghost.

## CHAPTER 14

AND it came to pass in Iconium, that they went both together into the synagogue of the Jews, and so spake, that a great multitude both of the Jews and also of the Greeks believed.

2. But the unbelieving Jews stirred up the Gentiles, and made their minds evil affected against the brethren.

reviled his person. **Blaspheming** does not mean to blaspheme God but to revile men.

46. Paul replied that it was the divine order that the Gospel should be offered first to the Jews that they might accept it and in turn evangelize the Gentiles. However, since they rejected the word of God and thereby judged themselves unworthy of the life of the age to come, Paul must himself turn to the Gentiles. Here **the word of God** includes much more than the Scriptures; it designates the proclamation of the gospel of the death and resurrection of Jesus. **Eternal life** is here the future possession rather than the present experience. The one, however, includes the other.

47. A prophecy from Isa 49:6, originally referring to the servant of the Lord, is here applied to the apostles, who were to bring light to the Gentiles. **48. Ordained to eternal life.** The primary significance of this reference to predestination is not theological but historical. As the Gospel moved out from its Jewish environment to the Gentile world, many **ordained to eternal life** received it and believed. This, however, does not involve minimizing the teaching of foreordination to life. Here is one of the recurring themes of Acts: At every new and strategic step the Gospel is rejected by the Jews but received by Gentiles.

50. **The Jews** not only rejected the Gospel; they initiated active steps to frustrate Paul's ministry. Among the God-fearers (cf. note on 10:2) attending the synagogue were **women of high standing.** These the Jews influenced to bring pressure on their husbands to drive Paul and Barnabas out of the area. Here is an authentic touch of local color; women did not exercise such influence in cities of Greece as they did here in Asia. **51,52.** Jesus had commanded his disciples to shake the **dust from their feet** when they were rejected (Lk 9:5; 10:11), thus indicating the breaking off of all intercourse. Among Jews such an action was equivalent to calling a man a heathen.

**14:1,2. Iconium** was the easternmost city of the district of Phrygia and lay in the Roman province of Galatia. Here the experience of Jewish opposition and Gentile faith was repeated. **3.** However, since it took a while for the opposition to become effective, the apostles were able to preach the word for a long period of time. This indefinite note of time is typical of Luke's method of writing. At a few points he gives us distinct chronologi-

3. Long time therefore abode they speaking boldly in the Lord, which gave testimony unto the word of his grace, and granted signs and wonders to be done by their hands.

4. But the multitude of the city was divided: and part held with the Jews, and part with the apostles.

5. And when there was an assault made both of the Gentiles, and also of the Jews with their rulers, to use *them* despitefully, and to stone them,

6. They were ware of *it*, and fled unto Lystra and Derbe, cities of Lycaonia, and unto the region that lieth round about:

7. And there they preached the gospel.

8. And there sat a certain man at Lystra, impotent in his feet, being a cripple from his mother's womb, who never had walked:

9. The same heard Paul speak: who steadfastly beholding him, and perceiving that he had faith to be healed,

10. Said with a loud voice, Stand upright on thy feet. And he leaped and walked.

11. And when the people saw what Paul had done, they lifted up their voices, saying in the speech of Lycaonia, The gods are come down to us in the likeness of men.

12. And they called Barnabas, Jupiter; and Paul, Mercurius, because he was the chief speaker.

13. Then the priest of Jupiter, which was before their city, brought oxen and garlands unto the gates, and would have done sacrifice with the people.

14. *Which* when the apostles, Barnabas and Paul, heard *of*, they rent their clothes, and ran in among the people, crying out,

15. And saying, Sirs, why do ye these things? We also are men of like passions with you, and preach unto you that ye should turn from these vanities unto the living God, which made heaven, and earth, and the sea, and all things that are therein:

cal references; but it is impossible from Luke's record to create a precise chronological table of Paul's travels and ministry. 4,5. The hostile Jews succeeded finally in inciting a riot and stirring up the rulers. And so Paul and Barnabas had to leave Iconium.

6. While Luke is often indefinite as to chronological references, he is often very definite in his geographical notes. This statement that **Lystra** and **Derbe** belonged to the region of **Lycaonia** implies that Iconium lay outside Lycaonia. Other writers of about Luke's time placed Iconium in the district of Lycaonia. Many scholars assumed that at this point Luke was inaccurate. Ramsay tells how this reference caught his attention and how careful examination vindicated Luke's statement. This was the beginning of Ramsay's change in attitude toward Acts, and he became one of the most vigorous and learned proponents of the accuracy of the book (see *The Bearing of Recent Discovery on the Trustworthiness of the New Testament*, chapter III).

11. In their excitement, the people fell into their native *Lycaonian* tongue, and Paul and Barnabas could not understand what was happening. Much of the Mediterranean world was bilingual, the people speaking the general language, Greek, and also their native dialect. 12. The two visitors were thought to be two gods. *Zeus* was the chief god of the Greek Pantheon, and *Hermes* was the herald of the gods. **Jupiter** and **Mercurius** (AV) are the Latin equivalents for the Greek names of these gods, but the Greek terms ought to be used. Since Paul was the spokesman of the two, the people called him Hermes; while Barnabas, the more silent partner who stood in the background, they called Zeus, the father of the gods. Legends existed that told of other occasions when these two gods visited people of this area.

13. **Before the city** probably refers to the temple located outside the city. The priest of Zeus prepared oxen adorned with woolen decorations to offer sacrifice to their unexpected visitors. The **gates** probably refer to the gates of the city near the temple. 14. Although the apostles could not understand the Lycaonian dialect, the actions of the priests soon indicated their purpose to sacrifice, and the apostles strongly protested. **They tore their clothes.** A Jewish gesture of horror at blasphemy (Mk 4:63).

15-17. Paul urged the people to worship the living God rather than His

16. Who in times past suffered all nations to walk in their own ways.

17. Nevertheless he left not himself without witness, in that he did good, and gave us rain from heaven, and fruitful seasons, filling our hearts with food and gladness.

18. And with these sayings scarce restrained they the people, that they had not done sacrifice unto them.

19. And there came thither *certain* Jews from Antioch and Iconium, who persuaded the people, and, having stoned Paul, drew *him* out of the city, supposing he had been dead.

20. Howbeit, as the disciples stood round about him, he rose up, and came into the city: and the next day he departed with Barnabas to Derbe.

21. And when they had preached the gospel to that city, and had taught many, they returned again to Lystra, and *to* Iconium, and Antioch,

22. Confirming the souls of the disciples, *and* exhorting them to continue in the faith, and that we must through much tribulation enter into the kingdom of God.

23. And when they had ordained them elders in every church, and had prayed with fasting, they commended them to the Lord, on whom they believed.

24. And after they had passed throughout Pisidia, they came to Pamphylia.

25. And when they had preached the word in Perga, they went down into Attalia:

emissaries. This sermon given to a purely pagan audience contrasts strikingly with the sermon delivered at Antioch in the Jewish synagogue. Before pagans can appreciate the mission of Jesus, they must recognize the oneness of God. Paul's sermon rests largely upon the evidences of natural theology which point to the existence of a Creator and Sustainer. Although God allowed men to go their own way, he provided for them a witness unto himself in granting the rains and harvest times to satisfy the human appetites. 18. Paul barely succeeded in persuading the people that he and Barnabas were not indeed divine beings.

19. No reference is made to a Jewish synagogue in Lystra, but probably such a synagogue existed, for Jews from Antioch and Iconium were able to raise up such opposition against Paul that he was stoned and dragged out of the city as dead. Paul refers to this event in II Cor 11:24,25. 20. The abruptness of these words suggests that a miracle took place. It is difficult to conceive of a man's undergoing such a stoning without receiving severe physical injury. "The marks of Jesus" (Gal 6:17) may well be the scars inflicted by these stones. Derbe. A frontier city of the province of Galatia.

21. No opposition in Derbe is recorded. The apostles made many disciples. This is the meaning of taught (AV). The apostles retraced their steps through the cities of Galatia. 22. The kingdom of God is here the future eschatological realm established by the return of Christ in glory. The very structure of things decrees that in this age the church must expect tribulation as it looks forward to the glory of the future kingdom. The faith is a synonym for the Gospel.

23. The apostles established a formal leadership in the several churches by the selection of elders, after the pattern of the Palestine churches (see note on 11:30). The method of choice is not clear, for the Greek word may describe either an election by the congregation or an appointment by the apostles. It does not designate formal ordination, as the AV suggests. The language suggests that there were several elders in each local church; but the church in a given city may have consisted of a number of house congregations with an elder ruling over each group.

24,25. Pisidia. The southernmost region of the province of Galatia. Pamphylia. A small province between Galatia

**26.** And thence sailed to Antioch, from whence they had been recommended to the grace of God for the work which they fulfilled.

**27.** And when they were come, and had gathered the church together, they rehearsed all that God had done with them, and how he had opened the door of faith unto the Gentiles.

**28.** And there they abode long time with the disciples.

### CHAPTER 15

AND certain men which came down from Judea taught the brethren, *and said*, Except ye be circumcised after the manner of Moses, ye cannot be saved.

and the Mediterranean Sea, of which Perga was the capital and Attalia the chief seaport.

**26-28.** The apostles now returned to Antioch in Syria, whence they had been sent upon this missionary venture. It is significant that no report was sent to Jerusalem. The church in Antioch had become independent of the mother church. They **abode long time;** this is one of Luke's characteristically indefinite notes of time. Probably the missionary journey in Galatia lasted about a year and the apostles now stayed in Antioch another year.

B. Problem of the Gentile Church, and Council in Jerusalem. 15:1-35. The success of the Gentile mission now brought to a head the most important problem in the early church—that of the relationship between Jewish and Gentile believers and the terms of admission of Gentiles into the church. In the earliest days, the church consisted of Jews, and the Gentile mission was not foreseen in spite of our Lord's commission. Philip took the Gospel to the Samaritans, and Peter, after being prepared by God, overcame his Jewish scruples and took the Gospel to Cornelius, entering into full fellowship with Gentiles. The establishment of a Gentile church in Antioch and the success of the Gentile mission in Galatia now focused attention upon a problem that had to be solved.

In the Jerusalem church existed a party which insisted that unless Gentiles were **circumcised after the custom of Moses,** they could not be saved and received into the church. Verse 5 indicates that these were converts from among the Pharisees, who were the strictest sect of the Jews. This party looked upon Christianity as a movement within Judaism. They retained all of the practices and customs of the Law, simply adding the gospel of the death and the resurrection of Jesus as the promised Jewish Messiah. It is apparent that no Jewish believers gave up their Jewish practices when they became Christians. However, Pharisee converts insisted that Gentiles must also become Jews in order to become Christians.

This problem had already been raised in the church. If, as seems likely, Gal 2:1-10 describes the famine visit of Acts 11:27-30 [For a statement of the alternative position, that Gal 2:1-10 describes an aspect of the council meeting of Acts 15, see under Gal 2:1 ff.—Editor.], then the leaders at Jerusalem had approved in

**2.** When therefore Paul and Barnabas had no small dissension and disputation with them, they determined that Paul and Barnabas, and certain other of them, should go up to Jerusalem unto the apostles and elders about this question.

principle Paul's mission to the Gentiles and did not insist upon circumcision for Gentile converts. Peter was in agreement with this policy; for some time later, when he came to Antioch, he showed that he had learned the lesson taught him by his vision from heaven, and freely entered into table fellowship with Gentile converts (Gal 2:11,12). Two different churches now existed: the Jewish church in Jerusalem, in which Jewish Christians were free to continue the practice of the OT Law, but as Jews and not as Christians; and the Gentile church in Antioch, where none of the Jewish ceremonial requirements were practiced. Peter approved of Gentile freedom from the Law; and when he was in a Gentile environment, he laid aside his Jewish practices for the sake of Christian fellowship.

The "right wing" party in Jerusalem saw something which was not evident to Peter: that the growth of the Gentile church must mean the inevitable end of the Jewish church. As intercourse increased between the two churches, Jewish Christians would have to follow Peter's example and lay aside their Jewish practices. Therefore, when certain men came from James to Antioch (Gal 2:12), they accused Peter of forsaking the Law and pointed out to him that his course of action meant the end of Judaism. Peter had not realized the consequences of his action. Therefore he withdrew from table fellowship with the Gentiles to reflect upon the situation. This immediately caused a breach in the church at Antioch. Paul recognized at once the implication of Peter's withdrawal; it meant nothing less than two separate churches—one Jewish and the other Gentile. Either Jewish Christians would have to lay aside Jewish practices and eat with Gentiles, or Gentiles would have to accept the entire law of Moses; otherwise there would be a divided church. Paul was quite willing for Jews as Jews to practice the law of Moses. But he insisted that when Jewish Christians came into a Gentile church, they must lay aside their Jewish scruples and enter into free fellowship with Gentiles. A divided church was unthinkable, and for Gentiles to accept the Law meant the end of salvation by grace. Paul's viewpoint apparently prevailed, but those of the Jewish party in Jerusalem were not satisfied. They came to Antioch again and insisted that Gentiles be circumcised to become Christians.

**2.** This caused such dissension that

3. And being brought on their way by the church, they passed through Phenice and Samaria, declaring the conversion of the Gentiles: and they caused great joy unto all the brethren.

4. And when they were come to Jerusalem, they were received of the church, and of the apostles and elders, and they declared all things that God had done with them.

5. But there rose up certain of the sect of the Pharisees which believed, saying, That it was needful to circumcise them, and to command *them* to keep the law of Moses.

6. And the apostles and elders came together for to consider of this matter.

7. And when there had been much disputing, Peter rose up, and said unto them, Men *and* brethren, ye know how that a good while ago God made choice among us, that the Gentiles by my mouth should hear the word of the gospel, and believe.

8. And God, which knoweth the hearts, bare them witness, giving them the Holy Ghost, even as *he did* unto us;

9. And put no difference between us and them, purifying their hearts by faith.

10. Now therefore why tempt ye God, to put a yoke upon the neck of the disciples, which neither our fathers nor we were able to bear?

11. But we believe that through the grace of the Lord Jesus Christ we shall be saved, even as they.

12. Then all the multitude kept silence, and gave audience to Barnabas and Paul, declaring what miracles and wonders God had wrought among the Gentiles by them.

13. And after they had held their peace, James answered, saying, Men *and* brethren, hearken unto me:

14. Simeon hath declared how God at the first did visit the Gentiles, to take out of them a people for his name.

the church at Antioch found it necessary to have the issue decided in Jerusalem. Therefore a delegation was appointed to go to the apostles and elders and achieve a settlement of the question. 3. We know nothing about the churches in Phoenicia. It was not Luke's purpose to relate a full history of the early church but only to trace the main lines of its rise and development.

4,5. The church in Jerusalem welcomed the delegation and listened to their story of the success of the Gentile church in Antioch and the Gentile mission in Galatia. Then criticism was voiced by converts from the Pharisees, who maintained their position that Gentile converts must become Jews and accept the law of Moses. 6. This led to a formal conference of the apostles and elders with the delegation from Antioch. Verses 12,22, however, show that the church as a whole participated in the decision.

7-9. Paul's rebuke of Peter in Antioch (Gal 2:11) had been effective. So now Peter, as leader of the apostles, reverted to the position taken after his mission to Cornelius — that God had accepted the Gentiles as Gentiles by faith alone and not on Jewish terms. 10,11. A yoke in Jewish thought does not necessarily mean a burden but designates an obligation. Here Peter asserts that Jewish legalism was an obligation and a burden that the Jews were unable to bear. In contrast to the burdensomeness of the Law, salvation is through grace both for Gentiles and for Jews. When Jews keep the Law, it is not as a means of salvation.

12. The assembly next listened to the report of Barnabas and Paul as they related the wonderful works of God among the Gentiles.

13-16. The last and decisive word was spoken by James, the brother of the Lord, who had come to assume a position of leadership among the elders and apostles in Jerusalem. He referred to Peter's mission to Cornelius and showed that the Gentile mission was in God's plan by quoting a passage from Amos 9:11,12. Some Bible students have seen in this quotation God's program for the end of the age. After the Gentile mission God will build again the tabernacle of David by restoring the fortunes of the Jewish nation (Acts 15:16). The result of the restoration of Israel at the end of the age will be a further salvation of the Gentiles (v. 17). This interpretation sees here three stages in God's program: 1. The calling out of a people for his name

15. And to this agree the words of the prophets; as it is written,

16. After this I will return, and will build again the tabernacle of David, which is fallen down; and I will build again the ruins thereof, and I will set it up:

17. That the residue of men might seek after the Lord, and all the Gentiles, upon whom my name is called, saith the Lord, who doeth all these things.

18. Known unto God are all his works from the beginning of the world.

19. Wherefore my sentence is, that we trouble not them, which from among the Gentiles are turned to God:

20. But that we write unto them, that they abstain from pollutions of idols, and *from* fornication, and *from* things strangled, and *from* blood.

(the church age); 2. The restoration and salvation of Israel; 3. The final salvation of the Gentiles.

However, the quotation from Amos was cited to illustrate and give Scriptural support for the mission of Peter to the Gentiles (v. 14). Verse 14 refers to Peter's mission to Cornelius. **And to this,** i.e., that **God first visited the Gentiles, to take out of them a people for his name,** agrees the prophecy in Amos. If the salvation of **the residue of men** (v. 17) refers to an event at the end of the age, the quotation from Amos has nothing to do with the present visitation of the Gentiles. But James quoted the OT for precisely this purpose — to show that the present salvation of the Gentiles is in God's predicted purpose and that the Gentiles should therefore be freely accepted into the church. **A people for his name** (v. 14). The usual OT word designating Israel as the true people of God. The Gentiles were now included in this **people.** The rebuilding of **the tabernacle of David** therefore must refer to the salvation of the believing Jewish remnant, the "Israel within Israel" (see Rom 9:8; 11:1-5). Scripture elsewhere makes it clear that promises to Israel are fulfilled in the Church. "They which are of faith, the same are the children of Abraham" (Gal 3:7). "He is a Jew, which is one inwardly; and circumcision is that of the heart, in the spirit and not in the letter" (Rom 2:28,29). This does not mean that Israel as a nation has no future. Romans 11 clearly affirms that all Israel shall be saved; God yet has a future for national Israel. However, this was not James' concern; he was citing Amos to prove that the successful mission to the Gentiles is in the purpose of God and was predicted by the OT.

19. James therefore rendered the judgment that they should no longer **trouble** the Gentiles by demanding that they accept circumcision and the law of Moses.

20. There remained another problem, that concerning fellowship between Jew and Gentile. Gentile practices were strongly offensive to Jews and to Jewish Christians. Therefore, as a modus vivendi and an expression of Christian charity, James recommended that Gentile Christians abstain from certain practices that would offend their Jewish brethren. **Pollutions of idols** is described in 15:29 as **meats offered to idols.** Often meat purchased in the market places had been sacrificed in pagan temples to heathen deities. The eating of such meat was of-

21. For Moses of old time hath in every city them that preach him, being read in the synagogues every sabbath day.

22. Then pleased it the apostles and elders, with the whole church, to send chosen men of their own company to Antioch with Paul and Barnabas; *namely*, Judas surnamed Barsabas, and Silas, chief men among the brethren:

23. And they wrote *letters* by them after this manner; The apostles and elders and brethren *send* greeting unto the brethren which are of the Gentiles in Antioch and Syria and Cilicia:

24. Forasmuch as we have heard, that certain which went out from us have troubled you with words, subverting your souls, saying, Ye *must* be circumcised, and keep the law; to whom we gave no *such* commandment:

25. It seemed good unto us, being assembled with one accord, to send chosen men unto you with our beloved Barnabas and Paul,

26. Men that have hazarded their lives for the name of our Lord Jesus Christ.

27. We have sent therefore Judas and Silas, who shall also tell *you* the same things by mouth.

28. For it seemed good to the Holy Ghost, and to us, to lay upon you no greater burden than these necessary things;

29. That ye abstain from meats offered to idols, and from blood, and from things strangled, and from fornication: from which if ye keep yourselves, ye shall do well. Fare ye well.

30. So when they were dismissed, they came to Antioch: and when they had gathered the multitude together, they delivered the epistle:

31. *Which* when they had read, they rejoiced for the consolation.

32. And Judas and Silas, being prophets also themselves, exhorted the brethren with many words, and confirmed *them*.

33. And after they had tarried *there* a space, they were let go in peace from the brethren unto the apostles.

34. Notwithstanding it pleased Silas to abide there still.

35. Paul also and Barnabas continued in Antioch, teaching and preaching the word of the Lord, with many others also.

36. And some days after, Paul said unto Barnabas, Let us go again and visit our brethren in every city where we have preached the word of the Lord, *and see* how they do.

fensive to sensitive Jewish consciences, for it smacked of taking part in the worship of the pagan deity. **Fornication** may refer either to immorality in general or to religious prostitution in pagan temples. Such immorality was so common among Gentiles that it merited special attention. **Things strangled.** Meats from which the blood had not been properly removed. Such meat was considered a delicacy by many pagans. **Blood** refers to the pagan custom of using blood as a food. The last two requirements involved the same offense, for the Jew who believed that "the life is in the blood" (Lev 17:11) regarded the eating of any blood particularly offensive. This decree was issued to the Gentile churches not as a means of salvation but as a basis for fellowship, in the spirit of Paul's exhortation that those who were strong in faith should be willing to restrict their liberty in such matters rather than offend the weaker brother (Rom 14:1 ff.; I Cor 8:1 ff.).

**21.** Abstinence of Gentile Christians from practices offensive to Jews was required by the fact that Jews were to be **found in every city,** and whether in the Palestinian or in the Diaspora **synagogues, Moses . . . is read . . . every sabbath day** and the requirements of the Law strictly observed.

**22. Judas called Barsabbas.** Apparently a brother of Joseph called Barsabbas (1:23). **Silas.** The *Silvanus* of I Thess 1:1; II Cor 1:19; I Pet 5:12, who later became Paul's companion.

**23.** The salutation of the letter designates two groups and not three: either **the apostles and elders, brethren;** or **the apostles and elder brethren. 24. Subverting your souls** is too strong a translation; *upsetting your minds* is better. The Jerusalem church as a whole did not back the position of the extreme Judaizing party.

**31-33.** The decision of the Jerusalem church and the letter to Antioch apparently solved the problem. After an interval of some time, Judas and Silas returned to Jerusalem, while Paul and Barnabas remained in Antioch.

**34.** This verse in the AV does not appear in the most ancient texts.

C. Second Mission: Asia Minor and Europe. 15:36—18:22. Luke now records the preparations for what we call the second missionary journey. After an indefinite period of time, Paul determined to revisit and to confirm the churches already established. An unfortunate rupture occurred just then between Paul and

37. And Barnabas determined to take with them John, whose surname was Mark.

38. But Paul thought not good to take him with them, who departed from them from Pamphylia, and went not with them to the work.

39. And the contention was so sharp between them, that they departed asunder one from the other: and so Barnabas took Mark, and sailed unto Cyprus;

40. And Paul chose Silas, and departed, being recommended by the brethren unto the grace of God.

41. And he went through Syria and Cilicia, confirming the churches.

## CHAPTER 16

THEN came he to Derbe and Lystra: and, behold, a certain disciple was there, named Timotheus, the son of a certain woman, which was a Jewess, and believed; but his father *was* a Greek:

2. Which was well reported of by the brethren that were at Lystra and Iconium.

3. Him would Paul have to go forth with him; and took and circumcised him because of the Jews which were in those quarters: for they knew all that his father was a Greek.

Barnabas. **Barnabas** wanted to take along John Mark, who had accompanied them on the first journey but had forsaken them when they had reached the mainland of Asia Minor, and had returned to Antioch. Paul regarded this as such a serious evidence of instability that he refused. The result was that Paul and Barnabas parted company. **Barnabas** and **John Mark sailed to Cyprus** to visit the churches established on the first missionary journey. Paul sent to Jerusalem for **Silas**, who had recently visited Antioch and in whom the apostle recognized a man of great promise.

41. Instead of traveling by ship, Paul and Silas set out by land toward Galatia. We know nothing about the establishment of **churches** in **Syria** and **Cilicia**, but we know from 15:23 that such churches existed. Possibly they were the result of Paul's work before he was brought to Antioch.

16:1. At **Lystra**, Paul selected **Timothy**, who had apparently been converted on the first mission, to be his traveling companion and one of his most important assistants. It was to this Timothy that Paul, toward the end of his life, wrote two of his last epistles. Timothy was of mixed parentage: his **father** was a **Greek** and his mother a **Jewess**. His mother, too, must have believed in Christ when Paul visited Lystra on his first journey; but his father, if he was still living, did not become a believer. We learn from II Tim 1:5 that the mother was named Eunice and that she had been a godly woman. 2. Since Paul's first visit, Timothy had gained a good reputation among the believers in Lystra and Iconium.

3. Because Timothy was half Jew, to make him acceptable as a traveling companion to the Jews to whom they would minister, Paul **circumcised** him. Although the young man had been brought up by his mother in the faith of the OT (II Tim 3:15), the Jews looked upon him as the uncircumcised son of a Greek. On the other hand, Gentiles would have regarded him as a Jew because of his religion. As a man professing adherence to the Jewish religion but who remained an uncircumcised Gentile, Timothy would have been offensive to the Jews Paul met in city after city and to whom he first preached the Gospel. Paul circumcised him as an act of expediency and not of religious principle. No conflict exists in the fact that Paul steadfastly refused to circumcise Titus (Gal 2:3); for Titus was altogether a Gentile, and there

4. And as they went through the cities, they delivered them the decrees for to keep, that were ordained of the apostles and elders which were at Jerusalem.

5. And so were the churches established in the faith, and increased in number daily.

6. Now when they had gone throughout Phrygia and the region of Galatia, and were forbidden of the Holy Ghost to preach the word in Asia,

7. After they were come to Mysia, they assayed to go into Bithynia: but the Spirit suffered them not.

8. And they passing by Mysia came down to Troas.

was no cultural reason to circumcise him. Timothy was circumcised therefore not as a Christian but as a Jew. This is an application of the principle that Paul expressed in I Cor 9:20: "And unto the Jews I became as a Jew, that I might gain the Jews; to them that are under the law, as under the law that I might gain them that are under the law." Where no essential principle was involved, Paul applied the principle of expediency and of conciliation in a way that many later Christians cannot understand or appreciate. It was probably at this time that Timothy was set aside for his mission by the elders in Lystra (I Tim 4:14).

6-8. These verses can be interpreted in two ways, depending on whether one follows the "North Galatian" or the "South Galatian" theory; and the interpretation depends upon the meaning of the word Galatia. (a) Galatia can refer to the northern part of the Roman province of Galatia, where the people of Gallic extraction lived. If so, Paul passed through the region of Phrygia (the cities of Iconium and Antioch) and planned to go directly westward to the great cities of the province of Asia. When the Holy Spirit forbade him to travel toward Asia, he turned north to Galatia, i.e., to the northern part of the Roman province. Then he traveled westward toward Mysia, which is the northermost part of the province of Asia, and attempted to go into the province of Bithynia, which lies between Galatia and the Black Sea. When he was hindered in this plan, he passed by Mysia and came to Troas on the Aegean Sea. There is one difficulty with this "North Galatian" theory: It seems strange that Luke gives no account of the formation of such important churches as those to which the Galatian epistle was written, and there is no positive evidence that such churches existed.

(b) Therefore it is easier to follow the "South Galatian" theory, which understands the region of Phrygia and Galatia not as two separate regions but as a single area—*Phrygian Galatia*. This would have been the southern part of the Roman province of Galatia, in which the region of Phrygia was located and which included the city of Antioch. According to this view, after visiting Derbe and Lystra, Paul entertained the purpose of moving through Phrygia and Galatia directly westward to the great cities of Asia. When the Holy Spirit showed by some undesignated means that this was inadvisable, Paul journeyed through

441

9. And a vision appeared to Paul in the night; There stood a man of Macedonia, and prayed him, saying, Come over into Macedonia, and help us.

10. And after he had seen the vision, immediately we endeavored to go into Macedonia, assuredly gathering that the Lord had called us for to preach the gospel unto them.

11. Therefore loosing from Troas, we came with a straight course to Samothracia, and the next *day* to Neapolis;

12. And from thence to Philippi, which is the chief city of that part of Macedonia, *and* a colony: and we were in that city abiding certain days.

13. And on the sabbath we went out of the city by a river side, where prayer was wont to be made; and we sat down, and spake unto the women which resorted *thither.*

14. And a certain woman named Lydia, a seller of purple, of the city of Thyatira, which worshipped God, heard *us:* whose heart the Lord opened, that she attended unto the things which were spoken of Paul.

*Phrygian Galatia* and then turned northward toward **Mysia** and **Bithynia.** When he approached Mysia, he tried to go into Bithynia, but again the Holy **Spirit** hindered him in this purpose. Consequently, he passed by **Mysia** and came to the seaport of **Troas.**

9. At **Troas** God revealed his purpose by sending a man who said, **Come over into Macedonia, and help us.** Such a request eliminates any problem as to how Paul recognized him as a man of Macedonia; his plea indicated his native country.

10. Here is the first of the famous "we" sections in Acts, where the narrative changes from the third person to the first person plural. The reason for this literary phenomenon has been vigorously debated, but the easiest explanation is that at this point the author of the record joined Paul and became his traveling companion. If this is the correct explanation, Luke joined Paul's company in Troas and traveled with him to Philippi (v. 16 is the end of this first "we" section), remaining in Philippi when Paul continued on his way.

11,12. Paul took ship from **Troas** and sailed to the island of **Samothrace** and the next day to **Neapolis,** which was the port of **Philippi,** a city lying ten miles inland. Macedonia was divided into four parts or **districts,** and Philippi was the chief city of one of these four districts. It was also a Roman **colony.** This word is a transliteration of the Latin term. "Colonies" were cities made up largely of Roman citizens and located at strategic points throughout the empire, which enjoyed special privileges, such as self-government, freedom from imperial taxation, and the same rights as citizens in Italy. Such a city was a little Rome far from the motherland.

13. Apparently there was no Jewish colony or synagogue in Philippi. Ten men were sufficient to constitute a synagogue. There was, however, an unofficial meeting place of a group of Jewish women and a number of God-fearers outside the city by the river. According to the best text, **where prayer was wont to be made** should be *where we supposed there was a place of prayer.* The word for *a place of prayer* is used in Jewish writings as a synonym for "synagogue." **We sat down.** The normal position for a Jewish teacher.

14. **Lydia** may be a proper name, or it may mean "the Lydian," designating the region in which Thyatira was situated.

15. And when she was baptized, and her household, she besought *us*, saying, If ye have judged me to be faithful to the Lord, come into my house, and abide *there*. And she constrained us.

16. And it came to pass, as we went to prayer, a certain damsel possessed with a spirit of divination met us, which brought her masters much gain by soothsaying:

17. The same followed Paul and us, and cried, saying, These men are the servants of the most high God, which show unto us the way of salvation.

18. And this did she many days. But Paul, being grieved, turned and said to the spirit, I command thee in the name of Jesus Christ to come out of her. And he came out the same hour.

19. And when her masters saw that the hope of their gains was gone, they caught Paul and Silas, and drew *them* into the market place unto the rulers,

20. And brought them to the magistrates, saying, These men, being Jews, do exceedingly trouble our city,

21. And teach customs, which are not lawful for us to receive, neither to observe, being Romans.

22. And the multitude rose up together against them; and the magistrates rent off their clothes, and commanded to beat *them*.

23. And when they had laid many stripes upon them, they cast *them* into prison, charging the jailer to keep them safely:

This area was famous for the manufacture and use of **purple** dye, and Lydia had brought this business to Philippi. This woman was a Gentile who had accepted the highest elements in Judaism. **15.** As a woman of means, Lydia had a family and servants, who followed her example in professing faith and being baptized. The phrase **household** may or may not include small children.

**16.** A spirit of divination. Literally, *a python spirit*. The priestess of Apollo at Delphi was called *python,* and the word was extended to soothsayers. A person having a python spirit was thought to be inspired by Apollo, who was associated with oracles. This girl was demon-possessed, and her uncontrolled utterances were regarded as the utterances of a god. Her owners made money for themselves by using her to tell fortunes. Just as a demon had recognized Jesus as the Holy One (Mk 1:24), so this demon recognized the divine power in Paul and his companions. **17. The most high God.** A designation used by pagans to indicate the supreme Jewish deity. **The way of salvation.** A common expression in Hellenistic religion, and a matter of great concern to many pagans.

**19.** Paul and Silas were seized not because they were preaching the Gospel but because they had disrupted a profitable business. Luke and Timothy for the time drop out of sight. Luke was concerned to trace the relations of Roman officials with the emissaries of the Gospel and to show that hostility came from other than official sources. **20.** The government of a Roman colony was vested in two **magistrates,** sometimes called "praetors." The Greek word translated "magistrate" is the equivalent of the Latin *praetor.*

**21.** Roman law permitted Jews to practice their own religion, but it forbade the propagating of foreign religions among Roman citizens. Paul and Silas were not recognized as Christians but as Jews who transgressed the prerogatives that Roman law allowed them.

**22,23.** No careful investigation was made of these charges. Mob action was roused, to which the magistrates yielded. Paul and Silas were stripped of their clothing and beaten. Verse 35 refers to the **sergeants** (AV) or *police* (RSV). This word designates lictors who attended the magistrates. Each lictor carried a bundle of rods with an axe inserted among them, symbolizing the power to inflict capital punishment. Paul and Silas were now

24. Who, having received such a charge, thrust them into the inner prison, and made their feet fast in the stocks.

25. And at midnight Paul and Silas prayed, and sang praises unto God: and the prisoners heard them.

26. And suddenly there was a great earthquake, so that the foundations of the prison were shaken: and immediately all the doors were opened, and every one's bands were loosed.

27. And the keeper of the prison awaking out of his sleep, and seeing the prison doors open, he drew out his sword, and would have killed himself, supposing that the prisoners had been fled.

28. But Paul cried with a loud voice, saying, Do thyself no harm: for we are all here.

29. Then he called for a light, and sprang in, and came trembling, and fell down before Paul and Silas,

30. And brought them out, and said, Sirs, what must I do to be saved?

31. And they said, Believe on the Lord Jesus Christ, and thou shalt be saved, and thy house.

32. And they spake unto him the word of the Lord, and to all that were in his house.

33. And he took them the same hour of the night, and washed *their* stripes; and was baptized, he and all his, straightway.

34. And when he had brought them into his house, he set meat before them, and rejoiced, believing in God with all his house.

35. And when it was day, the magistrates sent the sergeants, saying, Let those men go.

36. And the keeper of the prison told this saying to Paul, The magistrates have sent to let you go: now therefore depart, and go in peace.

37. But Paul said unto them, They have beaten us openly uncondemned, being Romans, and have cast *us* into prison; and now do they thrust us out privily? nay verily; but let them come themselves and fetch us out.

38. And the sergeants told these words unto the magistrates: and they feared, when they heard that they were Romans.

39. And they came and besought them, and brought *them* out, and desired *them* to depart out of the city.

beaten by the rods carried by these lictors. Paul tells us that he suffered this indignity on three different occasions (II Cor 11:25). This is the only such incident that Luke records. Paul and Silas were then locked up in the **inner prison** with their feet securely fastened in wooden stocks. The stocks could be so adjusted as to force a man's legs wide apart in a painful position.

26. Ramsay says that anyone who has seen a Turkish prison would not wonder at the effect of this earthquake. The door was sprung open and the stocks loosened from the walls. 27. When the jailer was awakened and discovered the prison doors open, he assumed that the prisoners had fled. He determined to follow the only honorable course of action left to him and commit suicide. 28. Although there was no light, Paul from the inner prison could see the outline of the jailer in the doorway, and he understood what the man was about to do. His call saved the jailer's life.

30. It is not clear what the jailer meant by his question about salvation. Had he listened to the preaching of Paul and Silas? Had he heard the fortuneteller declare that these men proclaimed the way of salvation? In any case, God blessed his modicum of faith, and he and his household were baptized. 34. A Roman jailer was free to treat his prisoners as he desired so long as he produced them upon demand. This jailer now received Paul and Silas as his guests.

35. In the morning the magistrates decided that the beating and the night's imprisonment were sufficient punishment for these two Jewish troublemakers. So they sent the lictors to the prison with a command that Paul and Silas should be released and ushered out of town.

37. Because Roman citizens were immune from certain forms of punishment, Paul now pointed out that his legal rights as a Roman citizen had been flagrantly violated. He and Silas had been punished without proper legal procedure, **uncondemned.** Paul insisted that the magistrates now treat them with the courtesy due to Roman citizens if they wished them to leave town. Paul doubtless took this position not for self-vindication but that the small Christian community in Philippi might not be left with a shadow hanging over it.

38,39. The magistrates were smitten with deep concern for their improper conduct, for it could conceivably have disqualified them from holding office.

**40.** And they went out of the prison, and entered into *the house of* Lydia: and when they had seen the brethren, they comforted them, and departed.

## CHAPTER 17

NOW when they had passed through Amphipolis and Apollonia, they came to Thessalonica, where was a synagogue of the Jews:

**2.** And Paul, as his manner was, went in unto them, and three sabbath days reasoned with them out of the Scriptures,

**3.** Opening and alleging, that Christ must needs have suffered, and risen again from the dead; and that this Jesus, whom I preach unto you, is Christ.

**4.** And some of them believed, and consorted with Paul and Silas; and of the devout Greeks a great multitude, and of the chief women not a few.

They therefore **apologized** (RSV) to Paul and Silas; and although they realized that they could not expel these Roman citizens from the city, they begged them to depart. **40.** The apostles accepted the apology, and after visiting the believers in the house of Lydia and encouraging them, they took their leave. Timothy accompanied Paul and Silas, but Luke remained in Philippi. He appears in 20:5 at the beginning of the second "we" section.

**17:1.** Paul, Silas, and Timothy journeyed westward along the great military road called the Via Egnatia. The fact that they **passed through Amphipolis** and **Apollonia** indicates that Paul was following the definite plan of planting the Gospel in strategic cities. He did not aim simply to preach the Gospel wherever he could find an audience. Rather, he was a missionary statesman with a program for establishing churches in key centers from which the surrounding countryside could be evangelized. **Thessalonica.** The chief city and capital of the province of Macedonia. In the epistle later written to the Thessalonian church, Paul indicated that the Gospel was sounded forth from them not only in Macedonia and in Achaia but in every place (I Thess 1:8).

**2.** The apostle followed his usual custom of preaching the Gospel first in the Jewish synagogue. This he did for **three** consecutive **sabbath days.** In the Thessalonian correspondence, he recalls that he engaged in his trade of tent-making that he might not be a burden to the believers (I Thess 2:9; II Thess 3:7-12). The three weeks, therefore, is not meant to indicate the extent of Paul's mission in Thessalonica.

**3.** Paul's method of preaching consisted of **opening** the OT and **proving** that **the Messiah must suffer and rise from the dead;** and that the Messiah is in fact **Jesus,** whom he was proclaiming. **Alleging** (AV). Literally, *setting alongside.* Paul cited OT Scriptures and set alongside of them the historical fulfillment in Jesus of Nazareth. The Jews did not know how the Messiah could be both a conquering king and a suffering servant, and they therefore were not accustomed to apply the predictions of suffering to the Messiah.

**4.** As usual, a few Jews were **persuaded** (RSV; a better translation than AV *believed*), and they cast their lot with Paul and Silas. But most of the converts came from the fairly large group of God-fearing Gentiles.

5. But the Jews which believed not, moved with envy, took unto them certain lewd fellows of the baser sort, and gathered a company, and set all the city on an uproar, and assaulted the house of Jason, and sought to bring them out to the people.

6. And when they found them not, they drew Jason and certain brethren unto the rulers of the city, crying, These that have turned the world upside down are come hither also;

7. Whom Jason hath received: and these all do contrary to the decrees of Caesar, saying that there is another king, *one* Jesus.

8. And they troubled the people and the rulers of the city, when they heard these things.

9. And when they had taken security of Jason, and of the others, they let them go.

**5.** The Jews went among the loafers hanging around the streets and stirred up a mob. **Lewd** (AV) simply means "wicked" or "evil." **Jason**, the Greek equivalent for Joshua, was apparently a believing Jew who had opened his house to Paul and Silas. The mob attacked Jason's house, intending to drag Paul and Silas out to trial. **People.** The general assembly of Greek people.

**6.** Jason had gotten wind of the mob and had removed Paul and Silas to safety. Instead of the evangelists, therefore, Jason and several brethren were brought before the city officials. **Rulers of the city.** Literally, *politarchs.* Since this term was long unknown in Greek literature, Luke was accused by some scholars of a gross inaccuracy. Inscriptions have now been found, however, which show that this term was the correct technical designation of city magistrates in cities of Macedonia. A list of such politarchs has been found engraved in a stone in an arch coming from the first century A.D. in Thessalonica.

**7.** Jason was charged with harboring men whose religious teaching had seditious political implications, for they proclaimed that **Jesus** was a **king** who would be a rival to the Roman emperor. **King.** The common Greek word to designate the Roman emperor (Jn 19:15; I Pet 2:13,17). This incident illustrates why the epistles of Paul as well as the Acts have relatively little to say about the kingdom of God. Much has been made of the fact that Paul almost never designates Jesus as King but rather calls him Lord. It has sometimes been said that Jesus is King of Israel but Lord of the Church, and that these two are entirely different concepts. This incident suggests that Paul laid little emphasis upon the kingship of Jesus and the kingdom of God because these ideas, familiar and precious to Jews, were subject to misunderstanding by Romans and suggested a rival political power. Such sedition was the charge brought against Jesus by Pilate (Lk 23:2). Rome was tolerant of many things but not of suspected sedition. Therefore Paul proclaimed Jesus to the Gentiles as Lord—a religious concept that was both familiar and acceptable to them and carried no political implications.

**8,9.** The politarchs were disturbed by this charge, but since Paul and Silas were not to be found, they settled the matter by making Jason and his companions responsible that no further breach of the peace should occur, and took a bond from

10. And the brethren immediately sent away Paul and Silas by night unto Berea: who coming *thither* went into the synagogue of the Jews.

11. These were more noble than those in Thessalonica, in that they received the word with all readiness of mind, and searched the Scriptures daily, whether those things were so.

12. Therefore many of them believed; also of honorable women which were Greeks, and of men, not a few.

13. But when the Jews of Thessalonica had knowledge that the word of God was preached of Paul at Berea, they came thither also, and stirred up the people.

14. And then immediately the brethren sent away Paul to go as it were to the sea: but Silas and Timotheus abode there still.

15. And they that conducted Paul brought him unto Athens: and receiving a commandment unto Silas and Timotheus for to come to him with all speed, they departed.

16. Now while Paul waited for them at Athens, his spirit was stirred in him, when he saw the city wholly given to idolatry.

17. Therefore disputed he in the synagogue with the Jews, and with the devout persons, and in the market daily with them that met with him.

18. Then certain philosophers of the Epicureans, and of the Stoics, encountered him. And some said, What will this babbler say? other some, He seemeth to be a setter forth of strange gods: because he preached unto them Jesus, and the resurrection.

them which would be forfeited in case of further trouble. This is probably the satanic hindrance to which Paul refers in I Thess 2:18, which made it impossible for him to return to Thessalonica and continue his ministry.

**10,11. Beroea** was some fifty miles to the west of Thessalonica. At this point Paul and Silas left the main military road and headed southward toward the province of Achaia. Here the Jews were not so prejudiced as those in Thessalonica. They showed openness of mind to test Paul's message by the OT Scriptures in order to decide whether or not it was true.

**13-15.** When hostile **Jews of Thessalonica** came to Beroea and stirred up opposition, some of the brethren accompanied Paul down to the seacoast and then to **Athens. As it were.** Rather, *as far as.* Silas and **Timotheus** did not accompany Paul to Athens but remained behind in Beroea under instructions to rejoin Paul as soon as possible in Athens.

**16. Athens** was not a city of great political or commercial importance, but it was the world's most famous intellectual center. Even young men of Rome often went to Athens for their university training. Paul's missionary strategy did not include the evangelizing of Athens. But as he waited there for Silas and Timothy, he was deeply moved by the evidence of **idolatry** he saw. The famous temples in Athens were works of art unsurpassed for beauty, but Paul saw behind the beauty the darkness of idolatry. **17.** Therefore he **argued** in the synagogue with the **Jews** and **devout** God-fearers, and he also engaged in discussion those whom he happened to meet in the market place.

**18.** Followers of the two most influential schools of philosophy of that day heard his message. The **Epicureans,** named after their founder Epicurus (341—270 B.C.), believed that the gods existed but had no interest whatsoever in the welfare of men. The chief end of life, the Epicureans held, was pleasure, which was to be sought in a happy and tranquil life, free from pain or trouble or fear, especially the fear of death. The **Stoics,** founded by Zeno (c. 300 B.C.), believed that God was the world's soul which indwelt all things, and that the happy life was that lived in accordance with nature. Since God was in all men, all men were brothers. Many Stoics were men of high moral principle. To these philosophers, Paul sounded like a **bab-**

19. And they took him, and brought him unto Areopagus, saying, May we know what this new doctrine, whereof thou speakest, *is?*

20. For thou bringest certain strange things to our ears: we would know therefore what these things mean.

21. (For all the Athenians, and strangers which were there, spent their time in nothing else, but either to tell or to hear some new thing.)

22. Then Paul stood in the midst of Mars' hill, and said, *Ye* men of Athens, I perceive that in all things ye are too superstitious.

23. For as I passed by, and beheld your devotions, I found an altar with this inscription, TO THE UNKNOWN GOD. Whom therefore ye ignorantly worship, him declare I unto you.

24. God that made the world and all things therein, seeing that he is Lord of heaven and earth, dwelleth not in temples made with hands;

25. Neither is worshipped with men's hands, as though he needed any thing, seeing he giveth to all life, and breath, and all things;

26. And hath made of one blood all nations of men for to dwell on all the face of the earth, and hath determined the times before appointed, and the bounds of their habitation;

bler. This word, which is literally *seed-picker*, was used to describe one who picked up scraps of undigested knowledge. **Jesus and the resurrection.** To the Greek ear, Jesus and *Anastasis* (**resurrection**) might sound like the names of a god and a goddess.

19. **Areopagus** may designate either the hill of Mars (v. 22, AV), which was situated between the market place and the Acropolis, or the council, which met in ancient times on Mars' Hill. Verses 22, 33 make the latter more probable. This council was not a trial court but a group of men who supervised religious and educational matters. Paul appeared before this council to give an account of his "philosophy," apparently to enable them to determine whether he should be permitted to teach in Athens. 21. The **Athenians** and the **foreign residents** were noted for their curiosity, being eager to know "the last new idea" (Lake and Cadbury). 22. **Mars' Hill** is the same word translated **Areopagus** in 17:19 and should be so rendered. Standing in the midst of this council, Paul attempted to make a point of contact by observing that they were **very religious.** This is a better translation than *too superstitious,* although both meanings are possible.

23. **Devotions** means *objects of worship.* No inscription has been found with the words **To an unknown God.** However, Greek writers tell us that altars to "unknown gods" were to be seen in Athens, and "if there were two or more altars each bearing an inscription 'to an unknown god,' these could well be referred to comprehensively as 'altars to unknown gods'" (F. F. Bruce, *Commentary*). In their religious zeal, the Athenians did not wish to omit from their worship any deity with whom they might not be acquainted. Paul asserted that there was indeed one whom they did not know, and this one he would declare to them.

24,25. Since this God is the creator of all things, Paul explained, and Lord of heaven and earth, he cannot dwell in any structure erected by men. Neither does he stand in need of anything that human service or worship can provide, for he himself is the source of all life.

26. Since God is the Creator, all men spring from a common source (AV **blood** is not in the best texts), and all men are dependent on him. He has provided them with the earth for a dwelling place and the **seasons** to supply their sustenance. This is the same thought that appears in 14:17 in the speech to the Greeks at

27. That they should seek the Lord, if haply they might feel after him, and find him, though he be not far from every one of us:

28. For in him we live, and move, and have our being; as certain also of your own poets have said, For we are also his offspring.

29. Forasmuch then as we are the offspring of God, we ought not to think that the Godhead is like unto gold, or silver, or stone, graven by art and man's device.

30. And the times of this ignorance God winked at; but now commandeth all men every where to repent:

31. Because he hath appointed a day, in the which he will judge the world in righteousness by *that* man whom he hath ordained; *whereof* he hath given assurance unto all *men*, in that he hath raised him from the dead.

Lystra. **Times** (AV) is the same word translated *seasons* in 14:17. **27.** The goodness of God manifested in the created world should lead men to seek God (see Rom 1:20).

**28.** The Lord is both a transcendent God who cannot be identified with his creation, and also the creating and the sustaining One, upon whom all men are dependent for their very physical life. The apostle illustrated this by words that appear to come from a Cretan poet named Epimenides. He then referred to the poet Aratus from his own country, Cilicia. Paul meant that all men are God's offspring in the sense that they are His creatures and dependent on Him for life. There is a Biblical doctrine of the universal fatherhood of God and brotherhood of man resting upon the fact of common creation rather than upon a spiritual relation, as this passage indicates. **29.** Since God is the creator of men, he must at least be greater than men. Therefore to identify the Deity with something man has made or imagined is the height of folly and the depth of sin (see Rom 1:22,23).

**30,31.** God **overlooked** (not *winked at*, AV) these **times of ignorance,** but has now given to men full knowledge of himself. Romans 3:25 refers to this patience of God for "the sins done aforetime," and Acts 14:16 alludes to the same patience. But God's patience will not last forever; because of the full knowledge now disclosed in Christ, he commands men to repent, and he has **appointed a day** when he will **judge the world in righteousness** by the man in whom this new light has come. The **pledge** (*assurance*) of this is provided by the resurrection of Jesus from the dead.

It has often been maintained that in Athens Paul attempted the intellectual approach and tried to be a philosopher among the philosophers rather than preaching the simple gospel of Jesus Christ. This is not a valid criticism, for the heart of the early Christian proclamation was the resurrection of Jesus Christ, and this was Paul's central emphasis in Athens. No message could have been more unpalatable to Greek philosophers than that of bodily resurrection from the dead and a day of judgment. A message of personal immortality in a disembodied state would have been acceptable, but the assertion of bodily resurrection was "untactful." Paul did not water down his gospel; he proclaimed the

**32.** And when they heard of the resurrection of the dead, some mocked: and others said, We will hear thee again of this *matter*.

**33.** So Paul departed from among them.

**34.** Howbeit certain men clave unto him, and believed: among the which *was* Dionysius the Areopagite, and a woman named Damaris, and others with them.

## CHAPTER 18

AFTER these things Paul departed from Athens, and came to Corinth;

**2.** And found a certain Jew named Aquila, born in Pontus, lately come from Italy, with his wife Priscilla, (because that Claudius had commanded all Jews to depart from Rome,) and came unto them.

truth that struck at the very heart of Greek philosophy.

**32-34.** Some ridiculed Paul's message; others were willing to discuss it further. This ended the hearing, and Paul went out from among the council men. He was not altogether without success, for some joined him, confessing faith in Christ. One believer was a member of the Areopagus itself. But there were few converts in Athens. Not only is there no reference to a church in Athens, but "the firstfruits of Achaia" (I Cor 16:15) were in Corinth and not in Athens. There is no adequate reason to feel that Paul's failure was due to a false method that he later abandoned; it was due rather to the character of the Athenians themselves. Paul had not planned any evangelistic or missionary program in that city.

**18:1.** The apostle **left Athens** for **Corinth,** where he awaited the arrival of Timothy and Silas from Macedonia. Corinth was the capital of the Roman province of Achaia. It was situated on an isthmus commanding the sea routes to east and west as well as the land routes to north and south. It was a prosperous commercial center, famous for its cosmopolitan character, and notorious for its immorality. According to Strabo, the temple of Aphrodite had a thousand religious prostitutes. The reputation of Corinth is illustrated by the fact that the verb "to act like a Corinthian" was used of practicing fornication, and the phrase "Corinthian girls" designated harlots. Little wonder that the Corinthian church was later plagued by problems of immorality.

**2.** Suetonius (*Life of Claudius* 25.4) tells us that the Jews were indulging in constant riots at the instigation "of Chrestus," and Claudius therefore banished them from Rome in A.D. 49. It is possible that *Chrestus* (meaning "the useful one") is a Roman misunderstanding of *Christus*, a term that was meaningless to Romans. If so, this means that the gospel of Christ was being preached in the Jewish synagogues in Rome and was meeting such strenuous resistance that Claudius ordered all Jews to leave the city. It is not clear whether **Aquila** and **Priscilla** (called Prisca in the epistles of Paul) were believers before they left Rome. Since nothing is said of Paul's preaching the Gospel to them, they probably had become Christians in Rome. We know nothing about the origin of the Roman church. These two Jews came to Corinth and set themselves up in their

3. And because he was of the same craft, he abode with them, and wrought: (for by their occupation they were tentmakers.)

4. And he reasoned in the synagogue every sabbath, and persuaded the Jews and the Greeks.

5. And when Silas and Timotheus were come from Macedonia, Paul was pressed in the spirit, and testified to the Jews *that* Jesus *was* Christ.

6. And when they opposed themselves, and blasphemed, he shook *his* raiment, and said unto them, Your blood *be* upon your own heads; I *am* clean: from henceforth I will go unto the Gentiles.

7. And he departed thence, and entered into a certain *man's* house, named Justus, *one* that worshipped God, whose house joined hard to the synagogue.

8. And Crispus, the chief ruler of the synagogue, believed on the Lord with all his house; and many of the Corinthians hearing believed, and were baptized.

9. Then spake the Lord to Paul in the night by a vision, Be not afraid, but speak, and hold not thy peace:

10. For I am with thee, and no man shall set on thee to hurt thee: for I have much people in this city.

11. And he continued *there* a year and six months, teaching the word of God among them.

trade. 3. **Tentmakers.** Either manufacturers of heavy cloth from goats' hair, from which tents and other articles were made; or "leather workers" (Lake and Cadbury). It was customary for Jewish rabbis not to receive pay for their teaching, and therefore Paul, who had been reared as a rabbi, had learned the trade of tentmaking. The apostle did not at once launch into the evangelization of Corinth but joined Aquila and Priscilla in practicing his trade during the week. 4. The Sabbaths he devoted to preaching in the synagogue. An inscription has been found in Corinth dating from the early first century, which reads, "Synagogue of the Hebrews."

5. Paul apparently planned to return from Corinth to Macedonia and continue his ministry in Thessalonica and Beroea after the arrival of Silas and Timothy. The Epistles tell us more about the movements of these two than does Acts. Paul had left them in Beroea with instructions to join him in Athens as soon as possible (17:15). They did, in fact, join Paul in Athens (I Thess 3:1), apparently bringing word that it was not safe for him to return to Macedonia. He therefore sent Timothy back to Thessalonica and Silas to some other city in Macedonia, possibly Philippi. Now Silas and Timothy joined him again in Corinth; and when they reported that Paul could not return to Macedonia, he devoted himself with fresh vigor to the evangelization of Corinth. **Pressed in the spirit,** according to the best texts, should be translated either *was constrained by the word,* or *was occupied in preaching.* Paul's message was that **Jesus was the Messiah.**

7. Next door to the Jewish synagogue was a house owned by one **Titus Justus,** a Gentile "God-fearer" (cf. note on 10:2) who attended the synagogue. He opened his house to Paul to preach the Gospel when the apostle left the synagogue. 8. The conversion of **Crispus, the ruler of the synagogue** (see 13:15) together with his family must have been a blow to the Jews and given a great impetus to Paul's mission. The baptism of Crispus is mentioned in I Cor 1:14.

9-11. Apparently Paul had not been sure that it was the Lord's will for him to devote himself to evangelizing Corinth. But God now reassured him by a **vision,** urging him **not to be silent** and assuring him that his mission would be attended with divine blessing and success. Paul therefore spent more time in Corinth than

12. And when Gallio was the deputy of Achaia, the Jews made insurrection with one accord against Paul, and brought him to the judgment seat,

13. Saying, This *fellow* persuadeth men to worship God contrary to the law.

14. And when Paul was now about to open *his* mouth, Gallio said unto the Jews, If it were a matter of wrong or wicked lewdness, O *ye* Jews, reason would that I should bear with you:

15. But if it be a question of words and names, and *of* your law, look ye *to it;* for I will be no judge of such *matters.*

16. And he drave them from the judgment seat.

17. Then all the Greeks took Sosthenes, the chief ruler of the synagogue, and beat *him* before the judgment seat. And Gallio cared for none of those things.

18. And Paul *after this* tarried *there* yet a good while, and then took his leave of the brethren, and sailed thence into Syria, and with him Priscilla and Aquila; having shorn *his* head in Cenchrea: for he had a vow.

was his custom, teaching the word of God for a year and a half

12. At the end of this period of time, a new **proconsul** came to the province of **Achaia,** of which Corinth was the capital city. Such provinces were under the supervision of the Senate and were governed by proconsuls, who filled a two-year term. **Gallio.** The brother of the philosopher Seneca. This provides the one relatively certain date in Paul's career, for Gallio arrived in Corinth in July of either 51 or 52, probably the former. Paul had already been in Corinth for a year and a half. **The Jews** seized the opportunity to try the mettle of this new proconsul, hoping that he might yield to their pressure. An unfavorable verdict from a Roman governor against Paul would have been effective not only in Corinth but throughout the entire province. Therefore they instigated a riot and brought Paul before Gallio's **judgment seat,** accusing the evangelist of propagating a religion that was **contrary** to the Roman law. Roman law recognized Judaism as a legitimate religion. The Jews accused Paul of teaching a new religion that was contrary to Judaism and therefore contrary to Roman law.

**14-16.** Gallio recognized that Paul was guilty of no **wrongdoing or vicious crime** (RSV). And the apostle's message, so far as he could tell, was only a variant form of Judaism and of interpretation of the Jewish law. Therefore he refused to render judgment against Paul and turned the accusers away.

**17.** The following incident reveals that there existed strong anti-Jewish feelings among the people. **Sosthenes** had succeeded Crispus as **ruler of the synagogue,** and the people set upon him and **beat him** in the presence of Gallio. That **Gallio cared for none of these things** does not mean that he was indifferent to spiritual values but that he deliberately *paid no attention* (RSV) to this mob action, which was technically a breach of the peace.

**18.** Paul now stayed in Corinth an indefinite period of time (**many days**), beyond the year and a half. Before leaving Corinth, he assumed a Nazarite vow (see Num 6:1-21) which was an OT act of thanksgiving or of dedication to God. During the period of the vow, the devotee allowed his hair to grow uncut, and at the end of the period he cut his hair. It is significant that while Paul steadfastly refused to permit the Law to be imposed on Gentiles, he himself, as a Jew, con-

**19.** And he came to Ephesus, and left them there: but he himself entered into the synagogue, and reasoned with the Jews.
**20.** When they desired *him* to tarry longer time with them, he consented not;
**21.** But bade them farewell, saying, I must by all means keep this feast that cometh in Jerusalem: but I will return again unto you, if God will. And he sailed from Ephesus.
**22.** And when he had landed at Caesarea, and gone up, and saluted the church, he went down to Antioch.
**23.** And after he had spent some time *there*, he departed, and went over *all* the country of Galatia and Phrygia in order, strengthening all the disciples.
**24.** And a certain Jew named Apollos, born at Alexandria, an eloquent man, *and* mighty in the Scriptures, came to Ephesus.
**25.** This man was instructed in the way of the Lord; and being fervent in the spirit, he spake and taught diligently the things of the Lord, knowing only the baptism of John.
**26.** And he began to speak boldly in the synagogue: whom when Aquila and Priscilla had heard, they took him unto *them*, and expounded unto him the way of God more perfectly.
**27.** And when he was disposed to pass into Achaia, the brethren wrote, exhorting the disciples to receive him: who, when he was come, helped them much which had believed through grace:
**28.** For he mightily convinced the Jews, *and that* publicly, showing by the Scriptures that Jesus was Christ.

tinued to practice many of its demands. As he came to Cenchrea, the eastern port of Corinth, on his way to Syria and Palestine, the time of his vow elapsed, and he therefore cut his hair.

**19-21.** Aquila and Priscilla separated from Paul at Ephesus and took up residence there. Paul engaged in a short ministry in the synagogue but refused to tarry. The words, I must by all means keep this feast that cometh in Jerusalem, are lacking in the majority of texts; but apart from this explanation, the reason for Paul's haste in returning to Palestine is unexplained.

**22,23.** These two brief verses summarize a long journey from Ephesus to Palestine and return. The church that Paul greeted was most certainly the church in Jerusalem, although this city is not mentioned. However, Antioch had sponsored the mission, and he spent some time in that city.

D. The Third Mission: Asia Minor and Europe. 18:23–21:17. Paul returned to Asia on what we call his third missionary journey, first traveling through the Phrygia-Galatia region, which he had visited on his second missionary journey (16:6).

**24,25.** Luke now interrupts his record of Paul's travels to relate an incident that took place in Ephesus. Jewish pilgrims who came to Jerusalem during the days of our Lord's ministry heard John the Baptist preach that the Messiah was soon to come. They recognized in the person and the works of Jesus the fulfillment of the OT Messianic prophecies. Such pilgrims would carry back home a report of the preaching of John and the life and ministry of Jesus, although they would not know of his death and resurrection and the coming of the Holy Spirit at Pentecost. The eloquent Apollos had accepted this good news about Jesus; and since he was mighty in the Scriptures, he was able to present the Messiahship of Jesus effectively to Jews.

**26.** When Priscilla and Aquila met him in Ephesus, they enlightened him more accurately about the Christian gospel, which included Christ's death and resurrection and the coming of the Holy Spirit. Quite likely, Apollos was now baptized by Aquila in the name of Christ. **27,28.** When he wished to go to Achaia, Aquila and Priscilla sent letters of recommendation for him, and he was able to reinforce Paul's work in Corinth, refuting the Jews by proving that Jesus

## CHAPTER 19

AND it came to pass, that, while Apollos was at Corinth, Paul having passed through the upper coasts came to Ephesus; and finding certain disciples,

2. He said unto them, Have ye received the Holy Ghost since ye believed? And they said unto him, We have not so much as heard whether there be any Holy Ghost.

3. And he said unto them, Unto what then were ye baptized? And they said, Unto John's baptism.

4. Then said Paul, John verily baptized with the baptism of repentance, saying unto the people, that they should believe on him which should come after him, that is, on Christ Jesus.

5. When they heard *this*, they were baptized in the name of the Lord Jesus.

6. And when Paul had laid *his* hands upon them, the Holy Ghost came on them; and they spake with tongues, and prophesied.

7. And all the men were about twelve.

8. And he went into the synagogue, and spake boldly for the space of three months, disputing and persuading the things concerning the kingdom of God.

was the Messiah. That some of the Corinthian Christians formed a party claiming Apollos as their leader (I Cor 1:12; 3:4) was probably not due to any improper conduct on his part.

**19:1.** Paul traveled from Galatia to Ephesus, following the higher road, which was more direct than the trade route that followed the valleys through Colosse and Laodicea. In **Ephesus** he found disciples who had the same partial knowledge of Jesus as Apollos had had. There is no good reason for rejecting the usual meaning of disciples: believers in Jesus.

**2.** The apostle recognized that the disciples' knowledge of Jesus was incomplete. He therefore asked, **Did you receive the Holy Spirit when you believed?** (RSV) The Greek participle is *having believed*, and it is capable of being translated either *since ye believed* (AV) or *when you believed* (RSV). Since the Holy Spirit was usually received at the time of belief in Christ, the latter is preferable. Their answer must mean that they had heard no distinctively Christian truth about the Holy Spirit, for any one familiar with the OT would have heard about the Holy Spirit. **3,4.** These disciples had not heard about Pentecost. They knew only the message of John the Baptist—that men should receive a baptism of repentance in anticipation of the coming One, **Jesus.** The word *Christ* (AV) is not found in the best texts.

**6,7.** This does not describe a new Pentecost but an extension of the Pentecostal experience to include all believers. No special significance is to be sought in the imposition of Paul's hands for the bestowal of the Spirit. This experience, like that of Peter and John in Samaria (8:16,17), is designed to illustrate the oneness of the Church. Since believers are baptized by one Spirit into one body (I Cor 12:13), there can be no such "splinter groups" as these disciples of John outside the Church. It is beside the point to debate whether or not these disciples were Christians before Paul met them, even as it is futile to question whether the apostles were saved before Pentecost. They were disciples of Jesus but with an incomplete knowledge of the Gospel.

**8,9.** Ephesus was the capital of the Roman province of Asia, where the Roman proconsul resided. It was the chief Asian city in the promotion of emperor worship. It was also an important commercial and trade center, with a busy seaport, and it enjoyed great

9. But when divers were hardened, and believed not, but spake evil of that way before the multitude, he departed from them, and separated the disciples, disputing daily in the school of one Tyrannus.

10. And this continued by the space of two years; so that all they which dwelt in Asia heard the word of the Lord Jesus, both Jews and Greeks.

11. And God wrought special miracles by the hands of Paul:

12. So that from his body were brought unto the sick handkerchiefs or aprons, and the diseases departed from them, and the evil spirits went out of them.

13. Then certain of the vagabond Jews, exorcists, took upon them to call over them which had evil spirits the name of the Lord Jesus, saying, We adjure you by Jesus whom Paul preacheth.

14. And there were seven sons of *one* Sceva, a Jew, *and* chief of the priests, which did so.

15. And the evil spirit answered and said, Jesus I know, and Paul I know; but who are ye?

16. And the man in whom the evil spirit was leaped on them, and overcame them, and prevailed against them, so that they fled out of that house naked and wounded.

17. And this was known to all the Jews and Greeks also dwelling at Ephesus; and fear fell on them all, and the name of the Lord Jesus was magnified.

18. And many that believed came, and confessed, and showed their deeds.

19. Many of them also which used curious arts brought their books together, and burned them before all *men:* and they counted the price of them, and found *it* fifty thousand *pieces* of silver.

20. So mightily grew the word of God and prevailed.

prosperity. Paul's message in the synagogue about the kingdom of God can hardly refer to the establishment of the kingdom at the second coming of Christ. The Christian gospel announces that the blessings of the kingdom of God have come to men in advance in the person of Jesus the Messiah (see Col 1:13). Most of the Jews accepted Paul's message in Ephesus; only some (*divers*, AV) were hardened and did not believe. However, this handful had such influence over the congregation (RSV) that Paul turned aside from the synagogue and engaged a school or lecture room belonging to one Tyrannus. One text says that Paul taught from 11 A.M until 4 P.M., when business was ordinarily suspended. He practiced his trade during the morning and preached the Gospel during the heat of the day. The Way. A technical phrase for Christianity in the early church.

10. During these two years Ephesus was the center for the evangelization of the entire area, and from it churches were established in Colosse, Laodicea, and Hierapolis (Col 2:1; 4:13). Probably the other churches mentioned in Rev 2:3 were brought into existence at this time. 12. The handkerchiefs or aprons were articles of clothing used in Paul's trade.

13. Luke cites one illustration to show the effectiveness of Paul's ministry in Ephesus. Traveling Jewish exorcists were common in the ancient world. In antiquity, the name of a person or of a deity was thought to have special power that could control the person concerned if the name were used in the right way. These Jewish exorcists, witnessing the miracles done by Paul in the name of Jesus, attempted to use the name in the practice of their magical spells. 14-16. No high priest by the name of Sceva is known. It may be that these seven Jews made a false claim to the priesthood and Luke merely reports their claim. Such a claim would be effective, for priests would certainly know how to use the divine name most effectively. The name of Jesus could not be used magically, and the demon recognized that these Jews had no right to use it.

18,19. The fate of the seven Jews led to the conversion of many other magicians. Confessing and divulging their practices (RSV) means that they forsook their magic, for it was believed that magical secrets lost their potency when they were made public. Other magicians brought their scrolls inscribed

21. After these things were ended, Paul purposed in the spirit, when he had passed through Macedonia and Achaia, to go to Jerusalem, saying, After I have been there, I must also see Rome.

22. So he sent into Macedonia two of them that ministered unto him, Timotheus and Erastus; but he himself stayed in Asia for a season.

23. And the same time there arose no small stir about that way.

24. For a certain *man* named Demetrius, a silversmith, which made silver shrines for Diana, brought no small gain unto the craftsmen;

25. Whom he called together with the workmen of like occupation, and said, Sirs, ye know that by this craft we have our wealth.

26. Moreover ye see and hear, that not alone at Ephesus, but almost throughout all Asia, this Paul hath persuaded and turned away much people, saying that they be no gods, which are made with hands:

27. So that not only this our craft is in danger to be set at nought; but also that the temple of the great goddess Diana should be despised, and her magnificence should be destroyed, whom all Asia and the world worshippeth.

with magic spells and charms and burned them publicly. A number of such magical papyri have been discovered. The volumes burned at Ephesus were worth at least ten thousand dollars.

21. Luke next relates Paul's purpose for his future ministry. **Purpose in the spirit** may refer either to Paul's spirit (AV) or to the leading of the Holy Spirit (RSV). The apostle planned to revisit the churches in **Macedonia** and **Achaia** to collect money for the needy saints in **Jerusalem** (II Cor 8; 9; Rom 15:25 ff.). After taking this collection to Jerusalem, he intended to visit **Rome**. He did not plan an extended ministry there, but wished to visit the Roman Christians on his way to Spain (Rom 15:24,28). It was his policy to preach the Gospel where it had not been heard, and not to build upon another man's foundation (Rom 15:20).

22. Paul sent **Timothy** and **Erastus**, two of his associates, ahead into **Macedonia**, intending to follow them shortly. Luke does not mention Timothy between the time he rejoined Paul at Corinth (18:5) and this point; but he had been with the apostle in Ephesus. Neither does Luke record events that took place between Paul and the Corinthian church while the missionary was in Ephesus. Paul had previously sent Timothy to Corinth to deal with certain problems in the church (I Cor 4:17; 16:10,11). In addition, the older missionary himself had paid a flying visit there as is reported in II Cor 12:14; 13:1.

23. Paul's decision to leave Ephesus was hastened by a riot that arose about **the Way** (RSV). Ephesus was the seat of the worship of the great goddess **Artemis** (*Diana* in AV, vv. 24,27,28, is an inaccurate use of the Latin equivalent for the Greek Artemis). Artemis was not the traditional Greek goddess of this name but the ancient mother-goddess of Asia Minor, commonly known as Cybele. The temple of Artemis, the foundations of which have been uncovered, was one of the seven wonders of the ancient world.

24-27. A profitable **business** was carried on by a guild of silversmiths who made and sold miniature silver shrines containing likenesses of the goddess. Paul's ministry was so effective that the sale of shrines was falling off. Therefore one **Demetrius** called a meeting of guildsmen and pointed out that the trade of the silversmiths was in danger of **coming into disrepute** (RSV) and that if the evangelists were not stopped, the

28. And when they heard *these sayings*, they were full of wrath, and cried out, saying, Great *is* Diana of the Ephesians.

29. And the whole city was filled with confusion: and having caught Gaius and Aristarchus, men of Macedonia, Paul's companions in travel, they rushed with one accord into the theatre.

30. And when Paul would have entered in unto the people, the disciples suffered him not.

31. And certain of the chief of Asia, which were his friends, sent unto him, desiring *him* that he would not adventure himself into the theatre.

32. Some therefore cried one thing, and some another: for the assembly was confused; and the more part knew not wherefore they were come together.

33. And they drew Alexander out of the multitude, the Jews putting him forward. And Alexander beckoned with the hand, and would have made his defense unto the people.

34. But when they knew that he was a Jew, all with one voice about the space of two hours cried out, Great *is* Diana of the Ephesians.

35. And when the townclerk had appeased the people, he said, Ye men of Ephesus, what man is there that knoweth not how that the city of the Ephesians is a worshipper of the great goddess Diana, and of the *image* which fell down from Jupiter?

36. Seeing then that these things cannot be spoken against, ye ought to be quiet, and to do nothing rashly.

37. For ye have brought hither these men, which are neither robbers of churches, nor yet blasphemers of your goddess.

38. Wherefore if Demetrius, and the craftsmen which are with him, have a matter against any man, the law is open, and there are deputies: let them implead one another.

goddess Artemis herself might be **deposed from her magnificence** (RSV). The worship of Artemis is known to have been practiced in at least thirty-three places in the ancient world.

**28-30.** The mob spirit of the silversmiths spread like a contagion throughout the city and gave rise to a public demonstration in the open-air **theatre.** The ruins of this theater have been uncovered; it could hold over twenty thousand people. Since Paul was not at the moment available, the crowd seized two of his associates; and when the apostle purposed to go out to face the crowd, other disciples would not let him do so.

**31. Asiarchs.** Provincial officials who supervised and promoted the cult of the worship of Rome and the emperor. Only one person filled the office at a time, but the title was retained in an honorary capacity by previous office holders. Paul had a number of friends among these **Asiarchs** (AV *chief of Asia* is a poor translation) who begged him not to **venture into the theater** (RSV).

**32.** Meanwhile complete confusion reigned in the theater, so that most people did not know the reason for the gathering. **33,34.** Some of the **Jews** in the crowd felt that they were in danger of being blamed for the riot. Therefore they put forward a man named **Alexander** to make a speech and clear them of guilt. But their spokesman was shouted down, and chaos prevailed.

**35.** Order was finally restored by the **town clerk,** the executive officer of the city assembly. As the liaison officer between Ephesus and the Roman governor, he was responsible for such a riotous gathering. When he had **quieted** (AV, *appeased)* the people, he reminded them that Ephesus was not in danger of being degraded, for it was famous throughout the world as the **temple keeper** (AV *worshiper* is inadequate) of Artemis. **The image which fell down from Jupiter** is the translation of a single Greek word meaning literally *from the sky,* and probably refers to a meteorite in which the worshipers of Artemis thought they detected a likeness of the goddess and which they worshiped in the temple.

**37,38.** These men, he said, had done nothing **sacrilegious** (the word literally is *robbers of temples)* nor **blasphemous.** Furthermore, there were regular court days (AV, **the law is open),** and there were **proconsuls** (AV, *deputies)* who were appointed to handle such matters. The silversmiths should **bring charges**

39. But if ye inquire any thing concerning other matters, it shall be determined in a lawful assembly.

40. For we are in danger to be called in question for this day's uproar, there being no cause whereby we may give an account of this concourse.

41. And when he had thus spoken, he dismissed the assembly.

## CHAPTER 20

AND after the uproar was ceased, Paul called unto *him* the disciples, and embraced *them*, and departed for to go into Macedonia.

2. And when he had gone over those parts, and had given them much exhortation, he came into Greece.

3. And *there* abode three months. And when the Jews laid wait for him, as he was about to sail into Syria, he purposed to return through Macedonia.

4. And there accompanied him into Asia Sopater of Berea; and of the Thessalonians, Aristarchus and Secundus; and Gaius of Derbe, and Timotheus; and of Asia, Tychicus and Trophimus.

(AV, *implead*) against one another through these regular channels. 39. Other matters should be settled in the regular assembly, not in an irregular gathering. Assembly is the Greek word *ekklēsia*, which designates the regular gathering of Greek citizens.

40,41. The silversmiths feared the loss of their business. The town clerk pointed out that their real danger lay in the possibility of their being accused by the Romans of rioting, since no reason could be given to justify the confused gathering. These words quieted the mob and dispersed the assembly.

20:1. The purpose of Paul to revisit Macedonia and Achaia, stated in 19:21, was now carried out. The apostle's departure from Ephesus is reflected in II Corinthians. When he arrived at Troas, a great opportunity to preach the Gospel presented itself to him, but his concern for the troubles in the Corinthian church did not give him freedom of spirit to take advantage of it. Paul had previously sent Titus to Corinth to deal with the serious problems among the believers there, and he expected to meet his fellow worker in Troas. The failure of Titus to arrive as expected burdened Paul's heart, and he therefore left Troas and headed for Macedonia to meet his helper (II Cor 2:12,13). When Titus finally came from Corinth, he brought the good news of improved conditions in the church (II Cor 7:5-16). At this time Paul wrote the second letter to Corinth, sending it in advance of his own arrival by the hand of Titus and another brother (II Cor 8:17-19).

2,3. Luke passes over all of these activities without a word. After visiting the churches in Macedonia, Paul arrived in Greece, or Achaia, and there spent three months, probably in Corinth. During this time he wrote the Epistle to the Romans, informing the believers in Rome of his purpose to visit Jerusalem and then to come to Rome (Rom 15:22-29). Luke fails to mention one of the main reasons for Paul's final journey to Jerusalem: the delivery of a generous collection of money which the saints in Macedonia and Achaia had made to aid the poor (Rom 15:25-27; II Cor 8; 9). As Paul was about to take ship from Corinth to Syria, he learned of a plot by the Jews to kill him on this voyage. He changed his plans and, traveling by land through Macedonia, retraced his steps. 4. Into Asia (AV) is from an inferior text; Paul's companions journeyed with him to Jeru-

5. These going before tarried for us at Troas.

6. And we sailed away from Philippi after the days of unleavened bread, and came unto them to Troas in five days; where we abode seven days.

7. And upon the first *day* of the week, when the disciples came together to break bread, Paul preached unto them, ready to depart on the morrow; and continued his speech until midnight.

8. And there were many lights in the upper chamber, where they were gathered together.

9. And there sat in a window a certain young man named Eutychus, being fallen into a deep sleep: and as Paul was long preaching, he sunk down with sleep, and fell down from the third loft, and was taken up dead.

10. And Paul went down, and fell on him, and embracing *him* said, Trouble not yourselves; for his life is in him.

11. When he therefore was come up again, and had broken bread, and eaten, and talked a long while, even till break of day, so he departed.

12. And they brought the young man alive, and were not a little comforted.

13. And we went before to ship, and sailed unto Assos, there intending to take in Paul: for so had he appointed, minding himself to go afoot.

14. And when he met with us at Assos, we took him in, and came to Mitylene.

15. And we sailed thence, and came the next *day* over against Chios; and the next *day* we arrived at Samos, and tarried at Trogyllium; and the next *day* we came to Miletus.

16. For Paul had determined to sail by Ephesus, because he would not spend the time in Asia: for he hasted, if it were possible for him, to be at Jerusalem the day of Pentecost.

17. And from Miletus he sent to Ephesus, and called the elders of the church.

18. And when they were come to him, he said unto them, Ye know, from the first day that I came into Asia, after what manner I have been with you at all seasons,

19. Serving the Lord with all humility of mind, and with many tears, and temptations, which befell me by the lying in wait of the Jews:

20. *And* how I kept back nothing that was profitable *unto you*, but have showed you, and have taught you publicly, and from house to house,

21. Testifying both to the Jews, and also to the Greeks, repentance toward God, and faith toward our Lord Jesus Christ.

salem. This party consisted of official representatives from the several churches that were sending money to the saints in Jerusalem.

5. Here begins a second "we" section, which continues to 20:15 and is resumed in 21:1. Luke had been left in Philippi on Paul's second journey (16:16). He now rejoined the apostle at Philippi and continued with him to Jerusalem. The rest of the party went on ahead and met Paul at Troas. 6. The apostle tarried at Philippi to observe the week of unleavened bread and then sailed with Luke to Troas to join the rest of the party.

7. The missionaries gathered with the believers at Troas on the first day of the week to preach and to celebrate the Lord's Supper. This is the earliest clear reference to the Christian practice of observing Sunday as a day of worship. The first Christians, as Jews, probably continued to observe the Sabbath as well as the first day of the week. We are not told when or how the practice of Sunday worship arose in the church. 8,9. The meeting was held in an upper room on the third floor. Illumination was provided by many smoky lamps, which made the air both stuffy and smoky. They (v. 8, AV) should read *we*. 11. Broken bread refers to the breaking of the bread of the Lord's Supper. Eaten refers to the *agape* or love feast, a fellowship meal that accompanied the Lord's Supper.

13-15. Luke and the other members of the party now took a ship from Troas around a promontory of land to Assos, while Paul traveled by land (AV, *afoot*). The apostle embarked with the rest of his party at Assos and sailed to Mitylene, the chief town of the island of Lesbos. From Mitylene, they sailed between the mainland and the islands of Chios and Samos until they came to Miletus.

16,17. Because Paul desired to reach Jerusalem by the day of Pentecost, he had taken a ship from Troas that stopped at Miletus but did not go to Ephesus. He did not wish now to visit Ephesus, for he did not have the time to become involved with the problems and the life of the church there. But since his ship was lying over in Miletus for several days, there was time to send to Ephesus and have the leaders of the church come to him for a brief visit.

18-35. Paul's sermon to the Ephesian elders is of great significance because it reflects the simplicity of the primitive church organization. Luke calls the Ephesian leaders elders or *presbyters* (v.

22. And now, behold, I go bound in the spirit unto Jerusalem, not knowing the things that shall befall me there:

23. Save that the Holy Ghost witnesseth in every city, saying that bonds and afflictions abide me.

24. But none of these things move me, neither count I my life dear unto myself, so that I might finish my course with joy, and the ministry, which I have received of the Lord Jesus, to testify the gospel of the grace of God.

25. And now, behold, I know that ye all, among whom I have gone preaching the kingdom of God, shall see my face no more.

26. Wherefore I take you to record this day, that I *am* pure from the blood of all *men.*

27. For I have not shunned to declare unto you all the counsel of God.

28. Take heed therefore unto yourselves, and to all the flock, over the which the Holy Ghost hath made you overseers, to feed the church of God, which he hath purchased with his own blood.

29. For I know this, that after my departing shall grievous wolves enter in among you, not sparing the flock.

30. Also of your own selves shall men arise, speaking perverse things, to draw away disciples after them.

31. Therefore watch, and remember, that by the space of three years I ceased not to warn every one night and day with tears.

32. And now, brethren, I commend you to God, and to the word of his grace, which is able to build you up, and to give you an inheritance among all them which are sanctified.

33. I have coveted no man's silver, or gold, or apparel.

34. Yea, ye yourselves know, that these hands have ministered unto my necessities, and to them that were with me.

35. I have showed you all things, how that so laboring ye ought to support the weak, and to remember the words of the Lord Jesus, how he said, It is more blessed to give than to receive.

17), while Paul calls them overseers (AV; *guardians,* RSV; v. 28). This word is *episcopoi,* later translated "bishops" (Phil 1:1; I Tim 3:1,2; Tit 1:7). Presbyter has a Jewish background, while overseer has a Greek background. It is clear that these two terms designate the same office of presbyter-bishop. Only at a later time does the bishop become a ruler distinct from the presbyters. Paul summarized his ministry in Ephesus by saying that he had testified the gospel of the grace of God (v. 24), preaching the kingdom of God (v. 25), two phrases which are here synonymous and interchangeable. Usually in the book of Acts the kingdom of God refers to the eschatological realm of salvation (14:22). But in this passage, the kingdom of God is the summary of Paul's entire message in Ephesus and refers to the present blessings of redemption in Christ.

22. Paul was going to Jerusalem under divine compulsion. The RSV is probably correct in translating bound in the Spirit, rather than following the AV, which refers only to Paul's inner compulsion. 23. The Holy Spirit had disclosed to Paul, possibly through the utterances of prophets (see 21:1-14), that bonds (the word often refers to the bonds of imprisonment) and afflictions lay ahead.

28. This verse presents a difficult textual problem. The best text and the most natural translation is that of the AV, which speaks of the church of God, which he hath purchased with his own blood. In this context, however, God refers to the Father, and nowhere does Scripture refer to the blood of God. Therefore important ancient texts read, *the church of the Lord* (RSV). This, however, is a decidedly inferior reading; the church of God must be preferred. It is possible to translate, *which he hath purchased with the blood of his Own,* as the margin of the RSV suggests (see Bruce, *Commentary).*

29,30. Paul predicted that troubles would come to the Ephesian church from two sources: fierce wolves would enter the church from without, and false teachers would arise from their own midst to turn disciples away from the faith. The growth of heresy at Ephesus is reflected in I Tim 1:3-7.

33-35. Paul reminded the Ephesians of his custom of making tents not only to support himself but to provide for the needs of others with him. He quoted a saying of the Lord which is not recorded in any of our Gospels, about the bless-

36. And when he had thus spoken, he kneeled down, and prayed with them all.

37. And they all wept sore, and fell on Paul's neck, and kissed him,

38. Sorrowing most of all for the words which he spake, that they should see his face no more. And they accompanied him unto the ship.

### CHAPTER 21

AND it came to pass, that after we were gotten from them, and had launched, we came with a straight course unto Coos, and the *day* following unto Rhodes, and from thence unto Patara:

2. And finding a ship sailing over unto Phenicia, we went aboard, and set forth.

3. Now when we had discovered Cyprus, we left it on the left hand, and sailed into Syria, and landed at Tyre: for there the ship was to unlade her burden.

4. And finding disciples, we tarried there seven days: who said to Paul through the Spirit, that he should not go up to Jerusalem.

5. And when we had accomplished those days, we departed and went our way; and they all brought us on our way, with wives and children, till *we were* out of the city: and we kneeled down on the shore, and prayed.

6. And when we had taken our leave one of another, we took ship; and they returned home again.

7. And when we had finished *our* course from Tyre, we came to Ptolemais, and saluted the brethren, and abode with them one day.

8. And the next *day* we that were of Paul's company departed, and came unto Caesarea; and we entered into the house of Philip the evangelist, which was *one* of the seven; and abode with him.

edness of giving. Very few authentic sayings of Christ have thus survived outside of our Gospels. The main objective of giving in the early church was to provide for the needs of poor brethren rather than to support the preaching of the Gospel, as is the case today.

36-38. The expectation of the Ephesian elders that they should see his face no more need not be understood as a hard and fast prophecy that Paul would never again visit Ephesus. The Pastoral Epistles indicate a further ministry after his release from imprisonment at Rome. It does, however, like 20:22,24, reflect the expectation that serious troubles and possible death lay ahead for Paul.

21:1,2. Paul and his party resumed their trip by boat, sailing between the islands and the mainland. Cos and Rhodes. Two islands where they anchored overnight. Rhodes was also the name of a city located on the island of the same name. At Patara, a city on the mainland, they found a ship that would sail directly across the sea to Phoenicia, leaving the island of Cyprus on their left. Apparently favorable conditions enabled them to make a rapid voyage, for after this point, Paul no longer appeared to be in haste to reach Jerusalem by Pentecost.

3-6. When they landed at Tyre, Paul had a bit of leisure, for seven days were required for the ship to unload its cargo. Disciples had come to Phoenicia as a result of the persecution following Stephen's death (11:19), and Paul now sought out the disciples in Tyre (RSV). In this church were prophets who disclosed through the Spirit that Paul faced serious dangers in Jerusalem. They therefore sought to dissuade him from his purpose. However, when Paul persisted, the entire church accompanied him to his ship, and after prayer on the seashore, the evangelist and his party embarked.

7. Continuing the journey, they sailed to Ptolemais, the southern port of Phoenicia, where Paul spent one day with the believers in that city.

8. Arriving at Caesarea, the apostle was entertained by Philip, who had gained a reputation as an evangelist. Philip, one of the seven chosen to supervise the ministry to the widows in the early church (6:3 ff.), had evangelized Samaria (8:5 ff.), the Ethiopian eunuch (8:26 ff.), and the coastal plain (8:40). He was last seen in Caesarea (8:40) and apparently made his permanent home in

9. And the same man had four daughters, virgins, which did prophesy.

10. And as we tarried *there* many days, there came down from Judea a certain prophet, named Agabus.

11. And when he was come unto us, he took Paul's girdle, and bound his own hands and feet, and said, Thus saith the Holy Ghost, So shall the Jews at Jerusalem bind the man that owneth this girdle, and shall deliver *him* into the hands of the Gentiles.

12. And when we heard these things, both we, and they of that place, besought him not to go up to Jerusalem.

13. Then Paul answered, What mean ye to weep and to break mine heart? for I am ready not to be bound only, but also to die at Jerusalem for the name of the Lord Jesus.

14. And when he would not be persuaded, we ceased, saying, The will of the Lord be done.

15. And after those days we took up our carriages, and went up to Jerusalem.

16. There went with us also *certain* of the disciples of Caesarea, and brought with them one Mnason of Cyprus, an old disciple, with whom we should lodge.

that city. He is called **Philip the evangelist** to distinguish him from Philip the apostle.

9. Philip's **four daughters** were endowed with the gift of prophecy. The fact that they were **unmarried** is only an interesting detail and carries no necessary religious significance.

10,11. Paul, no longer under pressure to reach Jerusalem, spent several days with Philip. **Agabus**, a prophet from Jerusalem (11:27,28), following the example of OT prophets, symbolically acted out the fate that he foresaw for the apostle in Jerusalem, and predicted that he would be delivered **into the hands of the Gentiles.** 12,13. Again the believers tried to dissuade Paul from going to Jerusalem. He replied that it was not important to him whether he lived or died, but their tears were in danger of "softening his will" (F. F. Bruce).

14. Paul's friends then acceded to the will of the Lord. There is no reason to think that Paul went to Jerusalem in violation of the will of God. We are to understand the several prophetic forecasts not as prohibitions from the Holy Spirit but as forewarnings of what lay ahead. As a result of these prophecies, Paul's friends tried to dissuade him from risking his life; but the apostle remained steadfast in accomplishing his course and in fulfilling the will of God in spite of personal danger. 15. The expression, **we took up our carriages,** is one of the most picturesque archaisms of the AV. The Greek word means simply to make preparations, and it might best be translated *when our preparations were completed.*

16. The Greek of this verse is a bit obscure and may be translated either **bringing us to the house of Mnason . . . with whom we should lodge** (RSV); or **brought with them one Mnason . . . with whom we should lodge** (AV). If the former is correct, Mnason lived somewhere between Caesarea and Jerusalem (a journey of sixty-five miles), and there the party spent the night. It is equally likely, however, that Mnason, a disciple from the earliest days (**an old disciple** has no reference to his age) but a Hellenistic Jew, owned a house in Jerusalem, where he planned to entertain Paul and his party. Paul was accompanied by Gentile Christians, and it was not clear how these Gentiles would be welcomed by the Jewish Christians in Jerusalem. The lodging provided by Mnason promised to avoid tensions that might arise

17. And when we were come to Jerusalem, the brethren received us gladly.

18. And the *day* following Paul went in with us unto James; and all the elders were present.

19. And when he had saluted them, he declared particularly what things God had wrought among the Gentiles by his ministry.

because of associations between Jewish and Gentile believers.

## V. Extension of the Church to Rome. 21:18—28:31.

Luke has related the extension of the church from Jerusalem through Judea and Samaria until a semi-independent Gentile church was established in Antioch. From Antioch the Gospel was carried by Paul on three missions through Asia and Europe. Evangelistic and missionary work was undoubtedly being carried on during this time by other apostles. We have, for instance, no account of the evangelization of Egypt, with its great center, Alexandria. Luke is concerned only to trace the main outlines of what he considers to be the most significant line of expansion—toward Rome. There remains only the need to record Paul's mission of taking the Gospel to Rome.

It is evident that it was not Luke's purpose to record the initial evangelization of Rome nor the beginnings of the church there, for he tells how Christian brethren welcomed Paul upon his arrival at the capital (28:15). We know that Paul had written a letter to the church at Rome (Rom 1:7), but Luke gives us no record of how the Gospel originally came to the Imperial City.

Since Luke's purpose was not to describe the initial evangelizing of Rome, it possibly was to show that although Paul first preached the kingdom of God to the Jews, he turned to the Gentiles when the Jews rejected his message (28:24-31). The geographical extension of the church was not Luke's main interest; it was rather **the movement of redemptive history from the Jews to the Gentiles.** In keeping with this purpose, Luke devotes considerable space to the record of Paul's last visit to Jerusalem, not because the visit was important in itself, but because it showed the final rejection of the Gospel by Jerusalem.

A. Rejection of the Gospel by Jerusalem. 21:18—26:32. **18,19.** Paul was received in Jerusalem by James, the brother of the Lord, who had become the leader of the Jerusalem church (15:13), and by the **elders.** Apparently none of the apostles was in Jerusalem at this time. Paul was cordially welcomed by the leaders of the church, to whom he related the success of the Gospel among the Gentiles. He made a statement to the effect that Gentile believers were introduced to the Christian life on the

20. And when they heard *it*, they glorified the Lord, and said unto him, Thou seest, brother, how many thousands of Jews there are which believe; and they are all zealous of the law:

21. And they are informed of thee, that thou teachest all the Jews which are among the Gentiles to forsake Moses, saying that they ought not to circumcise *their* children, neither to walk after the customs.

22. What is it therefore? the multitude must needs come together: for they will hear that thou art come.

23. Do therefore this that we say to thee: We have four men which have a vow on them;

24. Them take, and purify thyself with them, and be at charges with them, that they may shave *their* heads: and all may know that those things, whereof they were informed concerning thee, are nothing; but *that* thou thyself also walkest orderly, and keepest the law.

25. As touching the Gentiles which believe, we have written *and* concluded that they observe no such thing, save only that they keep themselves from *things* offered to idols, and from blood, and from strangled, and from fornication.

26. Then Paul took the men, and the next day purifying himself with them entered into the temple, to signify the accomplishment of the days of purification, until that an offering should be offered for every one of them.

basis of faith alone apart from the keeping of the Jewish law. The leaders of the Jerusalem church heartily approved of this procedure.

20,21. Although the leaders of the Jerusalem church were delighted with Paul's report, they had a word of caution for him. They told him that there were thousands of believing Jews who even as Christians continued to be zealous for the law of Moses, and that these had been informed that Paul not only preached to Gentiles a gospel of grace entirely apart from the Law, but also taught the Jews of the dispersion to forsake Moses and to neglect circumcision and the observance of the OT customs. This meant that Paul urged Jews to abandon Judaism and cease to be Jews, i.e., to become Gentiles.

22-24. James and the Jerusalem elders realized that this report was not true and that Paul permitted Jewish believers as Jews to continue in the Law. But they felt that something must be done to show the Jewish Christians that this report was false. The multitude must needs come together (AV) is not in the best texts. They suggested that Paul submit himself to the Law to prove to the Jews that he did not advocate the abolishment of the Law for Jewish Christians. There were four Jews who had taken a Nazarite vow. This ordinarily lasted thirty days, but they had incurred some defilement that had placed them in a condition of ceremonial impurity for seven days (v. 27). At the end of this period, they would shave their heads and offer certain sacrifices of purification to God. The elders suggested to Paul that he identify himself with these four and practice the common Jewish custom of paying the expenses for the sacrifices. This would prove to the Jewish church that Paul himself accepted the Jewish customs.

25. James assured Paul that this would not mean a modification of the decision rendered in the Jerusalem council that the Gentiles should be free from the Law but should only abstain from certain things that would give particular offense to their Jewish Christian brethren.

26. Paul accepted the counsel of the elders and for several successive days (the verb is in the imperfect tense) went into the Temple with the four Jews to offer a purifying sacrifice for each of them.

There is no fundamental inconsistency between Paul's willingness as a Jew to observe the Law and his inflexible insistence that Gentile believers should not

27. And when the seven days were almost ended, the Jews which were of Asia, when they saw him in the temple, stirred up all the people, and laid hands on him,

28. Crying out, Men of Israel, help: This is the man, that teacheth all *men* every where against the people, and the law, and this place: and further brought Greeks also into the temple, and hath polluted this holy place.

29. (For they had seen before with him in the city Trophimus an Ephesian, whom they supposed that Paul had brought into the temple.)

30. And all the city was moved, and the people ran together: and they took Paul, and drew him out of the temple: and forthwith the doors were shut.

31. And as they went about to kill him, tidings came unto the chief captain of the band, that all Jerusalem was in an uproar:

be brought under the Law, since they stood under grace. As a new creature in Christ Jesus, neither circumcision nor uncircumcision could have any vital importance to Paul (Gal 6:15). The evangelist considered such religious practices a matter of indifference, for the world had been crucified to him and he to the world (Gal 6:14). He himself said that if a man was converted as a Jew, he was to remain a Jew (I Cor 7:18), for circumcision in itself means nothing. Jewish Christians might keep the Law as Jews, not as Christians. But when efforts were made to impose the Law on Gentile Christians as a basis of salvation, Paul objected and insisted upon complete freedom from the Law. Undoubtedly if Jewish believers had desired to give up the practice of the Law, Paul would not have resisted them. Paul's position of letting expediency determine principle in certain areas is so delicate a matter that many have not understood him and have accused him unnecessarily of radical inconsistency.

27-29. Apparently Paul's course of action satisfied the Jewish Christians, but it aroused the enmity of a group of unbelieving **Jews from Asia** who had come to Jerusalem to worship at the feast of Pentecost. These men had known Paul in Asia, and they had seen him in Jerusalem in the company of **Trophimus,** a Gentile convert from Ephesus. Now when they saw the apostle in the court of Israel, where only Jews were permitted, they leaped to the conclusion that he had taken Trophimus into the temple court with him. The temple area included a vast court of the Gentiles in which non-Jews were free to come and go. Between this outer court and the court of Israel was a low parapet with inscriptions warning Gentiles not to venture into the court of Israel on pain of death. Two of these inscriptions have been found. The Asian Jews assumed that Paul had thus profaned the Temple and **defiled the holy place.**

30. A mob spirit quickly spread through the crowd, and Paul was dragged out of the court of Israel into the court of the Gentiles. Then the **gates** separating the two courts **were shut** to prevent further rioting within the sacred precincts.

31. Northwest of the temple area was the Tower of Antonia, which housed a cohort of Roman soldiers under a military tribune. This tower was connected with the temple court by two flights of stairs, by which quick access could be had in

32. Who immediately took soldiers and centurions, and ran down unto them: and when they saw the chief captain and the soldiers, they left beating of Paul.

33. Then the chief captain came near, and took him, and commanded *him* to be bound with two chains; and demanded who he was, and what he had done.

34. And some cried one thing, some another, among the multitude: and when he could not know the certainty for the tumult, he commanded him to be carried into the castle.

35. And when he came upon the stairs, so it was, that he was borne of the soldiers for the violence of the people.

36. For the multitude of the people followed after, crying, Away with him.

37. And as Paul was to be led into the castle, he said unto the chief captain, May I speak unto thee? Who said, Canst thou speak Greek?

38. Art not thou that Egyptian, which before these days madest an uproar, and leddest out into the wilderness four thousand men that were murderers?

39. But Paul said, I am a man *which am* a Jew of Tarsus, *a city* in Cilicia, a citizen of no mean city: and, I beseech thee, suffer me to speak unto the people.

40. And when he had given him license, Paul stood on the stairs, and beckoned with the hand unto the people. And when there was made a great silence, he spake unto *them* in the Hebrew tongue, saying,

## CHAPTER 22

MEN, brethren, and fathers, hear ye my defense *which I make* now unto you.

2. (And when they heard that he spake in the Hebrew tongue to them, they kept the more silence: and he saith,)

case of trouble. A **cohort** consisted of a thousand men. Now as Paul was about to be killed by mob action, word came to the chiliarch (AV, *chief captain;* RSV, *tribune*) of the garrison that a riot was occurring. 32. He took a band of at least 200 men with their **centurions** and intervened just in time to save Paul's life. 33. He **arrested** Paul, taking him into protective custody, and commanded that he be chained to two soldiers for safekeeping.

34. When the tribune tried to determine the cause of the riot, the shouts of the crowd were so contradictory that he could not find out what had happened. He therefore commanded that Paul be carried up the steps into the **barracks** (RSV). *Castle* (AV) reflects the old English idea of a military fortification. 35. But by the time they reached the **steps** leading to the Tower of Antonia from the temple area, the mob had become so violent that the soldiers had to pick up Paul and carry him.

37. As they came to the head of the stairs, Paul surprised the tribune by speaking to him in Greek.

38. Some three years before this time, an Egyptian Jew had stirred up a **revolt** by leading four thousand men out to the Mount of Olives, promising that the walls of the city would be leveled before them and that they would be able to overthrow the Roman garrison. The supporters of this revolt were called **assassins** (RSV; *murderers,* AV; literally, *sicarii*) because each carried a knife (*sica*) concealed in his garments with which he might assassinate political opponents. This revolt had been crushed by the Roman procurator Felix, but the Egyptian had escaped. The tribune for some reason identified his captive with that Jewish rebel.

39,40. When Paul assured the tribune that he, as a Jew, had a right to enter the temple precincts and that he was a citizen of the important city of Tarsus, the officer permitted him to try to quiet the mob. The apostle stood at the head of the stairs overlooking the court of the Gentiles, while the soldiers stood below him on the stairs. When Paul had captured the attention of the mob, he began to speak to them in the native **Aramaic** dialect, which was the common Jewish language of both Palestine and western Asia.

22:1,2. Many Jews of the Diaspora could speak only Greek; and so when the apostle unexpectedly addressed the crowd

3. I am verily a man *which am* a Jew, born in Tarsus, *a city* in Cilicia, yet brought up in this city at the feet of Gamaliel, *and* taught according to the perfect manner of the law of the fathers, and was zealous toward God, as ye all are this day.

4. And I persecuted this way unto the death, binding and delivering into prisons both men and women.

5. As also the high priest doth bear me witness, and all the estate of the elders: from whom also I received letters unto the brethren, and went to Damascus, to bring them which were there bound unto Jerusalem, for to be punished.

6. And it came to pass, that, as I made my journey, and was come nigh unto Damascus about noon, suddenly there shone from heaven a great light round about me.

7. And I fell unto the ground, and heard a voice saying unto me, Saul, Saul, why persecutest thou me?

8. And I answered, Who art thou, Lord? And he said unto me, I am Jesus of Nazareth, whom thou persecutest.

9. And they that were with me saw indeed the light, and were afraid; but they heard not the voice of him that spake to me.

10. And I said, What shall I do, Lord? And the Lord said unto me, Arise, and go into Damascus; and there it shall be told thee of all things which are appointed for thee to do.

11. And when I could not see for the glory of that light, being led by the hand of them that were with me, I came into Damascus.

12. And one Ananias, a devout man according to the law, having a good report of all the Jews which dwelt *there,*

13. Came unto me, and stood, and said unto me, Brother Saul, receive thy sight. And the same hour I looked up upon him.

14. And he said, The God of our fathers hath chosen thee, that thou shouldest know his will, and see that Just One, and shouldest hear the voice of his mouth.

15. For thou shalt be his witness unto all men of what thou hast seen and heard.

16. And now why tarriest thou? arise, and be baptized, and wash away thy sins, calling on the name of the Lord.

17. And it came to pass, that, when I was come again to Jerusalem, even while I prayed in the temple, I was in a trance;

18. And saw him saying unto me, Make haste, and get thee quickly out of Jerusalem: for they will not receive thy testimony concerning me.

in their own dialect, he captured their attention.

3. Paul attempted to win their sympathy by assuring them that he perfectly understood the Jewish faith. Although he was born in Tarsus, he had been **brought up** in Jerusalem at the feet of Gamaliel, who was one of the most famous rabbis of the time. He had thus been educated according to the **strict manner of the law** of the Jews and had been as **zealous toward God** as they themselves.

4,5. He further tried to win Jewish sympathy by reminding the crowd that, as a zealot for the Law, he had persecuted the followers of **this Way.** He reminded them that the **high priest and the whole council of the elders** (the Jewish Sanhedrin) could support his testimony, for they had given him letters of extradition to the Jewish brethren in Damascus to arrest Jewish believers who had fled to that city.

6-16. The apostle told the Jews what had turned him from his zeal for the Jewish traditions (cf. the earlier account of his conversion, Acts 9). He emphasized that his commission from the risen and ascended Christ · had come to him through a Jewish believer who was a **devout man according to the law,** and who had a good reputation among the Jews in Damascus. Ananias had told him that **the God of our fathers,** that is, the God of Israel, had chosen him to **know his will,** to **see the righteous One** (see 3:14; 7:52 for this title), and to be a witness to all men of what he had experienced. Ananias then exhorted Paul to be baptized in token of the washing away of his sins, calling upon the **name of the Lord.**

17-21. Paul told of a confirmation of this call given to him through a vision after he had returned to Jerusalem (9:26). Since Paul was not concerned to give a complete account of his experience, he omitted all mention of the three years he spent in Arabia (cf. Gal 1:17,18). He related another aspect of his experience in Jerusalem that Luke did not record in his earlier account. Acts 9 says that Paul was sent away from Jerusalem by the brethren to escape a plot to kill him (vv. 28-30). Here Paul tells us that he had left Jerusalem in response to a word from the Lord. While he was praying in the Temple as a faithful Jew, God had warned him in a trance that Jerusalem would not receive his message and that he therefore should **get quickly out of Jerusalem.** Paul protested that the

19. And I said, Lord, they know that I imprisoned and beat in every synagogue them that believed on thee:

20. And when the blood of thy martyr Stephen was shed, I also was standing by, and consenting unto his death, and kept the raiment of them that slew him.

21. And he said unto me, Depart: for I will send thee far hence unto the Gentiles.

22. And they gave him audience unto this word, and *then* lifted up their voices, and said, Away with such a *fellow* from the earth: for it is not fit that he should live.

23. And as they cried out, and cast off *their* clothes, and threw dust into the air,

24. The chief captain commanded him to be brought into the castle, and bade that he should be examined by scourging; that he might know wherefore they cried so against him.

25. And as they bound him with thongs, Paul said unto the centurion that stood by, Is it lawful for you to scourge a man that is a Roman, and uncondemned?

26. When the centurion heard *that*, he went and told the chief captain, saying, Take heed what thou doest; for this man is a Roman.

27. Then the chief captain came, and said unto him, Tell me, art thou a Roman? He said, Yea.

28. And the chief captain answered, With a great sum obtained I this freedom. And Paul said, But I was *free*-born.

29. Then straightway they departed from him which should have examined him: and the chief captain also was afraid, after he knew that he was a Roman, and because he had bound him.

30. On the morrow, because he would have known the certainty wherefore he was accused of the Jews, he loosed him from *his* bands, and commanded the chief priests and all their council to appear, and brought Paul down, and set him before them.

## CHAPTER 23

AND Paul, earnestly beholding the council, said, Men *and* brethren, I have lived in all good conscience before God until this day.

Jews' knowledge of his earlier zeal and sincerity in persecuting the Christians would convince them of the reality of his conversion. The Lord replied that he should leave Jerusalem, for he would be sent far away unto the Gentiles (RSV). The word *martys* (v. 20), translated thy martyr (AV), should be translated *thy witness* (RSV). *Martys* means "witness," and it only gradually came to designate a witness who sealed his witness with his blood.

22,23. The mob listened to him until he mentioned the Gentiles. The word Gentiles set the spark to the tinder of the Jews' wrath, and they began to shout for the captive's death, to wave their garments (RSV), and to throw dust into the air as a gesture of anger.

24. The tribune, realizing that he could gain no accurate information from the mob, decided to try to extort a confession from Paul by torture. Though scourging was a legal procedure with slaves, a free man could not legally be scourged. 25. As they tied Paul up and were about to scourge him, he asked if it was lawful to scourge a Roman citizen who had not even received a fair trial.

26-28. Roman citizenship could be obtained by birth from parents who were Roman citizens, or by purchase with money, or as a gift from the Roman government. After the abuse he had just suffered, Paul presented a rather sorry spectacle; and perhaps the words of the tribune implied that such a person must have obtained citizenship very cheaply. Paul replied that he did not buy citizenship but was born of parents who were already citizens. We do not know how his parents became citizens, but it is usually supposed that citizenship was given them as a reward for some service rendered to an earlier Roman ruler.

29. Upon these words, the soldiers who were about to torture Paul at once drew back from him. The tribune was stricken with fear because he had initiated an illegal procedure against a Roman citizen. 30. He decided that the proper course of action would be to ask the Jewish Sanhedrin to conduct a hearing and to determine if adequate grounds existed for legal procedures against Paul.

23:1. Paul began his defense before the Sanhedrin by claiming that he had acted in good conscience before God, not only in these affairs for which he was being accused but throughout his entire life. 2. Ananias was the high priest about A.D. 48–58. He was reputedly a

2. And the high priest Ananias commanded them that stood by him to smite him on the mouth.

3. Then said Paul unto him, God shall smite thee, *thou* whited wall: for sittest thou to judge me after the law, and commandest me to be smitten contrary to the law?

4. And they that stood by said, Revilest thou God's high priest?

5. Then said Paul, I wist not, brethren, that he was the high priest: for it is written, Thou shalt not speak evil of the ruler of thy people.

6. But when Paul perceived that the one part were Sadducees, and the other Pharisees, he cried out in the council, Men *and* brethren, I am a Pharisee, the son of a Pharisee: of the hope and resurrection of the dead I am called in question.

very greedy, insolent, overbearing man. Angered by this bold claim of Paul, he commanded some who stood near the apostle to **strike him on the mouth. 3.** Jesus in his trial had also been struck in the face (Jn 18:22) and had challenged the propriety of this blow.

With indignant words Paul now challenged this irregular conduct from a member of the Sanhedrin, accusing those who claimed they were enforcing the Law of actually violating the Law themselves. **Whited wall** suggests a tottering wall whose precarious position has been disguised by a generous coat of whitewash (Bruce, *Commentary*). The meaning is that although he held a high position, Ananias was bound to come to grief. In fact, Ananias was assassinated some eight years later.

**4,5.** When Paul was rebuked for speaking in such strong terms to **God's high priest,** he apologized, saying that he **did not know** that this man **was the high priest.** No explanation is given as to why Paul did not recognize the high priest, who usually presided over regular meetings of the Sanhedrin and therefore would be easily identifiable. Possibly this was not a regular session of the Sanhedrin and the high priest therefore was not occupying his usual position or wearing his official robes. Possibly Paul did not see from whom the command came to strike him. Some have thought that his words were ironical and mean that Paul did not think that a man who acted in this way could be the high priest.

6. This arbitrary and illegal conduct of the high priest made Paul realize that he could not expect a fair hearing from the Sanhedrin. Therefore he resorted to a strategem to divide his opposition. The Sanhedrin was composed of **Pharisees** and **Sadducees,** who differed on important points of doctrine. The Pharisees, who had developed an elaborate tradition based on the entire OT, believed in bodily resurrection and in an elaborate hierarchy of angels and demons in the spirit world. The Sadducees rejected the later developments in Jewish theology, denying both the doctrine of resurrection and the angelology and demonology. As a Pharisee, Paul had believed in the doctrine of resurrection. As a Christian, the teaching of resurrection took on new significance for him because it was linked inseparably with the resurrection of Jesus Christ. To Paul's mind, the Sadducean denial of resurrection would make Christianity utterly impossible, "for if the dead are not raised,

7. And when he had so said, there arose a dissension between the Pharisees and the Sadducees: and the multitude was divided.

8. For the Sadducees say that there is no resurrection, neither angel, nor spirit: but the Pharisees confess both.

9. And there arose a great cry: and the scribes *that were* of the Pharisees' part arose, and strove, saying, We find no evil in this man: but if a spirit or an angel hath spoken to him, let us not fight against God.

10. And when there arose a great dissension, the chief captain, fearing lest Paul should have been pulled in pieces of them, commanded the soldiers to go down, and to take him by force from among them, and to bring *him* into the castle.

11. And the night following the Lord stood by him, and said, Be of good cheer, Paul: for as thou hast testified of me in Jerusalem, so must thou bear witness also at Rome.

12. And when it was day, certain of the Jews banded together, and bound themselves under a curse, saying that they would neither eat nor drink till they had killed Paul.

13. And they were more than forty which had made this conspiracy.

14. And they came to the chief priests and elders, and said, We have bound ourselves under a great curse, that we will eat nothing until we have slain Paul.

15. Now therefore ye with the council signify to the chief captain that he bring him down unto you to-morrow, as though ye would inquire something more perfectly concerning him: and we, or ever he come near, are ready to kill him.

neither hath Christ been raised" (I Cor 15:16). The early Christians had met their first opposition from the Sadducees when they proclaimed in Jesus the doctrine of resurrection from the dead (4:1,2). Now Paul asserted that he was a Pharisee, that the fundamental question at stake was that of the resurrection of the dead, and that it was really because of this doctrine that he was on trial.

9. This served to divide the assembly. The scribes, i.e., the students of the Law, who belonged to the Pharisees' party, supported Paul to the point of suggesting that the two visions he had experienced near Damascus and in Jerusalem might have been the visitation of a spirit or an angel. The words, let us not fight against God (AV), are found only in the later Greek texts and were inserted in echo of Gamaliel's words in 5:39.

10. We may assume that the opposition to Paul from the orthodox Jews had been headed up by the priestly Sadducees because of the charge against Paul of polluting the Temple (21:28). Now that Paul had won the sympathy of the Pharisees, order gave way to chaos, and the prisoner was in danger of suffering bodily harm from the opposing elements in the Sanhedrin. Therefore the Roman tribune ordered the soldiers to intervene and to bring Paul to the Tower of Antonia (castle, AV).

11. These experiences made Paul feel that his worst forebodings of sufferings in Jerusalem (20:22-24) were likely to be realized. That night he was granted a reassuring vision in which he learned that he would not be killed in Jerusalem but would finally reach Rome.

12,13. Paul's fanatical opponents now contrived another way of trying to do away with him. A group of over forty Jews conspired together and bound themselves by a solemn oath that they would either kill Paul or starve to death. The extent of their fanaticism can be understood when we realize that the execution of this plot would certainly have meant the death of many of them at the hands of the strong Roman guard who protected Paul. However, this risk did not deter these fanatics.

14,15. In order to gain the co-operation of those priests and elders who had opposed Paul, they informed them of the plot. The priests were to summon a meeting of the council, which would ask the tribune to bring Paul a second time before the Sanhedrin under the pretense that they desired to determine the facts

16. And when Paul's sister's son heard of their lying in wait, he went and entered into the castle, and told Paul.

17. Then Paul called one of the centurions unto *him*, and said, Bring this young man unto the chief captain: for he hath a certain thing to tell him.

18. So he took him, and brought *him* to the chief captain, and said, Paul the prisoner called me unto *him*, and prayed me to bring this young man unto thee, who hath something to say unto thee.

19. Then the chief captain took him by the hand, and went *with him* aside privately, and asked *him*, What is that thou hast to tell me?

20. And he said, The Jews have agreed to desire thee that thou wouldest bring down Paul to-morrow into the council, as though they would inquire somewhat of him more perfectly.

21. But do not thou yield unto them: for there lie in wait for him of them more than forty men, which have bound themselves with an oath, that they will neither eat nor drink till they have killed him: and now are they ready, looking for a promise from thee.

22. So the chief captain *then* let the young man depart, and charged *him*, See *thou* tell no man that thou hast showed these things to me.

23. And he called unto *him* two centurions, saying, Make ready two hundred soldiers to go to Caesarea, and horsemen threescore and ten, and spearmen two hundred, at the third hour of the night;

24. And provide *them* beasts, that they may set Paul on, and bring *him* safe unto Felix the governor.

25. And he wrote a letter after this manner:

26. Claudius Lysias unto the most excellent governor Felix *sendeth* greeting.

27. This man was taken of the Jews, and should have been killed of them: then came I with an army, and rescued him, having understood that he was a Roman.

28. And when I would have known the cause wherefore they accused him, I brought him forth into their council:

29. Whom I perceived to be accused of questions of their law, but to have nothing laid to his charge worthy of death or of bonds.

30. And when it was told me how that the Jews laid wait for the man, I sent straightway to thee, and gave commandment to his accusers also to say before thee what *they* had against him. Farewell.

of the case more exactly. The conspiring Jews would waylay Paul and the Roman guards between the Tower of Antonia and the Council House and would kill him. Though this plot failed, these oath-bound Jews did not actually starve to death, for scribal casuistry had ways of relieving men from such an oath.

**16.** We know almost nothing about Paul's family. It is usually assumed that the apostle's words in Phil 3:8 that he had "suffered the loss of all things" mean that when he became a Christian, his family disinherited him. Paul never refers to any members of his family. We know, however, that he had a nephew, the son of a sister, who somehow learned of this plan of ambush (RSV). How he obtained this information we can only guess. However, he had such a warm feeling for Paul that he brought the word of the plot to the prisoner in the Tower of Antonia. Paul at once sent him to the tribune with his information.

**23,24.** The tribune, realizing that he had an explosive situation on his hands, determined to solve the problem by sending Paul under heavy guard to the Roman procurator in the capital at Caesarea. **The third hour of the night** was between 9:00 and 10:00 P.M. The word translated **spearmen** has not been found elsewhere, and its meaning is uncertain. Literally it means, *holding by the right*. This was an unusually strong guard, but the tribune was taking no chance that his prisoner might be assassinated and the responsibility fall on him. **25-30.** His letter to the procurator **Felix** explains his reason for sending Paul. For the first time we are given the name of the tribune, **Claudius Lysias.** The governor or **procurator** Felix is addressed as **most excellent** (AV) or *his Excellency* (RSV). This was the usual form of address for members of the Roman equestrian order and also for governors in certain provinces. It is the same title given to Theophilus in Lk 1:3. The tribune's explanation makes it appear that he recognized Paul as a Roman before he rescued him from the Jews (v. 27). Verse 28 suggests that the hearing before the Sanhedrin was not a formal trial but a preliminary investigation to determine the nature of the case. Lysias of course makes no reference to the fact that he had nearly scourged Paul.

**31. Antipatris** was some thirty-five to forty miles from Jerusalem. A forced march brought Paul with his heavy guard to this point by morning. **32,33.** Now the

**31.** Then the soldiers, as it was commanded them, took Paul, and brought *him* by night to Antipatris.

**32.** On the morrow they left the horsemen to go with him, and returned to the castle:

**33.** Who, when they came to Caesarea, and delivered the epistle to the governor, presented Paul also before him.

**34.** And when the governor had read *the letter*, he asked of what province he was. And when he understood that *he was* of Cilicia;

**35.** I will hear thee, said he, when thine accusers are also come. And he commanded him to be kept in Herod's judgment hall.

## CHAPTER 24

AND after five days Ananias the high priest descended with the elders, and *with* a certain orator *named* Tertullus, who informed the governor against Paul.

**2.** And when he was called forth, Tertullus began to accuse *him*, saying, Seeing that by thee we enjoy great quietness, and that very worthy deeds are done unto this nation by thy providence,

immediate danger of assassination was over, and the four hundred foot soldiers and spearmen returned to Jerusalem, while only the seventy cavalrymen accompanied Paul the remaining distance to Caesarea.

**34.** Antonius Felix was the governor or **procurator** of Judea between A.D. 52 and 58. Our historical sources refer to him as an evil man. Tacitus says that "with all manner of cruelty and lust he exercised the functions of a prince with the mind of a slave" *(Histories* 5.9). His period of office in Palestine was characterized by a growing spirit of insurrection, and he governed with a ruthless and heavy hand.

In a case such as this, he had to determine the province from which the prisoner had come, for an accused man might be tried either in his own native country or in the country in which the crime had been committed. Since **Cilicia** was a Roman province, it was proper for a Roman governor to carry out the examination without consultation with any native prince. When Jesus appeared before the procurator of Judea, Pontius Pilate, the procurator, sent him to Herod Antipas, who ruled over Galilee, from which Jesus had come. In the case of Paul, no such external consultation was found necessary.

**35.** Felix committed Paul to custody in **Herod's palace** (Gr. *praetorium*, RSV). Herod the Great had made Caesarea his capital for all Palestine and had built a palace in this city. This royal residence had been taken over by the Roman governors and made their residence and the seat of the administrative activities.

**24:1. Tertullus** was a common name in the Roman world. This Tertullus was an **advocate** or attorney (AV, *orator;* RSV *spokesman* is too colorless) familiar with Roman legal procedures, who provided professional counsel for **Ananias** and the **elders.** As the representative of his clients, he **made his charges** (AV *informed* is too colorless) to the governor against Paul.

**2.** Tertullus' use of the first person plural in his speech may indicate either that he was himself a Jew or merely that he was associating himself with his clients. The expression **our law,** if genuine, would suggest that he was in fact a Jew. Tertullus introduced his speech with customary expressions of flattery to the governor. According to the best texts, he recalled **reforms** that Felix had introduced on behalf of the Jews (RSV). **3.** The word translated

3. We accept *it* always, and in all places, most noble Felix, with all thankfulness.

4. Notwithstanding, that I be not further tedious unto thee, I pray thee that thou wouldest hear us of thy clemency a few words.

5. For we have found this man *a pestilent fellow*, and a mover of sedition among all the Jews throughout the world, and a ringleader of the sect of the Nazarenes:

6. Who also hath gone about to profane the temple: whom we took, and would have judged according to our law.

7. But the chief captain Lysias came *upon us*, and with great violence took *him* away out of our hands,

8. Commanding his accusers to come unto thee: by examining of whom thyself mayest take knowledge of all these things, whereof we accuse him.

9. And the Jews also assented, saying that these things were so.

10. Then Paul, after that the governor had beckoned unto him to speak, answered, Forasmuch as I know that thou hast been of many years a judge unto this nation, I do the more cheerfully answer for myself:

11. Because that thou mayest understand, that there are yet but twelve days since I went up to Jerusalem for to worship.

12. And they neither found me in the temple disputing with any man, neither raising up the people, neither in the synagogues, nor in the city:

13. Neither can they prove the things whereof they now accuse me.

14. But this I confess unto thee, that after the way which they call heresy, so worship I the God of my fathers, believing all things which are written in the law and in the prophets:

most noble Felix is the same word used in 23:26 and Lk 1:3, and should be translated *most excellent* Felix. 4. Clemency. Better, *kindness, moderation,* or *gentleness.* In fact, Felix was noted for his ferocity rather than for his gentleness.

5,6. Tertullus alleged a threefold accusation against Paul: 1. He was a pest who created dissension among the Jews throughout the world. 2. He was the ringleader of the sect of the Nazarenes. 3. He tried to profane the Temple. The word translated a **mover of sedition** (AV) may refer merely to dissensions among the Jews, but it may also carry a veiled hint that Paul was a leader of Jewish movements that were seditious against Rome. If so, this charge was entirely without foundation, for in every instance when Paul had appeared before Gentile rulers, he had been exonerated of any seditious tendency.

This is the only place in the NT where the followers of Jesus are called Nazarenes. The term continued to be a designation for Christians in Semitic speech, and it is used today in Hebrew and Arabic. **Sect** is the word used by Josephus to designate the various parties within Judaism, such as the Pharisees and Sadducees. The Christians were not yet recognized as a separate group but were regarded as a party within Judaism. Tertullus toned down the earlier charge (21:28) that Paul had actually defiled the Temple and alleged merely that he had attempted to do so. Actual conviction of defiling the Temple would have provided adequate ground for legal execution.

6b-8a. These words are not in the oldest texts, but they may well be authentic. Tertullus alleged that the Jewish Sanhedrin was handling Paul's case in perfectly legal fashion, when the Roman tribune, Lysias, without justification, intervened and by force took Paul out of their hands. This is, of course, a serious distortion of the facts; but Lysias was not present to give his side of the story.

10. Paul introduced his defense with a very modest compliment to Felix, implying that the governor's experience in ruling the Jews for so long a time would assure the accused a fair trial.

11-13. The apostle flatly denied the charge of stirring up dissension. 14,15. He admitted that he was a follower of the Way, but he claimed that this was the true fulfillment of the OT faith and was founded on the hope of the resurrection. Heresy (AV) is the same word translated "sect" in 24:5, and should be

**15.** And have hope toward God, which they themselves also allow, that there shall be a resurrection of the dead, both of the just and unjust.

**16.** And herein do I exercise myself, to have always a conscience void of offense toward God, and *toward* men.

**17.** Now after many years I came to bring alms to my nation, and offerings.

**18.** Whereupon certain Jews from Asia found me purified in the temple, neither with multitude, nor with tumult.

**19.** Who ought to have been here before thee, and object, if they had aught against me.

**20.** Or else let these same *here* say, if they have found any evil doing in me, while I stood before the council,

**21.** Except it be for this one voice, that I cried standing among them, Touching the resurrection of the dead I am called in question by you this day.

**22.** And when Felix heard these things, having more perfect knowledge of *that* way, he deferred them, and said, When Lysias the chief captain shall come down, I will know the uttermost of your matter.

**23.** And he commanded a centurion to keep Paul, and to let *him* have liberty, and that he should forbid none of his acquaintance to minister or come unto him.

**24.** And after certain days, when Felix came with his wife Drusilla, which was a Jewess, he sent for Paul, and heard him concerning the faith in Christ.

**25.** And as he reasoned of righteousness, temperance, and judgment to come, Felix trembled, and answered, Go thy way for this time; when I have a convenient season, I will call for thee.

so translated. It designates no "heretical" tendencies but only a legitimate party within Judaism. Nowhere in his epistles does Paul affirm the **resurrection** of both **the just and the unjust,** although his doctrine of the judgment of the unjust must imply it. In his epistles, Paul is primarily concerned with the resurrection of those who are in Christ. There is no necessity to conclude that Paul here suggests that the resurrection of all men will occur at a single time. I Cor 15:23,24 suggests that the resurrection of those who are in Christ occurs before "the end," when the final resurrection will occur.

**17,18.** Here is the one clear reference in Acts to the purpose of Paul's visit to Jerusalem, which occupies so large a place in his epistles. The evangelist had brought a collection from the Gentile churches to the impoverished Jewish Christians in Jerusalem.

**19-21.** Paul claimed that no proof had been brought of any wrongdoing on his part and that the only real charge brought against him was a doctrinal one concerning the resurrection of the dead. This was a matter in which a Roman court would have no interest or jurisdiction.

**22,23.** Felix already had a **rather accurate knowledge** (RSV) of this new sect in Judaism called **the Way.** Perhaps he had obtained this knowledge from his wife Drusilla (see v. 24). However, the statements of Tertullus and Paul embodied conflicting testimony, and therefore he adjourned the hearing until Lysias, the Roman tribune, should come to Caesarea, at which time he promised to **decide the case** (RSV). Paul was placed in a custody that allowed him considerable **liberty** and permitted his friends to minister to his needs. Luke does not inform us whether Lysias came to Caesarea and whether the promised hearing was conducted.

**24.** Drusilla was the youngest daughter of Herod Agrippa I (see 12:1). She had been married to the King of Emesa, a small state in Syria, but Felix had persuaded her to leave her first husband to marry him. The governor desired to improve his knowledge about the Way, and he therefore had Paul tell him further about **faith in Christ Jesus. 25.** Paul adapted his message to the situation, emphasizing the ethical implications of the Way. His message of **righteousness and self-control and coming judgment** understandably alarmed Felix, who dis-

26. He hoped also that money should have been given him of Paul, that he might loose him: wherefore he sent for him the oftener, and communed with him.

27. But after two years Porcius Festus came into Felix' room: and Felix, willing to show the Jews a pleasure, left Paul bound.

## CHAPTER 25

NOW when Festus was come into the province, after three days he ascended from Caesarea to Jerusalem.

2. Then the high priest and the chief of the Jews informed him against Paul, and besought him,

3. And desired favor against him, that he would send for him to Jerusalem, laying wait in the way to kill him.

4. But Festus answered, that Paul should be kept at Caesarea, and that he himself would depart shortly *thither.*

5. Let them therefore, said he, which among you are able, go down with *me,* and accuse this man, if there be any wickedness in him.

6. And when he had tarried among them more than ten days, he went down unto Caesarea; and the next day sitting on the judgment seat commanded Paul to be brought.

7. And when he was come, the Jews which came down from Jerusalem stood round about, and laid many and grievous complaints against Paul, which they could not prove.

8. While he answered for himself, Neither against the law of the Jews, neither against the temple, nor yet against Caesar, have I offended any thing at all.

missed the hearing until a later time.

26. The governor fully realized that there was no case against Paul and that he should be dismissed. Although accepting a bribe for the release of a prisoner was forbidden by Roman law, it was a common practice and quite consistent with Felix' character. The procurator, therefore, retained Paul as a prisoner and conversed with him frequently, hoping for a bribe.

27. At the end of two years, the governor was recalled to Rome by the emperor Nero under accusation by the Jews of bad administration. **Porcius Festus** succeeded him as procurator of Judea. Though Felix knew that justice required Paul's dismissal, he left him in prison because he saw that he could thereby ingratiate himself with the Jews. While this two-year incarceration must have been very trying to Paul, one redeeming feature was that throughout this entire time Luke was in Palestine with the apostle. Quite certainly Luke used this time to gather information about the life and ministry of Jesus and to compile notes about the life of the early church. This material later appeared in the Gospel of Luke and in the Acts.

25:1. Festus was a far more honorable and fair ruler than Felix. But by this time Palestine had become a hotbed of seething unrest, and he died in office without being able to settle the troubled conditions.

Festus came first to Caesarea, the capital of his province. However, since Jerusalem was the religious capital, he felt it advisable to make an early visit to that city to try to establish good relations with the leaders of his new subjects.

2,3. The Jewish rulers thought they saw in this visit an opportunity to put pressure on a new and inexperienced governor. They therefore **asked as a favor** that he send the prisoner Paul to Jerusalem. Perhaps the same forty Jews who had earlier entered into a plot now again plotted to kill Paul en route to Jerusalem. 4,5. Festus saw no reason to grant this favor. He intended shortly to return to Caesarea, and he invited **the men of authority** (RSV) or men of ability (AV, *them . . . which . . . are able*) to accompany him on his return and to accuse Paul in the capital.

6,8. Some ten days later, when the hearing was held in Caesarea, the Jewish leaders made **serious charges** (RSV)

9. But Festus, willing to do the Jews a pleasure, answered Paul, and said, Wilt thou go up to Jerusalem, and there be judged of these things before me?

10. Then said Paul, I stand at Caesar's judgment seat, where I ought to be judged: to the Jews have I done no wrong, as thou very well knowest.

11. For if I be an offender, or have committed any thing worthy of death, I refuse not to die: but if there be none of these things whereof these accuse me, no man may deliver me unto them. I appeal unto Caesar.

12. Then Festus, when he had conferred with the council, answered, Hast thou appealed unto Caesar? unto Caesar shalt thou go.

13. And after certain days king Agrippa and Bernice came unto Caesarea to salute Festus.

against the apostle for which they could bring no tangible proof whatever. Paul categorically denied that he had committed any offense against the Law, against the Temple, or against Caesar.

9. As a newcomer to Palestine, unfamiliar with Jewish affairs, Festus did not grasp the point of this argument (see v. 20). The accusations and the defense flatly contradicted each other. However, affairs were so unstable in Palestine that it seemed feasible for him to try to gain the good will of the Jewish leaders. They had previously urged that Paul be brought to Jerusalem for trial; Festus therefore suggested to the prisoner that the trial be transferred to Jerusalem to the scene of the alleged crimes.

10. This plan seemed utterly unreasonable to Paul. It was at Jerusalem that he had had to be rescued from a plot against his life, and it seemed the course of folly to risk such danger again. Although Paul had not been convicted of crime, Festus appeared willing to conciliate the Jews at the apostle's expense, and Paul doubtless feared what might be the end of such a conciliatory course. One course of action for avoiding this danger was open to him as a Roman citizen, i.e., appeal to Caesar. He was confident that in Rome he would receive a fair trial; but before the inexperienced Festus, he feared the influence of the Jews. 11. This verse suggests that real danger of death at the hands of the Jews awaited Paul in Jerusalem. The apostle asserted that he was quite willing to suffer the death penalty if he was convicted of wrongdoing. Death penalty, however, had to be imposed by Roman justice; it could not be imposed by the Jews. Therefore Paul appealed to Caesar.

12. The council (AV). Not the Jewish Sanhedrin but the circle of advisors who accompanied Festus. Apparently appeal to Caesar did not function automatically; but Festus, with the support of his council, granted this request.

13. Before Paul could be sent away, a native king, Agrippa, came to Caesarea to greet Festus as the new Roman governor. Herod Agrippa II was the son of the first persecutor of the church (ch. 12). When Agrippa I died, his kingdom was not bestowed upon his son but was placed under Roman governors. In A.D. 53 Agrippa II was given the former tetrarchies of Philip, and also Lysanias, a small area north of Palestine. Later, certain towns in Galilee and Perea were added to his domain. In addition, he was

476

14. And when they had been there many days, Festus declared Paul's cause unto the king, saying, There is a certain man left in bonds by Felix:

15. About whom, when I was at Jerusalem, the chief priests and the elders of the Jews informed *me*, desiring *to have* judgment against him.

16. To whom I answered, It is not the manner of the Romans to deliver any man to die, before that he which is accused have the accusers face to face, and have license to answer for himself concerning the crime laid against him.

17. Therefore, when they were come hither, without any delay on the morrow I sat on the judgment seat, and commanded the man to be brought forth.

18. Against whom when the accusers stood up, they brought none accusation of such things as I supposed:

19. But had certain questions against him of their own superstition, and of one Jesus, which was dead, whom Paul affirmed to be alive.

20. And because I doubted of such manner of questions, I asked *him* whether he would go to Jerusalem, and there be judged of these matters.

21. But when Paul had appealed to be reserved unto the hearing of Augustus, I commanded him to be kept till I might send him to Caesar.

22. Then Agrippa said unto Festus, I would also hear the man myself. To-morrow, said he, thou shalt hear him.

23. And on the morrow, when Agrippa was come, and Bernice, with great pomp, and was entered into the place of hearing, with the chief captains, and principal men of the city, at Festus' commandment Paul was brought forth.

24. And Festus said, King Agrippa, and all men which are here present with us, ye see this man, about whom all the multitude of the Jews have dealt with me, both at Jerusalem, and *also* here, crying that he ought not to live any longer.

25. But when I found that he had committed nothing worthy of death, and that he himself hath appealed to Augustus, I have determined to send him.

26. Of whom I have no certain thing to write unto my lord. Wherefore I have brought him forth before you, and specially before thee, O king Agrippa, that, after examination had, I might have somewhat to write.

27. For it seemeth to me unreasonable to send a prisoner, and not withal to signify the crimes *laid* against him.

entrusted with the important function of the supervision of the temple treasure in Jerusalem and with the appointment of the high priest. This gave him a large influence in Jewish affairs, and his interests thus overlapped with those of Festus. **Bernice,** sister of Herod, had been wife of an uncle, Herod of Chalcis. Her husband had died, and she was now living with her brother in Caesarea Philippi.

**14-21.** While Agrippa was in Caesarea, it occurred to Festus that here was an admirable opportunity to get help in formulating the report he must send to Caesar explaining Paul's case and the reason for his appeal to the emperor. Agrippa, who was familiar with the Jewish religion, would be able to analyze accurately the nature of the problem Festus could not understand. Therefore he outlined the case, indicating that the accusations seemed to involve no real crimes (v. 18) but only **disputations** about fine points of the Jewish religion (**superstition** is the root of the same word used in Acts 17:22) and about one Jesus whom Paul affirmed to have come back to life from the dead. The word translated **hearing** (v. 21, AV) later became a technical word for a legal decision. **Augustus** (AV) is a misleading translation. The word, which is a translation of the Latin *Augustus,* means "the revered" or "august one"; it was applied to all of the Roman emperors. Augustus was the first Roman emperor; at this time the emperor was Nero. The best modern equivalent for Augustus would be "his majesty."

**23.** A further hearing was therefore set up before Festus, Agrippa, Bernice, and an advisory council consisting of the military tribunes and the **principal men** of the city. **24-27.** Festus explained the purpose of this hearing. He had found no reason why he should accede to the demands of the Jewish leaders that Paul be put to death; but since the prisoner had appealed to the emperor, Festus had to compose a letter to explain the character of the charges that he did not understand. **Lord** (v. 26) is here applied to the emperor. This title was used in the Roman provinces of Asia to designate the emperors and carried a divine connotation. The emperor Caligula (A.D. 12−41) was the first to call himself *Dominus,* and the practice later became common.

**26:1.** When Agrippa granted Paul permission to speak for himself, the apostle **stretched forth the hand** in a gesture of

## CHAPTER 26

THEN Agrippa said unto Paul, Thou art permitted to speak for thyself. Then Paul stretched forth the hand, and answered for himself:

2. I think myself happy, king Agrippa, because I shall answer for myself this day before thee touching all the things whereof I am accused of the Jews:

3. Especially *because I know* thee to be expert in all customs and questions which are among the Jews: wherefore I beseech thee to hear me patiently.

4. My manner of life from my youth, which was at the first among mine own nation at Jerusalem, know all the Jews;

5. Which knew me from the beginning, if they would testify, that after the most straitest sect of our religion I lived a Pharisee.

6. And now I stand and am judged for the hope of the promise made of God unto our fathers:

7. Unto which *promise* our twelve tribes, instantly serving God day and night, hope to come. For which hope's sake, king Agrippa, I am accused of the Jews.

8. Why should it be thought a thing incredible with you, that God should raise the dead?

9. I verily thought with myself, that I ought to do many things contrary to the name of Jesus of Nazareth.

10. Which thing I also did in Jerusalem: and many of the saints did I shut up in prison, having received authority from the chief priests; and when they were put to death, I gave my voice against *them.*

11. And I punished them oft in every synagogue, and compelled *them* to blaspheme; and being exceedingly mad against them, I persecuted *them* even unto strange cities.

12. Whereupon as I went to Damascus with authority and commission from the chief priests,

13. At midday, O king, I saw in the way a light from heaven, above the brightness of the sun, shining round about me and them which journeyed with me.

14. And when we were all fallen to the earth, I heard a voice speaking unto me, and saying in the Hebrew tongue, Saul, Saul, why persecutest thou me? *it is* hard for thee to kick against the pricks.

salutation to the king, and made .his defense (RSV).

2,3. He expressed his gratification that he was able to make his defense before King Agrippa, because the king was an expert in Jewish customs and questions. Although Agrippa had received his throne from Rome and was pro-Roman in sympathy, he also understood the Jews and had a reputation for promoting Jewish interests so far as this was possible. Paul, therefore, believed he could convince Agrippa that his message was but the true fulfillment of the hereditary Jewish faith. The apostle outlined his upbringing, first in his own nation, in Tarsus of Cilicia, and then later at Jerusalem. (The AV omits an important connective between nation and Jerusalem.) All of the Jews knew that Paul was reared in the strictest party of the Jewish religion, that is, that he was a Pharisee.

6-8. A central doctrine in the faith of the Pharisees was that of the resurrection. The promise that God had made to the fathers was bound up with this hope in resurrection; and now it was because of this very hope which the Pharisees themselves entertained that Paul stood accused by Jews. To anyone who knew the promise given to the fathers, Paul said, it should not seem incredible that God raises the dead. The position of by Jews (v. 7) is very emphatic, suggesting that it is an utterly amazing thing that Jews who have hope in the resurrection should accuse Paul for entertaining this very hope.

9-11. Paul explained how he was brought to associate his faith in Jesus with the resurrection. He had not always been of this persuasion, for he was formerly convinced that he ought to oppose the name of Jesus of Nazareth. This account describes in greater detail than the earlier accounts Paul's persecution of the early church. The fact that some Christians were put to death is nowhere else mentioned in Acts. Paul's method was to try to make them blaspheme the name of Christ and thus renounce their faith. The tense of the Greek word indicates that Paul failed in his attempt. *Compelled them to blaspheme* (AV) says too much. To call Jesus accursed meant to renounce Christian faith.

12-14. This is the only one of the three accounts of Paul's conversion that contains the words, it is hard for thee to kick against the pricks. It is hard means "it is painful" rather than "it is difficult." Pricks. Goads, used to prod

15. And I said, Who art thou, Lord? And he said, I am Jesus whom thou persecutest.

16. But rise, and stand upon thy feet: for I have appeared unto thee for this purpose, to make thee a minister and a witness both of these things which thou hast seen, and of those things in the which I will appear unto thee;

17. Delivering thee from the people, and *from* the Gentiles, unto whom now I send thee,

18. To open their eyes, *and* to turn *them* from darkness to light, and *from* the power of Satan unto God, that they may receive forgiveness of sins, and inheritance among them which are sanctified by faith that is in me.

19. Whereupon, O king Agrippa, I was not disobedient unto the heavenly vision:

20. But showed first unto them of Damascus, and at Jerusalem, and throughout all the coasts of Judea, and *then* to the Gentiles, that they should repent and turn to God, and do works meet for repentance.

21. For these causes the Jews caught me in the temple, and went about to kill *me*.

beasts of burden. This was a proverbial saying, found in Greek and Latin but not at that time in Hebrew or Aramaic. It probably indicates that Paul had not been altogether at ease in his conscience in his persecution of Christians. We are not to think that Paul was under a great conviction of sin, for he elsewhere tells us that he persecuted the church in ignorance (I Tim 1:13). However, deep in his· mind was the nagging conviction that possibly Stephen and the other Christians were right; and the Lord now showed him that this was a divine pressure.

16-18. Before Herod there was no need to refer to Ananias as there had been earlier (22:14), when Paul was appealing to orthodox Jews. Paul therefore attributed his call directly to the Lord without mention of the human agency. His experience had convinced him that Jesus, whom he had persecuted, was alive, and had sent him both to **the people,** i.e., to the Jews, and also to **the Gentiles.** Paul laid before Agrippa the crucial issue: his message was not only for Israel but also for the Gentiles; both were to be enlightened, to turn **from darkness to light** and **from the power of Satan to God.** Thus they would receive **forgiveness of sins** and an inheritance **among those who are sanctified** by faith in Christ. This verse, which is the summary of Paul's message, is very similar to Col 1:12-14.

19,20. These verses are designed to give not a chronological outline but merely a rough summary of Paul's whole missionary career. Paul preached repentance and conversion first in Damascus, then in Jerusalem, then throughout the country of Judea, and also to the Gentiles, as he was commissioned to do. There is a problem in harmonizing this statement with Gal 1:22, which says that Paul was unknown personally to the churches of Christ in Judea. Possibly the correct text should have read, "in every land to both Jews and Gentiles" (see Bruce, *Commentary,* following Blass).

21. Festus had been unable to understand the basic reason for the animosity of the Jews against Paul. Paul explained that he had been proclaiming the fulfillment of the promise made to the fathers as including the Gentiles as well as the Jews. For this reason the Jews caught him in the Temple and tried to kill him. "Knowing the Jews as he did, perhaps Agrippa understood why they would cherish such animosity towards

22. Having therefore obtained help of God, I continue unto this day, witnessing both to small and great, saying none other things than those which the prophets and Moses did say should come:

23. That Christ should suffer, *and* that he should be the first that should rise from the dead, and should show light unto the people, and to the Gentiles.

24. And as he thus spake for himself, Festus said with a loud voice, Paul, thou art beside thyself; much learning doth make thee mad.

25. But he said, I am not mad, most noble Festus; but speak forth the words of truth and soberness.

26. For the king knoweth of these things, before whom also I speak freely: for I am persuaded that none of these things are hidden from him; for this thing was not done in a corner.

27. King Agrippa, believest thou the prophets? I know that thou believest.

28. Then Agrippa said unto Paul, Almost thou persuadest me to be a Christian.

a former rabbi who would offer Gentile believers spiritual privileges on the same footing as the chosen people" (F. F. Bruce).

**22,23.** Paul concluded by insisting that his message embodied nothing except that which Moses and the prophets had foretold; namely, that **the Messiah must suffer** and that **He should be the first that should rise from the dead** and should proclaim light both to the Jews and to the Gentiles. This explains why Paul previously placed such emphasis upon the Resurrection. The traditional Jewish hope of resurrection had now taken a new turn because of the resurrection of Christ. The resurrection of the Messiah was not an isolated event, but the beginning of the resurrection itself. Christ was "the firstfruits of them that sleep" (I Cor 15:20), "the firstborn from the dead" (Col 1:18).

**24.** To the Roman Festus, this line of thought was one which no sane man could pursue. Paul was obviously a man of extensive learning, but he must be insane to harbor such ideas of resurrection from the dead.

**25-27.** Paul replied that he was quite sane and was speaking **the sober truth.** He then appealed to King Agrippa to vouch for the sobriety and the sanity of what he had just said. He reminded Agrippa that the death and resurrection of Jesus had not **escaped** his notice, for they were **not done in a corner** where no one would behold them. When anyone compares these events with the prophets, he must be convinced of the soundness of Paul's position; and Paul therefore appealed directly to the king, **Do you believe the prophets? I know that you believe.** This appeal placed Agrippa in an uncomfortable dilemma. As a representative of Rome and a colleague of Festus in the administration of government, he did not wish to appear to Festus to share Paul's insanity, and therefore it would have been unpleasant to agree with Paul and admit that he believed the prophets. On the other hand, to deny that he believed the prophets would have seriously impaired his influence with the Jews. Agrippa therefore parried Paul's appeal with the response, **In short, you are trying to make me play the Christian.** The Greek phrase is very difficult and literally translated says, *In a little you are persuading me to make a Christian. In a little* may mean either, "in a little time" or "in brief." *To make a Christian* may mean either to become a Christian or to play the role of a

29. And Paul said, I would to God, that not only thou, but also all that hear me this day, were both almost, and altogether such as I am, except these bonds.

30. And when he had thus spoken, the king rose up, and the governor, and Bernice, and they that sat with them:

31. And when they were gone aside, they talked between themselves, saying, This man doeth nothing worthy of death or of bonds.

32. Then said Agrippa unto Festus, This man might have been set at liberty, if he had not appealed unto Caesar.

## CHAPTER 27

AND when it was determined that we should sail into Italy, they delivered Paul and certain other prisoners unto *one* named Julius, a centurion of Augustus' band.

2. And entering into a ship of Adramyttium, we launched, meaning to sail by the coasts of Asia; *one* Aristarchus, a Macedonian of Thessalonica, being with us.

Christian. The translation of the AV is certainly incorrect; Agrippa was not on the point of becoming a Christian. His remark may be a sarcastic parry of Paul's appeal: "In a short time, you think to make me a Christian!" (RSV). However, the rendition suggested above (that of F. F. Bruce) makes Agrippa brush aside Paul's appeal by replying that Paul is not going to make Agrippa play the role of a Christian and try to persuade Festus of the correctness of his prisoner's position.

29. Paul took Agrippa's light comment seriously and replied solemnly, **whether in short or at length** (literally, *in a little or in a great deal*) he wished that all men who heard him might become Christians as he was—with the exception of the chains he was wearing because he was a Christian.

30-32. When Paul ended his defense, Festus, Agrippa, and Bernice, together with their advisors, withdrew to deliberate on the matter. It was obvious that Paul had violated no law and deserved neither death nor imprisonment. He deserved only to be set free; but since he had appealed to Caesar, the legal processes had to be carried out and the appeal carried through. We are to suppose that Festus, with the aid of Agrippa, composed the letter to the emperor explaining the charges of the Jews and recommending Paul's dismissal.

B. Reception of the Gospel in Rome. 27:1–28:31. Luke now relates Paul's journey from Palestine to Italy and his reception in Rome. The fact that Luke tells in detail about this trip shows how important it was for his purpose. The motif of the journey, in Luke's account, is not the initial evangelization of the Roman capital but the rejection of the Gospel by the Jews in Rome and its acceptance by the Gentiles. This brings to a climax one of the central motifs of the entire book—the rejection of Israel and the rise of the Gentile church.

27:1,2. The account of Paul's journey begins with the third "we" section. The last "we" reference was 21:18, when Paul, accompanied by Luke, arrived in Jerusalem; and we must assume that during the two years of Paul's imprisonment, Luke was in the area of Caesarea. Luke now accompanied Paul, along with **Aristarchus** of Thessalonica (see 19:29; 20:4), who had come with the apostle from Thessalonica to Jerusalem. The Roman authorities delivered Paul to a

3. And the next *day* we touched at Sidon. And Julius courteously entreated Paul, and gave *him* liberty to go unto his friends to refresh himself.

4. And when we had launched from thence, we sailed under Cyprus, because the winds were contrary.

5. And when we had sailed over the sea of Cilicia and Pamphylia, we came to Myra, *a city* of Lycia.

6. And there the centurion found a ship of Alexandria sailing into Italy; and he put us therein.

7. And when we had sailed slowly many days, and scarce were come over against Cnidus, the wind not suffering us, we sailed under Crete, over against Salmone;

8. And, hardly passing it, came unto a place which is called the Fair Havens; nigh whereunto was the city *of* Lasea.

9. Now when much time was spent, and when sailing was now dangerous, because the fast was now already past, Paul admonished *them*,

centurion named Julius. The band called the **Augustan cohort** has not been identified with any certainty. The centurion was responsible for the safe delivery of Paul and some other prisoners. The point of embarkation is not mentioned, but it was probably Caesarea. Here they found a coasting vessel from **Adramyttium**, a port of Mysia lying south of Troas in Asia Minor. The course of this ship called for it to sail to the ports along the coast of Asia en route to its home port.

3. The first port of call was Sidon of Phoenicia. The centurion **Julius treated** Paul with special kindness, and gave him liberty to go ashore while the ship was unloading and also to visit his friends, who constituted the Christian community in that city, and receive their ministrations.

4. Since the prevailing summer winds blew from the west or the northwest, the ship sailed between **Cyprus** and the mainland rather than directly into the wind. 5. It was now necessary to leave the coast and to sail across the open sea westward below **Cilicia** and **Pamphylia**. **Myra** of Lycia was a port of call for large ships, especially grain ships, sailing between Egypt and Rome, which found it impossible to sail directly across the sea because of the northwesterly winds. 6. At **Myra** they changed ships, leaving the coasting vessel and taking a grain ship that was sailing from **Alexandria** to **Italy**. Egypt was the chief source of supply of grain for Rome, and the transportation of grain between Alexandria and Rome was an important business conducted under the supervision of the state.

7. The voyage from Myra into the face of the westerly winds was difficult. But after several days they arrived **with difficulty** at **Cnidus** on a promontory at the southwest tip of Asia Minor. From this point, they had the choice of waiting for a more favorable wind and sailing directly westward, or else sailing southward toward Crete. Since **the wind did not allow us to go on** (RSV), the writer says, they chose the latter alternative and sailed southward around **Salome** at the eastern end of Crete and then coasted along westward under the island.

8. After sailing along the coast **with difficulty** (*hardly passing it*, AV) they came to a port called **Fair Havens** midway in the island. 9. West of Fair Havens the coast of Crete falls off

10. And said unto them, Sirs, I perceive that this voyage will be with hurt and much damage, not only of the lading and ship, but also of our lives.

11. Nevertheless the centurion believed the master and the owner of the ship, more than those things which were spoken by Paul.

12. And because the haven was not commodious to winter in, the more part advised to depart thence also, if by any means they might attain to Phenice, *and there* to winter; *which is* a haven of Crete, and lieth toward the southwest and northwest.

13. And when the south wind blew softly, supposing that they had obtained *their* purpose, loosing *thence*, they sailed close by Crete.

14. But not long after there arose against it a tempestuous wind, called Euroclydon.

15. And when the ship was caught, and could not bear up into the wind, we let *her* drive.

16. And running under a certain island which is called Clauda, we had much work to come by the boat:

17. Which when they had taken up, they used helps, undergirding the ship; and, fearing lest they should fall into the quicksands, struck sail, and so were driven.

abruptly to the north, so that from that point a ship would be completely exposed to the northwest winds. The sailboats used in the ancient Mediterranean world were not large or sturdy enough to face the winter storms. The dangerous season for sailing began about September 14, and after November 11 all sailing came to an end for the winter. The fast to which Luke refers is the Day of Atonement, which fell at the end of September or early in October.

10,11. Paul, who was an experienced traveler (II Cor 11:25 says he was shipwrecked three times), advised against continuing the journey at this time lest there be much loss of life as well as of cargo. His advice was opposed by the captain (*master*, AV) who was in control of navigation and was the owner of the ship. The centurion in charge of the prisoners, being the highest official on ship, ranked as the commanding officer; and he followed the advice (*believed*, AV) of the shipmaster and owner rather than that of Paul, and decided not to stay at Fair Havens.

12. Fair Havens was not a suitable harbor to winter in, since it was quite exposed. Apparently the advice of all on shipboard was sought, and the majority advised that they sail from Fair Havens on the chance that they might reach the harbor of Phoenix, which lay further west in Crete, facing southwest and northwest.

13. Leaving Fair Havens, they were favored by a gentle south wind and were able to follow close along the shore of the island. 14. Suddenly, however, the gentle breeze turned into a tempestuous wind blowing from the northeast. Euroclydon, meaning "northeaster," is a hybrid word, partly Greek and partly Latin. 15. At this point they were not far from their destination of Phoenix; but when the ship could not head into the wind because of its violence, they had to surrender to the wind and be driven by it.

16. As they came opposite a small island called Cauda (other manuscripts read *Clauda*), they found it necessary to pull on board the small boat that was carried in tow behind the ship. By this time, this little boat was so waterlogged, that it was secured only with difficulty.

17. Measures were then taken to undergird the ship. The nature of this operation is not clear, but it perhaps consisted of running ropes underneath the boat to strengthen it. The ship was now being driven toward the southwest

18. And we being exceedingly tossed with a tempest, the next *day* they lightened the ship;

19. And the third *day* we cast out with our own hands the tackling of the ship.

20. And when neither sun nor stars in many days appeared, and no small tempest lay on *us*, all hope that we should be saved was then taken away.

21. But after long abstinence, Paul stood forth in the midst of them, and said, Sirs, ye should have hearkened unto me, and not have loosed from Crete, and to have gained this harm and loss.

22. And now I exhort you to be of good cheer: for there shall be no loss of *any man's* life among you, but of the ship.

23. For there stood by me this night the angel of God, whose I am, and whom I serve,

24. Saying, Fear not, Paul; thou must be brought before Caesar: and, lo, God hath given thee all them that sail with thee.

25. Wherefore, sirs, be of good cheer: for I believe God, that it shall be even as it was told me.

26. Howbeit we must be cast upon a certain island.

27. But when the fourteenth night was come, as we were driven up and down in Adria, about midnight the shipmen deemed that they drew near to some country;

28. And sounded, and found *it* twenty fathoms: and when they had gone a little further, they sounded again, and found *it* fifteen fathoms.

29. Then fearing lest we should have fallen upon rocks, they cast four anchors out of the stern, and wished for the day.

30. And as the shipmen were about to flee out of the ship, when they had let down the boat into the sea, under color as though they would have cast anchors out of the foreship,

31. Paul said to the centurion and to the soldiers, Except these abide in the ship, ye cannot be saved.

32. Then the soldiers cut off the ropes of the boat, and let her fall off.

in the direction of Cyrene. Off the north African shore was a dangerous quicksand called **Syrtis** (RSV), and since the sailors feared that they would be driven across the sea onto these shoals, they **lowered the gear** (RSV). This may mean that they *struck sail* (AV), or it may mean that they let out a sea anchor to slow their speed, or that they set storm sails. Nevertheless, they were driven on by the wind.

18. By the next day, the tempest had not weakened, and it was therefore necessary to **throw the cargo overboard** (literally, *they made an ejection*). 19. When the storm did not abate on the next day, they threw overboard all extra **tackle** and gear.

20. Since sailors were entirely dependent upon the sun and stars for navigation, hope was at last abandoned of being saved, since they had no idea where they were and where they were being driven by the tempest.

21-26. The combination of seasickness, pitching decks, and soaked provisions had caused them to go long without food. *Long abstinence* (AV) should not be understood to denote a deliberate fast. Finally, Paul offered a word of encouragement which he prefaced with the all-too-human reminder, "I told you so." He informed the crew and the passengers that an angel of God had appeared to him and assured him that he would escape this peril to **stand before Caesar**, and that his traveling companions would be saved along with him.

27. Experts have figured that it would take exactly fourteen days to drift the distance indicated in the narrative. **Up and down** (AV). Inaccurate. They were drifting *across the sea of Adria*. Adria does not refer to the Adriatic Sea but is a term commonly used of the entire eastern Mediterranean. Something now led the sailors to believe that (lit.) *some land was approaching*. Probably the sound of breakers resounded through the darkness and warned that they were approaching the land. 28. Soundings indicated that the water was growing increasingly shallow.

30. Some of the sailors decided to escape from the ship to the shore by a small boat rather than risk falling upon the rocks. Therefore, **under pretext** of casting anchors from the **bow**, they undertook to flee the ship. 31,32. Paul detected the plan and warned the **centurion** and the soldiers that safety lay in staying

33. And while the day was coming on, Paul besought *them* all to take meat, saying, This day is the fourteenth day that ye have tarried and continued fasting, having taken nothing.

34. Wherefore I pray you to take *some* meat; for this is for your health: for there shall not a hair fall from the head of any of you.

35. And when he had thus spoken, he took bread, and gave thanks to God in presence of them all; and when he had broken *it*, he began to eat.

36. Then were they all of good cheer, and they also took *some* meat.

37. And we were in all in the ship two hundred threescore and sixteen souls.

38. And when they had eaten enough, they lightened the ship, and cast out the wheat into the sea.

39. And when it was day, they knew not the land: but they discovered a certain creek with a shore, into the which they were minded, if it were possible, to thrust in the ship.

40. And when they had taken up the anchors, they committed *themselves* unto the sea, and loosed the rudder bands, and hoisted up the mainsail to the wind, and made toward shore.

41. And falling into a place where two seas met, they ran the ship aground; and the forepart stuck fast, and remained unmovable, but the hinder part was broken with the violence of the waves.

42. And the soldiers' counsel was to kill the prisoners, lest any of them should swim out, and escape.

43. But the centurion, willing to save Paul, kept them from *their* purpose; and commanded that they which could swim should cast *themselves* first *into the sea*, and get to land:

44. And the rest, some on boards, and some on *broken pieces* of the ship. And so it came to pass, that they escaped all safe to land.

## CHAPTER 28

AND when they were escaped, then they knew that the island was called Melita.

2. And the barbarous people showed us no little kindness: for they kindled a fire, and received us every one, because of the present rain, and because of the cold.

with the ship. The sailors' plan was frustrated when the soldiers cut away the ropes of the boat and thus let it fall away.

**33-36.** At daybreak, Paul advised the crew and passengers to break their involuntary fast and eat some food, that they might be strengthened by it, and he assured them that no one would perish in the landing that lay ahead. He then set the example by giving thanks to God and eating a substantial meal. All were encouraged and followed his example. **38.** After all had eaten their fill, they cast the rest of the cargo of wheat into the sea to lighten the ship in preparation for the landing.

**39.** When daylight came and they were able to see the shore, they did not recognize the land. But they observed a bay with a beach, where they planned to bring the ship ashore. **40.** Therefore they **cast off the anchors and left them in the sea** (RSV; this is a far more probable translation than that of the AV). **Rudders.** Two large steering oars on each side of the boat, which would have been lashed tight during the storm. Now these rudders were freed, a small **foresail** was raised to the wind (not *mainsail*, AV), and the ship headed toward the shore.

**41.** However, the men did not reach the shore, for the ship ran aground on a narrow strip of submerged land separating two stretches of deeper water (the Greek is, **a place of two seas**). The bow of the ship was stuck fast in this shoal, but the force of the waves against the stern was breaking the ship in two.

**42,43.** The soldiers guarding the prisoners wished to follow the traditional Roman discipline and kill their charges rather than risk the escape of any of them. But the centurion, who had become favorably disposed toward Paul and did not wish to see his death, forbade their doing this. Rather, he ordered all to escape to the shore either by swimming, by floating on planks, or by being carried on the backs of some of the crew (the Greek is, **on some of those from the ship; those** may be either neuter or masculine). Thus all safely reached the land.

**28:1.** After coming ashore, they discovered that the island was called **Melita** (AV; modern *Malta*, RSV) lying about a hundred miles directly south of Sicily. Melita (the Canaanite word for "refuge") was inhabited by people of Phoenician extraction. **2.** From the Roman and Greek point of view, every one who spoke a foreign language was called a barbarian.

3. And when Paul had gathered a bundle of sticks, and laid *them* on the fire, there came a viper out of the heat, and fastened on his hand.

4. And when the barbarians saw the *venomous* beast hang on his hand, they said among themselves, No doubt this man is a murderer, whom, though he hath escaped the sea, yet vengeance suffereth not to live.

5. And he shook off the beast into the fire, and felt no harm.

6. Howbeit they looked when he should have swollen, or fallen down dead suddenly: but after they had looked a great while, and saw no harm come to him, they changed their minds, and said that he was a god.

7. In the same quarters were possessions of the chief man of the island, whose name was Publius; who received us, and lodged us three days courteously.

8. And it came to pass, that the father of Publius lay sick of a fever and of a bloody flux: to whom Paul entered in, and prayed, and laid his hands on him, and healed him.

9. So when this was done, others also, which had diseases in the island, came, and were healed:

10. Who also honored us with many honors; and when we departed, they laded *us* with such things as were necessary.

11. And after three months we departed in a ship of Alexandria, which had wintered in the isle, whose sign was Castor and Pollux.

Barbarous people (AV) has no reference to fierce character or primitive culture, but merely indicates that their language (Phoenician) was not Greek or Latin. Since it was raining and cold, these natives showed no usual kindness by building a fire so that the chilled and soaked travelers might warm themselves.

3. A large fire for such a large company needed constant replenishing with fuel, and Paul set about gathering wood for the flames. In one bundle was a poisonous snake, stiff from the cold; and as the apostle stood by the fire warming his hands, the viper, revived by the heat, crawled away from the flames and sank its fangs into Paul's hand. 4. The natives interpreted this event in terms of their own superstition. They concluded that Paul actually was a murderer; and although he had escaped death in the sea, the goddess of justice, *Dike,* had now wrought a proper fate upon him. 5,6. When Paul shook the snake off into the fire without injury, the natives decided that they had been completely wrong. Instead of a victim of the gods, he was himself a divine being who could not be hurt by ordinary human misfortunes.

7. The chief man of the island. The leading official. The word used has been found in two inscriptions as a title for an official in the island. We do not know whether this chief man was a native official or a representative of Rome. This Publius had an estate in the neighborhood, where he entertained Paul and his companions for three days, showing them gracious hospitality.

8. Dysentery and fever were common on the island of Malta. 9,10. Healed in 28:9 is a different word from that in 28:8, and might better be translated *were cured* or *were treated.* It suggests not miraculous healings but medical treatment, probably at the hands of Luke the physician. Verses 10 and 11 suggest that this medical ministry lasted throughout the three months stay at Malta, so that when Paul and Luke left the island, they were honored with many honors, and their ship was loaded with everything they needed for the remaining journey.

11. The shipwreck had taken place during the first half of November. Three months later, or the middle of February, would still be considered early for safe sailing, but apparently an early spring had come. They found a ship sailing from Alexandria to Italy, which had spent the winter in the island. Ancient ships took

12. And landing at Syracuse, we tarried *there* three days.

13. And from thence we fetched a compass, and came to Rhegium: and after one day the south wind blew, and we came the next day to Puteoli:

14. Where we found brethren, and were desired to tarry with them seven days: and so we went toward Rome.

15. And from thence, when the brethren heard of us, they came to meet us as far as Appii Forum, and the Three Taverns; whom when Paul saw, he thanked God, and took courage.

16. And when we came to Rome, the centurion delivered the prisoners to the captain of the guard: but Paul was suffered to dwell by himself with a soldier that kept him.

their names from their figureheads. This ship had as its figurehead or sign (AV) the *Dioscuri,* a term meaning the "sons of Zeus," designating the two brothers, Castor and Pollux, who were regarded as the patron deities of sailors. 12. Sailing directly north, they came to Syracuse, the most important city of Sicily, located on the southeastern side of the island.

13. From Syracuse, since the winds were not favorable, it was necessary to make a circuit or tack back and forth in order to reach Rhegium on the toe of Italy. The quaint archaism of the AV, *fetched a compass,* has nothing to do with instruments of navigation. Here the party waited for a more favorable wind, and when the south wind arose on the next day, they easily came to Puteoli, on the bay of Naples, the regular port of arrival for grain ships coming from Alexandria.

14. Apparently Julius, the centurion in charge of the prisoners, had official business that detained him in Puteoli, and he permitted Paul to accept the invitation of Christian brethren in the city to spend the seven days with them. Similar permission had been granted in Sidon (27:3).

15. News of Paul's approach reached Rome during these seven days, and Christian brethren came down the Appian Way to meet Paul and Luke and to accompany them back to the city. The word rendered to meet is the same word used of the 'rapture' of believers to meet the Lord in the air at his second coming (I Thess 4:17). It is a term regularly used of the official welcome tendered by a delegation who went out to meet a visiting official and accompany him into the city. The Forum of Appius is some forty-three miles from Rome, and Three Taverns is about ten miles nearer. Both were stopping places on the Appian Way, with inns where travelers might lodge.

16. The statement, the centurion delivered the prisoners to the captain of the guard, is found in only a few of the ancient texts and is probably not authentic. Paul was not locked up in prison but was placed under the guard of a soldier who was responsible with his life to present the prisoner at the proper time. Paul was chained by the wrist to the soldier (see v. 20) but was permitted to maintain his own dwelling and to exercise a large measure of freedom. This is the last of the "we" sections. However, since Luke is mentioned in Paul's correspondence written from Rome (Phm

17. And it came to pass, that after three days Paul called the chief of the Jews together: and when they were come together, he said unto them, Men *and* brethren, though I have committed nothing against the people, or customs of our fathers, yet was I delivered prisoner from Jerusalem into the hands of the Romans:

18. Who, when they had examined me, would have let *me* go, because there was no cause of death in me.

19. But when the Jews spake against *it*, I was constrained to appeal unto Caesar; not that I had aught to accuse my nation of.

20. For this cause therefore have I called for you, to see *you*, and to speak with *you*: because that for the hope of Israel I am bound with this chain.

21. And they said unto him, We neither received letters out of Judea concerning thee, neither any of the brethren that came showed or spake any harm of thee.

22. But we desire to hear of thee what thou thinkest: for as concerning this sect, we know that every where it is spoken against.

23. And when they had appointed him a day, there came many to him into *his* lodging; to whom he expounded and testified the kingdom of God, persuading them concerning Jesus, both out of the law of Moses, and *out of* the prophets, from morning till evening.

24; Col 4:14), it is clear that he remained with the prisoner in Rome.

**17-20.** There were a number of Jewish synagogues in Rome, but since Paul was a prisoner, even though he enjoyed some freedom, it was not convenient for him to visit them. Therefore he called the leaders of the Jews together that he might present his case to them. He claimed that he had violated none of the Jewish customs and as an innocent man was delivered prisoner into the hands of the Romans. In spite of the fact that the Romans had wished to release him, the Jews had opposed their decision, and so Paul had felt that his only way of escape was to appeal to Caesar. However, Paul did not desire to make any accusation against the Jews for their treatment of him. He was a prisoner only because of **the hope of Israel.** By this, he meant that his Christian faith was the true fulfillment of the hope of God's people.

**21,22.** The Jewish leaders declared that they had received neither letters nor emissaries from Jerusalem charging Paul with any evil. Furthermore, they implied that they were not familiar with the **sect** to which Paul belonged but had only heard that it was strongly criticized everywhere. F. F. Bruce (*Commentary on Acts*) logically suggests that at this point the Jewish leaders were telling less than the whole truth. It would have been impossible for them to have been unfamiliar with the Christian church in Rome, since we know from Paul's letter to the Romans that a vigorous church existed there (see also 18:2). Furthermore, it was highly unlikely that word would not have reached the Roman Jews from Jerusalem, because constant communication was sustained. However, it was apparent that no sound case could be registered against Paul, and the Jews therefore felt it the better part of wisdom to dissociate themselves entirely from Paul's case and thus avoid incurring the wrath of the Roman government.

**23.** Some time later, the Jews came together again in the house where Paul was staying to listen to his opinions. Paul's message consisted of testifying **the kingdom of God, persuading concerning Jesus.** The **things concerning Jesus** and **the kingdom of God** are clearly synonymous concepts. Paul undertook to show that the things about Jesus and the kingdom of God were the true fulfillment of the law of Moses and the prophets and that the ancestral faith of Israel had

24. And some believed the things which were spoken, and some believed not.

25. And when they agreed not among themselves, they departed, after that Paul had spoken one word, Well spake the Holy Ghost by Esaias the prophet unto our fathers,

26. Saying, Go unto this people, and say, Hearing ye shall hear, and shall not understand; and seeing ye shall see, and not perceive:

27. For the heart of this people is waxed gross, and their ears are dull of hearing, and their eyes have they closed; lest they should see with *their* eyes, and hear with *their* ears, and understand with *their* heart, and should be converted, and I should heal them.

28. Be it known therefore unto you, that the salvation of God is sent unto the Gentiles, and *that* they will hear it.

29. And when he had said these words, the Jews departed, and had great reasoning among themselves.

30. And Paul dwelt two whole years in his own hired house, and received all that came in unto him,

31. Preaching the kingdom of God, and teaching those things which concern the Lord Jesus Christ, with all confidence, no man forbidding him.

found its fulfillment in the Christian faith.

**24-27.** The reaction of the Jewish leaders at Rome to Paul's message was the same as he had everywhere met. Some believed, but the majority rejected his message. Seeing this, Paul quoted from Isa 6:9,10, which describes the dullness and the spiritual hardness of God's people. Their plight is hopeless, and they are unable to turn to God to be healed.

**28.** The book of Acts comes to a climax with this statement: *The salvation of God is now sent to the Gentiles, who will listen to the message.* The last eight chapters of the book of Acts—over a quarter of the book—are devoted to a record of Paul's experiences in Jerusalem and of his journey to Rome. The question rises: Why did Luke devote so much space to these events when his earlier narrative passed over other equally important events with the barest summary? The answer must be that one of Luke's major purposes was to show that just as the Jewish nation rejected Jesus as her Messiah and sent him to a cross, so the leaders of the Jews, both in Jerusalem and in Rome, confirmed their apostate character by rejecting the greatest figure of the apostolic church and his gospel. On the other hand, everywhere Paul went, he was received by the Gentile worshipers in the synagogues and was extended the protection of the Roman authorities. This keynote of the obdurate character of Israel and the responsiveness of the Gentiles is summarized in Acts 28:25-28. These words stand as a formal pronouncement of the divine displeasure for the rebelliousness of Israel. Henceforth the Gospel was to find lodging among the Gentiles. Israel's rebellion was complete.

**30,31.** The ending of The Acts leaves the thoughtful reader with many unanswered questions in his mind. Paul lived in Rome for two whole years, not confined in prison but permitted to maintain **his own hired dwelling** under the custody of a Roman soldier. This did not permit him complete freedom of activity but did enable him to receive all who wished to converse with him and hear his message. Luke again summarizes Paul's ministry in Rome with the two phrases **preaching the kingdom of God, and teaching those things which concern the Lord Jesus Christ.** The obvious conclusion is that the good news about the kingdom of God is synonymous with the things which concern the Lord Jesus Christ. This is the same message he had preached to the Jewish leaders when they came to him upon his arrival in Rome (v. 23).

We are left with the questions: How did Paul's imprisonment end? What was the outcome of his appeal to Caesar? Was he found guilty and executed, or was he found innocent and dismissed; or was the case dismissed by default? The natural implication of 28:30 is that after the two years, the apostle was released from detention. Tradition tells us that he was executed in Rome about or shortly after A.D. 64. This leaves an interval of some two or three years between the end of Acts and Paul's death. The three Pastoral Epistles which claim to have been written by Paul reflect a ministry of traveling and preaching that cannot be fitted into the narrative of the book of Acts. In spite of arguments against the authenticity of the Pastoral Epistles, the most likely conclusion is that Paul was released after the two years of imprisonment, engaged in a further ministry, which is reflected in these letters, and finally suffered a second imprisonment in Rome, which is reflected in II Timothy.

The rather abrupt ending of the book of Acts has been variously explained. Some have maintained that Luke had intended to write a third volume to record the trial and release of Paul and his subsequent missionary travels, but for some reason was prevented from carrying out his purpose. Another possible explanation is that Acts was written during the two-year imprisonment, for we know from Phm 24 and Col 4:14 that Luke was with Paul during this interval in Rome. It is likely that Luke had gathered material for his narrative about the early church during the two years of Paul's detention in Caesarea and composed the book of Acts during these two years in Rome. In this case, the narrative ends as it does because it had caught up with history, and at the moment there was nothing more to record.

It is probable that the letters to the Philippians, Ephesians, and Colossians, and that to Philemon were written by Paul during his Roman detention. However, some scholars have felt that these "Prison Epistles" were written either from an imprisonment in Ephesus which is not mentioned in Acts, or possibly from the Caesarean imprisonment.

# BIBLIOGRAPHY

BLAIKLOCK, E. M. *The Acts of the Apostles (Tyndale Commentaries).* Grand Rapids: Wm. B. Eerdmans Pub. Co., 1959.

BRUCE, F. F. *Commentary on the Book of the Acts (The New International Commentary).* Grand Rapids: Wm. B. Eerdmans Pub. Co., 1954.

JACKSON, F. J. FOAKES, and LAKE, KIRSOPP. *The Beginnings of Christianity.* 5 vols. London: Macmillan and Co., 1933–1943.

RACKHAM, R. B. *The Acts of the Apostles (Westminster Commentaries).* London: Methuen and Co., 1908.

# THE EPISTLE TO THE ROMANS

## INTRODUCTION

*Original Readers.* One gains help in understanding the letters or epistles of the New Testament by learning as much as possible about the people who first received these writings. This is surely true regarding the letter to the Romans. Although most of the first eleven chapters of the book seem quite general, in the last five chapters the reader is made aware of a particular community with particular needs. Then we realize that the teaching of the first eleven chapters, though universal in outlook, contains certain emphases which Paul felt were especially needed by believers in Rome (the right basis of judgment of those who did not know the Jewish law, the relation of the Gentiles to Abraham and the patriarchs, etc.).

The apostle addresses his letter to believers — "To all those who are in Rome, beloved by God, called to be saints" (1:7). Paul's practice in writing to churches was to have the word "church" in the salutation (cf. I Cor 1:2; II Cor 1:1; Gal 1:2; I Thess 1:1; II Thess 1:1) or the word "saint" as the designation of those addressed (Eph 1:1; Phil 1:1; Col 1:2). The address here is a variation of the second of these procedures. The greeting in Romans does not imply a strongly knit church organization, and chapter 16 gives a picture of small groups of believers rather than of one large group.

Were these believers predominantly Jewish or Gentile? This question must be answered in the light of what Romans explicitly says. It is true that a good deal of the content relates to the Jewish people — God's dealing with them in the past, the present, and the future. But the readers are addressed in a manner which leaves no doubt that they were predominantly Gentile (see 1:5,6; 1:13; 11:13; 15:15,16). There probably were Jewish Christians in the church, but they constituted a minority.

It seems pertinent to ask how the church at Rome was founded. Unfortunately there are no documents from the first century that provide the answer.

A number of suggestions have been made. It has been asserted that the "strangers of Rome, Jews and proselytes," who witnessed the coming of the Holy Spirit (Acts 2:10) may have returned to the city and established a nucleus of believers there. However, the Christians after Pentecost did not immediately feel themselves distinct from Judaism nor begin to start local churches in distinction from the synagogues. Hence, the beginning of a Christian church in Rome right after Pentecost is unlikely. Others believe that the church in Rome was founded by missionaries from Antioch (cf. Hans Lietzmann, *The Beginnings of the Christian Church,* trans. Bertram Lee Woolf, pp. 111, 133, 199). Since Antioch was a missionary center, this is certainly plausible. But the best suggestion seems to be that the church was founded and enlarged by converts of Paul, Stephen, and the other apostles who traveled to the imperial city either on business or to live there.

When did Peter and Paul arrive at Rome? If one compares the statements in the early Church Fathers with the New Testament evidence, it seems unlikely that either apostle reached Rome before A.D. 60, several years after Romans was written. If Peter had been at Rome when Paul wrote this epistle, Paul certainly would have sent him greetings. Paul's longstanding desire to preach in Rome (Rom 1:11-13) and his policy of not building upon another man's foundation (15:20) make it seem unlikely that Peter was even in Rome before the time of the writing of Romans.

*Authorship and Date.* There is almost universal agreement that Paul was the author of this epistle. This is based on statements in chapters 1 and 15, on the style and argument put forth in the intervening chapters, and on the testimony of all from ancient times who quote the epistle.

The only questions raised regarding authorship concern chapter 16 and the doxologies. In 16:3-16 there is a long list of persons to whom greetings are sent. Priscilla and Aquila are mentioned in 16:3-5, but Acts 18:18,19 declares that Paul left them in Ephesus. Because of this, some have concluded that Romans 16, containing these names, originally was addressed by Paul to Ephesus. Epaenetus is mentioned in 16:5, where he is referred to as the first fruits of Asia (i.e., of Asia Minor). This also is assumed to support the conclusion that this section was written to Ephesus. But the evidence does not demand this conclusion. Priscilla and Aquila traveled a great deal. Since they originally came from Italy (Acts 18:2), it would not be strange for them to return. The fact that Epaenetus was the first convert of Asia Minor does not prove that he lived there all of his life. One of Paul's consistent practices was that he did not send greetings by name to individuals in places where he personally had ministered (cf. I Cor, II Cor, I and II Thess, Phil, Eph [Ephesus and Asia Minor], and Gal). But in Romans and Colossians he does greet persons by name. In these places where he had not been he could include everyone he knew, in order to establish rapport. Or if he made a selection, the purpose would be evident, so that no one would feel slighted.

In the Authorized (King James) Version of Romans, there are five doxologies or benedictions — 15:13; 15:33; 16:20; 16:24; 16:25-27. In each of these, either God or Christ is besought to do something, to be with the readers, or to provide the readers with grace. The first (15:13) concludes the section in which Paul sets forth the ethical conduct of a Christian and the need for Christians to live in harmony and understanding with each other. The second (15:33) ends a section where Paul tells of his travel plans and his bringing of a collection to Jerusalem, and asks prayer in regard to this collection and his coming to the Romans. The third (16:20) follows a warning against those whose actions and speech are contrary to that which they have been taught. Paul assures his readers that God, who brings peace, will soon crush Satan under their feet. Meanwhile, Paul expresses his earnest desire that the grace of the Lord Jesus may be their portion. The fourth in the Authorized Version (16:24), not having good manuscript evidence behind it, is omitted in all modern versions based upon a better Greek text. The last (16:25-27) is the

most interesting of all because it is found in various places in the ancient manuscripts. The Alexandrian textual family, and the Manuscript D from the Western textual family have this rather long doxology at the very end of chapter 16. This is where it belongs. Some other manuscripts place it after 14:23. A few put it both after 14:23 and at 16:25-27. One manuscript, G, omits this doxology altogether. The papyrus manuscript, $P^{46}$, puts it after 15:33.

Some scholars have tried to show that the content of this last doxology stamps it as having been composed in the second century as a liturgical formula of conclusion (cf. John Knox, "Romans," *The Interpreter's Bible,* IX, 365-68). Dr. Hort, almost a century ago, carefully compared its phrases with phrases in Paul's earlier and later epistles and found a remarkable number of similarities (F. J. A. Hort, "On the End of the Epistle to the Romans," in *Biblical Essays,* compiled by J. B. Lightfoot, pp. 324-329). Hence there is good evidence to support Paul's authorship of this final doxology beyond the fact that it is found at or near the end of Romans.

But why should this doxology at the end of Romans appear in different places in the various manuscripts? A number of factors may have played a part. Origen, in his commentary on the Epistle to the Romans, declares that the heretic Marcion (who flourished A.D. 138 — 150) cut away all of Romans from 14:23 to the end. Followers of Marcion would produce copies that stop at this point. Also, the section headings—terse phrases describing the content—are absent from the last two chapters in two manuscripts of the Vulgate—Codex Amiatinus and Codex Fuldensis. The omission of these chapters from public reading would have influenced the placing of the doxology. Again, Paul, or the Christians at Rome immediately after his death, may have shortened the epistle in order to circulate it to other churches. The very fact that we have so many early manuscripts of Romans permits us to see some of these deviations and to note what the best manuscripts have done. Whether we consider the manuscripts of highest quality (the most important) or their total quantity, most of them include all of Romans except 16:24, which was clearly not a part of the original text.

This letter was written by Paul on his third missionary journey. Since the apostle spent three months in Greece

(Acts 20:3) and he recommends Phoebe, the deaconess from Cenchrea (eastern seaport of Corinth) who probably carried the letter to Rome, it is very likely that the letter was written from Corinth. But it is possible that another Grecian city, such as Philippi, was the place. Dates for the epistle have ranged from A.D. 53 to A.D. 58. The years 55 or 56 seem to be the most likely dates for the letter.

*Occasion and Purpose for Writing.* The apostle planned to leave Greece and go to Palestine with the collection he had gathered from the Gentile churches. Paul wanted this collection to be presented to the poor saints at Jerusalem by him personally along with representatives from the Gentile churches. He felt that this gesture by the Gentiles would show their love for their Christian brothers in Palestine and demonstrate the unity of the church. He then intended to go to Rome. From Rome he wanted to go to Spain. Before Paul turned his back for a time on his westerly goals, he penned this mighty letter to the Romans and sent it westward.

What kind of a writing is Romans? It is a letter to a group (or groups) of believers in Rome. The fact that it expresses mighty, profound, and sublime thoughts about God does not invalidate the classification of this book as a letter. Paul had prayed for the readers unceasingly (1:9,10) and longed to have fellowship with them (1:11). He wanted them to pray for him because of the dangers that threatened (15:30-32). Hence Romans is not a systematic doctrinal treatise. Paul's thoughts are developed logically, but he surely does not try to present all of his doctrinal teaching. Nor is Romans a controversial essay—a polemic for Pauline Christianity against Jewish Christianity. The *unity* and *oneness* of believers is central in the metaphor of the olive tree in Romans 11.

Romans is a letter of instruction touching upon those main truths of the Gospel that Paul felt were needed by those in Rome. Since the needs of Gentiles were similar whether they were in Rome or Colosse, there is a universal note in the teaching. Romans is a summary of key truths that Paul taught in the churches where he spent some time proclaiming the Gospel. One reason this epistle has had such wide influence is that God guided his servant to present these superb thoughts in a letter so that scholar and layman alike could lay hold of truths that would shape their eternal destiny.

*Unfolding of the Thought.* Paul begins with some preliminary comments to prepare the reader for all that he intends to write (1:1-17), and so establishes excellent rapport between himself and his readers. Then he launches forth into the subject of the importance of righteousness in man's relations with God (1:18–8:39). He first graphically points out that man is not righteous, then carefully answers the question: How does a man become righteous before God? He re-enforces this with a discussion of how a man should live who has become righteous before God. Being a Jew, Paul looked at mankind as divided into two classes—Jew and Gentile. As a Christian, how should he look at these two divisions? He answers this when he surveys the plan of God for Jew and Gentile (9:1–11:36). Here he lays a distinct basis for a Christian philosophy of history. Then, coming to the area of application, he gives specific exhortations for Roman Christians concerning their outlook, attitude, and action (12:1–15:13). In conclusion he shows his deep interest in the Roman believers (15:14–16:27). They were in his territory and he intended to visit them. Until that was possible, he had to send greetings by mail, give a final warning, and commit them to God, who alone could establish them.

In studying Romans, we must not forget the whole of which each individual passage is only a part. To tear a passage out of its context is always harmful; in Romans it may bring a complete reversal of Paul's meaning.

# OUTLINE

I. Opening affirmations of Paul, the apostle. 1:1-17.
    A. Identity of the writer disclosed. 1:1.
    B. The Gospel identified with Jesus Christ. 1:2-5.
    C. Readers addressed. 1:6,7.
    D. Paul's interest in the Romans, part of a larger concern. 1:8-15.
    E. Nature and content of the Gospel summarized. 1:16,17.

II. Righteousness—the key to man's relationship to God. 1:18—8:39.
  A. Righteousness as the necessary status of men before God. 1:18—5:21.
    1. Man's failure to attain righteousness. 1:18—3:20.
      a. Default of the Gentiles. 1:18-32.
      b. Default of the man who judges in contrast with God's righteous judgment. 2:1-16.
      c. Default of the Jew. 2:17-29.
      d. Objections to Paul's teaching on man's default. 3:1-8.
      e. Default of all mankind before God. 3:9-20.
    2. Righteousness attained by faith, not by legalistic works. 3:21-31.
    3. Righteousness by faith in the life of Abraham. 4:1-25.
      a. His righteousness attained by faith, not by works. 4:1-8.
      b. Abraham made the father of all who believe by his faith prior to circumcision. 4:9-12.
      c. Realization of the promise brought by faith, not by law. 4:13-16.
      d. God, Master of death, the object of faith for both Abraham and the Christian. 4:17-25.
    4. Centrality of the righteousness by faith in individual lives and in the framework of history. 5:1-21.
      a. Effects of the righteousness by faith upon the recipients. 5:1-11.
      b. Effects of Adam's disobedience and Christ's obedience. 5:12-21.
  B. Righteousness as the manner of Christian living before God. 6:1—8:39.
    1. Fallacy of sinning that grace might abound. 6:1-14.
    2. Fallacy of sinning because believers are under grace, not law. 6:15—7:6.
      a. Allegiance, fruit, destiny. 6:15-23.
      b. Annulment and new alignment caused by death. 7:1-6.
    3. Questions raised by the struggle against sin. 7:7-25.
      a. Is the Law sin? 7:7-12.
      b. Is that which is good the cause of death? 7:13,14.
      c. How can the conflict within be resolved? 7:15-25.
    4. Victory through the Spirit connected with the purpose and action of God. 8:1-39.
      a. Deliverance from sin and death by the activity of Father, Son, and Spirit. 8:1-4.
      b. The mind-set of the flesh versus that of the Spirit. 8:5-13.
      c. Guidance and witness of the Spirit. 8:14-17.
      d. Completion of redemption awaited by creation and believers alike. 8:18-25.
      e. Intercessory ministry of the Spirit. 8:26,27.
      f. Purpose of God for those loving him. 8:28-30.
      g. Triumph of believers over all opposition. 8:31-39.
III. Israel and the Gentiles in the plan of God. 9:1—11:36.
  A. Concern of Paul for his own people, Israel. 9:1-5.
  B. God free, righteous, and sovereign in his dealing with Israel and with all men. 9:6-29.
    1. God's choice of Isaac rather than the other sons of Abraham. 9:6-9.
    2. God's choice of Jacob rather than Esau. 9:10-13.
    3. God's mercy toward Israel and hardening of Pharaoh. 9:14-18.
    4. God's control over vessels of wrath and mercy. 9:19-24.
    5. God's testimony in Hosea and Isaiah to an extension and limitation of his saving work. 9:25-29.
  C. Failure of Israel and success of the Gentiles. 9:30—10:21.
    1. Attainment by Gentiles of what Israel missed. 9:30-33.
    2. Israel's ignorance of God's righteousness. 10:1-3.
    3. Connection between the righteousness of faith and the object of faith. 10:4-15.
    4. Good tidings rejected. 10:16-21.
  D. Situation of Israel in Paul's day. 11:1-10.
  E. Israel's prospects for the future. 11:11-36.
    1. Degree of blessing from Israel's fall and fullness. 11:11-15.
    2. Individual Gentile's lack of grounds for boasting. 11:16-21.

        3. Goodness and severity of God disclosed by his response to belief and unbelief. 11:22-24.
        4. Salvation for the people of Israel. 11:25-27.
        5. God's mercy to all magnified by his action in history. 11:28-32.
        6. Excellence and glory of God—the Source, Sustainer, and Goal of all things. 11:33-36.
IV. Attitude and conduct expected of Christians at Rome. 12:1—15:13.
    A. Consecration of body and mind. 12:1,2.
    B. Humility in the use of God's gifts. 12:3-8.
    C. Character traits to be exemplified. 12:9-21.
    D. Submission to governmental authorities to be accompanied by a loving, upright manner of life. 13:1-14.
    E. Tolerance necessary for those with strong and weak consciences. 14:1—15:13.
        1. Differences of opinion over food or special days. 14:1-6.
        2. Judgment by the Lord, not by one's brother. 14:7-12.
        3. Removal of stumbling blocks. 14:13-23.
        4. The strong to help the weak rather than please themselves. 15:1-3.
        5. Glory brought to God by endurance, consolation, and harmony. 15:4-6.
        6. Ministry of Christ designed for both Jew and Gentile. 15:7-13.
V. Items of personal interest and care for the readers. 15:14—16:27.
    A. Paul's reason for writing boldly to mature readers. 15:14-16.
    B. Supernatural confirmation of Paul's pioneer missionary work. 15:17-21.
    C. Travel plans: Jerusalem, Rome, Spain. 15:22-29.
    D. Specific requests for prayer. 15:30-33.
    E. Recommendation of Phoebe. 16:1,2.
    F. Particular greetings to individuals and groups. 16:3-16.
    G. Dangerous character of those who teach false doctrine. 16:17-20.
    H. Greetings from Paul's associates in Corinth. 16:21-23.
    I. Establishment of believers by the sovereign God of history. 16:25-27.

# ROMANS

## CHAPTER 1

PAUL, a servant of Jesus Christ, called *to be* an apostle, separated unto the gospel of God,

2. (Which he had promised afore by his prophets in the holy Scriptures,)

3. Concerning his Son Jesus Christ our Lord, which was made of the seed of David: according to the flesh;

# COMMENTARY

**I. Opening Affirmations of Paul, the Apostle. 1:1-17.**

The length of the introduction shows that Paul attached great importance to this letter. Observe the spirit of dedication that permeates these opening lines. Note also how quickly he shifts from one thought to another.

A. Identity of the Writer Disclosed. 1:1. The word for **servant** really means a *slave*. For Paul, this expression said that he belonged to Jesus Christ. He was Christ's property, and, as such, he had a divinely appointed task to perform. His **call** to be an apostle came to him clearly in Damascus (Acts 9:15,16; 22:14,15; 26:16-18). He was **in a state of being set apart** unto the Gospel of God. In Galatians Paul traces this call back to his birth (Gal 1:15), but here in Romans he stresses the purpose for his being set apart: for **the good news** which God had brought into being. Paul had a divine Master, a divine office, and a divine message.

B. The Gospel Identified with Jesus Christ. 1:2-5. In these verses the Gospel is viewed in two dimensions — the historical and the personal.

2. Historically, God had **proclaimed** this **good news in advance**, by special agents, **his prophets**. The record of what they proclaimed is found **in the holy scriptures**. The latter is a technical designation for all the parts of Scripture, the Scripture as a whole.

3. God's good news is about his Son. Paul stresses first his humanity: **who was born from the seed of David as far as his physical descent was concerned.** Here is a stress upon his birth. He **became** man.

4. Next he stresses the quality of his being as Son of God: **who was powerfully declared to be Son of God by the resurrection of the dead.** In every instance where Paul uses the word "dead" after the word "resurrection," the Greek word "dead" is in the plural. Sometimes he explicitly means a resurrection of individuals (cf. I Cor 15:12,13,21,42). But here in Rom 1:4 and also in Acts 26: 23 he is referring to the resurrection of

4. And declared *to be* the Son of God with power, according to the Spirit of holiness, by the resurrection from the dead:

5. By whom we have received grace and apostleship, for obedience to the faith among all nations, for his name:

6. Among whom are ye also the called of Jesus Christ:

7. To all that be in Rome, beloved of God, called *to be* saints: Grace to you, and peace, from God our Father and the Lord Jesus Christ.

Jesus Christ. Yet the term "dead" is in the plural. Hence in the resurrection of this individual there is implicit the resurrection of all who will be raised by him. But explicitly in Rom 1:4 Paul is referring to the victory of Christ over death (cf. 6: 9). The use of the plural here is a stylistic trait of the writer.

**In accordance with the Spirit of Holiness.** The resurrection from the dead was a fact proclaimed by Christians. But the powerful declaration of Jesus as Son of God by his resurrection was the work of the Holy Spirit in illuminating the full meaning of the historical fact. Some scholars take "spirit of Holiness" to be a strengthened form of "the Holy Spirit" (see Arndt, *hagiōsynē*, p. 10). Others take the phrase to refer to Christ's human spirit, which was characterized by great holiness — "in relation to the (his) spirit of holiness" (see Sanday and Headlam, ICC, p. 9; cf. Arndt, *pneuma*, 2, p. 681). Another view equates "holiness" here with Deity or God. But the Spirit of God, according to this view, is not the Holy Spirit but the Creative Living Principle, God operative in human affairs (see Otto Procksch, TWNT, I, 116: "Christ's Deity becomes clear by the resurrection in which the new creation shows itself according to the Principle of ...Deity."). **Being born** (1:3; AV, *was made)* asserts origination. **Being declared** (v. 4) asserts the designation of what is. Hence the human and the divine are contrasted in these two verses. One must decide whether the phrase, *pneuma hagiōsynēs* (Spirit of Holiness, spirit of holiness, Creative Principle of Deity), modifies the declaration, or describes the person of Christ, or conveys the idea of the activity of God in the world. The first interpretation, which certainly appears to be the best, calls for the translation, "Spirit of Holiness."

5. Through the Son Paul had received **grace** and his **apostleship.** The phrase, **for his name** (AV), should be tied to apostleship—an apostleship, literally, *on behalf of his name.*

C. Readers Addressed. 1:6,7. It is clear from these verses that the "Romans" addressed were among the Gentiles. Twice Paul stresses the fact that they were **called.** They were called to be **saints.** The idea behind the word "saint" is not that of someone cut off from all association with others but of one who is *consecrated to God.* The impact on society of a group of believers who are conse-

8. First, I thank my God through Jesus Christ for you all, that your faith is spoken of throughout the whole world.

9. For God is my witness, whom I serve with my spirit in the gospel of his Son, that without ceasing I make mention of you always in my prayers;

10. Making request, if by any means now at length I might have a prosperous journey by the will of God to come unto you.

crated or dedicated to God ought never to be minimized. The words **grace** and **peace** represent a Christian formula of greeting in letters (see Rom 1:7; I Cor 1:3; II Cor 1:2; Gal 1:3; Eph 1:2; Phil 1:2; Col 1:2; I Thess 1:1; II Thess 1:2; Tit 1:4; Phm 3; I Pet 1:2; II Pet 1:2; I Tim 1:2; II Tim 1:2; II Jn 3). **Grace** (charis) is here used in place of a common Greek expression, chairein, which means "greetings." **Peace** has a Hebrew and Aramaic parallel, shalōm, which carries the complex idea of prosperity, good health, and success. But this Christian greeting stresses what God has done in the lives of believers. Yet the student must always remember that this is a formula of greeting — not an independent reference to grace and peace. The phrase must be taken as a whole: **May grace and peace be to you from God our Father and from the Lord Jesus Christ.**

D. Paul's Interest in the Romans Part of a Larger Concern. 1:8-15. Paul tells his readers about his longstanding desire to visit them. Such a visit, he felt, would help not only the Romans but also himself. Rome, with its cross section of humanity, epitomized the various kinds of people to whom the apostle had an obligation.

8. **I thank my God.** The frequency of thanksgivings at the beginnings of Paul's epistles is a testimony to Paul's closeness to God and his cheerful outlook (eucharisteō, "to give thanks": Rom 1:8; I Cor 1:4; Eph 1:16; Col 1:3; I Thess 1:2; II Thess 1:3; Phm 4; charin echō, "to be grateful, thankful": I Tim 1:12; II Tim 1:3). Note that thanks as well as petitions are rendered to God **through Jesus Christ.** The object for thanksgiving is specifically stated.

9. Observe the stress here on the inward aspect of service — **whom I serve in my spirit** (ASV). God, who knew the inward man, would testify to Paul's interest in the Romans.

10. Not only did the apostle mention the Romans frequently in his prayers, but he prayed always about coming to them. Here one sees that although Paul earnestly prayed to be in **the will of God** in this matter, he was not sure, at the time of writing, whether it was God's will for him to go to Rome. Here are his own words: **praying whether now at last I may perhaps succeed in coming . . . to you.** God had not said "No"; so Paul continued to pray.

11. For I long to see you, that I may impart unto you some spiritual gift, to the end ye may be established;

12. That is, that I may be comforted together with you by the mutual faith both of you and me.

13. Now I would not have you ignorant, brethren, that oftentimes I purposed to come unto you, (but was let hitherto,) that I might have some fruit among you also, even as among other Gentiles.

14. I am debtor both to the Greeks, and to the Barbarians; both to the wise, and to the unwise.

15. So, as much as in me is, I am ready to preach the gospel to you that are at Rome also.

11. The **spiritual gift** was what Paul desired to impart to the Romans for their strengthening. This was not some special gift, such as Paul lists in Rom 12:6-8, but rather a growing knowledge of various truths of God that would enable them to be better Christians.

12. Encouragement or comfort would come to Paul as well as to his readers if he could visit them. Even this great evangelist, who perhaps has never been equaled in spiritual stature, says plainly that he needed the encouragement that comes in Christian fellowship. Thus we dare not underestimate the importance of Christian fellowship for Christian growth. The mutual faith is simply the fact that both Paul and his readers were Christians. Observe how the pronouns make this faith personal — **your** faith and **mine**.

13. The last phrase in this verse should be tied to the verb "purposed." I **purposed** to come in order **that I might have . . . fruit among you . . .** The readers in Rome were Gentiles, and Paul hoped to have the same results from ministering to them as he had had with other Gentiles he had visited.

14,15. The apostle saw himself as a debtor to those who spoke Greek and to those who did not (**Barbarians**). This is a language-cultural division of mankind. The second pair of contrasts in 1:14 deals with intellectual learning and achievement. A **wise** man is one with a trained intellect. An **unwise** man or *unintelligent* man discloses his foolishness in what he does. Representatives of all of these classes were found in Rome. To all of these Paul felt impelled to proclaim the good news. Hence he speaks of his eagerness **to proclaim good tidings** there. It is important to note that he expected to reach all these classes as he ministered to Roman believers — **to you who are in Rome also.** Hence, although Christianity found most of its adherents among members of the lower strata of society (cf. I Cor 1:26-29), there was a compelling urgency to reach all classes of men.

E. Nature and Content of the Gospel Summarized. 1:16,17. In these verses one finds three factors: (1) Paul's attitude toward the Gospel; (2) the nature of the Gospel; and (3) the content of the Gospel. These verses indicate that the good news of the Christian faith is not a system of philosophy or a code of ethics.

16. In contrast to a series of abstract ideas, the Gospel or good news is dy-

16. For I am not ashamed of the gospel of Christ: for it is the power of God unto salvation to every one that believeth; to the Jew first, and also to the Greek.

17. For therein is the righteousness of God revealed from faith to faith: as it is written, The just shall live by faith.

namic. Paul was not ashamed of the Gospel. The phrase **of Christ** (AV) is not found in the best manuscripts and should be omitted. Paul was not ashamed of the Gospel because this good news is God's power, the purpose and goal of which is to bring about deliverance or salvation. A man obtains such salvation when his constant individual response to the Gospel is trust and belief — **to every one in the process of believing.**

The Greek word *pisteuō* is a profound word. Belief in the content of the Gospel is only part of its meaning. Above this it means trust or personal commitment, to the extent of handing over one's self to another person. Though belief does involve response to a truth or a series of truths, this response is not mere intellectual assent but rather wholehearted involvement in the truth believed. To believe in Christ is to commit oneself to him. To trust Christ is to become totally involved in the eternal truths taught by him and about him in the NT. Such total involvement brings moral earnestness, a dedication and consecration apparent in every aspect of life. Note that although the salvation spoken of here is to the Jew first, the Gentile experiences the same salvation.

**17. Therein.** In the Gospel the righteousness is revealed which God bestows, produces, imputes. The rest of Romans tells more about what is involved in this righteousness. Here Paul stresses that righteousness is **from faith to faith.** This righteousness (which God brings into being) comes to the Christian only because of faith. As the believer becomes increasingly aware of all that God's righteousness signifies, he must still commit himself if he is to receive God's righteousness.

The order of words in the last part of the verse is this: **the just by faith shall live.** Here one sees the danger of following the Greek word order too literally. It might imply that a man being just in some other way could not live even if he met the requirement of being just! Faith is put first for emphasis to show that faith is essential for a man to be just. Greek *dikaios*, **just**, may also be translated *upright* or *righteous;* hence the rendering: **the just** (*upright, righteous*) **shall live by faith.** Does the living referred to here describe the temporal sequence of life immediately ahead or does it refer only to eternal life? Bauer in the lexicon translated and edited by Arndt and Gingrich asserts that "the di-

**18.** For the wrath of God is revealed from heaven against all ungodliness and unrighteousness of men, who hold the truth in unrighteousness;

**19.** Because that which may be known of God is manifest in them; for God hath showed *it* unto them.

viding line between the present and the future life is sometimes non-existent or at least not discernible" (Arndt, *zaō*, 2. b., p. 337). He would translate this clause: **he that is just through faith will have life.** How great is the role of faith in a man's being just, in the life he now lives, and in the life which is to come!

## II. Righteousness — The Key to Man's Relationship to God. 1:18—8:39.

Here Paul grapples with great issues of life. How can a man be righteous in the sight of God? How is man affected by the action of Adam and of Christ? How should a man who is righteous live? How can he live in this way?

A. Righteousness as the Necessary Status of Men before God. 1:18—5:21. Righteousness is necessary for men. This necessity is grounded in the nature and being of God.

1) Man's Failure To Attain Righteousness. 1:18—3:20.
The reason why righteousness is so important is that man does not have it. First, he must be made aware that he does not have it. Throughout the ages there have been those who felt that God ought to be pleased with their character. In these chapters Paul proceeds to show the shallowness of such an outlook.

a) Default of the Gentiles. 1:18-32.
**18.** The righteousness and wrath of God both express divine action toward man. Righteousness is God's response toward faith or trust; wrath is his reaction to **godlessness** and **unrighteousness**. Both clearly **reveal** the response of God. What does a godless or unrighteous man do? He **holds down** or *suppresses* **the truth** (present participle) in the sphere of unrighteousness where he is living. He wants to avoid the truth about what he is and about what he is doing. So he foolishly tries to get rid of the truth.

**19.** The truth comes to man in his sphere of unrighteousness. **Because what can be known about God.** Here is the assertion that God is knowable. **Is manifest in them.** This could also be translated *is visible to them* (Arndt, *phaneros*, p. 860; *en*, IV, 4. a, p. 260) or *is manifest among them.* The context certainly favors the latter two. Why is God knowable? He acts. God has **made known** or *revealed* (AV, *shewed*) what can be known about himself to men. This

**20.** For the invisible things of him from the creation of the world are clearly seen, being understood by the things that are made, *even* his eternal power and Godhead; so that they are without excuse:

**21.** Because that, when they knew God, they glorified *him* not as God, neither were thankful; but became vain in their imaginations, and their foolish heart was darkened.

**22.** Professing themselves to be wise, they became fools,

**23.** And changed the glory of the uncorruptible God into an image made like to corruptible man, and to birds, and four-footed beasts, and creeping things.

revelation is a self-disclosure that God may carry out in any way he pleases.

**20. The invisible things of him.** This phrase refers to God's invisible nature or attributes. **From the creation of the world are clearly seen.** Paul makes a bold assertion here. From the time that God brought the world into being, his invisible attributes — characteristics which declare him to be God — are perceived clearly. By whom and how are they perceived clearly? **Being understood in the things that are made.** In is a better translation than the *by* of the AV. The invisible attributes of God are understood by men, who can engage in rational reflection and understanding. What is the basis for their understanding? It is **in the things that are made** (*poiēma*). The word *poiēma* means "what is made," "work," or "creation." Bauer translates it: *in the things that have been made* (Arndt, *kathoraō*, p. 393) or *by the things he has created* (Arndt, *poiēma*, p. 689). The noun is in the plural. In classical Greek the word is used in the plural to refer to works, to poems, to fiction, deeds or acts — i.e., anything made or done (LSJ. p. 1429). The word *poiēma* is found thirty times in the LXX. Except for one occurrence, it translates the Hebrew word *ma'aśeh*, "deed," or "work." In the one exception it translates the Hebrew *pō'al*, "doing," "deed," or "work." Therefore, it is clear that the things which God has created are said to testify to his invisible nature.

To what aspect of the invisible nature of God do they testify? Paul is specific —to **his eternal power.** In creation the everlasting or perpetual power of God is seen. As man's skill in exploring space and in analyzing the structure of the atom grows, so he ought to grow in his awareness of God's power. **And Godhead.** The Creator who has shown such unlimited power is the supreme Being with whom men must reckon. By observing his work, men are confronted with the living God. As a result, **they are without excuse.**

**21-23.** Paul enumerates the things men put in the place of the living God. What a tragic list of substitutions! **Because, although they knew God.** Here are men who were brought face to face with God's works and with God, so that they knew him. But they did not respond to this knowledge as they should have. They did not **glorify** (praise, honor, magnify) him as God; neither did they **return thanks** to him. These

24. Wherefore God also gave them up to uncleanness, through the lusts of their own hearts, to dishonor their own bodies between themselves:

25. Who changed the truth of God into a lie, and worshipped and served the creature more than the Creator, who is blessed for ever. Amen.

26. For this cause God gave them up unto vile affections: for even their women did change the natural use into that which is against nature:

27. And likewise also the men, leaving the natural use of the woman, burned in their lust one toward another; men with men working that which is unseemly, and receiving in themselves that recompense of their error which was meet.

failures show what should be man's chief end: to glorify the Lord for what he is and to return thanks for what he has done.

The thoughts of these Gentiles turned to worthless things. **Their senseless mind was darkened.** To reject God, to turn away from the light, naturally brings darkness. This darkness came into their inner being—the mind, reasonings, emotions, etc. In their idolatry, i.e., in their creating substitutes for the being of God, they actually thought they were wise. Worthless thoughts quickly brought worthless objects of worship.

**24,25.** Verses 24,26,28 all repeat the same solemn phrase: **God handed them over unto.** The Lord hands men over to the consequences of that which they have chosen for themselves. When men choose an evil manner of life, they also choose the consequences such a manner of life brings. This is proof that God has established a moral universe. **In the desires** (lusts, AV) **which originated from their hearts** (or, which their hearts produced, v. 24). The word translated "desire" may refer to that which is either good or bad. Here it is obviously an evil desire. The translation "lust" conveys the idea of sensuality, which fits into the context of uncleanness. Notice that God hands men over to the very things which they desire. As a result their bodies are dishonored among them. Idolatry consists in worshiping and serving the creature (v. 25); in sensuality man worships and serves himself.

**26,27.** Uncleanness always generates more uncleanness. Here is a divine judgment in which God handed the Gentiles over to **disgraceful passions.** Women are charged with homosexuality in verse 26 and men in verse 27. Paul uses straightforward language to condemn perversion of sex from its rightful place in the marriage relationship. He regards the union of the sexes in marriage as a natural relationship (AV, natural use). But here women exchanged natural sex relations for that which is contrary to nature. The men did the same thing. Paul pictures the depravity and degradation of men inflamed with sensual desire for each other. This is followed by the note of judgment. **In themselves . . . that recompense . . . which was necessary.** Paul does not go into detail as to the exact nature of the judgment—the psychological and physical consequences. But the nature of the penalty is said to correspond to

28. And even as they did not like to retain God in *their* knowledge, God gave them over to a reprobate mind, to do those things which are not convenient;

29. Being filled with all unrighteousness, fornication, wickedness, covetousness, maliciousness; full of envy, murder, debate, deceit, malignity; whisperers,

30. Backbiters, haters of God, despiteful, proud, boasters, inventors of evil things, disobedient to parents,

31. Without understanding, covenantbreakers, without natural affection, implacable, unmerciful:

32. Who, knowing the judgment of God, that they which commit such things are worthy of death, not only do the same, but have pleasure in them that do them.

## CHAPTER 2

THEREFORE thou art inexcusable, O man, whosoever thou art that judgest: for wherein thou judgest another, thou condemnest thyself; for thou that judgest doest the same things.

2. But we are sure that the judgment of God is according to truth against them which commit such things.

the enormity of the sin.

**28-32.** Those who did not see fit to have God in their knowledge were handed over by God to a reprobate mind. The Greek word has the meanings: "base," "unqualified," "worthless," "not standing the test," or "unapproved." Here is a mind with no stabilizing point on which inward harmony may be built. Such a mind can produce only that which is improper (AV, *not convenient)* or *those things which are not fitting.* The list in verses 29-31 shows that such a mind is at odds with itself and with its fellow men. Anarchy and chaos come from a mind that removes God from its knowledge. In some good manuscripts fornication (AV, v. 29) is not found. **Whisperers** (AV) are gossipers or secret slanderers. **Backbiters** (AV) are those who seek to ruin or defame someone's character—vilifiers of character. The man who ruins other people's reputations himself becomes repulsive. Note the unlovely combination set forth in verse 31: **Senseless, faithless, unloving, unmerciful. Implacable** is not found in the early, good manuscripts. Remember that the people described here had opportunity to know the requirements of God. Further, they knew that death is the penalty of evil action. Yet they not only sinned with pleasure but applauded others who were sinning. Their sin had reached a point where they received a vicarious satisfaction in the sinful deeds of others.

b) Default of the Man Who Judges in Contrast with God's Righteous Judgment. 2:1-16. The man Paul thinks of as judging is not named as a Jew or Gentile. It is likely that Paul had the Jew in mind, since the man who was judging had experienced God's goodness and forbearance in a distinct way. The Lord's recompense to each individual will be according to the man's works—not according to his privileges. God will judge fairly, whether a man lived under the Mosaic Law or apart from it.

**1-4.** The word **judge** (*krinōn*) occurs three times in verse 1. It means here to pass unfavorable judgment by criticizing or finding fault. The man who is inexcusable is the one who has great power of criticism but no self-discipline. The **judgment of God is rightly upon those doing such things. Such things.** The actions of the critic are identical with the actions of those whom he criticizes. The catalogue of sins in Romans 1 is fairly inclusive. Envy, gossip, and strife

505

3. And thinkest thou this, O man, that judgest them which do such things, and doest the same, that thou shalt escape the judgment of God?

4. Or despisest thou the riches of his goodness and forbearance and long-suffering; not knowing that the goodness of God leadeth thee to repentance?

5. But, after thy hardness and impenitent heart, treasurest up unto thyself wrath against the day of wrath and revelation of the righteous judgment of God;

6. Who will render to every man according to his deeds:

7. To them who by patient continuance in well doing seek for glory and honor and immortality, eternal life:

8. But unto them that are contentious, and do not obey the truth, but obey unrighteousness, indignation and wrath,

9. Tribulation and anguish, upon every soul of man that doeth evil; of the Jew first, and also of the Gentile;

10. But glory, honor, and peace, to every man that worketh good; to the Jew first, and also to the Gentile:

11. For there is no respect of persons with God.

are looked upon as faults in others, but the critic may excuse these things in himself as "a rightful sense of need," "a simple statement of fact," or "a courageous stand for the truth." Paul appeals to the man's conscience: **Do you really imagine . . . that you will escape the condemnation of God** (i.e., the sentence pronounced by him)? The translation **despise** (v. 4) may be too strong for *kataphroneō* in this context. It seems better to render it: **Or do you entertain wrong ideas about** (Arndt, p. 421) God's goodness, forbearance, patience? The word **repentance** involves much more than a turning away from a former practice. It involves the beginning of a new religious and moral life (see Arndt, pp. 513,514). Hence God's goodness in not bringing immediate punishment is no evidence that the Lord is indifferent to the sin. Far from it! By divine goodness he wants to lead men to a new way of life. To have wrong ideas about this is to rest in a false complacency. The judgment of God is sure.

**5-11.** The Almighty examines man's conduct and judges him accordingly. A man whose heart is hard and impenitent stores up divine anger or wrath for himself. **God's anger** stored up in heaven is the most tragic stockpile a man could lay aside for himself. Observe the note of individual judgment in verse 6. What is the mood or outlook of those who seek for glory, honor, and immortality? With an outlook characterized by **a perseverance in doing what is right** (v. 7), these contend for the goals listed. The outcome is that they receive from the Judge eternal life. Those who because of strife are disobedient to the truth and obey unrighteousness receive anger and wrath. Works are always central in the NT picture of judgment. They are an outward indication of an individual's inward trust or commitment. The Lord, of course, looks at both the inward and the outward. But the outward activity reveals the inward conviction. One needs only to compare the verb form in 2:9—**that constantly doeth evil**—with that in 2:10—**that constantly worketh the good**—to see that actions disclose convictions (or the lack of them). This does not mean that those who constantly do the good have a full understanding of God. But apart from a trust in God, which demands some knowledge, men will not carry out constantly and with determination that which God has said to be good.

**12-16.** Since there is no partiality with

12. For as many as have sinned without law shall also perish without law; and as many as have sinned in the law shall be judged by the law;

13. (For not the hearers of the law *are* just before God, but the doers of the law shall be justified.

14. For when the Gentiles, which have not the law, do by nature the things contained in the law, these, having not the law, are a law unto themselves:

15. Which show the work of the law written in their hearts, their conscience also bearing witness, and *their* thoughts the mean while accusing or else excusing one another;)

God, how does he treat those who sin apart from the law and those who sin under the law? The answer lies in the phrases—shall perish and shall be punished (v. 12). Both those living under the law and those living apart from the law are said to have sinned. The aorist tense here (*have sinned*, AV) stresses wholeness of action. It summarizes all the sins the individual has committed during his life. For the sum total of such sins, men who have not had the opportunity of living under the Mosaic law shall perish. Likewise, for the sum total of their sins, those who have lived under the law shall be punished. Although different language is used to describe God's judgment, this judgment is sure and fairly dispensed, whether the Mosaic law plays any part in the judgment or not. As far as judgment is concerned, what counts is performance, not the being aware of this or that statute. The doer of the law will be justified; i.e., *be acquitted, be pronounced righteous.*

At this point a profound question arises: Are the doers of the Law limited to those who know and carry out the Mosaic law? In 2:14 Paul answers "No" to this question and shows why. The Gentiles who have not the Mosaic law may do by nature the things contained in the law. The phrase by nature (*physei*) has been interpreted to mean "by following the natural order of things" (see Hans Lietzmann, *Der Brief and die Römer*, also *Handbuch zum Neuen Testament*. Excursus on Rom 2:14-16). But the context here does not make the same stress as in 1:20. Hence it seems much better to take by nature to mean "instinctively." What is involved in this type of response? When Gentiles do instinctively the requirements of the Law, they are law (2:14). These show the manifestation of the law written in their hearts. Such Gentiles have an internal norm or standard put in their hearts by God. This internal standard is the basis both for the response of their conscience and for their reasoning. The conscience (v.15) is an automatic intellectual response to a given standard. In contrast, reason engages in reflection. The thoughts resulting from such reflection represent a weighed value judgment in contrast to the automatic intellectual response of conscience. The consciences of many associated individuals bring about a mutual witnessing together. Similarly the combined value judgments of the group are circu-

**16. In the day when God shall judge the secrets of men by Jesus Christ according to my gospel.**

lated. The resulting decisions sometimes reproach the individuals of the group and sometimes speak in their defense. Although Paul does not describe the full content of this internal standard, he asserts that it exists. We do know that both the conscience and the reason can decide that certain action is bad and other action is good. Gentiles reacting correctly to this standard are thus not altogether without law. They are obedient doers of the law which God put in their hearts. It would seem best to connect 2:16 with 2:13: "The doers of the law will be justified . . . in the day in which God will judge the secrets of men."

This passage may shed some light upon the eternal destiny of those who have never heard the Gospel. How will God deal with such people in the day of judgment? These verses seem to indicate that he will observe their actions just as he will observe the actions of those who knew the Law, and those who have heard the Gospel, and that he will judge all accordingly. Then, does not obedience to this internal standard nullify the principle of salvation by faith? No. Faith is essential for those who obey the internal standard and for those who obey the Law or the Gospel. But how much richer and fuller is our knowledge of God as revealed through his Son! A seeking for **glory, honour,** and **immortality** (v. 7) could be mere selfishness. But a seeking of these things with a determination to do what is good (v. 7) means that the seeker is aware of a standard of goodness. If this standard were a mere abstraction, how very difficult it would be to persevere in goodness. But if the standard is God himself—even though imperfectly perceived (and who of us perceives God perfectly?), faith or committal to him will lay the basis for constant perseverance in that which is good. Why then should we eagerly take the Gospel to those who have never heard it? First of all, because God has commanded us to do so (Mt 28:19,20; Acts 1:8). Secondly, it is essential because of who God is that every individual be confronted with the knowledge of God (Isa 11:9; Hab 2:14; Isa 45:5,6; 52:10; 66:18,19; II Thess 1:8) and have opportunity to commit himself to Him, and to increase in knowledge of Him (Jn 14:7; 17:3; II Cor 2:14; Tit 1:16; I Jn 2:3-6; 5:19,20; Phil 3:8-10; II Pet 3:18). Finally, it is essential because of who Christ is—the climax of God's reve-

508

17. Behold, thou art called a Jew, and restest in the law, and makest thy boast of God,

18. And knowest *his* will, and approvest the things that are more excellent, being instructed out of the law;

19. And art confident that thou thyself art a guide of the blind, a light of them which are in darkness,

20. An instructor of the foolish, a teacher of babes, which hast the form of knowledge and of the truth in the law.

21. Thou therefore which teachest another, teachest thou not thyself? thou that preachest a man should not steal, dost thou steal?

22. Thou that sayest a man should not commit adultery, dost thou commit adultery? thou that abhorrest idols, dost thou commit sacrilege?

23. Thou that makest thy boast of the law, through breaking the law dishonorest thou God?

24. For the name of God is blasphemed among the Gentiles through you, as it is written.

25. For circumcision verily profiteth, if thou keep the law: but if thou be a breaker of the law, thy circumcision is made uncircumcision.

26. Therefore, if the uncircumcision keep the righteousness of the law, shall not his uncircumcision be counted for circumcision?

lation (Heb 1:1,2).

Since Christ is the supreme revelation of God, and since the NT is the record that confronts men with Christ, other methods of divine revelation are seen to be only fragmentary. This is especially true of two methods discussed in Romans 1;2: (1) the testimony of the things which are made (1:20); (2) the internal standard put in the hearts (2:14,15). Nevertheless, these are divinely chosen channels the existence and function of which Paul invites his readers to consider seriously.

c) Default of the Jew. 2:17-29. Here Paul vividly pictures the Jew's opportunities, and points out how even these did not bring the Jew to a life of obedience and fellowship with God.

17-20. The failure of the Jew was the more conspicuous because of his privileges and confidence. He **relied upon the** Law. He **boasted** (gloried, prided himself) in God. He knew God's will. He **accepted as proved by testing the things that really matter** (or those things which are essential). He could do this because he was orally instructed in the Law. He had heard the rabbis discuss the crucial points. Because of such a background, the Jew had confidence. He could give help and instruction to the rest of men because he was certain that he had **the embodiment** of knowledge and of truth in the Law (v. 20).

21-24. Paul presses home to the Jew his defeat by asking if his practice conforms to his teaching (2:21,22). **You, who teach another, teach yourself don't you?** (v. 21) Why, of course, he did. In the other three questions: **Do you steal? Do you commit adultery? Do you rob temples?** Paul does not say what kind of answer he expects. But he points out that the Jew, by transgressing the very Law of which he was so proud, dishonored God—the One who gave the Law. The name of God was blasphemed among the Gentiles because of the way the Jews acted. The last phrase—**just as it has been written**—does not refer to a particular OT passage that speaks of the sins of the Jews as causing God's name to be blasphemed. Rather, Paul seems to have put together Isa 52:5 and Ezk 36:21-23.

25-29. Here the apostle points out what it means to be a true Jew. He shows that a Gentile who keeps (the word *phylassō* may also be translated *observe*, or *follow*) **the requirements of the law**

**27.** And shall not uncircumcision which is by nature, if it fulfil the law, judge thee, who by the letter and circumcision dost transgress the law?

**28.** For he is not a Jew, which is one outwardly; neither *is that* circumcision, which is outward in the flesh:

**29.** But he *is* a Jew, which is one inwardly; and circumcision *is that* of the heart, in the spirit, *and* not in the letter; whose praise *is* not of men, but of God.

## CHAPTER 3

WHAT advantage then hath the Jew? or what profit *is there* of circumcision?

**2.** Much every way: chiefly, because that unto them were committed the oracles of God.

(v. 26) is a true Jew. The rite of circumcision declares only that a man is a Jew providing he practices the Law. For a Jew to become a transgressor of the Law is really in God's sight to become uncircumcised. Not only is a Gentile a true Jew if he observes the requirements of the Law, but he who is physically uncircumcised will sit in judgment over the Jew who has the physical qualifications but nothing by way of obedience (v. 27). This is an assertion of Paul, not a question. In verse 27 Paul stresses that the Jew whom the Gentile will judge is one who is a transgressor of the Law **though provided with the written code and with circumcision** (cf. *dia*, Arndt, III, 1, c, p. 179). Here is the tragedy of one who had an objective written law and the outward sign of God's covenant with his people, but who yet had never laid hold of the reality. In a final parting word to the Jew, Paul stresses that it is not in externals but rather in the inward condition of the heart that a man is a true Jew, i.e., a child of God (v. 29). True circumcision is a heart kind of circumcision (cf. Lev 26:41; Deut 10:16; 30: 6; Jer 4:4; 9:26; Acts 7:51). This true circumcision is not in the sphere of legality — a written code — but rather in the sphere of the spirit, i.e., the area of the will.

d) Objections to Paul's Teaching on Man's Default. 3:1-8. Paul is speaking mostly about objections from Jews. But the idea that God's righteousness is exalted by man's sin could come from any opponent of Paul's teaching.

**1-4.** What is the **advantage** of the Jew? What is the **use** of circumcision? These questions seem to be taken from Paul's experiences in proclaiming the Gospel. Paul's answer is: "Much in every respect" (v. 2). He reminds his questioner that to the Jews were committed **the oracles of God.** In classical Greek the word *logion* ("oracle") is used mostly of short sayings originating from a divinity (Arndt, p. 477). In Acts 7:38 the word is used of the revelations that came to Moses. In Heb 5:12 it is used in connection with the initial elements belonging to the oracles or sayings of God. The passage in Hebrews refers to a collective whole. Peter says that if any man speak who has received grace, he is to speak as the very oracles or sayings of God (I Pet 4:11). In Rom 3:2 the stress is on the promises of God to the Jews. In all contexts the "oracles" involve oral proclamation,

3. For what if some did not believe? shall their unbelief make the faith of God without effect?

4. God forbid: yea, let God be true, but every man a liar; as it is written, That thou mightest be justified in thy sayings, and mightest overcome when thou art judged.

5. But if our unrighteousness commend the righteousness of God, what shall we say? Is God unrighteous who taketh vengeance? (I speak as a man)

6. God forbid: for then how shall God judge the world?

7. For if the truth of God hath more abounded through my lie unto his glory; why yet am I also judged as a sinner?

and refer to the living voice of God and the truths which God spoke to men. God entrusted these truths to the Jews over long periods of time. The Jews collected them, and they are **recorded** throughout the OT. But the word *logion* itself stresses the particular utterance of God. The fact that all of these utterances came to the Jews was certainly to their advantage.

Paul begins verse 3 with a question: **What then is the situation? The Jews had these vital truths of God. But how did they respond? Since some became unfaithful, their unfaithfulness will not nullify the faithfulness of God, will it?** Paul quickly replies: **By no means** *(far from it)*. The word *some* does not necessarily mean a small part. The contrast is between "part" and "whole." Not only is God faithful but also he is true. In support of this the apostle quotes Ps 51: 4: "In order that you may be proved to be right in your words and may win when you are accused." God is faithful, true, and victorious, although the Jews, in large part, may have become unfaithful.

**5-8.** The translation **commend** is not satisfactory for *synistēmi*. The word really means to *demonstrate* or *bring out*. If our unrighteousness — that of Jew and Gentile — brings out the righteousness of God, what then? **God who inflicts wrathful punishment is not unrighteous, is he?** Paul tells us that he is speaking from a human point of view. Then he replies, **By no means** (v. 6). Paul is so concise in the beginning of verse 6 that the full force of his answer is lost. **For otherwise, if the Lord does not inflict wrathful punishment, how will God punish the world?** The fact that the divine righteousness shines more brightly against the dark background of man's unrighteousness has nothing to do with the Lord's righteousness in judging and the condemnation that must come. God must judge, condemn, and punish because he is a holy being. As a holy being he *must* deal with every violation of holiness. Paul asserts here the *must* without going into the why. In verse 7 he puts the objection of his questioner in a little different form, but it is the same objection. **But if by my lie the truthfulness of God has shown itself to be supremely great, to his glory** (cf. *perisseuō*, Arndt, p. 656), **why am I indeed still punished as a sinner?** Previously he dealt with the argument that the righteousness of God stands out clearer against the background of human sin. Here he attacks the argument that the truth of God becomes clearer when con-

8. And not *rather*, (as we be slanderously reported, and as some affirm that we say,) Let us do evil, that good may come? whose damnation is just.

9. What then? are we better *than they?* No, in no wise: for we have before proved both Jews and Gentiles, that they are all under sin;

10. As it is written, There is none righteous, no, not one:

11. There is none that understandeth, there is none that seeketh after God.

12. They are all gone out of the way, they are together become unprofitable; there is none that doeth good, no, not one.

13. Their throat *is* an open sepulchre; with their tongues they have used deceit; the poison of asps *is* under their lips:

14. Whose mouth *is* full of cursing and bitterness:

trasted with human falsehood. At this point Paul mentions the current caricature of his teaching concerning salvation by grace: **Let us do evil, that good may come** (v. 8). To those who respond in this way, Paul's only comment is: **Whose condemnation is deserved.** These two false arguments are based on the idea that the Lord needs sin in order to demonstrate that he is God. He needs nothing of the kind. Since he is God, he will in the presence of sin show himself to be what he is. But how much more glorious to see what and who he is in the sphere of eternal fellowship with him than in banishment from his presence, with all the consequences thereof.

e) Default of All Mankind Before God. 3:9-20. Paul concludes that this teaching agrees with the OT and the role of the Law, which is to bring about the consciousness of sin.

**9. What then?** (AV) ought to be expanded into: **What then are we to conclude?** Before giving that conclusion, Paul asks one more question. If this question — **Are we better than they?** (AV) — concerns the Jews with whom Paul has been dealing in the first part of chapter 3, the verb *proechometha* ought to be translated: **Are we (Jews) excelled?** That is, Are we Jews in a worse position than the Gentiles? To which Paul answers, **Not at all.** But if the question refers to the whole argument begun in 1:18, then taking *proechometha* to be in the middle voice, the translation should be: **Can we (the readers) hold anything before ourselves for protection?** The verb *proechō* in the middle means "to hold before oneself" (see LSJ, p. 1479). The question would then be: Do we have anything in ourselves to shield us from God's wrath? Paul's answer is: **Not at all. Because we have already charged that both Jews and Greeks are all under sin.** The sinner has no means within himself to deal with sin. He is **under sin,** i.e., under the power, rule, command, control of sin. He needs help from without. His own resources cannot set him free.

**10-18.** In these verses Paul quotes a number of OT passages: 3:10-12 from Ps 14:1-3; 3:13 a,b from Ps 5:9; 3:13 c from Ps 140:3; 3:14 from Ps 10:7; 3:15-17 from Isa 59:7,8; 3:18 from Ps 36:1. The apostle does not quote from the Hebrew text but from the Greek version of the OT, the Septuagint (LXX). Sometimes he quotes it exactly; other times he paraphrases or

15. Their feet *are* swift to shed blood:

16. Destruction and misery *are* in their ways:

17. And the way of peace have they not known:

18. There is no fear of God before their eyes.

19. Now we know that what things soever the law saith, it saith to them who are under the law: that every mouth may be stopped, and all the world may become guilty before God.

20. Therefore by the deeds of the law there shall no flesh be justified in his sight: for by the law *is* the knowledge of sin.

abridges it; occasionally he is quite free in his handling of the wording (see Sanday and Headlam, *The Epistle to the Romans*, ICC, pp. 77-79). But the thought of the OT is adequately conveyed. All these quotations come from the Psalms except one passage—Isa 59:7. In their original context not all of these verses stress the universality of sin. The first (Ps 14:1-3) does. The next three (Ps 5:9; 140:3; 10:7) deal with the condition, attitude, and conduct of the wicked. The passage from Isaiah (59:7,8) deals with the unrighteousness of Israel. Psalm 36:1 sets forth the wicked man's lack of respect for God. Hence this collection of OT quotations illustrates the various forms of sin, the undesirable characteristics of sinners, the effect of their action, and their attitude toward God. This is the same picture that Paul himself has been painting.

**19,20. Whatever** (*as many things as*) **the law says.** The word **law** here must refer to the various quotations Paul has just made. Since these come from the Psalms, except for the Isaiah passage, Paul does not here refer to the Mosaic law. These quotations come from "the Writings" and "the Prophets"—two major divisions of the OT—indicating that Paul means by the law the whole of the OT. Hence the OT speaks to **those who are subject to the law** (Arndt, *en*, 5. d., p. 259). This includes both Jews and Gentiles—any who take seriously the message of the OT. The teaching of the OT is such that **every mouth is closed**—has no defense to make—and **that all the world has become accountable to God.** In verse 20 Paul seems to return to the narrower and more frequent concept of law—the Mosaic law. By the works which the Mosaic law prescribed, **no person will be acquitted.** Paul has shown the failure of both Jew and Gentile. Therefore, the verdict of no acquittal is an important part of the picture. If the Law and what it prescribes does not bring acquittal, what does it bring? **Through the law is the consciousness** (cf. Arndt, *epignōsis*, p. 291) **of sin.** The word **sin** is in the singular. The Law makes man aware of the defects of his nature, character, or being. By virtue of what he is, man acts as he does. The Law makes man aware that he is not what he ought to be. To bring men to this recognition is a great task. Since Paul assigns to the Law such a task, he surely does not minimize law.

2) Righteousness Attained by Faith,

21. But now the righteousness of God without the law is manifested, being witnessed by the law and the prophets;

22. Even the righteousness of God *which is* by faith of Jesus Christ unto all and upon all them that believe; for there is no difference:

23. For all have sinned, and come short of the glory of God;

Not by Legalistic Works. 3:21-31.

If man has failed to attain righteousness, and if righteousness is necessary before God, then how is a man to attain righteousness? How can God be righteous when he acquits a man and declares him righteous? Paul has just made the problem more acute by showing that all men are sinners. So if God declares any man righteous, he is declaring one to be righteous who is unrighteous. Paul's answer shows God's wisdom and involvement in the matter of human sin.

**21. The righteousness of God.** Paul means the righteousness bestowed by God. Such a righteousness is **apart from the law** in the sense that it is not a righteousness deserved or achieved by keeping the Law. Apart from the Law the righteousness of God **has been revealed.** Here is righteousness sent by God and revealed by God. Though distinct from any righteousness sought by keeping the Law, it is testified to **by the law and the prophets.** The latter phrase means the whole OT (Mt 5:17; 7:12; 11:13; 22:40; Lk 16:16; Acts 13: 15; 24:14; 28:23). That God would reckon faith as righteousness is not foreign to the OT (see Rom 4).

**22-24.** If righteousness is bestowed, upon whom is it bestowed? This righteousness is realized through the efficient cause—faith, which has for its object, Christ. It is a righteousness **to all those in the process of trusting.** The present participle makes it clear that this is a lifelong committal to Christ seen in the day-by-day response of trust (see on 1:16). It is trust and only trust that is required. **There is no difference** between Jew and Gentile so far as sin is concerned (3:23). **Because all sinned** (see 2:12). This sin refers to the involvement of all men—both Jew and Gentile—in transgression. The tense brings together the individual personal transgressions into a collective whole.

**All men** manifest their involvement in Adam's departure from right by **constantly falling short of the glory of God. Falling short** means to lack or to be without. What is it that men fall short of and lack? The **glory of God** includes the splendor or radiance of God—the outward manifestation of what God' is. Majesty and sublimity are also part of the glory of God. Majesty involves power. Sublimity involves a superior and elevated position — that of the One who is supreme. Yet the glory of God is not only to be *seen* by those who believe

**24.** Being justified freely by his grace through the redemption that is in Christ Jesus:

**25.** Whom God hath set forth *to be* a propitiation through faith in his blood, to declare his righteousness for the remission of sins that are past, through the forbearance of God;

(Jn 11:40), but it is *received* and *made a part of* those who believe (II Cor 3:18) and is their destiny (I Thess 2:12; II Thess 2:14). It is not only ascribed to God by the great multitude in heaven because of his victory over sin (Rev 19:1), but it also characterizes the Holy City, the eternal dwelling place of God with his people (Rev 21:11,23). Men are constantly lacking God's glory because the continual practice of sin denies all that the glory of God means.

The righteousness of God which has been revealed, and which God bestows upon all those who are believing or trusting means that these **are acquitted** or **freely pronounced righteous** (Rom 3:24). How can this be? It is **by means of God's grace.** God is favorably disposed to do this, not because of any merit in men but because he is gracious and chooses to manifest his grace towards men. But can God do this simply by a decision of his will without any objective action on his part? Paul would answer, "No." Therefore, he adds the phrase, **through the redemption that is in Christ Jesus.** Men can be acquitted (pronounced righteous) because God has acted. He has provided **redemption.** Originally the word meant *the buying back* of a slave or captive, *the making him free* by the payment of a ransom (Arndt, *apolytrōsis*, p. 95). Here redemption refers to the release provided by Christ from sin and its consequences. This redemption or release is **in Christ Jesus.** To be in Christ is to belong to him and to be a part of all that he has done and brought into being through his redemptive work. Paul now proceeds to show just what this work involved.

**25,26.** This work is an objective transaction, a particular act of God which involved the person of his Son. It was a necessary act. The necessity was not imposed upon God from without, for then he would not have been God. It was imposed upon him from within, by virtue of his own nature. **Whom** (Christ Jesus) **God displayed publicly as a means of propitiation in his blood through faith.** Here Paul brings together God and Christ, the work accomplished, and man's response to this work. God publicly displayed Christ as a means of propitiation in or by his blood. The death of Christ was a fact to be observed by all. But the atoning aspect—that which propitiates sin—was the giving up of his life. This is seen in the fact that his blood was shed or poured out. These details are

**26. To declare, *I say*, at this time his righteousness: that he might be just, and the justifier of him which believeth in Jesus.**

**27. Where *is* boasting then? It is excluded. By what law? of works? Nay; but by the law of faith.**

**28. Therefore we conclude that a man is justified by faith without the deeds of the law.**

given not to arouse sympathy but to show the reality of this death. God was the offerer. Christ was the sacrifice. Human sin was covered, i.e., blotted out forever. Yet for this propitiation to be effective in the life of the individual, faith must be present. The faith or trust is in God, first of all, but it also involves what he has done. He took sin into his his own being (II Cor 5:21), dealt with it there objectively, and by doing this **gave proof of his righteousness. But did God let go unpunished the sins which happened** before Christ's death? The objective, public death of Christ at Calvary proves that the Lord did not let these sins go unpunished. We know that he was dealing with human sin there—with the past sins of mankind as well as with those presently being carried out, and those yet to be committed—because he declared it through his apostles and prophets. These past sins were done **in the sphere of God's forbearance** (Rom 3:25). The Lord did not forget these sins, although he did not deal with them immediately.

God's action in the cross was more than a vindication of himself in regard to past human history. It was also **the proof of his righteousness in the present** (3:26). The Lord must be just or righteous now as he declares righteous the one who believes in Jesus. He did not pass a law that he who believes in Jesus would be declared righteous simply because He said so. Rather, He acted. The Father, Son, and Holy Spirit entered into the arena of human sin. The Almighty laid the basis upon which he could forgive sin, and upon which he could declare sinners righteous and still himself be righteous.

**27-31.** Now Paul proceeds to the results of God's saving work in Christ at the cross. He contends that **boasting is eliminated.** How? **By what kind of a law?** By what kind of system, principle, code, or norm could boasting be eliminated? By **a system of works?** Oh, no. Such a system engenders pride. Rather, it is by a **faith kind of system.** A work-centered life is a self-centered life. But the law or code of faith brings about a God-centered life. Christianity is regarded here as a new law—a code of life with faith at its center. This idea of the word *law* is found in Rom 3:27; 8:2; Jas 1:25; 2:8,9; 2:12. The essence of **the law of faith** is that a man is **declared righteous by means of faith apart from the works of the law** (Rom 3:28).

**29.** *Is he* the God of the Jews only? *is he* not also of the Gentiles? Yes, of the Gentiles also:

**30.** Seeing *it is* one God, which shall justify the circumcision by faith, and uncircumcision through faith.

**31.** Do we then make void the law through faith? God forbid: yea, we establish the law.

### CHAPTER 4

WHAT shall we say then that Abraham our father, as pertaining to the flesh, hath found?

**2.** For if Abraham were justified by works, he hath *whereof* to glory; but not before God.

**3.** For what saith the Scripture? Abraham believed God, and it was counted unto him for righteousness.

**4.** Now to him that worketh is the reward not reckoned of grace, but of debt.

**5.** But to him that worketh not, but believeth on him that justifieth the ungodly, his faith is counted for righteousness.

The Lord is the one who declares men righteous. He is the God both of the Jews and of the Gentiles (v. 29). He declares the Jews to be righteous because of *(ek)* faith, the Gentiles through or by *(dia)* faith. In both instances faith is the cause of God's declaration. So both Jew and Gentile find acceptance with God in the same way—through a personal committal to him, a personal trust in him. This fact does not mean that the Law is nullified. Rather, **the law is** confirmed or made valid. It is confirmed in its role of making men conscious of sin (v. 20). The law confronts men not only with their sin but with the Law-giver as well. When men trust God, the Law-giver, they are at the place where law was meant to bring them.

3) Righteousness by Faith in the Life of Abraham. 4:1-25.

Paul's argument that we are declared righteous by faith was not something new. The object of faith for Paul was Christ. The clear presentation of faith in Christ as the way to righteousness makes the new covenant an everlasting covenant. But the old covenant did embody the principle of being declared righteous by faith. Who could better serve as an example than Abraham? He was the father of the Jewish people. So Paul looks carefully at his life.

a) His Righteousness Attained by Faith Not by Works. 4:1-8. **1.** Paul represents a Jew as raising the question: **What shall we say that Abraham, who physically is our forefather, has found?** These questions that Paul often raises probably are those put to him as he traveled from city to city. **2.** Assume for the moment that Abraham was justified by works; he could then boast. His boast, however, would not be in God but in himself. **3.** The testimony of the Scripture is the final authority to settle any point at issue. Abraham believed or trusted God. This belief or trust was **credited to him as righteousness** (Arndt, *dikaiosynē*, 3, p. 196; *eis*, 8.b., p. 229). Here Paul is quoting Gen 15:6.

**4,5.** **To one working, his pay is credited not as a favor but as due.** Wages earned have nothing to do with unmerited favor. **To one not working but trusting the one who pronounces righteous the godless, his faith or trust is credited to him as righteousness.** Here in a nutshell is the Pauline doctrine of justification by faith. Constant trust or committal to God is the first and sole re-

6. Even as David also describeth the blessedness of the man, unto whom God imputeth righteousness without works,

7. *Saying,* Blessed *are* they whose iniquities are forgiven, and whose sins are covered.

8. Blessed *is* the man to whom the Lord will not impute sin.

9. *Cometh* this blessedness then upon the circumcision *only,* or upon the uncircumcision also? for we say that faith was reckoned to Abraham for righteousness.

10. How was it then reckoned? when he was in circumcision, or in uncircumcision? Not in circumcision, but in uncircumcision.

11. And he received the sign of circumcision, a seal of the righteousness of the faith which *he had yet* being uncircumcised: that he might be the father of all them that believe, though they be not circumcised; that righteousness might be imputed unto them also:

quirement of the man who is declared righteous. This to the Jews was a scandal of no mean proportions. To them it was unthinkable that God should acquit a guilty, godless man. Two things were overlooked by Jews who objected to this as being a libel upon the being of God. First of all, the Jews rejected Jesus as the Messiah, and, therefore, they disregarded the redemptive transaction involving God and Christ. Secondly, they failed to see the significance of belief or trust on the part of one who was godless. Such trust shows that the man is no longer without God but is rather a person who has committed himself to all that God is, to all that God has done, and to all that God will do.

**6-8.** David also speaks of how blessed (fortunate) is the man **to whom God credits righteousness apart from works.** In so doing he confirms the earlier assertions made about Abraham. In the quotation from Ps 32:1,2, it is clear that righteousness is credited to a man, is put to his account. This same individual is pictured as having his lawless deeds forgiven and his sins covered. The Lord does not put sin to his account. In place of a debt which he can never pay, he has righteousness put to his account which he did not earn. How can a man be righteous in God's sight? God bestows His righteousness upon the one who trusts him (Phil 3:9). The OT asserts that God does this. The NT shows more clearly how he can.

b) Abraham Made the Father of All Who Believe by His Faith Prior to Circumcision. 4:9-12. If Abraham is a test case, how was his faith related to the rite of circumcision? He was the first to participate in this rite, and it became the sign of God's covenant with His people. This question was sure to come up in any discussion Paul had with the Jewish people. **9,10.** The apostle insists that the crediting of faith as righteousness took place prior to Abraham's circumcision. In fact, circumcision is looked upon in the Scriptures as **confirming the righteousness which belonged to the faith Abraham had while in uncircumcision** (v. 11). Hence circumcision was a sign to Abraham of the righteousness that God bestowed upon him because of his trust. Since the faith and the bestowal of righteousness occurred before circumcision, Abraham is the father of the Gentiles who believe but who do not have this religious symbol. The order in

12. And the father of circumcision to them who are not of the circumcision only, but who also walk in the steps of that faith of our father Abraham, which *he had* being *yet* uncircumcised.

13. For the promise, that he should be the heir of the world, *was* not to Abraham, or to his seed, through the law, but through the righteousness of faith.

14. For if they which are of the law *be* heirs, faith is made void, and the promise made of none effect:

15. Because the law worketh wrath: for where no law is, *there is* no transgression.

Abraham's case — faith and then righteousness credited to him — made it unmistakably clear that righteousness could be reckoned to the Gentiles who believed. The fact that circumcision was a sign of the righteousness imparted to Abraham because of his faith makes Abraham the father of Jews also, who — like him — receive circumcision, exercise faith, obtain a righteousness which God bestows, and regard circumcision as the sign of this faith and righteousness. **12.** Note that Abraham is not the father (in a vital, spiritual sense) of those who have only the external sign; but rather he is the father of those who walk in the faith that he had before he had any external sign. The Jews were to walk in the footprints of Abraham, the man of faith, not in the footprints of one who legalistically carried out a rite that God demanded of him.

c) Realization of the Promise Brought by Faith, Not by Law. 4:13-16. **13.** Paul asserts that it was **not through the law** that the promise came to Abraham or to his seed. What promise does Paul have in mind? It is the promise that **he** (Abraham) **should be the heir of the world.** This exact language is not found in the OT, but certainly Paul is speaking here of Abraham's being the father of a great posterity (Gen 15:5,6; 22:15-18). The great number of his seed — as the stars of the heaven and as the sand along the seashore (Gen 22:17) — was understood by the Jews to refer solely to his physical descendants. But in Rom 4:11 Paul says that Abraham is the father of those who believe among the Gentiles — "those believing in a state of uncircumcision." Hence Abraham is the heir of the world because he is the father of believers. This promise is **through the righteousness which faith bestows.** Of course, faith does not really bestow the righteousness. God bestows it on the ground of faith. **14.** What if we assume that those of the Law are heirs? **Faith is in a state of being invalid. The promise is in a state of being nullified.** Whenever the choice becomes either faith or law, then to choose law (legalism) as the basis of inheriting the world and pleasing God means the abandoning of faith and the promise based thereon. **15. The law produces** or **brings about wrath.** It does this by setting forth God's standard of conduct. Men who disregard this standard and act as they please place themselves directly under God's wrath. **Where there is no law,**

**16.** Therefore *it is* of faith, that *it might be* by grace; to the end the promise might be sure to all the seed; not to that only which is of the law, but to that also which is of the faith of Abraham; who is the father of us all,

**17.** (As it is written, I have made thee a father of many nations,) before him whom he believed, *even* God, who quickeneth the dead, and calleth those things which be not as though they were:

neither is there transgression (ASV). One is not usually charged with speeding if the state has no speed limit, if there are no posted limits along the road, and if there appears to be nothing unreasonable or improper about one's driving. The word **transgression** *(parabasis)* refers to an overstepping, a violation of specifically stated commandment. The role of the Law, then, is to make clear what God demands of men.

**16. The promise is from faith.** The **it** of the AV should be clearly designated as **the promise.** The promise has its source in faith in order to make clear that the content of the promise is **a favor**, not an earned, merited payment. Furthermore, the promise becomes certain **to all the seed.** Paul makes clear that the seed is not to be equated with those who lived under the Law. Rather, the seed refers to those who, like Abraham, believe God — to those who share Abraham's faith. If this is the definition of the word **seed**, then **Abraham** is truly **the father of us all.**

d) God, the Master of Death, the Object of Faith for Abraham and the Christian. 4:17-25. In this section the reader sees the God in whom Abraham believed. He also learns what obstacles and difficulties Abraham overcame because of his firm trust. Both Abraham and the Christian share the same conviction: God gives life to the dead.

**17.** A year before Isaac was born, God reappeared to Abraham, re-emphasized His covenant with him that he should be the father of many nations, and changed his name from Abram to Abraham (Gen 17:1-5). The apostle quotes the phrase, **I have made thee a father of many nations.** Paul pictures Abraham, at the time this declaration was made, as standing **before the God whom he trusted.** Two important things are said about the God in whom Abraham trusted: (1) He is **the one who brings the dead to life.** Abraham experienced this power in the birth of Isaac (cf. Rom 4:19). Paul was thinking of the Father especially as the one who raised up Christ (cf. v. 24). (2) He **calls the things which do not exist as if they did exist.** This is the Lord's power to create. It could also be translated: *God calls into being what does not exist as* (easily as he calls) *that which does exist.* No mortal can comprehend the divine creative power. The bringing of animate and inanimate objects into existence and

18. Who against hope believed in hope, that he might become the father of many nations, according to that which was spoken, So shall thy seed be.

19. And being not weak in faith, he considered not his own body now dead, when he was about a hundred years old, neither yet the deadness of Sarah's womb:

20. He staggered not at the promise of God through unbelief; but was strong in faith, giving glory to God;

21. And being fully persuaded, that what he had promised, he was able also to perform.

22. And therefore it was imputed to him for righteousness.

23. Now it was not written for his sake alone, that it was imputed to him;

24. But for us also, to whom it shall be imputed, if we believe on him that raised up Jesus our Lord from the dead;

25. Who was delivered for our offenses, and was raised again for our justification.

their maintenance is God's activity. The nature of the objects may be discussed — mind, matter, energy—but the why and how of their existence can be known accurately only to the extent that the Lord reveals them. 18. Because Abraham knew such a God, he was able, contrary to all human expectations, in hope to believe. His faith was directed to the purpose and goal of his being the father of many nations. 19. There were two great obstacles to his achieving this goal. He was physically incapable of fathering a child. His wife Sarah was physically incapable of conception and childbearing. Because Abraham was not weak in faith, he looked at with reflection (considered) his own body in a state of being impotent (v. 19). The AV has: He considered not his own body now dead. But this negative is not supported by the best manuscripts. Hence Paul pictures Abraham as fully facing the difficulty. He was about one hundred years old. He further considered the deadness of Sarah's womb. 20. But he was not at odds with himself over the promise of God because of unbelief. The word translated "to be at odds with oneself" (diakrinō) could also be translated "to doubt" or "to waver." For the patriarch, there was no uncertainty because of unbelief. In the face of these obstacles Abraham was strengthened because of faith or trust. Note here the effects of unbelief and belief. Unbelief puts one at variance with himself; belief brings strength to meet the obstacle. Abraham gave glory to God as he was strengthened. 21. He was convinced that what God had promised He was able to do. The verb "to promise" is in the perfect tense. This means Abraham had been in a state of possessing the promise, so great was his conviction that the promise would be realized. 22. This was the kind of faith credited to Abraham as righteousness. 24. The crediting of faith as righteousness was not for Abraham's benefit alone. The written record of this fact was because of us. Righteousness will be reckoned to those who are in the process of trusting in the One who raised up Jesus our Lord from the dead. There is a difference between Abraham and the Christian. Abraham believed or trusted God (v. 3). The Christian trusts the same God, but He is now known as the God who raised up Jesus Christ from the dead (v. 24). In this the Lord has revealed himself as acting on man's behalf in a most unusual way. 25. The center of his action is Christ, who was handed over because of our trans-

## CHAPTER 5

THEREFORE being justified by faith, we have peace with God through our Lord Jesus Christ:

gressions. The verb "to hand over" is in the passive, meaning that it was God who did the handing over (cf. 8:32). The same word is used of Judas and his betrayal of Christ. But although Judas was the human instrument who handed Christ over to the soldiers, and although Judas' sin was very great, it was God's purpose that Christ be handed over into the hands of sinners. (The word "to hand over," *paradidōmi*, is used in a number of interesting contexts. For a word study of this term see F. Buchsel, *TWNT*, II, 171-175; Karl Barth, *Church Dogmatics*, Vol. II, Part 2, *The Doctrine of God*, pp. 480-494). When we see that "our" transgressions necessitated Christ's being put to death, the death of Jesus appears in a different light. A detached observer might conclude that Christ died and rose again. But one who has committed himself to God says: "Jesus was handed over because of *my* transgressions." The plural pronoun **our** shows Paul's identification with his Roman readers. **He was raised because of our vindication.** The verb is again passive. God raised Christ from the dead. The resurrection here is said to be essential to our being declared righteous. The resurrection signaled not only Christ's victory over death but also his living to testify that he had completed the redemptive work laid out by God (the work for which he became man), and that he lives to plead the cause of those who believe in him and his saving work.

4) Centrality of the Righteousness by Faith in Individual Lives and in the Framework of History. 5:1-21.

In the first part of this chapter Paul examines the meaning of righteousness by faith for believers. What do they have? What should they do? How did God meet them and what is their future? Then he turns to a comparison of the effects of Adam's departure from God with the effects of Christ's reconciling work. The importance of righteousness in the last half of the chapter is made clear by the occurrence of the term in 5:17,18,19, 21.

a) Effects of the Righteousness by Faith upon the Recipients. 5:1-11. **1.** The participle speaks of action which has occurred. **Having been declared righteous by faith.** This has been the theme from 3:21 through 4:25. From this theme, certain conditions and responses follow. The main verb forms in 5:1,2,3 may be translated: "we have peace . . . we boast

2. By whom also we have access by faith into this grace wherein we stand, and rejoice in hope of the glory of God.

3. And not only so, but we glory in tribulations also; knowing that tribulation worketh patience;

4. And patience, experience; and experience, hope:

5. And hope maketh not ashamed; because the love of God is shed abroad in our hearts by the Holy Ghost which is given unto us.

in afflictions . . ." Or these verbs can be translated as exhortations: "Let us enjoy the peace we have . . . let us boast (glory) in the hope . . . let us boast (glory) in afflictions . . ." The verbs are all in the present tense and express constant activity. The **peace** a believer has is **peace with God.** This is an objective state for the one who is declared righteous. It is **through our Lord Jesus Christ.** Christ's redemptive work provided an atonement, a covering for the sin of the one declared righteous by faith. Such an one has been reconciled to God. Therefore the hostility and animosity between God and believers are gone. Instead there is blessed peace.

**2 a.** There is also fellowship — **through whom we have had the approach** or *access.* The wonder of being declared righteous consists in this open access to the presence of God. *Prosagōgē* can be translated "approach," "access," or "introduction" (see LSJ, p. 1500). But the idea of "introduction" goes hand in hand with "access" or "approach." One who came to see a king needed both access — the right to come, and an introduction — the proper presentation. The right or access is fundamental, the introduction more a matter of protocol. Hence the stress here ought to be on **access.** The access is **into this grace in which we have taken our stand. This grace** is the unmerited favor of God to declare righteous those who have put their trust in Jesus.

**2 b.** The translation **and rejoice in hope** (AV) fails to make clear to the reader that the same verb is used here as in 5:3 — "we glory in tribulations." Hence 5:2 really means: **And we are boasting (glorying) in the hope of the glory that God will manifest or display.** Hope plays a vital part in the life of believers, for it has to do with all that God has promised to do for them in Christ.

**3,4.** But this hope becomes clearer in the day-by-day pressures of life. The believer glories in tribulations because he knows they will bring clearer vision of what lies ahead — hope with conviction in it. The order of these verses is significant — **tribulation, endurance, character,** and then **hope.** Testing brings the response of endurance. Endurance produces character. The outcome of all of this is hope. **5. Hope does not disappoint.** Even though hope does center in God's future action (8:24,25), it has an important present possession—**God's love,** i.e., the love which God imparts, **is being poured out in our hearts through the Holy Spirit he gave to us.** The abun-

6. For when we were yet without strength, in due time Christ died for the ungodly.

7. For scarcely for a righteous man will one die: yet peradventure for a good man some would even dare to die.

8. But God commendeth his love toward us, in that, while we were yet sinners, Christ died for us.

9. Much more then, being now justified by his blood, we shall be saved from wrath through him.

10. For if, when we were enemies, we were reconciled to God by the death of his Son; much more, being reconciled, we shall be saved by his life.

dance of this love in the heart of justified men, and its outreach, are said by Christ to be the distinguishing trait of Christians (Jn 13:34,35).

This love, poured out in our hearts, with the hope that does not disappoint, has its supreme example in God's love for us (Rom 5:6-8). **6.** Indeed, **while we were still weak** [moral weakness], **at the right time Christ died for the godless.** There are rare examples of a person's dying for an upright man. That someone might dare to die **for** the good man because of the impact of his life is very plausible. But that God should demonstrate his love for us in that while we were sinners Christ should die **for** us is not only amazing but almost incredible. Four times in this section the preposition *hyper* occurs (vv. 6,7,7,8). It has such broad meaning that no one English word can convey it. It really involves in one unit the ideas of "for the benefit of," "on behalf of," and "instead of." If these ideas are put into the English word "for," then the full significance of Christ's death "for" us begins to dawn.

**9.** But Paul quickly shifts the scene from our former state as sinners to the now. If God loved us when we were sinners, if Christ died for us then, much more now, having been declared righteous by his blood, we shall be saved through him (Christ) from God's future wrath. Note that the ground for justification is Christ's blood. This future salvation is from God's wrathful punishment, spoken of in II Thess 1:9 as "an eternal destruction from the face of the Lord and from the glory of his strength." **10.** Those now justified are said to have been reconciled to God while they were **enemies.** The basis for this reconciliation is explicitly stated — **through the death of his Son** (ASV). We were reconciled by his death when we were enemies. This being true, the apostle concludes, much more is it true that **we shall be saved in** or **by his life.** Elsewhere Paul points out that the one who is joined to the Lord is one spirit (I Cor 6:17), i.e., he shares Christ's resurrected life and spiritual power. He also says: "When Christ, our life, shall appear, then shall ye also appear with him in glory" (Col 3:4). We shall be saved by Christ's life because we share this life. We belong to Christ. The writer of Hebrews stresses that Christ lives to make intercession for us (Heb 7:25). The intercessory life of Christ in glory plays a vital role in the salvation of believers. But the context here seems to put the

11. And not only *so*, but we also joy in God through our Lord Jesus Christ, by whom we have now received the atonement.

12. Wherefore, as by one man sin entered into the world, and death by sin; and so death passed upon all men, for that all have sinned:

stress on the believers' sharing in Christ's death and resurrected life. Believers will be saved (fut.) by their present and future participation in Christ's life.

11. The boasting or glorying in God by which the believer affirms his devotion to God is through the Lord Jesus Christ. Through him **we have now received the reconciliation** (ASV). God is the one who is active in reconciliation (II Cor 5:18,19), and men are said to be reconciled (Rom 5:10; II Cor 5:20), i.e., they are acted upon by God. Thus believers are said to receive reconciliation. They are recipients of a relationship of peace and harmony brought about by God.

b) Effects of Adam's Disobedience and Christ's Obedience. 5:12-21. This is one of the most difficult passages in the book of Romans, because Paul is so concise. The apparent repetition is only because of frequent mention of Adam and Christ — and those influenced by their action. Actually, Paul carefully develops his argument. He uses the argument *a fortiori* (with stronger reason, more conclusively): If Adam's sin resulted in this, how much more will Christ's redemptive work do this. Although Christ's redemptive work is far more potent than Adam's transgression, as the apostle shows, this does not mean that all men will be saved. For men to reign in life they must receive the abundance of grace and the righteousness that God makes available (v. 17).

12-14. *Universality of Sin and Death.*
12. **Through one man sin entered into the world and through sin, death.** The man is Adam. The tense of the verb indicates a distinct historic entrance. **World** refers to mankind (a common use of the word in Romans; cf. 1:8; 3:6; 3:19; 5:12,13). **Death passed through to all men because all sinned.** Physical death came to all men but not because they were all in the process of individually sinning. All men did sin (except for infants dying in infancy) experientially. But Paul is not talking about that here. The sin of the all is centered in that of the **one man** Adam. **Because all sinned.** Paul asserts that all men sinned when Adam sinned, but he does not explain how. Yet much has been written on the question of how. Paul's concept of racial solidarity seems to be a universalizing of the Hebrew concept of family solidarity. A tragic picture of family solidarity is seen in Josh 7:16-26, where Achan is discovered as the cause of Israel's defeat at Ai. He had appropriated

13. (For until the law sin was in the world: but sin is not imputed when there is no law.

14. Nevertheless death reined from Adam to Moses, even over them that had not sinned after the similitude of Adam's transgression, who is the figure of him that was to come.

15. But not as the offense, so also *is* the free gift: for if through the offense of one many be dead, much more the grace of God, and the gift by grace, *which is* by one man, Jesus Christ, hath abounded unto many.

for himself some of the spoil from Jericho contrary to the Lord's specific command (Josh 6:17,18). Achan blamed no one else — "I saw . . . I coveted . . . I took" (Josh 7:21). But in the administration of the punishment, not only Achan but also all his property, his sons, his daughters, his oxen, his asses, his sheep, his tent were destroyed. Everything connected with Achan was blotted out of Israel. Another example of family solidarity is found in Abraham's paying tithes to Melchizedek (Gen 14:18-20). The writer of Hebrews regards Levi as also paying tithes to Melchizedek although he was not born until approximately 200 years later. He regards Levi as being still in the loins of his father when Melchizedek met him (Heb 7:9,10). In the same sense Adam was both the individual and the race. His posterity are looked upon as acting with him because they are *his* posterity. As sons of Adam they constitute *Adam's* race.

13. From Adam's time to that of the Mosaic law, sin was in the world. It was present in men's acts and in their nature (i.e., in the principle of rebellion found in them). **But sin is not charged to an account while there is no law.** Adam's sin was charged to his account and to that of his posterity because he broke an explicitly stated command of God. Men from Adam to Moses without such explicit laws could not have sin charged to their account in the same way as Adam had. They did not have definite, specific statutes, such as those later given in the Mosaic code. 14. But these men shared in the effect of Adam's sin, because death reigned from Adam to Moses **even over those who did not sin in the likeness of Adam's transgression.** Looking at these men from the standpoint of racial solidarity, Paul sees men from Adam to Moses as involved both in Adam's initial sin and in its consequences. Those in this group who did not sin in breaking a specifically given command still died. Adam is called in this verse **the type of the one about to come.** Paul is not saying that there were no God-given commands known to men between Adam and the Law (cf. Gen 26:5). He does assert that an absence of a code of law — of a divinely given norm — affects the way sin is reckoned against men.

**15-17.** *Contrasting Results of Diverse Actions.* Paul points out the differences between Adam and Christ.

15. The transgression of the **one** (Adam) is contrasted with the grace of

16. And not as *it was* by one that sinned, *so is* the gift: for the judgment *was* by one to condemnation, but the free gift *is* of many offenses unto justification.

17. For if by one man's offense death reigned by one; much more they which receive abundance of grace and of the gift of righteousness shall reign in life by one, Jesus Christ.)

God and the gift in the sphere of grace which the one man Christ bestows. **The many died** because of the transgression of Adam. Since death passed through to all men (v. 12), it is clear that the phrase **the many** means "all men." **Much more.** The grace of God and the gift which is in the sphere of grace that Christ provides have abounded to the many. "The many" is the same group who were affected by Adam's transgression and therefore died. God's grace and the gift in the sphere of Christ's grace abound to all men. The gift is righteousness (see v. 17). Adam's act brought death. Divine grace abounds to those affected by Adam's act.

16. The verdict of condemnation stemming from one transgression is contrasted with the gracious gift that came into existence because of many transgressions. **Now the verdict indeed was from one transgression unto condemnation.** The verdict refers to God's sentence. The word for **condemnation** involves the ideas of "punishment" and "doom." So we ask: Condemned to what? The answer is, to divine punishment and doom. The seriousness of this condemnation cannot be overstated. **The gracious gift is because of many transgressions unto acquittal or justification.** The outcome of Adam's one transgression was condemnation. Many transgressions brought God's gracious gift into operation, and its outcome or goal is acquittal. How powerful must be this gracious gift when it is directed toward such an end!

17. The reign of death, because of the trespass of the one, is contrasted with the reign in life — on the part of those who receive the abundance of grace and the gift of righteousness. **Death reigned through the one.** Adam transgressed God's commandment that he must not eat of the tree of the knowledge of good and evil (Gen 2:17). This command was a test of man's obedience to God. With the coming of sin into man's experience, death also came. Death became king. It reigned supreme. Adam's action brought the reign of death. **Much more.** Here again is man's action; but this time it is man's action simply in response to what God has done. **Those who are receiving the abundance of grace and the gift, i.e., righteousness.** Here we see man obliged to make a response toward the action of God. The abundance of grace has to do with all that God has accomplished and promised to do in Christ. The gift is defined here as **the righteousness.** This is

18. **Therefore, as by the offense of one** *judgment came* **upon all men to condemnation; even so by the righteousness of one** *the free gift came* **upon all men unto justification of life.**

19. **For as by one man's disobedience many were made sinners, so by the obedience of one shall many be made righteous.**

the righteousness bestowed by God on the basis of faith (Rom 1:17; 3:21,22, 26; 5:17,21; 9:30; 10:3). Those who are receiving God's abounding favor toward them in Christ and the righteousness which he provides **will reign in life through the one man, Jesus Christ.** Because of what the one man, Jesus Christ, accomplished, death no longer reigns, but **men reign in life.** Why are there not as many who reign in life as there were under the reign of death? Because the abundance of grace and the gift of righteousness were rejected by many rather than received.

**18,19.** All men are affected by the one transgression (Adam's) and the one righteous deed (Christ's atoning death and resurrection). **So then** (*as a result then*). Paul is now ready to summarize his argument briefly. **As through one transgression the verdict came to all men unto condemnation.** The subject, **the verdict** (AV, *judgment*), must be supplied here from verse 16. The verb **come** is a satisfactory translation of the Greek verb *egeneto,* which should be supplied. **Thus also through the one righteous deed the gracious gift came unto all men unto the acquittal that brings life.** For the translation **one righteous deed,** see Arndt, *dikaiōma,* 2, p. 197. Romans 4:25 gives evidence that Paul conceived of Christ's death and resurrection as a unified whole. The subject, **the gracious gift** (AV, *the free gift*), must be supplied here from 5:16. This gracious gift comes to all men **for the purpose of** (*unto*) **acquittal that brings life** (see Arndt, *dikaiōsis,* p. 197). In both parts of this verse the same phrase occurs — **unto all men.** Through one transgression the verdict or sentence of judgment came **to all men.** So through one righteous deed the gracious gift of redemption (see Arndt, *charisma,* 1, p. 887) came **unto all men** for the purpose of acquittal that brings life. Paul asserts clearly that the effect of Christ's righteous deed extends just as far as the effect of Adam's transgression.

**19. Now just as through the disobedience of the one man the many were appointed** (AV, *were made*) **to be sinners, in this manner also through the obedience of the one the many will be appointed** (AV, *shall be made*) **to be righteous.** The disobedience of Adam is contrasted with the obedience of Christ. In the preceding verse Paul employs the vocabulary and setting of a law court — condemnation on the one hand and acquittal on the other. He retains this legal language in this

**20. Moreover the law entered, that the offense might abound. But where sin abounded, grace did much more abound:**

**21. That as sin hath reigned unto death, even so might grace reign through righteousness unto eternal life by Jesus Christ our Lord.**

verse as well. The verb *kathistēmi*, rendered by the AV as **be made**, is part of this language of law. In what sense *were the many* **made sinners**, and in what sense *will the many be* **made righteous?** The legal language suggests the following meanings: "appoint," "put down in the category of," "constitute," "establish." Because of Adam's disobedience, the many were appointed by God to be sinners. They were put down in the category of and constituted to be sinners. Because of Christ's obedience, the many will be appointed to be righteous. The verb is future because Paul was thinking of the future generations of believers who by trusting Christ will be declared righteous. Has the apostle changed the extent of **the many** in either side of this comparison? No, because he is showing in what categories God puts men when he views them in terms of the *actual* effect of Adam's disobedience and the *potential* effect of Christ's obedience. Paul is not teaching, as 5:17 shows, that all men will be saved. But in verse 19 he does assert that Christ's obedience encompasses all those affected by Adam's disobedience.

**20,21.** *The Reign of Sin Versus the Reign of Grace.* Here Paul concludes the argument he began in 5:12 on the question: Which is the more powerful—sin or grace?

**20.** The writer reminds us that although righteousness by faith is central in human history, the Law has an important place. The Law came **in order that the transgression might abound** (increase in number, multiply). **But where sin abounded.** The words **transgression** and **sin** are both personified here to make evil a distinct foe and not a mere abstraction. **Grace did much more abound.** Or, *was present in greater abundance.* Grace is much more powerful than sin. Yet when believers see what tremendous power sin has, they forget this truth.

**21.** Just as **sin reigned in the sphere of death**, grace abounds **in order that grace might reign through righteousness.** Sin is connected with death in this verse just as it was in 5:12. Grace reigns through the righteousness that God bestows. The fact that the righteousness of Christ is bestowed upon those who believe means not only that they are declared righteous but also that they belong to the reign and the triumph of grace. **Unto eternal life through Jesus Christ our Lord.** Grace reigns with a goal in view—eternal life. Eternal life is a quality of life; it is living by God's life and for God.

529

## CHAPTER 6

WHAT shall we say then? Shall we continue in sin, that grace may abound?

2. God forbid. How shall we, that are dead to sin, live any longer therein?

3. Know ye not, that so many of us as were baptized into Jesus Christ were baptized into his death?

Believers have this life now. But eternal life means not only living by God, and for him, but in an environment that he has made perfect — free from all sin. Hence eternal life is the believer's destiny as well as immediate reality. How will this life be achieved? It will be achieved through a person — through **Jesus Christ our Lord.**

B. Righteousness as the Manner of Christian Living Before God. 6:1—8:39. Thus far Paul has stressed that God is righteous or just (cf. 3:26) and that he bestows righteousness on those who believe (cf. 3:22). To the question as to how men become righteous before God, he has replied: "Not by works but by trust in God" (cf. 4:1-8). But the one who has the righteousness that God bestows must live a righteous life. Paul now shows what this means. First, he eliminates some wrong ideas regarding his teaching about grace. Next, he shows that in the struggle against sin, the believer must not condemn law. Then he pictures sin as a powerful tyrant that cannot be defeated by human effort alone. Paul concludes this section by pointing out how victory can be attained.

1) Fallacy of Sinning That Grace Might Abound. 6:1-14.

**1.** If grace is so powerful, could not a man remain in sin and still experience the delivering power of grace?. **2.** Paul's answer is emphatic: **By no means.** The one trusting Christ has identified himself with the Lord Jesus in His death. **We who died in reference to sin.** Verse 10 makes it clear that Paul is here speaking of Christ's death. But he uses the first person plural — *We* have died to sin. This is a past experience. Such being the case, how can we still live in sin when we have already died to it?

**3-5.** Having said that the believer died with Christ, Paul now refers to the ordinance of baptism. Here the apostle follows his familiar pattern of asserting a truth and then illustrating it. **3. As many as were baptized unto Christ Jesus were baptized unto his death.** The phrase for "to be baptized unto" (*baptizein eis*) can also be translated *to be baptized in* or *with respect to.* It is used in the sense of being baptized with respect to the name of someone (cf. Acts 8:16; 19:5; I Cor 1:13,15; Mt 28:19; see Arndt, *baptizō,* p. 131). The ordinance of baptism is focused upon the death of Christ—its meaning and outcome. But Paul here

**4.** Therefore we are buried with him by baptism into death: that like as Christ was raised up from the dead by the glory of the Father, even so we also should walk in newness of life.

**5.** For if we have been planted together in the likeness of his death, we shall be also *in the likeness* of *his* resurrection:

points to the implications of baptism with reference to the Romans' way of life. **4. Through baptism, therefore, we were buried together with him in respect to his death.** "Being buried together" stresses the reality of Christ's death. Christ died, and the believer really died with him. **Just as Christ was raised from the dead through the glory of the Father.** This is a comparative clause. The resurrection brought to the Lord Jesus a new manner of life. In a similar way **we also should live in newness of life.** Since we were identified with Christ in his death, we are identified with him in his resurrection. For the Saviour, the resurrection meant a new manner of life. We were buried with Christ in order that we, like him, should **live** in newness of life. The translation to *walk* (AV) *in newness of life* carries with it the day-by-day living in the ordinary routines of life. **5. Since we have become united with** (MM, p. 598) **the likeness of his death, we certainly shall be united with the likeness of his resurrection.** The word **likeness** is used with two words in the English rendering of this verse — **death** and **resurrection.** Though it occurs only once in the original text, it is clear that Paul meant it to apply to both death and resurrection. Some have wanted to supply a "him" in this verse — "Since we have become united with him in the likeness." But **his** death and resurrection makes it clear, nevertheless, that Christ is central here. The word **him** is not found in the text, and good sense can be made out of the text without it. The emphasis in the verse falls on the word **likeness** *(homoiōma)*. To sin in the likeness of Adam's transgression (5: 14) means to sin in a similar way, i.e., to break a specific command. It does not mean to sin the same sin. So the word may have the meanings of "representation," "copy," "facsimile," and "reproduction." (For an excellent treatment of the word and the various interpretations given to it in this context, see Johannes Schneider, TWNT, V, 191-195.) Since believers have had a death like Christ's, they will certainly have a resurrection like his. This does not mean that they will have the identical resurrection of Christ; rather, they will have a resurrection like his. In baptism believers are united with the representation of his death. To be united with the likeness of Christ's resurrection is a future hope that they are sure of. Both of these facts (baptism and resurrection) point to a changed manner of life between these

6. Knowing this, that our old man is crucified with *him*, that the body of sin might be destroyed, that henceforth we should not serve sin.

7. For he that is dead is freed from sin.

8. Now if we be dead with Christ, we believe that we shall also live with him:

9. Knowing that Christ being raised from the dead dieth no more; death hath no more dominion over him.

10. For in that he died, he died unto sin once: but in that he liveth, he liveth unto God.

11. Likewise reckon ye also yourselves to be dead indeed unto sin, but alive unto God through Jesus Christ our Lord.

12. Let not sin therefore reign in your mortal body, that ye should obey it in the lusts thereof.

13. Neither yield ye your members *as* instruments of unrighteousness unto sin: but yield yourselves unto God, as those that are alive from the dead, and your members *as* instruments of righteousness unto God.

two events – the walking in newness of life.

In verses **6-10,** as in verse 2, Paul points to the historic event of Christ's death. **Our old man.** The earlier or unregenerate man before he became a renewed, changed, transformed man. This unregenerated man was crucified with Christ **in order that the sinful body might be done away with.** The body is stressed here because of the role it plays in the man's carrying out of his sinful desires. **In order that we should not be in constant slavery to sin.** Sin is personified here. As a tyrant, it holds men in abject slavery.

**Now the one who died has been set free from sin.** A dead person cannot act in the daily events of life. One who has died to sin does not respond to the pattern of sinful living. **8. And since we died together with Christ.** Our dying with Christ is the basis for our belief that we will be raised with him. 9. Christ's death was in reference to sin. His victory over death is permanent. This occurred once for all. 10. Since the time of his death he lives solely for God, i.e., for God's advantage and glory. And he lived solely for God before his death. But when Jesus had accomplished the redemptive work that centered in his death, his living for God had a new outlook. He had dealt with the sin question once for all. He had conquered death. With sin and death defeated, he could live for God with these experiences behind him.

All of this had certain consequences for believers (6:11-14). **11. We are to keep reckoning** or *considering* **ourselves to be dead indeed to sin and living for God.** The fact that we must continue to reckon ourselves dead to sin shows that the possibility of sinning is ever present. But our reckoning is more than negative. We reckon ourselves to be alive (to be constantly living) for God. The phrase **in your mortal body** is made equivalent to **yourselves** (in v. 13). **Let not sin keep on reigning** in you, i.e., in your person, **with the result that you obey its evil desires.** If we are in Christ, we have the power to dethrone the sin in our lives. If a believer allows sin to reign, he obeys the evil desires that sin generates. **13. Stop handing over your members as weapons** (or *tools*) **of unrighteousness to sin.** When the tyrant, sin, reigns in the hearts of men, sinners freely hand over their hands, feet, eyes, and mind to the cause of unrighteousness. In place of this constant dedication to evil, Paul urges:

14. For sin shall not have dominion over you: for ye are not under the law, but under grace.

15. What then? shall we sin, because we are not under the law, but under grace? God forbid.

16. Know ye not, that to whom ye yield yourselves servants to obey, his servants ye are to whom ye obey; whether of sin unto death, or of obedience unto righteousness?

Hand over yourselves once for all to God . . . and your members as weapons of righteousness. Why should we hand over ourselves to God? Because those in Christ are living as having risen from the dead. We died with Christ. Hence we see life from a new perspective. We have dedicated ourselves to God. The self, of course, includes every member or part of us and every activity we may engage in. All that goes to make up the human personality will be either actively serving unrighteousness or actively serving righteousness. In whose service are our members employed? **14.** The abounding of grace is of such a nature that sin does not **lord it over** believers. We are not **under law** but **under grace.** Those in Christ are not under the regime of the Mosaic law as the means of attaining salvation. We are under the grace of God and of Christ. The whole of the OT — the Law, the Prophets, and the Writings (e.g., Psalms) — certainly brings the knowledge of sin (Rom 3:20; 5:20) when understood in the light of Christ's teaching and the teaching of the apostles after his death and resurrection. The OT also teaches Christians great truths about God. Paul regards what Christ taught and Christ himself as law. "Always bear one another's crushing weights, and in this fashion you will fulfill **the law of Christ**" (Gal 6:2). "I became to those without law as without law [to the Gentiles as a Gentile], though I do not reject God's law but *I am subject to the law of Christ* in order that I might gain those without law [the Gentiles]" (I Cor 9:21).

2) Fallacy of Sinning Because Believers Are Under Grace, Not Law. 6:15–7:6.

When we are under grace, we have a new owner. This fact changes all of a believer's conduct. Our status under grace is like that of a woman married to another man after the death of her husband. It involves a whole new manner of life. Thus, by analogy, Paul shows why being under grace never allows a believer to be indifferent to sin.

a) Allegiance, Fruit, Destiny. 6:15-23. Here Paul appeals to what his readers know. He reminds them of their former lives and the fruit they bore. He tells them the outcome of their new dedication. He contrasts the eternal results of two different kinds of allegiance. **15.** Should a man commit a sinful act because he is not under law but under grace? Paul replies: **By no means. 16.** He

17. But God be thanked, that ye were the servants of sin, but ye have obeyed from the heart that form of doctrine which was delivered you.

18. Being then made free from sin, ye became the servants of righteousness.

19. I speak after the manner of men because of the infirmity of your flesh: for as ye have yielded your members servants to uncleanness and to iniquity unto iniquity; even so now yield your members servants to righteousness unto holiness.

20. For when ye were the servants of sin, ye were free from righteousness.

21. What fruit had ye then in those things whereof ye are now ashamed? for the end of those things is death.

22. But now being made free from sin, and become servants to God, ye have your fruit unto holiness, and the end everlasting life.

reminds his readers that they are slaves to that one to whom they hand themselves over. If they hand themselves over to sin, the outcome is death. If they become slaves of obedience to God, the outcome is righteousness. The handing over is looked upon here as a constant process or allegiance.

17. They were formerly slaves of sin. Then there came a break with that bondage. **You obeyed from the heart the pattern of teaching unto which you were given over.** The pattern of teaching, of course, is Christianity. They were given over to it to learn its content. They responded with obedience — obedience that came from the depths of their being. This brought a decisive change. They were freed from sin. They became slaves to righteousness. Both sin and righteousness are personified, and this figure of speech — being a slave to sin or righteousness — helps us understand just what is at stake. **19. I speak in human terms because of the weakness of your flesh.** This human analogy is necessary, Paul says, because of the poor judgment of those who become willing instruments of sin. The man under the control of sin is "in the flesh." Formerly Paul's readers had presented their members as slaves to uncleanness and to one sinful deed after another. This proved their constant devotion to various forms of wickedness. **In this manner hand over your members once for all as slaves to righteousness for consecration.** With the same abandon with which men dedicated themselves to evil, they should now hand over their members as slaves to righteousness. The outcome is **consecration** or **holiness.** Consecrated to whom? To God. Holiness is the product of consecration to God. **20.** Paul contends that when the readers belonged to sin, they certainly did not have righteousness as their master. **21. What fruit did you have then?** (Note change in question from AV.) When you were slaves of sin, what fruit did you have? **You had fruit in those things of which you are now ashamed.** Sinners produce bad fruit (see Mt 7:16-20). **Now the end of those things is death.** By **death** Paul here means eternal death (see Arndt, *thanatos*, 2, b, p. 352; Rom 1:32; 6:16, 21,23; 7:5; II Cor 2:16; 7:10; II Tim 1:10; Heb 2:14 b; I Jn 5:16; Rev 2:11; 20:6,15; 21:8).

22. Being free from sin means being a slave to God. The immediate fruit produced is consecration. The final outcome of belonging to God is eternal life. **23.**

23. For the wages of sin *is* death; but the gift of God *is* eternal life through Jesus Christ our Lord.

## CHAPTER 7

KNOW ye not, brethren, (for I speak to them that know the law,) how that the law hath dominion over a man as long as he liveth?

2. For the woman which hath a husband is bound by the law to *her* husband so long as he liveth; but if the husband be dead, she is loosed from the law of *her* husband.

3. So then if, while *her* husband liveth, she be married to another man, she shall be called an adulteress: but if her husband be dead, she is free from that law; so that she is no adulteress, though she be married to another man.

4. Wherefore, my brethren, ye also are become dead to the law by the body of Christ; that ye should be married to another, *even* to him who is raised from the dead, that we should bring forth fruit unto God.

Now the compensation paid by sin (for services rendered to it) is death. Paul changes the analogy slightly here. Sin pays wages to those working for it. The wages paid is death. But the gracious gift of God is eternal life in Jesus Christ our Lord. God's gracious gift of deliverance from sin, his transforming of the sinner's whole being, is eternal life. Eternal life is a new kind of life. The sinner realizes this as an unmerited favor. This kind of life, this quality of existence, is found in only one person — in Jesus Christ. The last phrase — our Lord — is Paul's way of saying that the Lord belongs to us as we belong to him. We have made him our Lord by our act of commitment. His lordship extends to the manner of our living.

b) Annulment and New Alignment Caused by Death. 7:1-6. 1. The law, says the apostle, lords it over (*rules over*) a man as long as he lives. Paul lays down this axiom both for the sake of the illustration that he is about to use and to show that this is the nature of law. Its requirements remain in force as long as one lives under the regime of law. 2. The married woman is in a state of being bound by the law to the living husband. In the first verse Paul says that he is speaking to those who know law. Since the majority of the Romans were Gentiles, the law here is not the Mosaic Law in particular but merely the legal principle that a married woman is bound to her husband. Paul's handling of this particular command is certainly in the light of his Jewish background in the Mosaic law. If the husband dies, the woman is discharged from (*is released from*) this particular commandment about her husband. Death brings annulment of the whole former relationship regarding her marriage. 3. While her husband lives, she will be called an adulteress if she belongs to a different husband. The translation "to belong to" (cf. Arndt, *ginomai*, II, 3, p. 159) has the force of *being married to*. But after the death of her husband she may re-enter the marriage state without being charged with adultery. The living one (the wife) is free to belong to another.

4. When Paul applies the illustration to the relationship of an individual to the Law and to Christ, it is the one who dies (the believer who died with Christ) who is released from the Law and is free to belong to Christ. You were put to death to the disadvantage of the law through the

5. For when we were in the flesh, the motions of sins, which were by the law, did work in our members to bring forth fruit unto death.

6. But now we are delivered from the law, that being dead wherein we were held; that we should serve in newness of spirit, and not *in* the oldness of the letter.

body of Christ. The phrase **through the body of Christ** (ASV) refers to the believer's identification with Christ in his physical death. In 6:6 Paul has already said that our unregenerate person has been crucified with Christ. This death deprived the Law of its power over us and had as its end our **belonging to another — to the one who arose from the dead.** Here is the new alignment. We now belong to Christ, so that we may bring forth fruit to God. To translate the phrase, *eis to genesthai humas heterô,* "in order that you should be married to another," is certainly all right. It is part of Paul's analogy and agrees with his use of the comparison with marriage elsewhere (II Cor 11:2; Eph 5:25,29).

**5.** To be **in the flesh** means to be under the control and domination of sin. **The sinful passions,** which the Law made conspicuous by reminding men of God's standards, **were constantly at work** in their members. Dominated by these sinful passions, men brought forth fruit to the advantage of death. Death here is personified. It means eternal death (see 6: 21). **6. But now having been discharged from** (*released from*) **the law.** The Law was powerless to remove sinful passions. Being released from the Law is here made equivalent to being released from being in the flesh. **Because we died** [in regard to that] **in which** (referring to the Law) **we were held fast.** While under the Law, the believer died with Christ. He died to the Law's claim requiring condemnation. Paul speaks of this death to the Law in Gal 2:19. Being discharged from the Law opens a new relationship with a new attitude. The relationship is that of **constantly being a slave** to God. This means that we serve God, fully aware that we belong to him. He owns us because he redeemed us. We serve **in a new spirit, not in the old letter.** Or better, in newness of Spirit in contrast to the old legal code. In place of a legalism that enforces statutes, there is a spirit of love and dedication.

3) Questions Raised by the Struggle Against Sin. 7:7-25.

Here Paul unfolds his own inward struggles. He does not tell this as an interesting piece of autobiography, but because he knew that his readers had the same struggles. Paul controlled by sin did things that Paul controlled by God did not wish to do. Paul controlled by sin was not his true self but his false self. Nevertheless it was the same self. Paul

7. What shall we say then? *Is* the law sin? God forbid. Nay, I had not known sin, but by the law: for I had not known lust, except the law had said, Thou shalt not covet.

8. But sin, taking occasion by the commandment, wrought in me all manner of concupiscence. For without the law sin *was* dead.

9. For I was alive without the law once: but when the commandment came, sin revived, and I died.

was guilty when he was controlled by sin and holy when he was controlled by God. As a Jew he knew God's will (Phil 3:6; Acts 22:3; 26:4,5). To the extent that he carried out God's will, he was controlled by God. This did not make him a believer in Christ or a Christian. But it did make him aware of the struggle between doing right and doing wrong. When he became a Christian, the struggle was intensified. Every believer, aware of the righteousness that God bestows, and of righteousness as the manner of Christian living, can say when he reads this passage, "This is my experience." Paul also stands representatively for those Jewish people—the people of the Law—who passed from a place of complacency under the Law to a condition of concern with the deep struggles to which it gave rise, and then to a position of composure and victory in Christ.

a) Is the Law sin? 7:7-12. 7. If, when a man becomes a Christian, he is released or discharged from the Law, does that mean there is something wrong with the Law? Paul answers: **By no means.** The Law showed him (and it shows us) just what sin is. For example, Paul says: **I would not have felt guilty [in] desiring that which is forbidden if the law were not saying: you (sing.) shall not desire that which is forbidden.** The longing for that which is evil becomes apparent when the commandment declares: This evil thing is forbidden. Then the sinner wants it. 8. The apostle tells how sin took the commandment **as a base of operations** and wrought in him **desire of every kind** (for that which is forbidden). **Now without law, sin is dead.** Paul does not say that sin is not committed without law. He is saying that without law sin is not apparent to us. It takes a carpenter's level to make clear how far from straight a board really is.

9. **Indeed I was alive without the law at one time. But when the commandment came, sin became alive and I died.** The apostle here is talking about his own consciousness of sin. When he was a lad, the content of the Law did not really reach him. He did not understand the true purpose of law. This lack of understanding is not confined to children. An adult like the rich young ruler can assert confidently: "I have guarded (ASV, *observed*) all these things from my youth" (Mk 10:20; cf. Mt 19:20; Lk 18:21). 10. But there came a day in

10. And the commandment, which *was ordained* to life, I found *to be* unto death.

11. For sin, taking occasion by the commandment, deceived me, and by it slew *me.*

12. Wherefore the law *is* holy, and the commandment holy, and just, and good.

13. Was then that which is good made death unto me? God forbid. But sin, that it might appear sin, working death in me by that which is good; that sin by the commandment might become exceeding sinful.

14. For we know that the law is spiritual: but I am carnal, sold under sin.

Paul's life when the particular commandment, "You (sing.) shall not desire that which is forbidden," hit him right between the eyes. He knew he was desiring the forbidden. Paul became conscious of sin, and he knew that he was spiritually dead. This particular commandment ("Thou shalt not covet") not only made clear the sinfulness of desiring that which is forbidden but also told him how to live. It reminded him that he was not living the right way. 11. Sin had deceived him. As he understood the commandment, the extent of sin's deception became clear to him. The commandment made Paul see that sin had brought about his death. Sin first **deceives** and then **kills**. This order shows how tricky sin is and what is its objective—the eternal ruin of individuals.

b) Is that which is good the cause of death? 7:13,14. Paul asks this question about himself. He answers emphatically: **By no means.** God put things together in such a way that sin brought death through that which is good. **In order that sin through the commandment might become sinful to an extraordinary degree.** Because man is a sinner, he does not believe that sin is really what it is. The Law shows clearly what it is and what it intends to do.

Both the readers and the writer knew that **the law is caused by or filled with the** (divine) **Spirit** (see Arndt, *pneumatikos,* p. 685). The word *pneumatikos* can also be translated *pertaining* or *corresponding to the* (divine) *Spirit (ibid.).* Here is Paul's great tribute to the Law. It is caused by or filled with the Spirit of God. Paul condemns law only on one ground—legalism. He resists that view which regards law as a lien upon the being of God—by which God is obligated to do this or that for man (e.g., to save him) because man has kept certain statutes. In contrast to the Law, which is filled with or caused by God's Spirit, Paul sees himself as belonging to the flesh. He was one who was **in a state of being sold as a slave under the sovereignty of sin.** The apostle surely did not mean that he was entirely fleshly (see vv. 16,18,22). He did mean that he knew what it was to be under the domination of sin. Paul's battle was not a few isolated conflicts but a continual warfare.

c) How can the conflict within be resolved? 7:15-25. In this section the writer vividly paints the contest within

15. For that which I do, I allow not: for what I would, that do I not; but what I hate, that do I.

16. If then I do that which I would not, I consent unto the law that *it is* good.

17. Now then it is no more I that do it, but sin that dwelleth in me.

18. For I know that in me (that is, in my flesh,) dwelleth no good thing: for to will is present with me; but *how* to perform that which is good I find not.

19. For the good that I would, I do not: but the evil which I would not, that I do.

20. Now if I do that I would not, it is no more I that do it, but sin that dwelleth in me.

21. I find then a law, that, when I would do good, evil is present with me.

22. For I delight in the law of God after the inward man:

his own soul. He uses some expressions to describe his own person as serving self or sin. He uses others to describe himself as serving God. The conflict arises because he wants to serve God but finds himself serving self and sin.

15. **I do not know what I am doing.** This is a statement of one who is baffled. But he is not ignorant as to what is wrong. The problem is how to overcome what is wrong. **Because I am not doing this which I wish to do; but what I hate, this I am doing. 16.** Here is a person who has knowledge. He shows that he **agrees with the law that it is good** when he says he hates his actions that are contrary to law. Thus it was not Paul's true self that was doing evil but the sin dwelling within him (v. 17). Here the writer identifies his true self with "I" (*egō*). When he says that it is sin that is doing the evil, Paul is not waiving responsibility, but simply recognizing that it is sin that causes his self to become false.

18. **Because I know that in me (that is, in my flesh) dwells no good thing.** The phrases **in me** and **in my flesh** describe Paul as under the control of sin. The absence of good in the sphere of the flesh is another way of saying that oil and water do not mix. Where the flesh is powerful, the will to do good becomes powerless. **Now the wishing** or *willing* **to do is present with me but the doing the good, no.** Paul meant that he was in the process of willing but not in the process of doing. **19. Now, I am not doing good which I wish to do, but evil which I do not wish to do, this I am doing.** In doing of good, Paul felt he was making no achievement. But in the area of evil he was aware of his activities. **20.** This being true, he again concludes, as in verse 17, that it is no longer the **I** who is doing it, but **the sin dwelling in me.**

21. Hence the writer concludes that when he wills **to do good, evil is present with him.** His desire to do good is met by a vigorous opponent that he calls **the law** or **the principle.** Here it is sin that is called a law or principle because of the regularity of its action. **22.** On the encouraging side, Paul declares: **I joyfully agree with** (see Arndt, *synedomai*, p. 797) **the law of God according to the inward man.** Here is Paul's inner response to God's law as a child of God. The phrase "the inward man" occurs only three times in Paul's writings —Rom 7:22; II Cor 4:16; Eph 3:16. In

23. But I see another law in my members, warring against the law of my mind, and bringing me into captivity to the law of sin which is in my members.

24. O wretched man that I am! who shall deliver me from the body of this death?

25. I thank God through Jesus Christ our Lord. So then with the mind I myself serve the law of God; but with the flesh the law of sin.

the second and third of these passages, Paul speaks of the renewal of the inward man and the strengthening of the inner man. Here in Rom 7:22 one finds a spiritually healthy response to the law of God.

23. At the same time, Paul saw **a different law in his members**. His true self, the inward man, agreed with the law of God. But another law (the law of sin) brought the "me" into captivity, making him a prisoner. But before making Paul a prisoner, the law of sin **was at war** with **the law** of his **mind**. This law of his mind, together with the inward man, represents Paul's true self controlled by the being of God. Paul says that his true self was **being brought into captivity** to the law of sin in his members. If Paul had stopped here, he would have been at variance with his statement in 6:14. But he did not stop here. He asserts that sin in the members is a powerful force (and no one should try to deny that fact). 24. The thought that sin could make him captive causes him to cry out: **Wretched man that I am! Who will set me free from the body characterized by this spiritual death?** The body is the scene of this contest. Sin living in the members brings spiritual death to the body, and man becomes aware that he needs outside help. Paul cries out not for deliverance from the body as such, but for deliverance from the body characterized by this spiritual death—the doing of that which is evil in opposition to his desire to do that which is good. 25. **Thanks be to God through Jesus Christ our Lord.** Filled with emotion, the apostle does not round out a full reply to his question. He stresses the One to whom thanks should be rendered, emphasizing who the Deliverer is. The full statement would have been: "Thanks be to God; deliverance comes through Jesus Christ our Lord." In Romans 8 he tell more about this deliverance. But here he merely summarizes the argument of 7:7-25. With his **intellect** or **mind** he constantly serves the law of God. But with his **flesh** (the self controlled by sin) he serves the **principle** of sin.

The following expressions characterize Paul under the control of sin: "the sin dwelling in me" (vv. 17,20); "the law" (v. 21); "a different law in my members" (v. 23); "the law of sin which is in my members" (v. 23); "in me, that is, in my flesh" (v. 18); "in or with the flesh" (v. 25). The following expressions designate

## CHAPTER 8

THERE *is* therefore now no condemnation to them which are in Christ Jesus, who walk not after the flesh, but after the Spirit.

2. For the law of the Spirit of life in Christ Jesus hath made me free from the law of sin and death.

3. For what the law could not do, in that it was weak through the flesh, God sending his own Son in the likeness of sinful flesh, and for sin, condemned sin in the flesh:

Paul under the control of God: the emphatic "I" with the pronoun expressed (vv. 17,20); "the inward man" (v. 22); "the law of my mind" (v. 23); "in or with my mind" (v. 25).

4) Victory Through the Spirit Connected with the Purpose and Action of God. 8:1-39.

No one can appreciate the meaning of victory until he knows the nature of the opposition and the kind of struggle involved. In Romans 8 Paul shows what God has done to bring the Christian to victory over sin. He points out what God is now doing and what the believer must do. He examines the purpose of God and the crisis felt by both creation and the believer. He stresses the relation of the Spirit to the believer and the interrelation of the Spirit with Christ and the Father. He paints a glorious picture of the destiny of those who love God and shows that nothing can separate them from God's love. When a believer becomes occupied with himself, he can rise no higher than Rom 7:25. When he sees what God has done and is doing for him, he must respond in the language of 8:37-39.

a) Deliverance from Sin and Death by the Activity of Father, Son, and Spirit. 8:1-4. 1. **Therefore** goes back to the last verse of 7:25. Since the deliverance comes through Jesus Christ, there is no **condemnation** (involving punishment or doom) **to those who are in Christ Jesus.** Those in Christ are not condemned, because Christ was condemned in their stead. There is no punishment for them, because Christ bore their punishment. 2. But how about this contest with sin that Paul has been discussing? **Now the law,** i.e., **the Spirit of life in Christ Jesus freed you from the law,** i.e., **from sin and death.** Both the Spirit and sin and death are called **the law** because of the constancy of their influence and action. 3. **Law** here refers to the Mosaic Law, and the reader sees that God did what the Law could not do. The Law was up against *an impossibility.* It prescribed a way of life that men who were in the flesh could not follow. Legalistically, they might give the appearance of doing so, but they could never fulfill the terms of all that God demanded. God sent his son **in the likeness of sinful flesh.** The word **likeness** is important, for it signifies that Christ came in flesh like ours, and

4. That the righteousness of the law might be fulfilled in us, who walk not after the flesh, but after the Spirit.

5. For they that are after the flesh do mind the things of the flesh; but they that are after the Spirit, the things of the Spirit.

6. For to be carnally minded *is* death; but to be spiritually minded *is* life and peace.

7. Because the carnal mind *is* enmity against God: for it is not subject to the law of God, neither indeed can be.

8. So then they that are in the flesh cannot please God.

9. But ye are not in the flesh, but in the Spirit, if so be that the Spirit of God dwell in you. Now if any man have not the Spirit of Christ, he is none of his.

was true man, but not a sinful man. This is the difference between Christ and those whom he came to save: He was free from sin both in nature and in act. God condemned sin in his flesh. The phrase could be translated *in the flesh,* but the context favors his flesh. Here the word flesh refers to Christ's true humanity. 4. In this verse flesh refers to men who are living under the control of sin. Sin as a rebellious force against God was condemned in the flesh of Christ. God pronounced judgment on sin in the flesh of Christ in order that the requirements of the law might be fulfilled in us who are not walking *(living)* in accordance with the flesh but in accordance with the Spirit. The word translated requirements is in the singular. It means the complete requirement of God. God dealt with sin in the death of his Son so that those in Christ might understand the complete requirement of God as it is expressed in the Law. Those who realize this purpose of God live in accordance with the Spirit, not in accordance with the flesh.

b) The Mind-set of the Flesh Versus That of the Spirit. 8:5-13. 5. In 8:4 the picture is of those who live in accordance with the flesh or Spirit. Here the stress is on those who are in accordance with the flesh or with the Spirit. In one group are those occupied with all the particulars that go into a sinful life. In the other group are those occupied with all that goes into life under the direction and power of the Spirit. 6. Now the mind-set of the flesh is death, but the mind-set of the Spirit is life and peace. The flesh—the principle of rebellion within man—produces a certain pattern and way of thinking. Likewise, the Holy Spirit produces a certain pattern and way of thinking. The translation mind-set stresses the direction and the outlook of the mind. Spiritual death is made the equivalent of the mind-set of the flesh. Life and peace are equated with the mind-set of the Spirit. 7,8. The mind-set of the flesh is hostile to God, unwilling to subject itself to his law. Persons with such a nature cannot please God.

In verses 9-11 the apostle shows what makes the difference between those in the flesh and those in the Spirit. 9. His readers are "in the Spirit." He assumes that the Spirit of God dwells in them. The if so be that (AV) gives a false impression. Actually, the writer leaves no

10. And if Christ *be* in you, the body *is* dead because of sin; but the Spirit *is* life because of righteousness.

11. But if the Spirit of him that raised up Jesus from the dead dwell in you, he that raised up Christ from the dead shall also quicken your mortal bodies by his Spirit that dwelleth in you.

12. Therefore, brethren, we are debtors, not to the flesh, to live after the flesh.

13. For if ye live after the flesh, ye shall die: but if ye through the Spirit do mortify the deeds of the body, ye shall live.

doubt in his statement. If one does not have **the Spirit of Christ,** he does not belong to Christ. Those who belong to Christ do have the Holy Spirit. The fact that the Spirit is called the Spirit of God and then the Spirit of Christ shows that the Father and the Son are related to the Spirit in the same way. **10.** Not only is the Spirit said to dwell in the believers—you, but **Christ is in them.** For the believer to have the Spirit of Christ within is to have Christ himself within (cf. 8:16,17). Paul is speaking of the reality of God in the life of a Christian. Although filled with God in this fashion, he says, **the body is dead because of sin; but the Spirit is life because of righteousness.** Here the term **body** means the man under the control of sin—the idea usually expressed in "flesh." The false self is dead or useless because of sin. This self cannot be effective for God. But the spirit—the true self—is living because of the righteousness which God bestows. Of course, there are not two separate selves. When the self becomes false, it acts in accordance with the flesh. When the self is true, it acts in accordance with the Spirit.

**11.** The presence of the Spirit of God in believers guarantees that the God who raised up Christ from the dead will quicken the mortal bodies of believers **through his Spirit dwelling in** [them]. The role of the Holy Spirit in the resurrection of believers is a neglected theme. A mortal body is a body capable of dying. A body made alive by the Holy Spirit becomes immortal. The transition from mortality to immortality is the work of the Spirit.

**12.** Believers are in the Spirit, and the Spirit dwells in them. Through him they will have glorified bodies. These facts lead to one certain conclusion. **So then, brothers, we are under obligation, but not to the flesh, to live according to its demands** (see Arndt, *opheiletēs,* 2b, p. 603). **13.** Assuming that you live according to the flesh, Paul tells his readers, you are about to die. This is a spiritual death. But assuming that by the Spirit you keep putting to death the evil deeds (cf. Col 3:9) of the body, you will live. Both "ifs" in 8:13 assume the actuality of the thing stated. The conclusions logically follow. Their solemnity corresponds to the seriousness of the action in the "if" clauses. Since spiritual death here is viewed as climactic—the final banishment from God's presence—the life re-

14. For as many as are led by the Spirit of God, they are the sons of God.

15. For ye have not received the spirit of bondage again to fear; but ye have received the Spirit of adoption, whereby we cry, Abba, Father.

16. The Spirit itself beareth witness with our spirit, that we are the children of God:

17. And if children, then heirs; heirs of God, and joint-heirs with Christ, if so be that we suffer with *him*, that we may be also glorified together.

18. For I reckon that the sufferings of this present time *are* not worthy *to be compared* with the glory which shall be revealed in us.

ferred to must be the glorified life that awaits the believer.

c) Guidance and Witness of the Spirit. 8:14-17. **14. Sons of God** are defined as those who are led by the Spirit of God. The Spirit does the leading. The verb is in the present tense and in the passive —as **many as allow themselves to be led** (cf. Arndt, *agō*, 3, p. 14). **15.** The phrases **spirit of bondage** and **Spirit of adoption** are parallel. A better rendering would be: the *state of mind that belongs to slavery* and *the state of mind that belongs to adoption.* The outcome of the former is fear; the outcome of the latter is the ability to pray and to address God as Father. The word *Abba* is an Aramaic word put into Greek letters and then transliterated into English. It means "Father." The bringing together of both Jew and Greek (Gentiles) in Christ is seen in these opening words of address in prayer.

**16.** The Holy Spirit bears witness together **with our human spirit** that we are children of God. This really means that the Spirit bears witness with our very self (see I Cor 16:18; Gal 6:18; Phil 4:23). This witness is directed to every aspect of our personality that goes into the making of our self. The Spirit's testimony is to the person. **17.** It is noted that the believer is an **heir of God** and a **fellow heir of Christ.** We are heirs of all that God has to bestow, which means that we are fellow heirs with Christ, to whom the Father has given all things. But to be a joint heir with Christ means to be a fellow sufferer with Christ. The tense is present: **since indeed we are suffering together.** Suffering was the role that God had appointed for Christ (Lk 24:26,46; Acts 17:3; 26:23; Heb 2:9,10). It is also the God-ordained experience for believers in Christ (Mt 10:38; 16:24; 20:22; I Thess 3:3; II Thess 1:4,5; II Cor 1:5; Col 1:24; II Tim 3:12; I Pet 1:6; 4:12). Those who are fellow sharers with Christ in suffering will also be fellow heirs with him in glory (Rom 8:17). The experience of suffering precedes the experience of glory.

d) Completion of Redemption Awaited by Creation and Believers Alike. 8:18-25. How should one view the sufferings of the present? They are to be viewed in the light of **the glory that is about to be revealed in us** (v. 18). The sufferings are not to be compared with the coming glory, for they are not at all equal in intensity or value. **19.** Not only

19. For the earnest expectation of the creature waiteth for the manifestation of the sons of God.

20. For the creature was made subject to vanity, not willingly, but by reason of him who hath subjected *the same* in hope;

21. Because the creature itself also shall be delivered from the bondage of corruption into the glorious liberty of the children of God.

22. For we know that the whole creation groaneth and travaileth in pain together until now.

23. And not only *they*, but ourselves also, which have the firstfruits of the Spirit, even we ourselves groan within ourselves, waiting for the adoption, *to wit*, the redemption of our body.

24. For we are saved by hope: but hope that is seen is not hope: for what a man seeth, why doth he yet hope for?

is glory to be revealed to believers, but believers themselves are to be revealed. Paul says that this event is the eager expectation of the creation. The word **creation** (AV, *creature*, except in v. 22) found in 8:19-22 refers to all of God's creation below the human level, here personified to make clear the tensions and dislocation found in creation because of sin. Sin brought distortion not only into man's relation with God but into the universe in which he lives. **20. Creation was made subject to frustration against its own will.** Tornadoes, hurricanes, earthquakes, drought, floods are just a few evidences of the imbalance of nature. Paul says that nature was reduced to this state by God. Although the Lord brought this about, he did it **in hope,** i.e., with a definite hope for a future day when the frustration will be removed. **21. Because the creation itself also will be set free from the slavery to deterioration.** God has promised that the very creation which has been enslaved to deterioration and corruption will be set free from this condition. Its new condition is described as **the glorious freedom which belongs to the children of God. 22.** How different this is from the present situation—both for creation and for God's children. Creation groans and suffers agony together with the men who dwell upon the earth. **23.** Not only creation, but also believers who **have the first fruits of the Spirit** groan within themselves. **First fruits** here may mean the blessings and changes that the Spirit has already produced in the lives of believers. Or it can mean that the Spirit himself is looked upon as the first fruit (cf. II Cor 1:22; Eph 1:14). In the light of the context, the former interpretation seems best. The **groaning** of a believer has nothing to do with complaining. Rather, it is his sighing to himself because he lives in a sinful world. **The adoption** for which the believer awaits refers to **the redemption of our body,** its release from sin and finiteness, the pressure of which we constantly feel as long as we have our mortal body.

**24. Now we are saved for the hope.** The hope for which God saved us is deliverance from a body put under pressure by sin, and from a state of mortal finiteness in which we await the day when, clothed with immortality, we shall see God. What is hope? Paul says it is a confident expectation of promised blessings not now present or seen. This hope is not a wish for something too

25. But if we hope for that we see not, *then* do we with patience wait for *it.*

26. Likewise the Spirit also helpeth our infirmities: for we know not what we should pray for as we ought: but the Spirit itself maketh intercession for us with groanings which cannot be uttered.

27. And he that searcheth the hearts knoweth what *is* the mind of the Spirit, because he maketh intercession for the saints according to *the will of* God.

28. And we know that all things work together for good to them that love God, to them who are the called according to *his* purpose.

29. For whom he did foreknow, he also did predestinate *to be* conformed to the image of his Son, that he might be the firstborn among many brethren.

good to be true and unlikely to occur. The object or blessing hoped for (here, the redemption of the body) is real and distinct but not yet present. **25. But since we are hoping for what is not seen,** with *(dia;* see Arndt, III, 1, c, p. 179) **patience** (or *fortitude*) **we are eagerly awaiting it.** The redeemed body will be a glorified body, free from all sin. With such a hope before him, the believer awaits its realization with fortitude.

e) Intercessory Ministry of the Spirit. 8:26,27. **26. Likewise,** the Spirit helps our weakness. The weakness referred to is our inability to analyze situations and pray intelligently about them. We know this is the weakness referred to because of the next phrase. The Spirit is said **to plead** or *intercede* with sighs **too deep for words** (see *alalētos,* Arndt, p. 34). Sometimes we cannot pray because words cannot express the needs we feel. The Spirit's response of **sighs too deep for words** shows how God through his Spirit enters into our experiences. **27.** God the Father who investigates the hearts [of men] **knows what is the mind-set of the Spirit.** God knows the total response of the Spirit to any situation or issue. The intercession he makes on behalf of the saints is **in conformity with the being of God.** These words certainly declare that communication of thought and knowledge of each other is shared by two members of the Godhead—Father and Spirit (i.e., the Holy Spirit).

f) Purpose of God for Those Loving Him. 8:28-30. **28.** Paul begins with a basic axiom: **We know.** Then he states this truth: **To those loving God, he** (i.e., God) **works all things together for good.** Paul puts the phrase "to those loving God" first so that there will be no mistake about who are involved in "God works all things together for good." It is for those who continually express love for God both in attitude and action. These are further defined as **those who are called ones in accordance with** (God's) **plan** or *purpose.* The call and election are put side by side in II Thess 2:13,14; II Pet 1:10. The call may be focused upon the eternal destiny (II Thess 2:14) or on the earthly life of freedom and holiness (Gal 5:13; I Thess 4:7).

**29. Because whom he knew beforehand** or *foreknew.* The pronoun **whom** is plural, not singular. Paul is thinking of a group here—composed of individuals to be sure—but nevertheless a group of

**30.** Moreover, whom he did predestinate, them he also called: and whom he called, them he also justified: and whom he justified, them he also glorified.

**31.** What shall we then say to these things? If God *be* for us, who *can be* against us?

**32.** He that spared not his own Son, but delivered him up for us all, how shall he not with him also freely give us all things?

individuals who constitute a corporate whole. This is identical with the apostle's procedure in Eph 1:4, where he says: Just as he chose **us** (plural) in him (i.e., in Christ). Christ is the Elect or Chosen **one** (see Lk 9:35 [ASV; RSV]; 23:35; I Pet 2:4,6); and believers—those who belong to God—are elect or chosen **ones** in him (i.e., in Christ). The verb **foreknow** has as its basic ingredient knowledge. This group of individuals, the members of this corporate whole, are foreknown in what sense? They are foreknown as having a distinct place in God's plan or purpose (Rom 8:28). They have a role to play in God's plan. What is their destiny? **Whom** (pl.) **he knew beforehand, he decided upon beforehand to be conformed to the image of his son** (v. 29). God's decision here is that those composing this group shall be like his Son in form and appearance. The number is not small. God decided this beforehand in order that his Son might be the first-born **among many brothers.** The term **firstborn** means the one highest in rank or position. That Christ is supreme or first Paul makes very clear in Col 1:18: "And he is the head of the body, the church, [he] who is (the) beginning, (the) first-born from the dead; that he might come to have the first place in everything." The headship is over and in the midst of many brothers —those who receive the abundance of grace and the gift, i.e., righteousness (Rom 5:17). Christ's rank as first-born shows that he stands as the exalted head of the new humanity—as the second Adam (Rom 5:12-21; I Cor 15:22).

The stress in this section (Rom 8:28-30) lies upon the action of God—his plan and the accomplishment of his plan. **30.** The verbs: **he called, he acquitted** (or *justified*) and **he glorified** have to do both with the plan (eternal counsel of God) and the carrying out of this purpose. Because God has a plan, or purpose—to sum up all things, to bring all things together in Christ, things in the heaven and things upon earth (Eph 1:10, 11), he is able to work all things together for good to those loving him. Paul's emphasis here is on what God does for the many brothers. The only human response mentioned is that of love for God.

g) Triumph of Believers over All Opposition. 8:31-39. **31,32.** Paul now begins to point out the implications of his teaching. God became involved in man's dilemma in order to accomplish his plan. He

33. Who shall lay any thing to the charge of God's elect? *It is* God that justifieth.

34. Who *is* he that condemneth? *It is* Christ that died, yea rather, that is risen again, who is even at the right hand of God, who also maketh intercession for us.

35. Who shall separate us from the love of Christ? *shall* tribulation, or distress, or persecution, or famine, or nakedness, or peril, or sword?

36. As it is written, For thy sake we are killed all the day long; we are accounted as sheep for the slaughter.

37. Nay, in all these things we are more than conquerors through him that loved us.

38. For I am persuaded, that neither death, nor life, nor angels, nor principalities, nor powers, nor things present, nor things to come,

39. Nor height, nor depth, nor any other creature, shall be able to separate us from the love of God, which is in Christ Jesus our Lord.

## CHAPTER 9

I SAY the truth in Christ, I lie not, my conscience also bearing me witness in the Holy Ghost,

2. That I have great heaviness and continual sorrow in my heart.

handed over his Son on behalf of us all. Christ was handed over for our benefit, on our behalf, and in our stead. God could not spare his Son and carry out his plan of redemption. So he handed him over to death that we might be redeemed. Paul draws certain conclusions from this action by God. With Christ he will graciously give us all things, though we may not have all of them right now. **33,34.** No one can bring any charge against God's chosen or elect ones or condemn them, because God and Christ have participated in this divine action of handing over Christ.

**35,36.** Formidable obstacles cannot separate us from the love Christ extends to us. These difficulties are: **affliction, distress, persecution, famine, lack of clothing, danger, or sword** (i.e., violent death). The apostle quotes Ps 44:22 to show what difficulties the people of God have. **37.** His conclusion is that in all these difficulties **we are winning a most glorious victory through the one who loved us.** The meaning here is: "We are in the process of winning." In the external pressures of life we can be gaining the victory through the one who loved us. We are winning not through our own strength or brilliance but through Christ. **38,39.** Paul broadens out the experiences, the personalities, and the things that confront the believer: **death** or **life, angels** or **angelic rulers, space above the horizon** or **space below it,** or **any created thing.** Then he emphatically declares that none of these things shall be able to separate us from the love God manifests, this love that is in Christ Jesus our Lord. The power of God's love is a theme that can never be exhausted.

### III. Israel and the Gentiles in the Plan of God. 9:1–11:36.

Paul looks at the plan of God as it relates to the two divisions of mankind that he, as a Jew, saw — Israel or the Jewish people and the Gentiles.

### A. Concern of Paul for His Own People, Israel. 9:1-5.

**1,2.** This chapter begins with an array of proof that Paul had **great grief** and **unceasing pain** in his heart with reference to his own people. Here is the proof: he speaks truth in Christ; he is not lying; his conscience testifies for him in the presence of the Holy Spirit. The apostle told this because he knew how the Jews maligned him (see, e.g., Acts 21:28 — an event that occurred after he wrote

3. For I could wish that myself were accursed from Christ for my brethren, my kinsmen according to the flesh:

4. Who are Israelites; to whom *pertaineth* the adoption, and the glory, and the covenants, and the giving of the law, and the service *of God*, and the promises;

5. Whose *are* the fathers, and of whom as concerning the flesh Christ *came*, who is over all, God blessed for ever. Amen.

Romans but indicative of how the Jews felt.) 3. So deeply did Paul feel about his people that he here employs the language of an unattainable wish (potential imperfect in Greek): I could wish that I myself would be under a curse (and thus separated) from Christ for the sake of my brothers, my fellow countrymen with respect to earthly descent. The language here sounds like that of Moses when he pleaded that God would blot him out of His book (Ex 32:31,32).

Paul now lists the blessings that belonged to his fellow countrymen. 4. They were Israelites to whom belonged the adoption—i.e., a people whom God made his own (cf. Isa 43:20,21). They had the glory. This could be either the honor of being God's people or the glory of God that appeared in the midst of his people (Ex 24:16,17). The word covenants is in the plural because God spoke to his people about his covenant relation with them on a number of occasions. It might also be rendered *decrees* or *assurances*. To them also belonged the legislation, i.e., the Mosaic law, and the service or *worship* of God—the ritual of the Tabernacle and the Temple. They had the promises of God, especially the Messianic promises. 5. The fathers—Abraham, Isaac, and Jacob—also belonged to them. But the most important blessing was that Christ, with respect to his flesh, came from Paul's fellow countrymen, the Israelites. But this one (Christ), who on the human side came from Israel, was much more than a fellow Israelite; he was God over all, blessed forever. (For evidence that this last clause refers to Christ, see Sanday and Headlam, *Epistle to the Romans,* ICC, pp. 232-238). Knowing Christ's exalted place only increased Paul's anguish over the blindness of his people. They had refused such a Messiah. These lines are not a doxology to God, for that does not fit the train of thought. Rather, the lines show how exalted Christ is, which fits the train of thought perfectly.

B. God Free, Righteous, and Sovereign in His Dealing with Israel and with All Men. 9:6-29. From 9:6 to the end of chapter 11 Paul discusses a profound question: *How could God reject his elect people?* He points out to what extent the people have been rejected, why they have been rejected, the existence of a remnant, and what plans God has for the future of his people, Israel. In 9:6-29 the writer is answering an argument of his Jewish

3. For I could wish that myself were accursed from Christ for my brethren, my kinsmen according to the flesh:

4. Who are Israelites; to whom *pertaineth* the adoption, and the glory, and the covenants, and the giving of the law, and the service *of God*, and the promises;

5. Whose *are* the fathers, and of whom as concerning the flesh Christ *came*, who is over all, God blessed for ever. Amen.

opponents that went like this: "We have circumcision as a sign (cf. Gen 17:7-14) that we are God's elect people. Members of God's elect people will not perish. Therefore, we will not perish." Rabbinical evidence shows that this was the attitude of most Jews in Paul's day. Hermann L. Strack and Paul Billerbeck have prepared a *Commentary on the New Testament* in which they bring together parallels from the Talmud and Midrashim that shed light on the NT. In Vol. IV, Part 2, they have devoted an entire excursus (#31) to the subject of Sheol, Gehenna [place of punishment], and the Heavenly Garden of Eden (Paradise). The following quotations include names of tractates of the rabbinical writings from which their ideas about these places are drawn, as well as indicate the location in Strack-Billerbeck.

> Rabbi Levi has said: In the future (on the other side—what the Greeks called the spirit world) Abraham sits at the entrance of Gehenna and he allows no circumcised ones from the Israelites to enter into it (i.e., Gehenna). [Midrash Rabba Genesis, 48 (30ᵃ, 49) SBK, IV, Part ii, p. 1066]

In this same context the question is asked: How about those who sin excessively? The answer is: They are returned to a state of uncircumcision as they enter Gehenna. The next quotation deals with the question of what happens after death to an Israelite.

> When an Israelite goes into his eternal house (=grave), an angel is sitting over the heavenly garden of Eden, who takes each son of Israel who is circumcised for the purpose of bringing him into the heavenly garden of Eden (paradise). [Midrash Tanchum, Sade, waw, 145ᵃ, 35; SBK, IV, Part ii, p. 1066]

Again the question is raised: How about those Israelites who serve idols? As above, the answer is: They will be returned to a state of uncircumcision in Gehenna. Here is a quotation that looks at the Israelites as a group:

> All Israelites who are circumcised come into the heavenly garden of Eden (paradise). [Midrash Tanchuma, Sade, waw, 145ᵃ, 32; SBK, IV, Part ii, p. 1067]

It is clear from these quotations that most Jews believed and taught that all circumcised Israelites who have died are in paradise and that there are no circumcised Israelites in Gehenna.

To the claim that the Lord could not reject his elect people, Paul first of all

6. Not as though the word of God hath taken none effect. For they *are* not all Israel, which are of Israel:

7. Neither, because they are the seed of Abraham, *are they* all children: but, In Isaac shall thy seed be called.

8. That is, They which are the children of the flesh, these *are* not the children of God: but the children of the promise are counted for the seed.

9. For this *is* the word of promise, At this time will I come, and Sarah shall have a son.

10. And not only *this*; but when Rebecca also had conceived by one, *even* by our father Isaac,

11. (For *the children* being not yet born, neither having done any good or evil, that the purpose of God according to election might stand, not of works, but of him that calleth;)

12. It was said unto her, The elder shall serve the younger.

replies by emphasizing God's freedom, righteousness, and sovereignty. God *acts* freely, *acts* in righteousness, and *acts* sovereignly because he *is* free, righteous, and sovereign in his own eternal being.

1) God's Choice of Isaac Rather Than the Other Sons of Abraham. 9:6-9.

6. But it is by no means as if the word of God had come to failure. The present state of the Jews does not indicate that the divine promise has been rescinded. Not all those who are descended from Israel are really Israel. The promises of the Lord at any one period of history may actively involve as many of his people as he decides. 7. In the case of Abraham's children, God made a choice. In (through) Isaac you are to have your descendants (cf. *Kaleō*, Arndt, 1. a, p. 400). 8. Here a distinction is made between the children of the flesh, those born of Hagar and Keturah (Gen 16:1-16; 25:1-4), and Isaac, born according to promise. That is, not the children of the flesh are thereby children of God, but the children of the promise are looked upon as seed. The AV is unsatisfactory in verse 8. Paul puts the negative first to make clear that the children of the flesh do not automatically become children of God. Isaac was born because of promise. God chose through him to bring blessings to all of mankind.

2) God's Choice of Jacob Rather Than Esau. 9:10-13.

Paul's Jewish contemporaries might have replied: "We are children of Isaac; hence, we can be certain that God will not reject us." 10,11. But Paul shows that God made a choice between Isaac's two sons, even before the sons were born or had done anything good or bad. Such a choice occurred in order that the purpose or plan of God which operates by selection might continue not from works but from the one who calls. God's selection was not based upon legalistic works but upon himself and his plan for the world. 12,13. What did this selection involve? The older will be in subjection to the younger. Since this selection occurred before the twins were born (Gen 25:23), Paul was certainly thinking of two individuals here. In the quotation from Mal 1:2,3, which looks back to God's dealings with Jacob and Esau, the emphasis falls upon nations. What began in the lifetime of the founders of these peoples continued among their children. The selection had to do with the roles these

13. As it is written, Jacob have I loved, but Esau have I hated.

14. What shall we say then? *Is there* unrighteousness with God? God forbid.

15. For he saith to Moses, I will have mercy on whom I will have mercy, and I will have compassion on whom I will have compassion.

16. So then *it is* not of him that willeth, nor of him that runneth, but of God that showeth mercy.

17. For the Scripture saith unto Pharaoh, Even for this same purpose have I raised thee up, that I might show my power in thee, and that my name might be declared throughout all the earth.

two groups were to play in history. The Lord showed his love for Jacob by making the patriarch's descendants the channels through whom He spoke His oracles and made known His truth. God hated Esau in the sense that He did not make Esau's descendants channels of revelation but rather, as Malachi says: God "made his mountains a desolation and gave his heritage to the jackals of the wilderness" (Mal 1:3). In looking back upon Esau's history, Malachi also uses the word "hate" because of God's severity in dealing with Esau. The historical situation of both individuals and peoples certainly affects their eternal destiny. But **election** in Rom 9:10-13 is not selection for eternal salvation or damnation. Rather, it is selection for the roles God has called individuals and nations to play in their earthly life.

3) God's Mercy Toward Israel and Hardening of Pharaoh. 9:14-18.

**14. Therefore, what shall we say? There isn't unrighteousness with God is there? By no means.** The fact that God's selection is not based upon human works does not make the Lord unrighteous. He is free, righteous, and sovereign. **15.** These qualities are seen in his action toward Moses and Pharaoh. His declaration to Moses—**I will have mercy upon whomever I am having mercy and I will have compassion upon whomever I am having compassion** (Ex 33:19)—came *after* Israel's sin of the golden calf. At that point Israel could not possibly have deserved God's mercy. Such idolatry as theirs deserved only wrath. **16.** The "it" supplied by the AV refers to the mercy or compassion. **Mercy and compassion therefore do not belong to the one willing or the one running but to God who constantly has mercy.** That is, no one has a claim on God's mercy. God also pours out his wrath as he sees fit. **17.** The verb "to raise up" is better translated in this verse: **For this very reason I cause you to appear.** God brought Pharaoh upon the scene of history in Egypt for the purpose of showing His power and proving that His name would be proclaimed in all the earth. Pharaoh would still have been his own stubborn self if God had placed him in some obscure settlement up the Nile. But God put him over all Egypt in order to carry out His own purpose and plan. **18.** In looking back over these two cases of Moses and Pharaoh, Paul concludes: **Therefore, then, he shows mercy to whom he wishes and he hardens whom**

**18. Therefore hath he mercy on whom he will *have mercy,* and whom he will he hardeneth.**

he wishes. God was free and sovereign in the hardening of Pharaoh's heart, but He was not arbitrary.

A study of the Exodus narrative shows that Pharaoh hardened his own heart before God hardened it. And even after God hardened it, Pharaoh still had power to harden it further.

The Lord clearly predicted that he would harden Pharaoh's heart: "I will harden *(ḥāzāq,* piel, "make rigid, hard; harden") his heart" (Ex 4:21; cf. 14:4); "I will make hard *(qāshâh,* hiphil, "make hard, stiff, stubborn") the heart of Pharaoh" (Ex 7:3). But not until 9:12 does the record of Exodus say that God actually hardened the king's heart: "And Jehovah **hardened** *(ḥāzāq,* piel, "make rigid, hard; harden") the heart of Pharaoh."

The Scriptures have much to say about the fact that Pharaoh's heart was "growing hard," and about Pharaoh's "making his heart heavy, dull, unresponsive," even before they state that God hardened Pharaoh's heart. The phrase, "Pharaoh's heart grew hard," means that Pharaoh's moral character (see BDB, p. 525) grew hard. Moral character is a most important aspect of one's person. Hence, in a real sense Pharaoh grew hard as the result of his own activity. "And the heart of Pharaoh **grew hard**" *(ḥāzāq* qal, "grow stout, rigid, hard"; see Ex 7:13,22; 8:19 [Heb. text 8:15]). "The heart of Pharaoh is **hard**" *(kâbēd,* adj., "heavy," "dull," "hard"; see Ex 7:14). "The heart of Pharaoh **became hard**" *(kâbēd,* qal, "be heavy, insensible, dull, hard"; see Ex 9:7). "Pharaoh **made heavy** (or *dull, unresponsive;* all possible translations of *kâbēd,* hiphil) his heart" (see Ex 8:15 [Heb. text 8:11]; 8:32 [Heb. text 8:28]). After all this activity on the part of Pharaoh, "Jehovah **hardened** *(ḥāzāq,* piel, "make rigid, hard; harden") the heart of Pharaoh" (see Ex 9:12). But Pharaoh had the power to continue what he had been doing: ". . . he [Pharaoh] sinned more, and he **made heavy** (or *dull, unresponsive;* all possible translations of *kâbēd,* hiphil) his heart, he and his servants. And the heart of Pharaoh **grew hard**" *(ḥâzaq,* qal, "grow stout, rigid, hard"; see Ex 9:34 b,35 a).

Then Jehovah completed his judicial punishment of Pharaoh. "And Jehovah hardened *(ḥāzāq,* piel, "make rigid, hard"; "harden") the heart of Pharaoh," (see Ex 10:20,27; 11:10; 14:8). "And Jehovah said unto Moses: 'Go unto Pha-

19. Thou wilt say then unto me, Why doth he yet find fault? For who hath resisted his will?

20. Nay but, O man, who art thou that repliest against God? Shall the thing formed say to him that formed *it*, Why hast thou made me thus?

21. Hath not the potter power over the clay, of the same lump to make one vessel unto honor, and another unto dishonor?

raoh because **I am making heavy** *(dull, unresponsive;* all possible translations of *kâbēd,* hiphil) his heart and the heart of his servants' " (see Ex 10:1).

So the conclusion that God hardens whom he wishes is based upon his righteousness as well as upon his freedom in dealing with Pharaoh.

4) God's Control Over Vessels of Wrath and Mercy. 9:19-24.

Paul has been directing his argument to the Jews, who thought that, because they had circumcision and were. members of God's elect people, the Lord was duty-bound to grant them earthly prosperity and eternal bliss. The apostle has stressed the divine sovereignty and freedom as a corrective to this erroneous Jewish view. The Lord is duty-bound only to his own righteous being — not to claims put upon him by those who misunderstand his being and action.

19. At this point, Paul imagines that one of his opponents is saying: "Look what your argument leads to. The Lord hardens a man like Pharaoh and then finds fault with him. That doesn't make sense." The question is: **Why does he still find fault? Who can resist his will?** Paul's answer is phrased in terms suited to the man who makes the objection rather than in terms of an intellectual analysis of the man's counterargument. Paul writes (v. 20 a): **O man, on the contrary, who are you who answers back to God in this way?** A real knowledge of the true God makes such an objection preposterous. Paul turns to an illustration (vv. 20b,21): **What is moulded will not say to the moulder, why have you made me in this fashion, will it? Or, the potter has the right over the clay, doesn't he, to make from the same lump one vessel for honor and another for dishonor?** This illustration of the potter had been used very effectively by Jeremiah centuries before (Jer 18:4-6). Paul stresses the complete control of the potter over the clay in terms of that for which the vessel is to be used. A vessel is honored or dishonored by the use to which it is put (cf. Arndt, *timē,* 2, b, p. 825). One pot may be intended for carrying water and another for carrying away refuse. The same material is used for both. But they are to be made for different functions, and so the potter gives each one a shape that accords with its intended function.

Paul now applies this principle. He does this in one long sentence that extends from Rom 9:22 to 9:24. If a pot-

**22.** *What* if God, willing to show *his* wrath, and to make his power known, endured with much long-suffering the vessels of wrath fitted to destruction:

**23.** And that he might make known the riches of his glory on the vessels of mercy, which he had afore prepared unto glory,

ter may do what he wants with his vessels, certainly God may do what He wants with His vessels. Although Paul is still stressing God's sovereignty and freedom, he carefully avoids picturing the Lord as having the same relationship to the vessels of wrath as he does to the vessels of mercy. **Now if God, although he wished to show his anger and make known his power, bore patiently** (*endured*) **with much forbearance the vessels of wrath made ready** (*prepared*) **for destruction and** [if he did this] **in order that he might make known** (*reveal*) **the riches of his glory to vessels of mercy, which he prepared beforehand for glory, us whom also he called not only from the Jews but also from the Gentiles** [how can you (sing.; cf. v. 19) bring any objection against God's justice?] In the concessive clause beginning with "although," Paul certainly has in mind Pharaoh and others like him. The words **to show his anger and make known his power** are merely a variation of the language he used in verse 17: "in order that I might show in you my power." Paul was very eager to emphasize God's patience and forbearance with the vessels of wrath. **22.** These are described as **made ready** (*prepared*; see *katartizō*, LSJ, II, pass., p. 910) **for destruction.** Some Bible students, taking the participle to be in the middle voice, have translated: *those who have been in a state of preparing themselves for destruction.* Others have regarded the participle as passive and have said: *those who have been in a state of being prepared by God for destruction.* But the context certainly favors the passive without confining the agent to one being or thing. **23.** God is specifically connected with the preparing beforehand (active voice) of the vessels of mercy. But when it comes to the vessels of wrath, the student finds this indefinite passive. What operates on man to put him in a state of being **made ready** (*prepared*) for eternal destruction? The answer is complex. It includes his own sinful acts and rebellious nature. It involves his environment, which makes sin enticing, as well as the judicial judgments of God (cf. 1:24,26,28). These factors influence certain vessels to become vessels of wrath, i.e., objects that are in a state of being prepared for destruction. God specifically prepared beforehand vessels of mercy for glory, and he also revealed to them the riches of his glory. **Glory** refers to the radiance of the being of God. The outpouring of God's bounty

24. Even us, whom he hath called, not of the Jews only, but also of the Gentiles?

25. As he saith also in Osee, I will call them my people, which were not my people; and her beloved, which was not beloved.

26. And it shall come to pass, *that* in the place where it was said unto them, Ye *are* not my people; there shall they be called the children of the living God.

27. Esaias also crieth concerning Israel, Though the number of the children of Israel be as the sand of the sea, a remnant shall be saved:

28. For he will finish the work, and cut *it* short in righteousness: because a short work will the Lord make upon the earth.

means riches untold to the recipients. Who are these vessels of mercy? In 9:24 Paul defines the **us** as those whom God has called not only from the Jews but also from the Gentiles. The Lord's freedom, power, and sovereignty on the one hand are placed over against his forbearance, his revelation of the riches of his glory, and his preparation beforehand of the vessels of mercy (vv. 22-24). The destiny of those thus prepared is glory (cf. 8:30).

5) God's Testimony in Hosea and Isaiah to an Extension and Limitation of His Saving Work. 9:25-29.

The **us** in verse 24 refers to those whom God has called, not only from the Jews but also from the Gentiles. The writer now turns to the OT to show that it supports such a call.

**25,26.** Paul quotes Hos 2:23; 1:10, passages originally addressed to the ten tribes. The words **not my people** and **not beloved** were spoken to the ten tribes because of their departure from the Lord. They had become like the Gentiles. God promised the ten tribes that one day they would be called sons of the living God in the very place where they had been called "not my people." The apostle takes this quotation from the LXX and applies it to the Gentiles.

**27,28.** The writer turns to the testimony of Isaiah about Israel and quotes from Isa 10:22,23. He uses the LXX, which in Isa 10:23 is quite different from the Hebrew text. But on the main point for which Paul is quoting this passage, the Hebrew and LXX agree. Only a remnant **will be saved** (LXX), will *turn back*, (Heb text), *shall return* (AV), i.e., turn back to God. Paul develops this theme further in Romans 11. Difficulty has been found in interpreting Rom 9:28 because of the language and textual variation. The words "in righteousness: because a short work" of the AV are not found in the best texts. Here are two possible ways of translating and interpreting this verse (see Arndt, *suntemnō*, p. 800). (1) **The Lord will act by accomplishing his word and by shortening or cutting off.** The shortening can be construed as fulfilling the promises to a limited degree or as shortening the nation into a remnant. (2) **The Lord will act by closing the account and shortening** [the time]. This means that God will not prolong indefinitely the period of his long-suffering, but that his judgment will come. In Paul's context here, the second interpretation seems the

29. And as Esaias said before, Except the Lord of Sabaoth had left us a seed, we had been as Sodoma, and been made like unto Gomorrah.

30. What shall we say then? That the Gentiles, which followed not after righteousness, have attained to righteousness, even the righteousness which is of faith.

31. But Israel, which followed after the law of righteousness, hath not attained to the law of righteousness.

32. Wherefore? Because *they sought it* not by faith, but as it were by the works of the law. For they stumbled at that stumblingstone;

33. As it is written, Behold, I lay in Sion a stumblingstone and rock of offense: and whosoever believeth on him shall not be ashamed.

better.

29. Finally, in completing the OT picture of God's saving action, Paul quotes Isa 1:9 from the LXX. Where the LXX has "left us seed," the Hebrew text has "a very small remnant." If God had not left some, the nation Israel would have been blotted out.

C. Failure of Israel and Success of the Gentiles. 9:30—10:21.

Paul now takes up the relation of Israel and the Gentiles to righteousness, faith, and salvation. He shows that this is a crucial matter because the Jews believed that since they were marked by circumcision as God's elect people, the Lord could not reject them.

1) Attainment by Gentiles of What Israel Missed. 9:30-33.

30,31. Since God has called us, Christians (v. 24), from both Jews and Gentiles, what shall we say then about the attainment of righteousness by the Gentiles and Israel? The answer: We say or declare that the Gentiles, who were not striving for righteousness attained righteousness, that is the righteousness which is because of faith. But Israel, although pursuing law that would produce righteousness, did not attain to law producing righteousness. Paul is very concise here. Nevertheless, notice that in verse 30 the word **righteousness** occurs three times. Believing Gentiles had found the key to man's relationship with God—righteousness. They had found the righteousness that God bestows because of faith or trust (cf. 3:21-26). Israel had pursued the principle of law (the Mosaic code was Israel's most treasured embodiment of this principle) in order to obtain righteousness, but they never attained to that righteousness.

32. Why did Israel not attain to righteousness? Tragically the reply comes: **because not from faith but as by works** [they sought after righteousness]. Faith or trust is important because of the object (Christ) believed and trusted. Israel rejected the object. **They rejected** (or *stumbled at) the stone which causes men to stumble.* In the warning note of Isa 8:14, Jehovah is the stone of stumbling to the majority of those in both houses of Israel. In the NT it is Christ who is the stone of stumbling (here and in I Pet 2: 6-8). 33. Most of Paul's quotation in this verse is from the promise of Isa 28:16. But the apostle takes the language of warning from Isa 8:14—a **stumbling-**

## CHAPTER 10

BRETHREN, my heart's desire and prayer to God for Israel is, that they might be saved.

2. For I bear them record that they have a zeal of God, but not according to knowledge.

3. For they, being ignorant of God's righteousness, and going about to establish their own righteousness, have not submitted themselves unto the righteousness of God.

4. For Christ *is* the end of the law for righteousness to every one that believeth.

stone and rock of offence – and inserts this warning in the middle of the positive teaching about the stone in Isa 28:16, and then completes the verse. The last clause of Rom 9:33—And the one trusting in him will not be disappointed—introduces a ray of light into an otherwise dark picture. Such a positive response, however, was not that of Israel as a whole, for Israel stumbled at the stone that God placed in Zion.

2) Israel's Ignorance of God's Righteousness. 10:1-3.

1. The apostle again expresses his concern for his people. In place of for Israel the best texts have *on behalf of* them. Paul prayed on behalf of them for salvation—i.e., that they would appropriate this salvation for themselves. 2. Their zeal for God was not backed up with knowledge—in accordance with *(real)* knowledge (see Arndt, *epignōsis*, p. 291). 3. In the minds of Jewish readers a new question would naturally arise: Why were so many of Israel rejected in spite of their having the covenant of circumcision as a sign that they were members of God's elect people? Paul answers: Now being ignorant of the righteousness which God bestows and seeking to establish their own, they did not subject themselves to the righteousness of God. There are two contrasts in this verse. First, the Israelites sought to establish their own righteousness. Note their self-confidence in this. Secondly, they would not subject themselves to what God had provided—their wills were unyielded. Having stumbled at the stone of stumbling (Christ), they knew nothing of God's gift of righteousness.

3) Connection Between the Righteousness of Faith and the Object of Faith. 10:4-15.

In verse 4 two things are stressed: (1) what Christ is; (2) who is benefited by what Christ is. To every one in the process of trusting, Christ is the goal and termination of the law with respect to righteousness. The word end (AV)—*telos* —seems to combine the ideas of both goal and termination (see Arndt, *telos*, 1, a.b. c., p. 819). We cannot say, merely, that Christ is the goal and termination of the Law. Rather, he is the goal and termination of the Law with respect to righteousness. Before Christ came, believers in God were in a tension. That is, they were promised life on condition that they live

5. For Moses describeth the righteousness which is of the law, That the man which doeth those things shall live by them.

6. But the righteousness which is of faith speaketh on this wise, Say not in thine heart, Who shall ascend into heaven? (that is, to bring Christ down *from above:*)

7. Or, Who shall descend into the deep? (that is, to bring up Christ again from the dead.)

8. But what saith it? The word is nigh thee, *even* in thy mouth, and in thy heart: that is, the word of faith, which we preach;

9. That if thou shalt confess with thy mouth the Lord Jesus, and shalt believe in thine heart that God hath raised him from the dead, thou shalt be saved.

in a way that was unattainable by them. 5. Although Paul, in quoting Moses, changes Lev 18:5 somewhat from both the Hebrew and Greek texts, he gives substantially the sense of the verse. The man who practices [the righteousness that the Law demanded] will live by it (feminine pronoun, referring to righteousness). In the Greek text of Lev 18:5, the Jewish believer is commanded to guard all the ordinances and judgments. Though the one who trusted God did his best to fulfill the righteous demands of the Law, he was also aware of his failures. This inconsistency caused tension. Hence he faithfully presented his sin and trespass offerings. For this reason, the Jewish believer could not take Lev 18:5 as a legalistic guarantee of eternal life, but only as a promise of God involving a man's fellowship with Him. He could not take it as a legalistic prescription. To take this verse as such would have made the tension intolerable. Christ broke this tension. By his life and death he revealed the perfect righteousness of God, bestowed by the Father on the basis of faith in the Son. This was the goal to which the Law pointed. It terminated the tension brought about by the promise of life to man for doing what man could not do. Since man could not live as God demanded, salvation under the Old Covenant as well as under the New had to be by faith.

In Rom 10:6-8 Paul quotes Deut 30: 12-14, interspersing his own comments and phrases as he quotes. In the OT passage, the "it," in the questions concerning ascending or descending to bring "it" to men, refers to the commandment "to love the Lord thy God." It was this commandment of God that was in the heart and mouth of the Israelite. 6,7. But Paul takes the language of Deuteronomy and applies it to the righteousness that comes from faith. He refers the ascending and descending to Christ. 8. The word that is in the mouth and in the heart is the declaration about the faith. Paul is not saying that Moses in Deuteronomy predicted that righteousness was to come by faith. Rather he says, "Righteousness by faith must speak in this way" (10:6). The compatibility of the two covenants is shown by the fact that this righteousness finds the language of the OT so suitable.

9. Confession with the mouth and belief in the heart refer to the believer's outward and inward responses. His inward conviction must find outward expression. When he confesses that Jesus is Lord, he

10. For with the heart man believeth unto righteousness; and with the mouth confession is made unto salvation.

11. For the Scripture saith, Whosoever believeth on him shall not be ashamed.

12. For there is no difference between the Jew and the Greek: for the same Lord over all is rich unto all that call upon him.

13. For whosoever shall call upon the name of the Lord shall be saved.

14. How then shall they call on him in whom they have not believed? and how shall they believe in him of whom they have not heard? and how shall they hear without a preacher?

15. And how shall they preach, except they be sent? as it is written, How beautiful are the feet of them that preach the gospel of peace, and bring glad tidings of good things!

16. But they have not all obeyed the gospel. For Esaias saith, Lord, who hath believed our report?

is asserting Christ's deity and His exaltation, and the fact that he, the believer, belongs to Him. A man's belief in the Resurrection shows that he knows God acted and triumphed in the cross. The man who confesses that Christ is Lord and has such a belief or conviction will attain salvation. 10. This trust or belief is a constant activity and refers to righteousness; the confession is also a constant activity and refers to salvation. These confessed and believed truths are constant, lifelong convictions.

12. Since such confession and belief are the essentials for salvation, Paul's next statement is pertinent and almost self-evident. In the matter of obtaining salvation, there is no distinction (or *difference*) between Jew and Greek. Christ who is the same Lord of all is in the process of being rich (and *generous*) to all who are calling upon him. The NT writers made the name Lord (*kyrios*) one of their favorite titles of Jesus (see Arndt, *kyrios*, 2. c., pp. 460,61; Foerster, *TWNT*, III, 1087-94). Paul takes the OT quotation that speaks of Jehovah as Lord and applies the term to Jesus (cf. vv. 13 and 12). To call upon the name of the Lord means to call upon Jesus. Thus prayer to Jesus is explicitly referred to by this language.

14,15. The connection between the righteousness of faith and the object of faith is simple. Belief in the object of faith (Christ) brings the righteousness of faith to the believer. When men trust Christ, they call upon him. This leads Paul to questions about calling upon the name of the Lord There can be no *calling* without *belief* or *trust*. There can be no *belief* or *trust*, without *hearing*. There can be no *hearing* without *preaching*. There can be no *preaching* unless preachers have a *commission*. Note that reaching men for God begins with the commission of the messengers. Then through preaching, hearing, and trusting, men are brought to call upon the name of the Lord. The beauty of the feet of the messengers refers to their eagerness to carry the good tidings. The quotation from Isa 52:7 refers to the report of messengers that Jehovah had redeemed Jerusalem. Paul applies these words to the good tidings about Christ—the Gospel.

4) Good Tidings Rejected. 10:16-21.

16. Although good tidings are proclaimed, this does not mean that the hearers obey the good tidings. Paul quotes

17. So then faith *cometh* by hearing, and hearing by the word of God.

18. But I say, Have they not heard? Yes verily, their sound went into all the earth, and their words unto the ends of the world.

19. But I say, Did not Israel know? First Moses saith, I will provoke you to jealousy by *them that are* no people, *and* by a foolish nation I will anger you.

20. But Esaias is very bold, and saith, I was found of them that sought me not; I was made manifest unto them that asked not after me.

21. But to Israel he saith, All day long I have stretched forth my hands unto a disobedient and gainsaying people.

### CHAPTER 11

I SAY then, Hath God cast away his people? God forbid. For I also am an Israelite, of the seed of Abraham, *of* the tribe of Benjamin.

2. God hath not cast away his people which he foreknew. Wot ye not what the Scripture saith of Elias? how he maketh intercession to God against Israel, saying,

Isaiah as asking: "Lord, who has believed our preaching?" (cf. Isa 53:1) **17.** The apostle draws the conclusion that **faith** comes from **preaching** (the things heard). And **preaching** comes to be **through the message** *(command, order, direction)* **of Christ.** The AV has **God,** but the better manuscripts have **Christ. 18.** Since Israel has had both the messengers who proclaim good tidings and the good tidings themselves, why haven't the Jews obeyed? The apostle deals with two excuses that might be put forth. **It was not that they did not listen, was it?** No, they listened all right. He quotes Ps 19:4, which originally dealt with the universal proclamation of God's glory and power by the works of nature. He applies the words of this psalm to the Gospel—**their voice went forth into all the earth, and their words unto the extreme limits of the inhabited earth.** The second excuse deals with a failure of knowledge. **19. It was not that Israel did not know, was it?** No, they knew all right. Moses was the first to say that God would use an unintelligent nation or people to make the Jews jealous and angry (cf. Deut 32:21). The Jews had not only listened to the message about Christ but knew that God would deal with other peoples besides themselves. **20.** Paul quotes the prophet Isaiah as affirming this (Isa 65:1,2). Actually, the two verses quoted from Isaiah refer to disobedient Israel. But in Rom 10:20 the writer applies Isa 65:1 to the Gentiles. In Rom 10:21 he applies Isa 65:2 to Israel. Applying the language of Isa 65:1 to the Gentiles is similar to applying Hos 2:23 and 1:10 (cf. Rom 9:25, 26) to them. The apostle represents God as saying to the Gentiles: **I have let myself be found by those not seeking me; I revealed myself to those not inquiring after me. 21.** In contrast, the Lord implores Israel—He stretched forth his hands **to a disobedient and obstinate people.**

D. Situation of Israel in Paul's Day. 11:1-10.

**1.** Although Paul has just described the disobedience and obstinacy of his people, he now declares: **God has not repudiated his people, has he? By no means.** Because Paul himself was an Israelite, the idea that God should reject His people was abhorrent to him. By **his people** Paul means national Israel. **2a. God did not repudiate his people**

3. Lord, they have killed thy prophets, and digged down thine altars; and I am left alone, and they seek my life.

4. But what saith the answer of God unto him? I have reserved to myself seven thousand men, who have not bowed the knee to *the image of* Baal.

5. Even so then at this present time also there is a remnant according to the election of grace.

6. And if by grace, then *is it* no more of works: otherwise grace is no more grace. But if *it be* of works, then is it no more grace: otherwise work is no more work.

7. What then? Israel hath not obtained that which he seeketh for; but the election hath obtained it, and the rest were blinded

8. (According as it is written, God hath given them the spirit of slumber, eyes that they should not see, and ears that they should not hear;) unto this day.

9. And David saith, Let their table be made a snare, and a trap, and a stumbling-block, and a recompense unto them:

10. Let their eyes be darkened, that they may not see, and bow down their back alway.

whom he foreknew. The phrase **his people** emphasizes God's previous choice or selection. The verb **foreknew** indicates that the Lord knew beforehand that Israel would be disobedient and obstinate (cf. 10:21). God foreknows the sins of his people, but he does not directly decree them (see Jas 1:13).

**2b-5.** By showing that there is a remnant of Israelites who are faithful, Paul proves that God did not repudiate His people. The apostle reminds his readers that there was a godly remnant in Elijah's time, and declares that there is a similar remnant in his own time (Rom 11:5). **Therefore in this same fashion also in the present time a remnant exists** (see Arndt, *ginomai*, II, 5, p. 159) **according to selection by grace** (see Arndt, *eklogē*, 1, p. 242). Grace produces or brings into being this election or selection. **6.** This truth is restated. Selection is by God's grace or favor — not by men's works. Works suggest legalism and nullify grace.

**7.** What then are we to conclude? We are to conclude that in Israel there is now a faithful remnant and there is a faithless majority. **What Israel kept striving for, this she did not attain to; but those selected attained to it, and the rest were made dull.** An interpreter must ask, What was it that Israel strove for which she did not obtain? Paul has already answered this in 9:32 and 10:3. Israel strove for righteousness. But instead of submitting to the righteousness of God, she sought to establish her own. The selected ones did attain the righteousness that God bestows. **8.** The rest were **made dull.** These were made dull because they failed to submit themselves to the righteousness of God. Here is God acting again in judicial punishment. When a man is confronted with the righteousness of God, but is determined to go his own way, dullness, hardness, and blindness are the outcome. Paul applies the words of the OT to his own generation. His first quotation is from Deut 29:4, with a little of Isa 29:9,10 included. He intensifies this OT passage to emphasize the judicial hardening. God gives a spirit of stupor (cf. Isa 10), eyes for the purpose of not seeing, ears for the purpose of not hearing. **9,10.** Finally, the apostle cites Ps 69:22,23—the LXX translation—in which the psalmist pictures the table of his enemies as desolate, their eyes darkened, and their backs bent under toil. Thus, Paul is saying that although the majority of God's people are presently

11. I say then, Have they stumbled that they should fall? God forbid: but *rather* through their fall salvation *is come* unto the Gentiles, for to provoke them to jealousy.

12. Now if the fall of them *be* the riches of the world, and the diminishing of them the riches of the Gentiles; how much more their fulness?

13. For I speak to you Gentiles, inasmuch as I am the apostle of the Gentiles, I magnify mine office:

14. If by any means I may provoke to emulation *them which are* my flesh, and might save some of them.

15. For if the casting away of them *be* the reconciling of the world, what *shall* the receiving *of them be*, but life from the dead?

under divine judgment, the existence of the select minority is proof that the Almighty has not repudiated his people.

E. Israel's Prospects for the Future. 11:11-36.

Here Paul brings to a conclusion his discussion of the place of Israel and of the Gentiles in the plan of God. The purpose of God's action in history is that he might have mercy upon all — both Jew and Gentile. The role of Israel is most impressive whether in rejection or acceptance. Blended together in a sublime picture are the scope of history, the attitudes and response of Israel and the Gentiles, and the wisdom of God in the inter-relations of these two groups. In the metaphor of the olive tree we see the impressive unity of the people of God of both covenants.

1) Degree of Blessing from Israel's Fall and Fullness. 11:11-15.

11. Paul begins with his usual question. **They did not stumble once for all so as to fall into ruin, did they? By no means.** On the contrary, it was by means of Israel's sin (transgression) that salvation came to the Gentiles for the purpose of provoking Israel to jealousy. 12. What is this sin or transgression? It is the sin of unbelief: **Now if their sin** *(transgression)* **is the riches of the world, and their defeat the riches of the Gentiles, how much more** [will] **their** (the Jews') **fulfilling** (the divine demand) [bring wealth to the world]. Israel's sin (unbelief) and defeat were the means by which God brought blessing to the Gentiles. The apostle argues from the less to the greater; so we can see that the Jews' positive action — the fulfilling of God's demand (see *plērōma*, Arndt, 4, p. 687) — should bring even greater blessing. 13. The writer reminds the Gentiles that this blessing has come to them — **I am speaking to you** (pl.) **the Gentiles.** Paul magnifies the fact that his ministry is to the Gentiles. 14,15. He hopes thereby to provoke to jealousy his brothers in the flesh and bring some of them to salvation. **If their rejection is the reconciling of the world, what will their acceptance (by God) be except life from the dead?** Note that Paul continues the argument from the less to the greater. The rejection of Israel involved the reconciliation of the world. Both Jew and Gentile have been reconciled to each other and to God

16. For if the firstfruit *be* holy, the lump *is* also *holy:* and if the root *be* holy, so *are* the branches.

17. And if some of the branches be broken off, and thou, being a wild olive tree, wert graffed in among them, and with them partakest of the root and fatness of the olive tree;

18. Boast not against the branches. But if thou boast, thou bearest not the root, but the root thee.

19. Thou wilt say then, The branches were broken off, that I might be graffed in.

in Christ. This is a significant accomplishment. But the acceptance of Israel by God will bring about an even more significant accomplishment — **life from the dead.** This undoubtedly refers to the climax of reconciliation in the return of Christ, the resurrection of the dead, the deliverance of creation from slavery to deterioration or decay (8:21), and the glorious reign of Christ.

2) Individual Gentile's Lack of Grounds for Boasting. 11:16-21.

We must remember that Romans is a letter to a particular group of people at Rome. In verse 13 the writer clarifies this: "I am speaking to you (plural), the Gentiles." But in 11:17-24 he has in mind each individual Gentile reader. In these verses there are eight pronouns and thirteen verbs in second person singular form (the AV shows this clearly: *thou, thee* for singular; *you, ye* for plural). Although the majority of the Israelites had been defeated and rejected, no Gentile could dare to become proud or self-sufficient. Hence, Paul makes the Gentiles, individually, aware of where they stand in relation to Israel. Then in verse 25 he returns to the you (plural) and looks at the believing Gentiles and Israel as two groups.

**16.** Two metaphors are found here: **the first fruits of dough** and **the whole lump; the root** and **the branches.** The first fruits of dough and the root refer to Abraham and the other patriarchs, Isaac and Jacob (see Paul's stress on "the fathers" in 9:5 and 11:28). The whole lump and the branches refer to God's people Israel, who have come from the patriarchs. The holiness attributed to the part and the whole, the root and the branches, is that of being dedicated, consecrated, set apart to God. This is a legal holiness for the group by virtue of their being God's chosen people.

**17-24.** Paul develops the second metaphor in verses 17-24. Some of the branches were broken off (v. 17). The individual Gentile as a wild olive branch has been grafted in among the branches of the natural olive tree. Thus this branch, the individual Gentile, **participates in the rich root that belongs to the cultivated olive** (v. 17). But then Paul warns the individual Gentile to stop boasting against the branches. He has no grounds for boasting: **you** (sing.) **are not bearing the root but the root you** (sing; v. 18). The stress here is on the unity that character-

20. Well; because of unbelief they were broken off, and thou standest by faith. Be not high-minded, but fear:

21. For if God spared not the natural branches, *take heed* lest he also spare not thee.

22. Behold therefore the goodness and severity of God: on them which fell, severity; but toward thee, goodness, if thou continue in *his* goodness: otherwise thou also shalt be cut off.

izes the people of God from both covenants. The apostle then deals with the argument that the branches were broken off in order that I (the Gentile) might be grafted in. 20,21. Quite right, because of unbelief they were broken off and you (sing.) have taken your stand (*you stand firm*) because of faith. Stop feeling proud, but rather fear. If God did not spare the natural branches, neither will he spare you (sing.). The difference between the branches broken off and the branch grafted in consists in the presence of faith. Unbelief meant rejection. Faith meant acceptance. Instead of resting proudly in a false sense of security, the individual Gentile is to fear. Genuine fear of God and respect for him constitute the basis of true assurance. God broke off the natural branches because of their unbelief (v. 20). If he did not tolerate unbelief in them, neither will he tolerate it in you.

3) Goodness and Severity of God Disclosed by His Response to Belief and Unbelief. 11:22-24.

22. **Therefore.** The writer is concluding his extended metaphor of the root and the branches. **Behold, therefore, the goodness and severity of God. On the one hand, to those who fell, severity; but to you** (sing.) **the goodness of God, if you** (sing.) **continue in the sphere of** (God's) **goodness; for otherwise,** (if you do not continue in the sphere of God's goodness) **you** (sing.) **also will be cut off.** Paul urges the individual Gentile to continue in the goodness of God. This, of course, involves his continuing in faith (v. 20), but Paul stresses that God provides for those who trust or believe Him. Hence **to continue in God's goodness** expresses this very well. This goodness will be the portion of the Gentile if he **continues,** *persists, perseveres* (see Arndt, *epimenō*, 2., p. 296) in that goodness. Then comes a causal clause that involves contrast, **otherwise** (*epei*, see Arndt, 2., p. 283. With ellipsis **for** [if it were different], **for otherwise,** Rom. 3:6; 11:6, 22 etc.). As in the other contexts in Romans where this word **otherwise** (Gr. *epei*) appears, the reader, to get the meaning, must reverse the preceding thought and then draw the conclusion. Thus it would read, "Otherwise if you (sing.) do not continue in the sphere of God's goodness, you (sing.) **also will be cut off."** These solemn words of the apostle remind us of the words of Jesus: "Every branch in me not bearing fruit, he cuts it out" (Jn

23. And they also, if they abide not still in unbelief, shall be graffed in: for God is able to graff them in again.

24. For if thou wert cut out of the olive tree which is wild by nature, and wert graffed contrary to nature into a good olive tree; how much more shall these, which be the natural *branches*, be graffed into their own olive tree?

25. For I would not, brethren, that ye should be ignorant of this mystery, lest ye should be wise in your own conceits, that blindness in part is happened to Israel, until the fulness of the Gentiles be come in.

26. And so all Israel shall be saved: as it is written, There shall come out of Sion the Deliverer, and shall turn away ungodliness from Jacob:

15:2 a); "If anyone does not abide in me, he is thrown away as the branch" (Jn 15:6 a). To make sure this will be an effective warning, the Greek construction shows that Paul does not state whether or not the individual will continue: **If you** (sing.) **continue in God's goodness,** God's goodness will be your portion.

This same Paul wrote in Rom 8:28-30 that God's purpose for those loving him begins with his foreknowledge and foreordination and ends with their glorification. God has not revealed all the aspects of his purpose and all that is involved in his selection. What he has made known centers in the fact that believers are elect in Christ (Eph 1:4). It is very clear that the Lord has acted "for" and "in" those who are "in Christ." But it is equally clear that those "in Christ" must act: they must continue; they must bear fruit. Their action, the writer shows, is just as essential as God's action in bringing them to himself and putting them in Christ. If a teacher minimizes either of these two aspects — God's action or the believers' response — he has departed from the NT. If one thinks that he fully understands the relation between these two factors, he has forgotten that God has left some things to be revealed in the ages to come (cf. Eph 2:7).

**23,24.** If those from Israel do not continue or persist in unbelief, **they shall be grafted in.** Now Paul stresses God's ability. God is powerful, strong, mighty — able to graft these in again. Since, in the language of the metaphor, the Lord did what was contrary to nature, he can certainly put natural olive branches back into the natural olive tree. **24. Much more** shows Paul's confidence in God's plan.

4) Salvation for the People of Israel. 11:25-27.

**25.** The mystery of which Paul does not want his readers (note the **your**, pl.) to be ignorant is **that insensibility in part has happened to Israel until the full number of the Gentiles enters in** (comes to enjoy the promised blessing). Unless his readers realize this, they may become wise in their own estimation. **In part.** Characteristic Pauline understatement. The "part" is a very large part, but it is balanced off against the **full number** of Gentiles — those who are foreknown and foreordained by God (cf. 8:28-30).

**26. And in this fashion all Israel will be saved. All Israel.** National Israel. Com-

27. For this *is* my covenant unto them, when I shall take away their sins.

28. As concerning the gospel, *they are* enemies for your sakes: but as touching the election, *they are* beloved for the fathers' sakes.

29. For the gifts and calling of God *are* without repentance.

30. For as ye in times past have not believed God, yet have now obtained mercy through their unbelief:

31. Even so have these also now not believed, that through your mercy they also may obtain mercy.

pare the parallel **from Jacob** in the next quotation. **All.** Not necessarily every individual, but enough individuals to make the believers in Christ representative of the nation. The phrase **in this fashion** is correlated with the quotation from Isa 59:20,21 and Isa 27:9. The salvation of Israel is directly connected with the personal action of the deliverer, Jesus the Messiah. The **and** *(kai)*, which begins verse 26 is a co-ordinating conjunction. This suggests that the work of the Deliverer (Christ) in turning away ungodliness from Jacob and bringing all Israel to salvation goes hand in hand with the entering of the full number of the Gentiles into God's blessing and favor. After this glance into the future, Paul returns to his own day.

5) God's Mercy to All Magnified by His Action in History. 11:28-32.

**28.** The vast majority of contemporary Israelites, as far as the good news of Christ was concerned, were hostile toward the Roman Christians. But because the Jews were still God's elect people, the Roman Christians were to regard them as beloved because of their fathers. Observe here a group which, though elect, was far from God. Paul's Gentile readers stood in contrasting relation to the Jews. **On the one hand in respect to the gospel they were enemies because of you.** Having rejected the Gospel, most of the Jewish people became hostile to the Christians. Because God had rejected them but showed mercy to the Gentiles, they treated the Gentiles as enemies. **But on the other hand, as far as their** *(the Jews')* **election** *(by God)* **is concerned, beloved because of the fathers.** This refers to the election of the whole Jewish nation and to the fact that the people were beloved because God had chosen their fathers. Election may involve a whole nation, as here; it may involve a remnant, as in 11:5; it may involve a smaller group, such as the Twelve (Jn 6:71). In each of these cases, election concerned a specific task committed by God to the group.

**29.** Paul teaches the faithfulness of God when he says: **the gifts and calling of God are irrevocable. Gifts.** The privileges Israel enjoyed (cf. 9:4,5). **Calling.** God's declaration to Israel or Jacob that they were his people (cf. Isa 48:12). The Gentiles, who had been disobedient to God, obtained mercy because of, or by means of, the disobedience of Israel. Now,

32. For God hath concluded them all in unbelief, that he might have mercy upon all.

33. O the depth of the riches both of the wisdom and knowledge of God! how unsearchable *are* his judgments, and his ways past finding out!

34. For who hath known the mind of the Lord? or who hath been his counselor?

35. Or who hath first given to him, and it shall be recompensed unto him again?

36. For of him, and through him, and to him, *are* all things: to whom *be* glory for ever. Amen.

## CHAPTER 12

I BESEECH you therefore, brethren, by the mercies of God, that ye present your bodies a living sacrifice, holy, acceptable unto God, *which is* your reasonable service.

because of the mercy experienced by the Gentiles, the people of Israel are to experience mercy. **32.** Paul's conclusion is that **God imprisoned them all in disobedience in order that he might have mercy upon all.** Each all in this verse refers to both Jew and Gentile. God shuts up men for the purpose of setting them free. **Mercy upon all.** Not the salvation of all. Paul's teaching about those who despise the kindness of God also applies to those who despise his mercy (see 2:4).

6) Excellence and Glory of God – the Source, Sustainer, and Goal of All Things. 11:33-36.

God's plan in history enables him to show mercy to both Israel and the Gentiles that he may have mercy upon all. And he is able to make the rebellion of men serve a purpose in his plan. This causes Paul to break out in praise. **33. Depth.** God's riches, wisdom, and knowledge are inexhaustible. His **decisions** or *decrees* are beyond man's capacity to fathom. **His ways** – the whole of his conduct – cannot be followed through and tracked out. No man is great enough to observe all of God's actions and to follow them through. The OT quotations (Isa 40:13; Job 41:11) show God's independence from man. **36.** Finally, in one mighty surge of devotion, Paul attributes glory to God for ever, the God who is the Source, Sustainer, and Goal of all things.

### IV. Attitude and Conduct Expected of Christians at Rome. 12:1–15:13.

Evidently Paul had been well informed of the needs of believers at Rome. Although most of his exhortations fit any group of believers, many of them show that the apostle was thinking of a particular group as he wrote. The range of these exhortations is amazing. They touch almost every aspect of life. Christian living is simply being a Christian and acting as a Christian should in every part of life.

A. Consecration of Body and Mind. 12:1,2.

**1.** The language here is from the OT, and reminds us that Jewish believers presented sacrifices to the Lord. But Christian believers, instead of giving something outside themselves, are to offer their own bodies to God as living,

2. And be not conformed to this world: but be ye transformed by the renewing of your mind, that ye may prove what *is* that good, and acceptable, and perfect will of God.

3. For I say, through the grace given unto me, to every man that is among you, not to think *of himself* more highly than he ought to think; but to think soberly, according as God hath dealt to every man the measure of faith.

4. For as we have many members in one body, and all members have not the same office:

5. So we, *being* many, are one body in Christ, and every one members one of another.

holy, and acceptable sacrifices. This type of sacrifice is a spiritual service involving all of their rational powers. 2. Because of the dedication involved, believers are to cease being conformed to this age and let themselves be transformed by the renewing of their minds (12:2). Such transformation and renewal is to prove by testing (approve or discover) God's will as to what is good and well-pleasing and perfect.

B. Humility in the Use of God's Gifts. 12:3-8.

3. In introducing the matter of gifts, Paul speaks of the grace given to him that enabled him to be an apostle. Then he exhorts each of his readers not to be haughty, i.e., not to think too highly of himself. He resorts to a play on words, using various Greek terms having the word "mind" or "think" as the basic element — not to be high-minded beyond what is proper to mind *(think)*, but to set one's mind for the purpose of being of a sound *(well-balanced in evaluation)* mind. We are to make a self-evaluation as God has apportioned the measure of faith to each one. Paul is not here speaking of "saving faith" but rather "a working-for-God faith." "Saving faith" would be no standard for correct self-judgment. Only pride would say: "See how much saving faith I have." But it is a humbling experience to say: "Here is the faith I have for carrying out this or that particular task for God." This can only lead to the prayer, "Lord, increase our faith" (see Lk 17:5). In the account of the heroes of faith in Heb 11, we see that the measure of faith given corresponds to the task to be accomplished.

4,5. The one body of which the many are members, while at the same time being individually members of each other, is the Church universal, made up of all believers in Christ. (See I Cor 10:17; 12: 12,13,27,28; Eph 1:22,23; 2:15b,16; 4:3-6, 11-13, 15,16; 5:22-30; Col 1:17, 18, 24,25). The symbol of the body describes the Church as an organism, with every member drawing life from Christ (see Col 3:3). Since all the members draw their life from Christ, they all belong to each other. Local groups of believers are the local manifestation of Christ's body, the Church. Such a local group is body of Christ but not all of *the body* of Christ (see I Cor 12:27). *The body of Christ* consists of the totality of believers who are joined to Christ, the

6. Having then gifts differing according to the grace that is given to us, whether prophecy, *let us prophesy* according to the proportion of faith;

7. Or ministry, *let us wait* on *our* ministering; or he that teacheth, on teaching;

8. Or he that exhorteth, on exhortation: he that giveth, *let him do it* with simplicity; he that ruleth, with diligence; he that showeth mercy, with cheerfulness.

9. *Let* love be without dissimulation. Abhor that which is evil; cleave to that which is good.

10. *Be* kindly affectioned one to another with brotherly love; in honor preferring one another;

11. Not slothful in business; fervent in spirit; serving the Lord;

12. Rejoicing in hope; patient in tribulation; continuing instant in prayer;

13. Distributing to the necessity of saints; given to hospitality.

14. Bless them which persecute you: bless, and curse not.

Church's head.

6. **The grace** of God given to individual believers is shown in different gifts. Paul lists the gifts and then tells the way each is to be used. In each case the reader, to get the proper sense, should supply the verb, *let us use,* followed by the particular gift. **Whether prophecy, let us use prophesy in agreement with** or *in a right relationship to* **the faith.** Faith here means the body of faith, belief, or doctrine (see Arndt, *pistis,* 3, pp. 669-670). Prophecy, which is meant to exhort, encourage, and comfort (see I Cor 14:3), must do so in a right relationship to the revealed truth of God. **7.** The word *diakonia,* which in the AV is translated **ministry,** can be rendered *service* if one takes it in a general sense. If one takes it in a particular sense, it refers to **the office of a deacon.** The emphasis here is that these gifts are to be used. Those with gifts for **teaching** and **exhortation** should exercise them. **8. Giving** should be done with liberality. The word *proistēmi,* translated **ruling** (AV), may mean this or it can mean, **give aid.** This is to be done **diligently.** The one who has the gift for **showing mercy** should use the gift with **cheerfulness.** The gifts mentioned here are — (1) prophecy, (2) service or the office of a deacon, (3) teaching, (4) exhorting (possibly comforting, encouraging), (5) giving, (6) ruling or giving aid, (7) showing mercy. Each of these is a special talent for a particular type of activity.

C. Character Traits To Be Exemplified. 12:9-21.

We must meditate on this list if its full force is to strike home. **9. Love** is to be genuine (or sincere, without hypocrisy). Believers are commanded constantly abhor evil and to be attached constantly to the good. **10.** They are to be devoted to one another in brotherly love and they are to outdo one another in showing respect for each other. **11.** They are not to be indolent. They are to be **aglow** (RSV), literally, *boiling,* with the Spirit. They are to be continually serving the Lord. **12.** Believers are to rejoice in the **hope,** i.e., in all that God has promised to do for them in Christ. They are to endure affliction and always be in prayer. **13.** They are to provide for the needs of the **saints** (fellow believers) and to pursue or seek after hospitality. **14.** Believers are to bless their persecutors and stop cursing the rascals. **15.** They are to

15. Rejoice with them that do rejoice, and weep with them that weep.

16. *Be* of the same mind one toward another. Mind not high things, but condescend to men of low estate. Be not wise in your own conceits.

17. Recompense to no man evil for evil. Provide things honest in the sight of all men.

18. If it be possible, as much as lieth in you, live peaceably with all men.

19. Dearly beloved, avenge not yourselves, but *rather* give place unto wrath: for it is written, Vengeance *is* mine; I will repay, saith the Lord.

20. Therefore if thine enemy hunger, feed him; if he thirst, give him drink: for in so doing thou shalt heap coals of fire on his head.

21. Be not overcome of evil, but overcome evil with good.

### CHAPTER 13

LET every soul be subject unto the higher powers. For there is no power but of God: the powers that be are ordained of God.

2. Whosoever therefore resisteth the power, resisteth the ordinance of God: and they that resist shall receive to themselves damnation.

rejoice with those rejoicing and to weep with those sorrowing. To feel genuine joy for another's success is a mark of true spiritual maturity. **16.** Believers are to live in harmony with each other. Instead of striving after things that are too high for them, they are to accommodate themselves to humble ways and cease being wise in their own estimation. **17.** They are not to return evil in exchange for evil. Rather, they are to be concerned for what is morally good before all men. **18.** As far as that which proceeds from Christians is concerned, if it is possible, they are to keep the peace with all men. **19.** Believers are not to take their own revenge but rather to give the wrath of God an opportunity to work out its purpose (see Arndt, *topos*, 2.c, pp. 830-831). The OT points out that vengeance and recompense belong to God. **20.** Believers are to treat enemies in need as they would treat others in similar circumstances. By feeding them and giving them water to drink, believers heap up burning embers on their heads. This figure seems to mean that the enemy will blush with shame or remorse at such unexpected kindness. **21.** The last character trait mentioned in Romans 12 shows Paul's sense of a contest in the Christian life — "Cease being overcome by evil, but be in the process of overcoming the evil by the good."

D. Submission to Governmental Authorities To Be Accompanied by a Loving, Upright Manner of Life. 13:1-14.

How a Christian faces his responsibilities to government, how he acts toward his neighbor, and how he behaves in his personal life are all matters of great importance.

**1,2.** Obedience to the state is an ordinance of God. The opening words: **Let every person subject himself to the governing authorities** defines the obligation of the Christian. The rest of the first two verses shows why he has this obligation. **There is no human authority except by God and those which exist have been established by God.** The phraseology stresses both the officeholder and the office. Nothing is said here about form of government. The passage emphasizes government itself and its administrators when these function properly. To resist governmental authority is to resist the ordinance of God. Those who resist will receive condemnation.

**3,4.** Paul pictures the rulers in the

3. For rulers are not a terror to good works, but to the evil. Wilt thou then not be afraid of the power? do that which is good, and thou shalt have praise of the same:

4. For he is the minister of God to thee for good. But if thou do that which is evil, be afraid; for he beareth not the sword in vain: for he is the minister of God, a revenger to *execute* wrath upon him that doeth evil.

5. Wherefore *ye* must needs be subject, not only for wrath, but also for conscience' sake.

6. For, for this cause pay ye tribute also: for they are God's ministers, attending continually upon this very thing.

7. Render therefore to all their dues: tribute to whom tribute *is due;* custom to whom custom; fear to whom fear; honor to whom honor.

8. Owe no man any thing, but to love one another: for he that loveth another hath fulfilled the law.

9. For this, Thou shalt not commit adultery, Thou shalt not kill, Thou shalt not steal, Thou shalt not bear false witness, Thou shalt not covet; and if *there be* any other commandment, it is briefly comprehended in this saying, namely, Thou shalt love thy neighbor as thyself.

10. Love worketh no ill to his neighbor: therefore love *is* the fulfilling of the law.

rightful exercise of their prerogatives. Since rulers in their proper function bring terror to the evil worker — not to the good, the man who does not want to fear the ruler will constantly practice the good work. Paul pictures the man who acts thus as receiving praise from the authority. His description of the ruling authority as a *helper* or *agent* of God seems very strong to us. The one who does evil ought to fear. The authority does not carry the sword without a purpose. Here it is clear that God has ordained force (the sword) to be used by human authorities to prevent anarchy and the tyranny of evil in human society. For the second time in the verse (13:4), the ruler is called the agent of God. Then Paul adds — an avenger who brings (God's) wrath upon the evildoer.

5-7. Two reasons emerge for obedience to governmental authorities, and certain results follow. The reasons for obedience are: (1) God's wrath administered by the ruler will fall upon those who disobey; (2) the Christian's conscience declares that he must obey the ordinances of God. Submission to rulers is one of these ordinances. It involves paying one's taxes, paying customs duties, showing respect to those entitled to respect, and showing honor to those entitled to honor. These are obligations of believers to rulers.

Love is said to be the fulfillment of the Law (13:8-10). **8. Be indebted to no one in anything except the constant loving of each other.** Love is the only debt a believer cannot fully discharge. **8b. Now the one who is in the process of loving is in a state of having fulfilled the law. 9.** Paul shows that the commandments about adultery, murder, stealing, desiring that which is forbidden, and all other commandments that one might mention are summed up in the admonition to love one's neighbor as one's self. **10. Therefore love is the fulfilling of the law.** The commandment about loving one's neighbor as one's self is taken from Lev 19:18. In this OT passage there is found near the close of a series of injunctions a description of how the individual should act in regard to those with whom he lives. Whereas the OT *implies* that love is the fulfilling of the Law, Paul makes this *explicit*. Love clearly shows the believer's positive commitment and active obedience to God.

Upright conduct is essential because of the near approach of complete salvation (Rom 13:11-14). Love is a positive, creative outgoing of one's personality. Cer-

11. And that, knowing the time, that now *it is* high time to awake out of sleep: for now *is* our salvation nearer than when we believed.

12. The night is far spent, the day is at hand: let us therefore cast off the works of darkness, and let us put on the armor of light.

13. Let us walk honestly, as in the day; not in rioting and drunkenness, not in chambering and wantonness, not in strife and envying:

14. But put ye on the Lord Jesus Christ, and make not provision for the flesh, to *fulfil* the lusts *thereof.*

## CHAPTER 14

HIM that is weak in the faith receive ye, *but* not to doubtful disputations.

tain sins make this love impossible and must be avoided at all costs. **11.** The nature of the present time is such that believers must **be aroused from sleep.** Indifference to sin must be replaced by alertness. The salvation "which is nearer than when the readers first believed" refers to all that Christ will do for believers at his second advent. Certainly Paul hoped that Christ would come during his lifetime. **12.** The contrast between **night and day, light and darkness** is not only a familiar Biblical theme but is found in the Dead Sea scrolls as well. The people of God know there is a distinct line between evil and righteousness. Yet reminders are constantly necessary. **Therefore, let us lay aside for ourselves the works of darkness and let us clothe ourselves with the weapons of light. 13.** After Paul exhorts the readers to behave decently, as in the day, he lists specific activities that are to be avoided. These are carousings or revelries, and drunkenness, unlawful sexual activities and sensual indulgences, strife and jealousy. **14.** Finally, victory demands that the believer act. He is to clothe himself with the Lord Jesus Christ. He is to stop making provision (forethought) for the flesh to arouse desires for that which God has forbidden.

E. Tolerance Necessary for Those with Strong and Weak Consciences. 14: 1–15:13.

In this section Paul is discussing the attitudes that two kinds of Christians have toward each other. In regard to ceremonial matters—eating foods, observing days—the more mature Christian, in Paul's day, saw these things as unimportant. The weaker Christian, who did not yet have a firm standard for his conscience and was "feeling his way along," felt greatly disturbed at the actions of his stronger brother. The conscience is said to be strong if it has a sound standard for judgment and weak if it has an inferior standard.

1) Differences of Opinion over Food or Special Days. 14:1-6.

**1.** Paul first discusses whether the Christian group should receive into fellowship the one who is weak in knowledge of what it means to be a Christian and how to live as a Christian. The apostle states that such a one is to be received but **not for the purpose of getting into quarrels about opinions** (see

573

2. For one believeth that he may eat all things: another, who is weak, eateth herbs.

3. Let not him that eateth despise him that eateth not; and let not him which eateth not judge him that eateth: for God hath received him.

4. Who art thou that judgest another man's servant? to his own master he standeth or falleth. Yea, he shall be holden up: for God is able to make him stand.

5. One man esteemeth one day above another: another esteemeth every day *alike.* Let every man be fully persuaded in his own mind.

6. He that regardeth the day, regardeth *it* unto the Lord; and he that regardeth not the day, to the Lord he doth not regard *it.* He that eateth, eateth to the Lord, for he giveth God thanks; and he that eateth not, to the Lord he eateth not, and giveth God thanks.

7. For none of us liveth to himself, and no man dieth to himself.

8. For whether we live, we live unto the Lord; and whether we die, we die unto the Lord: whether we live therefore, or die, we are the Lord's.

9. For to this end Christ both died, and rose, and revived, that he might be Lord both of the dead and living.

10. But why dost thou judge thy brother? or why dost thou set at nought thy brother? for we shall all stand before the judgment seat of Christ.

11. For it is written, *As* I live, saith the Lord, every knee shall bow to me, and every tongue shall confess to God.

12. So then every one of us shall give account of himself to God.

Arndt, *diakrisis,* 1, p. 184). 2. The weaker Christian was the one who would eat only vegetables. The stronger Christian was the one who believed he could eat all things. 3. The one who ate was not to be **constantly despising** the one who did not eat. The one who did not eat was not to be **constantly condemning the one who did.** The eating or not eating of certain foods for the Christian is not in itself a moral matter. It is merely a matter of preference. Presently, however, Paul shows that this *may* become a moral matter. 4. The weaker Christian should not condemn another man's servant; that is the job of his master. Here Paul adds that the master is able to make him stand.

5. Paul next takes up the matter of special days. The weaker Christian **prefers one day above another.** The stronger Christian **holds every day in esteem.** The apostle does not take sides here but merely insists that each one **be fully convinced in his own mind.** This tacitly suggests that each one take thought about the basis for his own opinion.

6. Both groups, whether they observe a day or not, whether they eat or not, are giving thanks to God. Hence there is no question of their devotion to the Lord.

2) Judgment by the Lord, Not by One's Brother. 14:7-12.

7. In giving thanks to the Lord, we are reminded that believers cannot live or die to or for themselves. For them both life and death are focused upon the Lord. In every experience they belong to the Lord. 9. Christ died and arose so that he might have Lordship over the dead and the living. 10. If Christ is Lord, then why should the weaker Christian condemn his brother? If Christ is Lord, why should the stronger Christian despise his brother? Both the stronger and the weaker Christians—we all—must **stand before the judgment seat of God.** The AV has *judgment seat of Christ,* but all of the best manuscripts here read **God.** In II Cor 5:10, Paul speaks of the "judgment seat of Christ." The shift is of little importance, since Jesus himself told us that the Father judges no one but has given "all judgment to the Son" (see Jn 5:22,23,27,29). God judges men in the sense that he judges them through his Son. 11,12. Paul quotes Isa 45:23, from the LXX, to show that men must appear before God in judgment, then concludes:

13. Let us not therefore judge one another any more: but judge this rather, that no man put a stumblingblock or an occasion to fall in *his* brother's way.

14. I know, and am persuaded by the Lord Jesus, that *there is* nothing unclean of itself: but to him that esteemeth any thing to be unclean, to him *it is* unclean.

15. But if thy brother be grieved with *thy* meat, now walkest thou not charitably. Destroy not him with thy meat, for whom Christ died.

16. Let not then your good be evil spoken of:

17. For the kingdom of God is not meat and drink; but righteousness, and peace, and joy in the Holy Ghost.

18. For he that in these things serveth Christ *is* acceptable to God, and approved of men.

19. Let us therefore follow after the things which make for peace, and things wherewith one may edify another.

20. For meat destroy not the work of God. All things indeed *are* pure; but *it is* evil for that man who eateth with offense.

21. *It is* good neither to eat flesh, nor to drink wine, nor *any thing* whereby thy brother stumbleth, or is offended, or is made weak.

22. Hast thou faith? have *it* to thyself before God. Happy *is* he that condemneth not himself in that thing which he alloweth.

Each one of us will give an account of himself [to God]. **To God** ought to be supplied, but it is not a part of the original text.

3) Removal of Stumbling Blocks. 14: 13-23.

13. Paul urges his readers to stop condemning each other, and instead, **decide not to be putting an obstacle in their brother's way or a temptation to sin.** In verse 14 the apostle shows that he sides with the stronger Christian. He knows that nothing is unclean of itself. But to the man who thinks that something is unclean, to that one it is. 15. Nevertheless, food must not be the cause of hurting a brother's feelings (AV, **be grieved**). Such hurt feelings could push a man further and further from Christ. **By means of food do not bring about his ruin [the ruin of] that one on behalf of whom Christ died.** In discussing the word "to bring to ruin" *(apollumi),* Arndt lists Rom 14:15 under the heading, "With reference to eternal destruction" *(apollumi,* Arndt, 1. a., alpha, p. 94). Hence nonmoral issues can become moral if they destroy a man's fellowship with Christ. 16. Christian freedom is one of the good things of the Christian faith. But a Christian ought not to act in such a way that this good can be blasphemed.

17-19. Note that the kingdom or reign of God is a present reality. It is defined as Christian living: uprightness of conduct, peace or harmony, and joy. This is in the sphere of the Holy Spirit (cf. 8:9) who energizes believers to be **well pleasing to God** and **respected by men.** Instead of engaging in conflict, Paul urges the believers to be pursuing that which makes for the peace and edification of fellow believers.

20,21. **For the sake of food, stop tearing down the work of God.** Although all things are pure, they become **evil to the man eating with offence.** With offense to what or to whom? If it is with offense to the scruples of another, then it is the stronger Christian who is thought of as doing the eating. If it is with offense to himself, then it is the weaker Christian who is doing the eating. The context in verse 21 favors the former. **Or is made weak** is omitted by many early, good manuscripts.

22,23. **Faith.** Better, **conviction.** You (sing.), **keep to yourself the conviction which you have before God. Happy is the man who finds no fault with him-**

23. And he that doubteth is damned if he eat, because *he eateth* not of faith: for whatsoever *is* not of faith is sin.

## CHAPTER 15

WE then that are strong ought to bear the infirmities of the weak, and not to please ourselves.

2. Let every one of us please *his* neighbor for *his* good to edification.

3. For even Christ pleased not himself; but, as it is written, The reproaches of them that reproached thee fell on me.

4. For whatsoever things were written aforetime were written for our learning, that we through patience and comfort of the Scriptures might have hope.

5. Now the God of patience and consolation grant you to be likeminded one toward another according to Christ Jesus:

6. That ye may with one mind *and* one mouth glorify God, even the Father of our Lord Jesus Christ.

self in what he approves. But the one who is at variance with himself, if he should eat, he feels condemnation and stays in that state because his eating is not from conviction. And everything which is not from conviction is sin. Here it is made very clear that everyone must have a standard for his conduct. With the right one, there are no qualms of conscience with regard to eating; but with the wrong one, e.g., a standard carried over from a past manner of living, condemnation results. **Conviction** is the assurance that one's standard is right. Without a right basis for judgment the believer may be convicted of sin by his conscience where no sin is really involved. It is highly important that a believer provide the correct standard for his conscience, and that he help his fellow believers to have this standard too. He must shun anything that prevents a fellow believer from getting a correct standard and anything that separates a fellow believer from fellowship with Christ.

4) The Strong To Help the Weak Rather Than Please Themselves. 15:1-3.

**1.** To bear patiently with the over-conscientious scruples — **weaknesses—of those without strength** (Christian maturity) is the obligation of **those who are strong** (in faith). **2.** A believer is to please his neighbor for the neighbor's good and for his edification. **3.** The believer has his example in Christ, who did not please himself. Paul applies the words of David in Ps 69:10 to Christ. The reproaches which fell upon Christ are the evidence that he did not please himself.

5) Glory Brought to God by Endurance, Consolation, and Harmony. 15:4-6.

**4.** What value does the OT have for the Christian? It has instruction to give to Christian believers. In reading and responding to the OT Scriptures, the Christian learns both **endurance** and **consolation.** Instruction, endurance, and consolation are all essential elements for the Christian who has **hope** (v. 4). The OT can do this because it is a book about God and his people rather than about ideas. **5.** Paul prays that the God who brings endurance and consolation may help his readers live in harmony together, with Christ Jesus as the standard. **6.** The purpose of this harmony is that **with one mind and with one voice**

7. Wherefore receive ye one another, as Christ also received us, to the glory of God.

8. Now I say that Jesus Christ was a minister of the circumcision for the truth of God, to confirm the promises *made* unto the fathers:

9. And that the Gentiles might glorify God for *his* mercy; as it is written, For this cause I will confess to thee among the Gentiles, and sing unto thy name.

10. And again he saith, Rejoice, ye Gentiles, with his people.

11. And again, Praise the Lord, all ye Gentiles; and laud him, all ye people.

12. And again, Esaias saith, There shall be a root of Jesse, and he that shall rise to reign over the Gentiles; in him shall the Gentiles trust.

13. Now the God of hope fill you with all joy and peace in believing, that ye may abound in hope, through the power of the Holy Ghost.

14. And I myself also am persuaded of you, my brethren, that ye also are full of goodness, filled with all knowledge, able also to admonish one another.

[they] **may glorify the God and Father of our Lord Jesus Christ.** Note that unity of believers is essential if they are to bring glory to God.

6) Ministry of Christ Designed for Both Jew and Gentile. 15:7-13.

7. In concluding the question of the relation of the stronger and weaker Christians, Paul urges that they **receive each other** into their society **just as Christ receives** into fellowship with himself these same people. The outcome of such reception is glory to God.

8,9. For two reasons Christ became **a helper for the circumcision** (i.e., the Jews): (1) to prove that the promises made to the fathers were reliable; (2) to enable the Gentiles to glorify God for his mercy. In sharing the promises made to and through the Jewish people, the Gentiles have come to glorify God (cf. Rom 11:11-36; Eph 3:6, etc.). In becoming a helper to the Jewish people, Christ became a helper to all men. **9 b- 12.** Paul then makes four quotations from the Greek version of the OT (LXX). These quotations picture the Gentiles as listening to personal testimony (Ps 18:49), as rejoicing with God's people (Deut 32:4, LXX), as being exhorted to praise the Lord (Ps 117:1), and as being ruled over by the Messianic king and hoping in him (Isa 11:10).

13. After showing what is involved in Christian conduct, Paul concludes with a prayer for his readers. **And may the God who brings hope fill you with all joy and peace in trusting, in order that you may abound in hope by the power which the Holy Spirit bestows.** "Abounding in Christian hope" should be an apt description of every Christian. The Christian looks ahead with a contagious enthusiasm. God has filled him with hope.

### V. Items of Personal Interest and Care for the Readers. 15:14—16:27.

Paul's conclusion is long because he wanted to tell his readers about the goals he had as an apostle. He wanted his readers to feel that they had a part in his ministry. Along with his greetings he gives instructions, warnings, and specific teachings. This section surely makes clear that Romans is a letter.

A. Paul's Reason for Writing Boldly to Mature Readers. 15:14-16.

**14,15.** Though the apostle was confi-

15. Nevertheless, brethren, I have written the more boldly unto you in some sort, as putting you in mind, because of the grace that is given to me of God,

16. That I should be the minister of Jesus Christ to the Gentiles, ministering the gospel of God, that the offering up of the Gentiles might be acceptable, being sanctified by the Holy Ghost.

17. I have therefore whereof I may glory through Jesus Christ in those things which pertain to God.

18. For I will not dare to speak of any of those things which Christ hath not wrought by me, to make the Gentiles obedient, by word and deed,

19. Through mighty signs and wonders, by the power of the Spirit of God; so that from Jerusalem, and round about unto Illyricum, I have fully preached the gospel of Christ.

20. Yea, so have I strived to preach the gospel, not where Christ was named, lest I should build upon another man's foundation:

21. But as it is written, To whom he was not spoken of, they shall see: and they that have not heard shall understand.

22. For which cause also I have been much hindered from coming to you.

23. But now having no more place in these parts, and having a great desire these many years to come unto you;

24. Whensoever I take my journey into Spain, I will come to you: for I trust to see you in my journey, and to be brought on my way thitherward by you, if first I be somewhat filled with your *company*.

25. But now I go unto Jerusalem to minister unto the saints.

26. For it hath pleased them of Macedonia and Achaia to make a certain contribution for the poor saints which are at Jerusalem.

dent that the Roman Christians were full of goodness and *in a state of being filled* with Christian knowledge, yet he had written this letter to remind them of certain truths they already knew. Note Paul's modesty. His justification for writing to them **rather boldly on some points** was that he had received special grace for his office. **16.** He regarded his apostleship to the Gentiles as a priestly ministry, in which he ministered or served **the gospel of God as a priest.** The purpose for his ministry was that **the offering up** of the Gentiles might be acceptable because this offering had been consecrated by the Holy Spirit.

B. Supernatural Confirmation of Paul's Pioneer Missionary Work. 15:17-21.

**17.** Since Paul had received grace as an apostle, and since he ministered the gospel of God as a priest, he could declare: **Therefore, I may boast in Christ of my relation to God. 18,19.** Yet he did not boast in what he had done but in what Christ had accomplished through him by word and deed, by the power of signs and wonders, by the power of the Spirit. His goal was the obedience of the Gentiles — which the Gentiles were rendering even then. Paul looked at his territory thus far as having extended from Jerusalem to Illyricum (also called Dalmatia, a Roman province above Macedonia, extending along the eastern shore of the Adriatic — present day Yugoslavia). **20,21.** His ambition was to preach the Gospel where Christ was not named — i.e., was not known. He carried out the words of Isa 52:15, which refer to kings. But Paul applies them to Gentiles who believed when they heard the good news about Christ for the first time.

C. Travel Plans: Jerusalem, Rome, and Spain. 15:22-29.

**22. I have so often been prevented from coming to you.** Since Rome was the next step — just across the Adriatic — Paul had often expected to make the journey. **23. Place** (AV). Better, *opportunity.* In the territory where Paul had been he no longer had opportunity to preach Christ where He was not known. **24.** So the apostle hoped to see the Romans on the way to Spain. He announces his plan **to visit** them and **to be sent forth** by them after he has **enjoyed their company for a while.** **25,26.** But before Paul could come, he had to complete his immediate project. He had received contributions from

27. It hath pleased them verily; and their debtors they are. For if the Gentiles have been made partakers of their spiritual things, their duty is also to minister unto them in carnal things.

28. When therefore I have performed this, and have sealed to them this fruit, I will come by you into Spain.

29. And I am sure that, when I come unto you, I shall come in the fulness of the blessing of the gospel of Christ.

30. Now I beseech you, brethren, for the Lord Jesus Christ's sake, and for the love of the Spirit, that ye strive together with me in *your* prayers to God for me;

31. That I may be delivered from them that do not believe in Judea; and that my service which *I have* for Jerusalem may be accepted of the saints;

32. That I may come unto you with joy by the will of God, and may with you be refreshed.

33. Now the God of peace *be* with you all. Amen.

believers in Macedonia and Achaia for the poor saints in Jerusalem. He looked upon this collection as part of the Gentiles' spiritual obligation. 27. As they had shared in the spiritual blessings of Israel, certainly they should now minister to the Israelite Christians from their material things. 28. The apostle looked upon this fund as a sacred trust. **When I have placed the sum that was collected safely** (*sealed*) **in their hands, I shall come through you to Spain** (see Arndt, *sphragizō*, 2. d., p. 804). Paul mentions this collection in I Cor 16:1 and II Cor 8 and 9. 29. Note the writer's confidence that he would come in the **fullness of the blessing of Christ.** The word **gospel** (AV) is not found here in the best manuscripts. Paul did come with Christ's blessing, but he came as a prisoner. God fulfilled his desire, but in a way he did not foresee. He knew, however, that the way ahead would be difficult. Therefore he wanted his readers to pray for him.

D. Specific Requests for Prayer. 15: 30-33.

30. Paul appealed to his readers either by or through **our Lord Jesus Christ** and **the love which the Spirit produces** that they pray for him. He wanted earnest prayer—**contend along with me in prayer.** 31. He asked them to pray, in the first place, that he might be delivered from the disobedient Jews in Judea. He knew how much the unbelieving Jews in Palestine despised him. Also, he asked the Roman Christians to pray **that the contribution meant for Jerusalem** [might] **be acceptable to the saints.** Paul wanted the believing Jewish Christians to respond to this gesture of Christian love on the part of the Gentile Christians — the collection from all the Gentile churches. 32. Finally, they were to pray that in joy he might find refreshing with them when he came to them by the will of God. When Paul did reach Rome, he came as a prisoner, with no outward grounds of joy. He could not find refreshing with the Romans, since he was not free to go to them, although they were free to come to him. God's will overruled some of the details of this request, but the request itself was granted. 33. Since God is the only one who can really bring peace, how natural for Paul to close these prayer requests with a sentence prayer of his own for his readers: **May the God who brings peace be with you all, Amen.**

E. Recommendation of Phoebe. 16:1,2.

### CHAPTER 16

I COMMEND unto you Phebe our sister, which is a servant of the church which is at Cenchrea:

2. That ye receive her in the Lord, as becometh saints, and that ye assist her in whatsoever business she hath need of you: for she hath been a succorer of many, and of myself also.

3. Greet Priscilla and Aquila, my helpers in Christ Jesus:

4. Who have for my life laid down their own necks: unto whom not only I give thanks, but also all the churches of the Gentiles.

5. Likewise *greet* the church that is in their house. Salute my well-beloved Epenetus, who is the firstfruits of Achaia unto Christ.

1. In recommending Phoebe, Paul tells who she is and where she comes from. She was a deaconess of the church in Cenchrea. Her duties, like those of the deacons, were quite general. Material needs and also spiritual needs of others were met by believers like Phoebe. (cf. Acts 6:1-6 with Acts 6:8-15 and 7:1-60). 2. Paul requests the Romans to welcome Phoebe in the Lord in a manner worthy of the saints, and to help her in whatever undertaking she may have need. She deserves such a welcome, Paul declares, because she became a helper of many and of Paul himself as well. This chapter refutes the idea that the apostle resented women working in the churches or among believers. His tribute to Phoebe is followed by greetings to various people and groups. Among those greeted are eight women. Paul specifically comments on how much work five of these women did (Mary, v. 6; Priscilla, a fellow worker, v. 3; Tryphena and Tryphosa, v. 12; Persis, v. 12). The mother of Rufus was so dear to Paul that he calls her his mother as well (v. 13). Only two women are mentioned without any comment — Julia and the sister of Nereus (v. 15).

F. Particular Greetings to Individuals and Groups. 16:3-16.

The frequency of these names in the catacombs and inscriptions of ancient burial places in Rome and the significance of this information is discussed well by C. H. Dodd, *The Epistle to the Romans*, in *The Moffatt New Testament Commentary;* and William Sanday and Arthur C. Headlam, *The Epistle to the Romans*, in *The International Critical Commentary*. In these commentaries to the book of Romans, see the Introductions as well as the textual comments. 3. Paul starts with two of his dearest friends — Priscilla and Aquila. Ever since Paul had met them in Corinth on his second missionary journey, they had been hard at work in the service of God (see Acts 18:2,18,26; Rom 16:3,4; I Cor 16:19; II Tim 4:19). 4. Just how they risked their own necks for Paul's life, he does not say. But the fact that not only Paul but all the churches of the Gentiles gave thanks for them shows the extent of their efforts on behalf of Christ. 5 a. Paul greets the church in their house. This shows that the zeal of these two for Christ was no different in Rome than elsewhere. Household churches are probably also to be found in 16:10,11,14,15. If this is true, then the mention of five household

6. Greet Mary, who bestowed much labor on us.

7. Salute Andronicus and Junia, my kinsmen, and my fellow prisoners, who are of note among the apostles, who also were in Christ before me.

8. Greet Amplias, my beloved in the Lord.

9. Salute Urbane, our helper in Christ, and Stachys my beloved.

10. Salute Apelles approved in Christ. Salute them which are of Aristobulus' *household*.

11. Salute Herodion my kinsman. Greet them that be of the *household* of Narcissus, which are in the Lord.

12. Salute Tryphena and Tryphosa, who labor in the Lord. Salute the beloved Persis, which labored much in the Lord.

13. Salute Rufus chosen in the Lord, and his mother and mine.

14. Salute Asyncritus, Phlegon, Hermas, Patrobas, Hermes, and the brethren which are with them.

15. Salute Philologus, and Julia, Nereus, and his sister, and Olympas, and all the saints which are with them.

16. Salute one another with a holy kiss. The churches of Christ salute you.

17. Now I beseech you, brethren, mark them which cause divisions and offenses contrary to the doctrine which ye have learned; and avoid them.

18. For they that are such serve not our Lord Jesus Christ, but their own belly; and by good words and fair speeches deceive the hearts of the simple.

19. For your obedience is come abroad unto all *men*. I am glad therefore on your behalf: but yet I would have you wise unto that which is good, and simple concerning evil.

20. And the God of peace shall bruise Satan under your feet shortly. The grace of our Lord Jesus Christ *be* with you. Amen.

churches makes one realize that Christians in Rome were members of smaller groups rather than of one large assembly.

5 b. Epaenetus is greeted as the first convert of **Asia Minor**. The AV is wrong in its reading, *Achaia*. 7. Andronicus and Junias were Paul's fellow countrymen, who had been in jail with him at some time. Paul describes them as being prominent among the apostles and as having been Christians before him. This would mean they had been believers for about twenty-five years.

13. Since that which is chosen may be regarded as choice or excellent, **Rufus, the choice one in the Lord,** could also be translated as: *"Rufus, the outstanding Christian"* (Arndt, *eklektos,* 2, p. 242).

16. The command to **greet one another with a holy kiss** (cf. I Cor 16:20; II Cor 13:12; I Thess 5:26) or with a kiss of love (I Pet 5:14) shows that warm Christian fellowship was characteristic of the early church. Whatever in modern cultures is symbolic of the deep affection Christians ought to feel toward each other — a kiss on the cheek, a warm handshake, a grasping of both hands, etc. — is the equivalent of the apostolic command.

G. Dangerous Character of Those Who Teach False Doctrine. 16:17-20.

Paul is not saying that false teachers were already present among the Roman believers. But he knew what had happened elsewhere. 17. **Now I urge you, brothers, to look out for those making the dissensions and the temptations to sin contrary to the teaching you learned.** The teaching becomes the standard. Here is the authority of the apostolic message. Paul's readers are to turn away from those producing dissensions and providing temptations to sin. 18. Such people, instead of being slaves to Christ, are slaves to their own stomachs. But their manner captivates their audience. **By smooth, plausible speech and false eloquence, they deceive the hearts of the unsuspecting.** 19. Paul wanted his readers to stay wise in reference to the good, but innocent as far as participation in evil was concerned. Hence he gives this warning. 20. After the warning comes the promise: **the God who brings peace will crush Satan under your feet in a short time.** With final victory on the horizon, the prayer is very pertinent: **May the grace of our Lord Jesus be with you.**

H. Greetings from Paul's Associates in Corinth. 16:21-23.

21. Timotheus my workfellow, and Lucius, and Jason, and Sosipater, my kinsmen, salute you.

22. I Tertius, who wrote *this* epistle, salute you in the Lord.

23. Gaius mine host, and of the whole church, saluteth you. Erastus the chamberlain of the city saluteth you, and Quartus a brother.

24. The grace of our Lord Jesus Christ *be* with you all. Amen.

25. Now to him that is of power to stablish you according to my gospel, and the preaching of Jesus Christ, according to the revelation of the mystery, which was kept secret since the world began,

26. But now is made manifest, and by the Scriptures of the prophets, according to the commandment of the everlasting God, made known to all nations for the obedience of faith:

21. **Kinsmen** (AV). Rather, *fellow countrymen.* Timothy, Paul's fellow worker, is well known. For the other three, we have no positive identification. Lucius may be the Lucius of Cyrene (Acts 13:1). Jason seems to be the Jason mentioned in Acts 17:5-9. Sosipater looks like the Sosipater of Acts 20:4. **22,23.** The scribe, Tertius, to whom Paul dictated the letter, sends his own greetings. Gaius, who may be the Gaius mentioned in I Cor 1:14. is said to be not only Paul's host but the host for the whole church. This seems to indicate that the church met in his house. The fact that Erastus was the city treasurer shows that the Christian faith reached some people in the upper classes. Quartus, **our brother,** is the last to send greetings.

I. Establishment of Believers by the Sovereign God of History. 16:25-27.

See the Introduction for the discussion of the concluding prayers and doxology in regard to their location in the epistle. **25.** This doxology centers in God's ability or power to strengthen the readers. God's strengthening is **in accordance with Paul's gospel and the preaching about Jesus Christ.** This preaching is being carried on **because of the revealing of the mystery** or *secret.* Three things are said about the mystery or secret: (1) It was **concealed for long ages** or *long ages ago* (v. 25). (2) It has been **revealed now through the prophetic scriptures** (i.e., the OT) **by the command of the eternal God** (v. 26). (3) It **has been made known unto all the nations for the obedience which faith puts into operation** (v. 26). This mystery has to do with God's reaching both Jew and Gentile through the redemption that is in Christ Jesus (see Rom 9; 11; Eph 3:1-7; Col 1:26,27; 2:2,3; 4:3). In the language of Eph 3:6, the mystery consists of the Gentiles' being fellow heirs with the believing Jews, belonging to the same body with them, and being sharers together with them of the promise (cf. Rom 11:11-32).

**27. To God only wise, *be* glory through Jesus Christ for ever. Amen.**

Written to the Romans from Corinthus, *and sent* by Phebe servant of the church at Cenchrea.

An account of God's ability and plan precedes Paul's ascription of glory to God. In the very last verse (v. 27) there is a relative pronoun, **to whom,** which, although left out by one good manuscript and a few others, seems to be a part of what Paul originally wrote. But it is very difficult to put it in the text, simply because this whole doxology centers in God. Glory comes to the only wise God through Jesus Christ. This glory is forever and ever. Perhaps the sense of the text may best be seen if we read it thus: **May the glory for ever and ever [be] to the only wise God, through Jesus Christ, to whom [also] the glory forever and ever** [belongs]. **Amen.** In the original text the phrase **the glory forever and ever** occurs only once. The relative pronoun **to whom** follows Jesus Christ. The phrase **the glory forever and ever** follows the **to whom.** Since the doxology centers in God and this last clause centers in Christ, it seems best to conclude that Paul attributes eternal glory both to God and to Christ. How fitting that Romans should close with the theme, "Glory be to God forevermore!"

# BIBLIOGRAPHY

ALTHAUS, PAUL. *Der Brief an Die Römer. Das Neue Testament Deutsch.* Herausgegeben von Paul Althaus und Johannes Behm. Göttingen: Vandenhoeck und Ruprecht, 1949.

GODET, F. *Commentary on St. Paul's Epistle to the Romans.* Translated by A. Cusin. New York: Funk and Wagnalls, 1883.

HODGE, CHARLES. *Commentary on the Epistle to the Romans.* New Edition. New York: A. C. Armstrong and Son, 1890.

LAGRANGE, P. M. J. *Saint Paul Epitre Aux Romains.* Paris: J. Gabalda et Cie, 1950.

MEYER, H. A. W. *Critical and Exegetical Handbook to the Epistle to the Romans.* Translated by J. C. Moore and E. Johnson. New York: Funk and Wagnalls, 1884.

MURRAY, JOHN. *The Imputation of Adam's Sin.* Grand Rapids: Wm. B. Eerdmans Publishing Co., 1959.

PHILIPPI, FRIEDRICH ADOLPH. *Commentary on St. Paul's Epistle to the Romans.* Translated by J. S. Banks. 2 vols. Edinburgh: T & T Clark, 1878.

SANDAY, WILLIAM, and HEADLAM, ARTHUR C. *A Critical and Exegetical Commentary on the Epistle to the Romans.* New York: Charles Scribner's Sons, 1915.

SHEDD, RUSSELL PHILIP. "The Pauline Conception of the Solidarity of the Human Race in Its Relationship to the Old Testament and Early Judaism," *Man in Community.* London: The Epworth Press, 1958.

SHEDD, WILLIAM G. T. *A Critical and Doctrinal Commentary upon the Epistle of St. Paul to the Romans.* New York: Charles Scribner's Sons, 1879.

# THE FIRST EPISTLE
# TO THE CORINTHIANS

## INTRODUCTION

*The City of Corinth.* Corinth was a wealthy commercial center, situated on the narrow isthmus that connected the mainland of Greece and the Peloponnesus. Its history may be divided conveniently into two parts. The city, which according to legend was the place where Jason's Argo was constructed, was destroyed by the Roman consul Lucius Mummius Achaicus, in 146 B.C. This ended the first chapter of its history. It was inevitable, however, that a city so favorably located should have a resurrection. Hence, in 46 B.C., the new city was constructed by Julius Caesar and given the status of a Roman colony. It quickly regained its commercial importance and, in addition, became in many ways the leading city of Greece.

The importance of the city must have influenced the Apostle Paul in his missionary endeavors. Being the hub of commerce from the north to the south and from the east to the west and containing a population of mixed character — Roman, Greek, and Oriental — Corinth was a strategic center. In fact, it has been called "the Empire in miniature; — the Empire reduced to a single State" (ICC, p. xiii). A message heralded and heard in Corinth might find its way to the distant regions of the inhabited earth. It is no wonder, then, that Paul was "constrained by the Word" (Acts 18:5) to testify in Corinth. Added to the pressure within from the Lord and from the Word may well have been a pressure from without — the open door in cosmopolitan Corinth.

And finally, Corinth's moral character made it a fertile field for the glorious good news of the Messiah. The old city had contained the famous Temple of Aphrodite, where one thousand sacred prostitutes were made available to its cultists. The same spirit, if not the same temple, prevailed in the new city. The sexually-slanted proverb, "It is not given to everyone to visit Corinth," lived on (cf. MNT, p. xviii). The Greek word *Korinthiazomai*, meaning literally, *to act the Corinthian*, came to mean "to prac-

tice fornication" (cf. LSJ, p. 981). "Every Greek," wrote Moffatt, "knew what a 'Corinthian girl' meant" (MNT, *loc. cit.*). The popular Scottish commentator, William Barclay, has said, "Aelian, the late Greek writer, tells us that if ever a Corinthian was shown upon the stage in a Greek play he was shown drunk" (William Barclay, *The Letters to the Corinthians,* p. 3). It is needless to multiply references and illustrations; Corinth was a city noted for everything depraved, dissolute, and debauched. It was providential that Paul was in Corinth when he was writing the Epistle to the Romans. From no other city could he have received more of an incentive to write of the sin of man, and from no other city could he have seen more apt illustration of it. A gaze from Gaius' house may well have been the occasion of the great catalogue of man's wicked deeds set forth in Romans 1:18-32. From this background, then, came Paul's First Epistle to the Corinthians, the epistle of sanctification. It is as if one today were to address an epistle of holiness to a group of believers in Paris, or Singapore.

*Origin of the Church.* The story of the founding of the church at Corinth is told by Luke in Acts 18:1-17. Paul reached the city on his second missionary journey in A.D. 50, and soon became the first to preach Christ's gospel there. While living and working with Aquila and Priscilla, he began his ministry in the synagogue, a ministry that stretched over eighteen months. A striking insight into the apostle's method of preaching is afforded by the Western text of Acts 18:4, which reads, *And entering into the synagogue every sabbath he discoursed, inserting the name of the Lord Jesus, and tried to persuade not only Jews but also Greeks. Inserting the name of the Lord Jesus* must refer to the application of the Old Testament Scriptures to Christ. In other words, he preached Jesus of Nazareth as the fulfillment of Messianic prophecy. He, therefore, followed the methodology of the Lord himself, who, on the Emmaus Road with the two disciples, began at Moses and all the prophets and expounded unto them in all the Scriptures the things that concerned him (cf. Lk 24:27). The response to Paul's preaching was different from the response to Jesus' teaching. For the most part, the hearts of Paul's listeners did not burn with interest in the truth; they burned with opposition to the truth. And Paul was forced to leave (Acts 18:6). Moving next door to the house of Titus Justus (possibly the Gaius of I Cor 1:14 and Rom 16:23; William Ramsay, *Pictures of the Apostolic Church*, p. 205), Paul continued to preach "in weakness, and in fear, and in much trembling" (I Cor 2:3). And who would not fear under the circumstances? The meeting place of the little assembly was next door to the synagogue! The Lord, however, came to Paul in a vision and encouraged him with the promise that He had "much people" in Corinth (cf. Acts 18:9,10). This promise must have been of great comfort to the apostle in later years, when the believers' moral laxity might have given him reason to doubt the genuineness of the work there. After concluding his ministry in Corinth, Paul returned to Jerusalem and Antioch.

*Authorship of the Letter.* The external and internal evidences for the Pauline authorship of the letter are so strong that it is really unnecessary to give the subject more than cursory attention. Clement of Rome, writing about A.D. 95, refers the epistle to "the blessed Paul, the Apostle." This is the earliest instance of the quotation of a New Testament writer identified by name (ICC, p. xvii). Ignatius, Polycarp, and others provide abundant additional external evidence. The internal evidences — of style, vocabulary, and content — harmonize with what is known of both Paul and Corinth. This is a genuine product of Paul the Apostle.

*Place of Writing.* Paul wrote the letter from Ephesus (cf. I Cor 16:8), not from Philippi, as the AV subscription has it.

*Date of Writing.* The date cannot be fixed with absolute certainty, but it seems probable that the epistle was written during the latter part of Paul's prolonged stay at Ephesus (cf. Acts 19:1 – 20:1). That would put it about A.D. 55.

*Occasion of Writing.* Before suggesting the occasion of the letter, it would be wise to outline the order of Paul's contacts and correspondence with the Corinthian assembly. Though almost all points in the outline are disputed, defense of them is not within the purpose of this brief introduction.

1. Paul's initial contact was that referred to above, the visit in which the good news was first preached to the Corinthians. According to 2:1, 3:2, and 11:2, it seems that this was the only visit before the writing of the canonical I Corinthians.

2. After this initial visit Paul wrote the church a letter which has been lost (cf. 5:9).

3. When disturbing news came from the believers and a letter requesting information, Paul wrote I Corinthians.

4. Apparently the problems in the church were not solved by the epistle, for the apostle was forced to pay the church a hurried, painful visit (cf. II Cor 2:1; 12:14; 13:1,2).

5. Following this painful visit the apostle wrote the church a third letter of a very severe character, to which he refers in II Corinthians 2:4.

6. The apostle's anxiety for the church was so great that he could not wait in Troas for Titus, the bearer of the severe letter, but hurried on to Macedonia. There he met Titus and learned from him that the letter had produced results; all was well in Corinth. From Macedonia Paul wrote the canonical II Corinthians (cf. II Cor 2:13; 7:6-16).

7. He then followed up this last letter with his final recorded visit to the church (cf. Acts 20:1-4).

The occasion of the writing of I Corinthians may be traced to several things. In the first place, there had come to the apostle from two sources reports of divisions in the church (cf. I Cor 1:11; 16:17). The more serious of the alien elements may have been Judaists (cf. 1:12; 9:1). In the second place, there arrived in Ephesus from the Corinthian church Stephanas, Fortunatus, and Achaicus (cf. 16:17). The trio brought a letter from the believers in which were contained a number of questions for Paul to answer. The questions may be seen in the recurring key phrase, "now concerning" (*peri de;* see 7:1,25; 8:1; 12:1; 16:1,12). In the third place, certain subjects appear to be simply "the spontaneous outcome of the Apostle's anxious thoughts about the Corinthian Church" (ICC, p. xxi).

*Chief Characteristics of the Letter.* Perhaps the leading feature of this epistle is its emphasis upon the life of the local church. The order and the problems of a primitive church are before the reader. If Romans may be called a theological writing, I Corinthians is certainly a practical one. If in Romans Paul resembles the modern professor of Biblical Theology, in I Corinthians he resembles the pastor-teacher, faced with the care of the church on the firing line of Christian warfare.

On the other hand, the letter is not wholly practical in its emphasis. The most important chapter in the New Testament on the resurrection of Jesus Christ is probably I Corinthians 15, and certainly the most important section in the New Testament on spiritual gifts is found in I Corinthians 12; 13; 14.

And, of course, this great letter is known supremely for its great lyric on love, chapter 13. Here one sees to what heights a man may climb in spiritual writing when borne aloft by the Holy Spirit of God. The genius of the man Paul flashes forth here with indescribable effect.

Finally, it may be of interest to mention that this is Paul's longest epistle.

*Plan of the Letter.* The Pauline argument is plain and clear, subject following subject in orderly fashion, with the divisions being clearly marked. The following outline is utilized in the exposition.

# OUTLINE

# I CORINTHIANS

### CHAPTER 1

PAUL, called *to be* an apostle of Jesus Christ through the will of God, and Sosthenes *our* brother,

2. Unto the church of God which is at Corinth, to them that are sanctified in Christ Jesus, called *to be* saints, with all that in every place call upon the name of Jesus Christ our Lord, both theirs and ours:

# COMMENTARY

## I. Introduction. 1:1-9.

### A. The Salutation. 1:1-3.

The introduction, made up of salutation and thanksgiving, prepares the way for the discussion to follow and, in true Pauline fashion, contains important hints with reference to the burden of the letter.

1. **Called to be an apostle** (Gr., *an apostle by calling,* the force of the verbal adjective) stresses the divine initiative in Paul's summons to office. This phrase, together with the strengthening, **the will of God,** is a designed reference to those in Corinth who may have questioned his right to speak authoritatively (cf. 9:1). **Sosthenes our brother** (lit., *the brother*) may designate the ruler of the synagogue mentioned in Acts 18:17, but this cannot be proved. The definite article may mean nothing more that that he was a well-known Christian. If, however, this is the Corinthian Sosthenes of Luke's account, then the beating he received from the Greeks was a blessing; he became a Christian!

2. The church is **the church of God,** not of Cephas, or Apollos, or even Paul (cf. 1:12). **Sanctified in Christ Jesus** introduces an important doctrine, yet one very much misunderstood. The Greek word *hagiazō* means "to sanctify," not in the sense of "to make holy," but in the sense of "to set apart" for God's possession and use (cf. Jn 17:19). Christians are not sinless, although they should sin less. Biblical sanctification is fourfold: (1) primary, equivalent to the 'efficacious grace' of systematic theology (cf. II Thess 2:13; I Pet 1:2); (2) positional, a perfect standing in holiness, true of all believers from the moment of conversion (cf. Acts 20:32; 26:18); (3) progressive, equivalent to daily growth in grace (cf. Jn 17:17; Eph 5:26; II Cor 7:1); (4) prospective, or ultimate likeness to Christ positionally and practically (cf. I Thess 5:23). The use of the perfect participle here refers to positional sanctification. Christians are saints now, not by human canonization, but by divine operation. Paul's aim in

3. Grace *be* unto you, and peace, from God our Father, and *from* the Lord Jesus Christ.

4. I thank my God always on your behalf, for the grace of God which is given you by Jesus Christ;

5. That in every thing ye are enriched by him, in all utterance, and *in* all knowledge;

6. Even as the testimony of Christ was confirmed in you:

7. So that ye come behind in no gift; waiting for the coming of our Lord Jesus Christ:

8. Who shall also confirm you unto the end, *that ye may be* blameless in the day of our Lord Jesus Christ.

the letter was to bring the Corinthians' practical life into more definite conformity to their position in Christ. **With all that in every place call upon the name of Jesus Christ our Lord, both theirs and ours** does not extend the address to all Christians, but guards against the tendency to confine the teaching to Corinth only (cf. I Cor 4:17; 7:17; 11:16; 14:33, 36), a further confirmation of the oneness of the body.

3. The familiar **grace** and **peace** refer to grace and peace *in* the Christian life. They do not refer to the grace that brings a man *into* that life and the peace that follows thereupon (cf. Jn 1:16; 14:27).

### B. The Thanksgiving. 1:4-9.

The thanksgiving is not ironical, nor is it addressed only to a certain part of the assembly. Still less is it simply a courteous attempt "to win friends and influence people," although it is true that "blame comes best on the back of praise" (MNT, p. 7). It is, rather, a truthful estimate of the position of the Corinthians in Christ and forms the basis of Paul's appeal for practical conformity to this. The apostle singles out their gifts of utterance and knowledge for special emphasis. **4. Grace of God.** That which is responsible for the spiritual gifts mentioned later. **5. Utterance** probably includes more than the gift of tongues (cf. 12:8-10, 28-30). The Corinthians had a wide assortment of utterance gifts (see 14:26). **7.** The result of their enrichment is that they **come behind in no gift.** While the word *charisma*, translated **gift**, has a wide variety of meanings, it probably here refers to spiritual gifts in the technical sense (cf. 12:1 – 14:40). **Waiting**, a strong double compound word, meaning *to await ardently* or *eagerly* (Arndt, p. 82), expresses the believers' attitude as they use the gifts in God's service.

**8. Confirm** was used in Koine Greek as a technical legal term referring to a properly guaranteed security (*ibid.*, p. 138). They have God's guarantee that

9. God *is* faithful, by whom ye were called unto the fellowship of his Son Jesus Christ our Lord.

10. Now I beseech you, brethren, by the name of our Lord Jesus Christ, that ye all speak the same thing, and *that* there be no divisions among you; but *that* ye be perfectly joined together in the same mind and in the same judgment.

11. For it hath been declared unto me of you, my brethren, by them *which are of the house* of Chloe, that there are contentions among you.

12. Now this I say, that every one of you saith, I am of Paul; and I of Apollos; and I of Cephas; and I of Christ.

they shall be in his presence at Christ's return. **Blameless.** Literally, *chargeless,* or "unimpeachable" (Leon Morris, *The First Epistle of Paul to the Corinthians,* p. 37). "It implies not merely acquittal, but the absence of even a charge or accusation against a person" (W. E. Vine, *Expository Dictionary of New Testament Words,* I, 131; cf. Rom 8:33). 9. Everything is grounded on the fact that **God is faithful. Fellowship** has as its primary thrust the concept of having a share in, then a common share. Thus, all believers have a share in Christ and, consequently, a share in one another. This is the hinge upon which Paul attacks the party spirit, the climax of the attack being reached in 3:21-23.

## II. The Divisions in the Church. 1:10 –4:21.

### A. The Fact of the Divisions. 1:10-17.

The first major burden of the letter, dissension in the church, is now considered. The apostle will not leave it until he pens the words, "What will ye? shall I come unto you with a rod, or in love, and in the spirit of meekness?" (4:21) The opening verses of the passage (1:10-17) state the facts as reported by servants from Chloe's house. **10. Now** (adversative *de,* "but") introduces Paul's diagnosis. His initial words are an appeal for unity. **Perfectly joined together.** A versatile Greek word, used of the adjustment of parts of an instrument, of the setting of bones by a physician, of the mending of nets (Mk 1:19), as well as of the outfitting of a ship for a voyage. Adjustment with a view to unity is the appeal. **11. For.** Introducing the reason for the appeal. **Contentions.** A work of the flesh (cf. Gal 5:20), revealing the presence of divisions. **12. Now this I say.** Better, *Now I mean this.* The party of **Apollos** suggests a group who preferred the more polished style and rhetoric of the gifted Alexandrian. There are many modern members of this clique, such as the woman who confessed, "I almost weep every time I hear my minister pronounce that blessed word *Mesopotamia!*" The party of **Cephas** apparently doubted Paul's credentials, preferring the link with Jerusalem by Peter. The ones who were **of Christ** disdained all connections with the others, thus becoming a party themselves. The following words plainly presuppose the disapproval of this

13. Is Christ divided? was Paul crucified for you? or were ye baptized in the name of Paul?

14. I thank God that I baptized none of you, but Crispus and Gaius;

15. Lest any should say that I had baptized in mine own name.

16. And I baptized also the household of Stephanas: besides, I know not whether I baptized any other.

17. For Christ sent me not to baptize, but to preach the gospel: not with wisdom of words, lest the cross of Christ should be made of none effect.

group (cf. ICC, p. 12; II Cor 10:7) by Paul.

**13.** The interrogations make appeals to the unity of the body of Christ and to the believers' identification with him. Barclay comments on **in the name** (lit., *into the name*) as follows: "To give money into a man's name was to pay it into his account, into his personal possession. To sell a slave into a man's name was to give that slave into his absolute and undisputed possession. A soldier swore loyalty into the name of Caesar; he belonged absolutely to the Emperor" (*op. cit.*, p. 18).

**14,16.** Paul thank[s] **God** for the providence which led him to baptize so few at Corinth. It is clear that he does not here depreciate baptism; he simply puts it in its proper place, as a symbolic act pointing to the real fact of identification with Christ by faith. It is also clear that Paul *did* baptize. **17. For.** The reason he did not emphasize baptism. His primary task was to preach the good news. Could Paul have uttered these words if baptism were necessary for salvation? (cf. 4:15; 9:1,22; 15:1, 2) Hardly. His commission also involved no embellishment of the truth with the flowery speech of the professional rhetorician (cf. ICC, p. 15), thus emptying the Gospel of its content. The rendering **be made of none effect** leaves much to be desired. The verb *kenoō* means "to empty," that is, to deprive of substance. The Gospel's appeal is not to man's intellect, but to his sense of guilt by sin. The cross clothed in wisdom of words vitiates this appeal. The Gospel must never be presented as a human philosophical system; it must be preached as a salvation. **Wisdom of words** (lit., *wisdom of word*) marks the transition to Paul's analysis of the cause of the dissension at Corinth, this love of a false wisdom.

B. The Causes of the Divisions. 1:18—4:5.

In the first place, they have not understood the nature and character of the Christian message, the true wisdom (1:18—3:4). In the second place, their sectarian spirit indicates that they have no real understanding of the Christian ministry, its partnership under God in the propagation of the truth (3:5—4:5).

1) Cause one: Misconception of the Message. 1:18—3:4. First, the apostle shows that the Gospel is not a message

18. For the preaching of the cross is to them that perish, foolishness; but unto us which are saved, it is the power of God.

19. For it is written, I will destroy the wisdom of the wise, and will bring to nothing the understanding of the prudent.

20. Where is the wise? where is the scribe? where is the disputer of this world? hath not God made foolish the wisdom of this world?

21. For after that in the wisdom of God the world by wisdom knew not God, it pleased God by the foolishness of preaching to save them that believe.

22. For the Jews require a sign, and the Greeks seek after wisdom:

23. But we preach Christ crucified, unto the Jews a stumblingblock, and unto the Greeks foolishness;

24. But unto them which are called, both Jews and Greeks, Christ the power of God, and the wisdom of God.

25. Because the foolishness of God is wiser than men; and the weakness of God is stronger than men.

26. For ye see your calling, brethren, how that not many wise men after the flesh, not many mighty, not many noble, are called:

for the intellectual (1:18–25). This truth was amply demonstrated by the fact that the church at Corinth contained few worldly-wise persons (1:26-31) and that Paul preached no such message when in Corinth (2:1-5). Then, the apostle expounds the true wisdom of God, outlining its spiritual character (2:6-12), and its spiritual perception (2:13-16); and concludes with a frank statement that carnality accounts for the divisions (3:1-4).

18. For introduces the reason he did not come in wisdom of word. To the perishing, the cross must always appear to be foolishness. Preaching (lit., *word*) is evidently contrasted with words (v. 17; lit., *word*). Paul regarded the cross as God's saving instrumentality. Perish and saved (present tenses, but frequentative, rather than durative) vividly portray the constant stream of the lost toppling into eternity without Christ, and the fewer, but still constant, stream of the saved entering the door of eternal fellowship with Christ. 19,20. For it is written. An appeal to Scripture for support. Good Pauline practice (cf. Isa 29:14; 19:12; 33:18). The words are God's denouncement of the policy of the 'wise' in Judah in seeking an alliance with Egypt when threatened by Sennacherib.

21. Pleased is more than a statement of willingness; it refers to God's happy purpose and plan (cf. Eph 1:5). Preaching refers to the content of the proclamation, not the method of delivery (cf. I Cor 2:4); it is the message (AV, *preaching*) which saves, a message designed for those who simply believe. 22-25. In paradoxical fashion, Paul claims, the called (cf. v. 2) have obtained what the sign-seeking Jews and the wisdom-loving Greeks (v. 22), or Gentiles (v. 24; the AV has *Greeks* again, but the attestation is weak) were after, the power of God, and the wisdom of God. Christ crucified is the secret. Jews and Greeks would not recognize their sin. Christ crucified does; hence, he is the power and wisdom of God. The use of the word crucified without the article strongly emphasizes the character in which Paul preached Christ, *as* crucified (cf. 2:2; Gal 3:1). A Christ without a cross could not save.

26. For introduces the "unanswerable *argumentum ad hominem*" (ICC, p. 24). "Why, look at your own ranks, my brothers," is Moffatt's rendering (MNT, p. 19). A glance at their own church

27. But God hath chosen the foolish things of the world to confound the wise; and God hath chosen the weak things of the world to confound the things which are mighty;

28. And base things of the world, and things which are despised, hath God chosen, *yea*, and things which are not, to bring to nought things that are:

29. That no flesh should glory in his presence.

30. But of him are ye in Christ Jesus, who of God is made unto us wisdom, and righteousness, and sanctification, and redemption:

31. That, according as it is written, He that glorieth, let him glory in the Lord.

## CHAPTER 2

AND I, brethren, when I came to you, came not with excellency of speech or of wisdom, declaring unto you the testimony of God.

2. For I determined not to know any thing among you, save Jesus Christ, and him crucified.

would prove Paul's point, for there were not many of the wise and mighty among them. **Calling** continues the emphasis on God's initiative in man's salvation. In the Pauline tradition was the famous dying remark of John Allen of the Salvation Army, "I deserve to be damned; I deserve to be in hell; but God interfered!" **27,28.** The threefold **God hath chosen** continues the emphasis. **29.** The purpose of God's methodology is stated negatively here and positively in the last verse of the chapter. As Bengel once said, "Glory not *before* Him, but in Him." Jonah was absolutely right in saying, "Salvation is of the Lord" (Jon 2:9; cf. Jer 9:23,24).

30. **But** introduces the blessed contrast. **Of him** and not of wisdom are the Corinthians **in Christ Jesus.** Here is the only solid ground of boasting. Due to the construction of the Greek sentence, it is clear that wisdom is the dominant word, and that the nouns **righteousness, sanctification,** and **redemption** amplify and explain wisdom. Wisdom here, then, is not practical wisdom, but positional wisdom, God's wise plan for our complete salvation. **Righteousness** is forensic, the righteousness given in justification, or that which Paul expounds in Rom 1:1–5:21. **Sanctification** is used in its immediate and complete sense (cf. I Cor 1:2). Righteousness enables one to stand before God in the court of divine justice, while sanctification equips one to serve him in the temple of divine service. It is that which Paul outlines in Rom 6:1–8:17. **Redemption,** in view of the order of words, is probably the final redemption of the body (cf. Rom 8:23), that which occupies the apostle in Rom 8:18-39. **31. That.** The aim of this work of God is to glorify him in his grace, a purpose gloriously achieved. For the worldly-wise have been brought to nought, and the called who believe now enjoy a sovereignly given salvation sufficient for all the exigencies of time and eternity.

2:1-5. The theme continues, the writer now bringing forward his own witness among the Corinthians. It, too, was not based on worldly wisdom, either in its message (vv. 1,2), method (vv. 3,4), or motive (v. 5). **And I** makes the connection.

1,2. **Testimony** (internally preferable to *mystery*, the reading of many ancient manuscripts). There is no hint from this passage, nor from Acts 17, that Paul preached the simple message of Christ

3. And I was with you in weakness, and in fear, and in much trembling.

4. And my speech and my preaching *was* not with enticing words of man's wisdom, but in demonstration of the Spirit and of power:

5. That your faith should not stand in the wisdom of men, but in the power of God.

6. Howbeit we speak wisdom among them that are perfect: yet not the wisdom of this world, nor of the princes of this world, that come to nought:

7. But we speak the wisdom of God in a mystery, *even* the hidden *wisdom,* which God ordained before the world unto our glory;

8. Which none of the princes of this world knew: for had they known *it,* they would not have crucified the Lord of glory.

9. But as it is written, Eye hath not seen, nor ear heard, neither have entered into the heart of man, the things which God hath prepared for them that love him.

10. But God hath revealed *them* unto us by his Spirit: for the Spirit searcheth all things, yea, the deep things of God.

11. For what man knoweth the things of a man, save the spirit of man which is in him? even so the things of God knoweth no man, but the Spirit of God.

12. Now we have received, not the spirit of the world, but the Spirit which is of God; that we might know the things that are freely given to us of God.

crucified because of a sense of failure (as some have suggested) in the philosophical approach at Athens. As a matter of fact, the approach at Athens was not basically philosophical. Paul's sermon began with the Biblical revelation of creation (cf. Acts 17:24) and ended on the note of the Resurrection (Acts 17: 31). Moffatt is right in saying: "At Athens he had not been able to start from any belief in resurrection, as he could in a synagogue" (MNT, p. 22; cf. N. B. Stonehouse, *Paul Before the Areopagus and Other New Testament Studies,* pp. 25-27).

**3,4.** Instead of human persuasion, Paul's method involved the **demonstration of the Spirit and of power.** The word **demonstration** refers to the producing of proofs in argument in court (MM, pp. 60,61). The new life of the Corinthians was a conclusive proof of God's power in them (cf. I Thess 1:5). **5. That** introduces the motive. Paul's simple preaching was designed to prevent the Corinthians' holding a **faith** that rested upon logical and philosophical arguments, a faith at the mercy of other arguments of the same nature. "What depends upon a clever argument is at the mercy of a cleverer argument" (ICC, p. 34). A faith, however, that stands **in the power of God** has a solid and enduring foundation.

**2:6-12.** Someone might infer at this point that Paul had no use for wisdom and that he held Christian truth to be outside the realm of the intellect. The apostle meets this by pointing out that the Gospel does contain a wisdom, but a spiritual wisdom. The opening words, **but a wisdom we do speak,** make the connection (*sophian,* "wisdom," has the position of emphasis in the Greek text).

**6. Perfect,** mature in the things of God (cf. 14:20; Phil 3:15), is equated by Paul with **spiritual** (I Cor 2:15). The clause, **but a wisdom we do speak among the perfect,** may be a summary statement of the section. The **wisdom** would be the subject of verses 6-12, the *speaking,* or teaching, of it the subject of verse 13 (note the **we speak**), and **the perfect** the subject of the remainder of the section (F. Godet, *Commentary on St. Paul's First Epistle to the Corinthians,* I, 135). **7-9. A mystery.** Not something mysterious, but a divine secret, truth which is undiscoverable apart from divine revelation.

**10-12. To us** (emphatic position in the Greek text) contrasts believers with

13. Which things also we speak, not in the words which man's wisdom teacheth, but which the Holy Ghost teacheth; comparing spiritual things with spiritual.

14. But the natural man receiveth not the things of the Spirit of God: for they are foolishness unto him: neither can he know *them*, because they are spiritually discerned.

15. But he that is spiritual judgeth all things, yet he himself is judged of no man.

16. For who hath known the mind of the Lord, that he may instruct him? But we have the mind of Christ.

the world. To them **God has revealed** his wisdom **by his spirit,** who has been given that believers **might know the** things that are freely given by God.

13. Paul moves naturally to the method of communication. This wisdom, he says, **we speak in words which the Holy Ghost teacheth** — an emphatic declaration that the knowledge of divine truth is not traceable to intellect and mental capacity primarily. Paul traces it to the possession of the Spirit of God, the perfect Teacher and the perfect Judge of doctrine. **The words** have been used as support by proponents of verbal inspiration (a true doctrine). But Paul here writes **we speak,** not *we write,* thus referring to oral presentation. The final clause poses a difficult interpretive problem. **Comparing** (AV) may be correct, for the word means this in its only other NT occurrence (II Cor 10:12). The context, however, is decidedly against this unusual meaning of the word. It may also have the sense of "interpreting," or "explaining" (cf. Gen 40:8; Dan 5:15-17, LXX). The rendering would then be, *explaining spiritual things to spiritual men* (cf. RSV). Or, the usual meaning of the word, "combine," may be the sense, the rendering being, *combining spiritual things with spiritual words* (preserving the reference to *words* just preceding). This appears preferable, and Paul thereby refers to "wedding kindred speech to thought" (ExpGT, II, 783). The apostle received his truth from God and clothed it in language given by God's Spirit. His claim is that his utterance was God-given and Spirit-led.

14. The subjective perception of this truth now becomes the topic. **But** introduces the contrast with **the natural man,** the non-Christian (cf. Jude 19; Rom 8:9). The Greek word rendered **natural** means "dominated by the soul," the principle of physical life. This soulish man does not **receive** (lit., *welcome;* cf. Acts 17:11; I Thess 1:6) divine truth, nor **can he know** it, for it is **discerned** by the Spirit (cf. I Cor 2:10,11). Human ears cannot hear high-frequency radio waves; deaf men are unable to judge music contests; blind men cannot enjoy beautiful scenery, and the unsaved are incompetent to judge spiritual things, a most important practical truth.

15,16. The **spiritual** man has the potentiality to understand **all things.** He is **judged of no man** (who is not spiritual), for the unspiritual do not have the neces-

## CHAPTER 3

AND I, brethren, could not speak unto you as unto spiritual, but as unto carnal, *even* as unto babes in Christ.

2. I have fed you with milk, and not with meat: for hitherto ye were not able *to bear it*, neither yet now are ye able.

3. For ye are yet carnal: for whereas *there is* among you envying, and strife, and divisions, are ye not carnal, and walk as men?

sary relation to the Spirit to judge the spiritual. This explains why Christians are often enigmas to worldlings, and sometimes enigmas to carnally minded Christians. Much controversy among Christians can be traced to this principle.

**3:1-4.** The application to the Corinthians' condition, indicated by the change from the first person (2:6-15) to the second (3:1-4), is now made. **And I, brethren, could not speak unto you** makes the connection smoothly.

**1.** Their immaturity prevented Paul's feeding them meat on his first visit. The Greek word for **carnal** (from *sarkinos)* means literally, *made of flesh,* being the equivalent of the expression, *in the flesh* (A-S, p. 402). Back of *sarkinos* is the thought of weakness (cf. Mt 26:41), as **babes** confirms. At Paul's first visit the Corinthians were weak, for the simple reason that they were new believers. The apostle attaches no blame to those in this condition.

**2,3.** A serious charge of spiritual inability is made in **neither yet now are ye able** (a very strong expression in the Greek). The reason **(for)** is that they are **still carnal. Carnal** here is not *sarkinos,* but *sarkikos,* which means, literally, *characterized by the flesh,* being the equivalent of *after the flesh* (cf. Rom 8:4). Back of it is the thought of willfulness, and Paul does attach blame to those in this condition. Weakness prolonged becomes willfulness. Refusal to respond to the milk of the Word prevents reception of the meat of the Word. **And divisions** (AV) is not a genuine reading, although the thought is in the context (I Cor 3:4).

Paul has described four types of men. The first, *the natural man,* is the man without the Spirit, who needs the new birth (cf. Jn 3:1-8). The second is the *carnal-weak man* (I Cor 3:1), the babe in Christ, who needs growth through reception of the milk of the Word. The third type is the *carnal-willful man,* the older, yet immature, Christian, who needs restoration to fellowship, or the healthy condition conducive to the taking of nourishment, by confession of his willfulness, or sin (cf. I Jn 1:9). The fourth is the *spiritual* or *mature man,* who has responded to the milk and grown into spiritual adulthood, so that he is strong and able to take the meat of the Word (I Cor 2:15; 3:2). This is the man God would have every Christian to be. That Paul equates *the ma-*

4. For while one saith, I am of Paul; and another, I *am* of Apollos; are ye not carnal?

5. Who then is Paul, and who *is* Apollos, but ministers by whom ye believed, even as the Lord gave to every man?

6. I have planted, Apollos watered; but God gave the increase.

7. So then neither is he that planteth any thing, neither he that watereth; but God that giveth the increase.

8. Now he that planteth and he that watereth are one: and every man shall receive his own reward according to his own labor.

9. For we are laborers together with God: ye are God's husbandry, *ye are* God's building.

10. According to the grace of God which is given unto me, as a wise masterbuilder, I have laid the foundation, and another buildeth thereon. But let every man take heed how he buildeth thereupon.

11. For other foundation can no man lay than that is laid, which is Jesus Christ.

12. Now if any man build upon this foundation gold, silver, precious stones, wood, hay, stubble;

ture man with *the spiritual man* is evident from a comparison of 2:6 with 2:15 (cf. 3:1; he contrasts babes with the spiritual). He also states that the wisdom of God is for the perfect, but he never uses the term again in the section. Instead, he writes of the spiritual man (2:15; 3:1), who has unlimited capacity to judge all things. The analogy of the physical life with all of this is its best illustration.

2) Cause two: Misconception of the Ministry. 3:5 — 4:5. The second reason for divisions, misunderstanding of the Christian ministry, is now discussed. Ministers are simply servants; actually, it is God who works (3:5-9). They are responsible for the proper materials as they build in the temple of God, the Church (3:9-17). One must not glory in any one of such men, for they all belong to each believer (3:18-23) and will be judged by God alone (4:1-5).

5. Who. Literally, *what*. This draws attention from the men to their functions (Morris, *op. cit.*, p. 64). Paul and Apollos were nothing more than ministers, servants of God. 6. Paul planted and Apollos watered, but only God could make the seed grow. 8,9. In the work Paul and Apollos were *one*, that is, in harmony. However, in the matter of reward, distinctions will be made. Labourers together with God may mean that they were fellow workers with one another who belong to God, or fellow workers with God. The context favors the former.

10. God's building (v. 9) leads to a discussion of the construction of it. It must be emphasized that Paul had in mind *builders* and *works*, not *believers* and *life; service*, and not *salvation* is the theme. The grace of God is the divine enablement given Paul for the planting of the churches. God might have used angels, or even sinners, but to use the "chief" of sinners (cf. I Tim 1:15) was a never ending marvel to the beloved apostle. I have laid (aorist tense, emphasizing the event) points to the initial preaching, while another buildeth (present tense, indicating the continual building) includes Apollos' work (cf. I Cor 3:6). 11. One must be careful, for Jesus Christ is the one and only foundation (cf. Jn 8:12; 10:9; 14:6; Acts 4:12).

12. There are three types of builders — the wise man (vv. 12,14), the unwise (v. 15), and the foolish, who injures the

13. Every man's work shall be made manifest: for the day shall declare it, because it shall be revealed by fire; and the fire shall try every man's work of what sort it is.

14. If any man's work abide which he hath built thereupon, he shall receive a reward.

15. If any man's work shall be burned, he shall suffer loss: but he himself shall be saved; yet so as by fire.

16. Know ye not that ye are the temple of God, and *that* the Spirit of God dwelleth in you?

17. If any man defile the temple of God, him shall God destroy; for the temple of God is holy, which *temple* ye are.

18. Let no man deceive himself. If any man among you seemeth to be wise in this world, let him become a fool, that he may be wise.

19. For the wisdom of this world is foolishness with God: for it is written, He taketh the wise in their own craftiness.

20. And again, The Lord knoweth the thoughts of the wise, that they are vain.

21. Therefore let no man glory in men: for all things are yours;

22. Whether Paul, or Apollos, or Cephas, or the world, or life, or death, or things present, or things to come; all are yours;

23. And ye are Christ's; and Christ *is* God's.

## CHAPTER 4

LET a man so account of us, as of the ministers of Christ, and stewards of the mysteries of God.

building (v. 17). Three different results follow. Even among God's laborers two types of labor may be expended, the one solid and enduring, the other perishable and passing (the foolish laborer does not belong to God; v. 17). **13.** The phrase, **every man's work,** looks at individual responsibility. **The day** is the day of the judgment seat of Christ (cf. 4:5; II Cor 5:10), before which only believers appear. **Of what sort it is** indicates that the basis of judgment is *quality* of work, not *quantity,* a comforting thing for those of little gift (cf. I Cor 4:2).

**14.** Paul does not explain the nature of the reward (cf. II Jn 8). **15. Shall suffer loss.** Loss of reward, not loss of salvation. There are no differences among the Lord's *sheep;* there may be differences among his *servants* (cf. Lk 19:17). **He himself** (emphatic) contrasts the person with his work and pointedly upholds the believer's security. **By fire.** Better, *through fire.* The thought back of it is of one's rushing through fire to safety as the building crumbles (the preposition is local; cf. ICC, p. 65).

**16,17.** The third class of builder, who injures the building, is the non-Christian professor, who is not a possessor (cf. Gal 2:4; II Pet 2:1-22). **Defile** and **destroy** are renderings of the same Greek word, which is much stronger than **suffer loss** (I Cor 3:15). The **temple** is the local church, but surely the local church as the local manifestation of one true temple of God, the Church Invisible, composed of all true believers in Christ.

**18-23.** There follows a warning to those who think they are wise (vv. 18-20), and an exhortation to glory in the possession of all things, including Paul, Apollos, and Cephas (vv. 21-23). **Seemeth.** Better, *thinketh.* Each believer belongs to Christ, not to some human servant (rebuke to the followers of Paul, Apollos, and Cephas), and all believers belong to him (rebuke to the Christ party; cf. 1:12). Paul is a master teacher!

**4:1-5.** The analysis of the causes of division comes to a close here. God's ministers are servants, whose sole responsibility is to be faithful (vv. 1,2). Their judgment belongs only to the Lord (vv. 3,4). Therefore, all judgment must await his coming (v. 5). There was to be no pre-judgment seat judgment!

**1. Ministers** (different in the Greek from the word in 3:5) conveys the thought of subordination, the word originally referring to one who rowed in the

2. Moreover it is required in stewards, that a man be found faithful.

3. But with me it is a very small thing that I should be judged of you, or of man's judgment: yea, I judge not mine own self.

4. For I know nothing by myself; yet am I not hereby justified: but he that judgeth me is the Lord.

5. Therefore judge nothing before the time, until the Lord come, who both will bring to light the hidden things of darkness, and will make manifest the counsels of the hearts: and then shall every man have praise of God.

6. And these things, brethren, I have in a figure transferred to myself and to Apollos for your sakes; that ye might learn in us not to think of men above that which is written, that no one of you be puffed up for one against another.

lower tier of a trireme (cf. Lk 1:2). **Stewards** were administrators in charge of large estates; directed privilege is the thought. **2.** Reliability is the one necessary virtue for all servants and stewards, especially in the things of God.

**3.** Paul repudiates judgment by others, as well as judgment by himself. **Man's judgment** (lit., *man's day*) may glance back to 3:13. It means nothing to Paul that man has his day of judgment now. **4. For** explains his unconcern. **By myself** (lit., *against myself*) is a remarkable claim. Paul experienced unbroken fellowship (cf. 1:9); his practice conformed to his position. He had not failed as a steward. **5. Therefore** (the conclusion) since the Lord alone can judge, judgment must await him. At the proper **time** he will perform it capably and completely, probing into **the hidden things of darkness.** That time is his coming (cf. 1:7). And — wonder of wonders! — **every man** (believer) shall have some **praise from God.**

C. The Application and Conclusion. 4:6-21.

Paul now asks a number of indignant questions to demonstrate the pride of the Corinthian believers (vv. 6-13), and then concludes on a gentler note, reminding them of their relation to him (vv. 14-21). He was their father, and therefore they, the children, were to follow him. Otherwise he might have to use the rod when he visited them (v. 21).

**6. I have in a figure transferred** is the rendering of a verb which means "to change the outward appearance," the thing itself remaining the same (cf. Frederick Field, *Notes on the Translation of the New Testament*, p. 169). *I have adapted* would be a good translation. **These things** refers to 3:5—4:5, not to 1:10—4:5. Paul and Apollos were simply illustrations of the Corinthian situation. The writer omitted the names of the real culprits to prevent resentment. **Not to think of men above that which is written** is difficult. Perhaps a better rendering is, *not to go beyond that which is written;* or RSV, *to live according to scripture.* The apostle desired them to walk by the Word (cf. R. A. Ward, "Salute to Translators," *Interpretation,* 8:310, July, 1954; C. F. D. Moule, *An Idiom Book of New Testament Greek,* p. 64. A marginal gloss is their solution).

7. For who maketh thee to differ *from another?* and what hast thou that thou didst not receive? now if thou didst receive *it*, why dost thou glory, as if thou hadst not received *it?*

8. Now ye are full, now ye are rich, ye have reigned as kings without us: and I would to God ye did reign, that we also might reign with you.

9. For I think that God hath set forth us the apostles last, as it were appointed to death: for we are made a spectacle unto the world, and to angels, and to men.

10. We *are* fools for Christ's sake, but ye *are* wise in Christ; we *are* weak, but ye *are* strong; ye *are* honorable, but we *are* despised.

11. Even unto this present hour we both hunger, and thirst, and are naked, and are buffeted, and have no certain dwelling place;

12. And labor, working with our own hands: being reviled, we bless; being persecuted, we suffer it:

13. Being defamed, we entreat: we are made as the filth of the world, *and are* the offscouring of all things unto this day.

14. I write not these things to shame you, but as my beloved sons I warn *you.*

15. For though ye have ten thousand instructors in Christ, yet *have ye* not many fathers: for in Christ Jesus I have begotten you through the gospel.

16. Wherefore I beseech you, be ye followers of me.

17. For this cause have I sent unto you Timotheus, who is my beloved son, and faithful in the Lord, who shall bring you into remembrance of my ways which be in Christ, as I teach every where in every church.

7. For explains why pride is pointless. The pronouns are singular; Paul is addressing the individual. Augustine saw the truth of God's grace through the second question in this verse. 8. Now (MNT, *already,* p. 48) looks back to before the time (v. 5). The Messianic age, to begin after the judgment seat of Christ and his second coming to the earth, had begun for the Corinthians, Paul reproachfully wrote. "They (had) got a private millenium of their own" (ICC, p. 84). The verse affords some evidence for Paul's concept of the Kingdom.

9. The apostles, in sharp contrast, were far from entrance into the Kingdom. In fact, they were doomed to death, like the condemned criminals, or prisoners, who fought with wild beasts and seldom survived at the close of pagan festivals and exhibitions. Or, Paul may have had in mind the triumphal procession of a Roman general, at the end of which walked those captured soldiers who were being taken to the arena to fight with wild beasts (cf. 15:32; II Cor 2:14-17). In the arena of the world of men and angels, the doomed apostles were a spectacle (the English word *theater* is derived from the Greek word, making a vivid picture). 10-13. A series of caustic contrasts between the apostles and the Corinthians, designed to admonish the believers. The new dispensation had not begun for the apostles!

14. My beloved sons introduces the tender solicitude of a father for his spiritual children. 15. For. Paul explains why he may exhort them as a father. Instructors were Roman slave-guardians, responsible for general supervision of children until they reached adulthood and could put on the *toga virilis* (cf. Gal 3:24). It is as if the apostle were saying that the Corinthians had many supervisors of their spiritual life, but only one who brought them into that life. The begotten introduces a third figure of Paul's relation to them (cf. I Cor 3:6, "planted," and 3:10, "laid the foundation"). He did not bring them into life through good advice, but through the good news, through the gospel.

16. Paul was the rare preacher who could say, Be ye followers of me (lit., *imitators of me*). Most men must say, "Do as I *say,* not as I *do*" (cf. Barclay, *op. cit.,* p. 46). 17-20. Timothy was to bring them into remembrance. Dr. Johnson remarked that more people required

18. Now some are puffed up, as though I would not come to you.

19. But I will come to you shortly, if the Lord will, and will know, not the speech of them which are puffed up, but the power.

20. For the kingdom of God *is* not in word, but in power.

21. What will ye? shall I come unto you with a rod, or in love, and *in* the spirit of meekness?

## CHAPTER 5

IT is reported commonly *that there is* fornication among you, and such fornication as is not so much as named among the Gentiles, that one should have his father's wife.

2. And ye are puffed up, and have not rather mourned, that he that hath done this deed might be taken away from among you.

to be reminded than required to be instructed (MNT, p. 51). This is not true, but there is much need for the reminding ministry. **The kingdom of God** (cf. v. 8). The Corinthians' kingdom was a kingdom **in word**, not **in power**. 21. A challenge concludes. Will it be **the rod** of discipline that they will choose, or **love and the spirit of meekness** produced by the restoration of fellowship? The answer lies with them. **The rod** introduces the note of discipline, predominant in the next section of the letter.

### III. The Disorders in the Church. 5:1—6:20.

A. The Absence of Discipline. 5:1-13.

It is frequently said that the only Bible the world will read is the daily life of the Christian, and that what the world needs is a revised version! The next two chapters are designed by Paul to produce a Corinthian revised version, so that orthodoxy might be followed by orthopraxy (cf. Roy L. Laurin, *Life Matures,* pp. 103,104). Chapter 5 concerns a known case of incest in the church. The believers, rather than mourning over it, were complacently permitting the matter to go unjudged, perhaps even being proud of their liberty (vv. 1,2; cf. 6:12). Paul expresses his attitude in the matter (5:3-5), urges the church to exercise discipline (vv. 6-8), and concludes with a clarification of the previous letter's instruction (vv. 9-13). **Puffed up** (v. 2) marks a slight connection with the preceding (cf. 4:6,18,19), but the real connection is with what follows (cf. v. 1; 6:9,13-20). Both chapters deal with disorders. The lack of a connective in 5:1 confirms this, and also gives the opening words an explosive force in the ears of the serene Corinthians, coolly relaxing "at ease in Zion."

**1. Commonly.** Better, *actually* (cf. Arndt, p. 568). The **fornication** was incest, forbidden by the Law (Lev 18:8; Deut 22:22). **Have** (present tense) suggests some sort of permanent union (cf. Mt 14:4). The singling out of the man may suggest that the woman, his stepmother, was not a Christian. The father may have been dead or divorced. **Named.** Omit in view of weak textual attestation. The sin was prohibited by Roman law. **2.** Inflated by false liberty, the church was **puffed up.** A church can

3. For I verily, as absent in body, but present in spirit, have judged already, as though I were present, *concerning* him that hath so done this deed,

4. In the name of our Lord Jesus Christ, when ye are gathered together, and my spirit, with the power of our Lord Jesus Christ,

5. To deliver such a one unto Satan for the destruction of the flesh, that the spirit may be saved in the day of the Lord Jesus.

6. Your glorying *is* not good. Know ye not that a little leaven leaveneth the whole lump?

7. Purge out therefore the old leaven, that ye may be a new lump, as ye are unleavened. For even Christ our passover is sacrificed for us:

never prevent evil absolutely, but it should always practice discipline. **Be taken away from you** refers to ecclesiastical censure and excommunication. 3,4. Paul had already judged the matter in spirit. His words gave them directions regarding proper action.

5. The substance of his judgment is here. **To deliver** to Satan is difficult (cf. I Tim 1:20). It probably refers to committing the man to the world as belonging to Satan (cf. I Jn 5:19). **Destruction of the flesh** has been taken in the moral sense of the annulment of the fleshly appetites. **Destruction** is too severe for this view, although, of course, discipline is to be remedial. It is probably better to see here the thought of bodily chastisement, to which persistent sin leads, according to NT teaching, not only in this letter (cf. I Cor 11:30), but also elsewhere (cf. I Jn 5:16,17). The purpose of the action is given in the following clause.

6. The principle back of the need of discipline is here. "Never say by way of excuse that after all it's only one case. Only one, but it will infect **the whole group** (xv. 33)" (MNT, p. 57). Sin always spreads and contaminates if left alone, just as poison, weeds, and cancer do. **7. Therefore.** Decisive action is necessary. **As ye are unleavened** expresses the position of the believers, to which their condition is to correspond. Their cleansing is to be manifested in clean living. **For** explains. The background of the apostle's remarks is the Feasts of the Passover and Unleavened Bread. The Passover (cf. Ex 12:1-28) prefigured Christ as God's Lamb, who would take away the sin of the world by his sacrifice on Golgotha (cf. Jn 1:29). The Feast of Unleavened Bread (cf. Ex 12:15-20; 13:1-10), during which the Israelites were to have no leaven in their homes (leaven referring, of course, to sin typically), continued for the week following the slaying of the lamb. This feast prefigured the life of holiness that should follow the slaying and eating of the lamb, seven days being a complete circle of time. The Passover, then, is typical and illustrative of the work of Christ in dying for his own. This has taken place, so Paul writes **is sacrificed for us** (aorist tense, looking at the event as a once-for-all thing). The Feast of Unleavened Bread is illustrative of the believer's walk in holiness, a continuous thing, and so Paul writes **let us go on keeping the feast** (v. 8; present tense,

8. Therefore let us keep the feast, not with old leaven, neither with the leaven of malice and wickedness; but with the unleavened *bread* of sincerity and truth.

9. I wrote unto you in an epistle not to company with fornicators:

10. Yet not altogether with the fornicators of this world, or with the covetous, or extortioners, or with idolaters; for then must ye needs go out of the world.

11. But now I have written unto you not to keep company, if any man that is called a brother be a fornicator, or covetous, or an idolater, or a railer, or a drunkard, or an extortioner; with such a one, no, not to eat.

12. For what have I to do to judge them also that are without? do not ye judge them that are within?

13. But them that are without God judgeth. Therefore put away from among yourselves that wicked person.

## CHAPTER 6

DARE any of you, having a matter against another, go to law before the unjust, and not before the saints?

durative action). And just as a crumb of leaven in the house of the Israelite meant judgment (cf. Ex 12:15), so sin in the believer's life means judgment. Hence the need of discipline.

8. The conclusion (**therefore**) of Paul's exhortation is here. Purity and rectitude were to characterize the believer, not the wickedness of the man and the church in this matter of incest. These godly virtues were to be the food of the Christian's feast.

9. The apostle now clarifies instructions given in a previous letter (see Introduction), a letter now lost. **10,11.** A Christian must have some contact with the world; otherwise he would have to go out of the world, a manifest impossibility (at least before the advent of the space age!). The key to understanding the command of verse 9 is the verb **to company with** (vv. 9,11), which means literally *to mix up together with* (cf. Arndt, p. 792). The thought is that of familiar fellowship. The apostle knew that some fellowship with the world must take place in the daily pursuits of life. However, the brother under discipline was to be denied fellowship, and particularly were the believers not **to eat with such an one,** the most obvious act of fellowship.

12. **For** explains why Paul in the lost letter was not referring to the world, but to brethren, when he spoke of denial of fellowship. He was not concerned with the ones **that** [were] **without;** they were in God's province (cf. A. R. Fausset, in JFB V, 297). The Corinthians, however, were obligated to judge the ones within. 13. The **therefore** (AV) should be omitted, which gives the final sentence of excommunication an emphatic summary force (cf. Deut 24:7).

B. The Lawsuits Before the Heathen. 6:1-11.

The discussion of disorders continues. While there is no connecting particle in 6:1, the idea of *judging* clearly links the two chapters. The judicial competency of the church among its members is in view in both. Godet has put it well, " 'Not only do ye not judge those whom you have a mission to judge (**them that are within**); but, moreover, ye go to have yourselves judged by those who are beneath you (**them that are without**)!' " (*op. cit.*, I, 284). The question of lawsuits is introduced (v. 1) and then met (vv. 2-11). The solution features the

2. Do ye not know that the saints shall judge the world? and if the world shall be judged by you, are ye unworthy to judge the smallest matters?

3. Know ye not that we shall judge angels? how much more things that pertain to this life?

4. If then ye have judgments of things pertaining to this life, set them to judge who are least esteemed in the church.

5. I speak to your shame. Is it so, that there is not a wise man among you? no, not one that shall be able to judge between his brethren?

6. But brother goeth to law with brother, and that before the unbelievers.

7. Now therefore there is utterly a fault among you, because ye go to law one with another. Why do ye not rather take wrong? Why do ye not rather *suffer yourselves to* be defrauded?·

8. Nay, ye do wrong, and defraud, and that *your* brethren.

9. Know ye not that the unrighteous shall not inherit the kingdom of God? Be not deceived: neither fornicators, nor idolaters, nor adulterers, nor effeminate, nor abusers of themselves with mankind,

10. Nor thieves, nor covetous, nor drunkards, nor revilers, nor extortioners, shall inherit the kingdom of God.

11. And such were some of you: but ye are washed, but ye are sanctified, but ye are justified in the name of the Lord Jesus, and by the Spirit of our God.

threefold occurrence of **know ye not** (Gr., *ouk oidate;* vv. 2,3,9).

1. **Dare any of you** (very emphatic in the Greek text). What audacity for the *justified* (although Greeks were given to litigiousness) to go before the *unjustified* for justice! (cf. v. 11)· 2. The first point in the rebuttal is the known fact that **the saints shall judge the world,** because of their union with the Messiah, to whom all judgment is committed (cf. Jn 5:22; Mt 19:28). 3. The second point is the known fact that **we shall judge angels; how much more,** then, **things that pertain to this life** (cf. Jn 5:22; Jude 6; II Pet 2:4,9).

4. **Then** introduces an inference, somewhat clouded by a problem of translation. **Set to judge** may be taken as an imperative or as an indicative. If indicative, it may also be declarative or interrogative. Probably the indicative with interrogative force is to be preferred, the sense then being, **Are you setting them to judge who are least esteemed by the church?** 5. A very ironical suggestion that there may not be a **wise man** among the 'wise' Corinthians!

7,8. A better course is suggested. **Fault** may be rendered *defeat,* the point being made that resorting to law against a brother constitutes a loss of case already.

9. Paul's third point is an appeal to "wider principles" (ICC, p. 117). The unrighteous, or unjust, are not qualified to judge; only believers, the just, may judge. The negative is presented first (vv. 9,10), followed by the positive (v. 11). The emphasis in **kingdom of God** rests upon **God;** the unjust have no place in his kingdom. The following catalogue of sins proves that Paul and James are in basic agreement. Both affirm that genuine faith produces good works (cf. Eph 2:8-10), and that the absence of good works indicates lack of faith (cf. Jas 2:14-26). The prevailing moral laxity of the Greeks and Romans may have prompted the apostle's emphasis here upon unnatural vice. For example, Socrates, as well as fourteen of the first fifteen Roman emperors, practiced unnatural vice (cf. Barclay, *op. cit.,* p. 60).

11. The positive appeal is here. **And such were some of you** points to the depths from which the grace of God in Christ had rescued them. **Ye are washed.** Literally, *ye allowed yourselves to be washed* (a permissive middle voice), or, *ye washed yourselves* (a direct middle, stressing the active side of faith; cf. Acts

12. All things are lawful unto me, but all things are not expedient: all things are lawful for me, but I will not be brought under the power of any.

13. Meats for the belly, and the belly for meats: but God shall destroy both it and them. Now the body is not for fornication, but for the Lord; and the Lord for the body.

14. And God hath both raised up the Lord, and will also raise up us by his own power.

22:16; Gal 5:24). **Washed, sanctified,** and **justified** reflect the new position of the Corinthians. The mention of sanctification before justification is no problem, since Paul has in mind positional truth (see I Cor 1:2,30). The verbs refer to the same thing with differing emphases, the one stressing the believer's cleansing, the next the believer's new calling, and the final one the believer's new standing. **Justified** stands last, as a fitting climax to the argument about seeking justice before the unjust (vv. 1-8).

C. The Moral Laxity in the Church. 6:12-20.

Paul turns his attention to the moral laxity that polluted the church, apparently caused by the application of the truth of Christian liberty to the sexual realm. The question is: If there are no restrictions in food, one appetite of the body, why must there be in sexual things, another physical desire? Paul's reply, in which he begins with the principle of liberty and applies it to fornication specifically, again features the threefold occurrence of **Know ye not** (vv. 15,16,19).

12. The principle of liberty is stated, with two limitations: (1) expediency (cf. 10:23); (2) self-control. **Lawful** and **power,** from the same root, form a designed play on words: "All things are in my power, but I will not be brought under the power of anything." The indulgence in a habit which has one in its grip is not liberty but slavery.

13. While **meats** are **for the belly and the belly for meats** (necessary for one another), this relation is not true of the body and fornication. The body is designed to glorify the Lord, and the Lord is necessary to the body for this to take place. Paul uses the term **body** here in a broader sense than simply the physical tabernacle. It is almost equivalent to the man's personality, much like the use of the word *somebody,* or *everybody* (cf. MNT, pp. 68,69,71-73; Morris, *op. cit.,* p. 100; Moule, *op. cit.,* pp. 196,197). In verse 19 he appears to equate **body** with **you.** This, of course, is not always Paul's usage (II Cor 12:3). 14. A further difference between the body and the belly and the body and fornication lies in the fact that the body is destined for resurrection, while the belly is to be brought to nought (v. 13). The permanence of the body has more than theoretical sig-

**15.** Know ye not that your bodies are the members of Christ? shall I then take the members of Christ, and make *them* the members of a harlot? God forbid.

**16.** What! know ye not that he which is joined to a harlot is one body? for two, saith he, shall be one flesh.

**17.** But he that is joined unto the Lord is one spirit.

**18.** Flee fornication. Every sin that a man doeth is without the body; but he that committeth fornication sinneth against his own body.

**19.** What! know ye not that your body is the temple of the Holy Ghost *which is* in you, which ye have of God, and ye are not your own?

**20.** For ye are bought with a price: therefore glorify God in your body, and in your spirit, which are God's.

nificance. For example, what about the practice of cremation?

**15.** By reason of the believer's union with Christ (cf. 12:12-27), fornication robs the Lord of that which is his. **Take.** Better, *take away.* **16.** The second reason is expressed here. **What** should be omitted. **Or know ye not** is the preferred reading. Not only is the Lord robbed, but a new union takes place (cf. v. 15; Gen 2:24). The practical proof of this is that a new personality may result from the union. **17. One spirit.** One of the strongest expressions of unity and security in the Word of God. As one author has put it, "The sheep may wander from the shepherd, the branch may be cut off from the vine; the member may be severed from the body . . . but when two spirits blend in one, what shall part them?" (Arthur T. Pierson, *Knowing the Scriptures,* p. 146)

**18. Flee** (present tense for habitual action). The positive command. Morris suggests, "Make it your habit to flee" (*op. cit.,* p. 102). Someone has said, "While it is often claimed that there is safety in numbers, there are times when there is more safety in exodus!" Joseph's experience comes to mind (cf. Gen 39:1-12). The final phrases, **without the body** and **against the body,** are difficult. Perhaps the meaning is that other sins, such as drunkenness, have effects *on* the body, but fornication is a sin wrought *within* the body and involves a monstrous denial of union with Christ by union with the harlot.

**19.** The final reason is the fact that the **body is the temple of the Holy Ghost. Your body.** A "distributive" expression, i.e., *the body of each one of you* (cf. Charles J. Ellicott, *Paul's First Epistle to the Corinthians,* p. 107). The body of the individual believer is the Spirit's temple (cf. 3:16). How incongruous it is to hear, as one often does, believers praying for the coming of the Spirit!

**20. For** introduces the reason believers are not their own. The Spirit occupies that which God has obtained by purchase. One can demonstrate ownership by purchase and by occupancy. Both of these things God has done; hence Christians are not their **own,** but *His own* (cf. Jn 13:1). **Bought** (aorist tense) refers to Golgotha, where the price was paid. The figure is that of sacral manumission, whereby a slave, by paying the price of his freedom into the temple treasury, was regarded thereafter as the slave of the god and no longer the

## CHAPTER 7

NOW concerning the things whereof ye wrote unto me: *It is* good for a man not to touch a woman.

2. Nevertheless, *to avoid* fornication, let every man have his own wife, and let every woman have her own husband.

3. Let the husband render unto the wife due benevolence: and likewise also the wife unto the husband.

4. The wife hath not power of her own body, but the husband: and likewise also the husband hath not power of his own body, but the wife.

5. Defraud ye not one the other, except *it be* with consent for a time, that ye may give yourselves to fasting and prayer; and come together again, that Satan tempt you not for your incontinency.

6. But I speak this by permission, *and* not of commandment.

7. For I would that all men were even as I myself. But every man hath his proper gift of God, one after this manner, and another after that.

slave of his earthly master. **Therefore glorify**, the logical conclusion, is both negative and positive. Negatively, a believer should eliminate defiling things, such as fornication, and positively he should display the One who had come to dwell within. The terrible price of the priceless blood (cf. I Pet 1:18,19) demanded nothing less than this. **And in your spirit, which are God's** have weak manuscript support.

### IV. The Difficulties in the Church. 7:1—15:58.

A. The Counsel Concerning Marriage. 7:1-40.

Having discussed the things that came to him by way of report (cf. 1:11; 5:1), the apostle now turns to matters raised in correspondence (cf. 7:1, *peri de;* see Introduction). The problems of marriage are introduced first. The chapter, after a prologue dealing with general principles (vv. 1-7), contains discussions of the problems of the married (vv. 8-24) and of the unmarried (vv. 25-40).

1) The Prologue. 7:1-7. The apostle sets forth the general principle that, while celibacy is a matter of personal preference (vv. 6,7), yet marriage is a duty for those who do not have the gift of continence (vv. 1,2), a real marriage with due provision for the sexual needs of each partner (vv. 3-5). **1. Now concerning the things whereof ye wrote unto me.** The equivalent of our modern formula, *Regarding your letter.* It is possible that Paul had been asked to approve celibacy as a duty for all. He grants the state is **good. 2.** Marriage, however, is a duty for those to whom the evil society and habits of the day might prove too much. This is not a low view of marriage; it is an honest facing of the facts in order **to avoid fornication.** Literally, *fornications*, the plural referring perhaps to the many cases at Corinth (cf. 6:12-20). **3-5.** Genuine marriage, however, is a partnership, a union of two people who become "one flesh" (6:16), and involves mutual obligations, conjugal rights. **6,7.** The preceding words were spoken by concession (AV, *permission*), not by commandment. Marriage is a *may*, not a *must*. The leading of the Lord, one's gift from God, is the pre-eminent thing (cf. Mt 19:10-12).

2) The Problems of Marriage. 7:8-38.

8. I say therefore to the unmarried and widows, It is good for them if they abide even as I.

9. But if they cannot contain, let them marry: for it is better to marry than to burn.

10. And unto the married I command, *yet* not I, but the Lord, Let not the wife depart from *her* husband:

11. But and if she depart, let her remain unmarried, or be reconciled to *her* husband: and let not the husband put away *his* wife.

12. But to the rest speak I, not the Lord: If any brother hath a wife that believeth not, and she be pleased to dwell with him, let him not put her away.

13. And the woman which hath a husband that believeth not, and if he be pleased to dwell with her, let her not leave him.

14. For the unbelieving husband is sanctified by the wife, and the unbelieving wife is sanctified by the husband: else were your children unclean; but now are they holy.

15. But if the unbelieving depart, let him depart. A brother or a sister is not under bondage in such *cases:* but God hath called us to peace.

The writer now considers specific problems involving the married and the unmarried.

**8,9.** Addressed first are those who were unmarried at the time Paul wrote, but who had had sexual experience. **Unmarried,** probably widowers, being set over against **widows.** Unmarried men and virgins are dealt with elsewhere (vv. 1,2,25,28-38). **Abide** (aorist tense) is the lifelong and final decision. **10,11.** Paul's next word relates to the maintenance or severance of the marriage bond, in the case of believers' marriages (vv. 10,11) and mixed marriages (vv. 12-16). For believers the rule is, No separation, supported by the Lord's viewpoint, **yet not I, but the Lord** (cf. Mk 10:1-12). In the case of unapproved separation, Paul outlines two possibilities. The wife must **remain unmarried,** present tense, emphasizing the permanent state. Or she should **be reconciled,** aorist tense, emphasizing the once-for-all event, with no further separations.

**12.** But what of marriages in which one of the parties has become a Christian? Jewish law required the unbeliever to be put away (cf. Ezr 9:1—10:44). Again, the rule is, No separation (I Cor 7:12,13).

**14. For.** The first reason is that the unbelieving partner and the children of a mixed marriage are **sanctified.** This does not mean that a child born into a home where only one of the parents is a Christian is born "into the family of Christ" (cf. Barclay, *op. cit.,* p. 71). Paul simply means that the OT principle of the communication of uncleanness does not hold (cf. Hag 2:11-13). The union is lawful and confers privilege on the members (cf. ICC, p. 142), privileges such as the protection of God and the opportunity of being in close contact with one in God's family. This might ease the path to conversion for the unbelieving.

**15.** A second reason for the preservation of the union is found in the fact that God **has called to peace.** A curiously ambiguous situation, however, exists. Some interpreters feel that Paul here encourages the believer to permit the separation in the interests of preserving peace, if the unbeliever desires to depart. There might be war otherwise! On the other hand, Paul's thought may be that separation should be prevented if at all possible, since that would disrupt the peace of the marriage union. The general principle of the context (vv. 10,11)

16. For what knowest thou, O wife, whether thou shalt save *thy* husband? or how knowest thou, O man, whether thou shalt save *thy* wife?

17. But as God hath distributed to every man, as the Lord hath called every one, so let him walk. And so ordain I in all churches.

18. Is any man called being circumcised? let him not become uncircumcised. Is any called in uncircumcision? let him not be circumcised.

19. Circumcision is nothing, and uncircumcision is nothing, but the keeping of the commandments of God.

20. Let every man abide in the same calling wherein he was called.

21. Art thou called *being* a servant? care not for it: but if thou mayest be made free, use *it* rather.

22. For he that is called in the Lord, *being* a servant, is the Lord's freeman: likewise also he that is called, *being* free, is Christ's servant.

23. Ye are bought with a price; be not ye the servants of men.

24. Brethren, let every man, wherein he is called, therein abide with God.

25. Now concerning virgins I have no commandment of the Lord: yet I give my judgment, as one that hath obtained mercy of the Lord to be faithful.

26. I suppose therefore that this is good for the present distress, *I say*, that *it is* good for a man so to be.

27. Art thou bound unto a wife? seek not to be loosed. Art thou loosed from a wife? seek not a wife.

28. But and if thou marry, thou hast not sinned; and if a virgin marry, she hath not sinned. Nevertheless such shall have trouble in the flesh: but I spare you.

favors the second view, as well as the following verse. Nothing is said about a second marriage for the believer; it is vain to put words in Paul's mouth when he is silent. It is true that the verb "to depart" in the middle voice (it is middle in this verse) was almost a technical term for divorce in the papyri (MM, p. 695,696). This, however, really proves nothing here.

**16. For.** The third reason for no separation is that the salvation of the other member may be accomplished through preservation of the union. Others understand the statement to mean that separation should be willingly agreed to, since one can never know whether the partner will be converted or not. The general context favors the former view. But it is not easy to determine what Paul meant.

**17-24.** The apostle now summarizes, indicating that this principle of abiding in one's marital relationship is simply part of a more general principle touching every sphere of life. The rule in everything is to abide in one's calling, unless that calling be immoral. Three times Paul states the principle (vv. 17, 20,24), interspersing the declarations of principle with two illustrations, one religious (cf. Rom 2:28,29) and the other secular. The expression **with God,** which concludes the section, emphasizes the fact that the presence of God makes any secular work a work with God. In a sense, then, every Christian is engaged in "full-time Christian work." In the light of Paul's teaching here, is it not also a questionable thing to "pressure" young people into full-time service for God as missionaries, pastors, etc.? The thing of pre-eminent importance for every believer is to be in the calling of God for him.

**25. Now concerning** *(peri de)* indicates to the readers that an answer to another part of the church's letter follows. In the remainder of the chapter Paul deals with three groups: (1) the unmarried young (v. 25-35); (2) the parents (vv. 36-38); (3) widows (vv. 39,40). The section is bounded by two statements concerning the author's authority (vv. 25,40). The point of the paragraph is this: Celibacy is desirable, but not demanded.

**26-28. It is good for a man so to be.** Rather, *It is well for a person to remain as he is* (RSV). The first reason for remaining single is **the present distress,** a phrase probably referring to the pressure of the Christian life in an unfriendly

29. But this I say, brethren, the time *is* short: it remaineth, that both they that have wives be as though they had none;

30. And they that weep, as though they wept not; and they that rejoice, as though they rejoiced not; and they that buy, as though they possessed not;

31. And they that use this world, as not abusing *it:* for the fashion of this world passeth away.

32. But I would have you without carefulness. He that is unmarried careth for the things that belong to the Lord, how he may please the Lord:

33. But he that is married careth for the things that are of the world, how he may please *his* wife.

34. There is difference *also* between a wife and a virgin. The unmarried woman careth for the things of the Lord, that she may be holy both in body and in spirit: but she that is married careth for the things of the world, how she may please *her* husband.

35. And this I speak for your own profit; not that I may cast a snare upon you, but for that which is comely, and that ye may attend upon the Lord without distraction.

36. But if any man think that he behaveth himself uncomely toward his virgin, if she pass the flower of *her* age, and need so require, let him do what he will, he sinneth not: let them marry.

37. Nevertheless he that standeth steadfast in his heart, having no necessity, but hath power over his own will, and hath so decreed in his heart that he will keep his virgin, doeth well.

38. So then he that giveth *her* in marriage doeth well; but he that giveth *her* not in marriage doeth better.

world (cf. v. 28; II Tim 3:12). If the Christian life is difficult in itself, why impose more of a burden upon oneself with marriage? **29-31.** A second reason is suggested by the statement, **the time is short** (lit., *has been drawn together* so as to be short). The apostle refers to the time before the coming of the Lord (cf. Rom 13:11). All of life is to be lived in the light of this great fact. Then shall the fashion of this world pass away and a glorious new day dawn.

**32-35.** A third reason is found in these verses. It is expressed negatively in the words **I would have you without carefulness** (v. 32), and positively in the words **that ye may attend upon the Lord without distraction** (v. 35). A highly involved textual problem is posed by the words connecting verses 33 and 34. This may find its solution in modifying the words, **There is difference also between a wife and a virgin** (v. 34), to "Parted also by a similar division of interests are the married and the unmarried woman" (ICC, pp. 150,151). The point of the apostle is clear: Marriage is a distracting thing. This he states definitely at the end of verse 35. The words **that ye may attend upon the Lord without distraction** suggest the Lukan account of the incident of the Lord's visit to the house of Mary and Martha in Bethany. There are also several verbal connections in the Greek text between Luke's account and Paul's words (cf. Lk 10:38-42). It is as if Paul were tacitly saying that marriage makes Marthas out of Marys, thus preventing the choice of "that good part" — occupation with the Lord and his Word.

**36-38.** Parents are in view here. The passage must be understood in the light of the customs of the day. The father had control of the arrangements for his daughter's marriage. **Behaveth himself uncomely** refers to the withholding of marriage when there is evidence of the lack of the gift of continence. It is doubtful that Paul has in mind here "spiritual marriages," in which people went through a form of marriage and yet lived together as brother and sister (cf. Barclay, *op. cit.*, pp. 74,75; MNT, pp. 98-100). **Standeth stedfast,** i.e., does not think that he is behaving unseemly. **So then** introduces the summary, really a summary of the chapter. One does **well;** the other does **better.** The celibate state is not holier than the married state; celibacy simply has greater utility in serving the Lord. But even in marriage

39. The wife is bound by the law as long as her husband liveth; but if her husband be dead, she is at liberty to be married to whom she will; only in the Lord.

40. But she is happier if she so abide, after my judgment: and I think also that I have the Spirit of God.

## CHAPTER 8

NOW as touching things offered unto idols, we know that we all have knowledge. Knowledge puffeth up, but charity edifieth.

2. And if any man think that he knoweth any thing, he knoweth nothing yet as he ought to know.

everything, as far as possible, is to be in subjection to His interests. The word **giveth in marriage** (v. 38) always has this sense in the NT (cf. Mt 22:30; 24:38); it never means simply *to marry,* which appears to clinch the interpretation just given as being the true one.

3) The Postscript. 7:39,40. Widows are granted **liberty to be married,** but only **in the Lord,** i.e., to Christians. This seems to indicate clearly that Paul would never have approved of mixed marriages (marriages between believers and unbelievers), a truth which has a wide application today. Paul reverts again to utility, however, when he writes **but she is happier if she so abide** (cf. v. 8). The concluding words appear to indicate that Paul thought his words here had divine approval (the **also** may point to some in Corinth who claimed the Spirit's approval for their unscriptural attitudes); and the fact that they have been preserved in Holy Writ may confirm this viewpoint.

B. The Counsel Concerning Things Sacrificed to Idols. 8:1–11:1.

The *peri de* (AV, *Now as touching*) indicates that a new subject begins here. **Things offered unto idols** were the remainders of animals sacrificed to heathen gods. Whether an animal was offered as a private or a public sacrifice, portions of the meat remained for the offerer. If offered as a private sacrifice, the flesh might be used for a banquet, to which were invited friends of the offerer. If offered as a public sacrifice, the meat left after the magistrates took what they wanted might be sold to the markets for resale to the people of the city. The problems, then, were these: (1) Might a Christian partake of meat offered to a false god in a heathen feast? (2) Might a Christian buy and eat flesh offered to idols? (3) Might a Christian, when invited to the home of a friend, eat flesh which had been offered to idols?

1) The Principles. 8:1-13. Paul first sets forth general principles to guide the believer in these ticklish problems.

1. **We all have knowledge** may be a quotation from their letter to him. Christians do possess knowledge, but it may be only superficial and incomplete (cf. vv. 2,7). **Knowledge,** in addition, is not sufficient for the solution of all problems, for by itself it **puffeth up. 2. He know-**

3. But if any man love God, the same is known of him.

4. As concerning therefore the eating of those things that are offered in sacrifice unto idols, we know that an idol *is* nothing in the world, and that *there is* none other God but one.

5. For though there be that are called gods, whether in heaven or in earth, (as there be gods many, and lords many,)

6. But to us *there is but* one God, the Father, of whom *are* all things, and we in him; and one Lord Jesus Christ, by whom *are* all things, and we by him.

7. Howbeit *there is* not in every man that knowledge: for some with conscience of the idol unto this hour eat *it* as a thing offered unto an idol; and their conscience being weak is defiled.

8. But meat commendeth us not to God: for neither, if we eat, are we the better; neither, if we eat not, are we the worse.

9. But take heed lest by any means this liberty of yours become a stumblingblock to them that are weak.

10. For if any man see thee which hast knowledge sit at meat in the idol's temple, shall not the conscience of him which is weak be emboldened to eat those things which are offered to idols;

11. And through thy knowledge shall the weak brother perish, for whom Christ died?

eth nothing yet refers to the true knowledge of God. While here, man's knowledge of God is always incomplete (cf. 13:12). 3. To love God brings both a knowledge of God and a sense of God's knowledge of the individual. For example, in a palace everyone knows the king, but not everyone is known by the king. The second stage would indicate personal intimacy and consequent firsthand knowledge (cf. Godet, *op. cit.*, I, 410; Gal 4:9).

4. An idol is nothing in the world probably should be *there is no idol in the world.* An idol cannot really be a representation of God. How could wood or stone represent God's incorruptibility? 5. The apostle admits, however, that there are those called gods. 6. But to us marks a forceful contrast. Of whom are all things refers to the first creation; the Father is the source of all (cf. Gen 1:1). We in him (lit., *we for him*) refers to the Father as the goal of the new creation, the Church. The Church's function is to glorify him. By whom are all things points to the Lord Jesus Christ as the agent of God in creation (cf. Jn 1:3). We by him presents him as the agent responsible for the new creation (cf. Col 1:15-18).

7. From here to the end of the chapter Paul expounds the words, love builds up (v. 1; AV, *charity edifieth*). This is necessary, for not in every man is the knowledge of the one God and one Lord, which enables one to eat idol flesh without harm. With conscience of the idol has weak attestation. The preferable reading is *by reason of being long accustomed to idols.* 8. Paul points out that meat in itself will not bring believers near to God. Commendeth. The sense is *bring near.* "It is the clean heart, and not clean food, that will matter; and the weak brother confounds the two" (ICC, p. 170).

9. In the next few verses Paul warns the strong to take heed that their liberty (lit., *authority,* the exercise of their right) does not prove a stumbling block to the weak. In other words, knowledge will not solve the problem (cf. vv. 1-3). 10. Be emboldened (lit., *be built up*) is ironic. Fine edification this is; it builds up to sin!

11. And (lit., *for*) introduces the reason why the strong believer has become a stumbling block. The sentence should be punctuated with a period, not a question mark. The last clause has great appeal. If Christ loved the brother

**12.** But when ye sin so against the brethren, and wound their weak conscience, ye sin against Christ.

**13.** Wherefore, if meat make my brother to offend, I will eat no flesh while the world standeth, lest I make my brother to offend.

### CHAPTER 9

AM I not an apostle? am I not free? have I not seen Jesus Christ our Lord? are not ye my work in the Lord?

enough to die for him, then the strong believer ought to love him enough to give up his right to eat certain meat. **Perish** refers to bodily perishing, not eternal perishing. The weak brother, persistently violating his conscience by eating something he thinks he should not, sins and makes himself liable to sin unto death (cf. 5:5; 11:30; I Jn 5:16,17). The tense is present; the process of perishing is going on as long as he persists in eating. **12.** The worst consequence of this matter is that the strong believers **sin against Christ** in sinning against the brethren. The argument is based on the unity of the body of Christ (cf. 12:12, 13,26).

**13. Wherefore** leads to Paul's conclusion. *Love,* not *light* (knowledge), solves the problem. On moral matters, about which the Word has spoken, the Word is supreme. On morally indifferent matters, such as eating meat offered to idols, liberty is to be regulated by love. Several things must be kept in mind, however. In the first place, the passage does not refer to legalists desirous of imposing their narrow-minded scruples on others. Such are not weak brethren, but willful brethren desirous of glorying in the subjection of others to their tenets (cf. Gal 6:11-13). This is tyranny, and Christianity must always be on guard against this. In the second place, it should be noted in this verse that the decision to follow the path of love rests with Paul, not with the weak. The strong are to yield to love's appeal voluntarily, not because the weak demand it (legalists always demand subjection to their laws). Finally, it is significant that Paul, in dealing with fornication and meat sacrificed to idols, does not appeal to the decree of the Jerusalem Council (cf. Acts 15:19, 20). Instead, he appeals to loftier spiritual concepts, which the Greeks would appreciate.

2) *The Illustration of the Principles.* 9:1-27. Paul does not diverge from the subject here. Rather, he illustrates the principles just set forth by an appeal to his own experience. As an apostle and one who also possessed Christian liberty, he could claim financial support from those to whom he preached (vv. 1-14). Actually, however, he refused to exercise his rights in order to gain a reward (vv. 15-23). Such a decision demanded personal discipline and privation (vv. 24-27). The Corinthians, of course, were to apply the lesson of self-denial and

2. If I be not an apostle unto others, yet doubtless I am to you: for the seal of mine apostleship are ye in the Lord.

3. Mine answer to them that do examine me is this:

4. Have we not power to eat and to drink?

5. Have we not power to lead about a sister, a wife, as well as other apostles, and *as* the brethren of the Lord, and Cephas?

6. Or I only and Barnabas, have not we power to forbear working?

7. Who goeth a warfare any time at his own charges? who planteth a vineyard, and eateth not of the fruit thereof? or who feedeth a flock, and eateth not of the milk of the flock?

8. Say I these things as a man? or saith not the law the same also?

9. For it is written in the law of Moses, Thou shalt not muzzle the mouth of the ox that treadeth out the corn. Doth God take care for oxen?

10. Or saith he *it* altogether for our sakes? For our sakes, no doubt, *this* is written: that he that ploweth should plow in hope; and that he that thresheth in hope should be partaker of his hope.

discipline to the problem of meat sacrificed to idols.

**1. Am I not free?** This question precedes the question regarding apostleship in the leading manuscripts. There is an appropriateness in this order, too, for the advance from rights as a Christian to rights as an apostle provides a climactic opening of the section. **Have I not seen Jesus our Lord?** The basis of his qualification for the apostolate (cf. Acts 1:21,22). **Are not ye my work in the Lord?** Words designed to emphasize the genuineness of Paul's work among the Corinthians. **2,3.** The Corinthians were **the seal** of his apostleship. That is, they were the guarantee of spiritual fruit in his labors among them, or, in other words, the proof that God really "gave the increase" (cf. 3:5-7). **Them that examine me.** Those who questioned Paul's apostolic position and office. **This** looks backward (vv. 1-3), not forward (vv. 4-14).

**4.** Having settled the matter of apostleship, the apostle goes on to argue the authority or right of support, which was derived from the office. Compare 8:9, where the AV's "liberty" is the same word as **right** (AV, *power*) here. **To eat and drink** does not refer to idol meats, but to ordinary food and drink.

**5,6.** Five grounds for the right of maintenance can be discerned. The first, referred to here, might be called the example of others. **The brethren of the Lord,** who did not believe on him, were now missionaries (cf. Jn 7:5; Mt 13:55). The mention of **Cephas'** wife is interesting. If Peter was the first pope (he was *not,* of course), it is clear that he was a married one! (cf. Mt 8:14) Paul's right included support of his family. **7.** The second, the principle of common right, is presented by means of well-known illustrations — the soldier, the vine-planter, and the shepherd.

**8-10.** The third ground, the teaching of the Scriptures, is now introduced (cf. Deut 25:4). Paul claims that the OT teaches the right of maintenance for those who preach the Word. His use of Scripture here has often been impugned. It has been said that he shows disdain for the literal sense of the OT (cf. MNT, pp. 116,117). That is not true. All that Paul claims is that the passage in Deuteronomy has a deeper significance than the literal sense. Both senses, the literal and the allegorical (both are *spiritual* senses), are found in this passage. **Doth God take care for oxen?** The literal sense

11. If we have sown unto you spiritual things, *is it* a great thing if we shall reap your carnal things?

12. If others be partakers of *this* power over you, *are* not we rather? Nevertheless we have not used this power; but suffer all things, lest we should hinder the gospel of Christ.

13. Do ye not know that they which minister about holy things live *of the things* of the temple? and they which wait at the altar are partakers with the altar?

14. Even so hath the Lord ordained that they which preach the gospel should live of the gospel.

15. But I have used none of these things: neither have I written these things, that it should be so done unto me: for *it were* better for me to die, than that any man should make my glorying void.

16. For though I preach the gospel, I have nothing to glory of: for necessity is laid upon me; yea, woe is unto me, if I preach not the gospel!

17. For if I do this thing willingly, I have a reward: but if against my will, a dispensation *of the gospel* is committed unto me.

of the question must not be pressed. The Greek construction is such that the answer, "No," is expected. Paul means that God's care is not primarily for animals, but for men. However, God's care for animals is affirmed in many passages in the OT (cf. Ps 104:14,21,27; Mt 6:26). Luther's argument was bolder than Paul's. He said the passage in Deuteronomy was written altogether for our sakes, since oxen cannot read! The word **altogether** here probably has the sense of *doubtless* (ICC, p. 184).

**11-13.** The right of holy ministry, the fourth ground, is set forth here, and the argument turns on the greater value of the spiritual over the material. **Carnal things** are things for the body, the word carnal having here a neutral sense. **This power over you** is the teacher's privilege of partaking of the believers' material things. Apparently certain teachers had exercised their right over the Corinthians. But Paul triumphantly boasts that **we have not used this power.** His taking financial help might have **hinder**[ed] **the gospel of Christ,** for some might have thought he preached only for this. **Partakers with the altar** alludes to the rights of the priests of the old covenant (cf. Num 18:8-24). **14.** The command of the Lord, a fifth ground, concludes the claim to support from the church (cf. Mt 10:10; Lk 10:7).

**15.** The apostle now shows how love acted in his case, even though he had a perfect right to support from the Corinthians: He thus contrasts his personal sacrifice with the selfishness of those who were using their liberty in the matter of meats to the detriment of others. **But** marks the contrast, and the change to the first person marks the personal illustration, the illustration of knowledge regulated by love. **16.** The readers are led on to Paul's purpose in preaching without pay — namely, he desired a reward. **Necessity is laid upon me** refers to the call on the Damascus Road, a call he could not refuse.

**17. For if I do this thing willingly** introduces a supposition that could never be true of Paul. Thus, in his case there could be no reward for preaching, for he preached by necessity. The clue to Paul's argument is found in the expression, **a dispensation of the gospel is committed unto me.** A *stewardship* (AV, **dispensation**) was a work committed to one under an owner. The steward, therefore, was of the class of slaves (cf. Lk 12:42, 43). And a slave received no recom-

18. What is my reward then? *Verily* that, when I preach the gospel, I may make the gospel of Christ without charge, that I abuse not my power in the gospel.

19. For though I be free from all *men*, yet have I made myself servant unto all, that I might gain the more.

20. And unto the Jews I became as a Jew, that I might gain the Jews; to them that are under the law, as under the law, that I might gain them that are under the law;

21. To them that are without law, as without law, (being not without law to God, but under the law to Christ,) that I might gain them that are without law.

22. To the weak became I as weak, that I might gain the weak: I am made all things to all *men*, that I might by all means save some.

23. And this I do for the gospel's sake, that I might be partaker thereof with *you*.

pense; he had to work (cf. Lk 17:10). Paul, therefore, had to introduce the idea of preaching without pay. As Moffatt puts it, "His pay was to do it without pay" (*op. cit.*, p. 121). This is the way the apostle gained his reward. Thus, *light* is regulated by *love*. **18.** To proclaim the gospel of Christ without charge was his aim and the means of his reward. This, of course, is not a principle to be applied to all preachers of the Gospel. It is the voluntary choice of one who, although having a right to support, was compelled to proclaim the truth through a supernatural vision of the ascended Saviour.

**19.** Paul now adds other ways in which, for the sake of others, he refused to exercise his rights. **Free from all** refers to his lack of dependence on others in any way (cf. v. 1).

**20.** The principle that Paul espoused was mobility in methods, not mobility in morals. After the words **as under the law**, the Greek text adds, **though not being myself under law**, a remarkable statement which emphasizes how completely Paul had broken with the Law of Moses. It is difficult to find a stronger statement of this fact anywhere in his writings. **21. Them that are without law** refers to the Gentiles. **Being not without law to God, but under the law to Christ** is added to prevent misunderstanding. While Paul was not under law, he did not become an outlaw, or lawless. The law of love for Christ is a stronger motivation toward righteousness than the fear of the judgments of Sinai. Those who, while not under the Mosaic Law, walk by the Spirit of God with love toward the Lord Jesus Christ will fulfill the righteous requirement of the Law (cf. Rom 8:3; Gal 5:16-23).

**22. The weak** are the over-scrupulous referred to in 8:7, 9-12. Paul never strays far from the general subject of meats sacrificed to idols. **I am made all things to all men** expresses his principle. (The verb here is in the perfect tense, not aorist as in verse 20, expressing the permanent result of his past action). It is not the end justifying the means, but adaptability because of love within the Word. *Save* is stronger than **gain** (v. 19). *That I might . . . save some* does not remove salvation from the hands of God; it merely emphasizes the human cooperation of God's servant in the ministry of the truth.

**23. For the gospel's sake** does not mean in order to advance the Gospel, but be-

**24.** Know ye not that they which run in a race run all, but one receiveth the prize? So run, that ye may obtain.

**25.** And every man that striveth for the mastery is temperate in all things. Now they *do it* to obtain a corruptible crown; but we an incorruptible.

**26.** I therefore so run, not as uncertainly; so fight I, not as one that beateth the air:

**27.** But I keep under my body, and bring *it* into subjection: lest that by any means, when I have preached to others, I myself should be a castaway.

cause of its preciousness to the apostle. Omit the **with you**, which concludes the verse.

**24.** Paul's decision demanded personal discipline. When a man refuses to discipline himself by always exercising his liberty to the detriment of the weak, he injures not only the weak, but also himself. This is the burden of the remaining verses (vv. 24-27). The background of the section is the great athletic spectacle, the Isthmian games, held every two years near Corinth. **The prize** indicates that the apostle had in mind service and rewards, not salvation and life (cf. v. 17, "reward"; Phil 3:11-14). **25.** After the illustration in verse 24, there follows the application, containing both a comparison and a contrast. **Is temperate.** *Practices self-restraint* (MNT, p. 125). Paul's point is that athletes who expect to win must train diligently — a truth well illustrated in today's athletic endeavors, whether track, baseball, or some other sport. **A corruptible crown** brings in the contrast. Athletes discipline themselves to win an insignificant prize (in the Isthmian games it was a wreath of pine). How much more ought Christians to win **an incorruptible** one (cf. II Tim 4:8; I Pet 5:4; Rev 2:10; 3:11). **26,27.** Paul's conclusion follows, introduced by **therefore.** Paul ran, but **not uncertainly;** he knew where he was going (cf. Phil 3:14). He was not like the little lad learning to ride a bicycle, who proudly shouted to his sister, "I'm moving. I really am moving." The sister, coldly observing his wobbly progress, replied, "Yes, you are moving, but you are not going!" **Beateth the air** is a boxing metaphor. The statement has no reference to shadowboxing, a necessary and legitimate boxer's exercise; it has to do with wild misses during the actual contest. Paul was an accurate puncher, always on the mark. **I keep under my body** is the rendering of the text of a few weak manuscripts. The better attested reading is *buffet,* or *maul* (RSV has *pommel*). The thought, of course, is that of personal discipline. Walking with God demands personal sacrifice, sacrifice of things not necessarily evil, but which prevent the full devotion of the soul to God — such as, pleasures and worldly pursuits. In an age of luxury, like the present time, the words have real significance for the serious-minded servant of Christ. **I have preached to others.** A reference to the custom of having the competitors sum-

### CHAPTER 10

MOREOVER, brethren, I would not that ye should be ignorant, how that all our fathers were under the cloud, and all passed through the sea;

2. And were all baptized unto Moses in the cloud and in the sea;

3. And did all eat the same spiritual meat;

moned to the race by a herald (a *kēryx*, derived from the same root as the word **preached**). Paul summoned many to the race of the Christian life through the Gospel. He did not want to become a **castaway** after that. The word has no reference to loss of salvation. It means literally *disapproved*. Clearly the apostle was concerned lest he be rejected by the umpire for the prize. He had no fear of the herald's barring him from participation in the race. All run, but not all receive the prize; Paul wanted to win the prize.

3) The Admonition and Application to the Corinthians. 10:1–11:1. Paul concludes his discussion of meats offered to idols with admonition (vv. 1-13) and application (10:14–11:1). In the application he deals with participation in heathen religious festivals (vv. 14-22), with the eating of meat sold in the market place (vv. 23-26), and with the eating of meat in a private home (10:27–11:1).

**1.** The AV's **moreover** obscures an intimate connection that exists between chapter 9 and chapter 10. The Greek text has *for*. The writer has emphasized the need of personal discipline and the possibility of failure in the realm of rewards for the undisciplined. To show the reality of the possibility, he uses the nation Israel as an illustration of failure, and with this illustration he admonishes the Corinthians to "take heed" lest they fall also. Israel was **disapproved!** (9:27)

But first Paul must enumerate the Jews' advantages. **All**, repeated five times, emphasizes the universality in Israel of divine blessing, and, when considered with the fact that almost all (Caleb and Joshua excepted) perished, links this section very closely with 9:24. There Paul said, "Know ye not that they which run in a race run **all**, but **one** receiveth the prize?" **Were under the cloud** points to prolonged supernatural guidance (cf. Ex 13:21,22; 14:19; Mt 28:20). **Passed through the sea** points to a supernatural deliverance, the second privilege (cf. Ex 14:15-22; I Pet 1:18-20). **2. Baptized unto Moses**, their third privilege, refers to their union with their leader, who under God provided them with supernatural leadership (cf. Ex 14:31; Rom 6:1-10). **3. Did . . . eat the same spiritual meat.** The eating of the manna, "angels' food" (Ps 78:25), was the nation's fourth privilege. The people partook of supernatural food (cf. Ex

4. And did all drink the same spiritual drink; for they drank of that spiritual Rock that followed them: and that Rock was Christ.

5. But with many of them God was not well pleased: for they were overthrown in the wilderness.

6. Now these things were our examples, to the intent we should not lust after evil things, as they also lusted.

7. Neither be ye idolaters, as *were* some of them; as it is written, The people sat down to eat and drink, and rose up to play.

8. Neither let us commit fornication, as some of them committed, and fell in one day three and twenty thousand.

16:1-36; I Pet 2:1-3). **Spiritual** probably has the sense of *supernatural* (cf. ICC, p. 200).

**4. The same spiritual drink,** a fifth privilege, refers to the events mentioned in Ex 17:1-9 and Num 20:1-13 (cf. Num 21:16). The words **that spiritual rock that followed them** do not mean that Paul believed the rabbinical legend that a material rock followed the Israelites throughout their journey and that Miriam, above all others, possessed the secret of obtaining the water (cf. Godet, *op. cit.*, II, 56). Actually, the apostle says, **that Rock was Christ,** i.e., it was the visible means of the supply of water which came ultimately from Christ. Since the people of Israel obtained this water in the opening years of their wilderness wanderings (Ex 17:1-9) and in the closing years (Num 20:1-13), it is only natural to infer that he, Christ, the Supplier of the water, was with them all along the way. The literal sense of **that Rock was Christ** is no more to be pressed than is the literal sense of "I am the true vine" (Jn 15:1). The **was,** rather than *is,* may, however, point to Christ's pre-existence (cf. II Cor 8:9; Gal 4:4). Supernatural sustenance was Israel's fifth privilege. The parallel with the two ordinances of the Church may be intended.

**5.** One might think that such privileges must mean success. **But** introduces the sad contrast. Privileged people may experience divine displeasure. **With many** (RSV, *with most)* is an understatement; only Caleb and Joshua survived the displeasure. **Overthrown** may be rendered *strewn,* a vivid picture of a wilderness paved with bodies sated with angel's food and drink (cf. Num 14:29).

**6. Examples.** Probably the correct rendering of the Greek word *typoi;* not **types** in the technical sense (MNT, p. 131). The first reason for Israel's failure was that they **lusted** (cf. Num 11:4), preferring the food of the world, Egypt, to that of the Lord, the manna. **7.** They also became **idolaters,** the second cause for failure (cf. Ex 32:1-14, 30-35; I Jn 5:21). **8.** The third reason, **fornication,** is a reference to the incident involving Israel and the Moabite women (cf. Num 25:1-9). Immorality is always the natural consequence of idolatry (cf. Ps 115:8). **Three and twenty thousand** is not a mistake, although Moses wrote the number 24,000. Paul's **one day** should be noted. He refers to those slain by the plague in one day, while Moses' figure

9. Neither let us tempt Christ, as some of them also tempted, and were destroyed of serpents.

10. Neither murmur ye, as some of them also murmured, and were destroyed of the destroyer.

11. Now all these things happened unto them for ensamples: and they are written for our admonition, upon whom the ends of the world are come.

12. Wherefore let him that thinketh he standeth take heed lest he fall.

13. There hath no temptation taken you but such as is common to man: but God *is* faithful, who will not suffer you to be tempted above that ye are able; but will with the temptation also make a way to escape, that ye may be able to bear *it.*

14. Wherefore, my dearly beloved, flee from idolatry.

15. I speak as to wise men; judge ye what I say.

16. The cup of blessing which we bless, is it not the communion of the blood of Christ? The bread which we break, is it not the communion of the body of Christ?

includes the ones who died later from the effects.

9. Presumption, the fourth reason, is referred to by the words **tempt Christ** (cf. Num 21:4-9; Ps 78:19); they dared God to live up to his promise to discipline if they doubted his Word. This was the sin of "ungrateful suspicion" (MNT, p. 132). 10. **Murmured** introduces the fifth reason (cf. Num 16:41-50), and this may be a gentle Pauline allusion to the Corinthians' attitude to their own spiritual leaders in the matter of idol meats (the other four reasons can be linked with this problem).

11. While the events were **examples unto them,** the accounts of the events were **written for our admonition. The ends of the world** (lit., *the ages*) refers to the completion of the ages before the present one. Believers in this age are to reap the benefit of preceding ones (cf. ICC, p. 207).

12,13. Two final words conclude the admonitory section, the one for the self-assured, the strong who have no thought for the conscience of the weak (v. 12), and the other for the discouraged, who feel that the Christian life is so hard that they can never hope to survive its trials (v. 13). **Thinketh he standeth.** Written for the strong man who is using his liberty at the expense of the weak (8:9-13). **Fall.** Not from salvation, but into God's discipline, and thus become disapproved (9:27). **Common to man** is that which is incident to man (the Vulgate has *humana).* God does not treat believers as angels, or as demons, but as men (vv. 1-11). **But.** Better, *and;* the encouragement is continued. **Above that ye are able.** Not above that ye think ye are able! **A way to escape.** Literally, *the way out,* the suitable and necessary one. This is not an escape from temptation, nor simply a hope of strength to overcome in the future, but a present power to endure in the midst of temptation (cf. Heb 2:18), a glorious promise for the sorely tried.

14. **Wherefore.** *Dioper,* a strong conjunction, used in the NT only here and in 8:13. It introduces the application to the readers. Heathen religious festivals are considered first (10:14-22). **Flee from idolatry.** Literally, *Flee away from.* This command might surprise the ones who prided themselves on their liberty, but Paul commands the use of the way of escape immediately.

16. Partaking of a religious table, whether Christian (vv. 16,17), Jewish

17. For *being* many are one bread, *and* one body: for we are all partakers of that one bread.

18. Behold Israel after the flesh: are not they which eat of the sacrifices partakers of the altar?

19. What say I then? that the idol is any thing, or that which is offered in sacrifice to idols is any thing?

20. But *I say*, that the things which the Gentiles sacrifice, they sacrifice to devils, and not to God: and I would not that ye should have fellowship with devils.

21. Ye cannot drink the cup of the Lord, and the cup of devils: ye cannot be partakers of the Lord's table, and of the table of devils.

22. Do we provoke the Lord to jealousy? are we stronger than he?

23. All things are lawful for me, but all things are not expedient: all things are lawful for me, but all things edify not.

24. Let no man seek his own, but every man another's *wealth*.

25. Whatsoever is sold in the shambles, *that* eat, asking no question for conscience' sake:

26. For the earth *is* the Lord's, and the fulness thereof.

27. If any of them that believe not bid you *to a feast*, and ye be disposed to go; whatsoever is set before you, eat, asking no question for conscience' sake.

28. But if any man say unto you, This is offered in sacrifice unto idols, eat not for his sake that showed it, and for conscience' sake: for the earth *is* the Lord's, and the fulness thereof:

29. Conscience, I say, not thine own, but of the other: for why is my liberty judged of another *man's* conscience?

30. For if I by grace be a partaker, why am I evil spoken of for that for which I give thanks?

31. Whether therefore ye eat, or drink, or whatsoever ye do, do all to the glory of God.

32. Give none offense, neither to the Jews, nor to the Gentiles, nor to the church of God:

(v. 18), or heathen Gentile (vv. 19-21), involves fellowship in the being to whom the worship is directed. Therefore, a Christian must not partake of meat offered to idols in a pagan feast; there is no liberty here. **The communion** (lit., *communion;* there is no article in the Greek text). To partake is to share in, according to Paul. **17.** The apostle explains why (**For . . . for**) partaking signifies a share in, or union with, the deity. **18.** The example of Israel confirms the fellowship of the worshipers with the deity.

**19-21.** The example of Gentile festivals follows. **They sacrifice to demons** (ASV) does not mean that the idol is a deity after all. Rather, the writer means that, while idols and things sacrificed to them are nothing, yet they are used by demonic forces to lead men away from the true God (cf. Deut 32:17,21). **22.** Will the Corinthians **provoke the Lord** (*Christ* here, *Jehovah* in Deuteronomy) **to jealousy** as the fathers did? Can they risk his anger with impunity? (MNT, pp. 136,137)

**23.** Meat bought in shops is now considered. Paul repeats the general principle of liberty (cf. 6:12), subjecting it to the principle of benefit (**expedient**) and edification. **24.** This is the endeavor that builds up. **Wealth** (AV) is an archaism; *welfare* would be better today. **25,26.** Permission is here granted for eating any meat sold in the market (AV, *shambles*). No troubling of the conscience by the asking of questions about the meat is necessary.

**27.** Finally, the apostle considers the case of private dinner parties in the homes of unbelieving friends. The believers may **eat, asking no question for conscience sake. 28.** But if a "puritanic fellow guest" (MNT, p. 144) should nudge the believer and say, **This is offered in sacrifice to idols,** then he is to **eat not for his sake that shewed it.** In other words, the believer must voluntarily respect the weaker conscience. The quotation from Ps 24:1 is not in the better manuscripts. **29,30. For.** Paul explains the action. What good is there in his eating if it means his liberty is blamed? How can grace be said for that which offends a brother?

**31. Therefore** introduces the principle that is all-inclusive in the entire discussion. **The glory of God** is the ultimate aim. **32.** The good of others comes next, whether **Jews, Gentiles,** or **the church of God** (cf. Rom 14:21). Three separate

33. Even as I please all *men* in all *things*, not seeking mine own profit, but the *profit* of many, that they may be saved.

## CHAPTER 11

BE ye followers of me, even as I also *am* of Christ.

2. Now I praise you, brethren, that ye remember me in all things, and keep the ordinances, as I delivered *them* to you.

3. But I would have you know, that the head of every man is Christ; and the head of the woman *is* the man; and the head of Christ *is* God.

groups are in view. 33; 11:1. Paul concludes with the example of himself and the Lord. **Please** does not mean to curry favor, but to do that which is for men's **profit** (same root as **expedient**, v. 23). Our Lord is one who "pleased not himself" (Rom 15:3). This climactically concludes the discussion. The correct attitude in the matter, then, is liberty, the liberty of love for the Lord, for the truth, and for one's brother. Neither legality, nor license will do; conditioned liberty is the principle to follow.

C. The Counsel Concerning the Veiling of Women in Public Worship. 11:2-16.

In chapters 11 through 14 Paul turns to and discusses matters that concern primarily the public worship of the church. The section on spiritual gifts (12:1–14:40) was written in answer to a question from the church (cf. 12:1, *peri de*). The opening chapter is the result of personal report (11:18). The first matter for discussion is the veiling, or covering, of the heads of women, and Paul's ruling is that women must cover their heads during the meeting. He regarded the Corinthian innovation (apparently some were present in the meetings bareheaded) as "irreligious rather than indecorous" (MNT, p. 150), thus showing that his objections have nothing to do with social custom. (Some commentators have appealed to social custom in order to do away with Paul's decision here.) The worship meeting alone is in view. The apostle advances several reasons for his viewpoint.

1) The Theological Reason. 11:2-6. Paul first points out that in God's order the woman is under the man. This does not, of course, imply inequality of the sexes (cf. Gal 3:28; Eph 1:3). Subordination does not necessarily involve inequality. Headship is not the same as lordship. The clue to the standing of the sexes is found in the last words of I Cor 11:3. Man is head over the woman as the Father is head over the Son. There are four orders in the Word — personal, family, ecclesiastical, and governmental. Truth relative to each must be carefully distinguished.

2. **I praise you.** A general word of commendation, which sets the stage for particular failures. **Ordinances** (RSV, *traditions*). Oral teaching.

3. **The head of the woman is the man.**

4. Every man praying or prophesying, having *his* head covered, dishonoreth his head.

5. But every woman that prayeth or prophesieth with *her* head uncovered dishonoreth her head: for that is even all one as if she were shaven.

6. For if the woman be not covered, let her also be shorn: but if it be a shame for a woman to be shorn or shaven, let her be covered.

7. For a man indeed ought not to cover *his* head, forasmuch as he is the image and glory of God: but the woman is the glory of the man.

8. For the man is not of the woman; but the woman of the man.

9. Neither was the man created for the woman; but the woman for the man.

10. For this cause ought the woman to have power on *her* head because of the angels.

11. Nevertheless neither is the man without the woman, neither the woman without the man, in the Lord.

12. For as the woman *is* of the man, even so *is* the man also by the woman; but all things of God.

13. Judge in yourselves: is it comely that a woman pray unto God uncovered?

The theological basis for the wearing of a covering. Man's headship goes back to Gen 3:16. **4.** The man, too, has an order to follow; **his head** must not be **covered.** Men must not preach with their hats on! **5. Prayeth or prophesieth** does not mean that Paul approved these actions by women in public worship. Rather, he was simply referring to what was going on at Corinth unauthorized (cf. 14:34,35). **Her head.** The woman's physical head, not her husband. **6. Let her also be shorn.** A disgrace for a woman. Paul's ironical words to the rebellious. He is saying, "Make the reproach complete, then."

2) The Biblical Reasons. 11:7-12. The facts of creation (vv. 7-9,12,13) and the presence of angels at worship (v. 10) are brought forward.

**7. He is** (probably, *represents,* as in v. 25) **the image and glory of God.** This looks back to Gen 1:26,27. The male displays the authority of God on earth (cf. MNT, p. 151). **8,9.** The two prepositions **of** and **for** reveal the place of the woman. She has her origin and purpose of life in the man (cf. Gen 2:21-25). Every woman taking a new name at her marriage ceremony tacitly affirms the Pauline teaching. **10. Power,** or authority, means, by an unusual metonymy, sign of authority. The veil is the sign of the man's authority. The word for **angels** in the expression **because of the angels** does not refer to elders (cf. Rev 2:1. The same word refers to angels in I Cor 4:9). Nor does it refer to evil angels (cf. Gen 6:1-4). It refers to the good angels who are present in worship meetings, since they live in the presence of God (cf. I Cor 4:9; Lk 15:7,10; Eph 3:10; I Tim 5:21; Ps 138:1). The insubordination of women in refusing to acknowledge the authority of their husbands would offend the angels who, under God, guard the created universe (cf. Col 1:16; Eph 1:21), and know no insubordination.

**11,12.** Paul gives the other side of the truth here. The man and the woman are necessary for each other **in the Lord;** in fact, the man must always remember that he exists **by the woman.** And both are **of God.**

3) The Physical Reason. 11:13-16. Impropriety, based upon nature itself, argues for the covering. The word **comely** refers to a necessity founded upon an inner fitness of things (cf. Heb

14. Doth not even nature itself teach you, that, if a man have long hair, it is a shame unto him?

15. But if a woman have long hair, it is a glory to her: for *her* hair is given her for a covering.

16. But if any man seem to be contentious, we have no such custom, neither the churches of God.

17. Now in this that I declare *unto you* I praise *you* not, that ye come together not for the better, but for the worse.

18. For first of all, when ye come together in the church, I hear that there be divisions among you; and I partly believe it.

2:10; Mt 3:15). It is better rendered *proper*.

**14,15.** The fact of short hair for men and long hair for women is a divine suggestion in **nature itself** that the man and the woman are to heed in their dress in the assembly. The words **her hair is given her for a covering** do not mean that the woman's hair *is* her covering and that she needs no veil, a view vitiating the force of 11:2-14. The word **for** is to be rendered *answering to* (cf. Ellicott, *op. cit.*, p. 208).

**16. No such custom,** i.e., no custom of women worshiping without coverings. Some say that the custom was peculiar to Corinth, but Paul's words, **neither the churches of God,** argue against this view. Still others insist that the custom is not to be applied today (cf. Morris, *op. cit.*, p. 156; Barclay, *op. cit.*, p. 110). It should be noted, however, that each of the reasons given for the wearing of a veil is taken from permanent facts, lasting as long as the present earthly economy (cf. Godet, *op. cit.*, II, 133). Paul did carry his point, for early church history bears witness that in Rome, Antioch, and Africa the custom became the norm. A final word: In the final analysis, the hat, or veil, is not the important thing, but the subordination for which it stands. The presence of both is the ideal.

D. The Counsel Concerning the Lord's Supper. 11:17-34.

The Lord's Supper, the only act of worship for which Christ gave special direction, receives Paul's attention now. It is connected with the previous section by the fact that both matters concern public worship. It may help in reconstructing the situation to realize that in the early church the Supper was usually preceded by a fellowship meal, called the *Agape,* or Love Feast (cf. Jude 12). Disorders at the *Agape* called forth the apostle's indignation (vv. 17-22), a review of past teaching (vv. 23-26), and a stern application of the truth to the Corinthian assembly (vv. 27-34).

1) The Indignation of Paul. 11:17-22. The fellowship meal was primarily religious, not social, but abuses had made it a disgraceful farce.

**17. This** refers to the following instruction. Their meetings were **for the worse,** because they were incurring judgment as a result of the disorders (cf. v. 29). **18. Divisions.** Better, *parties.*

19. For there must be also heresies among you, that they which are approved may be made manifest among you.

20. When ye come together therefore into one place, *this* is not to eat the Lord's supper.

21. For in eating every one taketh before *other* his own supper: and one is hungry, and another is drunken.

22. What! have ye not houses to eat and to drink in? or despise ye the church of God, and shame them that have not? What shall I say to you? shall I praise you in this? I praise *you* not.

23. For I have received of the Lord that which also I delivered unto you, That the Lord Jesus, the *same* night in which he was betrayed, took bread:

24. And when he had given thanks, he brake *it*, and said, Take, eat; this is my body, which is broken for you: this do in remembrance of me.

25. After the same manner also *he took* the cup, when he had supped, saying, This cup is the new testament in my blood: this do ye, as oft as ye drink *it*, in remembrance of me.

These existed apparently because the rich, contrary to custom, greedily consumed their more bountiful provisions before all the poor came, so that they would not have to share their food in visible representation of the unity of the body. **19. Heresies.** *Factions,* groups with self-chosen views, is the emphasis and meaning of the word. These existed, Paul remarks somewhat resignedly, in order that the **approved** (cf. 9:27; 11:28) might be recognized.

**20.** It was a supper, but it was not **the Lord's** (the adjective is emphatic) **supper**; that is, it was not a real re-enactment of the Last Supper. **21,22.** The indignant question, **Have ye not houses to eat and to drink in?** was addressed to those who regarded the gathering simply as a social banquet and not as a spiritual fellowship meal.

2) The Review of Past Instruction. 11:23-26. The apostle justifies his rebuke by reviewing the real and true significance of the ordinance, tracing the teaching back to the Lord himself.

**23.** Paul could not praise them, **for** their conduct disagreed with that which he had received **of the Lord** (RSV, *from the Lord*). He does not make clear whether he received his instruction directly from the Lord or through a source. The latter is probable.

**24.** The words **take, eat,** and the word **broken,** occurring in the AV, do not appear in the best manuscripts. The bread is distributed first, since it represents the incarnation. Then the wine follows, representing the death that ends the old covenant and establishes the new. One thing is sure: in the words, **this is my body,** Paul is not teaching transubstantiation. The bread certainly was not the Lord's body at the moment he said this, nor is the cup the new covenant literally (v. 25). The word **is** has the common sense of "represents" (cf. v. 7; Jn 8:12; 10:9; I Cor 10:4), "as [the] German has it, not *'das ist,'* but *'das heiszt'*" (MNT, p. 168). **For you** emphasizes the sacrificial aspect. **In remembrance** involves more than just memory; the word suggests an active calling to mind. And the phrase **of me** is wider than *of my death*. The person who did the work is the object of the calling to mind. The present imperative **do** suggests that frequent attendance at the Lord's Supper is a divine command (cf. Acts 20:7).

**25. The new covenant** reminds the

26. For as often as ye eat this bread, and drink this cup, ye do show the Lord's death till he come.

27. Wherefore whosoever shall eat this bread, and drink *this* cup of the Lord, unworthily, shall be guilty of the body and blood of the Lord.

28. But let a man examine himself, and so let him eat of *that* bread, and drink of *that* cup.

29. For he that eateth and drinketh unworthily, eateth and drinketh damnation to himself, not discerning the Lord's body.

30. For this cause many *are* weak and sickly among you, and many sleep.

31. For if we would judge ourselves, we should not be judged.

32. But when we are judged, we are chastened of the Lord, that we should not be condemned with the world.

hearer of the old Mosaic covenant, which could only condemn. The Greek *diathēkē* in contrast to *synthēkē*, the usual OT word for "covenant," emphasizes the initiative of God in it. The new covenant provided an effective remission of sins. **In my blood** points to the sphere and basis of the covenantal blessings. Barclay's suggestive rendering is, "This cup is the new covenant and it cost my blood" (*op. cit.*, p. 114). The repetition of **in remembrance of me** is designed for the disorderly Corinthians; they needed to learn that *fellowship* with Christ, not *food,* was the important thing at the Supper.

**26. For** introduces the reason the Supper is continually repeated. It is an acted sermon, for it **proclaim**[s] (AV, *shew)* **the Lord's death.** The Supper has both a backward and a forward look, since it is to be observed **till he come** (cf. Mt 26:29).

3) The Application to the Corinthians. 11:27-34. Paul now applies the teaching to the disorderly believers.

**27. Wherefore** introduces the application, a consequence of the instruction. **Unworthily** does not refer to the person of the one partaking, but to the manner of his partaking. All are unworthy always. **Guilty of the body and blood of the Lord.** Guilty of sin against the body and blood. **28. But** introduces the proper alternative, self-judgment. There must be preparation before participation. **29. For.** The reason that self-judgment, or confession of sin, must precede the partaking is that otherwise the believer makes himself liable to **judgment** (the meaning of *krima;* the AV's *damnation* is misleading). Not **discerning** means not "rightly judging" (ICC, p. 252; the verb is found twice in v. 31). That is, the believer does not recognize the unity of **the body,** the Church (cf. 10:16,17; 11:20,21). **30.** Judgment had already come upon some **for this cause** — abuse of the Lord's Table. Some had committed sin unto death and already slept (the verb *koimaō,* **sleep,** when referring to death, always refers to the death of believers; cf. Jn 11:11,12; Acts 7:60; I Cor 15:6,18,20,51; I Thess 4:13,14, 15; II Pet 3:4). These believers had not lost their salvation, but they had lost the privilege of service on the earth. **31.** The preventive is to **judge ourselves** rightly. **32.** Even God's judgment, however, is not eternal; it is designed to be family discipline, a **chastening of the**

33. Wherefore, my brethren, when ye come together to eat, tarry one for another.

34. And if any man hunger, let him eat at home; that ye come not together unto condemnation. And the rest will I set in order when I come.

## CHAPTER 12

NOW concerning spiritual *gifts*, brethren, I would not have you ignorant.

Lord, to prevent condemnation with the world. Here Paul uses the strong *kata-krinō*, which does mean to condemn eternally. **33. Wherefore.** Concluding words follow, a practical appeal to the Corinthians to remember the unity of the body in their observance of the feast. **34. Condemnation** is incorrect. Read, instead, **judgment** (the word again is *krima*, as in v. 29). The rest of the details in connection with the Lord's Supper, Paul says, will be **set in order** at his next visit.

E. The Counsel Concerning Spiritual Gifts. 12:1–14:40.

With the familiar *peri de* (AV, "Now concerning") Paul refers to another question propounded by the Corinthians. The new subject, spiritual gifts, is linked, however, with the preceding section by the common relation to public worship. It is important to distinguish spiritual gifts from spiritual graces and spiritual offices. Spiritual graces are features of Christian character. Every believer is responsible for the development of all of them (cf. Gal 5:22,23). Spiritual offices are positions in the church for the administration of its affairs, whether spiritual oversight of the flock (elders) or spiritual oversight of temporalities (deacons; cf. I Tim 3:1-13). Only certain believers hold spiritual office. Spiritual gifts are divine enablements related to service in the local church, both unofficial and official service. Every believer possesses a spiritual gift, but not all believers possess the same gift (cf. I Cor 12:4-11). The church at Corinth, certainly no dead church, was in danger of abusing its privileges by an overemphasis on certain of the spectacular gifts. The apostle first sets forth the unity and diversity of the gifts (12:1-31 a), next the primacy of love over the seeking of gifts (12:31 b –13:13), and finally evaluation and regulation of the exercise of the gifts of prophecy and tongues (14:1-40).

1) The Validity of Utterance. 12:1-3. Paul gives the church an opening word of admonition to aid them in determining genuine spiritual utterance. The pagan background of the Corinthians would have been no help to them in this matter.

**1. Spiritual gifts** (lit., *the spiritual things*) does not refer to spiritual men (cf. F. W. Grosheide, *Commentary on*

2. Ye know that ye were Gentiles, carried away unto these dumb idols, even as ye were led.

3. Wherefore I give you to understand, that no man speaking by the Spirit of God calleth Jesus accursed: and *that* no man can say that Jesus is the Lord, but by the Holy Ghost.

4. Now there are diversities of gifts, but the same Spirit.

5. And there are differences of administrations, but the same Lord.

6. And there are diversities of operations, but it is the same God which worketh all in all.

7. But the manifestation of the Spirit is given to every man to profit withal.

8. For to one is given by the Spirit the word of wisdom; to another the word of knowledge by the same Spirit;

9. To another faith by the same Spirit; to another the gifts of healing by the same Spirit;

10. To another the working of miracles; to another prophecy; to another discerning of spirits; to another *divers* kinds of tongues; to another the interpretation of tongues:

the First Epistle to the Corinthians, p. 278, although Grosheide himself does not hold this view); nor simply to the spirituals (G. Campbell Morgan, *The Corinthian Letters of Paul,* pp. 145,146). The word gifts in verse 4, as well as Paul's words in 14:1 (the neuter gender should be noted), support the supplying of the word gifts (AV; RSV). 2,3. Wherefore, because of their need of instruction, they are to understand, that no man speaking by the Spirit of God calleth Jesus accursed (the negative criterion): and that no man can say that Jesus is the Lord, but by the Holy Ghost (the positive criterion). The apostle, of course, refers to utterance that comes from the heart (cf. Mt 26:22,25).

2) The Unity of the Gifts. 12:4-11. After the short digression Paul looks first at the unity of the gifts, a unity of source and purpose.

4-6. Gifts. Greek *charismatōn,* connected with the word *charis,* "grace," has been rendered grace-gifts not inappropriately. The word is used here in its technical sense of spiritual gifts. Viewed (1) as from the Spirit, they are gifts; (2) as from the Lord, administrations, or services, to the assembly; (3) as from the Father, operations, or supernatural workings. 7. Given to every man distinguishes gift from office (cf. I Pet 4:10).

8-10. Certain of the gifts are now listed. 8. The word of wisdom, probably a temporary gift like apostleship, had to do with the communication of spiritual wisdom, such as is contained in the Epistles. It was necessary in the early days when the church possessed no NT. The word of knowledge had to do with truth of a more practical character (the practical sections of the Epistles); it, too, was a temporary gift. The Word of God is sufficient now. 9. Faith. Not to be confused with saving faith, the possession of every Christian. This is the faith that manifests itself in unusual deeds of trust (cf. 13:2). The faith of a George Mueller, or of a Hudson Taylor, would qualify. Gifts of healing. Not to be confused with the work of so-called divine healers today. This gift of healing provided restoration of life, which is beyond the power of 'divine healers' (cf. Acts 9:40; 20:9). The Word teaches *divine healing* according to a pattern (cf. Jas 5:14,15); it does not contemplate 'divine healers.' 10. Prophecy. The gift of *foretelling* and *forth-*

11. But all these worketh that one and the selfsame Spirit, dividing to every man severally as he will.

12. For as the body is one, and hath many members, and all the members of that one body, being many, are one body: so also *is* Christ.

13. For by one Spirit are we all baptized into one body, whether *we be* Jews or Gentiles, whether *we be* bond or free; and have been all made to drink into one Spirit.

14. For the body is not one member, but many.

15. If the foot shall say, Because I am not the hand, I am not of the body; is it therefore not of the body?

16. And if the ear shall say, Because I am not the eye, I am not of the body; is it therefore not of the body?

17. If the whole body *were* an eye, where *were* the hearing? If the whole *were* hearing, where *were* the smelling?

18. But now hath God set the members every one of them in the body, as it hath pleased him.

19. And if they were all one member, where *were* the body?

20. But now *are they* many members, yet but one body.

*telling* new revelation from God was also temporary, needed when the canon was incomplete. No further revelation is now needed; the proclamation and teaching of the completed revelation is the task of the church today. **Discerning of spirits** is now done by the Spirit through the Word. **Tongues** and **interpretations** were also temporary (see following discussion), having to do with known languages rather than with ecstatic utterance, although the question of speaking in tongues is a moot one.

**11. As he will.** The Spirit is the sovereign dispenser of the gifts. The words are a key to the following section, showing those apparently more favored in the gifts that there is no self-merit in them, and those less favored that there is no lack of importance for them (cf. Godet, *op. cit.*, II, 206).

3) The Diversity of the Gifts. 12:12-31 a. Using the illustration of the human body, Paul describes the relation of gifted believers to one another and to Christ in the Church, his body.

**12. For** introduces the explanation of the unity in diversity and diversity in unity of believers in the body. That Christ gives his name to the body is seen in the words **so also is Christ** (lit., *the Christ*). **13. For** gives the reason for the union, the baptism of the Spirit **into one body. By one Spirit** (lit., *in one Spirit;* cf. Mt 3:11; Lk 3:16; Acts 1:5) expresses the sphere of the union effected by baptism. **One body** is the end to which the act is directed (cf. ICC, p. 272). The aorist tense in **baptized** clearly indicates that the action is a past fact true of all believers (even the carnal Corinthians; cf. I Cor 3:1-3), never to be repeated. In fact, the baptism that unites to Christ is not to be sought; it has been wrought already for all. As a consequence of this union with Christ, believers **have been all made to drink into one Spirit.** Union with him necessarily involves the Spirit's indwelling.

**14-20.** The illustration of the body is developed in these verses, with emphasis upon the diversity of the members for the sake of the apparently inferior ones, who thought their gifts were not important. The key thought is: **The body is not one member, but many** (v. 14), and the members have been **set . . . in the body, as it pleased him** (v. 18). Hence, the seemingly inferior were not to envy the seemingly superior.

**21-24.** The dependent relation of the

21. And the eye cannot say unto the hand, I have no need of thee: nor again the head to the feet, I have no need of you.

22. Nay, much more those members of the body, which seem to be more feeble, are necessary:

23. And those *members* of the body, which we think to be less honorable, upon these we bestow more abundant honor; and our uncomely *parts* have more abundant comeliness.

24. For our comely *parts* have no need: but God hath tempered the body together, having given more abundant honor to that *part* which lacked:

25. That there should be no schism in the body; but *that* the members should have the same care one for another.

26. And whether one member suffer, all the members suffer with it; or one member be honored, all the members rejoice with it.

27. Now ye are the body of Christ, and members in particular.

28. And God hath set some in the church, first apostles, secondarily prophets, thirdly teachers, after that miracles, then gifts of healings, helps, governments, diversities of tongues.

29. *Are* all apostles? *are* all prophets? *are* all teachers? *are* all workers of miracles?

30. Have all the gifts of healing? do all speak with tongues? do all interpret?

31. But covet earnestly the best gifts: and yet show I unto you a more excellent way.

### CHAPTER 13

THOUGH I speak with the tongues of men and of angels, and have not charity, I am become *as* sounding brass, or a tinkling cymbal.

members comes to the fore here. Seemingly superior members (having the more spectacular gifts) must not disdain the seemingly inferior. Actually, Paul says, the uncomely parts of the human body have the most attention (by way of clothing), and according to this analogy the seemingly inferior can expect from God the same equalization of dignity in the one body, the Church. In fact, this is just what God has done, for he has tempered the body together. Tempered refers to the mingling of two elements so that they become a compound, such as wine and water (A-S, p. 245). The body is a unity.

25. That. The purpose of the unity is (negatively) that there be no schism (cf. 1:10; 11:18), or division, in the body; and (positively) that the members should have the same care one for another. 26. The natural results of the perfect blending of the members are fellow suffering and fellow rejoicing.

27. The body of Christ (lit., *body of Christ*; there is no definite article) does not refer to the local church at Corinth, for there are not *many* bodies, a thought contrary to the context. Rather, it points to the quality of the whole, which each of them individually helps to constitute (ICC, p. 277). 28. A further listing of the gifts, including several not found in verses 4-11. First, secondarily, and thirdly refer to rank, but the after that and then probably do not.

29,30. The questions refer the reader to 12:14,27. And in these verses Paul strikes a deathblow to the theory that speaking in tongues is the sign of the possession of the Spirit, for the answer "No" is expected to each question (cf. Greek). 31. The best gifts (lit., *the greater gifts*) refers to teaching, helps, etc. Tongues is significantly put at the end of the list. This inferior significance of tongues Paul will develop in chapter 14. In the meantime, he says he will describe a pursuit that is more important than the pursuit of any spiritual gift.

4) The Primacy of Love over Gifts. 12:31 b–13:13. The last clause of chapter 12 has been misunderstood. Many feel that Paul is here showing *how* the gifts are to be ministered, i.e., in love. However, the use of way (*hodos*) in the sense of "a road" instead of way (*tropos*) in the sense of "manner," and the statement of 14:1, indicate that Paul is, rather, pointing out a path of life superior to a life spent in the seeking and

**2.** And though I have *the gift of* prophecy, and understand all mysteries, and all knowledge; and though I have all faith, so that I could remove mountains, and have not charity, I am nothing.

**3.** And though I bestow all my goods to feed *the poor*, and though I give my body to be burned, and have not charity, it profiteth me nothing.

**4.** Charity suffereth long, *and* is kind; charity envieth not; charity vaunteth not itself, is not puffed up,

displaying of spiritual gifts. In a sense, then, there is a parenthesis in the argument, but a closely related one. The thought is this: In all your exercise in gifts, be sure to understand their proper place in the over-all scheme of things. Love is the pre-eminent thing (31 b– 13:3), containing noble properties (vv. 4-7), and it abides permanently (vv. 8-13). It provides the answer to the age-long question, What is the *summum bonum?*

**1. Tongues of men and of angels.** Probably the gift of tongues. **Charity.** Better, **love,** but it is a love that includes charity! **Sounding brass** (MNT, *noisy gong*). Paul's point is that power of expression is not determined by diction, phraseology, and style; it is determined by depth of heart. 2. The apostle ascends from tongues to **prophecy, knowledge,** and **faith** (cf. 12:8-10). **Love** is greater than **faith,** because the end is greater than the means (cf. Lk 9:54). **Nothing.** "Not *outheis,* nobody, but an absolute zero" (A. T. Robertson, *op. cit.,* IV, 177).

**3.** The thought moves from gifts to acts which seem to be expressions of love, one a great act of philanthropy and the other an act of martyrdom. Instead of **to be burned,** many good manuscripts have, *that I may glory.* But on the whole it seems that the AV rendering represents the genuine reading. There may be an allusion here to the Indian, Zarmano-chegas, who burned himself in public on a funeral pyre and had the inscription put on his monument in Athens, "Zarmano-chegas, an Indian from Bargosa, according to the traditional customs of the Indians, made himself immortal and lies here" (Barclay, *op. cit.,* p. 132). Such exhibitionism, or 'showboating,' as moderns would say, was just egoism. The spirit of self can be introduced into the greatest of human acts. This **profiteth nothing.**

**4-7.** A description of the nature of love, with its noble properties, follows. One might almost say that love is personified here, since the description is practically a description of the life and character of Jesus Christ. However, the picture is directly related to the Corinthians. The observance of the truths of this chapter, as will be noted in the following remarks, would have solved their problems. **Charity suffereth long, and is kind** may be a summary statement of the section, with the next eight qualities related to longsuffering and the next

5. Doth not behave itself unseemly, seeketh not her own, is not easily provoked, thinketh no evil;

6. Rejoiceth not in iniquity, but rejoiceth in the truth;

7. Beareth all things, believeth all things, hopeth all things, endureth all things.

8. Charity never faileth: but whether *there be* prophecies, they shall fail; whether *there be* tongues, they shall cease; whether *there be* knowledge, it shall vanish away.

9. For we know in part, and we prophesy in part.

10. But when that which is perfect is come, then that which is in part shall be done away.

four to kindness. **Envieth not** (MNT, *knows no jealousy*) is related to the attitude of the brethren who felt that their gifts were inferior (12:14-17). Love would have solved that problem. **Vaunteth not itself.** Literally, does not *play the braggart.* This is related to 12:21-26. **Puffed up** clearly points to the opening section of the book (1:10—4:21).

5. The words **doth not behave itself unseemly** are clearly related to several sections in the book (cf. 7:36; 11:2-16,17-34). **Seeketh not her own** would have been the answer to the problem of meats sacrificed to idols (cf. 8:1—11:1). **Is not easily provoked** is not strong enough; there is no *easily* in the Greek text. A translator with a short temper must have been responsible for the AV rendering! This property of love would have solved the problem of the lawsuits (cf. 6:1-11). **Thinketh no evil.** Or, *plots no evil.* 6. **Rejoiceth not in iniquity** suggests the problem of immorality and lack of discipline of it in 5:1-13.

7. **Believeth all things** does not include gullibility. It means, rather, that the believer is not to be suspicious. If, however, sin is evident, the believer must judge it and support its discipline. From this description of love, it is evident that Moffatt is right in saying, "The lyric is thus a lancet." Paul was probing into the open sore of sin in the Corinthian church with this beautiful description of the one thing, love, that would have met all the believers' problems.

8-13. In the remaining verses the permanence of love is expounded. Love, unlike the gifts of prophecy, tongues, and knowledge, never fails, nor ceases its activity. The AV is weak in verse 8, being guilty of rendering two different Greek words by the same English word **fail**, as well as one Greek word occurring twice by two different English words, **fail** and **vanish away.** Fortunately the sense is not greatly affected by the variations. The point of verse 8 is that there will come a time when the gifts mentioned will be done away with, or cease.

9. The **for** introduces the explanation of why the gifts will pass away. A time of perfected knowledge and prophecy is coming. 10. **That which is perfect** cannot be a reference to the completion of the canon of Scripture; otherwise we now, living in the age of the completed canon, would see more clearly than Paul

11. When I was a child, I spake as a child, I understood as a child, I thought as a child: but when I became a man, I put away childish things.

12. For now we see through a glass, darkly; but then face to face: now I know in part; but then shall I know even as also I am known.

13. And now abideth faith, hope, charity, these three; but the greatest of these is charity.

did (v. 9). Even the most self-satisfied and opinionated of theologians would hardly admit that. The coming of that which is perfect can only be a reference to the Lord's second coming. That event will mark the end of the exercise of prophecy, tongues, and knowledge. How then can one speak of these gifts as temporary? The following verse will answer the question.

11. It is extremely important to an understanding of Paul's thought to notice the force of the illustration he introduces at this point. The illustration is designed to show the character of the period between the two comings of Christ. With reference to these particular gifts, it may be likened to the growing up of a person from infancy to manhood. The special and spectacular gifts were necessary in the early stages of the growth of the true church (cf. Eph 4:7-16) for purposes of authentication (cf. Heb 2:3,4) and edification (I Cor 14:3) when there was no NT to give light. They were the 'baby talk' of the church. As history has abundantly verified, with the Word and growing maturity, there came to be no need for such gifts. Today it is questionable that there exists anywhere the Scriptural exercise of the three gifts referred to by Paul in this passage. I spake (lit., was speaking, or used to speak) possibly refers specifically to tongues, I understood to prophecy, and I thought to knowledge. One cannot be dogmatic about it, however. I put away childish things (lit., have put away, the perfect tense stressing the results of the action) looks ultimately to the coming of that which is perfect (v. 10).

12. For. Paul explains that the present time is the infant stage. Now might be rendered at the present moment (the word arti usually refers to the present time in contrast to past or future time). In the light of the fact that the Corinthians saw only darkly and in part through the exercise of the gifts, why should they have gloried so in that which was fragmentary?

13. Now (nuni refers to time generally without reference to other times, but here it may well be logical and not temporal, being rendered so then) Abideth faith, hope, and love. These virtues outlast the gifts and, consequently, are to be cultivated more earnestly. It is not true that "Faith will vanish into sight, Hope will be emptied in delight," for all abide eternally. How shall faith

### CHAPTER 14

FOLLOW after charity, and desire spiritual *gifts*, but rather that ye may prophesy.

and hope abide? Godet has hit upon the meaning: "The permanent essence of the creature is to have nothing of its own, to be eternally helpless and poor. . . . It is not once for all, it is continually that in eternity faith changes into vision and hope into possession. These two virtues, therefore, abide to live again unceasingly" (*op. cit.*, II, 261). Love is the **greatest** force in the universe, and its true source and clearest expression is Golgotha. One under the spell of that love cannot help singing, with adoration:

"Were the whole realm of nature mine,
    That were a present far too small;
Love so amazing, so divine,
    Demands my soul, my life, my all."

5) The Superiority of Prophecy, and the Public Worship of the Church. 14:1-36. Apparently a major cause of the disorder in the church involved the misuse of the gift of tongues. The apostle deals with the matter in this chapter. He affirms the superiority of prophecy to tongues (vv. 1-25), then adds directions for the exercise of the gifts (vv. 26-33) and for the regulation of the participation of women in the assembly meeting (vv. 34-36). A résumé and a conclusion follow (vv. 37-40).

No one who has investigated the nature of the gift of tongues would care to be dogmatic about the matter. The present exposition of this chapter follows the view that the gift of tongues was the ability to speak in known languages, not in ecstatic speech. (The AV's *unknown* is not found in the Greek text, which reads simply **tongues,** or **tongue,** as the case may be.) Most modern commentators take the view that the gift involved ecstatic speech (cf. MNT, pp. 206-225; Morris, *op. cit.*, pp. 172, 173, 190-198). There are some factors, however, which cast some doubt on the correctness of this interpretation.

In the first place, it seems clear that the speaking in tongues recorded in Acts was in known languages (cf. Acts 2:4, 8,11). In view of the fact that Luke was a close companion of Paul (he may even have been in Corinth) and wrote Acts after the Corinthian correspondence, it would seem logical for him to note the distinction between the phenomenon in Acts and that in Corinth, if any existed. In other words, I Corinthians should be interpreted by Acts, the unknown by the known, a good

2. For he that speaketh in an *unknown* tongue speaketh not unto men, but unto God: for no man understandeth *him;* howbeit in the spirit he speaketh mysteries.

3. But he that prophesieth speaketh unto men *to* edification, and exhortation, and comfort.

4. He that speaketh in an *unknown* tongue edifieth himself; but he that prophesieth edifieth the church.

5. I would that ye all spake with tongues, but rather that ye prophesied: for greater *is* he that prophesieth than he that speaketh with tongues, except he interpret, that the church may receive edifying.

hermeneutical principle. Furthermore, the terminology of Paul is identical with that of Luke in Acts, although Luke further defines his terminology. Paul uses the Greek word *glōssa,* meaning tongue; Luke uses this word and further defines it as being a *dialektos* (Acts 1:19; 2:6,8; 21:40; 22:2; 26:14), a word which in every case refers to a language of a nation or a region (cf. Arndt, p. 184). It is quite unlikely that the phenomena, described by the two writers in identical terms, would be dissimilar.

Finally, the intent of the gift was that it should be a sign to the Jews (I Cor 14:21,22), as prophesied in the OT (cf. Isa 28:11), as well as a suggestion regarding the method of fulfilling the commission of Acts 1:8. At Pentecost there was inaugurated a work of the Spirit that would reverse the curse of Babel (cf. Gen 11:1-9), when there occurred the confusion of [known] tongues. Thus, there was a double edge in the conferring of the gift. It was a sign to provoke the Jews (in every case of the occurrence of the gift in Acts, Jews were present; cf. Acts 2:4 ff.; 8:17,18; 10:46; 19:6), and a signal of a work of God which would unite the redeemed under the banner of King Messiah in his coming kingdom. To introduce ecstatic language into the picture only serves to introduce confusion in more ways than one. Additional points in support of the thesis that the tongues were known languages are set forth in the exposition of the section.

1. The opening verse, which contains no connecting particle, is a reaffirmation of the content of 12:31 b — 13:13 with a view to transition. **Follow after** (lit., *pursue)* is stronger than **desire.** It appears from this statement that, while spiritual gifts are sovereignly bestowed, they are not necessarily granted in every case at conversion. **Rather** points to Paul's evaluation of prophecy in contrast to tongues. Speaking in tongues does not build up (vv. 2-5), does not benefit without interpretation (vv. 6-15); in fact, only befuddles (vv. 16-19). **2. An unknown tongue** (lit., *a tongue).* The words **for no man understandeth him** refer to speaking in the tongue without an interpreter. **3-5.** The apostle's evaluation is clear. Prophecy is greater than tongues **except he interpret.** In the case of interpretation, the speaking in tongues assumed practically the character of prophecy. (Is this why the two are often

6. Now, brethren, if I come unto you speaking with tongues, what shall I profit you, except I shall speak to you either by revelation, or by knowledge, or by prophesying, or by doctrine?

7. And even things without life giving sound, whether pipe or harp, except they give a distinction in the sounds, how shall it be known what is piped or harped?

8. For if the trumpet give an uncertain sound, who shall prepare himself to the battle?

9. So likewise ye, except ye utter by the tongue words easy to be understood, how shall it be known what is spoken? for ye shall speak into the air.

10. There are, it may be, so many kinds of voices in the world, and none of them is without signification.

11. Therefore if I know not the meaning of the voice, I shall be unto him that speaketh a barbarian, and he that speaketh *shall be* a barbarian unto me.

12. Even so ye, forasmuch as ye are zealous of spiritual *gifts*, seek that ye may excel to the edifying of the church.

13. Wherefore let him that speaketh in an *unknown* tongue pray that he may interpret.

14. For if I pray in an *unknown* tongue, my spirit prayeth, but my understanding is unfruitful.

15. What is it then? I will pray with the spirit, and I will pray with the understanding also: I will sing with the spirit, and I will sing with the understanding also.

16. Else, when thou shalt bless with the spirit, how shall he that occupieth the room of the unlearned say Amen at thy giving of thanks, seeing he understandeth not what thou sayest?

17. For thou verily givest thanks well, but the other is not edified.

18. I thank my God, I speak with tongues more than ye all:

19. Yet in the church I had rather speak five words with my understanding, that *by my voice* I might teach others also, than ten thousand words in an *unknown* tongue.

20. Brethren, be not children in understanding: howbeit in malice be ye children, but in understanding be men.

21. In the law it is written, With *men of* other tongues and other lips will I speak unto this people; and yet for all that will they not hear me, saith the Lord.

22. Wherefore tongues are for a sign, not to them that believe, but to them that believe not: but prophesying *serveth* not for them that believe not, but for them which believe.

connected in Acts? Cf. Acts 10:46; 19:6.)

**6-15.** The uselessness of tongues without interpretation Paul illustrates with facts drawn from life. **Revelation** precedes **prophesying** and **knowledge** precedes **doctrine** (lit., *teaching*).

**7. Distinction in the sounds** is necessary in music and in speaking; otherwise there is no understanding. **9. So likewise ye** introduces the application of the illustration. **10,11.** A further illustration in the realm of languages; and the point is, "Speech is useless to the hearer, unless he understands it" (ICC, p. 310). **12.** **Even so ye** introduces the conclusion of the argument from the illustrations. Edification is the aim of spiritual gifts.

**13,14.** There should be prayer for the gift of interpretation by the one speaking in tongues. Otherwise **my spirit prayeth, but my understanding** (lit., *my mind*) **is unfruitful.** That is, it gains no fruit in the understanding of the listeners. **15.** To **pray with the understanding** also means to pray so that there is fruit in the understanding of the hearers, as the following verses indicate. Intelligible speech is essential. **16. He that occupieth the room of the unlearned** probably refers to the one who does not have the gift of tongues or interpretation, or perhaps to one who is merely an inquirer (cf. F. F. Bruce, *Commentary on the Book of the Acts*, p. 102; Morris, *op. cit.*, pp. 195,196). The rank and file are referred to.

**18,19.** Paul's preference is clear. However much he may use tongues outside the assembly (publicly or privately), **in the church** (emphatic in the Greek) he must speak with **understanding** in order **to teach others.**

**20-25.** Paul has pointed out the superiority of prophecy for the insiders, and now he discusses its superiority for the outsiders.

**21,22.** The apostle introduces a free quotation from **the law** (the OT is indicated by law here) to show that tongues are intended to be a **sign** of God's presence with others than the Jews. In Isa 28:11,12, the place of the quotation, the Assyrians are referred to as the men **of other tongues.** Thus, the gift is designed primarily for the unbelieving. In the Acts this gift is mentioned four times ("saw" in Acts 8:18 seems to suggest that there was some outward sign in Samaria), and in each case Jews were present. It was the intention of God to indicate to this unbelieving group that he was with

23. If therefore the whole church be come together into one place, and all speak with tongues, and there come in *those that are* unlearned, or unbelievers, will they not say that ye are mad?

24. But if all prophesy, and there come in one that believeth not, or *one* unlearned, he is convinced of all, he is judged of all:

25. And thus are the secrets of his heart made manifest; and so falling down on *his* face he will worship God, and report that God is in you of a truth.

26. How is it then, brethren? when ye come together, every one of you hath a psalm, hath a doctrine, hath a tongue, hath a revelation, hath an interpretation. Let all things be done unto edifying.

27. If any man speak in an *unknown* tongue, *let it be* by two, or at the most *by* three, and *that* by course; and let one interpret.

28. But if there be no interpreter, let him keep silence in the church; and let him speak to himself, and to God.

29. Let the prophets speak two or three, and let the other judge.

30. If *any thing* be revealed to another that sitteth by, let the first hold his peace.

31. For ye may all prophesy one by one, that all may learn, and all may be comforted.

32. And the spirits of the prophets are subject to the prophets.

33. For God is not *the author* of confusion, but of peace, as in all churches of the saints.

the new movement. It is quite clear that known languages, such as were used at Pentecost, were the only suitable signs to hard-to-be-convinced Jews. Ecstatic language admits of too many natural explanations, not the least of which is the known historical fact that non-Christian groups have frequently so spoken (MNT, pp. 208,209).

23-25. Paul describes the differing effects of tongues and prophecy on outsiders, indicating the superiority of prophecy. There is no contradiction here with 14:22, as appears at first glance (tongues provide no help to the unbelieving, whereas prophecy seems to be a help to them). In the latter verse, individuals who have heard and rejected the truth are in view, as the comparison with the rebellious Israelites shows, whereas in the following verses first-time hearers are in view (ICC, p. 319). Prophecy leads to a conviction of one's sinful condition, a judgment (lit., *examined*), and a manifestation of the secrets of the heart. The result is worship, the true object of all ministry (cf. Mt 14:33).

26-33. Instruction for the exercise of the gifts is given here. The section is important because it is "the most intimate glimpse we have of the early church at worship" (Morris, *op. cit.*, pp. 198,199). What a contrast is found here with the formal and inflexible order of service that prevails in most of Christendom today! Barclay, in commenting upon this freedom and informality, points out two facts that emerge here. First, "Clearly the early church had no professional ministry" (*op. cit.*, p. 149). Second, in the service itself "there was clearly no settled order at all" (*ibid.*, p. 150). The early believers did not come to the worship meeting to hear a sermon from one man or simply to receive; they came to give. Much has been lost by the renouncement of these privileges.

26,27. Every one points to free participation, but because such freedom might lead to disorder, Paul counsels Let all things be done unto edifying. The speaking is to be by course (lit., *in turn*). 28,29. Tongues were not to be exercised unless an interpreter was present, and at the most only three were to participate. Apparently the directions for prophesying were more lenient. 32,33. The prophetic impulses are subject to the prophets, that is, the ones uttering the prophecies. Self-control must always be

34. Let your women keep silence in the churches: for it is not permitted unto them to speak; but *they are commanded* to be under obedience, as also saith the law.

35. And if they will learn any thing, let them ask their husbands at home: for it is a shame for women to speak in the church.

36. What! came the word of God out from you? or came it unto you only?

37. If any man think himself to be a prophet, or spiritual, let him acknowledge that the things that I write unto you are the commandments of the Lord.

38. But if any man be ignorant, let him be ignorant.

39. Wherefore, brethren, covet to prophesy, and forbid not to speak with tongues.

40. Let all things be done decently and in order.

## CHAPTER 15

MOREOVER, brethren, I declare unto you the gospel which I preached unto you, which also ye have received, and wherein ye stand;

present; otherwise **confusion** might result.

**34,35.** A word for the women is inserted here, possibly because of unwarranted intrusion of some into the worship of the church. They were to **keep silence** (cf. I Tim 2:12). Even if, as some think, women were permitted to pray and prophesy in the early church (cf. 11:5, although it must be remembered that prophecy was a temporary gift), other speaking was not allowed. Paul says nothing about spinsters who have no **husbands at home!**

**36.** The apostle gives an indignant response to the implied suggestion that Corinth had the right to be different from other churches. The Corinthian believers had no unique authority and place.

6) The Conclusion. 14:37-40. A Re sumé and conclusion, opening with a strong statement of authority. **38. Let him be ignorant.** The one ignorant of Paul's words was to be left in his condition. The correct translation, however, may be, *he is ignored,* i.e., by God (based upon a variant reading in good manuscripts). **40. Decently** may refer to the behavior of women and the observance of the Lord's Supper (11:2-34), and **in order** may refer to spiritual gifts (12:1—14:40).

F. The Counsel Concerning the Doctrine of the Resurrection. 15:1-58.

In approaching this chapter it is helpful to have some conception of the Greek view of life. In general the Greeks believed in the immortality of the soul, but they did not accept the resurrection of the body. To them the resurrection of the body was unthinkable in view of the fact that they held the body to be the source of man's weakness and sin. Death, therefore, was very welcome, since by it the soul would be liberated from the body; but resurrection was not welcome, because this would constitute another descent of the soul into the grave of the body. This was the skepticism that Paul faced at Athens (cf. Acts 17:31,32) and that the Christian faces in the modern world. James S. Stewart, Professor of New Testament at the University of Edinburgh, has put the timeless conflict succinctly, "Twenty centuries have echoed the laughter of Areopagus."

1) The Certainty of the Resurrection. 15:1-34. The problem at Corinth

2. By which also ye are saved, if ye keep in memory what I preached unto you, unless ye have believed in vain.

3. For I delivered unto you first of all that which I also received, how that Christ died for our sins according to the Scriptures;

4. And that he was buried, and that he rose again the third day according to the Scriptures:

developed in the Christian church. The believers had accepted resurrection, at least in the case of Christ; but under the influence of Greek thought, some doubted the bodily resurrection of Christians. Therefore, the apostle wrote to combat the doctrinal weakness. His method is fairly clear. He first considers the certainty of the resurrection, developing the necessary connection between Christ's resurrection and the resurrection of believers (vv. 1-34). He follows with a consideration of certain objections (vv. 35-57). Then he concludes with an appeal (v. 58).

**1,2. Moreover** introduces the new subject, the resurrection, an integral part of **the gospel. Ye are saved** (Gr., present tense) may refer to continual salvation from the power of sin in the lives of believers, or it may refer to the day-by-day salvation of the inhabitants of Corinth as they received the message and formed part of the church of Jesus Christ. **Believed in vain** does not indicate loss of salvation as a possibility. The apostle means either that a faith that does not persevere is not true saving faith, or that a faith lodged in a purported resurrection of the Messiah would be groundless if the message of Christ's resurrection were untrue. The latter interpretation is probably correct. If Christ was not crucified and resurrected, salvation is impossible.

**3,4. First of all** (lit., *among the first things*) refers to importance, not time. The substance of Paul's message is contained in the four *that*'s following **received,** and it includes Christ's death, burial, resurrection, and appearances. These things make up the Gospel. **For our sins according to the scriptures** must be understood in the light of passages such as Isaiah 53. The preposition **for** (Gr., *hyper,* which modern grammarians now recognize may denote substitution) suggests his death in our stead. The word **buried,** the only reference to his burial outside the Gospels, with the exception of Paul's words in Acts 13:29 (cf. Acts 2:29), blasts the swoon theory of our Lord's death. He really died. It also leads naturally to the empty tomb, a witness for the Resurrection which has never been effectively refuted. **Rose again,** a perfect tense, implies abiding results. (On the problem of translation in view of the definite time phrase, **the third day,** see James Hope Moulton's *A Grammar of New Testament Greek,* I, 137.)

5. And that he was seen of Cephas, then of the twelve:

6. After that, he was seen of above five hundred brethren at once; of whom the greater part remain unto this present, but some are fallen asleep.

7. After that, he was seen of James; then of all the apostles.

8. And last of all he was seen of me also, as of one born out of due time.

9. For I am the least of the apostles, that am not meet to be called an apostle, because I persecuted the church of God.

10. But by the grace of God I am what I am: and his grace which *was bestowed* upon me was not in vain; but I labored more abundantly than they all: yet not I, but the grace of God which was with me.

11. Therefore whether *it were* I or they, so we preach, and so ye believed.

12. Now if Christ be preached that he rose from the dead, how say some among you that there is no resurrection of the dead?

13. But if there be no resurrection of the dead, then is Christ not risen:

14. And if Christ be not risen, then *is* our preaching vain, and your faith *is* also vain.

15. Yea, and we are found false witnesses of God; because we have testified of God that he raised up Christ: whom he raised not up, if so be that the dead rise not.

**5. And that he was seen** introduces evidence outside the NT Scriptures. **6.** The reference to **the greater part** who **remain unto this present** has immense apologetic value. The resurrection story was undisputed, so far as we know, twenty-five years later! The appearance may be that of Mt 28:16-20. **7.** This **James** was probably the Lord's brother, and this appearance may have brought him to faith in Christ (cf. Jn 7:5; Acts 1:14).

**8. One born out of due time** (lit., *the miscarriage,* or *abortion*) does not refer to the taunts of his enemies, nor to the fact that he came to Christ before his nation, Israel, which will come to Christ in the future (cf. Rom 11:1-36). The **for** of the next verse explains. Paul regards himself in comparison with the other apostles as a miscarried infant would be regarded among perfectly formed infants, because he was lifted out of his role of persecutor into his office of apostle. The others responded to the loving call of the Saviour, but Paul's call on the Damascus Road had almost the element of force in it. Therefore, he magnifies **the grace of God** which came to him (cf. Eph 3:8; I Tim 1:15).

**10. Labored more abundantly than they all** is ambiguous. It may refer to the other apostles individually or collectively. The latter may be right, for history seems to support him in this. Under any circumstances the apostle emphasizes that he does not take credit for this personally. **11. So we preach** links the Resurrection with the apostolic message. **So ye believed** links the Corinthians with faith in Christ's resurrection. Taking their faith in the Lord's resurrection as a starting point, Paul will now prove that this logically involves faith in the bodily resurrection of all others who are *in him* (vv. 12-19).

**12,13.** The fact of Christ's resurrection involves belief in the bodily resurrection. There is no need to debate resurrection, since one has already been raised. It is obvious that Paul's argument turns on the humanity of Christ (cf. I Tim 2:5, "the *man* Christ Jesus"). **14. Vain.** Void of content (Gr., *kenos*). If there was no resurrection, the Gospel was empty of real content. And the Corinthians' faith did not take hold of a real fact; it was all a mirage. **15.** Furthermore, if there was no resurrection, the heralds of the Gospel were **false witnesses** against **God.**

16. For if the dead rise not, then is not Christ raised:

17. And if Christ be not raised, your faith *is* vain; ye are yet in your sins.

18. Then they also which are fallen asleep in Christ are perished.

19. If in this life only we have hope in Christ, we are of all men most miserable.

20. But now is Christ risen from the dead, *and* become the firstfruits of them that slept.

21. For since by man *came* death, by man *came* also the resurrection of the dead.

22. For as in Adam all die, even so in Christ shall all be made alive.

23. But every man in his own order: Christ the firstfruits; afterward they that are Christ's at his coming.

24. Then *cometh* the end, when he shall have delivered up the kingdom to God, even the Father; when he shall have put down all rule, and all authority and power.

17. Vain renders a different adjective here, meaning "void of useful aim or effect" (Gr., *mataios*). If Christ was not raised, their faith had failed to secure its end or aim, namely, salvation. There could be no assurance that he had not died for his own sin. The Resurrection was necessary to demonstrate the perfection of the character of the Redeemer (cf. Acts 2:24) and to demonstrate the acceptance of the Son's work by the Father (cf. Rom 4:25). As someone has said, the Resurrection is God's "Amen" to Christ's "It is finished." We observe the cross and see redemption effected; we see the Resurrection and know the redemption is accepted. 18,19. Without resurrection, believers who thought they were dying in Christ, with the expectation of resurrection blessedness, really perished (emphatic contrast). The bitter conclusion is reached that the denial of the Resurrection constitutes Christians the most miserable of men. They suffer here and now for a faith that is only a fiction (cf. Rom 8:18).

20. Paul, having established the fact that Christ arose and that the admission of his resurrection is inconsistent with the denial of the resurrection of the dead, now discusses the fruit and issue of the Lord's resurrection. Assumption departs and the facts come in with his words, but now is Christ risen. The word firstfruits, derived from the Feast of First fruits in Israel (cf. Lev 23:9-14), suggests the thoughts of an earnest and a sample.

21,22. There is a causal relationship between Adam and death and Christ and life. The apostle's thought moves in the realm of Romans 5. When Paul writes in Christ shall all be made alive, he is not teaching universalism (a heresy), nor universal resurrection (a truth, but not taught here), but universal resurrection in Christ. The two all's are not identical in quantity, being limited by the prepositional phrases in Adam and in Christ (cf. Rom 5:18). The word made alive is never used of the wicked in the NT (cf. Jn 5:21; 6:63; Rom 8:11; Gal 3:21; I Cor 15:45, the same context). The chapter contemplates the resurrection of believers only.

23. The order of resurrection is now discussed. Christ is first, followed by believers, them that are Christ's at his coming for the Church (cf. I Thess 4:13-18).

24. Then, Greek *eita*, covers an interval, just as the closely related *epeita*, after-

25. For he must reign, till he hath put all enemies under his feet.

26. The last enemy *that* shall be destroyed *is* death.

27. For he hath put all things under his feet. But when he saith, All things are put under *him, it is* manifest that he is excepted, which did put all things under him.

28. And when all things shall be subdued unto him, then shall the Son also himself be subject unto him that put all things under him, that God may be all in all.

29. Else what shall they do which are baptized for the dead, if the dead rise not at all? why are they then baptized for the dead?

30. And why stand we in jeopardy every hour?

ward, of the preceding verse, covers a long interval, the interval of the kingdom of Christ on earth. Every Pauline use of *eita* involves an interval. Note that the *epeita* of verse 23 has already covered an interval of at least 1900 years! **The end** refers to the end of the kingdom, as the following verse indicates. **25. For** gives the reason he cannot relinquish the kingdom until the end comes. The Son must reign as man under the Father (cf. Ps 110:1). Following this reign, the mediatorial kingdom will be merged with the eternal kingdom of the triune God. **26.** The annulling of **death** will take place at the Great White Throne Judgment, after the kingdom and final rebellion of Satan (cf. Rev 20:7-15). Here is the Christian answer to the Greek philosophers. They said that there is no resurrection, but Paul says there is no death (cf. ExpGT, II, 928). **27,28.** The statement that the **Son also himself** shall **be subject** to God has been thought by some to lower the dignity of the Son of God, as well as, possibly, to cast a reflection on his deity. The subjection, however, is not that of the Son *as Son,* but *as the incarnate Son.* This, of course, does not involve inequality of essence. The son of a king may be officially subordinate and yet equal in nature to his father (cf. Charles Hodge, *An Exposition of the First Epistle to the Corinthians,* pp. 333-335). Paul's point is this: The Son as incarnate Son has all power now (cf. Mt 28:18). When he delivers up the administration of the earthly kingdom to the Father, then the triune God will reign as God and no longer through the incarnate Son. Messiahship is a phase of the Son's eternal Sonship (cf. Moffatt, MNT, p. 249). **29-34.** After outlining the positive issues of resurrection (vv. 12-28), the apostle turns now to the negative side. **29. Baptized for the dead** is a difficult expression, which has been given many interpretations, some bizarre and heretical. For example, it is claimed by some that Paul refers to the practice of vicarious baptism, such as is observed by the Mormons, although he did not approve of it (cf. Morris, *op. cit.,* pp. 218-219). The practice, however, is known only as early as the second century, and then among heretics. Others feel that the apostle refers to those who were baptized on the basis of the testimony of some who had died. The prepo-

31. I protest by your rejoicing which I have in Christ Jesus our Lord, I die daily.

32. If after the manner of men I have fought with beasts at Ephesus, what advantageth it me, if the dead rise not? let us eat and drink; for to-morrow we die.

33. Be not deceived: evil communications corrupt good manners.

34. Awake to righteousness, and sin not; for some have not the knowledge of God: I speak *this* to your shame.

35. But some *man* will say, How are the dead raised up? and with what body do they come?

36. *Thou* fool, that which thou sowest is not quickened, except it die:

37. And that which thou sowest, thou sowest not that body that shall be, but bare grain, it may chance of wheat, or of some other *grain:*

sition *hyper,* rendered for in the AV, may mean "with regard to," although this is not the normal meaning. Still others feel that Paul refers to the baptism of young converts who took the place in the church of older brethren who had died. *Hyper* has the meaning "instead of" quite frequently, even in the NT, as II Cor 5:15 and Phm 13 indicate, although it is not the predominant meaning. The Greek expositors explained the expression as "baptized with an interest in (the resurrection of) the dead," but this is unnatural for several reasons (cf. ICC, pp. 359-360). The second and third suggestions are more in line with Pauline theology, but the interpretation remains difficult.

31. I die daily refers to the external perils Paul faced. It was a foolish thing to face them if there is no resurrection (cf. II Cor 1:8,9; 11:23). 32. I have fought with beasts at Ephesus is commonly thought to be a figurative reference to his persecutions from men (cf. 16:9). Let us eat and drink expresses the inevitable result of the denial of the future life — moral decay (cf. Isa 22:13).

33,34. After a subtle warning against association with those who were undermining the believers' faith in the resurrection, Paul tells the believers to awake to righteousness (lit., *sober up with righteous resolve*) and sin not (lit., *stop sinning*). The inevitable moral results of wrong doctrine are clearly seen here. He charges the Corinthians, who prided themselves on their knowledge, with lack of knowledge of God. No wonder he adds, I speak this to your shame.

2) The Consideration of Certain Objections. 15:35-57. The apostle deals with objections in this section. Two of them are referred to in the first verse. How are the dead raised up? questions the *possibility* of resurrection (not the method), and this objection is answered in verse 36. With what body do they come? concerns the nature of the resurrection body, and this problem is discussed in verses 37 through 49. The final problem, which is implied, is this: What happens to those who do not die? Paul deals with this in the remaining verses of the section (vv. 50-57). 35,36. The apostle's simple answer to the first question is that the body is not quickened (resurrected), except it die. Death, the body's enemy, is really the means to resurrection.

37-41. Illustrating from the natural

38. But God giveth it a body as it hath pleased him, and to every seed his own body.

39. All flesh *is* not the same flesh: but *there is* one *kind of* flesh of men, another flesh of beasts, another of fishes, *and* another of birds.

40. *There are* also celestial bodies, and bodies terrestrial: but the glory of the celestial *is* one, and the *glory* of the terrestrial *is* another.

41. *There is* one glory of the sun, and another glory of the moon, and another glory of the stars; for *one* star differeth from *another* star in glory.

42. So also *is* the resurrection of the dead. It is sown in corruption, it is raised in incorruption:

43. It is sown in dishonor, it is raised in glory: it is sown in weakness, it is raised in power:

44. It is sown a natural body, it is raised a spiritual body. There is a natural body, and there is a spiritual body.

45. And so it is written, The first man Adam was made a living soul; the last Adam *was made* a quickening spirit.

46. Howbeit that *was* not first which is spiritual, but that which is natural; and afterward that which is spiritual.

47. The first man *is* of the earth, earthy: the second man *is* the Lord from heaven.

48. As *is* the earthy, such *are* they also that are earthy: and as *is* the heavenly, such *are* they also that are heavenly.

49. And as we have borne the image of the earthy, we shall also bear the image of the heavenly.

world, Paul deals with two common errors. One is to regard the resurrection body the same as the original body, simply re-formed; the other is to regard it as a new body unrelated to the original. The fact is that there is continuity (v. 36), identity (v. 38), and yet diversity (vv. 39-41) between the two bodies. **Not that body that shall be** refutes the notion that the body will be the same body in its physical make-up. **38. His own body.** Just as in the case of the grain, each one preserves his personal identity.

**39,40. All flesh is not the same flesh.** In the light of the theory of evolution, this is an interesting statement. It is designed to preserve the element of diversity among believers' resurrection bodies. **Celestial bodies** are the sun, moon, stars, etc. **41.** The statement, **one star differeth from another star in glory,** may point to differing rewards among the glorified (cf. ICC, pp. 371,372).

**42. So also** introduces the Pauline application to the resurrection body. Four particulars are singled out, as the apostle labors to describe the indescribable and express the inexpressible. First, the body will be **raised in incorruption;** there will be no possibility of decay (cf. vv. 53,54). **43.** It will also be **raised in glory** and **raised in power.** There will be no more sin principle within it nor physical weakness. **44.** Finally, it will be **raised a spiritual body.** Apparently a reference to the body's use, not its substance. It will be formed to be the organ of the Spirit.

**45.** Paul points out that Scripture agrees with what he is saying, for **so it is written.** The two Adams stamp their characteristics on their races. The term, **the last Adam,** was coined by Paul (cf. MNT, p. 263) to indicate that there can be no third representative man, sinless and without human father, as were both Christ and Adam. Had God's last Adam failed, there would have been no other. **Quickening** (lit., *life-giving;* cf. Col 1:17; Phil 3:20,21). **47. The Lord from heaven** looks forward to his coming. **48,49. We shall also bear** is a ringing promise. Many excellent manuscripts have *let us bear,* but the reading is probably the result of an early corruption of the text. **The image of the heavenly** is the final note on the nature of the resurrection body. It is to be like Christ's own glorious body (cf. Lk 24:29-43; Phil 3:21; Ps 17:15).

**50.** The question Paul has next to an-

50. Now this I say, brethren, that flesh and blood cannot inherit the kingdom of God; neither doth corruption inherit incorruption.

51. Behold, I show you a mystery; We shall not all sleep, but we shall all be changed,

52. In a moment, in the twinkling of an eye, at the last trump: for the trumpet shall sound, and the dead shall be raised incorruptible, and we shall be changed.

53. For this corruptible must put on incorruption, and this mortal *must* put on immortality.

54. So when this corruptible shall have put on incorruption, and this mortal shall have put on immortality, then shall be brought to pass the saying that is written, Death is swallowed up in victory.

55. O death, where *is* thy sting? O grave, where *is* thy victory?

56. The sting of death *is* sin; and the strength of sin *is* the law.

57. But thanks *be* to God, which giveth us the victory through our Lord Jesus Christ.

swer is one that naturally follows. It is this: But what happens to those who do not die? In what way do they participate in the resurrection of the body? The principle is that there must be a transformation, for flesh and blood (he does not say *body*) cannot inherit the kingdom of God.

**51. Mystery** (cf. 2:7). Not all believers will **sleep** (die), but all shall be **changed,** i.e., have their bodies transformed. The all in the last clause negates the doctrine of a partial rapture of the Church. **52. In a moment.** From Greek *atmos,* "that which cannot be cut," from which is derived the word *atom.* In the **twinkling of an eye.** The fluttering of an eyelid. These phrases emphasize the suddenness of the change. The sounding of the **trumpet** points to the time (cf. I Thess 4:16). **53.** The dead and the living come before the writer here, **corruptible** referring to the dead and **mortal** referring to the living.

**54.** This glorious transformation in resurrection shall bring **to pass the saying that is written, Death is swallowed up in victory** (a free application of Theodotion's rendering of Isa 25:8). The consummation of Gen 3:15 is reached.

**55.** From the exultation of the resurrection triumph, Paul taunts death. The better manuscripts have the clauses reversed, with **death** being asked both the questions (Paul never uses *hades;* cf. Hos 13:14). **56.** A short and concise statement of the relation of **death, sin,** and **law,** suggested by the thought of death's **sting** being removed. **The sting of death is sin** because it is by sin that death gains authority over man, and it is by **the law** that sin gains its **strength.** Law gives sin the character of rebellion, conscious defiance (cf. Rom 4:15; 7:7-13). The Law, then, stirred up sin, which led to death. Christ, by entering death, overcame sin, so that believers may sing, "He death by dying slew."

**57.** The apostle leads the thanksgiving of the redeemed to the **God** who initiates and in grace **giveth us the victory. Through our Lord Jesus Christ** points to the divine instrumentality, the work of Christ; and the phrase is a short summary of all that is involved in verses 3-5,20-22. These words, concluding the resurrection argument, answer to the apostle's words elsewhere — "and so shall we ever be with the Lord" (I Thess 4:17).

3) The Concluding Appeal. 15:58

58. Therefore, my beloved brethren, be ye steadfast, unmovable, always abounding in the work of the Lord, forasmuch as ye know that your labor is not in vain in the Lord.

## CHAPTER 16

NOW concerning the collection for the saints, as I have given order to the churches of Galatia, even so do ye.

2. Upon the first *day* of the week let every one of you lay by him in store, as *God* hath prospered him, that there be no gatherings when I come.

3. And when I come, whomsoever ye shall approve by *your* letters, them will I send to bring your liberality unto Jerusalem.

4. And if it be meet that I go also, they shall go with me.

5. Now I will come unto you, when I shall pass through Macedonia: for I do pass through Macedonia.

6. And it may be that I will abide, yea, and winter with you, that ye may bring me on my journey whithersoever I go.

7. For I will not see you now by the way; but I trust to tarry a while with you, if the Lord permit.

8. But I will tarry at Ephesus until Pentecost.

9. For a great door and effectual is opened unto me, and *there are* many adversaries.

**Therefore** introduces the conclusion. As Robertson and Plummer put it, "Let there be less speculation and more work" (ICC, p. 379).

## V. The Conclusion: Practical and Personal Matters. 16:1-24.

### A. The Collection for the Poor. 16:1-4.

The last chapter of the letter is occupied with practical and personal matters, the first of which is the collection for the poor at Jerusalem. The chapter provides an illustration of the outworking of the great spiritual reality affirmed in 1:9—namely, that believers are called "into the fellowship of his Son Jesus Christ our Lord" (cf. 15:58). **1. Now concerning** introduces the subject as one mentioned in the Corinthians' letter to Paul. **2. The first day of the week,** or Sunday, was the day the believers met for worship. This is the earliest mention of the fact (cf. Acts 20:7). Giving was to be systematic. **As God hath prospered him** sets forth the NT measure of giving (cf. Acts 11:29). **By him** is probably a reference to the home; giving was to be private giving. Paul desired the collection to be taken before he came, that pressure might be absent (cf. II Cor 9:5). This system would revolutionize present church customs!

**3,4.** Paul's carefulness in money matters should be noted. He never appealed for money for himself and did not even desire to handle money for others if there could be the slightest question about it. **If it be meet** (lit., *worthy*), probably means, "If it is large enough to make it worthwhile for me to abandon other work and go with the gift" (cf. Rom 15:25).

### B. The Planned Visit of Paul. 16:5-9.

The apostle desired to spend some time among the Corinthians. Therefore, he planned to pass through Macedonia first rather than go to Corinth at once. This constituted a change in plans, for which he was later criticized by some in the church (cf. II Cor 1:15-17). **5,6. Bring me on my journey** does not involve their giving money to him (cf. 9:15). **7. If the Lord permit.** The apostle's acknowledgement of a will above his own. He held the reins of his life in a loose hand. **8,9. Door.** Figurative for an op-

10. Now if Timotheus come, see that he may be with you without fear: for he worketh the work of the Lord, as I also do.

11. Let no man therefore despise him: but conduct him forth in peace, that he may come unto me: for I look for him with the brethren.

12. As touching our brother Apollos, I greatly desired him to come unto you with the brethren: but his will was not at all to come at this time; but he will come when he shall have convenient time.

13. Watch ye, stand fast in the faith, quit you like men, be strong.

14. Let all your things be done with charity.

15. I beseech you, brethren, (ye know the house of Stephanas, that it is the firstfruits of Achaia, and that they have addicted themselves to the ministry of the saints,)

16. That ye submit yourselves unto such, and to every one that helpeth with us, and laboreth.

17. I am glad of the coming of Stephanas and Fortunatus and Achaicus: for that which was lacking on your part they have supplied.

18. For they have refreshed my spirit and yours: therefore acknowledge ye them that are such.

19. The churches of Asia salute you. Aquila and Priscilla salute you much in the Lord, with the church that is in their house.

20. All the brethren greet you. Greet ye one another with a holy kiss.

21. The salutation of me Paul with mine own hand.

portunity (cf. II Cor 2:12; Col 4:3). Many adversaries may be a motive for Paul's stay at Ephesus (cf. 15:32; Acts 19:1-41).

C. Commendations, Exhortations, Salutations, and Benediction. 16:10-24.

His planned visit reminds him of two helpers in the ministry to 'Corinth — Timothy and Apollos.

10,11. If Timothy come allows for possible difficulties along the way (cf. 4:17; Acts 19:22). Timothy was young and apparently somewhat timid (I Tim 4:12; 5:21-23; II Tim 1:6-8; 2:1,3,15; 4:1,2), but he was a faithful worker. It is difficult to conceive of a higher commendation than he worketh the work of the Lord, as I also do. 12. Although Paul may have had reason to envy Apollos (cf. 1:12), he was not jealous of the attractive and gifted Alexandrian. Nor did he have ultimate authority over Apollos, for although Paul greatly desired him to come, Apollos felt it was not the time to come and did not do so. His will refers to Apollos.

13. Here begins a series of exhortations addressed to the church. The first four are military words; in fact, quit you like men reminds one of the battle cry of the Philistines (cf. I Sam 4:9, AV). Each of the imperatives in this verse and the one in the following verse are in the present tense, expressing actions that are to be continuous. 15,16. The house of Stephanas (cf. 1:16). Addicted themselves (lit., appointed themselves) refers to "a self-imposed duty" (ICC, p. 395). 17,18. Stephanas and Fortunatus and Achaicus were probably the bearers of the Corinthian letter to Paul (cf. 7:1). My spirit and yours refers to Paul's refreshment and to theirs when they would hear the report of their representatives upon their return and read this letter.

19-24. Concluding salutations, warning, and benediction. Aquila and Priscilla, whether at Rome (Rom 16:3-5) or Ephesus, kept their home as a gathering place for the saints. 20. The holy kiss (cf. Rom 16:16; I Thess 5:26; II Cor 13:12; I Pet 5:14). An ancient custom. This is an implied exhortation to put away their divisions.

21,22. The apostle takes the pen from his amanuensis and inscribes the final words, the first statement of which comes in like a clap of thunder. Ana-

22. If any man love not the Lord Jesus Christ, let him be Anathema, Maranatha.

23. The grace of our Lord Jesus Christ *be* with you.

24. My love *be* with you all in Christ Jesus. Amen.

The first *epistle* to the Corinthians was written from Philippi by Stephanas, and Fortunatus, and Achaicus, and Timotheus.

thema. The Greek equivalent of the Hebrew *hērem*, meaning "a thing devoted to destruction, the object of a curse" (cf. Rom 9:3; Gal 1:8,9; I Cor 12:3). The word should be followed by a period. The following word, **Maranatha** (Gr. transliteration of an Aramaic expression) may mean "Our Lord, come," or "Our Lord is come" (the Incarnation in view), or "Our Lord cometh" (Second Coming). The context, with its note of warning, decides for the last translation (RSV, *Our Lord, come!*). **23,24.** The note of warning is not the final note, however. Even the benediction of grace is not adequate here; Paul must add the tender **My love be with you all**. His rebukes have been the rebukes of love, and his love extends to **all**, even the wayward and rebellious.

# BIBLIOGRAPHY

BARCLAY, WILLIAM. *The Letters to the Corinthians (The Daily Study Bible Series).* Philadelphia: Westminster Press, 1956.

FINDLAY, G. G. "St. Paul's First Epistle to the Corinthians," *The Expositor's Greek Testament.* Vol II. Grand Rapids: Wm. B. Eerdmans Publishing Co., n.d.

GODET, FREDERIC. *Commentary on St. Paul's First Epistle to the Corinthians.* 2 vols. Edinburgh: T. & T. Clark, 1880.

GROSHEIDE, F. W. *Commentary on the First Epistle to the Corinthians (The New International Commentary).* Grand Rapids: Wm. B. Eerdmans Publishing Co., 1953.

HODGE, CHARLES. *An Exposition of the First Epistle to the Corinthians.* Grand Rapids: Wm. B. Eerdmans Publishing Co., reprinted 1950.

IRONSIDE, H. A. *Addresses on the First Epistle to the Corinthians.* New York: Loizeaux Brothers, 1938.

MOFFATT, JAMES. *The First Epistle of Paul to the Corinthians (The Moffatt New Testament Commentary).* New York: Harper and Brothers, 1938.

MORRIS, LEON. *The First Epistle of Paul to the Corinthians (Tyndale New Testament Commentaries).* Grand Rapids: Wm. B. Eerdmans Publishing Co., 1958.

ROBERTSON, ARCHIBALD, and PLUMMER, ALFRED. *A Critical and Exegetical Commentary on the First Epistle of Paul to the Corinthians (The International Critical Commentary).* New York: Charles Scribner's Sons, 1911.

VINE, W. E. *First Corinthians.* London: Oliphants, 1951.

# THE SECOND EPISTLE TO THE CORINTHIANS

## INTRODUCTION

*The Occasion of the Writing.* The major matters pertaining to Paul's relations with the church at Corinth are dealt with more specifically in the Introduction to I Corinthians than they are here. The immediate occasion that prompted the writing of II Corinthians centered in certain crises that had arisen in the church after the dispatch of the first letter. To state the known facts concisely, it appears that Paul had sent Titus to Corinth to correct certain abuses and to encourage the believers there to complete their contribution for the poor saints at Jerusalem. Paul, troubled in spirit, had departed from Ephesus and had come to Troas with the expectation of finding Titus. Still more troubled because he did not find Titus in Troas, he departed hurriedly to Macedonia. There Titus, freshly returned from Corinth with encouraging news, met Paul. But things were not what they should have been in the Corinthian church. The encouraging news was all but dissipated by the fact that ominous thunderheads were lying along the horizon of the church life at Corinth. It was necessary for Paul to act quickly and sternly. He had to do three things: (1) present the Gospel more clearly to the Christians; (2) put pressure on them for the completion of their promised contribution; (3) pulverize all opposition by an unparalleled defense of his apostolic ministry and authority. These points form the framework around which all the thoughts in this second letter cluster.

*Date and Place of Writing.* There can be little doubt that this letter was written on Paul's third missionary journey (A.D. 57)—some months or possibly a year or more after I Corinthians. It was written from Macedonia, probably from Philippi.

*The Unity of the Writing.* Some modern scholars hold that II Corinthians is not a unified work. (1) They affirm that 6:14–7:1 is an interpolation, because it breaks the sequence of thought. But Paul's movements do not always correspond with modern ideas of development. An author dealing with an actual situation may have reasons for an apparent digression that are utterly unknowable to a modern critic. (2) Again these scholars claim that chapter 9 largely duplicates what is in chapter 8. However, if one will study these chapters carefully, apart from the influence of a preconceived theory, he will find that chapter 9 is anything but a repetition of chapter 8. (3) Most importantly, these objectors claim that the last section (10: 1 – 13:14) is so different in tone and thought from the earlier sections (1:1 – 9:15) that it must have belonged originally to some "lost" or "stern" letter that Paul sent to Corinth. The fatal objection to this popular theory is that there is absolutely no manuscript evidence for such a fragmentized or truncated epistle. Moreover, a closer study of this epistle will reveal to the diligent student a unity that is simply amazing. And obviously our knowledge of the total situation at Corinth is so nebulous that no modern scholar can safely affirm that any part of this epistle is either discordant with the rest of the epistle or irrelevant to the actual situation at Corinth.

*The Development of the Thought.* The progress of thought in this epistle is like the movement of a mighty army advancing over rugged terrain still inhabited by pockets of stubborn resistance. Paul never lays his armor down while such resistance to his ministry exists. His letter is, in fact, an ultimatum calling for total and unconditional surrender to the authority of Christ's apostle. In spite of its ruggedness, this letter is as beautiful in its symmetry as a mountain flower — and it carries far more spiritual fragrance. Our outline attempts to show this symmetry.

*Influence.* It is perhaps invidious to compare any one of Paul's epistles with another. Each one has its special characteristics that make it great in its field. But in II Corinthians we find certain features that are not so evident in Paul's other writings. As the great evangelist defends his apostolic authority against the subtle and insidious attacks of "the superlative apostles" who sought to free the Corinthians of his influence, he reveals his very soul and adds many details about his life that would otherwise be unknown. But this epistle is a monument to the fact that Paul, vital and inspired, was more than a match for "every high thing that is exalted against the knowledge of God" (II Cor 10:5, ASV).

# OUTLINE

I. The conciliation. 1:1—7:16.
  A. Paul's distress reciprocated. 1:1-7.
    1. Salutation. 1:1,2.
    2. Adoration. 1:3.
    3. Agonizing tribulation. 1:4-7.
  B. Paul's desperation relieved. 1:8-14.
  C. Paul's diversion justified. 1:15—2:17.
    1. The plan contemplated. 1:15,16.
    2. The plan criticized. 1:17.
    3. The plan comprehended. 1:18-22.
    4. The plan changed. 1:23—2:4.
    5. The plan chastened. 2:5-11.
    6. The plan consummated. 2:12-17.
  D. Paul's dispensation superior. 3:1-18.
    1. In documentation. 3:1-3.
    2. In dynamism. 3:4-6.
    3. In degree. 3:7-9.
    4. In destination. 3:10,11.
    5. In diagnosis. 3:12-17.
    6. In denouement. 3:18.
  E. Paul's dualism explained. 4:1-18.
    1. The hidden and the open. 4:1,2.
    2. The blinded and the enlightened. 4:3,4.
    3. Slaves and the Master. 4:5.
    4. Darkness and light. 4:6.
    5. The frail and the Mighty. 4:7.
    6. Trials and triumphs. 4:8-10.
    7. Death and life. 4:11,12.
    8. The written and the spoken. 4:13.
    9. The past and the future. 4:14.
    10. Grace and thanksgiving. 4:15.
    11. The outer and the inner man. 4:16.
    12. Affliction and glory. 4:17.
    13. The seen and the unseen. 4:18 a.
    14. The temporal and the eternal. 4:18 b.
  F. Paul's dedication motivated. 5:1—6:10.
    1. Motivated by knowledge. 5:1-9.
    2. Motivated by judgment. 5:10.
    3. Motivated by fear. 5:11.
    4. Motivated by unselfishness. 5:12,13.
    5. Motivated by love. 5:14,15.
    6. Motivated by regeneration. 5:16,17.
    7. Motivated by reconciliation. 5:18-21.
    8. Motivated by time. 6:1,2.
    9. Motivated by suffering. 6:3-10.
  G. Paul's dissuasion urged. 6:11—7:1.
    1. The thesis: Change your attitude toward me. 6:11-13.
    2. The antithesis: Change your attitude toward the world. 6:14-16.
    3. The synthesis: Obey and live. 6:17—7:1.
  H. Paul's delight exemplified. 7:2-16.

# II CORINTHIANS

## CHAPTER 1

PAUL, an apostle of Jesus Christ by the will of God, and Timothy *our* brother, unto the church of God which is at Corinth, with all the saints which are in all Achaia:

2. Grace *be* to you, and peace, from God our Father, and *from* the Lord Jesus Christ.

3. Blessed *be* God, even the Father of our Lord Jesus Christ, the Father of mercies, and the God of all comfort;

# COMMENTARY

### I. The Conciliation. 1:1—7:16.

A. Paul's Distress Reciprocated. 1:1-7.

1) Salutation. 1:1,2. **1.** The epithet **apostle,** used extensively in Paul's letters (cf. Eph 1:1; Col 1:1; I Tim 1:1; II Tim 1:1), tersely and trenchantly epitomizes Paul's commission and mission (cf. Gal 1:1). **Saints** is a parallel description of the Christian brotherhood (cf. Rom 1:7; I Cor 1:2; Eph 1:1; Phil 1:1; Col 1:1). The term is always reminiscent of the radical change that has taken place (cf. II Cor 5:17; I Cor 6:11). The territory included in **all Achaia** embraced Athens (cf. Acts 17:34) and Cenchrea (cf. Rom 16:1). **2.** In the protocol of salvation, recognized even in a salutation, **grace** always precedes **peace.** The former is the basis and foundation of the latter; therefore, the order cannot be changed. No man can have peace who has not previously experienced divine **grace** (cf. 8: 9). The deity of Christ is emphatically affirmed in the salutation and doxology (13:14) of this epistle. The single preposition **from** *(apo)* links together (see ASV) **God our Father** and **the Lord Jesus Christ** in an indissoluble union. The full title of Christ should be duly weighed.

2) Adoration. 1:3. The verbal adjective **blessed** *(eulogētos),* always applied to the divine persons in the NT (11:31; Mk 14:61; Lk 1:68; Rom 1:25; 9:5; Eph

4. Who comforteth us in all our tribulation, that we may be able to comfort them which are in any trouble, by the comfort wherewith we ourselves are comforted of God.

5. For as the sufferings of Christ abound in us, so our consolation also aboundeth by Christ.

1:3; Col 1:3; I Pet 1:3), describes the infinite felicity and blessedness existing in the Trinity. Paul here characterizes God (1) according to his internal nature — blessed; (2) according to his trinitarian relationship — the Father of our Lord Jesus Christ; and (3) according to his attributes — the Father of mercies, and the God of all comfort. The word *oiktirmos* means "pity, mercy, compassion"; it is always in the plural in the NT (Rom 12:1; Phil 2:1; Col 3:12; Heb 10:28) — possibly to express the variegated nature of the virtue.

3) Agonizing Tribulation. 1:4-7. 4. God comforts believers. God's comfort is: (1) active — who comforteth us; (2) extensive — in all our tribulation; (3) purposive — that we may be able; (4) specific — in any trouble; (5) reflexive — by the comfort wherewith we ourselves are comforted. Tribulation and trouble represent the same word (*thlipsis;* elsewhere in this epistle in 1:8; 2:4; 4:17; 6:4; 7:4; 8:2, 13). 5. Christ comforts believers. The as . . . so in the Greek here compares two things of equal rank or nature (as in Lk 11:30; 17:26; Jn 3:14; 14:31; Col 3:13). By the sufferings of (the) Christ we are to understand the suffering of the Messiah, the Anointed One (cf. Lk 24: 26,46; Phil 3:10; Col 1:24; I Pet 1:11). The verb abound (*perisseuō*) is somewhat typical of this epistle (II Cor 3:9; 4:15; 8:2,7,8,12).

6. And whether we be afflicted, *it is* for your consolation and salvation, which is effectual in the enduring of the same sufferings which we also suffer: or whether we be comforted, *it is* for your consolation and salvation.

7. And our hope of you *is* steadfast, knowing, that as ye are partakers of the sufferings, so *shall ye be* also of the consolation.

8. For we would not, brethren, have you ignorant of our trouble which came to us in Asia, that we were pressed out of measure, above strength, insomuch that we despaired even of life:

9. But we had the sentence of death in ourselves, that we should not trust in ourselves, but in God which raiseth the dead:

10. Who delivered us from so great a death, and doth deliver: in whom we trust that he will yet deliver *us;*

6. The better translation is given in the ASV and the RSV. Note the present passives in the original—*are being afflicted . . . are being comforted.* Whether **afflicted** or **comforted,** the result is always good for God's children. The words, **which is effectual,** translate the present middle participle of *energeō.* In the middle form it always implies some kind of mysterious or supernatural force (cf. 4: 12; Rom 12:6,11; Gal 5:6; Eph 3:20; Col 1:29; I Thess 2:13; II Thess 2:7; Jas 5:16). In the active form God is always the subject (cf. I Cor 12:6,11; Gal 2:8; Eph 1:11,20; Phil 2:13). **7.** The eschatological **our hope** (cf. I Thess 2:19) is based squarely on the fact that salvation is **stedfast** (*bebaios,* "reliable, dependable, certain" — Arndt). In **knowing** (i.e., "since we know") Paul states the objective cause of his assurance regarding the Corinthians (cf. I Thess 1:4). The **as . . . so** (as in II Cor 7:14; Eph 5:24) differs only slightly from the construction in verse 5. The word (*koinōnos*) back of **partakers** is used of physical companionship (cf. II Cor 8:23), moral participation (cf. Mt 23:30; I Cor 10:18,20; Heb 10:33), and spiritual union (cf. I Pet 5:1; II Pet 1:4).

B. Paul's Desperation Relieved. 1:8-14.

8. The nature of **our trouble** (*thlipsis;* see v. 4) that took place **in Asia** (i.e., the Roman province of Asia) has been debated at length. Some commentators look upon the mob violence at Ephesus (cf. Acts 19:23-41; I Cor 15:32) as the occasion of this **trouble.** Whatever it was — and the language used here puts it among the most excruciating of human experiences — it was one of those trials that Paul endured for the name of Christ (cf. Acts 9:16; also Ps 69:1ff.; Isa 43:2). **9.** Like Isaac (cf. Heb 11:17-19), Paul had a **sentence of death** hanging over him; and, like Abraham, he could now **trust** anew **in God which raiseth the dead** (cf. Gen 22:1-18). **10.** The verb (*rhuomai*) rendered **delivered** is used elsewhere of Lot (II Pet 2:7,9), Paul (II Tim 4:17), and believers (I Thess 1:10). The use of **out of** (ASV) rather than **from** is justified by the fact that the Greek here uses *ek,* "out of," rather than *apo,* "from." Paul actually went through and triumphantly came "out of" the trouble here described (cf. Rom 8:35-39; also Ps 66: 12; 69:14; 144:7). The descriptive **so great** (cf. its use in Heb 2:3; Jas 3:4; Rev 16:18) reveals the utter magnitude

11. Ye also helping together by prayer for us, that for the gift *bestowed* upon us by the means of many persons thanks may be given by many on our behalf.

12. For our rejoicing is this, the testimony of our conscience, that in simplicity and godly sincerity, not with fleshly wisdom, but by the grace of God, we have had our conversation in the world, and more abundantly to you-ward.

13. For we write none other things unto you, than what ye read or acknowledge; and I trust ye shall acknowledge even to the end;

14. As also ye have acknowledged us in part, that we are your rejoicing, even as ye also *are* ours in the day of the Lord Jesus.

of this trial. Paul's deliverance was (1) a wonderful providence — **who delivered us;** (2) a sure prophecy — **and will deliver** (ASV); (3) a bright promise — **on whom we have set our hope that he will also still deliver us** (ASV). The future deliverance was fulfilled in II Tim 4:17.

**11.** This verse can be variously translated (see ASV and RSV). The basic thoughts are these: (1) the efficacy of prayer in Paul's deliverance; (2) the **gift** granted to the apostle; (3) the consequent thanksgiving rendered by . . . **many** . . . **persons on our behalf** (ASV). Paul had great faith in intercessory prayer (cf. Rom 15:30,31; Phil 1:19; Col 4:12). The word *charisma* means "a gift (freely and graciously given), a favor bestowed" (Arndt). It is not limited to ministerial endowments (cf. Rom 1:11; I Cor 1:7; I Pet 4:10).

**12.** The word **rejoicing** *(kauchēsis)* is found seven times in this epistle (7:4, 14; 8:24; 9:4; 11:10,17), but only five times elsewhere in the NT. By **behaved ourselves** (ASV) Paul means that three judges determined his conduct: (1) his **conscience;** (2) God's **holiness and sincerity** (ASV); (3) the **world** and the Corinthians. Spiritual irreconcilables and incompatibles are represented by **fleshly wisdom** (cf. Jas 3:15) and **the grace of God** (cf. I Cor 3:10; 15:10; Eph 3:2,7, 8).

**13.** Paul was a consistent man, whether dealing with hostile Jews (cf. Acts 26:22) or with recalcitrant Christians. What he wrote in his letters could be easily **read** and *fully known* (so *epiginōskō,* here translated **acknowledge,** usually means; cf. I Cor 13:12, ASV). The Greek phrase *heōs telous* can be translated **unto the end** (AV; ASV) or *fully* (RSV). The fact that the word used here usually designates "the end" (cf. Mt 24:6,14; I Cor 15:24), plus the fact that the next verse refers to the Second Advent, seems to justify **unto the end** as the best translation (cf. I Cor 1:8). **14.** Paul's laudation over the Corinthians was made poignant by the fact that the true motivation of his ministry among them was "fully known" (the same verb as in v. 13) only **in part,** i.e., by some of them (see the same construction in Rom 11:25; I Cor 13:9). The Second Advent is called **the day** (as in I Cor 1:8; 3:13; 5:5; Phil 1:6,10; I Thess 5:2; II Thess 2:2).

C. Paul's Diversion Justified. 1:15—2:17.

15. And in this confidence I was minded to come unto you before, that ye might have a second benefit;

16. And to pass by you into Macedonia, and to come again out of Macedonia unto you, and of you to be brought on my way toward Judea.

17. When I therefore was thus minded, did I use lightness? or the things that I purpose, do I purpose according to the flesh, that with me there should be yea, yea, and nay, nay?

18. But as God is true, our word toward you was not yea and nay.

19. For the Son of God, Jesus Christ, who was preached among you by us, even by me and Silvanus and Timotheus, was not yea and nay, but in him was yea.

20. For all the promises of God in him are yea, and in him Amen, unto the glory of God by us.

21. Now he which stablisheth us with you in Christ, and hath anointed us, is God;

22. Who hath also sealed us, and given the earnest of the Spirit in our hearts.

1) The Plan Contemplated. 1:15,16. 15. The word *pepoithēsis*, translated here as **confidence**, is used in the NT only by Paul (3:4; 8:22; 10:2; Eph 3:12; Phil 3:4). The **second benefit** (*charis*, "grace") sums up the double blessing that would be theirs by his two visits (cf. Rom 1:11). 16. Paul's contemplated plan included four stages: (1) a direct trip to Corinth; (2) a land trip from Corinth to Macedonia; (3) a return trip to Corinth; (4) a trip from Corinth to Judea. Paul often gave his proposed itinerary (cf. Rom 1:10; 15:22; I Thess 2:18).

2) The Plan Criticized. 1:17. Paul answers the charges made against him— of vacillating and using fleshly methods— (1) by using logic (**therefore**; but in the Greek both *oun* and *ara* are used); (2) by an emphatic negative (*mēti*; cf. Mt 7:16; 26:22,25)); (3) by repetition (**yea, yea; and nay, nay**); (4) by the emphasis of order (which can be seen only in the Greek).

3) The Plan Comprehended. 1:18-22. 18. **But as God is true** may be taken as an adjuration (AV; ASV; RSV) or as a plain statement ("But God is faithful in that our word which was toward you is not yea and nay"). Paul often appeals to the faithfulness of God as a proof of the truthfulness of the Gospel he proclaimed (cf. I Cor 1:9; I Thess 5:24; II Thess 3:3). 19. This verse reveals (1) the person, (2) the preaching, (3) the preachers, and (4) the positiveness of the message: all having their unity in Christ. The difference between **was** (aorist of *ginomai*) in **was not** and the **was** (perfect of *ginomai*) in **was yea** should be noted: "became not yea and nay, but in him became (and remains as) yea" (cf. Jn 1:14; Rev 1:17,18). 20. Read as in the ASV. The **how many soever** (ASV) correctly represents the Greek pronoun used here (see its use in Mt 14:36; Jn 1:12; Acts 3:24; Rom 2:12; Phil 3:5). All of God's promises find their realization and fulfillment in Christ (cf. Rom 15:8,9). 21,22. We should not overlook the references to the Trinity in 1:18-22: (1) the certainty given by God (v. 18); (2) the centrality found in Christ (vv. 18-20); (3) the certification established by the Spirit (vv. 21,22). Paul appeals to a present experience (**stablisheth**, present tense of *bebaioō*; cf. its use in Mk 16:20; Rom 15:8; I Cor 1:6,8; Col 2:7; Heb 2:3; 13:9), which is confirmed by three simultaneous and decisive acts that took

23. Moreover I call God for a record upon my soul, that to spare you I came not as yet unto Corinth.

24. Not for that we have dominion over your faith, but are helpers of your joy: for by faith ye stand.

## CHAPTER 2

BUT I determined this with myself, that I would not come again to you in heaviness.

2. For if I make you sorry, who is he then that maketh me glad, but the same which is made sorry by me?

3. And I wrote this same unto you, lest, when I came, I should have sorrow from them of whom I ought to rejoice; having confidence in you all, that my joy is *the joy* of you all.

place at regeneration − **anointed . . . sealed . . . gave** (ASV; all in the aorist tense). The verb *(chriō)* translated **anointed** is used concerning the anointing of the Holy Spirit (cf. Lk 4:18; Acts 4:27; 10:38; Heb 1:9). The name *Christ* ("The Anointed One") comes from the same root. The **earnest** *(arrabōn;* used elsewhere in the NT only in II Cor 5:5; Eph 1:14) is the initial payment on a purchase: *a guarantee* (RSV).

4) The Plan Changed. 1:23−2:4. **23.** Paul gives a negative reason (**to spare you;** 1:23−2:4a) and a positive reason (**but that ye might know the love,** etc.; 2:4 b) why he changed his contemplated plan. **But I call God for a witness upon my soul** (ASV) correctly represents Paul's words (cf. 11:31; Rom 1:9; Phil 1:8; I Thess 2:5,10). The **not as yet** statement could be translated as "no more" − implying that Paul desisted from his visit to Corinth until certain things were corrected there (cf. II Cor 13:2,10). **24.** That the words "to spare you" might not be misunderstood, Paul reminds his readers that he is not seeking ecclesiastical tyranny over their **faith** (cf. 4:5; 11:20; I Pet 5:3). The word **joy** *(chara)* occurs as often in this epistle (1:24; 2:3; 7:4,13; 8:2) as in Philippians (1:4,25; 2:2,29; 4:1). We can read **by faith** (AV) or *in faith* (ASV; RSV) − the former indicating means; the latter, sphere. On **stand,** see also Rom 5:2; 11:20; I Cor 15:1; I Pet 5:9.

**2:1.** Paul's "determination" issued from the fact that **sorrow** (ASV) would have characterized his visit if his original plan (cf. 1:15,16) had been carried out. Endless debate has revolved around the words **come again.** The issue is made extremely complex by the fact that only one visit to Corinth is recorded in Acts (18:1-18) prior to this epistle. However, in II Cor 12:14; 13:1 it appears that the apostle's next visit was to be his third one. Some scholars hold that Paul made a second (unrecorded) visit. **2.** The **if** assumes the fact to be true (as in 2:5,9; 3:7,9,11; 5:14). Paul gets no sadistic delight out of pain he causes his converts: his sadness and joy are contingent on their spiritual state.

**3.** Which letter are we to understand by **I wrote?** Older commentators generally assumed that our I Corinthians is referred to here; more recent commentators think that Paul is referring to a "stern letter" (now lost or else found in chapters 10−13 of our present epistle) that

4. For out of much affliction and anguish of heart I wrote unto you with many tears; not that ye should be grieved, but that ye might know the love which I have more abundantly unto you.

5. But if any have caused grief, he hath not grieved me, but in part: that I may not overcharge you all.

6. Sufficient to such a man *is* this punishment, which *was inflicted* of many.

7. So that contrariwise ye *ought* rather to forgive *him*, and comfort *him*, lest perhaps such a one should be swallowed up with overmuch sorrow.

8. Wherefore I beseech you that ye would confirm *your* love toward him.

he wrote after he wrote I Corinthians. These same commentators also assume that an unrecorded visit took place prior to the "stern letter." One cannot be dogmatic on the circumstances surrounding Paul's relation to the church at Corinth.

**4.** Paul's emotional life is here epitomized in (1) depth — **much affliction and anguish of heart;** (2) its visible expression—**with many tears;** (3) its negative purpose — **not that ye should be grieved;** (4) its positive purpose — **that ye might know the love which I have more abundantly unto you.** The last clause gives Paul's positive reason (see 1:23) for changing his plan (cf. 1:15,16).

5) The Plan Chastened. 2:5-11. **5.** The reference of **any** hinges on the view one takes of Paul's visits and letters to Corinth. According to the older view, the incestuous person of I Cor 5:1-8 is referred to here. More recent commentators hold that a person or party (cf. II Cor 10:7; I Cor 1:12) had recently arisen there to challenge Paul's apostolic authority. The issue will probably never be settled until we possess more than the scanty facts we now have. In **overcharge** (*epibareō,* "to weigh down, burden" — Arndt) we have perhaps a polite understatement of Paul's concern (cf. the same word in I Thess 2:9; II Thess 3:8). **6.** The **punishment** was **sufficient.** "The punishment is severe enough" (Arndt). But the silence was polite (**such a man**) and ominous (**of many** — implying that a recalcitrant minority still rebelled against Paul).

**7.** Neither **ought** (AV) nor **should** (ASV; RSV) is required by the Greek. Plummer puts it thus: "So that on the contrary you may rather forgive him" (*A Critical and Exegetical Commentary on the Second Epistle of St. Paul to the Corinthians*). The verb **forgive** (*charizomai;* see its use in II Cor 1:10; 12:13; Rom 8:32; Gal 3:18; Eph 4:32; Col 2:13; 3:13) means "to give freely or graciously as a favor" (Arndt). It should be noted that this was the act of the whole church. The use of **lest by any means** (ASV), which translates *mē pōs* (cf. its use in II Cor 9:4; 11:3; 12:20; I Cor 8:9; 9:27), indicates that the action mentioned was within the range of possibility. **8. Confirm** (*kyroō;* elsewhere in NT only in Gal 3:15) means either "to reaffirm" (Arndt) or "to ratify" (Plummer). Their acceptance of him as a brother restored to Christian fellowship

9. For to this end also did I write, that I might know the proof of you, whether ye be obedient in all things.

10. To whom ye forgive any thing, I *forgive* also: for if I forgave any thing, to whom I forgave *it*, for your sakes *forgave I it* in the person of Christ;

11. Lest Satan should get an advantage of us: for we are not ignorant of his devices.

12. Furthermore, when I came to Troas to *preach* Christ's gospel, and a door was opened unto me of the Lord,

13. I had no rest in my spirit, because I found not Titus my brother; but taking my leave of them, I went from thence into Macedonia.

14. Now thanks *be* unto God, which always causeth us to triumph in Christ, and maketh manifest the savor of his knowledge by us in every place.

would be the public display of this "reaffirmation."

9. Paul indicates three reasons why he wrote: (1) to prepare them for his visit (2:3); (2) to manifest to them his love (2:4); (3) to test their obedience (2:9). The word **proof** *(dokimē)* is found four times in this epistle (2:9; 8:2; 9:13; 13: 3); elsewhere in the NT only in Rom 5:4; Phil 2:22. By **in all things** Paul shows that incomplete obedience is intolerable.

10. Read this verse in the ASV or the RSV. Paul ratifies the action of the Corinthian church in the corporate duty of "forgiving" (cf. Jn 20:23). On **forgive**, see II Cor 2:7. We can read the last statement as **in the person of Christ** (AV), i.e., acting as his representative; or *in the presence of Christ* (ASV; RSV), i.e., acting with him as our witness. 11. We have (1) a common foe — Satan; (2) a common danger — **get an advantage of us**; (3) a common protection — **we are not ignorant of his devices.** The verb *pleonekteō* (found elsewhere in the NT only in 7:2; 12:17,18; I Thess 4:6) means "to take advantage of, outwit, defraud, cheat" (Arndt). Here we may read: "that we may not be outwitted by Satan" (Arndt).

6) The Plan Consummated. 2:12-17. 12. From here to the end of the chapter Paul tells us how his changed plan was consummated in trial (vv. 12,13), in triumph (vv. 14-16), and in testimony (v. 17). What an opportunity—a **door!** What a privilege—**for me!** What a responsibility—**opened!** What a relationship—**in the Lord!** Paul's travels were always purposive and evangelistic — **for the gospel of Christ** (ASV). 13. Paul's disturbed **spirit** demanded his quick departure from Troas. To get news concerning the Corinthian church was his immediate obsession; all else — including the evangelization of Troas — was secondary. Who or what caused these two men — Paul and Titus — to "foul up" their plans is not revealed here. Shall we say that souls were lost in Troas because of somebody's failure? God overruled by granting Paul a ministry there on his return from Corinth (Acts 20:6).

14. The order in the Greek is emphatic: "But unto God be thanks" (cf. 8: 16; 9:15). This verse illustrates Rom 8: 28. The verb *thriambeuō* should be translated **leadeth us in triumph** (ASV; RSV). This verb is used elsewhere in the NT only in Col 2:15. Paul considers himself

**15.** For we are unto God a sweet savor of Christ, in them that are saved, and in them that perish:

**16.** To the one *we are* the savor of death unto death; and to the other the savor of life unto life. And who *is* sufficient for these things?

**17.** For we are not as many, which corrupt the word of God: but as of sincerity, but as of God, in the sight of God speak we in Christ.

## CHAPTER 3

DO we begin again to commend ourselves? or need we, as some *others*, epistles of commendation to you, or *letters* of commendation from you?

**2.** Ye are our epistle written in our hearts, known and read of all men:

**3.** *Forasmuch as ye are* manifestly declared to be the epistle of Christ ministered by us, written not with ink, but with the Spirit of the living God; not in tables of stone, but in fleshly tables of the heart.

as a slave (cf. Rom 1:1) being led triumphantly in the Messiah's conquered host (cf. Eph 4:8; after a victorious military campaign it was customary for Roman emperors to stage a "triumph," during which they paraded captives through the streets of Rome). Note the **always** *(pantote;* cf. II Cor 4:10; 5:6; 9:8) and **in every place** (cf. Acts 1:8; Rom 10:18; Col 1:6,23). The verb *(phaneroō)* translated **maketh manifest** is quite common in this epistle (3:3; 4:10,11; 5:10; 7:12; 11:6). The use of **savour** shows that Paul is continuing the picture of a triumphal procession. The word **knowledge** *(gnōsis)* is used twenty-nine times in the NT; Paul uses it twenty-three times. It is used elsewhere in this epistle in 4:6; 6:6; 8:7; 10:5; 11:6.

**15.** In the NT, salvation is described as (1) past (aorist tense: II Tim 1:9; Tit 3:5); (2) present (present tense: here and in I Cor 1:18; 15:2); (3) future (future tense: Rom 5:9,10; I Cor 3:5; II Tim 4:18); (4) completed (perfect tense: Eph 2:5,8). The verb **perish** *(apollumi;* cf. its use in II Cor 4:3; Jn 3:16; 10:28; 17:12; 18:9; II Thess 2:10) designates destruction and ruination rather than annihilation. **16.** The same **savour** is wafted to all by the messengers of the Gospel. To some it is fatal; to others it is lifegiving (cf. Jn 3:19; 9:39; 15:22; 16:8 ff.; Acts 13:46 ff.; 28:25-28). The transition from spiritual death (cf. Eph 2:1) to eternal death (cf. Rev 2:11; 20:14; 21:8) is probably indicated by **from death unto death** (ASV).

**17.** Paul's testimony is that he does not, like **many** (the false teachers, mentioned in 11:4,12-15), **corrupt** *(kapēleuō,* meaning "to trade in, peddle, huckster" — Arndt) **the word of God.** Paul's sincerity is evident in its (1) origin — **of God;** (2) manifestation — **in the sight of God;** (3) sphere of action — **speak we in Christ** (cf. 13:3).

D. Paul's Dispensation Superior. 3:1-18.

1) Superior in Documentation. 3:1-3. **1.** Paul vehemently exposes those who need **letters** of self-commendation (cf. 5:12; 10:12,18; 12:11). His mission and ministry did not need such conceited self-appraisal. **2.** On the contrary, Paul's letter is (1) personalized — **our epistle;** (2) permanent — **written in our hearts;** (3) public — **known and read of all men. 3.** The genuineness of the Corinthians as **an epistle of Christ** (ASV) is authenti-

4. And such trust have we through Christ to God-ward:

5. Not that we are sufficient of ourselves to think any thing as of ourselves; but our sufficiency *is* of God;

6. Who also hath made us able ministers of the new testament; not of the letter, but of the spirit: for the letter killeth, but the spirit giveth life.

7. But if the ministration of death, written *and* engraven in stones, was glorious, so that the children of Israel could not steadfastly behold the face of Moses for the glory of his countenance; which *glory* was to be done away;

cated (1) by their ministry — **ministered by us;** (2) by their supernatural origin — **with the Spirit of the living God;** (3) by their internal testimony — **in fleshy tables of the heart** (cf. Jer 24:7; 31:33; 32:39; Ezk 11:19; 36:26).

2) Superior in Dynamism. 3:4-6. **4.** This **trust** *(pepoithēsis;* see 1:15) is **through Christ.** The use of the definite article before **Christ** ("The Christ"; i.e., "The Anointed One") is quite common in this epistle (1:5; 2:12,14; 3:4; 4:4; 5:10, 14; 9:13; 10:1,5,14; 11:2,3; 12:9). On **through** *(dia),* see 5:18 in the ASV. **5.** Our **sufficiency** *(hikanotēs,* meaning "fitness, capability, qualification"—Arndt) is **of God.** The **of** *(ek)* indicates source (as in 4:7,18; Jn 10:47; 18:36,37. Cf. I Cor 15:10).

**6.** Follow the ASV translation: **who also made us sufficient as ministers.** The **new covenant** (ASV; cf. Mt 26:28; Heb 8:8,13) requires a "new man" (Eph 2:15; 4:24) who is a "new creature" (II Cor 5:17). This regenerated person has a "new name" (Rev 2:17), observes a "new commandment" (I Jn 2:7,8), sings a "new song" (Rev 14:3), looks for "new heavens and a new earth" (II Pet 3:13; Rev 21:1) where the "new Jerusalem" (Rev 21:2) is and where all things are "new" (Rev 21:5). The contrast between **the letter killeth** and **the spirit giveth life** is not a contrast between extreme literalism and a free handling of Scripture (as in the allegorical method of interpretation); the contrast is rather between the Law as a system of salvation requiring perfect obedience (cf. Rom 3:19,20; 7:1-14; 8:1-11; Gal 3:1-14) and the Gospel as God's gift of grace in Christ. Even the Law, however, could lead a soul to Christ (cf. Gal 3:15-29); but degenerate Judaism had turned it into a lifeless mass of forms (cf. Isa 1:10-20; Jer 7:21-26). The new age of "grace and truth" (Jn 1:17), already anticipated in the OT (cf. Ezk 37:1-14; 47:1-12), is now fully realized in the dynamic dispensation of grace (cf. Jn 4:23; 6:63; Rom 2:28; 7:6).

3) Superior in Degree. 3:7-9. **7.** Read Ex 34:29-35 for background material. The dispensation of "the letter" is inferior to the dispensation of "the spirit" in (1) essential nature — **death** (cf. Rom 7:5,10,11; Gal 3:10,21,22); (2) outward form — **engraven in stones** (cf. Ex 24:12; 31:18); (3) abiding merit — **which glory was passing away** (ASV). The verb *(katargeō)* in the last clause means "to

**8.** How shall not the ministration of the spirit be rather glorious?

**9.** For if the ministration of condemnation *be* glory, much more doth the ministration of righteousness exceed in glory.

**10.** For even that which was made glorious had no glory in this respect, by reason of the glory that excelleth.

**11.** For if that which is done away *was* glorious, much more that which remaineth *is* glorious.

**12.** Seeing then that we have such hope, we use great plainness of speech:

**13.** And not as Moses, *which* put a veil over his face, that the children of Israel could not steadfastly look to the end of that which is abolished:

abolish, wipe out, set aside" (Arndt); except for two places (Lk 13:7 and Heb 2:14), it is used exclusively in the NT by Paul (e.g., II Cor 3:1,13,14; I Cor 15:24,26; II Tim 1:10).

**8.** The negative **not** *(ouchi)* expects a strong positive answer (as in I Cor 9:1; 10:16,18). The argument used here is called *argumentum a minore ad majus:* if the lesser of two things be true, how much more shall the greater be true.

**9.** The old dispensation admittedly had its **glory** (cf. Rom 9:4,5); but the new dispensation must **exceed in glory** (cf. Heb 8:6ff.; 9:11-15). In the OT "everlasting righteousness" (Dan 9:24) was promised as a concomitant of the Messiah's advent (cf. Isa 51:5-8; 56:1; Jer 23:5,6). That **righteousness** was fulfilled by Christ (cf. II Cor 5:21; Mt 3:15; Rom 10:4) and is now imputed to all who believe on him (cf. II Cor 5:21; Rom 3:21-31; 4:1-13).

4) Superior in Destination. 3:10,11. **10.** The new dispensation is superior to the old in that the new is not subject to diminution and demolition. The **glory** of the old was but a reflection of the new; it was a "copy and shadow" (Heb 8:5; 10:1) of the new. **11.** The old "is being abolished" (ASV margin); the new remains. The verbs **done away** and **remaineth** are present participles. Cf. Heb 12:18-28.

5) Superior in Diagnosis. 3:12-17. **12.** The new far exceeds the old in clarity and perspicuity. The use of **such** calls up the inherent quality of the thing to which it is applied (as in Mt 19:14; Jn 9:16; Gal 5:21,23; Heb 13:16). Paul uses the word **hope** in all of his epistles except Philemon. **Plainness of speech** *(parrēsia;* cf. II Cor 7:4) describes the *boldness of speech* (ASV) that characterized the early Christians (cf. Acts 2:29; 4:13,29,31) and Paul (cf. Eph 6:19; Phil 1:20) in their testimony against Jews and Gentiles. The believers were not ashamed of the Gospel, because they knew it had an inner power and vitality that could not be found elsewhere (cf. Rom 1:16,17). **13.** Read this verse in the ASV or the RSV. We have here the reason for the "great boldness" of Christians. Moses *used to put* (the verb is in the imperfect tense) a veil on his face so that the Israelites could not see **the end of the fading splendor** (RSV). In Paul's inspired interpretation of the OT, the evanescent glory that shone from Moses' face after his

**14.** But their minds were blinded: for until this day remaineth the same veil untaken away in the reading of the old testament; which *veil* is done away in Christ.

**15.** But even unto this day, when Moses is read, the veil is upon their heart.

**16.** Nevertheless, when it shall turn to the Lord, the veil shall be taken away.

**17.** Now the Lord is that Spirit: and where the Spirit of the Lord *is*, there *is* liberty.

communion with God becomes typical of the passing glory of the old dispensation.

**14.** Paul here gives a spiritual application for the physical **veil** on Moses' face. That **veil** now becomes a **veil** that keeps the Jews from understanding the true import of **the old covenant** as they read it (ASV). The word *noēma*, here translated **minds,** is used almost exclusively in this epistle (2:11; 4:4; 10:5; 11:3; cf. Phil 4: 7). The cognate verb form *(noeō)* designates "rational reflection or inner perception" (Arndt; cf. its use in Jn 12:40; I Tim 1:7; Heb 11:3). The passive form **were blinded** denotes the judicial blindness that befell Israel when the nation rejected Christ (cf. Jn 12:40; Rom 11:7, 25). Such blindness may be due to God (cf. Rom 11:7,8), Satan (cf. II Cor 4:4), or man himself (cf. Heb 3:8). The clause, **which veil is done away in Christ,** can also be translated as in the ASV or as in the RSV. The verb **is done away** (present passive of *katargeō;* see II Cor 3:7 b) means that this **veil** of spiritual blindness is being removed from the hearts of believing Israelites the moment they "see" Christ as their Saviour (cf. Jn 9:40,41).

**15.** The Pentateuch was habitually read — **whensoever Moses is read** (ASV) — in the synagogues (cf. Acts 15:21). Paul had no question about its authorship (cf. Acts 26:22; 28:23; Rom 10:5,19; I Cor 9:9). It was even necessary for Christ to "open" the minds of his own disciples regarding the Messianic significance of the OT (cf. Lk 24:25,26,32,44,45). **16.** The **whensoever** (ASV) should be retained here. It is the same indefinite particle as is used in verse 15 (but nowhere else in the NT). The subject of **shall turn** may be either "the heart" or "he" (i.e., the individual Israelite). The verb **turn** *(epistrephō)* often designates conversion (cf. Lk 1:16,17; Acts 3:19; 26:20; I Thess 1:9). Whenever the soul believes, then "the veil is being removed" — the removal of the veil synchronizes with the act of saving faith (cf. Isa 25:7; Zech 12:10).

**17. The Lord is the Spirit** (ASV). This construction in the Greek, with the definite article preceding both subject and predicate (cf. I Jn 3:4), indicates identity of nature. By **Lord** here we are to understand Jesus Christ (so almost universally in Paul's writings; e.g., II Cor 5:6,8,11; 8:5; 10:8; 12:1,8). Paul is here teaching that Christ and the Spirit have the same essence (cf. Jn 10:30); their persons remain distinct. As announced prophetically (Isa 61:1,2; Joel 2:28-32), the new

**18.** But we all, with open face beholding as in a glass the glory of the Lord, are changed into the same image from glory to glory, *even* as by the Spirit of the Lord.

## CHAPTER 4

THEREFORE, seeing we have this ministry, as we have received mercy, we faint not;
**2.** But have renounced the hidden things of dishonesty, not walking in craftiness, nor handling the word of God deceitfully; but, by manifestation of the truth, commending ourselves to every man's conscience in the sight of God.
**3.** But if our gospel be hid, it is hid to them that are lost:
**4.** In whom the god of this world hath blinded the minds of them which believe not, lest the light of the glorious gospel of Christ, who is the image of God, should shine unto them.

dispensation was to be characterized by the outpouring of the Spirit. The Lord Jesus sent the Spirit (cf. Jn 16:7). **Where** and "whensoever" (II Cor 3:16) the Spirit regenerates the heart, there is real liberty (cf. Jn 8:32; Gal 5:1,13).

6) Superior in Denouement. 3:18. Here is the grand finale. Using Ex 34:29-35 as the background, Paul gives a summary of advantages possessed by the new dispensation: (1) liberty — **with unveiled face** (ASV); (2) intimacy—**beholding . . . the glory of the Lord** (cf. Ex 33:17-23, I Jn 3:1,2); (3) efficacy — **are** (being) **transformed into the same image** (ASV); (4) perfection—**glory to glory** (cf. Isa 66: 11,12); (5) supernatural origination—**even as from the Lord the Spirit** (ASV). The last statement, translated erroneously in the AV, equates Christ and the Spirit in the cooperative work of salvation (cf. II Cor 3:17; Jn 7:39; 15:26; 16:6-14).

E. Paul's Dualism Explained. 4:1-18.

1) The Hidden and the Open. 4:1,2. **1.** Note three things: (1) our riches — **we have this ministry**; (2) our reminder — **even as we obtained mercy** (ASV; cf. I Tim 1:13,16); (3) our resource — **we faint not** (cf. the same verb in II Cor 4:16; Lk 18:1; Gal 6:9; Eph 3:13; II Thess 3:13). **2.** The decisive act, **renounced**, is explained by two negative concomitants: (1) **not walking in craftiness**; (2) **nor handling the word of God deceitfully**. The resultant life is described according to its (1) means — **by the manifestation of the truth**; (2) method — **commending ourselves to every man's conscience**; (3) measure — **in the sight of God**. Christians should renounce (as here), repudiate (cf. 6:14-17), and reprove (cf. Eph 5:11) **the hidden things of shame** (ASV; cf. Rom 6:21; I Cor 4:5).

2) The Blinded and the Enlightened. 4:3,4. **3.** The **if** assumes the state to be real. **Our gospel.** The one and only **gospel** (cf. Gal 1:6 ff.). **Is veiled** (ASV). The perfect tense portrays the fixed state. The present participle is correctly rendered by **them that are perishing** (RSV; cf. 2:15). The AV's use of **hid** obscures the implicit reference to 3:13-18; the "veil" that "blinded" the Jewish mind has now become the "veil" that Satan uses to "blind" the **perishing** (RSV). **4.** Satan is here called *the god of this age* (so the Greek; cf. Jn 12:31; 14:30; 16:11; Eph 2:2). The word *image (eikōn)* is twice

5. For we preach not ourselves, but Christ Jesus the Lord; and ourselves your servants for Jesus' sake.

6. For God, who commanded the light to shine out of darkness, hath shined in our hearts, to *give* the light of the knowledge of the glory of God in the face of Jesus Christ.

7. But we have this treasure in earthen vessels, that the excellency of the power may be of God, and not of us.

8. *We are* troubled on every side, yet not distressed; *we are* perplexed, but not in despair;

9. Persecuted, but not forsaken; cast down, but not destroyed;

10. Always bearing about in the body the dying of the Lord Jesus, that the life also of Jesus might be made manifest in our body.

11. For we which live are alway delivered unto death for Jesus' sake, that the life also of Jesus might be made manifest in our mortal flesh.

elsewhere applied to Christ (Col 1:15; Heb 1:3). The verb shine (*augazō*) is found only here in the NT.

3) Slaves and the Master 4:5. Paul preached **Christ Jesus as Lord** (ASV). The supreme Lordship of Christ was central in apostolic preaching (cf. the same construction as here in the ASV translation of Rom 10:9; Phil 2:11). The original of **servants** is *slaves*. Paul repeatedly calls himself a "slave" (*doulos;* cf. Rom 1:1; Gal 1:10; Phil 1:1; Tit 1:1). Here he uses the term to describe his relationship to his converts at Corinth.

4) Darkness and Light. 4:6. The versions (AV, ASV, RSV) differ considerably here. The RSV seems to present the original most clearly. Paul goes back to creation (Gen 1:3) for a prototype of his own conversion (cf. Acts 9:3ff.). The God who created the physical light illuminates our minds in our re-creation when we savingly behold **the face of Jesus Christ.**

5) The Frail and the Mighty. 4:7. By **this treasure** Paul reminds us that the Gospel is a valuable jewel (cf. Mt 13:44, 52) committed to him (cf. Eph 3:1,2,7,8). Human nature in its weakness and frailty is pictured in the phrase **earthen vessels** (cf. Acts 9:15). The word **exceeding** (*hyperbolē*) means "excess, extraordinary quality or character" (Arndt). The word is used in the NT only by Paul (II Cor 1:8; 4:7,17; 12:17; Rom 7:13; I Cor 12:31; Gal 1:13).

6) Trials and Triumphs. 4:8-10. These verses may be summarized thus: (1) All the verbs in 8-10 a are present participles and are grammatically related to "we" in 4:7. They explain or illustrate Paul's secret of power in "earthern vessels." (2) These participles seem to go in ascensive order — like a swelling crescendo. (3) They are paradoxical and antithetical — contrasting nature with grace. (4) Moreover, although based on 2:14ff., they step up higher on the ladder that will lead us through 6:4-10 up to the climax in 11: 16-23. **Always bearing about in the body the dying of the Lord Jesus** (v. 10). Cf. Rom 8:36; I Cor 15:31; Gal 6:17; Col 1:24. Paul's great desire was that **the life also of Jesus may be manifested in our body** (ASV; cf. Gal 2:20; Phil 1:20).

7) Death and Life. 4:11,12. The thought of verse 10 is repeated, with the significant addition of **for Jesus' sake** (cf.

12. So then death worketh in us, but life in you.

13. We having the same spirit of faith, according as it is written, I believed, and therefore have I spoken; we also believe, and therefore speak;

14. Knowing that he which raised up the Lord Jesus shall raise up us also by Jesus, and shall present *us* with you.

15. For all things *are* for your sakes, that the abundant grace might through the thanksgiving of many redound to the glory of God.

16. For which cause we faint not; but though our outward man perish, yet the inward *man* is renewed day by day.

17. For our light affliction, which is but for a moment, worketh for us a far more exceeding *and* eternal weight of glory;

Acts 9:16; Phil 1:29). The apostle's life was a continuous exposure to death — we are always being given up to death (RSV; cf. II Tim 4:6, ASV). On worketh (*energeō*), see II Cor 1:6. God's power also worked in Paul (cf. Eph 3:20; Col 1:29).

8) The Written and the Spoken. 4:13. Paul, citing Ps 116:10 (LXX), gives the reason for his speaking. Having (ASV) equals "because we have." This verse implicitly teaches that the Holy Spirit is the Author of faith, Scripture, and testimony. The we is emphatic: Paul, like David, believes and speaks; the two dispensations are united in faith (cf. Heb 11:39,40).

9) The Past and the Future. 4:14. The resurrection of believers is here presented with reference to its (1) Author — he which raised up the Lord Jesus (cf. Acts 3:26); (2) time — shall raise up (cf. I Cor 15:51,52; I Thess 4:13ff.); (3) cause— also with Jesus (ASV; cf. I Cor 15:20-23); (4) purpose — shall present us with you (cf. Eph 5:27; I Thess 2:19,20).

10) Grace and Thanksgiving. 4:15. Paul's philosophy (all things . . . for your sakes) issues in a purpose (that) which finds a plenitude of grace that causes thanksgiving to abound unto the glory of God (ASV). On abound, see 1:5.

11) The Outer and the Inner Man. 4:16. Faint not. See 4:1. Is decaying (ASV) . . . is being renewed (RSV). The present tense in both verbs indicates simultaneous action. The outward man corresponds to the "earthen vessels" of 4:7 and the "earthly house" of 5:1. The seeds of decay and dissolution are in the body from birth. Read Rom 8:18-25 as an extended commentary on this verse. "For here we have no continuing city" (Heb 13:14).

12) Affliction and Glory. 4:17. We have here (1) the disparity, (2) the design, and (3) the denouement. The disparity is threefold: (1) in time — for a moment contrasted with eternal; (2) in magnitude — light contrasted with weight; (3) in character — affliction contrasted with glory. The design is found in worketh, a verb (*katergazomai*), which means "to bring about, produce, create" (Arndt). This verb is found seven times in this epistle (5:5; 7:10,11; 9:11; 12:12). The denouement is sounded in the more and more exceedingly (ASV), in which Paul

18. While we look not at the things which are seen, but at the things which are not seen: for the things which are seen *are* temporal; but the things which are not seen *are* eternal.

## CHAPTER 5

FOR we know that, if our earthly house of *this* tabernacle were dissolved, we have a building of God, a house not made with hands, eternal in the heavens.

2. For in this we groan, earnestly desiring to be clothed upon with our house which is from heaven:

3. If so be that being clothed we shall not be found naked.

4. For we that are in *this* tabernacle do groan, being burdened: not for that we would be unclothed, but clothed upon, that mortality might be swallowed up of life.

5. Now he that hath wrought us for the selfsame thing *is* God, who also hath given unto us the earnest of the Spirit.

almost exhausts the Greek language in his crescendo of superlatives.

13) The Seen and the Unseen. 4:18 a. **While we look** represents the present participle of *skopeō* (a verb that occurs elsewhere in the NT only in Lk 11:35; Rom 16:17; Gal 6:1; Phil 2:4; 3:17). One should not "keep one's eye on what can be seen" (Arndt). Consult Heb 11:1,7. 13-15,26 for the same thought.

14) The Temporal and the Eternal. 4: 18 b. The word **temporal** *(proskairos;* elsewhere in the NT only in Mt 13:21; Mk 4:17; Heb 11:25) defines the ephemeral and evanescent in contrast to the abiding and **eternal.** Eternity is the everlasting *now;* we live in the midst of it, although we cannot see it. In the glorified state we shall know fully (cf. I Cor 13: 12) and see fully (cf. I Jn 3:2). Now we walk by faith.

F. Paul's Dedication Motivated. 5:1– 6:10.

1) Motivated by Knowledge. 5:1-9. **1.** Christians can **know** *(oida;* the same verb is used in I Jn 2:21; 3:1,2) the truth about the unseen world (cf. II Cor 4:17, 18). The **if** *(ean;* cf. its use in I Jn 3:2) suggests uncertainty regarding the time but not concerning the fact. The **earthly house** (cf. II Cor 4:7) is called a **tabernacle** — very vulnerable and transitory. The verb **were dissolved** *(kataluō)* means "to tear down, demolish" (Arndt). The body's decomposition signalizes its exit from earth into a far more glorious state above (cf. Phil 1:23; 3:20,21; I Jn 3:2, 14). No philosophy can give the assurance found in **we have** (cf. *echō* in II Cor 3:4,12; 4:1,7,13; 7:1; 9:8 for a treasury of spiritual possessions).

**2.** Probably **tabernacle** (v. 1) is the antecedent of **this.** The use of **groan** *(stenazō;* cf. its use in Rom 8:23) suggests that there is something distasteful in the present state (cf. Phil 1:23). The adverb **earnestly** translates the preposition *epi* in *epipotheō*—a verb expressing vehemence of desire, as can be seen in such passages as Rom 1:11; Phil 1:8; II Tim 1:4. **3.** The meaning of **being clothed** and **naked** has been debated interminably. Such passages as Jn 11:25,26; I Cor 15: 37-49; Phil 1:21-23; 3:20,21; I Thess 4: 13-18; I Jn 3:1 ff.; Rev 6:9; 20:4 must be taken into account in our interpretation.

**4.** This verse restates and expands the previous verses. The transformation here

6. Therefore *we are* always confident, knowing that, whilst we are at home in the body, we are absent from the Lord:

7. (For we walk by faith, not by sight:)

8. We are confident, *I say*, and willing rather to be absent from the body, and to be present with the Lord.

9. Wherefore we labor, that, whether present or absent, we may be accepted of him.

10. For we must all appear before the judgment seat of Christ; that every one may receive the things *done* in *his* body, according to that he hath done, whether *it be* good or bad.

11. Knowing therefore the terror of the Lord, we persuade men; but we are made manifest unto God; and I trust also are made manifest in your consciences.

envisaged is that what is mortal may be swallowed up of life (ASV). "Death is swallowed up in victory" (I Cor 15:54). Compare the cases of Enoch (Gen 5:24) and Elijah (II Kgs 2:11). The absolute use of *the life* (so the Greek) must carry some significance here as in the other places where the definite article is used (II Cor 4:12; I Jn 1:2; 2:25; 3:14; 5:12). 5. The aorist **wrought** (ASV; see 4:17 for the verb) takes us back to God's decrees (cf. Rom 8:30; 9:23; I Cor 2:7-9). On earnest see 1:22.

6. The adverb **always** *(pantote)* is found in all of Paul's epistles. It is applied to such things as prayer (Rom 1:9), thanksgiving (I Cor 1:4), work (I Cor 15:58), and obedience (Phil 2:12). Cf. also II Cor 2:14; 4:10; 9:8. The verb *endēmeō* ("to be at home" — Arndt) should be consistently translated (as ᵢin ASV) here and in 5:8,9 (the only places where it is found in the NT). 7. **Walk** *(peripateō)*. A verb often used to describe the Christian's whole life (cf. Rom 6:4; 13:13). In II Cor 1:12 "we behaved ourselves" (ASV) is a comparable expression.

8. The thought of 5:6 is resumed. **Willing rather.** Paul does not mean that he is anxiously courting the opportunity to leave the present life (cf. the faulty rendering in the RSV). The verb translated **willing** *(eudokeō)* simply denotes that which brings pleasurable satisfaction (cf. its use in Mt 3:17; 12:18; 17:5). Cf. Phil 1:23. 9. The verb **labour** *(philotimeomai;* elsewhere in NT only in Rom 15:20; I Thess 4:11) means "to have as one's ambition" (Arndt). The word **accepted** *(euarestos)* is used in the NT only by Paul (Rom 12:1,2; 14:18; Eph 5:10; Phil 4:18; Col 3:20; Tit 2:9) and in Heb 13:21.

2) Motivated by Judgment. 5:10. This important verse may be summarized thus: (1) the plan — we must; (2) the parties — all; (3) the presence — appear; (4) the place — before the judgment seat of Christ (cf. Rom 14:10); (5) the purpose — that, etc. The purpose (1) includes all — every one; (2) recompenses all — may receive; (3) recalls all — the things done in his body; (4) discriminates between all — according to that he hath done, whether it be good or bad.

3) Motivated by Fear. 5:11. **Knowing** is definitely causal ("since we know"). *Phobos* (as in Acts 9:31; Eph 5:21) should be rendered as **fear** (ASV; RSV).

12. For we commend not ourselves again unto you, but give you occasion to glory on our behalf, that ye may have somewhat to *answer* them which glory in appearance, and not in heart.

13. For whether we be beside ourselves, *it is* to God: or whether we be sober, *it is* for your cause.

14. For the love of Christ constraineth us; because we thus judge, that if one died for all, then were all dead:

15. And *that* he died for all, that they which live should not henceforth live unto themselves but unto him which died for them, and rose again.

It denotes that reverential awe that should characterize the believer's life in view of his appearance before Christ as Judge. The order and emphasis of the original is like this: ". . . men we are persuading; but to God we have been made manifest, and I hope that in your consciences we have been made manifest." Paul sought to **persuade men** either (1) concerning the coming judgment (II Cor 5:10), or (2) of his own integrity as a minister, or (3) of the need of reconciliation (v. 5:18-21). Only (2) seems to be immediately relevant.

4) Motivated by Unselfishness. 5:12, 13. **12. Commend** (*sunistanō*). "To introduce or recommend someone to someone else" (Arndt). This verb is so characteristic of this letter (3:1; 4:2; 6:4; 7:11; 10:12,18; 12:11) that it occurs here more times than in all the rest of the NT. Evidently some at Corinth gloried **in appearance.** Paul wanted to give his converts a real **occasion** for **glorying** in his **behalf,** as one whose glory is truly in **heart,** i.e., in the inner reality. **13.** Plummer translates correctly thus: "For whether we went mad, (it was) for God; or whether we are in our right mind, (it is) for you." The "went mad" (aorist tense) may refer to some occasion when his enemies charged him with insanity (cf. Mk 3:21; Acts 26:24). It is strange how the world considers a man unbalanced when his life is fully consecrated to the Lord.

5) Motivated by Love. 5:14,15. **14. By the love of Christ** (cf. Rom 8:35; Eph 3:19) let us understand Christ's own love for us. The verb **constraineth** (*sunechō*) normally means "to hold together"; but here Arndt takes it to mean "urge on, impel." **Controls us** (RSV) seems to be justified in the light of the previous verse. Christ's love will keep any believer from insane extremes. Paul's judgment, made once for all at his conversion, was this: "One died for all; therefore, all died." The **for** in **one died for all** teaches substitution (as in Jn 10:15; 11:50,51; Rom 5:6ff.; Gal 1:4). The aorist tense in **all died** identifies the believer with Christ in his death (cf. Rom 6:2-11; Gal 2:19; Col 3:3). **15.** Those who have been redeemed by the One **who for their sakes died and rose again** (ASV) should now live wholly for their Lord, not for self (cf. Rom 14:7ff.; I Cor 6:19,20; I Thess 5:10; Rev 14:1-5).

16. Wherefore henceforth know we no man after the flesh: yea, though we have known Christ after the flesh, yet now henceforth know we *him* no more.

17. Therefore if any man *be* in Christ, *he is* a new creature: old things are passed away; behold, all things are become new.

18. And all things *are* of God, who hath reconciled us to himself by Jesus Christ, and hath given to us the ministry of reconciliation;

19. To wit, that God was in Christ, reconciling the world unto himself, not imputing their trespasses unto them; and hath committed unto us the word of reconciliation.

20. Now then we are ambassadors for Christ, as though God did beseech *you* by us: we pray *you* in Christ's stead, be ye reconciled to God.

21. For he hath made him *to be* sin for us, who knew no sin; that we might be made the righteousness of God in him.

6) Motivated by Regeneration. 5:16, 17. **16.** Before the crisis of his conversion, Paul knew Christ only **after the flesh** (i.e., as merely another man). After he knew the significance of Christ's death (5:15), he knew neither man nor Christ **after the flesh.** Spiritual insight had changed Paul's center of gravity; eternity had become the yardstick of all measurement. **17.** The believer now becomes a **new creature** (AV; ASV). On **new**, see 3:6. Read *passed away* instead of **are passed away.** The tense is aorist, and thus indicates the definitive change that took place at regeneration. The same verb *(parerchomai)* is used of the catastrophic passing away of heaven and earth at the final conflagration (Mt 5:18; Lk 21:32,33; II Pet 3:10). The perfect tense in **are become new** dramatizes the abiding change introduced by regeneration.

7) Motivated by Reconciliation. 5:18-21. **18. God** is the Author of **all things** (cf. Rom 11:36; Rev 4:11). Read thus: "who reconciled . . . and gave"; both acts belong to God. Reconciliation precedes donation. Sinners are reconciled by the death of Christ (cf. Rom 5:10). The word **ministry** *(diakonia)* is used often in this epistle (II Cor 3:7ff.; 4:1; 5:18; 6:3; 8:4; 9:1,12,13; 11:8). **19.** The comma after **Christ** in the AV is misleading. Read as in the ASV. The basic thought, **God was in Christ reconciling** (ASV), is explained negatively—**not imputing** and positively—**having committed** (ASV). Scripture teaches that there is a nonimputation of sin (Rom 4:8) and an imputation of righteousness (Rom 4:3,6,11, 22; Gal 3:6) to the one who believes in Christ.

**20.** This verse presents (1) the messengers—**we are ambassadors;** (2) the means—**as though God were entreating by us** (ASV); (3) the mediation— **we beseech you on behalf of Christ** (ASV); (4) the message — **become reconciled** (Alfred Plummer *(op. cit.).* The **as though** *(hōs)* does not express doubt; the thought could be more accurately rendered *seeing that.* **21.** The Greek runs like this: *The One who did not know sin for us sin was made, that we might become God's righteousness in Him.* The Sinless One became (by imputation) sin for the sinner, that the sinner might become (by imputation) sinless in the Sinless One. Here is the very heart of the Gospel, a verse that stands with Jn 3:16 in importance. In the OT, the imputation of God's righteousness to the believer is taught didactically

## CHAPTER 6

WE then, *as* workers together *with him*, beseech *you* also that ye receive not the grace of God in vain.

2. (For he saith, I have heard thee in a time accepted, and in the day of salvation have I succored thee: behold, now *is* the accepted time; behold, now *is* the day of salvation.)

3. Giving no offense in any thing, that the ministry be not blamed:

4. But in all *things* approving ourselves as the ministers of God, in much patience, in afflictions, in necessities, in distresses,

5. In stripes, in imprisonments, in tumults, in labors, in watchings, in fastings;

6. By pureness, by knowledge, by long-suffering, by kindness, by the Holy Ghost, by love unfeigned,

7. By the word of truth, by the power of God, by the armor of righteousness on the right hand and on the left,

8. By honor and dishonor, by evil report and good report: as deceivers, and *yet* true;

9. As unknown, and *yet* well known; as dying, and, behold, we live; as chastened, and not killed;

10. As sorrowful, yet alway rejoicing; as poor, yet making many rich; as having nothing, and *yet* possessing all things.

11. O *ye* Corinthians, our mouth is open unto you, our heart is enlarged.

12. Ye are not straitened in us, but ye are straitened in your own bowels.

13. Now for a recompense in the same, (I speak as unto *my* children,) be ye also enlarged.

(Gen 15:6; cf. Rom 4:3,9), prophetically (Isa 53:11; 61:10; Jer 23:6), and typically (Zech 3:1-5).

8) Motivated by Time. 6:1,2. **1.** The participle **working together** (ASV) represents *sunergeō* (a verb that occurs elsewhere in the NT only in Mk 16:20; Rom 8:28; I Cor 16:16; Jas 2:22). There is a true 'synergism' after salvation (cf. Phil 2:12,13). **In vain.** Cf. Gal 2:2; Phil 2:16; I Thess 3:5. Paul always seeks real evidence of the power of the Gospel among his converts (cf. I Thess 2:13). **2.** By a quotation from Isa 49:8 (LXX), Paul reinforces the urgency of **receive** in verse 1. Isaiah's statement referred originally to the Messiah; Paul applies it to believers (cf. Rom 10:15 for a similar application). The **now** (*nun;* cf. its use in Eph 3:5,10; Heb 12:26; II Pet 3:7) ends when the Gospel age is finished (cf. Heb 9:26-28).

9) Motivated by Suffering. 6:3-10. All the participles through 6:10 are to be attached to **we . . . beseech** in 6:1. **The ministry** will "not be vilified" (Plummer) when the minister gives **no occasion of stumbling in anything** (ASV). The negative thought of 6:3 is stated affirmatively in 6:4 a, and then, in 6:4 b-10, expanded antithetically and ascensively by the use (in ASV) of **in** (eighteen times), **by** (three times), and **as** (seven times). Here is a multicolored rainbow glowing with the graces of Paul's ministry. Cf. 2:14ff.; 4:8-10; 11:16-23.

### G. Paul's Dissuasion Urged. 6:11—7:1.

1) The Thesis: Change your attitude toward me. 6:11-13. The verb **is open** represents the perfect tense and thus indicates the abiding state—it stands **open** (cf. the same tense in Acts 10:11; Rev 4:1). The same is true of **is enlarged**—a verb *(platunō)* that occurs elsewhere in the NT only in II Cor 6:13 and Mt 23:5. It is evident that the **Corinthians** did not share these affirmations. **12.** The verb **straitened** is from *stenochōreō*, meaning "to crowd, cramp, confine, restrict" (Arndt). It pungently describes how the Corinthians were "tight" in their affections for the apostle. **13.** As amplified, read thus: "(Grant me) the same requital —as to children I am speaking—do you also open wide (your hearts)." Ill feeling against Paul had given the Corinthians a bad case of spiritual hardening of the heart.

14. Be ye not unequally yoked together with unbelievers: for what fellowship hath righteousness with unrighteousness? and what communion hath light with darkness?

15. And what concord hath Christ with Belial? or what part hath he that believeth with an infidel?

16. And what agreement hath the temple of God with idols? for ye are the temple of the living God; as God hath said, I will dwell in them, and walk in *them;* and I will be their God, and they shall be my people.

17. Wherefore come out from among them, and be ye separate, saith the Lord, and touch not the unclean *thing;* and I will receive you,

2) The Antithesis: Change your attitude toward the world. 6:14-16.

**14.** The command may be rendered: "Stop becoming heterogeneously yoked with unbelievers." The principle goes back to the Mosaic legislation (cf. Lev 19:19; Deut 22:10). Christians are "new creatures" (II Cor 5:17); they must not be united spiritually with dead unbelievers (cf. Eph 2:1). The word *(metochē)* translated **fellowship** is found only here in the NT; it means "sharing, participation" (Arndt). The word *(anomia)* back of **unrighteousness** really means "lawlessness" (Arndt). Cf. Heb 1:9 for a similar contrast. **Communion** *(koinōnia)* involves "close relationship" (Arndt), as in marriage or as in spiritual relationship with God (cf. II Cor 13:14; I Cor 1:9; I Jn 1:3,6). The contrast between **light** and **darkness** is especially prominent in NT literature (cf. Jn 1:5; 3:19; Eph 5:7, 11; Col 1:12,13; I Jn 1:6,7; 2:10,11) **15.** The word **concord** *(symphōnēsis)* is found only here in the NT. The holiness and purity of **Christ** cannot harmonize with the wickedness and impurity of **Belial** (a synonym for Satan). Cf. I Cor 10:21. The ASV correctly translates **what portion hath a believer with an unbeliever?** The two are spiritually incompatible. The word *(meris)* back of **portion** (ASV) suggests a deep sharing of things in common (cf. its use in Lk 10:42; Acts 8:21; Col 1:12).

**16.** The word **agreement** *(sunkatathesis)* climaxes the four previous words that Paul uses to express sinful union between the sons of God and the children of the devil. This word suggests a sympathetic union of mind and will in a plan mutually agreed to. The Temple *(naos)* is the inner sanctuary (as in I Cor 3:16,17; 6:19,20). In periods of apostasy, abominations were practiced in the holy place (cf. II Kgs 21:7; 23:6,7; Ezk 6:3-18). The heathen temple at Corinth was a cesspool of iniquity (cf. Rom 1:18-32). The quotation introduced by **even as God said** (ASV) is a composite drawn from the LXX of Lev 26:11,12; Ezk 37:27 (cf. also Ex 25:8; 29:45; Jer 31:1). We should note how Paul supports his command (II Cor 6:14 a): (1) by an appeal to five self-evident questions (vv. 14 b-16 a), (2) by an appeal to God (v. 16b), and (3) by an appeal to Scripture (v. 16 b).

3) The Synthesis: Obey and live. 6:17—7:1. **17. Wherefore** *(dio)* always intro-

18. And will be a Father unto you, and ye shall be my sons and daughters, saith the Lord Almighty.

## CHAPTER 7

HAVING therefore these promises, dearly beloved, let us cleanse ourselves from all filthiness of the flesh and spirit, perfecting holiness in the fear of God.

2. Receive us; we have wronged no man, we have corrupted no man, we have defrauded no man.

3. I speak not *this* to condemn *you:* for I have said before, that ye are in our hearts to die and live with *you.*

duces a logical conclusion (as in 2:8; 4:13,16; 5:9; 12:10). The aorist imperatives in **come out . . . be separate** (RSV) **. . . touch not** underscore the urgency and definitiveness of the act involved. The quotation is from Isa 52:11 (cf. Rev 18:4). The gender of **unclean** is ambiguous; it may be masculine or neuter (thing). On separation from evil, see Rom 13:11-14; Eph 5:3-14; I Pet 2:9-12; 4:1-5; I Jn 2:15-17. **I will welcome you** (RSV) introduces the first of three promises (cf. Ezk 20:34). God cannot lovingly entertain those who are knowingly and willingly involved in evil. **18.** The two promises here cited (based on such passages as II Sam 7:8,14; Isa 43:6; Hos 1:10) illustrate how promises originally made to Israel are now applied to Christians. For further illustration of this principle, cf. Ex 19:5 with I Pet 2:5,9,10; Hos 1:10 with Rom 9:25; Jer 31:31-34 with Heb 8:8-12.

**7:1.** Here is the conclusion of the apostle's sermonette (6:11 – 7:1). He gives the cause, the command, and the consequence. **Since we have these promises, beloved** (RSV) introduces the cause. **These** is quite emphatic in the original —the **promises** just mentioned. **Let us cleanse ourselves.** The aorist tense makes the act absolutely peremptory and final (cf. I Cor 6:11). On "cleansing from," see Heb 9:14; I Jn 1:7,9; also see Eph 5:26; Tit 2:14. The conclusion, **perfecting holiness,** emphasizes the fact that the process is continuous; for *epiteleō*, "to complete, accomplish, perform" (Arndt) is used here in the present tense. On **fear** in the believer's life, see Acts 9:31; Eph 5:21; Phil 2:12; I Tim 5:20; I Pet 1:17; 3:15.

### H. Paul's Delight Exemplified. 7:2-16.

1) Paul's High Regard for the Corinthians. 7:2-4. **2.** Hear the apostle's plea: "Make room for us" (so the Greek). Get rid of your petty peevishness and petulance; give us a place in **your hearts** (ASV). Hear his protestation: "None we wronged; none we corrupted; none we defrauded" (so the Greek order and tense). Cf. I Sam 12:3. Paul lived "soberly, righteously, and godly" (Tit 2:12) among them. No one could prove a case of moral laxness against him. **3.** The **before** recalls 6:11-13. Three things are latent here: (1) Paul's purpose—"You are in our hearts unto—*eis to*—dying together and living together"; (2) the indissoluble union between Paul and his converts—

4. Great *is* my boldness of speech toward you, great *is* my glorying of you: I am filled with comfort, I am exceeding joyful in all our tribulation.

5. For, when we were come into Macedonia, our flesh had no rest, but we were troubled on every side; without *were* fightings, within *were* fears.

6. Nevertheless God, that comforteth those that are cast down, comforted us by the coming of Titus;

7. And not by his coming only, but by the consolation wherewith he was comforted in you, when he told us your earnest desire, your mourning, your fervent mind toward me; so that I rejoiced the more.

8. For though I made you sorry with a letter, I do not repent, though I did repent: for I perceive that the same epistle hath made you sorry, though *it were* but for a season.

9. Now I rejoice, not that ye were made sorry, but that ye sorrowed to repentance: for ye were made sorry after a godly manner, that ye might receive damage by us in nothing.

to die together and live together (ASV); (3) the priority of "dying" to "living." To place "dying" before "living" may teach us either that one must really "die" before he lives (cf. Jn 12:24; Rom 6:1-14) or, equally probable, that physical death must precede eternal life in glory (cf. Jn 11:25,26; Heb 9:27,28). 4. Paul's objective attitude is expressed in **boldness** (see 3:12) and **glorying** (see 1:12); his subjective attitude is expressed in **I am filled** and **I overflow** (ASV). The "filling" (perfect tense, had become a settled state; the "overflowing" (present tense) was an ever-flowing river. On joy in **tribulation**, see II Cor 1:4; cf. Mt 5:12; Rom 5:3; Jas 1:2,3.

2) Reasons for Paul's High Regard for the Corinthians. 7:5-16. **5.** Verses 5-7 give Paul's first reason: Their regard for him. His "tribulation" (7:4), previously experienced at Ephesus (1:8) and Troas (2:12,13), followed him **into Macedonia.** It was incessant **(no rest)**, encircling **(on every side)**, external **(without)**, and internal **(within)**. 6. Does *tapeinos* (AV, **cast down**) mean *downcast* (RSV) or *lowly* (ASV)? Usage elsewhere in the NT (cf. 10:1; Mt 11:29; Lk 1:52; Rom 12:16; Jas 1:9; 4:6; I Pet 5:5) shows that it means "of low position, poor, lowly, undistinguished" (Arndt). The word **coming** *(parousia)* means both "arrival" and "presence." It often designates the Second Advent (e.g., I Thess 2:19; 3:13; 4:15; 5:23). 7. Three expressions—**your longing, your mourning, your zeal for me** (ASV)—set forth Paul's revived joy resulting from the arrival of Titus.

8. Verses 8-12 give Paul's second reason: Their response to his letter. Four matters in 7:8 need some clarification: (1) We should translate *metamelomai* as **regret** (ASV; RSV) rather than *repent* (AV). (2) The verb for **made . . . sorry** *(lupeō)* means "to grieve, pain" (Arndt). It does not necessarily carry an overtone of moral fault. (3) Some scholars hold that the **letter** mentioned here is a lost "stern letter"; others hold that our I Corinthians is referred to. Available information does not sanction a dogmatic decision about this. (4) If I Corinthians is meant, Paul's inspiration is in no wise impaired by his stating that, humanly speaking, he regretted that **his letter grieved them, though only for a while** (RSV). 9. Paul's joy had a negative side—not that ye were made sorry; a positive side—**but that ye were made sorry unto repentance** (ASV); an underlying reason

10. For godly sorrow worketh repentance to salvation not to be repented of: but the sorrow of the world worketh death.

11. For behold this selfsame thing, that ye sorrowed after a godly sort, what carefulness it wrought in you, yea, *what* clearing of yourselves, yea, *what* indignation, yea, *what* fear, yea, *what* vehement desire, yea, *what* zeal, yea, *what* revenge! In all *things* ye have approved yourselves to be clear in this matter.

12. Wherefore, though I wrote unto you, *I did it* not for his cause that had done the wrong, nor for his cause that suffered wrong, but that our care for you in the sight of God might appear unto you.

13. Therefore we were comforted in your comfort: yea, and exceedingly the more joyed we for the joy of Titus, because his spirit was refreshed by you all.

14. For if I have boasted any thing to him of you, I am not ashamed; but as we spake all things to you in truth, even so our boasting, which *I made* before Titus, is found a truth.

15. And his inward affection is more abundant toward you, whilst he remembereth the obedience of you all, how with fear and trembling ye received him.

16. I rejoice therefore that I have confidence in you in all *things*.

—for ye were made sorry after a godly manner; and an ultimate purpose—that ye might suffer loss by us in nothing (ASV). By suffer loss (ASV) Paul is thinking of the eternal damage that might result from his irresponsibility and leniency (cf. I Cor 3:15; Phil 3:8).

10. Follow the ASV or the RSV here. Note the contrasts: (1) **Godly** and **of the world**; (2) **salvation** and **death** (i.e., "the second death"—Rev 2:11; 20:6,14); (3) the two different verbs translated **worketh** — *ergazomai*, "to work" (as in I Thess 2:9), and *katergazomai* (see II Cor 4:17), "to produce" (as in 12:12). 11. The energy of this verse is almost untranslatable. Their **godly** sorrow **produced** (RSV; cf. v. 10) salvation (cf. Phil 2:12, where *katergazomai* is also used), not death. Paul arranges seven nouns in ascensive order to describe the explosive nature of their repentance. The Corinthians came out **pure in the matter** (ASV).

12. Whatever the wrong or whoever the wronged may have been, the apostle's chief concern in writing his letter to them was that **your earnest care for us might be made manifest unto you in the sight of God** (ASV; cf. 5:11; 11:6). Their obedience was Paul's primary concern (cf. 2:9; 7:15; 10:6).

13. In 7:13-16 Paul gives the third reason: Their reception of Titus. Here we enter the calm after the storm. Note the two perfects (**have been comforted . . . hath been refreshed**—ASV). Paul's joy was intensified by **the joy of Titus**. The **you all** reflects the unity of the church. 14. Three thoughts are here: (1) Paul's vulnerability — **if I have boasted**; (2) his veracity—**as we spake all things . . . in truth**; (3) his vindication—**so our glorying . . . was found to be truth** (ASV). On **as . . . so,** see 1:7. This is the only place in the NT where **truth** is a predicate noun after *ginomai* ("to become"). "Our glorying . . . became [cf. Jn 1:14] truth" —as if **truth** became incarnate before them!

15. Note the faculties of human personality: (1) the emotions—**his affection** (ASV); (2) the mind—**whilst he remembereth**; (3) the will—**how . . . ye received him.** The Corinthians had learned **obedience** (cf. Heb 5:8) . . . **with fear and trembling** (cf. Phil 2:12). 16. **Have confidence** (AV). *Tharreō* (used elsewhere in the NT only in 5:6,8; 7:16; 10:1,2; Heb 13:6) means here "to be able to depend on someone" (Arndt). **Perfect confidence** (RSV) is perhaps too **strong;** nevertheless, Paul's optimism here **is not**

## CHAPTER 8

MOREOVER, brethren, we do you to wit of the grace of God bestowed on the churches of Macedonia;

2. How that in a great trial of affliction, the abundance of their joy and their deep poverty abounded unto the riches of their liberality.

3. For to *their* power, I bear record, yea, and beyond *their* power *they were* willing of themselves;

4. Praying us with much entreaty that we would receive the gift, and *take upon us* the fellowship of the ministering to the saints.

5. And *this they did,* not as we hoped, but first gave their own selves to the Lord, and unto us by the will of God.

6. Insomuch that we desired Titus, that as he had begun, so he would also finish in you the same grace also.

7. Therefore, as ye abound in every *thing, in* faith, and utterance, and knowledge, and *in* all diligence, and *in* your love to us, *see* that ye abound in this grace also.

8. I speak not by commandment, but by occasion of the forwardness of others, and to prove the sincerity of your love.

altogether irreconcilable with his pessimism in 12:20,21. In brief, Paul felt that, in spite of seemingly insurmountable obstacles, no future emergency could permanently undermine his conviction that things would eventually work out for good.

## II. The Collection. 8:1—9:15.

A. The First Reason for Its Completion: The Example of the Macedonians. 8:1-8.

1. In make known (ASV; AV, *do . . . to wit)* we have a verb *(gnōrizō)* which occurs twenty-four times in the NT and is used eighteen times by Paul, usually in connection with some important revelation (e.g., Rom 16:26; I Cor 15:1; Eph 1:9; 3:3,5,10; Col 1:27). Paul often uses the verb *didōmi,* "to give," with *charis,* grace (cf. Rom 12:3,6; 15:15; I Cor 1:4; 3:10; Gal 2:9; Eph 3:2,8; 4:7). The perfect tense (hath been given—ASV) and the preposition in (ASV) make the present verse unique. The Macedonian churches had already received a deposit of the grace of God. 2. Affliction *(thlipsis).* See 1:4. Some severe test of affliction (RSV) had come upon the Macedonian churches (cf. Acts 16:20; 17:5,13; Phil 1:28; I Thess 1:6; 2:14; 3:3-9). There is a contrast here between great trial and abundance of . . . joy, between deep poverty (lit., "down-to-the-bottom poverty") and riches of . . . liberality.

3-5. These verses constitute one sentence, the main element of which is found in they gave themselves (RSV) in verse 5. Follow the ASV or the RSV. The "liberality" (8:2) of the Macedonians is expanded thus: (1) they gave sacrificially—beyond their means (RSV); (2) they gave willingly—of their own free will (RSV); (3) they gave eagerly—beseeching us with much entreaty (ASV); (4) they gave spiritually—first they gave their own selves to the Lord (ASV).

6. On as . . . so, see 1:5. Cf. Phil 1:6. By finish *(epiteleō;* see II Cor 7:1) let us understand that the same grace of giving must be "brought to an end" (Arndt). It appears (cf. 8:10; 9:2; I Cor 16:1-4) that the Corinthian church had dillydallied too long about this collection. 7. They were quite proficient in some graces (faith . . . utterance . . . knowledge . . . diligence); but they were quite deficient in one grace (this grace also). "One thing thou lackest" (Mk 10:21). 8. The word *(epitagē)* translated commandment is used in the NT exclusively

9. For ye know the grace of our Lord Jesus Christ, that, though he was rich, yet for your sakes he became poor, that ye through his poverty might be rich.

10. And herein I give *my* advice: for this is expedient for you, who have begun before, not only to do, but also to be forward a year ago.

11. Now therefore perform the doing *of it;* that as *there was* a readiness to will, so *there may be* a performance also out of that which ye have.

12. For if there be first a willing mind, *it is* accepted according to that a man hath, *and* not according to that he hath not.

13. For *I mean* not that other men be eased, and ye burdened:

14. But by an equality, *that* now at this time your abundance *may be a supply* for their want, that their abundance also may be *a supply* for your want; that there may be equality:

by Paul (Rom 16:26; I Cor 7:6,25; I Tim 1:1; Tit 1:3; 2:15). An "order" could not do what the *spoudē* ("eagerness, earnestness, diligence"—Arndt) of the Macedonians would do to prove "whatever is genuine in your love" (Plummer).

B. The Second Reason for Its Completion: The Example of Christ. 8:9.

9. Look at the wonderful truths here: (1) a knowledge given—ye know; (2) a state relinquished—though he was rich; (3) a reason offered—yet for your sakes; (4) a state assumed—he became poor; (5) a resource tapped—through his poverty; (6) an exaltation conferred—ye . . . might become rich (ASV). Cf. Phil 2:5-10. Give according to the magnitude of your wealth in Christ Jesus.

C. The Third Reason for Its Completion: The Requirements of Honor. 8:10—9:5.

10. My advice is reasonable: it is expedient (*sympherō*—a verb meaning "to confer a benefit, be advantageous"—Arndt) for you—you who were "such ones" (for so the who implies) as first to make a beginning a year ago (ASV). Let your performance now catch up with and match your willingness! 11. The now (*nuni;* cf. its use in I Cor 15:20; Eph 2:13; 3:10; Heb 8:6; 9:26) is more emphatic than the regular form (*nun;* cf. its use in II Cor 5:16; 6:2; 7:9). The *nuni* form is used in the NT exclusively by Paul (twenty-two times). The advice of 8:10 becomes a command—perform. The aorist of *epiteleō* (see 7:1) implies urgency and immediacy. 12. Follow the ASV or the RSV here. One's financial response must be according to what a man has (RSV); harsh legalism has no place in Christian giving. 13. Literally: *For not that* (might become) *relief* (*anesis*, as in 2:13; 7:5) *to others* (Jerusalem saints), (but) *to you affliction (thlipsis;* see 1:4). The Jerusalem saints were not to enjoy plush seats while the Corinthians sat on hard benches. Let there be no "fringe benefits" at your expense! 14. The desired equality (supplied by Corinthian abundance) will (1) supply their need; (2) make more palatable their supply of your (future) need; (3) produce an ethically satisfactory equality. The present passage gives no support either to communism or to works of supererogation. Not even

15. As it is written, He that *had gathered* much had nothing over; and he that *had gathered* little had no lack.

16. But thanks *be* to God, which put the same earnest care into the heart of Titus for you.

17. For indeed he accepted the exhortation; but being more forward, of his own accord he went unto you.

18. And we have sent with him the brother, whose praise *is* in the gospel throughout all the churches;

19. And not *that* only, but who was also chosen of the churches to travel with us with this grace, which is administered by us to the glory of the same Lord, and *declaration of* your ready mind:

20. Avoiding this, that no man should blame us in this abundance which is administered by us:

21. Providing for honest things, not only in the sight of the Lord, but also in the sight of men.

22. And we have sent with them our brother, whom we have oftentimes proved diligent in many things, but now much more diligent, upon the great confidence which *I have* in you.

23. Whether *any do inquire* of Titus, *he is* my partner and fellow helper concerning you: or our brethren *be inquired of, they are* the messengers of the churches, *and* the glory of Christ.

24. Wherefore show ye to them, and before the churches, the proof of your love, and of our boasting on your behalf.

Rom 15:27 is necessarily involved. Paul is speaking of a temporary disparity in the necessities of life existing at Jerusalem and Corinth. **15.** The apostle cites an incident in Israel's history (Ex 16:18) to support the principle of "equality" (II Cor 8:14).

**16.** On thanks, see 2:14. Literally: *But thanks (be) to God who keeps on giving the same diligence for you in the heart of Titus* (cf. 8:1). **17.** Titus' "heart" (v. 16) responded spontaneously: (1) he accepted Paul's exhortation; (2) he became very diligent; (3) of his own accord he went unto you. The verb being (present participle of *huparchō*) underscores real existence in the essential nature of a thing (cf. its use in Acts 2:30; 16:20; I Cor 11:7; II Pet 1:8; 2:19; 3:10).

**18.** Paul does not further identify the brother "whose praise in the gospel is through all the churches" (Plummer). No one can dogmatically assert that Luke is the brother here referred to. **19.** We have here (1) the past—chosen (by "raising the hand"); (2) the present—this grace "which is being ministered by us" (Plummer); (3) the future—"unto the (furtherance of the) glory of God and our readiness." The human and the divine are intermingled here.

**20.** This verse gives the negative side; the next presents the positive side. With such abundance Paul would avoid any cause of blame (same word as in 6:3) in the possible mismanagement of this fund (cf. I Thess 5:22). **21.** The verb (*proneō*) rendered forethought is used elsewhere in the NT only in Rom 12:17; I Tim 5:8. Paul made ample provision to insure his moral integrity in the sight of the Lord and in the sight of men (cf. Rom 14:18; Phil 4:8; I Pet 2:12,15,16).

**22.** A third brother, who had been often tested (RSV) and was now much more diligent, was going along in the party. **23.** Titus is described as Paul's partner and fellowhelper (cf. Rom 16:3; Col 4:11; Phm 17). The other two men are called messengers of the churches, the glory of Christ (RSV). The word (*apostolos*) rendered messengers is elsewhere in the AV translated *apostle* (except in Jn 13:16; Phil 2:25). **24.** Three parties are involved: (1) the Corinthians —ye; (2) the "messengers" (v. 23)—them; (3) the churches. All eyes were on Corinth to see how the Christians there would receive the "messengers." Two things were at stake: your love and our boasting.

## CHAPTER 9

FOR as touching the ministering to the saints, it is superfluous for me to write to you:

2. For I know the forwardness of your mind, for which I boast of you to them of Macedonia, that Achaia was ready a year ago; and your zeal hath provoked very many.

3. Yet have I sent the brethren, lest our boasting of you should be in vain in this behalf; that, as I said, ye may be ready:

4. Lest haply if they of Macedonia come with me, and find you unprepared, we (that we say not, ye) should be ashamed in this same confident boasting.

5. Therefore I thought it necessary to exhort the brethren, that they would go before unto you, and make up beforehand your bounty, whereof ye had notice before, that the same might be ready, as *a matter of bounty,* and not as *of* covetousness.

6. But this *I say,* He which soweth sparingly shall reap also sparingly; and he which soweth bountifully shall reap also bountifully.

7. Every man according as he purposeth in his heart, *so let him give;* not grudgingly, or of necessity: for God loveth a cheerful giver.

8. And God *is* able to make all grace abound toward you; that ye, always having all sufficiency in all *things,* may abound to every good work:

9:1. Literally: *For concerning the ministry* (which is) *unto the saints, unnecessary for me is the* (continued) *writing to you.* Nevertheless, he goes on to write more. 2. The Christians of Achaia (including the Corinthians) were characterized by **readiness** (ASV), preparation (**hath been prepared for a year past**—ASV), and **zeal.** The verb *(erethizō)* back of **provoked** is used here in a good sense—"stimulate." In the only other NT use (Col 3:21), it has a bad sense—"irritate, embitter" (Arndt).

3. Paul fully believed that means are necessary to secure the end. This verse has many spiritual applications (cf. Acts 27:24,31). 4. An undesirable contingency is expressed by **lest by any means** (ASV; *mē pōs;* cf. its use in 2:7; 11:3; 12:20). 5. The threefold use of *pro,* "before," is significant: **go before . . . make up before . . . aforepromised** (ASV). **Extortion** (ASV) and **exaction** (RSV) are too strong for *pleonexia.* It is better translated "greediness, insatiableness, avarice, covetousness" (Arndt).

D. The Fourth Reason for Its Completion: The Requirements of Stewardship. 9:6-15.

1) Principles Drawn from Nature. 9:6. The commensurate proportion between sowing and reaping finds expression in the spiritual realm: "He that soweth on the principle of blessings, on the principle of blessings shall reap" (Plummer; cf. Prov 11:24; Lk 6:38; Gal 6:7,8).

2) Principles Drawn from God's Nature. 9:7-10. 7. We may summarize thus: (1) the person—**every man;** (2) the proportion—**according as he hath purposed** (ASV); (3) the place—**in his heart;** (4) the perversion—**not grudgingly, or of necessity;** (5) the principle—**for God loveth a cheerful giver.**

8. Very literally: *Now God is able to cause to abound all grace unto you in order that you, always having all sufficiency in all things, might abound unto all good work.* Note the repetition of **all.** On **God is able,** see Mt 3:9; 10:28; Mk 2:7; Eph 3:20; Jude 24. The noun **sufficiency** *(autarkeia)* is used elsewhere in the NT only in I Tim 6:6 (but Paul applies the adjective to himself in Phil 4:11). This word, used by the Stoics, describes "a perfect state of life in which no aid or support is needed" (Thayer, *Lexicon*). The word "sufficiency" *(hikanotēs)* in II Cor 3:5 designates "ability or

9. (As it is written, He hath dispersed abroad; he hath given to the poor: his righteousness remaineth for ever.

10. Now he that ministereth seed to the sower both minister bread for *your* food, and multiply your seed sown, and increase the fruits of your righteousness:)

11. Being enriched in every thing to all bountifulness, which causeth through us thanksgiving to God.

12. For the administration of this service not only supplieth the want of the saints, but is abundant also by many thanksgivings unto God;

13. While by the experiment of this ministration they glorify God for your professed subjection unto the gospel of Christ, and for *your* liberal distribution unto them, and unto all *men;*

14. And by their prayer for you, which long after you for the exceeding grace of God in you.

15. Thanks *be* unto God for his unspeakable gift.

### CHAPTER 10

NOW I Paul myself beseech you by the meekness and gentleness of Christ, who in presence *am* base among you, but being absent am bold toward you:

competency to do a thing" (Thayer). The two terms are not identical; a person may have one without the other.

**9.** The apostle uses the exact construction **as it is written** twelve times in Romans, twice in I Corinthians, and twice in this epistle (8:15 and here). Nowhere else does he use it. The quotation is from Ps 112:9 (LXX). The **righteousness** that endures pertains to reward rather than to salvation (cf. II Tim 4:8; Rev 19:8; 22:11). **10.** Follow the ASV or the RSV. The plenitude in nature (**He who supplies** – RSV) is a guarantee for the plenitude in grace (**shall supply and multiply . . . and increase**–ASV). Cf. Isa 55:10; Hos 10:12.

3) Principles Drawn from Christian Nature. 9:11-15. **11.** The first principle is spiritual enrichment. Literally: *in every thing being enriched unto all liberality* (as in 8:2) *which is such as* (the qualitative relative, as in 8:10) *to produce* (see 4:17) *through us thanksgiving to God.* **12.** The second principle is **thanksgiving.** This **service** (*leitourgia;* cf. its use in Lk 1:23; Phil 2:17,30; Heb 8:6; 9:21) emphasizes the ministerial aspect of the contribution. The verb **filleth up** (ASV) translates *prosanapleroō,* which means "to fill up by adding to" (A. T. Robertson. Giving for the needs of others multiplies **many thanksgivings unto God** (ASV).

**13.** The third principle is obedience. The **test of this service** (RSV) brings two benefits: (1) Christians at Jerusalem **will glorify God by your obedience** (RSV); (2) they will thereby know "the sincerity of your fellowship" (Charles Hodge, *An Exposition of the Second Epistle to the Corinthians*) toward all believers.

**14.** The fourth principle is prayer. Follow the ASV. On **long after** (*epipotheō*), see 5:2. To understand **exceeding** (*huperballō*), consult the other places where it is used (3:10; Eph 1:19; 2:7; 3:19). The phrase **in you** is better translated as *upon you* (cf. the same preposition, *epi,* in 12:9; I Pet 4:14). **15.** The fifth principle is praise. Here we have Paul's "outburst of gratitude for the gift of his Son" (Hodge, *op. cit.*). Cf. Jn 3:16; Rom 6:23.

### III. The Credentials. 10:1–13:14.

A. Spiritual Armor. 10:1-6.

**1.** Note the emphatic **Now I Paul myself** – as if anticipating the defensive role he now assumes against those who would impugn his apostolic authority.

2. But I beseech *you*, that I may not be bold when I am present with that confidence, wherewith I think to be bold against some, which think of us as if we walked according to the flesh.

3. For though we walk in the flesh, we do not war after the flesh:

4. (For the weapons of our warfare *are* not carnal, but mighty through God to the pulling down of strongholds;)

5. Casting down imaginations, and every high thing that exalteth itself against the knowledge of God, and bringing into captivity every thought to the obedience of Christ;

6. And having in a readiness to revenge all disobedience, when your obedience is fulfilled.

7. Do ye look on things after the outward appearance? If any man trust to himself that he is Christ's, let him of himself think this again, that, as he *is* Christ's, even so *are* we Christ's.

8. For though I should boast somewhat more of our authority, which the Lord hath given us for edification, and not for your destruction, I should not be ashamed:

9. That I may not seem as if I would terrify you by letters.

10. For *his* letters, say they, *are* weighty and powerful; but *his* bodily presence *is* weak, and *his* speech contemptible.

On **in presence,** see 10:10; I Cor 2:3,4. **2.** Paul says he will act sternly against some at Corinth who were imputing worldly standards to him (cf. 13:2,10). **3. Flesh** should not be changed to **world** (RSV). On **walk,** see 5:7; cf. also 12:18. The apostle often uses the language of warfare (cf. Rom 13:12,13; Eph 6:13-17; I Tim 1:18; II Tim 2:3,4).

**4.** This parenthetic verse — with a possible allusion to the fall of Jericho (Josh 6:1-27) — describes the Christian's **warfare** both positively and negatively. **5.** Here we have a microscopic commentary on the book of Revelation. The military terminology reminds us of Eph 2:2; 6:12. Subjugation and submission are the main thoughts. That **high thing** *that is being exalted* (present passive of *epairō;* cf. *huperairō* in 12:7; II Thess 2:4) **against the knowledge of God** will be devastatingly destroyed. Note the twice-repeated **every** (ASV). On **thought** *(noēma)*, see 3: 14. All theories that are hostile to the word of God will come to nought.

**6.** The theological implications of 10: 5 would have a practical display at Corinth. Literally: *Having in a ready* (state) *to avenge every disobedience, whenever your obedience shall have been fulfilled.* **Whenever** *(hotan,* as in 12:10; 13:9; I Cor 15:24,27,28) makes the time, but not the act, indefinite. Two parties were at Corinth: one disobedient, the other seeking to obey.

B. Constructive Authority. 10:7-18.

**7.** Evidently some at Corinth measured a man by **outward appearance** (cf. I Cor 1:12; 3:3,4). The **if** assumes the situation as true (as in II Cor 5:17). The verb **trust** (second perfect of *peithō,* "to trust" —as in 5:11) sets forth an internal persuasion that results in outward conviction (cf. its use in Phil 3:4; II Tim 1:5, 12). No group can be more cocksure than those who are deluded by the devil (cf. II Cor 4:3,4; 11:13ff.). On **as . . . so,** see 1:5.

**8.** Here we have an **authority** (1) assumed — **for though I should boast,** (2) possessed — **our authority,** (3) received — **which the Lord hath given us,** (4) defined — **for edification,** and (5) justified — **I should not be ashamed.**

**9.** Notwithstanding sinister insinuations, Paul would not **terrify** *(ekphobeō;* only here in NT) his converts with his **letters. 10.** The subtle implication of the gossip at Corinth was that Paul's **presence** *(parousia;* see 7:6) was somewhat

11. Let such a one think this, that, such as we are in word by letters when we are absent, such *will we be* also in deed when we are present.

12. For we dare not make ourselves of the number, or compare ourselves with some that commend themselves: but they, measuring themselves by themselves, and comparing themselves among themselves, are not wise.

13. But we will not boast of things without *our* measure, but according to the measure of the rule which God hath distributed to us, a measure to reach even unto you.

14. For we stretch not ourselves beyond *our measure*, as though we reached not unto you; for we are come as far as to you also in *preaching* the gospel of Christ:

15. Not boasting of things without *our* measure, *that is*, of other men's labors; but having hope, when your faith is increased, that we shall be enlarged by you according to our rule abundantly,

16. To preach the gospel in the *regions* beyond you, *and* not to boast in another man's line of things made ready to our hand.

17. But he that glorieth, let him glory in the Lord.

18. For not he that commendeth himself is approved, but whom the Lord commendeth.

### CHAPTER 11

WOULD to God ye could bear with me a little in *my* folly: and indeed bear with me.

less effective than his **letters.** If natives of Lystra could call Paul Hermes (cf. Acts 14:12), it is likely that the inglorious **contemptible** arose from animosity rather than from actuality. Cf. II Pet 3:15,16. **11.** On **such,** see 3:12; cf. 12: 2,3,5. **What we are** (ASV) corresponds to the Greek *(hoioi esmen).* Paul's words and works corresponded — whether he was absent or present. Let his defamer beware!

**12.** Paul would not become a member of The Society of Self-Approved Scholars at Corinth. Such men (1) **commend** themselves; (2) **measure themselves by themselves;** (3) **are not wise** *(suniēmi;* cf. its use in Mt 13:13ff.; Acts 7:25,26; Rom 3:11 — they cannot put two and two together). The apostle had no use for the "all scholars are agreed" fetish. **13.** Paul would **not boast** as his opponents did (cf. 10:12). God **apportioned** (ASV) a territory or **province** (ASV) for him to evangelize (cf. Gal 2:7; Eph 3:1-9). In that territory, which included Corinth, he would boast.

**14.** Paul and his helpers did not presumptuously intrude themselves among the Corinthians. They came (1) by province — we **stretch not ourselves overmuch** (ASV); (2) by priority — **were the first to come** (RSV); (3) by proclamation — **in the gospel of Christ** (ASV). Paul uniformly speaks of the gospel of "the Christ"; i.e., the Anointed One (as in 2: 12; 4:4; 9:13; Rom 15:19; Gal 1:7; Phil 1:27; I Thess 3:2). **15,16.** These verses enunciate spiritual principles, such as these: (1) A minister should not **boast in other men's labours** or in **things made ready at hand.** (2) A church's faith (as **your faith groweth** — ASV) affects a minister's activity. (3) By spiritual growth a church can enable a minister to evangelize **even unto the parts beyond you** (ASV; cf. Rom 15:19-29).

**17.** Cited as Scripture in I Cor 1:31 (cf. Jer 9:24). In Paul's epistles, the **in** *(en)* in the phrase, **in the Lord,** always expresses an intimate and mystical relation with Christ. The phrase is somewhat like a spiritual trademark (e.g., Rom 16:12,13,22; Phil 4:1,2,4,10; Phm 20). No other NT writer uses it. **18.** Paul infinitely preferred Christ's "Well done!" (Mt 25:21,23) to all the plaudits of self-appointed scholars (cf. II Cor 10:12). On **Lord,** see II Tim 4:8,14,17,18,22.

C. Justifiable Apprehensiveness. 11:1-6.

**1.** Literally: *Would that ye tolerated*

2. For I am jealous over you with godly jealousy: for I have espoused you to one husband, that I may present *you as* a chaste virgin to Christ.

3. But I fear, lest by any means, as the serpent beguiled Eve through his subtilty, so your minds should be corrupted from the simplicity that is in Christ.

4. For if he that cometh preacheth another Jesus, whom we have not preached, or *if* ye receive another spirit, which ye have not received, or another gospel, which ye have not accepted, ye might well bear with *him*.

5. For I suppose I was not a whit behind the very chiefest apostles.

6. But though *I be* rude in speech, yet not in knowledge; but we have been thoroughly made manifest among you in all things.

7. Have I committed an offense in abasing myself that ye might be exalted, because I have preached to you the gospel of God freely?

8. I robbed other churches, taking wages *of them*, to do you service.

*me in a little something of folly but ye do indeed tolerate me.* The last clause may be understood somewhat ironically. Would that (ASV) expresses a strong emotional outburst (as in Rom 9:3). **2.** Here we have Paul's (1) passion — **I am jealous over you;** (2) position—**I espoused you to one husband** (ASV); (3) purpose — **that I might present you as a pure virgin to Christ** (ASV). The false teachers at Corinth were seeking to woo the church away from Christ. The 'espousal' took place at conversion; the 'presentation' will be consummated at the Second Coming (cf. Eph 5:26,27; Rev 21:2,9; 22: 17).

**3.** Follow the ASV. Paul's perturbation (**lest**; see 2:7) was enhanced by a parallel (**as the serpent beguiled Eve**; cf. Gen 3:4,13) which, in the case of the Corinthians, could cause a similar perversion (**your minds should be corrupted**). The verb **beguiled** represents a compound word *(exapataō)* which conveys the idea of utter or complete deception (cf. I Tim 2:14). On **minds,** see II Cor 3:14. The Greek of the last half reads thus: *your thoughts should be corrupted from the simplicity and the purity that is toward the Christ* (Plummer).

**4.** The ASV correctly translates the three aorists—**did . . . preach . . . did . . . receive, did . . . accept.** Paul is referring to the time of their conversion (cf. I Cor 15:1,2). We should read **different spirit** and **different gospel** (ASV; cf. Gal 1:6-8). **5.** It appears that by **these superlative apostles** (RSV) — a description by no means complimentary — Paul has in mind the false apostles of 11:13-15. **6.** The apostle admits a deficiency (**unskilled in speaking**—RSV). But he asserts a proficiency **in knowledge** (cf. I Cor 2:6-13; Gal 1:11-17; Eph 3:1-13) and an efficiency in making that **knowledge** "manifest among all men to youward" (Plummer; cf. Rom 16:26; Col 1: 26; 4:4; II Tim 1:10; Tit 1:1-3).

D. Reasonable Abasement. 11:7-15.

**7. Or did I commit a sin** (ASV) suggests the seriousness of the charge made against Paul. In **abasing myself** we see the teaching (Mt 18:4; 23:12) and example (Phil 2:8) of Jesus. The "exaltation" of the Corinthians was from the depths of pagan darkness to the heights of fellowship with God (cf. Eph 2:1ff.; I Pet 2:9,10). On **freely** see II Cor 12:14; Acts 20:33-35; I Cor 9:4-18; I Thess 2: 9. **8,9.** Paul's righteous indignation

9. And when I was present with you, and wanted, I was chargeable to no man: for that which was lacking to me the brethren which came from Macedonia supplied: and in all *things* I have kept myself from being burdensome unto you, and *so* will I keep *myself*.

10. As the truth of Christ is in me, no man shall stop me of this boasting in the regions of Achaia.

11. Wherefore? because I love you not? God knoweth.

12. But what I do, that I will do, that I may cut off occasion from them which desire occasion; that wherein they glory, they may be found even as we.

13. For such *are* false apostles, deceitful workers, transforming themselves into the apostles of Christ.

14. And no marvel; for Satan himself is transformed into an angel of light.

15. Therefore *it is* no great thing if his ministers also be transformed as the ministers of righteousness; whose end shall be according to their works.

against false insinuations prompted him to use strong language in his defense. (1) He took from other churches . . . wages. (2) His dire need at Corinth was supplied by some Macedonians (cf. Phil 4: 15,16). (3) His fixed policy was to keep himself from being burdensome unto them.

10. This verse is a strong statement, with emphasis on **is**: "Christ's truth is in me that this glorying shall not be blocked up against me in the regions of Achaia." The verb **stop** (*phrassō*) is used elsewhere in the NT in Rom 3:19; Heb 11:33. 11. Paul calls God to witness that he loves the Corinthians even while they impute wrong motives to him (cf. 12:15).

12. This verse has been subjected to various translations and interpretations. Follow the AV and the ASV rather than the RSV (which is almost a paraphrase). Three things are plain: (1) Paul would continue his policy of taking no funds from the Corinthians. (2) This financial policy was motivated by a desire to undermine the false teachers. (3) Having nothing to charge against Paul on this score, these false teachers would **be found even as we**, i.e., judged by the same standards; their boasted superiority would evaporate. 13. Paul describes his antagonists thus: (1) their character — **false apostles**; (2) their chicanery — **deceitful workers**; (3) their camouflage — **transforming themselves into the apostles of Christ**. On such, see 3:12. The verb *metaschēmatizo*, translated **transforming**, differs from the verb *metamorphoō* in 3: 18 as an outward change differs from an inner change.

14. It is no **marvel** (*thauma*; elsewhere in the NT only in Rev 17:6) that Satan *is transforming himself* (the habitual practice indicated by the present middle tense) **into an angel of light** (cf. Gen 3:5; Job 2:1; Isa 14:13ff.; Ezk 28:1-19; Mt 4:8,9; II Thess 2:4). 15. These Satanic **ministers** partake of their father's perversity (cf. Jn 8:44), parade in his theological paraphernalia, and perish in his predestinated perdition (cf. Mt 7:22,23; 25:41; Rev 20:10,15). How do such men, still with us today, **disguise themselves as ministers of righteousness** (RSV)? (1) By rejecting God's righteousness while insisting on the merit of man's righteousness. (2) By denying the fatal effects of sin on man's original righteousness while insisting that man's nature is still basically righteous. (3) By nullifying the imputed righteousness of Christ (cf. 5:21) while insisting that his death still has some moral effect on mankind. (4)

16. I say again, Let no man think me a fool; if otherwise, yet as a fool receive me, that I may boast myself a little.

17. That which I speak, I speak *it* not after the Lord, but as it were foolishly, in this confidence of boasting.

18. Seeing that many glory after the flesh, I will glory also.

19. For ye suffer fools gladly, seeing ye *yourselves* are wise.

20. For ye suffer, if a man bring you into bondage, if a man devour *you*, if a man take *of you*, if a man exalt himself, if a man smite you on the face.

21. I speak as concerning reproach, as though we had been weak. Howbeit, whereinsoever any is bold, (I speak foolishly,) I am bold also.

22. Are they Hebrews? so *am* I. Are they Israelites? so *am* I. Are they the seed of Abraham? so *am* I.

23. Are they ministers of Christ? (I speak as a fool,) I *am* more; in labors more abundant, in stripes above measure, in prisons more frequent, in deaths oft.

24. Of the Jews five times received I forty *stripes* save one.

25. Thrice was I beaten with rods, once was I stoned, thrice I suffered shipwreck, a night and a day I have been in the deep;

26. *In* journeyings often, *in* perils of waters, *in* perils of robbers, *in* perils by *mine own* countrymen, *in* perils by the heathen, *in* perils in the city, *in* perils in the wilderness, *in* perils in the sea, *in* perils among false brethren;

27. In weariness and painfulness, in watchings often, in hunger and thirst, in fastings often, in cold and nakedness.

28. Beside those things that are without, that which cometh upon me daily, the care of all the churches.

29. Who is weak, and I am not weak? who is offended, and I burn not?

30. If I must needs glory, I will glory of the things which concern mine infirmities.

31. The God and Father of our Lord Jesus Christ, which is blessed for evermore, knoweth that I lie not.

32. In Damascus the governor under Aretas the king kept the city of the Damascenes with a garrison, desirous to apprehend me:

By questioning the absolute righteousness of Christ while insisting that his life, though imperfect, is still worthy of our imitation.

E. Well-known Assiduity. 11:16-33.

16. The word fool (*aphrōn*) is uniformly translated "foolish" by the ASV (11:19; 12:6,11; Lk 11:40; 12:20; Rom 2:20; I Cor 15:36; Eph 5:17; I Pet 2:15). It means "mindless" — acting "without reflection or intelligence" (Thayer). 17. The RSV needlessly introduces here the idea of inspiration. By not after the Lord Paul simply means that his forced boasting has no basis in the life of Christ. 18. By after the flesh (cf. 5:16) such things as one's ancestry, achievements, and accolades are to be understood (cf. Phil 3: 4). Paul reluctantly resorted to the methods of the many that he might save his work at Corinth from utter ruin.

19. Literally: *For gladly you tolerated the senseless, (you) being sensible.* The biting irony of these words the sophisticated Corinthians could readily understand (cf. I Cor 4:8-10). 20. Five verbs, increasing in intensity, express the indignities which the sycophant Corinthians willingly endured at the hands of a false prophet. These men (1) degraded them — makes slaves of you (RSV); (2) devoured them — devour you; (3) defrauded them—takes advantage of you (RSV); (4) derided them — puts on airs (RSV); (5) defamed them — smite you on the face. The dupes of duplicity are the wildest defenders of the very men who debauch them! Cf. Mk 12:40; I Pet 5:2,3; II Pet 2:10-22; Jude 8-16.

21-31. In these verses we have (1) Paul's provocation (v. 21) — his unwilling defense of himself against unwarranted calumnies; (2) Paul's pretensions (vv. 22-24 a) — his superiority in all matters of human pride (cf. Phil 3:4ff.); (3) Paul's persecutions (II Cor 11:24b, 25) — his many sufferings for the sake of Christ; (4) Paul's perils (vv. 26,27)— his frequent dangers encountered on his journeys; (5) Paul's perturbations (vv. 28,29) — his uninterrupted anxiety for all the churches (ASV); (6) Paul's principle (v. 30)—his paradoxical glorying in his weakness; (7) Paul's protestation (v. 31) — his ultimate deference to God's knowledge for the truthfulness of his record.

32,33. The incident recorded here (which, on the surface, looks like an anticlimax) harmonizes beautifully (1) with the account in Acts 9:23-25, (2) with the

33. And through a window in a basket was I let down by the wall, and escaped his hands.

## CHAPTER 12

IT is not expedient for me doubtless to glory. I will come to visions and revelations of the Lord.

2. I knew a man in Christ above fourteen years ago, (whether in the body, I cannot tell; or whether out of the body, I cannot tell: God knoweth;) such a one caught up to the third heaven.

3. And I knew such a man, (whether in the body, or out of the body, I cannot tell: God knoweth;)

4. How that he was caught up into paradise, and heard unspeakable words, which it is not lawful for a man to utter.

5. Of such a one will I glory: yet of myself I will not glory, but in mine infirmities.

6. For though I would desire to glory, I shall not be a fool; for I will say the truth: but now I forbear, lest any man should think of me above that which he seeth me to be, or that he heareth of me.

7. And lest I should be exalted above measure through the abundance of the revelations, there was given to me a thorn in the flesh, the messenger of Satan to buffet me, lest I should be exalted above measure.

8. For this thing I besought the Lord thrice, that it might depart from me.

known facts of ancient history (Aretas reigned from 9 B.C. to A.D. 39), and (3) with the providence of God. Paul remembered this incident at the beginning of his ministry (cf. Gal 1:17) as the dramatic event that set the pattern of his life for all the years that followed.

F. Compensatory Affliction. 12:1-10.

1. Follow the ASV or the RSV. There was a certain "oughtness" (dei, as in Eph 6:20; Col 4:4) about Paul's boasting, even though it was not expedient (sumpherō; see 8:10; cf. same verb in Jn 11:50; 16: 7; 18:14; I Cor 6:12; 10:23). This verse expresses Paul's compulsion (I must needs glory—ASV), repulsion (though it is not expedient – ASV), and impulsion (but I will come, etc.–ASV).

2-4. The apostle objectified himself for the purpose of defending his visions and revelations from the false ecstasies of the false teachers. His vision was (1) personal – I know a man (ASV); (2) Christian – in Christ (therefore, not belonging to either Judaism or paganism); (3) historical – fourteen years ago (therefore, dated in history – not a fiction); (4) mysterious – whether in the body, etc.; (5) ecstatic – caught up to the third heaven (cf. Enoch, Elijah, Ezekiel); (6) revelatory – heard unspeakable words; (7) indelible – a "thorn" was placed in his flesh (v. 7).

5. Here and in verses 9,10; 11:30 infirmities should be translated weaknesses (ASV; cf. 12:9,10). 6. The thoughts here are mainly two: (1) If Paul wished to glory further, he would not be a fool; for he spoke truth (alētheia; cf. its use in 4:2; 6:7; 7:14; 11:10; 13:8). (2) He spared (pheidomai, as in 1:23; 13:2) them a further recital of his unique privileges for fear somebody might estimate him to be above what could be seen and heard from him. Paul had no desire to become a "superman" or encourage hero worship.

7. A classic passage. The magnitude of Paul's revelations (on abundance, see 4:7) caused the Lord to give to him a divine deterrent (a thorn) in order to deflate any tendency toward exaltation in pride. Paul needed some reminder that, in spite of his rapture to heaven, he still was a man among men. Our information is too scanty (cf. 1:8) to justify our dogmatizing regarding the exact nature of his thorn in the flesh. On exalted, see 10:5. 8. Paul prayed specifically (for this thing), entreatingly (I besought

9. And he said unto me, My grace is sufficient for thee: for my strength is made perfect in weakness. Most gladly therefore will I rather glory in my infirmities, that the power of Christ may rest upon me.

10. Therefore I take pleasure in infirmities, in reproaches, in necessities, in persecutions, in distresses for Christ's sake: for when I am weak, then am I strong.

11. I am become a fool in glorying; ye have compelled me: for I ought to have been commended of you: for in nothing am I behind the very chiefest apostles, though I be nothing.

12. Truly the signs of an apostle were wrought among you in all patience, in signs, and wonders, and mighty deeds.

13. For what is it wherein ye were inferior to other churches, except it be that I myself was not burdensome to you? forgive me this wrong.

14. Behold, the third time I am ready to come to you; and I will not be burdensome to you: for I seek not yours, but you: for the children ought not to lay up for the parents, but the parents for the children.

15. And I will very gladly spend and be spent for you; though the more abundantly I love you, the less I be loved.

the Lord), repeatedly (thrice), and purposively (that it might depart from me). On Lord, see 10:17,18.

9. The perfect tense in he hath said (ASV) registers Paul's complete acquiescence in Christ's definitive answer. Only here in the NT do we find my grace (cf. Phil 1:7 in ASV). The verb (arkeō), in the predicate is sufficient, indicates that Christ's grace is "possessed of unfailing strength" (Thayer). This verb is sometimes rendered be content (Lk 3:14; I Tim 6:8; Heb 13:5). The present passive of teleō (cf. the perfect tense in Jn 19:28,30; II Tim 4:17) means is being (continually) made perfect (cf. Heb 5:9). The verb may rest (episkēnoō) occurs only here in Biblical Greek. The simple verb skēnoō is found in Jn 1:14; Rev 7:15; 21:3. Plummer's rendering, "spread a tent over me," is reminiscent of OT phraseology (cf. Ex 33:22; Ps 90:17; 91:4; Isa 49:2; 51:16). 10. No one can take pleasure (eudokeō; see 5:8) in the five adverse things mentioned here unless it be for Christ's sake (cf. 5:20; Phil 1:29; Col 1:24; III Jn 7). On when (hotan), see II Cor 10:6.

G. Sufficient Attestation. 12:11-13.

11. A sudden realization (I have become a fool! — RSV) is justified (1) by the forced nature of the apostle's self-vindication; (2) by the superiority of his apostleship; and (3) by his essential humility (though I be nothing; cf. I Cor 15:9; Eph 3:8; I Tim 1:15). 12. The signs of an apostle could probably be summarized as (1) a divine call (Gal 1:15, 16); (2) a divine commission (Acts 9:5, 6,15 ff.); (3) a transformed life (I Tim 1:13-16); and (4) attesting miracles (Acts 5:12-16). On were wrought, see II Cor 4:17. Cf. Acts 2:22; II Thess 2:9; Heb 2:4. 13. Evidently the Corinthians developed an 'inferiority complex' because Paul did not burden (RSV) them financially. He prayed (ironically?) that this wrong (adikia, meaning "unrighteousness, wickedness, injustice" — Arndt) might be forgiven!

H. Beneficial Association. 12:14-18.

14. Paul gives here his purpose — to come to you, preparation — ready, precaution—I will not be burdensome to you, principle — for I seek not yours, but you, and precept—for the children, etc. cf. 13: 1. 15. Literally: But I, I will most gladly spend and be utterly spent out for your

16. But be it so, I did not burden you: nevertheless, being crafty, I caught you with guile.

17. Did I make a gain of you by any of them whom I sent unto you?

18. I desired Titus, and with *him* I sent a brother. Did Titus make a gain of you? walked we not in the same spirit? *walked we* not in the same steps?

19. Again, think ye that we excuse ourselves unto you? we speak before God in Christ: but *we do* all things, dearly beloved, for your edifying.

20. For I fear, lest, when I come, I shall not find you such as I would, and *that* I shall be found unto you such as ye would not: lest *there be* debates, envyings-wraths, strifes, backbitings, whisperings, swellings, tumults:

21. *And* lest, when I come again, my God will humble me among you, and *that* I shall bewail many which have sinned already, and have not repented of the uncleanness and fornication and lasciviousness which they have committed.

## CHAPTER 13

THIS *is* the third *time* I am coming to you. In the mouth of two or three witnesses shall every word be established.

2. I told you before, and foretell you, as if I were present, the second time; and being absent now I write to them which heretofore have sinned, and to all other, that, if I come again, I will not spare:

*souls. If more abundantly you I am loving, the less am I being loved?* Paul went beyond the love of parents for their children; but his love was reciprocated in inverse proportion to its intensity!

**16-18.** The apostle's detractors charged him with **crafty** deception. The subtle insinuation seems to have been that, although Paul was not a **burden** to them as a church, yet he had so maneuvered the collection fund as to get a heavy hand in the till. The apostle answers this scurrilous attack (1) by citing the scrupulously impeccable behavior of the two men he **sent** to Corinth, and (2) by affirming that his standard of conduct was of the same kind as theirs. The questions expect a negative answer. On **being** *(huparchō)*, see 8:17.

I. Warranted Anxiety. 12:19-21.

**19.** Follow the ASV or the RSV. Paul had not **been defending** (RSV) himself before the Corinthians as his judges (cf. I Cor 2:15). His whole ministry was conducted (1) **before God**, (2) **in Christ** (cf. II Cor 12:2), and (3) **for your upbuilding** (RSV).

**20.** Here the apostle reveals: (1) his subjective fear — the disparity between his ideal for the Corinthians and their actual condition; (2) his objective fear — the disparity between their estimate of him and his actual deportment, upon arrival, among them; (3) the reasons for both fears: the possible existence among them of eight evils — strife, suspicion, spleen, selfishness, slander, scandalmongering, superegoism, sulkiness! The serpent's hiss (cf. 11:3) could still be heard at Corinth! On **lest by any means** (ASV), see 2:7; 9:4. **21.** This verse graphically illustrates: the perturbation caused by sin —lest . . . I bewail (AV); sin's pertinacity —**have not repented**; depravity—**uncleanness ánd fornication and lasciviousness;** and practice — **which they have practiced** (RSV).

J. Defensible Asperity. 13:1-10.

**1.** Paul promised that, using a Scriptural method (cf. Deut 19:15; Mt 18: 16; Jn 8:17), he would thoroughly investigate every charge (cf. II Cor 13:1). **2.** The ASV brings out clearly the symmetry of Paul's Greek here. The doubt expressed by **if** *(ean;* see 5:1) concerns the time, not the fact, of his visit. Paul had previously spared them (cf. 1:23); now

3. Since ye seek a proof of Christ speaking in me, which to you-ward is not weak, but is mighty in you.

4. For though he was crucified through weakness, yet he liveth by the power of God. For we also are weak in him, but we shall live with him by the power of God toward you.

5. Examine yourselves, whether ye be in the faith; prove your own selves. Know ye not your own selves, how that Jesus Christ is in you, except ye be reprobates?

6. But I trust that ye shall know that we are not reprobates.

7. Now I pray to God that ye do no evil; not that we should appear approved, but that ye should do that which is honest, though we be as reprobates.

8. For we can do nothing against the truth, but for the truth.

judgment was at hand (cf. I Pet 4:17, 18).

3. Here is the reason why Paul cannot spare them: they are actually seeking a proof (dokimē; see 2:9) of the in-me-speaking Christ (so the Greek). This passage is a definite affirmation of the apostle's inspiration and authority. Rejection of him meant rejection of Christ. This same Christ is powerful in you (ASV), i.e., among you externally (cf. 11:12) and in you internally (cf. 5:17). 4. Omit though (AV). Follow the ASV. The through (ASV) indicates source (ek; cf. Gal 3:8). The contrast is threefold: (1) between weakness and God's power; (2) between Christ's death (he was crucified) and his resurrected life (yet he liveth); (3) between Paul's human weakness (we also are weak in him) and Paul's apostolic power through Christ (but we shall live with him by the power of God toward you). By the last statement we are to understand, not the resurrected life in glory, but rather the effectiveness of Paul's ministry as an ambassador of the risen Lord. Cf. I Cor 2:3-5.

5. Here Paul turns on his accusers and puts them through a grueling examination. (1) The men tested — yourselves (emphatic). (2) The method of testing—try . . . prove (ASV). The present imperatives express repeated action ("keep on . . ."). (3) The criteria of testing. The first is objective: Are you in the faith? Do you really belong to "the household of faith"? (Gal 6:10, ASV; cf. Acts 6:7; 14:22) The second is subjective: Is Jesus Christ really in you? (cf. Rom 8:10; Gal 2:20; Col 1:27) (4) The possible result of the test — except ye be reprobates. See next verse. This test was not beyond their ability, for they could "fully know" (epiginōskō; see II Cor 1: 13,14) these things. 6. The word (adokimos) back of reprobate (ASV) designates the opposite of "approved" (cf. 10:18; 13:7). It is used exclusively by Paul (Rom 1:28; I Cor 9:27; II Tim 3:8; Tit 1:16; Heb 6:8).

7. We have here (1) the prayer (Now we pray — ASV); (2) the purpose — stated negatively (that ye do no evil) and positively (do that which is honest); (3) the possibility — stated negatively (not that we should appear approved) and positively (though we be as reprobates). 8. By can do nothing Paul expresses a moral impossibility. The verb used here (dunamai) is often thus used (e.g., Rom 8:8; I Cor 2:14; II Tim 2:13;

9. For we are glad, when we are weak, and ye are strong: and this also we wish, *even* your perfection.

10. Therefore I write these things being absent, lest being present I should use sharpness, according to the power which the Lord hath given me to edification, and not to destruction.

11. Finally, brethren, farewell. Be perfect, be of good comfort, be of one mind, live in peace; and the God of love and peace shall be with you.

12. Greet one another with a holy kiss.

13. All the saints salute you.

14. The grace of the Lord Jesus Christ, and the love of God, and the communion of the Holy Ghost, *be* with you all. Amen.

The second *epistle* to the Corinthians was written from Philippi, *a city* of Macedonia, by Titus and Lucas.

3:7; Heb 3:19). On truth (*alētheia*), see II Cor 7:14; 12:6.

**9.** The paradox of Paul's being weak while the Corinthians are strong causes the apostle to rejoice (ASV); but still he continues to pray for their perfecting (ASV; see v. 11). **10.** Paul's present purpose in writing (I write these things) anticipates his imminent coming among them (being present); then he will exercise his delegated power (the authority which the Lord gave me — ASV) and his constructive prerogative (for building up and not for tearing down — RSV).

K. A Christian Adieu. 13:11-14.

**11.** The five precepts given here are all in the present imperative ("keep on . . ."). The precepts are: (1) farewell (*chairō*, meaning "to rejoice, be glad"; cf. its use in 2:3; 6:10; 7:7,9,13,16; 13:9); (2) be perfect (*katartizō*, meaning "to restore to its former position" — Arndt; cf. the noun form in v. 9); (3) be of good comfort (*parakaleō*; cf. its use in 1:4,6; 2:7; 7:6,7,13); (4) be of one mind (lit., *think the same thing*— as in Rom 12:16; 15:5; Phil 2:2; 4:2); (5) live in peace (*eirēneuō*; elsewhere in NT only in Mk 9:50; Rom 12:18; I Thess 5:13; Arndt here uses *keep the peace*). God's love (cf. Jn 3:16; I Jn 3:1; 4:9,10) and God's peace (cf. Rom 16:20; Phil 4:7; Heb 13:20) are united in a blessed promise of futurity and fruition. **12,13.** The holy kiss, later restricted because of abuses, was a symbol of Christian fellowship among the first believers (cf. Rom 16:16; I Cor 16:20; I Thess 5:26; I Pet 5:14). **14.** This wonderfully human letter closes with the most sublime of all doxologies. The epistle begins (cf. 1:2) and ends with an affirmation of the deity of Christ that is reminiscent of Mt 28:19. The genitives in this doxology are probably subjective — the grace which comes from the Lord Jesus Christ; the love which God bestows; the fellowship which the Holy Spirit (RSV) engenders. Thus ends a wonderful epistle!

# BIBLIOGRAPHY

DENNEY, JAMES. *The Second Epistle to the Corinthians (The Expositor's Bible).* New York: A. C. Armstrong and Son, 1900.

HODGE, CHARLES. *An Exposition of the Second Epistle to the Corinthians.* New York: A. C. Armstrong and Son, 1891.

MENZIES, ALLAN. *The Second Epistle of the Apostle Paul to the Corinthians.* London: The Macmillan Company, 1912.

PLUMMER, ALFRED. *A Critical and Exegetical Commentary on the Second Epistle of St. Paul to the Corinthians.* New York: Charles Scribner's Sons, 1915.

ROBERTSON, A. T. *The Glory of the Ministry.* New York: Fleming H. Revell Company, 1911.

TASKER, R. V. G. *The Second Epistle of Paul to the Corinthians* (Tyndale New Testament Commentaries.) Grand Rapids, Michigan: Wm. B. Eerdmans Publishing Co., 1958.

# THE EPISTLE
# TO THE GALATIANS

## INTRODUCTION

*Occasion of the Writing.* The Galatian churches had come into being as a result of Paul's missionary labors. Therefore the apostle was especially exercised in spirit when he learned that Jewish Christian agitators had circulated among these Gentile converts seeking to impose circumcision and the burden of the Mosaic law upon them as necessary for salvation (Gal 1:7; 4:17; 5:10). Writing under great stress (as is suggested by the omission of the usual thanksgiving), he met the issue squarely, and thus, in the epistle to the Galatians, gave to the Church a mighty polemic against the Judaizing error.

*Recipients of the Letter.* These churches were sufficiently close together and enough alike to be addressed as a group. In 3:1 Paul calls his readers "Galatians." In the middle of the first Christian century *Galatia* had more than one meaning. (1) It denoted the area in north central Asia Minor where the Gauls had settled after migrating from western Europe. The principal centers were Pessinus, Ancyra, and Tavium. (2) It also denoted the Roman province of Galatia. This the Romans had organized in 25 B.C. by adding to northern Galatia some territory to the south. The latter included the cities of Antioch, Iconium, Lystra, and Derbe, which were visited by the apostle on his first missionary journey. It is hardly likely that the epistle was addressed to Christians in both North Galatia and South Galatia (cf. 4:14).

The debate regarding the destination of this epistle goes on and on, and may never be settled. Lightfoot espoused the North Galatian theory. Most of the German commentators have continued to maintain this position (e.g., Schlatter, Lietzmann, Schlier), though some have remained noncommittal. Sir William Ramsay argued strongly for the South Galatian position, which has gained wide currency among English-speaking scholars. It has the advantage, if it be the correct viewpoint, of providing us with information about the founding of these churches (Acts 13; 14). On the other hand, Luke uses the term "Galatia" (lit., *Galatic region)* only when describing the progress of the missionaries beyond South Galatian territory (Acts 16:6; cf. 18:23). However, the circumstance that he does not mention *churches* in the North Galatian territory, but only *disciples,* favors the South Galatian theory (see Acts 18:23).

*Date and Place of Writing.* On the basis of the South Galatian theory, one might conclude that the epistle was written prior to the apostolic council described in Acts 15 (when an official pronouncement was made concerning the relation of Gentiles to the Law). Since Paul and Barnabas visited the churches twice on this first journey, the demands of Gal 4:13 could be considered met (there *first* means *former* of two visits), though it is by no means certain that Paul himself would consider this doubling back as a second visit. Many think that when Paul recounts a meeting with certain apostles in chapter 2, he can not be referring to the apostolic council, since he fails to mention the decree that was there drawn up, which would have been highly advantageous to his argument in the epistle. This argument is not decisive, since the purpose of the decree was not to lay down terms on which Gentiles might be admitted to the Church, but rather to facilitate relations between such Gentile converts and those who were of Jewish origin. So the decree did not bear directly on the argumentation of the letter.

Lightfoot emphasized the similarities between Galatians, Corinthians, and Romans. All deal with the Judaizing controversy to some degree. On this basis Galatians may be assigned to the period of Paul's third missionary journey and either to Ephesus or to Macedonia as its point of origin. This would date the epistle as late as A.D. 56. According to the alternative view, it was written in 48 or 49, probably from Antioch. An intermediate date of about 53, early in the ministry at Ephesus, is attractive. A reasonable interval between the letter to the Galatians and the letters to the Corinthians and the Romans is needed to account for differences in tone and treatment.

*Development of the Thought.* The first two chapters are devoted largely to setting forth the nature of Paul's apostleship. This explanation was vital to the apostle's gospel, for if his opponents could show that he had not been called and commissioned to preach the truth, then his hearers could justly question his message. Though it pained Paul to be so personal, he had to meet the challenge, which he did by showing that he had an independent apostleship fully on a par with that of the original apostles. He had received his gospel not through human instruction but through divine revelation, and it proved to be in agreement with that of the other apostles.

Next Paul passes to a statement of what the Gospel is (chs. 3; 4). It is a message of grace that calls for faith. The law does not produce faith, but rather works a curse, from which Christ had to redeem men.

Beyond the act of receiving the Gospel, lies the necessity of living it out (chs. 5; 6). Here the power of the cross and the energy of the Holy Spirit are presented as efficacious rather than efforts to keep the Law.

*Influence.* This letter contains the most emphatic statement of salvation apart from works to be found in Scripture. It revolutionized the thinking of Luther and played a strategic part in the Reformation. Luther declared that he was wedded to this book; it was his Katherine.

In the nineteenth century F. C. Baur made the book pivotal to his theory that the legalistic controversy was so severe as to rock the early church to its foundation. According to him, it affected the entire literature of the New Testament positively or negatively as men wrote in the interest of one viewpoint or the other, or else tried to conceal the fact of divergence between law and grace as means of salvation. Since Galatians exhibits this controversy in unmistakable fashion, its genuineness must be granted. This verdict has remained virtually unchallenged since Baur's day.

# OUTLINE

V. Conclusion. 6:16-18.
   A. Closing prayer. 6:16.
   B. Closing testimony. 6:17.
   C. Benediction. 6:18.

# GALATIANS

## CHAPTER 1

PAUL, an apostle, (not of men, neither by man, but by Jesus Christ, and God the Father, who raised him from the dead;)

2. And all the brethren which are with me, unto the churches of Galatia:

3. Grace *be* to you, and peace, from God the Father, and *from* our Lord Jesus Christ,

4. Who gave himself for our sins, that he might deliver us from this present evil world, according to the will of God and our Father:

# COMMENTARY

## I. Introduction. 1:1-9.

A. Salutation. 1:1-5. The conventional framework of letter-writing is here utilized but transcended, for the writer was an apostle with authority from the Godhead, and he addressed those who by grace had been delivered from this present age. They, too, were not ordinary men, for they were Christians.

1. **Apostle.** The meaning *sent one* will not suffice here. All believers have some such commission. Paul proceeds to defend his special authority as a Christian teacher, founder of churches, disciplinarian, and corrector of false teaching. **Not from men, neither through man.** The negative **not** sets the tone of the epistle; it is a polemic, an exposure of error in order to portray the truth to better advantage. If the Judaizers had any apostleship, it was from men. Paul's was not. It had a higher source. Nor was it **through** man. No person, apostle or other, had mediated Paul's authority (cf. 1:12). It came instead through the intervention in his life of **Jesus Christ.** The contrast makes Christ more than man. Behind him and on an equality with him stands **God the Father,** presented here as the one who **raised** Christ **from the dead.** It was the risen Christ who appeared to Paul and made him an apostle.

2. The identity of **the brethren** with Paul is unknown. For the location of **the churches of Galatia,** see the Introduction.

3. **Grace and peace** are twin gifts of God, never reversed in their order. The divine favor received makes possible a life of fullness and of harmony with God and fellow believers. These blessings come from the Lord Jesus Christ as well as from God the Father.

4,5. **Who gave himself.** An act of finality, purely voluntary. **For our sins. For** *(hyper)* is usually used of the persons benefited by Christ's work (cf. 3:13). Personal sin is not the only barrier between man and God. Man needs to be freed from his whole position in **this present evil age** (AV, *world*). The Gospel is not a message of improvement but of deliverance. **Age** is a time word and does not refer to nature or to man as

5. To whom *be* glory for ever and ever. Amen.

6. I marvel that ye are so soon removed from him that called you into the grace of Christ unto another gospel:

7. Which is not another; but there be some that trouble you, and would pervert the gospel of Christ.

such, but to the circumstances of man's life, corrupted as it is by sin and dominated by Satan, the god of this age (II Cor 4:4). Christ, in his redeeming work, acted in conjunction with God, according to his will (cf. II Cor 5:19). To God belongs the glory, the praise of saints, forevermore. Without affirming the deity of the Son, the apostle conveys the truth of it by linking Christ with the Father in the apostolic call, in the gift of grace and peace, and in the achieving of salvation.

B. Theme of the Epistle. 1:6-9. Instead of giving thanks to God for his readers, Paul expresses his amazement at their defection. He pronounces no blessing, but instead hurls a warning anathema.

6. **Are removed.** Rather, *are removing yourselves,* going over to another position and thus denying the very terms of the divine call to sonship, which is in **the grace** of Christ. **So soon.** Probably not a reference to recency of conversion, for young converts are the most liable to be swayed by false teaching. If this be interpreted temporally, it means so soon after the false teachers began their work, or so soon after the apostle left the Galatians. Perhaps *manner* is intended—*so readily,* with such an unresisting surrender. The removal was still going on, and so was not complete. There was still hope of turning the tide. But the seriousness of the defection is indicated. It was away from God, who called in grace, and it was unto **another,** i.e., a different **gospel.** Paul uses **gospel** by way of concession. Actually there is not **another,** a second gospel which one may choose and still have the divine message of eternal salvation.

7. While the responsibility for the defection belonged to the Galatians (**removing yourselves**), the explanation for it lay elsewhere, in those who were troubling them (cf. Acts 15:24), namely, the Judaizing teachers who were willing to **pervert** the Gospel by changing it into something quite different. Yet it was not theirs to alter, for it was the **gospel of Christ.** The privilege of declaring it does not include the right to change it.

8. But though we, or an angel from heaven, preach any other gospel unto you than that which we have preached unto you, let him be accursed.

9. As we said before, so say I now again, If any *man* preach any other gospel unto you than that ye have received, let him be accursed.

10. For do I now persuade men, or God? or do I seek to please men? for if I yet pleased men, I should not be the servant of Christ.

11. But I certify you, brethren, that the gospel which was preached of me is not after man.

12. For I neither received it of man, neither was I taught *it*, but by the revelation of Jesus Christ.

13. For ye have heard of my conversation in time past in the Jews' religion, how that beyond measure I persecuted the church of God, and wasted it:

8. Even, Paul says, if we (editorial plural here for Paul, the least likely on earth to change it, because of the circumstances of his call) or an angel from heaven (who would be even less likely to alter any divine message; cf. Mt 6:10), should proclaim as the Gospel something contrary to the word given out by us in Galatia, he must become *anathema*, accursed of God (cf. I Cor 16:22).

9. Paul had given such warning when in the Galatian churches. In this letter he did so again. He was a zealous guardian of the purity of the Gospel. In reiterating his strong statement, the apostle changes from the subjunctive mood of possibility to the indicative mood of actuality — if any man is preaching a different gospel (as the Judaizers are), let him be accursed.

II. Paul's Apostleship Defended. 1:10 —2:21.

A. A Special Apostleship Affirmed. 1: 10-17.

10. Since the apostle had spoken so harshly, he felt that it should be clear now that he was not seeking to persuade men in the sense of conciliating them or seeking their favor. He was concerned, rather, to be on good terms with God. Pleasing men by adjusting the message to suit their desires is inconsistent with being the servant of Christ.

11. As Christ's servant, the apostle could only make known the Gospel message. Though he preached it, he did not originate it, nor did any other man.

12. Since Paul came late into the apostolic ranks, men might have supposed that he received the Gospel from his predecessors or learned it through a course of instruction. Not so. He came into possession of it by revelation from Jesus Christ. This was the very highest authority. How, then, could his message be questioned?

13. Nothing less than direct intervention in Paul's life was required to open his heart to the truth of the Gospel. His pre-Christian manner of life was well known. The word conversation (Gr., *anastrophē*) means "life pattern." Everything in Judaism was prescribed. Anyone familiar with Pharisaism could predict what Saul's course of life would be. But in his case there was a special element that had become notorious. He was a persecutor of the Christians (not all Pharisees went this far in showing their devotion to Judaism). As the ravening wolf of Benjamin, he was engaged in

14. And profited in the Jews' religion above many my equals in mine own nation, being more exceedingly zealous of the traditions of my fathers.

15. But when it pleased God, who separated me from my mother's womb, and called *me* by his grace,

16. To reveal his Son in me, that I might preach him among the heathen; immediately I conferred not with flesh and blood:

17. Neither went I up to Jerusalem to them which were apostles before me; but I went into Arabia, and returned again unto Damascus.

laying waste the church, which he afterward recognized was the true congregation of Jehovah.

**14.** This unusual determination and excess of fury earned for Saul an exceptional reputation in Judaism. He kept advancing in devotion to his faith and its traditions, passing by men of his own age, and giving proof of his zeal by persecuting Christians. Humane considerations meant nothing to him compared with the fulfillment of his calling in behalf of his religion. He regarded his murderous activity as the Jews regarded their stoning of Stephen: It was done in the service of God (Jn 16:2; Acts 26:9-11). Clearly, then, Paul could not have been influenced in favor of the Gospel before his conversion, and he could not have received his message from men, as alleged by the Judaizers.

**15.** Paul's conversion was effected in line with God's purpose. The apostle, like Jeremiah (Jer 1:5), was set apart for his lifework from birth. His conversion was in the nature of a revelation of God's Son within his soul. This statement is not intended to create speculation as to the psychology of his conversion experience, but rather to certify the reality and depth of that transformation. Paul had been blind to the deity of God's Son. His prejudice against his own countrymen who looked to Jesus as their Messiah was due to his belief that the Nazarene was an impostor, a fraud.

**16,17.** The ultimate, divine purpose of this revelation within the soul of the apostle was that he should in turn proclaim this knowledge to others, especially to the Gentiles. The reality and sufficiency of his encounter with the risen Lord is seen in the fact that he did not confer with **flesh and blood** (an expression denoting humanity, with special emphasis on weakness and inadequacy) either locally, at Damascus, or in Jerusalem, the center of the church's life, where the **apostles** had their headquarters. If Paul had felt uncertain about his message, a journey to one of these centers would have been natural and necessary. But he was an apostle as truly as were the Twelve, fully in possession of the truth of the Gospel from the Lord himself.

The apostle mentions Arabia not as a place for preaching, because, even though preaching was in view in the call, it is not the subject under consideration at this point. Paul is discussing the *source* of his Gospel. He mentions Arabia

18. Then after three years I went up to Jerusalem to see Peter, and abode with him fifteen days.

19. But other of the apostles saw I none, save James the Lord's brother.

20. Now the things which I write unto you, behold, before God, I lie not.

21. Afterward I came into the regions of Syria and Cilicia;

22. And was unknown by face unto the churches of Judea which were in Christ:

in contrast to Jerusalem. No apostle was to be found there. No one was there who could inform him about the Lord and His saving work. It is probable that the new convert journeyed to Arabia to be alone with God, to think through the implications of the Gospel. There is no need to suppose that every aspect of the truth was flashed into his mind at the time of his conversion. From Arabia Paul returned to Damascus. This incidental reference confirms the information gleaned from Acts 9:3 that the conversion occurred near that city.

B. Lack of Early Contact with the Apostles at Jerusalem. 1:18-24. This was not a complete lack, to be sure, as Paul in frankness admits, but the contacts were brief, personal, and quite incidental.

18. How much of the three years belongs to Arabia and how much to Damascus we cannot tell, but the interval fortifies Paul's contention. If he had lacked the Gospel at his conversion, he would not have waited that long to be informed about it. To see Peter. The verb see (in the Greek) is in deliberate contrast to conferred (1:16), for the latter suggests conferring with a view to being enlightened on a subject, while the former refers to becoming acquainted with a person or thing. It is sometimes used of sightseeing. The visit was brief (fifteen days).

19. Paul saw no other apostle except James, the Lord's brother. This is the James who became the head of the Jerusalem church (cf. Acts 12:17).

20. The apostle declares himself willing to go on oath that he is telling the truth. No Jew dared to do this if he was about to speak a falsehood, for that would have been equivalent to inviting God to pour out His wrath upon him. The deep solemnity of Paul's declaration is the measure of the distrust of his word that the Judaizers had sown in the hearts of his converts.

21. Paul's next move, necessitated by the opposition to his preaching in Jerusalem (Acts 9:29,30), was to Syria and Cilicia. Obviously he had no opportunity in those remote areas to receive instruction from the apostles.

22. Probably the apostle mentioned the churches of Judea in order to strengthen his argument. It is likely that most of the apostles were in the outlying districts at this period, so Paul's lack of contact with the churches of Judea meant a lack of contact with the

23. But they had heard only, That he which persecuted us in times past now preacheth the faith which once he destroyed.

24. And they glorified God in me.

## CHAPTER 2

THEN fourteen years after I went up again to Jerusalem with Barnabas, and took Titus with *me* also.

apostles ministering there. The Twelve did not supervise the work in Syria; Barnabas was sent there (Acts 11:22-26). During the years when Paul ministered in this region, where he had been brought up, he was quite independent of the other apostles. His further purpose in mentioning the Judean churches was to underscore the greatness of the change his conversion had wrought in him. He now **preached the faith** he formerly had sought to tear down. The change meant peace for the believers in Palestine (Acts 9:31).

C. Failure of Later Contact to Question His Apostleship or Add to His Gospel. 2:1-10.

1. The differences between this later visit and the previous one are quite plain. This time Paul went not alone but in the company of Barnabas, and he went with the deliberate purpose of discussing the Gospel, more specifically the application of the Gospel to the Gentiles. It is not easy to fit this visit into the framework of the narrative of Acts. Those who favor identifying it with the so-called famine visit of Acts 11:27-30 can point to the fact that Barnabas accompanied Paul on that occasion. They hold that Paul was obligated to mention every contact he had with the Jerusalem church. But this reasoning is precarious. The only contacts that required notice were those that might have resulted in a communication to him of the Gospel. Since elders only are mentioned in connection with the reception of the gift by the Jerusalem church, it is unlikely that Paul had contact with the apostles at that time. This was a period of persecution for them (Acts 12:1-3), and so they may have been unavailable for consultation.

If the question of the admission of Gentiles into the Church was settled at the famine visit (which is involved in equating Acts 11 with Gal 2), then it is strange that another conference was necessary for the settlement of the very same question (Acts 15). Furthermore, it would have been highly discourteous for the apostles to insist that Paul should remember the poor (Gal 2:10) when he had just brought the gift of the Antioch church for the relief of the saints in the Holy City. Finally, to identify Galatians 2 with Acts 11 is virtually impossible chronologically. The famine visit took place about the time of Herod's death, which occurred in A.D. 44. By

**2. And I went up by revelation, and communicated unto them that gospel which I preach among the Gentiles, but privately to them which were of reputation, lest by any means I should run, or had run, in vain.**

adding fourteen years (Gal 2:1) to the three years of 1:18 and then subtracting the total of seventeen from 44, one arrives at the year 27 as the date of Paul's conversion, which is too early. Even if the fourteen years of Gal 2:1 refer to the conversion rather than to the first visit to Jerusalem, the dating of the conversion is still too early; it leaves no interval between the resurrection of Christ and the conversion of Paul.

The identification of Galatians 2 with Acts 15 has its strength in the fact that the subject of discussion is the same in both cases and in the fact that Peter and James, as well as Paul and Barnabas, are given prominence in both passages. There are difficulties in this identification, to be sure. Acts 15 gives the impression of a large public gathering, whereas Gal 2:2 pictures a private session. A harmonization is possible on the assumption that the friction cited in Acts 15:5,6 may have forced the leaders of the church to dismiss the council temporarily and move into a private session such as is described in Galatians 2. On the basis of the understanding reached there, Peter and James would then quite naturally have taken a leading part and a decisive role in the final public phase of the conference reported in Acts 15:7-21. It is possible that the word **them** (Gal 2:2) is a reference to the church as a whole in contrast to the apostles, with whom Paul and Barnabas proceeded to meet privately. A further difficulty to be faced is the failure of Paul to mention the so-called apostolic decree in Gal 2:1-10, whereas that decree is given considerable prominence in Luke's account (Acts 15:20,28,29; 16:4; 21:25). However, since Paul was concerned with the Gospel in this whole passage, and since the decree did not bear directly on the Gospel but simply provided for harmonious relations between Jewish and Gentile believers, he was not under obligation to include the decree in his argument.

**2.** Paul's second visit to Jerusalem was dictated by **revelation,** in line with the strong emphasis on the supernatural in the previous chapter. This intimation may have come before the decision of the Antioch church to send Paul, or it may have come afterward and sealed for him the decision of the church (Acts 15:2). He and Barnabas met with **them that were of reputation.** Literally, *those who seemed*, a rather curious term for

3. But neither Titus, who was with me, being a Greek, was compelled to be circumcised:

4. And that because of false brethren unawares brought in, who came in privily to spy out our liberty which we have in Christ Jesus, that they might bring us into bondage:

5. To whom we gave place by subjection, no, not for an hour; that the truth of the gospel might continue with you.

6. But of those who seemed to be somewhat, (whatsoever they were, it maketh no matter to me: God accepteth no man's person:) for they who seemed *to be somewhat* in conference added nothing to me:

7. But contrariwise, when they saw that the gospel of the uncircumcision was committed unto me, as *the gospel* of the circumcision *was* unto Peter;

8. (For he that wrought effectually in Peter to the apostleship of the circumcision, the same was mighty in me toward the Gentiles;)

the apostles. The same expression occurs twice in Gal 2:6 and again in 2:9, where the word "pillars" is added. Perhaps Paul felt that the church was in danger of idolizing these leaders by deferring to them overmuch. Did Paul really have a fear that he was running (pursuing his course of Christian service) in vain and had run in vain since his conversion, that he had possibly been wrong about the Gospel and now needed to be set right? By no means. But circumstances forced him to submit his message to the apostles, for only in this way could he hope to shut the mouths of his detractors, the Judaizers, and the mouths of those who had been taken in by their propaganda.

3-5. Now the reason for Paul's bringing Titus along (v. 1) becomes evident. He was to be a test case in the matter of Gentile reception into the Church. If he were compelled to be circumcised, the rite could not logically be withheld from other Gentile believers. If he emerged from the conference uncircumcised, all other Gentiles who had put their trust in Christ could enjoy their freedom without fear of successful challenge. Paul seems to say that some pressure was exerted here to have Titus circumcised (cf. Acts 15:5). It is highly unlikely that this pressure came from the apostles, for they stood with Paul (Acts 15:19). The culprits were the false brethren who had slipped into the ranks of the believers. They bore the name of Christian but were nevertheless opposed to granting that liberty which Paul's gospel proclaimed—freedom from bondage to the Law, including freedom from circumcision. Paul's resistance to these Judaizers was not dictated by stubbornness nor by a sense of superiority. He saw that the circumcision issue involved the truth of the gospel (Gal 2:5). To impose on a Gentile the sign of the covenant given to Abraham and his descendants was to set aside the simplicity of saving faith by introducing the necessity of a particular work. If this work had been found necessary for church membership, other works would have been found necessary, too.

6-8. In conference with Paul, the apostles could find no fault with his gospel. They added nothing to what he had already received by revelation from the Lord. But they perceived that to him had been committed the gospel of the uncircumcision. He was responsible for the Gentiles in a special sense (Rom

9. And when James, Cephas, and John, who seemed to be pillars, perceived the grace that was given unto me, they gave to me and Barnabas the right hands of fellowship; that we *should go* unto the heathen, and they unto the circumcision.

10. Only *they would* that we should remember the poor; the same which I also was forward to do.

11. But when Peter was come to Antioch, I withstood him to the face, because he was to be blamed.

12. For before that certain came from James, he did eat with the Gentiles: but when they were come, he withdrew and separated himself, fearing them which were of the circumcision.

1:5). For this reason the Lord did not permit him to labor in Jerusalem (Acts 22:17-21). This special call did not rule out a ministry to Jews when Paul labored in the synagogues, where both Jews and Gentiles (God-fearers) were assembled. Peter, charged with proclaiming the same gospel of grace, was to specialize in reaching the circumcision, the Jews. His Aramaic name, Cephas, is appropriately used here. The success of the two men in their respective spheres attested the divine call to them.

**9,10.** Paul's privilege as preacher of the Gospel to the Gentiles is called a grace (cf. I Cor 15:9,10; Eph 3:2). The Jerusalem leaders recognized this grace by extending the right hand of fellowship to Paul and to Barnabas. This was no mere formality, but a meaningful endorsement of the message of free grace that these two had been proclaiming among the Gentiles. The apostles endorsed also the division of labor that sent one group of evangelists to the Gentiles, the other to the Jews. However, they requested the missionaries to the Gentile world not to so divorce themselves from the Jewish believers — especially those at Jerusalem, who were notoriously **poor** (Rom 15:26)—as to forget their need. The proof of Paul's good faith in acceding to this request was that he raised a substantial fund among the Gentile churches for these people (I Cor 16:1-4), which he and others took to Jerusalem on the occasion of his last visit.

D. His Independent Authority Vindicated in the Encounter with Peter at Antioch. 2:11-21. This is the third occasion on which Paul came into contact with Peter. The first time he simply met Peter; the next time he discovered their unity and equality; this time he was moved to differ with him and rebuke him. This confirms the fact that Paul's purpose throughout the epistle to the Galatians is to demonstrate his independent apostleship.

**11,12.** He withstood Peter because Peter's conduct gave the false impression that he was renouncing the stand he had taken at Jerusalem. The action of the council in the matter of the decree (Acts 15:28,29) had opened the way for freedom of social intercourse between Jews and Gentiles in the church at Antioch, a freedom that Peter was glad to share. He even ate with the Gentiles (cf. Acts 10:28; 11:3). But the arrival of certain men from James, the acknowl-

13. And the other Jews dissembled likewise with him; insomuch that Barnabas also was carried away with their dissimulation.

14. But when I saw that they walked not uprightly according to the truth of the gospel, I said unto Peter before *them* all, If thou, being a Jew, livest after the manner of Gentiles, and not as do the Jews, why compellest thou the Gentiles to live as do the Jews?

15. We *who are* Jews by nature, and not sinners of the Gentiles.

edged head of the church at Jerusalem, awoke fear in Peter's heart, for he remembered that the mother church had rebuked him for associating and eating with Gentiles in the house of Cornelius (Acts 11:1-18). It is impossible to know in what relation these visitors stood to James and on precisely what mission they came. Peter separated himself from his Gentile brethren by degrees, as the original suggests, perhaps absenting himself from one meal one day, from two the next, and finally cutting himself off altogether.

13. Peter's example influenced others. The word **dissimulation** (AV, *dissembled*) ordinarily rendered *hypocrisy*, means a lack of correspondence between one's external acts or demeanor and his state of heart. In Pharisaism the outward acts were good but the state of heart was often corrupt. In Peter's case, his inward convictions were sound, for he endorsed Gentile equality in the Church, but his conduct belied his convictions. There is a plaintive note here—**even Barnabas**, as though Paul expected more of him than of the other Jewish believers.

14. The statement that Peter was not acting according to the truth of the Gospel needs explanation. He was a Jew and therefore not obliged to live **after the manner of the Gentiles**, as he had been doing in his table companionship. But now, having gone that far and then broken off, he was logically compelling Gentile believers to live as Jews, that is, to adopt circumcision and the dietary laws of the Jews and thus remove all barriers between themselves and men like Peter. But if the Gentile believers did this, they would sacrifice the truth of the Gospel, which had been affirmed at Jerusalem. The church had decided that no such burden of legal compliance was to be laid on Gentile believers. The whole principle of grace was at stake. The logical outcome of Peter's conduct was to make Jews out of Gentile Christians or else force the creation of a Gentile church alongside the Jewish church, which would break the unity of the body of Christ. So the truth of the Gospel was involved.

15-18. Paul extracted from Peter the acknowledgment that the two of them, being native Jews and having enjoyed the special advantages of Judaism, including the possession of the Law, had nevertheless been obliged to come to the place of simply trusting Christ for salvation, just as any poor Gentile had

16. Knowing that a man is not justified by the works of the law, but by the faith of Jesus Christ, even we have believed in Jesus Christ, that we might be justified by the faith of Christ, and not by the works of the law: for by the works of the law shall no flesh be justified.

17. But if, while we seek to be justified by Christ, we ourselves also are found sinners, is therefore Christ the minister of sin? God forbid.

18. For if I build again the things which I destroyed, I make myself a transgressor.

19. For I through the law am dead to the law, that I might live unto God.

20. I am crucified with Christ: nevertheless I live; yet not I, but Christ liveth in me: and the life which I now live in the flesh I live by the faith of the Son of God, who loved me, and gave himself for me.

21. I do not frustrate the grace of God: for if righteousness *come* by the law, then Christ is dead in vain.

to do. Peter was bound to agree, because of his own commitment to this position (Acts 15:11). The OT itself testifies that justification does not come from the works of the law (cf. Ps 143:2). To be justified means to be declared and considered righteous in God's eyes, to be vindicated of any charge of sin incident to failure to keep God's holy law. **The faith of Jesus Christ** means faith *in* Christ (Gr. objective genitive). This lowering of the Jew to the level of the Gentile seemed to involve Christ, making Him a **minister of sin** in that He released man from bondage to the Law, since faith in Christ for both Jew and Gentile on equal terms is the condition of salvation. But Paul rejected the conclusion, for it rested on a false premise, namely, the fancied superiority of Jew over Gentile. Here Paul delicately takes what belongs to Peter and refers it to himself. The real transgressor is not Christ, but the one who, like Peter, builds up again a distinction that has in fact been destroyed. Peter was doing just that by withdrawing from Gentile fellowship, making it appear that Jewish believers were a superior breed.

19-21. The Law had done a service for Paul even if it had not brought him justification. Through the Law he had become dead to that very Law, for the Law had wrought a consciousness of sin which prepared him to accept Christ. It had also brought Christ to the cross in order to redeem those who had broken that Law. Christ was Paul's representative in that death to the Law. The result was a new life **unto God. I am crucified with Christ.** The perfect tense emphasizes both the past event and its continuing effects. This death brought life, yet not the same old life in the feebleness of the natural man, but a life entirely new; not simply divine life impersonally granted, but rather the living Christ himself taking up his abode in the redeemed one. In this arrangement, however, there is no submerging of human personality—**the life which I now live.** The new life is lived on the principle of faith in Christ (cf. 2:16) rather than on that of legal obedience. This faith builds on the fact of the personal love of the Saviour for those on whose behalf he died (cf. Eph 5:2). Not to trust Christ in this way would **frustrate** (set aside) the grace of God. If righteousness could be obtained by law, the death of Christ would be unexplainable; it would be a wasted gesture.

## CHAPTER 3

O FOOLISH Galatians, who hath bewitched you, that ye should not obey the truth, before whose eyes Jesus Christ hath been evidently set forth, crucified among you?

2. This only would I learn of you, Received ye the Spirit by the works of the law, or by the hearing of faith?

3. Are ye so foolish? having begun in the Spirit, are ye now made perfect by the flesh?

4. Have ye suffered so many things in vain? if *it be* yet in vain.

5. He therefore that ministereth to you the Spirit, and worketh miracles among you, *doeth he it* by the works of the law, or by the hearing of faith?

6. Even as Abraham believed God, and it was accounted to him for righteousness.

7. Know ye therefore that they which are of faith, the same are the children of Abraham.

8. And the Scripture, forseeing that God would justify the heathen through faith, preached before the gospel unto Abraham, *saying,* In thee shall all nations be blessed.

9. So then they which be of faith are blessed with faithful Abraham.

## III. Paul's Gospel Explained. 3:1—4:31.

A. The Argument from Experience (of the Galatians). 3:1-5. The apostle here declares that the experience of his readers, starting with faith in Christ crucified and certified by the gift to them of the Holy Spirit, lay completely outside the sphere of the Law. Would they now renounce the perfection of the divine provision, he asks, for the folly of their own efforts?

1. They must have become **bewitched**, victims of an evil spell (cf. 1:7). In view of his dramatic preaching of Christ crucified when he was among them (cf. I Cor 1:23; 2:2), their change in attitude seemed strange. Had they forgotten their first vivid impression? 2,3. After the reception of Christ came the gift of the Spirit (cf. Gal 4:4-6; Eph 1:13), not at all based on law-keeping as an effort of the flesh (cf. Gal 5:18,19). 4. **Suffered** probably does not refer to persecution or the burden of law-keeping, but is used in a good sense — *experienced.* This interpretation is favored by the continuing mention of the Spirit in the next verse. 5. The ongoing work of the Spirit in **miracles**, like his advent into the hearts of the Galatians, depended not on works but on **the hearing of faith,** i.e., a faith response to the Gospel message preached to them.

B. The Argument from Scripture (the Case of Abraham). 3:6-9. The mention of faith invites an excursion into the OT to show that Abraham, the revered patriarch, depended on it for righteousness. Only those with like faith are truly blessed of God. Note the companion treatment in Rom 4:9-12.

6,7. Abraham was justified by faith (Gen 15:6; Rom 4:3; Jas 2:23). The real, children of Abraham are not his natural descendants (Mt 3:9), but those who share his **faith. 8.** This was anticipated in the very language of the Abrahamic covenant, which had **all nations** in view. The words **in thee** magnify Abraham as the exemplar of faith. **9.** He was **faithful** in the sense of being full of faith. His justification is available also to the nations. This is their promised blessing.

C. The Argument from the Law. 3:10 —4:11.

1) The Curse of the Law, from Which Christ Must Deliver. 3:10-14. Paul, hav-

10. For as many as are of the works of the law are under the curse: for it is written, Cursed *is* every one that continueth not in all things which are written in the book of the law to do them.

11. But that no man is justified by the law in the sight of God, *it is* evident: for, The just shall live by faith.

12. And the law is not of faith: but, The man that doeth them shall live in them.

13. Christ hath redeemed us from the curse of the law, being made a curse for us: for it is written, Cursed *is* every one that hangeth on a tree:

14. That the blessing of Abraham might come on the Gentiles through Jesus Christ; that we might receive the promise of the Spirit through faith.

ing disposed of the Jews' confidence that physical relation to Abraham meant justification, now proceeds to the other refuge of Judaism, the possession of the Law.

10. Faith brings blessing, but the Law produces a curse because of the requirement that one must *continue* to meet its demands faithfully (Deut 27:26). 11,12. To the practical impossibility of being justified by law is now added the truth that God uses another method anyway—the just shall live by faith. Judging from the context, the apostle's use of this quotation (Hab 2:4) is intended to stress the truth that one can become just in God's sight only by faith. On this basis alone can he truly live the life of God. A similar sense is demanded in Rom 1:17. Under law, one must *do* before he can *live* (Lev 18:5). Under the Gospel one gets life from God through faith, then begins to do the will of God in the energy of that faith. It may appear that the apostle excludes all blessing for those living under the Law in pre-Christian days. What about the first psalm? 13. The Law is both a mirror of the will of God for his covenant people and a taskmaster that brings a curse. But in this point Paul is not discussing this brighter aspect of the Law, for he confines himself to the Law as a means of condemnation (cf. II Cor 3:6-9). The curse of the Law was real. It took Christ to the cross. The inflexibility of the Law's demands is clearly seen in the fact that when Christ took the place of the lawbreaker, though he himself was perfectly holy, he had to endure exactly the same penalty as any other who came under the curse of the Law. The circumstance that Christ died by hanging on the **tree** of Calvary emphasized the element of curse (Deut 21:23).

14. The example of Abraham continues to furnish background for the thought here. The death of Christ operated to bring **the blessing of Abraham** (justification) on the Gentiles. God, having delivered his own covenant people (the Jews) from the curse of the Law, was free from all hindrance in dealing likewise in grace with the Gentiles. The token of acceptance with God is **the promise of the Spirit,** i.e., the promised Spirit (cf. 4:6; Acts 1:4,5). We includes both Jews and Gentiles.

2) The Inviolability of the Covenant of Promise and Its Priority to the Law. 3:15-18. By its very nature a covenant

15. Brethren, I speak after the manner of men; Though *it be* but a man's covenant, yet *if it be* confirmed, no man disannulleth, or addeth thereto.

16. Now to Abraham and his seed were the promises made. He saith not, And to seeds, as of many; but as of one, And to thy seed, which is Christ.

17. And this I say, *that* the covenant, that was confirmed before of God in Christ, the law, which was four hundred and thirty years after, cannot disannul, that it should make the promise of none effect.

18. For if the inheritance *be* of the law, *it is* no more of promise: but God gave *it* to Abraham by promise.

is something fixed, not subject to change, even when it is a human arrangement. The promise cannot be set aside by the Law, which came much later.

15. **I speak after the manner of men.** This is a technical expression, a kind of apology. The immutability of God's arrangements should be beyond debate, but Paul finds it necessary to discuss the matter to make it fully clear to his readers. Even in human arrangements, once confirmed, a party to an agreement cannot, by himself, set it aside as no longer binding, nor can he add to its provisions as one might do with a will.

16. God made **promises** (the same promise was repeated) to Abraham and to **his seed.** But how much is embraced in the word **seed?** Not all the descendants of Abraham were intended (it is not **seeds**), nor are all lines of descent in view. We are instructed to think of **seed** as a collective term. It includes the patriarchs, for the promises were spoken to them. But it also looks on to Christ and includes him, as is shown by 3:19, where he is called once more **the seed,** the one who brought to an end the age of law. This corporate sense of the term **Christ** is found again in I Cor 12:12.

17. The promise to Abraham enjoyed priority over the giving of the Law, since it came 430 years earlier. Paul seems to include here the continuation of the promise to the patriarchs who came later, for the interval between Abraham and the giving of the Law was even longer than this. The essential thing, in line with the truth of 3:15, is the consideration that the Law could not possibly set aside the previous arrangement that God had made and confirmed.

18. Another feature is brought forward. Law does not so condition promise as to change its character, for this would violate the unconditional nature of promise. The **inheritance** (the enjoyment of the blessings of the covenant with Abraham — that a justification like his own would be extended ultimately to all the families of the earth) has nothing to do with **law.** The two things, law and **promise,** are fundamentally different. If the inheritance were contingent on law, then the promise would be nullified because of the well-known character of law—that it is a yoke which none can bear. It is an indisputable fact that God gave the inheritance to Abraham by promise. Nothing can change that basic truth.

19. Wherefore then *serveth* the law? It was added because of transgressions, till the seed should come to whom the promise was made; *and it was* ordained by angels in the hand of a mediator.

20. Now a mediator is not *a mediator* of one, but God is one.

21. *Is* the law then against the promises of God? God forbid: for if there had been a law given which could have given life, verily righteousness should have been by the law.

22. But the Scripture hath concluded all under sin, that the promise by faith of Jesus Christ might be given to them that believe.

3) The Purpose of the Law — Temporary in Its Standing and Negative in Its Operation. 3:19-22. The apostle's apparent discounting of the Law leads to a necessary question.

19. If the Law did not set aside the promise of God or even condition it, then why was it given? It was added because of transgressions, i.e., to give sin the distinctive character of transgression (cf. Rom 4:15; 5:20). Till. The Law was to run a certain course, fulfilling its mission of preparing the way for the seed — Christ, who is "the end of the law for righteousness" (Rom 10:4). The Law was ordained by angels in the hand of a mediator. Not only was the Law temporary, but the very manner of its bestowal indicates its inferior character. It had a double mediation, through angels (Acts 7:53; Heb 2:2) and through Moses the lawgiver.

20. The very idea of mediation assumes two parties, and this was true at the giving of the Law. But God is one, and this is emphasized in the covenant with Abraham. God acted sovereignly. He needed no one to stand between him and the patriarch. Paul's point is that mediation is a mark of inferiority in the Law. It shows the deliberate remoteness of God in the whole scene. The mediation of Christ in the present dispensation is not thereby labeled as inferior, for he is not a third party between God and men. God was in Christ reconciling the world.

21,22. The Law is not properly thought of as opposing the promises of God, for it operated in a different sphere. Life could not come by the Law. Those who enjoyed spiritual life in the legal dispensation had it not because of the Law but because of the grace of God, which forgave the sins committed against the Law. Such OT passages as promise life in connection with keeping the commandments of God (e.g., Deut 8:1), are properly interpreted as referring to life in a temporal sense, the enjoyment of God's favor and blessing in this earthly existence. Righteousness (a righteous standing before God) was no more possible in terms of law in Moses' day than in Paul's. Further, the Law cannot be opposed to the promises, since it aids their fulfillment by shutting men up to their need of grace and showing them that they must put their trust in Christ (cf. Gal 3:19).

4) Sonship Not Through the Law But Through Faith. 3:23—4:7.

23. But before faith came, we were kept under the law, shut up unto the faith which should afterward be revealed.

24. Wherefore the law was our schoolmaster *to bring us* unto Christ, that we might be justified by faith.

25. But after that faith is come, we are no longer under a schoolmaster.

26. For ye are all the children of God by faith in Christ Jesus.

27. For as many of you as have been baptized into Christ have put on Christ.

28. There is neither Jew nor Greek, there is neither bond nor free, there is neither male nor female: for ye are all one in Christ Jesus.

29. And if ye *be* Christ's, then are ye Abraham's seed, and heirs according to the promise.

## CHAPTER 4

NOW I say, *That* the heir, as long as he is a child, differeth nothing from a servant, though he be lord of all;

2. But is under tutors and governors until the time appointed of the father.

3. Even so we, when we were children, were in bondage under the elements of the world:

23. **Before faith came.** The new dispensation of free grace brought men the first opportunity, historically speaking, to put faith in Christ. **24.** The age of law was a time of discipline, the Law serving as a **schoolmaster** (not teacher; in fact, only a teacher's aid, usually a slave whose task it was to insure the safe arrival of the child at the school). Christ is the real teacher, who takes us in hand and shows us the way of God in terms of grace. "A low view of law leads to legalism in religion; a high view of law makes a man a seeker after grace" (J. Gresham Machen, *The Origin of Paul's Religion*, p. 179).

25. The disciplinary function of the Law, in the historic sense, ceased with the coming of Christ. But the Law may still operate in an individual life to create a sense of sin and need, thus preparing the heart to turn to Christ.

26-29. **Ye . . . all.** Gentiles as well as Jews are welcomed into the family of God by faith. And thus they attain their position in Christ Jesus. **Baptized into Christ.** Water baptism brings a person into the fellowship of the Church, but behind this rite lies the more significant aspect of baptism—being set apart by the Spirit for living union with Christ and his body (cf. I Cor 12:13). **Have put on Christ.** The Lord Jesus becomes the secret and the sphere of a new life that is shared with other believers. **All one in Christ Jesus.** Sonship with God involves brotherhood in Christ. There is one new man in him (cf. Eph 2:15). The ordinary distinctions and divisions of life are swallowed up in this relationship. To be in Christ Jesus, belonging to him, makes one a part of **Abraham's seed,** since Christ is that, as already stated in Gal 3:16,19. Sonship makes the believer also an heir (cf. Rom 8:17).

4:1-7. The tension here is between the words **servant** and **son. 1.** I say, i.e., *I mean.* The subject has not changed. The **heir,** until he attains maturity, is treated like a **servant. 2.** There are those who direct and control him—**tutors** (guardians) and **governors** (managers)— until he is free to possess his inheritance at the time appointed in his father's will.

3. Application begins here. The time of childhood was the period of the Law's control, when there was **bondage under the elements of the world.** These are not the physical elements, as in II Pet 3:10,12, nor the heavenly bodies, nor the elemental spirits considered by the ancients to be associated with these

4. But when the fulness of the time was come, God sent forth his Son, made of a woman, made under the law,

5. To redeem them that were under the law, that we might receive the adoption of sons.

6. And because ye are sons, God hath sent forth the Spirit of his Son into your hearts, crying, Abba, Father.

7. Wherefore thou art no more a servant, but a son; and if a son, then an heir of God through Christ.

8. Howbeit then, when ye knew not God, ye did service unto them which by nature are no gods.

9. But now, after that ye have known God, or rather are known of God, how turn ye again to the weak and beggarly elements, whereunto ye desire again to be in bondage?

10. Ye observe days, and months, and times, and years.

bodies (Paul would never have agreed that he was serving such spirits when he lived under the Law). They are elements in the sense of *rudiments*, because they belong to the legalistic religion of Judaism, and not to Christianity, the more mature and spiritual faith. This view of the matter is confirmed by the use of the word **elements** in Gal 4:9.

**4,5.** The fulness of the time corresponds to "the time appointed of the father" (4:2). It suggests that the disciplinary and preparatory work of the Law required a long period. His Son. The appropriate means of bringing many sons into glory. Real sonship is impossible until the Son par excellence appears. Pre-existence is suggested here. **Made of a woman.** This is not a reference to the virgin birth (Mt 11:11). Paul's argument requires a stress on Christ's likeness to us, not on dissimilarity. Through His birth He entered into our humanity. **Made under the law.** Circumcised, presented, reared in terms of the Law's requirements, fulfilling all righteousness. It was necessary that he keep the Law perfectly in order to **redeem** his people from the bondage and curse of the Law and to secure for them **the adoption of sons.** This privilege came to them as a gift of grace and not as the result of a long period of tutelage under the Law.

**6,7.** This acceptance is attested by the testimony of the Spirit, called here **the Spirit of his Son,** since his mission is to further and apply the work of the Son. He begets in the believer assurance of acceptance with God by His testimony in the heart. Paul uses **Abba,** the Aramaic word for *father,* followed by its Greek equivalent (cf. Mk 14:36; Rom 8:15,16). Sonship rules out servanthood and includes heirship. The Holy Spirit is the guarantee of these future blessings (cf. Eph 1:13,14).

5) An Appeal Not To Return to Bondage. 4:8-11. The apostle turns back once more to consider in direct fashion the Galatians and their situation, as regards legalism and Christian liberty.

**8.** Before conversion they served beings that **by nature are no gods** (being idols). Such conduct is understandable, because at that time these people **knew not God. 9,10.** They knew him now because he had known them, as shown by his overtures of grace toward them. It is incredible that people with such a history would **turn again to weak and beggarly elements** (as con-

11. I am afraid of you, lest I have bestowed upon you labor in vain.

12. Brethren, I beseech you, be as I *am;* for I *am* as ye *are:* ye have not injured me at all.

13. Ye know how through infirmity of the flesh I preached the gospel unto you at the first.

14. And my temptation which was in my flesh ye despised not, nor rejected; but received me as an angel of God, *even* as Christ Jesus.

15. Where is then the blessedness ye spake of? for I bear you record, that, if *it had been* possible, ye would have plucked out your own eyes, and have given them to me.

16. Am I therefore become your enemy, because I tell you the truth?

17. They zealously affect you, *but* not well; yea, they would exclude you, that ye might affect them.

18. But *it is* good to be zealously affected always in *a* good *thing,* and not only when I am present with you.

trasted with the Gospel), putting great store by special seasons. Apparently the Judaizers first put forward the more pleasant side of obedience to the Law (the Galatians were actually observing these things when Paul wrote) as less burdensome and offensive than circumcision, which the Galatians had not yet wholly accepted (cf. 5:2). **11.** Paul feared that if this attachment to legalism should continue and increase, it would mean that his labor among them had gone for nothing.

D. The Argument from Personal Reception by the Galatians. 4:12-20. The attitude of these people toward Paul at the time of this writing was in stark contrast to their original appreciation of him as God's messenger.

**12,13.** A plea to abandon legalism and be as Paul was, enjoying his liberty in Christ, for he had become like them. That is, by abandoning his Jewish distinctives he became, as it were, a Gentile (cf. 2:15-18). However much he was pained now, he recalled that the Galatians did him no injury at the *first,* on his *former* (ASV marg.) visit, but overlooked his infirmity of the flesh which caused him to tarry in their midst, an ill man. He did not leave their area until he had acquainted them with the good news of the Gospel. **14.** His sickness constituted a **temptation** for them to think lightly of him and reject him. This they refused to do; instead, they received him as one would receive an angel, or even as they would have received Christ himself.

**15,16. Blessedness.** They congratulated themselves on being thus favored by an emissary of the Lord. Their gratitude was unbounded; they would have sacrificed their **eyes** for Paul. This is not necessarily proof that the apostle had eye trouble (cf. the Gr. of Acts 23:1). The eyes are probably singled out for mention because of their preciousness. It must be, Paul is saying, that the Galatians' present coolness toward him is due to the fact that he has spoken the **truth.** Alienated from truth by Judaizing error, they had turned against Paul as well as against his message.

**17,18.** In contrast to Paul's habit of speaking the truth, the errorists had resorted to flattery and fawning attention to win the Galatians. Lest it be thought that the apostle was writing out of rancor and self-interest, he made clear that he was not averse to having another

19. My little children, of whom I travail in birth again until Christ be formed in you,

20. I desire to be present with you now, and to change my voice; for I stand in doubt of you.

21. Tell me, ye that desire to be under the law, do ye not hear the law?

22. For it is written, that Abraham had two sons, the one by a bondmaid, the other by a free woman.

23. But he *who was* of the bondwoman was born after the flesh; but he of the free woman *was* by promise.

24. Which things are an allegory: for these are the two covenants; the one from the mount Sinai, which gendereth to bondage, which is Agar.

25. For this Agar is mount Sinai in Arabia, and answereth to Jerusalem which now is, and is in bondage with her children.

26. But Jerusalem which is above is free, which is the mother of us all.

man minister to them rather than himself, provided the ministry was of the right sort—aiding the cause of the truth. How different were the Judaizers, who would **exclude** all who came to minister the Word, seeking to keep their protégés away from the apostle and other heralds of grace!

**19,20.** Paul's pain and concern were like those of a mother in travail. Yet what he agonizingly sought for was not the new birth of his friends (they were his **children** already in the Lord), but the full forming of the new life in them (Eph 4:13; cf. Phil 3:10). Another visit, he felt, would be highly desirable. It would accomplish more than the pen. Then he could speak softly to them, as a mother to an erring but still beloved child, and thus **change** his **voice,** which now necessarily seemed harsh.

E. The Argument from the Covenant of Promise. 4:21-31. Having called his readers **children,** the apostle proceeded to tell them a story, one with a moral, in the hope that they would see their folly.

**21-23.** They seemed to desire to be under law. Then let them **hear the law** (the Genesis narrative was part of the Law in the broader sense, which included the whole Pentateuch). One son of Abraham was **born after the flesh**— in the ordinary course of things, with a possible suggestion of human expediency trying to help along God's announced plan. This was Ishmael, born of Hagar. The other, namely, Isaac, the son of Sarah, was given by **promise** from God.

**24,25. Which things are allegorized.** That is, they are capable of expressing something more than the simple historical account. Paul proceeds to bring out the features that bear on the Galatian situation. **These** (women) answer to the **two covenants,** Hagar denoting the one given on **mount Sinai,** the Mosaic code. As she left the place of blessing in Canaan and went to this bleak area (Gen 21:21), so the Galatians had done in departing from the grace of Christ. Sad to say, more were affected than the Galatians. The Jerusalem of the day was **in bondage with her children**—not the church at Jerusalem, but Judaism as centered in this city.

**26,27.** But there is another Jerusalem, the one above, which is the **mother of all** the children of grace. This is a reference not to the future New Jerusalem of the Apocalypse but to a present spir-

27. For it is written, Rejoice, thou barren that bearest not; break forth and cry, thou that travailest not: for the desolate hath many more children than she which hath a husband.

28. Now we, brethren, as Isaac was, are the children of promise.

29. But as then he that was born after the flesh persecuted him *that was born* after the Spirit, even so *it is* now.

30. Nevertheless what saith the Scripture? Cast out the bondwoman and her son: for the son of the bondwoman shall not be heir with the son of the free woman.

31. So then, brethren, we are not children of the bondwoman, but of the free.

## CHAPTER 5

STAND fast therefore in the liberty wherewith Christ hath made us free, and be not entangled again with the yoke of bondage.

2. Behold, I Paul say unto you, that if ye be circumcised, Christ shall profit you nothing.

3. For I testify again to every man that is circumcised, that he is a debtor to do the whole law.

4. Christ is become of no effect unto you, whosoever of you are justified by the law; ye are fallen from grace.

itual reality, the home of believers. This home answers to the "heavenlies" of Eph 1:3 and "the city of the living God" of Heb 12:22. At this point Paul quotes Isaiah as foreseeing glory and triumph for Israel on the basis of the expiatory work of the Suffering Servant after the barrenness of the days of siege and captivity (Isa 54:1). This change of fortune is put in language that reflects the history of Sarah, who, though barren at first and apparently forsaken in favor of another, came into her own, in God's good time, with a greater progeny than that of Hagar. The church was enjoying a rapid increase in apostolic days, whereas Judaism was largely static and was even losing ground because of the witness of Jewish believers to their faith in Christ.

**28-31.** The New Testament saints were **children of promise,** as Isaac was. Just as Isaac was subject to persecution from Ishmael (cf. Gen 21:9), so they were subject to persecution from the legalists. The pressure to have Titus circumcised was a case in point (Gal 2:3). Yet the trial did not last, for God commanded the expulsion of **the bondwoman and her son** (Gen 21:10). The Judaizers did not have the authority or the blessing of God. Their work must come to nought.

### IV. Paul's Gospel Practiced. 5:1—6:15.

A. The Gospel Practiced in Liberty. 5:1-12. Refusal to be circumcised was a prime token of the enjoyment of this liberty.

**1.** This transitional statement is not well rendered in the AV. **For liberty Christ set us free** is the apostle's statement of fact, followed by the appeal to stand in that liberty and not be involved again in bondage. In some ways it is easier to live as a slave than to make right use of one's freedom (e.g., Israel in the wilderness wishing to return to Egypt).

**2-4.** One must choose, Paul says, between **Christ** and **circumcision.** This is not spoken of Jews (cf. Acts 21:21), but of Gentiles, who had no background of circumcision. In their case the rite could only signify a deliberate attempt to create merit by adopting a legalistic position and seeking righteousness by works. In the beginning, circumcision had no such connotation, for with Abraham it was a sign and seal of the righteousness which he already had by faith (Rom 4:11). But

5. For we through the Spirit wait for the hope of righteousness by faith.

6. For in Jesus Christ neither circumcision availeth any thing, nor uncircumcision; but faith which worketh by love.

7. Ye did run well; who did hinder you that ye should not obey the truth?

8. This persuasion *cometh* not of him that calleth you.

9. A little leaven leaveneth the whole lump.

10. I have confidence in you through the Lord, that ye will be none otherwise minded: but he that troubleth you shall bear his judgment, whosoever he be.

in the course of time, it had become a badge of merit. This being so, Christ could not **profit** the recipient of circumcision, who had really placed himself under obligation **to do the whole law**, with a view to bring justified thereby. To assume circumcision meant to leave the ground of grace in Christ (**fallen from grace**) in favor of the lower and impossible ground of self-righteousness. The true believer stands in grace (Rom 5:2).

**5.** Whereas the legalist is bogged down in insecurity—for he cannot know when he has done enough to satisfy the standard of divine righteousness—those who are justified by faith, who have **the Spirit** as the pledge of their acceptance with God, confidently await **by faith** the consummation (**the hope of righteousness**) in glory (cf. Rom 8:10,11).

**6.** Having shown faith's upreach in hope, the apostle indicates its outreach in **love**. In Christ one is not advantaged by having circumcision; nor is he who lacks it at a loss. What counts is love, which sums up in itself all that the Law demands (Rom 13:9,10). Justifying faith does not set aside this cardinal consideration of love. On the contrary, faith, operating through love, is the only workable means whereby the demands of the Law may be met.

**7-10.** The spiritual progress of the Galatians had been arrested. Someone had hindered these converts by alienating them from **the truth**. Elsewhere (1:7; 5:12) a group of legalistic agitators is in view; here, however, an individual is indicated, presumably the leader. This propaganda did not emanate from the One who called and started them on their race (cf. 1:6). The readers had been deceived by listening to false teaching. And let no one of them claim that Paul was overwrought, that he was making too much of the troubles in Galatia. A proverb would emphasize their folly. **A little leaven leaveneth the whole lump.** Perhaps the actual converts to legalism were thus far only few in number. Nevertheless, the believers must be on their guard lest the error spread. If it was honestly faced, it could be stayed. Paul had confidence in a happy issue of the difficulty, not based on **his** converts or on his own ministry, but on **the Lord**. Nevertheless, a favorable turn of events would not lift the responsibility from the shoulders of him who had led the sheep astray. He must **bear his judgment**.

11. And I, brethren, if I yet preach circumcision, why do I yet suffer persecution? then is the offense of the cross ceased.

12. I would they were even cut off which trouble you.

13. For, brethren, ye have been called unto liberty; only *use* not liberty for an occasion to the flesh, but by love serve one another.

14. For all the law is fulfilled in one word, *even* in this; Thou shalt love thy neighbor as thyself.

15. But if ye bite and devour one another, take heed that ye be not consumed one of another.

11,12. "Some may contend," Paul says, "that I am inconsistent in arguing against circumcision." It was known, for example, that he had circumcised Timothy (Acts 16:3). But this was a special case, for the young man was a half-Jew whom his father, a Greek, had not circumcised. If Timothy had gone about with Paul in this condition, it would have created needless opposition among the Jews. No principle was violated in this particular circumcision. The proof that Paul did not preach **circumcision** lay in the fact that he continued to **suffer persecution** (from the Jews). If he had circumcised the Gentiles, these same Jews would have regarded him in a much more friendly light. But if he had preached circumcision, **the offence of the cross** would have **ceased** so far as his ministry was concerned. Grace involves the helplessness of man to participate in his own salvation. This truth counters his human pride. Paul found offense not in the cross but in those who *unsettle[d]* (ASV) his converts — which **trouble you** (AV). His indignation led him to make a strong statement: **I would they were even cut off,** or better, *would mutilate themselves* (RSV). As an emasculated man has lost the power of propagation, so should these agitators be reduced to impotence in spreading their false doctrine. Such is the fervent wish to which the Apostle Paul gives expression here.

B. The Gospel Practiced in Love. 5:13-15.

13. While liberty is inherent in the Christian call to salvation, it must not be converted into license. This is what happens when liberty is viewed as an opportunity for **the flesh** to satisfy its desires. The one effective countermeasure is the service of others by love. The thought may be paraphrased as follows: You profess to be very zealous for the Law, which I have told you is bondage. But if you are really seeking bondage, there is a type that is harmless, even beneficial. I commend that to you. Be in bondage to each other to demonstrate love (cf. Rom 13:8). 14. This is the OT requirement (Lev 19:18), and the NT knows nothing higher. 15. There was dire need for the exercise of love in the Galatian churches, for Paul implies that there was fighting and bitter strife among them. The sharp antagonism was probably between those who had succumbed to the propaganda of the legalists and those who had not. Paul's sympathies

**16.** *This* I say then, Walk in the Spirit, and ye shall not fulfil the lust of the flesh.

**17.** For the flesh lusteth against the Spirit, and the Spirit against the flesh: and these are contrary the one to the other; so that ye cannot do the things that ye would.

**18.** But if ye be led of the Spirit, ye are not under the law.

**19.** Now the works of the flesh are manifest, which are *these*, Adultery, fornication, uncleanness, lasciviousness,

were with the latter group, but he recognized that without love they could not win over those who were of the opposite persuasion. Argument without love results in continuing friction.

C. The Gospel Practiced in the Spirit. 5:16-26. Though not expressed here, freedom (5:1,13) has not been lost from view. "Love is the guard of Christian freedom. The Holy Spirit is its guide" (G. G. Findlay, *The Epistle to the Galatians* in *The Expositor's Bible,* p. 347). This section, with its contrast between flesh and Spirit, has been somewhat anticipated by the statement in 3:3. Life in the Spirit is seen now as the effective antidote to the movings of the flesh, the sinful principle that persists in the saints. So there is a legitimate and necessary warfare, in contrast to that hinted at in 5:15.

**16,17. Walk in** (better, *by*) **the Spirit.** Only in this way can believers rise above the limitations of the flesh and avoid fulfilling its desires. The promise is emphatic—**ye shall not at all fulfill. Flesh** and **Spirit** are opposites, locked in continual combat. If the Christian is walking by the power of the one, he cannot be in the control of the other. The statement, **and these are contrary the one to the other,** is somewhat parenthetical, and the conclusion of the verse depends directly upon the second of the two statements earlier in the verse. Behind the Spirit's resistance to the flesh is the divine purpose that believers should be kept from doing things they (otherwise) would do.

**18.** To realize the victory over the flesh, one must put himself under the leadership of the Spirit. The Law conducts a man to Christ (3:24). Then the Spirit assumes control and directs the child of God into the fullness of the life in our Lord. This fullness will inevitably result unless the Spirit is limited by sin in the believer (Eph 4:30). Instead of saying, in agreement with the first pronouncements of this section, that to be led by the Spirit means to be delivered from the flesh, the apostle draws an unexpected conclusion. To be led by the Spirit demonstrates freedom from **law.** Adherence to law means the multiplying of transgressions (cf. Gal 3:19) instead of their reduction. Evidently a close bond exists between law and flesh (cf. Rom 8:3).

**19-21.** The **works of the flesh** can be expected to spawn freely in the atmos-

20. Idolatry, witchcraft, hatred, variance, emulations, wrath, strife, seditions, heresies,

21. Envyings, murders, drunkenness, revelings, and such like: of the which I tell you before, as I have also told *you* in time past, that they which do such things shall not inherit the kingdom of God.

22. But the fruit of the Spirit is love, joy, peace, long-suffering, gentleness, goodness, faith,

23. Meekness, temperance: against such there is no law.

phere of legalism. A flash of irony is detectable here in the reference to **works** —"Look at the accomplishments of the flesh!" First come the sensual sins. **Adultery** is unlawful intercourse with a married person, **fornication** with one who is unmarried. **Uncleanness** covers all sorts of sexual defilement. **Lasciviousness** denotes brazen boldness in this sort of life. Next, religious sins are enumerated. **Idolatry** is devotion to idols. The Greek word rendered **witchcraft** yields the English term "pharmacy," and basically denotes the administering of drugs and magical potions. But it had come to stand for the whole practice of the magician's art (cf. "sorceries," and ASV "sorcery" in Rev 9:21; 18:23). Still a third class includes temperamental sins. These run the gamut from **hatred,** which is something latent, through **strife,** which is something operative (denoting in this case disputes due to selfishness), and **seditions** (better, *divisions)* and **heresies,** or displays of party spirit (**envyings** may be related to the foregoing as helping to produce divisions, or may equally well be associated with the next item), to **murders,** the climax of wrongly cherished antagonisms. In a fourth class may be put **drunkenness** and **revellings.** The list could be extended—**and such like.** Those who practice such things **shall not inherit the kingdom of God** (cf. I Cor 6:9,10). A believer may fall into such wrongdoing if he walks in accordance with the flesh. Hence the inclusion of this list in its present position in this letter, where the life of the Christian is under review.

**22,23.** Everything here stands in contrast to the foregoing: **fruit** instead of works; **the Spirit** instead of the flesh; and a list of virtues altogether attractive and desirable in place of the ugly things just cited. The word **fruit,** being singular, as usual in Paul's writings, tends to emphasize the unity and coherence of the life in the Spirit as opposed to the disorganization and instability of life under the dictates of the flesh. It is possible, also, that the singular may be intended to point to the person of Christ, in whom all these things are seen in their perfection. The Spirit seeks to produce these by reproducing Christ in the believer (cf. 4:19). Passages like Rom 13:14 suggest that the moral problems of redeemed men and women can be solved by the adequacy of Christ when he is appropriated by faith.

In the light of Paul's preference for the

**24.** And they that are Christ's have crucified the flesh with the affections and lusts.

**25.** If we live in the Spirit, let us also walk in the Spirit.

**26.** Let us not be desirous of vainglory, provoking one another, envying one another.

singular form of **fruit,** it is not necessary to resort to the expedient of putting a dash after love in order to make all the other items depend on this one. Love is crucial (I Jn 4:8; I Cor 13:13; Gal 5:6). **Joy** is conferred by Christ upon his own followers (Jn 15:11) and is mediated by the Spirit (I Thess 1:6; Rom 14:17). **Peace** is the gift of Christ (Jn 14:27) and includes inward repose (Phil 4:6) and harmonious relations with others (contrast Gal 5:15,20). **Longsuffering** relates to one's attitude toward others and involves a refusal to retaliate or work vengeance for wrong received. It is literally *long-spiritedness.* **Gentleness** is better rendered *kindness.* It is benevolence in action, a distinctly social virtue. **Goodness** is an uprightness of soul that abhors evil, a clean-cut honesty of motive and conduct. **Faith,** in this setting, means faithfulness (if it were *faith,* it would stand at the beginning of the list). For a parallel use, see Tit 2:10 ("fidelity"). **Meekness** is based on humility and denotes an attitude toward others in keeping with due denial of self. **Temperance** is better rendered *self-control* (lit., *a holding in with a firm hand*), or control of the self life by means of the Spirit. **Against such there is no law.** "Law exists for the purpose of restraint, but in the works of the Spirit there is nothing to restrain" (J. B. Lightfoot, *Galatians,* p. 213). The same truth is stated elsewhere, e.g., Rom 8:4.

**24-26.** Those who are truly Christ's must be like him in that they participate in his cross. They have **crucified the flesh.** Ideally, this points to their identification with Christ in his death (2:20). Practically, it emphasizes the need of carrying the cross principle into the redeemed life, since the flesh, with its **affections** and desires is still an ever present reality (cf. 5:16,17). The same tension between divine provision and human appropriation is found regarding the Spirit. We **live** in the Spirit by God's arrangement, by means of the gift of the Spirit at conversion. But we **walk** in the Spirit as a matter of personal volition, taking each step in dependence upon him. If one is walking thus, he will not be desirous of **vainglory**—ambitious for self and frustrated when unsuccessful. "Vainglorying challenges competition, to which the stronger-natured respond in kind, while those who are weaker are moved to envy" (Hogg and Vine, *Galatians,* p. 305).

## CHAPTER 6

BRETHREN, if a man be overtaken in a fault, ye which are spiritual, restore such a one in the spirit of meekness; considering thyself, lest thou also be tempted.

2. Bear ye one another's burdens, and so fulfil the law of Christ.

3. For if a man think himself to be something, when he is nothing, he deceiveth himself.

4. But let every man prove his own work, and then shall he have rejoicing in himself alone, and not in another.

5. For every man shall bear his own burden.

6. Let him that is taught in the word communicate unto him that teacheth in all good things.

7. Be not deceived; God is not mocked: for whatsoever a man soweth, that shall he also reap.

8. For he that soweth to his flesh shall of the flesh reap corruption; but he that soweth to the Spirit shall of the Spirit reap life everlasting.

**D. The Gospel Practiced in Service. 6:1-10.** Christians still have a law to fulfill, the law of Christ. They can fulfill it only in the power of the Spirit, as they serve one another in the fellowship of the Church.

**1-5. A man.** One of like passions with yourselves and therefore liable to fall. **Be overtaken.** Apprehended, taken by surprise, caught in the act. **Fault** should be more strongly worded. It is a lapse (cf. Rom 5:15). A sinning saint needs restoration as well as divine forgiveness. The one qualified to help him is **spiritual,** i.e., possessing to a notable degree the fruit of the Spirit, especially love (5:22) for the brother in trouble and also **meekness** (5:23), seeing that he himself could some day slip into sin and need the same loving ministration for himself. A true spirit of helpfulness should obtain in other matters also— **bear ye one another's burdens** (contrast Lk 11:46). The law of Moses is described as a burden (Acts 15:10), but **the law of Christ** is not so (I Jn 5:3). His burden is light (Mt 11:30). This sets the disciple free to minister to his fellows (Mk 10:43-45). The warning at the end of Gal 6:1 is carried on in 6:3. Over-evaluation of one's self is self-deception. Let a man put his own work to the test. If he finds anything there to give satisfaction, he can have **rejoicing in himself.** His feeling will be one of gratification and contentment rather than of pride and superiority over his brethren. Each had better evaluate himself aright now, in preparation for the Lord's judgment of him in the coming day, when he must **bear his own burden.** He will be held responsible for his own life and work (Rom 14:12).

**6-10.** Here the thought returns to bearing one another's burdens, but in the specific area of giving for the support of Christian work (cf. II Cor 11:9; II Thess 3:8). **6. Communicate** means to participate in something along with someone else. The one who is **taught in the word** shares his material goods with the one who teaches him. In this way he participates in the work of the Lord. This is the divine plan. Beware lest any try to set it aside. **7. God is not mocked.** The word for mockery is *turning up the nose.* No man can successfully snub God or evade his decree that, "whatsoever a man soweth, that shall he also reap"— the immutable law of life (cf. II Cor 9:6 in a similar connection). **8.** A selfish Christian **soweth to his flesh,** spending

9. And let us not be weary in well doing: for in due season we shall reap, if we faint not.

10. As we have therefore opportunity, let us do good unto all *men*, especially unto them who are of the household of faith.

11. Ye see how large a letter I have written unto you with mine own hand.

12. As many as desire to make a fair show in the flesh, they constrain you to be circumcised; only lest they should suffer persecution for the cross of Christ.

his resources to gratify his own personal desires. He may expect to **reap corruption.** That which might have brought reward by being invested in the Lord's work will be nothing but a decayed mass, a complete loss in terms of eternity. On the other hand, by responding to the Spirit in love and kindness, and gladly participating in the extension of the Gospel by supporting Christian workers, believers will be adding interest to the capital of eternal life. This passage is capable of broader application, in line with the proverbial character of the statement in verse 7. But **flesh** and **Spirit** suggest primary application to the believer (cf. 5:17,24,25), in line with the immediate context. 9. The specific issue of giving leads naturally to a consideration of the more general theme of doing good, which by implication is a sowing. The harvest will come **in due season.** One may well **faint** if he expects to see the harvest immediately. 10. Two spheres of Christian beneficence are suggested—**all** men and **the household of faith.** The latter group is **especially** the obligation of the children of God. If one neglects to care for his own (and believers are the family of God), he is worse than an unbeliever (I Tim 5:8).

E. The Gospel Practiced in Separation from the World. 6:11-15. Paul uses this final section as a means of underscoring some of the emphases of the epistle as a whole, stressing the centrality and sufficiency of the cross, and the division it creates between believers and men of the world.

11. **How large a letter** is not a good rendering. The apostle is not referring to length (Galatians is not a long letter), but to the size of the letters he used as he took the pen from the hand of the scribe and wrote these closing words himself for the sake of greater effectiveness. He returns to the subject of circumcision and exposes the motives of those who were troubling his readers. 12. They **desire**[d] **to make a fair show in the flesh,** in the only realm of life which they knew, since they did not walk by the Spirit. **Constrain** in this case means "seek to compel" (cf. 2:3). Pressure was being exerted. By stressing circumcision, and going among the Gentiles to urge it upon them, the Judaizers were hoping to escape the wrath of unbelieving Jews against themselves for having espoused the cause of Christ. They were afraid of **persecution for the cross of Christ** (cf. 5:11). Men of this type are

13. For neither they themselves who are circumcised keep the law; but desire to have you circumcised, that they may glory in your flesh.

14. But God forbid that I should glory, save in the cross of our Lord Jesus Christ, by whom the world is crucified unto me, and I unto the world.

15. For in Christ Jesus neither circumcision availeth any thing, nor uncircumcision, but a new creature.

16. And as many as walk according to this rule, peace be on them, and mercy, and upon the Israel of God.

17. From henceforth let no man trouble me: for I bear in my body the marks of the Lord Jesus.

18. Brethren, the grace of our Lord Jesus Christ be with your spirit. Amen.

Unto the Galatians written from Rome.

called "the concision" (cutting party) in Phil 3:2. 13. Having dealt with the real motive of the Judaizers, Paul now reveals their professed motive, which was zeal for the Law. They took one item, an external matter at that, and made it stand for the observance of the Law as a whole. They hoped to gain credit for bringing Gentiles under the Law as a system by forcing them to accept circumcision. They would glory in this mark made in the flesh of their converts. 14. Paul refused to boast in circumcision or in anything else except the cross by which (AV by whom, i.e., Christ) the world with all its craven motives was banished, crucified to him, utterly separated from his thought and way of life. Paul cared not for comfort or reputation, as the Judaizers did (cf. 1:10). 15. Why does the apostle here discount circumcision? Because it had been made a mere worldly ceremony by the crucifixion. What truly counts, he declares, is the new life that comes through being in Christ Jesus. This amounts to a new creation. The word new denotes what is superior to the old.

## V. Conclusion. 6:16-18.

A. Closing Prayer. 6:16. For those who walk according to the rule or canon just laid down, namely, the cross of Christ and the message of grace that centers there, Paul requests peace and that merciful loving-kindness which brings a continuance of the grace already received in the Gospel. He seeks the same blessing for the Israel of God. While it is possible that this refers to the whole church, in view of the and, the more probable reference is to Christian Jews, such as Paul himself. These are the real Israel, as opposed to those who merely bear the name (cf. Rom 2:29).

B. Closing Testimony. 6:17. If the Galatians had been troubled, so had Paul. But if any wished to question his devotion to Christ, let them realize that the marks of persecution which he bore in his body, scars suffered for the sake of the Lord Jesus, spoke more eloquently than the body marks (circumcision) which the Judaizers loved to impose on others as a proof of their zeal.

C. Benediction. 6:18. This parting word, with its emphasis on grace, summarizes the message of the epistle as a whole. Nothing could be more appropriate.

# BIBLIOGRAPHY

Burton, E. D. *The Epistle to the Galatians (International Critical Commentary).* New York: Charles Scribner's Sons, 1920.

Ellicott, C. J. *Commentary on St. Paul's Epistle to the Galatians.* Andover: Warren F. Draper, 1896.

Findlay, G. G. *The Epistle to the Galatians (The Expositor's Bible).* New York: A. C. Armstrong and Son, 1889.

Hogg, C. F., and Vine, W. E. *The Epistle of Paul the Apostle to the Galatians.* London: Pickering and Inglis, 1922.

Lightfoot, J. B. *St. Paul's Epistle to the Galatians.* London: Macmillan and Co., 1896.

Ramsay, W. M. *A Historical Commentary on St. Paul's Epistle to the Galatians.* New York: G. P. Putnam's Sons, 1900.

Ridderbos, H. N. *The Epistle of Paul to the Churches of Galatia.* Grand Rapids: Wm. B. Eerdmans Publishing Co., 1953.

# THE EPISTLE
# TO THE EPHESIANS

## INTRODUCTION

*Authorship, Date, and Place of Writing.* Few critics have seriously denied Paul's authorship of this epistle. More attack has been leveled against the traditional date and place of writing, as well as against the traditional destination (see below).

Ephesians is in the same chronological group of Paul's epistles as Colossians, Philemon, and Philippians, called collectively "The Prison Epistles" because written during Paul's first Roman imprisonment. Paul evidently arrived in Rome in the spring of 61. The Acts speaks of his living two whole years in his own hired house (Acts 28:30), which would bring him to the spring of 63. He was probably released before the burning of Rome in 64. In Philippians he was expecting such release (1:19-26), a hope to which he refers also in Philemon 22. Ephesians, Colossians, and Philemon were dispatched at the same time by the same messengers (Eph 6:21,22; Col 4:7-9; Phm 12,23,24).

Attempts to place these epistles at an earlier time from some other place of imprisonment, such as Caesarea or even Ephesus (George S. Duncan, *St. Paul's Ephesian Ministry*) have not been successful. There is no good reason for rejecting the traditional place of writing—Rome. This epistle, along with Colossians and Philemon, was probably written in the year 62.

*Destination of the Epistle.* Because the words in Ephesus (*en Ephesō*) do not occur in the original handwriting of Codex Sinaiticus (Aleph) and Codex Vaticanus (B), two of the oldest extant manuscripts of the New Testament, some deny that this epistle was addressed to Ephesus. Another point of difficulty is the fact that an epistle from Laodicea is mentioned in Col 4:16, but there is no mention of Ephesus. Some believe that this epistle may have been a circular letter addressed to a number of different churches. [This is the view most widely held today.—Ed.] It seems more likely, however, that a particular congregation was in view, and there is no strong reason for rejecting the traditional destination—Ephesus (see John W. Burgon, *The Last Twelve Verses of St. Mark*, 1959 edition, pp. 169-187). Even Aleph and B are headed by the title *To Ephesians* (*Pros Ephesious*). Paul had remained a comparatively long time in Ephesus while on his third missionary journey (Acts 19:1-20:1; 20:31). His association with the believers there had been most intimate, as his address to the Ephesian elders shows (Acts 20:17-38).

*Contents of the Epistle.* This epistle, along with Colossians, emphasizes the truth that the Church is the body of which Christ is the Head. While Paul had mentioned the same truth earlier, in Romans 12 and I Corinthians 12, he develops it more fully here. There is no higher point of revelation than is reached in this epistle which shows the believer as seated with Christ in the heavenlies and exhorts him to live in accordance with this high calling. Actually the epistle falls into two main parts of three chapters each. In Eph 1–3 the apostle tells believers what they are in Christ; In Eph 4–6 he tells them what they are to do because they are in Christ. It has often been suggested that the contents of the epistle can be summarized by the three words *sitting, walking,* and *standing.* By position, the believer is seated with Christ in the heavenlies (2:6); his responsibility is to walk worthy of the calling wherewith he has been called (4:1); and this walk is further seen as a warfare in which he is engaged against Satan and all his hosts and in which he is exhorted to stand against the wiles of the devil (6:11).

# OUTLINE

I. The believer's position in Christ. 1:1—3:21.
  A. Salutation. 1:1,2.
  B. All spiritual blessings. 1:3-14.
    1. Chosen by the Father. 1:3-6.
    2. Redeemed by the Son. 1:7-12.
    3. Sealed by the Holy Spirit. 1:13,14.
  C. Paul's first prayer. 1:15-23.
  D. Salvation by grace. 2:1-10.
    1. What we were in the past. 2:1-3.
    2. What we are in the present. 2:4-6.
    3. What we shall be in the future. 2:7-10.
  E. Oneness of Jews and Gentiles in Christ. 2:11-22.
    1. What the Gentiles were without Christ. 2:11,12.
    2. The one body. 2:13-18.
    3. The one building. 2:19-22.
  F. The revelation of the mystery. 3:1-13.
    1. The dispensation of the grace of God. 3:1-6.
    2. The fellowship of the mystery. 3:7-13.
  G. Paul's second prayer. 3:14-21.
II. The believer's conduct in the world. 4:1—6:24.
  A. The worthy walk. 4:1-16.
    1. The unity of the Spirit. 4:1-6.
    2. The gift of Christ. 4:7-12.
    3. The unity of faith and knowledge. 4:13-16.
  B. The different walk. 4:17-32.
    1. Description of the Gentiles' walk. 4:17-19.
    2. Putting off the old and putting on the new. 4:20-24.
    3. Practical application. 4:25-32.
  C. The loving walk. 5:1-14.
    1. Walking in love. 5:1-7.
    2. Walking in light. 5:8-14.
  D. The wise walk. 5:15—6:9.
    1. Being circumspect. 5:15-17.
    2. Being filled with the Holy Spirit. 5:18—6:9.
      a. Rejoicing and thanksgiving. 5:19,20.
      b. Submission in practical relationships. 5:21—6:9.
        (1) Wives and husbands. 5:21-33.
        (2) Children and parents. 6:1-4.
        (3) Servants and masters. 6:5-9.
  E. The Christian walk as a warfare. 6:10-20.
    1. Being strong in the Lord—the whole armor of God. 6:10-17.
    2. Prayer for all saints and for Paul. 6:18-20.
  F. Closing greetings. 6:21-24.

## EPHESIANS

### CHAPTER 1

PAUL, an apostle of Jesus Christ by the will of God, to the saints which are at Ephesus, and to the faithful in Christ Jesus:

## COMMENTARY

**I. The Believer's Position in Christ. 1:1—3:21.**

A. Salutation. 1:1,2. The salutations of all Paul's epistles are strikingly similar. Although this is the regular epistolary form, there is less of the personal element in Ephesians than in most of Paul's letters.

**1. Paul, an apostle of Jesus Christ by the will of God.** As in other epistles, Paul emphasizes that he has been appointed by God to the special office of apostle. **To the saints.** In the NT **saints** are those who are set apart, that is, all believers. **Which are at Ephesus.** See Introduction. **The faithful.** Believing ones (cf. Gal 3:9). The absence of the article before the word **faithful** in the original indicates that the saints *are* the believers. **In Christ Jesus.** An important phrase in this epistle. No matter what the geographical location of the saints, their real position in God's sight is in Christ Jesus. They have been put into a vital union with him so that they are identified with him (cf. Jn 14:20).

2. Grace *be* to you, and peace, from God our Father, and *from* the Lord Jesus Christ.

3. Blessed *be* the God and Father of our Lord Jesus Christ, who hath blessed us with all spiritual blessings in heavenly *places* in Christ:

4. According as he hath chosen us in him before the foundation of the world, that we should be holy and without blame before him in love:

**2. Grace be to you, and peace.** This same greeting is found in all of Paul's epistles, though the word *mercy* is added in the Pastorals. Grace must always precede peace. The Greek word for **grace,** *charis,* is related to the common Greek greeting, *chairein,* but gives to the salutation a distinctively Christian emphasis. **Peace** is the usual Hebrew greeting. **From God our Father, and from the Lord Jesus Christ.** The second **from** is not in the original. There is a very close connection here, which shows the identity of the Father and the Lord Jesus Christ in their essence.

**B. All Spiritual Blessings. 1:3-14.** The believer is seen as the recipient of **all spiritual blessings.** Hence he has no need to seek additional blessings from God. He must, instead, appropriate the ones that already have been provided. All three Persons of the Holy Trinity are seen to have a part in this provision of the spiritual blessings.

**1) Chosen by the Father. 1:3-6.** The work of the Father is mentioned first.

**3. Blessed be the God and Father of our Lord Jesus Christ.** "Almost all St. Paul's epistles begin with some ascription of praise" (Alf). Notice the play on words in the use of **blessed. Who hath blessed us.** We are called upon to bless God, who has already blessed us. But of course God has blessed us by what he has done, while our blessing of him is by words, that is, by our praise of him. He is **the God and Father of our Lord Jesus Christ.** This identifies him as the one true God, not some false or imaginary deity. The only way to know him is through Jesus Christ (cf. Jn 14:6). **In heavenly places.** Although the adjective occurs elsewhere, this phrase occurs only in Ephesians in the NT. It is found five times— 1:3; 1:20; 2:6; 3:10; 6:12. The word **places** is not in the original. Here it denotes the spheres or realms of our association in Christ. We are not yet actually in heaven, but our calling is heavenly; the power for our daily living is heavenly; God's provision is heavenly. Note the continual repetition in the epistle of the phrase, **in Christ.** It is only in him that we ever could have received these blessings.

**4. As he hath chosen us.** This is middle voice in Greek; that is, he chose us for himself. The Scripture has much to say about God's electing love. The doctrine of election is never presented in

5. Having predestinated us unto the adoption of children by Jesus Christ to himself, according to the good pleasure of his will,

6. To the praise of the glory of his grace, wherein he hath made us accepted in the beloved:

Scripture as something to be afraid of, but always as something for believers to rejoice in. Note that we are chosen **in him**, that is, in Christ, and that this choice took place **before the foundation of the world**. God's purposes are eternal. **That we should be holy and without blame before him.** This is the purpose for which God has chosen us in Christ (cf. Rom 8:29; Jude 24,25). The phrase **in love** probably belongs with what follows rather than with what precedes; that is, *in love having predestinated us* (Nestle).

**5. Having predestinated us.** God's choice of us in Christ was for a purpose that is eternal. **Unto the adoption of children.** The word translated **adoption of children** is used five times in the NT (Rom 8:15,23; 9:4; Gal 4:5; and here). It refers to our being placed in the position of sons. It is not the modern idea of adoption, but rather the placing of a child in the position of adult sonship. God's purpose is that all believers should be adult sons in his family, in which Christ is the "firstborn" (Rom 8:29). **According to the good pleasure of his will.** Any attempt to base God's election and predestination upon human merit, whether foreknown or otherwise, is unScriptural and futile. The cause of God's choice of us is not to be found in us, but in him alone (cf. Tit 3:5; Eph 2:8-10). The will of God is the determining factor.

**6. To the praise of the glory of his grace.** Note the threefold use of this expression (cf. vv. 12,14). The three occurrences of this phrase mark off the part each of the three Persons of the Godhead takes in our salvation in giving us the blessings that have come to us. The most important consideration in the universe is the glory of God. The Westminster Shorter Catechism expresses this well in its answer to the first question, "What is the chief end of man?" "Man's chief end is to glorify God, and to enjoy Him forever." **His grace.** "Grace is undeserved, unearned, and unrecompensed" (Chafer). It is God's self-dependent favor bestowed upon sinful men, who deserve only his wrath. **Wherein he hath made us accepted.** More literally, *which he has freely bestowed upon us.* There is another play on words in the original—"His grace which he graced." It is difficult to show this in English. This bestowal is **in the beloved**; that is, in the beloved one—namely, the Lord Jesus Christ (cf. Col 1:13; Mt 3:17).

7. In whom we have redemption through his blood, the forgiveness of sins, according to the riches of his grace;

8. Wherein he hath abounded toward us in all wisdom and prudence;

9. Having made known unto us the mystery of his will, according to his good pleasure which he hath purposed in himself:

10. That in the dispensation of the fulness of times he might gather together in one all things in Christ, both which are in heaven, and which are on earth; *even* in him:

11. In whom also we have obtained an inheritance, being predestinated according to the purpose of him who worketh all things after the counsel of his own will:

2) Redeemed by the Son. 1:7-12.

**7. In whom**—that is, Christ,—**we have redemption.** This is our present possession. **Through his blood.** The Scripture presents the blood of Christ as the infinite purchase price of our redemption (cf. Acts 20:28; I Cor 6:20; I Pet 1:18-20). Colossians 1:14 parallels this verse. **The forgiveness of sins.** The Pharisees rightly observed (for once) that no man can forgive sins but God only (Mk 2:7). The fact that the Lord Jesus Christ forgives is evidence that he is God. **According to the riches of his grace.** Again the emphasis on the utter absence of human merit (cf. Rom 5:21). Note the word **riches.** His grace is not limited.

**8. Wherein he hath abounded toward us.** God abounds in every respect. He is the infinite One. The **wisdom** of the Lord Jesus Christ is unlimited, and he has abounded in the sense that he has made this wisdom available to us, as the next verse indicates. **9. Having made known unto us.** The explanation of his abounding. **The mystery.** In the NT the word **mystery** (literally, *secret)* indicates something not clearly revealed before, but now made known. **According to his good pleasure which he hath purposed in himself.** Again we see that God is completely self-determining and self-sufficient.

**10. That in the dispensation of the fulness of times.** The word **dispensation** means "stewardship." It is used in the NT to refer to the different administrations of God's blessings. Evidently **the dispensation of the fulness of times** is the final stewardship committed to men, which will bring the purposes of God to fruition in human history. The purpose that has been referred to is summed up in the expression, **He might gather together in one all things in Christ.** This is a literary remark (Robertson) — "that he might head up everything in Christ" (cf. Col 1:18). **All things** includes the whole creation. Since Christ is pre-eminent in God's purpose in the universe and in the Church, the individual who does not have Christ pre-eminent in his life is entirely out of harmony with the purpose of the Father.

**11. In whom also we have obtained an inheritance.** There is difference of opinion concerning the Greek here— whether it is active or passive. The latter seems more probable, in which case we could translate it *in whom we have been made an heritage.* We are Christ's inheritance, as he is ours. **Being predestinated according to the purpose of him who worketh all things after the counsel of his own will.** The words **predestinated,**

12. That we should be to the praise of his glory, who first trusted in Christ.

13. In whom ye also *trusted*, after that ye heard the word of truth, the gospel of your salvation: in whom also, after that ye believed, ye were sealed with that Holy Spirit of promise,

14. Which is the earnest of our inheritance until the redemption of the purchased possession, unto the praise of his glory.

purpose, counsel, and will have an intimate connection. There is no clearer or more sublime statement anywhere in Scripture concerning the sovereignty of God. Running throughout the Bible are the parallel lines of God's sovereignty and man's responsibility. We cannot reconcile them, but we can believe both because both are taught in the Word.

**12. That we should be to the praise of his glory, who first trusted in Christ.** Some believe that **we** here refers to the Jews, because of the expression **first trusted.** This seems likely in view of the contrast between **we** in verse 12 and **ye** in verse 13. **To the praise of his glory.** This marks off the second section in this great triad.

3) Sealed by the Holy Spirit. 1:13,14. **13. In whom ye also trusted.** That is, you Gentiles, in contrast to the Jews. **After that ye heard the word of truth.** When you heard the word of truth, or word which consists of truth. This is equated further with **the gospel of your salvation**—the good news which brought you salvation. **In whom also after that ye believed.** Literally, *in whom also when you believed, you were sealed.* This sealing did not take place as something subsequent to salvation but was simultaneous with salvation. The sealing ministry of the Holy Spirit is mentioned several times in the NT (cf. II Cor 1:22; Eph 4:30). A seal indicates possession and security. The Holy Spirit himself is the seal. His presence guarantees our salvation. **That holy Spirit of promise. That** is simply *the* in the Greek text. The word **holy** should be capitalized, for this is the third Person of the Godhead, and the adjective is emphatic in the original. **Of promise.** The Holy Spirit himself is the object or content of the promise that was given.

**14. Who is the earnest of our inheritance.** That is, the pledge which guarantees that all the rest will follow. **Until the redemption of the purchased possession.** Jesus Christ has purchased us for himself and has given us the Holy Spirit as the pledge that the redemption which has been so wondrously begun will be completed. Again we have the refrain **unto the praise of his glory.** The repetition of this refrain reminds us again of the triune God—Father, Son and Holy Spirit, three Persons, yet one God.

C. Paul's First Prayer. 1:15-23. The prayer that follows is based upon the

15. Wherefore I also, after I heard of your faith in the Lord Jesus, and love unto all the saints,

16. Cease not to give thanks for you, making mention of you in my prayers;

17. That the God of our Lord Jesus Christ, the Father of glory, may give unto you the spirit of wisdom and revelation in the knowledge of him:

18. The eyes of your understanding being enlightened; that ye may know what is the hope of his calling, and what the riches of the glory of his inheritance in the saints,

19. And what *is* the exceeding greatness of his power to us-ward who believe, according to the working of his mighty power,

20. Which he wrought in Christ, when he raised him from the dead, and set *him* at his own right hand in the heavenly *places,*

paragraph just concluded. It is because God has done all of these things for the believer, carrying him from his eternal purpose in the past eternity to the completion of the redemption in the future eternity, that Paul can pray as he does. Note that in contrast to most of our prayers, Paul's intercession was primarily for the spiritual welfare of those for whom he prayed.

**15. After I heard of your faith in the Lord Jesus, and love unto all the saints.** Sometimes we forget that we should pray as .earnestly for people after they are saved, as we do for their salvation. The faith and love of these Ephesian believers was an incentive to Paul to pray for their continued spiritual growth. **16. Cease not to give thanks for you.** Thanks on your behalf; that is, thanks to God for what he had done for the Ephesians. **Making mention of you in my prayers.** Paul did not regard prayer as something vague and indefinite. He remembered them and their needs specifically before God.

**17. That the God of our Lord Jesus Christ** (cf. v. 3), **the Father of glory.** That is, the Father characterized by glory. **May give unto you the spirit of wisdom and revelation.** Probably this is objective; that is, the Holy Spirit who gives wisdom and revelation. **In the knowledge.** This word indicates full experiential knowledge. **18. The eyes of your understanding being enlightened.** Literally, *the eyes of your heart.* "The heart in Scripture is the very core and center of life" (Alf). **That ye may know.** It is only as God enlightens us that we actually can know what he wants us to know. **What is the hope of his calling.** Hope in Scripture is the absolute certainty of future good. **Riches of the glory of his inheritance in the saints.** Compare with the "riches of grace" in verse 7 (cf. also Deut 33:3,4).

**19. The exceeding greatness of his power.** The phrases that follow pile up words to denote the almightiness of God **to us-ward.** "No better rendering here could be devised than the *to us-ward* of the AV, which is wisely retained by the [English] RV" (Salmond). **20. Which he wrought in Christ when he raised him from the dead.** Frequently in the OT the standard of God's power referred to is the deliverance from Egypt, especially the crossing of the Red Sea. But here is a much greater standard of power. That very power of God that raised Christ from the dead is available to us, and we can know it in our experience.

21. Far above all principality, and power, and might, and dominion, and every name that is named, not only in this world, but also in that which is to come:

22. And hath put all *things* under his feet, and gave him *to be* the head over all *things* to the church,

23. Which is his body, the fulness of him that filleth all in all.

## CHAPTER 2

AND you *hath he quickened,* who were dead in trespasses and sins;

**And set him at his own right hand.** Probably the various references in the NT to Christ at the right hand of God go back to Psalm 110. **In the heavenly places.** In this second of the five uses of this phrase there is evidently a local sense: the Lord Jesus is literally and bodily in heaven.

**21. Far above all principality, and power.** All in the sense of "every." Different words are used in the NT for varying ranks and kinds of heavenly beings, both holy and fallen angels. For this exaltation of Christ compare Phil 2:8-11. **In this world.** This is a time word—*in this age.* **22. And hath put all things under his feet.** Again the allusion to Ps 110:1 (cf. also Ps 8:6). This indicates Christ's ultimate complete victory. **Gave him** (cf. Jn 3:16) **to be the head.** This is the first mention in the epistle of Christ as the Head of the Church, a truth that is developed quite fully (see Introduction).

**23. Which is his body.** While we speak of this as a figure, it is more than that. It denotes the complete union of the Church with the Lord Jesus, the absolute identification of believers with him (cf. I Cor 12:12). **The fulness.** That which is filled. "She [the Church] is the continued revelation of his divine life in human form" (JFB). It can be seen that true prayer includes an abundance of praise. Adoration of our wonderful God should take precedence over our own selfish and self-centered petitions. How different our lives would be if we were to pray like this for one another continually!

D. Salvation by Grace. 2:1-10. In this paragraph the apostle tells about our salvation by God's grace, showing what we were in the past, what we are now, and what we shall be in the future.

1) What We Were in the Past. 2:1-3. The opening statement of this section reminds the Ephesian believers of how desperately they once needed God's saving grace.

**1. And you hath he quickened.** There is a broken construction here. Note that the words **hath he quickened** are in italics, indicating that they are not in the original. Literally it is, *and you who were dead in trespasses and sins.* Verses 2 and 3, then, are parenthetical, and the main thought is resumed in verse 4. The contrast is between you, dead in trespasses and sins, and God, rich in mercy. The death referred to here is

2. Wherein in time past ye walked according to the course of this world, according to the prince of the power of the air, the spirit that now worketh in the children of disobedience:

3. Among whom also we all had our conversation in times past in the lusts of our flesh, fulfilling the desires of the flesh and of the mind; and were by nature the children of wrath, even as others.

4. But God, who is rich in mercy, for his great love wherewith he loved us,

5. Even when we were dead in sins, hath quickened us together with Christ, (by grace ye are saved;)

not physical, but spiritual; that is, separation from God.

**2. Wherein in time past ye walked.** Walking is used in Scripture to refer to daily conduct, manner of life (cf. the later portions of the epistle for the believer's walk). **According to the course of this world.** It is unusual to find the word *aion,* "age," and the word *kosmos,* "world," together—"the age of this world-system." Both of these words have acquired an ethical sense from their usage in the NT. **According to the prince of the power of the air.** This obviously refers to Satan. There is a paradox here in that dead people are represented as walking. Everyone apart from Christ is dead and is walking according to the prince of the power of the air. Satan is further described as **the spirit that now worketh in the children of disobedience;** that is, children characterized by disobedience. Ever since Adam's sin, men have been disobedient children.

**3. Among whom also we all had our conversation.** The word **conversation** means behavior, manner of life, or conduct. The **we** is in contrast to the **you** of 2:1. **Our flesh.** The term **flesh** in the NT is often used in an ethical sense to refer to the old nature, that which we inherited from Adam. **The desires of the flesh and of the mind.** Apparently the body and the mind are connected, both being a part of the flesh, that is, of the old nature. Many people are accustomed to think of sins of the flesh merely as various kinds of immorality, forgetting that there are also sins of the mind. **The children of wrath.** That is, those who are under wrath, whose destination is wrath, upon whom the wrath of God abides (cf. Rom 1:18; Jn 3:36; see also Heb 10:26,27).

2) **What We Are in the Present. 2:4-6.** God's Word is full of striking contrasts between man's inability and the Lord's sufficiency.

**4.** The writer now returns to the statement that was interrupted at verse 2. **But God.** This is the saving contrast. **Rich in mercy** (cf. riches of his grace and glory, 1:7,18). There is no limit to the mercy of God. **For his great love.** Literally, *because of his great love wherewith he loved us.* The Scripture repeatedly indicates that God's love toward us, not our love toward him, is the more important (cf. I Jn 4:9,10). **5. Dead in sins.** This looks back to the statement in 2:1. **Hath quickened us.**

6. And hath raised *us* up together, and made *us* sit together in heavenly *places* in Christ Jesus:

7. That in the ages to come he might show the exceeding riches of his grace, in *his* kindness toward us, through Christ Jesus.

8. For by grace are ye saved through faith; and that not of yourselves: *it is* the gift of God:

9. Not of works, lest any man should boast.

10. For we are his workmanship, created in Christ Jesus unto good works, which God hath before ordained that we should walk in them.

Made us alive. **Together with Christ.** There is a compound verb here which is joined with the word **Christ,** to show that our being made alive is in conjunction with his being made alive, that is, in his resurrection. The parenthesis, **by grace ye are saved,** is further explained and amplified in verse 8.

**6. And hath raised us up together, and made us sit together in heavenly places in Christ Jesus.** The Scripture teaches that we have been identified with the Lord Jesus Christ, not only in his death (Rom 6), but also in his resurrection and in his ascension to the right hand of the Father. The word **sit** is one of the great words in this epistle, indicating the position we have in Christ, as partakers of a finished, accomplished redemption and sharers in a victory. **In heavenly places.** The third use of this expression in the epistle. Because of our position in Christ, we are already potentially in heaven, where he is actually.

3) What We Shall Be in the Future. 2:7-10. The fact that God has made redeemed sinners an eternal object lesson of his grace is amazing but true.

**7. That in the ages to come he might show.** The Church is to be an eternal demonstration of the grace of God. **The exceeding riches of his grace** (cf. 1:7) **in his kindness** (cf. Tit 2:14; 3:4).

**8. For by grace are ye saved.** That is, *you have been saved.* God's grace is the source of our salvation. **Through faith.** Paul never says *on account of* faith, for faith is not the cause, only the channel through which our salvation comes. **And that not of yourselves.** The word **that** refers not to grace or to faith, but to the whole act of salvation—"That salvation not of yourselves." **The gift of God.** Cf. Rom 6:23. **9. Not of works.** This is the negative complement of the preceding statement. The Holy Spirit has been very careful to guard this precious doctrine of salvation by grace against all forms of heresy. **Works** in the Scripture are the product or fruit of salvation, not the cause of it. **Lest any man should boast.** There will be no boasting in heaven because there will be no one there who has anything to boast about (I Cor 4:7).

**10. We are his workmanship.** The **his** is emphatic in the original. **Created in Christ Jesus unto good works.** It is the purpose of our new creation that we should walk. The passage has now come full circle, for this walk is in direct contrast to the walk described in verse 2.

11. Wherefore remember, that ye *being* in time past Gentiles in the flesh, who are called Uncircumcision by that which is called the Circumcision in the flesh made by hands;

12. That at that time ye were without Christ, being aliens from the commonwealth of Israel, and strangers from the covenants of promise, having no hope, and without God in the world:

13. But now, in Christ Jesus, ye who sometime were far off are made nigh by the blood of Christ.

14. For he is our peace, who hath made both one, and hath broken down the middle wall of partition *between us;*

E. Oneness of Jews and Gentiles in Christ. 2:11-22. One of the great truths of this epistle is that Jew and Gentile are united in the body of Christ. That body has already been referred to in 1:23, and the union is described here, with further amplification in chapter 3.

1) What the Gentiles Were Without Christ. 2:11,12. The language in these verses paints a very dark picture of the Gentile position before Christ came.

**11. Wherefore remember.** Most of Paul's original readers were Gentiles. The apostle here reminds them of their position before they heard the Gospel. **In time past Gentiles.** In the sight of men they were still Gentiles, but not in the sight of God. God looks upon all men as either Jews, Gentiles, or the Church (I Cor 10:32). When one accepts the Lord Jesus Christ, whether he be Jew or Gentile, he is no longer such in the sight of God, but a member of the body of Christ. **Called Uncircumcision.** This was a contemptuous epithet applied by the Jews to the Gentiles. **12. Aliens from the commonwealth of Israel.** In the OT God had a covenant with the nation of Israel and governed that state directly. Those who were not Jews were foreigners or aliens. **Having no hope** and being **without God,** they could know the covenant and promises of the Lord only through Israel. The descriptive expressions become more and more serious.

2) The One Body. 2:13-18. Jew and Gentile have been united in Christ, and the latter is now as near to him as the former.

**13. But now.** This is emphatic. It indicates a contrast to their previous position. **In Christ Jesus.** Formerly they were **in the world** (v. 12). Their condition was hopeless. Now they are **in Christ,** with all the privileges of heaven. Note several contrasts in these verses—**in the world, in Christ Jesus; sometimes** (ASV, *once),* **now; far off, nigh. 14. He is our peace.** Observe the progress in this section: **He is our peace** (v. 14); **making peace** (v. 15); **preached peace** (v. 17; cf. Col 1:20). **Hath made both one.** That is, Jew and Gentile. **The middle wall of partition** may be here an allusion to the wall separating the Court of the Gentiles and the Court of the Jews in the Temple. An inscription on this wall warned Gentiles of the death penalty for entering the Court of the Jews. Now, in the sight of God, there is no distinction (see Rom 1; 2; 3).

15. Having abolished in his flesh the enmity, *even* the law of commandments *contained* in ordinances; for to make in himself of twain one new man, *so* making peace;

16. And that he might reconcile both unto God in one body by the cross, having slain the enmity thereby:

17. And came and preached peace to you which were afar off, and to them that were nigh.

18. For through him we both have access by one Spirit unto the Father.

19. Now therefore ye are no more strangers and foreigners, but fellow citizens with the saints, and of the household of God;

20. And are built upon the foundation of the apostles and prophets, Jesus Christ himself being the chief corner *stone;*

21. In whom all the building fitly framed together groweth unto a holy temple in the Lord:

**15. The enmity.** Perhaps in apposition to "the middle wall of partition." **One new man.** Not an individual but the new creation of which Christ is the Head. **16. Both.** Again a reference to Jew and Gentile. **Having slain the enmity thereby.** That is, by the cross. Verses 17, 18 further amplify this truth of the uniting of Jew and Gentile in Christ. **Far off.** The Gentiles. **Them that were nigh.** The Jews. **18.** Note the emphasis on the word both (vv. 14,16,18). Both made one, both reconciled to God, both having access.

3) The One Building. 2:19-22. The figure of the Church as a human body now shades into the figure of the Church as a great building. The human body is also described as a building in various passages (e.g., I Cor 6:19; II Cor 5:1).

**19. Now therefore.** The logical conclusion of what has been written. **No more strangers and foreigners.** The present position of these Gentiles is entirely reversed from their former condition described earlier in the chapter. **But fellow-citizens with the saints.** In Christ, Jews and Gentiles have a new citizenship (cf. Phil 3:20,21).

**20. And are built upon the foundation.** The Church, which is the body of Christ, is viewed here as a great building, a temple of God. **The apostles.** Men especially appointed by the Lord Jesus Christ in the beginning of the Church. They had no successors. **And prophets.** Not the OT prophets but the Christian prophets, the NT prophets, some of whom are mentioned and described in the book of Acts and in the epistles. **Jesus Christ himself being the chief corner stone.** Passages such as this and I Pet 2:5 help us to understand the meaning of Mt 16:18. Peter, being an apostle, was one of the foundation stones along with the other apostles and prophets, but the whole structure is built upon Christ. Compare what Paul says in I Cor 3:11.

**21. All the building.** In this context this translation seems preferable to *each several building* (ASV). "But *every building* here is quite out of place, inasmuch as the apostle is clearly speaking of one vast building, the mystical body of Christ" (Alf). This interpretation is confirmed by the language of the following verse. Israel in the OT had a temple of wood and stone. In contrast to this, the Church is a temple (cf. I Cor 3:16; I Pet 1:2-9). A temple is a dwelling place of God, as verse 22 mentions.

**22.** In whom ye also are builded together for a habitation of God through the Spirit.

### CHAPTER 3

FOR this cause I Paul, the prisoner of Jesus Christ for you Gentiles,

**2.** If ye have heard of the dispensation of the grace of God which is given me to you-ward:

**3.** How that by revelation he made known unto me the mystery; (as I wrote afore in few words;

**4.** Whereby, when ye read, ye may understand my knowledge in the mystery of Christ,)

F. The Revelation of the Mystery. 3:1-13. The Apostle Paul was chosen by God to make known and explain at least two great revelations. The first of these was the Gospel itself—good news of salvation through the death and resurrection of the Lord Jesus Christ. The second was the truth of the Church as the body of Christ. In the great Gospel epistles — Romans, I and II Corinthians, and Galatians—Paul develops at length this first revelation. In the epistles of the present chronological group, the "Prison Epistles," he deals to a very large extent with the second of these revelations—the Church as the body of Christ. Chapter 3 forms the climax of the first main division of the epistle, which gives us our position in Christ.

1) The Dispensation of the Grace of God. 3:1-6. Here is the mystery of the Church as the body of Christ.

**1. For this cause.** Referring to the whole preceding statement. **I Paul.** The writer's repetition of his name shows that he attached seriousness and importance to what he was about to write. **The prisoner of Jesus Christ.** Of course Paul was a prisoner of Christ in the sense that he had been captured by Christ, but that is not the primary thought here. He was a prisoner in Rome at the time he wrote, and it was for Christ's sake that he was a prisoner. **For you Gentiles.** Paul was specifically the apostle to the Gentiles by appointment of the Lord Jesus (cf. Rom 15:16).

**2. The dispensation of the grace of God.** The word **dispensation** means stewardship. The message of grace was a sacred trust given to Paul in order that he might make it known among the Gentiles. **Given me to you-ward.** It was not given to Paul for him to keep, but that he might give it out, particularly to the Gentiles. **3. How that by revelation he made known.** Paul always insisted upon his direct reception of the Gospel from the Lord Jesus himself, without any human intermediaries (cf. Gal 1:11,12). **The mystery.** See comment on 1:9. **As I wrote afore in few words.** Probably not a former letter but something already written in the present epistle (cf. 1:9 ff.).

**4.** This verse and the one following shed much light on the NT usage of the word **mystery.** The word means, not something mystical or magical, but a sacred secret which has not been previously revealed; when it is revealed, it is understood only by the initiated—here, those

5. Which in other ages was not made known unto the sons of men, as it is now revealed unto his holy apostles and prophets by the Spirit;

6. That the Gentiles should be fellow heirs, and of the same body, and partakers of his promise in Christ by the gospel:

7. Whereof I was made a minister, according to the gift of the grace of God given unto me by the effectual working of his power.

8. Unto me, who am less than the least of all saints, is this grace given, that I should preach among the Gentiles the unsearchable riches of Christ;

9. And to make all *men* see what *is* the fellowship of the mystery, which from the beginning of the world hath been hid in God, who created all things by Jesus Christ:

10. To the intent that now unto the principalities and powers in heavenly *places* might be known by the church the manifold wisdom of God,

11. According to the eternal purpose which he purposed in Christ Jesus our Lord:

12. In whom we have boldness and access with confidence by the faith of him.

who are saved. **5. Unto his holy apostles and prophets by the Spirit.** Just as holy men of God were inspired by the Holy Spirit in OT times (II Pet 1:20,21), so were the writers of the NT. **6. The Gentiles.** The mystery was not that the Gentiles should be saved—there is much in the OT concerning the salvation of the Gentiles, particularly in Isaiah—but that they should be joined with Jews in one body.

2) The Fellowship of the Mystery. 3:7-13.

**7. A minister.** Paul was made a servant by God's gift. This is the word transliterated in English as *deacon*—one who serves or waits on tables. Paul never considered his office something high, removing him from other men. He always spoke of himself humbly.

**8. Who am less than the least of all saints.** In several other places Paul, remembering what he had been before he was saved and what he had done to the church, speaks of himself in this self-abnegating way (cf. I Cor 15:9,10; I Tim 1:15). The expression rendered **less than the least** is an unusual form—a comparative of the superlative. The AV expresses it very well. **Is this grace given.** God's grace was given to Paul not in the main for his enjoyment, but that he might pass it on to others. **That I should preach among the Gentiles.** The Lord Jesus gave this word to Ananias concerning Paul (Acts 9:15). **The unsearchable riches.** Here again the word **riches** comes into prominence with an adjective denoting its limitless character. **9. And to make all men see.** To throw light on what is the fellowship of the mystery. Some manuscripts have *stewardship* rather than *fellowship*. **Has been hid from ages in God.** Further confirmation of the definition of "mystery" previously given. **Who created all things.** All that exists—not merely the physical creation or the spiritual creation alone.

**10. In heavenly places.** The fourth occurrence of the phrase in the epistle. Further indication that heavenly beings are observing the Church and seeing in the Church the unfolding of God's wisdom. Both good and evil angels are evidently amazed at the working of God as seen in redeemed men and women. **11. The eternal purpose.** Cf. Rom 8:29; Eph 1:11. **12. In whom.** That is, in Christ. **Access with confidence.** Apart from Christ we could not draw near. This has been shown in chapter 2. **The faith of him.** Objective genitive; mean-

13. Wherefore I desire that ye faint not at my tribulations for you, which is your glory.

14. For this cause I bow my knees unto the Father of our Lord Jesus Christ,

15. Of whom the whole family in heaven and earth is named,

16. That he would grant you, according to the riches of his glory, to be strengthened with might by his Spirit in the inner man;

17. That Christ may dwell in your hearts by faith; that ye, being rooted and grounded in love,

ing, *faith in Him*. Christ is the object of our faith.

13. **My tribulations for you.** Compare what Paul says in Acts 20:18-35 about his work in Ephesus; also in II Cor 1:8-11.

G. Paul's Second Prayer. 3:14-21. This is the second prayer of Paul for the Ephesians, and like the former one in Eph 1, it is concerned mainly with their spiritual welfare. Whereas the first prayer centers in knowledge, this prayer has its focal point in love.

14. **For this cause.** This takes up the thought begun in 3:1. Evidently the main thought in this chapter is the prayer, and 3:2-13 is explanatory. **I bow my knees.** While Scripture does not indicate that any one bodily posture is necessary in prayer, yet the bowing of the knee is indicative of true reverence. **The Father of our Lord Jesus Christ.** Some manuscripts omit the words **of our Lord Jesus Christ.** There is a play on words in the word **Father** in 3:14 and the word translated **family** (which is *fatherhood*) in 3:15.

15. **Of whom the whole family.** There are two possible explanations of this. Some would translate *every family*, with the idea that the concept of family or fatherhood comes from God. This is true, of course, although less common. Grammatically the other explanation seems to fit in better with the context of Scripture generally; that is, **the whole family.** The expression **in heaven and earth** seems to favor this. That is, the whole family of the redeemed—those who have gone before and those who are still alive here on earth—are under the one Father, who is the Father of our Lord Jesus Christ.

16. **According to the riches.** Again the abundant reference to what we have from God (cf. 1:7; 2:4; Phil 4:19). **Strengthened with might.** Parallel to the earlier prayer, which said much about God's power. **By his spirit.** The Spirit is the agent of the Godhead in applying our redemption to us. **In the inner man.** That is, our immaterial part, true personality.

17. **That Christ may dwell.** Not merely to live, but to be at home—to abide. This is what every Christian needs always, not praying that Christ may come in for the first time, for he already indwells every believer, but that he may be at home there in the sense that the believer has given over his whole life to him. **Being rooted and grounded in love.** A mixed metaphor referring to that which is planted and that which is built (cf.

18. May be able to comprehend with all saints what *is* the breadth, and length, and depth, and height;

19. And to know the love of Christ, which passeth knowledge, that ye might be filled with all the fulness of God.

20. Now unto him that is able to do exceeding abundantly above all that we ask or think, according to the power that worketh in us,

21. Unto him *be* glory in the church by Christ Jesus throughout all ages, world without end. Amen.

Col 2:2, which is somewhat parallel to this).

**18. May be able to comprehend with all saints.** A knowledge that every believer ought to have. **What is the breadth, and length, and depth, and height.** This sort of knowledge would be continually growing, for we could never measure the dimensions. **19. To know the love of Christ which passeth knowledge.** Some things we cannot know fully; often we have experiences that we cannot understand or explain. However, the same root is used here in the infinitive and in the noun, and the idea seems to be to know that which is essentially unknowable—yet to know it enough so that we can rejoice in it. **Filled with all the fulness of God.** God is infinite and we are finite. This is of course paradoxical, but it is an attempt to convey in language that will mean something to us, the superabundance of grace available to us from our heavenly Father through our Lord Jesus Christ.

**20.** This fullness is further described in the benediction that brings the first great division of the epistle to a close. **Now unto him.** Of course the verb and predicate are in the next verse. **Able.** There is no limit to what God can do. **Exceeding abundantly above.** Superlatives are piled one upon the other here to impress us with this truth. **All that we ask or think.** How limited we often are in our asking, thinking that God will not do some particular thing for us. He is able to do far more than we can ask; indeed, more than we could ever imagine. And he does it **according to the power that worketh in us.** That is, we have been strengthened by his Spirit. Consequently, this power is being energized in us. **21. Unto him be glory** may be taken as a statement—*unto him is the glory;* or as an imperative sentence—*unto him be the glory.* **In the church.** God's glory is being manifested throughout all eternity in the body which he has redeemed. **Throughout all ages, world without end.** Literally, *to all the courses of the age of the ages.* A very strong expression for eternity. With this prayer and benediction Paul concludes that portion of the epistle that tells us about what God has done for us and about our position in Christ.

**II. The Believer's Conduct in the World. 4:1—6:24.**

A. The Worthy Walk. 4:1-16. God always joins doctrine and practice, teach-

## CHAPTER 4

I THEREFORE, the prisoner of the Lord, beseech you that ye walk worthy of the vocation wherewith ye are called,

2. With all lowliness and meekness, with long-suffering, forbearing one another in love;

3. Endeavoring to keep the unity of the Spirit in the bond of peace.

4. *There is* one body, and one Spirit, even as ye are called in one hope of your calling;

ing and the practical results of the teaching. In Eph 1–3 he has told us of the riches of his grace and the riches of his glory through Jesus Christ. Now he exhorts us toward a worthy manner of life in this world.

1) The Unity of the Spirit. 4:1-6. God has brought about a wonderful unity which it is the responsibility of believers to maintain in experience.

**1. I therefore.** As is generally the case in Paul's epistles, this exhortation is made on the basis of the teaching that has preceded (cf. Rom 12:1). **The prisoner of the Lord.** That is, the prisoner for the Lord's sake (cf. Eph 3:1). **Beseech.** This word, which stands first in the original, for emphasis, is an entreaty, an encouragement. God, of course, has the right to command and to demand, but instead he entreats, he beseeches, because he wants willing surrender, willing service. **That ye walk worthy.** The word walk is used often in the Scripture for our conduct, our behavior, our manner of life (cf. Introduction). **Worthy.** Not that we ever could deserve what God has done, but that we should walk in a manner befitting what he has done for us. We do not become Christians by living the Christian life; rather, we are exhorted to live the Christian life because we are Christians, that our lives may measure up to our position in Christ (cf. Phil 1:27). **Vocation.** Our calling, which is described as a heavenly calling and a holy calling (cf. Heb 3:1; II Tim 1:9).

**2. Lowliness and meekness.** These virtues can be produced only by the indwelling Spirit of God. They are totally foreign to the flesh and unfortunately rare in the lives of many Christians. **Lowliness** carries the idea of humility; **meekness** connotes gentleness (see Trench). **Longsuffering** is preserving an even temperament in the face of adversity and persecution. **3. Endeavoring to keep.** God realized that this is not always possible because one person alone cannot keep the unity. Observe that Paul does not request the Christians to make the unity, for only God could make the bond; but it is the responsibility of believers to try to keep it. This is **the unity of the Spirit.** That is, the unity which has been forged by the Holy Spirit himself, and its bond or connection is a peaceable one.

**4. One body.** The organism composed of the Lord Jesus Christ as the Head and all true believers in him. It is the

5. One Lord, one faith, one baptism,

6. One God and Father of all, who *is* above all, and through all, and in you all.

7. But unto every one of us is given grace according to the measure of the gift of Christ.

8. Wherefore he saith, When he ascended up on high, he led captivity captive, and gave gifts unto men.

9. (Now that he ascended, what is it but that he also descended first into the lower parts of the earth?

10. He that descended is the same also that ascended up far above all heavens, that he might fill all things.)

11. And he gave some, apostles; and some, prophets; and some, evangelists; and some, pastors and teachers;

new creation, the body mentioned earlier in the epistle (1:23). **One Spirit.** The Holy Spirit himself is the life infusing every part of the body. **5. One Lord, one faith, one baptism.** Note the emphasis all the way through on the unity. The one baptism is undoubtedly the baptism of the Holy Spirit—that ministry of the Spirit by which we have been put into the body of Christ (I Cor 12:13).

6. The three Persons of the Godhead are mentioned in these verses in the reverse order to that usually given: **one Spirit** (v. 4); **one Lord** (v. 5), that is, the Lord Jesus; **one God and Father** (v. 6). **Who is above all,** etc. Here we have a threefold relationship of the one God and Father to all who are his. He is **above all.** This expresses his sovereignty, his transcendence. He is **through all,** "expressing the pervading, animating, controlling presence of that one God and Father" (Salmond). **In you all.** This is his constant indwelling in his people—all the Persons of the triune God are said in various passages of Scripture to indwell the believer.

2) The Gift of Christ. 4:7-12. The ascended Lord has given gifts to his Church for its upbuilding.

**7. To every one of us.** This is limited to believers in him. **Is given grace.** Not saving grace, but grace as a gift to believers—God's favor, unmerited and unrecompensed. **According to the measure.** A measure which is immeasurable.

**8. Wherefore he saith.** The quotation is from Ps 68:18. The connection is not altogether clear. But in his ascension the Lord Jesus is said to have **led captivity captive;** that is, he captured that which had captured us, and annulled its power. **And gave gifts.** In some passages of Scripture, gifts are mentioned which the Lord gave to individuals; e.g., I Cor 12. Here the gifts are those people of various capacities whom he has given to the church. **9.** The apostle, commenting on the quotation, mentions that the Lord Jesus had to descend first before he could ascend. Some take this to be a reference to the death of Christ and his so-called descent into Hades. It seems more likely, however, that it is simply referring to his coming down from heaven. He descended into **the lower parts** which consist **of the earth**—genitive of apposition (cf. Jn 3:13). **10. Far above all heavens.** Cf. Heb 4:14.

**11. And he gave some.** The various types mentioned are Christ's gifts to the

12. For the perfecting of the saints, for the work of the ministry, for the edifying of the body of Christ:

13. Till we all come in the unity of the faith, and of the knowledge of the Son of God, unto a perfect man, unto the measure of the stature of the fulness of Christ:

14. That we *henceforth* be no more children, tossed to and fro, and carried about with every wind of doctrine, by the sleight of men, *and* cunning craftiness, whereby they lie in wait to deceive;

church. **Apostles.** This was a special office at the beginning of the church. The apostles had no successors. They had a unique work from the Lord Jesus (cf. 2:20). **Prophets.** A prophet was a spokesman for God. As used ordinarily in the Scripture, this term refers to someone who has been given a direct revelation, which he is to pass on to men (cf. 2:20). In the strictest sense of the term this office also was temporary in the church, for there were no more prophets in the technical sense after the completion of the NT. **Evangelists.** Those who proclaim glad tidings—those who preach the Gospel. **Pastors and teachers.** These two terms go together. The first word means *shepherds.* Those who are the shepherds of the flock are also to be teachers. The true pastor should carry on an expository preaching ministry of the Word.

**12. For the perfecting of the saints, for the work of the ministry.** The two uses of **for** represent two different prepositions in the original. These gifts were given by God to the Church *for the perfecting of the saints unto the work of the ministry.* That is, it is the business of all the saints—not of a few leaders only—to carry on the work of the ministry. The leaders are for the purpose of perfecting or equipping believers to carry on this work. Most local churches today do not follow this NT idea. It is common practice to let the pastor do the ministering. Sometimes the pastor temporarily may find it easier to do the work himself than to train others to do it. But his job is to train up workers, and in the long run his ministry will be more effective if he does so.

3) The Unity of Faith and Knowledge. 4:13-16. The unity of believers in Christ tends toward a unity in faith and knowledge.

**13. The unity of the faith.** The faith itself is one body of truth. As we hold to this, we in turn are united to one another. **Unto a perfect man.** A reference not to the individual believer but to the composite man; that is, the body of which Christ is the Head.

**14. That we henceforth be no more children.** Literally, *babies.* **Tossed to and fro.** Driven by the wind, which is here used, of course, figuratively — *wind of teaching.* **By the sleight of men.** The word translated **sleight** originally meant dice-playing. Then it came to mean trickery of any kind, because of the various tricks that were used to cheat in

15. But speaking the truth in love, may grow up into him in all things, which is the head, *even* Christ:

16. From whom the whole body fitly joined together and compacted by that which every joint supplieth, according to the effectual working in the measure of every part, maketh increase of the body unto the edifying of itself in love.

17. This I say therefore, and testify in the Lord, that ye henceforth walk not as other Gentiles walk, in the vanity of their mind,

18. Having the understanding darkened, being alienated from the life of God through the ignorance that is in them, because of the blindness of their heart:

19. Who being past feeling have given themselves over unto lasciviousness, to work all uncleanness with greediness.

the game of dice. The only way to be able to detect error is to know the truth; hence, we must come to the knowledge of the Son of God, to Christian maturity. A person does not have to study every counterfeit bill in order to know that some particular bill is counterfeit. He needs only to know the genuine article.

**15. But speaking the truth in love.** It is possible to speak the truth without speaking it in love. Literally, *holding the truth.* We may grow up into him. God wants us to be mature or full-grown, to be adults. We have an absolutely perfect Head, Christ himself.

**16.** Note the perfection of the body. How intricately the human body is fitted together! It is therefore an apt illustration of the body of Christ. Someone has said that not everyone can be one of the larger members, but the joints are very important too. All parts work together (cf. I Cor 12; Rom 12).

B. The Different Walk. 4:17-32. The Scriptures, in both the Old and New Testaments, emphasize that God's people are to be different from the people of the world.

1) Description of the Gentiles' Walk. 4:17-19. The Gentiles are "as sheep going astray" (I Pet 2:25; cf. Isa 53:6). Believers have a great and good Shepherd to follow.

**17. This I say therefore.** The Christian's walk is described in various ways in the passage. Here we have a negative description. **Testify.** Protest, exhort, or beseech. **Henceforth.** Their lives are to be different now. **Walk not as other Gentiles walk.** This walk has been described in 2:2. Most of the Ephesians were Gentiles in background. Some manuscripts do not have any word for **other.** Hence, *Walk not as the Gentiles walk.* In the sight of God, believers in the Lord Jesus Christ are no longer either Jews or Gentiles (cf. I Cor 10:32). **In the vanity of their mind.** The word for **vanity** seems to mean perverseness or depravity in this connection. **18. Understanding darkened.** Cf. II Cor 4:4. **Alienated from the life of God.** Cf. 2:12. **Blindness of their heart.** Literally, *hardness* or *dull perception* (cf. Mk 3:5).

**19. Past feeling.** Cf. I Tim 4:2. **Uncleanness.** Impurity in general. Not merely indulging in impurity but indulging in it with a greedy desire to have more. A graphic statement of the insatiable nature of sinful desire.

20. But ye have not so learned Christ;

21. If so be that ye have heard him, and have been taught by him, as the truth is in Jesus:

22. That ye put off concerning the former conversation the old man, which is corrupt according to the deceitful lusts;

23. And be renewed in the spirit of your mind;

24. And that ye put on the new man, which after God is created in righteousness and true holiness.

25. Wherefore putting away lying, speak every man truth with his neighbor: for we are members one of another.

26. Be ye angry, and sin not: let not the sun go down upon your wrath:

27. Neither give place to the devil.

28. Let him that stole steal no more: but rather let him labor, working with *his* hands the thing which is good, that he may have to give to him that needeth.

2) Putting Off the Old and Putting On the New. 4:20-24. The Christian life is compared to putting off one garment and putting on another. This is not a reference to our position in Christ, but to our experience. It is possible to be a new man in Christ Jesus and yet be living like an "old man"; that is, having on the garment of the "old man."

**20. But ye.** A contrast with the preceding. **Have not so learned Christ.** This is the grandest subject that one could study. **21. If so be that ye have heard him, and have been taught by him, as the truth is in Jesus.** That which they had learned after hearing of the Lord Jesus Christ should have caused them to improve their lives, for Christians ought to act like Christians, not like pagan non-Christians. **22. According to the former conversation.** For **conversation** see note on 2:3. **The old man.** That is, the Adamic nature, that which we are in ourselves. **Corrupt according to the deceitful lusts.** Scripture teaches that in the old nature is no good thing (cf. Rom 7:18). **23. And be renewed.** Cf. Rom 12:2. **24. Put on the new man.** Correlative of the preceding, the product of the new birth. For the conflict between the old and the new, compare Rom 7 and Gal 5:16,17. **After God.** According to God. God is the Creator of the new man.

3) Practical Application. 4:25-32. God in his Word never teaches the truth abstractly, but always makes concrete application.

**25. Wherefore.** On the basis of what precedes; that is, our standing in Christ. **Putting away lying.** Note the negative and the positive. It is not enough simply to abstain from lying; one must also tell the truth (cf. Zech 8:16). **We are members.** Members not only of Christ but of each other (Rom 12:5). **26. Be ye angry, and sin not.** There is such a thing as righteous anger, although the term is much abused. The apostle is saying that if you are angry, be sure it is the kind of anger that is not sinful. **Let not the sun go down.** "Even a righteous wrath by overindulgence may pass all too easily into sin" (Salmond). **27. Neither give place to the devil.** Cf. II Cor 2:10, 11; Eph 6:10 ff.

**28. Rather let him labour.** A Christian is not only to refrain from stealing but is to provide for himself and his family through his own work. The Scripture everywhere commends honest toil (cf. I Thess 4:11,12). In fact, the apostle lays

29. Let no corrupt communication proceed out of your mouth, but that which is good to the use of edifying, that it may minister grace unto the hearers.

30. And grieve not the Holy Spirit of God, whereby ye are sealed unto the day of redemption.

31. Let all bitterness, and wrath, and anger, and clamor, and evil speaking, be put away from you, with all malice:

32. And be ye kind one to another, tenderhearted, forgiving one another, even as God for Christ's sake hath forgiven you.

## CHAPTER 5

BE ye therefore followers of God, as dear children;

down the principle that he who will not work should not eat (II Thess 3:10). **To give to him that needeth.** Here is the basis for genuine Christian charity.

**29. No corrupt communication.** The word for **corrupt** originally meant *rotten* or *putrid.* Again we see the positive emphasized—but that which is good.

**30. And grieve not the holy Spirit of God.** That which grieves the Holy Spirit is sin. The remedy is confession (cf. I Jn 1:9). Although the Holy Spirit may be grieved, yet he will never leave the believer. He is our seal. We have been sealed by him **unto the day of redemption** (cf. Eph 1:13). He is the guarantee that our redemption will be completed. **31.** Some of the sins that grieve the Holy Spirit are now particularized. While some Christians would classify as sins only those grosser iniquities which even the world recognizes as wrong, God mentions matters of the mind and spirit as well as those of the body.

**32.** The theme of putting on as well as putting off is prominent throughout the section. Living the Christian life is not just observing a list of prohibitions; it is cultivating positive virtues. **And be ye kind.** The verb here means *keep on proving yourselves to be kind* to one another. **Tenderhearted.** The English translation is very good. The word in the original has been much misunderstood, as is shown by its frequent translation elsewhere as *bowels.* "Heart" is correct. In the classical Greek this word referred to the organs of the upper body cavity; specifically the heart, lungs, and liver, as distinguished from the organs of the lower cavity (see the lexicons). **Forgiving one another.** The only way we can be enabled to forgive is through the forgiveness which we ourselves already have received for Christ's sake. As God's love produces our love, so our realization of God's forgiveness produces our forgiveness of others (cf. I Jn 4:19).

C. The Loving Walk. 5:1-14. Christian living involves not only walking worthy of our calling and walking in a manner different from that of the Gentiles, but also walking in love.

1) Walking in Love. 5:1-7. Because believers are God's "dear children" and have experienced his love, they have a standard to uphold, a path to follow. **1. Be ye therefore.** Literally, *become therefore,* or *prove yourselves to be therefore.* **Followers.** Literally, *imitators.* **As dear children.** Just as little children learn

2. And walk in love, as Christ also hath loved us, and hath given himself for us an offering and a sacrifice to God for a sweet-smelling savor.

3. But fornication, and all uncleanness, or covetousness, let it not be once named among you, as becometh saints;

4. Neither filthiness, nor foolish talking, nor jesting, which are not convenient: but rather giving of thanks.

5. For this ye know, that no whoremonger, nor unclean person, nor covetous man, who is an idolater, hath any inheritance in the kingdom of Christ and of God.

6. Let no man deceive you with vain words: for because of these things cometh the wrath of God upon the children of disobedience.

7. Be not ye therefore partakers with them.

8. For ye were sometime darkness, but now *are ye* light in the Lord: walk as children of light;

9. (For the fruit of the Spirit *is* in all goodness and righteousness and truth;)

to do things by imitating their parents, so we are to be imitators of God. **2. And walk in love.** This is descriptive of our whole manner of life. **As Christ also hath loved us and gave himself for us.** That is, he delivered himself on our behalf (cf. Gal 2:20). **An offering and a sacrifice to God.** Cf. Ps. 40:7, which is quoted in Heb 10:7. **For a sweetsmelling savour.** Reminiscent of the sweet savor offerings of the book of Leviticus, which prefigured Christ's voluntary sacrifice of himself to God.

**3. But fornication.** General term for sexual immorality. **Let it not be once named among you.** The connection with what precedes is clear. Love will not gossip about the sins of others (cf. I Cor 13:4-8). There is danger of one's experiencing a morbid satisfaction in discussing other people's sins. **As becometh saints.** We are to know what is fitting and proper in our high position. **4. Nor foolish talking, nor jesting.** These words do not preclude spontaneous Christian gaiety and a sense of humor, but they indicate that Christians are not to indulge in empty frivolity. In the Greek they connote the sort of jesting that is vulgar and unclean. The antidote for the Christian is thanksgiving.

**5. For this ye know.** Cf. I Cor 6:9,10. **Nor covetous man.** It is interesting to see that this type of sinner is included in the same classification with immoral and unclean persons. God's way of distinguishing between sins is not like ours. In his sight all sins are hateful. We must learn to look on sins as he does. **6. With vain words.** That is, empty words, meaningless words. **The children of disobedience.** Literally, *the sons of disobedience* (cf. 2:2, where the same expression is used). **7. Be not ye therefore partakers.** The use of the present imperative with this form of the negative *(mē)* indicates the prohibition of something already in progress; literally, *stop becoming fellow partakers with them.*

2) Walking in Light. 5:8-14. Love and holiness (often symbolized by light in Scripture) must not be separated, the apostle explains. The loving walk is also the holy walk.

**8. Ye were sometimes darkness.** A beautiful expression of the contrast between our past and our present (cf. the same sort of contrast in I Cor 6:9-11; I Thess 5:5). **Walk as children of light.** God always places the fact of our position before us as the basis for our behavior. **9. The fruit of the Spirit.** Some

10. Proving what is acceptable unto the Lord.

11. And have no fellowship with the unfruitful works of darkness, but rather reprove *them.*

12. For it is a shame even to speak of those things which are done of them in secret.

13. But all things that are reproved are made manifest by the light: for whatsoever doth make manifest is light.

14. Wherefore he saith, Awake thou that sleepest, and arise from the dead, and Christ shall give thee light.

15. See then that ye walk circumspectly, not as fools, but as wise,

16. Redeeming the time, because the days are evil.

17. Wherefore be ye not unwise, but understanding what the will of the Lord *is.*

18. And be not drunk with wine, wherein is excess; but be filled with the Spirit;

manuscripts read *the fruit of light* (cf. Gal 5:22,23). **10. Proving what is acceptable.** That is, putting it to the test. Acceptability to the Lord is the criterion (cf. II Cor 5:9, where the same expression is used).

**11. Do not have fellowship.** Again, literally, *stop having fellowship.* **But rather rebuke.** If a Christian is in fellowship with his Lord, his very life will be a reproof to the world. **12. For it is a shame** (cf v. 3 above). Dr. A. C. Gaebelein called public discussion of secret sins the "communion of sinners," as contrasted with the Scriptural communion of saints. **13. Are made manifest by the light.** Cf. Jn 3:19-21; I Jn 1:5-7. **14. Wherefore he saith.** The quotation that follows is difficult to identify. It is possibly a combination of several different references (cf. Isa 26:19; 60:1).

D. The Wise Walk. 5:15—6:9. The apostle next describes how the life of a believer is to be circumspect. He enjoins the Ephesians to be filled with the Holy Spirit and shows them the result of that filling in the practical relations of life.

1) Being Circumspect. 5:15-17. A careful walk depends upon wisdom, which can come only from knowing the Lord's will.

**15. See then.** That is, look to it in view of what has just been said. **That ye walk circumspectly.** Diligently, carefully. **16. Redeeming the time.** Buying up the opportunity. **Because the days are evil.** Cf. Gal 1:4. **17. Be ye not unwise** (AV). Again the command to stop that which is already in progress—*stop becoming foolish.* **But.** Strong adversative in Greek (*alla*).

2) Being Filled with the Holy Spirit. 5:18—6:9. No believer in Christ is ever commanded to be indwelt by the Spirit. His indwelling is certain and permanent (Jn 14:16,17). Nor is a believer commanded to be baptized with the Spirit. This has already been done (I Cor 12:13). But believers are commanded to be filled with the Spirit. Hence there is individual responsibility; there are conditions to be met if we are to experience the Spirit's control in our lives.

**18. And be not drunk with wine.** There are repeated warnings in the Scripture against drunkenness (cf. Prov 23:31). **But be filled with the Spirit.** As in most contrasts, there is some point of comparison. A person intoxicated with wine acts

19. Speaking to yourselves in psalms and hymns and spiritual songs, singing and making melody in your heart to the Lord;

20. Giving thanks always for all things unto God and the Father in the name of our Lord Jesus Christ;

21. Submitting yourselves one to another in the fear of God.

22. Wives, submit yourselves unto your own husbands, as unto the Lord.

in an unnatural manner that is evil; a person filled with the Holy Spirit acts in an unnatural manner that is good. Compare what was said to the apostles on the day of Pentecost (Acts 2:13). **Be filled with the Spirit.** Keep on being filled; be continuously filled with the Spirit. A believer can never obtain more of the Holy Spirit, for he indwells the Christian's life in all his fullness. But the Holy Spirit can get more of the believer; that is, he can exercise complete control of the life that is yielded to him.

a) Rejoicing and Thanksgiving. 5:19, 20. One of the evidences of the filling of the Holy Spirit is that exuberance of life that shows itself in rejoicing and in continual thankfulness to God.

19. **Speaking to yourselves.** The result of the Spirit's filling is praise and thanksgiving as well as submission in the ordinary relationships of life (vv. 19-21). **Psalms.** This word usually indicates songs set to instrumental accompaniment, as does also the participle translated **making melody** (*psallontes*). **In your heart to the Lord.** Some people are not able to make much melody outwardly. But even they, if they are filled with the Spirit, will be making music in their hearts. **20. Giving thanks always.** No limit on the time (cf. I Thess 5:18). **For all things.** No limit on the extent. Some would restrict this to the blessings mentioned in the epistle, but it seems better to take it in its widest sense (cf. Rom 8:28).

b) Submission in Practical Relationships. 5:21—6:9. Another result of the Spirit's filling, besides praise and thanksgiving, is submission. This is a statement of what we should do in our earthly relationships. "In contrast with pagan self-seeking and self-assertion" (Salmond; cf. I Pet 5:5).

(1) Wives and Husbands. 5:21-33. The first human relationship mentioned, also the most intimate one, in which the filling of the Holy Spirit is to be manifested, is the marriage relationship.

21. **One another.** Note the mutuality of this submission. **In the fear of Christ.** The NT as well as the OT speaks of fear of God—that is, a reverence toward him that makes one afraid of displeasing him (cf. II Cor 5:11).

22. The apostle now shows the outworking of this mutual submission in the three most common relationships of life —marriage, family, and employment.

23. For the husband is the head of the wife, even as Christ is the head of the church: and he is the saviour of the body.

24. Therefore as the church is subject unto Christ, so *let* the wives *be* to their own husbands in every thing.

25. Husbands, love your wives, even as Christ also loved the church, and gave himself for it;

26. That he might sanctify and cleanse it with the washing of water by the word,

27. That he might present it to himself a glorious church, not having spot, or wrinkle, or any such thing; but that it should be holy and without blemish.

28. So ought men to love their wives as their own bodies. He that loveth his wife loveth himself.

29. For no man ever yet hated his own flesh; but nourisheth and cherisheth it, even as the Lord the church:

30. For we are members of his body, of his flesh, and of his bones.

**Wives, submit yourselves unto your own husbands.** This passage is an expression of God's ideal for marriage. The marriage relationship was designed by him to be symbolic of the spiritual relationship between Christ and the Church. The apostle points this out in verse 32. **23. For the husband is the head.** The reason for the subjection of the wife is found in this relationship which God has ordained. **24. But as the church is subject to Christ.** Even though there is a difference between the position of the husband toward the wife and that of Christ toward the Church, yet this does not affect the relation of headship which the husband holds to the wife. **25. Husbands, love your wives.** The obligations are not merely one-sided. The husband's responsibility is just as binding as that of the wife. This is not a reference to normal marital love, which would not need to be commanded, but to that volitional love which stems from God and resembles his own love. In contrast to normal sexual desire, which by its nature is self-seeking, this love is unselfish. **As also Christ loved the church.** While human husbands can never attain the degree of love Christ manifested, yet they are exhorted to have the same kind of love, which is demonstrated in the clause that follows, **and gave himself for it.**

**26. That he might sanctify and cleanse it.** This was his purpose in giving himself to die for the Church. **With the washing of water by the word.** Probably water and word are used synonymously. This clearly cannot be a reference to baptism or baptismal regeneration. Just as water washes the body, so the Word of God washes the heart (cf. Ezk 36:27). **27. That he might present it.** The ultimate object for which Christ gave himself. The word **sanctify** shows the immediate object (cf. II Cor 11:2). **A glorious church.** The adjective is predicative rather than attributive; that is, *that he might present the church as glorious.* **Not having spot.** Further explanation of the word **glorious** as descriptive of the "bride" of Christ.

**28. So ought husbands to love their wives as their own bodies.** That is, as if they were their own bodies. **Love** which is natural, not merely from a sense of duty. God said, "They [two] shall be one flesh" (Gen 2:24). **29. For no man.** The reason for the preceding statement.

**30. For we are members of his body.** The thought shifts back and forth between the marriage relationship and the

31. For this cause shall a man leave his father and mother, and shall be joined unto his wife, and they two shall be one flesh.

32. This is a great mystery: but I speak concerning Christ and the church.

33. Nevertheless, let every one of you in particular so love his wife even as himself; and the wife *see* that she reverence *her* husband.

## CHAPTER 6

CHILDREN, obey your parents in the Lord: for this is right.

2. Honor thy father and mother; which is the first commandment with promise;

3. That it may be well with thee, and thou mayest live long on the earth.

4. And, ye fathers, provoke not your children to wrath: but bring them up in the nurture and admonition of the Lord.

relationship between Christ and the Church. **31. For this cause.** A free quotation from Gen 2:24. It sets forth the Scripture basis of marriage as a natural result of woman's creation. The marriage bond is stronger than that between parent and child, establishing such close intimacy as to be called in the Scripture, *oneness*—unity rather than union. **32. This is a great mystery.** That is, although the explanation of this meaning of the marriage relationship had been intimated in the OT (cf. the Song of Solomon), it was not clearly revealed until the NT was given. Paul directs our thoughts from the marriage unity itself to that which it symbolizes. **33.** Summary of the mutual submissiveness God expects in this relationship as a normal result of the filling of the Holy Spirit.

(2) Children and Parents. 6:1-4. The apostle now goes on to another specific relationship, that of parents and children, with the obligations entailed upon both sides.
**1. Children, obey your parents in the Lord.** *Obedience* is a stronger term than *submission*, which was given as the duty of the wife. **In the Lord.** "The sphere in which it is to move, a Christian obedience fulfilled in communion with Christ" (Salmond). **For this is right.** This is shown to be an eternal principle of God.
**2. Honor thy father and mother.** Paul shows that the Law had the same injunction. All the Ten Commandments except the fourth are restated and applied under grace. **The first commandment with promise.** That is, a promise is given for obedience. **3. That it may be well with thee.** This must be taken as a continuation of the quotation from the Law and not as a direct application to the believer in the present dispensation. Although the principle is always true, the soon coming of the Lord, rather than long life, is the Christian's blessed hope.
**4. And, ye fathers.** As before, there is a second side to the responsibility. It is stated at first negatively, and then affirmatively. **But bring them up.** Cf. Deut 6:7. A parallel passage is Col 3:20,21.

(3) Servants and Masters. 6:5-9. A third set of relationships is now discussed —that of masters and servants. Slavery existed as an institution in NT days. It was not the function of the Gospel to overthrow slavery, although a by-product of Christianity has been the gradual abolition of that institution.

5. Servants, be obedient to them that are *your* masters according to the flesh, with fear and trembling, in singleness of your heart, as unto Christ;

6. Not with eyeservice, as menpleasers; but as the servants of Christ, doing the will of God from the heart;

7. With good will doing service, as to the Lord, and not to men:

8. Knowing that whatsoever good thing any man doeth, the same shall he receive of the Lord, whether *he be* bond or free.

9. And, ye masters, do the same things unto them, forbearing threatening: knowing that your Master also is in heaven; neither is there respect of persons with him.

10. Finally, my brethren, be strong in the Lord, and in the power of his might.

**5. Servants.** Literally, *slaves.* However, the principles apply to any kind of employees and employers. **In singleness of your heart.** In reality and sincerity— not in hypocrisy. **As unto Christ.** Cf. I Pet 2:18; Col 3:22-25. **6. Not with eye-service, as men-pleasers.** An amplification of the foregoing. The word **men-pleasers** occurs in the Septuagint, but is found in the NT only here and in Col 3:22. **Doing the will of God from the heart.** Literally, *from the soul*—that is, with one's whole being. **7. With good will doing service.** A Christian who is a bond servant is to recognize that his primary responsibility is to the Lord Jesus Christ. When he does the work he is expected to do and does it well, he is pleasing the Lord. **8. Knowing that.** This is a causal connective—*because we know* there is a reward for faithfulness in serving Christ. **Whether he be bond or free.** A person's standing in this world has nothing to do with his faithfulness and with the reward for faithfulness.

**9. And, ye masters.** Here the duties of employers are emphasized. **Do the same things to them.** The positive side, showing the mutuality of the obligation. **Forbearing threatening.** What the masters are not to do. **Knowing.** That is, *because you know.* **That your master.** These masters have a Master of their own. This is the Lord *(Kurios).* There is no respect of persons with him (cf. Col 4:1). All of these practical relationships flow from the filling of the Holy Spirit, enjoined in Eph 5:18.

E. The Christian Walk as a Warfare. 6:10-20. Throughout this whole division of the epistle a great deal has been said about practical Christian living. In this paragraph the walk of a Christian is described as a warfare, a deadly conflict in which he is engaged against the power of Satan and his hosts.

1) Being Strong in the Lord—the Whole Armor of God. 6:10-17. Because this walk is a warfare, as it is here described, a Christian must be prepared and equipped. This passage on the whole armor of God shows what wonderful provision God has made for his warriors.

**10. Finally.** Here are the general concluding exhortations of the epistle. **My brethren.** Paul reminds his readers of their relationship in the Lord. **Be strong in the Lord.** The Lord Jesus had said, "Without me, ye can do nothing" (Jn 15:5; cf. also Phil 4:13). **And in the**

11. Put on the whole armor of God, that ye may be able to stand against the wiles of the devil.

12. For we wrestle not against flesh and blood, but against principalities, against powers, against the rulers of the darkness of this world, against spiritual wickedness in high *places*.

13. Wherefore take unto you the whole armor of God, that ye may be able to withstand in the evil day, and having done all, to stand.

14. Stand therefore, having your loins girt about with truth, and having on the breastplate of righteousness;

15. And your feet shod with the preparation of the gospel of peace;

power of his might. Three words are used in the verse for **power** or *strength*. First, the imperative verb, *be empowered* or *be enabled*, is used, then the word for *force*, and finally the word for *strength—in the force of his strength*.

**11. Put on the whole armour of God.** While God has provided this, the individual Christian has the responsibility of putting it on; that is, he must consciously appropriate the power the Lord Jesus Christ makes available to him. **The whole armour of God.** The armor is described in detail, as well as the foes a believer must face. **That ye may be able to stand.** Without this armor of God, the Christian is not able to stand. One who is seated with Christ in the heavenlies and walking in this world must now also take a stand **against the wiles**—the methods or stratagems—**of the devil.**

**12. For we wrestle not.** The reason that we need the whole armor of God. **With flesh and blood.** The Israelites under Joshua had to fight against flesh and blood in order to conquer the land of Canaan. Ours is a spiritual warfare rather than a physical one. **But against principalities.** Not a comparative, but an absolute negation. Different ranks are seen among the hosts of Satan. It is not possible to make clear distinctions between the various types of foes mentioned here. **Against the rulers of the darkness of this world.** Literally, *the world rulers of this darkness*. **Against spiritual wickedness.** This rendering is unsatisfactory. It is *against spiritual forces of wickedness in the heavenly places*. **High places**, in the AV is the same Greek word translated "heavenly places" elsewhere in the epistle. This is the last of the five occurrences of *en tois epouraniois*, "in the heavenlies."

**13. Wherefore.** Because our enemies are such as have just been described. **Take unto you the whole armour.** Again the human responsibility is emphasized. **Able to withstand.** Note that the passage speaks both of withstanding and of standing. The former is the ability to win the fight, to hold one's position; the latter shows the result of the conflict.

**14. Stand therefore.** In this and the following verses the armor is described in detail. All of these things speak in a certain sense of the Lord Jesus Christ himself, who is our defense. **Your loins girt about with truth.** One who has his loins girded is prepared for activity (cf. I Pet 1:13). **The breastplate of righteousness.** Cf. Isa 59:17. **15. And your feet shod.** Much of the language in this sec-

**16.** Above all, taking the shield of faith, wherewith ye shall be able to quench all the fiery darts of the wicked.

**17.** And take the helmet of salvation, and the sword of the Spirit, which is the word of God:

**18.** Praying always with all prayer and supplication in the Spirit, and watching thereunto with all perseverance and supplication for all saints;

**19.** And for me, that utterance may be given unto me, that I may open my mouth boldly, to make known the mystery of the gospel,

**20.** For which I am an ambassador in bonds; that therein I may speak boldly, as I ought to speak.

**21.** But that ye also may know my affairs, *and* how I do, Tychicus, a beloved brother and faithful minister in the Lord, shall make known to you all things:

tion is taken from various passages in the OT (cf. Isa 52:7). **The preparation.** That is, that which prepares us. This would correspond to the shoes or boots. **The gospel of peace.** The good news characterized by peace or resulting in peace.

**16. Taking the shield of faith.** The genitive of apposition; that is, *the shield which consists of faith* or *is faith.* **Fiery darts of the wicked.** The word **wicked** is singular and undoubtedly masculine rather than neuter—hence, the *wicked one*—that is, Satan himself. The full dress of a Roman soldier is indicated in this passage, and the various parts are applied spiritually. **17. And take the helmet of salvation.** Again, the helmet *which is salvation.* **The sword of the Spirit.** Not the same type of genitive as before; perhaps an ablative of source or origin. That is, *the sword supplied by the Spirit.* **Which is the word of God.** God's word is a piercing sword. Here *hrēma*, "word" as utterance, is used. In a similar passage in Heb 4:12 *logos*, "word" as concept or idea, is used. The Scriptures are both *hrēma* and *logos.* All of the parts of the armor mentioned up to this point are defensive. The sword of the Spirit is the only offensive as well as defensive weapon.

2) Prayer for All Saints and for Paul. 6:18-20.

**18. Praying always.** The panoply of God must always be worn in connection with believing prayer (cf. I Thess 5:17; Col 4:2). **Prayer and supplication.** The former word is used for prayer in general, the latter for petition. **In the Spirit.** The same Holy Spirit who wields the sword of the Word must also be active in our praying. **For all saints.** Paul would not restrict their praying specifically to himself, although he does mention himself in the next verse. **19. And for me.** That is, for me in particular; this in view of Paul's circumstances at the time. **That utterance may be given unto me.** Even in his imprisonment Paul was not thinking primarily of his own welfare but of his testimony for the Lord Jesus Christ. We read in Acts 28:30,31 of Paul's speaking to all who came to him while he was a prisoner in his own hired house in Rome. **To make known with boldness the mystery of the gospel.** Not that the Gospel is any longer a secret to those who will receive it.

F. Closing Greetings. 6:21-24.
**21. But that ye also may know my**

22. **Whom I have sent unto you for the same purpose, that ye might know our affairs, and** *that* **he might comfort your hearts.**

23. **Peace** *be* **to the brethren, and love with faith, from God the Father and the Lord Jesus Christ.**

24. **Grace** *be* **with all them that love our Lord Jesus Christ in sincerity. Amen.**

Written from Rome unto the Ephesians by Tychicus.

**affairs.** One of the few personal references in this epistle. **Tychicus.** Evidently the bearer of the letter (cf. Col 4:7). **22. Whom I have sent.** Epistolary aorist tense. Paul is sending him, but at the time they read the letter he will have been sent. As in writing to the Philippians, Paul wants them to know how it is with him, and he wants to know about them.

**23. Peace be to the brethren, and love with faith.** Only God can give these qualities. **24. Grace.** Literally, *the grace;* that is, the grace beside which there is no other. **With all them that love our Lord Jesus Christ.** That is, believers.

# BIBLIOGRAPHY

ALFORD, HENRY. "The Epistle to the Ephesians," *The Greek Testament.* Vol. III. Chicago: Moody Press, 1958.

CHAFER, LEWIS SPERRY. *The Ephesian Letter Doctrinally Considered.* Chicago: The Bible Institute Colportage Assn., 1935.

ERDMAN, CHARLES R. *The Epistle of Paul to the Ephesians.* Philadelphia: Westminster Press, 1931.

FINDLAY, G. G. The Epistle to the Ephesians. *(Expositor's Bible.)* New York: A. C. Armstrong & Son, 1903.

HARRISON, NORMAN B. *His Very Own.* Chicago: The Bible Institute Colportage Assn., 1930.

MOULE, HANDLEY C. G. *Ephesian Studies.* London: Hodder & Stoughton, 1900.

PAXSON, RUTH. *The Wealth, Walk, and Warfare of the Christian.* New York: Fleming H. Revell Co., 1939.

SALMOND, S. D. F. "The Epistle to the Ephesians," *The Expositor's Greek Testament.* Vol. III. Grand Rapids: William B. Eerdmans Pub. Co., n.d.

SIMPSON, E. K. *Commentary on the Epistles to the Ephesians and Colossians (New International Commentary).* Grand Rapids: William B. Eerdmans Pub. Co., 1957.

WESTCOTT, B. F. *St. Paul's Epistle to the Ephesians.* Grand Rapids: William B. Eerdmans Pub. Co., 1950.

# THE EPISTLE
# TO THE PHILIPPIANS

## INTRODUCTION

*Founding of the Church.* In response to the Macedonian call, Paul and his companions had crossed the Aegean Sea from Troas to Neapolis and followed the renowned Egnatian Way some eight to ten miles up and over the coastal range to the city of Philippi. Philippi (named after Philip of Macedon, the father of Alexander the Great) was famous for its gold mines and its strategic location as the gateway to Europe. It was a miniature Rome, a proud Roman colony, exempt from taxation and modeled after the capital of the world. With the conversion of Lydia, the slave girl, and the jailer (Acts 16), it became the "birthplace of European Christianity." Soon Paul moved on towards Thessalonica, leaving Luke behind to care for this flock that held such a special place in his affections.

*Authorship.* Apart from F. C. Baur and several other German critics, the Pauline authorship has never been seriously doubted. External evidence is both early and strong. Some find allusions to it in the letter of Clement of Rome to the Corinthians (c. A.D. 96). Towards the middle of the second century Polycarp wrote to the Philippians, "Paul . . . when he was absent wrote letters to you" (iii. 2).

*Place of Writing.* That Philippians was written from prison is quite clear. Just where that prison was is another matter. If we assume that Luke mentions all of Paul's imprisonments, then Rome is the most probable answer. (Philippi is out of the question, and Paul's expectation of a speedy release seriously undermines the Caesarean hypothesis.)

However, in recent times an Ephesian origin has been advanced, and the theory has gained considerable ground. The argument is of many strands, the more important being:

(1) The plausibility of an Ephesian imprisonment (I Cor 15:30-32; II Cor 1:8-10).

(2) Inscriptional evidence of the presence of a detachment of the "praetorian guard" as well as members of "Caesar's household" in Ephesus (A. H. McNeile, *St. Paul*, p. 229, notes 1 and 2) — formerly advanced as irrefutable evidence of a Roman origin.

(3) The affinity of Philippians with Paul's earlier letters, namely, Romans and I Corinthians.

(4) The greater ease with which the frequent communications implied in Philippians could have been conducted (Ephesus to Philippi was a journey of seven to ten days, while Rome to Philippi involved a land journey totaling some eight hundred miles, plus an ocean crossing that would be suspended in winter; cf. Acts 27:12).

(5) Paul's avowed purpose to push on to the west which, if the imprisonment had been in Rome, would have been contradicted by his plans to revisit Philippi (1:25; 2:24) upon release. (For a concise presentation of this position, see the introduction to J. H. Michael's *The Epistle of Paul to the Philippians* in *The Moffatt New Testament Commentary*. Cf. also G. S. Duncan, *St. Paul's Ephesian Ministry.* For an important discussion which gives arguments for the Roman origin and which treats the evidence for the Ephesian origin as indecisive, see C. H. Dodd, *New Testament Studies*, pp. 85-128.)

Fortunately the interpretation of the epistle does not depend upon its point of origin. While the Ephesian hypothesis itself commends itself with greater force, it makes little difference in our understanding of this remarkable letter from prison.

Assuming an Ephesian origin, the date of composition would be about A.D. 54. (A Roman origin would give a date of 61-62.)

*Occasion.* The popular view that Philippians was primarily a thank-you letter is unlikely. Would Paul have waited until the very last moment (4:10-20) before expressing his appreciation for the gift from the believers at Philippi? The immediate purpose was to send a note of commendation and explanation along with Epaphroditus so as to head off any criticism that he was returning prematurely from his charge. This, in turn, allowed Paul the opportunity to assure the church of his grateful appreciation for their gift and to correct such minor disorders in the church as pessimism over Paul's continued imprisonment, timidity in the face of pagan hostility, the threat of Judaizers, and (especially) the shadow of disunity that was beginning to fall across the church. While these trends were not yet pronounced, if allowed to continue unchecked they would soon have undermined the cause of Christ at Philippi.

*Chapter 3 — Interruption or Interpolation?* Because of the unexpected and abrupt change of tone and subject matter at 3:2, many have suggested that Philippians is a composite of two or more of Paul's letters. The fatal weakness of the partition theory is the hopeless difference of opinion among the critics as to where the interpolation ends (3:19? 4:9? 4:20? etc.). A far more natural interpretation is that Paul was interrupted in his writing (perhaps by some depressing news of Judaizing activity), and when he returned, he picked up the new subject without transition.

*Characteristics.* Philippians is the most personal of Paul's writings. It breathes an air of confidence and strong personal attachment. There is a marked absence of formal doctrine. Even the great Christological hymn in chapter 2 is brought in indirectly to buttress an exhortation to humility. The dominant note of the letter is joy. It reveals the apostle Paul as "radiant amid the storm and stress of life."

*Outline.* Since Philippians is an extremely personal letter, it resists all attempts to force it into a logical outline. The flow of thought is natural and spontaneous. A descriptive analysis might be:

# OUTLINE

I. Salutation. 1:1,2.
II. Thanksgiving and prayer. 1:3-11.
III. The unconquerable Gospel. 1:12-14.
IV. Unprincipled preaching. 1:15-18.
V. Life or death? 1:19-26.
VI. Exhortation to steadfastness. 1:27-30.
VII. An appeal to Christian experience. 2:1-4.
VIII. The supreme example of self-renunciation. 2:5-11.
IX. Continued exhortation. 2:12-18.
X. Plans for reunion. 2:19-30.
XI. An interrupted conclusion. 3:1-11.
XII. The homestretch. 3:12-16.
XIII. A Christian commonwealth. 3:17-21.
XIV. Apostolic advice. 4:1-9.
XV. Appreciation for the gift. 4:10-20.
XVI. Greetings and benediction. 4:21-23.

# PHILIPPIANS

## CHAPTER 1

PAUL and Timotheus, the servants of Jesus Christ, to all the saints in Christ Jesus which are at Philippi, with the bishops and deacons:

2. Grace *be* unto you, and peace, from God our Father and *from* the Lord Jesus Christ.

# COMMENTARY

## I. Salutation. 1:1,2.

Ancient letters usually began, "A to B, Greetings." While following the conventional pattern, Paul could not help transforming this somewhat vague expression of good will into a meaningful Christian blessing.

**1. Paul,** who alone was the author, graciously added the name of **Timothy** (who was with him at the time of the writing and may have acted as his secretary). Together they were **servants of Christ Jesus.** *Douloi* literally means *slaves,* but there is no thought of cringing submission here. With cheerful abandon they had given themselves to the service of the One to whom they belonged. The term **saints** does not designate a level of ethical achievement, but persons who **in Christ Jesus** have been set apart unto the new life. Just why **with the bishops and deacons** is added is not clear. It may have been an afterthought, calling attention to those who had supervised (*episcopos* is best translated "overseer") the collection of money sent to Paul as a personal gift (4:10-19). Since the terms "bishop" and "presbyter" are virtually synonymous (cf. J. B. Lightfoot, *St. Paul's Epistle to the Philippians,* p. 96 ff.), and since there were several "bishops" (note plural) at Philippi, it would be unwise to contend for a first century episcopacy on the basis of this verse.

**2. Grace unto you and peace.** Paul's Christian version of the combined Greek

**3.** I thank my God upon every remembrance of you,

**4.** Always in every prayer of mine for you all making request with joy,

**5.** For your fellowship in the gospel from the first day until now;

and Hebrew greetings. Not *chairein*, "greetings," but *charis*, "grace" — the spontaneous, undeserved, loving-kindness of God towards men. **Peace** is more than inner composure; it has theological overtones that speak of restored fellowship between man and God on the basis of Christ's reconciling work. These spiritual blessings find their ultimate source in **God our Father and the Lord Jesus Christ.**

## II. Thanksgiving and Prayer. 1:3-11.

Paul lifts his heart in gratitude and prayer for the partnership of the Philippian Christians in the work of the Gospel and expresses his deep yearning that they continue to grow in love and discernment.

**3.** Thanksgiving with joy is an undercurrent that runs through all of Paul's writings. (Only in Galatians is it momentarily eclipsed by the seriousness of the Judaizing menace.) Nowhere does it burst to the surface more expressively than in Philippians. Even in prison Paul's thoughts were directed towards others. In his continuing **remembrance** of them (not isolated instances, as the AV suggests) he gave thanks to God. The singular **my God** betrays a profound and intimate relationship.

**4.** This verse is parenthetical. **Always in every supplication of mine** goes with what follows rather than paralleling verse 3 (cf. J. J. Müller, *The Epistles of Paul to the Philippians and to Philemon*, p. 40, n. 4). For Paul, to remember was to pray. The nature of his intercession is pointed up by the choice of *deēsis* (a prayer of petition) instead of the more general *proseuchē*. The studied repetition of the word **all** (1:4,7,8,25; 2:17, 26; 4:4) is Paul's gentle reminder that there is no place for partisanship in the Christian community. Intercession is not a burden to be borne but an exercise of the soul to be performed **with joy.**

**5.** The occasion for the thanksgiving is the Philippians' "sympathetic cooperation towards the furtherance of the gospel." *Koinōnia* is poorly translated by the English word **fellowship.** It comes from a verb meaning "to have in common" and may be defined in the NT as "that Christian corporate life and mutual belonging which grows out of the common sharing of Christ and his benefits" (C. E. Simcox, *They Met at Philippi*, p. 28). Even though the immediate ref-

6. Being confident of this very thing, that he which hath begun a good work in you will perform *it* until the day of Jesus Christ:

7. Even as it is meet for me to think this of you all, because I have you in my heart; inasmuch as both in my bonds, and in the defense and confirmation of the gospel, ye all are partakers of my grace.

8. For God is my record, how greatly I long after you all in the bowels of Jesus Christ.

9. And this I pray, that your love may abound yet more and more in knowledge and *in* all judgment;

10. That ye may approve things that are excellent; that ye may be sincere and without offense till the day of Christ;

erence may be to the gift of money (*koinōnia* is so used in the papyri), the expression is not exhausted by this one act. The gift is only a symbol of a far deeper concern for the propagation of the Gospel. The desire to share had been characteristic of the Philippians **from the first day**. One gift had reached Paul when he had gone no further than Thessalonica (4:16). **6.** Paul's confidence that their partnership in the Gospel would continue rested upon the faithfulness of God who, having begun a good work, would most certainly bring it to completion. To the convert from paganism the semitechnical terms **began** and **complete** would call to mind the initiation into and ultimate goal of the mystery religions. **Good work.** That total action of divine grace in their midst. The **day of Jesus Christ.** NT equivalent for the OT "day of the Lord."

**7.** It was right for Paul to think of them in this way because he had them in his **heart.** This bond of affection is made evident by their partnership with him both in his **imprisonment** and before the court. (Papyri discoveries show that both *apologia,* **defense,** and *bebaiōsis,* **confirmation,** were legal terms.) They were partakers with him **in grace,** not, *of* his *grace.* To suffer for Christ is a special favor of God. **8. I yearn for you all** reveals a deep sense of Christian family affection. Michael comments that the AV translation **bowels of Jesus Christ** "is as inexact as it is inelegant" (p. 19). *Splagchnos* (lit., heart, lungs, liver, etc.; not intestines) refers metaphorically to the feelings of love and tenderness believed to arise from the inward parts. Paul's affection had a divine origin; in fact, it was actually the indwelling Christ who was loving through him (cf. Gal 2:20).

**9.** Paul does not disparage the warmth of their affection but prays that their love may abound more and more in **precise knowledge** (*epignōsis*) and **moral discernment** (*aisthēsis*). Love must comprehend with accuracy and apply the truth with discrimination and ethical common sense. **All discernment.** Discernment for all kinds of situations. **10.** To **approve things that are excellent** (interpreting *ta diapheronta* as "things which transcend") is to give one's entire support to that which through testing has proved to be essential and vital. The result of intelligent love is a right sense of values. This, in turn, enables one to be **pure** (one derivation of *eilikrineis* sug-

11. Being filled with the fruits of righteousness, which are by Jesus Christ, unto the glory and praise of God.

12. But I would ye should understand, brethren, that the things *which happened* unto me have fallen out rather unto the furtherance of the gospel;

13. So that my bonds in Christ are manifest in all the palace, and in all other *places;*

14. And many of the brethren in the Lord, waxing confident by my bonds, are much more bold to speak the word without fear.

gests the meaning of "flawless when tested against the light") and without offense to others (taking *aproskopoi* as transitive). This becomes a vital concern in view of the coming day of Christ. 11. Filled with the fruit of righteousness. Discerning love will also result in a bumper crop (note sing., *karpos*) of uprightness. But even this depends upon the righteousness by faith—that which comes through Jesus Christ. The goal of all Christian activity is to bring recognition and homage (*epainos*) to the divine perfections (*doxa*) of a redeeming God.

### III. The Unconquerable Gospel. 1:12-14.

The Philippians were greatly distressed at the news of Paul's imprisonment. What would happen to the cause of Christ now that the chief apostle was in chains? Paul wrote encouragingly that what might have appeared as a setback was in reality an important advance. Not only had the entire Praetorian Guard learned of Christ, but the local church had been emboldened to proclaim the Gospel openly and fearlessly.

12. Six times in this one letter Paul addresses the recipients as **brethren.** The term denotes a strong sense of unity and spiritual comradeship. The circumstances (*ta kat' eme*) that had befallen Paul had unexpectedly proved to advance the Gospel actively. *Prokopē* (**furtherance** or *advance*) is from a verb used originally of a pioneer cutting his way through brushwood (Souter, *Pocket Lexicon,* p. 216). 13. The advance had been on two fronts: the Gospel had come to the Praetorian Guard (v. 13), and the Christians had been stirred to more fearless witnessing (v. 14). *Praitōrion* here refers not to the official residence of the governor (thus AV, **palace**) but to the imperial guard (RSV and most commentators; cf. Lightfoot's famous note *op. cit.,* pp. 99-104). Even professional guards could not resist speaking of this remarkable prisoner and the reason for his imprisonment. Soon the entire city (**all the rest,** ASV) knew that Paul was in chains for the cause of **Christ.**

14. The majority of the brethren were "infected with the contagion of Paul's heroism" (Rainey in ExpB, p. 52). It is better to take **in the Lord** as representing the sphere of their confidence than to make it modify **the brethren.** The occasion of the confidence was Paul's **bonds.** The end result was that they dared more fearlessly than ever to speak out (*laleō* denotes the sound produced) the **word of God.**

15. Some indeed preach Christ even of envy and strife; and some also of good will:

16. The one preach Christ of contention, not sincerely, supposing to add affliction to my bonds:

17. But the other of love, knowing that I am set for the defense of the gospel.

18. What then? notwithstanding, every way, whether in pretense, or in truth, Christ is preached; and I therein do rejoice, yea, and will rejoice.

## IV. Unprincipled Preaching. 1:15-18.

Not all preached out of pure motives; but in that Christ was being preached, Paul rejoiced.

15. The identity of the some who preached Christ from impure motives cannot be established with certainty. However, they were not the Judaizing party (as Lightfoot and Moule contend), because they preached Christ, not "another gospel" (cf. Gal 1:6-9). Would it have been like Paul to tolerate one day what he had utterly repudiated the day before? Neither were they the minority implied in Phil 1:14, because they were by no means reticent to preach. More probably the antagonists were a group within the church who, envious of Paul's influence (in prison or out) and stirred by a quarrelsome spirit, had increased their missionary activity with a desire to add to the annoyance of the imprisoned apostle. The good will of the others refers to their motives in preaching.

16. The Received Text, following inferior authorities, has transposed verses 16 and 17 to avoid the supposed irregularity of dealing with the two groups of verse 15 in reverse order. Out of love refers both to their concern for the progress of the Gospel and to their personal attachment to Paul. *Keimai*, I am set *(here)*, pictures a sentry *posted* for duty. In the present context it may have the more metaphorical meaning of being *destined* for the vindication of the gospel. 17. The preaching of the second group arose out of selfish ambition *(eritheia* was used by Aristotle to denote "a self-seeking pursuit of political office by unfair means," Arndt, p. 309). Their real interest was to win against Paul and in the process to annoy him in prison. *Thlipsis*, affliction, literally means *friction*. "To rouse friction by one's chains" is a vivid way of portraying the consternation of a person who cannot rectify a situation because of some limitation which has been placed upon him.

18. But what was Paul's reaction? Regardless of the motive, if Christ was being preached, he rejoiced. Even though the Gospel may have been used as a camouflage for personal gain, it was still "the power of God unto salvation." Michael understimates the apostle when he says that "Paul's spirit was fretful as he wrote" and that 1:18 was "a deliberate attempt . . . to curb his agitated spirit" *(op. cit.*, p. 45). And will rejoice

19. For I know that this shall turn to my salvation through your prayer, and the supply of the Spirit of Jesus Christ,

20. According to my earnest expectation and *my* hope, that in nothing I shall be ashamed, but *that* with all boldness, as always, *so* now also Christ shall be magnified in my body, whether *it be* by life, or by death.

21. For to me to live *is* Christ, and to die *is* gain.

22. But if I live in the flesh, this *is* the fruit of my labor: yet what I shall choose I wot not.

does not belong to verse 18 as expressing a strong determination not to lapse into irritation at the deceptive conduct of his antagonists, but introduces the further grounds for rejoicing given in verses 19,20.

### V. Life or Death? 1:19-26.

While the apostle's personal desire was to go home to Christ, the need of the church convinced him that he would soon be released and continue working for their advancement in the faith.

19. Paul believed that the present opposition would work out for good because the Christians were praying. As a result, the **Spirit of Jesus Christ** (the Holy Spirit, not a Christlike spirit) would grant a **bountiful supply** of that which was necessary for the existing emergency. *Sōtēria* is best taken as **deliverance** (RSV) from prison, although many commentators understand it in a wider sense. Some detect a quotation from Job 13:16 (LXX), and interpret Paul's hope of vindication as resting on his consciousness of integrity (cf. Michael, *in loc.*). 20. *Apokaradokia,* **earnest expectation,** is a striking word, perhaps coined by Paul. Literally it means to *look intently into the distance with outstretched head.* The apostle's expectation was twofold: that he would not be **ashamed** (i.e., be disappointed by the failure of divine help), and that **Christ** would **be magnified** (note the sensitive substitution of the third person passive for the first person active) in his **body** (the natural sphere for the outward expression of the inner man). The emphasis upon **now** implies that the hour of crisis was near. **Whether by life or by death** does not reflect indifference on Paul's part about his fate but concern that in either case Christ be honored.

21. Paul's own life had been so completely taken up into the person and program of his Lord that he could say, **For to me to live is Christ.** Christ was the sum total of his existence. **To die is gain** because in the absence of life's limitations union with Christ will be completely realized. No sense of world-weariness should be read into these words. 22. The lack of continuity within verse 22 reflects Paul's perplexity. Of the several possibilities, the elliptical construction — **If, however** *(it is granted to me)* **to live in the flesh, this** *(will result in)* **fruitful labor for me**—is preferable. The choice of **flesh** instead of "body" em-

**23.** For I am in a strait betwixt two, having a desire to depart, and to be with Christ; which is far better:

**24.** Nevertheless to abide in the flesh *is* more needful for you.

**25.** And having this confidence, I know that I shall abide and continue with you all for your furtherance and joy of faith;

**26.** That your rejoicing may be more abundant in Jesus Christ for me by my coming to you again.

**27.** Only let your conversation be as it becometh the gospel of Christ: that whether I come and see you, or else be absent, I may hear of your affairs, that ye stand fast in one spirit, with one mind striving together for the faith of the gospel;

phasizes the weak and transitory nature of physical life. Paul does not venture to decide between the alternatives (in this context *gnōrizō* means "to make known one's decision"), but will leave it with the Lord.

**23.** I am immobilized by two opposing considerations. *Synechomai (I am in a strait)* is a strong expression meaning "to be held together." With the addition of *betwixt two*, it means "hemmed in and under pressure from both sides." Contemplating the possibility of either release or the sword, Paul is prevented from inclining in either direction. His personal desire is to depart *(analyō* pictures a vessel weighing anchor or a soldier breaking camp; it is a euphemism for "to die") and be with Christ. That would be by far the best—a doubly strengthened comparative ("a bold accumulation," Moule, *op. cit.)* expressing the surpassing excellence of being with Christ. **24.** The greater obligation is *to continue on in this present life.* The preposition compounded with the simple verb, *epi — menō,* gives it the special thought of persistence. Personal desire gives way to spiritual need.

**25.** Persuaded of this (i.e., the total thrust of vv. 19-24), Paul knows (personal conviction, not prophetic insight) that he shall abide and remain beside *(to serve)* them. The result will be joyful progress (the two nouns can hardly be separated) in the faith (both objectively — the creed and subjectively — the believer's apprehension). **26.** So that marks a specific purpose—the giving to them of an abundant ground for boasting. Even in English, "boasting" may mean "speaking in exulting language of another." In Christ is the sphere of their glorying. In me is the occasion, explained by the following phrase as by my return.

### VI. Exhortation to Steadfastness. 1:27-30.

Lest their boasting lead to carelessness in the conflict against paganism, Paul sounds a note of warning. With unity and steadfastness they were to go on contending for the faith.

**27.** They were to live as worthy citizens of the kingdom of heaven. Paul's use of *politeuomai,* "to live as a citizen," "to fulfill corporate duties," instead of the more usual *peripateō,* "to walk," would be noted and appreciated in a Roman colony like Philippi. The word stresses the effect of the Christian community in a

28. And in nothing terrified by your adversaries: which is to them an evident token of perdition, but to you of salvation, and that of God.

29. For unto you it is given in the behalf of Christ, not only to believe on him, but also to suffer for his sake;

30. Having the same conflict which ye saw in me, and now hear to be in me.

## CHAPTER 2

IF there be therefore any consolation in Christ, if any comfort of love, if any fellowship of the Spirit, if any bowels and mercies,

2. Fulfil ye my joy, that ye be likeminded, having the same love, being of one accord, of one mind.

pagan society. Whether I come . . . or . . . am absent does not indicate doubt concerning the future but is an attempt to disengage them from undue dependence upon him. The thought of gladiatorial combat runs throughout these verses: They are to take a firm stand (stēkō), join in combat (synathleō), and not be frightened (ptyreomai, v. 28). One spirit designates a unified offensive; one soul (seat of affections) indicates that unity must extend to inward disposition.

28. The verb, to be terrified, pictures frightened horses about to stampede. The opponents were not the Judaizers but members of a violently hostile element at Philippi. The fearlessness of the Christians was a clear omen to the adversaries that their attempts to thwart the Gospel were futile and only led to their own destruction. It also revealed to them that God was on the other side (reading of your salvation, not to you of salvation). 29. It is given could be more literally translated, It has been graciously conferred (charizomai is the verb form of charis, "grace"). "The privilege of suffering for Christ is the privilege of doing the kind of work for him that is important enough to merit the world's counterattack" (Simcox, op. cit., p. 61). To suffer for Christ (in the interest of his cause) is a favor granted only to those who believe in him. 30. Connect with verse 28 a. The Philippians were involved in the same sort of conflict (agōn; cf. our word agony) in which Paul had been (Acts 16:19 ff.) and still was engaged.

### VII. An Appeal to Christian Experience. 2:1-4.

In four compact conditional clauses Paul sets forth a powerful motive for harmony in the Christian community.

1. First class conditional clauses (if) assume the premise to be true, and the if may often be translated since. Consolation in Christ. Ground for appeal because of being in Christ. Comfort of love. The incentive furnished by the bond of love. Fellowship of the Spirit. The mutual concern effected by God's Spirit. Tender compassion (joining the two nouns). An appeal to human kindness. 2. Paul's joy would be complete if the Philippians would continue (note present tense) in harmony of thought and disposition. The apostle's earnestness is seen in his almost redundant enlargement—by having the same love and by being knit together

3. *Let* nothing *be done* through strife or vainglory; but in lowliness of mind let each esteem other better than themselves.

4. Look not every man on his own things, but every man also on the things of others.

5. Let this mind be in you, which was also in Christ Jesus:

6. Who, being in the form of God, thought it not robbery to be equal with God:

7. But made himself of no reputation, and took upon him the form of a servant, and was made in the likeness of men:

in soul (*sympsychē*), considering the one and same thing.

3. Selfish ambition (cf. 1:17) and vain conceit (*kenodoxia* combines the two words "hollow" and "opinion") were the headstrong and treacherous foes of the life of the church. They must give way to lowliness of mind (the Greeks took self-assertion so much for granted that a new word had to be coined) and thoughtful consideration (verb form, *esteem*) for others (*as*) better than oneself (not necessarily as essentially superior but as worthy of preferential treatment). Müller describes humility as "insight into one's own insignificance" (*op. cit.*, p. 75). 4. As humility (v. 3 a) is the antithesis of vain conceit, consideration for others (v. 4) is the antithesis of selfish ambition.

### VIII. The Supreme Example of Self-renunciation. 2:5-11.

Paul draws upon an early hymn of the church which eloquently portrays the divine condescension of Christ in His incarnation and death in order to buttress his appeal for self-forgetful and sacrificial living. (For a recent and excellent treatment of this much discussed passage cf. V. Taylor, *The Person of Christ*, pp. 62-79.) The interpretation that follows sees a basic contrast between the two Adams, and understands the "self-emptying" of Jesus in terms of the Suffering Servant (cf. A. M. Hunter, *Paul and His Predecessors*, pp. 45-51, for an able presentation of this approach). If it be remembered that the language of 2:5-11 is that of poetry, not of formal theology, many of the problems raised by kenotic (lit., *emptying*) speculation will correctly appear as irrelevant to the essential teaching of the passage.

5. **Let this mind . . .** (AV). Better, *Maintain that inner disposition towards one another which was exemplified* (the verb must be supplied) **by Christ Jesus.** 6. **Being in the form of God** (AV). Better, *Though in his pre-incarnate state he possessed the essential qualities of God, he did not consider his status of divine equality a prize to be selfishly hoarded* (taking *harpagmos* passively). *Morphē*, **form**, in verses 6 and 7 denotes a permanent expression of essential attributes, while *schēma*, **fashion** (v. 8), refers to outward appearance that is subject to change.

7. **But he emptied himself.** *Ekenōsen* is not intended in a metaphysical sense (i.e., that he gave up divine attributes), but is a "graphic expression of the com-

8. And being found in fashion as a man, he humbled himself, and became obedient unto death, even the death of the cross.

9. Wherefore God also hath highly exalted him, and given him a name which is above every name:

10. That at the name of Jesus every knee should bow, of *things* in heaven, and *things* in earth, and *things* under the earth;

11. And *that* every tongue should confess that Jesus Christ *is* Lord, to the glory of God the Father.

pleteness of his self-renunciation" (M. R. Vincent, *A Critical and Exegetical Commentary on the Epistles to the Philippians and to Philemon,* p. 59). Note the allusion to Isa 53:12, "he hath poured out his soul unto death." Christ emptied himself **by becoming a servant** (the use of *morphē,* **form,** here indicates the reality of his servanthood) **and appearing upon the scene as mortal man.** Unlike the first Adam, who made a frantic attempt to seize equality with God (Gen 3:5), Jesus, the last Adam (I Cor 15:47), humbled himself and obediently accepted the role of the Suffering Servant (cf. the contribution of R. Martin in ExpT, March '59, p. 183 f.). **8.** The act of voluntary humiliation did not stop with the Incarnation but continued to the ignominious depths of death by crucifixion. The omission of the article before *staurou,* **cross,** emphasizes the shameful nature of the death — even a **cross death.** (For the Roman view of crucifixion cf. Cicero *In Verrem* 5. 66). **He humbled himself.** He put aside all personal rights and interests in order to insure the welfare of others.

**9.** As a consequence, **God highly exalted him** (the Ascension and its concomitant glory) **and graciously conferred upon him the supreme name** (either LORD, *kurios,* the OT name for God; or to be understood in the Hebrew sense of denoting rank and dignity). Verses 9-11 answer to verses 6-8, and are best accounted for in the present context (the interrupted exhortation is resumed at 2:12) as the remainder of a hymn originally quoted for the thrust of its first strophe. **10.** Drawing from Isa 45:23, where the Lord prophesies that universal worship will one day be given him, the author writes that **in the name of Jesus** (not *at,* AV, which might suggest mechanical genuflection at the mention of the name, but **in connection with** all the name represents) **the totality of created rational beings will pay due homage. Those in heaven, on earth, and underground** is an expression of universality and should not be forced to support elaborate theories of classification. **11.** The compound verb for **confess** *(exomologeō)* may mean "confess with thanksgiving"—although this would seem strange if **every tongue** includes the lost as well as the saved. **Jesus Christ is Lord** is the earliest creed of the primitive church (cf. Rom 10:9; I Cor 12:3). The Lordship of Christ is the core of Christianity.

**12.** Wherefore, my beloved, as ye have always obeyed, not as in my presence only, but now much more in my absence, work out your own salvation with fear and trembling:

**13.** For it is God which worketh in you both to will and to do of *his* good pleasure.

**14.** Do all things without murmurings and disputings:

**15.** That ye may be blameless and harmless, the sons of God, without rebuke, in the midst of a crooked and perverse nation, among whom ye shine as lights in the world;

**16.** Holding forth the word of life; that I may rejoice in the day of Christ, that I have not run in vain, neither labored in vain.

## IX. Continued Exhortation. 2:12-18.

Christ's great example of self-renunciation led Paul to admonish his Philippian brethren further.

**12. My beloved.** A favorite expression (occurring twice in 4:1) that betrays a warm love for his converts. He urges them to **work out their own salvation,** especially now in his absence. The passage relates primarily to the community rather than to the individual (cf. Michael, *op. cit.,* p. 98 ff.). Salvation is corporate. The Philippians were to carry through (*katergazomai,* **keep on working out,** is continuous present) the deliverance of the church into a state of Christian maturity. **Fear and trembling** seems to be an idiomatic expression for a humble frame of mind (cf. I Cor 2:3; II Cor 7:15; Eph 6:5). **13.** Humility in reference to their deliverance was in place because, in spite of their co-operation, it was **God** (note emphatic position) who created within them both the will and the power (he "energizes"—*energeō*) **to do his pleasure** (or, *to promote the good will,* viz., harmony in the Philippian church).

**14.** The exhortation against **murmurings and disputings** (*dialogismos* is used in the papyri to denote litigation) reflects as a background the grumblings of the Israelites in their wilderness wandering. (However, to picture Paul as consciously comparing himself with Moses as he delivered his final injunctions is more imaginative than probable.) **15.** By not grumbling they would **become** (*ginomai*) **blameless** (before others) **and innocent** (*akeraios,* lit., *unadulterated* — denoting simplicity of charcter). **Unblemished,** *amōmos,* is used almost invariably in the LXX of sacrificial animals. **A crooked and perverse generation** (an adaptation of Deut 32:5) is a result of moral and intellectual distortion. In this dark world Christians are to **shine as lights** (cf. Mt 5:16).

**16.** If Paul is continuing the same metaphor, *epechontes,* etc. will be translated **holding forth** (like a torch held out before the bearer) **the word** (that brings) **life;** but if the final clause of verse 15 is parenthetical (Lightfoot) and the apostle is contrasting the Christians with the perverse generation, it will be translated **holding fast. Run** reflects the activity of the stadium. **Labor.** Deissmann sees here the discouragement of having woven a piece of cloth only to have it rejected (LAE, p. 317). Perhaps Herklotz is right in referring to Paul as "the master of

17. Yea, and if I be offered upon the sacrifice and service of your faith, I joy, and rejoice with you all.

18. For the same cause also do ye joy, and rejoice with me.

19. But I trust in the Lord Jesus to send Timotheus shortly unto you, that I also may be of good comfort, when I know your state.

20. For I have no man likeminded, who will naturally care for your state.

21. For all seek their own, not the things which are Jesus Christ's.

22. But ye know the proof of him, that, as a son with the father, he hath served with me in the gospel.

23. Him therefore I hope to send presently, so soon as I shall see how it will go with me.

24. But I trust in the Lord that I also myself shall come shortly.

25. Yet I supposed it necessary to send to you Epaphroditus, my brother, and companion in labor, and fellow soldier, but your messenger, and he that ministered to my wants.

the mixed metaphor" (H.G.G. Herklotz, *Epistle of St. Paul to the Philippians,* p. 74).

**17.** A metaphor built on sacrificial ritual. The **faith** of the Philippians (and all that involves in terms of life and activity) was their **sacrifice and priestly service.** Paul's lifeblood would be a libation poured upon their offering. If that was what the future held, then even in this Paul rejoiced. He would **rejoice with** them *(sygchairō)* because a double sacrifice afforded the opportunity for further fellowship. **18.** They were to adopt the same outlook and join their rejoicing with his.

### X. Plans for Reunion. 2:19-30.

Paul hoped to send Timothy before long with the news of the court's decision and then to come himself as soon as possible. In the meantime he would send back Epaphroditus—their messenger to Paul in his distress—to ease the Philippians' concern and restore their cheerfulness.

**19.** Although the apostle had urged them to take their own affairs in hand (v. 12), he would not leave them without guidance. The purpose of sending Timothy was that Paul might **be cheered** *(eupsycheō,* lit., *to be stouthearted)* by news of them, and vice versa (implied by **I also).** **20. No one.** Not a sweeping condemnation of his fellow laborers. But of those available there was no one who, like Timothy, would be **genuinely** *(gnēsiōs,* lit., *born in wedlock;* thus, "like a brother") concerned for their welfare. **21.** Paul felt a bit like the 'deserted'. *Elijah.* **22.** Timothy's **character** *(dokimē,* "approval gained through testing") was well known to the Philippians, because they had observed him (Acts 16) as he labored with Paul **as a son with a father in** (the interest of) **the gospel.**

**23.** It is **this one** (note emphatic position of *touton),* viz., Timothy himself, whom Paul hoped (his plans were still somewhat unsettled) to send as soon as he could get a clear perspective *(aphoraō,* "to see," means lit., *to look from)* on the outcome of his imprisonment. **24.** However, he was persuaded that **before long** *(tacheōs* is a reasonably flexible term) he, too, would come to them. **In the Lord.** All Paul's plans were conditioned by his relationship to Christ.

**25. Epaphroditus** *(charming)* is one of the most attractively heroic characters of the NT. He had been delegated to bring the gift of money (4:18) and to

**26.** For he longed after you all, and was full of heaviness, because that ye had heard that he had been sick.

**27.** For indeed he was sick nigh unto death: but God had mercy on him; and not on him only, but on me also, lest I should have sorrow upon sorrow.

**28.** I sent him therefore the more carefully, that, when ye see him again, ye may rejoice, and that I may be the less sorrowful.

**29.** Receive him therefore in the Lord with all gladness; and hold such in reputation:

**30.** Because for the work of Christ he was nigh unto death, not regarding his life, to supply your lack of service toward me.

serve Paul on behalf of the Philippians. Paul calls him a **brother** (emphasizing the bond of Christian family love), **fellow worker** (a term borrowed from the workshop and stressing the spirit of comradeship), and **fellow soldier** (*systratiōtēs* pictures Christians fighting side by side against the onslaughts of heathenism. Phillips translates, *comrade-in-arms*). **I supposed.** In ancient correspondence it was customary for the writer to adopt the reader's perspective (cf. also **I sent,** v. 28). **26.** Epaphroditus' eager longing for the Christians back at Philippi had turned to distress upon his learning that news of his illness had reached them. The verb for **full of heaviness** (AV) is usually derived from *adēmos*, "not at home," viz., "not inwardly at home"; hence **distraught, beside oneself.** It is used, for instance, to portray the profound consternation of Gethsemane (Mk 14:33). **27.** The apostle affirms the seriousness of the crisis. Epaphroditus' condition had been like death (taking *paraplesion*, **nigh to,** adverbially). But God had had mercy on them both: Epaphroditus had recovered, and bereavement had not been added to Paul's other concerns. **Sorrow upon sorrow** means "wave upon wave of distressing circumstances." **28. Rejoice again.** The AV and RSV are mistaken in taking **again** with the participle **seeing.** Lightfoot (p. 124) translates, *may recover your cheerfulness.* The alleviation of their anxiety would lessen Paul's. Thus he sent Epaphroditus back **more quickly** (or *spoudaiaterōs* may indicate "with greater eagerness"; cf. RSV) than he might have done.

**29.** Some commentators see a note of apprehension in Paul's "letter of recommendation." Would there not be some at Philippi who would judge that, by returning prematurely, Epaphroditus had deserted his charge? However, the verse need not be taken as an appeal. Moule suggests, "Accept him as my gift to you" (p. 54). **30.** He was worthy of honor because in the fulfillment of his obligations he almost died. **Unto death** reflects an attitude like that of Christ (cf. same phrase in 2:8). And this was in order to complete their service to Paul. The context shows that Epaphroditus' critical condition was due to overexertion rather than to persecution or the hazards of the journey. **Having gambled with his life.** From *parabolos*, "venturesome, reckless." In Alexandria there grew up an association of men known as the *Parabolani.* Among the hazardous duties of

### CHAPTER 3

FINALLY, my brethren, rejoice in the Lord. To write the same things to you, to me indeed *is* not grievous, but for you *it is* safe.

2. Beware of dogs, beware of evil workers, beware of the concision.

3. For we are the circumcision, which worship God in the spirit, and rejoice in Christ Jesus, and have no confidence in the flesh.

this "suicide squad" was the nursing of the sick during epidemics.

### XI. An Interrupted Conclusion. 3:1-11.

As Paul begins to bring his letter to a close, some sort of interruption breaks his train of thought. When he returns to dictating, he digresses to warn the Philippians against Judaizers and self-complacent antinomianism. By 4:4 (or 4:8) he has worked his way back to the original theme.

**1. Finally.** W. S. Tindal is quoted as saying that Paul is "the father of all preachers who use 'finally, my brethren' as an indication that they have found their second wind" (Herklotz, *op. cit.*, p. 16). **The same things.** Those central truths of life and doctrine to which Paul makes repeated reference. In the present context they can refer to his teaching ministry while with them or to prior correspondence of which we have no further information. The theory that one such letter has found its way back into the text and accounts for the abrupt change in style and subject at 3:2 (or 3:1 b?) is by no means necessary to explain what is at most only a "curious digression" (Plummer, p. 66. Cf. "Lost Epistles to the Philippians," Lightfoot, pp. 138-142; Vincent, xxxi f.).

**2.** The warning is not against three types of people (e.g., heathen, self-seeking Christian teachers, and Jews), but against one kind from three angles: their character (**dogs**), conduct (**evil workers**), and creed (**concision**. Cf. Robertson in *Abingdon Bible Commentary*, p. 1246). According to Mosaic law the dog was an unclean animal (Deut 23:18). In Eastern cities he was a scavenger and usually diseased — a "despised, shameless, and miserable creature" (SBK, I, 722). Paul reverses this term of contempt which had long been applied to the Gentiles by the Jews (cf. Mt 15:27) and says that it is the Christians who are feasting at the spiritual banquet table, while the Jews are those who eat the "garbage of carnal ordinances" (Lightfoot). The dogs are either extreme Judaizers or antagonistic Jews (the line becomes rather thin). With a bitter play on words Paul designates them the **concision** *(katatomē)* rather than the **circumcision** *(peritomē)*. They are "those who mutilate the flesh" (RSV). The verb is used in the LXX of cuttings forbidden by Mosaic law.

**3.** Not they, but **we are the** true **circumcision.** The new Israel is comprised,

4. Though I might also have confidence in the flesh. If any other man thinketh that he hath whereof he might trust in the flesh, I more:

5. Circumcised the eighth day, of the stock of Israel, *of* the tribe of Benjamin, a Hebrew of the Hebrews; as touching the law, a Pharisee;

6. Concerning zeal, persecuting the church; touching the righteousness which is in the law, blameless.

7. But what things were gain to me, those I counted loss for Christ.

8. Yea doubtless, and I count all things *but* loss for the excellency of the knowledge of Christ Jesus my Lord: for whom I have suffered the loss of all things, and do count them *but* dung, that I may win Christ,

first, of those who **worship by the Spirit of God.** That the early church made this claim is most certainly implied in the verse. The AV here follows the inferior reading, which, however, rather happily maintains a contrast between that which is external and that which takes place in the domain of the spirit. Again, true Israel is made up of those who **boast in Christ Jesus. Boast** is a favorite expression of Paul's. He uses it thirty times in his epistles, though it appears only twice elsewhere in the NT. Here the meaning is "to glory" or "to exult." Third, the new Israel is made up of those who **have no confidence in the flesh,** viz., in external privileges.

4. The writer, for the moment, places himself on the same ground as his antagonists to show that even according to their standards, he had superior **ground for confidence** (taking *pepoithēsis* objectively). 5. Paul sets forth his credentials. **Circumcised on the eighth day.** He was a true Israelite from birth (Ishmaelites, whose Jewish blood was mixed with Egyptian, were not circumcised until they were 13). He was no proselyte, but **of the stock of Israel.** In fact, he belonged to the honored **tribe of Benjamin,** which gave to Israel its first king. In contrast with Greek-speaking Jews (Hellenists), he came from a family that had retained Hebrew customs and spoke the Hebrew (or Aramaic) language. In addition to these inherited privileges, there were matters that had involved his personal choice. In his relationship to the Law he was a **Pharisee** — a "passionate adherent of the strictest religious tradition among the Jews" (Müller, p. 110). 6. **Law righteousness.** "Righteousness" that consists in obedience to external commands. **Blameless.** A remarkable claim when one considers the minutiae of Pharisaic legislation.

7. Whatever **gains** (note plural) Paul may have had (the privileges mentioned in vv. 5,6), he counted as **loss** (sing.). They were worse than useless—actually a hindrance—because they had to be unlearned. 8. Here the writer enlarges the preceding thought and protects it against misinterpretation. He says that he is **counting** (present tense indicates that v. 7 was no isolated and impulsive act of the past) **all things** (not only his former ground of confidence) **as loss** in comparison with the surpassing worth of "experiential knowledge of God" (the key thought of vv. 8-11). He not only counted them as loss, but they were

9. And be found in him, not having mine own righteousness, which is of the law, but that which is through the faith of Christ, the righteousness which is of God by faith:

10. That I may know him, and the power of his resurrection, and the fellowship of his sufferings, being made conformable unto his death;

11. If by any means I might attain unto the resurrection of the dead.

12. Not as though I had already attained, either were already perfect: but I follow after, if that I may apprehend that for which also I am apprehended of Christ Jesus.

13. Brethren, I count not myself to have apprehended: but *this* one thing *I do*, forgetting those things which are behind, and reaching forth unto those things which are before,

actually confiscated. The AV regards *skybalon* as that rejected by the body, i.e., **dung.** Lightfoot favors a derivation from *es kunas,* "that which is thrown to the dogs," *refuse* (RSV). The motive for this unprecedented *volte-face* was to **gain Christ.**

9. Paul discounted all personal achievement that he might be found in Christ. The parallel clauses contrast works-righteousness, which is based on law, with faith-righteousness, which is given by God. Here is Paul's most concise statement of justification by faith. 10. The passionate expression of Paul's deepest longings. To **know him** is to experience the power that flows from union with the resurrected Christ and to enter into fellowship with **his sufferings** (all the hardships to be endured for the cause of Christ; cf. Acts 9:16). That these are two aspects of the same experience is indicated by the single article in Greek. **Being conformed** (pres. participle) **to his death** further defines the experience as one of continual dying out to self. 11. **If by any means.** An expression of humility, not of uncertainty. The **resurrection from** (*ek,* "out of") **the dead** is the resurrection of believers, not a general resurrection.

## XII. The Homestretch. 3:12-16.

Lest he leave the impression of having already arrived, Paul carefully indicated that he was still very much involved in the race of life. This caution against misinterpretation was called forth by the spreading influence of complacent perfectionists in the church at large.

12. That which Paul had not **already attained** was the experience of complete and final knowledge of his Lord (vv. 8-11). **Already perfect** further defines his goal. Perfection here would be full knowledge and perfect conformity. Verse 12 b may be paraphrased, "but I press on strenuously if somehow I may **overtake and lay hold of** (*katalambanō* is used in the papyri of colonists appropriating land) that for which I was **taken captive** (same verb as above) **by Christ Jesus** on the Damascus road." God had a purpose in Paul's conversion, and Paul desired intensely that it might be fully realized in his experience. Many commentators take *eph' hō* to mean "because," which would then stress the *motive* (not the goal) of Paul's exertion (cf. C.F.D. Moule, *Idiom Book,* p. 132).

13. Verses 13,14 enlarge the thought

**14.** I press toward the mark for the prize of the high calling of God in Christ Jesus.

**15.** Let us therefore, as many as be perfect, be thus minded: and if in any thing ye be otherwise minded, God shall reveal even this unto you.

**16.** Nevertheless, whereto we have already attained, let us walk by the same rule, let us mind the same thing.

**17.** Brethren, be followers together of me, and mark them which walk so as ye have us for an ensample.

of 3:12. The **not yet** state of Christian perfection destroys complacency and demands strenuous pursuit. **I myself** may imply a contrast with the self-appraisal of others. The metaphor is one of a foot-race. The concise, **but one thing,** expresses "singleness of purpose and concentration of effort" (Michael, p. 160). "I do" is added in the English. **Forgetting what lies behind.** The past accomplishments of his Christian career, which might induce self-satisfaction and a slackening of pace. **Straining forward** graphically portrays a runner who draws upon all his remaining strength and stretches out toward the goal (thus, our homestretch). **14. Mark** (*skopos*, from *skopeō*, "to gaze at"). That upon which the eye has been fixed. Distraction would be fatal. (Some suggest that the metaphor is that of a chariot race.) If ultimate perfection is the aim of the runner (that which keeps him from deviating from his course), it is also his **prize.** The prize belongs to those who respond wholeheartedly to God's **upward call,** (away from self and toward new heights of spiritual attainment) **in Christ Jesus.**

**15.** To be **perfect.** To be mature. In the mystery religions it designated the fully instructed as opposed to the novices. There is no indication here of "reproachful irony" (so Lightfoot). **Be thus minded.** Have this basic attitude of disposition, i.e., that past success does not remove the necessity for future striving. **If in anything ye be otherwise minded,** Paul adds by way of encouragement. "If you are not quite convinced that this point of view should be applied to *every* area of life, God will reveal **even this unto you.**" **16.** While the precise meaning of this compressed verse is doubtful, the general idea is clear: "Let us not deviate from those principles that have brought us safely to our present stage of Christian maturity." The condition for future enlightenment is to walk according to present light.

### XIII. A Christian Commonwealth. 3:17-21.

The presence of those whose sensual manner of life was undermining the effectiveness of the Gospel led Paul to exhort the Philippians to imitate him and others who also lived as citizens of the heavenly state.

**17.** They were to join with one another in imitating Paul and the others who, after close inspection (*skopeō;* see on v. 14), proved to be living on the same high plane. *Typos* (**ensample**) was origi-

18. (For many walk, of whom I have told you often, and now tell you even weeping, *that they are* the enemies of the cross of Christ:

19. Whose end *is* destruction, whose God *is their* belly, and *whose* glory *is* in their shame, who mind earthly things.)

20. For our conversation is in heaven; from whence also we look for the Saviour, the Lord Jesus Christ:

21. Who shall change our vile body, that it may be fashioned like unto his glorious body, according to the working whereby he is able even to subdue all things unto himself.

## CHAPTER 4

THEREFORE, my brethren dearly beloved and longed for, my joy and crown, so stand fast in the Lord, *my* dearly beloved.

nally the mark left by a blow, and then a "pattern" or "mold." **18.** Those here described were not Judaizers (v. 2 ff.) nor heathen (this would have elicited a different reaction than **weeping**), but antinomian libertines who were in some way connected with the church. They misinterpreted Christian liberty as freedom from all moral restraint. They **are** (not "live as") **the enemies** (note definite article) **of the cross.** They were at enmity with everything for which the cross stands. **19.** Their **end** (better, *destiny*) **is perdition**, the antithesis of salvation. Their **god**, the supreme object of their concern, was **the belly.** The reference is not only to gluttony but to all sensual indulgences. Their supposed liberty was really bondage to shameful lusts, and they were disposed to dwell on sordid and earthy matters.

**20.** In contrast with these licentious profligates, the mature Christians lived as a colony of heavenly citizens whose temporary abode was on earth. While *politeuma* (the only occurrence in the NT) may indicate the pattern of life followed by a citizen (thus AV, **conversation**), here it means the state to which the citizen belongs (*commonwealth*, RSV). Roman citizens living at the outpost of Philippi would immediately grasp the point. *Apekdechometha* (rather mildly translated as **we look**, AV, or *we await*, RSV) denotes eager expectation. Inscriptions show that *sōtēr*, **savior**, was widely used in the Greco-Roman world to designate kings and emperors. Here it extends the preceding metaphor and reflects the attitude of the primitive church toward the return of Christ.

**21.** At his appearance Christ will **refashion** (*metaschēmatizō*) our **lowly body**, the body which now clothes our lowly state of mortal existence. Not *vile body*, as if Paul shared the Stoic contempt for all things material. **That it may be conformed** (*symmorphon*; for *schēma* and *morphē*, cf. 2:6) to **his glorious body**, the body in which Christ is clothed in his glorified estate. This transformation requires an act of supernatural power, that very power necessary to bring about universal dominion. *Energia* is used only by Paul and nearly always denotes God in action.

### XIV. Apostolic Advice. 4:1-9.

The apostle admonishes two women to drop their differences, shows that prayer is the cure for anxiety, and urges a more noble sphere for the life of the mind.

2. I beseech Euodias, and beseech Syntyche, that they be of the same mind in the Lord.

3. And I entreat thee also, true yokefellow, help those women which labored with me in the gospel, with Clement also, and *with* other my fellow laborers, whose names *are* in the book of life.

4. Rejoice in the Lord always: *and* again I say, Rejoice.

5. Let your moderation be known unto all men. The Lord *is* at hand.

6. Be careful for nothing; but in every thing by prayer and supplication with thanksgiving let your requests be made known unto God.

7. And the peace of God, which passeth all understanding, shall keep your hearts and minds through Christ Jesus.

1. **Therefore.** In view of your heavenly citizenship and the glorious transformation it will involve. The exhortation to **stand fast** is both a conclusion to chapter 3 and an introduction to what follows. Note the six terms of endearment in this one verse. *Stephanos,* **crown,** was a woven wreath awarded to a winning athlete. It was also used of the garland placed on the head of a guest at a banquet. Thus it signified both triumph and festivity.

2. *Euodia* (not *Euodias,* AV, which is a man's name) **and** *Syntyche* were two prominent women in the Philippian church who had lately begun to irritate each other. The repeated **I beseech** indicates Paul's impartiality. **Be of the same mind.** Cultivate harmony of thought and disposition (cf. 2:2). **3.** To help effect the reconciliation Paul appeals to *Syzygos,* who, true to the meaning of his name, was a **genuine yokefellow.** *Syzygos* is best understood as a proper name taken by some convert at baptism. If only an epithet, conjectures as to whom it designates run all the way from Silas to Paul's wife — Lydia? *Synēthlēsan.* **They labored** (fought) **side by side,** is a metaphor from the arena (cf. 1:27). The mention of **Clement** may be added to recall a specific occasion. The reference to **the book of life,** in which are listed the members of the heavenly commonwealth, suggests that Clement and others may have given up their lives on this occasion.

4. *Chairete* was the common expression for farewell. The addition **always** indicates that Paul had its deeper meaning, **rejoice,** in mind. The repetition suggests that conditions at Philippi were such as to make such an exhortation seem unreasonable. Christians can be commanded to rejoice, because their ground for rejoicing is not in circumstances but **in the Lord. 5.** The somewhat elusive *epieikes,* **moderation** (AV), indicates readiness to listen to reason, a yieldingness that does not retaliate. The motive for this "sweet reasonableness" is the imminent return of Christ. **The Lord is at hand.** The watchword of the early church (cf. the Aramaic equivalent, *maran atha,* in I Cor 16:22).

6. The hostility of heathendom (cf. 1:28) would give rise to anxiety. This was to be dispelled by prayer. "To care is a virtue, but to foster cares is sin" (Müller, *op. cit.,* p. 141). **In everything.** Anything sufficient to cause anxiety if not prayed about. **With thanksgiving.** Thankfulness for what God has already done is the proper spirit in which to make new requests. **7.** The **peace of God** is that tran-

8. Finally, brethren, whatsoever things are true, whatsoever things *are* honest, whatsoever things *are* just, whatsoever things *are* pure, whatsoever things *are* lovely, whatsoever things *are* of good report; if *there be* any virtue, and if *there be* any praise, think on these things.

9. Those things, which ye have both learned, and received, and heard, and seen in me, do: and the God of peace shall be with you.

10. But I rejoiced in the Lord greatly, that now at the last your care of me hath flourished again; wherein ye were also careful, but ye lacked opportunity.

quillity of spirit that God enjoys and only God can give. The phrase, **which passes all understanding,** is usually taken as indicating the utter inability of man's mind to fathom God's peace. More probably it means that God's peace far surpasses all our careful planning and clever ideas as to how we can resolve our own anxieties. **Shall keep.** *Phroureō,* "keep," is a military term meaning "to guard or garrison." With striking metaphor Paul here portrays the peace of God as a sentinel standing watch over the citadel of man's inner life — mind, will, and affections.

8. In this "paragraph on mental health" (Simcox) Paul draws up a list of virtues which might well have come from the pen of a Greek moralist. Two of the eight do not occur elsewhere in the NT, and one occurs only here in Paul's writings. **True.** Belonging to the nature of reality. **Honest.** Worthy of reverence, august. **Just.** In accordance with the loftiest conception of what is right (Michael). **Pure.** Not mixed with elements that would debase the soul. **Lovely.** That which inspires love. **Of good report.** Better than this rather tame translation is *that which has a good ring* (Michael). **If there be any virtue.** Lightfoot paraphrases, "Whatever value may reside in your old heathen conception of virtue" (p. 162), in order to stress Paul's concern not to omit any possible ground of appeal. They are to **take into account** *(logizomai;* AV, *think on)* these virtues of pagan morality. 9. In addition they are to **keep on practicing** (AV, *do;* the imperative *prassete* is present tense) all the distinctively Christian ethics and morality they have learned from the apostle's life and teaching. Not only the "peace of God" (v. 7) but also the **God of peace** will be with them.

## XV. Appreciation for the Gift. 4:10-20.

To borrow Paul's expression, **now at length** he thanks them formally for their gift. While not dependent upon the gift, or even seeking it, he rejoices in that such sacrifices are pleasing to God and beneficial for the giver.

10. If Philippians were actually a "thank you letter," we would expect words of appreciation much sooner. That they appear almost as a postscript lends plausibility to Michael's conjecture that Paul had already paid his thanks and was now clarifying some statement that had evidently caused offense (p. xxi f.; p. 209 ff.). *Anathalō,* "to cause to bloom again," pictures a tree putting on new foliage in

11. Not that I speak in respect of want: for I have learned, in whatsoever state I am, *therewith* to be content.

12. I know both how to be abased, and I know how to abound: every where and in all things I am instructed both to be full and to be hungry, both to abound and to suffer need.

13. I can do all things through Christ which strengtheneth me.

14. Notwithstanding, ye have well done, that ye did communicate with my affliction.

15. Now ye Philippians know also, that in the beginning of the gospel, when I departed from Macedonia, no church communicated with me as concerning giving and receiving, but ye only.

16. For even in Thessalonica ye sent once and again unto my necessity.

17. Not because I desire a gift: but I desire fruit that may abound to your account.

18. But I have all, and abound: I am full, having received of Epaphroditus the things which were sent from you, an odor of a sweet smell, a sacrifice acceptable, well-pleasing to God.

19. But my God shall supply all your need according to his riches in glory by Christ Jesus.

the spring. Some, to avoid what seems to be a mild reproach, understand **flourished again** as indicating recovery from a period of dire poverty. The lack of **opportunity** would then be a lack of means. However, it probably means that no one was available for the trip.

11. Paul quickly corrects any false impression that he is complaining of want. *Autarkēs.* **Content.** Better, *self-sufficient.* A favorite term of the Stoics, who conceived of man as possessing the intrinsic ability to resist all external pressures. 12. **In any and all circumstances** (no matter how distressing any one might be or how comprehensive the sum of them all) Paul had been **initiated** (a technical term in the mystery religions) into the secret of facing both lack and abundance. 13. The profound difference between Paul and the Stoics is that while they held themselves to be *self-*sufficient, Paul's sufficiency lay in Another — the One who **infuse[d]** strength in him (AV, *strengtheneth me*).

14. Nevertheless, in unitedly entering into fellowship with his misfortune, the Philippians had done a **noble thing** (*kalōs; ho kalos* is the renowned Greek concept of "the beautiful").

15. **The beginning of the gospel.** When the Gospel was first proclaimed in Macedonia. **When I departed** probably refers to a gift given at the time of departure (cf. Acts 17:14) rather than subsequently (in which case see II Cor 11:9). **Giving and receiving.** The first of several allusions to financial transactions. It may be a gentle reminder that material payment for spiritual goods is not at all out of line (cf. I Cor 9:11). 16. Almost before he was out of sight (even in Thessalonica; cf. Acts 17) they had **more than once** sent him help.

17. Again he was anxious not to leave the impression that he coveted their material help. What he really desired was "the interest that accumulates in this way to (their) divine credit" (Moffatt). Or, less technically, **fruit** may be that greater "capacity for human sympathy" (Scott in IB, XI, 126) which is the inevitable result of sacrificial living. 18. *Apechō.* Possibly, "paid in full" (so used in the papyri, MM, p. 57), or "I have all that I could wish for" — in fact, he continues, **even more.** *Osmē euōdias,* **an odor of a sweet smell,** is used frequently in the LXX for an offering pleasing to God (cf. Gen 8:21).

19. As *you* have responded to *my* needs, so *my* **God shall supply** all of yours. A tit-for-tat arrangement that offers little comfort for "close" Christians. In

20. Now unto God and our Father *be* glory for ever and ever. Amen.

21. Salute every saint in Christ Jesus. The brethren which are with me greet you.

22. All the saints salute you, chiefly they that are of Caesar's household.

23. The grace of our Lord Jesus Christ *be* with you all. Amen.

It was written to the Philippians from Rome by Epaphroditus.

glory. Either "in a glorious manner," or eschatologically, "in the glorious future age." **According to his riches.** On a scale commensurate with his wealth. **In Christ Jesus.** In union with the One who mediates God's blessings to man. **20. Unto God and our Father.** Better, *to God, even our Father!* It is the thought of God's fatherly care that gives rise to the doxology. **For ever and ever.** Literally, *unto the ages of the ages* — an endless succession of indefinite periods.

### XVI. Greetings and Benediction. 4:21-25.

**21.** Probably added by Paul's own hand (cf. Gal 6:11). **Saint.** Only here in the NT does *hagios* occur in the singular (fifty-seven times in the plural), and even here it is prefaced by **every** — a strong reminder that Christianity is essentially a corporate affair. Those whom Paul commands to do the greeting are probably the elders of the church, who would read the letter aloud to the congregation.

**22.** Both Paul's personal companions (**brethren,** v. 21) and the entire church (**all the saints**) send their greetings. **Those of Caesar's household.** Not (as formerly thought) the emperor's family, but all those employed in the service of the government. As these were not confined to Rome, the expression does not argue a Roman origin for the epistle. Synge detects a touch of humor: the English euphemism for a prisoner is "his majesty's guest" (*Torch Series,* p. 49).

**23. Grace . . . be with your spirit** (note singular). Even in the benediction the central theme of harmony reappears.

# BIBLIOGRAPHY

HERKLOTZ, H. G. G. *Epistle of St. Paul to the Philippians.* London: Lutterworth Press, 1946.

KENNEDY, H. A. "The Epistle to the Philippians," *The Expositor's Greek Testament.* Edited by W. Robertson Nicoll. Vol. III. Grand Rapids: Wm. B. Eerdmans Publishing Co., n.d.

LIGHTFOOT, J. B. *Saint Paul's Epistle to The Philippians.* London: The Macmillan Co., 1868 (12th ed., 1896).

MICHAEL, J. H. *The Epistle of Paul to the Philippians (The Moffatt New Testament Commentary).* London: Hodder and Stoughton, 1928.

MOULE, H. C. G. *The Epistle of Paul the Apostle to the Philippians (Cambridge Greek Testament for Schools and Colleges).* Cambridge: The University Press, 1897.

MULLER, J. J. *The Epistles of Paul to the Philippians and to Philemon (The New International Commentary on the New Testament).* Grand Rapids: Wm. B. Eerdmans Publishing Co., 1955.

SCOTT, E. F. *The Epistle to the Philippians (The Interpreter's Bible).* New York: Abingdon Press, 1955.

SIMCOX, C. E. *They Met at Philippi.* New York: Oxford University Press, 1958.

VINCENT, M. R. *A Critical and Exegetical Commentary on the Epistles to the Philippians and to Philemon (The International Critical Commentary).* Edinburgh: T. & T. Clarke, 1897.

Significant works published since this commentary was written:

BEARE, F. W. *The Epistle to the Philippians (Harper's New Testament Commentaries).* New York: Harper & Brothers, 1959.

HUNTER, A. M. *The Letter of Paul to the Philippians (The Layman's Bible Commentary).* Vol. 22. Richmond: John Knox Press, 1959.

MARTIN, R. P. *The Epistle of Paul to the Philippians (Tyndale New Testament Commentaries).* Grand Rapids: Wm. B. Eerdmans Publishing Co., 1959.

# THE EPISTLE
# TO THE COLOSSIANS

## INTRODUCTION

*The Occasion.* First century Colosse, an ancient but declining commercial center some hundred miles eastward from Ephesus, was situated on the Lycus Valley caravan route, near the cities of Laodicea and Hierapolis (cf. Col 4:13). Although an earlier evangelization (by the Galatian Christians?) cannot be excluded, the Colossians may have first heard the Christian message during Paul's Ephesian ministry (c. A.D. 53-56; cf. Acts 19:10).

Paul possibly passed through Colosse on his way to Ephesus, but he was personally unacquainted with the Christians there (cf. Col 2:1). His co-worker, Epaphras, who ministered to this church, visited the apostle and made known to him both the progress of the believers and an erroneous teaching that was subverting them.

Jews had been resident in this province of Phrygia for two centuries (Jos *Antiquities* 12. 147). Evidently less than orthodox, they receive this comment in the Talmud: "The wines and baths of Phrygia had separated the ten tribes from their brethren" (Shabbath, 147b). The accommodation to Gentile practices left its mark on Jews embracing Christianity. In the bordering province of Galatia the infant faith was threatened by legalism, a Judaizing heresy; here, as in Ephesus (cf. Acts 19:14,18), the danger lay in a Jewish-Hellenistic religious syncretism. To meet the former situation Paul had earlier addressed an epistle to the Galatians; to meet the equally grave peril in Colosse he wrote the present letter.

*The Heresy at Colosse.* In the church of the second century there appeared a heretical movement known as Gnosticism. Some of its basic principles were already known in the first century, not only in the Christian church but in the Judaism of the Diaspora as well (cf. R. McL. Wilson, *The Gnostic Problem;* C. H. Dodd, *The Interpretation of the Fourth Gospel,* p. 97 ff.; Rudolf Bultmann, "Gnosis," *Bible Keywords,* II). This incipient Gnosticism was more a religio-philosophical attitude and tendency than a system, and it could adapt itself to Jewish, Christian, or pagan groups as the occasion required. Nevertheless, certain ideas appear to be generally characteristic of the Gnostic mind: metaphysical dualism, mediating beings, redemption through knowledge or *gnōsis*. All religions, Gnostics held, which are manifestations of one hidden verity, seek to bring men to a knowledge of the truth. This knowledge or *gnōsis* is not intellectual apprehension but the enlightenment derived from mystical experience. Because man is bound in the world of evil matter, he can approach God only through mediating angelic beings. By the aid of these powers and through allegorical and mythical interpretations of the sacred writings, spiritual enlightenment can be achieved and one's redemption from the world of sin and matter be assured.

Naturally and perhaps inevitably some in the early church sought to enrich or accommodate their faith to current religious ideas; converts with an imperfect grasp of Christianity may unconsciously have merged earlier beliefs with Christian concepts. This may well have been the origin of the Gnostic influences that appeared in a number of the Pauline churches. In Corinth, for example, the desire for speculative wisdom (I Cor 1:7 ff.) and the disregard for the body (reflected in the denial of resurrection, in asceticism, and in sexual license; cf. I Cor 15:5,7), represent a Gnostic attitude.

The Colossian heresy combined Jewish and Hellenistic elements. Dietary and Sabbath observances, circumcision rites, and probably the mediatorial function of angels are reminiscent of Jewish practice and belief (Col 2:11,16,18); the emphasis on "wisdom" and "knowledge," the *plērōma* of cosmic powers, and the abasement of the body reflect Greek thought (2:3,8,23). Some Jewish converts probably brought this mixture from a heterodox Judaism and developed it further after they became Christians. In a strategy used elsewhere, Paul takes the terminology of the errorists to attack their teaching and, in the process, develops the doctrine of the 'cosmic Christ.' In Christ, the one mediator, dwells all wisdom and knowledge; in his death and resurrection all powers of the cosmos are defeated and subjected to himself (2:3,9,10,15). Any teaching which detracts from the centrality of Christ under the pretense of leading men to maturity and perfection is a perversion that threatens the very essence of the faith. The apostle thus identifies and exposes the root of the error at Colosse.

*Origin and Date.* Colossians, like Ephesians, Philippians, and Philemon, was written from prison and was delivered with the Epistle to Philemon and (possibly) Ephesians by Tychicus and Onesimus (4:3, 7-9; Phm 12; Eph 6:12). The mass of early tradition fixes its origin in Rome during the imprisonment of Acts 28 (c. A.D. 61–63). Although this view remains dominant, a number of scholars suggest that earlier imprisonments in Caesarea (c. A.D. 58-60) or Ephesus (c. A.D. 55/56) offer a more likely occasion for the writings. Caesarea has few advocates today, but the Ephesian imprisonment theory has attracted considerable attention. It has been most recently argued by G. S. Duncan *(St. Paul's Ephesian Ministry)*, who points out that: (1) Second Corinthians (6:5; 11:23), written at the close of the Ephesian ministry, indicates that Paul had been in prison a number of times unmentioned in Acts; if I Cor 15:32 is interpreted literally, as seems most reasonable, at least one of these imprisonments occurred in Ephesus. (2) The visit of Epaphras (Col 1:7; 4:12) and the presence of the runaway slave Onesimus are more in keeping with an Ephesian setting than with far distant Rome. (3) Paul plans a visit to the Lycus Valley upon his release (Phm 22), but according to tradition Paul proceeded westward to Spain after the Roman imprisonment (cf. Rom 15:24). Duncan's arguments have been more persuasive in the case of Philippians, but the view remains a live option for the other Prison Epistles as well. Those continuing to favor the Roman origin consider the arguments for other cities given above as inconclusive, and point to the weight of early tradition and to a more developed theology (especially) in Colossians and Ephesians. Could it have been propounded at such an early date as the Ephesian ministry?

*Authorship.* The Pauline authorship continues to be denied in some quarters, but the majority opinion is in the other direction. A few students, influenced by the fact that one-fourth of Colossians is found in Ephesians, have viewed the former as an expanded version of genuine Pauline correspondence. The relation between the two letters, however, is adequately and most easily explained as the—conscious or unconscious—working of the mind of the apostle himself as he writes upon similar themes.

Chief objections to Pauline authorship have been these: (1) The thought and emphasis of the letter do not conform to that of Romans, Corinthians, and Galatians; (2) The Colossian heresy could not possibly have developed so quickly. It is a mistake, however, to approach Paul as if his mind were in a strait jacket; changed circumstances offer a satisfactory answer for the change of theme and vocabulary. Recent investigations have shown quite conclusively that Gnosticism, at least in the incipient form appearing in Colossians, was already a potent force in the first century. The unanimous and early voice of church tradition joins the majority of present-day scholars in affirming the genuineness of the letter; one may place considerable confidence in this verdict.

*Themes and Development of Thought.* The structure of the epistle follows the familiar Pauline pattern, in which a doctrinal section (what to believe) is followed by an exhortation (how to act). In opposing false teaching, Paul emphasizes the exalted nature of the lordship of Jesus Christ and its significance for those who have been joined to Him. As lord of creation, Jesus embodies the fullness of deity; as head of the Church and reconciler of his people, he effectively mediates in his person the redemptive relation of man to God (Col 1:15-22; 2:9). To establish the sole sufficiency of Jesus as Lord and Redeemer (in opposition to the Gnostic substitution of redeeming disciplines and a *plērōma*, or plenitude, of mediating powers), Paul stresses both aspects of Christ's character.

Important in this regard is the concept of the 'Body of Christ,' with which the Colossians undoubtedly were familiar (1:18,24; 2:17; 3:15). This mysterious and unique relationship, which is exclusive of every other, makes anathema any belief or practice that displaces the centrality of Jesus as Redeemer and Perfecter of his people. The 'Body of Christ' is a motif deeply embedded in the substructure of New Testament theology. Some have sought its origin in the thought of Paul, but probably its roots lie in the teaching of the Lord himself (cf. Mk 14:58; Jn 2:19-22; E. E. Ellis, *Paul's Use of the Old Testament*, p. 92). Members of a community conceived of as parts of a body was a metaphor not unknown in the Greek world, e.g., among the Stoics. Paul's use of the figure, however, goes beyond mere metaphor and is to be understood in the framework of the ancient and realistic Hebrew concept of corporate solidarity (see R. P. Shedd, *Man in Community*).

In I Cor 12:12-21 the 'body' (of Christ) is pictured as including the 'head'. Hence a Christian can be described as an eye or an ear as well as a hand. In Colossians and Ephesians, where *Christ* is described as the 'head' of the body, the image, at first, appears to be substantially altered. If so, the diverse imagery is an accommodation to the apostle's desire to emphasize in these epistles the intimate relation of Christ to His people and not simply a longtime development of his earlier concept. In the complex of images Paul uses, each must be understood within its own framework and "a single over-all conceptual analysis will be about as useful for the interpretation of the apostle's writings as a bulldozer for the cultivation of a miniature landscape garden" (A. Farrar, *The Glass of Vision*, p. 45).

It is probable, however, that the divine Head is not a variant image of the 'Body' at all, but rather a complementary image. The concept of Christ as the head (*kephalē*) of the Church is analogous to that of I Cor 11:3: "Christ is the head of every man." More specifically: "The husband is the head of the wife, even as Christ is the head of the church: . . . he is the saviour of the body" (Eph 5:23). The 'head' imagery, as it relates to Christ and the Church, is to be understood in terms of the husband-wife analogy. It expresses Christ's union with the Church, for the husband and wife are 'one flesh.' But, more importantly, it pictures Christ's distinction from, his authority over, and his redemption of

his body, the Church (cf. Col 2:10). The definition of the Church as the extension of the Incarnation does not reflect sufficiently this aspect of the Pauline imagery.

In the Pauline writings the Christian's relation to the new age is viewed both as a past event and as a future hope. In the past, Christians were crucified with Christ, raised to new life, translated into his kingdom, glorified, and made to sit with him in heaven (Eph 2:5-7; Col 1:13; 2:11-13; Rom 8:30). Yet Paul, toward the end of his life, expressed his yearning to "know him, and the power of his resurrection, and the fellowship of his sufferings, being made conformable unto his death; if by any means I might attain unto the resurrection of the dead" (Phil 3:10-14). The meaning of these different chronological perspectives, and their relationship, is of central importance for understanding Paul's thought-world (cf. E. E. Ellis, *Paul and His Recent Interpreters*, pp. 37-40). Briefly, we may suggest that the concept of the 'Body of Christ' provides a clue to their meaning. When Paul speaks of Christians having died and risen to new life, he speaks of a corporate reality experienced by Jesus Christ individually in A.D. 30, but mediated to the Christian corporately by the indwelling Spirit. Having been incorporated into Christ's body and destined to be conformed individually to Christ's image, the Christian is now to actualize in his individual life the "in Christ" life into which he has been brought. While the self in its mortality will "put on immortality" only at the *parousia*, the Lord's return, (I Cor 15:51-54), the self in its ethical and psychological expression begins to actualize the new-age realities in the present life: "If ye be dead with Christ . . . why . . . are ye subject to ordinances?" "If ye then be risen with Christ, seek those things which are above." "Ye have put off the old man . . . and have put on the new. . . . Put on therefore kindness . . . " (Col 2:20; 3:1,9,10). The character and mind of Christ and, in the resurrection, his immortal life are to be realized in his Body. Within this framework Paul's 'exhortation' is seen to be intimately related to his theological teaching.

# OUTLINE

I. Introduction. 1:1,2.
II. The nature of Christ's lordship. 1:3—2:7.
   A. Thanksgiving for the Colossians' faith in Christ. 1:3-8.
   B. Prayer for their growth in Christ. 1:9-14.
   C. Christ as Lord. 1:15-19.
      1. Lord of creation. 1:15-17.
      2. Lord of the new creation. 1:18,19.
   D. Christ as God's reconciler. 1:20-23.
      1. Reconciler of all things. 1:20.
      2. Reconciler of the Colossian Christians. 1:21-23.
   E. Paul: Christ's minister of reconciliation. 1:24-29.
      1. Sharer of Christ's sufferings. 1:24.
      2. Proclaimer of the Christian mystery. 1:25-27.
      3. Instructor of the saints. 1:28,29.
   F. Paul's concern for the Lycus Valley Christians. 2:1-7.
III. Christ's lordship and the false teaching at Colosse. 2:8—3:4.
   A. The sole sufficiency of Christ. 2:8-15.
      1. Christ: Lord of every power and authority. 2:8-10.
      2. Christ: Source of the Christian's new life. 2:11-14.
      3. Christ: Conqueror of all cosmic powers. 2:15.
   B. The Colossians' practices as a denial of Christ's lordship. 2:16-19.
      1. Fixation upon ritual, a retreat into the old age. 2:16,17.
      2. Subservience to angelic powers, a departure from Christ. 2:18,19.
   C. The Colossians' practices as a contradiction of their corporate life in Christ. 2:20—3:4.
      1. Death with Christ means death to the regulations of the old age. 2:20—23.
      2. Resurrection with Christ demands a "new-age" world and life view 3:1-4.
IV. Christ's lordship in the Christian life. 3:5—4:6.
   A. The Christian imperative: Actualize individually the 'in Christ' reality. 3:5-17.
      1. The character of the old age to be put off. 3:5-9.
      2. The character of the new age to be put on. 3:10-17.
   B. Special precepts. 3:18—4:6.
      1. The Christian home. 3:18—4:1.
      2. Prayer. 4:2-4.
      3. Relation to non-Christians. 4:5,6.
V. Conclusion. 4:7-18.
   A. Commendation of the bearers of the letter. 4:7-9.
   B. Greetings from Paul's co-workers. 4:10-14.
   C. The apostle's greetings and blessings. 4:15-18.

# COLOSSIANS

## CHAPTER 1

PAUL, an apostle of Jesus Christ by the will of God, and Timotheus *our* brother,

# COMMENTARY

## I. Introduction. 1:1,2.

1. As in a number of other letters—II Corinthians, Philippians, I and II Thessalonians, Philemon—Paul associates Timothy in the salutation of Colossians, but he reserves to himself the title **apostle.** This term conveys the ideas of mission, authorization, and responsibility. And its NT meaning probably is to be derived from the Hebrew word *shālah,* "to send." (See J. B. Lightfoot, *St. Paul's Epistle to the Galatians,* p. 92 ff.; R. H. Rengsdorf, "Apostleship," *Bible Keywords II,* ed. J. R. Coates.) The substantive *shāliah,* a virtual equivalent of the NT word "apostle," is not uncommon in rabbinical writings. It was primarily a legal term, signifying authorized representation. As in the modern law of agency, the one sent was held to be equivalent to the sender himself. To dishonor the king's ambassador was to dishonor the king (II Sam 10; cf. I Sam 25:5-10,39-42). Although the term, **apostle of Jesus Christ,** has other secondary usages (Phil 2:25; II Cor 8:23), it appears to apply primarily to those directly commissioned as apostles by the risen Lord (cf. I Cor 9:1; 15:8-10). Thus Paul exercised the function of an apostle **by the will of God.**

2. To the saints and faithful brethren in Christ which are at Colosse: Grace be unto you, and peace, from God our Father and the Lord Jesus Christ.

3. We give thanks to God and the Father of our Lord Jesus Christ, praying always for you,

4. Since we heard of your faith in Christ Jesus, and of the love *which ye have* to all the saints,

5. For the hope which is laid up for you in heaven, whereof ye heard before in the word of the truth of the gospel;

6. Which is come unto you, as *it is* in all the world; and bringeth forth fruit, as *it doth* also in you, since the day ye heard *of it*, and knew the grace of God in truth:

7. As ye also learned of Epaphras our dear fellow servant, who is for you a faithful minister of Christ;

8. Who also declared unto us your love in the Spirit.

2. All Christians are saints or holy by virtue of their relation to God in Christ; the use of the appellation for a particularly devout person is a later development. Paul uses the ancient Hebrew greeting, peace, but alters the customary Greek *chaire,* "hail," to *charis,* grace, giving the phrase a distinctively Christian ring.

## II. The Nature of Christ's Lordship. 1:3–2:7.

A. Thanksgiving for the Colossians' Faith in Christ. 1:3-8.

An ancient Greek letter opens:

Apion to Epimachus his Father and Lord, many greetings *(chairein).* Before all things I pray that thou art in health, and that thou dost prosper and fare well continually. . . . I thank the Lord Serapis that, when I was in peril in the sea, he saved me immediately. . . . (Deiss, LAE, p. 169).

In opening his letters (except Galatians) with a thanksgiving, Paul follows this literary custom, but he significantly alters the content.

3-6. Paul gives thanks for the triad of graces present among the Colossians. Their faith Christward (and in the 'Christ sphere'), which lies in the past, and their love manward, manifest in the present, have for their foundation the hope that is to be actualized in the future. By hope Christ himself may be meant (cf. 1:27). The three go together: If we have hope only in this life, we are to be pitied (I Cor 15:19), but if our hope resides in heaven, where the new age is actualized in the person of Christ, it will manifest itself in love and bring forth fruit in the present world (cf. Col 1:13; 3:14; Eph 6:12; Mk 4:20).

7. Only here does Paul designate a co-worker as a fellow slave (Gr. *sundoulos*) of Christ; this also may be the sense of "fellow prisoner" in 4:10. Epaphras, the minister or deacon *(diakonos)* of the Colossians may have been the organizer of this Lycus Valley church. Doubtless the apostle had learned from him about the errors threatening the Christians there, as well as about their love for Paul in the Spirit. The latter probably refers to the sphere of the Spirit or new age, although *spiritual love* and *love from the Spirit* are possible translations (cf. Rom 8:9; Eph 1:3).

B. Prayer for Their Growth in Christ. 1:9-14.

The prayers of Paul not only provide

9. For this cause we also, since the day we heard *it*, do not cease to pray for you, and to desire that ye might be filled with the knowledge of his will in all wisdom and spiritual understanding;

10. That ye might walk worthy of the Lord unto all pleasing, being fruitful in every good work, and increasing in the knowledge of God;

11. Strengthened with all might, according to his glorious power, unto all patience and long-suffering with joyfulness;

12. Giving thanks unto the Father, which hath made us meet to be partakers of the inheritance of the saints in light:

13. Who hath delivered us from the power of darkness, and hath translated *us* into the kingdom of his dear Son:

rare insight into the apostle's faith; they offer valuable lessons for all concerning the meaning of Christian prayer. When compared with the Lord's Prayer, they provide an index to the way Christ's instruction, "after this manner pray ye" (Mt 6:9), was applied in the early church. After the initial thanksgiving, Paul begins a petition that merges into thanksgiving as the prayer moves into a paean of praise to the exalted Christ.

9,10. Pray. See on 4:2. C. Masson (*L' Epître de Saint Paul aux Colossiens*) suggests that **filled with the knowledge** (*epignōsis*) should be understood as "mature with regard to knowledge." There is probably a subtle contrast here with the knowledge (*gnōsis*) of the Gnosticizing advocates: Paul emphasizes neither an abstract intellectualism nor an occult experience of the 'powers,' but a thorough knowledge (*epignōsis*) of God's will in accordance with wisdom (*sophia;* cf. I Cor 1:24-30) and perception. Although in using these terms the apostle may have been influenced by the vocabulary of his opponents, he turns the meaning of the words against the false teachers. He prays that the Colossians may undergo God's psychiatric therapy, which will transform their world and life view (cf. Rom 12:1,2). A mental transformation is prerequisite to, and the basis for, ethical renewal; in turn, as they are **fruitful in every good work,** their **knowledge of God** will be further augmented.

11. To intensify a concept, the apostle reiterates: **Strengthened . . . might . . . power.** At work in the Christian is no less than the power of Almighty God himself, not at present to exalt, but to give **patience,** fortitude, and endurance. The Stoic philosophers also enjoined these virtues but, like the traditional poker-faced Indian, coupled them with an attitude of complete detachment. Paul means hopeful waiting and suffering with **joyfulness.** This is the Christian distinctive! Joy not rooted in the soil of suffering is shallow (C. F. D. Moule, *The Epistles of Paul the Apostle to the Colossians and to Philemon*).

12-14. God's power has **made us meet** (AV), that is, *qualified us* (RSV), **to be partakers,** i.e., has empowered us (MM) and made us worthy. **Light** and **darkness** are common theological terms used in many religions, and found most recently in the Dead Sea Scrolls. Here Paul seems to be contrasting the realm or sphere of the new age — **light,** with

**14. In whom we have redemption through his blood, *even* the forgiveness of sins:**

that of the present age, the evil sphere or authority *(exousia)* of **darkness.** Elsewhere this evil sphere is equated with the power of Satan (cf. 2:15; Lk 22:53; Acts 26:18; Eph 2:2).

These verses, which posit a past deliverance and transference into Christ's **kingdom** and a redemption which Christians **have** as a present possession, are the hallmarks of 'realized eschatology,' i.e., that the new age arrived with Christ's resurrection and that Christians enter it at conversion. The relation of the realized kingdom and the future kingdom has been long debated and variously understood. Are they mutually exclusive concepts representing stages of doctrinal development in the minds of NT writers? Since virtually all strata of the NT literature contain both concepts, this solution appears to be forced. Is the present aspect of the kingdom a partial realization of the future fulfillment? Paul seems to regard Christians to be fully within the sphere of the new age in their corporate status in Christ, which is mediated to individuals by the Holy Spirit; the new-age sphere of being, however, will become fully actualized individually only at the parousia, i.e., Christ's return. (See Introduction.)

In later Gnosticism a distinction was made between forgiveness, as an initial stage, and redemption, as the escape of the soul to immortal realms. Paul here speaks of **redemption** which effects the forgiveness of sins. (See Leon Morris, *The Apostolic Preaching of the Cross,* p. 43.)

C. Christ as Lord. 1:15-19.

The startling aspect of the ascriptions in this passage is their application to a young Jew who was executed as a criminal only thirty years previously. Jesus Christ is pictured in phrases reminiscent of the divine Wisdom in the OT (cf. Prov 8:22-30; Ps 33:6), in inter-Testamental literature, and in similar NT passages (cf. Jn 1:1; I Cor 1:30; Heb 1:1 ff.). Here Jesus' not merely mediates the creation but is the goal of the whole created order. The awesomeness of this stark contrast is captured by the one who wrote:

Who is He on yonder tree
   Dies in grief and agony?
'Tis the Lord! O wondrous story!
   'Tis the Lord, the King of Glory!
At His feet we humbly fall;
   Crown Him! Crown Him Lord
   of all!

**15.** Who is the image of the invisible God, the firstborn of every creature:

**16.** For by him were all things created, that are in heaven, and that are in earth, visible and invisible, whether *they be* thrones, or dominions, or principalities, or powers: all things were created by him, and for him:

**17.** And he is before all things, and by him all things consist:

**18.** And he is the head of the body, the church: who is the beginning, the firstborn from the dead; that in all things he might have the preeminence.

**19.** For it pleased *the Father* that in him should all fulness dwell;

**15-17. Image** of God reflects upon the Adam-Christ typology (cf. Gen 1:27; Ps 8; Heb 2:5-18), in which Christ is viewed as the first true man who fulfills God's design in creation. Thus to be in the image of Christ is the goal of all Christians (cf. Rom 8:28; I Cor 11:7; 15:49; II Cor 3:18; 4:4; Col 3:10). The divine Son, however, is the archetype, the effluence of God's glory and not, as other men, its reflection (Heb 1:3). It is because man "bears the image of his creator that it was possible for the Son of God to become incarnate as man and in his humanity to display the glory of the invisible God" (Bruce in *The Epistles to the Ephesians and the Colossians* by E. K. Simpson and F. F. Bruce).

**Firstborn** (prōtotokos) was interpreted by the Arians to mean "first of a kind," i.e., Christ was the first creature. The word can have this meaning (cf. Rom 8:29); but such a reading is not consistent with Paul's theme, which here stresses a Messianic priority and primacy (cf. Ps 89:27): Christ is 'chief' because **in him** (RSV) — the sphere of his domain or perhaps through his instrumentality—the created order came into being (cf. Jn 1:3; Heb 1:2), and **for him** it exists. Whatever cosmic **powers** there may be, they have nothing to offer or deny a Christian; in Christ he has all things (cf. Rom 8:38; Eph 1:10).

**18.** The terms **head, beginning, firstborn,** express the pre-eminence of Christ in the new creation, which has its birth in his resurrection (I Cor 15:22; Rev 1:5; 3:14). Although the **head** as *locus* of control of the body was not unknown to first century medical writers, the OT meaning of "chief" or "origin" is the sense of the word here. As the **body** of Christ (not 'body of Christians') the **church** is not merely a 'society' but is defined in terms of its organic communion with Christ (see Introduction).

**19.** As the present cosmos was created in and through Christ, so also is the new creation. Both are inclusive, in Paul's mind, of far more than mankind (cf. Rom 8:22,23). Yet the **fulness** (*plērōma*) of all dwells in Christ. It has been suggested that *plērōma* means here, as in later Gnostic usage, the totality of cosmic powers who mediate redemption to men; all these, says Paul, in opposition to the Gnostic teaching, belong to and reside in Christ. In view of the use of the Greek word in the LXX and elsewhere in Paul's writings, however, this technical meaning is unlikely. The proper interpretation is in-

**20.** And, having made peace through the blood of his cross, by him to reconcile all things unto himself; by him, *I say,* whether *they be* things in earth, or things in heaven.

**21.** And you, that were sometime alienated and enemies in *your* mind by wicked works, yet now hath he reconciled

**22.** In the body of his flesh through death, to present you holy and unblamable and unreprovable in his sight:

**23.** If ye continue in the faith grounded and settled, and *be* not moved away from the hope of the gospel, which ye have heard, *and* which was preached to every creature which is under heaven; whereof I Paul am made a minister;

**24.** Who now rejoice in my sufferings for you, and fill up that which is behind of the afflictions of Christ in my flesh for his body's sake, which is the church:

dicated in Col 2:9, where *plērōma* can only mean the fullness of the powers and attributes of God. In this book Christ is regarded as containing and representing all that God is. Moreover, fulness, as "image" (cf. 1:15), is predicated elsewhere of Christians in view of their final glorified state in Christ (Eph 3:19; 4:12,13; cf. Jn 17:22,23).

D. Christ as God's Reconciler. 1:20-23.

**20.** In Eph 2:14-18 Paul views the peace effected by Christ's **blood** sacrifice as encompassing and unifying Jew and Gentile. Here it is primarily mankind and **all things** in the cosmos (cf. Isa 11:6-9; Rom 8:19-23) that are in view. The fact that God through Christ will **reconcile** the universe was equated by Origen (on Jn 1:35) with universal redemption. Whether the meaning here is "reconciled to God" or (more **probably**) "reconciled in Christ," that is, brought into a unity that has its goal in Christ, is not certain (cf. Arndt). But Origen's view scarcely does justice to the Pauline teaching (and that of the NT generally) concerning the judgment of God. The Colossians were reconciled through redemption, but Col 2:15 suggests that other evil beings and powers are 'reconciled' through defeat and destruction (cf. I Cor 15:24-28). For some the cross is "a savour of death unto death" (II Cor 2:16).

**22,23. Body of his flesh** and **present** have sacrificial connotations (cf. Rom 12:1,2) and accent the believer's identity with Christ in his death. **If ye continue.** Here is the "proof of the pudding." Paul addresses his hearers as Christians but always recognizes 'existential' factors which prevent any complacency even for himself (cf. I Cor 9:27; II Cor 13:5). For the apostle, assurance always had to be present tense. And, while God's election is not vacillating, it can be affirmed only in terms of profession (cf. Rom 10:9), conduct (cf. I Cor 6:9), and the witness of the Spirit (cf. Rom 8:9). **To every creature** (*ktisis*) may be a reference, as the context would admit, to the cosmic scope of the proclamation (cf. II Pet 3:9). If Paul is here speaking of the Roman citizenry, he may be allowed a hyperbole inevitable to a "born" evangelist.

E. Paul: Christ's Minister of Reconciliation. 1:24-29.

**24.** Earlier Paul prayed that the Colossians might endure with joyfulness (1:11);

**25.** Whereof I am made a minister, according to the dispensation of God which is given to me for you, to fulfil the word of God;

**26.** *Even* the mystery which hath been hid from ages and from generations, but now is made manifest to his saints:

**27.** To whom God would make known what *is* the riches of the glory of this mystery among the Gentiles; which is Christ in you, the hope of glory:

**28.** Whom we preach, warning every man, and teaching every man in all wisdom; that we may present every man perfect in Christ Jesus:

he now affirms this as his own experience. The striking concept that Paul's sufferings *(pathēma),* borne on behalf of the Colossians, **complete what is lacking** (RSV) in Christ's **afflictions** *(thlipsis)* is not limited to this passage (cf. II Cor 1:5-7; 4:12; 13:4; Phil 3:10; I Pet 4:13; 5:9; Rev 1:9). This idea is to be understood from the standpoint of the Hebrew concept of corporate personality illustrated in Jesus' graphic statement concerning his **church,** "Why persecutest thou *me?"* (Acts 9:4). And some interpret Col 1:24 to mean that in God's purpose the corporate Christ, the Messianic community, is destined to suffer a quota of 'birth pangs' in bringing in the Messianic age. Probably more central is the idea that union with Christ involves *ipso facto* union with Christ's sufferings: "If we suffer with him, we shall be glorified with him" (Rom 8:17). The corporate "in Christ" reality (Gal 2:20) is to be actualized in individual Christians; thus Paul can speak even of his own death as a sacrifice (Phil 2:17; II Tim 4:6). It is to be noted, however, that in this context, as elsewhere, the sole redemptive sufficiency is in Christ and his atonement. Christians share Christ's sufferings because they have been redeemed, not as an aid to their redemption. (Thus, in the imitation of Christ, stressed by Anabaptists, "the crown of thorns stands over the crown of glory." See Robert Friedmann, "Conception of the Anabaptists," *Church History,* IX (1940), 358; cf. Walther von Loewenich, *Luthers Theologia Crucis;* Dietrich Bonhoeffer, *The Cost of Discipleship;* Elisabeth Elliot, *Through Gates of Splendor).*

**25-27.** Paul's dispensation or assignment in God's redemptive plan was, specifically, to make salvation known to the **Gentiles.** In the world of the first century **mystery** *(mystērion)* meant (1) something mysterious, (2) an initiatory religious rite, (3) a secret known only by divine revelation (Dan 2:28-30,47). The broad Pauline usage falls into the last category (cf. I Cor 15:51; Eph 5:32; II Thess 2:7). But in relation to God's redemptive plan, the mystery is the corporate union with Christ, **Christ in you,** by which God gives righteousness and salvation. In Ephesians (3:6) the focus is upon the inclusion of the Gentiles in the Body, and this aspect of the mystery is not absent here.

**28,29.** The 'doctor of souls' has a **warning** and **teaching** ministry, not self-centered but patient-centered. Paul's goal was to **present every man perfect** *(teleios)* or

29. Whereunto I also labor, striving according to his working, which worketh in me mightily.

## CHAPTER 2

FOR I would that ye knew what great conflict I have for you, and *for* them at Laodicea, and *for* as many as have not seen my face in the flesh;

2. That their hearts might be comforted, being knit together in love, and unto all riches of the full assurance of understanding, to the acknowledgment of the mystery of God, and of the Father, and of Christ;

3. In whom are hid all the treasures of wisdom and knowledge.

4. And this I say, lest any man should beguile you with enticing words.

5. For though I be absent in the flesh, yet am I with you in the spirit, joying and beholding your order, and the steadfastness of your faith in Christ.

6. As ye have therefore received Christ Jesus the Lord, *so* walk ye in him:

7. Rooted and built up in him, and stablished in the faith, as ye have been taught, abounding therein with thanksgiving.

mature in Christ, always striving but also recognizing that the power is His who worketh in me (Phil 2:12,13).

F. Paul's Concern for the Lycus Valley Christians. 2:1-7.

Like *teleios* above, several words here – mystery, wisdom, knowledge, head (v. 10), dear to the Gnostics, are turned into effective instruments of Christian truth. This transition section moves from a presentation of Christ's Lordship to an attack upon the insidious doctrines which were endangering that Lordship in the Colossian church.

1-3. The conflict. The picture suggested by the Greek is drawn from an athletic contest. The word primarily describes, as does the verse above, the apostle's spiritual warfare in prayer against principalities and powers (cf. Eph 6:12). Paul did not command fire to come down in judgment (Lk 9:54) but, positively, prayed that the *Colossians* and *Laodiceans*, who apparently were threatened with the same heresy, might be comforted (v. 2), i.e., strengthened, through exhortation, by ethical renewal (love) and spiritual apprehension (understanding). Orthodoxy without love is sterile, and love apart from truth becomes "mush"; but together they issue in spiritual apprehension, knowledge of the mystery of God. If there is a secret, Paul says, Christ is it – Christ as the embodiment of God's wisdom (Moule, *op. cit.*), Christ as the sole mediator of God's gifts to men (cf. Prov 2:3-9).

4-7. As a member of Christ's body present with them in the spirit, Paul now makes clear the purpose of the preceding comments. He fears that enticing words, i.e., persuasive reasoning (*pithanologia*), will disrupt their order and stedfastness. These paired words are military terms conveying the thought of an enemy breeching a formerly solid formation of troops. The errorists' appeal to philosophy and wisdom (cf. 2:8,23), is an approach not entirely unknown in the present day. Paul did not answer false reasoning with obscurantism nor with a command to believers to shut their ears, but with a reasoned appeal to them to return to that positive Christ-centered tradition through which they had received the Gospel (cf. 2:8). From this starting point the emptiness of the Gnostic reasoning would become apparent to them.

III. Christ's Lordship and the False Teaching at Colosse. 2:8–3:4.

**8.** Beware lest any man spoil you through philosophy and vain deceit, after the tradition of men, after the rudiments of the world, and not after Christ.

**9.** For in him dwelleth all the fulness of the Godhead bodily.

**10.** And ye are complete in him, which is the head of all principality and power:

**11.** In whom also ye are circumcised with the circumcision made without hands, in putting off the body of the sins of the flesh by the circumcision of Christ:

**12.** Buried with him in baptism, wherein also ye are risen with *him* through the faith of the operation of God, who hath raised him from the dead.

A. The Sole Sufficiency of Christ. 2: 8-15.

The apostle begins his argument with a reassertion of the uniqueness of Christ and of the believer's relation to Him. As the head and conqueror of every authority and as the very sphere of the Christian's new-age existence, Christ's place in the Christian life is all-inclusive, and it is exclusive of all others.

**8.** The Colossian heresy was a "philosophy" after the tradition (*paradosis*) of men and rudiments of the cosmos (cf. 2:20). Paul does not condemn tradition in itself but rather contrasts with this heresy the tradition after Christ, which the Colossians had received (2:7). There is then a proper tradition — to which the apostle elsewhere expresses indebtedness (e.g., Rom 6:17; I Cor 11:2,23; 15:3; Phil 4:9) — the essence of which lies in its apostolicity (see on Col 1:1). Apostolic tradition has the status of revelation, for in it the exalted Christ himself speaks through his authorized representatives (cf. Oscar Cullmann, "Tradition," *The Early Church*, pp. 59-99).

**9,10.** The Greek word for **Godhead** or *deity* is the abstract noun for God (Arndt) and includes not only the divine attributes but also the divine nature (Beng). Opposing the Docetic idea that matter is evil is the Biblical assertion that deity itself has been manifest in **bodily** (*sōmatikōs*) or material reality (Lightfoot; cf. Jn 1:14). Others (e.g., Moule) interpret *sōmatikōs* to mean: (1) one organism of Christ in contrast to the multitudinous *plērōma* of cosmic powers; or, less probably, (2) the Body of Christ, i.e., the Church. The fullness (*plērōma;* cf. note on 1:19) that inheres in Christ infuses those in union with him so as to **complete** (**peplērōmenoi**) them or bring them to fullness (cf. Eph 1:23). Union with Christ alone is sufficient, for he is **head** of all other authorities; they can add nothing to holiness or to redemption.

**11,12.** In the NT **made without hands** is a quasi-technical term used of corporate new-age realities in contrast to the institutions and rituals of the old covenant. It refers most often to the Church as God's true temple brought into being in Christ's death and resurrection (Mk 14:58; Jn 2:19-22; Acts 7:48; II Cor 5:1; Heb 9:11, 24). Here it identifies Christ's death and resurrection as the true **circumcision** (cf. Phil 3:3), in which Christians, as Christ's Body, participated. Both concepts are, for Paul, expressions of **the corporate reality** implicit in the Christian's **faith** — union

**13.** And you, being dead in your sins and the uncircumcision of your flesh, hath he quickened together with him, having forgiven you all trespasses;

**14.** Blotting out the handwriting of ordinances that was against us, which was contrary to us, and took it out of the way, nailing it to his cross;

**15.** *And* having spoiled principalities and powers, he made a show of them openly, triumphing over them in it.

with the Saviour's death and resurrection. (see Introduction). **Putting off the body of flesh** (RSV). See on 2:15. **Baptism** may refer primarily to Christ's baptism of death (cf. Mk 10:38; Lk 12:50), although Christian baptism is not to be excluded (cf. Rom 6:4). There is no direct analogy between Christian baptism and the 'old age' rite of circumcision. Circumcision here is the death of Christ, by which he wrought severance from the old age, cleansing of sin, and reconciliation to God (cf. Deut 30:6; Jer 4:4; 9:25,26). It is to this that Christian baptism is to be related.

**13.** For the Gentiles the figure of Christ's death as circumcision had particular significance: their former alienation from the people of God was symbolized in their literal **uncircumcision** (cf. Eph 2:11). However, the use here of **flesh**, i.e., man under sin, to indicate a moral uncircumcision is possible. Resurrection, viewed as a corporate action **together with Christ**, finds its realization through God's gracious forgiveness (cf. Eph 2:1-10).

**14.** A **handwriting** is a certificate of debt (Deiss, BS, p. 247) and presumably refers to the written Mosaic law. For Gentiles it may include also the law to which their consciences assent (cf. Rom 2:14,15; Ex 24:3; Eph 2:15). This obligation which, unfulfilled, stood **against us** was discharged on **his cross.**

**15.** **Spoiled,** or better, *stripped (apekdyomai)* is a compound not essentially different from another Pauline expression, *ekdyō.* The latter, as used in the LXX (and classical Greek) of the defeating or "stripping" of enemies in war, provides a clue to the meaning here.

In OT times captives were stripped of most or all clothing. This action came to symbolize defeat, and for the prophets it signified the judgment of God (cf. Ezk 16:39; 23:26). In the NT this idea moves into the realm of 'last things,' when the righteous will be clothed, in contrast to the wicked, who will stand stripped and naked under God's judgment (cf. Mt 22:11; Rev 3:17,18; 16:15; II Cor 5:3,4). The present verse, picturing Christ as "stripping" **principalities and powers** through his death and resurrection, probably refers, on one hand, to angelic powers (through whom the **handwriting of ordinances** had been given, Gal 3:19) who control human rulers, and on the other hand, to such personified evils as death. Christ died, "that through death he might destroy him that had the power of death,

**16.** Let no man therefore judge you in meat, or in drink, or in respect of a holyday, or of the new moon, or of the sabbath *days:*

**17.** Which are a shadow of things to come; but the body *is* of Christ.

**18.** Let no man beguile you of your reward in a voluntary humility and worshipping of angels, intruding into those things which he hath not seen, vainly puffed up by his fleshly mind,

that is, the devil, and deliver them who through fear of death were all their lifetime subject to bondage" (Heb 2:14,15). For the individual, death remains to be destroyed (I Cor 15:25,26); "in Christ" its destruction occurred when, in his triumphant ascension, the Saviour led captive this and all other powers (Eph 4:8). Similarly, stripping or **putting off** (*apekdyomai*) the body of flesh (Col 2:11, RSV) may refer to the corporate judgment on the cross of the Adamic **body of flesh**, i.e., the whole man under sin, under judgment, under death. If so, this phrase stands in contrast to the 'body of Christ' (cf. I Cor 15:22; Robinson, *The Body*, p. 31). God's gracious forgiveness (Col 2:13) is to be understood in the light of the meaning of the cross: in it man's debt is cancelled and the powers holding man captive are themselves **openly** defeated and made captive. Realizing this, the absurdity of turning, as an aid to redemption, from the triumphant Christ to the subjected powers becomes apparent.

B. The Colossians' Practices as a Denial of Christ's Lordship. 2:16–3:4.

**16,17. Therefore.** Paul pounds the table and drives home the conclusions following from his argument. The objectionable observances, which evidently had been imposed by the false teachers, not only flew in the face of Christian freedom (cf. Rom 14; Gal 5) but, as among the Galatians (3:1-12; 4:9,10), threatened to draw them from Christ back into the **shadow** of the former age (cf. Heb 10:1-10). Paul points out that shadowy symbolisms and prohibitions have faded before Christ, the daylight reality. To impose such laws (today we call them by different names) on others as tests of spiritual maturity are most evident signs of Christian immaturity and error. **Body** is usually interpreted as "reality" or "substance," in contrast to the OT 'type' (Lightfoot), but **body of Christ** should not be limited to this. " 'Substance,' 'Church' and 'final perfect sacrifice' may all be ideas which would have crowded into the writer's mind . . ." (Moule).

**18,19** The description reflects an athletic contest in which the contestant is disqualified (RSV) or deprived of **reward** because of some impediment (cf. I Cor 9:24; Gal 5:7; Phil 3:14; II Tim 4:7). The false teachers either (1) hindered the Colossians in their Christian race or (2) intimidated them by declaring them disqualified if they did not follow the prescribed course. **Humility**, which in Col

19. And not holding the Head, from which all the body by joints and bands having nourishment ministered, and knit together, increaseth with the increase of God.

20. Wherefore if ye be dead with Christ from the rudiments of the world, why, as though living in the world, are ye subject to ordinances,

21. (Touch not; taste not; handle not;

22. Which all are to perish with the using;) after the commandments and doctrines of men?

3:12 is a virtue, is here condemned because of the object toward which this submissive attitude and activity is directed. Worship of *the* angels *(tōn aggelōn)*. Whatever the mediatorial function of angels in the old age (cf. Gal 3:19), it is now obviated by the indwelling Christ. For Paul, angels may still have had a ministerial function (I Cor 11:10; cf. Mt 18:10; Heb 1:14; II Pet 2:11; Jude 8,9), but the heretical teaching seems to have gone beyond OT and Jewish reverence for angels — even beyond more extravagant rabbinic speculations — to an activity of worship which, like the devotion of present-day Roman Catholics to the Virgin Mary, displaced the centrality of Christ Ernst Percy *(Die Probleme der Kolosser und Epheserbriefe,* pp. 168,169), pointing to the virtual identity of **worshipping of angels** with **humility** (cf. Col 2:23), views Paul as saying: "Your legalistic practices amount to a worship of angels." But something more than this is involved (cf. Bruce).

The basis of the error is the egoistic or **fleshly mind** (see on 2:15) that spends its time elucidating **visions** (RSV) **which he hath seen** (ASV). (A difficult clause. See Bruce, Moule.) Such a mind fails to hold to Christ, the **Head**, from whom the **body**, i.e., the Church, is nourished in true and godly growth. In contrast to the earlier use, **Head** here reflects not *authority* so much as the *origin* or *source* of the Church's health and life.

C. The Colossians' Practices as a Contradiction of Their Corporate Life in Christ. 2:20—3:4.

**20-22.** The **rudiments** *(stoicheia)* or *elemental spirits* (RSV) are identified (1) with demonic powers to whom have been delegated authority in the cosmos and, therefore, over men (cf. 2:15), or (2) with angelic powers generally who mediated the law and exercised in the old age a certain suzerainty over men. [The reader is referred to the careful discussion in E. D. Burton, *Galatians,* pp. 510-518. Ed.] A few commentators (e.g., Moule) translate the phrase *elemental teaching,* i.e., a Jewish or pagan ritualism that stands over against the freedom of the spirit. On Calvary the Christian died **with Christ** to the old age, and so he must not live as though the **world** *(kosmos)* or its **ordinances** still had a claim upon him (cf. Rom 6). To submit to things which **perish** is to admit that one belongs to the perishing old age, the mortal Adamic race (cf. I Cor 15:45-50); and it is a de-

**23.** Which things have indeed a show of wisdom in will-worship, and humility, and neglecting of the body; not in any honor to the satisfying of the flesh.

### CHAPTER 3

IF ye then be risen with Christ, seek those things which are above, where Christ sitteth on the right hand of God.

**2.** Set your affection on things above, not on things on the earth.

**3.** For ye are dead, and your life is hid with Christ in God.

**4.** When Christ, *who is* our life, shall appear, then shall ye also appear with him in glory.

nial of the new-age life into which, in Christ's risen body, the Christian has been incorporated.

**23.** Perfection of Christian character through rules is the doctrine of men (cf. Col 2:8). Although observing taboos gives a man a reputation for spiritual **wisdom** and sacrificial **humility,** such taboos in actual practice "do honor, not to God, but to man's own pride" (Phillips' trans.). Phillips, probably correctly, understands **flesh** as "the old man," man in his sinful rebellion, and not merely as a sensual term (cf. 2:18). In contrast, *severity to* (ASV) the **body,** is to be understood literally of ascetic practices.

**3:1–3.** The Christian has not only died but also **risen with Christ.** In his true existence he resides "in heavenly places." (Eph 2:6). The old age still manifests itself in the individual Christian — he sins, gets sick, dies; the new age remains **hid,** realized only in the body of the Saviour. Nevertheless, in A.D. 30 his old-age existence died, crucified with Christ (cf. II Cor 5:14; Gal 2:20). This demands that the Christian **seek** (in the set of his will) and direct his **affection** *(phroneite,* in the set of his mind) to the new-age reality **above** (cf. Rom 12:1,2). "Above" and "below" (or **on the earth**) in the writings of Paul and John do not primarily indicate spatial contrasts, although this mode of expression naturally is involved in reference to Christ and to heaven. The terms express a crucial contrast in the temporal relationship — the old age and the new age. In A.D. 30 the new age burst into history in Christ's resurrection. But Christ, in whom the new age presently inheres, is above, whereas the world continues in the death grip of the old age. Christians at present exist "above," that is, in the new age, only "in Christ" and through the indwelling Holy Spirit. But their corporate existence in Christ is no less a reality than their individual existence. A Christian's citizenship is in the "Jerusalem which is above" (Gal 4:26), and this demands a continuing transformation of his mind and will to that reality. Conformation to the ritual, the ceremony, the mediatorial 'powers' of the old age is a denial of one's corporate resurrected life with Christ.

**4.** In the sense in which **Christ is our life,** a Christian even now 'realizes' the consummation of his union with Christ. But in the *parousia,* i.e., when Christ comes again,

5. Mortify therefore your members which are upon the earth; fornication, uncleanness, inordinate affection, evil concupiscence, and covetousness, which is idolatry:

6. For which things' sake the wrath of God cometh on the children of disobedience:

the Christian will be with him not merely in a corporate sense but in individually fulfilled glory (cf. Rom 8:18; II Cor 3:18). This is the 'futurist' aspect of Paul's eschatological teaching. **Appear** (*phaneroō*), although not as common as *parousia*, is used in a number of passages to denote Christ's second advent (II Thess 2:8; II Cor 5:10; I Tim 6:14; II Tim 4:1,8; cf. I Pet 5:4; I Jn 2:28; 3:2).

## IV. Christ's Lordship in the Christian Life. 3:5—4:6.

In the Pauline pattern (cf. Rom 12:1; Eph 4:1), a transition from the doctrinal indicative mode to the ethical imperative now occurs. There is, of course, no absolute dichotomy in the doctrine-ethics sequence. If Paul is saying anything by this literary form, it is that doctrine is the basis for ethics: What a man believes does determine in substantial measure how he acts.

A. The Christian Imperative: Actualize Individually the 'in Christ' Reality. 3:5-17.

5. **Members . . . upon the earth** probably refers not to literal bodily organs being used immorally (Moule; cf. I Cor 6:15) but to bodily attitudes and actions as expressive of "the old man" (Bruce; cf. Rom 7:23; 8:13). Thus included (as much as **fornication**) is the sin of **covetousness**: acquisitive desire or self-seeking. Perhaps most needed in modern materialistic American Christendom is a vow to own nothing and a prayer to be delivered from things and from ambition. (The thought is A. W. Tozer's.) To call covetousness **idolatry** is not too strong if we realize that, when we (strongly desire to) *own* a thing, it actually owns a part of us.

6. **Wrath** (*orgē*; cf. TWNT, V, esp. pp. 419-448) is often associated with anger (*thymos*), occasionally when attributed to God (Rom 2:8; cf. Rev 16:19; 19:15). For man, wrath is not absolutely forbidden, as it was in the Stoic doctrine of *apatheia* (see Eph 4:26; cf. I Cor 14:20; Jn 2:13-17; Jas 1:19,20). Nevertheless, Paul does describe it as characteristic of the "old man" (Eph 4:31; Col 3:8; cf. Rom 12:19).

The concept of God's wrath is not a leftover from a primitive OT ideology. God's wrath is the basis for the fear of God (Heb 10:31; Jas 4:12; Mt 10:28); and it is to be understood not as

7. In the which ye also walked sometime, when ye lived in them.

8. But now ye also put off all these; anger, wrath, malice, blasphemy, filthy communication out of your mouth.

9. Lie not one to another, seeing that ye have put off the old man with his deeds;

10. And have put on the new *man*, which is renewed in knowledge after the image of him that created him:

11. Where there is neither Greek nor Jew, circumcision nor uncircumcision, Barbarian, Scythian, bond *nor* free: but Christ *is* all, and in all.

a momentary emotion but as a settled disposition, a principle of retribution (Rom 1:18; 3:5; 9:22; cf. Jn 3:36; Heb 3:11), not unlike that of an earthly ruler (Rom 13:4,5; cf. Heb 11:27). It is often associated with the day of judgment (Rom 2:5; I Thess 1:10). Far from negating God's love, his wrath confirms it. For without justice mercy loses its meaning. (Cf. R. V. G. Tasker, *The Biblical Doctrine of the Wrath of God.*)

7,8. Cf. 2:6. Out of your mouth may refer to all of the sins listed. Expressed sin is contagious, and the control of sin's expression is a long step toward deliverance from it.

9,10. Put off *(apekdysamenoi)*, referring to the point of conversion, conveys the ideas of divesting, as of a garment, and of passing judgment upon the old man, i.e., by identification with Christ in his death (see on 2:15). *Neon* (new) or, as elsewhere, *kainos* (e.g., Eph 4:24) is interpreted by the following being renewed (RSV). That is, the corporate "in Christ" existence is increasingly actualized in the individual Christian (cf. II Cor 3:18; see Introduction). Thus the image of God, which the first Adam failed to realize, is to be fulfilled in the sons of the second Adam (cf. Gen 1:26; Heb 2:5 ff.; Rom 8:29; I Cor 15:45 ff.). This means that believers not merely put on new attributes, but are undergoing a psychological transformation which, at Christ's *parousia*, i.e., his second coming, will be seen in its radical and comprehensive character (Rom 12:2; I Cor 15:53). Christians, as the second century Epistle to Diognetus expresses it, belong to a 'new race.' Knowledge. See on 1:9.

11. Scythian. The lowest type of barbarian slave. In Christ all distinctions are transcended; at the foot of the cross the ground is level. It is not, however, the leveling of the modern socialist ethic, which may only produce Djilas' 'new class.' It is not a uniformity of status in the present world order, but a change in attitude by which the stigma of being different is loved away. It is "a unity in diversity, a unity which *transcends* differences and works within them, but never a unity which *ignores* or *denies* differences or necessarily seeks to erase them" (E. E. Ellis, "Segregation and the Kingdom of God," *Christianity Today*, I, 12. March 18, 1957, p. 8). Thus the apostle, who declared that in Christ there is "no male or female," "no Jew or Greek," at the

12. Put on therefore, as the elect of God, holy and beloved, bowels of mercies, kindness, humbleness of mind, meekness, longsuffering;

13. Forbearing one another, and forgiving one another, if any man have a quarrel against any: even as Christ forgave you, so also *do* ye.

14. And above all these things *put on* charity, which is the bond of perfectness.

15. And let the peace of God rule in your hearts, to the which also ye are called in one body; and be ye thankful.

16. Let the word of Christ dwell in you richly in all wisdom; teaching and admonishing one another in psalms and hymns and spiritual songs, singing with grace in your hearts to the Lord.

17. And whatsoever ye do in word or deed, *do* all in the name of the Lord Jesus, giving thanks to God and the Father by him.

same time instructed women to be silent in the churches and observed Jewish rites which he forbade to Gentiles (Gal 3:28; I Cor 11:3 ff.; 14:34; Acts 16:3; 18:18; Rom 14; Gal 5:2,3). See on 3:18ff.

12-14. To the Church, the true Israel, belong the titles given to OT Israel: **elect, holy, beloved** (cf. Rom 2:29; 9:6; Gal 3:29; 6:16; Phil 3:3). The virtues listed here, which emphasize the relations of Christians in a situation fraught with friction, reflect the character of **Christ,** whose example is cited (cf. II Cor 8:9; Mt 6:12). The virtue which sums up, gives meaning to, and cements the rest is **love** (Rom 13:9,10).

15,16. The **peace of Christ** (RSV). That peace which Christ mediates to those in union with him (cf. Jn 14:27; Rom 5:1). It is to **rule** in the sense of arbitrating differences that arise in the **body** (Bruce). Similarly, the indwelling **word of Christ,** i.e., his teaching, exercises a transforming influence on a believer's life.

It has been the testimony of Christians from earliest times that "Christ put a song in my heart." And it is no exaggeration to say that **songs** have taught more theology to new converts than textbooks. In the Pauline church oracular utterance sometimes occurred in hymn form (I Cor 14:15), and a number of NT passages may reflect a hymn origin (cf. Phil 2:5-11; Eph 5:14; E. G. Selwyn, *The First Epistle of Peter,* p. 273 ff.). **Grace.** The grace of God (Lightfoot) or the grateful attitude of the Christian (Moule).

17. To live **in the name of the Lord Jesus** obviates the necessity for rules; inward motivation replaces external norms. Thus Christ's Lordship of the whole of life is expressed. His Lordship implies not only a mode of conduct but an attitude toward life: in conscious reflection upon the will of Christ, one's actions become an act of thanksgiving to Christ. External rules, even when good, are not adequate for every situation; the 'rule' of the indwelling Christ is the only sufficient guide (cf. I Cor 10:31; Gal 5:18).

B. Special Precepts. 3:18—4:6.

The present section illustrates how the principles of 'life in Christ' may be expressed in everyday affairs. One sees here not only how a Christian household functioned but also what early Christian society was like. The earliest church included persons of wealth as well as

18. Wives, submit yourselves unto your own husbands, as it is fit in the Lord.

19. Husbands, love *your* wives, and be not bitter against them.

20. Children, obey *your* parents in all things: for this is well-pleasing unto the Lord.

21. Father, provoke not your children *to anger*, lest they be discouraged.

22. Servants, obey in all things *your* masters according to the flesh; not with eye-service, as menpleasers; but in singleness of heart, fearing God:

23. And whatsoever ye do, do *it* heartily, as to the Lord, and not unto men;

the more numerous poor, masters as well as slaves (3:18–4:1). Besides pointing out the nature of the Christian home, Paul pays particular attention to the central importance of prayer (4:2-4) and the relation of Christian to non-Christian (4:4-6).

The conduct of the household was a much discussed subject in both Jewish and pagan writers (e.g., the apocryphal Ecclesiasticus, 30:1-13; 42:5 ff.). And it appears to have been a regular item in the Pauline teaching (cf. Eph 5:22-33; I Tim 6:1-8; Tit 2:1-10). In contrast to Jewish and pagan teaching, Paul emphasizes the mutuality of rights and responsibilities. A second Christian distinctive is the motivation urged upon the reader. Since unity in Christ does not negate the diversity of function and status in the world (see on Col 3:11), the Christian, as much as the pagan, should have concern for proper social order and custom. The Christian, however, is motivated by his relationship to Christ and his responsibility to God (e.g., 3:18, 20, 22-25).

18,19. The wives' submission is to be reciprocated in the husbands' **love.** As Eph 5:28 makes explicit, **love** here denotes not mere affection but an outgoing concern for the wife's whole person.

20,21. **All things.** The child is even to gain his understanding of God's will through his parents' counsel. In a Christian family it is not proper to suggest a conflict between duty to parents and duty to God (T. K. Abbott, *The Epistles to the Ephesians and to the Colossians*). **Pleasing in the Lord** (ASV) probably refers to obedience as motivated by love for Christ; it does not limit the child's responsibility to Christian parents. Although in an extreme case a young person may have to choose Christ's will in opposition to that of non-Christian parents (cf. Lk 14:26), this course should be taken only after sober thought and Christian counseling. "Don't overcorrect your children" (Phillips). The purpose of discipline is to develop a Christian man, not to produce a hangdog. "Don't," here, as much as in Christian ethics generally (cf. Col 2:21), must be subordinated to a positive "discipline and instruction of the Lord" (Eph 6:4, RSV).

22,23. **Servants** — today, employees — are to work not only when the boss is watching, and with the motivation his watching supplies, but to work with **singleness of heart,** i.e., in honest dedi-

24. Knowing that of the Lord ye shall receive the reward of the inheritance: for ye serve the Lord Christ.

25. But he that doeth wrong shall receive for the wrong which he hath done: and there is no respect of persons.

## CHAPTER 4

MASTERS, give unto *your* servants that which is just and equal; knowing that ye also have a Master in heaven.

2. Continue in prayer, and watch in the same with thanksgiving;

3. Withal praying also for us, that God would open unto us a door of utterance, to speak the mystery of Christ, for which I am also in bonds:

4. That I may make it manifest, as I ought to speak.

5. Walk in wisdom toward them that are without, redeeming the time.

6. Let your speech *be* always with grace, seasoned with salt, that ye may know how ye ought to answer every man.

cation. All service, for the Christian, is primarily **to the Lord,** who judges in all fairness and justice.

**24.** The faithful 'slave' of Christ receives a son's portion – the **inheritance.** Reward *(exact requital,* Lightfoot) is not, as critics use the term, "pie in the sky by and by." Rather, it is the ice cream reserved for the little girl who, rushing into her father's arms, cries, "See, Daddy, I cleaned up my playroom like you told me to." The real reward is the father's approval; the ice cream is mere trimming – but quite proper trimming. The prayer-song which requests that we "may feast in paradise with thee," is unspiritual only to a Platonist. But motivation is necessary; mercenary-mindedness excludes one from true Christian reward (cf. Acts 8:18 ff.).

**25. Receive.** That is, get back, whether in the present life or at the day of judgment. God is here viewed as the guarantor of justice (cf. Rom 12:19; II Cor 5:10. On 'just desert' as a proper measuring stick in criminal punishment, compare C. S. Lewis, "The Humanitarian Theory of Punishment," *Res Judicate,* VI, 1953-54, 224-230. Also see commentary on Col 3:6). **No respect of persons** refers to both slave and master, and provides a transition to the next section (cf. Eph 6:9; Lev 19:15).

**4:1.** The admonition brings to mind the teaching of the Sermon on the Mount: "Forgive us our debts as we forgive our debtors"; "With what judgment ye judge ye shall be judged" (Mt 6:12; 7:2. See on Col 3:11).

**2-4.** Christian **prayer** *(proseuchē;* cf. Trench) should be characterized by a spirit of thankfulness (see on 1:11). **And watch** *(grēgoreō,* "watchful") adds the thought of awareness or alertness (cf. Mk 14:37,38). Christian prayer is to be marked not by ceremonial stupor nor intoxicating verbosity, but by concern and sobriety (cf. I Pet 5:8). **Watch** *(grēgoreō)* is used frequently with reference to the Christian's attitude toward Christ's return (e.g., Mk 13:33ff.; I Thess 5:6; Rev 16:15). **Door of utterance.** An opportunity or, more probably, an ability to declare the **mystery** clearly (cf. 1:26; Eph 6:19,20).

**5,6. Wisdom** includes not only the apprehension of and ability to communicate the mystery (1:9) but also the knowledge of how to communicate it successfully. Only thus will the redemptive purpose of this **time,** which God has designated

7. All my state shall Tychicus declare unto you, *who is* a beloved brother, and a faithful minister and fellow servant in the Lord:

8. Whom I have sent unto you for the same purpose, that he might know your estate, and comfort your hearts;

9. With Onesimus, a faithful and beloved brother, who is *one* of you. They shall make known unto you all things which *are done* here.

10. Aristarchus my fellow prisoner saluteth you, and Marcus, sister's son to Barnabas, (touching whom ye received commandments: if he come unto you, receive him;)

11. And Jesus, which is called Justus, who are of the circumcision. These only *are my* fellow workers unto the kingdom of God, which have been a comfort unto me.

12. Epaphras, who is *one* of you, a servant of Christ, saluteth you, always laboring fervently for you in prayers, that ye may stand perfect and complete in all the will of God.

13. For I bear him record, that he hath a great zeal for you, and them *that are* in Laodicea, and them in Hierapolis.

14. Luke, the beloved physician, and Demas, greet you.

15. Salute the brethren which are in Laodicea, and Nymphas, and the church which is in his house.

16. And when this epistle is read among you, cause that it be read also in the church of the Laodiceans; and that ye likewise read the *epistle* from Laodicea.

"the opportune season" *(kairos;* cf. O. Cullmann, *Christ and Time,* p. 39 ff., 225), be used effectively. An offensive or insipid manner is not likely to accomplish much. Therefore, in life and speech the Christian witness should be appetizing — not to other Christians but to non-Christians.

## V. Conclusion. 4:7-18.

A. Commendation of the Bearers of the Letter. 4:7-9.

The bearers of the letter, **Tychicus** and **Onesimus**, would convey information not contained in it and doubtless would interpret it to the recipients, answering any questions they might have. Onesimus, subject of the Philemon correspondence, has been suggested as the collector of the Pauline corpus of letters (cf. John Knox, *Philemon Among the Letters of Paul,* p. 98ff.). Paul's commendation of him here served to ease the return of this runaway slave and to remind the readers that he was now a brother in Christ.

B. Greetings from Paul's Co-Workers. 4:10-14.

**Epaphras.** See on 1:7. Of the other companions, **Mark** (ASV) and **Aristarchus** are known from Acts (15:36-39; 19:29; 20:4; 27:2). The former, after his lapse on Paul's first mission (Acts 15:36-39), was now restored to the apostle's favor. In spite of the doubts of F. C. Grant (*The Earliest Gospel,* pp. 52,53), Mark is almost certainly to be identified with the companion of Peter (I Pet 5:13) and the author of the Second Gospel. Luke, then, has a personal, as well as a literary, relation to Mark. Since Luke is not included among those of the **circumcision,** it is usually inferred that he was a Gentile—the only NT writer so identified. His identity as a **physician** finds confirmation in the vocabulary of Luke-Acts. **Demas.** Cf. II Tim 4:10,11.

C. The Apostle's Greetings and Blessings. 4:15-18.

15. The 'house-church' was widespread, both in the Pauline congregations and in general (Acts 12:12; 16:15,40; Rom 16:5,23; I Cor 16:19; Phm 2).

16. Paul's 'Letter to the Laodiceans' has been the subject of much speculation. In the second century an apocryphal epistle was composed to fill the gap; in recent times the letter has been identified with Ephesians (e.g., Lightfoot; so Mar-

17. And say to Archippus, Take heed to the ministry which thou hast received in the Lord, that thou fulfil it.

18. The salutation by the hand of me Paul. Remember my bonds. Grace be with you. Amen.

Written from Rome to the Colossians by Tychicus and Onesimus.

cion, A.D. 140) or Philemon (e.g., Goodspeed).

17. The personal note to **Archippus,** who may have been the son of Philemon (Phm 2), is reminiscent of the apostle's charge to Timothy (II Tim 1:6). **In the Lord** identifies Archippus' *ministry* as a 'spiritual gift' rather than merely an organizational function (cf. Rom 12:6-8; I Cor 12:5; Eph 4:12). The concern that Paul voices is ever present in the life of the church: the danger is not a lack of spiritual gifts but spiritual gifts which because of personal sin, organizational pressures, or non-spiritual influences are smothered, warped, and unfulfilled.

18. After dictating the letter, Paul confirmed its genuineness, as was his custom (cf. I Cor 16:21; Gal 6:11; II Thess 3:17; Phm 19), with a greeting in his own hand (cf. Deiss, LAE, pp. 171,172). Referring to his **bonds,** Paul reminds his readers that "he who is suffering on behalf of Christ has a right to speak on behalf of Christ" (Lightfoot). On this moving note the apostle closes his letter.

# BIBLIOGRAPHY

ABBOTT, T. K. *The Epistles to the Ephesians and to the Colossians.* Edinburgh: T. & T. Clark, n.d.

DIBELIUS, M. *An die Kolosser, Epheser, und Philemon.* Tuebingen: Mohr, 1953.

HANSON, S. *The Unity of the Church in the New Testament: Colossians and Ephesians.* Uppsala: Almquist & Wiksells, 1946.

LIGHTFOOT, J. B. *St. Paul's Epistles to the Colossians and to Philemon.* London: Macmillan, 1886.

MASSON, C. *L'Epître de Saint Paul aux Colossiens.* Paris: Delachaux et Niestle, 1950.

MOULE, C. F. D. *The Epistles of Paul the Apostle to the Colossians and to Philemon.* Cambridge: The University Press, 1957.

ROBINSON, J. A. T. *The Body.* London: SCM Press, 1952.

SIMPSON, E. K. and BRUCE, F. F. *The Epistles to the Ephesians and the Colossians.* Grand Rapids: Eerdmans Publishing Co., 1957.

# THE FIRST EPISTLE
# TO THE THESSALONIANS

## INTRODUCTION

*Occasion of the Writing.* The church at Thessalonica was a fruit of Paul's second missionary journey (Acts 17:1-9). Miraculously released from imprisonment at Philippi, Paul and his companions, Silas and Timothy, trekked southward and then westward along the great Roman highway to the Macedonian capital and commercial center, Thessalonica. There, in spite of dogged opposition, they founded the second European church. Harassed by the Jews in Thessalonica and Berea (Acts 17:10-15), Paul fled to Athens, where concern for the spiritual welfare of the Thessalonian believers prompted him, at some personal sacrifice, to dispatch Timothy to buttress the church against the waves of persecution (I Thess 3:1-3). Timothy rejoined Paul at Corinth with the welcome report that the Gospel seed had fallen on good soil. Paul then penned I Thessalonians to commend his faithful brethren for their stalwart dedication to Christ and to one another and to encourage them to further progress in love and holiness.

*Date and Place of Writing.* Thanks to Luke's penchant for historical details, the dates of these letters may be fixed with reasonable certainty. Luke's reference to Gallio, proconsul of Achaia, in connection with Paul's sojourn at Corinth (Acts 18:12) has been illuminated by the discovery at Delphi of an inscription which dates Gallio's proconsulship within the reign of the emperor Claudius. The inscription seems to indicate that Gallio assumed office in the summer of A.D. 51. Since Luke apparently suggests that Paul had stayed in Corinth about eighteen months before Gallio came to power (Acts 18:11), the apostle probably arrived in Corinth early in A.D. 50. Not long after this, Silas and Timothy returned from Macedonia with the report which issued in Paul's writing I Thessalonians (Acts 18:5; I Thess 3:1-6) probably about the middle of A.D. 50. A few months later II Thessalonians followed, in response to reports that certain problems were not yet solved.

*Development of the Thought.* The first three chapters are personal and reflective. Paul recalls the warm reception the Macedonian believers gave the Gospel and reminds them of the difficult circumstances in which he brought the word of God to them. His vital concern was evidenced by his willingness to part with his needed companion, Timothy, in order to strengthen the oppressed church.

Timothy's positive report lifted the apostle's burden and evoked from him a series of practical exhortations. Aware of the temptations that stalked believers in a pagan culture, the apostle warns them about the menace of sexual impurity and the dangers of strife and factiousness.

Paul's teaching on the return of Christ while at Thessalonica had spawned two special problems: lack of industry in view of Christ's imminent coming and a fear that dead believers would be robbed of the rights of participation in the glories of that grand event. With characteristic directness Paul meets these problems with admonitions to diligence and with a dramatic description of the roles of living and dead saints in Christ's coming. The book concludes (ch. 5) with a challenge to alertness and with some practical advice concerning Christian attitudes and spiritual gifts.

*Importance.* The early date of these epistles allows us to get a glimpse of the uncomplicated structure of the primitive church. There was no complex organization; the glue that held the believers together was a common faith, love, and hope. An unofficial leadership had arisen within the church, yet the Christians were desperately dependent upon the apostolic circle. In few New Testament writings is there found more forceful testimony to the power of the Gospel, which turned the pagans to God from idols, kept their love warm in the midst of strife, and anchored them in hope in spite of relentless onslaughts of persecution.

In these letters Paul lays bare not so much his subject as his soul: Here the beat of the apostle's warm heart is audible. He compares himself to a gentle nurse (I Thess 2:7), a firm father (2:11), and a homeless orphan (in the Greek of 2:17). He shows himself ready to spend and be spent for the spreading of the Gospel. It is Paul, the *man*, who confronts us, gentle in his strength, loving in his exhortations, dauntless in his courage, guileless in his motives — a man (as Carl Sandburg said of Abraham Lincoln) "of steel and velvet, hard as rock and soft as drifting fog."

The eschatological teachings in these letters enhance their importance. Nowhere else does the apostle deal at such length with the sequence of events at Christ's second coming and the role of dead believers in that advent. Furthermore, only in II Thessalonians 2 does Paul allude to the paragon of evil who will set himself up as God at the end of history — the Antichrist.

# OUTLINE

I. Introduction. 1:1.
   A. Author.
   B. Recipients.
   C. Blessing.
II. Personal reflections. 1:2—3:13.
   A. Paul's commendation of the church. 1:2-10.
      1. For their reception of the Gospel. 1:2-5 a.
      2. For their testimony to the world. 1:5 b-10.
   B. Paul's founding of the church. 2:1-16.
      1. Purity of the apostle's motives. 2:1-6.
      2. Extent of the apostle's sacrifice. 2:7,8.
      3. Integrity of the apostle's conduct. 2:9-12.
      4. Reliability of the apostle's message. 2:13.
      5. Result of the apostle's message: persecution. 2:14-16.
   C. Timothy's strengthening of the church. 2:17—3:13.
      1. Paul's concern. 2:17—3:5.
      2. Timothy's welcome report. 3:6-10.
      3. Paul's prayer. 3:11-13.
III. Practical exhortations. 4:1—5:22.
   A. Abstain from immorality. 4:1-8.
   B. Love one another. 4:9,10.
   C. Mind your own affairs. 4:11,12.
   D. Comfort one another with the hope of the Second Coming. 4:13-18.
   E. Live as children of the day. 5:1-11.
   F. Abstain from evil; embrace the good. 5:12-22.
      1. In relation to others. 5:12-15.
      2. In basic attitudes. 5:16-22.
IV. Conclusion. 5:23-28.
   A. Closing prayer. 5:23,24.
   B. Request for prayer. 5:25.
   C. A final salute. 5:26.
   D. Command to read the letter. 5:27.
   E. Benediction. 5:28.

# I THESSALONIANS

## CHAPTER 1

PAUL, and Silvanus, and Timotheus, unto the church of the Thessalonians *which is* in God the Father, and *in* the Lord Jesus Christ: Grace *be* unto you, and peace, from God our Father, and the Lord Jesus Christ.

# COMMENTARY

## I. Introduction. 1:1.

A. Author. **Paul** did not need to defend his apostleship, so firm was his friendship with the Macedonian churches. **Silvanus** (Silas), who had replaced Barnabas on the second missionary journey (Acts 15:39,40), and **Timothy,** who had joined the company at Lystra (Acts 16:1-3), are mentioned because they were partners in the founding of the church (Acts 17:1-9) and were at Corinth at the time of composition of the epistle. Timothy, though subordinate to the others, was probably especially dear to the Thessalonians because of his mission (I Thess 3:1-10). The mention of Paul's associates serves more to buttress the apostle's authority than to divide it.

B. Recipients. The mode of address, **unto the church,** etc., is unparalleled (though cf. Gal 1:2). The emphasis seems to be on the local assembly rather than on the universal church as it is found in any particular place. **In God the Father**

2. We give thanks to God always for you all, making mention of you in our prayers;

3. Remembering without ceasing your work of faith, and labor of love, and patience of hope in our Lord Jesus Christ, in the sight of God and our Father;

4. Knowing, brethren beloved, your election of God.

shows the new relationship between the believers and God.

C. Blessing. Paul's characteristic greeting, **grace and peace**, combines Greek and Hebrew salutations enriched with theological significance. God's act of unmerited favor in Christ (**grace**) brings in its wake complete spiritual welfare (**peace**).

## II. Personal Reflections. 1:2–3:13.

A. Paul's Commendation of the Church. 1:2-10. The rehearsal of the Thessalonians' reception of the Gospel evokes the apostle's thankful prayer. The Spirit who attested God's election by his convicting power also enabled the Thessalonians to face affliction with such steadfastness and joy that reports of their dynamic conversion, stalwart service, and vibrant hope had sped throughout the Mediterranean area.

1) For Their Reception of the Gospel. 1:2-5a. 2. We give thanks. We is probably editorial, referring to Paul alone, as in 3:1. **Always.** Whenever he prayed, he thanked God for **all** of them. There was no disloyal group for which he could not give thanks.

3. **Without ceasing** probably belongs with **making mention** in 1:2. Here, as in 5:17, the word *adialeiptōs* means "without let up." In a non-Biblical papyrus it describes the annoying persistence of a cough. The first reason for Paul's constant thanksgiving is his recollection of the faith, love, and hope of the Thessalonians. This is Paul's first mention of these three graces (cf. 5:8; Rom 5:2-5; and especially I Cor 13:13). The order is logical and chronological: **faith** relates to the past; **love** to the present; **hope** to the future. **Work of faith** — faith has produced good works; **labor of love**—love has led them to fatiguing toil for one another; **patience of hope** — hope in Christ's second coming undauntedly endures in persecution. **In the sight of God** should possibly be limited to the final phrase, **patience of hope,** but may also refer to the other achievements of the church, which was aware of and sensitive to God's presence (cf. 2:19; 3:9,13).

4. A second reason for thanksgiving is the apostle's assurance of the Thessalonians' **election.** Paul's oneness with this Gentile church is shown by the frequent appearance of the word **brethren.** Election stems from God's love (cf. Eph 1: 4,5). The believers are called **beloved of**

5. For our gospel came not unto you in word only, but also in power, and in the Holy Ghost, and in much assurance; as ye know what manner of men we were among you for your sake.

6. And ye became followers of us, and of the Lord, having received the word in much affliction, with joy of the Holy Ghost:

7. So that ye were ensamples to all that believe in Macedonia and Achaia.

8. For from you sounded out the word of the Lord not only in Macedonia and Achaia, but also in every place your faith to Godward is spread abroad; so that we need not to speak any thing.

9. For they themselves show of us what manner of entering in we had unto you, and how ye turned to God from idols to serve the living and true God;

God, the phrase of God belonging with beloved rather than with election, as in the AV. Note the OT background: Gentiles have joined Israel as objects of God's elective love. 5a. Proof of their election was the fact that the Spirit drove the Gospel home to their hearts. Our gospel reveals Paul's personal commitment to his message. Not mere words, it carries its own divinely supplied power (cf. Rom 1:16; I Cor 2:4). Preached by men, it is ratified by the Holy Spirit. This divine unction caused the Gospel to be received in much assurance, i.e., with full certainty that it was the word of God.

2) For Their Testimony to the World. 1:5b-10. 5b. What manner of men. The apostles practiced what they preached. The Holy Spirit had changed their lives; their lives reinforced their message. 6. Followers. *Imitators.* Responding to the Gospel in spite of much affliction, the new believers followed in the train of the apostles and their Master. Affliction cannot dampen the true joy of the Spirit (Jn 16:33; Acts 16:23-25; Gal 5:22; Heb 12:2; I Pet 2:19-21). Affliction. *Tribulation*, the relentless pressure to which a believer may be exposed in a world opposed to Christ.

7. Accordingly, this church became an ensample (singular is preferable to plural) a *pattern* or *model* for the believers in Macedonia and Achaia, the northern and southern provinces, standing for all of Greece. 8. Sounded out. Like a trumpet or a clap of thunder. Word of the Lord has an OT prophetic ring and points to the divine authority behind the message. In every place. Probably hyperbole, but the strategic location of Thessalonica enabled the report to spread far and wide, and speedily. Possibly Priscilla and Aquila brought this news from Rome to Corinth (Acts 18:2). Your faith, i.e., the report of your faith. This sentence should have ended after every place, but Paul rushes on to underscore his statement. He delighted to spread the report, for the Thessalonians were his joy (2:19). But wherever he went, the news had preceded him.

9. They themselves. Probably people in general, wherever Paul went. What manner of entering in. Both the welcome reception accorded the apostles and the success of their mission. Turned to God from idols indicates the thoroughness of their conversion and the predominantly Gentile nature of the church. To serve, in complete subjection like slaves, the

10. And to wait for his Son from heaven, whom he raised from the dead, *even* Jesus, which delivered us from the wrath to come.

## CHAPTER 2

FOR yourselves, brethren, know our entrance in unto you, that it was not in vain:

2. But even after that we had suffered before, and were shamefully entreated, as ye know, at Philippi, we were bold in our God to speak unto you the gospel of God with much contention.

living (not lifeless idols) **and true God** (not false gods, who were shams).

**10. To wait** *(anamenein)* implies patient, confident waiting for the expected coming. **His son.** The only direct reference to Christ's sonship in I and II Thessalonians, which stress rather his Lordship. The Resurrection was the prelude to Christ's return, and the guarantee of God's power to rescue those who are his and judge those who are not (Acts 17:31). **Delivered** should be present tense, the participle *(ruomenon)* being timeless here —*rescuing.* **Wrath.** God's wrath as in I Thess 2:16, and Rom 3:5; 5:9; 9:22; 13:5. **To come** and **to wait** clearly indicate that Paul refers to God's final judgment. This wrath is God's personal retribution against sin, his holiness in action. Though the final period of tribulation is to be a time of wrath, God's ire will not then be exhausted; for Christ's coming itself will be a display of wrath against the wicked and unbelieving nations (Mt 24:30 Rev 19:11-15).

**B. Paul's Founding of the Church. 2: 1-16.** Paul recalls the hardships of his visit and the integrity of his motives and conduct. Undoubtedly he was deliberately refuting accusations of the Jews, who were using every possible emotional lever to pry the new converts from the rock of their Christian confession.

**1) Purity of the Apostle's Motives. 2: 1-6. 1. For yourselves, brethren.** Paul appeals both to the unquestionable reality of their own experience and to the intimacy of his relationship with them. **Entrance in** *(eisodos)* is the same word translated "entering in" at 1:9. Paul calls the believers to affirm personally what others had said about them. **Was not in vain.** The perfect tense of the Greek verb **was** shows that the results of Paul's ministry were still in effect. He uses an understatement. His mission was anything but fruitless. **2. But.** The Greek word is strong, underscoring the success of the visit in spite of both physical (**suffered**) and mental (**shamefully entreated**) illtreatment at Philippi (Acts 16:19-40). **We were bold.** This verb virtually always in the NT refers to open, fearless preaching (e.g., Acts 13:46; 18:26). The evangelists' confidence was rooted **in our God,** the source of their courage, power, and message. Opposition dogged their tracks, so that in Thessalonica, as in Philippi, the Gospel was preached **with much contention.** This expression recalls ath-

3. For our exhortation *was* not of deceit, nor of uncleanness, nor in guile:

4. But as we were allowed of God to be put in trust with the gospel, even so we speak; not as pleasing men, but God, which trieth our hearts.

5. For neither at any time used we flattering words, as ye know, nor a cloak of covetousness; God *is* witness:

6. Nor of men sought we glory, neither of you, nor *yet* of others, when we might have been burdensome, as the apostles of Christ.

7. But we were gentle among you, even as a nurse cherisheth her children:

8. So being affectionately desirous of you, we were willing to have imparted unto you, not the gospel of God only, but also our own souls, because ye were dear unto us.

letic contests where competitive struggle (**contention**) preceded every prize.

**3. Our exhortation** suggests the urgency of Paul's manner of preaching. **Deceit.** False teachers are deceivers and deceived (II Tim 3:13), but Paul was neither. In a world where religion was often coupled with immorality, he kept himself free from **uncleanness**. As the Master was guileless (I Pet 2:22), so the servant could not resort to an atmosphere of guile (in contrasted with of deceit) to snare unsuspecting followers. **4. Allowed by God.** *Tested and approved by God.* Paul's singleness of eye (Mt 6:22) was based on the double premise that he was commissioned by God and that only God could test his heart, examine his inner motives (I Cor 4:4). **Heart** in Biblical thought is the seat not so much of emotions as of volition and intellect, the center of moral decision. Paul refutes the Jewish charge that he was preaching an 'easy' message, **pleasing men** by removing the yoke of the Law (see Gal 1:10).

**5. Flattering words,** standard equipment of demagogues of every era, found no place in Paul's arsenal. Nor did he conceal **covetousness** with the cloak of pretended unselfishness. His hearers could vouch for absence of flattery, and **God is witness** that no greed lurked beneath the mantle of altruism. **6.** Paul coveted neither material gain nor the **glory** or praise of men, even though as an apostle, dispatched on his missions by **Christ,** he had a right both to financial aid and to personal respect (I Cor 9:1-14; Gal 6:6; *et al.*). **Burdensome,** i.e., insisting on being supported by the church.

2) Extent of the Apostle's Sacrifice. 2:7,8. **7. But.** A strong contrast. **Gentle** *(ēpioi).* Many excellent manuscripts have **babes** *(nēpioi),* the idea being that Paul, far from being highhanded, actually became as a child, using baby talk to communicate with the infant church. Whichever reading is preferred, Paul, instead of being a burden, put himself out to help. **As a nurse.** Better, *a nursing mother.* **Cherisheth.** Warmly and tenderly cares for **her** own **children.** Paul maintained a dual relationship to his converts: before God he and they were brethren (I Thess 1:4; 2:1; *et al.*); yet they were his children (cf. 2:11), whom he had brought into the life of faith and for whom he was obliged to care. **8. Affectionately desirous.** A word used only here in the NT, indicating warm affection, longing. The apostles were **willing,** *well pleased,* to share themselves, their very

9. For ye remember, brethren, our labor and travail: for laboring night and day, because we would not be chargeable unto any of you, we preached unto you the gospel of God.

10. Ye *are* witnesses, and God *also*, how holily and justly and unblamably we behaved ourselves among you that believe:

11. As ye know how we exhorted and comforted and charged every one of you, as a father *doth* his children,

12. That ye would walk worthy of God, who hath called you unto his kingdom and glory.

13. For this cause also thank we God without ceasing, because, when ye received the word of God which ye heard of us, ye received *it* not *as* the word of men, but, as it is in truth, the word of God, which effectually worketh also in you that believe.

lives, because of their love for the new converts (cf. I Jn 3:16).

3) Integrity of the Apostle's Conduct. 2:9-12. 9. Labor and travail are also paired in II Thess 3:8 and II Cor 11:27, where the AV "weariness and painfulness" highlights the emphases of the two words. Night and day. Paul probably began his tent-making (Acts 18:3) before dawn in order to be able to take some time off for preaching. Chargeable. *Burdensome,* as in 2:6. 10. Both the Thessalonians, who could judge Paul's actions, and God, who could test his motives (2:4), were witnesses to the apostle's sterling conduct. Holily and justly stresses the positive quality of Paul's life before God and men. The former (*hosiōs*) probably refers to religious purity; the latter (*dikaiōs*) to moral integrity. Unblameably states the same thing negatively. You that believe. Only the faithful can judge the faithful. The verdict of unbelievers is frequently too biased to be counted.

11. In another striking simile (cf. 2:7) Paul likens himself to a father, charged not with the nursing but with the training of his children. Three verbs summarize this ministry: exhorted (cf. 2:3), calling to decisive action; comforted (cf. 5:14; Jn 11:19,31) — Paul was tenderly appreciative of their hard lot; charged, reminding of the solemn nature of Christian duty (cf. "testify" in Eph 4:17).

12. This fatherly counsel had one aim: to encourage the Thessalonians to live (walk) worthily of God (cf. Eph 4:1). Better manuscripts read *who calls you* for who called you. God's call confronts men continually. The kingdom has both present and future aspects. It is God's active sovereignty over those who submit to him; yet this submission is neither as complete nor as extensive as it will be. Both the epistle's eschatological tone and the close connection between kingdom and glory (linked with one definite article in Greek) indicate the future aspect (as in I Cor 6:9; 15:50; Gal 5:21; II Thess 1:5; II Tim 4:1,18) rather than the present (as in Rom 14:17; I Cor 4:20; Col 1:13). Glory is future (cf. Rom 5:2; 8:18), referring to the full revelation of God's majestic character.

4) Reliability of the Apostle's Message. 2:13. For similar thanksgiving see 1:2. Two words are translated received: the former (*paralambanō*) means to accept formally and outwardly; the latter (*dechomai*), to receive willingly and inwardly, to welcome. The apostle's mes-

**14.** For ye, brethren, became followers of the churches of God which in Judea are in Christ Jesus: for ye also have suffered like things of your own countrymen, even as they *have* of the Jews:

**15.** Who both killed the Lord Jesus, and their own prophets, and have persecuted us; and they please not God, and are contrary to all men:

**16.** Forbidding us to speak to the Gentiles that they might be saved, to fill up their sins always: for the wrath is come upon them to the uttermost.

**17.** But we, brethren, being taken from you for a short time in presence, not in heart, endeavored the more abundantly to see your face with great desire.

sage was the **word of God** (repeated for emphasis) not of man. Compare the stress on the **gospel of God** (2:2,8,9). **Effectually worketh.** The verb should probably be understood as passive—*is set in operation.* God is the source of the power; the word is his instrument (cf. Rom 1:16; Heb 4:12; Jas 1:21; I Pet 1:23).

5) Result of the Apostle's Message: Persecution. 2:14-16. **14. Followers.** *Imitators,* as in 1:6. The churches of God were geographically **in Judea** and spiritually **in Christ Jesus.** The imitation consisted in their suffering **like things** (*the same things*) from their neighbors as the Judean Christians suffered from theirs. **Countrymen** (*tribesmen*) is used here in a local rather than an ethnic sense; probably both pagans and Jews in Thessalonica persecuted the church.

**15.** Paul indicts his countrymen with a vigor unique in his writings: they killed the one who was both **Lord,** sovereign over creation and history, and **Jesus,** the human Saviour, kinsman to them (the Greek word order stresses both names; cf. Acts 2:36); they killed or persecuted the **prophets** (**prophets** may be taken as the object of either verb, but it seems preferable to link it with **persecuted;** cf. Mt 5:12); they **persecuted** or *drove out* the apostles (**us**). Paul may have been recalling the parable in Mk 12:1 ff. **Please not God.** A forceful understatement meaning "to displease." (Cf. II Thess 3:2). **Contrary to all men.** By opposing the Gospel the Jews were working against the good of mankind, which so desperately needs salvation. **16. To fill up,** etc., refers to God's sovereign purpose worked out in the lives of the Jewish persecutors. In continuing their rejection of Christ and increasing their opposition, they heaped sin upon sin. The wording recalls Gen 15:16. Especially pertinent are the words of Christ in Mt 23:31,32. **Wrath.** See note on I Thess 1:10. **Is come** emphasizes the completeness and certainty of judgment. Wrath for them was inescapable. (Cf. Rom 1:24,26,28).

C. Timothy's Strengthening of the Church. 2:17—3:13. Paul explains his involuntary absence and the reasons for Timothy's mission. Grateful for Timothy's report, he prays that God will cause the church to continue to flourish.

1) Paul's Concern. 2:17—3:5. **17. Being taken from you.** Literally, *orphaned, bereft,* reflecting the warm tie between Paul and the church. Compare II Cor

18. Wherefore we would have come unto you, even I Paul, once and again; but Satan hindered us.

19. For what *is* our hope, or joy, or crown of rejoicing? *Are* not even ye in the presence of our Lord Jesus Christ at his coming?

20. For ye are our glory and joy.

## CHAPTER 3

WHEREFORE when we could no longer forbear, we thought it good to be left at Athens alone;

2. And sent Timotheus, our brother, and minister of God, and our fellow laborer in the gospel of Christ, to establish you, and to comfort you concerning your faith:

11:28, where the writer numbers among his burdens the *anxiety for* (RSV) *all the churches.* **Endeavored the more abundantly** and **with great desire** are strong attempts by Paul to convey his earnest yearning for fellowship. He even uses the graphic word **desire,** *epithymia,* which in the NT usually connotes lusting or coveting. **18. Even I Paul** points out his personal concern. **Once and again** is, literally, *both once and twice,* meaning "repeatedly." **Satan hindered.** This title stresses the devil's role, as adversary of God and His people. How was Paul hindered? By illness (II Cor 12:7; Gal 4:13) or by opposition in Athens that made it impossible for him to leave (I Thess 3:1)? Some think the hindrance was the security taken from Jason *et al.,* that Paul would not return (Acts 17:9). Firmly believing in God's sovereignty, the apostle never minimized the reality of evil, especially as it was summed up in Satan (I Thess 3:5; II Cor 4:4; Eph 2:2; 6:12).

**19.** Paul's emotional attachment to the Thessalonians becomes almost exuberant. **Are not even ye.** This seems to be a parenthesis within the major question: "What is our hope . . . . in the presence . . . ?" **Crown of rejoicing.** An allusion to the wreath or garland of victory awarded to winners in the games or to distinguished public servants. Paul's **hope, joy,** and only grounds for boasting **(rejoicing)** were the thought of the souls he would present to Christ (cf. II Cor 1:14; 11:2; Phil 2:16). **Coming** *(parousia)* originally meant "presence" or "arrival," but later took on a technical sense referring to the visit of a king or official. New Testament writers frequently use it for Christ's second coming (I Thess 2:19; 3:13; 4:15; II Thess 2:1; Jas 5:7,8; II Pet 1:16; I Jn 2:28; *et al.*). **20.** The writer makes doubly sure that the Thessalonians know the answer to his question. **For** has a confirmatory sense — "truly" or "indeed." **Ye** is emphatic: you alone.

**3:1. Could no longer forbear.** Could bear up under the strain of separation no longer. Though Paul uses **we** here, as throughout these epistles, it seems probable that the **we** is editorial. **Alone** seems to confirm this. **2. Our brother.** Timothy was Paul's son in the faith (I Tim 1:2); but because of this mission, Paul stresses partnership, not dependence (cf. II Cor 1:1; Col 1:1; Phm 1:1). Manuscript evidence indicates that **minister of God and our fellow laborer** is an expansion of an original statement: either *minister of God* or *fellow laborer of God.* The former

3. That no man should be moved by these afflictions: for yourselves know that we are appointed thereunto.

4. For verily, when we were with you, we told you before that we should suffer tribulation; even as it came to pass, and ye know.

5. For this cause, when I could no longer forbear, I sent to know your faith, lest by some means the tempter have tempted you, and our labor be in vain.

6. But now when Timotheus came from you unto us, and brought us good tidings of your faith and charity, and that ye have good remembrance of us always, desiring greatly to see us, as we also to see you:

has slightly better support, while the latter is more startling (although see I Cor 3:9) and is less likely to be a scribal correction. In either case Paul emphasizes Timothy's fitness to perform his mission.

The concern throughout these epistles is the spiritual rather than the physical welfare of the believers. Timothy's purpose was to establish (*strengthen*) and comfort (*actively encourage*) them concerning (as Milligan notes, *for the furtherance of*) their faith, which here is active — the experience of believing.

3. Timothy's purpose is further explained: to prevent their seduction by Jews, who might seize the opportunity afforded by affliction to try to lure the believers from their faith. **Moved** (*sainesthai*) probably retains some of its original meaning, *to wag the tail,* and, therefore, to "beguile" or "flatter." (Arndt, however, prefers *move.*) Afflictions are part and parcel of Christian experience (Jn 16:33; Acts 14:22). Note the **we.** Paul, who had suffered more than his share, here groups himself with the suffering believers. 4. An essential element in the apostle's message to the Thessalonians was the redemptive suffering of Christ (Acts 17:3). The church was born in suffering (Acts 17:6). Paul bore marks of his shameful treatment at Philippi when he evangelized the Thessalonians. Hence, suffering should not have caught them by surprise. **We told you.** The imperfect tense indicates that Paul had reminded them repeatedly.

5. Compare 3:1. **To know.** *To find out.* **Faith.** See note on 3:2. **Tempter** shows the seductive aspect of Satan's work. The devil tried to use Christ's physical difficulties to defeat him spiritually (Mt 4:3), and he did the same to the Thessalonians. The verb **have tempted** is aorist indicative and shows that the tempter was already at work, while the verb **be** is subjunctive, casting doubt upon Satan's success.

2) Timothy's Welcome Report. 3:6-10. After re-creating his personal anguish over the church's lot, Paul expresses his complete release from this burden at Timothy's return.

6. **But now** brings out the contrast between Paul's past concern and his present confidence, and indicates that Timothy had just arrived (cf. Acts 18:5). **Good tidings.** The Greek root means "to evangelize" and suggests that Timothy's report was virtually a 'gospel' to Paul's anxious soul. The good news was threefold: (1) **faith** was firm—this had

7. Therefore, brethren, we were comforted over you in all our affliction and distress by your faith:

8. For now we live, if ye stand fast in the Lord.

9. For what thanks can we render to God again for you, for all the joy wherewith we joy for your sakes before our God;

10. Night and day praying exceedingly that we might see your face, and might perfect that which is lacking in your faith?

11. Now God himself and our Father, and our Lord Jesus Christ, direct our way unto you.

12. And the Lord make you to increase and abound in love one toward another, and toward all *men*, even as we *do* toward you:

been Paul's principal concern (I Thess 3:5,7); (2) love was constant — in spite of the trials which could have frayed the edges of their dispositions; (3) their remembrance (recollection) of the apostles was always good — despite the reproach and persecution which the evangelists' visit had produced.

7. Comforted, i.e., encouraged (cf. 3:2). Paul's own lot had not been a happy one, even while he awaited news from Macedonia. Persecution at Philippi, Thessalonica, and Berea was followed by loneliness and indifferent response at Athens (3:1; Acts 17:32-34). Such dogged opposition plagued him at Corinth that he had to be divinely reassured (Acts 18: 6-10). No wonder he speaks of affliction (choking pressures) and distress (overbearing tribulation). 8. We live. New vitality had come into Paul's flagging body with the good news of the Thessalonians' faith and remained with him while he wrote (now). This would pale, however, unless the Thessalonian believers would stand fast in their relation to the Lord. The verb form seems to show that Paul confidently expected them to stand firm.

9. Paul took no credit for the soundness or growth of the church. It was God who gave the growth (I Cor 3:7). Not boastful but thankful (cf. I Thess 1:2 ff; 2:13 ff.), he rejoiced (cf. 5:18) before our God, because He made such joy possible. 10. Timothy's news relieved Paul's concern but did not lessen his desire to see them (cf. 2:17,18; 3:6), a desire prompted by the strong emotional tie (the wish to see your face) and by the need for mending the gaps in their faith. Perfect (katartizō) means to fit a thing for its full and proper use.

3) Paul's Prayer. 3:11-13. 11. Himself. Paul's destiny was in God's control. Christ's full title stresses His majesty. He is associated closely with God as the recipient of prayer and as the co-subject of the verb direct, the singular form of which (kateuthynai) yokes the subjects God and Christ together intimately. 12. The Lord, i.e., Christ. Abound in love. Cf. Phil 1:9. Love has the capacity for growing endlessly. It increases in intensity toward an individual and expands to embrace others. Christian love is first directed toward believers (one toward another) and then reaches out like God's love toward all men. This love can be produced only by the Spirit of God (Col 1:8; Gal 5:22). More than sentiment or warm feeling, Christian love is the selfless desire for the total welfare of

**13.** To the end he may stablish your hearts unblamable in holiness before God, even our Father, at the coming of our Lord Jesus Christ with all his saints.

### CHAPTER 4

FURTHERMORE then we beseech you, brethren, and exhort *you* by the Lord Jesus, that as ye have recieved of us how ye ought to walk and to please God, *so* ye would abound more and more.

**2.** For ye know what commandments we gave you by the Lord Jesus.

others. **Even as we.** God's love had been reflected in the apostle's gracious words and deeds.

**13.** Note the connection between **love** and **holiness.** If love is the Christian law (Gal 5:14), then one's **holiness** (separation to God) is measured chiefly by love. Selfishness blemishes this holiness; so Paul prays that the Thessalonians may live in love and be spotless (**unblameable**) in holiness **before God,** who, being completely holy, is the only adequate judge of holiness. God judges not as a brutal critic but as a loving **Father.** The time of reckoning is the coming (*parousia;* cf. I Thess 2:19) of Christ. **Saints.** Literally, *holy ones.* It probably includes holy angels as well as dead believers clothed in bodies "not made with hands" (II Cor 5:1), awaiting the resurrection of their earthly bodies. For other graphic pictures of Christ's coming with his whole heavenly entourage see Mt 24:30,31 and Rev 19:11-14. The OT background is Zech 14:5. According to Rev 19–20 this glorious coming paves the way for the Millenial kingdom.

### III. Practical Exhortations. 4:1–5:22.

Paul would not have been true to his pastoral calling nor to his parental concern if he had not seized every opportunity for spiritual instruction. To fulfill the law of love he had to say the needful things. Timothy's report was mainly encouraging, but undoubtedly included certain questions that Paul hastened to settle.

**A. Abstain from Immorality. 4:1-8.** No temptation faced by the early church was more vexing than that of immorality. The edict of the Jerusalem Council lists fornication with the ceremonial prohibitions placed upon Gentile believers, so generally accepted was this practice among the pagans (Acts 15:29). Paul makes the strongest possible case for morality by grounding it within the will and calling of God and the nature of the indwelling Holy Spirit.

**1. Furthermore then.** *Finally.* The word marks a major transition in subject matter and suggests that the letter's conclusion is approaching. **Beseech.** *Request.* **Exhort** is stronger (cf. 2:11 and 3:2). **Walk** equals *live,* as in 2:12. The essence of Paul's command is that the Thessalonians should do what they are doing, only more so. **Abound.** See 3:12 and 4:10 "increase" for other uses of *perisseuō.* **2.** Paul's ministry included

3. For this is the will of God, *even* your sanctification, that ye should abstain from fornication:

4. That every one of you should know how to possess his vessel in sanctification and honor;

5. Not in the lust of concupiscence, even as the Gentiles which know not God:

6. That no *man* go beyond and defraud his brother in *any* matter: because that the Lord *is* the avenger of all such, as we also have forewarned you and testified.

ethical instruction as well as evangelism. His **commandments** (orders or military commands) were stamped with the authority of Jesus who is **Lord**, the exalted Ruler of all of life.

**3.** After a general word of encouragement, in which he also establishes his authority, the apostle tackles the problem at hand — fornication. He begins positively: God both commands and enables your **sanctification.** In contrast with 3:13, where holiness (*hagiōsynē*) is viewed as a state, here **sanctification** (*hagiasmos*) is seen as a process—the act of being sanctified, set apart for God's service. **Abstain from.** *Keep completely separate from.* **4.** Amplification of abstain, etc. The meaning of **vessel** is difficult. Many commentators and translators (e.g., Moffatt, RSV) interpret **vessel** as "wife," appealing to certain Jewish usage, according to which a wife is likened to a vessel. Milligan, Morris, Phillips, and others understand **vessel** as "body," after the analogy of II Cor 4:7. This rendering seems preferable because it avoids the low view of the woman's role in marriage implied in the former interpretation. If **vessel** means "body," *ktasthai* must mean **possess** (as in AV and certain papyri) rather than the more frequent *acquire.*

**5.** The **sanctification** and **honor** in which the believer controls himself contrast directly with the **lust,** etc. In I Cor 7:2,3,9 Paul indicates that marriage gives opportunity to control passions, not to give them unbridled vent. **Lust of concupiscence.** Or, *passion of lust* (RSV). This implies the willful desire to yield to base sexual drives. Paul's definition of **Gentiles** is classic—**which know not God.** It is not superior self-control that separates Christian from pagan, but intimate acquaintance with God (cf. Ps 79:6; Jer 10:25). Hosea and Jeremiah both stress the essentiality of the knowledge of God (Hos 4:6; 6:6; Jer 4:22), involving love and obedience. It is the essence of salvation (Jn 17:3).

**6.** The social significance of chastity. **Go beyond,** i.e., *overstep* the bounds of human decency and social regulations. **Defraud** or *take advantage of* his brother. Not merely his Christian brother but his fellow man. **In any matter.** *In the matter* or *in this matter.* The Greek definite article links this statement with the subject of this paragraph—sexual purity. In this verse Paul gives a practical illustration of both the law of love and the connection between love and holiness

7. For God hath not called us unto uncleanness, but unto holiness.

8. He therefore that despiseth, despiseth not man, but God, who hath also given unto us his Holy Spirit.

9. But as touching brotherly love ye need not that I write unto you: for ye yourselves are taught of God to love one another.

10. And indeed ye do it toward all the brethren which are in all Macedonia: but we beseech you, brethren, that ye increase more and more;

11. And that ye study to be quiet, and to do your own business, and to work with your own hands, as we commanded you;

stressed in 3:12,13. Judgment day casts its lengthy shadow over all of life. **The Lord is the avenger,** who sees to it that full justice is done.

7. The emphasis is on **called** (cf. 2:12). Salvation is purposeful, and **uncleanness,** moral pollution, is not its purpose. Paul here reiterates the thought of 4:3. The will of God designs that a believer should live in **sanctification** (*hagiasmos*). This is the process (cf. 4:3) rather than the state of being sanctified (cf. 3:13). 8. To **despise** (*reject, treat as worthless*) the command to purity is to break divine law; for God has placed the Holy Spirit within a believer to make him holy. The emphasis is on **holy:** "It is not for nothing that the Spirit God gives us is called the *Holy* Spirit" (Phillips). Those whom he indwells are called to reflect his holiness. **Unto us** should read *unto you,* with the best manuscripts. The statement is pointedly personal.

B. Love One Another. 4:9,10. A second temptation hounded the early church —factiousness and petty strife. The situation at Corinth exemplifies the primitive believers' battle against their pagan environment (I Cor 3:1 ff.). Christianity sprang up in a land and culture where clan ties were strong and society was more corporate than individualistic. Not so the Greco-Roman culture; hence, Paul's constant emphasis on love.

9. **Brotherly love** (*philadelphia*) is clan love, the love between members of a family. For early believers, accepting Christ often meant severing family ties. But the Christians joined a new family, for they were now God's sons, and brothers of all believers. **Taught of God.** Both by God's gracious example (Jn 3:16) and by the Spirit, who pours God's love into our hearts (Rom 5:5). 10. The extensive (**all** brethren in **all** Macedonia) loving deeds (cf. 1:3) of the Thessalonians were proof that they had learned well God's lesson of love. But there was no room for complacency. Paul tenderly (**brethren**) urges them to **increase** their love **more and more** (cf. 3:12; 4:9,10).

C. Mind Your Own Affairs. 4:11,12. This section should be coupled closely with the previous, for selfless industry is a manifestation of Christian brotherly love.

11. **Study.** *Philotimeomai* originally meant *be ambitious,* but in the NT (cf. Rom 15:20; II Cor 5:9) it means "to

**12. That ye may walk honestly toward them that are without, and** *that* **ye may have lack of nothing.**

**13. But I would not have you to be ignorant, brethren, concerning them which are asleep, that ye sorrow not, even as others which have no hope.**

strive eagerly," "aspire." The clause is graphic: *strive eagerly* **to be quiet.** They were to strive for two other goals: **to do,** etc. (mind you own affairs and not somebody else's) and **to work,** etc. Apparently some believers were both meddlesome and lazy. Hope of the imminent Second Coming became an excuse for idleness (cf. II Thess 3:11). Greeks shunned manual labor, and Paul had taught the Thessalonians by word (the Lord was a carpenter) and by example (the apostle was a tent-maker) that the Christian doctrine of *creation* implies the Christian doctrine of *vocation:* God made everything good; therefore, man can perform the most menial tasks knowing that he is in touch with the Creator's handiwork; further, he can do them to God's glory.

**12.** The double purpose of dedicated industry: to live fittingly or becomingly (**honestly**) before non-Christians (**them that are without,** those outside the pale of salvation); to enjoy the freedom which personal financial sufficiency gives. Their diligence would enhance their testimony with outsiders; their "honorable independence" (Phillips) would help them fulfill the law of love by not sponging on fellow believers.

**D. Comfort One Another with the Hope of the Second Coming. 4:13-18.** Among the problems brought to Paul's attention by Timothy was the role of the dead believers at Christ's second advent. In Paul's discussions, the emphasis seems to have been on the imminence of the return. But persecution and affliction apparently took their toll of believers' lives. What would be the lot of such? Would death have robbed them of participation in the Grand Event? On the contrary, Paul says, they are to share fully in the glories of that day. Christ's death and resurrection are the guarantee of this. These comforting words of Paul were not intended to give a systematic picture of the last things, but were geared to the problem at hand.

**13. I would not,** etc. Compare Rom 1:13; 11:25; I Cor 10:1; 12:1; II Cor 1:8, where, as here, the statement introduces a new and important subject. In each instance **brethren** is used to add a note of tenderness. **Asleep.** To be "dead in Christ" (4:16) is to be **asleep,** for Christ by his death and resurrection (4:14) has taken the sting out of death. No allusion to 'soul sleeping' is involved. Paul had in mind the *bodies* of dead believers. **Others.** Rather, *the others,*

**14.** For if we believe that Jesus died and rose again, even so them also which sleep in Jesus will God bring with him.

**15.** For this we say unto you by the word of the Lord, that we which are alive *and* remain unto the coming of the Lord shall not prevent them which are asleep.

**16.** For the Lord himself shall descend from heaven with a shout, with the voice of the archangel, and with the trump of God: and the dead in Christ shall rise first:

those outside of Christ (cf. 4:12). **No hope.** This could well be the epitaph of unbelievers. **Hope** refers to the Second Coming, with all its attendant blessings. Sadness and loneliness are death's inescapable companions, but bitter grief and desperate hopelessness should play no role in the emotions of a bereaved believer, because he knows in advance the final chapter of history's plot.

**14. If we believe.** "And we *do* believe" is the idea conveyed by the Greek construction. **Jesus died.** "Sleep" will not do here. Christ took the full cup of death that he might triumph over it (Heb 2:14,15). **And rose again.** His triumph assures ours (cf. I Thess 1:10). **God** is emphatic here. He who raised Jesus is the Guarantor and Agent of our resurrection. **Sleep in Jesus** is *sleep through Jesus,* the idea being that through him death is transformed into sleep. **With him.** Paul answers the major question: Dead believers will not miss the *parousia;* God will see to it that they accompany Christ on his triumphal return (3:13).

**15. By the word,** etc., gives authority to Paul's statements (cf. I Cor 7:10). The source of the **word** is uncertain. Among the possible sources: (1) **Mt** 24:30,31 and parallel passages; (2) **an** unrecorded saying of Christ (cf. **Acts** 20:35); (3) a special revelation from the Lord (cf. II Cor 12:1; Gal 1:12,16; 2:2). **We which are alive.** Paul frequently stresses the imminence of Christ's return (I Cor 7:29; Phil 4:5). Like all believers, he hoped to live to share in the event (I Cor 16:22; Rev 22:20). Without stating that Christ *would* come during his lifetime, he seemed to welcome the possibility (cf. I Cor 15:51 ff.). **Shall not.** *By no means.* **Prevent.** *Come before, precede.*

**16.** The all-important fact is that the Second Advent centers in the activity of **the Lord himself.** The terse phrases add to the drama: (1) **with a shout,** a *call of command* like that of an officer to his soldiers, probably given by the Lord; (2) **with the voice,** etc., may be an explanation of the **shout;** both **voice** and **archangel** are indefinite in the Greek, and the idea is probably *a voice such as an archangel uses,* as Milligan suggests; (3) **with the trump of God,** *a trumpet dedicated to God's service* (Milligan); in I Cor 15:52 Paul twice mentions a trumpet in connection with the Second Coming (cf. Joel 2:1; **Isa** 27:13; Zech 9:14 for OT background). These three phrases convey the splendor

17. Then we which are alive *and* remain shall be caught up together with them in the clouds, to meet the Lord in the air: and so shall we ever be with the Lord.

18. Wherefore comfort one another with these words.

## CHAPTER 5

BUT of the times and the seasons, brethren, ye have no need that I write unto you.

2. For yourselves know perfectly that the day of the Lord so cometh as a thief in the night.

of the scene and the Lord's majestic authority. **Dead in Christ.** The bodies of dead believers. **First.** Dead believers will precede living ones.

**17. We which are alive.** See 4:15. **Shall be caught up.** *Snatched up suddenly and forcibly, raptured.* **Together with them.** Members of Christ's body will be reunited with each other as well as with their great Head. **The clouds** add to the mystery and drama of the event (cf. Mt 24:30; Acts 1:9; Rev 1:7). **In the air.** The absolute pre-eminence of Christ is underscored by his using the dwelling place of evil spirits (Eph 2:2; 6:12) for this rendezvous. **With the Lord.** The heart of the passage—endless fellowship with Christ. **Where?** Does the whole retinue ascend to heaven or return to earth? Any answer given will depend on the total interpretation of NT eschatology adopted. Pre-tribulationists posit an ascension with a subsequent return to earth. Post-tribulationists hold that a descent to earth follows this reunion.

**18.** To a church struggling to maintain itself in a society that was at best heedless and at worst hostile, these were comforting words indeed. We should note that Paul does not discuss here the relation of the Rapture to the Tribulation.

**E. Live as Children of the Day. 5:1-11.** The discussion of the participants in the *parousia* leads to questions about the time and the signs of the *parousia*. In response to these, Paul alerts the believers to constant readiness. Vigilance and sobriety are the proper attitudes, while faith, love, and hope are the Christian's arsenal.

**1.** Paul had undoubtedly relayed personally to the Thessalonians the important words of Christ: "but of that day . . . knoweth no man . . . " (Mk 13:32, 33). Nothing need or can be said about the time of the Second Coming. **Times** (*chronōn*, length of time) signifies the chronological periods which are to elapse before the Second Coming; while **seasons** (*kairōn*, kind or quality of time) refers to the significant events, the pregnant opportunities that transpire during these epochs (cf. Acts 1:7).

**2. Yourselves know perfectly.** Paul had carefully informed the believers that constant preparedness was the Christian's obligation. **The day of the Lord** must be viewed against its OT background. The term was current in Israel before the time of Amos but was applied only to God's judgment of the Gentiles. In a

3. For when they shall say, Peace and safety; then sudden destruction cometh upon them, as travail upon a woman with child; and they shall not escape.

4. But ye, brethren, are not in darkness, that that day should overtake you as a thief.

5. Ye are all the children of light, and the children of the day: we are not of the night, nor of darkness.

6. Therefore let us not sleep, as *do* others; but let us watch and be sober.

graphic passage, not unlike I Thess 5:2-4, Amos corrects this misinterpretation, pointing out that a righteous God judges sin wherever it is found—even in Israel (Amos 5:18-20). Cf. Joel 1:15; 2:1,2, 31,32; Zeph 1:14 ff. The day is the time of God's righteous intervention in history, when he will exact his rightful due from mankind. In II Thess 2:2 ff. this day is connected with the great apostasy and the revelation of Antichrist, i.e., the Tribulation period. **Thief**, etc., recalls Mt 24:43 and Lk 12:39. The figure depicts the unexpectedness of the event.

**3.** The fact that **for** is not found in the better manuscripts indicates that this is to be closely connected with the preceding. **They**, i.e., unbelievers. **Peace and safety** calls to mind OT passages like Amos 5:18,19; Mic 3:5-11; Ezk 13:10, which describe a false sense of peace and security. **Destruction.** To be the object of God's righteous wrath is to be completely and hopelessly destroyed, perhaps by separation from God (II Thess 1:9). **As travail.** This comparison is frequent in the OT (Isa 13:8; Hos 13:13; Jer 4:31) and in the Gospels (ASV, Mt 24:8; Mk 13:8). It is not pain but the suddenness and relentlessness of the day that Paul is stressing. Once labor sets in, there is no escape. **Shall not.** *By no means* (cf. 4:15).

**4. But ye, brethren,** emphasizes the strong contrast between believers and unbelievers. **Darkness** is more than ignorance; it is the unbelievers' moral and spiritual separation from God (cf. Jn 3:19,20; II Cor 6:14; Eph 5:8; Col 1:12,13). **5.** Having stated what the believers are *not*, Paul turns to what they *are*, and adds **all** to make the statement more inclusive. To be **sons of light** is to be characterized by light. Luke 16:8 and Eph 5:8 contain examples of this Semitic idiom. God, the source of light, is called "the Father of lights" (Jas 1:17). **Children** (sons) **of the day** not only reemphasizes the preceding phrase but recalls the **day** of the Lord. Believers are sons of that day because they share in its glory and triumph.

**6. Therefore.** Since we are sons of the day. **Sleep.** Not physically but morally and spiritually, as in Mk 13:36; Eph 5:14. **Others.** Cf. I Thess 4:13. **Watch** recalls Christ's injunctions about his coming in Mt 24:42; 25:13, etc. Mental and physical awareness is implied. **Be sober** (cf. II Tim 4:5; I Pet 1:13; 4:7; 5:8) speaks not so much of freedom from drunkenness as of rigidly disciplining *all*

7. For they that sleep sleep in the night; and they that be drunken are drunken in the night.

8. But let us, who are of the day, be sober, putting on the breastplate of faith and love; and for a helmet, the hope of salvation.

9. For God hath not appointed us to wrath, but to obtain salvation by our Lord Jesus Christ,

10. Who died for us, that, whether we wake or sleep, we should live together with him.

11. Wherefore comfort yourselves together, and edify one another, even as also ye do.

of one's life so as to be well balanced in every phase. **7.** Sleeping and drunkenness are habits customarily performed at night. Therefore, they have no place in the lives of sons of the day. There is no need for figurative interpretation here. **8. But let us** (in contrast with the "others") **be sober.** Sobriety must be a believer's habit, since he belongs to the day. Paul frequently speaks of spiritual equipment in terms of the armory (cf. II Cor 6:7; 10:4; Eph 6:13 ff.; the OT source is Isa 59:17). The trinity of virtues (cf. I Thess 1:3) protects the believer against the complacency and despair that characterize the sons of the night. **Hope of salvation** is the eager expectation of being rescued from God's final wrath (1:10) and destined for endless glory and fellowship with God.

**9.** The reason for this hope (5:8) is that God has destined believers for it rather than for **wrath** (cf. 1:10). **Appointed** (*etheto*), though lacking the definiteness of "predestinated" (Rom 8:29 ff.), nevertheless attributes salvation to "the direct purpose and action of God" (Milligan). **To obtain** implies that the believer has an active response to make. Salvation is made available **by** (through) **our Lord Jesus Christ.** The full title conveys the majesty of Jesus the Messiah. **10.** Salvation includes not only rescue from wrath (1:10; 5:9) but bestowal of life and promise of eternal fellowship. The cost of this legacy must not be taken for granted, as **who died for us** reminds us. **Wake** and **sleep** here are figurative for "live" and "die." The triumphant death of Christ perforates the once heavy line between life and death (4:14,15; cf. also Christ's promise in Jn 11:25,26).

**11. Edify.** *Build up,* a favorite expression of Paul's for "promoting spiritual growth and maturity" (cf. I Cor 3:9 ff.; 14:4; Eph 2:21 ff.). This metaphor and that of the armor (I Thess 5:8) are reminders that Paul, a citizen of "no mean city," drew his figures of speech largely from urban rather than from rural scenes. **Even as also ye do.** Paul's tact combined forceful exhortation with fervent praise.

F. Abstain from Evil; Embrace the Good. 5:12-22. Paul closes his letter with brief exhortations dealing with social, personal, and spiritual attitudes.

1) In Relation to Others. 5:12-15. The apostle lays down a few guiding principles for believers to follow in relation to their spiritual leaders, fellow Christians, the weak and helpless, and all men.

12. And we beseech you, brethren, to know them which labor among you, and are over you in the Lord, and admonish you;

13. And to esteem them very highly in love for their work's sake. *And* be at peace among yourselves.

14. Now we exhort you, brethren, warn them that are unruly, comfort the feebleminded, support the weak, be patient toward all *men.*

15. See that none render evil for evil unto any *man;* but ever follow that which is good, both among yourselves, and to all *men.*

16. Rejoice evermore.

12. **Know** here must mean "know the value of," "appreciate." **Labor.** Cf. 1:3; 2:9. Leading an afflicted, struggling church has seldom proved easy. **Over you.** The term used here is apparently not technical but refers to a general, informal type of leadership. However, it is probable that elders (presbyters) are meant (cf. Acts 20:17; 21:18; I Tim 5:17,19). **In the Lord** shows that Paul is speaking of spiritual authority, which involves admonishing or warning, especially where blameworthy conduct is involved (cf. I Thess 5:14; II Thess 3:15). 13. **In love** (AV) gives the setting and context for this high esteem; **for their work's sake** gives the reason. The task of maintaining and strengthening the believers is worthy of respect in itself. **Be at peace.** To degrade leadership or to cavil with authority is to sow seeds of strife. The well-being of the Christian community (**among yourselves**) is dependent on cordial cooperation between followers and leaders. 14. Directed to the leaders of the church and to the spiritually mature. **Warn.** Cf. "admonish" in 5:12. **Unruly.** *Out of order.* A military word describing soldiers who fail to remain in the ranks. This disorderliness is probably willful negligence of Christian duty, including the duty to work (4:11,12; II Thess 3:6-15). **Feebleminded.** *Fainthearted* (RSV), i.e., despairing in the face of adverse circumstances. **Support the weak.** Give those who are spiritually frail (cf. Rom 14:1; I Cor 8:9,11) a helping hand. **Be patient toward all.** This sums up the basic attitude that must prevail as one seeks to help the unruly, disheartened, and fragile brethren (cf. Eph 4:2), and thus reflect God's own attitude (Rom 2:4; 9:22; I Pet 3:20). 15. Vindictiveness and retaliation should find no lodging within the household of faith, for the Master clearly forbade them (Mt 5:43 ff.). **Follow.** *Pursue, set out after.* **Good.** In a kind, helpful, useful sense. **All men** includes unbelievers (cf. I Pet 2:17).

2) In Regard to Basic Attitudes. 5:16-22. In staccato-like statements Paul drives home his final exhortations.

16. Christian joy is not dampened by affliction or other harsh circumstances, because it is rooted in one's unassailable relationship to God (cf. Phil 2:18; 3:1; 4:4). In fact, joy may thrive in tribulation when a believer discerns the glorious purposes of God (Rom 5:3-5; Jas 1:2 ff.).

17. Pray without ceasing.
18. In every thing give thanks: for this is the will of God in Christ Jesus concerning you.
19. Quench not the Spirit.
20. Despise not prophesyings.
21. Prove all things; hold fast that which is good.
22. Abstain from all appearance of evil.

Such joy is not self-generated but is the Spirit's fruit (Gal 5:22). **17.** Prayer is attitude as well as activity. The attitude of devotion to God can be **without ceasing** (cf. note on 1:3), if the activity cannot. Paul illustrates his own command, for his letters are scented with the fragrance of prayer. **18. Everything.** All circumstances, even hardships and affliction. **This,** though singular, seems to embrace the three commands of 5:16,17,18. God's will includes constant joy, ceaseless prayer, and boundless thanks, attitudes made both necessary and possible **in Christ Jesus.**

**19. The** Greek construction suggests the translation: *Stop quenching the Spirit.* **Quench** aptly describes the hindering of the Spirit, whose nature has been likened to fire (Mt 3:11; Acts 2:3,4). In light of 5:20, this verse seems to indicate that some cautious believers had questioned the use of spiritual gifts in the church. This situation would be the opposite of that in I Cor 12–14, where we find ungracious zeal to outdo each other in exercising spiritual gifts. It is possible, however, that Paul's statement here is general, forbidding them to check the Spirit's refining and convicting work in their lives (cf. Eph 4:30). **20.** In I Cor 14:1 believers are urged to seek the gift of prophecy, the Spirit-guided public utterances of deep truths. This gift may have been abused; but abuse does not preclude use. The predictive element in Biblical prophesying should neither be overstressed nor minimized. The prophet's task is to tell what God has told him, including things to come. For NT references to a prophetic ministry, see I Cor 12:28 and Eph 2:20; 3:5; 4:11.

**21. All things** refers primarily to sayings that purport to be prophecies. They must not be accepted with credulity but are to be tested by more objective revelation and especially by the touchstones of Christ's Lordship (I Cor 12:3) and incarnation (I Jn 4:1-3). **Good,** i.e., genuine, not counterfeit.

**22.** Paul's negative command is actually: *Abstain from every kind of evil.* *Eidos* (**appearance,** AV) is often used in the papyri of the Greco-Roman period to denote "class," "sort," "kind." It has frequently been noted that while "the good" in verse 21 is singular, **evil** is said to take many different forms. The wording recalls Job 1:1,8; 2:3.

**IV. Conclusion. 5:23-28.**

**A.** Closing Prayer. 5:23,24. Paul em-

23. And the very God of peace sanctify you wholly; and *I pray God* your whole spirit and soul and body be preserved blameless unto the coming of our Lord Jesus Christ.

24. Faithful *is* he that calleth you, who also will do *it*.

25. Brethren, pray for us.

26. Greet all the brethren with a holy kiss.

27. I charge you by the Lord, that this epistle be read unto all the holy brethren.

braces all his exhortations in a prayer for sanctification, and assures the believers that a faithful God will answer it.

**23. The very God of peace** is *God himself who alone bestows peace,* a characteristic Pauline title of God (cf. Rom 15:33; 16:20; II Cor 13:11; Phil 4:9; II Thess 3:16). Though human surrender and obedience are necessary, sanctification is essentially a divine work (cf. Rom 15:16; Eph 5:26). **Wholly** (*holoteleis*) implies that no part is lacking; the whole person is to be kept **blameless. Spirit and soul and body** should probably not be interpreted as a definitive analysis of the nature of man. The three words are used to indicate the whole being of a person, "whether on its immortal, personal, or bodily side" (Milligan). Paul prays that they may be preserved **(kept)** from judgment at **(unto)** Christ's coming. **24. Faithful is he** can only refer to God (cf. I Cor 1:9; 10:13; II Cor 1:18; II Thess 3:3; II Tim 2:13; Heb 10:23; 11:11). The only guarantee that any believer will have a worthy report at the final judgment is God's faithfulness. His calling carries with it the successful completion of his purposes (Rom 8:30; Phil 1:6).

**B. Request for Prayer. 5:25.**

A tender plea revealing Paul's dependence on his **brethren** in Christ (cf. Rom 15:30; Eph 6:19; Col 4:3 ff.; II Thess 3:1 ff.).

**C. A Final Salute. 5:26.**

A fitting conclusion to a letter filled with expressions of affection. Paul includes **all the brethren,** even those who caused the problems. **Holy kiss.** Its character was completely divorced from the sensual. A pure display of the deep emotion of Christian love, this type of kiss remained a Christian custom until abuse and heathen misunderstanding caused the practice to be curtailed. For other NT references to the **holy kiss,** see Rom 16:16; I Cor 16:20; II Cor 13:12; also I Pet 5:14 ("kiss of love").

**D. Command to Read the Letter. 5:27.**

**I charge.** *I adjure you, put you under oath.* Paul wanted to make sure that the letter was read in the hearing of **all the brethren** (holy being omitted in the best manuscripts). The language is strong, and the switch to **I** from "we" reinforces the command. Paul may have anticipated some factiousness which would have made fraudulent use of his letter (cf. II Thess 2:2). But it is more

I THESSALONIANS 5: 28

**28. The grace of our Lord Jesus Christ *be* with you. Amen.**

The first *epistle* unto the Thessalonians was written from Athens.

likely that his urgent desire for fellowship pressed him to make sure that no one was left out.

E. Benediction. 5:28.

Paul ends as he began — with a prayer for **grace**, i.e., Christ's continued favor. Note that the apostle emphasizes the majesty of Christ by giving his full title — **Lord Jesus Christ.** The Amen and the subscription naming Athens as the place of writing, as in the AV, are omitted from the better manuscripts (cf. e.g., the ASV).

# BIBLIOGRAPHY

ANDREWS, SAMUEL J. *Christianity and Anti-Christianity in Their Final Conflict.* 2nd ed. Chicago: Bible Institute Colportage Association, 1898.

BAILEY, JOHN W. "I-II Thessalonians," *Interpreter's Bible.* Vol. XI. New York: Abingdon Press, 1955.

BARCLAY, WILLIAM. *The Mind of St. Paul.* New York: Harper and Brothers, 1958.

BICKNELL, E. J. *I-II Thessalonians (Westminster Commentary).* London: Methuen and Co., 1932.

BRUCE, F. F. "I and II Thessalonians," *New Bible Commentary.* Edited by F. Davidson, A. M. Stibbs, and E. F. Kevan. Grand Rapids: Wm. B. Eerdmans, 1953.

DENNEY, JAMES. *The Epistles to the Thessalonians (Expositor's Bible).* New York: A. C. Armstrong and Son, 1903.

FINDLAY, GEORGE G. *The Epistles to The Thessolonians (Cambridge Bible for Schools and Colleges).* Cambridge: University Press, 1900.

FRAME, J. E. *Epistles of St. Paul to the Thessalonians (International Critical Commentary)* Edinburgh: T. and T. Clark, 1912.

HENDRIKSEN, WILLIAM. *Exposition of I-II Thessalonians (New Testament Commentary).* Grand Rapids: Baker Book House, 1955.

HUBBARD, DAVID A. "Antichrist," *Dictionary of Theology.* Edited by E. F. Harrison. Grand Rapids: Baker Book House, 1959.

MILLIGAN, GEORGE. *St. Paul's Epistles to the Thessalonians.* New York: The Macmillan Co., 1908.

MOFFATT, JAMES. "The First and Second Epistles to the Thessalonians," *Expositor's Greek Testament.* Vol. IV. Grand Rapids: Wm. B. Eerdmans, reprinted 1952.

MORRIS, LEON. *The Epistles of Paul to The Thessalonians (Tyndale New Testament Commentary).* London: Tyndale Press, 1956.

VOS, GEERHARDUS. *The Pauline Eschatology.* Grand Rapids: Wm. B. Eerdmans, 1952.

WALVOORD, JOHN F. *The Thessalonian Epistles.* Findlay, Ohio: Dunham Publishing Co., 1956.

# THE SECOND EPISTLE TO THE THESSALONIANS

## INTRODUCTION

*Development of the Thought.* Grateful for the believers' faith, love, and endurance in persecution, Paul explains the purpose of this persecution, which refines believers for future glory and seals the doom of God's enemies. Christ's coming will reverse the present situation, bringing rest to the afflicted, and separation from God to their troublers.

Despite contrary reports, the Day of the Lord has not yet come (ch. 2). The rebellion and the man of lawlessness will appear first. All forms of worship, true and false, will be replaced by the worship of this lawless one. His day will be short in spite of his deceitful Satanic power. As darkness is dissolved by light, he will be slain at Christ's coming, when his deluded followers also will be judged.

The believers' destiny is different because God has called them to salvation. This sense of calling, coupled with the Spirit's ministry, will hold them firm in troubled times. Paul, too, faces opposition in his ministry and comforts himself and his friends with a reminder of God's loving faithfulness and Christ's patient steadfastness (ch. 3).

Industry, not sloth, is the hallmark of Christian conduct, as Paul had taught by instruction and example. Where there prevailed misinterpretation of the imminence of Christ's advent, or spiritual pride that disdained manual labor, firm but loving pressure should be brought to bear on the unruly. (For discussion of date, occasion of writing, etc., see Introduction to I Thessalonians.)

## OUTLINE

I. Introduction. 1:1,2.
   A. Authors. 1:1a.
   B. Recipients. 1:1b.
   C. Blessing. 1:2.
II. Encouragement in persecution. 1:3-12.
   A. Commendation for steadfastness. 1:3,4.
   B. Explanation of the purpose of persecution. 1:5-10.
   C. Intercession for continued spiritual growth. 1:11,12.
III. Instruction concerning the Day of the Lord. 2:1-12.
   A. To come in the future. 2:1,2.
   B. To be preceded by definite signs. 2:3-12.
IV. Thanksgiving and exhortation. 2:13-17.
   A. Praise for their calling. 2:13-15.
   B. Prayer for their comfort and stability. 2:16,17.
V. Confession of confidence. 3:1-5.
   A. Request for prayer. 3:1,2.
   B. Reminder of God's faithfulness. 3:3-5.
VI. Commandments to work. 3:6-15.
   A. Shun the idle. 3:6.
   B. Imitate us. 3:7-9.
   C. Work or do not eat. 3:10.
   D. Exhort the idle. 3:11-13.
   E. Warn and discipline the disobedient. 3:14,15.
VII. Conclusion. 3:16-18.
   A. Blessing. 3:16.
   B. Paul's signature. 3:17.
   C. Benediction. 3:18.

# II THESSALONIANS

### CHAPTER 1

PAUL, and Silvanus, and Timotheus, unto the church of the Thessalonians in God our Father and the Lord Jesus Christ:

2. Grace unto you, and peace, from God our Father and the Lord Jesus Christ.

3. We are bound to thank God always for you, brethren, as it is meet, because that your faith groweth exceedingly, and the charity of every one of you all toward each other aboundeth;

4. So that we ourselves glory in you in the churches of God, for your patience and faith in all your persecutions and tribulations that ye endure:

5. *Which is* a manifest token of the righteous judgment of God, that ye may be counted worthy of the kingdom of God, for which ye also suffer:

# COMMENTARY

### I. Introduction. 1:1,2.

This letter begins like I Thessalonians. The only addition is the mention of **God our Father and the Lord Jesus Christ** as the givers of **grace** and **peace** (1:2).

### II. Encouragement in Persecution. 1:3-12.

A. Commendation for Steadfastness. 1:3,4. The edge of Paul's gratitude has not been dulled since the writing of the first epistle. He warmly commends the believers for their faith, love, and stability in the midst of ruthless persecution.

3. **We are bound** conveys Paul's sense of personal debt to God because of the growth of the Thessalonians. **It is meet.** That is, "Your conduct merits such thanksgiving." **Your faith groweth exceedingly.** Concerned in the first letter about their faith (I Thess 3:5,10), the apostle rejoices here at its exceptional growth. Having encouraged them to increase their love (I Thess 3:12), he here notes that it (**charity**) **aboundeth** among them. In I Thess 1:3 he commends them for their **patience of hope.** Is such a statement absent here because the central problem of this letter is a misinterpretation of the hope?

4. **Clory in you.** Boast about you. He anticipated his boasting at Christ's coming (I Thess 2:19) by boasting of the Thessalonians among the churches where he labored. **Patience,** i.e., steadfastness, as in I Thess 1:3. **Faith** *(pistis)* sometimes means "faithfulness" (e.g., Rom 3:3; Gal 5:22). Though this meaning would fit well here, it is likely that **faith** refers to the act of trusting, as in II Thess 1:3 and everywhere else in these epistles. **Persecutions** *(diōgmois)* is a specific term, referring to attacks by opponents of the Gospel (cf. Acts 8:1; 13:50), while **tribulations** *(thlipsesin)* are more general pressures (cf. Mt 13:21 and Mk 4:17). The present tense of **ye endure** suggests that this bitter opposition was a present reality.

B. Explanation of the Purpose of Persecution. 1:5-10. Trust and stability in persecution are the evidence of the righteous judgment of God, who is preparing the righteous sufferers for his Kingdom and their opponents for his wrath.

5. **Which is a manifest token** refers not so much to persecution as to their faith and steadfastness in persecution. This stalwart response is *clear evidence*

6. Seeing *it is* a righteous thing with God to recompense tribulation to them that trouble you;

7. And to you who are troubled rest with us, when the Lord Jesus shall be revealed from heaven with his mighty angels,

8. In flaming fire taking vengeance on them that know not God, and that obey not the gospel of our Lord Jesus Christ:

9. Who shall be punished with everlasting destruction from the presence of the Lord, and from the glory of his power;

or a *plain indication* that God's **righteous judgment** will be favorable in their case (cf. II Cor 4:16 ff. and Phil 1:28). Though this righteous judgment will be culminated at the end, it is in operation already (Jn 3:19). Judgment is said to have a definite purpose in the lives of believers: **that ye may be counted worthy.** "It is part of God's *righteous judgment* to use tribulations to bring His own people to perfection" (Morris). **Kingdom.** See note on I Thess 2:12. **For which,** i.e., *on behalf of which.* Cf. Christ's beatitudes in Mt 5:10-12. **6.** Final judgment will bring a righteous reversal of present circumstances: troublers will be troubled, while their victims will receive rest. **Seeing,** i.e., *since indeed* (RSV). **It is a righteous thing.** God's righteousness would be blighted if this sort of wicked opposition were allowed to flourish permanently. **Trouble,** i.e., *bring tribulation upon.*

**7. Rest.** *A relaxing of the tensions.* **With us** apostles, who were strangers neither to tribulation nor to the longing for **rest. Revealed.** *Unveiled* (cf. I Cor 1:7 and especially Lk 17:30). **Mighty angels** is literally, *angels of his power.* That is, angels who are both symbols of and ministers of his power. See note on I Thess 3:13. The kingdom parables of Christ (cf. Mt 13:41,49; 25:31,32) also connect angels with the Judgment. **8. In flaming fire.** For OT background see Isa 66:15 and Dan 7:10,11. The subject of **taking** (*giving*) **vengeance** (*complete punishment*) is the **Lord Jesus** from II Thess 1:7. The Father has entrusted all judgment to him (Jn 5:22,27). The objects of Christ's wrath are **them that know not God and that obey not the gospel.** Some have suggested that two groups — Gentiles (cf. I Thess 4:5) and Jews — are indicated. More likely this is a blanket reference to all who refuse to act on what they know about God and who, more specifically, reject his revelation in Christ.

**9.** The nature of the vengeance: they **shall be punished** (*shall pay a penalty*) **with everlasting destruction.** Annihilation is not the thought but rather total ruin, the loss of everything worthwhile. Specifically, it is separation **from the** presence (*face*) **of the Lord,** the true source of all good things. New Testament descriptions of the pangs of hell are numerous: "furnace of fire" (Mt 13:42); "lake of fire and brimstone" (Rev 20:10); "outer darkness" (Mt 25:30), etc. But

10. When he shall come to be glorified in his saints, and to be admired in all them that believe (because our testimony among you was believed) in that day.

11. Wherefore also we pray always for you, that our God would count you worthy of *this* calling, and fulfil all the good pleasure of *his* goodness, and the work of faith with power:

12. That the name of our Lord Jesus Christ may be glorified in you, and ye in him, according to the grace of our God and the Lord Jesus Christ.

none is more graphic than this picture of endless, utter exclusion from him who is life, light, and love. **The glory of his power.** The "visible manifestation of the greatness of God" (Morris).

**10. When** *(hotan)* is *Whenever.* The time is indefinite. **In his saints.** Believers are the sphere in which Christ will **be glorified** when he comes. "He will be glorified in them, just as the sun is reflected in a mirror" (Alf). This is the culmination of a process already begun (Jn 17:10; II Cor 3:18). **To be admired.** This revelation of Christ's glory in believers will be amazing and wonderful to all who behold it. **In that day** is to be connected with **to be admired.** The intervening clause is parenthetical and difficult to relate to the verse. Perhaps the best suggestion is that it is a condensed expression to be rendered as Phillips does: "to all who believe — including you, for you have believed the message that we have given you."

C. Intercession for Continued Spiritual Growth. 1:11,12. Having clarified for the Thessalonians God's sovereign purposes in their persecution and its glorious outcome, the apostle reaffirms his constant, prayerful concern that the dedication of the believers shall match the designs of God.

**11. Wherefore.** *To this purpose,* relating to the entire section from 1:5-10. **Calling** usually refers to God's initial call to salvation, but the idea here probably includes the culmination of that initial act (cf. I Thess 2:12). **Good pleasure of goodness (his** is not in the Greek text) refers to the Thessalonians, not to God. Paul prays that God will **fulfill** *(carry out to completion)* their delight (**good pleasure**) in **goodness.** *Agathōsynē (goodness)* is never applied to God in the NT (cf. Rom 15:14; Gal 5:22; Eph 5:9). Kindness combines with righteousness in **goodness. Work of faith.** Cf. I Thess 1:3. **With power** describes the manner in which God can fulfill these two petitions.

**12.** The final petition recalls 1:10. **Name** is the revelation of the whole personality, in keeping with Biblical and general Semitic usage. The believers are to reflect continually that glory which shall be fully revealed in them at Christ's coming. **And ye in him** points up the intimacy of union between Christ and his Church. As Christ reveals his glory in the Church, so the only glory the Church can claim is in him. That such a sharing of glory can take place is due to (**according to**) divine **grace.**

## CHAPTER 2

NOW we beseech you, brethren, by the coming of our Lord Jesus Christ, and *by* our gathering together unto him,

2. That ye be not soon shaken in mind, or be troubled, neither by spirit, nor by word, nor by letter as from us, as that the day of Christ is at hand.

3. Let no man deceive you by any means: for *that day shall not come*, except there come a falling away first, and that man of sin be revealed, the son of perdition;

### III. Instruction Concerning the Day of the Lord. 2:1-12.

A. To Come in the Future. 2:1,2. Paul plunges into the problem which called forth the letter — the reports that the afflictions endured by the believers were sure signs that the Day of the Lord had already come. This Paul categorically denies.

1. By *(hyper)* the coming *(parousia;* see note on I Thess 2:19) should be translated *as regarding the coming* (Milligan). So also by our gathering together (cf. Mk 13:27; I Thess 4:17). 2. Soon here means "hastily," or almost "easily." Shaken in mind. Thrown off the course of sound thinking and reasoning. Be troubled. The present tense suggests "be kept in a state of agitation or panic." Three upsetting means are suggested: (1) spirit — report of a special revelation given to Paul; (2) word — a report of a sermon preached by Paul; (3) letter — a false epistle. As from us, *purporting to be from us* (RSV), probably applies to all three. The gist of these false reports was that the day of the Lord (*Christ* does not have good manuscript support) had arrived. The verb *(enestēken)* means "is present" (cf. Rom 8:38; I Cor 3:22; Heb 9:9), not is at hand. Day of the Lord. See note on I Thess 5:2.

B. To Be Preceded by Definite Signs. 2:3-12. The day will be initiated by an outburst of rebellion and by the revelation of the man of lawlessness. The vanguard of the Satanic army is on the march, but the dreadful, doomed leader has not yet come into view.

3. Let no man deceive. See Mt 24:4 ff. By any means. Those in II Thess 2:2 or others. That day shall not come does not occur in the Greek text, but something like it must be supplied. A falling away, literally, the *apostasy*. The meaning of the word was known to Paul's readers, but we are not so fortunate. *Apostasia* usually means "rebellion," whether in a political or religious sense. The reference here is probably to the marshaling of the powers of evil against the people and purposes of God. Christ and Paul both warned against this final wicked conspiracy (e.g., Mt 24:10 ff.; I Tim 4:1-3; II Tim 3:1-9; 4:3 ff.). Apparently it will be of sufficient scope and intensity to mark itself off from the spirit of general opposition to God (mystery of lawlessness, II Thess 2:7) which characterizes the world's attitude. The capstone of the rebellion will be the revelation of

**4.** Who opposeth and exalteth himself above all that is called God, or that is worshipped; so that he as God sitteth in the temple of God, showing himself that he is God.

**5.** Remember ye not, that, when I was yet with you, I told you these things?

**6.** And now ye know what withholdeth that he might be revealed in his time.

the man of lawlessness. **Be revealed** suggests that he is waiting behind the scenes until the time for his public appearance is ripe. In the NT only John uses the term "antichrist" (I Jn 2:18,22; 4:3; II Jn 7), but there can be no doubt as to whom Paul had in mind. **Son of perdition** (cf. Jn 17:12) points both to the nature and to the fate of the lawless one. His actions seal his doom. For **son of,** see note on I Thess 5:5.

**4. Antichrist's Work. Opposeth.** As Satan's minister, Antichrist will carry out his master's work (I Tim 5:14). **All that is called God.** The true, living God (I Thess 1:9) and all false gods. **That is worshipped,** i.e., every object held sacred — temples, shrines, etc. Antichrist will take his place **as God in the temple,** probably the Jerusalem temple, as the close connection between this passage and the description of Antiochus Epiphanes (Dan 11:36 ff.) suggests (cf. also Mk 13:14, where the masculine participle may indicate a person rather than an image). Revelation 13:4-15 describes Antichrist's cult. **Shewing himself.** Better, *proclaiming himself,* in accordance with the Hellenistic meaning of *apodeiknymi.*

**5. I told you.** The imperfect tense indicates that more than once Paul had discussed these events.

**6. What withholdeth** and the related **who letteth** (v. 7; i.e., "restrains") are exceedingly difficult to interpret confidently because of Paul's brief treatment. That the Thessalonians knew what he meant is of little comfort to us. Certain observations may be made: (1) The present tense of the two participles shows that the arresting force or person was already in operation. (2) The change from neuter (v. 6) to masculine (v. 7) suggests that the restrainer can be spoken of as a thing or person. (3) The restraining influence will be removed in God's **(his)** time, and Antichrist will be revealed. Dispensationalist interpreters (e.g., C. I. Scofield, L. S. Chafer, and J. Walvoord) have identified the restrainer as the Holy Spirit, a view supported by the fact that the Spirit may be described in both neuter and masculine genders. Removal of the Spirit takes place when the Church, his temple, is raptured (I Thess 4:13-17). However, why would Paul speak of the Spirit in such veiled terms? Furthermore, how can the revelation of Antichrist be a sign to the church that has already been raptured? Many Biblical commentators from Tertullian (c. A.D. 200) on have identified the restrainer as the Roman

7. For the mystery of iniquity doth already work: only he who now letteth *will let,* until he be taken out of the way.

8. And then shall that Wicked be revealed, whom the Lord shall consume with the spirit of his mouth, and shall destroy with the brightness of his coming:

9. *Even him,* whose coming is after the working of Satan with all power and signs and lying wonders,

10. And with all deceivableness of unrighteousness in them that perish; because they received not the love of the truth, that they might be saved.

Empire. The neuter participle would refer to the state; the masculine, to the emperor. This view leans upon Paul's charitable attitude toward government as a means of maintaining law and order so that the church may do its work (cf. Rom 13:1-7; Tit 3:1; I Pet 2:13,14,17). But the Roman Empire has long since faded away, and the lawless one has not yet been revealed. Thus it seems probable that the restraining influence refers to the principle of human government manifest in the Roman state. Human institutions are part of God's program of common grace, whereby he bridles the forces of evil to provide the proper setting for the revelation of his special, redemptive grace. Totalitarian in the extreme (cf. Rev 13:15-17), Antichrist's government is so diabolical in nature and so ruthless in practice that it utterly disqualifies itself for being considered a God-ordained human institution. In **his** (God's) **time** shows that God is in ultimate control.

7. **Mystery** indicates that the wicked spiritual principle already at work had been revealed to believers (cf. the use of *mystērion* in Mk 4:11; Rom 16:25, etc.). **Iniquity.** *Lawlessness.* Matthew 24:24 and I Jn 2:18 mention Antichrist's forerunners, who are embodiments of this principle of lawlessness. **He who letteth.** See note on 2:6. **Taken out of the way.** Probably by God, although not so stated. 8. **Wicked.** Literally, *lawless*—Antichrist's basic characteristic, as "man of lawlessness" and "mystery of lawlessness" (vv. 3,7, RSV) show. No sooner is his unveiling **(revealed)** mentioned than his doom is described. **Consume.** Better manuscripts read *slay.* **Spirit,** i.e., *breath.* See Isa 11:4 for OT background. **Destroy.** *Render useless, make powerless.* **Brightness** (*epiphaneia*) or *manifestation* speaks of the brilliant display of Christ's power at his coming (cf. II Thess 1:7,8; Rev 19:11-21).

9. Antichrist has his **coming** as Christ has His. Satan's **working** (*power in operation*) is Antichrist's dynamic (cf. Rev 13:2). His coming reveals itself in **all power** (to work miracles) and **signs** (significant, meaningful miracles) and **wonders** (amazing their observers). In the Greek, **lying** seems to apply to all three: the miracles are steeped in falsehood. Cf. Acts 2:22; Rom 15:19, etc., for the three words describing miracles. 10. **Deceivableness of unrighteousness.** Deceit stemming from unrighteousness. **Them that perish.** The present participle (*apollymenois*) suggests that the process

11. And for this cause God shall send them strong delusion, that they should believe a lie:

12. That they all might be damned who believed not the truth, but had pleasure in unrighteousness.

13. But we are bound to give thanks always to God for you, brethren beloved of the Lord, because God hath from the beginning chosen you to salvation through sanctification of the Spirit and belief of the truth:

14. Whereunto he called you by our gospel, to the obtaining of the glory of our Lord Jesus Christ.

15. Therefore, brethren, stand fast, and hold the traditions which ye have been taught, whether by word, or our epistle.

is already in operation (cf. I Cor 1:18). **Received.** Welcomed. **Truth,** i.e., of the Gospel.

**11. God shall send** indicates God's sovereignty, controlling the destinies not only of his own but of his enemies. Rejected light results in greater darkness, as Mt 13:10 ff. and Rom 1:24-32 demonstrate. Effectively deceived, they trust **the lie,** not **the truth** (2:10,12). Satan's lie consists in getting men to believe him instead of God (cf. Gen 3:1 ff.; Jn 8:44). **12. Damned.** *Judged.* The verdict of guilty is implied, not expressed. **Pleasure in unrighteousness.** Not helpless victims, they willingly side with Satan against God and will share their captain's fate (Jn 16:11).

### IV. Thanksgiving and Exhortation. 2:13-17.

A. Praise for Their Calling. 2:13-15. In marked contrast with the dark portrait of Antichrist and his followers are the bright prospects of those whom God has called.

**13. Bound to give thanks.** See note on 1:3. **Beloved.** See note on I Thess 1:4. **From the beginning** seems to reflect the Pauline view of an election prior to creation (Eph 1:4). Some manuscripts read *first fruits* for **from the beginning.** This reading, adopted by some editors (e.g., Nestle, Moffatt), would be fitting, because the Thessalonians were among the earliest of Paul's European converts. **Chosen** (*heilato;* cf. LXX, Deut 26:18) reminds us that believers have joined Israel as God's elect people (cf. I Pet 2:9, 10). **Sanctification** (cf. I Thess 4:3,7) **of the spirit** stresses the Spirit's role in separating believers from Satan's sphere of control to God's (I Pet 1:2). **Belief of the truth** emphasizes the human response of faith to the truth of the Gospel (Rom 10:17). **14. Whereunto** refers to God's act of salvation described in 2:13. **Called.** Cf. I Thess 2:12; 5:24. **Our gospel.** Cf. I Thess 1:5. **Obtaining** (cf. I Thess 5:9) **of the glory** is a further description of the meaning of salvation. See note on 1:10.

**15. Traditions.** Almost none of the NT existed in written form. The basis of instruction was the authoritative oral record (**word**) of the Gospel events and interpretation (cf. I Cor 11:2,23; 15:3). **Epistle** probably refers to I Thessalonians. The content of the tradition is discernible in the sermons in Acts (2:14 ff.; 7:2 ff.; 13:16 ff., etc.) and the creedal

16. Now our Lord Jesus Christ himself, and God, even our Father, which hath loved us, and hath given *us* everlasting consolation and good hope through grace,

17. Comfort your hearts, and stablish you in every good word and work.

## CHAPTER 3

FINALLY, brethren, pray for us, that the word of the Lord may have *free* course, and be glorified, even as *it is* with you:

2. And that we may be delivered from unreasonable and wicked men: for all *men* have not faith.

3. But the Lord is faithful, who shall stablish you, and keep *you* from evil.

4. And we have confidence in the Lord touching you, that ye both do and will do the things which we command you.

5. And the Lord direct your hearts into the love of God, and into the patient waiting for Christ.

statements embedded in the epistles (I Cor 15:3 ff.; I Thess 1:9,10, etc.).

B. Prayer for Their Comfort and Stability. 2:16,17. Paul, as was his custom, seals his exhortation with a prayer. **16.** Compare the very similar phrasing of I Thess 3:11. Note the honor paid to Christ by the position accorded him in this verse. **Consolation** (*paraklēsin*) includes strength as well as comfort. **Good hope** speaks of the worthy character of the believer's confident expectation, as well as of the joyous outcome (cf. I Thess 1:3). **Through grace** reminds us that these and all of God's blessings are undeserved, and it stifles pride (cf. 1:11,12). **17. Comfort and stablish.** Cf. I Thess 3:2. **Every good word and work.** Whatever you do or say.

## V. Confession of Confidence. 3:1-5.

A. Request for Prayer. 3:1,2. The request of I Thess 5:25 is repeated, with an added note of urgency due to the militant opposition of faithless men.

**1. May have free course** is literally *may run*, stressing both the vital, active nature of **the word of the Lord** (i.e., Christ's word) and the urgency with which the apostles desired to spread it (cf. Ps 147:15). **Be glorified.** By being received and obeyed (cf. Acts 13:48; Tit 2:10). **With you.** See I Thess 1:6; 2:13 for their wholehearted reception of the Gospel. **2. Delivered.** See note on I Thess 1:10. **Unreasonable.** *Perverse, improper.* **Wicked,** in an actively, deliberately harmful sense. See Acts 18:6,12 for glimpses of this Jewish opposition. **Have not faith.** An understatement; these men not only refused to believe but threatened all who did.

B. Reminder of God's Faithfulness. 3:3-5. This opposition was marked for failure because a faithful God is stronger than faithless men. **3.** See I Thess 5:24. **Stablish.** Cf. I Thess 3:2; II Thess 2:17. **Keep,** i.e., guard, protect. **From evil.** *From the evil one,* Satan (cf. Mt 6:13). **4. In the Lord.** The faithfulness of God helps to assure the obedient response of the Thessalonians both in the present (**ye both do**) and in the future (**will do**). **Which we command you** seems to refer to the instructions to follow (3:6 ff.). **5.** Paul pauses to utter one of his most touching prayers. **The Lord,** i.e., Christ. **Direct** (*kateuthynai,* as in I Thess 3:11) means to "clear the way of obstacles,"

6. Now we command you, brethren, in the name of our Lord Jesus Christ, that ye withdraw yourselves from every brother that walketh disorderly, and not after the tradition which he received of us.

7. For yourselves know how ye ought to follow us: for we behaved not ourselves disorderly among you;

8. Neither did we eat any man's bread for nought; but wrought with labor and travail night and day, that we might not be chargeable to any of you:

9. Not because we have not power, but to make ourselves an ensample unto you to follow us.

10. For even when we were with you, this we commanded you, that if any would not work, neither should he eat.

11. For we hear that there are some which walk among you disorderly, working not at all, but are busybodies.

"open a direct path." **Hearts.** See note on I Thess 2:4. **Love of God.** God's love is a tremendous source of stability and security (Rom 8:37-39). **Patient waiting for Christ.** *The steadfastness of Christ* (RSV). Christ's example of unflagging endurance is a prime source of inspiration to troubled believers (Heb 12:1,2).

## VI. Commandments to Work. 3:6-15.

With apostolic authority Paul attacks the problem of laziness which was plaguing the Thessalonian church. Reminding his friends of his own diligence, he commands firm yet loving discipline of the idle.

A. Shun the Idle. 3:6.
**We command,** as an officer his troops. **Brethren.** Paul's sternness does not throttle his affection. The apostle derived his authority from the **Lord. Disorderly.** Out of rank; cf. "unruly" in I Thess 5:14. **Tradition** (cf. II Thess 2:15) includes both Paul's personal example and his written instruction (I Thess 4:11,12).

B. Imitate Us. 3:7-9.
**7. Follow.** *Imitate, emulate* (Arndt). **Behaved not ourselves disorderly** is an understatement. Paul's example of industry was not only untarnished but brilliant. **8. Eat bread** means to gain a livelihood (cf. II Sam 9:7; Amos 7:12). **For nought.** Without cost. This verse resembles I Thess 2:9 but stresses Paul's example of diligence rather than his integrity of purpose. **9. Power,** i.e., apostolic authority to gain his living from his hearers (cf. I Thess 2:6). **Ensample.** Example, pattern (cf. I Thess 1:7). **Follow.** Cf. II Thess 3:7.

C. Work or Do Not Eat. 3:10.
The imperfect tense of **we commanded** shows that more than once Paul had urged them to diligence with these words: **If any would not work,** etc. **Would not** shows that this is willful inactivity. This saying may be based on Jewish interpretation of Gen 3:19.

D. Exhort the Idle. 3:11-13.
**11. We hear.** Unhappy news spread as easily as the report of the believers' faith (I Thess 1:8,9). **Disorderly.** Cf. II Thess 3:6,7. The force of the nice pun is brought out by Ellicott (cited in Milligan): "doing no business (**working**

12. Now them that are such we command and exhort by our Lord Jesus Christ, that with quietness they work, and eat their own bread.

13. But ye, brethren, be not weary in well doing.

14. And if any man obey not our word by this epistle, note that man, and have no company with him, that he may be ashamed.

15. Yet count *him* not as an enemy, but admonish *him* as a brother.

16. Now the Lord of peace himself give you peace always by all means. The Lord *be* with you all.

17. The salutation of Paul with mine own hand, which is the token in every epistle: so I write.

18. The grace of our Lord Jesus Christ *be* with you all. Amen.

The second *epistle* to the Thessalonians was written from Athens.

not at all) but being busybodies." **12.** Paul addresses the troublemakers. **We command.** Cf. 3:6,10 for similar tone of authority. **Exhort** (cf. I Thess 2:11) adds a note of tenderness but retains the urgency. **By our Lord,** etc. Paul views himself as Christ's spokesman. **With quietness.** In contrast to the disorder frequently noted (3:6,7,11). **Eat.** Cf. 3:8.

**13. But ye.** The whole church. Regardless of the conduct of the indolent, **be not weary,** i.e., do not flag or become slack. The aorist tense suggests that they had not yet begun to do so. To do the right thing (**well doing**) is never easy, but it becomes exceedingly difficult under irritating circumstances such as these.

E. Warn and Discipline the Disobedient. 3:14,15.

14. This epistle is Paul's last word on this matter of laziness. Anyone who disobeys is to be a 'marked man' (**note that man**) with whom believers are not to mix (**company**). The purpose of this ostracism was not punitive but corrective, Paul's hope being that the sense of shame would bring the offender into line. Such social pressure is especially effective in a close-knit, clan-like society, such as this company of believers. **15.** Love is to prevail. The idle loafer is not to be considered an **enemy** but a **brother. Admonish.** Cf. I Thess 5:12,14.

**VII. Conclusion. 3:16-18.**

A. Blessing. 3:16.
Human effort alone cannot bring spiritual well-being (**peace**). This is a gift of Christ, who promised his disciples peace (Jn 14:27; 16:33) and is here called **Lord of peace** (cf. note on I Thess 5:23). **Always by all means.** Continually in any kind of circumstance. **With you all.** Even with the idlers.

B. Paul's Signature. 3:17.
**The token.** Paul's handwriting at the close of his letters was the sign of their authority (cf. I Cor 16:21; Gal 6:11; Col 4:18). **So I write.** Calling to their attention his style of handwriting, a necessary precaution (cf. II Thess 2:2).

C. Benediction. 3:18.
See note on I Thess 5:28. **All.** This blessing includes even the troublemakers.

# BIBLIOGRAPHY

For bibliography see under *I Thessalonians*.

# THE FIRST
# EPISTLE TO TIMOTHY

## INTRODUCTION

*Authorship*. The Pauline authorship of the Pastorals (I, II Timothy and Titus) is contested. However, the *prima facie* evidence of the writings themselves indicates that Paul is the writer, since his name appears in the salutation of each, and autobiographical remarks fit the life of Paul as recorded elsewhere: e.g., I Tim 1:12,13; II Tim 3:10,11; 4:10,11, 19,20.

The basic rule of evidence regarding genuineness of documents was stated long ago by Simon Greenleaf: "Every document, apparently ancient, coming from the proper repository or custody, and bearing on its face no evident marks of forgery, the law presumes to be genuine, and devolves on the opposing party the burden of proving it to be otherwise" (*An Examination of the Testimony of the Four Evangelists*, London, 1847, p. 7).

We have in the Pastorals ancient books, coming from the proper custody, the church. The church always accepted them as Pauline; there is no dissenting voice until modern times. What then does criticism offer to offset the *prima facie* evidence and the unanimous voice of tradition? Alleged marks of non-genuineness or forgery are four: (1) non-Pauline language and style; (2) the opposition of the Pastorals to second-century Gnosticism; (3) discrepancies between the Pastorals and Acts—it is assumed that Paul was put to death at the end of the one and only Roman imprisonment, as recorded in Acts, and hence it is concluded that Paul cannot be the author of the Pastorals; (4) advanced ecclesiastical organization, beyond the time of Paul, reflected in the Pastorals.

These arguments do not overcome the positive evidence. (1) The linguistic argument is inconclusive because psychologically absurd as well as difficult, if not impossible, to prove. Would a forger, seeking to have a book accepted as a work of Paul, introduce non-Pauline vocabulary at the rate of seventeen words per page of Greek text, and refer to incidents and persons which did not enter the known life of Paul? The unhesitating and unanimous reception of the books by the ancient church, under such conditions, would be impossible to explain. Indeed, this unhesitating reception is very good evidence that the epistles were well known to be genuine. The linguistic data may conceivably point to the joint authorship of Luke and Paul (Moffatt, *Introduction to the Literature of the New Testament*, 3rd ed., p. 414), but it is well to remember that at best the dating of literature by limiting a writer's language and style is only conjecture. The readers of Paul's Pastoral Epistles were different from those of any other epistles. Timothy and Titus had been intimately associated with Paul's life and thought for fifteen to twenty years. We should therefore not be surprised if Paul chose to speak in language and style different from that used in addressing churches. Paul was encouraging and exhorting his sons in the faith, not correcting quarreling or wavering churches.

(2) The assumption in this objection is that if the Pastorals refute second-century Gnosticism, they must be second-century documents. Given the clear *prima facie* evidence of Pauline authorship, if there are statements answering later Gnosticism, the inference is that Paul has foreseen such developments, which is not impossible even from the standpoint of mere human sagacity. However, Paul has elsewhere in other epistles claimed, by inspiration, to foresee and predict the future. To deny that he could is to beg the whole question of the possibility of supernatural revelation. Moreover, Paul may not have been fighting in these epistles a Gnosticism as advanced as some have argued.

(3) That the names, places, and incidents alluded to in the Pastorals cannot be fitted into the outline of Acts, is a very good reason for extending the life of Paul beyond the narration of Acts. The Pastorals, then, would be the product of

Paul's fourth missionary journey and a second imprisonment.

(4) The elements of ecclesiastical organization found in the Pastorals are found elsewhere in the New Testament. Some have thought that the ranking of Luke's Gospel as Scripture (I Tim 5: 18) is an indication of late date. "By the time the author of the pastorals wrote, either Luke's gospel or some evangelic collection containing Luke 10:7 was reckoned as *graphē*" (*Ibid.*, p. 401f.). This argument also assumes the point to be proved, namely, that the book could not have been inspired and known to be inspired from the time of its writing and reception.

Fuller answers to these arguments have been worked out in the standard conservative commentaries and introductions. See especially Hendriksen, *New Testament Commentary: Exposition of the Pastoral Epistles*, pp. 4-32.

*Date.* The first letter to Timothy and the one to Titus were written during the period of travel and missionary work between Paul's two Roman imprisonments. A date somewhere between A.D. 61 and 63 cannot be far wrong. The second epistle to Timothy contains the last words found from the apostle; they were written from prison shortly before his martyrdom (4:6-8). We should view them, as Calvin expresses it, "as written not with ink but with Paul's own blood." The date of the apostle's death is generally set sometimes between A.D. 65 and 68.

*Occasion and Message.* As Moses gave the charge to Joshua, and the Lord to his apostles, so Paul gives the charge to Timothy and Titus. Likewise, as Moses ended with an exhortation to all Israel, and Christ to all the Church, so Paul concludes his charge with the benediction, "Grace be with you" ("you" is plural; I Tim 6:21; II Tim 4:22) and "Grace be with you all" (Tit 3:15). The occasion for writing the epistles was no less than the need to maintain the faith, to insure the continuity of the Church of Jesus Christ. The solemn charge — "That good thing which was committed unto thee, keep by the Holy Ghost which dwelleth in us" (II Tim 1:14) — is the heart of the Pastoral Epistles. Here Timothy and Titus, together with all the Church, are charged to keep "the faith," "the deposit," the written record, by the work of the Holy Spirit. The outwork-

ing of this charge is not only the maintaining of the faith through good works and right conduct in the house of God, but also the resisting of that which is false. The more immediate need for the first two epistles—I Timothy and Titus — lay, no doubt, in the fact that many things at Ephesus and Crete needed adjustment. Paul, however, having intended to advise his sons in the faith, determined to advise others at the same time.

*Structure and Theme. I Timothy.* This first of the Pastoral Epistles falls into a literary pattern that is probably not accidental. In its briefest form, it can be indicated thus: (A) Charge, (B) Praise, (A) Charge. Stated in another way it is: (A) Prose, (B) Poetry, (A) Prose. This simple pattern of a solemn charge in two parts, bound together by a doxology or hymn of praise, is repeated three times—in the introduction, the body, and the conclusion. The epistle summarized according to this pattern offers a greater unity than is generally recognized. In the introduction, following the salutation, we find the charge to Timothy, with a longer explanatory portion (1:3-16) and a briefer concluding word (1:18-20). These two parts are bound together by the terse but weighty doxology of verse 17. The initial part leading up to the doxology includes an outline—only briefly suggested—of the main topics of the epistle. All is so skillfully woven together that the many themes presented only serve to focus attention on Paul's charge to Timothy. Then follows the doxology, which gives solemn weight to the final part of the charge.

At the conclusion of the epistle, there is another charge, again twofold, with its parts bound together by the doxology of verse 16b. Again the same proportions are preserved: the first is a longer section (6:3-16a) with a recapitulation of the principal themes of the epistle; the shorter portion (6:17-21) concludes with the deeply moving appeal, "O Timothy, guard the deposit."

In like manner, the major portion of the epistle (2:1-6:2) is subdivided by a transitional paragraph (3:14–4:5), at the center of which are the lines of the ancient Christian hymn of which Paul is probably the author (3:16). The first section of this major portion deals with official or public aspects of the Church, the House of God, culminating in the memorable lines of the hymn. In the second portion, individual and personal aspects are stressed, paralleling to a remarkable degree the themes stated in the first section. For example, the reference to women in the first part sets forth the principle of masculine leadership in the Church; whereas, the reference to women in the second part, deals with the individual and personal problem of dependent widows. It appears that one section is intended to balance the other. But more important, the whole structure of the epistle is designed to throw into prominence the great hymn of praise at the center, which presents succinctly and beautifully the person and work of Christ.

*II Timothy.* In Paul's second epistle to his "dearly beloved son," he seems to be following essentially the same literary pattern as in the first. This time it occurs in its simplest possible form, namely, a solemn charge in two parts, bound together by a hymn. All is prefaced with a salutation and thanksgiving, and concluded with personal notes and prayer. Again the whole structure is designed to highlight the great hymn of doctrinal truth which appears at the

center (2:11-13). The chief point on which the structure turns is Paul's presentation of the Gospel as a trust to be preserved, cherished, and committed to faithful men. His words gain peculiar solemnity and weight because they were the last to come from his pen; he wrote knowing that his "departure" was "at hand."

*Titus.* The theme of this epistle is like that of all the Pastorals in emphasizing the connection of doctrine, committed to faithful men, with godliness of life. In this letter, Paul most memorably links grace, as the great doctrine of salvation, to good works in the balancing passages, 2:11-15 and 3:4-8. In the one passage grace appears, in the other, kindness and love appear. Both stress the blessed hope (2:13; 3:7b); both conclude with the emphasis on good works.

*Note on Commentary.* In the commentary that follows an effort has been made to give not merely explanatory words on a given text, but, far more important, the citation of parallel texts which, if patiently searched out, will give the Scripture's own commentary.

# OUTLINE

3. The motives of the man of God. 6:11-15 a.
B. Doxology. 6:15b,16.
C. Return to the solemn charge. 6:17-21.
  1. Right use of possessions. 6:17-19.
  2. Final appeal: A summation. 6:20,21.

# I TIMOTHY

## CHAPTER 1

PAUL, an apostle of Jesus Christ by the commandment of God our Saviour, and Lord Jesus Christ, *which is* our hope;

2. Unto Timothy, *my* own son in the faith: Grace, mercy, *and* peace, from God our Father, and Jesus Christ our Lord.

# COMMENTARY

## I. Salutation and Introduction. 1:1-20.

A. Salutation, with Special Notes of Authority and Hope. 1:1,2. **1.** Paul's apostolic authority was based on the deity and command of Christ. Compare Gal 1:1: " . . . not from men or through a man but through Jesus Christ and God the Father." The divine authorization is further emphasized (1) by the word **commandment:** it suggests a royal command which is to be obeyed; and (2) by the fact that it is the command of both God the Father and Christ Jesus. In thus linking equally the names of the Father and Christ, as in verse 2, Paul leaves no doubt as to the full deity of Christ (see Warfield, *Biblical and Theological Studies,* Ch. III). God is characterized by the name **Saviour,** an exalted title reminding one of Isa 45:21, and similar passages. Jesus is distinguished by the appellation, **our hope,** a succinct way of tying all eschatology to the person of Christ, for Timothy's encouragement. **2.** Also for Timothy's encouragement, no doubt, the apostle adds the word **mercy** to the ordinary formula of **grace and peace.** Only in the Pastorals does Paul thus depart from his usual custom.

B. Paul's Charge to Timothy, Presenting Principal Topics of the Epistle. 1:3-16. Paul's method, apparently, is to present the problems and topics he wishes to discuss, and then to revert to these topics later in order to add details. Hence he first treats the basic matter of sound doctrine. Paul did not need to expound doctrines in detail for Timothy, but it was necessary to remind him of the strategic importance of doctrine for life, and as the correlate, the necessity for obedience to doctrine. This leads to a discussion of one side of the doctrine of the Law, its relation to the cases of outbreaking, flagrant vice here mentioned. The writer briefly sums up the relation of the Law to the believer in the phrase, "The end of the command is love" (v. 5). Paul then encourages Timothy with a superb testimony and doxology, and gives a solemn charge and illustration of

**3. As I besought thee to abide still at Ephesus, when I went into Macedonia, that thou mightest charge some that they teach no other doctrine,**

**4. Neither give heed to fables and endless genealogies, which minister questions, rather than godly edifying which is in faith:** *so do.*

**5. Now the end of the commandment is charity out of a pure heart, and** *of* **a good conscience, and** *of* **faith unfeigned:**

**6. From which some having swerved have turned aside unto vain jangling;**

**7. Desiring to be teachers of the law; understanding neither what they say, nor whereof they affirm.**

the results of not holding a good conscience.

1) Sound versus False Teaching. 1:3,4. The heretical teaching and attention to myths and endless genealogies produced useless speculations and controversies instead of Gospel godliness. Verses 3,4 form the dependent clause of a sentence the main clause of which is verses 5-7. The relation can be seen by (1) omitting *so do*, which has been supplied by the translator, (2) punctuating with a comma instead of a semicolon after faith, (3) omitting *now* of verse 5. The thought would then be: "Just as I exhorted you . . . the end (purpose) of my charge is love. . . ." See comment on II Tim 1:3. **4.** The myths and genealogies were probably Gnostic or proto-Gnostic teachings. Gnosticism had two extremes: asceticism, as in 4:3, and antinomian license, as the context intimates here. Erroneous discourses on law, and Gnostic speculations left plain matters of immorality uncorrected. The **dispensation of God** (ASV; AV, *godly edifying)* is the proper issue of sound teaching, and therefore parallels the "love" of verse 5, and the "good warfare" of verse 18. Love is Paul's summary of religious and ethical duty (Rom 13:10; Gal 5:6). The sound teaching brings *God's ordering* or *God's superintendence* of the life.

2) The Purpose of Sound Teaching. 1: 5-7. These verses are the main clause of the sentence mentioned above. **5. Commandment.** *Charge* (ASV). The word is the noun cognate to the verb **charge** of verse 3. **Faith** is used in the sense of "the faith," sound doctrine. The charge relates to the sources of love: a pure heart, a good conscience, and sound doctrine. **6. Which.** A plural form referring to the heart, conscience, faith just mentioned. It is when these guides of the moral and ethical life have been impaired either by false teaching or disobedience, that people turn to vain jangling. **7. Teachers of the law.** One word. Used of Gamaliel (Acts 5:34) and of eminent teachers (Lk 5:17). Paul seems to refer to

8. But we know that the law *is* good, if a man use it lawfully;

9. Knowing this, that the law is not made for a righteous man, but for the lawless and disobedient, for the ungodly and for sinners, for unholy and profane, for murderers of fathers and murderers of mothers, for manslayers,

10. For whoremongers, for them that defile themselves with mankind, for menstealers, for liars, for perjured persons, and if there be any other thing that is contrary to sound doctrine;

11. According to the glorious gospel of the blessed God, which was committed to my trust.

12. And I thank Christ Jesus our Lord, who hath enabled me, for that he counted me faithful, putting me into the ministry;

13. Who was before a blasphemer, and a persecutor, and injurious: but I obtained mercy, because I did *it* ignorantly in unbelief.

the ambitious pride of the false teachers, and exposes their utter incompetence.

3) The True Doctrine of the Law. 1: 8-11. The apostle takes up the relation of the Law to the lost. Again these verses are one sentence. The connection is: "We know that the Law is good, if one uses it lawfully . . . in accordance with the Gospel." Paul discusses this function of the Law in detail in Rom 7:7-25: "It brings the knowledge of sin and makes sin exceedingly sinful, all with the end of bringing a man to Christ.

9,10. The law is not made for a righteous man. "The Law does not condemn a righteous man." The expression is a relative negative, to be taken in context. It does not mean that the Law has no relation to the righteous; for him, it is a righteous rule which he joyfully obeys in the Spirit. The catalogue of sins here given is not the same as lists given elsewhere. Probably this one contemplated special problems in Ephesus. 11. With the mention of the Gospel, Paul makes his exultant transition to his testimony of what the Gospel did in his case, emphasizing the things needed to encourage Timothy.

4) Paul's Testimony and Gospel. 1: 12-16. The writer's testimony is in two parts: (1) 12-14; (2) 15,16. These parts run parallel, in that Paul's preconversion condition is stressed; and also in each section the turning point and contrast comes with the words, "but I received mercy." The heartfelt doxology of the Introduction to the book (v. 17) comes as a fitting climax to Paul's testimony.

12. It is striking that in all Paul's recorded words only here does he give thanks directly to Christ, and only here does he use the eloquent language appropriate to the deep thankfulness he feels as he recalls his own salvation and call. Faithful (cf. I Cor 7:25). The basis of Christ's counting Paul faithful was His mercy. Paul was faithful to the trust he had received (I Tim 1:11).

13. Injurious. A violent, proud, insolent person; the "despiteful" of Rom 1:30. Paul characterizes his lost condition in three terrible words: blasphemer, persecutor, injurious. Against this self-condemnation, in dramatic contrast, stands the simple word, "I received mercy." Though Paul persecuted the church in ignorance, thinking he was doing God service (Acts 26:9), he does not minimize his sin. Even sins of ignorance need atone-

**14.** And the grace of our Lord was exceeding abundant with faith and love which is in Christ Jesus.

**15.** This *is* a faithful saying, and worthy of all acceptation, that Christ Jesus came into the world to save sinners; of whom I am chief.

**16.** Howbeit for this cause I obtained mercy, that in me first Jesus Christ might show forth all long-suffering, for a pattern to them which should hereafter believe on him to life everlasting.

**17.** Now unto the King eternal, immortal, invisible, the only wise God, *be* honor and glory for ever and ever. Amen.

**18.** This charge I commit unto thee, son Timothy, according to the prophecies which went before on thee, that thou by them mightest war a good warfare;

ment (Heb 9:7; Lev 5:15-19). The mention of ignorance emphasizes the pitiable, guilty blindness of sin (Eph 4:18; I Pet 1:14). "Paul was deeply penitent for having persecuted the church of God, but apparently he did not lay to his charge the black sin of having carried on the persecution in the face of better conviction" (J. Gresham Machen, *Origin of Paul's Religion*, p. 61).

**14.** Not a separate sentence, but the completion and climax of the statement begun at verse 12. In his sin, Paul found in Christ mercy, grace, faithfulness, love; and this grace overflowed and abounded exceedingly. **15. Saying.** "Faithful is the message and worthy of full acceptance." The message is not merely a **saying**, but is based on the words of Christ (Lk 19: 10), and is equivalent to the truth of the Gospel. It appears in this form here and in I Tim 4:9. In the simple words, **Faithful is the message** (at 3:1; II Tim 2:11; Tit 3:8, as here in verse 15), Paul underscores his lost condition. **Of whom I am chief.** This is parallel to **blasphemer, persecutor, injurious**; and it is climactic.

**16. I obtained mercy.** Again Paul gives the dramatic contrast between his unworthiness and Christ's mercy, adding here, **for this cause,** pointing to the explanatory **that** which follows: *that in me as chief might Jesus Christ show forth all his longsuffering* (ASV). Paul purposed his testimony as an encouragement to Timothy, who faced the sin mentioned above, plus false teaching in the church. Paul, in effect, says, "If the Lord saved me, who was worse than any others, none need despair; and you may be assured that my Lord can enable you, too."

C. Doxology. 1:17. To the double testimony just given, the doxology of praise comes as the climax and the welling-up of Paul's deep adoration and thankfulness. God the Father has not been mentioned in the context, so this doxology to God may possibly be taken as directed to Christ or to the Triune God.

D. Charge and Encouragement to Timothy. 1:18-20. The charge is the whole responsibility for the Gospel ministry, in accordance with prophetic utterances given at Timothy's ordination. The details of the charge are given in the rest of the epistle and summed up again at 6:13,14.

**18. By them.** By the prophecies, by the reminder of responsibility and trust reposed in him, Timothy may be chal-

19. Holding faith, and a good conscience; which some having put away, concerning faith have made shipwreck:

20. Of whom is Hymeneus and Alexander; whom I have delivered unto Satan, that they may learn not to blaspheme.

## CHAPTER 2

I EXHORT therefore, that, first of all, supplications, prayers, intercessions, *and* giving of thanks, be made for all men;

lenged and encouraged to remain fruitful in his difficult task. See notes on II Tim 1:4,5. **19. Holding faith and a good conscience.** The whole Gospel message embraces both doctrine and obedience thereto. The **faith** is what we believe about Christ; **good conscience** is not allowing the conscience to be defiled by sinful practices contrary to the doctrine. See note on II Tim 1:3. **Which.** Refers to the **good conscience.** If true doctrine is not obeyed, it is in effect denied and becomes a "dead faith," and men make **shipwreck.** Reshaping their doctrine to fit their sinful course, they proceed to teach a false doctrine. Hence the words: "There is danger lest faith be sunk by a bad conscience, as by a whirlpool in a stormy sea" (Calvin).

**20.** Paul cites two specific examples of **shipwreck.** Alexander is probably the Alexander of II Tim 4:14, who opposed the apostolic teaching (see Zahn's detailed discussion in *Introduction to the New Testament,* II, 108-110). Hymenaeus is mentioned at II Tim 2:17 and the heresy specified. **Delivered unto Satan.** This has been interpreted by some to mean the apostolic imposition of some extraordinary chastisement (Acts 5:5; 13:11; Job 2:6 — though God's delivering Job to Satan is not analogous to Paul's dealing with a fornicator or heretic). However, a comparison with I Cor 5:3-5 makes excommunication the more probable meaning. He who does not belong to the Church, the body of Christ, is under the dominion of Satan. Blasphemy is any violation of the third commandment, any light and sinful use of God's name (see *Westminster Larger Catechism,* Questions 112, 113).

**II. Exhortations and Instructions to the Church of the Living God. 2:1– 6:2.**

The topics Paul discusses in this section are readily distinguished, as indicated in the general outline. Not so readily distinguished is the point of view governing the choice of these topics and their order. The key idea of the epistle is the preservation of the faith and witnessing. It is not surprising, then, that at the very center of the letter stands the paragraph that presents the Church as **the pillar and ground of the truth,** as the agency which defends and spreads the Gospel message (see Introduction, *Structure and Theme. I Timothy*). Following this paragraph, at 4:6, comes a natural division.

2. For kings, and *for* all that are in authority; that we may lead a quiet and peaceable life in all godliness and honesty.

3. For this *is* good and acceptable in the sight of God our Saviour;

4. Who will have all men to be saved, and to come unto the knowledge of the truth.

Up to this division Paul appears to discuss aspects of the witness of the whole Church. After it he speaks to individuals and particular classes of individuals, selecting his exhortations with reference to witness and testimony.

A. To the Witnessing Church. 2:1—3:13. In general, the point of view here is the church in its public and corporate aspects: worship and officers.

1) Public Prayer as Related to the Missionary Purpose of the Church. 2:1-8. Paul's first topic is prayer for all, and for all in authority. The universal emphasis is clear from the *all's* in verses 1, 2, 4, 6, and from the apostolic, missionary note of verse 7. Paul does not here enter on a complete discussion of the relation of the Christian to civil authority, but only exhorts that prayer be made for those in authority, that believers may lead a quiet and peaceful life. This is conducive to the larger purpose of bringing salvation to men.

**1. Supplications, prayers, intercessions, and giving of thanks.** These words for prayer are the same as those found in Phil 4:6 and frequently in the NT, with the exception of **intercession,** which appears only here and in I Tim 4:5 (the cognate verb appears in Acts 25:24; Rom 8:27,34; 11:2; Heb 7:25).

**3. This.** Refers primarily to the prayer, but must include the contemplated result as well. Each has its place in bringing the message to men. **Saviour.** Repeats the theme of the salvation (1:1) and emphasizes the kindness and love of God to all. The emphasis in this passage is on the universal sufficiency, applicability, and offer of the Gospel. This is shown by Paul's characterizing Christ's giving himself as a witness, and by his stressing his own position of trust as preacher, apostle, and teacher of Gentiles. Verses 3-7 form the expansion of an important background thought in the apostolic exhortation to prayer. The writer's plea for prayer is directed toward missions. It is appropriate that missions should be set on its deepest basis: the genuineness of the offer to all, its applicability, and its sufficiency, as found in the work of Christ. Our prayer is good and acceptable to God because it is a prayer for all men and those in authority, to the end that the Church may witness effectively. God desires that through this witness all men may be saved and may come to the knowledge of the truth. **4. Will have.** *Would have*

5. For *there is* one God, and one mediator between God and men, the man Christ Jesus;

6. Who gave himself a ransom for all, to be testified in due time.

7. Whereunto I am ordained a preacher, and an apostle, (I speak the truth in Christ, *and* lie not,) a teacher of the Gentiles in faith and verity.

8. I will therefore that men pray every where, lifting up holy hands, without wrath and doubting.

9. In like manner also, that women adorn themselves in modest apparel, with shamefacedness and sobriety; not with braided hair, or gold, or pearls, or costly array;

10. But (which becometh women professing godliness) with good works.

(ASV). Not to be interpreted to mean "decreed," since not all men are saved.

**5.** An earlier verse (1:1) spoke of "God our Saviour." Here Paul uses the terse formula, "One there is who is God; One also there is who is mediator of God and men, the man Christ Jesus." In Mt 19:17 the order of words and thought is the same. "One there is who is good" (ASV). The predicating of the **good,** and **God,** and **mediator** is exclusive and can be said of only one. Here is the sharpest and most unequivocal assertion of the deity and humanity of Christ. It is also involved in the idea of the one true and perfect mediator that he must be God (cf. Heb 7:22; 8:6; 9:15; 12:24). This one gave himself a substitute-ransom for all. **6. Ransom.** Occurs only here in the NT, but it combines the two elements of Christ's ransom-saying in Mt 20:28; Mk 10:45. The preposition **for** and the noun **ransom** of the Gospel saying are here combined in one word. (See notes on I Tim 2:3 above for light on **a ransom for all.**) **To be testified in due time.** Christ, very God and truly man, gave himself as a ransom for all, *as the witness at the proper time.* In the fulness of time God sent forth his Son.

**7. Whereunto I am ordained a preacher,** etc. "Unto which (witness) I was appointed a preacher and apostle . . ." Paul's emphatic and earnest exaltation of his office shows the direction of his thought: it is because of this witness to Christ's Gospel, and for its success that he enjoins prayer.

**8.** Here Paul completes the paragraph on prayer. Earnest lifting up of hands, either literal or figurative, signifies earnest entreaty (Ps 28:2; 68:31; 134:2; 143:6; Prov 1:24). **Without wrath and doubting.** *Without wrath and disputing* (ASV); i.e., united (cf. Mt 18:19).

2) Conduct of Women as Related to the Testimony of the Church. 2:9-15. The **in like manner** probably carried on to women what has been said about men, namely that their lives, too, are to be characterized by prayer and devotion to the Gospel.

**9,10.** The remarks on women's dress are paralleled by I Pet 3:3-5. The compressed style heightens the contrast between attending to ostentatious dress and attending to good works. The implication is that the opposite of the former is the wearing of modest and appropriate clothing—a species of the genus "good works," the proper accompaniment of a

11. Let the woman learn in silence with all subjection.

12. But I suffer not a woman to teach, nor to usurp authority over the man, but to be in silence.

13. For Adam was first formed, then Eve.

14. And Adam was not deceived, but the woman being deceived was in the transgression.

15. Notwithstanding she shall be saved in childbearing, if they continue in faith and charity and holiness with sobriety.

## CHAPTER 3

THIS is a true saying, If a man desire the office of a bishop, he desireth a good work.

true confession of godliness.

**11,12.** The remainder of the chapter discusses official relations of women in the church. These two verses must be taken together: women are not to assume either leadership or the teaching office in the church. **13.** To illustrate the principle of masculine leadership, Paul cites the order of creation, as establishing the man's natural headship (I Cor 11: 8, 9). **14. Adam was not deceived.** This is to be taken relatively; Adam was deceived, but not so completely as the woman. The same Greek word is used of the woman, but in an intensified form. Adam followed deliberately instead of assuming leadership to repel the tempter's suggestions.

**15. She shall be saved in childbearing.** Paul's language in this section has echoes of the LXX reading of Genesis 2 and 3; and here he may play on the idea of Gen 3:15,16, to point to the incarnation of Christ. Through this **childbearing** the woman who believes and continues in godliness shall be saved.

3) Qualifications of Church Officers. 3: 1-13. **1 a.** The opening words of this section probably belong with the last thought of chapter 2, as is suggested in the ASV margin. All the other occurrences of the saying (I Tim 1:15; 4:9; II Tim 2:11; Tit 3:8) seem to follow or precede weighty statements of Gospel doctrine. It is so here, also, if the **childbearing** of 2:15 be taken to refer to the birth of the Saviour. This seems the preferable interpretation.

Paul then begins a consideration of an elder's qualifications, which he treats in orderly fashion: personally (vv. 2,3), as regards his family (vv. 4,5), as regards the church (vv. 5,6), and as regards the heathen world (v. 7). In the second half of this section the apostle deals with deacons and deaconesses (vv. 8-13), whose qualifications are parallel to those of elders. (For classic discussions of the function and office of elder, see Charles Hodge, *Church Polity*, Index, "Elder"; D. D. Bannerman, *The Scripture Doctrine of the Church*, Part VI, ch. iv; and also Lightfoot's essay, "The Christian Ministry," *Commentary on Philippians*, pp. 181-269).

**1. Office of a bishop.** One word; it also occurs at Lk 19:44, Acts 1:20, and I Pet 2:12. (The English sometimes reads "visitation.") The cognate verb occurs at Heb 12:15, suggesting that the basic function is a responsibility of every be-

**2.** A bishop then must be blameless, the husband of one wife, vigilant, sober, of good behavior, given to hospitality, apt to teach;

**3.** Not given to wine, no striker, not greedy of filthy lucre; but patient, not a brawler, not covetous;

**4.** One that ruleth well his own house, having his children in subjection with all gravity;

**5.** (For if a man know not how to rule his own house, how shall he take care of the church of God?)

**6.** Not a novice, lest being lifted up with pride he fall into the condemnation of the devil.

liever. The word **bishop** occurs at Acts 20:28; Phil 1:1; Tit 1:7; I Pet 2:25. The office of elder and bishop are the same; in Tit 1:5,7 both words are used of the same people in successive verses. In Acts 20:28 it is the elders whom the Holy Spirit has set as bishops (AV, *overseers*) in the Church. **If a man desire the office . . . he desireth,** etc. Two words are used for **desire** here. The first is used only here, in 6:10, and in Heb 11:16. A man's earnest desire for the office should be like Abraham's desire for the heavenly country. The other word is used more frequently, but also expresses earnest desire (Heb 6:11; I Pet 1:12; Lk 22:15).

**2. Blameless.** Irreproachable; the same Greek word is used in 5:7 and 6:14. **Vigilant.** ASV, *temperate.* Originally meant "temperate in use of wine," but here it is to be taken figuratively, since the next verse forbids intemperance. The cognate verb means to be self-controlled or self-possessed. **Sober.** *Sober-minded* (ASV); see also Tit 1:8; 2:2,5. **Of good behaviour.** *Orderly* (ASV); used of women's clothing in 2:9. **Hospitality.** Used in Tit 1:8; I Pet 4:9. A similar noun is used in Rom 12:13; Heb 13:2. **Apt to teach.** Used only here and in II Tim 2:24: in the one place of the elder, in the other of the minister.

**3. Not given to wine.** *No brawler* (ASV); *not quarrelsome over wine* (ASV margin); *no drunkard* (RSV). **No striker.** Not pugnacious or a bully. Used only here and Tit 1:7. **Not greedy of filthy lucre.** Does not belong in the text at this point because it does not appear in the best manuscripts. It obviously duplicates the **covetousness** at the end of the verse. Perhaps it was taken from the similar list of virtues in Tit 1:7. **Patient.** *Gentle* (ASV) or yielding (Phil 4:5; Tit 3:2; Jas 3:17; I Pet 2:18). **Not a brawler.** *Not contentious* (ASV), as in Tit 3:2. **Not covetous.** *No lover of money* (ASV). Used only here and in Heb 13:5.

**4,5. Ruleth.** To be at the head of. Leadership and direction are prominent in the word, as indicated in the following clause, and in 3:5. The verb in 3:5 (used elsewhere only in Lk 10:34,35) is explanatory of the **ruleth** of verse 4, with increased emphasis on the tender care implied. **6. Not a novice.** Not newly-converted. Occurs only here in the NT. "But, instead of being a *neophytos,* one of whose behaviour in his new faith little can be known, he must also have a good testimony (not only from those within the

7. Moreover he must have a good report of them which are without; lest he fall into reproach and the snare of the devil.

8. Likewise *must* the deacons *be* grave, not double-tongued, not given to much wine, not greedy of filthy lucre;

9. Holding the mystery of the faith in a pure conscience.

10. And let these also first be proved; then let them use the office of a deacon, being *found* blameless.

church, but) from those without" (C. J. Ellicott, ed., *A Bible Commentary for English Readers*, Vol. VII). **Pride.** Puffed up by too rapid advancement. **Condemnation.** See 3:7.

7. **He must have a good report of them which are without.** See Ellicott's paraphrase above (v. 6). The same thought is found in Rom 12:17 b, which is quoted from Proverbs. Note the ASV margin: *Let not kindness and truth forsake thee . . . so shalt thou find favor and good repute in the sight of God and man* (Prov 3:3,4). Notice the warning against pride in the same OT context (Prov 3:7), also quoted in Rom 12:16 b. **Reproach.** This is a parallel to the condemnation pronounced upon Satan because of pride (see Isa 14:12-15). **Snare.** Used in I Tim 6:9 and II Tim 2:26. Pride was the cause of Satan's fall, and is the snare he sets for men (I Jn 2:16).

8. **Likewise.** In like manner. The principal thought seems to be that there should be the same kind and degree of gifts and qualifications for deacons as for elders. **Grave.** Honorable, commanding respect. **Not double-tongued.** Truthful. **Not given to much wine.** The Bible testimony is consistently against the use of strong drink. The practical application of the principle in modern society is total abstinence. **Filthy lucre.** Used also in Tit 1:7, and the adverb in I Pet 5:2. A compound word, the two components of which are used separately in Tit 1:11. In I Pet 5:2 the word is opposed to *willingly*. The subject of economic motives is discussed more fully by Paul in I Tim 6:5-10; 17-19 (see below). The truism holds: not money, but love of it, is a root of all kinds of evil. The admonition is particularly relevant to the kind of responsibilities the deacon has.

9. **Faith.** Here again is th eunion of the doctrinal and practical aspects of Christianity: the faith is to be held in an obedient conscience, not defiled by disobedience. The expression **mystery of the faith** does not mean that there is some esoteric secret known only to the initiated. Paul's usage starts with the appearance of Christ in the flesh, as in verse 16 below. The mystery is not a secret to be kept, but a message to be proclaimed (Rom 16:25; Col 4:3).

10. **Proved.** Not necessarily by a formal test, but by the approval of the church. The **then** is significant: it appears to mean that candidates are to be approved before taking office, then serve; not to be proved in office.

11. Even so *must their* wives *be* grave, not slanderers, sober, faithful in all things.

12. Let the deacons be the husbands of one wife, ruling their children and their own houses well.

13. For they that have used the office of a deacon well purchase to themselves a good degree, and great boldness in the faith which is in Christ Jesus.

14. These things write I unto thee, hoping to come unto thee shortly:

15. But if I tarry long, that thou mayest know how thou oughtest to behave thyself in the house of God, which is the church of the living God, the pillar and ground of the truth.

**11. Their wives.** *Women* (AV). The context makes this most naturally refer to women who are acting in the capacity of deacons, as deaconesses. The apostle immediately returns to the subject of deacons in general and completes his remarks concerning them. The word **grave** and related words occur frequently in the Pastorals. The same virtue is required of deacons (v. 8) and elderly men (Tit 2:2). **Slanderers.** The Greek word for "slanderer" is *diabolos* (Eng., "devil"), the name given to Satan in the NT; he is the slanderer *par excellence*. Here, in II Tim 3:3, and in Tit 2:3, the word is used of men. **Sober.** As in I Tim 3:2 and Tit 2:2. **Faithful.** Believing, believer, or (as in the faithful sayings) trustworthy, faithful. The corresponding noun, **faith**, is enumerated in the fruit of the Spirit in Gal 5:22. The noun, like the adjective, can mean either faith in the active sense, "believing," or that "faithfulness" which produces confidence on the part of others and may help to inspire faith. **12.** See verses 4,5 above; the same words are used.

**13.** Paul closes this section as he began it in verse 1, with an argument designed to encourage the aspiring church leader. Those who serve well purchase or gain for themselves a good **standing** (ASV). The word **boldness** here probably means "ground of" or "cause for" boldness. Thus it could be parallel to, and explanatory of, the preceding **standing** (which is literally a *step* or *foundation* on which one stands). One who serves well finds the Lord faithful: he purchases for himself a good foundation and ground of boldness in the faith (fulness), which is in Christ Jesus. *They* **that have used the office . . . well.** Probably refers not only to the deacons but to the elders as well.

B. To the Church as Pillar and Ground of the Truth. 3:14—4:5.

1) Its Exalted Position as Organ of the Gospel Doctrine. 3:14,15. Paul makes clear why he thought it important to write to Timothy even though he might be with him again soon. One of the major emphases of the epistle is right conduct as a testimony to the truth. So the behavior of Christians in the government of the Church is of first importance, for the Church is the support and foundation of the truth; that is, in its sphere of testimony to the world. Christ, himself the truth, is the one foundation of the Church (I Cor 3:11). In Heb 3:6; 10:21, the

**16. And without controversy great is the mystery of godliness: God was manifest in the flesh, justified in the Spirit, seen of angels, preached unto the Gentiles, believed on in the world, received up into glory.**

Church is referred to as the "house" of Christ or "of God"; also cf. Eph 2:19,20. **The truth.** Most of the occurrences of this word in the NT are found in the writings of Paul and John. The term is often equivalent to "the gospel" or "the message (Rom 2:2,16; Col 1:5; Gal 2:14), as in this context, where it is clearly parallel to the following verse, which gives the substance of the Gospel.

2) Hymn of Praise: Poetic Statement of True Doctrine. 3:16. **Mystery.** See verse 9 above. **Godliness.** This significant word in the Pastorals and in this period of church history is found in I Tim 2:2; 3:16; 4:7,8; 6:3,5,6,11; II Tim 3:5; Tit 1:1; II Pet 1:3,6,7; 3:11; Acts 3:12; (the verb) Acts 17:23; I Tim 5:4; (the adjective) Acts 10:2,7; II Pet 2:9; (the adverb) II Tim 3:12; Tit 2:12. Its area of meaning emphasizes godly conduct, suggesting reverence and loyalty. This aptly stresses Paul's major emphasis in the Pastorals: sound doctrine and faithful living. The context makes it plain that Paul is referring to Christ when he says: **He who was manifest in the flesh** (ASV). Beginning here and in the remainder of the verse, the lines are in regular pattern, such as poetry or a hymn would furnish. It suited Paul's purpose well to tie his thoughts to something well known and current, since the message would then be remembered better. Many of the references to songs and singing in the NT are in connection with Paul (Eph 5:19; Col 3:16; Acts 16:25; I Cor 14:15). Hence it is not difficult to believe that Paul himself wrote this early Christian hymn, assuming, of course, that these lines (and Eph 5:14 also) are taken from a hymn. All the leading words occur elsewhere in Paul's writings. **Flesh.** Paul frequently emphasizes the humanity of Christ by the use of this word (Rom 1:3; 8:3; 9:5; Eph 5:15; Col 1:22; Heb 5:7; 10:20), so here of the incarnation, in harmony with the doctrine of the Virgin Birth. **Justified.** In the sense of being declared righteous, vindicated (Rom 3:4; Lk 7:29, 35). By the presence of the Spirit in Christ's ministry he was vindicated and proved true in all his claims (Rom 1:4; Lk 4:18,19; 10:21; Mt 12:18, 28; and especially Rom 8:10, 11). **Seen.** Translated "appeared" elsewhere, so here, "appeared to angels." The Spirit's final vindication of Christ was his resurrection: the mention of justification in the Spirit thus leads to his appearance to angels at resurrection, ascension, and entrance into

## CHAPTER 4

NOW the Spirit speaketh expressly, that in the latter times some shall depart from the faith, giving heed to seducing spirits, and doctrines of devils;

2. Speaking lies in hypocrisy; having their conscience seared with a hot iron;

3. Forbidding to marry, *and commanding* to abstain from meats, which God hath created to be received with thanksgiving of them which believe and know the truth.

4. For every creature of God *is* good, and nothing to be refused, if it be received with thanksgiving:

5. For it is sanctified by the word of God and prayer.

6. If thou put the brethren in remembrance of these things, thou shalt be a good minister of Jesus Christ, nourished up in the words of faith and of good doctrine, whereunto thou hast attained.

heaven (I Pet 3:22). **Preached unto the Gentiles.** Preached among the nations (ASV): the expression is a summary of the entire present era of missionary work (Rom 16:26; Col 1:6). **Believed.** A summary of the results of preaching. **Received.** Refers particularly to the Ascension, but includes all the subsequent exhibition of his glory. This is suggested by the historical and logical progressions of the poem: the whole messianic work of Christ is summed up in it.

3) Prophetic Warning of False Doctrine. 4:1-5. Gnosticism, one of whose characteristics was the asceticism here described, flooded the church in the second century, and no doubt was in evidence at the time Paul wrote.

**1. The faith.** The true doctrine of Christ as against the Satanic teaching. More details about the character and methods of the false teachers are found in II Pet 2 and in Jude. **2,3 a.** Characteristics of false teachers are seen in **hypocrisy, seared conscience,** and false attitudes toward the supports and blessings of this life: marriage and food.

**3 b-5.** The principles governing the right use of the supports of this life are: (a) God is the Creator and his creation is good; (b) He created food for men, and those who believe and know the truth about eternal salvation will have the right attitude toward the necessities of this life, and will neither deify the created thing nor degrade and despise it, but will accept it thankfully as the Father's wise provision (cf. Mt 6:31-33). **Sanctified.** The things God has provided by his creative word are set apart by his directions for their use (Gen 1:29-31; 2:4,5), and are further sanctified as a testimony of our heavenly Father's faithfulness and care when received with prayer, thankfulness, and understanding (cf. I Tim 6:17).

C. To the Witnessing Individual. 4:6 –6:2.

1) To Timothy as a Good Minister. 4:6-16.

**6. Put the brethren in remembrance.** Implies enjoining and teaching or demonstrating: it includes what is more fully stated in verse 11, **command and teach.** Throughout the section (vv. 6-16), the effect of the Gospel on both Timothy and his people is in view. Timothy himself is to be nourished by the words of the faith and good doctrine. **The faith** is the whole

7. But refuse profane and old wives' fables, and exercise thyself *rather* unto godliness.

8. For bodily exercise profiteth little: but godliness is profitable unto all things, having promise of the life that now is, and of that which is to come.

9. This *is* a faithful saying, and worthy of all acceptation.

10. For therefore we both labor and suffer reproach, because we trust in the living God, who is the Saviour of all men, specially of those that believe.

11. These things command and teach.

12. Let no man despise thy youth; but be thou an example of the believers, in word, in conversation, in charity, in spirit, in faith, in purity.

body of truth and knowledge of God. **7.** In contrast to the revelation from God are placed the **old wives' fables** (lit., *myths*) which dominate and confuse the minds and conduct of men. **Refuse.** The same word is used in II Tim 2:23. **Exercise.** This is probably to be taken in a comprehensive sense of all efforts advancing the Gospel. It applies to bodily exercise in the next verse, and to all effort in verse 10.

**8. Little.** *For a little* (ASV); the reference to the present life and to the life to come suggests that it means "little while," in other words, this life. **Godliness.** This word is used only by Paul and Peter in the NT, and is a comprehensive word for obedience to the Gospel in all areas of life. It implies a basis of sound doctrine (Tit 1:1). See I Tim 3:16. **The life . . . to come.** This and similar expressions are basic in Paul's theology and eschatology. **9. Saying.** Gospel message, word. As in 3:1, here the expression sums up what has been discussed. "Word" in one accepted English sense is "an utterance as implying the faith or authority of the person who utters it" *(Webster's New International Dictionary,* sec. ed.).

**10. Trust.** Have set our hope on. Setting one's hope on the living God, who is able to make good his promises in this life and the next, is a great motive for a life of toil and conflict in the advancement of the Gospel. **Suffer reproach.** *Strive* (ASV); God's servant is forbidden to "strive" in the sense of II Tim 2:24, where a different word is used, meaning to "quarrel." Here, as in Jude 3, it means to "contend earnestly." **Saviour** (Gr. *Soter).* Used in the sense of "deliverer"; the word can have a wider and a narrower meaning. *Soter* was an epithet of guardian deities, especially Zeus; men offered sacrifice to him after a safe voyage, etc. Paul's conception of God is such that all the blessings, deliverances, and kindly providences which men experience are to be attributed only to him (Mt 5:45). In a special and higher sense, he is the deliverer of those who believe unto eternal salvation.

**11. Command and teach.** Here Paul takes up and emphasizes his **put the brethren in remembrance** of verse 6, and points forward to the emphatic conclusion of the whole paragraph in verse 16. The form of the verbs emphasizes the progressive and continuous nature of the work.

**12.** So far from his youth's being a hindrance, Timothy might be an example

13. Till I come, give attendance to reading, to exhortation, to doctrine.

14. Neglect not the gift that is in thee, which was given thee by prophecy, with the laying on of the hands of the presbytery.

15. Meditate upon these things; give thyself wholly to them; that thy profiting may appear to all.

16. Take heed unto thyself, and unto the doctrine; continue in them: for in doing this thou shalt both save thyself, and them that hear thee.

### CHAPTER 5

REBUKE not an elder, but entreat *him* as a father; *and* the younger men as brethren;

2. The elder women as mothers; the younger as sisters, with all purity.

3. Honor widows that are widows indeed.

4. But if any widow have children or nephews, let them learn first to show piety at home, and to requite their parents: for that is good and acceptable before God.

5. Now she that is a widow indeed, and desolate, trusteth in God, and continueth in supplications and prayers night and day.

to believers in word (speech), conversation (manner of life), charity (love), faith (faithfulness), purity (strictly, "chastity"; but here in the sense of "propriety" or "careful observance of religious duties"). In spirit is not in the better texts.

13. Here are emphasized things which demand special attention among the people: reading (public reading of Scripture), exhortation (comfort, encouragement, admonition, exhortation, the whole area of ministry which would today be described as counseling, but here the context favors the ministry of preaching, expounding the Scriptures), doctrine (teaching). 14. Gift. Teaching and counseling are mentioned together (Rom 12:7,8); teachers are among the gifts of the Spirit to the Church (I Cor 12:28); pastors and teachers are mentioned as a unit (Eph 4: 11). This word meaning "gift of grace" can be applied to any gift of God through the Spirit. Here it seems to imply a charge given at ordination. Paul reiterates it and reminds Timothy here and at 1:18. Presbytery (used only in Lk 22:66, Acts 22:5, and here) refers to a group of representative spiritual leaders, chosen and proved.

15. Meditate. Practice, cultivate, or take pains with; used only here and in Acts 4:25. Profiting. Advancement. 16. Thyself. The minister needs to be reminded of his own needs in connection with doctrine; in feeding others, he too must seek a blessing. Continue. This is one of the basic words used to describe the steadfast walk of a Christian (Gal 3:10; Heb 8:9; Jas 1:25; Acts 14:22; Col 1:23). Basically it is the same as "abide" in John 15 and I John. Save is used in the sense of the "work out your own salvation" of Phil 2:12.

2) To Men. 5:1. Rebuke not. The violent rebuke or attack is forbidden.

3) To Women, Especially Widows. 5: 2-16.

2. Purity. Propriety.

3. Indeed (cf. vv. 5,16). Those who are widows and desolate — alone in the world — should be cared for by the church. The whole discussion should be considered in the light of OT teaching, where care for the widow is emphasized (also cf. Jas 1:27). 4. Nephews. Grandchildren. At home. *Toward their own family* (ASV).

5. Here is a description of the true widow, who may serve the church and be cared for by the church (cf. Lk 2:36,37).

6. But she that liveth in pleasure is dead while she liveth.

7. And these things give in charge, that they may be blameless.

8. But if any provide not for his own, and specially for those of his own house, he hath denied the faith, and is worse than an infidel.

9. Let not a widow be taken into the number under threescore years old, having been the wife of one man,

10. Well reported of for good works; if she have brought up children, if she have lodged strangers, if she have washed the saints' feet, if she have relieved the afflicted, if she have diligently followed every good work.

11. But the younger widows refuse: for when they have begun to wax wanton against Christ, they will marry;

**6. Liveth in pleasure.** This is the contrasting mention of unacceptable widows; more details are added later. This expression occurs only here and in Jas 5:5 and means voluptuous and indulgent living, which indicates a state of spiritual death. **7. Give in charge.** Paul is keenly conscious of the effect on the testimony of a failure at the home level. Hence these things are to be **commanded** (same verb as in 4:11), as Paul himself solemnly charges Timothy (6:13). **8.** Failure to provide is a denial of faith. **Infidel.** *Unbeliever.*

**9.** Here and in the next verse specific details are given about the qualifications of the widow the church is to support. **Not . . . under threescore years old.** Calvin gives two reasons why Paul does not wish any to be admitted under sixty years of age. First, "Being supported at the public expense, it was proper that they should have already reached old age." Second, there was a mutual obligation between the church and these widows: the church was to relieve their poverty, they were to consecrate themselves to the ministry of the church "which would have been altogether intolerable, if there were still a likelihood of their being married." **Having been the wife of one husband.** "It may be regarded as a sort of pledge of continence and chastity, when a woman has arrived at that age, satisfied with having had but one husband. Not that [Paul] disapproves of a second marriage, or affixes a mark of ignominy to those who have been twice married; (for, on the contrary, he advises younger widows to marry;) but because he wished carefully to guard against laying any females under a necessity of remaining unmarried, who felt it to be necessary to have husbands" (Calvin).

**11. Wax wanton.** This occurs only here and in Rev 18:7. Such conduct is incompatible with salvation and would suggest that Paul does not consider these "widows indeed." The idea of widowhood may have a wider application than actual bereavement; it may mean separation from a husband. For OT background, see II Sam 20:3 and Isa 54:4-6. Israel is a rejected, adulterous wife and widow because of separation, not because of the death of the husband. Hence these women, who are further described as having set aside their first pledge (faith, promise, I Tim 5:12) and as having turned aside to Satan (v.

12. Having damnation, because they have cast off their first faith.

13. And withal they learn *to be* idle, wandering about from house to house; and not only idle, but tattlers also and busybodies, speaking things which they ought not.

14. I will therefore that the younger women marry, bear children, guide the house, give none occasion to the adversary to speak reproachfully.

15. For some are already turned aside after Satan.

16. If any man or woman that believeth have widows, let them relieve them, and let not the church be charged; that it may relieve them that are widows indeed.

17. Let the elders that rule well be counted worthy of double honor, especially they who labor in the word and doctrine.

15) may be unfaithful wives who have been divorced. **12. Damnation.** Remarriage under conditions of separation for unfaithfulness would bring the condemnation of the Lord (Lk 16:18). **First faith.** First pledge or promise. So leaving one's "first love" (Rev 2:4) may be parallel and equal to spiritual unfaithfulness.

**14. Younger women.** These are probably the younger widows who are eligible, except for their age, not the ones described in verse 12. **Guide the house.** This verb is used only here in the NT. The high estimate of woman's place and ability is paralleled in the classic passage in Prov 31:10-31. **Give none occasion.** "Pretext" or "opportunity." "Let them, in order to shut the mouth of evil speakers, choose a way of life that is less liable to suspicion" (Calvin). The **adversary** is Satan, mentioned immediately following. **To speak reproachfully.** *For reviling* (ASV). Either, unbecoming behavior is a reviling of the truth by those who live thus and gives Satan occasion for further work against the church; or, such behavior gives Satan an opportunity to revile and so harms the church's testimony. **15.** This is not a separate sentence in the punctuation of Nestle's *Greek New Testament,* but is a specific example of the principle just stated.

**16. Man** should be omitted. **If any woman that believeth** (ASV). Even a woman might be in a position where it would be her responsibility to care for a widow rather than throw the burden on the church, which is to care for those who are **desolate** *(left alone,* v. 5). The governing principle is stated in verse 8.

4) To Elders. 5:17-25. Paul has already discussed some of the elders' official relationships in chapter 3. Here he deals with more detailed and individual relationships, and his style is marked by frequent imperatives and personal exhortations to Timothy. This is Paul's usual way of handling doctrine in his epistles: first a discussion of principle, and then the practical application, with an earnest exhortation to godly living. So in the present section Paul returns to the subject of elders to give further counsel.

**17. Rule well.** An important qualification of an elder (3:4,5) is that he govern (direct or manage) properly. This is among the basic gifts for the well-being of the church (Rom 12:8; I Thess 5:12). **Double honor. Honor** has two meanings:

18. For the Scripture saith, Thou shalt not muzzle the ox that treadeth out the corn. And, The laborer *is* worthy of his reward.

19. Against an elder receive not an accusation, but before two or three witnesses.

20. Them that sin rebuke before all, that others also may fear.

21. I charge *thee* before God, and the Lord Jesus Christ, and the elect angels, that thou observe these things without preferring one before another, doing nothing by partiality.

22. Lay hands suddenly on no man, neither be partaker of other men's sins: keep thyself pure.

"Honor" and "honorarium" or "compensation." Both meanings are doubtless intended here. In the case of those who labor in preaching and teaching, their whole time is thus devoted, and they are deserving of compensation from the church (see I Tim 5:18). The word **double** seems to argue for a sufficient or appropriate recompense, rather than a double amount. In the LXX, in Isa 40:2, the same word is used, and it carries in context the idea of "full equivalent." Note also Paul's parallel usage of **honor** in 6:1, where it is "all" or "full honor." (See William Hendricksen, *New Testament Commentary: Exposition of the Pastoral Epistles,* pp. 180,181.)

**18.** There are two quotations here: Deut 25:4 and Lk 10:7. **Muzzle the ox.** The content in Deuteronomy 25 deals with equitable relations among men; the verse is an aphorism quoted by Moses to prove a principle, and is so understood by Paul, who discusses the same principle at Rom 13:7 and I Cor 9:7-11, and quotes the same passage from Deuteronomy. **Laborer.** The exact original form of the quotation is found only in Luke. The citation here, **the scripture** saith, shows that Luke's Gospel was in existence and was regarded as Scripture.

**19. Before two or three witnesses.** The rule of evidence given by Moses (Deut 19:15), and used by the Lord (Mt 18:16). **20. Them that sin** (the Greek implies "those who persist in sin") **rebuke before all,** as Paul himself rebuked Peter (Gal 2:14). A godly man when so admonished publicly will take the lesson to heart (Prov 9:8).

**21.** Paul here uses the solemn charge, an entreaty, to reinforce the importance of the command against partiality. The same verb is used in II Tim 4:1 and again in II Tim 2:14, where Timothy himself is commanded to entreat others with the same earnestness.

**22. Lay hands suddenly.** This is often understood as forbidding hasty ordination. However, qualifications and ordination were discussed earlier. Locke suggests (ICC, p. 64) that it refers to the overhasty receiving of an offender back into communion. **Hands** (plural) may also mean "violent measures," "force." Here it would be another caution regarding Timothy's dealing with men who were to be rebuked. He should use no partiality, no violent measures, or unnecessary severity, nor, on the other hand, undue leniency, so as to be a partaker of their sins. **Pure.** This and related words are

23. Drink no longer water, but use a little wine for thy stomach's sake and thine often infirmities.

24. Some men's sins are open beforehand, going before to judgment; and some *men* they follow after.

25. Likewise also the good works *of some* are manifest beforehand; and they that are otherwise cannot be hid.

## CHAPTER 6

LET as many servants as are under the yoke count their own masters worthy of all honor, that the name of God and *his* doctrine be not blasphemed.

those generally translated "holy," "sanctify," "saint." Sometimes it has the specific meaning of chastity, but generally seems to refer to the right conduct of the Christian life. The closest parallel to pure, as used here, is "clear," as employed in II Cor 7:11. So perhaps here it should read: "Keep yourself clear [of other men's sins]." This discussion of others' sins is resumed and concluded in verses 24,25.

23. Drink no longer water. *No longer drink only water* (RSV). Paul's prohibitions are interpreted by context and sometimes are not absolute. To be a "water-drinker" in common usage seems to imply excessive severity and self-denial. The antiascetic principle is stated in 4:3-5. At that point Paul quickly shifted from general principle to specific, practical advice to Timothy (on bodily exercise, v. 8). So here, in speaking of general principles of avoidance, it is in point to warn against excessive frugality and severity. Wine is used for a wide variety of products of the grape; medicinal qualities are implied (Lk 10:34). Paul's prescription for Timothy's ailments is not a general rule of "moderate use" for all and sundry. General Biblical rules still apply (Hab 2:5,15; Prov 20:1; 23:31).

24. This and the next verse are to be kept in the context of neither be partaker of other men's sins (v. 22) and that in relation to the office of elder. The principle is: "By their fruits ye shall know them." Connect this with the warning against hasty action (v. 22). Some men's sins are open and lead to the appropriate decision; in the case of others, the evidence will be manifest in time.

25. *So also good deeds are conspicuous; and even when they are not, they cannot remain hidden* (RSV).

5) To Servants. 6:1,2. The context and the comparison with I Pet 2:18 suggest that two classes of masters are here dealt with: the believing and the unbelieving. Paul does not discuss the ultimate question of the right and wrong of slavery, but stresses the obligations resting on the slave, and the opportunity even in that situation to "adorn the doctrine" (Tit 2:10). The character of God and the Gospel teaching will be hurt by wrong conduct. And those who have believing masters are not to fail to give full honor, but are to serve them all the better, since it is a Christian brother who is devoting himself to (or benefiting by) good service.

**2.** And they that have believing masters, let them not despise *them,* because they are brethren; but rather do *them* service, because they are faithful and beloved, partakers of the benefit. These things teach and exhort.

**3.** If any man teach otherwise, and consent not to wholesome words, *even* the words of our Lord Jesus Christ, and to the doctrine which is according to godliness;

**4.** He is proud, knowing nothing, but doting about questions and strifes of words, whereof cometh envy, strife, railings, evil surmisings,

**5.** Perverse disputings of men of corrupt minds, and destitute of the truth, supposing that gain is godliness: from such withdraw thyself.

**6.** But godliness with contentment is great gain.

**7.** For we brought nothing into *this* world, *and it is* certain we can carry nothing out.

**8.** And having food and raiment, let us be therewith content.

**9.** But they that will be rich fall into temptation and a snare, and *into* many foolish and hurtful lusts, which drown men in destruction and perdition.

**10.** For the love of money is the root of all evil: which while some coveted after, they have erred from the faith, and pierced themselves through with many sorrows.

### III. Conclusion. 6:2 d-21.

A. A Solemn Charge. 6:2 d-15 a. **These things teach and exhort.** This is a basic theme in the Pastorals, which appears at 4:11 as well as here. Right teaching was a principal reason for leaving Timothy at Ephesus (1:3).

1) Warnings Against False Teachers. 6:3-5. **Wholesome words.** Healthy, sound, because they promote health. This expression is peculiar to the Pastorals, emphasizing Paul's plea for sound doctrine. **Even the words of our Lord Jesus Christ.** This is another indication (see 5:18) that written Gospel narratives were well known and in circulation. **And to the doctrine.** This *and* could better be rendered **even,** since the words of Christ are the basis and substance of the doctrine which accords with **godliness** (practically a synonym for "Christianity"; see notes on 3:16). For the importance in Paul's writings of the teaching and life of Jesus, see Machen, *Origin of Paul's Religion,* pp. 147-152.

**4. He is proud.** Used three times in the NT, all three occurring in the Pastorals (I Tim 3:6; 6:4; II Tim 3:4). The word combines the ideas of conceit and folly. The rejection of the evidence of the Gospel is rooted in pride and is the utmost folly. **Knowing nothing.** This is the only time Paul uses this word meaning "to understand." **Doting.** The word is literally "sick," "ailing"; having *a morbid craving for controversy and for disputes about words* (RSV). **Surmisings.** Suspicions, conjectures or guesses. **5. Supposing that gain is godliness.** *Supposing that godliness is a way of gain* (ASV). **From such withdraw thyself.** Omit, as in the ASV.

2) Right Attitudes of True Teachers. 6:6-10. **6. Great gain.** This word appears to have the uniform meaning, "way of gain," "means of livelihood," which yields a better sense here. Paul means to say: "The Christian faith with sufficiency for this life is a mighty way of gain." He has already said (in 4:8, which is parallel and a good commentary) that godliness is profitable in every respect, giving the promise not only for this life but also for the life to come. It is this eschatological emphasis which Paul proceeds to stress in the rest of the epistle. In verses 7,8 the apostle shows the folly of setting one's hopes and desires on this

11. But thou, O man of God, flee these things; and follow after righteousness, godliness, faith, love, patience, meekness.

12. Fight the good fight of faith, lay hold on eternal life, whereunto thou art also called, and hast professed a good profession before many witnesses.

13. I give thee charge in the sight of God, who quickeneth all things, and *before* Christ Jesus, who before Pontius Pilate witnessed a good confession;

world, which is temporary. One should be content with food and raiment. In verses 9,10 he develops the thought of the folly of concentrating on the accumulation of wealth as an end in itself. The rendering of Hendriksen (*op. cit.*) seems preferable: *For a root of all the evils is the love of money.* Which (referring to money) while some coveted after, they have erred from the faith. Love of money is idolatry (Col 3:5; Eph 5:5; I Jn 2:15) and leads away from the true hope of the Christian.

3) The Motives of the Man of God. 6:11-15 a. Paul proceeds to outline the things a Christian should be cherishing. Central are the life to come and the return of Christ.

**11. Follow after.** Pursue, keep pursuing. Vigor and intensity are suggested both in fleeing things that lead from the faith and in pursuing things pertaining to the faith. Paul has a striking number of these suggestive lists of virtues, no two identical and none exhaustive of the possibilities of the "weightier matters of the law." **Righteousness** may be thought of as a comprehensive name for all the fruit of the Spirit. **Godliness** means "godly faith," "true religion." In Paul, this expression is found only in the Pastorals (see note on 3:16). **Faith** may mean "believing" or "faithfulness." A full realization of **love** means the experience of God's love for us, as well as our loving him and others. **Patience** means "endurance," and **meekness** seems to go back to the Lord's teaching and example (Mt 5:5; 11:29).

**12. Fight.** Compare the use of the same verb with an intensifying prefix in Jude 3. The later epistles of Paul and others had as one of their purposes to inform and prepare Christians for the rising tide of opposition and persecution which was to come in the ages immediately following. The **good fight** involves holding fast the faith and committing it to others. In this context it is closely related to **holding fast** and **laying hold** of eternal life. The same word translated **fight** is used by the Lord in Lk 13:24 as "strive" in a parallel context. **Called.** Calling is the gracious work of the Spirit in bringing us to faith in Christ. **Professed.** The same word is also translated "confess" (Rom 10:9). This is a basic doctrine in the Lord's teaching (Mt 10:32).

**13. I give thee charge.** The solemn charge which begins here is one sentence running through the doxology of verses 15 and 16. It characterizes God as the

14. That thou keep *this* commandment without spot, unrebukable, until the appearing of our Lord Jesus Christ:

15. Which in his times he shall show, *who is* the blessed and only Potentate, the King of kings, and Lord of lords;

16. Who only hath immortality, dwelling in the light which no man can approach unto; whom no man hath seen, nor can see: to whom *be* honor and power everlasting. Amen.

17. Charge them that are rich in this world, that they be not high-minded, nor trust in uncertain riches, but in the living God, who giveth us richly all things to enjoy;

one who gives life to all things (cf. Rom 4:17 for the same emphasis on God's sovereign power and purposes in salvation). Paul had just spoken of eternal life in the preceding sentence; here it is emphasized that God is the one who gives it by effectual calling. Christ is characterized as the one who gave a good confession before Pilate. Just as Timothy had been called to life and had given a good confession, so Paul refers first to the Giver of all life and then to One who gave the good confession before Pilate. The **good confession** is to confess Jesus as Lord (Rom 10:9); such was the Lord's claim before Pilate and others. God and Christ are the witnesses of Paul's charge to Timothy.

**14. That thou keep this commandment. Commandment** seems to be used here as a comprehensive word for the Gospel, as Christ used it in Jn 12:50 (see also I Jn 3:23; II Jn 6). Keeping the commandment spotless and without reproach means both teaching and living above reproach. **Until the appearing of our Lord Jesus Christ.** Here is the high point of Paul's eschatological emphasis mentioned above (v. 6; cf. also II Tim 4:1, notes). The apostle uses it as the climax of his solemn charge to Timothy and as the transition to his great song of praise to the triune God. **In his times.** This expression is identical with "in due time" in 2:6 and Tit 1:3; *in its own times* (ASV); at the proper time, in the fulness of time as known to God.

B. Doxology. 6:15b,16. The triune God is the one who will reveal the appearing of Christ (cf. I Cor 15:28). God is here characterized by an accumulation of titles and ascriptions of majesty and power noteworthy even in Paul, and, indeed, in the entire Scripture. The ideas are parallel to 1:17 but are more fully expressed. Paul's thought moves from God's manifestations to men as Potentate ing King through his sovereign prerogative of immortality, back to his mysterious and inscrutable being, and leads to the final ascription of honor and eternal omnipotent sway.

C. Return to the Solemn Charge. 6: 17-21.

1) Right Use of Possessions. 6:17-21. **This world.** *This present world* (ASV). Paul's eschatological horizon has in view the age to come, the new heavens and new earth. **High-minded.** *Proud.* The ex-

18. That they do good, that they be rich in good works, ready to distribute, willing to communicate;

19. Laying up in store for themselves a good foundation against the time to come, that they may lay hold on eternal life.

20. O Timothy, keep that which is committed to thy trust, avoiding profane *and* vain babblings, and oppositions of science falsely so called:

21. Which some professing have erred concerning the faith. Grace *be* with thee. Amen.

The first to Timothy was written from Laodicea, which is the chiefest city of Phrygia Pacatiana.

pression is a single verb in Greek, combining two elements found in both Rom 11:20 and 12:16. **Trust.** *Have hope set on* (ASV). **Enjoy.** God has given all he has created for blessing and pleasure, which is realized only when possessions are put in the right relation to him; they are a stewardship from him. Two pairs of statements follow (v. 18), indicating how to use wealth. To **do good** and to **be rich in good works** are parallel; to be **ready to distribute** and **willing to communicate** (be liberal or sharing) are also parallels. In thus regarding and using wealth, one lays up a good foundation and lays hold on the life to come. **Laying up in store . . . a good foundation against the time to come** is a commentary on and parallel to Mt 6:19-21. **Eternal life.** "The life which is truly life." The adverb "truly" is used four times in I Tim out of the six times Paul uses it, and is emphatic of truth and real existence.

2) Final Appeal: A Summation. 6:20, 21. With deep emotion and personal appeal Paul begins his final exhortation: **O Timothy** (the interjection is especially frequent in Paul's epistles; see Rom 2:1,3; 9:20; Gal 3:1). He then briefly reiterates the principal themes of the entire epistle: (a) **Keep** the deposit of truth. The whole phrase is the rendering of three words: *guard the deposit.* This is the central message of the Pastorals: Guard the Gospel tradition by life and sound teaching, (b) **avoiding** false doctrine. There are two forms of learning which obscure the Gospel: (1) **profane** (implies blasphemous desecration of holy things) **and vain babblings,** consisting of high-sounding, empty words and speculations used for purposes of ostentation: and (2) **science** (lit., *knowledge*) **falsely so called.** Paul makes it plain that he is able to distinguish solid learning and fact from speculations without evidence, mere myth and fancy, **which some professing** (lit., *promising*) **have erred.** "Some, promising these fictions as truth and reality, leave the pledge and promise of God, which is the faith" (cf. II Pet 2:19). **Grace be with thee.** This is the characteristic ending to all Paul's epistles (II Thess 3:17,18; the briefest form is found here and in Col 4:18). The better text has the plural *you* (ASV), which intimates that the contents were intended for all the churches at Ephesus, and not for Timothy alone.

# BIBLIOGRAPHY

(for I Timothy, II Timothy, and Titus)

ALFORD, HENRY. *The Greek Testament.* Vol. III. Chicago: Moody Press, reprinted with revisions, 1958.

CALVIN, JOHN. *Commentaries on the Epistles to Timothy, Titus and Philemon.* Grand Rapids: Wm. B. Eerdmans Publishing Co., reprinted 1948.

HARRISON, P. N. *The Problem of the Pastoral Epistles.* Oxford: The University Press, 1921.

HENDRICKSEN, WILLIAM. *New Testament Commentary: Exposition of the Pastoral Epistles.* Grand Rapids: Baker Book House, 1957.

LOCKE, WALTER. *A Critical and Exegetical Commentary on the Pastoral Epistles.* New York: Charles Scribner's Sons, 1924.

PALEY, WILLIAM. "Horae Paulinae," *Works.* Philadelphia: Religious Tract Society, 1850.

PLUMMER, ALFRED. "The Pastoral Epis-

tles," *The Expositor's Bible.* Vol. 6. Grand Rapids: Wm. B. Eerdmans Publishing Co., reprinted 1943.

SALMON, GEORGE. *An Historical Introduction to the Study of the Books of the New Testament.* 9th ed. London: John Murray, 1904.

WARFIELD, B. B. *Faith and Life.* New York: Longmans Green, 1916.

——————— *Inspiration and Authority of the Bible.* Philadelphia: Presbyterian and Reformed Publishing Co., 1948.

——————— *The Lord of Glory.* New York: American Tract Society, 1907.

——————— *The Person and Work of Christ.* Philadelphia: Presbyterian and Reformed Publishing Co., 1950.

ZAHN, THEODOR. *Introduction to the New Testament.* Vol. II. Grand Rapids: Kregel, reprinted 1953.

# THE SECOND
# EPISTLE TO TIMOTHY

## OUTLINE

(For the general introduction to this epistle, see Introduction to I Timothy.)

# II TIMOTHY

## CHAPTER 1

PAUL, an apostle of Jesus Christ by the will of God, according to the promise of life which is in Christ Jesus,

2. To Timothy, *my* dearly beloved son: Grace, mercy, *and* peace, from God the Father and Christ Jesus our Lord.

# COMMENTARY

### I. Salutation and Introduction. 1:1-18.

#### A. Salutation of Special Authority and Affection. 1:1,2.

**1.** The special matters put with great terseness and brevity are: (1) Paul's apostleship from Christ Jesus; (2) that this was through the will of God; (3) that his apostleship was in accordance with God's promise of life in Christ Jesus. In I Tim 1:1 we find the expression, "Lord Jesus Christ, our hope." Here it is **the promise of life which is in Christ Jesus.** In Titus the ideas are expressed more elaborately (Tit 1:2). The supernatural evidence and attestation in Paul's apostleship corresponds to the fact of the promise in the Scriptures. **2.** God the Father and Christ Jesus our Lord are the single source of grace, mercy, and peace. **Mercy** is added only in the Pastoral Epistles, apparently for the encouragement of Paul's **dearly beloved son,** Timothy, and his "own son after the common faith," Titus (see Tit 1:4 and notes on I Tim 1:1,2).

#### B. Thanksgiving for Timothy's Faith. 1:3-5. Only in Galatians and Titus does

3. I thank God, whom I serve from *my* forefathers with pure conscience, that without ceasing I have remembrance of thee in my prayers night and day;

4. Greatly desiring to see thee, being mindful of thy tears, that I may be filled with joy;

5. When I call to remembrance the unfeigned faith that is in thee, which dwelt first in thy grandmother Lois, and thy mother Eunice; and I am persuaded that in thee also.

6. Wherefore I put thee in remembrance, that thou stir up the gift of God, which is in thee by the putting on of my hands.

7. For God hath not given us the spirit of fear; but of power, and of love, and of a sound mind.

Paul omit the formal thanksgiving or eulogy.

3. **God, whom I serve from my forefathers.** Paul knew of at least two previous generations who were intensely loyal to the faith, paralleling the subsequent mention of two generations of godly forebears in Timothy's case (v. 5). This is ground for encouragement that we are not following fables; the faith has endured and has borne its fruits. **With pure conscience.** See notes on I Tim 1:5,19; 3:9; 4:2. The Greek word is the exact counterpart of the Latin *con-science,* "a knowing with," a shared or joint knowledge. It is our awareness of ourselves in all the relationships of life, especially ethical relationships. We have ideas of right and wrong; and when we perceive their truth and claims on us, and will not obey, our souls are at war with themselves and with the law of God, as portrayed in Romans 7. To have a good, or pure, conscience does not mean that we have never sinned or do not commit acts of sin. Rather, it means that the underlying direction and motive of life is to obey and please God, so that acts of sin are habitually recognized as such and faced before God (I Jn 1:9). **I thank God.** The thing Paul is thankful for is the unfeigned faith in Timothy and his mother and grandmother. The clauses lying between give the other circumstances for Paul's thankfulness. **That,** in II Tim 1:3, is better translated as, *I unceasingly remember.* **That,** in verse 4, is better translated, *so that I am filled with joy.* This last phrase is placed between the ideas of Paul's remembering Timothy's tears and his remembering the unfeigned faith. The tears were tears of love and loyalty to Paul and the Lord, and so were cause for joy and led to the apostle's deep thanksgiving to God for the genuine faith expressed in tears.

C. Reminder of Responsibility for the Gospel. 1:6-18.

(1) The Gift of God. 1:6,7. The sequence of thought in verse 5 in referring to **faith,** and the reference to the **spirit** in verse 7 indicate that the **gift** of verse 6 is the Holy Spirit, or some special aspect of his work. This would explain Paul's reference to the conferring of the gift by the laying on of his hands. The Holy Spirit in special manifestations was given by the laying on of hands of the Apostles (Acts 8:17; 19:6). **Stir up.** Use the gift, engaging in appropriate activi-

8. Be not thou therefore ashamed of the testimony of our Lord, nor of me his prisoner: but be thou partaker of the afflictions of the gospel according to the power of God;

9. Who hath saved us, and called *us* with a holy calling, not according to our works, but according to his own purpose and grace, which was given us in Christ Jesus before the world began;

10. But is now made manifest by the appearing of our Saviour Jesus Christ, who hath abolished death, and hath brought life and immortality to light through the gospel:

11. Whereunto I am appointed a preacher, and an apostle, and a teacher of the Gentiles.

12. For the which cause I also suffer these things: nevertheless I am not ashamed; for I know whom I have believed, and am persuaded that he is able to keep that which I have committed unto him against that day.

13. Hold fast the form of sound words, which thou hast heard of me, in faith and love which is in Christ Jesus.

14. That good thing which was committed unto thee keep by the Holy Ghost which dwelleth in us.

ties of the ministry. **Fear.** Romans 8:15 is the commentary on this thought (cf. **Heb** 2:15; I Pet 3:14; I Jn 4:18). **Sound mind.** This and related words are especially frequent in the Pastorals (I Tim 2:9, 15; 3:2; Tit 2:2,4-6,12) and are closely parallel to the "minding" of the Spirit of Rom 8:5,6,9.

2) Challenge to Endure Afflictions Incident to the Ministry. 1:8-12. In the Greek text these verses are one continuous movement of thought and one sentence. The four imperatives in this and the following challenge contain the main point of Paul's reminder to Timothy: Be not ashamed (v. 8); Be partaker (v. 8); Hold fast (v. 13); Guard the deposit (v. 14). The exposition of the Gospel in verses 9-12 gives the ground for these exhortations. **The testimony of our Lord** is the Gospel he has given to his Church. **The afflictions** which the propagation of the Gospel entails must be borne in the power of God. **9.** Saving and calling are parallel activities of the Holy Spirit. **Given us.** Here, as always, Paul's reference to predestination is designed to strengthen and comfort. God's eternal purposes will not fail. **10. Manifest.** It is his grace (the gift of life) which was ours in his purpose from eternity, and which has now been manifested in the saving work of Christ. The same word, which implies "stands fully revealed," is used in Rom 3:21 and 16:26. **11. Whereunto** refers to the Gospel, of which Paul was appointed an apostle. **12. Cause.** Because of the Lord's commission. **These things.** Imprisonment and bonds. We can without shame endure any unfair and adverse circumstances if we know that in them all the Lord is keeping our deposit: that is, the Gospel he has entrusted to us. **Persuaded.** This passage closely parallels Paul's exposition of Abraham's experience in Rom 4:21.

3) Challenge To Hold Fast the Form of Sound Words. 1:13,14. The necessity of putting the basic outline of doctrine in concrete, easily remembered form is reiterated by Paul (cf. Rom 6:17) in another imperative (II Tim 1:13): **Hold fast the form of sound words,** or the outline of doctrine. The confession of faith was characteristic of the Church from earliest times, and was soon formulated in the Apostles' Creed. In Christ and in his Spirit are the **faith** (fulness) and **love** to insure our keeping the faith. **14. Good thing** means *good deposit*. The

15. This thou knowest, that all they which are in Asia be turned away from me; of whom are Phygellus and Hermogenes.

16. The Lord give mercy unto the house of Onesiphorus; for he oft refreshed me, and was not ashamed of my chain:

17. But, when he was in Rome, he sought me out very diligently, and found *me*.

18. The Lord grant unto him that he may find mercy of the Lord in that day: and in how many things he ministered unto me at Ephesus, thou knowest very well.

## CHAPTER 2

THOU therefore, my son, be strong in the grace that is in Christ Jesus.

2. And the things that thou hast heard of me among many witnesses, the same commit thou to faithful men, who shall be able to teach others also.

3. Thou therefore endure hardness, as a good soldier of Jesus Christ.

4. No man that warreth entangleth himself with the affairs of *this* life; that he may please him who hath chosen him to be a soldier.

5. And if a man also strive for masteries, *yet* is he not crowned, except he strive lawfully.

6. The husbandman that laboreth must be first partaker of the fruits.

7. Consider what I say; and the Lord give thee understanding in all things.

same word is used in verse 12 and in the LXX at Lev 6:2,4. The Spirit will keep the deposit. The intimate connection of the work of Christ and that of the Spirit are evident here as elsewhere in Paul's writings (Rom 8:9-11; II Cor 3:17, 18).

4) Personal Illustrations of Loyalty and Opposition. 1:15-18. Here are instances of those who helped and those who opposed the great apostle. They serve as warning and encouragement to Timothy. Paul's method was similar in I Tim 1:19,20.

## II. The Gospel: A Trust Requiring Faithfulness. 2:1—3:17.

A. To Be Diligently Committed to Others. 2:1-7. An all-important detail in guarding the deposit is to teach it faithfully to others who shall themselves be able to teach.

1. To this end, Paul says, the Christian teacher is to **be strong.** All NT occurrences of this word are in connection with Paul or used by him (Acts 9:22; Rom 4:20; Eph 6:10; Phil 4:13; I Tim 1:12; II Tim 4:17). **Grace** is an all-inclusive word for the power and gifts of the Spirit (see Charles Hodge, *Systematic Theology*, II, 654,655).

The three famous metaphors setting forth the relation of the Christian teacher to the faith are given in this passage: (1) The teacher as a soldier (vv. 3,4). **Endure hardness** is more accurately *suffer hardship with me* (ASV). **Please** is almost entirely a Pauline word in the NT; see the force of the cognate noun in Col 1:10. (2) The teacher as an athlete (v. 5). **Strive lawfully.** This implies both the training for the contest and the rules governing it. **Crowned** is used only here and in Heb 2:7,9 in the NT; the noun is used in II Tim 4:8. The crown is elsewhere defined as "incorruptible" (I Cor 9:25), "of righteousness" (II Tim 4:8), "of life" (Jas 1:12; Rev 2:10), "unfading" (I Pet 5:4). (3) The teacher as a farmer (v. 6). This principle (more fully discussed at I Cor 9:1-14 and I Tim 5:17, 18) may be applied to include remuneration and maintenance, but here the spiritual benefit to Timothy himself is stressed. He should know the blessings of the message he is giving to others (cf. I Tim 4:15,16).

7. **Consider what I say.** Or, *take note, think it over,* and the Lord give thee un-

8. Remember that Jesus Christ of the seed of David was raised from the dead, according to my gospel:

9. Wherein I suffer trouble, as an evildoer, *even* unto bonds; but the word of God is not bound.

10. Therefore I endure all things for the elect's sake, that they may also obtain the salvation which is in Christ Jesus with eternal glory.

derstanding. *Shall give* (ASV) is correct.

B. To Be Firmly Guarded and Cherished. 2:8-26.

1) The Central Truth of the Gospel. 2:8. The ASV has the correct word order in this verse. **Remember** stresses the continuity of the action: *Be continually remembering.* **Jesus Christ.** In the Gospels this is a rare but direct and solemn designation of Jesus, occurring at Mt 1:18; Mk 1:1; Jn 1:17; 17:3. This last passage is especially significant because the Lord used it of himself. This is the basis of the usage in Acts in the early church. Paul is emphasizing the apostolic message of Jesus Christ risen (see B. B. Warfield, *Lord of Glory,* pp. 184-186). **Raised** (ASV, *risen*) underscores the fact that he rose and now lives. The word is that used most frequently in the Lord's own teaching and in the Gospel accounts of his resurrection. Paul's use of the word here, in I Cor 15:4,12, and elsewhere, carries the testimony back exactly in its earliest form. **From** is properly translated *out from among.* **Dead** is not used figuratively, but literally means *dead people.* All the dead are referred to; Jesus rose as the first fruits, out from them. Paul preached that Christ died and was buried, eliminating any figurative interpretation in **risen** or **dead.** **Of the seed of David.** The apostle refers to Christ in this way here, in Rom 1:3, and in Acts 13:23. This term has the triple advantage of stressing Jesus' true humanity, his Messianic lineage, and his sovereign authority. For this last point, note especially Rev 3:7; 5:5; 22:16. Paul's usual term for this idea is "Lord." Peter connects these ideas in Acts 2:30,36. Paul uses **my gospel** here as he used **my deposit** in II Tim 1:12. The force of it is that the trust or deposit given to Paul is the Gospel, for which he was responsible and for which he was a competent eyewitness. Paul disclaims originality: these were the facts as known to him and to those from whom he had received them (cf. I Cor 15:3,11; see B. B. Warfield, *The Person and Work of Christ,* pp. 535-546).

2) Paul's Example of Faithfulness. 2:9,10. **Wherein I suffer trouble.** The troubles, opposition, and imprisonment Paul experienced stemmed directly from his unswerving testimony to the Resurrection (see J. O. Buswell, *Behold Him!* pp. 42-

11. *It is* a faithful saying: For if we be dead with *him*, we shall also live with *him:*

12. If we suffer, we shall also reign with *him:* if we deny *him*, he also will deny us:

13. If we believe not, *yet* he abideth faithful: he cannot deny himself.

14. Of these things put *them* in remembrance, charging *them* before the Lord that they strive not about words to no profit, *but* to the subverting of the hearers.

49). The two clauses of verse 10 are parallel to the two corresponding clauses of verse 9: suffer trouble answers to endure all things, with the added thought for the elect's sakes. The word of God is not bound answers to that they may obtain the salvation.

3) The Truth Embodied in a "Faithful Saying." 2:11-13.

11a. Paul used a faithful saying to introduce matters of great importance (see note on I Tim 3:1). Here he uses it to introduce words taken, most probably, from a familiar hymn (see note on I Tim 3:16). This is the heart of what Paul wanted to say; hence he sets it off in memorable form. The poem has a balanced structure. The first clause and the last receive the emphasis through the conjunction which is here translated *indeed* and *for:*

> If indeed we died with him, we shall also live with him;
> If we endure, we shall also reign with him;
> If we shall deny, he too will deny us;
> If we are faithless, he abideth faithful,
> For himself he cannot deny.

11b. If we be dead. *Died* (ASV) is correct. Our justification and forgiveness is a death to sin and the curse of the Law. Live with him looks to the ultimate goal—eternal life, while including our present walk. 12. Suffer means *endure* (ASV); the thought is parallel to that in Rom 8:16,17. Reign further suggests what is involved in living with Christ. Deny is a clear reference to Mt 10:33. There is a double incentive to remain faithful: the hope of reigning with him, and the certainty that if we deny him, he will deny us. 13. Believe not means to be *faithless* (ASV). This last sentence seems to suggest not an emphasis on his denial, if we deny him, but that if Christians sin, his faithfulness is the ultimate reliance: He cannot deny himself. The thought is similar to that of I Jn 2:1, involving the confession and forgiveness of sin (see the entire sermon "Communion with Christ," Warfield, *Faith and Life,* pp. 415-427).

4) The Truth Rightly Handled. 2:14-19. Empty discussions would unsettle those who heard; but Timothy was to proceed according to the Word, avoiding vanities, remembering the marks of the

**15.** Study to show thyself approved unto God, a workman that needeth not to be ashamed, rightly dividing the word of truth.

**16.** But shun profane *and* vain babblings: for they will increase unto more ungodliness.

**17.** And their word will eat as doth a canker: of whom is Hymeneus and Philetus;

**18.** Who concerning the truth have erred, saying that the resurrection is past already; and overthrow the faith of some.

**19.** Nevertheless the foundation of God standeth sure, having this seal, The Lord knoweth them that are his. And, Let every one that nameth the name of Christ depart from iniquity.

**20.** But in a great house there are not only vessels of gold and of silver, but also of wood and of earth; and some to honor, and some to dishonor.

**21.** If a man therefore purge himself from these, he shall be a vessel unto honor, sanctified, and meet for the master's use, *and* prepared unto every good work.

sure foundation, and seeking, by right conduct, to be useful to the Lord. **14.** Timothy was to give others the same charge Paul was giving him (4:1). The same word is used—charging them. It was to be done **before the Lord,** who would then witness to the grave responsibility conferred. **Strive not about words** is one word in the Greek text; the corresponding noun is used at I Tim 6:4. Both forms seem to imply quibbling over words and not seeking truth. **15. Study to show thyself approved.** *Give diligence to present thyself approved* (ASV). **Rightly dividing.** *Handling aright* (ASV), as a master workman would his tool. **16. Vain babblings.** Omit vain, as in the ASV. This is a further characteristic of the strifes about words. **They** refers to babblings. **Ungodliness.** Diverting the attention from solid truth would allow error in conduct. **17. Their word** seems to mean the doctrine of those who engage in such discussions. **Canker** is a spreading ulcer. **Hymenaeus** is associated with Alexander in I Tim 1:20, where the reason for his departure from the faith lies in his failure to hold a good conscience. **Philetus** is not mentioned elsewhere; nothing more is known of him. **18. Resurrection.** The Gnostics conceived of resurrection allegorically, as referring to an acquaintance with truth, occurring at baptism.

**19.** Here the ASV translation is preferable. **Foundation** seems to imply both the foundation and the temple, the church, as in I Tim 3:15; Eph 2:20; Mt 16:18. **Seal.** A mark of ownership and authentication. **Knoweth.** This quotation is taken from the LXX of Num 16:5, with allusions to verses 26,27 of the same passage (cf. Mt 7:23; Jn 10:14). **Every one that nameth the name** means every one who names the name of Christ as his Lord. No one distinct passage is cited in this statement, but the sense of many passages is compressed in it.

5) The Truth Applied to the Life. 2:20-26. The truth of separation from evil is applied in balanced and positive fashion in the rest of the chapter.

**20. The great house.** Probably the church in its visible aspect as seen by the world (cf. I Tim 3:15). The connection of thought seems to be that in the visible church there is false profession, from which one should purge himself. **Honour** is parallel to the expression in Rom 9:21. **21. These.** The dishonorable

22. Flee also youthful lusts: but follow righteousness, faith, charity, peace, with them that call on the Lord out of a pure heart.

23. But foolish and unlearned questions avoid, knowing that they do gender strifes.

24. And the servant of the Lord must not strive; but be gentle unto all *men*, apt to teach, patient;

25. In meekness instructing those that oppose themselves; if God peradventure will give them repentance to the acknowledging of the truth;

26. And *that* they may recover themselves out of the snare of the devil, who are taken captive by him at his will.

## CHAPTER 3

THIS know also, that in the last days perilous times shall come.

vessels as well as their doctrines and practices. **Purge** is closely related to the word used by the Lord in Jn 15:2,3, and suggests the same doctrine. **Sanctified** implies continuance of the state of being set apart. **Master's.** *Despot's.* An expressive divine title used in Lk 2:29; Acts 4:24; II Pet 2:1; Jude 4; Rev 6: 10. It is closely related to "housemaster" in Mt 10:25; Lk 13:25; 14:21; and especially in Mt 13:27,28. It means absolute owner.

**22. Charity.** Love. **Pure heart** is an expression very similar to that in the beatitude of Mt 5:8, and repeats the thought of **purge** (II Tim 2:21). **Call on the Lord** is parallel to "nameth the name" (v. 19). The preceding verse calls for separation from evil company; this verse calls for fellowship with the Lord's people and seeking the graces of the Spirit.

**23,24.** Again false doctrine and unprofitable discussions are mentioned, as in verses 14,16-18. **Strive.** A different word from that used in verse 5. Here it is the verb corresponding to "strifes" of the verse preceding, and is used in a bad sense. **Servant** refers still to the figure of the great house and the servants in it. **Patient.** *Forbearing.* **25,26.** This truth harmonizes with the truth of separation taught above: there should still be the meek attempt to instruct, in hope that God will give them repentance, though they are now in Satan's snare. Pride is indicated as the cause of rejection of truth and falling into Satan's snare (I Tim 6:4; 3:6). **Recover.** "Come to their senses"; parallel to "repentance" of the preceding verse.

C. To Be Recognized as a Bulwark. 3:1-17. As the writer contrasts truth and error, devotion to the Lord on one side, and obedience to sin and Satan on the other, he brings his thoughts to a climax in the detailed description of sins that will characterize a future departure from the faith. With this he contrasts the example of his own experience and the great stronghold of the faithful, the Scriptures. In order that Timothy may be the more encouraged to fight, he makes it clear (v. 9) that the truth of God will prevail.

1) Against Apostasy. 3:1-9. It is noteworthy that the severest opposition is to come from those who have a form of godliness only (v. 5). **1. The last days** probably is not here limited to the eschatological age-end, but includes the Gnostic

**2.** For men shall be lovers of their own selves, covetous, boasters, proud, blasphemers, disobedient to parents, unthankful, unholy,

**3.** Without natural affection, trucebreakers, false accusers, incontinent, fierce, despisers of those that are good,

**4.** Traitors, heady, high-minded, lovers of pleasures more than lovers of God;

**5.** Having a form of godliness, but denying the power thereof: from such turn away.

**6.** For of this sort are they which creep into houses, and lead captive silly women laden with sins, led away with divers lusts,

**7.** Ever learning, and never able to come to the knowledge of the truth.

**8.** Now as Jannes and Jambres withstood Moses, so do these also resist the truth: men of corrupt minds, reprobate concerning the faith.

attack on the Church then developing. **2. Lovers of their own selves** is one word in the Greek, used only here in the NT. It is significant that men should be characterized as lovers of self at the beginning of this passage. Then follows (through v. 5) a list of sins flowing from the corrupted hearts that love self rather than God. Most of the following adjectives are compounded of two parts, so that each has the effect of a compressed sentence, combining subject and predicate.

**Covetous.** The word used of the Pharisees (Lk 16:14). **Boasters** is used only here and in Rom 1:30 in the NT. **Proud** is also in Rom 1:30, Jas 4:6, and I Pet 5:5. **Blasphemers** is used by Paul of himself in I Tim 1:13. **Disobedient to parents,** as in Rom 1:30 (cf. Tit 1:16; 3:3; Acts 26:19). **Unthankful** occurs only here and in Lk 6:35, but the idea is expressed otherwise, as in Rom 1:21. **3. Without natural affection,** as in Rom 1:31. **Trucebreakers** means *implacable* (ASV), as in Rom 1:31. **False accusers** is generally used of Satan as *diabolos* (cf. Rev 12:10; also I Tim 1:10; Tit 2:3). **Incontinent** is *without self-control* (ASV). **Despisers of those that are good.** *No lovers of good* (ASV). **4. Heady.** *Head-strong* (ASV). **Highminded.** Puffed up (I Tim 3:6; 6:4). This sums up the sins flowing from the love of self and is in sharp contrast to **lovers of God.**

**5.** The terrifying fact is that such people are professing Christians, who very probably wish to be considered religious and holy. They have, however, only a **form of godliness,** only the external appearance of following Gospel doctrine and practice; the **power** is lacking. Only the Holy Spirit makes profession a reality; the faith without the works and fruit of the Spirit is dead. **Denying,** a strong word, implies knowing and yet decisively rejecting the truth. **From such turn away.** The expression may mean "repel them from you" as a good soldier repels a foe.

**6-9.** Their true character is shown by their sinful acts. **6. Creep into houses.** Enter families and homes. **7. Ever learning** refers to the women. **Knowledge of the truth** includes knowledge of sin (Rom 3:20) on the one side, as well as the knowledge of the truth, according to godliness, on the other (Tit 1:1); it implies a coming short of salvation (Heb 10:26). The implication here may be that these people do not come to a knowledge of their sinful condition even under the testimony of the church. **8. Jannes and Jambres** are names of two of the

**9.** But they shall proceed no further: for their folly shall be manifest unto all *men*, as theirs also was.

**10.** But thou hast fully known my doctrine, manner of life, purpose, faith, longsuffering, charity, patience,

**11.** Persecutions, afflictions, which came unto me at Antioch, at Iconium, at Lystra; what persecutions I endured: but out of *them* all the Lord delivered me.

**12.** Yea, and all that will live godly in Christ Jesus shall suffer persecution.

**13.** But evil men and seducers shall wax worse and worse, deceiving, and being deceived.

**14.** But continue thou in the things which thou hast learned and hast been assured of, knowing of whom thou hast learned *them;*

magicians alluded to in Ex 7:11,22. There were probably more, and the mention of these is simply a way of designating the magicians of Egypt. The mention of Satan earlier (II Tim 2:26) and the extreme corruption of the people here described, as well as the working of Satanic wonders, suggest a parallel to II Thess 2:9-12. **These** (II Tim 3:8) are not the women of verse 7, but those false teachers who seduce them, who deliberately oppose the truth. **Reprobate** seems clearly to imply a lost condition (cf. II Cor 13:5; Heb 6:8; Tit 1:16). The **faith** equals the Gospel. **9.** Paul's encouraging message is that, as the truth of God prevailed against the tricks of the magicians of Egypt, even so the Gospel will triumph over every kind of error that may arise.

2) In Defense of the Faithful. 3:10-12. The full exposure of the senseless opposition to the truth will be fulfilled completely in the time of the return of Christ. **10.** But Paul uses himself as an illustration of God's ability to deliver even now (cf. 4:17). **11.** He encourages Timothy by recalling events of the first missionary journey. Timothy is first mentioned in the second journey at Lystra, but Paul's remarks refer to the earlier visit. Timothy would have been the more affected by the remarks because he had seen the work at Lystra prosper and endure in spite of opposition. **12. Godly** is the adverb related to "godliness" (3:5; Tit 1:1, and frequently in I Tim). Paul must mean that to **live godly** involves the aggressive kind of witness he gave at Lystra, which roused opposition in addition to winning souls.

3) The Inspired Scriptures: Our Confidence. 3:13-17. As opposition increases, the Scriptures become the believer's reliance, his bulwark. Paul's characterization of this age as one of increasing wickedness is in accord with the picture given by the Lord in the Olivet Discourse. **13. Seducers.** Used in the sense of "wizard," and also of "juggler," or "cheat." In this context the emphasis is on deceit. **14.** In sharp contrast to this opposition of the world and its deceit, Timothy was to continue in the sound Scripture doctrine, in reliance on God. An important element in continuing is **knowing of whom** one has learned. The character of the teacher and witness is important in establishing the truth of the Gospel. Paul would have included him-

**15.** And that from a child thou hast known the holy Scriptures, which are able to make thee wise unto salvation through faith which is in Christ Jesus.

**16.** All Scripture *is* given by inspiration of God, and *is* profitable for doctrine, for reproof, for correction, for instruction in righteousness:

**17.** That the man of God may be perfect, thoroughly furnished unto all good works.

## CHAPTER 4

I CHARGE *thee* therefore before God, and the Lord Jesus Christ, who shall judge the quick and the dead at his appearing and his kingdom;

self and Timothy's parents, but the whom of the original text could also point to the Scriptures as the highest proof of the truth of the doctrines. **15.** Timothy had a lifetime of acquaintance with the Scriptures to teach him their power.

Paul then gives the reason for this efficacy of Scripture: it is of divine origin. **16. Inspiration of God** is a simple word, meaning, *God-breathed*. It comes with full divine authority because of full truthfulness, and is therefore profitable. The alternative translations of the original as **all Scripture** or *every Scripture* (ASV) are both possible and imply the same thing: If every Scripture is inspired, then all is. The Greek sentence has no verb expressed. Should the adjective "God-breathed" stand with the subject, or be a part of the predication made about the subject? The AV is more accurate than the ASV here, since the ASV seems to admit the possibility, absurd in Paul's case, that there could be Scripture which is not inspired. Warfield's paraphrase relieves the ambiguity: "Every Scripture, seeing that it is God-breathed, is as well profitable . . ." ("Inspiration," ISBE, III, 1474 a). **Doctrine** is emphasized in the Pastoral Epistles (nineteen of the twenty-one occurrences of *doctrine* in the NT are found in Paul's writings, and of the nineteen, fifteen are in the Pastoral Epistles.) **Reproof** is closely related to "reprove" of Jn 16:8. The Scripture is the Spirit's instrument in conviction. **Correction** conveys the idea of improvement. **Instruction in righteousness** indicates training or education that is to be found in the way of righteousness, or in "the faith" (cf. ASV: *instruction which is in righteousness*). The word for **instruction** is found only in Paul; it is translated "nurture" in Eph 6:4. In Heb 12:5,7, 8,11 it is rendered "chastening." **17. Man of God.** Paul had Timothy especially in mind (cf. I Tim 6:11). This is an OT phrase meaning prophet (Deut 33:1; Josh 14:6; I Sam 6:9; I Kgs 12:22; 13:1). **Perfect** and **throughly furnished** (equipped) are from the same root; the ASV has correctly translated it: *complete, furnished completely* (cf. Eph 6: 13-17).

**III. Charge to Timothy, and Conclusion. 4:1-22.**

A. The Solemn Charge. 4:1-5.

1) God and Christ: Witnesses of Timothy's Responsibility. 4:1. The idea of

2. Preach the word; be instant in season, out of season; reprove, rebuke, exhort with all long-suffering and doctrine.

3. For the time will come when they will not endure sound doctrine; but after their own lusts shall they heap to themselves teachers, having itching ears;

charging or commanding the passing on of the testimony is emphasized in outstanding Scriptures: Moses charged Israel (Deut 29:1,10; 30:11,16); Moses charged Joshua (Deut 31:7,8,23); Joshua charged Israel (Josh 23:2,6; 24:1,26,27); Samuel charged Israel (I Sam 12:1-25); David charged Solomon (I Kgs 2:1-9; I Chr 28:2-10,20); Ezra charged Israel (Neh 8—10); Jesus charged the apostles (Jn 13:34; 14-17). **Judge.** The right and ability to judge all men belongs to God alone; Christ clearly claimed it (Mt 7:21,22; Jn 5:25-30). **At his appearing.** The sanction of the charge is the appearing of Christ. The ASV translates correctly: *by his appearing and his kingdom.* God and Christ are the divine witnesses; the appearing and the kingdom are the most solemn of incentives to fidelity. **Appearing** means "manifestation" and is used of both the first coming (II Tim 1:10) and the second (4:1,8; Tit 2:13). **Kingdom** has different phases: judgment (Mt 25:31,34,40); Millennial reign (I Cor 15:24,25); eternal in new heavens and earth (Rev 22:3).

2) Five Imperatives. 4:2. These five terse imperatives, which are matched by four more in verse 5, sum up the work of the ministry: (1) **Preach.** Foremost is the great basic work of delivering the fundamental message, as Paul himself did (I Cor 15:1-11), and Jesus (Lk 5:1; 8:11, 21). (2) **Be instant.** Be ready, be at hand, both when it is convenient and when it is not. (3) **Reprove,** closely related to the idea in **reproof** (3:16; see note), is the same word used in Tit 1:9 ("convince"), 13 ("rebuke"); 2:15 ("rebuke"); I Tim 5:20 ("rebuke"). (4) **Rebuke** is translated *charge* in Mt 12:16; Mk 8:30; 10:48; Lk 9:21. It means to lay a value or charge on. The essential idea is often the implied demand for restitution when error is pointed out. (5) **Exhort** is often translated *comfort* or *beseech.* It is an earnest entreaty in any of life's circumstances, and is possible because of the presence of the Comforter, whose name is a different form of the same word. The phrase, **with all longsuffering and doctrine** (teaching), is not to be taken with the last of the imperatives only, but is to accompany all five commands. Punctuate as in the ASV. Patient teaching is the most solid basis for ultimate success in the ministry (cf. 2:25).

3) Turning from the Truth; Turning to Myths. 4:3,4. **3.** The insistence on faith-

**4. And they shall turn away** *their* **ears from the truth, and shall be turned unto fables.**

**5. But watch thou in all things, endure afflictions, do the work of an evangelist, make full proof of thy ministry.**

fulness and sound teaching is the more necessary because of the danger of apostasy in the churches. **Itching ears.** People will wish to hear what satisfies their sinful desires. Isaiah powerfully characterizes the attitude in 30:9-11. **Teachers.** The principle is Hosea's: "like people, like priest" (Hos 4:9; Jer 5:30,31). **Heap** means to multiply, have an abundance of false teachers. **4. Truth.** Very wonderful is the Bible's constant orientation to the **truth,** a comprehensive word for God's revelation, centering in Jesus Christ. **Fables.** Turning from the only basis of life, their hopes and conduct will be built on the sand, on myths (see note on I Tim 4:7). In II Pet 1:16 myths are contrasted with the written truth of God. Therefore, the more urgent is the need for much sound teaching.

4) Four Imperatives. 4:5. These conclude Paul's commands to Timothy. (1) **Watch.** Literally, *abstain from intoxicating drinks,* but in all NT occurrences the idea of watchfulness and alertness is stressed. The parallel expressions linked to it are self-explanatory: "watch and be sober" (I Thess 5:6); "be . . . sober, and .watch" (I Pet 4:7); "be sober, be vigilant" (I Pet 5:8). (2) **Endure afflictions.** All three Pauline uses of this word are in II Tim: "endure hardness" (2:3); "suffer trouble" (2:9). Note also the same word compounded with the preposition **with** in 1:8: "partaker (sharer) of the afflictions." (3) **Do the work of an evangelist.** If this is meant to indicate a special office (Acts 21:8), the list in Eph 4:11 is noteworthy, for it is fuller than the parallel list in I Cor 12:28: prophets, evangelists, pastors, teachers are mentioned as compared with prophets, teachers. Probably these functions would overlap; the evangelist might well stand between prophet and pastor-teacher. Timothy's life had included much itinerant evangelism, joined with pastoral and teaching work. (4) **Make full proof of thy ministry.** *Fulfill* (ASV) or "fulfill completely thy ministry" gives the thought. It is the command to teach and evangelize given by the Lord, and as such it stands as the climactic and comprehensive imperative of the whole series (cf. Paul's great text, Acts 20:24).

B. Paul's Final Testimony. 4:6-8. This eloquent and confident testimony touches on the main points Paul has endeavored to say to Timothy: confidence in the grace of Christ; faithful transmis-

6. For I am now ready to be offered, and the time of my departure is at hand.

7. I have fought a good fight, I have finished *my* course, I have kept the faith:

sion of the faith to others; the steadfast reliance on the blessed hope.

1) Paul's Calm Facing of Death. 4:6. **Ready to be offered** (lit., *I am being poured out*). This verb, occurring only here and in Phil 2:17, is used by Paul in a figurative sense. Literally it is used in connection with a libation or drink offering (Gen 35:14). But Paul was thinking of his imminent death as an offering in the service of Christians and their faith. His whole life had been a sacrifice (Rom 12:1), and now his death would complete the life with a drink offering. **The time of my departure is at hand** is a parallel statement of his approaching death, under a different figure. He uses the same metaphor in Phil 1:23, where the verb of the same root is used. Christ (Lk 9:31) and Peter (II Pet 1:15) spoke of death with a similar figure, using the word "exodus."

2) The Testimony of One Who Has Fulfilled His Task. 4:7. **Fight** is rendered "conflict" (Phil 1:30; Col 2:1), "contention" (I Thess 2:2), "race" (Heb 12:1), "fight" (I Tim 6:12). For Paul it was more than a grim and momentous battle; it was a contest, a race that demanded all the enthusiasm of a fervent, consecrated spirit (cf. Acts 20:24). To have fought the **good** fight implies having won. This fits Paul's figure well, and adds irony: though he appears to be conquered and to be about to die a felon's death, yet he has conquered, for he has finished the course Jesus set before him; he has kept the faith by committing it to faithful men and establishing churches. All those who die in faith (Heb 11:13) will ultimately receive the promise and carry off the prize (I Pet 1:9; 5:4; Heb 10:30). **Course** is used only by Paul in the NT (Acts 13:25; 20:24). The word may mean a lap in a race. Paul may be thinking of the transmission of the faith through the centuries as a relay race: he has successfully finished his course and passed on the faith to others. The figure of the relay race seems to fit the following verse, for not Paul only, but the whole 'team' will receive the prize. **Kept.** *Keep* means not only "guard" but also "observe and do." For a believer to persevere and be faithful unto death is a triumph of grace (Rev 2:10). The **faith** is the whole Gospel testimony, going back to the words of Jesus committed to his followers (Rom 10:17; Heb 2:3, 4; Rev 14:12).

8. Henceforth there is laid up for me a crown of righteousness, which the Lord, the righteous judge, shall give me at that day: and not to me only, but unto all them also that love his appearing.

9. Do thy diligence to come shortly unto me:

10. For Demas hath forsaken me, having loved this present world, and is departed unto Thessalonica; Crescens to Galatia, Titus unto Dalmatia.

11. Only Luke is with me. Take Mark, and bring him with thee: for he is profitable to me for the ministry.

12. And Tychicus have I sent to Ephesus.

13. The cloak that I left at Troas with Carpus, when thou comest, bring *with thee*, and the books, *but* especially the parchments.

14. Alexander the coppersmith did me much evil: the Lord reward him according to his works:

3) The Blessed Hope Undimmed. 4:8. Instead of being depressed, Paul is only the more confident. The greater the trial, the clearer the promise shines. The **crown** which is the prize is described in various ways: it is a crown of "righteousness," "life" (Rev 2:10), "rejoicing" (I Thess 2:19); "glory" (I Pet 5:4). **The righteous judge** may suggest that many of the decisions Paul had received in this life were unfair, but the Lord is the Judge who can make no mistake. **Not to me only.** Paul's thought is not of himself alone, but of all the redeemed. **Love.** "Who have set their love upon." The verb form implies steadfast maintaining of love for Christ's appearing.

C. Conclusion: Final Notes of Love and Concern. 4:9-22. Dwelling on the welfare of individuals is characteristic of Paul (see Rom 16). **9. Diligence.** Paul relied on the loyalty of Timothy. **10. Demas** (Col 4:14; Phm 24) . . . **loved this present world.** The strength of the blessed hope shines through as the apostle sadly mentions one so foolish as to set his affections on the things of this world. **Crescens** is mentioned only here. **Titus** had rejoined Paul since receiving the epistle addressed to him and had gone on to Dalmatia, also known as Illyricum (modern Yugoslavia; cf. Rom 15:19). Paul seems to have sent Titus to new territory, beyond where he himself had gone. **11. Mark** had proved himself in Paul's estimation since the time some twenty years before when the apostle had refused to take him on the second journey (Acts 15:37-39). **12.** Paul probably meant that **Tychicus** was to relieve Timothy, who probably was still at Ephesus, so that Timothy could join the apostle in Rome. This would suggest that Tychicus was the bearer of the letter (see note on Tit 3:12).

**13. Cloke.** A thick upper garment Perhaps Paul passed through in the summer, when it was not needed, but now winter was approaching. **Carpus** is mentioned only here. **The books.** Probably papyri copies of the Scriptures or Scripture portions. **The parchments.** Perhaps vellum codices, the earliest form of books. **14. Alexander.** Probably the same as the one mentioned in I Tim 1:20 (see note there). **Did.** From a Greek word elsewhere translated *show* (see Tit 2:10; 3: 2; Heb 6:11). Alexander "showed" evil to Paul in the sense that he revealed an evil heart in his opposition to the Gospel. Paul's wish, then, is not an expression of

15. Of whom be thou ware also; for he hath greatly withstood our words.

16. At my first answer no man stood with me, but all *men* forsook me: *I pray God* that it may not be laid to their charge.

17. Notwithstanding the Lord stood with me, and strengthened me; that by me the preaching might be fully known, and *that* all the Gentiles might hear: and I was delivered out of the mouth of the lion.

18. And the Lord shall deliver me from every evil work, and will preserve *me* unto his heavenly kingdom: to whom *be* glory for ever and ever. Amen.

19. Salute Prisca and Aquila, and the household of Onesiphorus.

20. Erastus abode at Corinth: but Trophimus have I left at Miletum sick.

21. Do thy diligence to come before winter. Eubulus greeteth thee, and Pudens, and Linus, and Claudia, and all the brethren.

22. The Lord Jesus Christ *be* with thy spirit. Grace *be* with you. Amen.

The second *epistle* unto Timotheus, ordained the first bishop of the church of the Ephesians, was written from Rome, when Paul was brought before Nero the second time.

personal vindictiveness (in II Tim 4:16 he shows compassion for those who have forsaken him); but, like the imprecatory psalms, it is a prayer for justice for those who reject the Gospel. **15. Be thou ware also.** Paul commands Timothy to avoid Alexander, who has openly attacked the truth.

Zahn argues convincingly (*Introd. to NT*, II, 12-14) that verses **16,17** contain a reminiscence of the earlier trial at Rome alluded to in Philippians. Paul was **delivered out of the mouth of the lion** and resumed his work, so that the preaching might be fully known. **18.** Now, however, in the face of imminent death, Paul was confident of ultimate victory — not that he would escape death, but that God would keep him faithful **unto his heavenly kingdom.** This is a general term for all phases of God's future rule on this earth, and in the new earth. **Amen.** After ascribing glory to God, the seal of sincerity and fervency follows; it serves as a characteristic mark of Paul's whole life: the sincere and wholehearted devotion to the will of God.

Paul concludes with a few personal matters, the benediction and amen. **19. Prisca and Aquila** were the companions whom Paul had first met at Corinth after their expulsion from Rome (Acts 18:18, 19,26). They were at Ephesus when I Corinthians was written (I Cor 16:19) and at Rome when Romans was written (Rom 16:3). Now they had returned to Ephesus. **20. Erastus** is mentioned in Rom 16:23 as city treasurer of Corinth. **Trophimus** was not left at Miletus in the journey of Acts 20:4, since he was at Jerusalem later (Acts 21: 29). Paul is referring to a later occasion. **Winter** explains the request for the cloke of II Tim 4:13. The persons who send greetings are mentioned only here in the NT. **22. Lord Jesus Christ** should be *Lord* only (see ASV). **Thy spirit** is for Timothy, primarily, and the **you** (plural) is for all of Paul's readers, the Christians at Ephesus.

# BIBLIOGRAPHY

For Bibliography see under *I Timothy.*

# THE EPISTLE TO TITUS

## OUTLINE

(For the general introduction to this epistle, see Introduction to I Timothy.)

I. Salutation. 1:1-4.
II. Titus' mission: To set matters in order. 1:5—3:11.
  A. The appointment and need of the teaching elder. 1:5-16.
    1. Qualifications of elders. 1:5-9.
    2. Need for elders to combat error. 1:10-16.
  B. The pastoral work of the teaching elder. 2:1—3:11.
    1. Application of sound doctrine to particular cases. 2:1-10.
    2. Proclamation of sound doctrine: The grace of God. 2:11-15.
    3. Demonstration of sound doctrine: The root and the fruit. 3:1-11.
III. Conclusion, emphasizing good works. 3:12-15.

## TITUS

### CHAPTER 1

PAUL, a servant of God, and an apostle of Jesus Christ, according to the faith of God's elect, and the acknowledging of the truth which is after godliness;

2. In hope of eternal life, which God, that cannot lie, promised before the world began;

## COMMENTARY

### I. Salutation. 1:1-4.

Paul's first utterance in his epistles reveals his point of view and attitude. 1. Servant of God is put forward here, but coupled with it is the authority of apostleship. In Romans, in II Timothy, and here, the apostle states the two aspects of his office together (Rom 1:1,5; II Tim 1:1-3). Elsewhere he uses one or the other alone. To the Philippians he was a servant; to the Galatians and Corinthians, who needed rebuke and authoritative instruction, he was an apostle. To Titus, who especially needed to be armed with Paul's authority before the Cretans, he is both servant of God and apostle of Jesus Christ. The faith of God's elect is the body of revealed truth and promise that God's people have cherished through the ages. Acknowledging. *Knowledge* (ASV). The idea is parallel to the faith just mentioned; both ideas are governed by the according to. Both faith and knowledge have their basis in a factual message that can be known and believed. Truth has the implication of "God's faithful revelation," so that Jesus Christ could say, "I am . . . the truth." It is according to godliness, a word of frequent occurrence in the Pastoral Epistles (I Tim 3:16, note).

2. Hope is connected with Paul's service and apostleship; he was an apostle of hope, the hope of eternal life, which God promised before the world began, to our Saviour Jesus Christ (II Tim 1:9), to be given to us through the message. 3. Due times. Cf. I Tim 2:6. The eternal

**3.** But hath in due times manifested his word through preaching, which is committed unto me according to the commandment of God our Saviour;

**4.** To Titus, *mine* own son after the common faith: Grace, mercy, *and* peace, from God the Father and the Lord Jesus Christ our Saviour.

purposes come to fruition in the history of this world through **preaching** *(the message,* thing preached). **Commandment.** Cf. I Tim 1:1. Paul was an apostle by commandment; by commandment he received his message. **Word** is equivalent to the **promise** of the preceding verse. The idea is that God made good his promise; he fulfilled his word in the Gospel. **Saviour** is the great comprehensive word for Deliverer; both God and Christ are so named. **4. Son.** Or, *child* (ASV). A term of affection used by Paul of Timothy, Titus, and Onesimus. **The common faith** was shared by Paul, Titus, and all Christians. The apostle may be using the analogy of inheritance: the faith is an estate or trust belonging to all; Titus is being entrusted with the administration of it. **Mercy** is added only in the Pastoral Epistles (see I Tim 1:2, note). **From** governs both God and Lord: together they constitute the one divine source of all blessings. The ASV correctly omits **Lord**: Christ Jesus our Saviour.

II. Titus' Mission: To Set Matters in Order. 1:5—3:11.

A. The Appointment and Need of the Teaching Elder. 1:5-16.

1) Qualifications of Elders. 1:5-9. **5.** For the possible order of events referred to, see 3:12. Paul left Titus in Crete and may have proceeded toward Nicopolis in Epirus, near Dalmatia (II Tim 4:10), where later Titus joined him and went on to Dalmatia. **Wanting** implies things

5. For this cause left I thee in Crete, that thou shouldest set in order the things that are wanting, and ordain elders in every city, as I had appointed thee:

6. If any be blameless, the husband of one wife, having faithful children not accused of riot or unruly.

7. For a bishop must be blameless, as the steward of God; not self-willed, not soon angry, not given to wine, no striker, not given to filthy lucre;

8. But a lover of hospitality, a lover of good men, sober, just, holy, temperate;

9. Holding fast the faithful word as he hath been taught, that he may be able by sound doctrine both to exhort and to convince the gainsayers.

10. For there are many unruly and vain talkers and deceivers, specially they of the circumcision:

11. Whose mouths must be stopped, who subvert whole houses, teaching things which they ought not, for filthy lucre's sake.

12. One of themselves, *even* a prophet of their own, said, The Cretians *are* always liars, evil beasts, slow bellies.

13. This witness is true. Wherefore rebuke them sharply, that they may be sound in the faith;

left undone. **Every city** suggests an extensive but rapid evangelization of the island, leaving further organizational work to be done. **Elders** or *presbyters* here means the teaching elders or pastors, judging from the context. This commission in Crete did not give Titus dictatorial power to appoint ministers. Rather, as Paul and Barnabas ordained elders (Acts 14:23) who had been chosen by the people, so Titus was to do, keeping in mind the proper qualifications. Paul gives three general qualifications (v. 6), a list of negatives (v. 7), and a list of positive qualifications (vv. 8,9). The whole section is closely parallel to I Tim 3:2-4. **9.** The ASV is preferable in word choice and order: *holding to the faithful word which is according to the teaching, that he may be able both to exhort in the sound doctrine, and to convict* [as in Jn 16:8] *the gainsayers.*

2) Need for Elders To Combat Error. 1:10-16. As verse 9 suggests, doctrine has a double application: exhortation and conviction — to instruct believers, and to convict gainsayers. **10. Unruly.** Used here, in 1:6 and in I Tim 1:9. The suggestion is of willful unbelief and rejection of truth. **Vain talkers** and **deceivers** (cf. related verb in Gal 6:3). Used only here in the NT. **Circumcision.** Unbelieving Judaism seemed to be moving into a more and more complete rejection of the truth. At a somewhat later time John spoke of Jews who were of the "synagogue of Satan" (Rev 2:9; 3:9). **11. Mouths must be stopped.** The principal end of contending for the faith (Apologetics) is to exhort and convict. The evidence should be so clearly presented that rejecters should at least be left without an excuse or answer. In Crete the situation was aggravated by the avaricious Judaizers and other false teachers, who subverted whole households in their desire to win favor and financial gain.

**12.** The rebuke is severe, but it comes from one of the Cretans' own number. Paul did not object to using fragments of truths gleaned from heathen authors (Acts 17:28; I Cor 15:33). **Slow bellies** equals *idle gluttons* (ASV). **13. This witness is true.** Paul presumably had been on the island for a time and could endorse the statement. Since the Cretans were liars, and were rejecting truth, their message had to be refuted. But also Titus was to **rebuke sharply** (same word as "convince" in v. 9) those professing believers who listened and believed. This

14. Not giving heed to Jewish fables, and commandments of men, that turn from the truth.

15. Unto the pure all things *are* pure: but unto them that are defiled and unbelieving *is* nothing pure; but even their mind and conscience is defiled.

16. They profess that they know God; but in works they deny *him*, being abominable, and disobedient, and unto every good work reprobate.

## CHAPTER 2

BUT speak thou the things which become sound doctrine:

2. That the aged men be sober, grave, temperate, sound in faith, in charity, in patience.

3. The aged women likewise, that *they be* in behavior as becometh holiness, not false accusers, not given to much wine, teachers of good things;

4. That they may teach the young women to be sober, to love their husbands, to love their children,

5. *To be* discreet, chaste, keepers at home, good, obedient to their own husbands, that the word of God be not blasphemed.

6. Young men likewise exhort to be soberminded.

7. In all things showing thyself a pattern of good works: in doctrine *showing* uncorruptness, gravity, sincerity,

8. Sound speech, that cannot be condemned; that he that is of the contrary part may be ashamed, having no evil thing to say of you.

9. *Exhort* servants to be obedient unto their own masters, *and* to please *them* well in all things; not answering again;

makes it clear that Paul here turns his attention from the unbelievers to the professing Christians. **14. Fables.** *Myths.* **Commandments of men** is reminiscent of Mt 15:9, and its source in Isa 29:13. False authority and fear of men is involved in rejection of the truth of God.

**15.** Here the teaching is parallel to that of I Tim 4:2-5. **All things** is to be taken in context as equivalent to "every creature of God" (I Tim 4:3,4). For those who reject God's sovereignty, and worship the creature, all things are defiled, even their mind and conscience. **16. Profess** (cf. II Tim 3:5). The works are the decisive evidence of the condition of the heart (Mt 7:20; I Jn 4:20). **Reprobate.** Unfit for any good work.

B. The Pastoral Work of the Teaching Elder. 2:1–3:11.

1) Application of Sound Doctrine to Particular Cases. 2:1-10. The instruction of this chapter is addressed to Titus directly in verses 1,7,8,15; but through Titus Paul was instructing the whole church of Crete. His central theme is sound doctrine applied, resulting in good works. (1) To Titus (v. 1) the primary responsibility was to preach and teach the truth, that which was in accord with sound doctrine (*healthful;* see 1:9,13; 2:1; and the adjective in 2:8). The use of this word in the Pastorals, always in connection with doctrine, shows Paul's emphasis on correct teaching. (2) To **aged men** (v. 2), who were actually or potentially teachers, life and doctrine were to stand together. This is an important consideration with each of these classes of people. Additional counsel is given in I Tim 5:1. (3) To **aged** and **young women** (vv. 3-5) considerable emphasis is placed on the foundation of the home. The details are reminiscent of Prov 31: 10-31. The honor of the Word of God is the supreme sanction for right conduct.

(4) To **young men** (vv. 6-8) the key virtue singled out for emphasis is sobermindedness or discretion, as in the case of young women (v. 5). The same emphasis is seen in the exhortations to young men in Proverbs (1:4; 2:11; 3:21; 5:2). To Titus himself the apostle gives the appropriate admonition for a young man and minister (Tit 2:7,8). The constant challenge of properly instructing unbelievers is included. (5) To **servants** (vv. 9,10) two common faults are singled out: **answering again**, contradicting or disputing; and **purloining**, stealing (used

10. Not purloining, but showing all good fidelity; that they may adorn the doctrine of God our Saviour in all things.

11. For the grace of God that bringeth salvation hath appeared to all men,

12. Teaching us that, denying ungodliness and worldly lusts, we should live soberly, righteously, and godly, in this present world;

13. Looking for that blessed hope, and the glorious appearing of the great God and our Saviour Jesus Christ;

14. Who gave himself for us, that he might redeem us from all iniquity, and purify unto himself a peculiar people, zealous of good works.

only of Ananias and Sapphira in Acts 5: 2,3). **Fidelity** is the word frequently used for faith in the NT.

Paul epitomizes the whole section, indeed the entire epistle, when he points out that good works **adorn the doctrine of God our Saviour.** James said that faith (doctrine) without (good) works is dead, just as the body without spirit is dead also. It is a most ennobling thought that our good works adorn the testimony of our God (Mt 5:16).

2) Proclamation of Sound Doctrine: The Grace of God. 2:11-15. **Grace** (Pastorals: I Tim 1:14; II Tim 1:9; 2:1; Tit 3:7) is always the great key word in salvation. **That bringeth salvation** is all one word, meaning "saving." **All men** sounds the universal, evangelistic note so prominent in the Pastorals. It **appeared** in Jesus Christ (II Tim 1:10). All God's promises and saving work from the beginning of the race have revealed his grace; all his blessings and gifts have been designed to lead men to repentance (Rom 2:4).

**12. Teaching.** Grace saves, but also teaches and trains in sober and godly living. **Denying.** The same strong decisive rejection that refuses grace (I Tim 5:8; II Tim 2:12; 3:5; Tit 1:16). **Soberly, righteously, and godly.** These three words skillfully reiterate the theme of all the Pastorals. **Present world.** Used once in each of the Pastorals (see I Tim 6:17; II Tim 4:10). These words show the basic orientation of Paul's thought — life consists of this world, as well as the world to come.

**13.** Paul expresses the rest of the thought by the great event of the world to come: the coming of Christ. **Hope . . . appearing** is one concept, as in the ASV: *the blessed hope and appearing.* **God . . . Saviour** is correctly translated: *"our great God and Saviour Jesus Christ"* (ASV margin). Again two ideas form one concept, much as do the compound divine names of the OT. **14. Who gave himself for us.** The atonement has both the particular reference to the elect and the universal reference to all (see note on I Tim 2:6). **Redeem.** Ransom or deliver by payment of a price (used in Lk 24:21; I Pet 1:18; and here). Purchase is stressed in the atonement (cf. Gal 3:13; Rev 5: 9). Deliverance from guilt and condemnation is not foremost here, but rather deliverance from ungodly walk. Thus the peculiar mark of God's people appears— their zeal for good works. **Peculiar** is used

**15.** These things speak, and exhort, and rebuke with all authority. Let no man despise thee.

## CHAPTER 3

PUT them in mind to be subject to principalities and powers, to obey magistrates, to be ready to every good work,

**2.** To speak evil of no man, to be no brawlers, *but* gentle, showing all meekness unto all men.

**3.** For we ourselves also were sometime foolish, disobedient, deceived, serving divers lusts and pleasures, living in malice and envy, hateful, *and* hating one another.

**4.** But after that the kindness and love of God our Saviour toward man appeared,

**5.** Not by works of righteousness which we have done, but according to his mercy he saved us, by the washing of regeneration, and renewing of the Holy Ghost;

in the LXX of Ex 19:5. This and the word translated "peculiar" in I Pet 2:9 both imply a possession or purchase. Good works are the fruit of the Spirit, the seal of God's ownership.

**15. These things speak.** The grace of God is the basis of good works, but it is essential for the minister continually to proclaim this grace, exhorting and reproving, with the authority of God's Word. Let not our ministry be such as would give men reason to despise us.

3) Demonstration of Sound Doctrine: The Root and the Fruit. 3:1-11. Paul here introduces another paragraph discussing righteous living, which, he declares, should be inspired by the example of our own unworthiness and God's dealing with us in kindness and love. He makes it clear (v. 8) that the intention of Christian doctrine is that believers should demonstrate good works. The grace of God is the root; the good works are the fruit. It is not surprising, then, that we find here another remarkable doctrinal summary (paralleling the one in the last chapter on the grace of God). This gem, this brilliant description of God's goodness to us (vv. 4-7), is placed in the setting of the believer's responsibility to demonstrate good works before men.

Paul's first emphasis falls on civic and public virtues and duties. There is also a brief added note about the government of the church (vv. 9-11) which supplements 1:5-16. **1. Principalities.** Rather, *rulers* (ASV). **Powers.** *Authorities* (ASV). **Obey magistrates** should read, *be obedient* (ASV). The same verb is used in Acts 5:29,32. **2.** The virtues listed are similar to those commanded previously, but are here oriented to the unbelieving world. **3. We ourselves also.** Paul never lost his memory of what he once was, and it moved him to compassion for the lost. **4. Kindness and love** are used only here and in Acts 28:2. Pity is also suggested by the context. These graces appeared supremely in Christ, though they are manifested in all God's natural benevolences (Acts 14:17). This whole passage forms a balance and complement to Tit 2:11-14. **5. Works of righteousness.** The ASV gives it correctly: *Not by works done in righteousness, which* [works] *we did ourselves.* This eliminates all works whatsoever; not only those done by an unsaved man in self-righteousness, but also the works done in true righteousness. Over against all works is the free mercy

6. Which he shed on us abundantly through Jesus Christ our Saviour;

7. That being justified by his grace, we should be made heirs according to the hope of eternal life.

8. *This is* a faithful saying, and these things I will that thou affirm constantly, that they which have believed in God might be careful to maintain good works. These things are good and profitable unto men.

9. But avoid foolish questions, and genealogies, and contentions, and strivings about the law; for they are unprofitable and vain.

10. A man that is a heretic, after the first and second admonition, reject;

11. Knowing that he that is such is subverted, and sinneth, being condemned of himself.

of God, exhibited in the work of the Spirit. Washing . . . renewing. The Holy Spirit renews us in regeneration. These two ideas are closely linked together as two ways of expressing the one work of the Spirit. 6. Shed on us. Poured out. The symbolism of water is often used of the Spirit. Jesus is the one through whom the Spirit is given (Jn 4:10; 7:37). Abundantly. Richly. The Spirit is true riches in that he is the earnest of our inheritance and the source and creator of all blessings. 7. That gives the result of the gift of the Spirit: "so that in being justified by his grace, we become heirs according to the hope, eternal life."

8 a. Faithful saying. This is one of the noteworthy sayings of the Pastorals (I Tim 1:15; 3:1; 4:9; II Tim 2:11, note). It not only gives weighty emphasis to the doctrinal statement just uttered (vv. 4-7), but it also calls attention to the succinct, powerful restatement of the message of the whole epistle which follows. Affirm constantly is one emphatic verb used only in I Tim 1:7 and here. The inculcation of Gospel truth requires patient repetition. They which have believed . . . maintain good works. The grace of God, producing faith, comes first; good works should follow: the root and then the fruit. 8b,9. Good and profitable of verse 8 contrasts with unprofitable and vain of verse 9, where the Apostle lists things that distract attention from the truth. These should be avoided, as should also those individuals who, having been admonished by the church, still perversely cling to them. 10. Heretick is used either in the strict sense or of one causing division. Admonition is a most important aspect of church discipline. The noun is used here, in I Cor 10:11, and in Eph 6:4; the verb in Acts 20:31; Rom 15:14; I Cor 4:14; Col 1:28; 3:16; I Thess 5:12,14; II Thess 3:15. 11. Subverted connotes "permanently turned," "set on a wrong course." Sinneth implies willfully sinning, as in Heb 10:26. Condemned of himself. Such a one, who has received knowledge of the truth and stubbornly rejected it, is himself the witness that he has twice rejected an earnest explanation and appeal.

12. When I shall send Artemas unto thee, or Tychicus, be diligent to come unto me to Nicopolis: for I have determined there to winter.

13. Bring Zenas the lawyer and Apollos on their journey diligently, that nothing be wanting unto them.

14. And let ours also learn to maintain good works for necessary uses, that they be not unfruitful.

15. All that are with me salute thee. Greet them that love us in the faith. Grace *be* with you all. Amen.

It was written to Titus, ordained the first bishop of the church of the Cretians, from Nicopolis of Macedonia.

## III. Conclusion, Emphasizing Good Works. 3:12-15.

After a few personal notes, Paul gives the final reiteration of the main burden of his letter—that the believers should be careful to maintain good works. **12. Artemas** is not mentioned elsewhere; **Tychicus** appears in Acts 20:4; Eph 6:21; Col 4:7; II Tim 4:12. **Nicopolis** is in Epirus. Titus is instructed to join the apostle there (II Tim 4:10, note). **13. Zenas** appears only here. **Apollos** was an Alexandrian; it is possible that the journey alluded to was to Alexandria by way of Crete. **14. Maintain** may mean "to be concerned with," but as used elsewhere in the Pastorals, it means "to lead or rule." There is the suggestion that Christians should be in the lead in doing good works. **15. Grace.** This is the characteristic conclusion of all Paul's epistles (see comment on I Tim 6:21).

# BIBLIOGRAPHY

(For bibliography, see under I Timothy)

# THE EPISTLE TO PHILEMON

## INTRODUCTION

*The Occasion and Theme.* Paul wrote this letter on behalf of Philemon's slave, Onesimus, who, after escaping from his master, had been converted under Paul's ministry. A recent conjecture of the noted contemporary writer, John Knox *(Philemon Among the Letters of Paul),* makes Archippus the slave owner (and principal addressee of the letter) and Philemon merely an overseer of the churches in Lycus Valley. The traditional view, however, which considers Archippus the son of Philemon and Apphia, remains the more convincing.

In the providence of God several factors were important in the church's recognition of this letter not merely as the private correspondence of Paul, but as apostolic teaching to be received as Scripture: (1) "The church" is included in the address. (2) The master-slave relationship posed a problem important for the whole of the church, not only for Philemon personally. (Philemon was not the only slaveholder in the Colossian church; cf. *Kyrioi,* Col 4:1.) By returning the slave, who, after absconding, had become a Christian and a servant to Paul, the apostle not only instructs us concerning the principles governing the relations of Christian brothers but reminds us that these principles are not to be realized "by compulsion, but by your own free will" (Phm 14, RSV). In Christ there is a completely new frame of reference that transforms all earthly relationships: brotherhood is the focus upon which all other relationships must be evaluated. Paul does not direct a polemic against slavery, but in the course of the passing centuries, the Christian faith has come to view the practice of slavery as incompatible with the principles Paul here enunciates. For the origin and date of the letter, see Introduction to Colossians.

## OUTLINE

I. Introduction. Phm 1-3.
II. Thanksgiving. Phm 4-7.
III. Paul's appeal for Onesimus. Phm 8-21.
IV. Conclusion. Phm 22-25.

# PHILEMON

PAUL, a prisoner of Jesus Christ, and Timothy *our* brother, unto Philemon our dearly beloved, and fellow laborer,

2. And to *our* beloved Apphia, and Archippus our fellow soldier, and to the church in thy house:

3. Grace to you, and peace, from God our Father and the Lord Jesus Christ.

4. I thank my God, making mention of thee always in my prayers,

5. Hearing of thy love and faith, which thou hast toward the Lord Jesus, and toward all saints;

6. That the communication of thy faith may become effectual by the acknowledging of every good thing which is in you in Christ Jesus.

7. For we have great joy and consolation in thy love, because the bowels of the saints are refreshed by thee, brother.

8. Wherefore, though I might be much bold in Christ to enjoin thee that which is convenient,

# COMMENTARY

## I. Introduction. Phm 1-3.

1. In contrast to the more usual term, "apostle," Paul's designation of himself as **prisoner for Jesus Christ** (RSV; cf. v. 13) has a direct bearing on the theme of the letter (see on Col 4:18). **2,3.** The addressee was not only this Christian family, but **the church** in their home. It was customary, and sometimes necessary, for the local churches to assemble in the home of one of the members (cf. Acts 18:7).

## II. Thanksgiving. Phm 4-7.

**4,5.** In Paul's prayers the **mention of** Philemon *(sou)* always brought to the apostle's lips a word of thanksgiving. Philemon was characterized by **love and faith**: these attitudes were directed primarily toward *(pros)* Christ but found their outworking in *(eis)* the church (cf. J. B. Lightfoot, *St. Paul's Epistles to the Colossians and to Philemon, in loco*). **6,7.** To be **effectual**, the **communication** or *sharing* (RSV) of **faith** must be in *knowledge (epignōsis;* see on Col 1:9; 2:1-3); i.e., a believer must have proper perception of the **good** that he has in **Christ**. The verse is difficult; compare Moule's discussion (C. F. D. Moule, *The Epistles to Colossians and Philemon*). Philemon's ministry was energized by his apprehension of Christian **love** and truth. Paul rejoices in this and desires that this motivation may influence Philemon's attitude toward his runaway slave. **Bowels** *(splagchna;* cf. vv. 12,20). The inmost feelings, "the very self" (Moule).

## III. Paul's Appeal for Onesimus. Phm 8-21.

**8,9.** Paul refrains from invoking apostolic authority to **enjoin** Philemon to do

9. Yet for love's sake I rather beseech *thee*, being such a one as Paul the aged, and now also a prisoner of Jesus Christ.

10. I beseech thee for my son Onesimus, whom I have begotten in my bonds:

11. Which in time past was to thee unprofitable, but now profitable to thee and to me:

12. Whom I have sent again: thou therefore receive him, that is, mine own bowels:

13. Whom I would have retained with me, that in thy stead he might have ministered unto me in the bonds of the gospel:

14. But without thy mind would I do nothing; that thy benefit should not be as it were of necessity, but willingly.

the **convenient**, i.e., the proper, thing. Rather, he appeals to his friend in **love**, as one who has grounds to be heard: he is Paul, "an ambassador" *(presbytēs)* and now a prisoner for Jesus Christ. Although *presbytēs* means strictly **aged** or old man, here the variant spelling and meaning is probably correct (cf. Eph 6:20). Whether the apostle is distinguishing between apostolic authority and the kind of authority exercisable by other Christian leaders is uncertain. In any case, he does illustrate the most effective way true Christian leadership can function.

**10,11.** As elsewhere (I Cor 4:15; cf. Gal 4:19) Paul refers to his convert as **begotten** by him. Although a slave in a Christian household, presumably Onesimus did not embrace the Christian faith until as an escapee he came under the influence of Paul. As a Christian, **Onesimus**, i.e., *Useful* (a not uncommon name for a slave in that time and region), who formerly was useless, now lived up to his name. John Knox speculates that Paul may have given the name "Onesimus" to the slave at his conversion (cf. Isa 62:2; Gen 17:5,15; 32:28; Acts 13:9). The custom of giving one a new name at conversion exists among Christians in non-Christian cultures today.

**12.** The verb translated **sent back** (ASV) can have the technical judicial meaning of "to refer a case," i.e., to allow Philemon himself to judge in the matter of Onesimus' freedom (cf. Lk 23:7,11; Acts 25:21). But the ordinary meaning is more probable here. Paul equates sending the slave with *sending my very heart* (RSV).

**13,14.** Onesimus had been of considerable help to Paul in his **bonds** or imprisonment for **the gospel.** The apostle desired to retain his services—services which Philemon would have gladly approved. But Paul, being sensitive to the ethics of the situation, refused to presume upon Philemon's love. He wanted his friend to make up his own **mind** and act **willingly**, without being manipulated or forced into a corner. When a man performs some 'Christian service' because friends have made it difficult for him to say *no*, his service is not genuinely Christian. Did Philemon free Onesimus and send him back to Paul? Did the former slave become a minister and, later, bishop of the church at Ephesus (cf. the letter of Ignatius to the Ephesians, 1)? Knox *(in loc.)* and Harrison (P. N. Harrison, "Onesimus and Philemon," AThR, XXX-

15. For perhaps he therefore departed for a season, that thou shouldest receive him for ever;

16. Not now as a servant, but above a servant, a brother beloved, specially to me, but how much more unto thee, both in the flesh, and in the Lord?

17. If thou count me therefore a partner, receive him as myself.

18. If he hath wronged thee, or oweth *thee* aught, put that on mine account;

19. I Paul have written *it* with mine own hand, I will repay *it:* albeit I do not say to thee how thou owest unto me even thine own self besides.

20. Yea, brother, let me have joy of thee in the Lord: refresh my bowels in the Lord.

21. Having confidence in thy obedience I wrote unto thee, knowing that thou wilt also do more than I say.

III (Oct., 1953) think so. While no certain answer can be given to these questions, the supposition raised by them is appealing.

**15,16. Season.** Literally, *for an hour.* An insignificant loss resulted in an immeasurable gain. **For ever.** *Permanently.* The term is reminiscent of the provision for voluntary slavery in Ex 21:6 (cf. SBK, IV, 746; Lev 25:46). But no longer is the relationship to be viewed in terms of master and servant. To be a Christian is to be a **brother** to other believers. And this is the determinative factor in all other human relationships, whether they be **in the flesh,** i.e., on the natural plane, or **in the Lord,** i.e., on the spiritual plane, in the sphere of the 'new age' (see Introduction to Colossians). Yet, relations on both planes must be carried on simultaneously. Philemon was both brother and master; Onesimus was both brother and slave. Such dual relationships gave rise to difficult problems within the early church. And such problems still complicate the economic and social relations of Christians today (I Tim 6:2; see on Col 3:11).

**17.** Having related the story and having gently restated some Christian principles, Paul now makes a direct appeal: "**Receive** Onesimus as you would **myself** [cf. Mt 25:40; Acts 9:4]; for your sake I would keep him **in thy stead** [Phm 13], but rather I send him to you in my stead." **Partner** *(koinōnon).* Not only a fellow Christian, but one with whom many experiences had been shared.

**18,19.** Paul does not mention Onesimus' actual offense, but it seems to have been more than mere escape. Paul's offer to **repay** suggests that a monetary loss was involved—through theft, embezzlement, or perhaps simply careless handling of funds. **Thine own self.** Apparently Philemon also was a convert of the apostle. This gentle reminder was designed to hush any demands for 'justice' and bring Philemon and Onesimus closer together; they had the same spiritual father.

**20,21.** By showing Christian love to Onesimus, Philemon would **refresh** and bring **joy** to Paul himself. On this note the apostle rests his appeal in **confidence** of a good response. **More than I say.** This may refer to (1) giving Onesimus his freedom or (2) returning him to Paul (cf. vv. 13,14).

**IV. Conclusion. Phm 22-25.**

**22.** Paul's **trust** that he will be re-

22. But withal prepare me also a lodging: for I trust that through your prayers I shall be given unto you.

23. There salute thee Epaphras, my fellow prisoner in Christ Jesus;

24. Marcus, Aristarchus, Demas, Lucas, my fellow laborers.

25. The grace of our Lord Jesus Christ *be* with your spirit. Amen.

Written from Rome to Philemon, by Onesimus a servant.

leased from this imprisonment echoes his sentiment in Phil 1:25,26 (see Introduction to Colossians). **Through your prayers.** It is noteworthy that the apostle who is most insistent about the sovereignty of God (cf. Gal 1:15,16; Rom 8:29) is equally convinced that God accomplishes His purposes through human instruments. The apostle does not request prayer; he takes for granted that his "partner" (Phm 17) remembers him in his prayers.

**23,24.** See on Col 4:10-14,15-17.

**25. Your** *(hymōn)* **spirit** (cf. Gal 6:18; II Tim 4:22). The plural reference is to the whole group included in the salutation (vv. 1,2). **Spirit** appears to be a term for the whole man—in his 'new age' status or outlook (cf. I Pet 4:6; II Cor 2:13; ⸢7:5; I Cor 2:11-16, Phillips).

# BIBLIOGRAPHY

HARRISON, P. N. "Onesimus and Philemon," *AThR*, XXXII (October, 1953), pp. 268-294.

KNOX, JOHN. *Philemon Among the Letters of Paul.* Chicago: University of Chicago Press, 1935.

LIGHTFOOT, J. B. *St. Paul's Epistles to the Colossians and to Philemon.* London: The Macmillan Company, 1886.

MOULE, C. F. D. *The Epistles to Colossians and Philemon.* Cambridge: The University Press, 1958.

MUELLER, J. J. *The Epistles of Paul to the Philippians and to Philemon.* Grand Rapids: Wm. B. Eerdmans Publishing Co., 1955.

RADFORD, L. B. *The Epistle to the Colossians and the Epistle to Philemon.* London: Methuen, 1931.

# THE EPISTLE
# TO THE HEBREWS

## INTRODUCTION

*Introductory Statement.* The student of this epistle must understand its uniqueness. It is like no other New Testament epistle, and it poses problems that are peculiar to itself. In form of construction, in style, in argument, and in relation to other books of the Bible, Hebrews stands apart.

Its history has been one of controversy. It has been ignored, challenged as to its authority, questioned as to canonicity, and studied relentlessly to determine its authorship. More recently, critical analysis has raised questions concerning certain portions of the epistle, notably chapter 13. Whether this chapter was added in whole or in part or whether it was a part of the original letter is a problem currently under study.

Increased interest in the Hellenistic period in relation to the history of civilization has also influenced the study of the Epistle to the Hebrews. Some of the mysteries of the epistle are now being set against the Hellenistic culture of the post-Alexandrian eastern Mediterranean world. Some scholars feel that the persons for whom the Epistle to the Hebrews was written were directly influenced by Hellenistic culture, and perhaps were thoroughly Hellenized. Such a view tends to suggest possible revisions of older views as to the recipients of the epistle and its purpose.

It has been said that the Epistle to the Hebrews is the least known of all New Testament epistles. The close reasoning, the sacrificial and priestly terminology, and the reigning idealism of the author are given as the reasons (Purdy and Cotton, *Epistle to the Hebrews,* Vol. XI, IB). This may be, but one thing seems more certain. The Epistle to the Hebrews is best comprehended when the five books of Moses are familiar ground. The inseparable tie of close reasoning from the Levitical system links the Pentateuch to the Hebrews letter.

The problems posed by the book are challenging. In sum, they concern its authorship, readers, destination, date, reason for having been written, and relationship to first century Christianity, Judaism, and the Hellenistic culture.

*Occasion of the Writing—Why Written.* The classical formulation for the occasion of the epistle is as follows. Jewish Christians, whether of a single congregation or in larger numbers and of broader geographical spread, were in danger of apostasy from Christ back to Moses. This condition of apostasy was an immediate danger (2:1), based upon unbelief (3:12). Conduct intimated such a possible going back (5:13,14). Neglect of public worship (10:25), weakness in prayer (12:12), a certain instability in doctrine (13:9), refusal to teach others as mature believers ought (5:12), and neglect of the Scriptures (2:1) were other symptoms of spiritual weakness. The danger was that those who were "holy brethren, partakers of the heavenly calling" (3:1) might "fall away" (6:6) or "depart from the living God" (3:12).

To forestall such a development, the author of Hebrews stressed the superiority of Christ in a series of contrasts to the angels, Moses, Aaron, Melchisedek, and the Levitical system. The object of such contrasts was to show the inferiority of Judaism and the superiority of Christ.

As the writer develops his thoughts, he weaves together three concepts. The first is exhortation (13:22); the second is a series of warnings, five in number (2:1-4; 3:7-19; 6:4-12; 10:26-31; 12:15-17); and the third is consolation or assurance, gathered around the thought introduced in the word "consider" (3:1), which reaches its culmination in the phrase, "consider him that endured . . ." (12:3). On the basis of these concepts, the writer argues against the tendency toward apostasy.

The line of reasoning developed by the reader—hearers was attractive. If following Christ brought persecution, and the older way of the Jewish practice did not, why not return to Judaism, retain a religion and at the same time be free from persecution? Attractive options, to be sure. The answer to all this is set forth in the Epistle to the Hebrews, as the superiority of Christ is argued point by point against the claims of Judaism.

More recently, this classical view of Hebrews has been questioned. Alexander C. Purdy, in his introductory comment to the *Epistle to the Hebrews* (IB, XI, 591,592), argues that this traditional view is only inferred. He gives nine reasons against the traditional view and then writes, "As it stands, then, Hebrews is an argument for the finality of Christianity resting on the valid foreshadowing in the Old Testament institution of sacrifice of the fundamental need for access to God, which has been brought out of the shadows for all men, Jew and Gentile alike, in the sacrifice of Christ." The marked Jewishness of Hebrews, according to Purdy, belongs to the form rather than to the actual content of its thought. He then goes on to argue that the author of Hebrews was fighting a Jewish-Christian form of Gnosticism and Hellenism rather than Judaism as such, but acknowledges that his view is still only hypothetical.

If we concede to Purdy that the author of Hebrews was writing against Jewish-Christian Gnosticism centered in a Hellenistic culture, it still seems necessary to face the fact that the main themes of the book have a Jewish character and argument. In fact, Hebrews binds together the Old Testament and the New Testament in the person and work of Jesus Christ. Hebrews might be said to be tne logical extension of John 17 in that it serves to correlate the high priestly prayer with the high priestly ministry of Christ. As the prayer of John 17 records our Lord's concern that believers should be active in the world, so it also records the petition, ". . . that thou shouldest keep them from the evil one" (Jn 17:15, ASV). The Hebrews epistle tells of such keeping, under the stresses and strains of persecution and of temptation to apostatize. To encourage such keeping, the author of Hebrews balanced the doctrinal and the hortatory, the pastoral and the practical, the word of consolation and the word of exhortation.

Judaism, a "cradle of convenience" for persecuted Christians of Jewish nationality, was thus opposed by contrast. The writer determined to help these early believers face the options with knowledge of the difference between Judaism and the work of Christ for and in the believer. All of this was designed to convince people under trial of the superiority of Jesus Christ.

At the same time, this letter of encouragement to first century believers contains help for today. No other New Testament epistle so clearly answers the "why" of the sacrifice of Christ, and of the redemption offered through this sacrifice. No other New Testament epistle so clearly links the twofold ministry of Christ as the eternal Son of God and the suffering Son of Man. Sin, guilt, atonement, and forgiveness are more fully comprehended through the Hebrews epistle. This writing also helps the readers gain a better understanding of Old Testament truths or incidents. Also, the difference between Judaism and Christianity becomes clear in the teaching of the Hebrews epistle.

Johannes Schneider has written: "Hebrews is very sober in the appraisal of the actual life of the churches. It knows the dangers which threaten God's people on this earth. Therefore it admonishes to hold fast to the faith and not be disloyal to Christ" (*The Letter to the Hebrews*, p. 8). With its emphasis upon the priestly ministry of Christ, and the privileges of the believer in relation to Christ, and its strong admonitions to develop a virile faith, Hebrews still speaks today.

*Date and Destination — To Whom Written.* A number of factors regulate the date for the Epistle to the Hebrews. The most important of these factors seems to be the Jewish-Roman conflict after A.D. 68 and the destruction of the Temple in A.D. 70. Nothing is mentioned concerning the conflict, the Temple, or the destruction of Jerusalem. Because of this silence, the letter is considered to have been written before 68 or after 80. The earlier dating is preferable, but must be looked at in relation to the mention of Timothy (13:23) and the mention of "they of Italy" (13:24). Also, the knowledge of Hebrews shown in the Epistle of Clement of Rome to the Corinthians (A.D. 95) has some bearing upon the date of Hebrews and perhaps upon its destination.

The argument for the late date of Hebrews is best stated in the IB, *Introduction*, XI, pp. 593,594. By a combination of reasoned arguments and the use of I Clement as a point of reference, the IB generalizes a date somewhere between the late seventies and the very early nineties, but then concludes that the actual date is uncertain.

In contrast, Canon Farrar, *Cambridge Greek Testament* (hereafter referred to as CGT), representing nineteenth century views, and Gleason L. Archer, in *The Epistle to the Hebrews, A Study Manual*, both argue for a date between A.D. 64 and A.D. 68. The latter writer then narrows this period of time to the actual date of 65 or 66 as the time most reasonable, according to internal and external evidence. All views of the date of the epistle stress the importance of the silence of the letter concerning events at Jerusalem in the sixth decade of the first century.

As for destination, three primary theories have prevailed, each of them pointing to a major city in the Roman and Mediterranean world. Some add a fourth view, which is really a modification of one of the main theories.

(1) Jewish Christians in and around Jerusalem were the recipients of the letter.

(2) It was sent to Jewish Christians who lived in Alexandria. This view tends to be held by those who support the argument for a strong Alexandrian flavor· for the Hebrew letter.

(3) It was intended for a congregation of Jewish Christians worshiping in the city of Rome, who were under severe trial and persecution. The "church at Rome" view also tends to hold to the "single congregation" theory, that the original recipients of the letter were a small congregation, or a "house church" in Rome.

(4) A modification of (3). The congregation addressed in Hebrews was small, but it might have been anywhere in the Roman Empire, and not necessarily at Rome.

Cogent arguments are offered for all views; all are beset with significant difficulties. The internal evidence of the letter itself contributes little in resolving the issues between the various theories. Jerusalem is mentioned by implication (13:12) in a manner that would be understood by all Hebrews. The reference to Italy (13:24) is general and therefore gives little actual aid in the question of destination.

One thing is clear. Those to whom this epistle was written were Hebrews by national identity and Christians by profession. As Downer has suggested, He-brews were in view, and the Hebrew point of view prevails (Arthur Cleveland Downer, *The Principles of Interpretation of the Epistle of the Hebrews,* p. 8). These Hebrew Christians had suffered losses, they had been much under trial and difficulty, they had suffered reproach, loss of privilege, persecution, ridicule, and open hatred from fellow Jews. But these conditions could have prevailed anywhere in the Roman world of the first century.

The fact is that all arguments and theories have ingredients of possibility and impossibility in almost equal measure. Discussion of the problem of destination may be examined at length in Farrar, CGT; A. B. Davidson, *The Epistle to the Hebrews;* Archer, *The Epistle to the Hebrews, A Study Manual;* William Manson, *The Epistle to the Hebrews, An Historical and Theological Reinterpretation;* and IB, XI. As for the present weight of opinion, the "Jerusalem" theory is defended best by William Leonard, *Authorship of the Epistle to the Hebrews: Critical Problem and Use of the Old Testament.* The "Rome" and "single congregation" theory is best defended by William Manson *(op. cit.),* who suggests that the files of correspondence of a Roman congregation first held this letter of exhortation and warning. But even this statement is conjecture.

*Authorship — By Whom Written.* Who wrote the Epistle to the Hebrews still remains the greatest single problem for the student of this book. The suggested authors are many, and opinions favoring one possible author over another are also many. The Apostle Paul, Apollos, Barnabas, Luke, Timothy, Aquila and Priscilla, Silas, Aristion, and Philip the Deacon have all been proposed for authorship, with supporting arguments. Examination of the tradition of the early church and of the church Fathers, both East and West, proves only that opinions vary.

The epistle itself does not name an author or even hint at one. Two main views have predominated in establishing its authorship. (1) The Pauline authorship. The argument supporting this view is also expanded to include a possible unknown writer who had been instructed and influenced by the Apostle Paul, and so gave Hebrews a distinctly Pauline cast. (2) The Alexandrian tradition and influence, based upon the use of the Old

Testament mainly in a typological manner. The reasoning here traces certain of the analogies of Hebrews to like analogies in the work of Philo of Alexandria. This is a view held by few at the present time. As noted in SHERK, II, 877, the influence of Philo upon the author of Hebrews is discounted by most scholars, while at the same time his influence upon the Alexandrian Fathers is generally acknowledged.

The Pauline authorship argument rests strongly upon the last chapter (13) of the epistle. The personal quality of this chapter is typical of the Apostle Paul, as is the epistolary style. The references to Timothy and to Italy (13:23,24) are seemingly direct links to the apostle. In addition, there is marked similarity between the language of this book and that of recognized Pauline letters (e.g., 1:4; 2:2; 7:18; 12:22); and the Christological argument is like that of Paul elsewhere. Much of this argument is inferential, and the same similarities could be noted of any Christian teacher of the early days of Christianity. In support of the Pauline authorship perhaps no work surpasses the definitive work of William Leonard in his *Authorship of the Epistle to the Hebrews: Critical Problem and Use of the Old Testament.*

Weighing against Pauline authorship are the following considerations: (1) failure of the book to name the Apostle Paul specifically, as is done in the recognized Pauline epistles; (2) the use of language that rises above the Pauline norm in construction, use, and style; and (3) logical development of the argument, which is not characteristically Pauline. The rhythm of Hebrews is rhetorical and Hellenic, and the style, in general, is much more calm and reasoned than the Apostle's style usually is.

As for doctrinal differences, these are evident in (1) the treatment of faith, (2) the eschatological view of chapter 12, (3) the applied use of the Mosaic code, and (4) the concept of the sanctuary. Leonard even points out that the habit of regarding the Old Testament Scriptures as an "arsenal of types" (*op. cit.,* p. 19), is not characteristic of the Pauline literature.

But what is known of the author? He was a man of considerable knowledge of the Scriptures, a Biblical theologian who thought in terms of redemptive history, and a person acquainted with the Greek Old Testament (LXX). Though a Jew, he was thoroughly familiar with Hellenistic culture as well as with Jewish tradition. He was an independent thinker who may have been influenced by the Apostle Paul and by the Alexandrian thinkers. He originated a unique literary form, quite different from that of other New Testament writings.

He was completely devoted to his subject of explaining the relationship of Judaism to Christianity, arguing constantly for the absolute superiority of the latter. Perhaps he was a preacher-teacher, familiar with the speaker-hearer relationship and thus committed to the exhortation-explanation-warning style which he used so effectively. In his use of this method, he exhibits more than passing acquaintance with the thinking of the Apostle Paul.

Notwithstanding all this, the actual identity of the author remains unknown. In conclusion, perhaps Origen (third century), as quoted by Eusebius (fourth century) can hardly be improved on in regard to his statement of the problem:

The style of the Epistle with the title, "To The Hebrews," has not that vulgarity of diction which belongs to the apostle, who confesses that he is but common in speech, that is, in his phraseology. But that this epistle is more pure Greek in the composition of phrases, every one will confess who is able to discern the difference of style. Again, it will be obvious that the ideas of the epistle are admirable, and not inferior to any of the books acknowledged to be apostolic. Every one will confess to this, who attentively reads the apostle's writings.

Then Eusebius adds, or includes:
But I would say, that the thoughts are the apostle's, but the diction and phraseology belong to some one who has recorded what the apostle said, and as one who noted down at his leisure what the master dictated. If then, any church considers this epistle as coming from Paul, let it be commended for this, for neither did those ancient men deliver it without cause. But who it was that really wrote the epistle, God only knows (Eusebius, *Ecclesiastical History*).

*Tradition and the Early Church — Acceptance of What Was Written.* The first mention of the Epistle to the Hebrews outside of the New Testament appears in the *Epistle to the Corinthians* written by Clement of Rome. Hebrews was known to both the Eastern and Western churches, but seems to have been less well known in the West until after the fourth century. The Alexandrian Fathers were actively interested in the problems of Hebrews, and both Clement of Alexandria and Origen commented upon the epistle and discussed it at length. The title "To The Hebrews" appeared by the end of the second century, and has been commonly used since.

From the outset, Hebrews has been accepted as being in the canon. No ancient authority, except Tertullian, failed to include this epistle in the New Testament canon.

At the end of the fourth century the West became more actively interested in the epistle, with Jerome in his *Epistle 129* plainly stating that he unquestionably accepted Hebrews in the New Testament canon. This view was consistently held by medievalists, and humanist scholarship adopted it. Erasmus, the humanist scholar, and Luther, the Reformationist, both accepted Hebrews as being in the New Testament, though they disagreed as to the author's identity. Post-Reformation scholarship has not challenged the canonicity of Hebrews successfully, but has been more occupied with the question of authorship.

*The Argument of the Epistle — Theme of the Writer.* The thesis of the writer of Hebrews seems to be captured in two main ideas, which are explained and illustrated in the logic of the argument. The first idea is expressed in the word "consider," used in 3:1 and 12:3. In each instance the admonition is to consider Christ. In 3:1, he is to be considered as the "Apostle and High Priest of our confession," and in 12:3 he is to be considered as the one who endured, as the ultimate example of the faith life. By the term "consider," the writer means reflect, study, examine attentively, think on with care. Note that the believers are reminded to consider Christ himself, and not merely the logical reasons why he should be considered, as set forth in the Hebrew letter.

Through the reasoning of the epistle, the readers are led to "consider him" in his priesthood and sacrifice. The contrasts drawn throughout the letter establish conclusively the superiority of Christ over angels, Moses, Aaron, Melchisedek, the Levitical system, and finally even over the greatest examples of the faith life that the Old Testament records (cf.

Heb 11). As the priest of God and as the sacrifice acceptable to him, Christ now speaks from within the sanctuary, guaranteeing to every believer an entrance into the very presence of God, and an immediate hearing for petitions and requests (4:14-16).

The second idea is found in the word **exhortation** *(paraklēsis)*, with its companion verb, "I exhort" (13:22). This has been called the informal title of the Hebrews letter. Farrar (CBSC) suggests that all of the information in the epistle is to serve the purpose of exhorting the readers. The persecution, trials, and difficulties would be made easier if these Christians, who were also Jews, would "consider him" (12:3), and "bear with the word of exhortation" (13:22, ASV). The supporting argument to this twofold or two-part theme is then built up by the Christianity-superior-over-Judaism argument to which the exhortation is directed.

The whole purpose of this letter was to inform the discouraged Christians and also to encourage them, and to support both approaches by innumerable examples both of Christ and of those who had successfully lived by faith. Central to the whole, the writer placed the eternity (therefore unchangeableness) of the priesthood of Christ, "after the order of Melchisedek" (ch. 7).

*The Author's Ideas and Concepts: Sources and Use.* Distinctive form and style (see next section of this Introduction) set Hebrews apart from other New Testament epistles. The author employs method, organization, and technique unlike those of any other New Testament writer. He also expresses ideas and combinations of thoughts and events peculiar to himself. Since the main thrust of the epistle is practical, to achieve practicality, he brings all of his theological concepts into this special frame of reference of exhortation, warning, and comfort. His concentration is upon those theological ideas and concepts he regards as significant. His reasoning in behalf of the readers is that this is what this community of believers needs above all else to make them strong in faith.

He approaches these ideas as a speaker would approach them, building one truth upon another in support of the main arguments. Interspersed are the warnings, which seem particularly designed to impress the hearers (readers) with the consequences of failing to comprehend the truth concerning Christ.

Considerable literary skill is demonstrated by the author. Evidently his background gave him a sense of proportion in literary composition. His Greek is perhaps the best in the New Testament, comparable to that of Luke. Cultural depth and familiarity are also evident. The writer seems to realize and reflect the influence of the Greek way of life (Hellenization) upon Judaism and upon the Mediterranean world.

In actual expressed ideas, the writer bases his theological discussion on the Scriptures and develops it by setting the shadowy realm of earth against the realm of reality, or heaven. The Old Testament or Scriptural source he used was the Greek version or LXX. In some instances the word used in the LXX does not even appear in the Hebrew text as we have it. In proving that the heavenly realm is the realm of reality, the author makes all possible passages apply to Christ. The entire Old Testament, as the writer of the Hebrews uses it, is a continuous exposition revealing the person and work of the Lord Jesus Christ. Access to the heavenly realm and understanding of the heavenly realm are also in Christ.

The author of Hebrews is the only New Testament writer who discusses certain of the subjects he takes up. No other writer, for instance, discusses the significance of Melchisedek (7:1-14). A new estimate of the patriarchs is also supplied in chapter 11. Some aspects of Moses' life are stressed in Hebrews which are not mentioned elsewhere. The subject of repentance is approached differently (12:17), as is the subject of deliberate sin (10:26). Many of the individual concepts of the author have posed problems of interpretation to later generations.

The most highly developed of all the ideas in Hebrews is that of the priesthood of Christ. Unique to the epistle, it is the most important concept to be grasped. In presenting this concept, three "sources" are apparent: (1) The Old Testament institution of the priesthood and sacrifice, or Levitical system; (2) Judaism; and (3) primitive or apostolic Christianity. Whatever other influences there may have been, these three are paramount.

As priest, Christ was divinely called, and is one with humanity (2:14-18; 4:15,16; 5:1-3). He met the needs of the people (2:17,18). He opened the

way into the presence of God (10:19,20), and made available the "sanctuary" (AV, heavens) and the "throne of grace" (4:14-16). He became the perfect and final sacrifice (10:18). Because of the priestly ministry of Christ, the believer has strength of faith and the privilege of worship. Perhaps no book in the New Testament better sets forth fellowship with God through worship than does Hebrews.

The Christology of Hebrews is rich, but it is mainly set forth in the ministry and function of Christ as priest. Christ is first presented as the revealer of God (1:1) and the agent of creation (1:1-4). The significance of the word charaktēr (AV, **express image**) in 1:3 should not be missed. After this preliminary statement or prologue, the Christology flows quickly into the main argument of the priestly ministry of Christ.

The ethical teaching of Hebrews is of the highest standard and fully Christian, though general in the main body of the argument. Only in chapter 13 does the ethical teaching become specific and pointed. Brotherly love (13:1), kindness to strangers (13:2), kindness to the less fortunate (13:3), honorable marriage relationships (13:4), a right attitude toward material wealth (13:5), honor to overseers (13:7,17), doing good (13:16), are there positively enjoined. In these the Christian does not have a choice. Much of the earlier ethical injunction in the epistle is found in the priestly analogy, and therefore is not as readily apparent as in the Synoptics or in some of the Pauline literature.

As for its practical value, Hebrews rests solidly upon the unquestioned premise that Christ meets the needs of all men at all times (including those of modern man). Men come to God through Christ in every age. In this concept is expressed the unity of history as lineal and redemptive, with God through Christ working out man's destiny according to His plan and will. Hebrews does not set up a philosophy of history different from that of the other books of the New Testament.

*Form and Style: The Author's Organization and Methods.* Only the section from 13:17 to 13:25 qualifies Hebrews as an epistle. But the literary genre of the book constitutes a problem. It begins like a treatise, continues like a sermon, and ends like a letter. The present beginning is the only beginning the book has ever had. In it there are no greetings, salutations, or personal references whatever. Within the literary form, certain habits are constant. In using the Old Testament, the writer may employ a reference either literally, historically, or typologically. His consistency lies only in that his use of the Old Testament text supports his main argument at the point where it is introduced.

It has been suggested that the exhortations and warnings in Hebrews class the book as polemic in nature, with the epistolary ending added as a way of concluding the polemic. If this is true, then the author is amazingly apt at avoiding reference to himself in the polemic. Autobiographical references are non-existent, and the metaphors employed strengthen the polemic without revealing a single clue as to the polemicist.

The opinion has been expressed that the basic literary form of Hebrews follows the Alexandrian patterns set by Philo (see J. Herkless [ed.], *Hebrews and the Epistles General of Peter, James and John;* also IB). The way the author contrasts the heavenly and the earthly realms, the "shadowy" and the real or the realm of the heavenly and the true is thought by some to be a technique "borrowed" from Philo of Alexandria. The IB calls this a "two-story" view of reality, which controls the whole thought of Hebrews (XI, 583).

Other opinions expressed are (1) that the influence of Philo is negligible, or (2) that the theory that he influenced the writer is a false premise entirely. Manson tends to minimize Philo's influence (William Manson, *The Epistle to the Hebrews, An Historical and Theological Reinterpretation*). A. B. Davidson, referring to the author of Hebrews *(op. cit.)*, speaks of traces of the influence of "the Alexandrian culture . . . upon his language," but presents no argument favoring this Philonic technique. In one sense, then, the origin of the form of Hebrews remains an open question. (3) Spicq, however *(L' épître aux Hébreux)*, notes considerable evidence which he regards as indicative of Philonic background.

What is clear, however, is that the writer systematically establishes a basic set of ideas, upon which he brings to bear Old Testament passages and arguments. To win acceptance of these basic ideas is not his objective, but rather to lead the believers to understand them fully and then act upon them. William

Leonard *(op. cit.,* p. 221) identifies seven such ideas: (1) the Sonship of Christ; (2) the priesthood of Christ, the basis for cleansing from sin; (3) the priest at God's right hand, the basis of Christian hope; (4) the promise made to Abraham; (5) the permanence of the promised "Sabbath-rest"; (6) the consequences of apostasy; and (7) the exhortations to virtuous living in light of the future. The IB *(loc. cit.)* lists thirteen such basic ideas, which cover the above seven, but include such additions as the promise of Christ's return, the defeat of Satan, the victory over death, and the promised deliverance of believers from bondage. These ideas are the constants; and, both in form and in the style of presentation, everything is made to refer to one or more of them.

Central to these basic ideas is the one concept of Christ as the perfect priest of God establishing the new covenant both by his priestly work and by his sacrificial death. There is no question about the high Christology of the Epistle to the Hebrews. But despite so much information from the Old Testament to support the Christology and other ideas central to the epistle, the enigma of the epistolary ending from 13:17 on still remains. Four possible solutions of the enigma are suggested: (1) That the author wrote to a specific group and from the beginning had such an ending in mind; (2) That the original letter was sent to a second audience, and that the new ending was added to accommodate this group; (3) That a person other than the author added the present ending when forwarding it to another group; (4) That the ending was added by another person to bolster the concept of the Pauline origin of the entire letter. Of these theories, the first and the fourth are the most reasonable or plausible.

Certain habits of style are also evident. The writer makes it a practice to introduce Old Testament quotations by "God says" (see 4:3; 5:5,6; 8:10), and by "the Holy Spirit says" (3:7). He also introduces parts of his argument some time before he proceeds to develop it fully. And so every larger argument in the epistle has its preliminary statement. At all points he makes reference to the ritual law rather than to the moral law or to the social or visual force of the Law, as on the feast days. Characteristically he employs the name "Jesus" rather than the full title used by the

Apostle Paul. Further, in presenting "Jesus" as the "new and living way," the writer does not stray from the thought nor does he leave the argument incomplete. He seems to be the complete master of himself and of his techniques.

# OUTLINE

I. Prologue. 1:1-4.
  A. Christ superior to the prophets. 1:1,2.
  B. Christ, the "imprint" of God. 1:3,4.
II. The main arguments introduced and explained. 1:5–10:18.
  A. Christ "greater than"; the argument for superiority. 1:5–7:28.
    1. Superior to angels. 1:5-14.
    2. The greater salvation, and a warning against neglect. 2:1-4.
    3. Christ as the perfect man. 2:5-18.
    4. Christ superior to Moses. 3:1-6.
    5. The superiority of the rest of Christ over the rest of Israel under Moses and Joshua. 3:7 – 4:13.
    6. Christ as high priest in the order of Melchisedek, superior to Aaron. 4:14 – 5:10.
    7. A rebuke for lack of understanding and for immaturity. 5:11 – 6:20.
    8. The priesthood of Melchisedek. 7:1-28.
  B. Christ, the minister and high priest of the new covenant. 8:1 – 10:18.
    1. The new covenant in relation to the old. 8:1-9.
    2. The better covenant explained. 8:10-13.
    3. The new sanctuary and the perfect sacrifice. 9:1-28.
    4. The new covenant complete, perfect, and at work. 10:1-18.
III. The elements of the faith life. 10:19–13:17.
  A. The description of the faith life. 10:19-25.
  B. A description of those who spurn this "new and living way." 10:26-39.
  C. Examples of the life of faith. 11:1-40.
  D. Christ, the supreme example of the faith life. 12:1-4.
  E. The Father's love known through chastisement. 12:5-11.
  F. Christian conduct under the new covenant. 12:12-29.
  G. The Christian life in daily practice. 13:1-17.
IV. Personal epilogue. 13:18-25.

# HEBREWS

### CHAPTER 1

GOD, who at sundry times and in divers manners spake in time past unto the fathers by the prophets,

2. Hath in these last days spoken unto us by *his* Son, whom he hath appointed heir of all things, by whom also he made the worlds;

# COMMENTARY

**I. Prologue. 1:1-4.**

The writer breaks the form of letter writing customarily identified with the letters of the NT by giving no salutation or opening sentences of greeting and introduction (see Introd.) He moves immediately to his subject, which is the person and work of the Lord Jesus Christ in relation to the Levitical system and the old covenant.

A. Christ Superior to the Prophets. 1:1,2. The implied question dealt with here is: Who was the last and most authoritative spokesman for God?

1. **In many parts** (*polymerōs*), or part by part, fragmentarily, and **in many manners** (*polytropōs*), or many and varied ways, God (Jehovah) spoke in the OT days through **the prophets,** many of whom tell in their writings by what methods he communicated with them. *Prophētais* is an all-inclusive word for all whom God used in OT times. 2. **At the end of these days** is the literal rendering of a common Hebrew expression found in Num 24:14, having Messianic overtones. God has spoken **unto us** through one who stands in the relation of a son, having complete authority as a spokesman. In this relationship, Christ is unique and is here so described in the classic sense, as under divine appointment because a **Son.** He is both **heir** and *agent* of creation. **Worlds.** Greek *aiōnes*, "ages," including the world of space (cf. 11:3).

B. Christ, the "Imprint" of God. 1:3,4.

3. **Light from light,** or *effulgence* (ASV). The shining forth to the world of the very character of God in Jesus

3. Who being the brightness of *his* glory, and the express image of his person, and upholding all things by the word of his power, when he had by himself purged our sins, sat down on the right hand of the Majesty on high;

4. Being made so much better than the angels, as he hath by inheritance obtained a more excellent name than they.

Christ. He is the essential being of God. In the same way **express image** is used, as in Mt 22:20, where it refers to the image on the Roman coin. Christ is *the stamp* or impress of God *(charaktēr);* the essence of God. The whole force of the first two clauses of this verse stresses this one concept.

He is also *creator,* both as the "creative Word" (CGT, p. 31) and as Sustainer — the one **bearing them up** (AV, *upholding all things).* Creation and preservation are by God in Jesus Christ, and the **word of his power.** The word of the Son *is* the power to preserve and sustain, but this creative power resolves itself into the greater ministry of redemption. In making purification, or purging of **our sins,** Christ purged the great mass of the world's accumulated sins and uncleanness, which God sees. In Christ the penalty for sin is fully discharged and cleansing is provided. The idea is found in the words of Cowper's hymn:

There is a fountain filled with blood
  Drawn from Immanuel's veins;
And sinners plunged beneath that flood,
  Lose all their guilty stains.

Having this power and authority as creator and sin-bearer, Christ occupies the place of authority at the right hand of God. As both high priest and sin-bearer, he can present a finished redemption. His work is completed, and he can, therefore, sit down. As the Son of man he occupies this place by the act of God the Father. This is not a place of repose, but of activity for the divine mediator, high priest, and intercessor. In fulfillment of Ps 110:1, he is Lord of all.

4. The first of the contrasts showing the superiority of Christ is then introduced. The idea of contrast in the thought of **superior** *(kreitōn,* "superior," "becoming superior") is used thirteen times. Angels were important in delivering God's message to men. From the giving of the Law on Sinai to the assistance of angels accorded Daniel and the later prophets, these messengers of God served God, but as subordinates. Christ is superior to the angels in his person, name, function, power, and dignity. As for his name, he alone can save the lost (Acts 4:12), and his is the name above every name (Phil 2:10). By his name his reputation is established, for his is a mighty name.

**II. The Main Arguments Introduced and Explained. 1:5—10:18.**

5. For unto which of the angels said he at any time, Thou art my Son, this day have I begotten thee? And again, I will be to him a Father, and he shall be to me a Son?

6. And again, when he bringeth in the first-begotten into the world, he saith, And let all the angels of God worship him.

7. And of the angels he saith, Who maketh his angels spirits, and his ministers a flame of fire.

8. But unto the Son *he saith*, Thy throne, O God, *is* for ever and ever: a sceptre of righteousness *is* the sceptre of thy kingdom.

9. Thou hast loved righteousness, and hated iniquity; therefore God, *even* thy God, hath anointed thee with the oil of gladness above thy fellows.

10. And, Thou, Lord, in the beginning hast laid the foundation of the earth; and the heavens are the works of thine hands.

11. They shall perish, but thou remainest: and they all shall wax old as doth a garment;

A. Christ "Greater Than"; The Argument for Superiority. 1:5—7:28.

The thought introduced in 1:4 is now expanded by a series of seven quotations from the OT. Of these, five show the superiority of Christ.

1) Superior to Angels. 1:5-14.

5. The thought presented is an argument from silence, and the he is God. Never did God say to any angel that he was a Son; only to and of Christ did he say that (see Ps 2:7; II Sam 7:14). In both passages the immediate meaning is given an exalted or higher meaning, which imparts to these passages (and others to follow) a typological sense. In Ps 2:7 an anniversary celebration (Heb 1:5 a ff.) is made to speak of Christ. And the words spoken of Solomon in II Sam 7:14 are applied to Jesus the Son as being even more true of him. In this use the typology is correct; for Christ is the antitype, a fact that is true throughout Hebrews in the typological interpretation of the writer.

6. Both Deut 32:43 (LXX) and Ps 97:7 speak of angels worshiping Christ the Son. And the psalmist also speaks of a display of glory (97:6), which corresponds to the brightness of Heb 1:3.
7. Two concepts are presented: (1) that angels are inferior or created beings —Who maketh; and (2) that angels are servants, as winds and fire are servants. The idea is thus re-emphasized that angels worship the Son because they are subordinate to him. Psalm 104:4 is thus presented as evidence of angelic subordination.

8,9. Christ is addressed as God and as king, or sovereign. As promised in the Davidic covenant, here is David's greater Son ruling as king, and his rule is eternal. The qualities of his kingship are justice, righteousness, and hatred of wickedness — qualities which can only characterize a just reign. In this position Christ is above or superior to all, and particularly to angels. To this exalted and honored position Christ has been anointed rather than appointed, and this anointing is that of *Christus Victor* — the victorious one ruling eternally.

10-12. From Ps 102:25-27. Spoken of Christ the Son, who as the Creator has made the world and who is the unchangeable one in the midst of things that will change. This also portrays a sharp contrast between Christ and an-

12. And as a vesture shalt thou fold them up, and they shall be changed: but thou art the same, and thy years shall not fail.

13. But to which of the angels said he at any time, Sit on my right hand, until I make thine enemies thy footstool?

14. Are they not all ministering spirits, sent forth to minister for them who shall be heirs of salvation?

## CHAPTER 2

THEREFORE we ought to give the more earnest heed to the things which we have heard, lest at any time we should let *them* slip.

gels. They are created material, and serve in the world as messengers of God. Christ is eternal, above the world, as being before it and after it. This argument is drawn from a LXX translation of a psalm not considered Messianic by rabbinic interpreters. So used by the writer, it further illustrates the superiority of Christ. **Thy years shall not fail.** They shall never cease or be discontinued.

13. In contrast to the angels, who were never told to sit at God's right hand, Christ now sits there as ruler and king, the God-man, the unchangeable and eternal Messiah. So he will sit until his ultimate triumph, when his enemies shall be made the **footstool of his feet.** This concept goes back to Joshua, who set his foot on the necks of vanquished kings as the ultimate sign of victory. So the passage gives hope to all believers in all ages that Christ will triumph over unrighteousness.

14. Angels serve, as shown by the inclusive **all**; but theirs is a sacred service or a "liturgic" service *(leitourgika)*, and a service to men *(diakonian)*. Angels are thus **ministering spirits,** who serve those who are **heirs of salvation,** or godly persons. This ministry of angels is implied as still continuing. The word salvation *(soterian)* is reserved by the author for development in another place.

2) The Greater Salvation and a Warning Against Neglect. 2:1-4.

The premise has already been stated in the reference to salvation (1:14). This salvation is by Christ, the exalted and anointed Son. It is therefore infinitely more important to heed God's revelation, **the things which we have heard** *(akousthesin)* or the Gospel. This is a solemn warning, greater than that of Deut 4:9.

1. **Therefore** relates to the Son as well as to the salvation which he gives. **The things that we have heard.** The Gospel, which provides a fixed point to which believers are referred. Here only is the place of safety. Nothing should be permitted to cause us to **drift past** *(pararyō-men)* this one fixed point of safety. No calamity, influence, force, or circumstance should be tolerated that weakens us with reference to the hope of salvation. A vessel launched unpiloted into midstream is made to **drift past** its landing point on the opposite shore by the currents at work in the stream. So the

2. For if the word spoken by angels was steadfast, and every transgression and disobedience received a just recompense of reward;

3. How shall we escape, if we neglect so great salvation; which at the first began to be spoken by the Lord, and was confirmed unto us by them that heard *him;*

4. God also bearing *them* witness, both with signs and wonders, and with divers miracles, and gifts of the Holy Ghost, according to his own will?

5. For unto the angels hath he not put in subjection the world to come, whereof we speak.

currents of life work against us unless we take heed. This is a warning directed specifically to those for whom the epistle was intended, signifying that the warning was necessary.

**2. For if . . .** Argument in the rabbinic style, from the lesser to the greater; from the giving of the Law by angels to the greater giving of the Gospel by Christ. The Law was vindicated by severe judgments (Lev 10:1-7; Num 16; Josh 7). It carried its penalties with it, and they were faithfully enacted. **3.** If the message of the Law was so jealously guarded, how much more strictly must the message of the Gospel be guarded. It was spoken by the Lord Jesus Christ, and it was established by those who heard him, who served as first-hand witnesses. And thus this Gospel message was both **steadfast** and **confirmed.** This being the case, how is there a way to **make good our escape** if we neglect this salvation? Escape is impossible because the message is of transcendent excellence and eternal importance. A greater message implies a greater judgment.

**4.** God himself joins in the witness by **signs** *(sēmeia),* **miracles** *(terata)* and **powers** *(dynameis).* These are the confirming evidences by no means to be slighted in weighing the authenticity of the Gospel. These evidences were further extended by the giving of **gifts** to believers by the Holy Spirit. Such signs, wonders, powers, and gifts are faithfully recorded in the four Gospels and in the record in the Acts. The gifts are mentioned in Rom 12; 13; I Cor 7:7; I Cor 12. Not the least of the reinforcing witnesses was the oneness of believers of every racial and national background. The implication is transparent. God was in Christ and in the Gospel, and therefore this message of salvation was to be heeded. To fail to pay attention held the threat of judgment. It is so today.

3) Christ as the Perfect Man. 2:5-18. Having issued the warning, the writer resumes the theological argument. The subject is the humanity and humiliation of Christ, centered in the phrase, "Thou madest him a little lower than the angels" (v. 7).

**5. The world to come** *(oikoumenēn tēn mellousan).* The future world, the inhabited earth of the future; the world future to the generation receiving this epistle and also future to us. This world will not be subject to angels, but it will be subject to Christ in its totality, and

6. But one in a certain place testified, saying, What is man, that thou art mindful of him? or the son of man, that thou visitest him?

7. Thou madest him a little lower than the angels; thou crownedst him with glory and honor, and didst set him over the works of thy hands:

8. Thou hast put all things in subjection under his feet. For in that he put all in subjection under him, he left nothing *that is* not put under him. But now we see not yet all things put under him.

9. But we see Jesus, who was made a little lower than the angels for the suffering of death, crowned with glory and honor; that he by the grace of God should taste death for every man.

10. For it became him, for whom *are* all things, and by whom *are* all things, in bringing many sons unto glory, to make the captain of their salvation perfect through sufferings.

11. For both he that sanctifieth and they who are sanctified *are* all of one: for which cause he is not ashamed to call them brethren,

12. Saying, I will declare thy name unto my brethren, in the midst of the church will I sing praise unto thee.

13. And again, I will put my trust in him. And again, Behold I and the children which God hath given me.

14. Forasmuch then as the children are partakers of flesh and blood, he also himself likewise took part of the same; that through death he might destroy him that had the power of death, that is, the devil;

15. And deliver them, who through fear of death were all their lifetime subject to bondage.

also to the redeemed. An entirely new condition will prevail, as Christ, with the saints, will rule in a harmony heretofore unknown.

**6-9.** A quotation from Ps 8:5-7 introduced by the indefinite one ... somewhere (ASV). This quotation is the proof of the statement concerning "the world that is to be." The quotation establishes the humanity of the Son, who was made a little lower than the angels in order to taste death for every man. Now he is being exalted and crowned with glory and with honor' because in his humanity he bore the humiliation of death (Phil 2:5-8). Because he suffered he is now exalted. Because he temporarily subjected himself to the limitations of humanity, he is now crowned with glory.

**10.** This meant suffering, and he did suffer. By this suffering his human experience was made complete. He *tasted* of the whole of human life, from birth to death. Thus was Christ perfected through suffering, and therefore he can identify himself with the needs of every man. Because he suffered he is now fully qualified to serve as captain (*archēgos*, "leader," 12:2) of man's salvation.

**11.** As the Son of God sent from the Father *into* humanity, Christ does not hesitate to identify himself with his own. We are his brethren. Jesus Christ, who sanctifies, and believers, who are sanctified, are one. **12,13.** A further illustration of the unity of the Saviour and the saved. This is set forth in pertinent OT passages from Ps 22:22; Isa 8:17,18. These "prove," as it were, that the Lord Jesus Christ and Christians are brothers. And he is not ashamed to call them brethren (v. 11). Both of the quoted passages from Isaiah are typologically applied.

**14,15.** The defeat of Satan and of death testifies that the atoning work of Christ is effectual. But not only is there defeat; there is also deliverance. Though fear can enslave, and the fear of dying has long plagued humanity, Christ has settled the problem by his own death and resurrection. As a man he died. He partook of flesh and blood and thus he died, but by his death came deliverance. Therefore, the power of Satan has been rendered inoperative (*katargeō*), and Christ has made an atonement for sin fully satisfying to God (Isa 53:11). What great victory is His! And what great victory all believers have in him! Satan and death are defeated and the fear of death is gone! That man who is

16. For verily he took not on *him the nature of* angels; but he took on *him* the seed of Abraham.

17. Wherefore in all things it behooved him to be made like unto *his* brethren, that he might be a merciful and faithful high priest in things *pertaining* to God, to make reconciliation for the sins of the people.

18. For in that he himself hath suffered being tempted, he is able to succor them that are tempted.

## CHAPTER 3

WHEREFORE, holy brethren, partakers of the heavenly calling, consider the Apostle and High Priest of our profession, Christ Jesus;

2. Who was faithful to him that appointed him, as also Moses *was faithful* in all his house.

3. For this *man* was counted worthy of more glory than Moses, inasmuch as he who hath builded the house hath more honor than the house.

4. For every house is builded by some *man;* but he that built all things *is* God.

5. And Moses verily *was* faithful in all his house as a servant, for a testimony of those things which were to be spoken after;

free in Christ is indeed the most free of men.

**16-18.** Here is the first mention of the subject that occupies the central place in the argument of the epistle — the ministry of Christ as high priest. In this office Jesus' humanity is again in view, but here only a hint is given as to the full significance of Christ as high priest.

Meanwhile he ministers and succors men by taking them **by the hand** (better than taking on the "nature of," AV). This he can do as their elder Brother and the captain of their salvation. Two words indicate the helping quality in the high-priestly function. These are **compassionate** *(eleēmōn)* and **faithful** *(pistos).* To men Christ is compassionate and to God he is faithful. Indeed, mercy and truth have met together in him. His faithfulness is shown in his being steadfast under the temptation which was a part of his suffering. Now he is able to come to the aid of all who are tempted because he has passed through the same tests and emerged victorious, and as Man he knows our need. **Propitiation** for our sins. See I Jn 2:2; 4:10; Rom 3:25; and CGT, p. 55.

4) Christ Superior to Moses. 3:1-6.

A comparison of two demonstrations of faithfulness is now introduced, and for the first time the readers are directly addressed in the phrase **holy brethren.** The parallels in structure between chapters 1 and 2 and chapters 3 and 4 are evident (CGT, p. 56).

**1,2.** The key to the understanding of Hebrews may rest in the thought of **consider** him. From *katanoēsate,* "observe attentively, fix your thoughts, mark with attention." This same thought appears again in 12:3. In 3:1,2 the emphasis is upon Christ as being faithful; in 12:3 it is upon his having endured. Here the **brethren** are encouraged to look to Jesus as **Apostle** ("messenger"; only here is this title used of Christ in the NT) and **High Priest,** an office that is more and more fully explained to the readers. **Confession** *(homologias)* rather than *profession* (AV). The term relates to believers confessing to Christ as their high priest.

**3-5.** The common metaphor is that of a **house.** The difference? Christ built the **house;** Moses served in the **house.** As in Jn 1:17, the juxtaposition of Moses and Christ is clearly stated. In the same fashion the juxtaposition of the old covenant and the new covenant is intimated. The emphasis is upon faithfulness, however.

6. But Christ as a son over his own house; whose house are we, if we hold fast the confidence and the rejoicing of the hope firm unto the end.

7. Wherefore as the Holy Ghost saith, To-day if ye will hear his voice,

8. Harden not your hearts, as in the provocation, in the day of temptation in the wilderness:

9. When your fathers tempted me, proved me, and saw my works forty years.

10. Wherefore I was grieved with that generation, and said, They do always err in *their* heart; and they have not known my ways.

11. So I sware in my wrath, They shall not enter into my rest.

12. Take heed, brethren, lest there be in any of you an evil heart of unbelief, in departing from the living God.

13. But exhort one another daily, while it is called To-day; lest any of you be hardened through the deceitfulness of sin.

Incomparable in position, Christ is faithful as a son, over his house (ASV, v. 6).

6. Whose house are we refers to believers, the company of the redeemed of God, whose faith is a continuing faith. Their faith is manifested in a joyful confidence *(parrēsian,* "free speech, outspokenness"; and thus outspoken or cheerful confidence) which becomes a glorying of our hope in the Son. Christ is the object as well as the basis of their confidence and their hope. Unto the end *(mechri telous).* Until hope becomes reality.

5) The Superiority of the Rest of Christ over the Rest of Israel under Moses and Joshua. 3:7—4:13.

The principle of rest is faith. This was true for the Israelites as they came to Canaan, and it is true for believers today. The *rest of faith* has both a present meaning and a future meaning. Psalm 95:7-11 is used to show how both threat and promise were related to Israel's rest in Canaan. Entrance into the promised land was conditioned on obedience.

7-11. The wilderness generation suffered the consequences of the threat made by God. That they perished in the wilderness was not an accident (see Num 14 and 21). As this psalm indicates, the children of Israel challenged God's sovereign authority by their rebellion in the wilderness (Num 20). The lesson is obvious. True obedience of heart goes beyond merely receiving instructions. One generation of Israelites perished because they rebelled in willful disobedience, and this in spite of a full revelation at Mount Sinai.

12. Here the truth of Ps 95:7-11 is given a present (to the original readers) and pertinent application. Willful neglect and disobedience, an evil heart of unbelief, can cause one to fall short or apostatize from God. This warning is made both individual and personal to encourage self-examination. A contrast between the faithfulness of Christ and the faithlessness of apostates is suggested. The apostasy is from the living God *(theou zōntos),* who carries out his judgments; therefore the warning is even more pointed. 13-19. The way to avoid both apostasy and consequent judgment is through daily exhortation. Believers are to warn and admonish one another to hope and confidence in Christ. The later warning against failure to assemble together touches upon the same subject (10:25). Such assembling includes the

14. For we are made partakers of Christ, if we hold the beginning of our confidence steadfast unto the end;

15. While it is said, To-day if ye will hear his voice, harden not your hearts, as in the provocation.

16. For some, when they had heard, did provoke: howbeit not all that came out of Egypt by Moses.

17. But with whom was he grieved forty years? *was it* not with them that had sinned, whose carcasses fell in the wilderness?

18. And to whom sware he that they should not enter into his rest, but to them that believed not?

19. So we see that they could not enter in because of unbelief.

## CHAPTER 4

LET us therefore fear, lest, a promise being left *us* of entering into his rest, any of you should seem to come short of it.

opportunity for exhortation. Mutual strength comes through such exhortation, which is the effective countermeasure against hardened hearts and sin. This is one specific responsibility believers are to exercise until the coming of Christ.

By so exhorting one another and thus encouraging faith and obedience, Christians show themselves to be **partakers with Christ** in the blessings of the promised rest. The test of a believing heart is **confidence firm unto the end.** The generation in the wilderness failed to enter into the Canaan rest (v. 19) **because of unbelief** (*di'apistian*). Can the warning be more plainly stated?

Notice that the children of Israel that perished in the wilderness left only two spokesmen, only two representatives of their faithless and therefore silent generation — Caleb and Joshua. And it was the *faith* of these two that protected them and that speaks to our hearts even today.

The perished generation failed on two counts — (1) hardness of heart, and (2) unbelief. This led them into error and finally to judgment. Their unbelief was manifested in attitudes still common. They murmured or complained; they set up alternate plans and sought alternate leadership; they openly rebelled against God; they expressed dissatisfaction with God's provision; and, finally, they grudgingly accepted their place in God's plan. The record plainly written in Num 14 — 21 and commented upon in Psalm 95 served the writer of Hebrews well in his repeated warnings against such hardness and unbelief as were evidenced in the perished generation (3:12,13,18, 19; 4:6,7,11).

**4:1-10.** There is no break between chapters 3 and 4. The example of the wilderness experience is applied immediately to the lives of believers. The heart attitude of the readers is discussed in relation to 'the rest of faith,' a phrase often used in relation to this passage of Scripture. Two basic views prevail with regard to the promised **rest.** The first places the **rest** in the future as a heavenly rest, or entrance into the Kingdom of God (see Gleason L. Archer, Jr., *The Epistle to the Hebrews: A Study Manual,* pp. 28,29; Charles R. Erdman, *The Epistle to the Hebrews,* pp. 49,50). The second view places more emphasis upon the present rest than upon the promised rest of the future, though the latter is not disregarded. This 'rest of faith' is spoken of as a "full surrender," which is

2. For unto us was the gospel preached, as well as unto them: but the word preached did not profit them, not being mixed with faith in them that heard *it*.

3. For we which have believed do enter into rest, as he said, As I have sworn in my wrath, if they shall enter into my rest: although the works were finished from the foundation of the world.

4. For he spake in a certain place of the seventh *day* on this wise, And God did rest the seventh day from all his works.

5. And in this *place* again, If they shall enter into my rest.

6. Seeing therefore it remaineth that some must enter therein, and they to whom it was first preached entered not in because of unbelief:

7. Again, he limiteth a certain day, saying in David, To-day, after so long a time; as it is said, To-day if ye will hear his voice, harden not your hearts.

8. For if Jesus had given them rest, then would he not afterward have spoken of another day.

9. There remaineth therefore a rest to the people of God.

10. For he that is entered into his rest, he also hath ceased from his own works, as God *did* from his.

11. Let us labor therefore to enter into that rest, lest any man fall after the same example of unbelief.

12. For the word of God *is* quick, and powerful, and sharper than any two-edged sword, piercing even to the dividing asunder of soul and spirit, and of the joints and marrow, and *is* a discerner of the thoughts and intents of the heart.

considered a unique experience (Erdman, *Ibid.*). This second position emphasizes the present reality of 'the rest of faith' as a ceasing from our works which puts the believer into a closer relationship to Christ.

**1,2.** The promised **rest** is still available. The promise of God was not used up on the wilderness generation. Only the failure to remain steadfast in faith limits entering into this rest. This is the direct application of the warnings against unbelief in the previous statements. **We are those who have been "gospeled"** (AV, *unto us was the gospel preached*) resolves itself into a statement difficult to translate because of variant readings, but not difficult to understand. The faith of the believer exercised in relation to the promise of God guarantees the rest. (For a discussion of the variant readings of *sugkekerasmenous tē pistei tois akousasin*, see Alf and ExpGT on Heb 4:2 b.)

**3,4.** Downer suggests a twofold rest (*Principles of Interpretation*). Here the writer discusses spiritual repose for the persecuted and harassed believers to whom this letter is addressed. This is a present personal experience — **we which have believed do enter into rest** (*eiserchometha*, "we enter into"). This is the word of encouragement to troubled Christians. The second, or sabbath rest, is then introduced by the clause, **God did rest the seventh day from all his works.** This is the *sabbatismos* of verse 9, the *sabbath rest*.

**5-10.** God has provided **rest,** and this rest is to be occupied or entered into. Unbelief blocks entrance into God's rest, while faith opens wide the entrance; and so this rest is available only to true Christians. Joshua did not give this rest to his generation only; therefore the promised rest is still open. **There remaineth therefore a rest to the people of God** appointed for believers today. It is a rest both present and future that depends not upon "works," but upon the faith of the believers. **11.** Here is the "word of exhortation" concerning entering into God's rest (see 13:22) through earnest striving (lit., *give diligence*).

**12,13.** The offering of *rest* is reinforced by reference to the word of God, that is, reference both to Christ as the living Word and to the revelation, or written word. Five assertions are made concerning the **word of God** (*logos tou theou*): (1) it is *living*; (2) it is the

13. Neither is there any creature that is not manifest in his sight: but all things *are* naked and opened unto the eyes of him with whom we have to do.

14. Seeing then that we have a great high priest, that is passed into the heavens, Jesus the Son of God, let us hold fast *our* profession.

15. For we have not a high priest which cannot be touched with the feeling of our infirmities; but was in all points tempted like as *we are, yet* without sin.

16. Let us therefore come boldly unto the throne of grace, that we may obtain mercy, and find grace to help in time of need.

word of power, or creative energy; (3) it *severs*, separating even the closest of relationships; (4) it is a judge of the innermost thoughts; and (5) it is the agency by which God deals directly with the *creature*. In this way the word of God reveals the whole man, particularly in relation to his heart attitudes, and his believing faith, that which will enable him to *enter into rest*. The word of God examines, judges, and admonishes the Christian to holy living and to believing faith.

6) Christ as High Priest in the Order of Melchisedek, Superior to Aaron. 4:14—5:10.

Now the theme first suggested in 2:17 and 3:1 is reintroduced for more extensive discussion. Here the preliminary statement concerning Christ in the sanctuary is made. What will follow will be a constant contrast between the earthly sanctuary or tabernacle and the "true" or heavenly sanctuary, and between the Aaronic or Levitical priesthood and the eternal priesthood of Christ "after the order of Melchisedek." At this point the place and ministry of Christ is explained.

14-16. He is in the sanctuary as our high priest. His right to this position is guaranteed by his death (including the shedding of his blood) and resurrection. He has **passed through the heavens** into the presence of God. He is there not only as the Son of God, but also as the Son of man. In his perfect humanity he is familiar with our needs, cares, temptations, and problems, because he was tempted without succumbing to the temptation. He knows all about sin without having sinned. His final familiarity with sin came when he took our sin upon himself at Calvary.

Now, because he is in God's presence, we can come to God boldly. The **throne of God** (AV, *of grace*), has been changed from a throne of judgment to a throne of mercy because the blood of Jesus has been "sprinkled" upon it. The symbolism is taken from the ark of the covenant in the Tabernacle and from the Day of Atonement (Lev 16). This symbolism and the replacement of the OT practice is explained point by point in the subsequent argument of the writer. For the moment, the author stresses the truth that there is help for the weak, mercy for the wretched, and **strength** (AV, *grace*) **to help,** because Christ our high

## CHAPTER 5

FOR every high priest taken from among men is ordained for men in things *pertaining* to God, that he may offer both gifts and sacrifices for sins:

2. Who can have compassion on the ignorant, and on them that are out of the way; for that he himself also is compassed with infirmity.

3. And by reason hereof he ought, as for the people, so also for himself, to offer for sins.

4. And no man taketh this honor unto himself, but he that is called of God, as *was* Aaron.

5. So also Christ glorified not himself to be made a high priest; but he that said unto him, Thou art my Son, to-day have I begotten thee.

6. As he saith also in another *place*, Thou *art* a priest for ever after the order of Melchisedec.

7. Who in the days of his flesh, when he had offered up prayers and supplications with strong crying and tears unto him that was able to save him from death, and was heard in that he feared;

priest at the throne of God meets our every need. This continual help is available instantly to each Christian, with no formalities save to "call upon the name of the Lord." Perhaps few passages in the NT are so rich as this one in the promise of help and comfort for Christians. Properly understood, this is one of the sublime truths in the Scripture concerning Christ and believers. Here it must be noted that everything relating to Christ as high priest is explained more fully in the passages that follow, up to Heb 10:18; also the comparison with Moses is now concluded.

**5:1-10.** The qualifications for the office of the high priest are next presented. Aaron serves as the model, since he was first to serve in the office of high priest.

**1,2. Chosen from among men** to represent man to God. The humanity of the high priest is basic and essential. He is also **appointed,** or *set apart*, to minister both before God and to men. Being a man, he can understand human weakness and minister to the erring and the ignorant. The high priest must deal with sinners as well as represent sinners. He must also offer sacrifice for his own sins as well as for those of the people. The picture is that of one totally involved as a man with the needs of men. **3.** Yet the personal needs of the appointed high priest were not forgotten. As he offered sacrifice for the people, so he offered for himself, representing his own needs to God through the blood of the sacrifice.

**4.** Aaron, the first high priest, was called of God to this office. He did not seek it nor did he merit it. He was appointed by God. The fate of those who sought to serve in this office apart from God's appointing is sufficiently illustrated by Korah (Num 16:40). **5,6.** So Christ was appointed high priest. The writer quotes Ps 2:7 with the meaning of, "This day I have appointed you to the office of a priest." He was fully qualified to hold the office and did not seek it for himself. He was appointed to this position of **glory** (*edōxasen*) by God the Father.

**7-10.** Christ's human experience is described here. It was an experience of learning and of limitations. This humiliation (Phil 2:7) was his time of learning to obey in the sphere of man. By this he was made complete. This was the time of his being in the flesh. The specific reference in Heb 5:7,8 is to the hours of agony in Gethsemane. The passage depicts anguish in the words **pray-**

8. Though he were a Son, yet learned he obedience by the things which he suffered;

9. And being made perfect, he became the author of eternal salvation unto all them that obey him;

10. Called of God a high priest after the order of Melchisedec.

11. Of whom we have many things to say, and hard to be uttered, seeing ye are dull of hearing.

12. For when for the time ye ought to be teachers, ye have need that one teach you again which *be* the first principles of the oracles of God; and are become such as have need of milk, and not of strong meat.

13. For every one that useth milk *is* unskilful in the word of righteousness: for he is a babe.

14. But strong meat belongeth to them that are of full age, *even* those who by reason of use have their senses exercised to discern both good and evil.

ers, supplications, strong crying, and tears. The enemy he faced was death — both physical and, because he was the sinbearer, spiritual, in that he bore the full wrath of God reserved for sinners. His request for deliverance was granted fully in the Resurrection, with its proclamation of death defeated. Through this experience Christ learned obedience as he would not have known it otherwise. Literally, *He learned from the things which he suffered* (v. 8), which is a play on words caught up in the Greek proverb *emathen — epathen.*

Now qualified perfectly as high priest, Christ provides **eternal salvation** (*sōtērias aiōniou*, v. 9), the eternal aspect of which is related to the priesthood of Melchisedek. In contrast to Aaron, Melchisedek is a priest of God eternally, a subject developed fully in chapter 7.

7) A Rebuke for Lack of Understanding and for Immaturity. 5:11—6:20.

Before developing his argument from the Melchisedekian priesthood, the writer again pauses to introduce exhortation and warning, including rebuke.

**11-14.** This is a strong rebuke. The writer plainly states that his readers are in no condition to receive the teaching he feels obligated to give them. He calls them **immature, backward, untaught,** and **dull of hearing.** Because of this condition, the typology concerning Melchisedek might be beyond their understanding. Jonathan Edwards once preached a sermon on Heb 5:12 entitled: "The Importance and Advantage of a Thorough Knowledge of Divine Truth." He noted that the rebuke in the passage seems to include all the readers addressed in the epistle, that these believers had made no progress either doctrinally or experimentally, that they did not understand Melchisedek, and furthermore, what they should have known, they did not *(The Works of President Edwards,* IV, 1-15).

The writer's conclusion that they were unqualified to be teachers of others seems self-evident. Further, they were actually qualified to receive only elementary truth or **milk.** As **babes** (nēpios, "sucklings"), they could not take stronger food; moreover, they lacked not only knowledge of the truth, but also experience of the truth. But those of **full age** or adulthood (*teloi,* "mature") were like **fully trained athletes** (*gegymnasmena*) ready for the contest because spiritually disciplined. Those so trained were spiritually sensitive and able to dis-

## CHAPTER 6

THEREFORE leaving the principles of the doctrine of Christ, let us go on unto perfection; not laying again the foundation of repentance from dead works, and of faith toward God,

2. Of the doctrine of baptisms, and of laying on of hands, and of resurrection of the dead, and of eternal judgment.

3. And this will we do, if God permit.

4. For *it is* impossible for those who were once enlightened, and have tasted of the heavenly gift, and were made partakers of the Holy Ghost,

5. And have tasted the good word of God, and the powers of the world to come,

6. If they shall fall away, to renew them again unto repentance; seeing they crucify to themselves the Son of God afresh, and put *him* to an open shame.

7. For the earth which drinketh in the rain that cometh oft upon it, and bringeth forth herbs meet for them by whom it is dressed, receiveth blessing from God:

8. But that which beareth thorns and briers *is* rejected, and *is* nigh unto cursing; whose end *is* to be burned.

cern between truth and error when under instruction. (Throughout the passage the figures of speech are mixed; see Alf, IV, 103.)

**6:1-3.** The exhortation continues. Having learned already the basic principles concerning Christ, they were not to stop with them but to go on to gain *full stature* and *maturity.* to exhibit full spiritual growth. They were to continue to discern between living truths and lifeless forms, such as were found in Judaism in the washings, baptisms, and rituals. In verse 3 the writer identifies himself with his readers and reveals his own dependence upon God.

**4-8.** Some had gone on to maturity; others had fall[en] away. These are now mentioned to enforce the warning that has just been given—to go on to maturity. Properly, this passage should be interpreted not from within a theological system but from within its own context. First principles learned is the subject. Now the writer speaks of those who, having received such instruction in first principles, had turned away from Christ. They were now enemies of Christ and of the salvation that is in him.

It was the writer's purpose to portray extreme peril so that those tempted to apostasy might have the strongest possible example. The issues were plain: Christ or no Christ, saving faith or unbelief, suffering his reproach or joining his betrayers and murderers. The words used are strong terms. *Hapax phōtisthentas* means **once for all enlightened.** *Tasted* is translated *come to know* in newer lexicons. **Partakers,** from Greek *metochous,* means real sharers (Alf, IV, 109). All these terms indicate a great deal of knowledge and participation on the part of those **once . . . enlightened.** Even miracles were familiar to those now shown to be hostile to Christ.

A somewhat different point of view is possible regarding the passage. It may be rendered, *if they fall away* (cf. the RSV, *if they commit apostasy).* In that case the writer is not thinking of specific instances of apostasy, least of all among the readers (v. 9), but is warning that refusal to progress in the Christian life leads logically to retrogression, of which the ultimate end may be apostasy. If one should go to the extreme of falling away after tasting the heavenly gift, his falling away cannot be classed with ordinary sin, for it involves a repudiation of God's provision in Christ (crucifying the Son of God afresh). Therefore, for

9. But, beloved, we are persuaded better things of you, and things that accompany salvation, though we thus speak.

10. For God is not unrighteous to forget your work and labor of love, which ye have showed toward his name, in that ye have ministered to the saints, and do minister.

11. And we desire that every one of you do show the same diligence to the full assurance of hope unto the end:

12. That ye be not slothful, but followers of them who through faith and patience inherit the promises.

13. For when God made promise to Abraham, because he could swear by no greater, he sware by himself,

14. Saying, Surely blessing I will bless thee, and multiplying I will multiply thee.

15. And so, after he had patiently endured, he obtained the promise.

16. For men verily swear by the greater: and an oath for confirmation is to them an end of all strife.

17. Wherein God, willing more abundantly to show unto the heirs of promise the immutability of his counsel, confirmed it by an oath:

18. That by two immutable things, in which it was impossible for God to lie, we might have a strong consolation, who have fled for refuge to lay hold upon the hope set before us:

19. Which hope we have as an anchor of the soul, both sure and steadfast, and which entereth into that within the veil;

20. Whither the forerunner is for us entered, even Jesus, made a high priest for ever after the order of Melchisedec.

him, the hope of renewal vanishes, for God does not have some other cure for sin when Calvary is rejected.

In choosing to reject Christ, the apostates most resembled a field that yields only thorns and thistles, though the rains falling upon it and the farmers tilling were intended to produce beneficial herbs. There can be no mistaking the direct and strong warning to readers tempted to turn away from Christ. Indeed, what was true for these first century believers is still true for believers today.

9-12. But all of the above is not true of those addressed, the writer explains. This is the conclusion of the matter so far as his speaking directly to his readers is concerned. Though he has just spoken in *severe words of warning (houtōs laloumen)*, he says he is **convinced of the better things** (*ta kreissona*) of them. God would not **forget in a moment** (*epilathesthai*) all they had done in word and deed in ministering to their Christian brethren, nor that they continued so to minister. This was a sign of their earnestness; now they were to keep this same earnest spirit and attitude all their lives (v. 11). They were to keep before them the splendid example of all who so earnestly persevered (v. 12), and they would enjoy the fulfilled promises of God. They must copy the faith and practices of those who were strong in faith.

13-20. They had the firm guarantee of the covenant made with Abraham, as their assurance. Abraham is introduced here as an example of perseverance. And Abraham persevered because God guaranteed by His own name the covenant He made with him. Having sworn by His own name, God could not then lie to Abraham, because both His authority and His integrity were at stake. God is unchangeable, and we have as strong an encouragement as Abraham had in his day. Our assurance is in Jesus, who is in the heavenly sanctuary already. By oath and by promise those whose hope is in Christ as the **anchor of the soul** will realize their hope of passing through the veil (symbolic, veil of Tabernacle) because Jesus has already **entered for us.**

As the eternal high priest in the sanctuary, Christ fulfills the priestly type of Melchisedek, and the writer returns to the interrupted theme of the person of Christ **after the order of** or *just like* Melchisedek.

## CHAPTER 7

FOR this Melchisedec, king of Salem, priest of the most high God, who met Abraham returning from the slaughter of the kings, and blessed him;

2. To whom also Abraham gave a tenth part of all; first being by interpretation King of righteousness, and after that also King of Salem, which is, King of peace;

8) The Priesthood of Melchisedek. 7:1-28.

Melchisedek is clearly a type of Christ. Everything known about Melchisedek is found in two passages of the OT—Gen 14:17-20 and Ps 110:4. In both instances his position as a priest of God is clear. Also his life story is related entirely in the Genesis passage. Nothing more is known about him, and it is not completely clear that the reference to Salem is to be interpreted as a reference to Jerusalem (Alf, IV, 125). However, there is no mistaking Melchisedek as a type of the eternal or everlasting priesthood of Christ. This thought serves to open up the whole discussion of the Levitical system.

Leonard designates 7:1—10:18 as the heart of the epistle. He speaks of it as a unique section, having few if any parallels in the NT, since it develops a comparative estimate of the priestly mediators of the two covenants (op. cit., p. 32).

The importance of Melchisedek and the significance of the comparison of Melchisedek and Christ has been the subject of much discussion. Opinions about these considerations vary widely. Cotton and Purdy (IB, XI, 660,661) speak of the "Melchisedek speculation," and of the "Alexandrian method of allegorical interpretation," which means, they say, "practically to play fast and loose with historical fact." And yet their comment on the passage goes on to point out clearly that Melchisedek establishes the "validity and dignity of Christ's priesthood," and that Melchisedek is "the prototype of the Son . . . He [the writer of Hebrews] has established proof that Jesus is the Son; he must now show that He is Priest."

A. B. Davidson in his *The Epistle to the Hebrews* (pp. 129, 146 ff.) discusses the whole subject of the priesthood of Christ, including the Melchisedek question. He rightly establishes the basic principle. With Melchisedek, the function of the priesthood is not under discussion, but the personnel of the priesthood. The ministry for all priests is essentially the same, being merely extended for the high priest in relation to the Day of Atonement. The writer thus relates Christ to Melchisedek in order to emphasize that *Christ is a priest forever*.

1-3. The historical incident recorded in Gen 14:17-20 is reviewed. The writer indicates that Melchisedek was a king and therefore received tribute of Abra-

3. Without father, without mother, without descent, having neither beginning of days, nor end of life; but made like unto the Son of God; abideth a priest continually.

4. Now consider how great this man *was*, unto whom even the patriarch Abraham gave the tenth of the spoils.

5. And verily they that are of the sons of Levi, who receive the office of the priesthood, have a commandment to take tithes of the people according to the law, that is, of their brethren, though they come out of the loins of Abraham:

6. But he whose descent is not counted from them received tithes of Abraham, and blessed him that had the promises.

7. And without all contradiction the less is blessed of the better.

8. And here men that die receive tithes; but there he *receiveth them*, of whom it is witnessed that he liveth.

9. And as I may so say, Levi also, who receiveth tithes, paid tithes in Abraham.

10. For he was yet in the loins of his father, when Melchisedec met him.

11. If therefore perfection were by the Levitical priesthood, (for under it the people received the law,) what further need *was there* that another priest should rise after the order of Melchisedec, and not be called after the order of Aaron?

12. For the priesthood being changed, there is made of necessity a change also of the law.

13. For he of whom these things are spoken pertaineth to another tribe, of which no man gave attendance at the altar.

14. For *it is* evident that our Lord sprang out of Juda; of which tribe Moses spake nothing concerning priesthood.

15. And it is yet far more evident: for that after the similitude of Melchisedec there ariseth another priest,

16. Who is made, not after the law of a carnal commandment, but after the power of an endless life.

17. For he testifieth, Thou *art* a priest for ever after the order of Melchisedec.

18. For there is verily a disannulling of the commandment going before for the weakness and unprofitableness thereof.

ham; but more important, he was **priest of God Most High** (ASV), and therefore received tithes of Abraham. The point of this is made later with reference to Melchisedek's being a priest of God before the Levitical priesthood was established (vv. 4-6). In the parenthetical portion of verses 2, 3, notice is taken of the fact that Melchisedek had no recorded genealogy or succession. Neither is his birth mentioned or his death recorded. His is a record of one having **neither beginning of days nor end of life, but made like unto the Son of God** (ASV). This lack of birth data strengthens the typology of Melchisedek in relation to Christ. Thus Ps 110:4 emphasizes the eternity of the priesthood of Melchisedek, as does *eis tō diēnekes*, "in perpetuity," **continually** (Heb 7:3).

**4-14.** What does all of this discussion of Melchisedek mean spiritually? **Observe**, or **contemplate** *(theōreite)* the greatness of the one whom Abraham acknowledged to be superior by giving him tithes. The important truth is that the priesthood of Melchisedek was greater than the priesthood of Aaron and the Levites because (figuratively) the later priesthood offered tithes to God through the earlier, or Melchisedekian, priesthood in the person of Abraham. In this way **the less**, i.e., the Levites, **is blessed of the better**, i.e., Melchisedek. The implications are all intended to demonstrate the superiority and eternity of the priesthood of the latter, who functioned as a priest when he blessed Abraham and (figuratively) Aaron and the Levites.

In this sequence the relation of the Levitical priesthood to Christ is discussed (vv. 11-14). Jesus was not of Levi but of Judah. This debarred him from the order of priests under the Law. His humanity related him to the tribe of Judah, and therefore (v. 13) he could not qualify on the human plane to serve before the altar as a priest, for Moses uttered not one word giving Judah priestly authority or function.

**15-28.** The technical question of whether Christ was/is a priest resolves itself because he is of another order of priesthood. This order is adjudged superior in every point to the Levitical priesthood, and this order is eternal. **16. The power of an endless life** *(akatalytos)* appears in no other place in the NT.

**18-20.** The Law of Moses referred to in the phrase **disannulling of the commandment**, or *disannulling of a foregoing commandment* (ASV) is abrogated or

19. For the law made nothing perfect, but the bringing in of a better hope *did*; by the which we draw nigh unto God.

20. And inasmuch as not without an oath *he was made priest:*

21. (For those priests were made without an oath; but this with an oath by him that said unto him, The Lord sware and will not repent, Thou *art* a priest for ever after the order of Melchisedec:)

22. By so much was Jesus made a surety of a better testament.

23. And they truly were many priests, because they were not suffered to continue by reason of death:

24. But this *man*, because he continueth ever, hath an unchangeable priesthood.

25. Wherefore he is able also to save them to the uttermost that come unto God by him, seeing he ever liveth to make intercession for them.

26. For such a high priest became us, *who is* holy, harmless, undefiled, separate from sinners, and made higher than the heavens;

27. Who needeth not daily, as those high priests, to offer up sacrifice, first for his own sins, and then for the people's: for this he did once, when he offered up himself.

28. For the law maketh men high priests which have infirmity; but the word of the oath, which was since the law, *maketh* the Son, who is consecrated for evermore.

## CHAPTER 8

NOW of the things which we have spoken *this is* the sum: We have such a high priest, who is set on the right hand of the throne of the Majesty in the heavens;

2. A minister of the sanctuary, and of the true tabernacle, which the Lord pitched, and not man.

set aside in that Christ is the priest of God sealed with an oath (Ps 110:4). **22.** Christ is the **surety** or pledge *(engyos)* that God's oath will be kept in the promises and assurances of the new covenant.

**23-28.** Christ **lives forever** and is not subject to death. The grave has been conquered. He can therefore save **to the uttermost,** completely and to the ultimate, i.e., eternally, whoever calls upon him. In the same fashion his intercession for his own is unceasing. These ministries are guaranteed by his own character (holy, guileless, undefiled, separated from sinners, ASV), his function (as the atoning sacrifice), and his relationship.

B. Christ, the Minister and High Priest of the New Covenant. 8:1—10:18.

The new covenant, the Levitical system of the old covenant, and the priestly ministry of Christ are now brought together in the concluding statements of the main argument of the epistle. In summation, direct reference is made to the tabernacle in the wilderness in order that the contrast with the heavenly sanctuary might be introduced. Christ is in the heavenly sanctuary, his presence there being earlier described (4:13-16). He is there as high priest performing priestly service based upon the sacrifice, he being also the sacrifice. Three concepts are thus combined, namely, atoning sacrifice, priestly service, and the heavenly sanctuary.

1) The New Covenant in Relation to the Old. 8:1-9.

Jeremiah mentioned a new covenant centuries before this discussion of its import (Jer 31:31 ff.). In Heb 8:8, both Israel and Judah are named as being the recipients of blessing and divine help in the promised new covenant. The new covenant is clearly contrasted with the old covenant (vv.8,9). It is shown to be inclusive, as well as a **better covenant** because guaranteed by **better promises** (v. 6).

**1-5.** The new covenant was established by Christ, who is its **minister** *(leitourgos)*. He ministers the **holy things** in the **true tabernacle,** which is built by **the Lord** *(kyrios,* evidently the Father, Alf). Here Christ ministers as high priest, having full authority (vv. 1,2). His position in the heavenly sanctuary is in perfect order. He offered to

3. For every high priest is ordained to offer gifts and sacrifices: wherefore *it is* of necessity that this man have somewhat also to offer.

4. For if he were on earth, he should not be a priest, seeing that there are priests that offer gifts according to the law:

5. Who serve unto the example and shadow of heavenly things, as Moses was admonished of God when he was about to make the tabernacle: for, See, saith he, *that* thou make all things according to the pattern showed to thee in the mount.

6. But now hath he obtained a more excellent ministry, by how much also he is the mediator of a better covenant, which was established upon better promises.

7. For if that first *covenant* had been faultless, then should no place have been sought for the second.

8. For finding fault with them, he saith, Behold, the days come, saith the Lord, when I will make a new covenant with the house of Israel and with the house of Judah:

9. Not according to the covenant that I made with their fathers, in the day when I took them by the hand to lead them out of the land of Egypt; because they continued not in my covenant, and I regarded them not, saith the Lord.

10. For this *is* the covenant that I will make with the house of Israel after those days, saith the Lord; I will put my laws into their mind, and write them in their hearts: and I will be to them a God, and they shall be to me a people:

11. And they shall not teach every man his neighbor, and every man his brother, saying, Know the Lord: for all shall know me, from the least to the greatest.

12. For I will be merciful to their unrighteousness, and their sins and their iniquities will I remember no more.

13. In that he saith, A new *covenant*, he hath made the first old. Now that which decayeth and waxeth old *is* ready to vanish away.

the Father both sacrifices and service. He offered himself as the one acceptable sacrifice (an idea developed more fully in chs. 9; 10), and his service is that of the high priest before God, serving in the sanctuary. In verse 4 there is a possible indication that this epistle was written before the fall of Jerusalem in A.D. 70, in the thought that earthly priests still serve who offer gifts according to the law. These serve only in the copy and shadow (ASV) given to Moses, who saw the real or true (heavenly) sanctuary on Mount Sinai (Ex 25:40).

6-9. The contrast is then sharpened (v. 6). A better service, or ministry the more excellent . . . a better covenant (ASV); and all based on better promises. If the old covenant had been satisfactory, God would not have been found fault with it nor would he have spoken of replacing it as he did through Jeremiah, the prophet (Jer 31:31 ff.). The prophet reported the giving of the old covenant, the failure of Israel to observe it, and the decision to replace it at some time future to Jeremiah.

2) The Better Covenant Explained. 8:10-13.

The writer appropriates the prophecy of Jeremiah to explain the nature and provisions of the new covenant. Under the new covenant: (1) God puts new laws in the hearts and minds of the people (accomplished by Christ through the new birth, thus establishing the new covenant as a covenant of relationship). (2) He establishes a new relationship with them—I will be to them a God, they . . . to me a people. (3) The people have a new function — teach every man . . . Know the Lord (v. 11). (4) And God's truth has a new outreach — all shall know me. (5) A new cleansing is provided, with sins and iniquities forgiven through Christ, the sacrifice and guarantor of the new covenant (v. 12). The old is replaced by the new, and the old is at the point of completely disappearing (v. 13).

3) The New Sanctuary and the Perfect Sacrifice. 9:1-28.

Familiarity with the functions of the Aaronic priesthood as described in the latter half of Exodus and in Leviticus greatly aids in understanding these verses. The service of the priest in the Tabernacle is described in summary fashion in relation to the various pieces of furniture and their functions. As in the

## CHAPTER 9

THEN verily the first *covenant* had also ordinances of divine service, and a worldly sanctuary.

2. For there was a tabernacle made; the first, wherein *was* the candlestick, and the table, and the showbread; which is called the sanctuary.

3. And after the second veil, the tabernacle which is called the holiest of all;

4. Which had the golden censer, and the ark of the covenant overlaid round about with gold, wherein *was* the golden pot that had manna, and Aaron's rod that budded, and the tables of the covenant;

5. And over it the cherubim of glory shadowing the mercy seat; of which we cannot now speak particularly.

6. Now when these things were thus ordained, the priests went always into the first tabernacle, accomplishing the service *of God.*

7. But into the second *went* the high priest alone once every year, not without blood, which he offered for himself, and *for* the errors of the people:

8. The Holy Ghost this signifying, that the way into the holiest of all was not yet made manifest, while as the first tabernacle was yet standing:

9. Which *was* a figure for the time then present, in which were offered both gifts and sacrifices, that could not make him that did the service perfect, as pertaining to the conscience;

10. *Which stood* only in meats and drinks, and divers washings, and carnal ordinances, imposed *on them* until the time of reformation.

11. But Christ being come a high priest of good things to come, by a greater and more perfect tabernacle, not made with hands, that is to say, not of this building;

12. Neither by the blood of goats and calves, but by his own blood he entered in once into the holy place, having obtained eternal redemption *for us.*

13. For if the blood of bulls and of goats, and the ashes of a heifer sprinkling the unclean, sanctifieth to the purifying of the flesh;

former chapter, the purpose is again to make plain the contrast between the superior service of Christ as high priest in the heavenly sanctuary and Aaron as high priest on earth.

**1-10.** The old practices are explained as the ordinances of the earthly sanctuary. The writer sees to it that his readers do not mistake the location of Levitical priestly service. He names the items of furniture in the Tabernacle and identifies them locationally by holy place, sanctuary, ASV, AV *(hagia);* and holy of holies, holiest of all, ASV, AV *(hagia hagiōn).* The former was the first room in the earthly Tabernacle, and the latter was the second or inner room. This careful description is important for an understanding of the activities of the Levitical priests and of the high priest in relation to the two rooms. The ministrations of the priests were clearly of greater importance than the furniture, as is indicated by the phrase, of which things we cannot now speak severally, or *individually* (ASV, v. 5).

The Levitical priests ministered daily in the Holy Place, but they did not go through the veil into the Holy of Holies. Ceremonial cleansing was obtained for the people as the priests daily ministered at the altar of incense in the Holy Place. Atonement or forgiveness was obtained only once each year, on the Day of Atonement (see Lev 16), when the high priest went through or beyond the veil to the mercy seat carrying the blood of the sacrifice. But these were carnal ordinances (Heb 9:10), because the earthly Tabernacle, its furniture and its service, were imperfect. The veil hung between the two rooms of the sanctuary in the Tabernacle bore perpetual witness that the way directly to God was not yet open (see 4:13-16). To this fact the Holy Spirit bore witness (9:8). Also there was a specific time limit as to how long the Levitical priesthood and the earthly Tabernacle were to serve (v. 10). There was to be a time of reformation.

**11-14.** Christ inaugurated this time of reformation by entering as a high priest into the heavenly tabernacle, or greater and more perfect tabernacle, and presenting his own blood on the heavenly mercy seat as an atonement. An eternal redemption was once for all accomplished by the eternal sacrifice of the Son of God. No repetition of this action is necessary or possible. The contrast between the blood of goats and bulls annually offered and the other ceremonial sym-

14. How much more shall the blood of Christ, who through the eternal Spirit offered himself without spot to God, purge your conscience from dead works to serve the living God?

15. And for this cause he is the mediator of the new testament, that by means of death, for the redemption of the transgressions *that were* under the first testament, they which are called might receive the promise of eternal inheritance.

16. For where a testament *is*, there must also of necessity be the death of the testator.

17. For a testament *is* of force after men are dead: otherwise it is of no strength at all while the testator liveth.

18. Whereupon neither the first *testament* was dedicated without blood.

19. For when Moses had spoken every precept to all the people according to the law, he took the blood of calves and of goats, with water, and scarlet wool, and hyssop, and sprinkled both the book and all the people,

20. Saying, This *is* the blood of the testament which God hath enjoined unto you.

21. Moreover he sprinkled likewise with blood both the tabernacle, and all the vessels of the ministry.

bols of the Levitical system and the atoning death of Christ is again explained. Of how much greater import is the blood of Christ who through the eternal Spirit offered himself (*dia pneumatos aiōniou*). Through the eternal Spirit probably means *his eternal Spirit* (ASV marg.), and refers to the consent of his own will in the offering of himself in relation to his position in the Godhead. In this way his was an eternal and not a temporal sacrifice. The exact interpretation of eternal Spirit is difficult to determine (cf. Davidson, *Epistle to the Hebrews*, p. 178; CGT, p. 119).

This redemptive and atoning work of Christ satisfies both legal requirements under the Law and personal requirements in a cleansed conscience. It provides internal purity as well as outward and eternal deliverance. This was a particularly important argument in light of the temptation to apostatize on the part of at least some of the readers of this epistle. As sinners delivered and cleansed, they, especially, were obligated to render service to God rather than return to the dead works of Judaism.

15-28. The way into the heavenly sanctuary is by atoning death. This is the functional meaning of mediator of a new covenant. This is true because a death has taken place, the death of Jesus Christ upon the cross. A transaction took place there which fully satisfied all redemptive requirements, and this issues in forgiveness and an eternal inheritance.

16. This new covenant may be viewed as a testament sealed by the death of him that made it. In OT times the blood of animal sacrifice sealed a covenant to its makers. The death of Christ seals the new covenant. 17. Here is added argument to strengthen the fact under consideration. The emphasis is upon testament (*diathēkē;* cf. Alf) sealed by death and by shedding of blood. This is the only way in which a covenant can be in force. And this is a better covenant. All along through these verses the point made is that death is necessary.

18-22. The blood of animal sacrifices was inseparably linked to the earthly or first Tabernacle. After God gave the promises and instructions to Moses, then Moses took the blood of sacrifices and sprinkled everything symbolically involved in the first covenant. Hence this is called the blood of the covenant. By this action these earthly things were cleansed and then maintained as clean and identified with God and his covenant

22. And almost all things are by the law purged with blood; and without shedding of blood is no remission.

23. *It was* therefore necessary that the patterns of things in the heavens should be purified with these; but the heavenly things themselves with better sacrifices than these.

24. For Christ is not entered into the holy places made with hands, *which are* the figures of the true; but into heaven itself, now to appear in the presence of God for us:

25. Nor yet that he should offer himself often, as the high priest entereth into the holy place every year with blood of others;

26. For then must he often have suffered since the foundation of the world: but now once in the end of the world hath he appeared to put away sin by the sacrifice of himself.

27. And as it is appointed unto men once to die, but after this the judgment:

28. So Christ was once offered to bear the sins of many; and unto them that look for him shall he appear the second time without sin unto salvation.

### CHAPTER 10

FOR the law having a shadow of good things to come, *and* not the very image of the things, can never with those sacrifices, which they offered year by year continually, make the comers thereunto perfect.

2. For then would they not have ceased to be offered? because that the worshippers once purged should have had no more conscience of sins.

3. But in those *sacrifices there is* a remembrance again *made* of sins every year.

with Israel. This was necessary because there is no remission apart from the blood of the sacrifice. The fundamental truth over which many stumble is the statement of verse 22 that without shedding of blood there is no remission (cf. Ex 24:3-8).

23-28. The finality of the atoning work of Christ is explained more fully. 23. Again, better sacrifices is the key. Heaven itself is free from the taint of human sin because the blood of Christ was shed (cf. Moll in J. P. Lange's *Commentary on the Holy Scriptures;* or, Ex 24:3-8).

24-26. Finality. Christ is in the holy place or heavenly sanctuary, appearing there in our behalf (v. 24). He does not go in and come out annually, for his sacrifice is complete (v. 25). He suffered only once; his blood was shed once; and in his suffering and death, sin was once and for all time conquered. This event is identified with the end of the world (AV) or age (ASV). This time designation and the almost immediate reference to the Second Coming (v. 28) suggest that God's people in the early generations after Christ linked the Lord's death with his return as events close to each other in import, if not in time.

27,28. A physical death precedes judgment. Christ suffered this death, and in so doing he died once and for all. In so doing he took sin upon himself—the sins of many (v. 28). And he will come a second time not to bear sin, but to meet sinners whose sins are washed away in his atoning blood. These are the redeemed of God who wait for him. Believers will then enter into full salvation and the actual presence of God. Those who know the joy of salvation should also know the hope of the Lord's coming.

4) The New Covenant Complete, Perfect, and at Work. 10:1-18.

How can sins be removed? The old covenant offered a way of forgiveness of sins. Was it satisfactory? Did the method work? These questions form the basis for the final phase of the argument.

1-4. The old covenant failed. It was a mere shadow *(skia)* of the better things to come, an image *(eikōn)* of the real. Because of this, it was ultimately futile in that it never made anyone mature in faith and trust. If it had made perfect believers, it would not have been replaced. The sin problem would have been solved. The fact clearly stated is that yearly offerings and the blood of animal

4. For *it is* not possible that the blood of bulls and of goats should take away sins.

5. Wherefore, when he cometh into the world, he saith, Sacrifice and offering thou wouldest not, but a body hast thou prepared me:

6. In burnt offerings and *sacrifices* for sin thou hast had no pleasure.

7. Then said I, Lo, I come (in the volume of the book it is written of me) to do thy will, O God.

8. Above when he said, Sacrifice and offering and burnt offerings and *offering* for sin thou wouldest not, neither hadst pleasure *therein;* which are offered by the law;

9. Then said he, Lo, I come to do thy will, O God. He taketh away the first, that he may establish the second.

10. By the which will we are sanctified through the offering of the body of Jesus Christ once *for all.*

11. And every priest standeth daily ministering and offering oftentimes the same sacrifices, which can never take away sins:

12. But this man, after he had offered one sacrifice for sins for ever, sat down on the right hand of God;

13. From henceforth expecting till his enemies be made his footstool.

14. For by one offering he hath perfected for ever them that are sanctified.

15. *Whereof* the Holy Ghost also is a witness to us: for after that he had said before,

16. This *is* the covenant that I will make with them after those days, saith the Lord; I will put my laws into their hearts, and in their minds will I write them;

17. And their sins and iniquities will I remember no more.

18. Now where remission of these *is, there is* no more offering for sin.

sacrifices cannot take away sin. The vital word in verse 4 is **impossible** *(adynaton).* This is a strong, conclusive, and true statement.

**5-10.** Psalm 40:7-9 is here used typologically. David is quoted as having spoken of the Messiah and his entrance into the world in human form. The will of God for Messiah was to make a full atonement for sin. This necessitated sacrifice and shedding of blood and therefore the **body . . . prepared** so that he might suffer. In suffering and death the will of God was fully accomplished and the second or better covenant was fully established. As a result, believers have been changed because cleansed and sanctified by the **offering of the body of Jesus Christ** once for all (v. 10). By this offering, atonement was made, pleasing a holy God perfectly.

**11-13.** The ultimate triumph of the Messiah is seen in that he does not come repeatedly, nor does he stand to symbolize an incomplete redemption; but upon offering himself, Christ **sat down on the right hand of God.** Again reference is made to the position occupied by Christ, the place of authority and of priestly service. For believers, he both rules and intercedes, two aspects of the ministry of Christ continually held before those tempted to apostatize back into Judaism and mere legalism and ritual. The rule of Christ will become actual. Meanwhile he patiently waits for the time when his enemies will be vanquished. There will then be no more opposition to Christ or to his rule.

**14-18.** Jeremiah's covenant prophecy has been fulfilled. Believers in Christ are now perfected, cleansed, purified, fitted for perpetual communion and fellowship with God. The word **perfected** *(teteleiōken)* means "completed." That is, the end in view is achieved; the believer is prepared for entrance into the sanctuary, and his earthly hope of this is assured (cf. ExpGT). This signifies growth and also enjoyment of privileges.

The writer again quotes Jer 31:33 ff., to indicate how the heart of a believer is changed by faith in Christ, and his very nature is transformed. Jeremiah foretold that it would be so as the Holy Spirit spoke through him. Remission of sins is now complete, and what Jeremiah spoke of in prophecy is now reality. Sins are not even remembered, and lives are fully transformed by all that Christ has accomplished in atoning death. The work is done.

19. Having therefore, brethren, boldness to enter into the holiest by the blood of Jesus,

20. By a new and living way, which he hath consecrated for us, through the veil, that is to say, his flesh;

21. And *having* a high priest over the house of God;

## III. The Elements of the Faith Life. 10:19—13:17.

Now an exhortation brings to a close the last thoughts of the writer. This closing section is an exhortatory composition with all the thoughts centered in the one word — faith. The exhortation is to constancy of faith, with accompanying warnings about the outcome if the life of faith is either rejected or despised. The thought of faith carries through to the personal epilogue with which the epistle finally ends. The thought of an active life of faith seems to be a focal point around which the writer gathers his final arguments and warnings. The thought introduced by **Let us draw near with a true heart in full assurance of faith** permeates all that follows. By description, warning, example, and other means that seem to come to mind, the writer states the case plainly in the phrase, **full assurance of faith.**

A. Description of the Faith Life. 10: 19-25.

The life of faith must first be understood. If a teacher finds that the believers' faith is weak, then he must speak much of an assured faith that makes strong, confident believers. This assurance is founded upon the eternal guarantee that Christ has entered into the sanctuary and into the presence of God, making it possible also for every believer to enter into the sanctuary and into God's presence. If this is the privilege of believers, and it is, then believers should take every advantage of the privilege. They should exercise the prerogative of drawing near, because Christ, the Son over God's house and the high priest in eternal (Melchisedekian) generation, has made this possible. In this expansion of 4:13-16, the writer bids us to be bold.

**19. Boldness,** or confidence. Because of all that the Lord Jesus Christ has done, we have boldness. This is free access **by the blood of Jesus;** the way is already opened. **20, 21.** Here is the means of access, **by a new** (*prosphaton*) **and living way** . . . , or **consecrated** way. The veil no longer blocks access to God, nor does human nature, symbolized by the reference to flesh (*sarx*). Christ's suffering in the flesh forever removes this barrier. As his body was torn on the cross, so the veil between God and men was torn, giving immediate access to God. And Christ is the **great high priest,** or **great priest,**

22. Let us draw near with a true heart in full assurance of faith, having our hearts sprinkled from an evil conscience, and our bodies washed with pure water.

23. Let us hold fast the profession of *our* faith without wavering; for he *is* faithful that promised;

24. And let us consider one another to provoke unto love and to good works:

25. Not forsaking the assembling of ourselves together, as the manner of some *is;* but exhorting *one another:* and so much the more, as ye see the day approaching.

as in 4:14, doing the work of a great priest in the sanctuary.

22. **Draw near,** bears the idea of coming to God frequently, openly, intimately, and unhesitatingly, but always with a cleansed heart, **true heart; hearts sprinkled** and a fully formed assurance that the way to God is opened to us. The cleansed heart and the fully assured faith are the predominant ideas; the secondary emphasis falls on the triad of cleansed heart, body, and conscience. 23. **Confession of our hope** (ASV). An unwavering confession of faith in the living Christ. God undergirds our hope by his own promises, **for he is faithful who promised.** This then speaks of further affirmation based upon faith in the faithfulness of God.

24. With assurance comes concern for others. This is manifested by the willingness of believers to assemble together (v. 25) and also by their willingness both to give and to receive helpful exhortation and instruction. **To provoke.** To stimulate through provocation and encouragement *(paroxysmos, paroxysm).* **Love** and **good works** are to be awakened toward fellow believers. 25. Assembly and fellowship are two evidences of vital faith. When zeal flags and faith weakens, the desire to fellowship with other believers weakens also. Through such assembly the provocation of verse 24 is possible. When Christians meet together, they exhort each other to fruitful service and unbroken fellowship. The danger of apostasy lurks in the failure of believers to meet together for mutual help *(parakalountes,* "mutual encouragement").

**The day.** The shortest of all the references to the coming again of the Lord Jesus Christ. A direct reference to the Second Coming. The urgency of the passage concerning exhortation is due to the imminence of this Day of Christ. At this point, some difficulty arises in relation to the fall of Jerusalem. The primary reference of this statement may be to the impending judgment of Jerusalem. But it is evident that the fall of Jerusalem can not completely fufill this promise. So the statement seems to presuppose a second or final judgment as well.

B. A Description of Those Who Spurn This "New and Living Way." 10:26-39.

The exhortation to constancy is continued with a negative application or warning. Alternatives are described in sharp contrast as belief or unbelief, faith

26. For if we sin wilfully after that we have received the knowledge of the truth, there remaineth no more sacrifice for sins,

27. But a certain fearful looking for of judgment and fiery indignation, which shall devour the adversaries.

28. He that despised Moses' law died without mercy under two or three witnesses:

29. Of how much sorer punishment, suppose ye, shall he be thought worthy, who hath trodden under foot the Son of God, and hath counted the blood of the covenant, wherewith he was sanctified, an unholy thing, and hath done despite unto the Spirit of grace?

30. For we know him that hath said, Vengeance *belongeth* unto me, I will recompense, saith the Lord. And again, The Lord shall judge his people.

31. *It is* a fearful thing to fall into the hands of the living God.

32. But call to remembrance the former days, in which, after ye were illuminated, ye endured a great fight of afflictions;

33. Partly, whilst ye were made a gazingstock both by reproaches and afflictions; and partly, whilst ye became companions of them that were so used.

34. For ye had compassion of me in my bonds, and took joyfully the spoiling of your goods, knowing in yourselves that ye have in heaven a better and an enduring substance.

and practice or fearful judgment, acceptance or rejection in the light of Calvary.

26. Sin wilfully *(hamartanontōn,* "as long as we are sinning wilfully") and knowledge *(epignōsis,* "full knowledge") govern this passage. In this case there is no lack of *understanding* of the truth, just as in the case of false teachers mentioned in II Pet 2:20,21, where the same strong word for knowledge is twice used. The basic thought in this climactic warning passage is the same as in Heb 6:4-6. A deliberate rejection of the cross by one who knows the way leaves God with no alternative. When mercy is rejected, judgment must fall.

27-29. Judgment follows. The practice under Mosaic law is cited in order to establish the contrast. This judgment will come upon the adversaries of God, and the rejection of verse 26 apparently places the rejectors among those adversaries. This will be a fearful, frightful judgment, because the one atoning sacrifice has been rejected.

The threefold charge follows: (1) contempt for Christ in the thought of trampling under foot; (2) rejecting the blood-bought covenant as worthless and unholy; (3) despising the person and work of the Holy Spirit.

30,31. From such ultimate condition there is neither remedy nor escape. Only vengeance awaits such persons, declares the inspired writer, quoting Deut 32:35, 36 as supporting evidence. This hopeless apostasy and ultimate and irrevocable rejection leads only to the fiercest judgment from God. Psalm 135:14 is also noted as supporting evidence for these statements.

32-34. Again, the writer draws a contrast. Continuing his exhortation, he describes strong faith and patience under trial and difficulty. He reminds the believers of their early faith and the first blessing of knowing Christ. In the joy of this newly found faith they regarded afflictions, temptations *(athlēsis,* such as the struggles of an athlete), sufferings, and reproaches as nothing. The kind of struggle — whether sympathizing with others under trial or suffering personal loss for Christ — makes little difference. Faith was strong; affliction was welcomed, and confidence in Christ was firm and constant. A gazingstock. They were made a theater, or set upon a stage *(theatrizomenoi)* for all to look upon; but they did not waver. In thus encouraging

**35.** Cast not away therefore your confidence, which hath great recompense of reward.

**36.** For ye have need of patience, that, after ye have done the will of God, ye might receive the promise.

**37.** For yet a little while, and he that shall come will come, and will not tarry.

**38.** Now the just shall live by faith: but if *any man* draw back, my soul shall have no pleasure in him.

**39.** But we are not of them who draw back unto perdition; but of them that believe to the saving of the soul.

### CHAPTER 11

NOW faith is the substance of things hoped for, the evidence of things not seen.

the believers to recall former days, the writer personalizes his exhortation.

**35-37.** Patience, or confidence, in the light of the things recalled, should not now be forgotten, or cast away; for this is a confidence based upon assurance, a boldness of vital faith, an assured victory. And this patience is the greatest need. Rather than turning back to an easier way, the believers are to keep both faith and hope high in a steadfast patience, for the reward is certain. To do the will of God must be their ruling desire on earth, that their heavenly reward may be the more blessed (cf. Mt 7:21). They must be patient, and carry the load, not cast it off *(hypomenēs)*. And they are to remember the words of Hab 2:3, for he shall surely come and will not delay.

**38-39.** Faith is the keynote of this passage. Those who live by faith and die in faith will ultimately rejoice in the final salvation guaranteed in Christ. As Habakkuk admonishes, men are not to shrink back (ASV), for then God is obliged to act as described in Heb 10:26-31. True believers will not be guilty of such shrinking back. Their faith is a faith unto the saving of the soul (ASV). In his description of the faith of the true believer, the writer has introduced in a quiet manner the next phase of his exhortation.

C. Examples of the Life of Faith. 11:1-40.

Having introduced the faith life as the subject of his final exhortation, and having described it both as to its elements and its opposites, the writer now brings to his argument the example of numerous people who lived such a life of faith. It is as though someone who had followed all the careful reasoning of the author now requested some evidence or proof to substantiate the claims made. Have any persons ever lived like this? Assuredly! Who are they? Heb 11:1–12:4 is the writer's answer.

**1-7.** He first explains the nature of true faith, giving not so much a definition as a description. Faith is trust in the unseen. It is *not* trust in the unknown, for we may know by faith what we cannot see with the eye. Those to whom the writer was directing his thoughts would now have the added assistance of the record of the heroes of the OT who lived with trust in the unseen, or by

2. For by it the elders obtained a good report.

3. Through faith we understand that the worlds were framed by the word of God, so that things which are seen were not made of things which do appear.

4. By faith Abel offered unto God a more excellent sacrifice than Cain, by which he obtained witness that he was righteous, God testifying of his gifts: and by it he being dead yet speaketh.

5. By faith Enoch was translated that he should not see death; and was not found, because God had translated him: for before his translation he had this testimony, that he pleased God.

6. But without faith *it is* impossible to please *him:* for he that cometh to God must believe that he is, and *that* he is a rewarder of them that diligently seek him.

7. By faith Noah, being warned of God of things not seen as yet, moved with fear, prepared an ark to the saving of his house; by the which he condemned the world, and became heir of the righteousness which is by faith.

8. By faith Abraham, when he was called to go out into a place which he should after receive for an inheritance, obeyed; and he went out, not knowing whither he went.

9. By faith he sojourned in the land of promise, as *in* a strange country, dwelling in tabernacles with Isaac and Jacob, the heirs with him of the same promise:

10. For he looked for a city which hath foundations, whose builder and maker *is* God.

11. Through faith also Sarah herself received strength to conceive seed, and was delivered of a child when she was past age, because she judged him faithful who had promised.

12. Therefore sprang there even of one, and him as good as dead, *so many* as the stars of the sky in multitude, and as the sand which is by the seashore innumerable.

faith. Faith is the ultimate assurance and the ultimate evidence that things not seen are realities *(pragmata)*. The continuity of men who have believed in things not seen, heroes of faith, is unbroken.

By the act of believing, God's children know that the Lord made the worlds by his word. The OT great ones lived by faith. Abel, Enoch, and Noah are mentioned as precise examples of men acting by faith. Also, the generation receiving the exhortation was to live by faith. And each succeeding generation also must live by things hoped for until the coming of Christ.

Abel made an acceptable offering, which was a blood sacrifice. And this offering typologically established blood sacrifice as the basis of entrance into the life of faith. The faith life becomes a life only by an atonement made. So Abel continues to speak. Enoch lived a righteous life. His goal was to please God at any cost, and he succeeded; before his translation he had been well-pleasing unto God (ASV). This should still be the goal of every true believer, and it is impossible to please God apart from faith. Abel brought an acceptable offering, and Enoch lived a life of unbroken fellowship. Noah believed that God would judge the earth, and this became an incentive for his life of faith. He built the ark as an evidence of his faith. He activated his faith in the light of judgment.

Noah lived to see his faith and practice vindicated. On the one hand, he exhibited his faith by building the ark; on the other, he saw his faith vindicated in his deliverance from the Flood. Thus he joined that glorious company of the just who live by faith through a righteousness which is according to faith (ASV).

8-31. The later patriarchs also bore the same witness. Abraham, Sarah, Isaac, Jacob, Joseph, and Moses all exemplify the life of faith. Abraham and Moses serve as the better examples because they played such an important part in the purposes of God in the earth. Abraham exemplifies obedience in the life of faith. When God called him out of Ur of the Chaldees, he became a dweller in tents and a sojourner, a spiritual pilgrim, with his eye fixed upon a city as yet unseen.

Later he willingly gave Isaac to God, fully persuaded that the seed of Abraham, through Isaac, predestined to bless the world, would be under no jeopardy if

13. These all died in faith, not having received the promises, but having seen them afar off, and were persuaded of *them*, and embraced *them*, and confessed that they were strangers and pilgrims on the earth.

14. For they that say such things declare plainly that they seek a country.

15. And truly, if they had been mindful of that *country* from whence they came out, they might have had opportunity to have returned.

16. But now they desire a better *country*, that is, a heavenly: wherefore God is not ashamed to be called their God: for he hath prepared for them a city.

17. By faith Abraham, when he was tried, offered up Isaac: and he that had received the promises offered up his only begotten *son*,

18. Of whom it was said, That in Isaac shall thy seed be called:

19. Accounting that God *was* able to raise *him* up, even from the dead; from whence also he received him in a figure.

20. By faith Isaac blessed Jacob and Esau concerning things to come.

21. By faith Jacob, when he was a dying, blessed both the sons of Joseph; and worshipped, *leaning* upon the top of his staff.

22. By faith Joseph, when he died, made mention of the departing of the children of Israel; and gave commandment concerning his bones.

23. By faith Moses, when he was born, was hid three months of his parents, because they saw *he was* a proper child; and they were not afraid of the king's commandment.

24. By faith Moses, when he was come to years, refused to be called the son of Pharaoh's daughter;

Isaac should die. In faithfulness to His covenant promise of a seed, God would raise him up. Even the birth of Isaac, the son of promise, was an evidence of faith on the part of Abraham and Sarah. For their son was born when they were physically too old for such an occurrence.

**13-16.** For true believers, to live by faith is to die **in faith**. The faith life is a pilgrimage. Heaven is the only home of faithful believers. It is the **better country** to which those who live by faith are fully committed. And because they are committed to God, God is committed to them. **God is not ashamed of them** (ASV), and he proves this by providing a city or place of habitation for his own (Jn 14:1,2).

**17-19.** From Genesis 22 we see the faith of Abraham in offering up Isaac on Mount Moriah. The faith of Abraham was tested in at least two ways: (1) he was required to offer to God the best and dearest of his possessions; and (2) he was required to offer to God the son of promise. Abraham's future was assured to him only through Isaac. If Isaac were to die, what of the promise of God to Abraham? In making his offering, Abraham demonstrated in practical fashion his belief that death is no problem to God. Death can be neither barrier nor deterrent to His keeping a covenant promise—**God was able to raise him up, even from the dead. Figure.** Parable, similitude, as though Isaac were actually returned from the dead; a resurrection.

**20.** Isaac blessed Jacob and Esau in the covenant promise made to Abraham, but still future to Isaac, thus concerning things to come (see Gen 27).

**21,22. By faith Jacob . . . By faith Joseph.** Evidence of the faith of the patriarchs in the promise made to Abraham. Jacob, by blessing the sons of Joseph, perpetuated the promise and evidenced both faith and submission as he worshiped. Joseph demonstrated his faith in the covenant promise to Abraham by requesting that his body (**bones**) be buried in the land of promise (Gen 48; 50).

**23-29.** In many ways Moses exemplified the life of faith. By faith his parents hid him in defiance of a specific royal command (Ex 1:16-22). He was a **proper** or beautiful child, thus a portent of future blessing from God. Later, Moses himself, by faith, made proper choices. **Son of Pharaoh's daughter.** A phrase symbolic of rank, indicating the rank of

25. Choosing rather to suffer affliction with the people of God, than to enjoy the pleasures of sin for a season;

26. Esteeming the reproach of Christ greater riches than the treasures in Egypt: for he had respect unto the recompense of the reward.

27. By faith he forsook Egypt, not fearing the wrath of the king: for he endured, as seeing him who is invisible.

28. Through faith he kept the passover, and the sprinkling of blood, lest he that destroyed the firstborn should touch them.

29. By faith they passed through the Red sea as by dry *land:* which the Egyptians assaying to do were drowned.

30. By faith the walls of Jericho fell down, after they were compassed about seven days.

31. By faith the harlot Rahab perished not with them that believed not, when she had received the spies with peace.

32. And what shall I more say? for the time would fail me to tell of Gideon, and *of* Barak, and *of* Samson, and *of* Jephthah; *of* David also, and Samuel, and *of* the prophets:

33. Who through faith subdued kingdoms, wrought righteousness, obtained promises, stopped the mouths of lions,

34. Quenched the violence of fire, escaped the edge of the sword, out of weakness were made strong, waxed valiant in fight, turned to flight the armies of the aliens.

35. Women received their dead raised to life again: and others were tortured, not accepting deliverance; that they might obtain a better resurrection:

36. And others had trial of *cruel* mockings and scourgings, yea, moreover of bonds and imprisonment:

37. They were stoned, they were sawn asunder, were tempted, were slain with the sword: they wandered about in sheepskins and goatskins; being destitute, afflicted, tormented;

38. Of whom the world was not worthy: they wandered in deserts, and *in* mountains, and *in* dens and caves of the earth.

39. And these all, having obtained a good report through faith, received not the promise:

prince. Moses chose God's people and the promises of God even though this meant affliction and adversity. In this, Moses became the deliverer of a hopeless people (Ex 2). He also chose not to enjoy the temporary pleasures of sin (Alf, p. 224). The reproach of Christ. Moses seemingly comprehended Messianic truth; hence his choice of faith in the Messiah. This reproach was borne by Christ, and it is likewise borne by those who faithfully serve him. This passage suggests that Moses had Christ in view.

Moses also chose to leave Egypt. Again, with Christ in view, he discounted both the riches of the land of his birth and the power and prestige of its Pharaoh, or king. This statement refers to the exodus of Israel from Egypt with Moses as the leader. Moses gave further evidence of his faith by keeping the Passover, thus indicating that deliverance is by the shedding of blood (Ex 12). Notice the reference to faithful continuance—he endured—a thought developed more fully in Heb 12:1-4. Furthermore, Moses and the people together by faith witnessed the miracle of the Red Sea—a deliverance for Israel, a judgment upon the Egyptians.

30,31. Jericho fell victim to the faith of Joshua and the children of Israel, and Rahab participated in Israel's blessing by her faith. The memorial to the faith of Rahab is read in Mt 1:5, where she is listed in the genealogy of Christ.

32-38. The writer now resorts to piling up examples, because of the impossibility of taking each case separately. The list is impressive, including some of the Judges, the greatest of Israel's kings—David, and one of her greatest prophets—Samuel.

The list of deeds is equally impressive. In some cases the incidents referred to are well known; in others they are more obscure. In each instance, however, something typical of those who live by faith is brought out. The faith life makes such deeds possible, deeds of valor, might, courage, or perseverance. And these are the kinds of experience that those who live by faith are called upon to endure. All of the history of Israel is encompassed in these few brief sentences. By a careful search of the OT, it is possible to find many of the events mentioned.

39,40. But in spite of all this evidence that men and women of the OT lived lives of faith, the fact remains that they

**40. God having provided some better thing for us, that they without us should not be made perfect.**

## CHAPTER 12

**WHEREFORE, seeing we also are compassed about with so great a cloud of witnesses, let us lay aside every weight, and the sin which doth so easily beset *us*, and let us run with patience the race that is set before us,**

did not know the full blessings of sins forgiven and of fellowship with God through the provisions of Calvary. They lived in anticipation of the new covenant, but without its full provisions. They had a positive and effective witness, **a good report through faith,** or as in the CGT, *having been borne witness to through their faith,* an attestation by God himself.

God unveiled a better plan, or at least a more complete plan, in the generations after the patriarchs and particularly regarding the generations since Calvary. Perfection had to await these generations, **that they without us should not be made perfect** (*teleiōthōsin, teleioō,* "to make perfect, or complete"). The whole of the completed redemption is in view.

Each of the people mentioned in this chapter illustrates some phase or aspect of the life of faith—whether obedience, acting on promises of things to come, separation from the world system (Moses), or some other. But the writer still has not completed his argument concerning the superiority of the life of faith over the practice of Mosaic legalism. One example remains, the Lord Jesus Christ. The final phase of the argument by example culminates in the "consider him" statement of Heb 12:3. Having considered all of these other witnesses, the readers are now to "consider him that endured . . . lest ye be weary and faint in your minds."

D. Christ, the Supreme Example of the Faith Life. 12:1-4.

**1, 2.** The exhortation is now renewed with vigor because of the examples given in the previous chapter. **Wherefore** includes all the heroes of chapter 11 who, together with us, will be **made perfect.** They are **witnesses,** who, like spectators in a vast arena, watch us progress in the course of the life of faith. **Let us run with patient endurance** (Davidson, *Epistle to the Hebrews,* p. 232) combines exhortations to run and to endure in the light of the example of those who have already run this course faithfully. **Every weight.** The superfluous and unnecessary that might hinder must be cast aside. Each individual must decide what is superfluous. But what is clearly **sin** allows of no individual choice; it must be cast aside immediately upon recognition, as it springs from its ambush to entrap (*euperistatos,* "to ambush, to encircle, to entrap") the unwary. This kind of sin

2. Looking unto Jesus the author and finisher of *our* faith; who for the joy that was set before him endured the cross, despising the shame, and is set down at the right hand of the throne of God.

3. For consider him that endured such contradiction of sinners against himself, lest ye be wearied and faint in your minds.

4. Ye have not yet resisted unto blood, striving against sin.

5. And ye have forgotten the exhortation which speaketh unto you as unto children, My son, despise not thou the chastening of the Lord, nor faint when thou art rebuked of him:

6. For whom the Lord loveth he chasteneth, and scourgeth every son whom he receiveth.

7. If ye endure chastening, God dealeth with you as with sons; for what son is he whom the father chasteneth not?

8. But if ye be without chastisement, whereof all are partakers, then are ye bastards, and not sons.

would impede our running, or slow us down; so away with it.

**Looking unto Jesus.** A reference to the supreme or ultimate example available to us. What did he do? He **endured.** In this he is **leader** or *author,* and **perfecter** or *finisher* of our faith. This concept is then expanded in the following passages. In them is set forth the example of patient endurance to which each believer is called — that of Christ himself (12:1). The reward for Christ's endurance is the position of authority and his occupation thereof. In this position his **joy** is complete, and so will our joy be complete when we are in his presence before God. At God's right hand Christ performs all the functions of ruler, high priest, and advocate, yet he came to that place through suffering and endurance, i.e., by way of the cross.

**3,4. Consider** *(analogizomai,* "compare yourself with," "think over") **him that endured.** A further enlargement on verse 2. **Contradiction** *(antilogia)* is a contrary argument. Christ was literally a contradiction to his enemies, who expressed themselves in open hatred and hostility. **That ye wax not weary, fainting in your souls** (ASV, the best rendering of the text. See CGT, p. 154). The first clause suggests a sudden breakdown in endurance, the second a more gradual relaxation of vigilance.

**Ye have not yet resisted unto blood.** They had not yet realized the full extent of the struggle. No martyrdom had as yet occurred; no extreme measures, such as wholesale taking of life, had been employed against them. Finally, they were to remember that sin is the antagonist. They were to continue to strive **against sin,** particularly the sin of unbelief, which destroys faith.

E. The Father's Love Known Through Chastisement. 12:5-11.

**5-9.** The writer uses Prov 3:11 ff. to remind the reader-hearers that chastening is a part of the love relationship, and he also describes this relationship by means of the analogy of father and son. The exhortation begins at the end of the quotation. Sons who are worthy of their sonship must endure or bear chastening. Sometimes we do not understand chastening, but we are still to accept it and endure it as a necessary part of our training. For by it we are acknowledged as true sons, rather than spurious sons

9. Furthermore, we have had fathers of our flesh which corrected *us*, and we gave *them* reverence: shall we not much rather be in subjection unto the Father of spirits, and live?

10. For they verily for a few days chastened *us* after their own pleasure; but he for *our* profit, that *we* might be partakers of his holiness.

11. Now no chastening for the present seemeth to be joyous, but grievous: nevertheless, afterward it yieldeth the peaceable fruit of righteousness unto them which are exercised thereby.

12. Wherefore lift up the hands which hang down, and the feeble knees;

13. And make straight paths for your feet, lest that which is lame be turned out of the way; but let it rather be healed.

14. Follow peace with all *men*, and holiness, without which no man shall see the Lord:

(v. 8) or **bastards** (*nothos*).

Since a worthy earthly father corrects his sons, it should not surprise the spiritual sons of God to learn that their heavenly Father chastens them. Such knowledge will help believers to be genuinely **in subjection** or submissive as true sons.

**10, 11.** The illustration leads into a contrast. **They . . . he.** Earthly fathers exercise their fatherly prerogative only for a short time and for immediate ends, but God has both holy lives and eternal ends in view.

Neither in the earthly sphere nor in the heavenly sphere is chastening appreciated at the time, but the final results more than warrant the discipline. In the heavenly or spiritual realm it yields **peaceable fruit, even that of righteousness.** Adversity and chastening, then, are a form of training.

F. Christian Conduct Under the New Covenant. 12:12-29.

The first thing for believers to do is to put away discouragement and complaining in adverse circumstances. The life of faith is not easy, nor does it become easier.

**12, 13.** They are to accept the discipline of adversity and be strengthened through it. They are to be strong in the midst of trial. **Lift up the hands.** Or, *make straight, strengthen,* as one made strong through difficulty. Relaxed hands and **palsied knees,** or *stumbling* knees, do not describe the patient endurance required to finish the course. In so strengthening the hands and knees, any lameness brought on by disuse will be healed. There is a possible suggestion here that joints not firmly held and muscles not properly tensed might suffer dislocation, or a sprain (*ektrapē*). True strength of character is shown in so gathering oneself together in time of adversity.

**14, 15.** Human relationships improve when the nature of adversity is understood. **Follow after peace with all men** (ASV). As one seeking harmony, as one having a peaceful spirit, and as one who desires unity and fellowship among the righteous. **Men.** Better omitted. **And holiness.** The covering or comprehensive term (*hagiasmon,* "sanctification"). **Lord** (*kyrion*) is more probably God than Christ. Certainly one of the essential proofs of new life in Christ lies in the

15. Looking diligently lest any man fail of the grace of God; lest any root of bitterness springing up trouble *you*, and thereby many be defiled;

16. Lest there *be* any fornicator, or profane person, as Esau, who for one morsel of meat sold his birthright.

17. For ye know how that afterward, when he would have inherited the blessing, he was rejected: for he found no place of repentance, though he sought it carefully with tears.

18. For ye are not come unto the mount that might be touched, and that burned with fire, nor unto blackness, and darkness, and tempest,

19. And the sound of a trumpet, and the voice of words; which *voice* they that heard entreated that the word should not be spoken to them any more:

20. (For they could not endure that which was commanded, And if so much as a beast touch the mountain, it shall be stoned, or thrust through with a dart:

21. And so terrible was the sight, *that* Moses said, I exceedingly fear and quake:)

22. But ye are come unto mount Sion, and unto the city of the living God, the heavenly Jerusalem, and to an innumerable company of angels,

23. To the general assembly and church of the firstborn, which are written in heaven, and to God the Judge of all, and to the spirits of just men made perfect,

24. And to Jesus the mediator of the new covenant, and to the blood of sprinkling, that speaketh better things than *that of* Abel.

way believers get along with each other.

The antithesis follows. Here is one who comes short, who fails because deep within him is a **root of bitterness** that poisons everything and everyone—thereby **many be defiled.** This root of bitterness is like an infection that spreads through the whole community *(hoi polloi)* of believers. Notice, this describes a breakdown in human relations among believers because one believer has become bitter.

**16, 17.** Esau serves as the example of the hopelessness of such a condition. By his own choice he became a **profane person**, or lover of the earthly and sensual, so that he lost both birthright and spiritual sensitivity. This latter condition, particularly, is the antithesis of the standard held up in verse 14. Esau exchanged peace and holiness for immediate and earthly pleasures.

When Esau attempted to change his condition, he found it impossible to do so. Whether the blessing of God or repentance was the object of his **tears**, it was too late. Esau was guilty of willful sin, from the consequences of which he found no deliverance. This is the lesson to the Hebrews who were contemplating an act of willful sin in the form of apostasy back to Mosaic tradition. To the writer the illustration-warning seemed obvious.

**18-24.** The exhortation continues with what Davidson calls "a grand finale to the strain . . . to hold fast their confession." Sinai and Mount Zion are placed in contrast to each other. The setting of the giving of the Law was (1) a mount **that burned with fire**, enveloped in **blackness, darkness, tempest,** and (2) **the sound of a trumpet, and the voice of words.** In this setting Moses was so overcome by the presence of God that he greatly feared and trembled (cf. Ex 19:12 ff. and Deut 9:19).

**But ye are come** introduces all the blessed realities and personages of the new covenant. Heaven is set against earth, the phenomenal against the superearthly, the glory of Sinai against the infinitely greater glory of the blood-sprinkled way. **Zion . . . the city of the living God, the heavenly Jerusalem . . . hosts of angels . . . the church of the firstborn . . . God the Judge . . . just men made perfect . . . Jesus the mediator of a new covenant** (ASV order) — these make a purposely impressive list because of the contrast intended. Again, the thought is transparent. Surely these marvels and

**25.** See that ye refuse not him that speaketh: for if they escaped not who refused him that spake on earth, much more *shall not* we *escape*, if we turn away from him that *speaketh* from heaven:

**26.** Whose voice then shook the earth: but now he hath promised, saying, Yet once more I shake not the earth only, but also heaven.

**27.** And this *word*, Yet once more, signifieth the removing of those things that are shaken, as of things that are made, that those things which cannot be shaken may remain.

**28.** Wherefore we receiving a kingdom which cannot be moved, let us have grace, whereby we may serve God acceptably with reverence and godly fear:

**29.** For our God *is* a consuming fire.

### CHAPTER 13

LET brotherly love continue.

**2.** Be not forgetful to entertain strangers: for thereby some have entertained angels unawares.

**3.** Remember them that are in bonds, as bound with them; *and* them which suffer adversity, as being yourselves also in the body.

blessings far outweigh the temporary respite to be gained through returning to Judaism to escape persecution. Men of faith have this bright hope under the new covenant. Men of faith have already entered that glad company of the firstborn, the just men made perfect *(prōtotokōn* and *teteleiōmenōn,* "firstborn and perfected," as in Alf and Arndt. See also Davidson, *Epistle to the Hebrews,* pp. 245-250).

**25-29.** Heed Christ. Do not refuse the voice of Christ speaking through the Gospel. If peril came to those who refused the voice of God at Sinai, how much greater peril must come to those who refuse or reject God's messenger, his own Son (1:2). This refusal is akin to that of the men invited to the "great supper" of Luke 14:16, who "all . . . began to make excuses" *(paraiteomai).* See Lk 14:18, where the same word appears (Arndt).

Judgment is then described, perhaps the last judgment. The earth will be shaken, and the impermanent will vanish in the shaking; only the permanent and eternal will remain — a kingdom that cannot be shaken (ASV). This kingdom will be given by God, not conceived by man. Membership in it through faith in Christ ought to result in glad service and reverent worship on the part of all.

The final word is again that of warning. **For indeed our God is a consuming fire** (cf. Deut 4:24). Fire is the final form of judgment (Rev 20:10,14).

G. The Christian Life in Daily Practice. 13:1-17.

The Christian life is sketched out in its bearing on the believer's relations with other people.

**1-6.** The normal situations are mentioned first. As in the later epistle of I John, **love of the brethren,** or *your brotherly affection* (CGT) is to **continue.** One of the constant evidences of a healthy Christian life is the manner in which Christian brethren get along with one another. Because of the lack of public resting places, hospitality is also enjoined, particularly with reference to strangers who know Christ. Matthew 25:35-40 offers the closest parallel to **entertained angels unawares** *(elathon,* "unconsciously").

These social duties or human relations are further expanded to include persons in prison — **them that are in bonds.** The expression **as bound with them** carries

4. Marriage *is* honorable in all, and the bed undefiled: but whoremongers and adulterers God will judge.

5. *Let your* conversation *be* without covetousness; *and be* content with such things as ye have: for he hath said, I will never leave thee, nor forsake thee.

6. So that we may boldly say, The Lord *is* my helper, and I will not fear what man shall do unto me.

7. Remember them which have the rule over you, who have spoken unto you the word of God: whose faith follow, considering the end of *their* conversation.

the thought of both sympathy and identity. Believers are to share with the prisoner as though they themselves were prisoners. The modern use of "identify" covers the idea. As long as believers are confined in the earthly body, it is possible for each one to suffer either adversity or imprisonment. Therefore, they must be sympathetic.

Then, of course, the closest human relationship, marriage, ought to exhibit to all the graces of the Christian life. If these Hebrews were in Rome or in some of the more notorious cities of the Mediterranean East, they were in a society in which chastity and honor in marriage were commonly disregarded. On the other hand, some religious sects or groups taught celibacy and asceticism. Celibacy is not a safeguard against immorality; but rather honorable marriage is the most wholesome life. Chastity in the bonds of marriage constitutes strong Christian witness. Profligate and licentious people must someday face their sins and practices before God.

As regards money, the writer warns: **Be ye free from the love of money** (ASV). *Aphilargyros* means "not money-loving," rather than *not covetous,* as in the AV. The manner of life (**conversation,** AV) or disposition to be cultivated is contentment with things present, or **such things as ye have.** If the torrents of abuse flung at these Jewish Christians by others more prosperous included references to their lack of prosperity, this came as a very practical and thoroughly NT bit of advice. It is still timely. Instead of taking comfort in possessions, Christians are to derive their comfort from God's own presence and provision, for he neither leaves them nor fails them. Thus **we may boldly say ... I will not fear. What shall man do unto me?** The last clause is properly a question (ASV). Joshua 23:14 and Psalm 118:6 testify to the faithfulness of God.

**7-9.** In the Church, especially, all the Christian graces ought to be found. Remember the example, says the author, of those who first taught you Christian truth. They were noted for presenting a true message and a godly example. They spoke God's word and lived holy lives right up to their "exit" or the end of life on the earth. **Imitate their faith** (ASV).

Their example and yours, he continues, is the unchanging person of the Lord Jesus Christ. He is the same; his purposes are the same; his goals are un-

8. Jesus Christ the same yesterday, and to-day, and for ever.

9. Be not carried about with divers and strange doctrines: for *it is* a good thing that the heart be established with grace; not with meats, which have not profited them that have been occupied therein.

10. We have an altar, whereof they have no right to eat which serve the tabernacle.

11. For the bodies of those beasts, whose blood is brought into the sanctuary by the high priest for sin, are burned without the camp.

12. Wherefore Jesus also, that he might sanctify the people with his own blood, suffered without the gate.

13. Let us go forth therefore unto him without the camp, bearing his reproach.

14. For here have we no continuing city, but we seek one to come.

15. By him therefore let us offer the sacrifice of praise to God continually, that is, the fruit of *our* lips, giving thanks to his name.

16. But to do good and to communicate forget not: for with such sacrifices God is well pleased.

17. Obey them that have the rule over you, and submit yourselves: for they watch for your souls, as they that must give account, that they may do it with joy, and not with grief: for that *is* unprofitable for you.

18. Pray for us: for we trust we have a good conscience, in all things willing to live honestly.

changing. **Jesus Christ** [is] **the same yester-day, and to day, and for ever,** thus sustaining and supporting the claims of verse 7. Allegiance to Christ, who is unchanging, should result in clarity of doctrine. Then none will be **carried away,** or turned aside by strange teaching or strange practice in the name of the Gospel. The contradictions of human teachers, externalism, and the embryonic works-righteousness practice of abstaining from certain foods should be avoided.

10-17. We do not now make sacrifice; we have a sacrifice already made for us in Christ; hence **we have an altar.** The OT ordinances as here described no longer avail. When Christ suffered death **outside the gate** on the cross, one of the things accomplished was the setting aside of the Levitical customs. They are now superfluous. The believer's identification is with Christ *outside* or **without the gate.** This means rejection of Judaism on the one hand and rejection by the Jews on the other. For these Hebrew Christians, this was the **reproach** they were to bear.

Because of Christ's death as a sin offering, or **through him,** believers are to demonstrate conduct befitting redeemed ones (vv. 14-17). (1) They are to fix their hope not in the OT ordinances, but in the heavenly city and in the heavenly prospect; (2) they are to give praise and thanksgiving to God, since the fruit of the lips ought to be the overflow of the full heart; (3) they must show benevolence of all sorts or kinds, which God will not forget; and (4) they are to be obedient and submissive. Pleasing God might ultimately be reduced to three fundamental practices or attitudes, all of which are named in this passage — praise, obedience, and submission. These need little comment in light of NT truth. Benevolence naturally follows. In verse 17 submission practically relates to the attitude of believers to their own leaders. With these words of responsibility laid on followers and leaders alike, the writer closes the practical or exhortatory composition that began with 10:19. The rest is personal.

### IV. Personal Epilogue. 13:18-25.

With a few personal requests, a subscription and salutations, and a brief benediction, the writer concludes.

18,19. **Pray for us.** A personal request. The writer asks to be remembered as to

**19.** But I beseech *you* the rather to do this, that I may be restored to you the sooner.

**20.** Now the God of peace, that brought again from the dead our Lord Jesus, that great shepherd of the sheep, through the blood of the everlasting covenant,

**21.** Make you perfect in every good work to do his will, working in you that which is well-pleasing in his sight, through Jesus Christ; to whom *be* glory for ever and ever. Amen.

**22.** And I beseech you, brethren, suffer the word of exhortation: for I have written a letter unto you in few words.

**23.** Know ye that *our* brother Timothy is set at liberty; with whom, if he come shortly, I will see you.

**24.** Salute all them that have the rule over you, and all the saints. They of Italy salute you.

**25.** Grace *be* with you all. Amen.

Written to the Hebrews from Italy by Timothy.

(1) his personal life, testimony, and service; and (2) his desire that he might soon be among them in person. This was a specific prayer request.

**20,21.** He promises that he, in turn, will pray for them, particularly concerning their obedience to the will of God. This subscription in the form of a prayer should have been a particular blessing to those who heard or who read it. It speaks of:

(1) Comfort, for, in and under persecution, they had access to and fellowship with the **God of peace.**

(2) Hope in Christ resurrected; literally, **brought up from the dead.**

(3) Personal and pastoral care in **our Lord Jesus, that great shepherd of the sheep.**

(4) Doctrine and theology. All of the comfort, hope, and pastoral care is sealed and guaranteed by the **blood of the everlasting covenant.**

Certain personal requests and wishes follow:

(1) **Make you perfect in every good work** (v. 21) or more correctly, *God make up to you,* or *in you, what you lack.* This request conveys the writer's desire that the believers might be fully fitted for their task, having no weaknesses, faults, or lacks. Believers need to be **made complete** *(katartizo).*

(2) To know and to be doing the whole will of God. Because God works in us, we desire to work for him in devoted surrender and obedience.

(3) To please God through Jesus Christ. Only the indwelling Son working in us by the Holy Spirit and through the Word of God can so make us pleasing to God. Let this request be the cry of our hearts.

**22-25.** Perhaps we have here the key verse of the epistle (see Introd., *The Argument of the Epistle)* as the writer begs his readers to accept his **exhortation.** He expresses the hope that he and Timothy may soon be able to visit them. He sends a general Christian greeting to them, and adds the indefinite **they of Italy salute you,** or *those who are from Italy salute you,* a general statement indicating that friends from Italy known to the writer wished to be included in the Christian greeting.

The closing words are a benediction in the form of a brief prayer, **Grace be with you all. Amen.**

941

# BIBLIOGRAPHY

ARCHER, GLEASON L., JR. *The Epistle to the Hebrews: A Study Manual.* Grand Rapids: Baker Book House, 1957.

BRUCE, A. B. *The Epistle to the Hebrews: The First Apology for Christianity.* Edinburgh: T. & T. Clark, 1899.

DAVIDSON, A. B. *The Epistle to the Hebrews.* Edinburgh: T. & T. Clark, 1921.

DELITZSCH, FRANZ. *Commentary on the Hebrews.* 2 vols. Grand Rapids: Wm. B. Eerdman's Publishing Company, reprinted 1952.

DOWNER, ARTHUR CLEVELAND. *The Principles of Interpretation of the Epistle of the Hebrews.* London: Charles Murray, n.d.

FARRAR, F. W. *The Epistle of Paul the Apostle to the Hebrews (Cambridge Bible for Schools and Colleges).* Cambridge: The University Press, 1883.

———. *The Epistle of Paul the Apostle to the Hebrews.* Cambridge: The University Press, 1896.

HERKLESS, J. (ed.). *Hebrews and the Epistles General of Peter, James and Jude.* London: J. M. Dent, 1902.

LEONARD, WILLIAM. *Authorship of the Epistle to the Hebrews: Critical Problem and Use of the Old Testament.* Vatican: Polyglot Press, 1939.

MANSON, WILLIAM. *The Epistle to the Hebrews, An Historical and Theological Reinterpretation.* London: Hodder and Stoughton, 1951.

MICKELSEN, A. BERKELEY. "Hebrews," *The Biblical Expositor: The Living Theme of the Great Book.* Vol. III. Philadelphia: A. J. Holman, 1960.

MOLL, CARL BERNHARD. "Epistle to the Hebrews," *Commentary on the Holy Scriptures, Critical, Doctrinal and Homiletical.* Edited by John Peter Lange. Grand Rapids: The Zondervan Publishing House, reprint.

NAIRNE, ALEXANDER. *The Epistle of Priesthood: Studies in the Epistle to the Hebrews.* Edinburgh: T. & T. Clark, 1913.

PURDY, ALEXANDER C. and COTTON, J. HARRY. "The Epistle to the Hebrews," *Interpreter's Bible.* Vol. 11. New York: Abingdon, 1955.

SCHNEIDER, JOHANNES. *The Letter to the Hebrews.* Grand Rapids: Wm. B. Eerdman's Publishing Company, 1957.

WESTCOTT, BROOKE FOSS. *The Epistle to the Hebrews.* Grand Rapids: Wm. B. Eerdman's Publishing Company, reprinted 1950.

# THE EPISTLE OF JAMES

## INTRODUCTION

*Authorship*. The superscription indicates that the author of the Epistle of James was **James, a servant of God and of the Lord Jesus Christ.** But who was this James? Of the numerous men bearing this name in the New Testament, only two have been proposed as the author of this epistle—James, son of Zebedee, and James, the Lord's brother. The former is an unlikely candidate. He was martyred in A.D. 44, and there is no evidence that he had attained a position of leadership in the church that would warrant his writing a general letter. Although Isidore of Seville and Dante thought him to be the author of the book, this identity has not been widely accepted in any age of the church. The traditional view identifies the author with James, the Lord's brother. The similarity of the language of the epistle with James' speech in Acts 15, the heavy dependence of the writer on Jewish tradition, and the consistency of the contents of his letter with the historical notices in the New Testament concerning James, the Lord's brother, all tend to support the traditional authorship.

*Date and Place of Writing*. A wide range of opinion prevails on the date of James. Those who accept the traditional authorship usually date it either in the middle forties or early sixties (just before James' death). It has been dated as late as A.D. 150 by those who hold to the "unknown James" or pseudonymous authorship theory.

Although we cannot be dogmatic about the time of writing, a number of factors point toward an early date. The social conditions revealed in the epistle, especially the sharp cleavage between the rich and poor, suggest a date before the destruction of Jerusalem. The eschatology revealed also points to an early date. The expectation of the Lord's return rates in intensity with that found in I and II Thessalonians. There is no suggestion of belief in a delayed return, such as we find in some of the late books of the New Testament; and there are no apocalyptic visions or similar developments, such as those found in late apocalyptic literature. James' readers were living in the active and powerful expectation of Christ's imminent return. There is nothing in the Christian literature of the second century that can match the simple and powerful eschatological teaching of this epistle.

The most crucial passage for dating the book is the famous one on faith and works (Jas 2:14-26). To understand these verses the reader must be acquainted with certain Pauline formulas; yet it is hard to believe that the author of 2:14-26 is refuting Paul. This would involve an almost inconceivable miscomprehension of the Pauline doctrine of justification by faith. The passage is best explained as having been occasioned by a misunderstanding of Paul, not on the part of the author of the epistle, but on the part of his readers. Such misunderstanding would most likely have arisen at the very outset of Paul's public preaching ministry. According to the book of Acts, Paul's first extended public preaching occurred at Antioch (Acts 11:26). This year-long ministry took place before the famine visit to Jerusalem of about 46 (cf. Acts 11:27-29; Gal 2:1-10) and the Herodian persecution of 44. How long it was before the misunderstanding and misapplication of Paul's doctrine of justification by faith came to the attention of James, we do not know. In view of the fact that Jews, both Christian and non-Christian, from all over the Mediterranean world, were constantly moving in and out of Jerusalem, it probably was not long. A date of about 44 for the epistle, during or immediately following the Herodian persecution, would best fit all the known factors.

Although a number of opposing suggestions have been made from time to time, there can be little doubt that James was written from Palestine. Especially in the local coloring suggested, the writer indicates that he is a Palestinian (cf. 1:10,11; 3:11,12; 5:7).

*The Recipients of the Letter*. The only direct hint in the book which possibly suggests who the readers were is found in the superscription: **James, a servant of God and of the Lord Jesus Christ, to the twelve tribes which are scattered abroad, greeting.** Traditionally the phrase, **the**

**twelve tribes,** was used to indicate the entirety of the Jewish nation (cf. the noncanonical Ecclesiasticus 44:23; The Assumption of Moses 2:4,5; Baruch 1:2; 62:5; 63:3; 64:3; 77:2; 78:4; 84:3; also see Acts 26:7). But since the entire Jewish nation, no matter how widely it may have been scattered in the Diaspora, could not have been considered to have its entire existence outside of Palestine, it seems best to understand the superscription symbolically. James was writing to the entire church, considered as the New Israel (cf. Gal 3:7-9; 6:16; Phil 3:3), dispersed in an alien and hostile world (cf. I Pet 1:1,17; 2:11; Phil 3:20; Gal 4:26; Heb 12:22; 13:14). There are many indications in the epistle, however, that it is addressed primarily to Jews who are Christians. This may be a further indication of an early date, since the only time in the history of the church when one could address the entire church and be speaking almost exclusively to Jews, was *before* Paul's first mission to the Gentiles—which occurred about 47.

*Contents.* The Epistle of James is a plea for vital Christianity. Herder caught the tenor of this book when he wrote: "What a noble man speaks in this Epistle! Deep unbroken patience in suffering! Greatness in poverty! Joy in sorrow! Simplicity, sincerity, direct confidence in prayer! How he wants action! Action, not words . . . not dead faith!" (quoted by F. W. Farrar in *The Early Days of Christianity*, p. 324).

In the true spirit of the Wisdom literature, James handles many different subjects. His short, abrupt paragraphs have been likened to a string of pearls—each is a separate entity in itself. There are some logical transitions, but for the most part transitions are abrupt or missing entirely. This phenomenon makes an outline in the usual sense impossible. There follows, however, a listing of the subjects dealt with in the order of their occurrence in the epistle.

# OUTLINE

# JAMES

## CHAPTER 1

JAMES, a servant of God and of the Lord Jesus Christ, to the twelve tribes which are scattered abroad, greeting.

2. My brethren, count it all joy when ye fall into divers temptations;

# COMMENTARY

### I. Salutation. 1:1.

James simply calls himself a servant of God and of the Lord Jesus Christ. His readers are the twelve tribes which are scattered abroad, a symbolic designation for the Christian church conceived of as the New Israel, its members scattered abroad in an alien and hostile world. Thus James does not have in mind a single congregation but the church at large throughout the Mediterranean world. His salutation (chairein) is the typical one found in Greek letters and the same one used in the letter that was sent out from the Jerusalem church over which James presided (Acts 15:23).

### II. Trials. 1:2-8.

2. James frequently (at least sixteen times) addresses his readers as brethren.

3. Knowing *this*, that the trying of your faith worketh patience.

4. But let patience have *her* perfect work, that ye may be perfect and entire, wanting nothing.

5. If any of you lack wisdom, let him ask of God, that giveth to all *men* liberally, and upbraideth not; and it shall be given him.

6. But let him ask in faith, nothing wavering: for he that wavereth is like a wave of the sea driven with the wind and tossed.

7. For let not that man think that he shall receive any thing of the Lord.

8. A double-minded man *is* unstable in all his ways.

9. Let the brother of low degree rejoice in that he is exalted:

He and his readers were bound together by a common loyalty to Jesus Christ. His first word is one of encouragement—count it all joy when ye fall into divers temptations. The RSV renders more adequately, *when you meet various trials.* The word *peirasmos* ("trial") has two meanings. Here it means "external adversities," whereas in verses 13,14 it means "inner impulse to evil," "temptation."

3. The Christian is to be joyful *in* trial not *because of* trial. There was a great need in the early days of the church for teaching along these lines because of the successive waves of persecution. The fruit of trial is patience (*hypomonē*), or better, *endurance.* James Moffatt (*The General Epistles,* p. 9) calls it "the staying power of life." 4. This endurance must be allowed to have its full scope (**perfect work**). It is a process that goes on in the life of a Christian, its goal being perfection (*teleios* is better rendered *maturity*). The writer may have had in mind the words of our Lord recorded in Mt 5:48.

5-8. There seems to be a connection between this paragraph and what precedes. James has been talking about the purpose of trial. He anticipates that some of his readers will say that they cannot discover any divine purpose in their hardships. In that case, he says, they are to ask God for wisdom, i.e., practical insights into life (not theoretical knowledge), and God will grant such a request **liberally** (RSV, *generously*), and will not upbraid or reproach them. There is, however, a condition set down. The request must be made **in faith, nothing wavering** (RSV, *with no doubting*). The man who comes to God with his request must be sure that he wants what he requests. James likens a doubting man to a **wave of the sea driven** to and fro by the wind. Such a man "cannot hope to receive anything from God" (Phillips). He is a **double minded man,** i.e., a man of divided allegiance. He has mental reservations both about prayer itself and about the requests he makes of God.

### III. Poverty and Wealth. 1:9-11.

9. This paragraph arises out of James' discussion of trial. Poverty is an external adversity. The poor Christian is to **rejoice** in his new status in Jesus Christ. This relationship has brought him true wealth. He is an heir of God and a joint heir with Jesus Christ!

10. But the rich, in that he is made low: because as the flower of the grass he shall pass away.

11. For the sun is no sooner risen with a burning heat, but it withereth the grass, and the flower thereof falleth, and the grace of the fashion of it perisheth: so also shall the rich man fade away in his ways.

12. Blessed *is* the man that endureth temptation: for when he is tried, he shall receive the crown of life, which the Lord hath promised to them that love him.

13. Let no man say when he is tempted, I am tempted of God: for God cannot be tempted with evil, neither tempteth he any man:

14. But every man is tempted, when he is drawn away of his own lust, and enticed.

15. Then when lust hath conceived, it bringeth forth sin; and sin, when it is finished, bringeth forth death.

**10,11.** A rich Christian, on the other hand, is to rejoice "that in Christ he has been brought down to a level where the 'deceitfulness of riches' (Mk 4:19) and the anxiety to amass and retain them are no longer primary or even relevant considerations" (R. V. G. Tasker, *The General Epistle of James,* p. 43). Furthermore, riches are temporary. They are like the green grass and its flowers, which quickly turn brown under the heat of the Palestinian sun. *Kausōn* (**burning heat**) is used here simply of the heat of the sun and not of the sirocco, the hot desert wind that blows across Palestine from the east (cf. J. Schneider, TWNT, III, 644).

## IV. Trial and Temptation. 1:12-18.

**12.** The reward for faithfully enduring trials is stated in terms both of the present and of the future. The man who endures is truly happy now; but also he **shall receive the crown of life, which the Lord hath promised to them that love him.** The genitive (**of life**) is in apposition to **crown.** The crown consists of life, a gift to all those who love God. Tasker (*op. cit.,* p. 45) pointedly comments that although neither our faith nor our love wins for us eternal life, yet it is "an axiom of the Bible that God has abundant blessings in store for those who love him, keep his commandments, and serve him faithfully whatever the cost may be (cf. Mt. 19:28; I Cor. 2:9)."

**13.** James now makes the transition from outward to inner trials, i.e., temptations. The word **temptation** (v. 12) carries the idea of luring one into sin. James probably had in mind the Jewish doctrine of the *Yetzer ha ra'*, "evil impulse." Some Jews reasoned that since God created everything, he must have created the evil impulse. And since it is the evil impulse that tempts man to sin, ultimately God, who created it, is responsible for evil. James here refutes that idea. **God cannot be tempted with evil, neither tempteth he any man. 14.** Instead of blaming God for evil, man must take personal responsibility for his sins. It is his own **lust** by which he is **drawn away** and **enticed.** These are primarily hunting and fishing words, used metaphorically here. **15.** When evil desire arises in the mind, it does not stop there. **Lust** gives birth to sin, and sin produces death. "Death is thus the mature or finished product of sin" (Moffatt, *op. cit.,* p. 19). Death is here spiritual death in contrast to the

16. Do not err, my beloved brethren.

17. Every good gift and every perfect gift is from above, and cometh down from the Father of lights, with whom is no variableness, neither shadow of turning.

18. Of his own will begat he us with the word of truth, that we should be a kind of firstfruits of his creatures.

19. Wherefore, my beloved brethren, let every man be swift to hear, slow to speak, slow to wrath:

20. For the wrath of man worketh not the righteousness of God.

21. Wherefore lay apart all filthiness and superfluity of naughtiness, and receive with meekness the engrafted word, which is able to save your souls.

life God gives to those that love him (1:12).

**16,17.** The point the writer makes is that God, instead of being the source of temptation, as some were contending, is the source of all good in the experience of men. James was especially desirous that his readers realize this, and so he addressed them with the tender, **my beloved brethren. Father of lights** is a reference to the creative activity of God. Such a title for God was not unknown in Jewish thought (cf. SBK, III, 752). Although there is considerable question as to the correct reading of the last part of verse 17, the meaning is clear enough: God is completely consistent; he does not change.

In James 1:18 the writer climaxes his refutation of the idea that God is the author of temptation. He has already shown that such a charge is contrary to the nature of God (1:13) and to His consistent goodness (1:17). Now he appeals to his readers' experience in the Gospel. J. B. Mayor (*The Epistle of St. James*, p. 62) aptly states the point of this verse: "So far from God's tempting us to evil, His will is the cause of our regeneration." These early Christians were called **firstfruits** because they were a guarantee of many more to come.

## V. Reception of the Word. 1:19-25.

**19.** There is a possible connection between this paragraph and what precedes. The strong admonition to be **swift to hear, slow to speak, slow to wrath** may be a reference to the readers' accusations against God. Or it may be simply a general statement about hearing and speaking. **20.** When a Christian gives vent to **wrath,** he is incapable of acting justly or righteously; and in addition, he prevents, or at least hinders, the vindication of God's righteousness in the world. **21. Lay apart all filthiness.** Since the Word is a seed, it must have good soil in which to thrive. "Have done, then," says James, "with impurity and every other evil" (Phillips). **Superfluity of naughtiness** might suggest that only excess of evil is to be put away. However, Tasker rightly takes **superfluity** to mean "remainder." "Every converted Christian brings with him into his new life much that is inconsistent with it. This has to be laid aside, that he may give himself more completely to the positive work of receiving **with meekness the engrafted** (RV, rightly *implanted*) **word**" (*op. cit.*,

22. But be ye doers of the word, and not hearers only, deceiving your own selves.

23. For if any be a hearer of the word, and not a doer, he is like unto a man beholding his natural face in a glass:

24. For he beholdeth himself, and goeth his way, and straightway forgetteth what manner of man he was.

25. But whoso looketh into the perfect law of liberty, and continueth *therein*, he being not a forgetful hearer, but a doer of the work, this man shall be blessed in his deed.

26. If any man among you seem to be religious, and bridleth not his tongue, but deceiveth his own heart, this man's religion *is* vain.

27. Pure religion and undefiled before God and the Father is this, To visit the fatherless and widows in their affliction, *and* to keep himself unspotted from the world.

p. 51). This word is **able to save** his **soul. 22.** Christianity is a religion of action. As important as it is to listen (cf. 1:19), one must not stop there. Doing must follow listening. To be a hearer only is a form of self-deception.

**23,24.** The hearing-but-not-doing man is like a person who sees the reflection of his own face in a mirror. "He sees himself, it is true, but he goes on with whatever he was doing without the slightest recollection of what sort of person he saw in the mirror" (Phillips). The tenses in this verse are interesting: **beholdeth** (aorist), **goeth** (perfect), **forgetteth** (aorist). "By the aorists he [James] shows that the impression was momentary, and the oblivion instantaneous; by the perfect he implies a continuing condition of absence from the mirror" (H. Maynard Smith, *The Epistle of St. James*, p. 85).

**25.** The mirror, which reveals the imperfections of the outer man, is now contrasted with the **perfect law,** the law of freedom, which reflects the inner man. This is the first reference to law in the epistle (cf. 2:8-12; 4:11). James uses the term to denote the ethical side of Christianity, the *didachē,* "teaching." Here he calls the law **perfect.** Compare Ps 19:7: "The law of the Lord is perfect, converting the soul." James, as a Jew, writing to Jews, is deliberately ascribing to *didachē* the attributes of the law. To James it is perfect because it was made perfect by Jesus Christ. **Law of liberty** probably means that it is a law that applies to those who have the status of freedom, not from law, but from sin and self, through the word of truth. The man who looks into this law and makes a habit of doing so *(parameinas)* will become a **doer of the work** and find true happiness (**shall be blessed in his deed**).

### VI. True Religion. 1:26,27.

**26.** The author now moves from the more general "not hearing but doing" to the more specific "not mere worship but doing." The word **religious** *(thrēskos)* means "given to religious observances." In this context it refers to attendance at worship services and to other observances of religion, such as prayer, almsgiving, and fasting. A man who is scrupulous in these observances but fails to control his speech in everyday life deceives himself, and his religion is vain (Moffat, *futile*).

**27.** "This is not a definition of religion, but a statement . . . of what is better than external acts of worship. James had

## CHAPTER 2

MY brethren, have not the faith of our Lord Jesus Christ, *the Lord* of glory, with respect of persons.

2. For if there come unto your assembly a man with a gold ring, in goodly apparel, and there come in also a poor man in vile raiment;

no idea of reducing religion to a negative purity of conduct supplemented by charity-visiting" (James H. Ropes, *The Epistle of St. James*, p. 182). Since orphans and widows were not provided for in ancient society, they were typical examples of those who needed help. In addition to extending charity, maintaining personal purity is another way in which true religion expresses itself. The world here and in 4:4 refers to pagan society opposed, or at least alien, to God.

### VII. Social Distinctions and "The Royal Law." 2:1-13.

**1.** The emphasis on the importance of conduct is continued in this paragraph. Here it is applied to partiality. **My brethren** marks the transition to a new subject (cf. 1:2,19; 2:14; 3:1; 5:1). The AV rightly translates the verb in the imperative (the other possibility being the indicative) in keeping with James' direct manner of writing. It is not certain how the genitive **Lord Jesus Christ** qualifies **faith.** G. Rendall suggests the possibility of regarding the genitive as qualitative, "as defining the particular character of their faith in God. 'The faith in God which has for its support and content our Lord Jesus Christ,' that is the Christian kind of faith in God" (*The Epistle of St. James and Judaic Christianity*, p. 46). It is probably easier, however, to take the genitive as objective — "your faith in our Lord Jesus Christ." Whichever way it is taken, the faith is dynamic faith, trust, directed towards the Lord Jesus Christ. It has nothing whatever to do with the later idea of faith as a body of doctrine to be believed. In the last part of the verse the AV has **the Lord of,** which does not occur in the original. Jesus is here called simply "the glory," an obvious reference to the Shekinah (cf. Jn 1:14; II Cor 4:6; Heb 1:3). The main point of this verse is that it is inconsistent to hold to the Christian faith and at the same time show partiality.

**2.** The writer now cites an illustration to drive home the point. A wealthy man wearing a **gold ring** and dressed in fine clothing (ASV) and a **poor man** dressed in **vile,** *shabby* (RSV), clothing enter into the Christian assembly (*synagōgē*). The use of this word for the Christian place of meeting has given rise to much conjecture about the author and the readers of the epistle; but as Blackman says, "It must be remembered that the two words *synagōgē* and *ekklēsia* are roughly synon-

3. And ye have respect to him that weareth the gay clothing, and say unto him, Sit thou here in a good place; and say to the poor, Stand thou there, or sit here under my footstool:

4. Are ye not then partial in yourselves, and are become judges of evil thoughts?

5. Hearken, my beloved brethren, Hath not God chosen the poor of this world rich in faith, and heirs of the kingdom which he hath promised to them that love him?

6. But ye have despised the poor. Do not rich men oppress you, and draw you before the judgment seats?

7. Do not they blaspheme that worthy name by the which ye are called?

8. If ye fulfil the royal law according to the Scripture, Thou shalt love thy neighbor as thyself, ye do well:

9. But if ye have respect to persons, ye commit sin, and are convinced of the law as transgressors.

10. For whosoever shall keep the whole law, and yet offend in one *point*, he is guilty of all.

ymous, and it is conceivable that *synagōgē* and not *ekklēsia* might have become the Church's regular term for itself. Thus it is possible to take the use of the word here by James as a survival from the time when usage was fluid" (*The Epistle of James*, p. 77). The author uses *ekklēsia* in 5:14. **3.** The rich man is given preferential treatment. He is offered the best seat (*kalōs*). There is a possibility that *kalōs* should be translated "please," as in the RSV. In either case the rich man gets special treatment, while the poor man is abruptly told to stand, or at best, to sit on the floor **under my footstool,** i.e., in a lowly place.

**4.** The verb translated, **Are ye not then partial . . . ?** is passive and should be translated as in the ASV margin, "Are ye not divided?" The division is "between profession and practice, between the profession of Christian equality and the deference to rank and wealth" (Richard Knowling, *The Epistle of St. James*, p. 44). By such action they also reveal themselves to be judges *with* (not of) **evil thoughts,** i.e., false-value judges.

**5.** Those who grant special treatment to the rich fail to take into consideration that **God** has **chosen the poor of this world** (*poor as to the world*, RV) to be **rich in faith, and heirs of the kingdom which he hath promised to those that love him. 6.** Another reason why it is inconsistent to show special favor to the rich is that they have been the very ones who have persecuted the Christians. **Judgment seats** is a reference to Jewish courts allowed and recognized under Roman law. **7.** The climax of James' argument against favoring the rich is that **they blaspheme that worthy name.** It is not the name 'Christian' that is blasphemed but the name of Jesus Christ, the **worthy name by the which ye are called** (ASV, *which was called upon you*).

**8.** **The royal law** is connected with the statement in 2:5, where James reminds his readers that God has chosen the poor to be **heirs of the kingdom. The royal law,** then, is for those of God's kingdom. By translating the Greek particle *mentoi* "really," the RSV rightly points out that James thinks that his readers, by showing partiality to the rich, are not fulfilling this law. **9.** For love shows no **respect of persons.** Indeed, partiality is **sin.** The **law** here is not the OT law as such (although Lev 19:15 deals with partiality) but the *didachē*, the whole spirit of which is contrary to partiality.

**10.** The idea of the solidarity of the

11. For he that said, Do not commit adultery, said also, Do not kill. Now if thou commit no adultery, yet if thou kill, thou art become a transgressor of the law.

12. So speak ye, and so do, as they that shall be judged by the law of liberty.

13. For he shall have judgment without mercy, that hath showed no mercy; and mercy rejoiceth against judgment.

14. What *doth it* profit, my brethren, though a man say he hath faith, and have not works? can faith save him?

law is found in the rabbinical writings (cf. SBK, III, 755). James adopts this idea but baptizes it into Christ. A. Cadoux writes: "James looks on the law, not as a number of injunctions, but as a personal relationship . . . not like an examination, where nine right answers will secure a pass, despite a wrong one, but like a friendship, where a hundred faithfulnesses cannot be set against one treachery" (*The Thought of St. James*, p. 72). This idea is closely associated with the Christian concept of fellowship with Christ. Transgression of one precept of the Christian rule of faith is a breach of the whole, because it breaks fellowship with the object of faith.

**11.** The order of the two commandments cited (the seventh before the sixth) is probably due to the order of the LXX in Codex Alexandrinus. If this is the reason, then subtle interpretations of this verse are excluded. It simply buttresses by specific example what the author has said by way of general principle in the preceding verse.

**12.** James comes now to his summary exhortation. Believers are to speak and act (with special reference towards behavior to the poor) as **they that shall be judged by the law of liberty.** There is a judgment for the Christian, and it will be based on his relation to the Christian ethical standard, the law that free men accept without compulsion (cf. Rom 14:10; II Cor 5:10). **13.** This verse is a warning that God shows no mercy toward those who are merciless (cf. Mt 18:21-35). And conversely *mercy triumphs over judgment* (RSV), i.e., by merciful acts God's judgment is deterred.

## VIII. Faith and Works. 2:14-26.

This is the best known and most widely debated passage in the epistle. These were the verses, more than any others, that caused Martin Luther to describe this book as a "right strawy epistle." Most of the difficulties in the interpretation of 2:14-26 have arisen out of a failure to understand that: (1) James was not refuting the Pauline doctrine of justification by faith but rather a perversion of it. (2) Paul and James used the words **works** and **justification** in different senses. These will be discussed in the commentary.

**14.** The answer which the two questions of this verse expect is a resounding "No!" It is important to note that the faith under discussion is a so-called, or spurious, faith. This is made clear by (1)

952

15. If a brother or sister be naked, and destitute of daily food,

16. And one of you say unto them, Depart in peace, be ye warmed and filled; notwithstanding ye give them not those things which are needful to the body; what *doth it* profit?

17. Even so faith, if it hath not works, is dead, being alone.

18. Yea, a man may say, Thou hast faith, and I have works: show me thy faith without thy works, and I will show thee my faith by my works.

19. Thou believest that there is one God; thou doest well: the devils also believe, and tremble.

20. But wilt thou know, O vain man, that faith without works is dead?

the statement, if a man say he hath faith, and (2) the use of the definite article with the word faith in the last clause (RSV, *Can his faith save him?*). It is only a false faith that does not issue in works and that is incapable of saving. By works James does not have in mind the Jewish doctrine of works as a means of salvation, but rather works of faith, the ethical outworking of true piety and especially the "work of love" (cf. 2:8).

15,16. An example is now cited. The "ill clad" (RSV) and hungry person is a brother or sister, i.e., a member of the Christian community. The needy brother is sent away with the empty words, Depart in peace, be ye warmed and filled, without so much as a hand being lifted to meet his urgent needs. James indignantly asks: "What on earth is the good of that?" (Phillips). The movement from the singular to the plural *(ye)* may indicate that "James assumes that all members of the brotherhood would be responsible for these callous remarks even though only one of them might give utterance to them" (Tasker, *op. cit.*, p. 64).

17. The faith under discussion, which is really not faith at all, is not merely useless or unacceptable, but dead. A faith that does not concern itself, by active participation, in the needs of others is not faith at all.

18. The difficulties in this verse arise out of the fact that the ancient Greek MSS had neither punctuation nor quotation marks. The objector is introduced by a man may say, a form often found in ancient synagogue sermons (cf. A. Marmorstein, "The Background of the Haggadah," *Hebrew Union College Annual,* VI (1929), p. 192). How much of the verse is to be considered as the words of the objector is open to doubt, but it is probably best to include only, Thou hast faith, and I have works. James refutes this attempt to separate faith and works by the challenge: Show me thy faith without thy works. This he certainly believes to be impossible.

19. Belief in the unity of God *(that God is one,* RSV) was a fundamental article of the creed of the Jews. James holds that such a belief is good. However, if it is lacking in deeds, it arises no higher than the faith of the demons. They, too, are monotheists, but this only makes them tremble (RSV, *shudder),* presumably in view of God's judgment (cf. Mk 5:7; Mt 8:29).

20. James reaches a new point in his argument with the words, But wilt thou

21. Was not Abraham our father justified by works, when he had offered Isaac his son upon the altar?

22. Seest thou how faith wrought with his works, and by works was faith made perfect?

23. And the Scripture was fulfilled which saith, Abraham believed God, and it was imputed unto him for righteousness: and he was called the Friend of God.

24. Ye see then how that by works a man is justified, and not by faith only.

25. Likewise also was not Rahab the harlot justified by works, when she had received the messengers, and had sent *them* out another way?

26. For as the body without the spirit is dead, so faith without works is dead also.

know. He is now ready to adduce Scriptural arguments to buttress his case for a working faith. Moffatt renders **O vain man** more pointedly, *You senseless fellow.* The ASV and RSV both follow the rendering *barren* rather than **dead**, and rightly so, because the latter is the result of conforming to 2:26. *Argē (barren)* in this context is probably best taken to mean "unproductive of salvation."

**21.** The Scriptural example given is **Abraham our father.** That he was considered to be the ancestor of all true Christians is clear from Gal 3:6-29. The use of the word **justified** here is not to be confused with Paul's use of the term in relation to Abraham (cf. Rom 4:1-5). Paul points to Abraham's initial justification when he "believed God, and it was reckoned unto him for righteousness" (cf. Gen 15:6). James is referring to an event that took place many years later, when Abraham was instructed to offer up his son Isaac. By this act he demonstrated the reality of the Genesis 15 experience.

**22.** Abraham's life thus remarkably exemplifies the impossibility of severing faith from works, or vice versa (cf. 2:18). In his case the two went hand in hand. Works brought faith to completion. **23.** In Abraham's act of obedience the **scripture** (Gen 15:6) **was fulfilled. Friend of God** was a title commonly applied to Abraham (cf. Isa 41:8; II Chr 20:7; also the noncanonical Jubilees 19:9; 30:20; Testament of Abraham, *passim).* **24.** This verse is the conclusive reply to the question of verse 14. Bare, unproductive faith, cannot save a man. True faith will demonstrate itself in works, and only such a faith brings justification.

**25.** James' second Scriptural example stands in marked contrast to Abraham. **Rahab** was a woman, a Gentile, and a prostitute. She was chosen to show that James' argument covered the widest ranges of possibilities (thus the use of *kai* with *hē pornē,* "even though a prostitute"). She, like Abraham, evidenced her justification by action (cf. Josh 2:1-21).

**26.** The concluding statement to the teaching of 2:14-26, shows that the relation between faith and works is as close as that between the body and the spirit. Life is the result of the union in both instances. When the two elements are separated, death results. "False faith is virtually a corpse" (F. J. A. Hort, *The Epistle of St. James,* p. 45).

## CHAPTER 3

MY brethren, be not many masters, knowing that we shall receive the greater condemnation.

2. For in many things we offend all. If any man offend not in word, the same *is* a perfect man, *and* able also to bridle the whole body.

3. Behold, we put bits in the horses' mouths, that they may obey us; and we turn about their whole body.

4. Behold also the ships, which though *they be* so great, and *are* driven of fierce winds, yet are they turned about with a very small helm, whithersoever the governor listeth.

5. Even so the tongue is a little member, and boasteth great things. Behold, how great a matter a little fire kindleth!

6. And the tongue *is* a fire, a world of iniquity: so is the tongue among our members, that it defileth the whole body, and setteth on fire the course of nature; and it is set on fire of hell.

## IX. The Tongue. 3:1-12.

1. The subject of speech is one of the most prominent in this book (cf. 1:19, 26; 4:11,12; 5:12). This, however, is the classic passage, and it is addressed to *teachers* (the AV's masters is misleading). James first warns his readers that they should not be overeager to become teachers, because of the responsibility involved.

2. Because a teacher constantly uses words, there is a particular danger in this area for him. In many things we offend (RSV, *make mistakes),* but the most difficult mistakes to avoid are those that involve the tongue. Thus the man who successfully controls his tongue is styled a perfect man. Having tamed the most difficult member, he is able also to bridle the whole body.

3. "It is with men as with horses: control their mouth and you are masters of all their action" (Ropes, *op. cit.,* p. 229). David, in Ps 39:1, uses the figure of the bridle in relation to control of speech. 4. This further illustration points out the power of the tongue. It is like the small helm (RSV, *rudder)* that controls a great ship. The point of the phrase, and are driven of fierce winds, is not clear unless and is taken to mean "even." Then the meaning would be that the rudder turns the ship even during fierce storms. The antique whithersoever the governor listeth is modernized by the RSV's *wherever the will of the pilot directs.*

5. From the governing or controlling power of the tongue, the author now turns to its destructive power. It may be a little member, but it can boast of great things. And this is not an empty boast! Matter *(hylēn)* probably means *forest* (RSV) here. A small spark can set ablaze an entire forest. 6. In the punctuation of this verse, it is best to follow the RSV, which places a full stop after fire. This eliminates the need for the added so in the AV. Tasker *(op. cit.,* p. 76) takes world of iniquity (RSV, *unrighteous world)* to mean "all the evil characteristics of a fallen world, its covetousness, its idolatry, its blasphemy, its lust, its rapacious greed." These all find expression through the tongue, and consequently it defileth the whole body.

The tongue also sets on fire the course of nature. Hort calls this one of the most difficult phrases in the Bible. Although the phrase is probably a technical one,

7. For every kind of beasts, and of birds, and of serpents, and of things in the sea, is tamed, and hath been tamed of mankind:

8. But the tongue can no man tame; *it is* an unruly evil, full of deadly posion.

9. Therewith bless we God, even the Father; and therewith curse we men, which are made after the similitude of God.

10. Out of the same mouth proceedeth blessing and cursing. My brethren, these things ought not so to be.

11. Doth a fountain send forth at the same place sweet *water* and bitter?

12. Can the fig tree, my brethren, bear olive berries? either a vine, figs? so *can* no fountain both yield salt water and fresh.

13. Who *is* a wise man and endued with knowledge among you? let him show out of a good conversation his works with meekness of wisdom.

14. But if ye have bitter envying and strife in your hearts, glory not, and lie not against the truth.

15. This wisdom descendeth not from above, but *is* earthly, sensual, devilish.

which originated outside of Palestine, James uses it here in a nontechnical sense to mean "the whole of human existence." This tremendous power for evil possessed by the tongue comes straight from **hell** (*Gehenna*).

**7,8.** God's command to man (Gen 1:26) to have dominion over the fish of the sea, etc., has been successfully carried out, **but the tongue can no man tame.** But certainly God can tame it! **Unruly** (RSV follows the better reading, *restless*) **evil** though it be and **full of deadly poison,** the Lord has controlled it in the lives of many to bring great blessing to mankind. **9,10.** The tongue is also inconsistent. It is used to fulfill its highest purpose, namely to **bless God,** but it is also used to curse men. Such inconsistency, especially in the case of Christians (**My brethren**), **ought not so to be. 11,12.** The illustrations of the fountain, fig tree, and vine show that "such incongruity of behavior is a revolt against nature, where everything pursues an orderly course of good or bad" (B. S. Easton, *The Epistle of James*, p. 48).

### X. The Two Wisdoms. 3:13-18.

**13.** Although the entire Epistle of James is Wisdom literature, wisdom (*sophia*) is expressly mentioned only in this passage and in 1:5. It is important that the Jewish (not Greek) idea of wisdom be kept in mind. Hort defines wisdom in James as "the endowment of heart and mind which is needed for the righteous conduct of life" (*op. cit.,* p. 7). **Wise man** (*sophos*) is the technical term for teacher, and **knowledge** (*epistēmōn*) for expert knowledge. By his **good conversation** (RSV's *life* is better) the **wise man** is to demonstrate **his works with meekness of wisdom.** The pride of knowledge has always been the besetting sin of professional teachers.

**14.** Pride of knowledge in the case of James' readers gave vent to **bitter** jealousy and *selfish ambition* (RSV), which resulted in boasting (**glory not**) and being thus *false to the truth* (RSV). The author does not mean here that the teachers were departing from orthodox doctrine, but rather that by their inconsistent living they were giving a lie to the truth of the Gospel.

**15.** This "false" wisdom is characterized as **not such as comes down from above** (RSV), i.e., does not have its origin in God (cf. 1:5). Instead it is **earthly, sensual, devilish.** "These three

16. For where envying and strife *is*, there *is* confusion and every evil work.

17. But the wisdom that is from above is first pure, then peaceable, gentle, *and* easy to be entreated, full of mercy and good fruits, without partiality, and without hypocrisy.

18. And the fruit of righteousness is sown in peace of them that make peace.

## CHAPTER 4

FROM whence *come* wars and fightings among you? *come they* not hence, *even of* your lusts that war in your members?

2. Ye lust, and have not: ye kill, and desire to have, and cannot obtain: ye fight and war, yet ye have not, because ye ask not.

words . . . describe the so-called wisdom, which is not of divine origin, in an advancing series—as pertaining to the earth, not to the world above; to mere nature, not to the spirit; and to the hostile spirits of evil instead of to God" (Ropes, *op. cit.*, p. 248). 16. The conjunction **for** indicates that what follows is proof for what has just been said. False wisdom produces **confusion** (RSV, *disorder*)—probably a reference to squabbles in the church—and **every evil work**. God is neither a God of confusion (I Cor 14:33) nor sympathetic to evil (I Jn 1:5). Thus "wisdom" that causes such a situation cannot come from God.

17. In contrast is **the wisdom that is from above**. It is the gift of God; it is practical wisdom, wisdom that preserves unity and peace. Because of the attributes ascribed to it—**pure, peaceable, gentle, easy to be entreated** (RSV, *open to reason*), **full of mercy and good fruits, without partiality** (RSV, *uncertainty*) or **hypocrisy** (RSV, *insincerity*)—some commentators have concluded that wisdom here is in reality Christ. In the light of the early identification of Christ with the Wisdom of God, this is not impossible. 18. The **fruit of righteousness** is probably best taken to mean "the fruit which is righteousness." The statement then is in contrast to 1:20: **The wrath of man worketh not the righteousness of God.** The latter is achieved by peacemakers who sow in peace.

### XI. The World and God. 4:1-10.

1. **Wars and fightings** are suggested by contrast with the preceding **peace.** James had in mind not wars between nations but quarrels and factions among Christians. The source of these is to be found in **your lusts** (*hēdonōn*, which really means *pleasures*) **that war in your members.**

2. The RSV punctuation is to be preferred, which brings out the parallelism of the verse: *You desire and do not have; so you kill. And you covet and cannot obtain; so you fight and wage war.* It is not necessary either to weaken or emend the reading **ye kill.** Ropes rightly says: "James is not describing the condition of any special community, but is analysing the result of choosing pleasure instead of God" (*op. cit.*, p. 255). Thus the force is almost conditional, "If you desire . . . If you covet . . ."

One reason their desires (in this case the legitimate ones) were not being real-

3. Ye ask, and receive not, because ye ask amiss, that ye may consume *it* upon your lusts.

4. Ye adulterers and adulteresses, know ye not that the friendship of the world is enmity with God? whosoever therefore will be a friend of the world is the enemy of God.

5. Do ye think that the Scripture saith in vain, The spirit that dwelleth in us lusteth to envy?

6. But he giveth more grace. Wherefore he saith, God resisteth the proud, but giveth grace unto the humble.

7. Submit yourselves therefore to God. Resist the devil, and he will flee from you.

8. Draw nigh to God, and he will draw nigh to you. Cleanse *your* hands, *ye* sinners; and purify *your* hearts, *ye* double-minded.

ized was that they did not ask God, who alone can fully satisfy human desires. **3.** A second reason is found in the unacceptable motive of those who do ask—that ye may consume it upon your lusts. The essential condition of all prayer is found in I Jn 5:14: "If we ask anything according to his will, he heareth us."

**4.** The AV's **Ye adulterers** is not found in the best manuscripts and so should be omitted. The fact that James addresses his readers as **adulteresses**, after the fashion of the OT prophets who spoke of Israel as the wife of Jehovah (cf. Isa 54: 5; Jer 3:20; Ezk 16:23; Hos 9:1, etc.), is strong evidence for both a Jewish author and Jewish readers. To maintain **friendship** with **the world** "is to be on good terms with persons and forces and things that are at least indifferent toward God if not openly hostile to him" (Ropes, *op. cit.*, p. 260), and thus to be at **enmity with God.**

**5.** A further reason why a Christian cannot be a friend of the world is adduced from Scripture. There are a number of possible translations of the words that follow, but it is in keeping with the context to follow the RSV, which makes God, not **spirit**, the subject of the verb: *He yearns jealously over the spirit which he has made to dwell in us.* God is a jealous God (cf. Ex 20:5; 34:14; Deut 32:16; Zech 8:2; I Cor 10:22), and hence he will not tolerate divided allegiance. No specific OT passage contains the words of this verse, but many passages express a similar sentiment.

**6.** The difficulties of living wholly for God in a wicked world are many, **but he giveth more grace,** which here seems to mean "gracious help." And this gracious aid God makes available, as Prov 3:34 declares, not to **proud,** self-sufficient persons, but to **humble,** dependent men.

**7.** The call to **submit yourselves . . . to God** (the first of eight closely following imperatives) follows logically the promise of grace to the humble. Calvin pointedly remarks: "Submission is more than obedience; it involves humility." The devil, the enemy of God, **is to be resisted,** and when he is, **he will flee from you** (cf. Mt 4:1-11). These are both important steps in avoiding the sin of worldliness.

**8.** The imperatives continue with **Draw nigh to God.** Close communion with God assures his friendship (**and he will draw nigh to you**), and estranges one from the world. That worldliness is sin is graphically shown by the following imperatives: **Cleanse your hands,** a refer-

9. Be afflicted, and mourn, and weep: let your laughter be turned to mourning, and *your* joy to heaviness.

10. Humble yourselves in the sight of the Lord, and he shall lift you up.

11. Speak not evil one of another, brethren. He that speaketh evil of *his* brother, and judgeth his brother, speaketh evil of the law, and judgeth the law: but if thou judge the law, thou art not a doer of the law, but a judge.

12. There is one lawgiver, who is able to save and to destroy: who art thou that judgest another?

13. Go to now, ye that say, To-day or to-morrow we will go into such a city, and continue there a year, and buy and sell, and get gain:

14. Whereas ye know not what *shall be* on the morrow. For what *is* your life? It is even a vapor, that appeareth for a little time, and then vanisheth away.

15. For that ye *ought* to say, If the Lord will, we shall live, and do this, or that.

ence to outward conduct; purify your hearts, a reference to inner motives. A double minded man is characterized by divided allegiance. And according to this passage, worldliness is basically divided allegiance. Kierkegaard's famous essay, "Purity of Heart Is to Will One Thing," arose out of this verse.

9. Here is a call to repentance in the face of serious sin. Be afflicted, i.e., "make yourselves wretched" (cf. Rom 7:24), mourn, and weep. These attitudes are more fitting than laughter or joy (i.e., the frivolity and lightness of the world) in view of the circumstances. Heaviness (RSV, *dejection)* "is the downcast, subdued expression of those who are ashamed and sorry" (Moffatt, *op. cit.,* p. 64). 10. James returns to his initial exhortation in the series (4:7) with the words, Humble yourselves. With this is coupled the promise, and he shall lift you up.

### XII. Judging. 4:11,12.

11. The author again returns to the subject of the abuse of speech. In this passage the interest of the brother and the interest of the law seem to be identi·fied. To speak evil against one's brother or to judge him is to speak evil against the law and to become a judge of the law. 12. Superiority to the law belongs only to God. He is the one lawgiver and judge, and in his hands are the issues of life and death. In view of this, James asks, Who art thou that judgest another?

### XIII. Sinful Self-confidence. 4:13-17.

13. The attitude of the merchants described here is another expression of the worldliness that brings estrangement from God. The itinerant merchants addressed were Jews who carried on a lucrative trade throughout the Mediterranean world. They are depicted as making careful plans for their business enterprises, declaring, To day or tomorrow we will go into such a city, etc. 14. There is nothing wrong with such planning in itself. However, the planners were ignoring two considerations. The first is the finiteness of human beings, which limits their knowledge—ye know not what shall be on the morrow. The second is the uncertainty of life, which James likens to a vapour, or a puff of smoke. 15. A Christian man, in making his plans, ought to acknowledge his dependence upon God and say, *Deo volente,*

16. But now ye rejoice in your boastings: all such rejoicing is evil.

17. Therefore to him that knoweth to do good, and doeth *it* not, to him it is sin.

## CHAPTER 5

GO to now, *ye* rich men, weep and howl for your miseries that shall come upon *you.*

2. Your riches are corrupted, and your garments are moth-eaten.

3. Your gold and silver is cankered; and the rust of them shall be a witness against you, and shall eat your flesh as it were fire. Ye have heaped treasure together for the last days.

4. Behold, the hire of the laborers who have reaped down your fields, which is of you kept back by fraud, crieth: and the cries of them which have reaped are entered into the ears of the Lord of Sabaoth.

5. Ye have lived in pleasure on the earth, and been wanton; ye have nourished your hearts, as in a day of slaughter.

If the Lord will. 16. But acknowledgment of dependence upon God was not the case among James' readers. Rather, they *boast*[ed] in their *arrogance* (RSV). This braggart talk James denounces as evil. 17. A concluding warning is sounded for the self-confident merchants. They are Christians. Hence they know that humility and dependence upon God are essential in Christian living. To *know* this and not to *do* it, is sin.

### XIV. Judgment of the Unscrupulous Rich. 5:1-6.

1. The rich addressed here are not Christians but, nevertheless, the warning sounded applies to all men, including Christians. James is consistent with the NT teaching generally in attacking the rich not simply because they are rich, but because they have failed in their stewardship. The weeping and howling are not signs of repentance but expressions of remorse in the face of judgment.

2. Both of the verbs in this verse and the first verb of the following verse are in the perfect tense. Ropes aptly describes them as "picturesque, figurative statements of the real worthlessness of this wealth to the view of one who knows how to estimate permanent, eternal values" (*op. cit.*, p. 284). Wealth is to be used for good purposes, not hoarded.

3. The rust of the hoarded wealth will be a witness against the rich, because God meant wealth to be used for the good of mankind. It also will destroy the rich themselves—shall eat your flesh as it were fire. The phrase, for the last days probably should be changed to in the last days. It points to the fact that, though the rich did not realize it, the last days were already present.

4. Another sin of rich men was the cruel defrauding of poor farm laborers. This action was particularly serious because it was explicitly contrary to the Mosaic law (cf. Deut 24:14,15). God, who is here called Lord of sabaoth, a title that suggests his sovereign omnipotence, was not oblivious to this injustice. His ears were open to the cries of the poor workmen.

5. A third sin of the rich was their luxury and pleasure. Extravagant living was simply fattening them up for the day of slaughter. This phrase is taken from Jeremiah (12:3). In the inter-Testament period (cf. I Enoch 94:9) it took on an eschatological significance, and in

6. Ye have condemned *and* killed the just; *and* he doth not resist you.

7. Be patient therefore, brethren, unto the coming of the Lord. Behold, the husbandman waiteth for the precious fruit of the earth, and hath long patience for it, until he receive the early and latter rain.

8. Be ye also patient; stablish your hearts: for the coming of the Lord draweth nigh.

9. Grudge not one against another, brethren, lest ye be condemned: behold, the judge standeth before the door.

10. Take, my brethren, the prophets, who have spoken in the name of the Lord, for an example of suffering affliction, and of patience.

11. Behold, we count them happy which endure. Ye have heard of the patience of Job, and have seen the end of the Lord; that the Lord is very pitiful, and of tender mercy.

this passage it is used of the day of judgment.

6. The **just** man is not Jesus but the poor man (used generically), who has been treated without mercy by the rich. Moffatt (*op. cit.*, p. 70) points out that the word **murdered** had a wider range of meaning in Jewish ethics than it has today. Particularly relevant are the statements in the apocryphal Ecclesiasticus 34:21,22: "The bread of the needy is the life of the poor; whoever deprives them of it is a man of blood. To take away a neighbor's living is to murder him; to deprive an employee of his wages is to shed blood." Here the reference in James is probably to "judicial murders," since the statement follows the word **condemned.** Poor people are haled into court (cf. Jas 2:6) and can do nothing to defend themselves. They are completely at the mercy of the unscrupulous rich men. Despite all of this mistreatment, the poor do not **resist.**

**XV. Patience until Christ's Return. 5:7-11.**

7. James turns now from addressing the wicked rich to counseling the oppressed poor. His instruction is that the poor should bear patiently their social and economic situation in view of the imminent return of the Lord. There is no suggestion here of the forceful overthrow of the rich. As an example of one who must exercise patience, James cites the case of the farmer who waits for **the precious fruit of the earth.** In Palestine the **early** rain (October–November) came after the crops were planted, and tht **latter rain** (April–May) when they were maturing. Both were crucial for the success of the crops.

8. So the Christian, James says, is not to lose patience in the face of adversities but is to stablish his heart in view of the fact that **the coming of the Lord draweth nigh. 9.** Adversities cause tensions, and these in turn express themselves in human relations. James therefore warns, **Grudge not** (Better, *Do not grumble,* RSV) **one against another.** Such action places them in danger of judgment, and the **judge standeth before the door.**

**10,11.** In addition to farmers, the prophets are now cited as illustrations of **suffering and patience** (RSV). It is strange that Christ's example is not cited here as it is in I Pet 2:21-23. Job was traditionally considered to be a prophet, and here he is explicitly cited as an example of

12. But above all things, my brethren, swear not, neither by heaven, neither by the earth, neither by any other oath: but let your yea be yea; and *your* nay, nay; lest ye fall into condemnation.

13. Is any among you afflicted? let him pray. Is any merry? let him sing psalms.

14. Is any sick among you? let him call for the elders of the church; and let them pray over him, anointing him with oil in the name of the Lord:

15. And the prayer of faith shall save the sick, and the Lord shall raise him up; and if he have committed sins, they shall be forgiven him.

16. Confess *your* faults one to another, and pray one for another, that ye may be healed. The effectual fervent prayer of a righteous man availeth much.

steadfastness. This is the only place in the NT where Job is mentioned. The main point of the illustration of Job is that "patient endurance can sustain itself on the conviction that hardships are not meaningless, but that God has some end or purpose in them which He will accomplish . . ." (Moffatt, *op. cit.*, p. 74).

## XVI. Oaths. 5:12.

It is doubtful whether this verse has any connection with what precedes. **Above all things** is probably best taken as a hyperbole used for emphasis. The subject under discussion is not profanity, but truthfulness. Easton paraphrases the verse: "Abstain from all oaths, for they weaken a man's sense of obligation to speak the truth on all occasions; learn to make a simple 'Yes' or 'No' completely binding" (*op. cit.*, p. 69).

## XVII. Prayer. 5:13-18.

13. **Suffering** (RSV; calamity of any sort) calls forth prayer; a joyful heart, praise. **Let him sing psalms** is too limited a translation of *psalletō*.

14. In the case of serious illness, James counsels, the **elders** (a reference to definite officers) of the church should be called. Their prayers were to be accompanied by anointing **with oil in the name of the Lord.** In some cases oil may have therapeutic value, but in most cases its use is best understood as an aid to faith. 15. It is clear from this verse that it is not the oil that heals the sick man, but rather **the Lord shall** raise him up in answer to the **prayer of faith.** This is not to suggest that God always answers believing prayer. All prayer, including prayer for healing, is subject to the will of God. Sometimes, certainly not always, sickness is the result of personal sin. Perhaps this is what is meant by **if he have committed sins.** In any event, the sick man is assured of forgiveness.

16. Prayer, to be most effective, must be intelligent. Thus we find the exhortation, **Confess your faults one to another.** This does not mean that Christians are to indulge in indiscriminate public or even private confessions. And certainly the passage has nothing to do with secret confessions to a priest. Believers are to confess their faults only that they may **pray one for another.** There is no unanimity as to how to render the last part of this verse, but the meaning is clear: a good man has great power in prayer.

17. Elias was a man subject to like passions as we are, and he prayed earnestly that it might not rain: and it rained not on the earth by the space of three years and six months.

18. And he prayed again, and the heaven gave rain, and the earth brought forth her fruit.

19. Brethren, if any of you do err from the truth, and one convert him;

20. Let him know, that he which converteth the sinner from the error of his way shall save a soul from death, and shall hide a multitude of sins.

17. The example is Elijah, a man of like nature with ourselves (RSV). His prayers both brought the drought and caused its end. James seems to be drawing on other sources than the OT, since Elijah's prayers for the drought and its cessation are not mentioned in the OT account. The length of the drought as being three and one half years is also not found in the OT.

## XVII. Reclaiming the Sinning Brother. 5:19,20.

The statement, **Brethren, if any of you do err from the truth,** and the two references to bringing him back (cf. RSV) seem clearly to indicate that the man under discussion is a Christian. **Convert** is misleading. If a fellow Christian sees that his brother has left the great doctrines of the Christian faith and the moral responsibilities that spring from these, and is able to bring him back into fellowship with Christ and His Church, the consequences will be twofold: (1) **he shall save a soul** (the sinner's) **from death,** and (2) **shall hide a multitude of sins.** Since the NT teaches the security of the believer in Christ, it is best to take the reference to death as physical death. The early church believed and taught that persistence in sin could cause premature physical death (cf. I Cor 11:30). The sins that are hidden are not those of the reclaiming brother (this suggests the Jewish doctrine that good works offset bad ones) but of the erring man. They are hidden from the sight of God, which is simply another way of saying they are forgiven.

# BIBLIOGRAPHY

CARR, A. *Epistle of St. James. (The Cambridge Greek Testament for Schools and Colleges).* Cambridge: The University Press, 1895.

EASTON, B. S. *The Epistle of James. (The Interpreter's Bible).* Vol. 12. New York: Abingdon, 1957.

HORT, F. J. A. *The Epistle of St. James, 1:1—4:7.* London: Macmillan and Co., 1909.

KNOWLING, RICHARD. *The Epistle of St. James. (Westminster Commentaries).* 2nd ed. London: Methuen, 1910.

MAYOR, JOSEPH B. *The Epistle of St. James.* 3rd ed. London: Macmillan and Co., 1913.

MOFFATT, JAMES. *The General Epistles James, Peter, and Judas. (The Moffatt New Testament Commentary).* Garden City, New York: Doubleday, 1928.

PLUMMER, ALFRED. *The General Epistles of St. James and St. Jude. (The Expositor's Bible).* London: Hodder and Stoughton, 1897.

PLUMTRE, E. H. *The General Epistle of St. James. (The Cambridge Bible for Schools and Colleges).* Cambridge: The University Press, 1909.

ROPES, JAMES H. *A Critical and Exegetical Commentary on the Epistle of James. (International Critical Commentary).* New York: Charles Scribner's Sons, 1916.

ROSS, ALEXANDER. *The Epistles of James and John. (The New International Commentary on the New Testament).* Grand Rapids: Eerdmans, 1954.

TASKER, R. V. G. *The General Epistle of James. (Tyndale New Testament Commentaries).* Grand Rapids: Eerdmans, 1956.

# THE FIRST
# EPISTLE OF PETER

## INTRODUCTION

*The Writer.* This letter claims to have been written by the Apostle Peter (1:1). The author also calls himself an elder and a witness of the sufferings of Christ (5:1). He writes with the help of one Silvanus (5:12) and speaks of a dear one, Marcus, as being with him (5:13).

In dealing with any ancient writing, the writer is at the outset assumed to be intelligent and straightforward. His statements of matters ostensibly lying within his knowledge, and particularly any affirmations about himself or his activities, are regarded as reliable. The given literary work is further studied for internal consistency, and the writings of contemporary and later authors are scanned for direct references to this author or his work and for possible allusions to it, quotations from it, or other evidence of their acquaintance with it. The original assumption of genuineness and accuracy is not properly altered unless these further studies reveal very compelling evidence to the contrary.

With reference to the sacred Scriptures, there is for Christian scholars a further important factor operative in their studies. The historic church has always believed firmly that the canonical writings are not only the result of careful reporting by honest men, but that they embody also the element of divine miracle; they are "God-breathed" (II Tim 3:16), and sometimes even transcend the understanding of their human writers (I Pet 1:10-12).

I Peter clearly claims to have been written by the Apostle Peter, and there seem to be no considerations of content or style that refute such a claim. Indeed, it contains statements here and there which are strongly reminiscent of expressions of Peter reported in the Acts. The writer's reference to the Father as judging "without respect of persons" (1:17) recalls Peter's earlier word to Cornelius and the group of Gentiles in his house (Acts 10:34). The allusions to God as having raised Christ from the dead (I Pet 1:21, *et al.*) remind one of the apostle's characteristic resurrection wit-

ness in the Acts (2:32; 3:15; 10:40). And the proclamation of Christ as Isaiah's prophetically seen "chief cornerstone" in I Pet 2:7,8 is very similar to Peter's words to the Sanhedrin in Acts 4:11.

Scholars have pointed out similarities to the Pauline writings (Harnack thought I Peter too deeply imbued with the spirit of Pauline Christianity to have been the work of Peter), the relation of the epistle to James, and its undoubted affinity with Hebrews. Still other scholars, notably Dr. Charles Bigg (*St. Peter and St. Jude,* in the *International Critical Commentary*), argue that such similarities may be interpreted as reflecting the borrowing of these other writers from Peter as reasonably as the reverse, that they can well be taken as representing points of view and ways of speaking which were common among the Christians of apostolic times, and that there is nothing here to cast doubt on the individuality of the writer of I Peter or to show that this writer could not have been the Apostle Peter, as claimed in the epistle's opening verse.

The references to persecution and suffering, so prominent in I Peter, have been studied closely by scholars to see how they correspond with what is known from history about the persecutions of the early Christians. Dr. S. J. Case ("Peter, Epistles of," in HDAC) distinguishes three principal waves in the early persecutions: these occurring in the reigns of Nero (A.D. 54–68), Domitian (A.D. 81–96), and Trajan (A.D. 98–117). He follows those scholars who see I Peter as reflecting not only an advanced and severe stage of persecution but one which had spread to the provinces of Asia Minor mentioned in I Pet 1:1.

Referring to Pliny's correspondence with the emperor Trajan regarding the punishment of Christians during Pliny's propraetorship (beginning A.D. 111) of Pontus and Bithynia, two of the provinces to which I Peter is addressed, Case considers this to be the setting that best corresponds to the statements of

I Peter on persecution. To follow such a line of reasoning to its conclusion, placing the writing of this epistle during the reign of Trajan, would make it too late to have been the work of St. Peter. Dr. Case himself, in view of other lines of evidence, does not adopt this conclusion.

Other scholars interpret I Peter as an anticipatory warning against approaching persecution, toward which things were even then moving. Bigg points out that the early persecutions were largely inspired by the Jewish Sanhedrin, but that the Romans were quick to see that here was a way of life incompatible with paganism, and which, from their point of view, must be stopped. The persecution of Paul and Silas in Philippi seems to have been on this basis and without Jewish instigation. The missionaries had impaired the livelihood of the pagan fortunetellers. And Roman law protected the right of each man to make a living without interference.

Dr. Bigg feels that I Peter belongs in this earlier stage of pagan opposition, antedating even the Neronian persecution which followed the burning of Rome (A.D. 64), for which Nero blamed the Christians. Certainly this earlier dating is not impossible nor unreasonable, and it accords best with the epistle's claim to Petrine authorship. This is not to say, of course, that Pliny's letters to Trajan do not contain items that help us greatly in our study of persecution as seen in I Peter.

External evidence strongly supports the genuineness of this epistle. Although Irenaeus (c. 130–216) was the first whom we know to have quoted Peter by name, New Testament scholars have found allusions to I Peter and parallelisms with it in the Epistle of Barnabas (c. A.D. 80), in the work of Clement of Rome (A.D. 95–97), in the *Shepherd of Hermas* (early second century), and in later patristic writings. Polycarp, who was martyred in A.D. 155, quotes from I Peter, although not naming its author. Eusebius (c. A.D. 324) says that Papias (who wrote c. A.D. 130–140) "used witnesses from the first epistle of John and similarly from Peter" (*Ecclesiastical History* 3.39.17). He counts I Peter among the books received without doubt by the whole church. Moreover, I Peter is found in the Syriac version of the Bible, called the Peshito, and in the Coptic, Ethiopic, Armenian, and Arabic versions. Its external attestation is strong indeed, and bears out the claim of this epistle to the authorship of the Apostle Peter.

*The Time and Place of the Writing.* The time and the place of the writing of I Peter, granting its Petrine authorship, are closely connected. From 5:13 it appears that the epistle was written from "Babylon." There was an Assyrian refugee settlement by that name in Egypt, where modern Cairo is located. But during the first century it was just a military post, and there is no traditional support for Peter's residence there.

Babylon on the Euphrates is known to have sheltered a Jewish congregation in A.D. 36, and there were Babylonian Jews in Jerusalem at Pentecost. There may well have been a Christian church there subsequently. But toward the end of the reign of Caligula (d. A.D. 41) the Jewish colony in Babylon was scattered by violent persecution and massacre. It seems quite improbable that this epistle was written from there.

There was an early and strong tradition for Peter's residence in Rome during the latter part of his life. This idea was generally held throughout the church prior to the Reformation. It is, perhaps, not impossible that the reformers, in urging Assyrian Babylon as the interpretation of Peter's reference in I Pet 5:13, may have been motivated partly by their opposition to the claim that the Roman papacy had come down from Peter. But the symbolic use of Old Testament names for existing cities was well known in apostolic times. Paul likened Hagar and Mount Sinai to Jerusalem (Gal 4:25). In Rev 11:8 Jerusalem is called "Sodom and Egypt," and in Rev 17:18 it is made clear that the scarlet lady called "Babylon" is a reference to Rome. To the recipients of I Peter, who would have known at once from the bearer whence the letter had come, there would have been no problem about this discreetly veiled reference to Rome.

Peter's arrival in Rome is calculated by Chase (*op. cit.*) to have been about the end of A.D. 63. Lightfoot sets it early in A.D. 64. Paul's coming to Rome as a prisoner had occurred earlier, in A.D. 61 or 62. There is a tradition that Paul was released after two years in Rome, and that II Timothy was written shortly before his execution, later, outside Rome, which is thus dated in A.D. 67 or 68. This second imprisonment is disputed, however, and those who dispute it place the writing of II Timothy about two years after Paul's arrival in Rome and assign a date of A.D. 63 or 64. This would come shortly before Paul's martyrdom, and at about the time Peter is thought to have arrived in Rome. It is interesting to note that Mark, who was summoned to Rome by Paul (II Tim 4:11), was present with Peter when this first epistle was written, as was also Silas, Paul's friend and one-time companion in travel (I Pet 5:12, 13).

This epistle, then, may well have been written from Rome at about the time of the outbreak of the Neronian persecution in A.D. 64. To place it shortly after the beginning of this persecution seems warranted by the epistle's vivid references to the fiery crucible of suffering.

*The Message of the Epistle.* Written to the Christians in the five provinces of Asia Minor, the epistle addresses its readers as scattered sojourners and foreigners, a figure very familiar to dispersed and downtrodden Israel, but also entirely apt for Peter's many Gentile Christian readers. That he had these Gentile Christians in mind is abundantly clear from the letter. He reminds them that although formerly "not a people," they are now the people of God (2:10). He describes their past life as having been lived in the sinful lusts of the Gentiles (4:3,4).

And why this interest on the part of Peter? Many from these provinces of Asia had heard his sermon at Pentecost (Acts 2:9), and many had doubtless gone back to their home territory as spiritual colonists. Paul had later carried on evangelistic labors in Asia, but to a limited extent only, having been forbidden by the Holy Spirit to work Asia intensively (Acts 16:6-8). Perhaps this was because of the splendid start already made by the Gospel in these parts.

Peter could well recall his Lord's injunctions, "When thou art converted, strengthen thy brethren" (Lk 22:32), and again, "Lovest thou me . . . ? Feed my sheep" (Jn 21:15-17). "When thou art converted," indeed! For the pre-Pentecost Peter, far from being a spiritual rock, was a shifting compound of human loyalty to Christ and treacherous self-interest. "Not the cross!" had been his advice to his Lord (Mt 16:22). And as Jesus went toward that instrument of suffering, in his Father's will, he did so without the company of Peter.

But Pentecost, with the Spirit's mighty filling, had brought a radical change. And now Peter, who had already endured beating and had faced death at Herod's hands, comes forward to encourage and strengthen his dear brethren of Asia to face the impending Calvary which he—perhaps already involved in the cruel Neronian persecution—could see coming upon them.

# OUTLINE

Theme: Suffering in the life of the believer.
Key verse: I Peter 4:1.
I. Comfort and reassurance in suffering. 1:1-25.
    A. Salutation. 1:1,2.
    B. Reassurance in the realized facts of Christ's gospel. 1:3-12.
    C. Reassurance in divinely bought holiness of life. 1:13-25.
II. The chastened response of practical holiness. 2:1–3:22.
    A. The negative and positive bases of holiness. 2:1-3.
    B. The readers' participation in a holy community, the Church. 2:4-10.
    C. Unimpeachable living, the answer to persecution. 2:11–3:13.
        1. Deference to statutes, officers, fellow citizens. 2:11-17.
        2. Submission by servants, even to injustice. 2:18-25.
        3. Deference of wives to husbands. 3:1-6.
        4. Consideration for wives. 3:7.
        5. Divine love among the saints. 3:8-13.
    D. Victory in unjust suffering. 3:14-22.
        1. Basic blessedness, freedom from terror. 3:14,15 a.
        2. Respectful apologetic supported by probity of life. 3:15 b-17.
        3. Christ the believer's example. 3:18-21.
        4. Christ the believer's reassurance. 3:22.
III. The spiritual significance of suffering. 4:1-19.
    A. Physical suffering a type of death to the flesh life. 4:1-6.
        1. Christ's death the example and empowerment. 4:1 a.
        2. Dying to the sin nature; alive to God. 4:1 b-6.

B. The "crucified life" characterized by divine love. 4:7-11.
C. The fires of persecution seen as purifying. 4:12-19.
IV. Divine love as a guide in church life. 5:1-11.
    A. Elders to rule in love. 5:1-7.
    B. The devil to be resisted through divine grace. 5:8-11.
V. Closing salutations and benediction. 5:12-14.

## I PETER

### CHAPTER 1

PETER, an apostle of Jesus Christ, to the strangers scattered throughout Pontus, Galatia, Cappadocia, Asia, and Bithynia,

2. Elect according to the foreknowledge of God the Father, through sanctification of the Spirit, unto obedience and sprinkling of the blood of Jesus Christ: Grace unto you, and peace, be multiplied.

## COMMENTARY

I. Comfort and Reassurance in Suffering. 1:1-25.

A. Salutation. 1:1,2.

1. **Peter, an apostle of Jesus Christ.** This is a straightforward claim by the epistle to the authorship, humanly speaking, of Peter the apostle. Only one person could have been thus identified. To negate this claim is to mark the epistle as a "pious fraud" and to raise a serious question about how a writing so authored can be depended upon for ethical and spiritual direction. **To the strangers scattered.** The Greek may be rendered, *to the foreign residents of the dispersion.* These were not strangers to Peter, but temporary residents in the provinces of Asia Minor here named by Peter. Their real citizenship was in heaven (cf. Phil 3:20, Gr.). The apostle, writing expressly to comfort these pilgrims, some of whom had no doubt been converted as a result of his sermon at Pentecost, immediately takes knowledge of the separation and even ostracism that marked them among their neighbors. The expression "dispersion" was fraught with poignant meaning for the scattered Jews. Peter adapts this figure to his Gentile readers.

2. **Elect according to the foreknowledge of God.** The Holy Spirit helped Peter, even in his introductory words, to advance a sound basis for encouragement to these Christians who were finding themselves increasingly alone. These were actually the ones who were chosen and preferred by Him whose favor is all-important. As elsewhere in the NT, the doctrine of election is made compatible with personal responsibility, as it is qualified by God's foreknowledge (see Rom 8:29), and is seen as operating in real life through imparted holiness (**sanctification of the Spirit,** II Thess 2:13). The result is **obedience** to God and cleansing from incidental defilement through the continuing **sprinkling of the blood** of Jesus Christ (Heb 12:24). To his dear brethren thus addressed Peter wishes **grace** (the Greek word being suggestive of the Gentile

**3. Blessed** *be* **the God and Father of our Lord Jesus Christ, which according to his abundant mercy hath begotten us again unto a lively hope by the resurrection of Jesus Christ from the dead,**

**4. To an inheritance incorruptible, and undefiled, and that fadeth not away, reserved in heaven for you,**

**5. Who are kept by the power of God through faith unto salvation ready to be revealed in the last time.**

greeting *Chaire!* "Be of good cheer!") and **peace** (reminiscent of the Oriental greeting *Shalom!* "Peace!"). Note, too, the inclusion of reference to all three persons of the Trinity in this salutation.

B. Reassurance in the Realized Facts of Christ's Gospel. 1:3-12.

**3. Blessed be the God and Father of our Lord Jesus Christ.** Beginning properly with this ascription of praise and credit to God, the source of every benefit, Peter begins to build up a picture of the spiritual wealth of his readers, a wealth that remains secure for them despite all tests and indignities. First comes the fact of the new birth, God having **begotten us anew** (Gr.), **in terms of the greatness of his mercy,** with the resultant possession of a **living hope,** this hope and assurance centering about the fully attested and often-proclaimed fact of Christ's **resurrection.**

**4.** The result of a new birth is a new **inheritance,** which is described as **incorruptible** (indestructible), **undefiled** (unstained), **that fadeth not away** (fresh of color), and **reserved** (kept under watch) **in heaven for you.** To Peter's readers, who had already resigned their part in Israel's earthly inheritance, the promised land of the fathers, and who were also to know the proscription and the spoiling of earthly goods (see Heb 10:34), this thought of the sure inheritance would give comfort and balance. How reminiscent of our Lord's admonitions to his followers to convert their worldly possessions into true riches! (e.g., Lk 12:33,34) **5. Who are kept by the power of God.** This kept inheritance is "for you the kept (i.e., by a military garrison) ones." The word for **kept** is the same Greek word used by Paul in Phil 4:7—"The peace of God . . . shall keep your hearts and minds." **Through faith.** This is the Christian's response to God's provision (cf. Heb 10:38,39). **Unto salvation ready to be revealed in the last time.**

Here is a salvation now enjoyed, the

6. Wherein ye greatly rejoice, though now for a season, if need be, ye are in heaviness through manifold temptations:

7. That the trial of your faith, being much more precious than of gold that perisheth, though it be tried with fire, might be found unto praise and honor and glory at the appearing of Jesus Christ:

8. Whom having not seen, ye love; in whom, though now ye see *him* not, yet believing, ye rejoice with joy unspeakable and full of glory:

9. Receiving the end of your faith, *even* the salvation of *your* souls.

10. Of which salvation the prophets have inquired and searched diligently, who prophesied of the grace *that should come* unto you:

11. Searching what, or what manner of time the Spirit of Christ which was in them did signify, when it testified beforehand the sufferings of Christ, and the glory that should follow.

full significance of which awaits an ultimate revelation (Gr., *apocalypse*).

6. **Wherein ye greatly rejoice, though now . . . in heaviness.** Here is the Christian's joy, independent of circumstances, paradoxical to the world. This is why Paul and Silas could sing with lacerated backs. It should be emphasized that this joy is not simply an intellectual anticipation of future possessions but a present appropriation of God's wealth through the Holy Spirit. Joy is one element in the fruit of the Spirit (Gal 5:22). **Through manifold temptations** or testings (Gr., *peirasmos*). These were more than the ordinary vicissitudes of life. Here is a reference to the weight of persecutions even then being felt by the Christians.

7. **The trial of your faith.** This word for **trial** is closely related to the idea of approval. The end result, not the process, is in focus. This demonstration of the eternal quality of their faith, shown forth brightly as a result of the testings, far excels the gleam of fire-refined gold, perishing in its nature, and will be **found unto praise and honour and glory at** (or *by*) **the appearing** (*revelation*) **of Jesus Christ.** Here is a double significance. Not only will this trying of faith be found rewarding to the Christians at Christ's coming, but it is presently found glorifying to Christ because of his unveiling (Gr., *apocalypsis*) in their suffering (cf. Paul in Gal 3:1). Compare these references to the second coming of Christ in verses 5 and 7 with those in Peter's sermon in the Temple (Acts 3:20,21) and in his message in the house of Cornelius (Acts 10:42).

8. **Whom . . . ye love; in whom . . . ye rejoice.** Christ personally, realized through faith, is the believer's unspeakable joy (see also Col 1:27). 9. **Receiving** (getting) **the end of your faith . . . salvation.** This is not a future but a present reference. In their love of and faith in Christ they have him who is salvation and joy (Jn 17:3).

10. **Of which salvation the prophets have inquired.** Literally, they *sought out and investigated.* They were intrigued by God's plan of salvation. 11. **Searching . . . the sufferings of Christ, and the glory.** The idea of salvation made available through a suffering Messiah was to them, indeed to all the Jews, a mystery (Col 1:26,27). Peter's introduction of the prophecies of glory through suffering must have greatly encouraged his readers. This was the way prohesied in Scripture, the way their Lord had trod, and

12. Unto whom it was revealed, that not unto themselves, but unto us they did minister the things, which are now reported unto you by them that have preached the gospel unto you with the Holy Ghost sent down from heaven; which things the angels desire to look into.

13. Wherefore gird up the loins of your mind, be sober, and hope to the end for the grace that is to be brought unto you at the revelation of Jesus Christ;

14. As obedient children, not fashioning yourselves according to the former lusts in your ignorance:

15. But as he which hath called you is holy, so be ye holy in all manner of conversation;

16. Because it is written, Be ye holy; for I am holy.

17. And if ye call on the Father, who without respect of persons judgeth according to every man's work, pass the time of your sojourning *here* in fear:

the way they themselves were now being called upon to traverse. **12. Not unto themselves, but unto us they** (the prophets) **did minister.** An important principle in inspiration. God has sometimes chosen to reveal through the sacred Scriptures mysteries beyond the comprehension of the writers (cf. Dan 12:8,9). Here, then, is a gospel given through the prophets, proclaimed by preachers endued with the Holy Spirit, a wonder to angels.

C. Reassurance in Divinely Bought Holiness of Life. 1:13-25.

**13. Wherefore gird up the loins of your mind.** He exhorts them to be encouraged in the realization of God's love (cf. Heb 12:12,13). **Be sober.** An injunction to sane appraisal of the facts, without undue emotion and panic (repeated in 4:7; 5:8). **Hope to the end.** The words **to the end** are better translated *perfectly, maturely.* There is a spiritual quality to the Christian's endurance. His is the "patience of hope in our Lord Jesus Christ, in the sight of God" (I Thess 1:3). **The grace that is to be brought** (Gr., *that is being brought*). Doubtless we cannot comprehend this fully. Certainly it includes the redemption of the body (Phil 3:21; Rom 8:23). Compare the statement in verse 5 above. It may be a reference to dying grace ministered divinely to the martyrs.

**14. As obedient children.** Literally, *children of obedience.* **Not fashioning yourselves.** Actually, "not conforming yourselves" (cf. Rom 12:2) "to your strong desires in your former ignorance" (cf. Eph 2:3). The Christian's desire life has been changed; but unless he is watchful, he may yet be "drawn away with his own desire, and enticed" (Jas 1:14). **15, 16. As he which hath called you is holy.** Christ's imminent return, the believer's precious hope, also is a strong incentive to holiness (I Jn 3:3). For Christ is holy. Recall Peter's embarrassing realization of his own sinfulness and truancy when suddenly confronted by the risen Christ while fishing on the Sea of Galilee one morning (Jn 21:7). This was reminiscent of a similar realization when he had first been called by the Lord (Lk 5:8). **Conversation.** Better, *deportment, manner of life.* **Be ye holy.** This was a commandment very well known to all who knew the Pentateuch (Lev 11:44; 19:2; 20:7; cf. Mt 5:48).

**17. If ye call on the Father.** Peter speaks to praying people, who call on

18. Forasmuch as ye know that ye were not redeemed with corruptible things, *as* silver and gold, from your vain conversation *received* by tradition from your fathers;

19. But with the precious blood of Christ, as of a lamb without blemish and without spot:

20. Who verily was foreordained before the foundation of the world, but was manifest in these last times for you,

21. Who by him do believe in God, that raised him up from the dead, and gave him glory; that your faith and hope might be in God.

22. Seeing ye have purified your souls in obeying the truth through the Spirit unto unfeigned love of the brethren, *see that ye love one another with a pure heart fervently:*

23. Being born again, not of corruptible seed, but of incorruptible, by the word of God, which liveth and abideth for ever.

24. For all flesh *is* as grass, and all the glory of man as the flower of grass. The grass withereth, and the flower thereof falleth away:

25. But the word of the Lord endureth for ever. And this is the word which by the gospel is preached unto you.

### CHAPTER 2

WHEREFORE laying aside all malice, and all guile, and hypocrisies, and envies, and all evil speakings,

God for deliverance from unjust persecution, but who should realize that God himself is a judge. **In fear.** This realization will cause a godly carefulness. The wise man is known by what and whom he fears (Mt 10:28).

**18,19. Not redeemed with corruptible things.** These were simple and poor folk. For the second time (cf. v. 7) Peter makes a scornful reference to temporal wealth as compared with the priceless heritage of salvation. **From your vain conversation.** More accurately, *from your foolish way of life inherited from your parents.* **The precious blood of Christ.** The word precious (Gr., *timios*) is peculiarly Petrine. The sinlessness of the Lamb, the vicariousness of his suffering, provide the basis for a new and heavenly scale of values. **20,21. Foreordained . . . manifest.** Christ's suffering was no emergency. It was God's best plan in view of man's sin. This would have been a comforting thought for saints now hard-pressed themselves. **For you.** Better, *through you.* Christ is actually manifested through them as they trust and hope in the same God who raised him from the dead.

**22. Seeing [that] ye have purified your souls.** Peter appeals to the genuineness of their conversion, an actuality well realized by his readers. They had indeed been changed, **purified.** This change of heart had issued in "unhypocritical brotherly love" (Gr., *philadelphia*). He exhorts them to follow and practice the same principle: **See that ye love one another** *from your heart, earnestly.* **23-25. Being born again . . . by the word of God.** How tenuous a matter regeneration seems to the human mind, resting, as it does, only on God's word. But Peter quotes Isaiah's grand assertion that this seemingly frail, invisible entity—God's word—will outlast all natural phenomena (Isa 40:6-8). And this is the word that gives significance to their faith and to themselves.

### II. The Chastened Response of Practical Holiness. 2:1–3:22.

A. The Negative and Positive Bases of Holiness. 2:1-3.

**1. Laying aside all malice.** There is a negative and purging phase in holiness (Eph 4:22 ff.; Col 3:9 ff.). Here are ugly qualities centering in self-love: **malice,** more exactly, *evil-spiritedness;* **guile,** which hides the unworthy motive it seeks to further; **hypocrisies,** which feign an

972

2. As newborn babes, desire the sincere milk of the word, that ye may grow thereby:

3. If so be ye have tasted that the Lord *is* gracious.

4. To whom coming, *as unto* a living stone, disallowed indeed of men, but chosen of God, *and* precious,

5. Ye also, as lively stones, are built up a spiritual house, a holy priesthood, to offer up spiritual sacrifices, acceptable to God by Jesus Christ.

unfelt righteousness; **evil speakings,** which hurt another to advance one's self.

**2. As newborn babes, desire.** The Greek words suggest the voracious, hungry impatience of a baby at its mealtime. Peter has been speaking of the word of God as operative in their regeneration (1:23-25). Now he urges the newborn ones to cultivate a healthy appetite for this word, which, while mighty, is *simple* or *unadulterated* (translated, sincere) and elementary, like milk. In this way his readers will grow "unto salvation." These latter words, found in some of the best manuscripts, refer to the believer's ultimate deliverance (cf. 1:5,13). **3. If so be ye have tasted.** Here is another reminder of the grace they have already experienced (cf. Ps 34:8).

B. The Readers' Participation in a Holy Community, the Church. 2:4-10.

**4. To whom coming, as unto a living stone.** Peter is now coming to that grand and comforting assurance that his readers, who are scorned and ostracized as a motley and negligible folk (cf. "foreigners," 1:1) by their neighbors, are members of a holy and glorious community, the Church. He begins rightly with the matter of personal relationship to Christ, Himself rejected as they are, but like them **chosen** (*elect*, cf. 1:1) **of God, and precious** (again this word "precious"; cf. 1:19 and below). **5. Ye also, as lively** (living) **stones.** Here is an identity in nature with Christ. The same words are used of the believers as of the Lord. The passage clearly recalls the Lord's words to Peter, "Thou shalt be called . . . a stone" (Jn 1:42); and again, "Thou art Peter (*a stone*), and upon this rock (*rock formation*) I will build" (Mt 16:18). Note that in the present passage Peter makes his Lord, not himself, pre-eminent in this holy building which is the Church. **Are being builded a spiritual house.** Compare Eph 2:19-22. The Church is seen as transcending the glory of the Jewish Temple. The argument in this part of the chapter, to I Pet 2:10, may intimate that the indignities and pressures being experienced by the believers were at the instigation of the Jews, though taken up likewise by the Gentiles, as so often happened in the early days of the church. **An holy priesthood, to offer up spiritual sacrifices, acceptable to God by Jesus Christ.** The offering of Christ is seen as opening the Holy of Holies to all be-

6. Wherefore also it is contained in the Scripture, Behold, I lay in Sion a chief corner stone, elect, precious: and he that believeth on him shall not be confounded.

7. Unto you therefore which believe *he is* precious: but unto them which be disobedient, the stone which the builders disallowed, the same is made the head of the corner,

8. And a stone of stumbling, and a rock of offense, *even to them* which stumble at the word, being disobedient: whereunto also they were appointed.

9. But ye *are* a chosen generation, a royal priesthood, a holy nation, a peculiar people; that ye should show forth the praises of him who hath called you out of darkness into his marvelous light:

10. Which in time past *were* not a people, but *are* now the people of God: which had not obtained mercy, but now have obtained mercy.

lievers and as superseding the Jewish sacrifices. Through Christ, once-sinful man can now make an acceptable offering to a holy God (cf. Rom 12:1,2).

**6. It is contained in the scripture.** Peter now cites his source, Isa 28:16. It is interesting to note that in this verse in Isaiah the stress is upon the function of the stone as "a sure foundation" (cf. I Cor 3:11). No doubt Peter's feeling for this figure went back to our Lord's use of it (Mt 21:42), following the wording in Ps 118:22,23. Peter himself had used it with the Sanhedrin: "This is the stone which was set at nought of you builders" (Acts 4:11).

**7,8. Unto you the believing** (Gr) . . . **precious: but unto them which be disobedient . . . a rock of offence.** The noun form of "precious" is here used; literally, *an honor, a thing prized.* Here is a simple representation of Christ as Saviour and Judge. Mercy rejected becomes condemnation. This, again, was Christ's doctrine (Mt 21:44; Jn 12:48). In the present passage the **believing** are contrasted with the **disobedient.** Faith, then, appears as a basic obedience or willingness (cf. "obedient to the faith," Acts 6:7). **Whereunto also they were appointed** (Gr., *set*). The same divine purpose which, on the basis of God's foreknowledge, chose Peter's readers as His own children, has sadly ordained the disobedient to their only alternative.

**9,10. But ye are a chosen** *(elect)* **generation** (Gr., *genos,* "race, kind"). This is very reminiscent of Christ's own teaching. His reference to the rejected cornerstone was in connection with his parable of the rebellious husbandmen who had slain the son of the owner of the vineyard. At the same time and along with his reference to the rejected stone, he said to the Jewish leaders, "The kingdom of God shall be taken from you, and given to a nation bringing forth the fruits thereof" (Mt 21:43). Peter is now writing to this "nation," whose evident royalty and worth at once mark them as the King's children and reflect credit upon him who called them from the world's darkness to his light. The words translated **peculiar people** literally mean *a people for a gain-making* (Gr., *peri-poiēsis*). Sometimes the word indicates the securing of a desired possession ("purchase to themselves," I Tim 3:13; "he purchased through his own blood." Acts 20:28). Sometimes it means a preservation or salvation. In Heb

11. Dearly beloved, I beseech *you* as strangers and pilgrims, abstain from fleshly lusts, which war against the soul;

12. Having your conversation honest among the Gentiles: that, whereas they speak against you as evildoers, they may by *your* good works, which they shall behold, glorify God in the day of visitation.

13. Submit yourselves to every ordinance of man for the Lord's sake: whether it be to the king, as supreme;

14. Or unto governors, as unto them that are sent by him for the punishment of evildoers, and for the praise of them that do well.

15. For so is the will of God, that with well doing ye may put to silence the ignorance of foolish men:

10:39 it is translated "saving" and contrasted with "perdition." Here is a tremendous word of encouragement. These are a people greatly prized, a people to be saved, a people for a possession. Peter rounds off this doctrine in the words of Hosea (1:6,9; 2:23). These once **not a people**—very probably a reference to their Gentile ancestry—are now **the people of God.**

C. Unimpeachable Living, the Answer to Persecution. 2:11—3:13.

**11. As strangers and pilgrims, abstain.** Peter sweeps aside the picture of their royalty, turns the page, addresses them once more as pilgrims. He picks up again the thought in 2:11 and bids them "hold themselves away" from carnal desires **which war against the soul.** The figure "to war against" is not that of hand-to-hand fighting, but of a planned expedition against a military objective. We might liken it to Delilah's cool exploitation of Samson's appetites for his destruction. **12. Having your conversation** (way of life) **honest** (the same word is used in "good works" later in the verse). Though a chosen race, they lived among the Gentiles, who were bent to **speak against** them **as evildoers.** Christianity by its very essence opposed the vanities of paganism at every turn. Hence it was in itself a crime, "everywhere spoken against" (Acts 28:22). Like righteous Noah, it "condemned the world" (Heb 11:7). This was the basic explanation for the willingness of the pagans to notice and persecute this insignificant people. And Peter knew that the best answer was probity of life, God-given and wringing unwilling praise from the very enemies of the cross (cf. Jesus' teaching in Mt 5:16). **In the day of visitation** is better rendered *the day of observation* (official inspection or cognizance).

**13,14. Submit yourselves to every ordinance . . . to the king . . . unto governors.** A Christian is law-abiding, meticulous, and self-disciplined. This doctrine is comparable with Paul's teaching in Rom 13:1-7 and Tit 3:1,2. It is, of course, not to be understood as compelling compliance with evil. Peter's own words to the Sanhedrin answer this: "Whether it be right in the sight of God to hearken unto you more than unto God, judge ye" (Acts 4:19). **15. With well doing . . . put to silence the ignorance of foolish men.** Pliny, in his report

**16.** As free, and not using *your* liberty for a cloak of maliciousness, but as the servants of God.

**17.** Honor all *men.* Love the brotherhood. Fear God. Honor the king.

**18.** Servants, *be* subject to *your* masters with all fear; not only to the good and gentle, but also to the froward.

**19.** For this *is* thankworthy, if a man for conscience toward God endure grief, suffering wrongfully.

**20.** For what glory *is it,* if, when ye be buffeted for your faults, ye shall take it patiently? but if, when ye do well, and suffer *for it,* ye take it patiently, this *is* acceptable with God.

**21.** For even hereunto were ye called: because Christ also suffered for us, leaving us an example, that ye should follow his steps:

**22.** Who did no sin, neither was guile found in his mouth:

**23.** Who, when he was reviled, reviled not again; when he suffered, he threatened not; but committed *himself* to him that judgeth righteously:

to Trajan about the Christians in Pontus and Bithynia, two of the provinces mentioned in 1:1, speaks of the "crimes clinging to the name" of Christian. Although coming at a considerably later time (c. A.D. 112), this is illustrative of the ignorant and unfair way in which a group of people may be assumed to be criminal. The answer of a good life would be the best defense.

**16. As free.** Spirit-impelled self-control is the only lasting basis of freedom: "If ye be led of the Spirit, ye are not under the law" (Gal 5:18). **But as the servants** *(slaves)* **of God.** The man wholly mastered of God is truly free. God then works in such a one the willing and the doing of His good will. It is this God-implanted love for His way that makes Christ's yoke easy, His burden light.

**17. Honour . . . love . . . fear.** Here is expressed self-abnegation and willingness to give to each his due. The word for **honor** is related to the word "precious," and suggests the Christian's high regard for human personality. The word for **love** indicates the divinely given *agapē* of I Cor 13. This was the love with which Christ had twice challenged Peter in Jn 21:15,16, a challenge from which honest Peter swerved with the reply, "I love (Gr., *philo,* "to love humanly") thee."

**18-20. Servants, be subject . . . also to the froward.** The Spirit-filled man is enabled to meet demands unreasonable, yes, quite impossible on any other basis. "Love your enemies," "turn the other cheek"—these are encompassed only through the complete mastery of him who prayed for his crucifiers, "Father, forgive them." **This is thankworthy.** Reward begins where the reasonable ends. He who serves God without transcendent divine love builds wood, hay, and stubble. **What glory is it . . . ?** Compare Jesus' questions in Lk 6:32-36. **Acceptable with God.** The word **acceptable** is the Greek *charis,* which has a beautiful double force of "grace" and "favor." It can give the sense, "When ye do well, and suffer . . . patiently, this is grace with God" or "this is favor with God."

**21-23. Christ also suffered.** Here, of course, is the personification of divine love. Here is our pattern. **Who did no sin.** Hence all punishment and indignity to him was without reason. **Who . . . reviled not again . . . but committed himself.** Here is the perfect fulfillment

24. Who his own self bare our sins in his own body on the tree, that we, being dead to sins, should live unto righteousness: by whose stripes ye were healed.

25. For ye were as sheep going astray; but are now returned unto the Shepherd and Bishop of your souls.

## CHAPTER 3

LIKEWISE, ye wives, *be* in subjection to your own husbands; that, if any obey not the word, they also may without the word be won by the conversation of the wives;

2. While they behold your chaste conversation *coupled* with fear.

3. Whose adorning, let it not be that outward *adorning* of plaiting the hair, and of wearing of gold, or of putting on of apparel;

4. But *let it be* the hidden man of the heart, in that which is not corruptible, *even the ornament* of a meek and quiet spirit, which is in the sight of God of great price.

5. For after this manner in the old time the holy women also, who trusted in God, adorned themselves, being in subjection unto their own husbands:

6. Even as Sarah obeyed Abraham, calling him lord: whose daughters ye are, as long as ye do well, and are not afraid with any amazement.

of the principle seen in Rom 12:19,20: "Vengeance is mine . . . saith the Lord. Therefore if thine enemy hunger, feed him." Here is perfect love for God and man. **24. Who . . . bare our sins in his own body.** Peter reminds his readers that this was done for them. **That we, being dead to sins, should live unto righteousness.** He implies that Christ's death was more than an example. By sharing his cross they will share his triumphant life. **By whose stripes . . .** Selwyn (*The First Epistle of St. Peter,* p. 95) calls attention to three strands in St. Peter's thought about the atonement: the paschal lamb "without blemish and without spot" (1:19), the suffering servant of Isa 53, "by whose stripes ye were healed," and the scape goat, "who his own self bare our sins in his own body on the tree." **25. For ye were as sheep . . . but . . .** Peter has been urging upon his readers a sharing of Christ's sufferings. Even as He commanded (Lk 14:27, etc.), they are to follow Him, taking up the cross. But they have already made an initial step in this sharing of the cross; once wayward sheep, they have been converted to the **Shepherd and Bishop** (caretaker) of their souls.

**3:1-6. Likewise, ye wives.** Leaving the implications of holiness for slaves, Peter addresses the married women. These he directs, **Be in subjection to your husbands** (cf. Eph 5:22; Col 3:18). The rule of divine love is still the background. The husband is recognized as leader in the home, and the wife's **chaste conversation,** her prudent and self-controlled conduct in the home, will win some to Christ. She is not to seek attention by the artificialities of coiffure, jewelry, or ostentatious dress, but to be distinguished by that **meek and quiet spirit** so rare in the world and so prized by God. The wives of the patriarchs are seen as examples of this deportment (v. 5). Apparently gaudy and showy adornment is viewed as contrary to the spirit of self-effacement and modesty toward husbands. The same implication appears in I Tim 2:9-12. Modesty of woman's dress is associated with becoming modesty of deportment. Apparently Christian faith implies a different standard of dress and adornment from the world's. Sara is seen as deferring to Abraham's leadership, **calling him lord** (Gen 18:12). Verse 6 reminds these Christian women that they are adopted daughters of Sara: "Whose children you became, doing good and

7. Likewise, ye husbands, dwell with *them* according to knowledge, giving honor unto the wife, as unto the weaker vessel, and as being heirs together of the grace of life; that your prayers be not hindered.

8. Finally, *be ye* all of one mind, having compassion one of another; love as brethren, *be* pitiful, *be* courteous:

9. Not rendering evil for evil, or railing for railing: but contrariwise blessing; knowing that ye are thereunto called, that ye should inherit a blessing.

10. For he that will love life, and see good days, let him refrain his tongue from evil, and his lips that they speak no guile:

11. Let him eschew evil, and do good; let him seek peace, and ensue it.

12. For the eyes of the Lord *are* over the righteous, and his ears *are open* unto their prayers: but the face of the Lord *is* against them that do evil.

13. And who *is* he that will harm you, if ye be followers of that which is good?

14. But and if ye suffer for righteousness' sake, happy *are ye:* and be not afraid of their terror, neither be troubled;

15. But sanctify the Lord God in your hearts: and *be* ready always to *give* an answer to every man that asketh you a reason of the hope that is in you, with meekness and fear:

not being subject to inordinate fear."

**7. Likewise, ye husbands.** Passing now to the implications of holiness in the husband, Peter enjoins that the marriage relationship be seen in terms of consideration, **according to knowledge.** Here is the opposite of selfishness. **Giving honour unto the wife.** The word for giving (Gr., *aponemō*) indicates a deliberate assignment, a purposeful channeling of honor (related to "precious") to the wife, who is in God's grace an equal heir. **That your prayers be not hindered.** Feelings of resentment, growing from selfish conduct in the home, make effective prayer impossible. Effective prayer must be "without wrath" (I Tim 2:8).

**8,9. Be ye all of one mind.** This recalls the "one accord" of Pentecost, or Paul's injunctions to the Philippians to be "in one spirit" (Phil 1:27) and "likeminded, having the same love, being of one mind, of one spirit" (Phil 2:2), followed closely by his gripping outline of the mind of Christ. Peter's catalog of accompanying graces reads like the gracious self-effacing aspects of the fruit of the Spirit (Gal 5:22,23) or of the "wisdom that is from above" (Jas 3:17).

**10-12. For he that will love life.** The apostle cites Ps 34:12-16 in substantiation of his teaching that this Spirit-directed and empowered way of self-emptying is really the life of blessing, the outcomes of which are guarded by the Lord, whose **eyes . . . are over the righteous, and his ears . . . open unto their prayers. 13. Who . . . will harm you . . . ?** This reminds us of Paul's postscript to the description of the fruit of the Spirit—"against such there is no law" (Gal 5:23). As a general principle, allowing for exceptions occasioned by the adversary's wrath, people are not punished for doing good. This very principle assures that undeserved suffering will not continue long.

D. Victory in Unjust Suffering. 3:14-22.

**14,15 a. But . . . if ye suffer for righteousness' sake, happy** *(blessed).* This beatitude, of course, recalls our Lord's beatitude in Mt 5:11,12. Peter then cites God's words to Isaiah (8:12,13), the complete passage reading, "Neither fear ye their fear, nor be afraid. Sanctify the Lord of hosts himself; and let him be your fear, and let him be your dread." This again brings to mind Christ's warning as to whom to fear (Mt 10:28).

**16. Having a good conscience; that, whereas they speak evil of you, as of evildoers, they may be ashamed that falsely accuse your good conversation in Christ.**

**17. For it is better, if the will of God be so, that ye suffer for well doing, than for evildoing.**

**18. For Christ also hath once suffered for sins, the just for the unjust, that he might bring us to God, being put to death in the flesh, but quickened by the Spirit:**

**19. By which also he went and preached unto the spirits in prison;**

**20. Which sometime were disobedient, when once the long-suffering of God waited in the days of Noah, while the ark was a preparing, wherein few, that is, eight souls were saved by water.**

There was real danger of defection in the face of death. Pliny describes how curtly the alternative was given to the Christians to curse Christ or die, and how not a few turned back. Peter's attitude here is not so quick and confident as it was when he told his Lord, "Though all men shall be offended because of thee, yet will I never be offended" (Mt 26:33).

**15 b,16. Be ready always to give an answer.** The attitude depicted is one of meekness and fear, yet of readiness. This, too, is a Spirit-given quality. Recall Christ's admonition: "Whatsoever shall be given you in that hour, that speak ye; for it is not ye that speak, but the Holy Ghost" (Mk 13:11). Recall the unanswerable apologetics of Stephen (Acts 6:10) and Paul (Acts 24:25; 26:24-28). **Having a good conscience.** As above, probity of life is seen as the basic defense. **17,18. It is better. . . . For Christ also hath once suffered for sins, the just for the unjust.** God-permitted suffering for welldoing is in prospect. Christ is again brought forward as the example (cf. 2:24), the outcome of whose suffering was reconciliation of lost men to God, along with his own vindication through his resurrection by the Holy Spirit's power.

**19,20. By which** (i.e., the Spirit) **also he went and preached.** Here follows a digression the interpretation of which is obscure. Some scholars, of whom Lange is an example, contend that the only straightforward and natural inference here is that Christ, after his crucifixion, descended into Hades and "proclaimed to these spirits in the prisons of Hades the beginning of a new epoch of grace" (J. P. Lange, *Commentary on the Holy Scripture*, IX, p. 64). He avers that no doubt many were saved because of this second chance. This view raises the difficult question as to why, of all unbelievers, the antediluvians were granted this reprieve, and raises the possibility (which is contrary to the clear teaching of the NT) that other sinners unrepentant at death would have a later chance to believe on Christ. Some take the view that Christ's preaching in Hades was condemnatory, but this is not the usual implication of the Greek word, which means to *herald, announce*, and is often used with the Gospel. John Owen, Calvin's translator and editor (John Calvin, *Commentaries on the Catholic Epistles*, p. 116, note), cites the explanation adopted by Beza, Doddridge, Macknight,

**21.** The like figure whereunto *even* baptism doth also now save us, (not the putting away of the filth of the flesh, but the answer of a good conscience toward God,) by the resurrection of Jesus Christ:

**22.** Who is gone into heaven, and is on the right hand of God; angels and authorities and powers being made subject unto him.

### CHAPTER 4

FORASMUCH then as Christ hath suffered for us in the flesh, arm yourselves likewise with the same mind: for he that hath suffered in the flesh hath ceased from sin;

and Scott, that the time of the action was in the ministry of Noah, when Christ by the Spirit ("by which") preached through Noah to the wicked who at Peter's later writing were spirits in Hades. And all this while **the longsuffering of God waited,** delaying the flood. The reference to the time spent in building the ark seems to corroborate this interpretation. Reference to the small number of those saved would encourage the "little flock" in Asia.

**21. Baptism doth also now save us.** The variant *by which* (Gr., *hô*), that is, "by water," is preferred for the beginning of this sentence. We read, then, "by which (water) baptism, as an anti-type, now saves us — not the putting off of the dirtiness of the physical flesh but the asking after" (better than "answers of") "a good conscience toward God." Compare Heb 10:22. The meaning seems to be that water baptism symbolizes spiritual cleansing. The connection of water baptism and the baptism of the Spirit with cleansing is everywhere apparent in the Scripture, relating to the sharing of Christ's death and his resurrection power. Those who believe in baptismal regeneration will perhaps be inclined to make something of the verb **save** here. Others will aver that it is the cleansing of the heart, not the outward ceremony, which saves. **22. Who is gone into heaven.** Resuming the theme of Christ's resurrection, left after verse 18, Peter mentions our Lord's present triumph and recognition as a strong encouragement to the godly who follow their Master in suffering. Selwyn makes a point of the fact that the early Christians often solemnized baptism at Easter time. He feels that the reference to baptism in verse 21, as well as the several allusions to Christ's sufferings, resurrection, and second coming, indicate that I Peter was written as an Easter epistle (*op. cit.,* p. 62).

### III. The Spiritual Significance of Suffering. 4:1-19.

A. Physical Suffering a Type of Death to the Flesh Life. 4:1-6.

**1 a. As Christ hath suffered . . . arm yourselves . . . with the same mind.** Philippians 2:5 uses the verbal form of "mind" and urges, "Be minded the same." The thought here is very similar. A different Greek word is used, suggesting the individuality of both Peter and Paul. Christ

2. That he no longer should live the rest of *his* time in the flesh to the lusts of men, but to the will of God.

3. For the time past of *our* life may suffice us to have wrought the will of the Gentiles, when we walked in lasciviousness, lusts, excess of wine, revelings, banquetings, and abominable idolatries:

4. Wherein they think it strange that ye run not with *them* to the same excess of riot, speaking evil of *you:*

5. Who shall give account to him that is ready to judge the quick and the dead.

6. For, for this cause was the gospel preached also to them that are dead, that they might be judged according to men in the flesh, but live according to God in the spirit.

is seen as the believer's example and empowerment for us in suffering. **1b, 2. He that hath suffered in the flesh hath ceased from sin.** Peter is now looking at death as encountered by man (cf. Rom 7:1-4), freeing him from all desire and commitment of sin. He immediately drives the spiritual parallel. He who has shared Christ's cross no longer is alive to the pull of sin through the ordinary human desires, but is alive only to the pull of God's will (Gal 6:14).

**3,4. The time past of our life may suffice.** Literally, *sufficient the bygone time to have wrought the will of the Gentiles.* Then follows a catalog of the ugly sins observable outside of God's grace. This reminds one of Paul's enumeration of the works of the flesh in Gal 5:19-21. **They think it strange . . . speaking evil.** The changed lives of the believers mark them as strange, almost as "foreigners," bringing to the heathen condemnation and a self-defensive and contemptuous defamation of the Christians. **5. Who shall give account.** But it is to God and not to men that such are answerable. And God's judgment will apply both to those now living and to those now dead. Dependent upon one's treatment of verse 6, this judgment may be considered both a vindication of believers and a condemnation of unrepentant sinners. In the OT, particularly in the Psalms, judgment is often seen as vindication for the righteous.

**6. The gospel preached also to them that are dead.** Some connect this with 3:19,20. Lange sees both passages as referring to a postcrucifixion evangelization of the unbelieving antediluvians by Christ, a further offer of salvation doubtless accepted by many of them. There are various other shades of interpretation. To us there seems to be solid merit in the suggestion of Scott, as modified by John Owen (*op. cit.*, p. 127), whose sense is: "With this end in view (i.e., the final judgment just mentioned) was the gospel preached also to those (martyrs) now dead, that they might be (as they were) judged in the flesh (and condemned to martyrdom) after the fashion of men, but might live in the Spirit according to God." Here, then, is the teaching that, in view of final judgment, the martyred dead are better off than the unbelieving Gentiles of verse 3.

**B. The "Crucified Life" Characterized by Divine Love. 4:7-11.**

7. But the end of all things is at hand: be ye therefore sober, and watch unto prayer.

8. And above all things have fervent charity among yourselves: for charity shall cover the multitude of sins.

9. Use hospitality one to another without grudging.

10. As every man hath received the gift, *even so* minister the same one to another, as good stewards of the manifold grace of God.

11. If any man speak, *let him speak* as the oracles of God; if any man minister, *let him do it* as of the ability which God giveth; that God in all things may be glorified through Jesus Christ: to whom be praise and dominion for ever and ever. Amen.

12. Beloved, think it not strange concerning the fiery trial which is to try you, as though some strange thing happened unto you:

13. But rejoice, inasmuch as ye are partakers of Christ's sufferings; that, when his glory shall be revealed, ye may be glad also with exceeding joy.

14. If ye be reproached for the name of Christ, happy *are ye;* for the Spirit of glory and of God resteth upon you: on their part he is evil spoken of, but on your part he is glorified.

7. **The end . . . is at hand.** With the focus still on the Judgment, the apostle enjoins an attitude of self-control (**be ye therefore sober**), and calmness (better than **watch**) and recourse to **prayer.** 8. **Have fervent** (intense) **charity.** Here again is divine love (Gr., *agapē*) as in I Corinthians 13, love which overlooks the sins and wrongs of others. 9. Here is a love which uses **hospitality . . . without grudging.** Literally, *loving of guests without murmuring.* There is here a giving of self and substance gladly. 10. **As every man hath received . . . so minister.** The "gift" received is a *charisma*, a grace, which makes its possessors **stewards of the manifold grace of God.** This grace is to be **minister**[ed] (Gr., *diakoneō;* cf. "deacon") to others, the best method also for its continued enjoyment by the original possessor. Here again is loving sharing of spiritual blessings. 11. **If any man speak.** The apostle extends the idea of stewardship introduced in verse 10. The speaker in the church must be careful to present God's sayings (Gr., *logia*), not his own. The caretaker (AV, **minister**; Gr., **deacon**) must serve in the strength (better than AV *ability*) which God abundantly supplies. Always the end in view must be **that God in all things may be glorified through Jesus Christ.** Here Peter inserts a benediction, himself giving glory to God as he has just enjoined.

C. The Fires of Persecution Seen as Purifying. 4:12-19.

12. **Think it not strange concerning the fiery trial.** Peter warns his readers against being taken by surprise, apparently indicating a test more severe than any they had yet experienced. This verse well befits the Neronian persecution, when Christians were nightly burned as torches in the emperor's gardens. Peter, in Rome, feared that soon this virulence would spread to the provinces. 13. **Rejoice . . . partakers of Christ's sufferings.** Here was that physical sharing of Christ's cross for which the spiritual sharing (2:24) was an adequate preparation. The admonition to joy recalls Jesus' words in Mt 5:12. **When his glory shall be revealed.** Or, *in the unveiling* (Gr., *apocalypsis) of his glory.* A "better resurrection" (Heb 11:35) was in prospect for them.

14. **Reproached for the name• of Christ, happy** *(blessed).* Here is another beatitude. **The spirit of...God resteth** *(is*

15. But let none of you suffer as a murderer, or *as* a thief, or *as* an evildoer, or as a busybody in other men's matters.

16. Yet if *any man suffer* as a Christian, let him not be ashamed; but let him glorify God on this behalf.

17. For the time *is come* that judgment must begin at the house of God: and if *it* first *begin* at us, what shall the end *be* of them that obey not the gospel of God?

18. And if the righteous scarcely be saved, where shall the ungodly and the sinner appear?

19. Wherefore, let them that suffer according to the will of God commit the keeping of their souls *to him* in well doing, as unto a faithful Creator.

### CHAPTER 5

THE elders which are among you I exhort, who am also an elder, and a witness of the sufferings of Christ, and also a partaker of the glory that shall be revealed:

2. Feed the flock of God which is among you, taking the oversight *thereof*, not by constraint, but willingly; not for filthy lucre, but of a ready mind;

3. Neither as being lords over *God's* heritage, but being ensamples to the flock.

4. And when the chief Shepherd shall appear, ye shall receive a crown of glory that fadeth not away.

5. Likewise, ye younger, submit yourselves unto the elder. Yea, all *of you* be subject one to another, and be clothed with humility: for God resisteth the proud, and giveth grace to the humble.

6. Humble yourselves therefore under the mighty hand of God, that he may exalt you in due time:

*pausing)* **upon you.** God stands with his martyrs. The Holy Spirit ministers special grace. Recall Stephen's dying radiance (Acts 6:15; 7:55). While men gnash and blaspheme, the martyr's serenity glorifies his God. **15. Let none . . . suffer as a murderer.** Peter warns against sin, which nullifies the witness of suffering. **16. If . . . as a Christian.** Pliny, writing later, speaks of a punishment because of the "name itself" (i.e., "Are you a Christian?"). Under such circumstances, Peter enjoins, **Let him not be ashamed; but let him glorify God** in this name (ASV, better than AV, *on this behalf*).

**17,18. Judgment must begin at the house of God.** Alluding perhaps to Ezk 9:6, the apostle regards these persecutions as a divinely permitted purging of the suffering believers, and as a harbinger of awful doom to the ungodly (cf. Lk 23:28 ff.). **19. Let them that suffer . . . commit.** Let them rest their case with their Maker, even as did Christ (2:23). To do so betokens the calmness of that divinely implanted love that casts out fear (cf. I Jn 4:18).

**IV. Divine Love as a Guide in Church Life. 5:1-14.**

A. Elders To Rule in Love. 5:1-7.

**1.** But this dying grace is also a wonderful principle for living. Peter addresses the elders. He calls himself **also an elder, and a witness** (Gr., *martys*, "martyr") **of the sufferings of Christ,** and a sharer of the coming glory. **2-4. Feed the flock.** Does not this recall Christ's words to Peter, "Feed my sheep"? (Jn 21:15-17) Perhaps the ministerial designation "pastor" *(shepherd)*, as applied to "elders" may have come from here. **Not by constraint** (forcibly) **but willingly** *(by consent)* **according to God** (added by certain good MSS); **not greedily but with a free will; neither as being lords over** *(lording it over)* **the premises** (more accurate than AV *God's heritage)* **but as examples** *(types)* **of the flock. When the chief Shepherd shall appear.** This recalls our Lord's discourse on the good shepherd (Jn 10:1-16), doubtless heard by Peter. Christ shall bestow upon his undershepherds **the unfading crown of glory** (RSV).

**5-7. Likewise, ye younger, submit.** The spirit of the elders is to be loving and deferential, an example making it easy and natural for the younger to follow. All are to be **clothed** *(girded about)* **with humility,** and thus to expect God's grace,

# I PETER 5:7-12

7. Casting all your care upon him; for he careth for you.

8. Be sober, be vigilant; because your adversary the devil, as a roaring lion, walketh about, seeking whom he may devour:

9. Whom resist steadfast in the faith, knowing that the same afflictions are accomplished in your brethren that are in the world.

10. But the God of all grace, who hath called us unto his eternal glory by Christ Jesus, after that ye have suffered a while, make you perfect, stablish, strengthen, settle *you*.

11. To him *be* glory and dominion for ever and ever. Amen.

12. By Silvanus, a faithful brother unto you, as I suppose, I have written briefly, exhorting, and testifying that this is the true grace of God wherein ye stand.

which is both the cause and the result of humility. Peter quotes Prov 3:34 (LXX) in support of this teaching (cf. Jas 4:6), and reinforces his admonition to humility (cf. Jas 4:10). It is the graciously humble who may relax, **casting all your care upon him; for he careth for you** (*it concerns him for you*).

B. The Devil To Be Resisted Through Divine Grace. 5:8-11.

**8,9. Be sober** (*calm*), **be vigilant** (*watchful*) . . . **your adversary** (opponent in a lawsuit) . . . **as a roaring lion, walketh about, seeking whom he may devour** (closer, *someone to devour*). This passage may well be a veiled reference to Nero or to his amphitheater with its lions. Seen behind all is a personal devil. **Whom resist.** Compare Jas 4:7. Christian determination triggers divine counterforce. And the knowledge that the members of **the brotherhood throughout the world** share **the same kinds of afflictions** tends to make the hard-pressed Christians **stedfast in the faith.**

**10. But the God of all grace.** Peter has enjoined upon them the graces consistent with their calling. He now commits them to the God of all grace **who hath called us unto his eternal glory by Christ Jesus.** This closing mention of God's call reminds us of his opening thought of their election (1:2). This glory, again, is to be **after . . . ye have suffered a while.** The verbs which follow are simple futures: **shall fit you out completely** (or, make you what you ought to be), **shall fix you firmly** (Christ's word used to Peter, "Strengthen thy brethren," Lk 22:32), **shall fill you with might, shall put you upon a firm foundation.**

**11. To him be . . . dominion for ever and ever** (*to the ages of the ages*). Peter closes his message with a benediction.

### V. Closing Salutations and Benediction. 5:12-14.

**12. By Silvanus . . . I have written.** Some argue that Silvanus was only the courier, but this statement seems broad enough to suggest the probability that Silvanus — generally agreed to have been the Silas of Paul's second missionary journey — actually served as a secretary in the writing of I Peter. **This is the true grace of God wherein ye stand.** The apostle thus sums up the matter of his encouragement and witness to his readers.

13. The *church that is* at Babylon, elected together with *you*, saluteth you; and *so doth* Marcus my son.

14. Greet ye one another with a kiss of charity. Peace *be* with you all that are in Christ Jesus. Amen.

13. At Babylon, elected together with you. Peter here brings greetings from *the fellow elect* (feminine gender) *in Babylon*. The translators of the AV made it "the fellow-elect church." Some think it to have been a greeting from Peter's wife, a noble person who accompanied Peter on his journeys and who, tradition says, was martyred before her husband. She would have been well known to Peter's readers. **And . . . Marcus my son.** Doubtless an indication that John Mark was with Peter at the time.

14. **Greet ye one another with a kiss of charity** (Gr., *agapē*, "divine love"). **Peace be with you all that are in Christ Jesus.** The letter closes on its keynote of divine love and of peace in Christ, superior to all opposing forces and considerations.

# BIBLIOGRAPHY

(for I and II Peter)

BIGG, CHARLES. *A Critical and Exegetical Commentary on the Epistles of St. Peter and St. Jude (The International Critical Commentary).* Edinburgh: T. & T. Clark, 1901.

CALVIN, JOHN. *Commentaries on the Catholic Epistles.* Translated and edited by John Owen. Grand Rapids: Wm. B. Eerdmans Publishing Co., reprinted 1948.

CASE, S. J. "Peter, Epistles of," *Dictionary of the Apostolic Church.* Edited by James Hastings. Edinburgh: T. & T. Clark, 1918.

CHARLES, R. H. (ed.). *The Apocrypha and Pseudepigrapha of the Old Testament in English.* London: Oxford University Press, 1913.

LANGE, JOHN P. *Commentary on the Holy Scriptures.* Translated and edited by Philip Schaff. Grand Rapids: Zondervan Publishing House, reprint, n.d.

MAYOR, JOSEPH B. *The Epistle of St. Jude and the Second Epistle of St. Peter.* London: Macmillan and Company, 1907.

ORR, JAMES (ed.). *International Standard Bible Encyclopedia.* Chicago: Howard Severance Company, 1930. James M. Gray, "Peter Simon"; William G. Moorehead, "Peter, The First Epistle of," "Peter, The Second Epistle of."

SELWYN, EDWARD G. *The First Epistle of St. Peter.* London: Macmillan and Company, 1958.

TENNEY, MERRIL C. "Bible Book of the Month: II Peter," *Christianity Today,* December 21, 1959.

# THE SECOND
# EPISTLE OF PETER

## INTRODUCTION

*The Writer.* At the outset this epistle, using a slightly different wording from that in I Peter, claims to be the writing of Symeon (Symeon appears in some of the better manuscripts; the AV has Simon Peter; cf. Acts 15:14), "a slave and an apostle of Jesus Christ" (II Pet 1:1). Simply and without affectation, the writer again identifies himself with the apostles (3:2). He is acquainted with the Pauline writings and expresses full accord with his "beloved brother Paul" (3:15,16). He refers to Christ's transfiguration with the quiet assurance of an eyewitness. He calls this letter a "second epistle" (3:1). He declares that the violent death predicted for him by his Lord (Jn 21:18) is in early prospect (II Pet 1:13,14). Here then, apparently, is a claim to authorship identical with that of I Peter, and certainly a claim to identity with St. Peter the Lord's apostle.

Are there internal difficulties that compel the honest reader to regard this as a spurious claim? From earliest times critics have called attention to a divergence in style between this epistle and I Peter. There is in II Peter a lack of the simplicity and ease of expression that characterize I Peter. The writer of I Peter was apparently not a Greek (e.g., he makes no use of the particle *an*), but he had an undoubted feeling for the correct use of the language. The style of II Peter does not evince the same familiarity with the language medium. It employs fewer participles than are seen in I Peter and does not use the *men* particle.

This difference in style caused some of the ancients and some of the reformers to question the authenticity of II Peter. Jerome (A.D. 346–420), the translator of the Vulgate version of the Bible, while accepting II Peter along with the other six 'catholic,' or general, epistles (*Epistle to Paulinius*), at the same time recognized that some scholars have doubted its genuineness because of this variation in style (*Catalogus Scrip-*

*torum Ecclesiasticorum*). Elsewhere (*Epistle to Hedibia*, 120) he explains this difference as resulting naturally from Peter's use of different interpreters for the two epistles.

In the same context he mentions Paul's use of Titus as an interpreter and Peter's dictation to Mark of material for the Gospel which was to bear Mark's name. To some with a very literalistic concept of inspiration, the idea of such an editorial function by Silas (I Pet 5:12), impairs the letter's inspiration and authority, despite the clear knowledge that ready scribes have often assisted the inspired writers (Jer 36:2,4; Rom 16:22; and the traditional notes following I and II Cor, Eph, Phil, Col, and Phm). Others have felt that here is no difficulty; the Holy Spirit helped Silas to write as He helped Peter to dictate. The great majority of the historic church have taken the latter attitude.

Another internal matter which has been urged against the Petrine authorship of this epistle is the asserted familiarity of its writer with the Pauline epistles, which, together with his reference to the authority of Paul's writings (II Pet 3:15,16), is taken as an indication that the NT canon had been pretty well established by the time II Peter was written, thus seeming to the holders of this view to make this epistle too late to have been the work of the apostle.

Such a line of reasoning seems gratuitous indeed, for if Peter reached Rome just two or three years subsequent to Paul's arrival as a prisoner, he certainly would have had a natural opportunity to learn of Paul's epistles and might conceivably have had fellowship with Paul himself. Anyway, there seems to be reasonable evidence that Paul's letters were copied and circulated from church to church immediately on their receipt (see Col 4:16).

One further matter of internal study should be considered, namely, the similarity of certain statements in II Peter to statements in Jude. Three of the most important parallelisms follow: (1) II Peter 2:4 and Jude 6 refer to the punishment of the fallen angels, an allusion to a statement in the apocryphal book of Enoch. (2) II Peter 2:11 and Jude 9 speak of the unwillingness of angels to bring a railing accusation against Satan, the Jude statement apparently adding an allusion to the apocryphal *Assumption of Moses,* where Satan is represented as claiming the body of Moses. (3) II Peter 3:3,4 and Jude 17,18 tell of the coming of scoffers in the last days. II Peter refers to this as in the future. Jude refers to it as a present reality, having been prophesied by the apostles, of whom Peter, of course, was one.

Dr. Charles Bigg (*St. Peter and St. Jude,* pp. 216,217), who accepts the Petrine authorship of this epistle, argues convincingly for the priority of II Peter. It is well to keep in mind, too, that there are plausible considerations for the early dating of the epistle of Jude itself. It is assigned a date as early as A.D. 65, and those who set its date as late as A.D. 80 or 90 must reckon with an account of Hegesippus (reported by Eusebius) that two grandsons of Jude were brought before Domitian, who reigned A.D. 81–96, these being described as grown men, horny-handed farmers, at that time. Recall that Jude was a brother of our Lord. The similarities between II Peter and Jude do not seem to require a post-Petrine date for the former.

What, then, of external testimony? This epistle is not quoted directly in the Church Fathers prior to the beginning of the third century, although there are possible allusions in some of the earlier writings. Eusebius (*Ecclesiastical History* 6.14.1), writing about A.D. 324, says that Clement of Alexandria (who died c. A.D. 213) in his *Hypotyposes* had compiled summaries of all the inspired Scriptures, including those whose authenticity was contested, among these the 'catholic' or general epistles.

Origen, who died in A.D. 253, although recognizing the question about II Peter, accepted the book as genuine. Origen's friend and pupil Firmilian, Bishop of Caesarea in Cappadocia A.D. 256, strongly corroborates the Petrine authorship of II Peter when in a letter to Cyprian he speaks of one Stephanus as "gainsaying the blessed apostles Peter and Paul . . . who in their epistles pronounced a curse upon heretics and warned that we shun them" (Cyprian, *Letters,* No. 75). It is in II Peter, not I Peter, that heretics are mentioned.

Eusebius himself, commissioned by the emperor Constantine to prepare fifty copies of the sacred Scriptures, refers to James, Jude, and II Peter as contested but well known to the majority of Christians.

Jerome (c. A.D. 346–420), commenting upon the question of the epistle's authenticity, says that the question arises because of the difference between its style and that of I Peter, and he offers the explanation already noted. He himself accepted II Peter and included it in his Vulgate version of the Bible. It was recognized by the Council of Laodicea (c. 372), and was formally acknowledged as belonging to the canon by the Council of Carthage (397).

This epistle is not found in the Muratorian fragment, a list of the NT Scriptures which dates about the end of the second century. This list is in a somewhat mutilated condition. As we now have it, there is no reference to Hebrews, I or II Peter, James, or III John. It is conceivable that some or all of these may have been included in parts which are missing; but, lacking these, it is certainly clear from the history of the development of the canon that the Muratorian list was not accepted as definitive and final by the church.

Neither was II Peter included in the Syriac Bible called the Peshito. The Old Testament of the Peshito was translated very early. The New Testament is probably the work of Rabbula, bishop of Edessa in Syria from 411–435. This version omits II Peter, II and III John, Jude, and Revelation. It is quite possible that the earliest New Testament of the Syrian church omitted all seven of the 'catholic' epistles.

Some speculate that because of the practical and disciplinary emphasis of these general epistles, they may have been regarded as "un-Pauline" in a region where Paul's name was held in high esteem because of his personal membership in the Antiochean church, and his championing the freedom of Gentile believers from Jewish laws at the Jerusalem council. Others surmise that the inclusion of references to apocryphal writings by some of the general epistles may have caused their rejection by the Christians of the Syrian church, who were particularly allergic to the extremes of Jewish angelology reflected in some of the apocryphal books.

Perhaps some mention should be made of the arguments of the British scholar Joseph B. Mayor (*The Epistle of St. Jude and the Second Epistle of St. Peter*), who regards I Peter as the work of the apostle whose name it bears but holds II Peter to be spurious.

He bases his opinion upon internal rather than external evidence. After reviewing the external evidence, with its references bearing for and against the acceptance of the epistle as genuine, Mayor summarizes by saying, "If we had nothing else to go upon in deciding the question of the authenticity of II Peter except external evidence, we should be inclined to think that we had in these quotations ground for considering that Eusebius was justified in his statement that our epistle "having appeared useful to many, was respected along with the other scriptures" (*op. cit.*, p. cxxiv; translation ours).

Mayor sets forth a minute study of vocabulary differences and lists 369 words used in I Peter but not in II Peter, and 230 words used in II Peter but not in I Peter. He finds 100 rather solid words (practically all nouns and verbs) used in both epistles. He then, amazingly, seems to set it down as an argument against their common authorship that "the number of agreements is 100 as opposed to 599 disagreements, i.e., the latter are just six times as many as the former" (*op. cit.*, p. lxxiv).

How could one possibly expect any greater vocabulary coincidence in two short epistles, written several years apart with different themes, occasions, and settings? This is argument from silence to a most precarious degree. Certainly two short epistles like these would not begin to tax an intelligent man's vocabulary. The very fact that one-sixth of the words are used in both epistles will certainly appeal to most persons as an argument for, rather than against, a common authorship.

He proceeds to a very scholarly examination of the grammar and style of the two epistles, an area in which their divergence has been a matter of note from earliest times, and on which we have already commented. Mayor's conclusion is moderate: "There is not the chasm between them which some would try to make out" (*op. cit.*, p. civ). Again, "The difference of style is less marked than the difference in vocabulary, and that again less marked than the difference in matter, while above all stands the great difference in thought, feeling, and character, in one word of personality." It should be interjected that differences in subject matter, thought, and feeling do not necessarily reflect a different personality. The same personality, for differing purposes, can write with vastly differing mood and matter.

Mayor, then, seems to place crucial weight upon his judgment as to the difference in feeling between the two epistles—a very precarious sort of thing, since a man's feeling may vary greatly from one occasion to another for any number of reasons. Beginning at page lxxvi of his Introduction, he deals with the matter of reminiscences from the life of Christ which are to be observed in I and II Peter. He observes that II Peter shows fewer of these and that they are "of a far less intimate nature than those in (I) Peter" (*op. cit.*, p. lxxvii). He then proceeds to a discussion in general of the tender spirit of I Peter, contrasting II Peter, which he says "lacks that intense sympathy, that flame of love, which marks I Peter."

Mayor carries this same type of criticism into the references of the two epistles to the Second Coming and to Noah's flood. But is not all this to be expected fully in view of the different purposes of the two epistles? I Peter comforts those who are in suffering; II Peter warns the believers of spiritual perils and exhorts them to holiness. Naturally the tone of the former is tender; of the latter, driving. The amazing thing is that with such differing objectives the appeal is made to the same basic facts—the centrality of Christ and the certainty of his second coming. In this great coming event the suffering believer receives hope, and the potential backslider, warning.

As to the mention of Noah's flood in I Peter (3:20) with emphasis on God's mercy and in II Peter (2:5; 3:6) with emphasis on God's judgment (although II Peter 2:5 also says that God "saved Noah"), this too fits admirably the different purposes just mentioned. And the fact that the same illustration is appealed to in its different facets tends to confirm the identity of authorship of the two epistles rather than the contrary.

Mayor is very fair in setting forth the whole picture. He proceeds to note, without any discounting observations, the agreement of I and II Peter regarding the spoken and written prophetic word, observing that in this they agree closely with the words of Peter in Acts 3:18-21 and of Paul in Acts 26:22,23. He also pays attention to the close correspondence of I and II Peter in their idea of Christian growth (I Peter 2:2; II Peter 3:18). One leaves Mayor's discussion of the authorship of I and II Peter with the feeling that this scholar has corroborated rather than weakened the claim of II Peter to its apostolic authorship.

Why, then, does Mayor reject this claim? One cannot escape the feeling that his position is dictated in large measure by the critical consensus of New Testament scholars and especially by the conclusion of Dr. F. H. Chase, whom he knew personally and quotes frequently, and whose articles on Peter and Jude in HDB he terms "by far the best introduction known to me on the two epistles here dealt with" (op. cit., p. vii).

Suffice it to say that in these considerations there seem to be no compelling reasons for refusing to accept the claims of II Peter to the authorship of the apostle whose name it bears.

*The Time and Place of the Writing.* The epistle was very possibly written to the Christians in Asia Minor (3:1) when the memory of I Peter was still rather fresh in their minds. If we judge that I Peter was written from Rome about A.D. 64, it seems reasonable to regard II Peter as written from Rome toward the end of Nero's reign, say A.D. 67.

*The Message of the Epistle.* The specific burden of Peter's heart at this time appears to have been the growth of a spirit of lawlessness and antinomianism in the churches, and also an attitude of skepticism toward Christ's second coming. Some feel that the false teachers described in the epistle were representatives of the Gnostic heresy in its early stages.

But while greatly concerned with the menace of these false teachers, and speaking with some emphasis to this point, the apostle realized that the basic need of his readers was for spiritual upbuilding and strength which would make them superior to such dangers. He, therefore, both opens and closes his letter with encouragement to spiritual conquest, inserting his warnings against the false teachers in the middle chapter of the three.

# OUTLINE

Theme: The imperative of spiritual conquest.
Key verse: II Peter 3:18.
  I. Peter's readers urged to go forward in grace. 1:1-21.
    A. Salutation and prayer for their spiritual advancement. 1:1,2.
    B. Reminder of the present reality of their spiritual inheritance. 1:3,4.
    C. Challenge to press into its full implications. 1:5-11.
    D. Peter's feeling of responsibility thus to challenge them. 1:12-21.
      1. Because of their need of intensified motivation. 1:12.
      2. Because of the imminence of his departure. 1:13-15.
      3. Because of the complete authenticity of the Gospel. 1:16-21.
  II. Peter's warning against the perils of false teachers. 2:1-22.
    A. The inevitability of false teachers. 2:1-3 a.
    B. The judgment of the false teachers. 2:3b-9.
    C. The characteristics of the false teachers. 2:10-22.
      1. Their fleshly self-indulgence and impudence. 2:10-12.
      2. Their perversion of Christian conviviality. 2:13.
      3. Their moral instability. 2:14.
      4. Their crassly selfish motivation. 2:15,16.
      5. Their spiritual barrenness and blight. 2:17-19.
      6. Their basic apostasy. 2:20-22.
  III. Christ's second coming an imperative to spiritual conquest. 3:1-18.
    A. Christ's coming in glory previously intimated to the readers. 3:1,2.
    B. The Second Coming an object of skepticism. 3:3-9.
    C. The Second Coming to be catastrophic. 3:10.
    D. An incentive to holy living. 3:11-18 a.
  IV. The apostolic benediction. 3:18 b.

## II PETER

### CHAPTER 1

SIMON Peter, a servant and an apostle of Jesus Christ, to them that have obtained like precious faith with us through the righteousness of God and our Saviour Jesus Christ:

2. Grace and peace be multiplied unto you through the knowledge of God, and of Jesus our Lord,

## COMMENTARY

**I. Peter's Readers Urged To Go Forward in Grace 1:1-21.**

A. Salutation and Prayer for Their Spiritual Advancement. 1:1,2.

**1. Simon** *(Symeon)* **Peter, a servant** *(slave)* **and an apostle of Jesus Christ.** This epistle clearly sets forth its authorship by the Apostle Peter. The title, *slave and apostle,* well illustrates Christ's rule: "He that is greatest among you shall be your servant" (Mt 23:11). **To them that have obtained like precious faith with us.** The expression **like precious** (in the original a single word meaning "equally precious") reminds us at once of the use in I Peter of the related words meaning "precious," "in honor," "preciousness or honor" — just one indication of the continuity between the two epistles. Harnack, though denying the Petrine authorship of both I and II Peter, held that the person who wrote II Peter had also authored the opening and closing parts of I Peter. The apostle here assigns great value to faith, and why not? It is the "coin of the realm" in God's kingdom. The writer finds the basis for faith, and its attainment by men in, **the righteousness of God and our Saviour Jesus Christ.** This, of course, is the foundation of the entire ethical universe. It is not a theoretical and juridical righteousness only, but a warm, loving, providential righteousness embracing God's entire redemptive plan. It is only "in the righteousness of God" that faith is possible. And again, it is through this faith, increasingly exercised, that God's righteousness is revealed (Rom 1:17).

**2. Grace and peace be multiplied.** The same greeting as used in I Peter, a characteristically Christian greeting (see commentary on I Pet 1:2). **Through the knowledge of God, and of Jesus our Lord.** The use here of the Greek word *epignōsis* ("precise and correct knowledge"— Thayer) is of interest. This epistle contains strong warnings against false teachers. Some conclude these to have been Gnostics, and use this as an argument for assigning to II Peter a postapostolic date, say, during the second century, when the Gnostic controversy was at its height. Others, like Bigg, fail to see in the epistle the sure marks of anti-Gnostic apologetic. Perhaps there is a reasonable middle ground. Certainly Gnosticism was a real issue in apostolic times and in Asia Minor,

3. According as his divine power hath given unto us all things that *pertain* unto life and godliness, through the knowledge of him that hath called us to glory and virtue:

4. Whereby are given unto us exceeding great and precious promises; that by these ye might be partakers of the divine nature, having escaped the corruption that is in the world through lust.

as is witnessed by Paul's Colossian letter, addressed largely to this incipient heresy. A key word in Colossians is the Greek *epignōsis*, "precise and correct knowledge," generally connected with God or Christ (Col 1:9,10; 2:2; 3:10). The Gnostics held to a highly intricate and extra-Scriptural system of doctrine, giving a great deal of attention to angels and to ascetic practices, tending to detract from the godhead of Christ, and withal assuming superior wisdom for their initiates. The Colossian letter from its beginning exalts Christ, the center of "all wisdom and knowledge," fully identified with God. This apologetic was doubtless shared by the other apostles, and may well be reflected here (as in II Pet 1:3,8; 2:20).

B. Reminder of the Present Reality of Their Spiritual Inheritance. 1:3,4.

3. **As his divine power hath given unto us all things.** Just as Peter opens his first letter, the aim of which was to encourage the Christians in their sufferings, by reminding them of their great spiritual wealth, their stake in remaining true, so he also opens the present epistle, aimed to brace them against plausible false doctrine. Those who are spiritually wealthy have much to lose by revolution and defection. **Through the knowledge of him.** To know Christ is life itself to a Christian (cf. Jn 17:3). **That hath called us.** Again, as in I Peter (e.g., 1:2), the apostle reminds his readers that they are a chosen people. **To glory and virtue** (generally signifying excellence). The original here seems to call for the meaning *by his own glory and virtue.* Either translation is possible and meaningful. It is by Christ's glory and excellence that we are drawn, and again these are the end product of the Christian life.

4. **Whereby** (*through which*, i.e., through the glory and virtue). The glory and excellence of Christ, reproduced in the characters of the saints, and thus rendered up as an offering to him whose they are, constitute the all-inclusive goal of Christian living. Ours is a goal of character: "We shall be like him" (I Jn 3:2). And in this goal are included all worthwhile things (cf. Mt 6:33). **Are given.** Not the usual word for "give," but a more rich and munificent word,

5. And besides this, giving all diligence, add to your faith virtue; and to virtue, knowledge;

6. And to knowledge, temperance; and to temperance, patience; and to patience, godliness;

7. And to godliness, brotherly kindness; and to brotherly kindness, charity.

"to endow," "to furnish with an estate." **Exceeding great and precious.** Literally, *the precious and greatest.* Again note the word "precious," so prominent in I Peter. **Promises.** Not the usual term indicating a quiet private agreement, but a heraldic word implying emphatic and public announcement—a very comfortable word for those concerned. **Partakers of the divine nature, having escaped the corruption that is in the world through lust.** On the basis of these publicly declared divine commitments, the believer becomes a sharer of that richest of all treasures, the nature and life of God. "If any man have not the Spirit of Christ, he is none of his" (Rom 8:9). This new life of the Spirit is none other than "Christ in you." It requires a yielding, an obedience, a walk (Gal 5:25). This new life removes us from the living death of bondage to carnal desire (Rom 8:11-13).

C. Challenge to Press into the Full Implications of Their Inheritance. 1:5-11.

**5-7. And beside this . . . add.** Peter urges these young believers to move on from step to step in divine grace. He tells them to bring to bear on their walk in grace all eagerness. **Add to your faith virtue.** "In your faith provide an ample supply of basic (Christian) excellence." This excellence is the quality of one who diligently practices the basic rudiments and implications of his calling. To virtue, the Christians are urged to add **knowledge.** Here is growth in awareness through study and experience. Next comes **temperance** (self-control). This is the Spirit-aided discipline of the Christian soldier. Then **patience,** the quality of a veteran's ability to see beyond current pressures in view of known resources. In patience the Christian adds **godliness** (Gr., *eusebeia*), a spirit of reverence and deference to God in all matters. In reverence he adds **brotherly kindness** (Gr., *philadelphia*). Deference to God and enduement with his love is the only basis for genuinely altruistic kindness to fellow men. In brotherly kindness, **charity** (Gr., *agapē*, "divine love," as in I Cor 13) is the Christian's quest. It would be amiss to picture these beautiful graces as compartmentalized and attainable only in their order. No, their presentation here seems to observe an order from the more elemental to the more advanced, but they are all of them facets

8. For if these things be in you, and abound, they make *you that ye shall* neither *be* barren nor unfruitful in the knowledge of our Lord Jesus Christ.

9. But he that lacketh these things is blind, and cannot see afar off, and hath forgotten that he was purged from his old sins.

10. Wherefore the rather, brethren, give diligence to make your calling and election sure: for if ye do these things, ye shall never fall:

11. For so an entrance shall be ministered unto you abundantly into the everlasting kingdom of our Lord and Saviour Jesus Christ.

12. Wherefore I will not be negligent to put you always in remembrance of these things, though ye know *them*, and be established in the present truth.

13. Yea, I think it meet, as long as I am in this tabernacle, to stir you up by putting *you* in remembrance;

14. Knowing that shortly I must put off *this* my tabernacle, even as our Lord Jesus Christ hath showed me.

15. Moreover I will endeavor that ye may be able after my decease to have these things always in remembrance.

of the Spirit's work in the life of a believer, aspects of the glory of the indwelling Christ, his character shown in the Christian's character.

**8,9. If these things be in you, and abound.** The word translated *be in* means "to be under one as a foundation or basis." This is implied in regeneration, in the Spirit's presence in the heart. But the matter of "abounding" implies Christian growth and the Spirit's fullness or full control as experienced by believers at Pentecost and since. **Neither . . . barren** (unworking) **nor unfruitful.** The fruit of the Spirit, if we rightly apprehend, is the character of Christ realized in the Christian. In the description of this fruit in Gal 5:22,23, divine love *(agapē)* is mentioned first; and the other graces, seven in number, are subsumed under it. These are closely related in their spirit and tenor to Peter's list above. In Col 3:14 Paul mentions divine love last as the comprehensive summation of the graces, somewhat as does Peter. The Father is glorified as the believer bears much fruit (Jn 15:8). **In the knowledge of our Lord.** Better, *Unto the precise and correct knowledge of our Lord.* This is a statement of the direction in which Christian conquest bears. The alternative is then mentioned. It is blindness and spiritual myopia, and a weakened sense of spiritual reality and life.

**10. Give diligence** *(make it your business)* **to make your calling and election sure** *(firm).* Here is personal responsibility with reference to God's call and choice of them. **If ye do** *(keep on doing)* **. . . ye shall never fall** *(stumble).* Obedience is not optional in any consideration of Christian safety. **11. An entrance shall be ministered unto you abundantly** *(richly).* Here is an intimation that heaven's society will not be classless. Good stewardship of Christ's riches will bear eternal proceeds. The Christian, endowed with wealth through Christ's provision, invests and saves for future wealth (cf. I Tim 6:19).

**D. Peter's Feeling of Responsibility Thus To Challenge Them. 1:12-21.**

**12. I will not be negligent to put you always in remembrance . . . though ye know . . . and be established.** The sense in the Greek is, "I will be intending to remind you always." Even where knowledge and establishment exist, there is need for motivation and exhortation. **13-15. As long as I am in this taber-**

16. For we have not followed cunningly devised fables, when we made known unto you the power and coming of our Lord Jesus Christ, but were eyewitnesses of his majesty.

17. For he received from God the Father honor and glory, when there came such a voice to him from the excellent glory, This is my beloved Son, in whom I am well pleased.

18. And this voice which came from heaven we heard, when we were with him in the holy mount.

19. We have also a more sure word of prophecy; whereunto ye do well that ye take heed, as unto a light that shineth in a dark place, until the day dawn, and the day-star arise in your hearts:

20. Knowing this first, that no prophecy of the Scripture is of any private interpretation.

21. For the prophecy came not in old time by the will of man: but holy men of God spake as they were moved by the Holy Ghost.

## CHAPTER 2

BUT there were false prophets also among the people, even as there shall be false teachers among you, who privily shall bring in damnable heresies, even denying the Lord that bought them, and bring upon themselves swift destruction.

2. And many shall follow their pernicious ways; by reason of whom the way of truth shall be evil spoken of.

3. And through covetousness shall they with feigned words make merchandise of you: whose judgment now of a long time lingereth not, and their damnation slumbereth not.

nacle. Christ, in his postresurrection commissioning of Peter, had intimated that the apostle would die a martyr's death (Jn 21:18). This is probably that to which Peter refers in verse 14. A sense of the brevity of his tenure adds weight to his feeling of responsibility for his readers. After my decease. Peter's epistles would serve to extend his care and admonition for his brethren.

16-18. We have not followed cunningly devised fables . . . but were eyewitnesses. The authenticity of the apostolic witness urges this reinforcement of it. Peter here speaks of a previous ministry to these people. This may be a reference to his sermon on Pentecost, when some of them had been present, or it may refer to labors among them in Asia Minor. This is my beloved Son. This reference to the Transfiguration scene may well have implied a rebuke to the false teachers who, if Colossians describes a parallel situation, were inclined toward the adoration of angels, thus reducing the pre-eminence of Christ. Since only Peter, James, and John were present with Christ on the mount, this also constitutes a reinforcement of the epistle's claim to Petrine authorship.

19-21. We have also a more sure word of prophecy. Taken with what is said in verse 21, the reference of these verses seems to be to the OT Scriptures. It is an amazing assessment of the validity of holy Scripture that Peter declares it to be more dependable than a voice from heaven heard with the natural ear. By implication, here is a rebuke for those teachers who went far beyond Scripture, constructing cunningly devised mystical theories. Holy men of God spake as they were moved by the Holy Ghost, or spake from God, being borne along by the Holy Spirit. This passage strongly recalls the comment on prophetic inspiration recorded in I Pet 1:10-12, another link between the two epistles.

II. Peter's Warning Against the Perils of False Teachers. 2:1-22.

A. The Inevitability of False Teachers. 2:1-3 a.

1-3 a. There shall be false teachers among you. Having just mentioned the prophets who spoke for God, Peter refers to the fact that these faced the opposition of false prophets. He warns the believers (somewhat after the manner of Acts 20:29,30; I Tim 4:1-6; II Tim 3:1-5—

994

4. For if God spared not the angels that sinned, but cast *them* down to hell, and delivered *them* into chains of darkness, to be reserved unto judgment;

5. And spared not the old world, but saved Noah the eighth *person*, a preacher of righteousness, bringing in the flood upon the world of the ungodly;

6. And turning the cities of Sodom and Gomorrah into ashes condemned *them* with an overthrow, making *them* an ensample unto those that after should live ungodly;

7. And delivered just Lot, vexed with the filthy conversation of the wicked:

8. (For that righteous man dwelling among them, in seeing and hearing, vexed *his* righteous soul from day to day with *their* unlawful deeds:)

9. The Lord knoweth how to deliver the godly out of temptation, and to reserve the unjust unto the day of judgment to be punished:

though the error here seems to have been in the area of life rather than of doctrine — I Jn 2:18-20; and Jude 3ff.) against false teachers who were perhaps even then known by the apostle to be at work in certain areas of the church. These would deny the Lord that bought them; they would gain a following and cast a shadow on the way of truth. Their purpose would be mercenary; they would be motivated through covetousness.

B. The Judgment of the False Teachers. 2:3b-9.

3b. Whose judgment . . . lingereth not. Here seems to be an intimation that these hardened and deliberate heretics had passed the probationary season of possible repentance. Their doom was now inexorable.

4. If God spared not the angels that sinned. Peter, at the very outset of his consideration of the false teachers, sets up a picture of the God of judgment. This is both encouragement to the faithful and warning to any inclined toward apostasy (cf. vv. 7-9 below). Chains of darkness. The reading *pits of darkness* (Gr., *sirois* or *seirois* instead of *seirais*) seems preferable. Although Peter seems here to refer to the apocryphal Book of Enoch, with its elaborate discussion of the sin of the fallen angels, their reservation unto judgment, and finally their judgment (this verse seems to reflect Enoch 21), yet there is an absence of that rather wild and questionable theorizing and intrusion of non-spiritual concept which is evident even to the casual reader of Enoch. 5. And spared not the old world, but saved Noah. Another reference to the severity, as well as to the goodness, of God. 6-8. Turning the cities of Sodom and Gomorrha into ashes . . . delivered just Lot. Still another illustration of God's judgeship of his creation. This reference to Lot's unhappiness with the developments connected with his choice of Sodom as a residence, because of his basic loyalty to God, whether considered as reflecting ancient tradition or as revelatory, is an interesting supplement to the OT picture of that patriarch.

9. The Lord knoweth how to deliver . . . and to reserve . . . to be punished. While in the supporting instances, Peter shows more interest in God's condemnation of wickedness than in his vindication of righteousness (this because of his preoccupation with the false teachers), in this final recapitulation he adduces

10. But chiefly them that walk after the flesh in the lust of uncleanness, and despise government. Presumptuous *are they,* self-willed, they are not afraid to speak evil of dignities.

11. Whereas angels, which are greater in power and might, bring not railing accusation against them before the Lord.

12. But these, as natural brute beasts made to be taken and destroyed, speak evil of the things that they understand not; and shall utterly perish in their own corruption;

13. And shall receive the reward of unrighteousness, *as* they that count it pleasure to riot in the daytime. Spots *they are* and blemishes, sporting themselves with their own deceivings while they feast with you;

14. Having eyes full of adultery, and that cannot cease from sin; beguiling unstable souls: a heart they have exercised with covetous practices; cursed children:

15. Which have forsaken the right way, and are gone astray, following the way of Balaam *the son* of Bosor, who loved the wages of unrighteousness;

16. But was rebuked for his iniquity: the dumb ass speaking with man's voice forbade the madness of the prophet.

first God's mercy to his own, a comfort to the readers. The epistle of Jude parallels very closely the present discussion of false teachers and their punishment. Peter speaks of their activities as being shortly at hand ("there shall be false teachers," 2:1); Jude treats these as present ("there are certain men crept in unawares," Jude 4).

C. The Characteristics of the False Teachers. 2:10-22.

10-12. Them that walk after the flesh ... and despise government. The picture is one of fleshly self-indulgence and carnal impudence. Not afraid to speak evil of dignities. . . . Whereas angels . . . bring not railing accusation. Peter warns against rash and self-confident speech, even as pertaining to evil powers. His reference to the angels is parallel to that of Jude 9, which seems to reflect a contest between Michael and the devil, related in the Assumption of Moses, an apocryphal writing known among the Jews. Peter's reference is discreet, causing some critical scholars to think that II Peter followed here the more specific reference in Jude. Bigg holds the contrary, feeling that Peter's statement was sufficient for his purpose, and that Jude's came a little later and particularized upon it. Speak evil of the things that they understand not. Their self-assurance was matched by their ignorance. This recalls the reference in Col 2:18. The characteristic of modern 'liberal' critical teachers which amazes one most is their absolute confidence in their own conclusions, based upon evidence however trivial, and involving tremendously important departures from tenets maintained for centuries by the historic church.

13. Sporting themselves with their own deceivings. Peter speaks of an abuse of Christian conviviality. Always eager for a good dinner, they make of such occasions an opportunity for raucous mirth and continued false teaching. Jude's reference to eating together by Christians as "feasts of charity" (lit., "your loves" or "occasions of love," Jude 12) sets a far different standard.

14-16. Having eyes full of adultery. Here is a picture of moral instability which finds too great a substantiation in the church today. A heart exercised in covetousness (ASV) ... following the way of Balaam. It is well known that eagerness for financial remuneration and desire for the large and popular churches have

17. These are wells without water, clouds that are carried with a tempest; to whom the mist of darkness is reserved for ever.

18. For when they speak great swelling *words* of vanity, they allure through the lusts of the flesh, *through much* wantonness, those that were clean escaped from them who live in error.

19. While they promise them liberty, they themselves are the servants of corruption: for of whom a man is overcome, of the same is he brought in bondage.

20. For if after they have escaped the pollutions of the world through the knowledge of the Lord and Saviour Jesus Christ, they are again entangled therein, and overcome, the latter end is worse with them than the beginning.

21. For it had been better for them not to have known the way of righteousness, than, after they have known *it*, to turn from the holy commandment delivered unto them.

22. But it is happened unto them according to the true proverb, The dog *is* turned to his own vomit again; and the sow that was washed to her wallowing in the mire.

## CHAPTER 3

THIS second epistle, beloved, I now write unto you; in *both* which I stir up your pure minds by way of remembrance:

caused many a modern prophet to **forsake the right way** and **to follow the way of Balaam.** And even in evangelical circles, an inordinate concern over financial return, or carelessness in the use of funds, has negated the work of some princes of the pulpit whose words were irresistibly powerful. **The dumb ass . . . forbad the madness.** In the light of eternal outcomes, the sad folly of such a perversion of purpose invites the scorn of even the most simple. Recall that the donkey was permitted to see that which evaded the myopic vision of Balaam "the seer" (Num 22:25).

**17-19. Wells without water.** The basic condemnation of false doctrine is its utter spiritual barrenness. It is this feature of the movement known as 'religious liberalism' that has caused great numbers of spiritually hungry people to desert coldly formal churches. It has also finally given rise to defection from 'liberalism,' even by intellectuals and scholars. This defection, known as "neo-orthodoxy," is a reactionary movement which, sadly enough, is still unwilling to own the full authority of Scripture. **Promise them liberty . . . servants** (*slaves*) **of corruption.** Theologians of a half century ago were drinking deep of the heady wine of freedom from the authority of Scripture and even of God. Said Prof. Walter Rauschenbusch, "The worst thing that could happen to God would be to remain an autocrat while the world is moving toward democracy. He would be dethroned with the rest" (*Theology of the Social Gospel*, p. 178). Said Prof. Hugh Hartshorne, "We no longer derive our ethical standards from established authorities, whether of church, state, family, convention, or philosophical system" (*Jour. of Ed. Soc.*, Dec., 1930, p. 202). Today the nation faces a tremendous harvest of increased crime and delinquency. The false teachers described by Peter were themselves examples of spiritual bondage (cf. Jn 8:34).

**20-22. Better for them not to have known.** This is a solemn assessment of the awful responsibility of apostasy, and it constitutes an implicit warning to the believers to remain steadfast.

**III. Christ's Second Coming, an Imperative to Spiritual Conquest. 3:1-18.**

A. Christ's Coming in Glory Previously Intimated to the Readers. 3:1,2.

**1. This second epistle.** Most naturally

2. That ye may be mindful of the words which were spoken before by the holy prophets, and of the commandment of us the apostles of the Lord and Saviour:

3. Knowing this first, that there shall come in the last days scoffers, walking after their own lusts,

4. And saying, Where is the promise of his coming? for since the fathers fell asleep, all things continue as *they were* from the beginning of the creation.

5. For this they willingly are ignorant of, that by the word of God the heavens were of old, and the earth standing out of the water and in the water:

6. Whereby the world that then was, being overflowed with water, perished:

7. But the heavens and the earth, which are now, by the same word are kept in store, reserved unto fire against the day of judgment and perdition of ungodly men.

taken as a reference to I Peter. **I stir up your pure minds.** Literally, *by a reminder I wake up your pure minds.* The word pure (Gr., *eilicrinēs*), while of disputed derivation, probably means "sun-judged," as a vase which, when held up to the sun, reveals no hidden flaws. As such flaws were often concealed by skillful patching with wax, the word is elsewhere (Phil 1:10) translated by the AV "sincere" (Lat., *sine cera,* "without wax"). Some take the word to refer, instead, to a sifting, as of grain.

2. **The holy prophets . . . us the apostles.** Peter claims a continuity and congruity with the witness of the OT Scriptures, the principal authentication for genuine Christian preaching in the apostolic age, and also with the witness of his fellow apostles. This incidental and unaffected claim to apostleship—as though the writer realized that it was well known to all his readers—is a strong corroboration of the Petrine authorship of this letter. The Second Coming was a subject greatly relished by the apostle. It underlies the exhortation and encouragement of his first letter (e.g., I Pet 1:5,7,10-13; 4:7,13; 5:1,4). He knew that his readers were familiar with this truth.

B. The Second Coming an Object of Skepticism. 3:3-9.

3,4. **There shall come . . . scoffers . . . Where is the promise of his coming?** It may be questioned whether this is a further reference to the false teachers of chapter 2, or simply a statement that the delay in Christ's return would cause many to abandon and even to scorn the Church's glorious hope.

5,6. **Willingly . . . ignorant.** Literally, *this escapes the notice of them willing.* A case of judicial blindness. They did not want the thing to be true. **By the word of God.** Peter goes back to the dependability and stability of God's word as demonstrated in creation. Literally, *it consisted in* (or *by*) *the word of God.* **Whereby** (Gr., *through which things,* i.e., through the word of God and the flood water) **the world that then was . . . perished.** God's judging word, like his creative word, was final. 7. **The heavens and the earth, which are now, by the same word are kept in store.** God's promise of fiery judgment upon sinners and upon the world is to be received respectfully. The apocryphal writings prior to the Christian era went into considerable

8. But, beloved, be not ignorant of this one thing, that one day *is* with the Lord as a thousand years, and a thousand years as one day.

9. The Lord is not slack concerning his promise, as some men count slackness; but is long-suffering to us-ward, not willing that any should perish, but that all should come to repentance.

10. But the day of the Lord will come as a thief in the night; in the which the heavens shall pass away with a great noise, and the elements shall melt with fervent heat, the earth also and the works that are therein shall be burned up.

11. *Seeing* then *that* all these things shall be dissolved, what manner *of persons* ought ye to be in *all* holy conversation and godliness,

detail about these matters. Our Lord, while on earth, spoke of a fiery destiny for the sinner (e.g., Lk 16:24).

**8,9. One day . . . with the Lord.** Peter now comes to the point at which he is aiming, namely, that the delay in Christ's return, cited by the skeptics, is no proper basis for doubt as to His coming. This has already been hinted at in his reference to the Noahic flood. It, too, was a long time coming, and its plausibility was quite belittled by the people of those days; but it came, exactly as God had said it would. This is Peter's third reference to Noah (I Pet 3:20; II Pet 2:5), another nice index of the unity of I and II Peter. Peter's comment on the equivalence between one day and a thousand years with God is a beautiful statement of God's eternity, his superiority to time-space limitations (cf. Ps 90:4). And it is exciting to think how such a concept contracts the period of waiting for his return. We accomplish quickly enough our years of this pilgrimage. But then, once "with the Lord" and freed from time-space limitations, it is but a day or two—figured even from apostolic times—until his kingdom comes with all its joys. **That all should come to repentance.** God's waiting is redemptive in its purpose; his basic will is that all might turn from their sin unto him.

C. The Second Coming To Be Catastrophic. 3:10.

**10. The day of the Lord will come as a thief.** Despite all apparent delay, God's word will again be demonstrated as valid. That day will come. The sudden, never-expected visit of the night burglar was a favorite simile with Christ, taken up by the apostles. **The elements shall melt . . . the earth . . . be burned up.** Here may be another allusion to the Book of Enoch, with its description of the "mountains of the seven metals" and their destruction. There seems to have been a general expectancy among the religious Jews that there would be an ultimate fiery cleansing of the earth. This, of course, looks beyond the reference of Scripture to the Millennium.

D. An Incentive to Holy Living. 3:11-18 a.

**11,12. What manner of persons ought ye to be . . . ?** Just as in his first epistle (1:14-16), Peter here uses the theme of the Christian's apocalyptic hope as a

12. Looking for and hasting unto the coming of the day of God, wherein the heavens being on fire shall be dissolved, and the elements shall melt with fervent heat?

13. Nevertheless we, according to his promise, look for new heavens and a new earth, wherein dwelleth righteousness.

14. Wherefore, beloved, seeing that ye look for such things, be diligent that ye may be found of him in peace, without spot, and blameless.

15. And account *that* the long-suffering of our Lord *is* salvation; even as our beloved brother Paul also according to the wisdom given unto him hath written unto you;

16. As also in all *his* epistles, speaking in them of these things; in which are some things hard to be understood, which they that are unlearned and unstable wrest, as *they do* also the other Scriptures, unto their own destruction.

powerful incentive to holiness. **Looking for and hasting unto the coming of the day of God.** What a picture of "loving his appearing"! (cf. II Tim 4:8) Not like those who dread that awful day, those who, when overtaken, will call for rocks and mountains to hide them from it (Rev 6:15-17), the Christian eagerly awaits it. The words **hasting unto the coming of the day of God** are capable also of the translation *hastening the coming.* . . . Those who help forward God's redemptive work can reasonably feel a partnership in its denouement.

13. **We . . . look for new heavens and a new earth, wherein dwelleth righteousness.** This had been a theme of the prophets (e.g., Isa 2:4; 11:6-9; Mic 4:1-5); it was **according to his promise.** It was a hope and vision shared by Abraham and the patriarchs (Heb 11:10). It is that which makes Christians of all ages "pilgrims and strangers." Compare Paul's mention of this in Rom 8:19-25. Like Lot in Sodom, the Christian cannot but groan at the prevalence of sin and its results. The name assigned to Jehovah by millennial Israel was Jehovah-Tsidkenu, "The Lord our Righteousness."

14. **Wherefore . . . seeing . . . ye look for such things.** A repeated urging of the Christian's hope as a motive for careful and holy living. **Be diligent** can be read, *make it your business.* **Peace** and holiness are associated in Heb 12:14. **15. Account that the longsuffering of our Lord is salvation.** Peter urges upon his readers the reasonableness of God's delays, a theme mentioned before, in verse 9. God waits that he may be gracious. **As our beloved brother Paul . . . hath written.** Peter knew the Pauline letters, although they were very nearly contemporary with his own. There seems no reason for interpreting this statement as indicating that the NT canon was becoming formalized when this was written. The phrase **our beloved brother** seems to refer naturally to a contemporary. **16. Which they that are unlearned and unstable wrest, as they do also the other scriptures.** Peter refers to those who quibbled about the authority of the Pauline writings as being spiritually illiterate and undependable. The apostle assigns to the letters of this man who was his contemporary and who at times had been critical of him a place among the *other* sacred writings. Compare Paul's own claim that his injunctions *when first written* were the commandments of God (I Cor 14:37; I Tim 6:3).

17. Ye therefore, beloved, seeing ye know *these things* before, beware lest ye also, being led away with the error of the wicked, fall from your own steadfastness.

18. But grow in grace, and *in* the knowledge of our Lord and Saviour Jesus Christ. To him *be* glory both now and for ever. Amen.

17. Beware lest ye . . . fall from your own stedfastness. A repeated and final admonition to faithfulness. Their advance knowledge gave them an advantage. Forewarned is forearmed (cf. I Thess 5:4). But there was real danger of their being involved in the error of lawless men. 18 a. But grow in grace. Life is never static. One must go forward or he will go backward. Peter closes upon the same note with which he began this epistle (1:5-11), that is, with a challenge to spiritual conquest through the knowledge of our Lord and Saviour Jesus Christ. To know him is to live; to grow in that acquaintance is to grow in the Spirit (cf. Phil 3:10).

### IV. The Apostolic Benediction. 3:18 b.

18 b. To him be glory both now and for ever. To Christ, the beginning, the process, and the fulfillment of our great salvation, is ascribed eternal praise.

# BIBLIOGRAPHY

For bibliography see under I Peter.

# THE FIRST EPISTLE OF JOHN

## INTRODUCTION

### (to I, II, III John)

*The Life of John.* The apostle's life divides itself into two periods. The first concludes with his departure from Jerusalem some time after the ascension of Christ, and the second continues from that time to his death. John was evidently much younger than Jesus. He may have been born in Bethsaida (Jn 1:44). The son of Zebedee and Salome, he apparently came from a fairly well-to-do family; for they had servants (Mk 1:20), his mother helped with the financial support of Christ (Mk 15:40,41), and John knew the high priest, who was chosen from the upper classes (Jn 18:15). His younger brother was James. Though John probably did not attend the rabbinical schools (Acts 4:13), his religious training in his Jewish home would have been thorough.

Galileans were industrious and hardy men of action and John was no exception. Though artists have pictured him as an effeminate person, the Bible describes him quite differently. He was known as one of the "sons of thunder" (Mk 3:17), who on occasion acted in bigotry (Mk 9:38; Lk 9:49), vindictiveness (Lk 9:54), and scheming (Mt 20:20,21; cf. Mk 10:35). It was the power of Christ that changed this typical Galilean into "the apostle of love."

How long John remained in Jerusalem after Pentecost is uncertain. He was evidently not there when Paul first visited the city (Gal 1:18,19), although he may have been there later as one of the members of the council (Acts 15:6). The evidence that he spent the latter part of his life in Asia Minor, and chiefly at Ephesus, is too strong to be shaken by other conjectures. Justin Martyr (*Dialogue with Trypho*, LXXXI), Irenaeus (Eusebius *Ecclesiastical History* V. xx. 4,5), Polycrates (*Ibid.* V. xxiv. 3), and the strong inference of The Apocalypse that it was written by a church leader in Asia Minor all attest to this fact. Extra-Biblical literature is replete with accounts of John's activities during this period, the most famous stories being about Cerinthus in the bath and a young lad (one of the apostle's converts) who became a bandit and was later restored to the church (cf. A. Plummer, *The Gospel According to S. John, Cambridge Greek Testament*, pp. xvii,xviii).

John is best known as "the apostle of love," but he was also a stern man who even in his later years was intolerant of heresy. Both these aspects of his character, sternness and love, are prominently displayed in the First Epistle. *Intense* is the single word that best describes the man. In actions, in love for the brethren, in condemnation of heresy, John was the intense apostle.

*The City of Ephesus.* Ephesus, John's home during his later life, is situated in a fertile plain near the mouth of the Cayster River. In Paul's day it was a center of trade, both of the eastern Aegean region and of that which passed through Ephesus from the East. Since the city was the capital of the province of Asia Minor, the Roman proconsul resided there. Democratic assemblies were allowed the people of Ephesus (Acts 19:39). Christianity came to the city about 55 through the ministry of Paul, and he wrote a circular letter to Ephesus and other churches about eight years later. Before John went to the city, many had labored there for the cause of Christ (Aquila and Priscilla, Acts 18:19; Paul, Acts 19:3-10; Trophimus, Acts 21:29; the family of Onesiphorus, II Tim 1:16-18; 4:19; and Timothy, I Tim 1:3).

Morality in Ephesus was low. The magnificent temple of Diana, with its 127 columns 60 feet high surrounding an area 425 by 220 feet, was like a magnet drawing people to the Ephesian cesspool. It was a house of prostitution in the name of religion. And yet in spite of the iniquitous idolatry of that place, it was a Mecca or Rome of religious worship, and the people delighted to call themselves "temple-keepers" of the great Diana (Acts 19:35).

*Gnosticism.* Gnosticism, a philosophy of existence or being, in its early form was making inroads into the Asia Minor church of John's day. It involved speculations concerning the origin of matter and how human beings can be free from matter. The name is Greek, but its main elements were Greek and Oriental; Jewish and Christian features were added to the mixture. In particular, Gnosticism held that knowledge is superior to virtue, that the nonliteral sense of Scripture is the true meaning and can be understood only by a select few, that evil in the world precludes God's being the creator, that the Incarnation is incredible because deity cannot unite itself with anything material—such as a body, and that there is no resurrection of the flesh. This teaching resulted in Docetism, asceticism, and antinomianism. Extreme Docetism held that Jesus was not human at all but was merely a prolonged theophany, while moderate Docetism considered Jesus the natural son of Joseph and Mary, upon whom Christ came at the time of baptism. Both forms of heresy are attacked by John in the First Epistle (2:22; 4:2,3; 5:5,6). Some Gnostics practiced asceticism because they believed all matter to be evil. Antinomianism, or lawlessness, was the conduct of others, since they held knowledge to be superior to virtue (cf. 1:8; 4:20). John's principal answer to these Gnostic errors is to emphasize the Incarnation and the ethical power of the example of the life of Christ.

*The Authorship of the Epistles.* The question raised concerning the authorship of First John is whether the John who wrote both the Gospel and the Epistle was really John the son of Zebedee or John the elder. Literature mentions a presbyter John in Ephesus, and some have been led to conclude that John the son of Zebedee was a different person from the John of Ephesus, and that it was the latter who wrote these books (Irenaeus in Eusebius, *op. cit.*, V. viii and xx; Papias in *Ibid.*, III, xxxix; Polycrates in *Ibid.*, V. xxiv; The Canon of Muratori).

The standard argument for the Johannine authorship of the Gospel is based on internal evidence. This argument is in the nature of three concentric circles. (1) The largest circle proves that the author was a Palestinian Jew. This is demonstrated by his use of the Old Testament (cf. Jn 6:45; 13:18; 19:37), and by his knowledge of Jewish ideas, traditions, expectations (cf. Jn 1:19-49; 2:6,

13; 3:25; 4:25; 5:1; 6:14,15; 7:26 ff.; 10:22; 11:55; 12:13; 13:1; 18:28; 19:31, 42), and by his knowledge of Palestine (Jn 1:44,46; 2:1; 4:47; 5:2; 9:7; 10:23; 11:54). (2) The middle circle proves that the author was an eyewitness. This is indicated by the exactness of the details of time, place, and incidents given in the Gospel (cf. Jn 1:29,35,43; 2:6; 4:40,43; 5:5; 12:1,6,12; 13:26; 19:14,20,23,34,39; 20:7; 21:6), and by the character sketches (e.g., Andrew, Philip, Thomas, Nathanael, the woman of Samaria, Nicodemus) which are peculiar to this Gospel. (3) The third circle concludes that the author was John. The method followed is first to eliminate all others who belonged to the inner circle of disciples and then to cite confirmatory evidence to show that only John could have been the author.

The arguments for the common authorship of the Gospel and the Epistle are conclusive. This evidence is built on the parallel passages (e.g., Jn 1:1 and I Jn 1:1), common phrases (e.g., "only begotten," "born of God"), common constructions (use of conjunctions instead of subordinate clauses), and common themes (*agapē*, "love"; *phōs*, "light"; *zōē*, "life"; *menō*, "abide"). Thus the basic question remains: Was the author of both writings John the apostle or John the elder?

Some of the reasons for distinguishing John the apostle from John the elder and thus favoring the authorship of these books by the latter are: (1) an unlettered man (Acts 4:13) could not have written anything so profound as the Fourth Gospel; (2) a fisherman's son would not likely have known the high priest; (3) an apostle would not have called himself an elder, as the writer of the Epistle does; (4) since the writer of the Gospel used Mark as a source, that writer could not have been John, since an apostle would not have used the work of one who was not an apostle. To these arguments the answers which support the case for authorship by John the apostle are not difficult to find. (1) *Unlettered* stands for lack of formal training in the rabbinic schools and does not mean "unlearned"; (2) it must not be assumed that all fishermen were from the lower classes; (3) the Apostle Peter called himself an elder (I Pet 5:1), so why should not John have used the same title? (4) Matthew, an apostle, used Mark as a source, according to the critics, but that is not ordinarily used as an argument against Matthean authorship of the First Gospel. Furthermore, if John the elder is the author of the Fourth Gospel and the same as the beloved disciple, it becomes very difficult to explain why such an important person as John the son of Zebedee is never mentioned in that Gospel. The evidence clearly points to one writer of Gospel and Epistles, John the apostle, the son of Zebedee, who is one and the same as John the elder who spent his later years in Ephesus.

*Dates and Place of Writing.* The dates for the writing of the Epistles are related to the date assigned to the writing of the Gospel. Those who assign a date between 110 and 165 for the Gospel and assume that John was not the author find themselves facing a dilemma. If the Gospel was published that late, allegedly but not actually by John, why did not the hundreds of living Christians who had known John during his later years denounce it as a forgery? Or at least, why did not someone mention that it did not come from John himself? If it was not published until some time between 140 and 165, how could it have been universally accepted by 170, as it was? The fact that the

Rylands fragment of John found in Egypt dates from A.D. 140 or earlier requires that the date of the composition of the book be set near the turn of the century or earlier. It is evident in the Gospel that the author is looking back (Jn 7:39; 21:19), which means that since John was the author, the Gospel must have been published between 85 and 90 (although the actual writing may have been done before that time). It was undoubtedly produced at the insistence of the elders of the churches of Asia Minor, who wanted those things which John had been teaching them orally to be put in writing before he died. Since the message of I John seems to presuppose a knowledge of the contents of the Gospel, and since there is no mention of the persecution under Domitian in 95, the First Epistle was probably written about A.D. 90. Second and Third John may also be dated about the same time as the First Letter, i.e., about 90. All the Epistles were written from Ephesus, according to reliable tradition.

# OUTLINE

IV. Fellowship's cautions. 4:1-21.
    A. A caution concerning lying spirits: false prophets. 4:1-6.
        1. The existence of lying spirits. 4:1.
        2. The examination of lying spirits. 4:2-6.
    B. A caution concerning a loving spirit: false profession. 4:7-21.
        1. The ground of love. 4:7-10.
        2. The glories of love. 4:11-21.
 V. Fellowship's cause. 5:1-21.
    A. Faith in Christ proved by the conduct we exhibit. 5:1-5.
    B. Faith in Christ proved by the credentials we exhibit. 5:6-12.
        1. The evidence of the credentials. 5:6-8.
        2. The effect of the credentials. 5:9-12.
    C. Faith in Christ proved by the confidence we exhibit. 5:13-21.
        1. Confidence in prayer. 5:13-17.
        2. Confidence in knowledge. 5:18-21.

# I JOHN

### CHAPTER 1

THAT which was from the beginning, which we have heard, which we have seen with our eyes, which we have looked upon, and our hands have handled, of the Word of life;

2. (For the life was manifested, and we have seen *it*, and bear witness, and show unto you that eternal life, which was with the Father, and was manifested unto us;)

# COMMENTARY

Introduction. 1:1-4.

Unlike most other NT epistles this one has no salutation at the beginning and no benediction at the conclusion. These four verses of introduction correspond to the opening eighteen verses of the Gospel and three verses of the Revelation. They tell us the writer's subject, namely, the Word, who is life.

A. The Person. 1:1,2. This is **that which** the apostle has to declare.

**1. Was.** Not "came into existence" but **was** in existence already *(ēn)*. **From [*the*] beginning.** The absence of the article is idiomatic. Meaning is always determined by the context. In this instance the phrase means a beginning prior to creation, and the meaning is determined by **was with the Father** in verse 2. This is a sweeping claim for the eternity of Christ. **Which we have heard.** Perfect tense, indicating permanent result of a past action. **Seen with our eyes.** John would have us know that the seeing is no figure of speech but a literal fact. **Looked upon, and . . . handled.** The tense is changed to aorist and indicates a special manifestation of Christ. **Handled** is the same word used by Christ in one of his post-resurrection appearances (Lk 24:39). Evidently John is referring to that here. **Word of life. Word** is a name rather than merely the idea of revelation, and **life** indicates work rather than being a name for Christ (though in v. 2 it is practically a name).

**2.** The **life** which Christ **manifested** was **eternal life** because Christ was **with the Father.** The phrase shows the distinct personality of Christ, who is the life; and

3. That which we have seen and heard declare we unto you, that ye also may have fellowship with us: and truly our fellowship *is* with the Father, and with his Son Jesus Christ.

4. And these things write we unto you, that your joy may be full.

the preposition with shows the equality of Christ with the Father, as in Jn 1:2.

B. The Purpose. 1:3,4. This is *why* the apostle declares this message.

3. Seen and heard. The Incarnation is the basis for fellowship. Unto you (also). Who have not seen and heard. Fellowship. This is the purpose (*hina*, "in order that") of John's message and is the theme of the epistle. The word is chiefly used by Paul in the NT, except for this chapter. It is both divine — with God, and human — with us. It is proved by exhibiting joy (v. 4) and by generosity (Acts 2:45; Rom 15:26; II Cor 8:4; 9:13; I Tim 6:18). Fellowship is best pictured in the Lord's Supper (I Cor 10:16). With the Father, and with his Son Jesus Christ. "Thus two fundamental truths, which the philosophical heresies of the age were apt to obscure or deny, are here clearly laid down at the outset: (1) the distinctness of personality and equality of dignity between the Father and the Son; (2) the identity of the eternal Son of God with the historical person Jesus Christ" (Plummer, *op. cit.*, p. 20).

4. That your joy may be full. Better, *that our joy may be fulfilled.* Fellowship is the basis of joy. The readers' joy depended on it and so did the apostle's. (It is difficult to reach a positive decision, as to the reading, between *our joy* and your joy.)

I. Fellowship's Conditions. 1:5-10.

A. Conformity to a Standard. 1:5-7. This section directly contradicts the Gnostic doctrine that moral conduct is a mat-

5. This then is the message which we have heard of him, and declare unto you, that God is light, and in him is no darkness at all.

6. If we say that we have fellowship with him, and walk in darkness, we lie, and do not the truth:

7. But if we walk in the light, as he is in the light, we have fellowship one with another, and the blood of Jesus Christ his Son cleanseth us from all sin.

8. If we say that we have no sin, we deceive ourselves, and the truth is not in us.

ter of indifference to the enlightened one.

**5. Of him.** From Christ. **God is light.** No one tells us so much about God as John does. He is spirit (Jn 4:24); he is light (I Jn 1:5); and he is love (I Jn 4:8). These statements concern what God is, not what he does. Thus, light is his very nature. Holiness is the principal idea, and its use here at the beginning of the epistle lays the foundation for the Christian ethics of the letter.

**6. If we say.** Greek third class condition, but including the writer — a very delicate way to state the possibility. **Walk in darkness.** Out of the will of God, who is light. **Do not the truth.** Truth is not only what one says but what he does.

**7. If we walk . . . as he is in the light.** God is light; we walk in it. The requirement for fellowship is to let the light reveal right and wrong and then to respond to that light continually. The Christian never becomes light until his body is changed, but he must walk in response to light while here on earth. Two consequences follow — first, fellowship, then cleansing. **Fellowship one with another.** The reference is to our brethren and not to God, as in 3:11,23; 4:7,12; II Jn 5. **And.** The cleansing of Christians is a consequence of walking in the light; the clause is coordinate and indicates a second result of walking in the light. **Blood of Jesus Christ.** In both OT and NT blood stands for death — usually a violent one. **Cleanseth us.** Walking in the light shows up our sins and frailties; thus we need constant cleansing, and this is available on the basis of the death of Christ. The verb is in the present tense and it refers to the cleansing in sanctification. **From all sin.** Sin is singular, indicating the principle of sin, but the addition of **all** (or *every*) shows that it has many forms.

B. Confession of Sin. 1:8-10. The mention of cleansing from sin in verse 7 leads to the thought of this section.

1) Confession of the Principle of Sin. 1:8.

**If we say.** The second of three false professions in this chapter (cf. vv. 6, 10). **No sin.** The phrase **to have sin** is peculiar to John in the NT (cf. Jn 9:41; 15:22, 24; 19:11). It refers to the nature, principle, or root of sin, rather than to the act. The consequences of not confessing that we have sin are two: (1) **we deceive ourselves,** literally, *lead ourselves astray,* do-

9. If we confess our sins, he is faithful and just to forgive us *our* sins, and to cleanse us from all unrighteousness.

10. If we say that we have not sinned, we make him a liar, and his word is not in us.

## CHAPTER 2

MY little children, these things write I unto you, that ye sin not. And if any man sin, we have an advocate with the Father, Jesus Christ the righteous:

ing for ourselves what Satan endeavors to do for us; (2) **the truth is not in us**; we shut out the light and live in an atmosphere of self-made darkness.

2) Confession of Particular Sins. 1:9. To admit the truth of verse 8 may not cost much, but to do what is required in verse 9 may. **Confess.** Literally, *say the same thing.* "Having the same medium of vision that God has" (Candlish, p. 49). But it is not mere outward agreement; rather, it includes forsaking, for that is God's attitude for us concerning sin. The confession is to God. **Faithful and just.** Better, *faithful and righteous.* God keeps his word and is just in all his actions, including the way he forgives sins, which is on the basis of the death of his Son. **Forgive . . . cleanse.** Forgiveness is absolution from sin's punishment, and cleansing is absolution from sin's pollution.

3) Confession of Personal Sins. 1:10. One may admit the truths of verses 8 and 9 in the abstract but never admit being personally involved in sin. **If we say.** This is the third false profession. **Have not sinned** refers to the act of sin, not the state, as in 1:8. **Make him a liar.** Because everywhere God says man has sinned. **His word is not in us.** The word of God in both OT and NT.

Thus fellowship depends on responding to the standard of light and realizing our sinful state. The victorious Christian life is a life of no unconfessed sins; and genuine confession includes forsaking, and thus produces growth.

**II. Fellowship's Conduct. 2:1-29.**

The writer now deals with the conduct of the believer who walks in the light. There is no break in thought between the chapters.

A. The Character of Our Conduct: Imitation. 2:1-11.

1) The Principle of Imitation — "That ye sin not." 2:1,2. The assurance of forgiveness of sins (1:9) and the statements of its universality (1:8,10) might lead some to take a light view of sin. Therefore, John shows the standard of conduct and the nature of the remedy for sin in order that his readers might not sin. **1. Little children.** A term of endearment, not an indication of age. **That ye**

2. And he is the propitiation for our sins: and not for ours only, but also for *the sins of the whole world*.

3. And hereby we do know that we know him, if we keep his commandments.

4. He that saith, I know him, and keepeth not his commandments, is a liar, and the truth is not in him.

5. But whoso keepeth his word, in him verily is the love of God perfected: hereby know we that we are in him.

sin not. The aorist tense cannot mean "that ye continue not in sin," but rather "that ye sin not at all." Though this can never be completely true until we see Him (3:2), it should be our aim always. **And if any man sin.** The aorist again shows that it is a particular act of sin. **We have.** John includes himself. **Advocate.** Literally, *one summoned alongside*, especially to serve as a helper — a patron. The word is used in the NT only by John (Jn 14:16,26; 15:26; 16:7; and here). The advocate pleads the cause of the believer against Satan, his accuser (Rev 12:10). He is **Jesus Christ the righteous. Righteous** indicates the particular characteristic of our Lord which gives effectiveness to his advocacy (cf. Heb 7:26). Because he is righteous he can plead with the righteous Father.

**2. He.** He *himself*, emphatic personal pronoun. **Propitiation.** This is the basis of his advocacy, and although the latter is for believers only, propitiation is for all men. **Propitiation** means satisfaction (used here and in 4:10 only). Christ himself is the satisfaction (note the present tense). "Christ is said to be the 'propitiation' and not simply the 'propitiator' (as He is called the 'Saviour' iv. 14), in order to emphasize the thought that He is Himself the propitiatory offering as well as the priest (comp. Rom. iii. 25). A propitiator might make use of means of propitiation, outside himself" (B. F. Westcott, *The Epistles of St. John*, p. 44). **For our sins. For** (*peri*). Concerning, not "in behalf of." **But also for the whole world.** There is no limitation on the satisfaction which Christ *is* concerning sin. **World.** *Kosmos* in this case, as in Jn 3:16, means the human race.

2) The Pattern for Imitation — "Even as he walked." 2:3-6.

a) The Word of Christ. 2:3-5. Imitation involves keeping his commandments.

**3. Hereby,** i.e., **if we keep his commandments. We do know.** We perceive. **That we know him.** Have come to a knowledge of him. **Keep his commandments.** Contrary to Gnosticism, which concerned itself with intellectual attainment, Christianity requires moral conduct. **4. Is a liar.** His whole character is false. Truth as an active principle is not in such a man and hence cannot regulate his whole life. **5.** This verse is the opposite of 2:4 as 2:4 is the opposite of 2:3. **Word.** Wider than **commandments,** covering all of God's revelation of his will. **Love of**

6. He that saith he abideth in him ought himself also so to walk, even as he walked.

7. Brethren, I write no new commandment unto you, but an old commandment which ye had from the beginning. The old commandment is the word which ye have heard from the beginning.

8. Again, a new commandment I write unto you, which thing is true in him and in you: because the darkness is past, and the true light now shineth.

9. He that saith he is in the light, and hateth his brother, is in darkness even until now.

10. He that loveth his brother abideth in the light, and there is none occasion of stumbling in him.

God. Probably man's love for God (objective genitive) here as in 2:15; 4:12; 5:3. The opposite (God's love for man, subjective genitive) is seen in 4:9.

b) The Walk of Christ. 2:6.

6. He that saith. To declare oneself on Christ's side binds one morally to imitate him. Abideth. A favorite word with John, defined in 3:24 as habitual fellowship maintained by keeping his commandments. Ought. Is bound; an obligation represented as a debt (cf. Lk 17:10). Even as. Kathōs, not merely hōs, indicating that the imitation must be exact and in all things. The pattern of Christ as set forth in the NT is everywhere humiliation and self-sacrifice. This should be the focus of the Christian's imitation (cf. Mt 11:29; Jn 13:15; Rom 15:2; Phil 2:5 ff.; Heb 12:2; I Pet 2:21).

3) The Proof of Imitation—Love. 2: 7-11.

The life of Christ was one of self-sacrificing love; therefore, the proof of imitating him is exhibited in love. Love is that which seeks the highest good in the one loved; and since the highest good is the will of God, love is doing the will of God.

7. Brethren. Better, beloved. First occurrence of the word in this epistle. Commandment. To walk as he walked (v. 6) and to love the brethren (vv. 9-11). These are essentially the same. From the beginning. This could mean the beginning of the race, or the beginning of the Law (Lev 19:18) or, best, the beginning of the Christian life. 8. Which thing is true. The best translation seems to be, A new commandment write I unto you, namely, that which is true. Is past. Better, is passing away (present tense). Because the darkness is passing away and the true light is shining, John bids his readers walk as children of light. The true light. The revelation of God in Christ.

9. He that saith. This is the fifth time John points out a possible inconsistency between profession and conduct (1:6,8,10; 2:4; cf. 4:20). Brother. Fellow Christian, not fellow man (though sometimes in the NT "brother" means fellow man, as Mt 5:22; Lk 6:41). Is in darkness. This false profession involves existence in the exactly opposite state from that which is claimed. 10. He that loveth. This is not mere profession, as in verse 9, but the actual truth. There is none occasion of stumbling in him. There is in him noth-

**11.** But he that hateth his brother is in darkness, and walketh in darkness, and knoweth not whither he goeth, because that darkness hath blinded his eyes.

**12.** I write unto you, little children, because your sins are forgiven you for his name's sake.

**13.** I write unto you, fathers, because ye have known him *that is* from the beginning. I write unto you, young men, because ye have overcome the wicked one. I write unto you, little children, because ye have known the Father.

ing likely to cause others to stumble. This follows the general NT meaning of *skandalon,* occasion of stumbling, for it is used of offense caused to others. "Want of love is the most prolific source of offences" (Westcott, p. 56). **11. Is in darkness, and walketh in darkness, and knoweth not.** Darkness is the home and sphere of activity and the blinding agent of the one who hates his brother.

B. The Commandment for Our Conduct: Separation. 2:12-17.

1) The Address of the Commandment. 2:12-14.

The ground of the appeal to separation which follows in 2:15-17 is found in the character and position of those addressed in these verses. **12. Little children.** All of John's readers are being addressed, but with special emphasis in this word on the kinship they have one to the other because of the forgiveness of their sins. **For his name's sake.** By believing on the name of Christ (and thus the person for whom the name stands) they experienced forgiveness. **13. Fathers.** The address is now made to the older ones in the congregation and those who were prominent by reason of their position. **Ye know** (ASV). You have come to know through abiding in the commandments of the Christian life. **Him that is from the beginning,** i.e., Christ (cf. Jn 1:1-14). **Young men.** The younger ones in the group. **Have overcome.** Perfect tense, expressing the abiding result of past action. Strength, which is characteristic of youth, is necessary for victory in spiritual battles. **The wicked one.** The form could be either masculine (the evil one, i.e., the devil) or neuter (evil). Since the address to the youth is personal, very likely the reference here is also to the personal devil. "The abruptness with which the idea of 'the evil one' is introduced shews that it was familiar" (Westcott, p. 60). **Little children.** The same group as addressed in 2:12, though the word here is *paidia* and the emphasis is on subordination rather than on relationship, as in *teknia* of verse 12. Age distinctions are not apparent in these words as they are in "fathers" and "young men"; hence the reference is to the entire group. **I write.** Literally, *I wrote,* changing to the aorist tense here and in verse 14 from the present tenses in 2:12,13 a. The change has been variously explained. It is probably to be accounted for by a

14. I have written unto you, fathers, because ye have known him *that is* from the beginning. I have written unto you, young men, because ye are strong, and the word of God abideth in you, and ye have overcome the wicked one.

15. Love not the world, neither the things *that are* in the world. If any man love the world, the love of the Father is not in him.

change in John's viewpoint as he wrote. Through 13 a he was looking at the letter as still incomplete, and from 13 b he viewed it as finished, and so employed these epistolary aorists. **Known the Father.** The use of **Father** in the address to **little children** reinforces the idea of subordination. The term **Father** occurs more often in John's writings than in all three Synoptic Gospels added together.

**14. Word of God.** The reason the young men could overcome the devil was that the word of God abode in them. They did the will of God as revealed in his word.

2) The Appeal of the Commandment. 2:15-17.

a) The Nature of the Appeal. 2:15 a.

In the addresses of 2:12-14, John reminded his readers of their privileges as Christians. Their sins had been forgiven, they knew Him who is the truth, and they had experienced spiritual victory. In these verses he exhorts them to walk worthy of this high calling by not loving the world nor the things in it. Loving God is incompatible with loving the world.

**15. Love not.** The command is addressed to all (not to one particular class) and appears abruptly in the text. **The world** (*kosmos*, the opposite of *chaos*). The world is that organized system which acts as a rival to God. It is that "which finds its proper sphere and fulfillment in a finite order and without God" (Westcott, p. 63). Though God loves the world of men (Jn 3:16), we must not love that which organizes them against God. A truly religious man keeps himself from the world (Jas 1:27), since friendship with it is enmity with God (Jas 4:4). The world lies in the lap of the wicked one (I Jn 5:19), and John uses the world as a synonym for darkness (Jn 3:19). The command is not, "Love not too much," but "Love not at all." **Neither the things that are in the world.** Love nothing in the sphere of the *kosmos*. We must use the things in the world, but when we love them in place of God, we abuse their use (I Cor 7:31).

b) The Reasons for the Appeal. 2:15 b-17.

**15 b.** This thought of supplanting God in our affections with the things of the world is stated in the last phrase of the verse. **If any man love the world.** It is the principle of not serving two masters (Mt 6:24; Jas 4:4). Since the world is the same as darkness, it must exclude God,

16. For all that *is* in the world, the lust of the flesh, and the lust of the eyes, and the pride of life, is not of the Father, but is of the world.

17. And the world passeth away, and the lust thereof: but he that doeth the will of God abideth for ever.

18. Little children, it is the last time: and as ye have heard that antichrist shall come, even now are there many antichrists; whereby we know that it is the last time.

who is light. This is the first reason for not loving the world.

16. The second reason for not loving the world is that the things of the world are not of the Father. **For.** Better, *because*. Verse 16 gives the detailed reasons for the statement of 2:15 b. **Lust of the flesh.** The genitive, **flesh,** is subjective here, as it is normally when used with **lust.** Thus the meaning is not lust for flesh but the flesh's lusts, or those lusts which have their base in the flesh. Flesh used in this ethical sense (as opposed to the material sense, meaning body) is the old nature in man, or his capacity to do that which is displeasing to God. **Lust of the eyes.** The eyes are the gate from the world to the flesh. In the phrase, **lust of the flesh,** the thought is of physical pleasure; while in **lust of the eyes,** the thought is of mental, physical, or aesthetic pleasure. **Pride of life.** The word **pride** occurs elsewhere only in Jas 4:16, where it is translated "boastings." The idea in the word is pretentious ostentation which results from not seeing the real emptiness of the things of the world. **Life.** *Bios,* not *zōē.* The latter means the vital principle of life, while the former means possessions. Thus the "pride of life" is ostentatious pride in the possession of worldly goods. **Is not of the Father. Of,** *ek,* "origin." None of these things originates from the Father but rather from the world.

17. The third reason for not loving the world is that it is transitory. **Is passing away.** Present tense, a process now going on. **The lust thereof.** The lust which belongs to and is stimulated by the world. If all this is passing away, how foolish to fix one's affections on that which is already in the process of dissolution. **But he that doeth.** The Christian is not disturbed. **Doeth.** Not saith, or even loveth, but doeth. **The will of God.** The opposite of all that is in the world. **For ever.** Doing the will of God proves the possession of eternal life, which means abiding forever.

C. The Creed for Our Conduct: Affirmation. 2:18-29.

1) The Necessity for a Creed. 2:18-21.

a) The Last Hour. 2:18 a.

**Little children.** This is a general address to all of John's readers, regardless of age, by one who has the authority of age and experience. **It is the last time.**

19. They went out from us, but they were not of us; for if they had been of us, they would *no doubt* have continued with us: but *they went out,* that they might be made manifest that they were not all of us.

20. But ye have an unction from the Holy One, and ye know all things.

21. I have not written unto you because ye know not the truth, but because ye know it, and that no lie is of the truth.

The statement arises out of the preceding idea of the passing away of the world. Literally, *a last hour.* The time of this present age which will grow more troublesome immediately preceding the second advent of Christ. A time of trouble and persecution.

b) The Many Antichrists. 2:18b-21.

18 b. Antichrist . . . antichrists. Only John uses the term (here; 2:22; 4:3; II Jn 7). In this verse alone John affirms the presence of many antichrists in his own day and anticipates the coming of the Antichrist in a future day (as described by him in Rev 13:1-10). *Anti* means "opposed" to Christ. Thus, an antichrist is one who opposes Christ under the guise of Christ. Such are empowered by superhuman Satanic forces; they may be part of the Christian assembly outwardly; and they teach false doctrine (2:19; II Jn 7). The presence of antichrists in the world proves that it is a last hour. Since they were present in John's day and have been present throughout church history, the "last hour" must be the entire period between the first and second advents of Christ.

19. They went out from us. They belonged outwardly to the church. They were not of us. Never organically united to the body. Continued with us. Their very separation from the Christian group proved their false profession, and their departure showed them up as antichrists. Apostasy is possible for those who have never really made Christ their own Saviour. 20. Unction. Anointing. Even if these antichrists had not separated themselves, believers have within themselves the power to discover them, that is, to discern between truth and error because of the anointing. Anointing designates something for sacred use. The words Christ and anoint are from the same root; therefore, John seems to be drawing a contrast here between Antichrist and his antichrists on one hand and Christ and his christs (anointed ones) on the other. Ye know all things. Particularly the difference between true and false teaching (cf. RSV, you all know).

21. I have not written. Epistolary aorist tense, referring to this Epistle (not the Gospel) and particularly to this section concerning antichrists. John states two reasons for writing: because his readers know the truth and because no lie is of the truth. These reasons establish a bond of sympathy and point of contact between writer and readers. Ye know it.

**22.** Who is a liar but he that denieth that Jesus is the Christ? He is antichrist, that denieth the Father and the Son.
**23.** Whosoever denieth the Son, the same hath not the Father: [*but*] *he that acknowledgeth the Son hath the Father also.*
**24.** Let that therefore abide in you, which ye have heard from the beginning. If that which ye have heard from the beginning shall remain in you, ye also shall continue in the Son, and in the Father.
**25.** And this is the promise that he hath promised us, *even* eternal life.
**26.** These things have I written unto you concerning them that seduce you.

John appeals to the knowledge they possess. **No lie is of the truth.** Every lie has its origin from the devil and therefore is alien to the truth which the readers know.

· 2) The Nature of the Creed. 2:22-29.
**22.** **Who is a liar?** Literally, *Who is the liar?* Abruptly introduced without any connecting particles. **He that denieth that Jesus is the Christ.** The background of this denial is Gnosticism, not Judaism. If it were Judaism, the denial would be similar to that against which the early apostles preached (Acts 5:42, etc.) — namely, that Jesus of Nazareth was not the Christ of the OT. But the Gnostic heresy against which John is here writing was that Christ came upon Jesus at his baptism and departed before his death. This was the liar's denial that Jesus was truly the God-man. This is the teaching of the antichrist. **That denieth the Father and the Son.** Gnosticism considered Christ and Jesus as two distinct entities. Thus, to deny that Jesus is the Christ is to deny the Son, the God-man. And to deny the Son is to deny the Father, because the Son is the revelation of the Father without whom the Father cannot be known (Mt 11:27).
**23.** The previous statement is now emphasized. **Hath not the Father.** In verse 22 John says that to deny the Son is to deny the Father. Here he says that to deny the Son is to have not the Father; to deny the Son is to forfeit the right to become a child of God (Jn 1:12) and to possess the Father as a living friend. It is a living relationship that is in view here, not merely a creedal assent. **He that acknowledgeth.** The positive statement of the same truth. The last part of the verse is apparently a genuine part of the original text and should not be italicized (as in the AV) as if it were not genuine.
**24.** **Let that . . . abide in you** (AV). In the Greek the sentence opens with emphasis on **you** — "As for you . . . ," and contrasts the true believers and the false teachers. **Which ye have heard from the beginning.** That is, the foundational truths of the Gospel. Abiding in them brings abiding in the Son and the Father. **25.** **This** refers to eternal life, which is the promise. But this is the same as abiding in him in the preceding verse.
**26.** **These things** concerning the false teachers. **Seduce.** Lead astray; present participle, indicating habitual effort. **27. And as for you** (ASV). Emphatic position

27. But the anointing which ye have received of him abideth in you, and ye need not that any man teach you: but as the same anointing teacheth you of all things, and is truth, and is no lie, and even as it hath taught you, ye shall abide in him.

28. And now, little children, abide in him; that, when he shall appear, we may have confidence, and not be ashamed before him at his coming.

29. If ye know that he is righteous, ye know that every one that doeth righteousness is born of him.

of the pronoun, as in verse 24. **Anointing.** The gift of the Holy Spirit which the believers received when they were converted (cf. v. 20). **From him.** Source of the gift of the Spirit. **Need not that any man teach you.** Because this is the Spirit's work (Jn 16:13 ff.). **As the same anointing teacheth you of all things.** A re-emphasis of the preceding statement. **Teacheth.** Present, continuous teaching of the truth. **Ye abide** (*shall* should be omitted). The verb could be indicative or imperative (as Jn 5:39; 12:19; 14:1; 15:18,27). If indicative, John is merely assuming the truth of the statements he has made concerning his readers. If imperative, he is commanding them to experience these things.

**28. Abide.** A command to keep His commandments (3:24). **When.** Best texts read *If (ean).* That *if,* does not throw doubt on the fact of his coming but only raises questions as to certain circumstances surrounding his coming; e.g., the time of it. Abiding results in (1) having **confidence** and (2) not being **ashamed. Confidence.** Boldness *(parrēsia);* literally, *freedom in speaking* or *readiness to say anything.* **When he shall appear.** We should be able to have unreserved utterance as we give account of our stewardship to him. **Not be ashamed before him.** Literally, *not shrink with shame from him* as a guilty person surprised at his coming. **Coming.** *Parousia.* The only occurrence of the word in John's writings. Often it is used in connection with judgment which accompanies his return (Mt 24:3,27,37; I Cor 15:23; I Thess 2:19; 3:13; 5:23; Jas 5:7,8).

**29. He is righteous.** The preceding verse speaks of Christ; thus it seems logical to refer the *he* of this verse to Christ. **Righteous.** Compare 2:1; 3:7. **Every one that doeth righteousness.** The verb is present — "doeth habitually." **Born of him.** Does this mean born of Christ, as would be indicated if the references in verses 28 and 29 a are to Christ? If so, this is the only reference to Christ's work of begetting (though begotten of God and of the Spirit are Scriptural ideas; cf. Jn 1: 13; 3:6,8). "The true solution of the difficulty seems to be that when St. John thinks of God in relation to men, he never thinks of him apart from Christ (comp. v. 20). And again he never thinks of Christ in His human nature without adding the thought of His divine nature. Thus a rapid transition is possible from the one aspect of the Lord's divine-human Person to the other" (Westcott, p. 83).

## CHAPTER 3

BEHOLD, what manner of love the Father hath bestowed upon us, that we should be called the sons of God: therefore the world knoweth us not, because it knew him not.

III. Fellowship's Characteristics. 3:1-24.

A. In Relation to Our Prospect — Purity. 3:1-3. The thought of 2:29 — born of him — is now developed. "Born of him! That is what awakens John's grateful surprise, and occasions his exclamation, 'Behold, what manner of love!' His discourse now is an expansion of that thought" (Robert S. Candlish, *The First Epistle of John*, p. 227.)

1) The Reasons for Purity. 3:1-3 a, John states two reasons why the Christian ought to be pure. One is related to a past work of God and the second to a future work.

**1. Behold.** The word is plural — "all of you behold what I have just seen" (2: 28). Some take **what manner of** to imply something foreign; i.e., "what kind of foreign or other-worldly love" (cf. Kenneth S. Wuest, *In These Last Days*, p. 142). Others see no such significance in the word as used in the NT (A. Plummer, *The Epistles of S. John, Cambridge Greek Testament*, p. 71). The word does imply astonishment and admiration (cf. Mt 8: 27; Mk 13:1; Lk 1:29; II Pet 3:11 for the only other uses in the NT). **Hath bestowed.** Literally, *hath given.* The perfect tense indicates further that the gift is a permanent possession of the child of God. **Sons.** Literally, *born ones* or *children. Huios*, adult son, presents the legal side

**2.** Beloved, now are we the sons of God, and it doth not yet appear what we shall be: but we know that, when he shall appear, we shall be like him; for we shall see him as he is.

**3.** And every man that hath this hope in him purifieth himself, even as he is pure.

of sonship (and is used only by Paul of believers). This word *(teknon)* emphasizes the natural side, birth into the family of God. Yet both terms are suitable for expressing adoption (Jn 1:12; Rom 8:14-17). After **sons of God** should be inserted the words *and we are.* For this cause (ASV; AV, *therefore*)—because we are children of God—**the world knoweth us not.** The world does not know by experience what sort of people the children of God are. The world cannot have such experiential knowledge because it knows not Christ as Saviour (cf. I Cor 2:14). **2. Now are we . . . and.** "The two thoughts of the present and future condition of God's children are placed side by side with the simple conjunction **and,** as parts of one thought. Christian condition, now and eternally, centers in the fact of being children of God. "In that fact lies the germ of all the possibilities of eternal life" (M. R. Vincent, *Word Studies in the New Testament.* II, p. 344). **Like him.** The likeness of the full reflection of the glory of God in the believer. This includes the physical change to a resurrection body as well as the full spiritual change, which includes purity (v. 3), no sin (v. 5), and righteousness (v. 7). **The** reason for this change is our seeing him at the translation of the church. "The sight of God will glorify us" (Plummer, *Epistles of S. John,* p. 74). **3. Hope in him.** Literally, *on (epi) him,* i.e., hope resting on him.

---

### 1. Righteousness. 3:4-9.

| Characteristics | Consequences |
|---|---|
| a. Does not do sin (4). | a. Is not lawless (4). Does not set at nought Christ's mission (5). |
| b. Does not sin as a prevailing habit (6). | b. Proves abiding and knowledge of him (6). |
| c. Does righteousness (7). | c. Is righteous and imitates Christ (7). |
| d. Does not do sin (8). | d. Is not of the devil and has entered into the victory Christ gives (8). |
| e. Does not practice sin (9). | e. Is begotten of God (9). |
| f. Cannot sin (9). | f. Proves being born of God (9). |

### 2. Love. 3:10-18.

| Characteristics | Consequences |
|---|---|
| a. Brother love (10) | a. Origin is of God (10). |
| b. Unlike Cain (11,12). | b. Will not lead to murder (11,12). |
| c. Hated by the world (13). | c. Not to be surprised (13). |
| d. Brother love (14) | d. Proof of having passed from death to life (14). |
| e. No hate (15). | e. Not a murderer and has life (15). |
| f. Lays down life for brethren (16). | f. Knows love in its essence (16). |
| g. Shares goods (17,18). | g. Love of God dwells in him (17,18). |

---

4. Whosoever committeth sin transgresseth also the law: for sin is the transgression of the law.

5. And ye know that he was manifested to take away our sins; and in him is no sin.

6. Whosoever abideth in him sinneth not: whosoever sinneth hath not seen him, neither known him.

7. Little children, let no man deceive you: he that doeth righteousness is righteous, even as he is righteous.

Him refers to Christ. **Purifieth.** Present tense, "constantly purifies himself." Personal effort is necessary, but it must be based on resting in our hope (cf. Jn 15:5).

2) The Meaning of Purity. 3:3 b.

The thought behind purity is of ceremonial purification required before appearing in God's presence (cf. Jn 11:55; Heb 10:19 ff.; Ex 19:10). But the idea in the word is not only of outward purification but also of inner cleansing (cf. Jas 4:8; I Pet 1:18,19). Thus, it means that the hopeful Christian should be completely pure, just as Christ was entirely pure. He is ever the standard which John holds before the believer (cf. I Jn 2:6).

B. In Relation to Our Position — Righteousness and Love. 3:4-18. Our position demands a certain practice, and John proceeds to emphasize the characteristics of that practice in two ideas — righteousness and love. Verse 3 is thus explained by expansion and contrast in 3:4-18, and perhaps the best way to follow the writer's thought is to present a chart of these verses. See bottom of page 10.

4. **Committeth sin.** Literally, *doeth the sin*. The idea is of sinning continually and as completely as possible. **Sin is the transgression of the law.** Literally, *sin is lawlessness*. The terms are interchangeable (because of the use of the article with both words). Sin is lawlessness and lawlessness is sin. Law is used in its broadest concept here and includes natural law (Rom 2:14), the Mosaic law, the law of Christ (Rom 8:2; I Cor 9:21). 6. **Abideth . . . sinneth not.** Both words are in the present tense and indicate the habitual character of the person. The person who is abiding in Christ is not able to sin habitually. Sin may enter his experience, but it is the exception and not the rule. If sin is the ruling principle of a life, that person is not redeemed (Rom 6); thus a saved person cannot sin as a habit of life. When a Christian does sin, he confesses it (I Jn 1:9) and perseveres in his purification (3:3). The continuous sinner has not known God and is therefore an unregenerate person.

7. **Little children.** "The tenderness of the address is called out by the peril of the situation" (Westcott, p. 105). **Deceive.** Literally, *lead astray*. **Doeth.** Present tense; "habitually doeth." **Is righteous.** Righteous deeds spring from a righteous character and are the proof of regeneration. **As.** Christ, as always, is the example.

8. He that committeth sin is of the devil; for the devil sinneth from the beginning. For this purpose the Son of God was manifested, that he might destroy the works of the devil.

9. Whosoever is born of God doth not commit sin; for his seed remaineth in him: and he cannot sin, because he is born of God.

10. In this the children of God are manifest, and the children of the devil: whosoever doeth not righteousness is not of God, neither he that loveth not his brother.

11. For this is the message that ye heard from the beginning, that we should love one another.

12. Not as Cain, *who* was of that wicked one, and slew his brother. And wherefore slew he him? Because his own works were evil, and his brother's righteous.

13. Marvel not, my brethren, if the world hate you.

14. We know that we have passed from death unto life, because we love the brethren. He that loveth not *his* brother abideth in death.

15. Whosoever hateth his brother is a murderer: and ye know that no murderer hath eternal life abiding in him.

8. **Committeth.** Present tense; "he who is continually doing sin." This is his habit of life, not merely a single act. **Of the devil.** Satan is the source of these sinful desires. "Habitual actions again are an index of character, and here, of source" (Wuest, pp. 148,149). **Son of God.** This is John's first use of this title in the epistle, and it particularly expresses dignity and authority. **Destroy.** Literally, *loose.* Christ in his death has undone the bonds by which the works of the devil were held together. Satan can no longer present a solid front in his attacks on the Christian.

9. **Is born.** Perfect participle — past action with results continuing to the present — "has been and remains born" (cf. 2:29; 4:7; 5:1,4,18). **Doth not commit sin . . . cannot sin.** Present tenses, indicating again habitual sinning. **Seed.** The principle of divine life given the one born of God (Jn 1:13; II Pet 1:4). This makes it impossible for the Christian to live habitually in sin. **10. In this** looks back to the preceding verses, though the same teaching is reiterated in the last part of verse 10; that is, "in this life of victory over sin . . ." **The children of God . . . the children of the devil.** This is the only place in the NT where these two phrases stand side by side (cf. Acts 13:10; Eph 2:3). All mankind is apparently of one family or the other; and until one receives Christ, he is a child of the devil (Eph 2:3 and here). **He that loveth not his brother.** "This clause is not a mere explanation of that which precedes but the expression of it in its highest Christian form" (Westcott, p. 109).

12. Love for the brother suggests hate of a brother, and thus the example of Cain is cited. He is said to have belonged to the family of the **wicked one. Slew.** Originally the Greek word (used here and in Rev 5:6,9,12; 6;4,9; 13:3,8; 18:24 only) meant "to cut the throat," and later it meant "to slay with violence." **13. Marvel not.** Literally, *stop marveling.* John's readers evidently could not understand why the world should hate them. **14.** Love means life and hate means death. The test of being born again is not that the world hates us but that **we love the brethren. 15. Murderer.** This is not to be understood figuratively as meaning a murderer of the soul or character, but literally, because of verse 12. God looks on the heart, and the heart that is full of hate is potentially capable of murder. Compare the Lord's teaching

16. Hereby perceive we the love *of God*, because he laid down his life for us: and we ought to lay down *our* lives for the brethren.

17. But whoso hath this world's good, and seeth his brother have need, and shutteth up his bowels *of compassion* from him, how dwelleth the love of God in him?

18. My little children, let us not love in word, neither in tongue; but in deed and in truth.

19. And hereby we know that we are of the truth, and shall assure our hearts before him.

20. For if our heart condemn us, God is greater than our heart, and knoweth all things.

21. Beloved, if our heart condemn us not, *then* have we confidence toward God.

in Mt 5:21,22. "He who falls under a state, falls under the normal results of that state carried out to its issue" (Alford, *The Greek Testament*, IV, 474). Should the occasion arise, the person who habitually hates his fellow man would act just as Cain did. Such a person is unsaved.

16. Cf. 2:6. Self-sacrificing love is required of the believer. 17. Not many are called to lay down their lives for others, but all can follow the instructions of this verse. John suggests "that there is a danger in indulging ourselves in lofty views which lie out of the way of common experience. We may therefore try ourselves by a far more homely test. The question is commonly not of dying for another but of communicating to another the outward means of living" (Westcott, p. 114). **Good.** The necessities of life. **Bowels.** The seat of tender affections; better rendered *heart*.

C. In Relation to Our Prayers—Answers. 3:19-24. The foregoing teaching would naturally raise misgivings in some minds. So John hastens to add that the fruit of love is confidence, and confidence expresses itself in prayer, and confident prayer is answered.

1) Answers Dependent on Confidence. 3:19-21.

19. Hereby. *In this,* i.e., the love of the brethren. **Assure.** Literally, *persuade* or *tranquilize.* Persuade our heart of what? That it need not **condemn us.** Thus the AV **assure** is a correct interpretive translation. **Before him.** It is in God's presence that assurance comes. 20. For if, i.e., "whereinsoever," balancing the **all things** of the last part of the verse. In what things our heart condemns us, **God is greater** . . . . In examining our brotherly-love life, our hearts may be either too strict or too lenient. But God is greater and knows all things; therefore, we appeal to him for the truth about ourselves, and remember that he is the all-compassionate One. This results in correct judgment and confidence for our hearts. 21. An a fortiori argument: "If before God we can persuade conscience to acquit us, when it upbraids us, much more may we have assurance before Him, when it does *not* do so" (Plummer, *The Epistles of S. John*, p. 89). **Condemn us not.** Not sinless perfection, but no unconfessed sin in the life. **Confidence.** Literally, *boldness* or *freedom in speaking.*

22. And whatsoever we ask, we receive of him, because we keep his commandments, and do those things that are pleasing in his sight.

23. And this is his commandment, That we should believe on the name of his Son Jesus Christ, and love one another, as he gave us commandment.

24. And he that keepeth his commandments dwelleth in him, and he in him. And hereby we know that he abideth in us, by the Spirit which he hath given us.

## CHAPTER 4

BELOVED, believe not every spirit, but try the spirits whether they are of God: because many false prophets are gone out into the world.

2. Hereby know ye the Spirit of God: Every spirit that confesseth that Jesus Christ is come in the flesh is of God:

2) Answers Dependent on Obedience. 3:22-24.

**22.** Answered prayer is now conditioned on the habitual keeping of commandments and doing the things that please Him. **Keep** and **do** are both in the present tense. **23.** The commandment is to **believe** and **love.** Faith is a work, as in Jn 6:29. **Believe on the name.** Literally, *believe the name.* It means to believe all that Christ is, as represented by his name. Since this is addressed to Christians, it is an exhortation to believe him for all that he provides for the Christian life. **24.** Obedience also results in abiding. **Dwelleth.** This word is translated "abide" in Jn 15. Thus, the sentence is a definition of abiding. To abide is to keep his commandments. And the Holy Spirit bears witness to the fact that Christ abides in us.

**IV. Fellowship's Cautions. 4:1-21.**

A. A Caution Concerning Lying Spirits: False Prophets. 4:1-6.

1) The Existence of Lying Spirits. 4:1. The mention of the Holy Spirit in 3:24 leads to defining false spirits. This is another example of John's method of using antithesis. **Beloved.** The address of tenderness again reminds the reader that the subject matter is important. **Believe not.** Literally, *stop believing.* Evidently some of his readers were being carried away with Gnostic teaching. **Try.** *Dokimazō,* which means to put to the test for the purpose of approving. This word generally implies testing with the hope that the thing tested will pass, while *peirazō* ("try" or "tempt") generally means to try with the purpose that the thing tried will be found wanting. The reason for testing is simply that **many false prophets** are in the world. False prophets are false teachers (II Pet 2:1) and wonder workers (Mt 24:24; Acts 13:6; Rev 19:20). The test concerns their origin, **whether they are of God.**

2) The Examination of Lying Spirits. 4:2-6.
a) Their Creed To Be Examined. 4:2,3.
**2.** If a teacher confesses **that Jesus Christ is come in the flesh,** he is a true prophet. He must openly acknowledge (the meaning of **confess**) the person of the incarnate Saviour. This involves the mode of his coming (**in the flesh**) and permanence of the incarnation (perfect tense of **come**). If he had not taken

3. And every spirit that confesseth not that Jesus Christ is come in the flesh is not of God: and this is that *spirit* of antichrist, whereof ye have heard that it should come; and even now already is it in the world.

4. Ye are of God, little children, and have overcome them: because greater is he that is in you, than he that is in the world.

5. They are of the world: therefore speak they of the world, and the world heareth them.

6. We are of God: he that knoweth God heareth us; he that is not of God heareth not us. Hereby know we the spirit of truth, and the spirit of error.

7. Beloved, let us love one another: for love is of God; and every one that loveth is born of God, and knoweth God.

8. He that loveth not, knoweth not God; for God is love.

upon himself a human body, he could never have died and been the Saviour. From this verse we are not to suppose that this is the only test of orthodoxy, but it is a major one and it was the most necessary one for the errors of John's day.

**3.** Negative statement of the truth of verse 2. **Not.** The position of the negative following the relative pronoun requires the translation: "Every spirit who is of such kind as not to confess." **That spirit of antichrist.** The AV rightly supplies **spirit**, though the omission of it in the Greek text indicates a breadth of thought. Such a false prophet is influenced by many forces and spirits, including demonic ones, and all of these reveal the action of antichrist. Superhuman forces are behind these false teachers.

b) Their Crowd To Be Examined. 4:4-6.

**4. Ye.** In contrast to false teachers. **Them.** The false prophets themselves, not the spirits behind them. **He that is in you.** Undefined as to which particular person of the Godhead John has in mind, though the mention of the Spirit in 3:24 would indicate that the indwelling of the Holy Spirit is referred to. **He that is in the world.** Satan, the prince of the world and the energizing force behind all false spirits and prophets (Jn 12:31). **5. They.** The false teachers. **Speak they of the world.** The world is their source of speech, not their subject matter. The world system headed by Satan is the source of all heresy. **6. We.** Intensive—"As for us, we . . ." **Knoweth . . . heareth.** Both verbs are present, indicating progressiveness. He that is increasing in the knowledge of God continues to hear us. **Hereby.** That is, the apostles speak the truth because God's people hear them, while the false prophets speak error because the world hears them.

B. A Caution Concerning a Loving Spirit: False Profession. 4:7-21.

1) The Ground of Love. 4:7-10.
a) Love is of God. 4:7,8.
**7.** "The transition seems abrupt, as if the Apostle had summarily dismissed an unwelcome subject" (Plummer, *The Epistles,* p. 99). This is the third section on love (cf. 2:7-11; 3:10-18). **Love is of God.** Origin. **Begotten.** Perfect tense—"hath been begotten and remains his child." **8. Loveth not.** Present participle—"habitually loveth not." **God is love.**

9. In this was manifested the love of God toward us, because that God sent his only begotten Son into the world, that we might live through him.

10. Herein is love, not that we loved God, but that he loved us, and sent his Son *to be* the propitiation for our sins.

11. Beloved, if God so loved us, we ought also to love one another.

12. No man hath seen God at any time. If we love one another, God dwelleth in us, and his love is perfected in us.

13. Hereby know we that we dwell in him, and he in us, because he hath given us of his Spirit.

14. And we have seen and do testify that the Father sent the Son *to be* the Saviour of the world.

15. Whosoever shall confess that Jesus is the Son of God, God dwelleth in him, and he in God.

The third of John's three great statements concerning the nature of God (Jn 4:24; I Jn 1:5). The absence of the article (God is *the* love) indicates that love is not simply a quality which God possesses, but love is that which he is by his very nature. Further, because God is love, love which he shows is occasioned by himself only and not by any outside cause. The word **God** is preceded by an article, which means that the statement is not reversible; it cannot read, "Love is God."

b) Love is of Christ. 4:9,10.
9. The manifestation of God's love in our case (**toward us**) was in the giving of his Son. **Only begotten.** Not only did God send his Son, but it was his only begotten Son whom he sent. Christ is the only born Son in the sense that he has no brothers (cf. Heb 11:17). **That we might live.** The purpose of the sending of Christ. **10. Herein is love.** Literally, *. . . the love;* i.e., the love which is the nature of God. And such love is unrelated to anything human beings could do, but it is expressed in the gift of Christ. **Propitiation.** Satisfaction.

2) The Glories of Love. 4:11-21.
a) It causes us to love others. 4:11,12.
**11. So.** If God loved us to the extent of giving his only Son, we **ought** (moral obligation) **to love one another.** False teachers were not concerned with teaching any moral obligations. **12. God** is in the emphatic position. Translate: **God no man hath beheld at any time.** The connection between this thought and the context seems to be this: Since no one has seen God ever, the only way he who is love can be seen is by his children's loving one another and thus showing the family likeness. **His love** could refer to his love for us or to our love for him (Plummer, p. 103) or to his nature (Westcott, p. 152; Wuest, p. 166). It is probably not his love for us. If it is our love for him, this is **perfected** (matured) as we love the brethren. If it is the love which is his nature, that is **perfected** (or accomplishes its full purpose) as believers love one another.

b) It causes us to know the indwelling of God. 4:13-16.
**13.** Since we cannot see God, he has given us evidence of his presence with us through his Spirit, who dwells within. **Of his Spirit.** Not that we receive part of the Third Person of the Trinity, but that we receive certain of the many gifts of the Spirit. **15. Confess.** Say the same

16. And we have known and believed the love that God hath to us. God is love; and he that dwelleth in love dwelleth in God, and God in him.

17. Herein is our love made perfect, that we may have boldness in the day of judgment: because as he is, so are we in this world.

18. There is no fear in love; but perfect love casteth out fear: because fear hath torment. He that feareth is not made perfect in love.

19. We love him, because he first loved us.

20. If a man say, I love God, and hateth his brother, he is a liar: for he that loveth not his brother whom he hath seen, how can he love God whom he hath not seen?

21. And this commandment have we from him, That he who loveth God love his brother also.

## CHAPTER 5

WHOSOEVER believeth that Jesus is the Christ is born of God: and every one that loveth him that begat loveth him also that is begotten of him.

thing; i.e., agree with some authority outside of one's self. **Son of God.** "This confession of the deity of Jesus Christ implies surrender and obedience also, not mere lip service" (A. T. Robertson, *Word Studies in the New Testament*, VI, 234).

**16. Love that God hath to** (literally, *in*) **us.** Love becomes a force working in us.

c) It causes us to have boldness in the day of judgment. 4:17.

**Our love.** The text literally reads *the love with us.* It is the love which God, who is love, has produced in us through begetting us and placing his spirit in us. **Boldness in the day of judgment.** The believer who has perfected God's love in his earthly life will be able to approach the judgment seat of Christ without any shame. Such assurance is not presumption, because **as he is, so are we in this world.** The ground of boldness is our present likeness to Christ in this life, and particularly, according to this context, our likeness in love.

d) It casts out fear. 4:18.

The thought of boldness brings to mind its opposite, **fear.** Since love seeks the highest good of another, fear, which is shrinking from another, cannot be a part of love. **Torment.** Better, *punishment.*

e) It proves the reality of our profession. 4:19-21.

**19. We love him.** The word **him** is not in the best texts, and the verb is subjunctive. Therefore, translate: *Let us love, because he first loved us.* **20, 21.** Our love for our brethren, a visible thing, proves our love for God, an invisible entity. It is easy to say piously, "I love God"; John says that real piety is shown in brotherly love. Furthermore, he drives the point home by declaring in verse 21 that this is a commandment of Christ (Jn 13:34).

### V. Fellowship's Cause. 5:1-21.

Believing in Christ is the ground of our fellowship. The word **believe** has occurred only three times so far in the epistle, but it appears six times in 5:1-13. "St. John now traces the foundations of spiritual kinsmanship" (Westcott, p. 176). The fact that the Christian has exercised faith in Christ is proved in three ways, according to the teaching of this chapter.

A. Faith in Christ Proved by the Con-

2. By this we know that we love the children of God, when we love God, and keep his commandments.

3. For this is the love of God, that we keep his commandments: and his commandments are not grievous.

4. For whatsoever is born of God overcometh the world: and this is the victory that overcometh the world, *even* our faith.

5. Who is he that overcometh the world, but he that believeth that Jesus is the Son of God?

6. This is he that came by water and blood, *even* Jesus Christ; not by water only, but by water and blood. And it is the Spirit that beareth witness, because the Spirit is truth.

duct We Exhibit. 5:1-5.

1) As begotten ones we love the brethren. 5:1-3.

**1.** The Gnostics denied that Jesus of Nazareth was the Christ. John makes faith in this truth an essential test of being begotten of God. **Him that begat** is God. **Him** also that is begotten is the believer. **2.** The converse of 4:20,21 is here stated. It is equally true to say that he who loves God loves His children, and he who loves God's children loves God. **When.** Literally, *whenever*. **3. Grievous.** Heavy, an oppressive and exhaustive burden. **Love** makes the commandments of God light.

2) As believing ones we live victoriously. 5:4,5.

**4.** Keeping the commandment to love the brethren is possible because of the **victory** which the Christian has over the world. **Overcometh.** Present tense, implying a continuous battle. **Victory that overcometh.** Here the verb is aorist, indicating the assuredness of the victory. The victory that overcame the world is our **faith. 5.** Our faith is in the fact that **Jesus is the Son of God.** It is the belief in the full deity (Son of God) and true humanity (Jesus) of the God-man. "Our creed is our spear and shield" (Plummer, *The Epistles of S. John*, p. 112).

B. Faith in Christ Proved by the Credentials We Exhibit. 5:6-12.

1) The Evidence of the Credentials. 5:6-8.

**6. Water and blood.** These have been interpreted to mean (1) the baptism and death of Christ; (2) the water and blood which flowed from Christ's side on the cross; (3) purification and redemption; and (4) the sacraments of baptism and the Lord's Supper. The last two interpretations are symbolical; and there is no call for such interpretations here because **came** is aorist, referring to actual event. The first two make the phrase refer to actual events in the Lord's life. The second is not to be preferred because the order of the words is reversed (cf. Jn 19: 34). The first is the most satisfactory explanation. Christ came **through** (*dia*, "by means of") baptism, which marked him off and associated his ministry with righteousness; and through blood, his death, which paid the penalty for the sins of the world. His ministry was also exercised in (the second and third **by** in the verse) the sphere of what his baptism and his

7. For there are three that bear record in heaven, the Father, the Word, and the Holy Ghost: and these three are one.

8. And there are three that bear witness in earth, the spirit, and the water, and the blood: and these three agree in one.

9. If we receive the witness of men, the witness of God is greater: for this is the witness of God which he hath testified of his Son.

10. He that believeth on the Son of God hath the witness in himself: he that believeth not God hath made him a liar; because he believeth not the record that God gave of his Son.

11. And this is the record, that God hath given to us eternal life, and this life is in his Son.

12. He that hath the Son hath life; *and* he that hath not the Son of God hath not life.

13. These things have I written unto you that believe on the name of the Son of God; that ye may know that ye have eternal life, and that ye may believe on the name of the Son of God.

14. And this is the confidence that we have in him, that, if we ask any thing according to his will, he heareth us:

15. And if we know that he hear us, whatsoever we ask, we know that we have the petitions that we desired of him.

death stood for. The Holy Spirit continues to bear witness of this truth. Baptism and death were the two termini of our Lord's ministry.

**7.** The text of this verse should read, **Because there are three that bear record.** The remainder of the verse is spurious. Not a single manuscript contains the trinitarian addition before the fourteenth century, and the verse is never quoted in the controversies over the Trinity in the first 450 years of the church era. **8.** The three witnesses are **the spirit, and the water, and the blood: and these three agree in one.** "The trinity of witnesses furnish one testimony" (Plummer, *The Epistles,* p. 116), namely that Jesus Christ came in the flesh to die for sin that men might live.

2) The Effect of the Credentials. 5:9-12.

**9.** A threefold witness is all that is necessary for men (cf. Deut 19:15; Mt 18:16; Jn 8:17). God has given us three witnesses in the Spirit, water, and blood which we must **receive. 10. In himself.** The witness is not only external but also internal. "That which for others is external is for the believer experimental" (Westcott, p. 186). **Made him a liar.** Because the unbeliever makes God out to be a liar about his entire plan of redemption. **11. Record.** Literally, *witness.* The content of the external and internal witness is that God gave his divine Son that men might have eternal life. **12.** A deduction from verse 11. If the Son has life, then he who has the Son also has life. **Life.** Literally, *the life.*

C. Faith in Christ Proved by the Confidence We Exhibit. 5:13-21.

1) Confidence in Prayer. 5:13-17.
**13. These things.** The whole epistle. **That ye may know.** The conscious knowledge of the possession of eternal life is the basis for the joy of fellowship, which is the theme of the epistle (1:4).
**14. Boldness.** This is the fourth mention of it (cf. 2:28; 4:17 in connection with judgment; and 3:21,22 and here in connection with prayer). **According to his will.** The limitation is gracious because his will is always best for his children. The promise is that God hears us, and this includes the idea that he also grants the petition (cf. Jn 9:31; 11:41, 42). **15. Whatsoever we ask** is synonymous with the **according to his will** of verse

**16.** If any man see his brother sin a sin *which is* not unto death, he shall ask, and he shall give him life for them that sin not unto death. There is a sin unto death: I do not say that he shall pray for it.

**17.** All unrighteousness is sin: and there is a sin not unto death.

**18.** We know that whosoever is born of God sinneth not; but he that is begotten of God keepeth himself, and that wicked one toucheth him not.

**14.** The believer who is in fellowship with God will not ask anything that is contrary to God's will.

**16.** Prayer is limited not only by the will of God but also by the actions of others. "Man's will has been endowed by God with such royal freedom, that not even His will coerces it. Still less, therefore, can a brother's prayer coerce it. If a human will has deliberately and obstinately resisted God, and persists in doing so, we are debarred from our usual certitude. Against a rebel will even the prayer of faith in accordance with God's will (for of course God desires the submission of the rebel) may be offered in vain" (Plummer, *The Epistles of S. John,* p. 121). **Sin a sin.** Literally, *sinning a sin.* The supposed case is one in which the brother is seen in the very act of sin. **He shall give him life for them that sin not unto death.** The pronouns are ambiguous. The sentence may mean that God shall give the intercessor life, or it can be taken to mean that the intercessor will give the sinner life through his prayers (similar to Jas 5:20). It is difficult to decide which is preferred, for both ideas are Scriptural.

**A sin unto death.** The translation **a sin** is too definite. There is *sin unto death,* which implies not a single act but acts which have the character of sin unto death. These may not always be outward so that they can be recognized and known, since John says we cannot know what to pray. Neither is the sin unto death the rejection of Christ, for the context is dealing with Christians. It must be similar to the cases cited in I Cor 5 and 11:30. Concerning prayer for such a brother, John is very guarded in what he recommends. He does not forbid intercession nor does he encourage it. Individual fellowship will determine the proper course of action. **17. All unrighteousness is sin.** John warns against the lax thinking that some sins are permissible and others (**unto death**) not.

2) Confidence in Knowledge. 5:18-21.

**18. We know.** With certain, positive knowledge. **Sinneth not.** Present tense; habitual sinning. "The power of intercession to overcome the consequences of sin might seem to encourage a certain indifference to sin" (Westcott, p. 193). "The condition of Divine sonship is incompatible, not merely with sin unto death, but with sin of any description" (Plummer, p. 125). **Toucheth.** Occurs in

19. *And* we know that we are of God, and the whole world lieth in wickedness.

20. And we know that the Son of God is come, and hath given us an understanding, that we may know him that is true; and we are in him that is true, *even* in his Son Jesus Christ. This is the true God, and eternal life.

21. Little children, keep yourselves from idols. Amen.

John only in Jn 20:17, and means not a mere superficial touching but a grasping hold of. Satan cannot grasp and hold on to the one begotten of God. **19.** The second fact in our knowledge. **The whole world.** The order of words indicates that **the world** with its thoughts, ways, methods, etc., is meant. **20.** Third fact. **Is come.** The verb (*hēkei* rather than *erchomai*) includes the ideas of his coming at the incarnation and his presence now in believers. **That we may know.** Know experientially through the appropriation of knowledge.

**21. Keep.** A different word (*phylassō*) from that used in 5:18 (*tēreō*). It means guard as a garrison does. **Idols.** "An 'idol' is anything which occupies the place due to God" (Westcott, p. 197). Ephesus abounded with idols and idolatrous practices; so the warning was most appropriate.

# BIBLIOGRAPHY

ALEXANDER, WILLIAM. *The Epistles of St. John.* New York: George Doran, n.d.

ALFORD, HENRY. *The Greek Testament,* IV, 421-528. London: Rivingtons, 1875.

CAMERON, ROBERT. *The First Epistle of John.* Philadelphia: A. J. Rowland, 1899.

CANDLISH, ROBERT S. *The First Epistle of John.* Grand Rapids: Zondervan Publishing House, n.d.

FINDLAY, GEORGE. *Fellowship in the Life Eternal.* London: Hodder and Stoughton, n.d.

IRONSIDE, H. A. *Addresses on the Epistles of John.* New York: Loizeaux Brothers, n.d.

KELLY, WILLIAM. *An Exposition of the Epistles of John the Apostle.* London: T. Weston, 1905.

LAW, ROBERT. *The Tests of Life.* Edinburgh: T. & T. Clark, 1909.

PLUMMER, A. *The Epistles of S. John. (Cambridge Greek Testament).* Cambridge: The University Press, 1886.

ROBERTSON, A. T. *Word Studies in the New Testament,* VI, 199-266. New York: Harper & Brothers, 1933.

ROSS, ALEXANDER. *The Epistles of James and John.* Grand Rapids: Wm. B. Eerdmans Publishing Co., 1954.

SMITH, DAVID. "The Epistles of John," *The Expositor's Greek Testament,* V, 151-208. Grand Rapids: Wm. B. Eerdmans Publishing Co., n.d.

STEVENS, G. B. *The Johannine Theology.* London: Richard B. Dickinson, 1894.

VINCENT, MARVIN R. *Word Studies in the New Testament,* II, 303-404. Grand Rapids: Wm. B. Eerdmans Publishing Co., 1946.

WESTCOTT, BROOKE FOSS. *The Epistles of St. John.* Cambridge: The Macmillan Company, 1892.

WUEST, KENNETH S. *In These Last Days.* Grand Rapids: Wm. B. Eerdmans Publishing Co., 1954.

# THE SECOND EPISTLE OF JOHN

## INTRODUCTION

Neither II nor III John contains any intimation of time or place of writing. In view of this silence and in absence of any evidence to the contrary, it seems probable that the circumstances were the same as those of the First Epistle. The destination of the Second Epistle is enigmatic. Some hold that the phrase **elect lady** (v. 1) is a figurative way of designating the whole church, or at least some particular church group. Such a metaphorical use may be paralleled by Eph 5:22-33 and Rev 21:9. In such a view **elect sister** (v. 13) would refer to John's own congregation. However, "the simplicity of the little letter precludes the possibility of so elaborate an allegory, while the tenderness of its tone stamps it as a personal communi-cation" (David Smith, ExpGT, IV, 162). Others hold that the letter is addressed to an individual lady and her family. Whether or not her name was Kyria is an open question (cf. alternate constructions in III Jn 1 and I Pet 1:1). Whatever her name, she evidently resided near Ephesus and was well known in her community (perhaps her home was the meeting place for the local church). A sister of hers, presumably deceased, had a family resident at Ephesus and connected with John's congregation. Apparently several of the "elect lady's" sons had visited their cousins in Ephesus. Having become acquainted with them, John wrote their mother this letter.

## OUTLINE

# II JOHN

THE elder unto the elect lady and her children, whom I love in the truth; and not I only, but also all they that have known the truth;

# COMMENTARY

**I. Introduction. 1-3.**

A. Author. 1.

**The elder.** See Introduction to I John. Perhaps the informal and more intimate use of **elder** instead of "apostle" lends support to the view that the letter is addressed to an individual rather than to a church. On the word **elder** used with reference to age, see I Tim 5:1,2; I Pet 5:5; and with reference to office, see Acts 11:30; 14:23; 15:4,6,23; 16:4; 20:17; I Tim 5:17,19; Tit 1:5; Jas 5:14; I Pet 5:1.

B. Address. 1.

**Elect lady.** See Introduction. **Whom** refers to mother and children. **In the truth.** Better, *in truth*, "in all Christian sincerity." **All they . . .** All Christians would love the family if they had the same relationship as John did.

2. For the truth's sake, which dwelleth in us, and shall be with us for ever.

3. Grace be with you, mercy, *and* peace, from God the Father, and from the Lord Jesus Christ, the Son of the Father, in truth and love.

4. I rejoiced greatly that I found of thy children walking in truth, as we have received a commandment from the Father.

5. And now I beseech thee, lady, not as though I wrote a new commandment unto thee, but that which we had from the beginning, that we love one another.

6. And this is love, that we walk after his commandments. This is the commandment, That, as ye have heard from the beginning, ye should walk in it.

C. Greeting. 2,3.

**2. For the truth's sake.** Cf. Jn 15:6; 16:6. The Truth (or Christ) and the Spirit make love for the elect lady and her family possible. The Truth is the foundation of love for all believers. **With us.** Emphatic position in clause.

**3.** Translate: **There shall be with us grace . . .** Unusual mode of greeting, probably suggested by **with us** in the preceding verse. It is a confident assurance of blessing. **Grace.** The favor of God toward sinners. The word occurs elsewhere in John only in Jn 1:14,16,17; III Jn 4; Rev 1:4; 22:21. **Mercy** is the compassion of God for us in our misery. John uses this word only here. **Peace** is the resultant state of wholeness when sin and misery are removed. **From God . . . and from the Lord.** The repetition of from (*para*) emphasizes the distinctiveness of the persons of the Father and the Son. **The Son of the Father.** A unique expression apparently connecting the revelation of the Father closely with the Son.

**II. Warning Concerning Heresy. II John 4-11.**

Truth and love mentioned in verse 3 are now developed. The walk of the lady's children in truth is commended, and loving one another is commanded.

A. The Content of the Heresy. 4-6.

**4. Rejoiced.** Aorist, perhaps epistolary —"rejoice"; or better, expressing the initial act of joy. **Found.** Perfect tense; what John found continued to be true. **Walking.** *Peripateō,* including every activity of life (cf. I Jn 1:7). **In truth.** The whole character and conduct of their lives was in truth; i.e., in conformity with the whole tone of Christianity. Some, of course, did not walk in truth, and this was the heresy.

**5. And now.** This introduces a practical exhortation based on verse 4. " 'It is my joy at the Christian life of some of thy children, and my anxiety about the others, that move me to exhort thee' " (Plummer, p. 135). **I beseech.** *Erōtaō,* a personal request, rather than *parakaleō,* a general request (which word is never used by John). **That we love one another.** These words probably depend on **I beseech thee,** the intervening clause being parenthetical.

**6. This is love.** The love that John refers to consists in this. In verse 5 the commandment is to love; in verse 6 love is obeying His commands. "This is no

7. For many deceivers are entered into the world, who confess not that Jesus Christ is come in the flesh. This is a deceiver and an antichrist.

8. Look to yourselves, that we lose not those things which we have wrought, but that we receive a full reward.

vicious logical circle, but a healthy moral connexion . . . Love divorced from duty will run riot, and duty divorced from love will starve" (Plummer, pp. 135,136). Love is not merely a matter of feeling; it is the action of doing the will of God. This word would be particularly necessary when writing to a woman, who by nature is more emotional. **In it.** In love, which is His commandment.

B. The Cause of the Heresy. 7.

Some were spreading heresy rather than walking in truth. The heresy consisted in denying the truth of the commandments of the incarnate Christ, and it was due to a denial of the Incarnation. If Christ was not truly human, then there is no basis for Christian ethics (cf. I Jn 2:6). And certainly there is no example of self-denying love if he was merely a phantom or theophany.

**7. Deceivers.** Those who lead astray. **Confess not.** Not to affirm is the same as to deny. **Is come.** Literally, *coming* (a participle). The emphasis is not simply on the past fact of the coming of Christ in flesh, but also on the continuance of his humanity and even on the future manifestation of the Lord. Christ is never said to come *into* flesh, but *in* flesh; the former would leave room for saying that deity was united with Jesus sometime after his birth. **An antichrist.** Better, *the antichrist.* The one about whom they had already heard. See notes on I Jn 2:28.

C. The Consequences of Heresy. 8-11.

The presence of heretical teaching calls for examination.

1) Examination of Self. 8.

The danger was personal as well as external; therefore, self-examination is called for as well as examination of the heretics.

**Look to yourselves.** Cf. Mk 13:9. **We lose not.** Better MSS support *ye lose not.* **We have wrought**; i.e., the apostles. **We receive.** Better MSS read *ye receive.* Thus the sentence reads: *that ye lose not those things which we have wrought, but that ye receive a full reward.* The readers are warned to take heed that the deceivers do not undo the work which the apostles and evangelists had done, so that they might receive a full reward. **Full reward.** No element lacking in rewarding of God's people in the life to come.

2) Examination of Others. 9-11.

**9.** Others should be examined on the

9. Whosoever transgresseth, and abideth not in the doctrine of Christ, hath not God. He that abideth in the doctrine of Christ, he hath both the Father and the Son.

10. If there come any unto you, and bring not this doctrine, receive him not into *your* house, neither bid him God-speed:

11. For he that biddeth him God-speed is partaker of his evil deeds.

12. Having many things to write unto you, I would not *write* with paper and ink: but I trust to come unto you, and speak face to face, that our joy may be full.

13. The children of thy elect sister greet thee. Amen.

basis of their abiding in the teaching of Christ. **Transgresseth.** Better, *goeth on*, i.e., in the profession of Christianity without the reality of abiding in the doctrine of Christ. **Doctrine of Christ.** That which he taught at his coming. **He hath both the Father and the Son.** The fuller expression in the positive part of the verse shows that, in the negative statement that precedes it, not to have God is also not to have Christ.

10. **If there come any.** The **if** assumes the case, not merely expresses the possibility. In other words, such people were coming into Christians' homes under a friendly guise (cf. Didache 11). **Unto you.** To the elect lady and her children. **Receive him not . . . neither bid** (say). Present imperatives, forbidding the continuance of what was customary. The injunction is to refuse such ones Christian hospitality. This is a severe measure, particularly when one remembers that hospitality is generally enjoined in the NT. **Neither bid him God speed.** Do not say a greeting of sympathy. **God speed** is a good translation of the broad idea contained in the word *chairein* (cf. Acts 15:23; 23:26; Jas 1:1). 11. **Partaker.** One who fellowships. The one who bids God speed actually fellowships in the work of the antichrist. **Evil deeds.** Literally, *his deeds, his* **evil** *deeds.* Emphasis on the evil character of his works.

### III. Conclusion. II John 12,13.

The conclusion is very similar to that of the Third Epistle and evidently indicates that the two letters were written at the same time. John has dealt with the main purpose for writing and reserves other subjects for a personal interview.

12. **Many things.** Perhaps the same subjects discussed in the First Epistle. 13. **Elect sister.** See Introduction to II John. The adjective **elect** is used by John only here, in verse 1, and in Rev 17:14.

# BIBLIOGRAPHY

For Bibliography, see after I John.

# THE THIRD EPISTLE OF JOHN

(See Introduction to II John)

## OUTLINE

I. Introduction. 1-4.
    A. Personal salutation. 1.
    B. Personal sentiments. 2-4.
II. The duty of hospitality. 5-8.
    A. The reward of hospitality. 5.
    B. The report of hospitality. 6.
    C. The reasons for hospitality. 7,8.
III. The danger of haughtiness. 9-12.
    A. Haughtiness exemplified. 9.
    B. Haughtiness condemned. 10.
    C. Haughtiness contrasted. 11,12.
IV. Conclusion. 13,14.

## III JOHN

THE elder unto the well-beloved Gaius, whom I love in the truth.

## COMMENTARY

### I. Introduction. 1-4.

This epistle presents one of the most vivid glimpses in the New Testament of a church in the first century. The characters, Gaius, Diotrephes, and Demetrius, are sketched with bold strokes of the apostle's pen. Characteristics of church life are also clearly seen in the epistle. The independence of the believers is outstanding, and their personalities, as well as their doctrinal problems, are patent. This brief and very personal letter shatters the notion that the state of things was ideal, or nearly so, in the first century. Contrariwise, it reveals the problems of a vigorously growing faith.

A. Personal Salutation. 1.
The salutation is brief in contrast with the salutations of other personal letters in the NT. **Elder.** See II Jn 1. This was evidently the usual way John designated himself. **The wellbeloved Gaius.** Since Gaius was one of the most common names of the time, it is impossible to identify him with any other Gaius mentioned in the NT (cf. Acts 19:29; 20:4; Rom 16:23; I Cor 1:14). **Beloved** expresses the common sentiment that others shared about Gaius. **Whom I love in the truth** expresses John's personal feelings. The I is emphatic, as if implying that there were some who were hostile to Gaius.

2. Beloved, I wish above all things that thou mayest prosper and be in health, even as thy soul prospereth.

3. For I rejoiced greatly, when the brethren came and testified of the truth that is in thee, even as thou walkest in the truth.

4. I have no greater joy than to hear that my children walk in truth.

5. Beloved, thou doest faithfully whatsoever thou doest to the brethren, and to strangers;

6. Which have borne witness of thy charity before the church: whom if thou bring forward on their journey after a godly sort, thou shalt do well:

B. Personal Sentiments. 2-4.

**2. Above all things.** No such meaning for *peri pantōn* is found in the NT or in the LXX. Better rendered *in all things.* It refers to the whole sentence in general. **Prosper.** Only here, in Rom 1:10, and in I Cor 16:2. **Be in health.** Paul sometimes uses the word metaphorically of sound doctrine, but here the sense is of sound physical health, as in Lk 5:31; 7:10; 15:27. It may indicate that Gaius had been ill. The phrase **even as thy soul prospereth** shows that **prosper** and **be in health** refer to temporal blessings, and this verse gives us the authority for praying for such for our friends.

**3. Came.** Present tense; not on one occasion but on several reports came. **The truth that is in thee, even as thou walkest . . .** The brethren had repeatedly witnessed to Gaius' Christianity, as proved by his doctrine and his walk. The verse may also imply that Gaius had withstood some false teaching. **4.** The literal order is bold: **Greater than these** (tidings of your stand) **I have no joy.** Some manuscripts read *grace* instead of **joy.** The result of these reports was that John might hear that his children were walking (as the habit of their lives) in truth.

## II. The Duty of Hospitality. 5-8.

Apparently Gaius had been censured by some for his hospitality to strange brethren. John approves of his actions and enjoins such hospitality as a Christian duty.

A. The Reward of Hospitality. 5.

**Beloved** marks a new section. **Thou doest faithfully** (*piston poieis*). Literally, *thou doest a faithful thing,* or *thou makest sure.* That is, any good done for or to the brethren will surely be rewarded (cf. Mt 26:10; Rev 14:13). Hospitality will have its reward. **And to strangers.** The addition of this phrase would indicate that this was the particular point for which Gaius was being taken to task.

B. The Report of Hospitality. 6.

**Which have borne witness.** Those who had experienced Gaius' hospitality had testified of it before the church, probably at Ephesus, where John was. **Thou shalt do well.** John urges Gaius to continue his good work. **Bring forward.** See Acts 15:3; Tit 3:13, where the idea of supplying provisions for the journey is included.

7. Because that for his name's sake, they went forth, taking nothing of the Gentiles.

8. We therefore ought to receive such, that we might be fellow helpers to the truth.

9. I wrote unto the church: but Diotrephes, who loveth to have the preeminence among them, receiveth us not.

10. Wherefore, if I come, I will remember his deeds which he doeth, prating against us with malicious words: and not content therewith, neither doth he himself receive the brethren, and forbiddeth them that would, and casteth *them* out of the church.

C. The Reasons for Hospitality. 7,8.

7. Three reasons are given for hospitality. First, these brethren **went forth** for the sake of the **Name**, i.e., Jesus Christ (cf. Acts 5:41; Jas 2:7). Second, they took **nothing** of unconverted Gentiles. The participle is present, indicating that it was their practice to take nothing. 8. Third, through hospitality Christians can become fellow workers for the truth. **Ought.** Bound to, as in I Jn 2:6.

## III. The Danger of Haughtiness. 9-12.

### A. Haughtiness Exemplified. 9.

The RSV has, *I have written something to the church*, i.e., a few words. *Ti*, "something," indicates that John viewed his letter lightly. It, of course, has not been preserved. **Unto the church.** The church to which Gaius belonged. But its purpose had failed. **Who loveth to have the pre-eminence among them.** The word occurs nowhere else in the NT. It does not imply doctrinal defection (cf. II Jn 9) but rather proud ambition and the desire to promote personal authority. Plummer makes an interesting suggestion: "Perhaps the meaning is that Diotrephes meant to make his Church independent; hitherto it had been governed by S. John from Ephesus, but Diotrephes wished to make it autonomous to his own glorification" (Plummer, p. 149). **Receiveth us not.** That is, Diotrephes did not receive John's wishes in the matter of hospitality. The improbability that any Christian would have withstood the apostle's authority is one of the internal arguments used against the Johannine authorship of this letter. It is thought to be inconceivable that a Christian would disregard the commandments of a genuine apostle if he were the author. However, Paul's apostolic authority was often challenged.

### B. Haughtiness Condemned. 10.

**If I come.** No doubt because of verse 14 (cf. I Jn 2:28 for similar construction). **I will remember.** Bring these things to his notice and the notice of others. **Prating.** Used only here, though the adjective form occurs in I Tim 5:13. Literally, *to talk nonsense*. **With malicious words.** Diotrephes' talk was both senseless and wicked. His actions included not being hospitable himself, forbidding those who would be, and casting them out of the church. Evidently he had sufficient authority in the congregation to do this excommunicating, of whatever sort it was.

11. Beloved, follow not that which is evil, but that which is good. He that doeth good is of God: but he that doeth evil hath not seen God.

12. Demetrius hath good report of all *men*, and of the truth itself: yea, and we *also* bear record; and ye know that our record is true.

13. I had many things to write, but I will not with ink and pen write unto thee:

14. But I trust I shall shortly see thee, and we shall speak face to face. Peace *be* to thee. *Our* friends salute thee. Greet the friends by name.

**C. Haughtiness Contrasted. 11,12.**

**11. Beloved** again marks the transition. **Follow.** Literally, *imitate*. **Evil.** *Kakos*, "bad." Rarely used by John. **Is of God.** The source (*ek*, "of") of his life is God; i.e., he is a child of God. He imitates his Master (Acts 10:38). **Hath not seen God.** Cf. I Jn 3:6. The question of hospitality is no longer the only specific matter in view, but doing good or evil in general and as the habit of one's life.

**12.** From the evil Diotrephes John turns to the good Demetrius. All we know of him we learn from this brief mention. It is conjecture that he is the same Demetrius, though now converted, of Acts 19:24. Demetrius' good testimony was witnessed to by three sources: (1) all men, (2) the truth, that is, the standard of Christianity, and (3) John and those with him.

**IV. Conclusion. 13,14.**

The similarity to the conclusion of II John supports the view that they were written about the same time.

**13. I had.** Imperfect, referring to the time when he began the letter. **Pen.** Literally, *reed*. **14.** See verse 10.

**15.** Note the division of verse 14 in the AV into verses 14 and 15 in the RSV and in editions of the Greek text. **Peace be to thee.** Ordinary blessing which was suitable either for a greeting or for a farewell. **Friends.** It is a question whether John means his friends (thus supply "our" as AV does) or Gaius' (thus supply "thy"). **By name.** The phrase occurs elsewhere only in Jn 10:3. The salutation was to be given to each individual separately. "S. John as shepherd of the Churches of Asia would imitate the Good Shepherd and know all his sheep by name" (Plummer, p. 153).

# BIBLIOGRAPHY

For Bibliography, see after I John.

# JUDE

## INTRODUCTION

*Authorship and Date.* The Epistle of Jude, the last of the "general" or "catholic" epistles, is declared to have been written by "Jude, the servant of Jesus Christ, and brother of James." Dispute over the authenticity of the claim is as old as Eusebius, who placed this letter, along with Hebrews, under suspicion. However, the soundest historical and internal evidence supports the truthfulness of the text. Matthew 13:55 and Mark 6:3 name Judas (Jude) and James as brothers of Jesus. That James is identified so simply in this epistle is evidence that he was Jesus' brother. Some scholars allege that "Jude" is a borrowed or pen name, but this is open to question. Apart from being the author of this letter, Jude had no special reputation or authority in the early church; therefore little reason existed for a forger to use Jude's name. Though the date of composition cannot be fixed with certainty, it would not be inaccurate to assign it to the latter half of the first century. It is listed in the Muratorian Canon (second century), and mentioned by Tertullian, Clement, and Origen (third century). Although it suffered a diminished status because of its citations from the non-canonical books of Enoch and the Assumption of Moses, its right to inclusion in the canon was universally recognized by A.D. 350.

*Purpose.* Apparently a general letter to Christians of the first century, the Epistle of Jude warns against the incipient heresy of Gnosticism, a philosophy that distinguished sharply between matter, as being inherently evil, and spirit, as being good. Such a system of thought had serious implications for Christian life and doctrine. It challenged the Biblical doctrine of creation. And it gave rise to the idea that Christ's body was only apparent, not real, for if Christ had had a real body, it would have been evil. In its effect on Christian ethics, Gnosticism prompted two quite different results: on the one hand antinomianism, the belief that one is not under obligation to obey the moral law, and on the other a form of abuse of the body to promote spirituality. Both are opposed by Scripture. It may be inferred from the epistle that the readers were guilty, in varying degrees, of rebellion against authority, irreverence, presumptuous speech, and a libertine spirit. Jude's tone is polemic, for he rebukes false teachers who deceive unstable believers and corrupt the Lord's table.

While no outline is finally authoritative, this epistle falls easily into four sections:

I. Identification, salutation, and purpose. Jude 1-4.

II. Admonitions against false teachers. Jude 5-16.

III. Exhortations to Christians. Jude 17-23.

IV. Benediction. Jude 24, 25.

# JUDE

JUDE, the servant of Jesus Christ, and brother of James, to them that are sanctified by God the Father, and preserved in Jesus Christ, *and* called:

2. Mercy unto you, and peace, and love, be multiplied.
3. Beloved, when I gave all diligence to write unto you of the common salvation, it was needful for me to write unto you, and exhort *you* that ye should earnestly contend for the faith which was once delivered unto the saints.
4. For there are certain men crept in unawares, who were before of old ordained to this condemnation, ungodly men, turning the grace of our God into lasciviousness, and denying the only Lord God, and our Lord Jesus Christ.

# COMMENTARY

I. Identification, Salutation, and Purpose. Jude 1-4.

1. Jude identifies himself as the writer, describes his relationship to Christ and to James, and defines his readers, all in one short sentence. **Jude,** or Judas, is a popular name in the Hebrew tradition. A frequent Pauline word — **slave,** or *bond servant* — is used, and it speaks of Jude's devotion to Christ. The writer's blood relationship to Jesus is of secondary importance. The sovereignty of God and the centrality of Christ are expressed in the election and preservation of the readers. The verb translated **kept** (ASV) points forward to Christ's return.
2. Jude's trilogy of **mercy . . . peace,** and **love** is distinctly Semitic, and corresponds closely to Paul's "grace, mercy, and peace" (II Tim 1:2).
3. The purpose of the letter is plainly stated, and the polemic point of view indicated. Jude does not harshly demand, but lovingly appeals to these Christians to recall their **common salvation.** The Greek adverb *hapax,* **once for all** (Heb 6:4; 10:2; I Pet 3:18), affirms the finality of the revelation of God in Christ in redemptive history. It is the fixed, nonrepeatable point of our faith. This revelation accomplished its goal, for it was delivered **to the saints.**
4. The occasion for the letter was the intrusion of ungodly persons into the fellowship of the church. These heretics are open to four charges: they entered secretly; they were previously appointed to condemnation; they are ungodly, i.e., irreverent; and they deny Christ as Master and Lord. To deny is positively to disbelieve what Christ testified about himself. Gnostic antinomianism is implied in **licentiousness** (AV, *lasciviousness),* which connotes sexual debauchery.

5. I will therefore put you in remembrance, though ye once knew this, how that the Lord, having saved the people out of the land of Egypt, afterward destroyed them that believed not.

6. And the angels which kept not their first estate, but left their own habitation, he hath reserved in everlasting chains under darkness unto the judgment of the great day.

7. Even as Sodom and Gomorrah, and the cities about them in like manner, giving themselves over to fornication, and going after strange flesh, are set forth for an example, suffering the vengeance of eternal fire.

8. Likewise also these *filthy* dreamers defile the flesh, despise dominion, and speak evil of dignities.

9. Yet Michael the archangel, when contending with the devil he disputed about the body of Moses, durst not bring against him a railing accusation, but said, The Lord rebuke thee.

10. But these speak evil of those things which they know not: but what they know naturally, as brute beasts, in those things they corrupt themselves.

11. Woe unto them! for they have gone in the way of Cain, and ran greedily after the error of Balaam for reward, and perished in the gainsaying of Core.

## II. Admonitions Against False Teachers. Jude 5-16.

5. Again the adverb *hapax* is used (cf. v. 3); here it refers to the readers' knowledge of the Gospel. Jude's argument is that a man's *profession* of faith does not establish him as righteous before God. The possibility of lapsing is illustrated by the example of disbelieving Israelites who were saved out of Egypt but subsequently destroyed.

6. A further illustration is the fall of the rebellious angels, who erred from their calling by exalting themselves. Jude's language here may reflect the influence of the book of Enoch, which contains an elaborated description of the disobedient angels. Genesis 6:1-4 provides the original Biblical account.

7. Lastly, Jude cites the history of **Sodom and Gomorrha** to enforce his moral. Throughout Scripture these cities are symbolic of divine judgment executed by fire. So their fate is a foretaste of the fate of professing believers who do not persevere in rightousness.

8. Irreverence is the chief sin of the **ungodly persons** of verse 4. The sense of the word **dignities** (AV), or *the glorious ones* (RSV), is not clear; it may refer to Christian leaders.

9. Jude amplifies his plea for reverence by citing the apocryphal story of Michael and the devil, taken from the pseudepigraphical Assumption of Moses. Although Jude quoted both this book and Enoch, it is not a supportable inference that he ascribed canonical status or historicity to them. The moral that Jude points up is that Michael showed restraint even in his relations with the devil, whereas the false teachers exhibit no reverence for any authority.

10. Lacking the spiritual insight to recognize the "glorious ones," these evil men scoff at them. With irony Jude destroys the Gnostic claim to superior spiritual knowledge by stating that they possess only irrational animal instincts. Dependence upon knowledge gained only by the brute senses leads to sure destruction.

11. Jude pronounces a woe, again employing a triad of historical examples — **Cain, Balaam,** and **Korah.** Cain is typical of unrighteousness, Balaam of the spirit of deceit and covetousness (cf. Num 22–24), and Korah (or Core) of

12. These are spots in your feasts of charity, when they feast with you, feeding themselves without fear: clouds *they are* without water, carried about of winds; trees whose fruit withereth, without fruit, twice dead, plucked up by the roots;

13. Raging waves of the sea, foaming out their own shame; wandering stars, to whom is reserved the blackness of darkness for ever.

14. And Enoch also, the seventh from Adam, prophesied of these, saying, Behold, the Lord cometh with ten thousands of his saints,

15. To execute judgment upon all, and to convince all that are ungodly among them of all their ungodly deeds which they have ungodly committed, and of all their hard *speeches* which ungodly sinners have spoken against him.

the rebellion of malcontents against duly constituted authority (cf. Num 16). These kinds of sin undermine the spiritual health of the whole church and destroy those who practice them.

12. The author heightens his condemnation of false teachers by turning from Biblical to natural analogies, of which there are five. **Love-feasts** were meals eaten in connection with worship services or the Eucharists, and their intent was to enrich the believers' Christian fellowship and strengthen their sense of union with Christ. Apparently the Gnostic heretics had corrupted such feasts into gluttonous orgies, thereby perverting their purpose. These fed themselves without concern for the spiritual welfare of the Church. **Waterless clouds** is highly descriptive of these men; they carried no spiritual burden, and were blown along as though without weight. Autumn is the time of fruit gathering. But false teachers produce no fruit, and such trees, being doubly dead, are destined for destruction.

13. The lives of the ungodly are like the restless, **raging waves of the sea** that litter the seashores with their refuse. Such lives bring not only future condemnation but present shame and ignominy. Lastly, Jude describes the heretics as **wandering stars.** He implies that theirs is a pointless, useless existence, which will terminate in eternal oblivion. Enoch 18:12-16 may have influenced Jude's thought here.

14,15. A problem arises in these verses because of the quotations from Enoch. Jude says: **Enoch in the seventh generation from Adam prophesied** (RSV). The difficulty is that Jude apparently ascribes this prophecy of apocryphal Enoch to the Enoch of Gen 5. Since there is no Biblical account of any prophecy of Enoch, Jude either regarded apocryphal Enoch as canonical, or else was guilty of obvious error. However, a solution to the problem may rest in the fact that this alleged prophecy is a citation not from a single passage in Enoch, but from several, and it is probable that Jude also quoted the line "the seventh generation from Adam" from Enoch 60:8. Thus Jude did not intend to refer to the Enoch of Gen 5, but referred entirely, even in the introductory line, to words found in the apocryphal Enoch. While the prophecy has no canonical status, its predictions are paralleled and supported by numerous Biblical passages, such as, Mt 25:31-46.

16. These are murmurers, complainers, walking after their own lusts; and their mouth speaketh great swelling *words*, having men's persons in admiration because of advantage.

17. But, beloved, remember ye the words which were spoken before of the apostles of our Lord Jesus Christ;

18. How that they told you there should be mockers in the last time, who should walk after their own ungodly lusts.

19. These be they who separate themselves, sensual, having not the Spirit.

20. But ye, beloved, building up yourselves on your most holy faith, praying in the Holy Ghost,

16. After affirming the doom of false teachers, Jude describes their character in three ways. They are grumblers, i.e., furtive complainers; they are malcontents, whose sole guide is their passions; and they are given to noisy boasting, with a view to securing gain for themselves. The language reflects the thought of the Assumption of Moses 5:5.

### III. Exhortations to Christians. Jude 17-23.

17. Although this letter was written to Christians, in verses 5-16 Jude defined the errors of false teachers. Now he turns his attention to his readers in a direct exhortation. They will guard themselves from error by recalling the apostles' **predictions** that false teachers would arise in the very church itself. By so doing they will properly "contend for the faith" (v. 3).

18. II Peter 3:3 uses almost identical language. Both passages may look back to a current oral tradition of the teaching of the apostles. **In the last time** sets the tone and points out that at the end of the age desperate lack of spirituality will characterize people. To scoff is to act impiously towards holy things, and **scoffers** (AV, *mockers*) do not obey the law of the Spirit, but follow the law of fleshly passion.

19. Jude continues his indictment against false teachers on two counts: they are divisive, and they are without the Spirit of God. The Greek verb *to separate* suggests setting up lines of demarcation that give rise to a factious spirit. Moreover, it bespeaks a sense of superiority on the part of these false teachers. With fine irony Jude accuses the Gnostics, who regarded themselves as spiritual, of **having not the Spirit.** He affirms that spirituality is a quality of life produced by the Spirit of God, and not by religious exercises known only to the initiated few.

20. Again a direct charge is made to the readers. Purity of life commences with sound doctrine, which is the "faith once for all delivered to the saints" (v. 3). A key to what is meant by **building up yourselves** is given in the following phrase: **praying in the Holy Spirit.** The strong implication is that the truly spiritual are not the exclusive, self-righteous persons (v. 19), but those who pray in the Holy Spirit.

21. Keep yourselves in the love of God, looking for the mercy of our Lord Jesus Christ unto eternal life.

22. And of some have compassion, making a difference:

23. And others save with fear, pulling *them* out of the fire; hating even the garment spotted by the flesh.

24. Now unto him that is able to keep you from falling, and to present *you* faultless before the presence of his glory with exceeding joy,

25. To the only wise God our Saviour, *be* glory and majesty, dominion and power, both now and ever. Amen.

21. Arndt paraphrases as follows: "Keep yourselves from harm by making it possible for God to show his love for you in the future also." The present environment of the Christian is the love of God, and the future expectation is the guarantee of eternal life with Jesus Christ.

22. The Greek text is difficult in Jude 22, 23. In v. 22 the better attested verb is **eleeō**, "to succor," "show compassion." The object of compassion is those who doubt. Thus, in this passage, Jude urges Christians to respond to both the intellectual and the moral doubts of those affected by false teachers. The end in view is not expulsion and condemnation of the doubters but their restoration to fellowship.

23. Zechariah 3:2-4 may have influenced Jude's thoughts here, for he writes of **snatching them out of the fire.** Fire may suggest sensual passion, but more likely it alludes to eternal judgment. It is difficult to know whether the writer intended to draw a sharp distinction between two classes of people by the double use of "some," or simply used the expression in an enumerative sense. However the words are to be understood, the Christian attitude is one of mercy towards the sinner, coupled with abhorrence of his sin.

### IV. Benediction. Jude 24,25.

24,25. One of the great and lofty benedictions of the NT is the one at the end of this short epistle. Two comparable Pauline benedictions are Rom 16:25 and I Tim 6:14-16. Vital to all exhortations to believers is the reminder of the infinite resource of God himself, who alone is competent to keep us from falling in this life and to bring us to himself in the last day. He will perfect the work of sanctification so that the believer will be **faultless,** or *without blemish* (ASV). This word looks back to the description of sacrificial animals in the OT. Jude 25 teaches both the oneness of God and the equality of Jesus Christ with God the Father. Thus it militates against the view that the deity of Christ was an invention of the post-apostolic church. God is spoken of as **Saviour** seven times in the NT. Here his saving power is shown in the Person of his Son, whom the Church acknowledges as "Lord," i.e., God. The final ascription of glory, majesty, dominion, and authority is Jude's testimony to the gracious character of God, who wrought our salvation through Christ.

# BIBLIOGRAPHY

BIGG, CHARLES. *A Critical and Exegetical Commentary on the Epistles of St. Peter and St. Jude. (International Critical Commentary).* New York: Charles Scribner's Sons, 1901.

MANTON, THOMAS. *Exposition of the Epistle of Jude.* London: James Nesbet & Co., 1871.

MAYOR, J. B. *Epistle of St. Jude and the Second Epistle of St. Peter.* London: Macmillan and Company, 1907.

MOFFAT, JAMES. *The General Epistles. (Moffat New Testament Commentary).* Vol. 15. Garden City, New York: Doubleday, Doran and Company, 1928.

# REVELATION

## INTRODUCTION

*Note.* At the beginning of this brief commentary on the inexhaustible concluding book of the New Testament Canon, a word is probably in order regarding two features that will be noticed throughout. In the first place, proportionately more space is given to introductory matters than is normally assigned in either a brief or longer treatment of this book. This is done because the writer believes the study of the book of Revelation calls for more preliminary consideration than that of any other book in the Bible. The better a reader has fixed in his mind certain fundamental principles of interpretation, the more readily will he understand these confessedly difficult chapters. In the second place, there is incorporated in these pages a good deal of material from the more important commentaries on Revelation written during the last century, some of the superbly concise and penetrating statements of great scholars of the Christian church concerning subjects touched upon in the book.

There is something almost paradoxical about the book of Revelation. It is a volume of acknowledged difficulty, and yet down through the ages it has been like a magnet, irresistibly drawing to its study Christians of every school of thought, laymen, clergy, and professors. R. H. Charles is right when he opens his *Lectures on the Apocalypse* with this statement: "From the earliest ages of the Church, it has been universally admitted that the Apocalypse is the most difficult book of the entire Bible" (p. 1). Calvin refused to write a commentary on Revelation, and gave it very little consideration in his massive writings. Luther for years avoided its teachings. At the same time, the book has compelled men to give prolonged study to its prophecies, and to go back again and again for a reconsideration of its themes and for a new grasp of its revelations. One testimony will suffice, from the one who is generally acknowledged to have been the most gifted Biblical expositor in the first quarter of our century, G. Campbell Morgan: "There is no book in the Bible which I have read so often, no book to

which I have tried to give more patient and persistent attention. . . . There **is** no book in the Bible to which I turn more eagerly in hours of depression than to this, with all its mystery, all the details of which I do not understand" *(Westminster Bible Record,* Vol. 3 [1912] 105,109).

*The Importance of the Book.* (1) The New Testament Scriptures would have been incomplete, would have left readers in a more or less depressed mood, had this book not been written and included in the Canon. It is not only the last book in the canonical arrangement of our Bible, but it is the necessary conclusion to God's revelation to men. This truth was brilliantly set forth by T. D. Bernard in his famous Bampton Lectures for 1864, *The Progress of Doctrine in the New Testament:* "I know not how any man, in closing the Epistles, could expect to find the subsequent history of the Church essentially different from what it is. In those writings we seem, as it were, not to witness some passing storms which clear the air, but to feel the whole atmosphere charged with the elements of future tempest and death. Every moment the forces of evil shew themselves more plainly. They are encountered, but not dissipated. . . . The last words of St. Paul in the second Epistle to Timothy, and those of St. Peter in his second Epistle, with the Epistles of St. John and St. Jude, breathe the language of a time in which the tendencies of that history had distinctly shewn themselves; and in this respect these writings form a prelude and a passage to the Apocalypse.

"Thus we arrive at this book with wants which it is meant to supply; we come to it as men, who not only personally are in Christ, and who know what as individuals they have in him; but who also, as members of his body, share in a corporate life, in the perfection of which they are to be made perfect, and in the glory of which their Lord is to be glorified. For this perfection and glory we wait in vain, among the confusions of the world, and the ever-active, ever-changing forms of evil. What is the meaning of this wild scene? What is to be its issue? And what prospect is there of the realization of that which we desire? To such a state of mind as this, and to the wants which it involves, this last part of the teaching of God is addressed, in accordance with that system of progressive doctrine which I have endeavoured to illustrate, wherein each stage of advance ensues in the way of natural sequence from the effect of that which preceded it."

(2) Of all the books of the Bible, this is the one that certainly may be considered as *the* book for the end of the age. And it would seem that in these last thirty years, the Western world itself, including its statesmen, scientists, economists, and essayists, has consciously, or unconsciously, recognized this. This is especially true in regard to the use of the word *apocalypse*. This word has come to stand for an age of upheaval, world conditions fraught with fearful consequences, the unleashing of vast powers which man himself seems unable to control. The author of the book on Revelation in the Moffatt Commentary, Martin Kiddle, refers to "the remarkable relevance" of the message of this book "to the church in our own day. It is only one more example of the divine sanction, and the timeless significance of John's visions. Whenever there is a world crisis, whenever the State exalts itself and demands an allegiance which Christians know they cannot pay without abandoning their very souls, whenever the Church is threatened by destruction, and faith is dim and hearts are cold, then the Revelation will admonish and exhort, uplift and encourage all who heed its message" (p. xlix).

(3) This is supremely the book of one world, and surely now, in the middle of this twentieth century, we are approaching a one-world condition. Frequently in the Apocalypse we come upon such a phrase as "many peoples, and nations, and tongues, and kings" (10:11; 11:9; 17:15), which suggests the universal scope of the vision. When kings are introduced, they are the "kings of the whole world" (16:14; 17:2,18; 18:9; 19:19). Of Satan it is said that he is "the deceiver of the whole world" (12:9). All the nations commit fornication with the harlot (18:3,23). The economic boycott enforced by the beast covers all mankind (13:16,17). In fact,

the beast from the sea has given to him "authority over *every* tribe and people and tongue and nation" (13:7); and of him it is said, "All that dwell on the earth shall worship him" (13:8). There is great significance in the fact that when the time comes for Christ to assume his rightful place as King of kings and Lord of lords, the word for the government of this world is in the singular, "the *kingdom* of the world" (11:15).

(4) This is pre-eminently a book for a troubled age, for an age in which the darkness deepens, fear spreads over all mankind, and monstrous powers, godless and evil, appear on the stage of history (as they appear in this book). But there is comfort and encouragement here: God knows all things from the beginning, even the tribulations of his own people. However, the ultimate end of this conflict, persecution, tribulation, martyrdom, is determined by Christ, when he, finally, will be victorious. Sin and Satan and all Satan's cohorts will be eternally defeated; and believers will be with the Son of God in glory forever.

(5) Even if all these things were not true, and especially true for our age, we should not forget that this is the only book in the Bible that pronounces a beatitude regarding the hearing, reading, and obeying of its words: "Blessed is he that readeth, and they that hear the words of the prophecy, and keep the things that are written therein" (1:3; 22:7).

(6) Finally, it is in this book that some of the greatest themes of divine revelation are brought to a climactic conclusion. Here the prophecies concerning Christ as King of kings are unfolded in fullness, and are seen coming to pass. Here such words as *tabernacle, temple, paradise, Babylon,* etc., take on their supremely spiritual connotation. Here all the promises of a life in glory are concentrated in the marvelous picture of the Holy City. Here we have the final doom of Satan, Antichrist, false prophets, and all the enemies of God. Here the rebellious kings of Psalm 2 find themselves under the feet of the Lamb of God.

*The Author.* Through the ages some doubt has been cast upon the authenticity of this book. In this commentary there is not space for presenting and answering the arguments against Johannine authorship, but we should consider

1047

the facts testifying to the Apostle John as the writer. (1) Four times in this book the author's name is inserted (1:1, 4,9; 22:8). (2) As early as the first half of the second century, it was the conviction of the Church that John was the author. Justin Martyr frankly states, "And with us a man named John, one of the Apostles of Christ, who in the revelation made to him . . . ." *(Dialogue with Trypho the Jew,* ch. 81). The great historian Eusebius repeatedly assigns this book to John *(Ecclesiastical History* III. xxiv, xxxix); likewise Tertullian *(Contra Marcion* 3:14,24).

(3) Whatever may be the grammatical peculiarities of this book, there are innumerable similarities between the vocabularies of John's Gospel and the Apocalypse. "One important link connecting these writings," Gloag points out, "is the application of the term Logos to Jesus Christ. This term is undoubtedly Johannine; it is not elsewhere employed in Scripture, and yet it occurs in the Apocalypse: 'He is arrayed in a garment sprinkled with blood: and His name is called the Word of God' (Rev. 19:13). So also the word 'the Lamb,' as denoting not merely the emblem or symbol of Christ, but Christ Himself, is peculiar to John; as when in the Gospel it is said, 'Behold the Lamb of God,' and in the Apocalypse, 'I saw in the midst of the throne and of the four living creatures, and in the midst of the elders, a Lamb standing as though it had been slain' (5:6). It is true that the Greek word is different, *ho amnos* being used in the Gospel and *to arnion* in the Apocalypse; but the idea that Jesus Christ is the Lamb is common to both. The word *alēthinos,* 'that which is true,' is used ten times in the Apocalypse, nine times in the Fourth Gospel, four times in the Epistle, and only once in the Pauline Epistles. So also 'he that overcometh' *(nikos),* a favourite expression in the Epistle, is of frequent occurrence in the Apocalypse, as in the conclusion of the Epistles to the Seven Churches and elsewhere throughout the work: 'He that overcometh shall inherit all things' (21:7). The verb *skēnoō,* 'to tabernacle,' only found in the Johannine writings, is used in the Gospel, with evident reference to the Shekinah, of the Logos tabernacling among men (1:14), and is four times employed in the Apocalypse with reference to God: 'Behold the tabernacle of God is with men, and He shall dwell (tabernacle) with them' (21:3)" (P. J. Gloag: *Introduction to the Johannine Writings,* pp. 306,307).

*The Date of Composition.* There have been two different major convictions concerning the time this book was written. Some have placed it as early as the reign of Nero, in the seventh decade of the first century. But for many reasons it seems that this is too early. The unanimous verdict of the early church was that the Apostle John was banished to the Isle of Patmos by the emperor Domitian (A.D. 81 to 96), some writers placing the exile in the fourteenth year of his reign, A.D. 95. (For the early evidence for this, see, e.g., Revere F. Weidner, *Annotations on the Revelation of St. John the Divine,* pp. xiv-xvii).

The Apocalypse clearly reveals that it was written in a time of great persecution. The persecution under Nero was more or less confined to Rome, but that under Domitian reached to other parts of the Roman empire. Domitian banished men to various places of exile, but Nero did not. Furthermore, the seven churches in Asia here show a mature development, which could hardly have existed as early as A.D. 65. Moreover, we have no evidence whatever that the Apostle exercised any authority over the churches of Asia before the destruction of Jerusalem. With this view agree such writers as Lange, Alford, Elliott, Godet, Lee, Milligan, and others.

*Title of the Book.* The word *Revelation* is derived from the Latin *revelatio* (from *revelare,* "to reveal or unveil that which has previously been hidden"). This was the title assigned to the book in the Latin Vulgate. The Greek title is *Apocalypse,* taken directly from the first word in the Greek text, *apokalypsis.* In this noun form the word is not found anywhere else in Greek literature, but as a verb it is continually used in the Gospels and the Epistles, in many different ways, especially in reference to some form of divine revelation to man (as of the Son of Man, in Lk 17:30). It is used by Paul in referring to the same coming event (Rom 8:18; I Cor 1:7; II Thess 1:7), and frequently in I Peter (1:7,13; 4:13; 5:1). In the Greek text of Daniel this word is often found referring to the uncovering of secrets, or the interpretation of dreams, or the revelation of God (see Dan 2:19,22,28,

29,30,47; 10:1; 11:35).

*The Theme.* The Apocalypse is a book of prophecy. In its unfolding of the future, it particularly emphasizes the repeated and increasingly violent world-wide attempts of earthly personalities and peoples, energized and directed by demonic powers and led by Satan, to oppose and prevent the execution of the declared intention of Christ to establish His kingly rule on earth. It makes clear that this conflict is certain to end in the complete overthrow of these evil forces and the establishment of the everlasting kingdom of Christ. This age-long conflict, even involving war in heaven, is made up of a series of plots on the part of the enemies of Christ to defeat the King of kings. Each plot ends in failure, followed by fearful divine judgment. And the long conflict terminates in the final judgment of the Great White Throne, the appearance of the New Jerusalem, and the beginning of eternity.

*A Book of Visions.* The book of Revelation, above every other book of the Bible, is a record of what the author had revealed to him in visions. All of us know how difficult it is at times to record what we have *seen*, especially when the sight is spectacular. How would anyone adequately describe a glorious sunset, or the majesty of the Alps? The many different Greek verbs meaning, "to see," "behold," or "perceive," occur 140 times in this book, beginning with "what thou *seest* write in a book" (1:11). Immediately afterwards, John says: "I turned to *see* the voice that spoke with me and having turned, I *saw*," etc. (v. 12). At the beginning of chapter 4, a voice is heard from heaven saying to John, "Come up hither, and I will show thee the things which must come to pass hereafter" (4:1). From this point on, there are numerous paragraphs, right down to the end of the book, beginning, "And I saw."

Not only do we have here a series of visions, but the book is saturated with symbolic language, and these symbols must be given careful consideration. Especially is this true of numbers. First of all, there is the constant repetition of the number *seven*. In regard to the symbolism of numbers in the book, inserted here are the concise and comprehensive summaries of Moorehead and Weidner.

"This number [seven] is not only em-

ployed to denote so many individual objects," Moorehead explains, "but it enters very largely into the whole plan of the book. Seven is the number of completeness, of perfection, and of dispensational fullness. All readers know that there are four sets of sevens that cover a very considerable section of the book. These are the seven messages to the seven churches (chaps. 2,3). The vision of the seven seals, which embraces 6—8:1 (with an episode between the sixth and the seventh of the series, viz.: vii). The vision of the seven trumpets, 8:2—11:16 (with an episode between the sixth and the seventh, 10—11:13). The vision of the seven vials, 15:5-16. Thus nearly one-half of the book belongs to this fourfold series. . . . It enters into passages where no direct mention of it is made. Thus, in 5:12, seven attributes of praise are ascribed to the Lamb that was slain; the white-robed company in 7:12 worship God with the like number of ascriptions. Chapter 14:1-20 consists of seven parts, viz.: the Lamb with His glorious company on mount Zion: the everlasting gospel: Babylon's fall: the solemn threat against any fellowship with the Beast: happy lot of those who die in the Lord from henceforth: the harvest: the vintage. Besides, the chapter mentions six angels, and One like the Son of Man. The place of honor is given the Son of Man—three angels are on each side of Him, and He is in the midst, presiding over the vast movements. The climax of the series is in the number four, where He sits on the white Cloud. The 'seven spirits before the throne' (1:4) express the infinite perfection of the Holy Spirit. The 'seven stars' in Christ's right hand (1:16) denote the complete authority He has over the churches. The Lamb has 'seven horns and seven eyes' (5:6), which denote the almighty power, the supreme intelligence, and the perfect omniscience with which He is endowed" (Wm. G. Moorehead, *Studies in the Book of Revelation*, pp. 30-32).

"The *half of seven* is used in the Old Testament," says Weidner, "to signify a time of tribulation. It appears in various forms, both in the Old and New Testament. The famine in Elijah's time lasted three and a half years (I Kings 17:1; Lk. 4:25; Jas. 5:17); the same period is the 'time and times, and half a time' of Dan. 7:25 and Dan. 12:7; 'the half of the week' referred to in Dan. 9:27. This same period of time appears in Revelation under the form of forty-two months (Rev. 11:2; 13:5), or 1,260 days (Rev. 11:3; 12:6), or 'a time and times, and half a time' (Rev. 12:14). The *two witnesses* also lay dead 'three days and a half' (Rev. 12:9,11). This *broken number* is therefore a symbol of great significance, and has been taken to be the 'signature' of the broken covenant or of suffering and disaster. . . . *Ten* is the symbolical representation of absolute perfection and complete development, whether referred to God or to the world. It is the 'signature' of a complete and perfect whole. *Ten* is the number of the Commandments; the Holy of Holies was a cube, each side being of ten cubits; *ten times ten*, or 100, is the number of God's Flock (Lk. 15:4,7); and the cube of *ten*, or 1,000, is the length of the reign of the saints (Rev. 20:4). The *tenth* generation means 'for ever' (compare Deut. 23:3 with Neh. 13:1). *Ten* is also the number of worldly completion, symbolizing perfect power. The *ten* Egyptian plagues symbolized the complete outpouring of divine wrath; the fourth beast of Daniel had *ten* horns (Dan. 7:7,24); the Red Dragon of the Apocalypse has *ten* horns (Rev. 12:3), as well as the First Beast or Antichrist (Rev. 13:1).

"*Twelve* is emphatically the number referring to the kingdom of God, the 'signature' of God *(three)* multiplied by the 'signature' of the world *(four)*. Lee holds that while *seven* is the sacred number of Scripture, *twelve* is the number of the Covenant People in whose midst God dwells, and with whom He has entered into Covenant relations. *Twelve* are the tribes of Israel: there were twice *twelve* courses of the priests; four times *twelve* cities of the *Levites; twelve* is the number of the Apostles; twice *twelve* is the number of the Elders who represent the Redeemed Church; the woman of Rev. 12:1 had a crown of *twelve* stars on her head; the New Jerusalem has *twelve* gates (Rev. 21:12), the wall of the city has *twelve* foundations (21:14), and the tree of life bears *twelve* names of fruits (22:2)" (Weidner, *op. cit.*, pp. xxxix, xl).

In the symbolism of colors, white is pre-eminently the color of innocence, purity, and righteousness, as well as of spiritual age, maturity, and perfection; black denotes famine, distress, suffering; blood red may, like blood itself, denote war, murder, or sacrificial death; purple is the color of royalty or voluptuous ease; and pale yellow is the color of expiring life and the kingdom of the dead (6:8). (See the excellent treatment of the symbolism of colors in John Peter Lange, *The Revelation of St. John,* pp. 16-18.)

*Vocabulary.* There are 916 different words in the Greek text of the Apocalypse; of these 416 are also found in the Fourth Gospel; 98 occur only once elsewhere in the New Testament; while there are 108 words that are not found anywhere else in the New Testament. There are numerous words here that speak of authority. For example, the word for *throne* occurs 44 times; *king, kingdom,* and *rule,* 37 times; *authority* and *power* 40 times. The many words translated to *see, to perceive,* etc., occur nearly 150 times. The words meaning *to write,* and the result of writing, i.e., a *book,* are found 60 times.

*The Use of the Old Testament in the Apocalypse.* This last book of the Bible forms an amazing mosaic, as it were, of Old and New Testament themes. In the appendix to Westcott and Hort's *Greek New Testament* (pp. 184-188), it is estimated that of 404 verses in this book, 265 contain lines which embrace approximately 550 references to Old Testament passages: there are 13 references to Genesis, 27 to Exodus, 79 to Isaiah, 53 to Daniel, etc. Many would agree with the late Professor Briggs that "the eschatology discourse of Jesus [Mt 24:25; Mk 13; Lk 21] is, to our mind, the key to the Apocalypse. This book is the work of a Jew saturated with Old Testament prophecy, under the guidance of the word of Jesus and the inspiration of God. It is the climax of the prophecy of the Old and New Testaments."

This extended incorporation of Old Testament material is seen in large sections, separate verses, and individual phrases. Thus the description of Babylon in chapter 18 has innumerable parallels with Jeremiah 51. The two beasts of chapter 13, with their ten horns which are ten kings, derive directly from the beast visions of Dan 7, 8. The vision of the two olive trees and two candlesticks (ch. 11) is a reframing of a vision of Zechariah (Zech 4). The time periods in the book of Revelation derive from Daniel, as time, times, and half a time (12:14, from Dan 12:7). Many of the judgments of the trumpets are amazingly parallel with the plagues of Egypt, which we shall consider in some detail in the exposition of that passage. Even in the first chapter, verse 6 refers back to Ex 19:6; verse 7 to Dan 7:13 and Zech 12:10,12; verse 14 consists of two passages taken from Dan 7:9,13; 10:5. Verse 15 derives from Dan 10:6; Ezk 1:24; verse 16 from Isa 11:4; 49:2; verse 17 from Isa 44:6; 48:12; and verse 18 from Isa 38:10. Many of the titles of deity used in this book are found originally in the Old Testament: "the Almighty" of 1:8, etc., in Gen 17:1; "Alpha and Omega," as above. (A good chapter on this subject will be found in Merrill C. Tenney's *Interpreting Revelation*, pp. 101-116.)

*The Relation of the Revelation to the Olivet Discourse.* That there are many lines of thought in the Apocalypse bearing strong resemblance to subjects touched upon in our Lord's Olivet Discourse, all would agree. Some have pressed this too far, it seems to me, and have forced the Revelation into a mold constructed from the threefold division of the Olivet Discourse. The events of the Olivet Discourse may be divided chronologically into three periods — pre-Tribulation, Tribulation, and post-Tribulation. It would be difficult to form a similar outline for the book of Revelation. However, there are many parallel passages, particularly those depicting physical and economic disturbances that are to take place toward the end of the age, e.g., Lk 21:9-11. War, famine, pestilence, and earthquakes appear in the first four judgments of the seals, wars often from Rev 16:12 to the end of chapter 19, and earthquakes in 16:18 and 18:8. The subject of martyrdom, as in Lk 21:12-16, is often introduced into the book, as in Rev 6:9-11; 11:7-10; 13:7,15; 16:6; 17:6; 18:24. The Great Tribulation is referred to in 7:14. False christs and false prophets appear in their final form in chapter 13. The celestial disturbances of Lk 21:25-28 are in Rev 6:12-14 ff. The coming of the Son of Man is announced in Rev 1:7, and is consummated when the Word of God descends from heaven at the time of the battle of Armageddon. (For a chapter on this subject, see my volume, *A Treasury of Books for Bible Study*, pp. 235-242. Some years ago Henry W. Frost wrote an entire book on this subject, *Matthew Twenty-Four and the Revelation*, New York, 1924.)

*The Principle of Anticipation.* Through-out this book, over and over again the author uses what is known as prolepsis; that is, early in the book he uses a phrase which reappears later, and generally with fuller development. Thus, e.g., Christ is called "the faithful witness" at the beginning (1:5), but he reappears as the Faithful Witness in 3:14; 17:6; 20:4 He is initially assigned the title, "the ruler of the kings of the earth" (1:5). But when we draw near the end of the age, when the prerogatives of this title are actually to be exercised, we find him again so designated (17:14; 19:16). It is announced at the beginning (1:6) that Christ has made us kings and priests; but this reappears at the end of the book (20:6). So likewise the title, "the Alpha and the Omega," is found at the beginning (1:8), and at the end (21:6; 22:13), as well as the title, "the Almighty" (1:8; 19:6,15; 21:22). The command to keep the words of this prophecy is given in the introduction, but this is exactly the command that we find repeatedly at the end of the book (22:7,10,18).

The promises made to believers in the seven epistles of chapters 2 and 3 reappear with amazing reiteration when the great struggles on earth are over, and the children of God are in the resurrection glory of the New Jerusalem. Thus, the promise of "the tree of life" (2:7) is found again at the very end of the book (22:2,14). Deliverance from the second death is promised to the faithful at Smyrna (2:11), and is referred to again at the Last Judgment (20:6,14). "The Spirit" declares, in the fourth epistle, that Christ will rule the nations "with a rod of iron" (2:27); and this is exactly what he is said to do at the battle of Armageddon (19:15). The promise of the "morning star" to those who are faithful (2:28) reappears in 22:16. The idea of walking with Christ "in white" is presented not only to the faithful of Sardis and Laodicea, but to the believers at the end of the age (3:4,5,18; 19:14). The "book of life" (3:5) reappears four times, beginning with the period of tribulation (13:8; 17:8; 20:12,15; 21:27). To the city of Philadelphia there is a fourfold promise (3:12), each phrase of which reappears at the end of the book: "He that overcometh, I will make him a pillar in the temple of God . . . and I will write upon him the name of my God [22:4], and the name of the city of my God [21:2,10], the new Jerusalem ... [21:2,10], and mine own new name." Finally, the promise to the overcomers in Laodicea, that they would sit down with Christ on his throne, reappears at the beginning of the description of the New Jerusalem (20:4).

*Alternating Scenes in Heaven and Scenes on Earth.* A fundamental factor in this book, too often passed over by commentators, is of great help in understanding these chapters when it is recognized. That is, many scenes of this book are located in heaven, while the judgments themselves take place on this earth; and the scenes in heaven always precede the earthly events to which they are attached. Thus, the messages to the seven churches are preceded by a vision of the ascended Lord. The opening of the six seals in chapter 6 is preceded by a vision of the Lamb in heaven, worthy to open the book (chs. 4; 5). The judgments accompanying the blowing of the seven trumpets are preceded by a heavenly scene extending from 7:1 to 8:5. The dreadful events of chapters 11; 12; 13 are again preceded by a heavenly scene of instructions to John. The devastations accompanying the seven plagues (chs. 15; 16) are preceded by the announcements of the angels and the showing of "the temple . . . in heaven." And, after the final judgment of chapter 20, the book concludes with a picture of the heavenly home of the redeemed.

I have always felt that there are two great truths to be drawn from this phenomenon. First, what is about to take place on earth, though unknown to man and unexpected by him, is fully known to those in heaven—the ascended Lord, the angels, the twenty-four elders, the living creatures, and the others. Secondly, what is to take place on earth is under the complete control and direction of heaven, so that we may safely say, judging from this book, as well as from other prophetic books in the Scripture, that everything that takes place on this earth only fulfills the Word of God. This principle is remarkably set forth in the preliminary announcements concerning the kings of the earth going forth to make war with the Lamb. Though we read of the ten kings satanically inspired, having one mind and giving their power and authority unto the beast (17:12,13), nevertheless, it is God who "did put in their hearts to do his mind, and to come to one mind, and

to give their kingdom unto the beast, until the words of God should be accomplished" (17:17).

*The Book of Judgment.* From the beginning of this book to almost the very end, we must ever keep in mind the fact that *the book of Revelation is a book of judgment,* therefore, a book involving destruction, havoc, death, pain, tribulation. The very description of the Lord Jesus as he is about to send messages to the churches contains some factors that indubitably speak of judgment—eyes "as a flame of fire," feet "like unto burnished brass," out of whose mouth proceeds "a sharp two-edged sword." The following passages bear especially on this theme of judgment: 6:16,17; 11:17,18; 14:7,10; 16:5,7; 18: 8,10,20; 19:2; and 20:11-15.

*Canonicity.* The Western Church early believed that the book of Revelation should be included in the canonical books of the New Testament, and it was publicly read in the churches. But the Eastern Church seemed reluctant to adopt the same position, and did not agree on the canonicity of the Apocalypse until the fourth century. The Muratorian Canon, compiled about 200, includes the book in its list. By the middle of the third century, the Bishop of Alexandria accepted the book as canonical. It was omitted from the Vulgate Syriac Version. The Third Council of Carthage (397) accepted the book as canonical, and the entire volume appears in the early manuscripts, the Codex Sinaiticus, the Codex Vaticanus, and the Codex Alexandrinus. Luther greatly erred in placing the book of Revelation, along with the epistles of James, Jude, and Hebrews, in an appendix. For centuries the Protestant Church universal and the Eastern and Western Churches have agreed that it is a canonical work. (This entire subject has been treated with great thoroughness in a volume by Ned B. Stonehouse: *The Apocalypse in the Ancient Church,* Goes, Holland, 1929.)

*The Four Principal Schools of Interpretation.* The book of Revelation is the only large portion of the Word of God concerning which four basic differing systems of interpretation have been developed. The system of interpretation a Bible student adopts will make an enormous amount of difference in what he believes the book teaches.

(1) *The Spiritual Scheme of Interpretation.* From the time of Augustine, there have always been some Biblical scholars who have insisted that the purpose of this book is not to instruct the church regarding the future, not to predict specific events, but simply to teach fundamental spiritual principles. This is the view expressed over and over again by Milligan (W. Milligan, *Lectures on the Apocalypse*), though at times he contradicts his own conviction. He says in one place: "The Apocalypse does deal in a most distinct and emphatic manner with the Second Coming of the Lord." Gloag insists upon the same view: "The book is designed to teach us the spiritual history of the Church of Christ, to warn us of those spiritual dangers to which we are exposed, to inform us of the spiritual trials to which we are liable, to describe the great contest with evil, and to comfort us with the assurance of the final victory of Christ over the powers of darkness." Now all of this is true. The book does teach principles, spiritual principles; it does bear a message of comfort in its assurance of the ultimate victory of Christ. But everything in the book contradicts the view that it does not unfold the prophetic future. The book itself claims to be genuine prophecy. "Evil," as Moorehead says, "ever seeks to concentrate in a person or system; so does good. Revelation shows us evil centralized in the beast and in the false prophet." Certainly the return of Christ is in this book, and that is a prophecy of a future event; likewise, the resurrection of believers and the judgment of the Great White Throne. (This is the view held by most commentators of the Reformed faith, Peters and others.)

(2) *The Preterist Scheme of Interpretation.* This system of interpretation of Revelation insists that the author describes only events taking place on earth in the Roman Empire during his own time, especially toward the end of the first century. This was a view developed principally in the seventeenth century by a Jesuit scholar, Alcazar, in an attempt to reply to the arguments of the Reformers, who insisted that the book predicted the corruption and doom of the Roman Catholic Church, especially in the two chapters devoted to Babylon. Alcazar's view has been adopted by a number of modern writers—Moses Stu-

art, A. S. Peake, Moffatt, Sir William Ramsay, Simcox, and others. These men hold that the ruler whose deadly wound was healed refers to Nero, and that Domitian was the beast of chapter 13. It is true that the preterist view must be applied in our interpretation of the seven churches. But to say that the remainder of the book refers only to the events of the first century is really to deny its prophetic character, and to force many of its statements into a mold too small to contain them. As Milligan has said, "The whole tone of the book leads to the opposite conclusion. It treats of much that was to happen down to the very end of time, until the hour of the full accomplishment of the Church's struggle, of the full winning of her victory, and of the full attainment of her rest. The Apocalypse bears distinctly upon its face that it is concerned with the history of the Church until she enters upon her heavenly inheritance" *(op. cit.,* p. 41).

(3) *The Historicist Scheme of Interpretation.* In the history of the interpretation of the Apocalypse, probably more great names are attached to this scheme than to any other one view, with the exception of the futurist. According to this conception, the book of Revelation, especially in the prophecies of the seals, the trumpets, and the bowls, sets forth particular events in the history of the world *from the first century down to modern times.* The greatest work based on this theory is the four-volume study by Elliott (E. B. Elliott, *Horae Apocalypticae*), which may be taken as an illustration of this scheme. He says that the trumpet judgments cover the period from A.D. 395 to 1453, that the first trumpet refers to the invasion of the Goths, the third to the Huns under Attila, the fifth to the hordes of Moslems pouring into the West in the sixth and seventh centuries, etc. To take another illustration, Mede, in his famous work, says that the sixth seal predicts the overthrow of paganism under Constantine, that the second vial refers to Luther, the third to events in the reign of Queen Elizabeth I, etc. Many of those who belong to this school insist that the earthquake in 11:19 refers to the French Revolution; others find Napoleon Bonaparte in the book of Revelation, etc., etc.

Now, apart from all other objections to this scheme, it is admitted on every hand that it offers no fundamental principle or criterion of judgment by which we are able to determine exactly what historical events are referred to in a given passage. And this has led to a vast morass of confusion and contradiction among those who hold this view.

Milligan, in a powerful criticism of this whole scheme, says: "We may indeed admit that the events found in it by the historical interpreter would have been instructive or consolatory to the early Christian, if he could have thoroughly apprehended them. But the real difficulty lies in this, that such apprehension was then impossible. . . . While thus useless to the men first addressed by them, the visions of the Apocalypse would, upon this system, have been equally useless to the great body of the Christian Church, even after they had been fulfilled, and their fulfillment recognized by a few competent inquirers. The poor and the unlearned have always known, and will probably always know, little of the historical events supposed to be alluded to. Could it be a part of the Divine plan to make the understanding of a revelation so earnestly commended to us dependent on an acquaintance with the ecclesiastical and political history of the world for many hundred years? The very supposition is absurd. It is inconsistent with the first promise of the book, 'Blessed is he that readeth, and they that hear the words of the prophecy!' . . . The selection of historical events made by the system is in a high degree arbitrary, and cannot be said to correspond to the degree of importance which these events have vindicated for themselves in the course of history" (op. cit., p. 131).

(4) *The Futurist Scheme of Interpretation.* It can hardly be doubted that the Revelation is a book of predictive prophecy. To deny this is to disregard the style, the theme, and the future events of the Apocalypse. Certainly the Second Advent, the final conflict of Christ with the forces of evil, the Millennium, the final judgment, are events still future. The futurist scheme of interpretation insists that, for the most part, the visions of this book will be fulfilled toward the end and at the end of this age. The futurist view was long ago excellently defined as that scheme which "looks for the fulfillment of these predictions, neither in the early presentations and heresies of the church, nor in the long series of centuries from the first preaching of the Gospel until now, but in the events which are immediately to precede, to accom-

pany, and to follow the Second Advent of our Lord and Saviour" (*Lectures on the Apocalypse,* p. 68).

It is strange to find Gloag (in 1891) saying that "this system has not many supporters" (*op. cit.,* p. 372). The fact is, it has a great many supporters, among whom are some of the outstanding Biblical expositors of modern times and some of the most distinguished students of prophecy. Among them are Todd, Benjamin Wills Newton, Seiss, William Kelly, Peters, practically all of those writing within the circumference of the Plymouth Brethren, e.g., S.P. Tregelles, Nathaniel West, A. C. Gaebelein, Scofield, Moorehead, Walter Scott, Alford, and others. Theodor Zahn's notable commentary on Revelation (not yet translated into English) takes the futurist position, and Zahn is recognized as the greatest conservative New Testament scholar of Europe towards the close of the nineteenth century. Simcox, who is no futurist himself, frankly admits "from the time of Tertullian and Hippolytus—not to say Justin and Irenaeus—we have a consistent expectation of the course of events that will precede the last judgment" (G. A. Simcox, *The Revelation of St. John the Divine* in CBSC, p. xliv).

There is, of course, an extreme futurism which must be emphatically rejected. Some futurists go so far as to say that the seven churches of Asia will be reorganized and re-established at the end of the age, at which time the predictions concerning them will be fulfilled—a view wholly unnecessary and unreasonable.

The objection so often heard, that it is strange to have in our New Testament a book which, for the most part, contains matters pertaining to the end of the age, does not hold when one reviews the fundamental factor regarding the basic far-reaching prophecies of the Scriptures, namely, that from earliest times they point to the end of the age for their fulfillment. Is not this true of the very first prophecy of the Bible—"and I will put enmity between thee and the woman, and between thy seed and her seed: he shall bruise thy head, and thou shalt bruise his heel" (Gen 3:15)? Is not this a prophecy of Messianic victory which still awaits its final fulfillment? The extended prophecy of Jacob in Genesis 49 refers to "the last days," as it says. Over and over again in the Book of Daniel, we are told that its prophecies refer to "the end" (7:26; 9:26,27; 11:13,27; 12:8,13).

Does not our Lord's Olivet discourse point directly to the *end* of the age, and Christ's still future Second Advent? (Mt 24:3,14; also his prophetic parables, e.g., Mt 13:39,40) So with Paul speaking to the Thessalonians regarding the man of sin; Peter's account of the apostasy of the last days; Paul's great eschatological prophecy in II Timothy 3, and the whole body of prophecy in the familiar resurrection chapter, I Corinthians 15. All these require a futurist interpretation. It is not unreasonable that the Bible should conclude with a book of prophecies which, for the most part, will be fulfilled at the great final consummation of this age—the end of the revolt against God, and the beginning of that age of righteousness for which all just men long.

Of course, there is some truth in each of these systems of interpretation. The first three chapters must be interpreted historically. There *are* great spiritual principles set forth in the judgments, promises, prophecies, and Messianic victories of this book. For the most part, however, the Apocalypse will be most correctly interpreted if the futurist scheme is adopted.

*The Apocalypse and Apocalyptic Literature.* When the gift of true prophecy ceased in the Old Testament with Malachi, about 400 B.C., there was developed within the Jewish commonwealth a body of literature a part of which is called apocalyptic. This literature was written in symbolic, pictorial language. It was composed, for the most part, in times of persecution, especially in the days of Antiochus Epiphanes in the second century, as well as in the first century of this era, when the Hebrew people saw the destruction of their holy city. Apocalyptic literature is, principally, eschatological. It concentrates on those future events when the enemies of Israel, and those of our Lord, will be destroyed, and Israel herself will be restored to her former glory.

The Apocalypse of the New Testament is distinctly different, on the whole, from the preceding apocalyptic literature. As George Ladd has well pointed out: (1) The author designates his book as a prophecy (1:3; 22:7, etc.), and the book is thus a product of the prophetic spirit. (2) John does not take the name of some great former prophet of Israel, but uses his own name. (3) John does not retrace history under the guise of

prophecy, but looks prophetically into the future himself. (4) John's book, while filled with dark and ominous passages, does not convey the mood of pessimism, as so many of the apocalypses did, but of optimism, for the seer constantly reiterates the great truth that Christ will conquer all enemies, and that the kingdoms of this world will become the kingdom of our Lord and Saviour Jesus Christ. (5) Finally, the Apocalypse presses upon its readers great ethical demands. There is a sense of moral urgency here. Salvation is not something automatically conferred but that which will be given to those who bear the marks of true children of God (G. E. Ladd: "Apocalyptic, Apocalypse," in *Baker's Dictionary of Theology,* 1960, pp. 50-54).

*Prolonged Study Needed for the Understanding of This Book.* Because of its symbolism, its saturation with Old Testament passages and themes, the various schemes of interpretation that have developed concerning this book through the ages, and the profundity and vastness of the subjects that are here unveiled, I believe that the Apocalypse, above every other book of the Bible, will yield its meaning only to those who give it prolonged and careful study. Professor William Milligan has challengingly reminded us that, "The book is there, and it must either be excluded from the NT, or the Church must continue her struggle to comprehend it until she succeeds in doing so. Consider —1. In the first place, that we start with the supposition—a supposition denied by none of those to whom these lectures are addressed—that the Revelation of St. John is part of the Word of God. This consideration settles the whole question. The simple fact that a book has been given by the Almighty to man constitutes man's obligation to make every effort to understand it. It may be hard to do so. We may be long defeated. Not less is the effort one that we are bound to make; using all the appliances in our power, and watching, if we still feel that we are in darkness, for the first symptoms of light. Nothing is more certain than that, had it not been intended that we should use this book, the exalted Redeemer would not have given it by revelation to His servant John" (*Lectures On the Apocalypse,* p. 4).

Many students, both before and since

Lange, have voiced the same hope he expressed in 1870: "Doubtless, in the future, the importance and influence of this Book will constantly increase with the increasing confusion and gloom of the times, with the increasing danger which they offer to sound and sober faith" *(Revelation,* p: 63).

*The Outline of the Book.* Many different schemes have been proposed for arranging or classifying the twenty-two chapters of the Apocalypse, some of them quite fantastic. It is my opinion that those schemes which attempt to base an outline upon seven sevens in this book are strained and artificial. Thus, e.g., is Benjamin Warfield's outline: the seven churches (1:1–3:22); the seven seals (4:1–8:1); the seven trumpets (8:2–11:19); the seven mystic figures (12:1–14:20); the seven vials (15:1–16:21); the seven fold judgment of the harlot (17:1–19:10), and the seven fold trumpet (19:11–22:5). All would agree that four of these divisions are inescapable: the seven churches, the seven-sealed book, the seven trumpets, and the seven vials of judgment. But the concept of *seven* is not stated in the other sections. After I had studied this volume for years, there finally opened out to me an outline which, I think, is not strained, and yet is easy to remember. Apart from the prologue (1:1-8) and the epilogue (22:6-21), the book may be logically divided as follows:

I. The letters to the seven churches of Asia. 1:9–3:22.
II. The seven-sealed book and the earthly events it announces. 4:1–

6:17.
III. The judgments announced by seven trumpets. 7:1–9:21.
IV. The darkest hour of world history. 10:1–13:18.
V. The seven vials of judgment. 14:1 –16:21.
VI. Babylon and Armageddon. 17:1– 19:21.
VII. The Millennium; the Last Judgment; the New Jerusalem and Eternity. 20:1–22:5.

Note that these divisions occur in the following sequence of blocks of chapters –3-3-3-4-3-3-3.

*The Text.* The translators responsible for the epochal King James (Authorized Version of the New Testament used for their authority the Greek text as constructed by Erasmus. For the Apocalypse Erasmus had only one Greek manuscript, a cursive of the thirteenth century, and even this was of inferior quality. For this reason there are many words and passages in the AV that do not rest upon the more ancient and authoritative manuscripts. Since then the great Greek manuscripts of the New Testament, as the Sinaiticus, the Alexandrian, etc., have become known and have been thoroughly studied. Consequently, for all purposes of serious study of the Apocalypse, one must use the RV of 1891, or one of the later versions. (The great value of the now famous Chester Beatty Papyrus of the Apocalypse, probably of the early third century, does not require consideration in our necessarily brief commentary).

# THE REVELATION

## COMMENTARY

### CHAPTER 1

THE Revelation of Jesus Christ, which God gave unto him, to show unto his servants things which must shortly come to pass; and he sent and signified *it* by his angel unto his servant John:

2. Who bare record of the word of God, and of the testimony of Jesus Christ, and of all things that he saw.

3. Blessed *is* he that readeth, and they that hear the words of this prophecy, and keep those things which are written therein: for the time *is* at hand.

4. JOHN to the seven churches which are in Asia: Grace *be* unto you, and peace, from him which is, and which was, and which is to come; and from the seven Spirits which are before his throne;

5. And from Jesus Christ, *who is* the faithful witness, *and* the first-begotten of the dead, and the prince of the kings of the earth. Unto him that loved us, and washed us from our sins in his own blood,

6. And hath made us kings and priests unto God and his Father; to him *be* glory and dominion for ever and ever. Amen.

## I. The Letters to the Seven Churches. 1:1—3:22.

**1:1-8.** Though the exact idea of *letters* to the seven churches is not actually found in chapter 1, in verse 4 we do have the phrase, **John to the seven churches which are in Asia,** and later (v. 11) John receives the command to write what he sees and send it to the seven churches. The location of the seven churches is considered in the commentary on chapter 2.

Chapter 1 contains a rich, almost blinding revelation of Jesus Christ himself. Verses 4-8 present three basic descriptions of Christ. John seems to be describing the Christ he *knows,* for there is no indication that he has been given a special revelation here. This is the Christ of the past, present, and future, as set forth in the phrase, **who is and who was and who is to come** (v. 4, ASV). In the past, Christ was **the faithful witness** and **the firstborn from among the dead;** in the present, he is the one who **loveth us, and loosed us from our sins** (v. 5, ASV); in the future, **he cometh with the clouds**

7. Behold, he cometh with clouds; and every eye shall see him, and they *also* which pierced him: and all kindreds of the earth shall wail because of him. Even so, Amen.

8. I am Alpha and Omega, the beginning and the ending, saith the Lord, which is, and which was, and which is to come, the Almighty.

9. I John, who also am your brother, and companion in tribulation, and in the kingdom and patience of Jesus Christ, was in the isle that is called Patmos, for the word of God, and for the testimony of Jesus Christ.

10. I was in the Spirit on the Lord's day, and heard behind me a great voice, as of a trumpet,

11. Saying, I am Alpha and Omega, the first and the last: and, What thou seest, write in a book, and send *it* unto the seven churches which are in Asia; unto Ephesus, and unto Smyrna, and unto Pergamos, and unto Thyatira, and unto Sardis, and unto Philadelphia, and unto Laodicea.

12. And I turned to see the voice that spake with me. And being turned, I saw seven golden candlesticks;

13. And in the midst of the seven candlesticks *one* like unto the Son of man, clothed with a garment down to the foot, and girt about the paps with a golden girdle.

14. His head and *his* hairs *were* white like wool, as white as snow; and his eyes *were* as a flame of fire;

15. And his feet like unto fine brass, as if they burned in a furnace; and his voice as the sound of many waters.

16. And he had in his right hand seven stars: and out of his mouth went a sharp two-edged sword: and his countenance *was* as the sun shineth in his strength.

and every eye shall see him . . . and all the tribes of the earth shall mourn over him (v. 7, ASV). The statement that Christ has made us to be a kingdom of priests unto God (v. 6) is from the basic declaration in Ex 19:6, quoted centuries later by Peter (I Pet 2:5,9). The passage referring to the future has a double OT reference: in Dan 7:13 the Son of man is depicted as coming with clouds, and the fact that all shall then see him is declared in Zech 12:10,12. The word here translated **pierced** occurs elsewhere in the NT only in Jn 19:37 (cf. Zech 12:10).

I have always thought that the phrase, **the ruler of the kings of the earth** (1:5), is the key title of Christ for the book of Revelation. Many other kings are referred to in this book: kings of nations that go out to war against the Lamb, the king of the abyss, etc. There is no indication until the end of the book that the kings of the earth acknowledge Christ as King of kings. In fact, the book of Revelation is almost a record of Christ's enforcing this title, and finally assuming the pre-eminence to which the title points.

**9-11.** We have here the words Christ *spoke* to the apostle, a brief command to record what he is about to see, and instructions for sending the transcription when it is finished. There is little doubt that **the Lord's day** here (v. 10) refers to the day we know as Sunday.

**12-19.** In this description of the ascended Lord, the Christ John *saw* is seen walking in the midst of the **seven golden lampstands,** which symbolically represent the seven churches (see v. 20). Here as in Dan 7:13, our Lord is called **the Son of man** (Rev 1:13), a title found only once elsewhere in this book (14:14). The various phrases used in describing Christ are taken principally from Dan 7:9,13; 10:5,6; Ezk 1:24. The entire description gives us first an overwhelming impression of omnipotence, and then certain symbols pointing to judgment, as the flame of fire, burnished brass, and a sharp two-edged sword.

Christ identifies himself with the title **the first and the last** (Rev 1:17), a title used of God himself in Isa 44:6; 48:12. Observe what Christ presents as the reasons why those who are his should **Fear not:** (1) He is the First and the Last, and **the Living one;** (2) He was dead, and became alive again; and (3) He has the keys of death and of

17. And when I saw him, I fell at his feet as dead. And he laid his right hand upon me, saying unto me, Fear not; I am the first and the last:

18. *I am* he that liveth, and was dead; and, behold, I am alive for evermore, Amen; and have the keys of hell and of death.

19. Write the things which thou hast seen, and the things which are, and the things which shall be hereafter;

20. The mystery of the seven stars which thou sawest in my right hand, and the seven golden candlesticks. The seven stars are the angels of the seven churches: and the seven candlesticks which thou sawest are the seven churches.

Hades (vv. 17,18). If he is the First and Last, then he is the Christ of creation in the past, and the one who will bring all things to their divinely ordained consummation at the end. He will abide when all of his enemies have been defeated, and Satan and all his cohorts have been put away forever. The fact that he was dead identifies Christ with the most tragic of all man's experiences. No mere human being can conquer death —but Christ did. As he was dead but is now alive, so we who are his, though we die, will yet be forever alive with him. That he has the **keys of death and of Hades** certainly implies that the destiny of human souls is entirely under the jurisdiction of Jesus Christ.

Verse 19 has been taken by many as indicating a threefold division of the book of Revelation, in which **the things which thou sawest** refers to chapter 1, **the things which are,** to the seven churches in chapters 2 and 3, and **the things which shall come to pass hereafter,** ASV, to the remainder of the book. Actually, this classification does not help much in interpretation. It should be remembered, moreover, that the words here translated **hereafter,** *meta tauta,* occur nine other times in the book of Revelation (4:1; 7:1; 7:9; 9:12; 15:5; 18:1; 19:1; 20:3).

20. We are not absolutely sure what John means by the statement **the seven stars are the angels of the seven churches.** This word translated **angel** occurs seventy-six times in the Revelation. Fundamentally, the word means *messenger.* Some believe this simply refers to some leading person in each church; others say that this implies that each church has its representative angel in heaven. These "angels" are at least the ones through whom these messages are to be conveyed to the seven churches.

The term **Asia** (v. 11) has had various meanings throughout the centuries. In NT times **Asia** was the name of the Roman province located in the westernmost part of what is now Asia Minor. It was the largest and most important of all the Roman provinces of that area, embracing the districts of Caria, Lydia, and Mysia. The seven churches addressed in these letters were all located in the west-central part of this province. Beginning at **Ephesus** in the southwest and moving northward, we come to **Smyrna** and **Pergamum;** turning east and south, we arrive at **Thyatira, Sardis, Philadelphia,**

## CHAPTER 2

UNTO the angel of the church of Ephesus write; These things saith he that holdeth the seven stars in his right hand, who walketh in the midst of the seven golden candlesticks;

2. I know thy works, and thy labor, and thy patience, and how thou canst not bear them which are evil: and thou hast tried them which say they are apostles, and are not, and hast found them liars:

3. And hast borne, and hast patience, and for my name's sake hast labored, and hast not fainted.

4. Nevertheless I have *somewhat* against thee, because thou hast left thy first love.

5. Remember therefore from whence thou art fallen, and repent, and do the first works; or else I will come unto thee quickly, and will remove thy candlestick out of his place, except thou repent.

6. But this thou hast, that thou hatest the deeds of the Nicolaitans, which I also hate.

7. He that hath an ear, let him hear what the Spirit saith unto the churches; To him that overcometh will I give to eat of the tree of life, which is in the midst of the paradise of God.

8. And unto the angel of the church in Smyrna write; These things saith the first and the last, which was dead, and is alive;

9. I know thy works, and tribulation, and poverty, (but thou art rich) and *I know* the blasphemy of them which say they are Jews, and are not, but *are* the synagogue of Satan.

10. Fear none of those things which thou shalt suffer: behold, the devil shall cast *some* of you into prison, that ye may be tried; and ye shall have tribulation ten days: be thou faithful unto death, and I will give thee a crown of life.

11. He that hath an ear, let him hear what the Spirit saith unto the churches; He that overcometh shall not be hurt of the second death.

and **Laodicea.** A circle embracing these cities would have a radius of not more than sixty miles. That these letters from the risen Lord should be addressed to churches in Asia is not hard to understand, since that is where John had been living for many years, and no doubt he was well known to the churches of this area. Why these particular churches were chosen, we cannot be sure. Paul spent a long period of time at Ephesus on the third missionary journey (Acts 19; 20:16,17); Lydia was from Thyatira (Acts 16:14); and Epaphras labored at Laodicea (Col 2:1; 4:12-16). However, we know nothing of Paul's labors in six of these seven cities, and four of them appear nowhere else in the NT. Furthermore, we know there were churches existing at the end of the first century in some cities of Asia that are never referred to in the NT. Before Paul had completed his third missionary journey, "all who dwelt in Asia heard the word of the Lord, both Jews and Greeks" (Acts 19:10,26).

All of these letters follow the same sequence. Each begins with a phrase descriptive of the exalted Christ, who is addressing the churches; and each descriptive phrase is found in the preceding chapter in John's account of his vision of the risen Christ. In each letter, with the exception of the ones to Laodicea and Sardis, Christ's first words are those of commendation. This commendation is always followed by some details regarding the condition of the church, leading to a rebuke and warning —with the exception of Philadelphia and Smyrna, which receive no rebuke. Each letter concludes with a promise to those believers who overcome.

Note the many references to things of Satan: twice we read of "the synagogue of Satan" (2:9; 3:9); at Pergamum was "the throne of Satan" (2:13); in the letter to Thyatira mention is made of "the deep things of Satan" (2:24); in connection with Smyrna, the warning is given that the devil would cast some of them into prison. In addition, we find references to the curse of the Nicolaitans, the presence of the pernicious teachings of Balaam (2:14), and the rebuke of Thyatira for suffering the presence of one called Jezebel (2:20).

For three reasons I am refraining in this brief survey of the Apocalypse from a detailed examination of each of these letters: In the first place, these two

12. And to the angel of the church in Pergamos write; These things saith he which hath the sharp sword with two edges;

13. I know thy works, and where thou dwellest, *even* where Satan's seat *is:* and thou holdest fast my name, and hast not denied my faith, even in those days wherein Antipas *was* my faithful martyr, who was slain among you, where Satan dwelleth.

14. But I have a few things against thee, because thou hast there them that hold the doctrine of Balaam, who taught Balak to cast a stumblingblock before the children of Israel, to eat things sacrificed unto idols, and to commit fornication.

15. So hast thou also them that hold the doctrine of the Nicolaitans, which thing I hate.

16. Repent; or else I will come unto thee quickly, and will fight against them with the sword of my mouth.

17. He that hath an ear, let him hear what the Spirit saith unto the churches; To him that overcometh will I give to eat of the hidden manna, and will give him a white stone, and in the stone a new name written, which no man knoweth saving he that receiveth *it.*

18. And unto the angel of the church in Thyatira write; These things saith the Son of God, who hath his eyes like unto a flame of fire, and his feet *are* like fine brass;

19. I know thy works, and charity, and service, and faith, and thy patience, and thy works; and the last *to be* more than the first.

20. Notwithstanding I have a few things against thee, because thou sufferest that woman Jezebel, which calleth herself a prophetess, to teach and to seduce my servants to commit fornication, and to eat things sacrificed unto idols.

21. And I gave her space to repent of her fornication; and she repented not.

22. Behold, I will cast her into a bed, and them that commit adultery with her into great tribulation, except they repent of their deeds.

23. And I will kill her children with death; and all the churches shall know that I am he which searcheth the reins and hearts: and I will give unto every one of you according to your works.

24. But unto you I say, and unto the rest in Thyatira, as many as have not this doctrine, and which have not known the depths of Satan, as they speak; I will put upon you none other burden.

25. But that which ye have *already*, hold fast till I come.

chapters do not present major eschatological problems, while the exact meaning of some of the promises found here, if considered at all, would require extended discussion. In the second place, these letters are more widely used in expository series of messages than any other part of this book, and are somewhat familiar to most Bible students. Thirdly, to discuss the relevant historical data for each of these cities would compel abbreviation in the later treatment of basic problems of prophetic interpretation.

**2:1-7. Ephesus** was the largest city in Asia. It is the only one of these seven which has a treble place in NT literature: it is given extensive prominence in the Acts (18:18—19:41); to this church Paul wrote one of his epistles; and to it the ascended Lord sent a letter. After commending the church for its labor, patience, and intolerance of pseudo-apostles, the Lord refers to one tragic defect—she had left her **first love** (v. 4).

G. Campbell Morgan relates this passage to Paul's words of warning to the Corinthian church: " 'For I espoused you to one husband, that I might present you as a pure virgin to Christ. But I fear, lest by any means, as the serpent beguiled Eve in his craftiness, your minds should be corrupted from the simplicity and the purity that is toward Christ'. . . . The elements of first love then are simplicity and purity. . . . The love of the Church to Christ is typified by the love of the wife for the husband. What then is the love of Christ to the Church? Unselfish love, love in which there was no single thought of self. What then is the Church's love for Christ? The response of love to the mystery of love, the submission of love to perfect love. First love is the love of espousal. Its notes are simplicity, and purity, marital love, the response of love to love, the subjection of a great love to a great love, the submission of a self-denying love to a love that denies self. First love is the abandonment of all for a love that has abandoned all" (*A First Century Message to Twentieth Century Christians*, pp. 40-42).

**8-11.** The word **Smyrna** is related to the word *myrrh,* which in turn is symbolic of death. Smyrna's history has been one of successive sackings, fires, destructions. Polycarp, one of the more famous of the earlier martyrs, was Bishop of Smyrna. This city is the only one of

26. And he that overcometh, and keepeth my works unto the end, to him will I give power over the nations:

27. And he shall rule them with a rod of iron; as the vessels of a potter shall they be broken to shivers: even as I received of my Father.

28. And I will give him the morning star.

29. He that hath an ear, let him hear what the Spirit saith unto the churches.

## CHAPTER 3

AND unto the angel of the church in Sardis write; These things saith he that hath the seven Spirits of God, and the seven stars; I know thy works, that thou hast a name that thou livest, and art dead.

2. Be watchful, and strengthen the things which remain, that are ready to die: for I have not found thy works perfect before God.

3. Remember therefore how thou hast received and heard, and hold fast, and repent. If therefore thou shalt not watch, I will come on thee as a thief, and thou shalt not know what hour I will come upon thee.

4. Thou hast a few names even in Sardis which have not defiled their garments; and they shall walk with me in white: for they are worthy.

5. He that overcometh, the same shall be clothed in white raiment; and I will not blot out his name out of the book of life, but I will confess his name before my Father, and before his angels.

6. He that hath an ear, let him hear what the Spirit saith unto the churches.

7. And to the angel of the church in Philadelphia write; These things saith he that is holy, he that is true, he that hath the key of David, he that openeth, and no man shutteth; and shutteth, and no man openeth;

8. I know thy works: behold, I have set before thee an open door, and no man can shut it: for thou hast a little strength, and hast kept my word, and hast not denied my name.

9. Behold, I will make them of the synagogue of Satan, which say they are Jews, and are not, but do lie; behold, I will make them to come and worship before thy feet, and to know that I have loved thee.

10. Because thou hast kept the word of my patience, I also will keep thee from the hour of temptation, which shall come upon all the world, to try them that dwell upon the earth.

the seven still in flourishing condition.

12-17. Of **Pergamum** an ancient writer said it was "given to idolatry more than all Asia." The high hill behind it was adorned with numerous temples, among which was the great temple to Zeus, who was called *Soter Theos*, the Saviour God. Pergamum was the first city in Asia to erect a temple to Augustus. It was famous for its medical schools; and Asclepius, god of health, symbolized by a serpent, was worshiped there. Ramsay says, "Beyond all cities in Asia Minor, it gives the traveller the impression of being the home of authority." How appropriate, then, that here, as we are told, was Satan's throne. A great deal of discussion has arisen over exactly who are meant by the Nicolaitans (here, and in 2:6). In some manner they encouraged some in the church to return to pagan laxity of morals.

18-29. In **Thyatira**, the smallest of these seven cities, the church had allowed a false prophetess to instruct her, leading members into practices of immorality and idolatry. For this reason the Christ who addresses her is described as one coming to execute judgment. To the overcomers of this city Christ promises privileges similar to those he himself exercises (see 12:5; 19:15; 22:16).

3:1-6. In John's day, **Sardis**, once the capital of the ancient kingdom of Lydia, was comparatively insignificant. Even the church there partook of this abasement—thou hast a name that thou livest, and thou art dead (v. 1).

7-13. Only the letter to the church at **Philadelphia** contains no word of rebuke. Even today this Asian city has a Christian group. Though so worthy, this church was nevertheless to know a time of severe trial. Note carefully that the word is trial here, not *tribulation*. But in the trial the believers were to be divinely kept (see Jn 17:15).

3:14-22. The last letter is to **Laodicea**, which receives no commendation. The unfavorable condition in this church was lukewarmness: the members were **neither cold nor hot** (v. 15). The lukewarm person does not become greatly disturbed at hearing heretical teaching, and is not vigorous in the defense of the truth. This spirit of indifference is the most tragic thing that can happen to a church. The close of this letter is different from the conclusions of the other six in that it makes an application to the individual: **If any man hear my voice, and open the**

11. Behold, I come quickly: hold that fast which thou hast, that no man take thy crown.

12. Him that overcometh will I make a pillar in the temple of my God, and he shall go no more out: and I will write upon him the name of my God, and the name of the city of my God, *which is* new Jerusalem, which cometh down out of heaven from my God: and *I will write upon him* my new name.

13. He that hath an ear, let him hear what the Spirit saith unto the churches.

14. And unto the angel of the church of the Laodiceans write; These things saith the Amen, the faithful and true witness, the beginning of the creation of God;

15. I know thy works, that thou art neither cold nor hot: I would thou wert cold or hot.

16. So then because thou art lukewarm, and neither cold nor hot, I will spew thee out of my mouth.

17. Because thou sayest, I am rich, and increased with goods, and have need of nothing; and knowest not that thou art wretched, and miserable, and poor, and blind, and naked:

18. I counsel thee to buy of me gold tried in the fire, that thou mayest be rich; and white raiment, that thou mayest be clothed, and *that* the shame of thy nakedness do not appear; and anoint thine eyes with eye-salve, that thou mayest see.

19. As many as I love, I rebuke and chasten: be zealous therefore, and repent.

20. Behold, I stand at the door, and knock: if any man hear my voice, and open the door, I will come in to him, and will sup with him, and he with me.

21. To him that overcometh will I grant to sit with me in my throne, even as I also overcame, and am set down with my Father in his throne.

22. He that hath an ear, let him hear what the Spirit saith unto the churches.

**CHAPTER 4**

AFTER this I looked, and, behold, a door *was* opened in heaven: and the first voice which I heard *was* as it were of a trumpet talking with me; which said, Come up hither, and I will show thee things which must be hereafter.

door, I will come in to him, etc. (v. 20).

Through the centuries, various students have held four different views of the deeper implications of this series of seven letters. First, there is the historical interpretation—that these churches did exist at the time John wrote and bore characteristics such as those here depicted. Secondly, there is the view—no doubt correct—that these churches are not only historic, but are representative of different types of churches down through the ages. Accordingly, they manifest both the good and the tragic characteristics present in churches century after century. The warnings and promises here, then, are for all ages. There is a third, and rather fantastic, view that these prophecies are to be interpreted futuristically; that is, that all these cities are to be literally restored at the end of the age, and then the predictions will be truly fulfilled. A fourth view, held by many, is that these seven churches represent seven successive periods of church history, extending from the first century to the end of this age. I personally do not follow this interpretation, and a study of the writings of its proponents will reveal confusion upon confusion. Virtringa, e.g., identifies the sixth church with the first century of the Reformation, and the seventh with the Reformed church of his own day. Generally, writers who take this view claim that they are in the Laodicean period. The only aspect of this fourth explanation that I think may have some virtue is the interpretation of Laodicea. It seems that lukewarmness and indifference will mark the church at the end of the age, particularly indifference as to the great doctrines of the faith and unwillingness to defend them.

**II. The Seven-Sealed Book and the Earthly Events It Announces. 4:1–6:17.**

Though there are some eschatological elements in the portrait of Christ in the first chapter, and some predictive elements in the letters to the seven churches, but *not* extending to the end of the age, the truly prophetic portion of the Apocalypse begins with the section we are now about to consider. As noted in the Introduction, the larger part of this section is introductory in nature, for the scene recorded in chapters 4 and 5 is a heavenly one. Actually, predictions of far future events do not begin until chapter

2. And immediately I was in the Spirit: and, behold, a throne was set in heaven, and *one* sat on the throne.

3. And he that sat was to look upon like a jasper and a sardine stone: and *there was* a rainbow round about the throne, in sight like unto an emerald.

4. And round about the throne *were* four and twenty seats: and upon the seats I saw four and twenty elders sitting, clothed in white raiment; and they had on their heads crowns of gold.

5. And out of the throne proceeded lightnings and thunderings and voices: and *there were* seven lamps of fire burning before the throne, which are the seven Spirits of God.

6. John now beholds a door opening in heaven, and hears a voice saying, "Come up hither, and I will show thee the things which must come to pass hereafter." (ASV; on other openings of heaven, see Ezk 1:1; Mk 1:10; Jn 1:51.) Many commentators place the 'rapture' of the Church between chapters 3 and 4 of this book, but inasmuch as the text itself is silent on such a subject, one questions the wisdom of even discussing it here.

4:1-3. Just as the book of Revelation opens with a reference to the throne of God, and the letter to the last of the seven churches closes with a reference to the throne of Christ, so here the first great prophetic vision begins with the statement, **there was a throne set in heaven** (see Dan 7:9). A **throne** is the symbol of government and power. John attempts to record a vision of God similar to that beheld by Moses (Ex 19:9,19), by Isaiah (6:5), and by Ezekiel (1:26-28). The seer likens what he saw to three stones: the **jasper,** a transparent stone like glass or rock crystal; the **sardius,** red in color; and the **emerald,** green. In the breastplate of the high priest the first and last stones were sardius and jasper (Ex 28:17,20). It has been suggested that these stones stand for holiness, wrath, and mercy. Around the throne was a **rainbow,** which speaks of grace, or, as Hengstenberg says, "of grace returning after wrath."

4,5. The first great heavenly company of this book is now introduced: twenty-four **elders** sitting on twenty-four thrones situated around the throne of God (see also 11:16), arrayed in white garments and wearing **crowns** *(stephanoi)* of gold. *Stephanoi* were crowns bestowed on victors. There have been many identifications of these elders, but most would agree with Govett that they are "councillors of the thrones, conversant with the purposes of the king, and able to impart intelligence to John as the servant of God" (Robert Govett, *Lectures on the Apocalypse, in loco).* Twenty-four as a symbolic number is found only in the Apocalypse, and there only in relation to these elders (5:8; 11:16; 19:4). (For a detailed discussion of the identity of the elders, see G. H. Lang, *The Revelation of Jesus Christ,* pp. 124-136.) From the throne proceeded lightnings, voices, and thunder, and, in addition, John saw seven lamps of fire, which he identifies as symbols of **the seven Spirits of God.**

6. And before the throne *there was* a sea of glass like unto crystal: and in the midst of the throne, and round about the throne, *were* four beasts full of eyes before and behind.

7. And the first beast *was* like a lion, and the second beast like a calf, and the third beast had a face as a man, and the fourth beast *was* like a flying eagle.

8. And the four beasts had each of them six wings about *him*; and *they were* full of eyes within: and they rest not day and night, saying, Holy, holy, holy, Lord God Almighty, which was, and is, and is to come.

9. And when those beasts give glory and honor and thanks to him that sat on the throne, who liveth for ever and ever,

10. The four and twenty elders fall down before him that sat on the throne, and worship him that liveth for ever and ever, and cast their crowns before the throne, saying,

11. Thou art worthy, O Lord, to receive glory and honor and power: for thou hast created all things, and for thy pleasure they are and were created.

## CHAPTER 5

AND I saw in the right hand of him that sat on the throne a book written within and on the back side, sealed with seven seals.

2. And I saw a strong angel proclaiming with a loud voice, Who is worthy to open the book, and to loose the seals thereof?

3. And no man in heaven, nor in earth, neither under the earth, was able to open the book, neither to look thereon.

4. And I wept much, because no man was found worthy to open and to read the book, neither to look thereon.

5. And one of the elders saith unto me, Weep not: behold, the Lion of the tribe of Juda, the Root of David, hath prevailed to open the book, and to loose the seven seals thereof.

The concept of the seven Spirits of God certainly refers to the perfection and fullness of the activities of the Third Person of the Godhead.

**6,7.** Before the throne was a sea of glass (cf. Ex 24:10), indicating, it would seem, that all that the sea once stood for —storms and treacherous waves, symbolical of agitation among the peoples of the earth—had now been subdued. Another group, **four living creatures,** is introduced—one like a lion, one like a calf, one with the face of a man, and one like a flying eagle (similar to those in Ezk 1:5-14, 15-22; 10:20-22). Swete, with characteristic succinctness, rightly says, "The four forms suggest what is noblest, strongest, wisest and swiftest in animate nature. Nature, including man, is represented before the throne taking its part in the fulfillment of the Divine will and the worship of the Divine majesty" (H. B. Swete, *The Apocalpse of St. John, in loco*) These reappear in Rev 6:7; 7:11; 14:3; 15:7; 19:4.

**8-11.** With the introduction of the four living creatures, we have the first of twenty hymns, as they might be called, sung by various heavenly groups throughout the book of Revelation. Five of them are in these two chapters prefacing the opening of the seals. The first two are hymns to God: one sung by the living creatures ascribing holiness to God (4:8) and the other by the twenty-four elders acknowledging God as Creator. The opening words of the first hymn remind us of Isa 6:3, technically known in ancient hymnology as the *Trisagion*. The third and fourth are hymns to the Lamb, sung by the two groups just mentioned, acknowledging that the Lamb is worthy to open the book (Rev 5:9,10; 5:11,12). The fifth hymn is sung to both God and the Lamb by "every created thing in heaven, on the earth, and under the earth" (v. 13), and ascribes to them blessing, honor, glory, and dominion.

**5:1-5.** John adds some details regarding the One sitting upon the throne, who is said to hold in his right hand a **book written within and on the back, close sealed with seven seals** (ASV). Whether this is a book in codex form, like our books today, with the seven seals somewhat equally distributed on the sides, top, and bottom, or a scroll with the seven seals in one continuous line, we are not told. Another voice is heard, that of a strong angel, asking who is **worthy** to open this book (v. 2). The answer is that no one

6. And I beheld, and, lo, in the midst of the throne and of the four beasts, and in the midst of the elders, stood a Lamb as it had been slain, having seven horns and seven eyes, which are the seven Spirits of God sent forth into all the earth.

7. And he came and took the book out of the right hand of him that sat upon the throne.

8. And when he had taken the book, the four beasts and four *and* twenty elders fell down before the Lamb, having every one of them harps, and golden vials full of odors, which are the prayers of saints.

9. And they sung a new song, saying, Thou art worthy to take the book, and to open the seals thereof: for thou wast slain, and hast redeemed us to God by thy blood out of every kindred, and tongue, and people, and nation;

10. And hast made us unto our God kings and priests: and we shall reign on the earth.

11. And I beheld, and I heard the voice of many angels round about the throne, and the beasts, and the elders: and the number of them was ten thousand times ten thousand, and thousands of thousands;

12. Saying with a loud voice, Worthy is the Lamb that was slain to receive power, and riches, and wisdom, and strength, and honor, and glory, and blessing.

13. And every creature which is in heaven, and on the earth, and under the earth, and such as are in the sea, and all that are in them, heard I saying, Blessing, and honor, and glory, and power, *be* unto him that sitteth upon the throne, and unto the Lamb for ever and ever.

14. And the four beasts said, Amen. And the four *and* twenty elders fell down and worshipped him that liveth for ever and ever.

in the universe is worthy. Then one of the elders (v. 5) announces that the Lion of the tribe of Judah (Gen 49:9), the Root of David (Isa 11:1,10) is worthy to open this book, for two reasons: first, he has overcome, which would seem to refer to his defeat, while on earth, of Satan and every evil power; and, secondly, by his redemptive work he has purchased us unto God, with his blood (Rev 5:9). Note the universality of the redeemed in verse 9.

6,7. It is not without great significance that the redemptive work of Christ is revealed as of pre-eminent importance in the thought of these heavenly creatures and in the program of God to be consummated in this book. The word here translated slain (v. 6) occurs only here, in verses 9, 12, and in 13:8. "It is 'blood' even more than 'death' that connotes sacrifice; for one may die without being slain and may be slain without being made a sacrifice" (R. C. H. Lenski, *The Interpretation of St. John's Revelation, in loco*).

8-14. Here the harp is mentioned for the first time (reappearing in 14:2 and 15:2). This idea of a new song is found frequently in the OT, as in Ps 33:3; 40:3; 96:1; 98:1; 149:1. Revelation 5:10 is practically a reaffirmation of the truth expressed in 1:6. Here, I think, for the first time we have the concept of the reigning of saints and a kingdom. Carefully note the statement, they reign[ed] upon the earth.

We are now ready for the actual opening of these seals, but before beginning the study of chapter 6, note—a point often overlooked—that while the seals are opened, that is, stripped from the book, the book itself is never opened. This, of course, leads to many suggestions as to the contents of the book. Simcox says, certainly in error, it is the Book of Life. Irenaeus insisted that it contained "the things of Christ." Swete is safe in saying that its contents cover the unknown future, and he thus calls it "the book of destiny." Milligan says it contains "the whole counsel of God." Only six seals are opened in this chapter; the seventh is not opened until the trumpet judgments are about to be announced (8:1). Of these six seals, the first four form a group; the fifth and sixth stand by themselves. Each of the first four is introduced with a rider on a horse, from which derives the famous phrase, used in many ways in numerous literatures, "the

## CHAPTER 6

AND I saw when the Lamb opened one of the seals, and I heard, as it were the noise of thunder, one of the four beasts saying, Come and see.

2. And I saw, and behold a white horse: and he that sat on him had a bow; and a crown was given unto him: and he went forth conquering, and to conquer.

3. And when he had opened the second seal, I heard the second beast say, Come and see.

4. And there went out another horse *that was* red: and *power* was given to him that sat thereon to take peace from the earth, and that they should kill one another: and there was given unto him a great sword.

5. And when he had opened the third seal, I heard the third beast say, Come and see. And I beheld, and lo a black horse; and he that sat on him had a pair of balances in his hand.

6. And I heard a voice in the midst of the four beasts say, A measure of wheat for a penny, and three measures of barley for a penny; and *see* thou hurt not the oil and the wine.

7. And when he had opened the fourth seal, I heard the voice of the fourth beast say, Come and see.

8. And I looked, and behold a pale horse: and his name that sat on him was Death, and Hell followed with him. And power was given unto them over the fourth part of the earth, to kill with sword, and with hunger, and with death, and with the beasts of the earth.

four horsemen of the Apocalypse."

**6:1-8.** The identity of the first horse will in large part be determined by the identification of the following three. The second horse and its rider are said to take peace from the earth, and this, with the words slay and sword, indicates war. The third horse and its rider surely represent scarcity of food, though not altogether a famine. (The Roman coin *denarius,* here translated shilling (ASV), was the equivalent of a man's wages for a day of work. One measure of barley or grain was the average daily consumption of workmen.) The fourth horse and its rider, more dreadful than any of the others, bear the very name Death. To them was given authority over the fourth part of the earth, to kill with sword, and with famine, and with death, and by the wild beasts of the earth (ASV).

In the light of the meaning of the second, third, and fourth riders, it would seem unreasonable to identify the first rider with the Lord Jesus Christ, who is the rider on the white horse in Revelation 19. When Christ does come, "conquering and to conquer," there will be no subsequent judgments, such as the second, third, and fourth horses represent. Swete is correct in saying of the first horse, "A vision of the victorious Christ would be inappropriate at the opening of a series which symbolizes bloodshed, famine, pestilence." Even Torrance discerns this, though he adopts a strictly spiritual scheme of interpretation: "Can there be any doubt that this is the vision of antiChrist? It so resembles the real Christ that it deceives people, even many a reader of this passage! . . . It applies whenever evil is mounted upon good and wherever spiritual wickedness conquers by borrowing from the Christian Faith" (Thomas F. Torrance, *The Apocalypse Today,* p. 44).

Note that in these first four scenes there are no names of individuals, human or superhuman, no geographical terms, and no specific events. The judgments are, as it were, of a general nature: wars have occurred often on earth, and they are often accompanied by pestilence and by scarcity of food, if not famine conditions. This would seem to be, then, just a preliminary phase of the more terrible judgments to follow.

**9-11.** The opening of the first four seals forms a unit. In the opening of the fifth seal we have what I would call the first truly difficult problem in the book

9. And when he had opened the fifth seal, I saw under the altar the souls of them that were slain for the word of God, and for the testimony which they held:

10. And they cried with a loud voice, saying, How long, O Lord, holy and true, dost thou not judge and avenge our blood on them that dwell on the earth?

11. And white robes were given unto every one of them; and it was said unto them, that they should rest yet for a little season, until their fellow servants also and their brethren, that should be killed as they *were*, should be fulfilled.

12. And I beheld when he had opened the sixth seal, and, lo, there was a great earthquake; and the sun became black as sackcloth of hair, and the moon became as blood;

13. And the stars of heaven fell unto the earth, even as a fig tree casteth her untimely figs, when she is shaken of a mighty wind.

14. And the heaven departed as a scroll when it is rolled together; and every mountain and island were moved out of their places.

15. And the kings of the earth, and the great men, and the rich men, and the chief captains, and the mighty men, and every bondman, and every free man, hid themselves in the dens and in the rocks of the mountains;

16. And said to the mountains and rocks, Fall on us, and hide us from the face of him that sitteth on the throne, and from the wrath of the Lamb:

17. For the great day of his wrath is come; and who shall be able to stand?

of Revelation. Here are the souls of men who were slain for the word of God, and for the testimony which they held. In other words, these are martyrs, and they ask the risen Lord, How long . . . dost thou not judge and avenge our blood on them that dwell on the earth? The reply is twofold. First, they are each given a white robe (v. 11), a symbol of the righteous acts of the saints (cf. 19:8), so that even before the end these martyrs in some way have a foretaste of the glory to come. They are told that they must abide as they are until their fellow servants also and their brethren are slain. Though it is not specifically said in what period of time these martyrs are to be placed, the sixth seal certainly speaks of tremendous celestial aberrations that have never yet taken place but will occur at the end of this age. Consequently, these, I judge, had suffered martyrdom in the days immediately preceding the Tribulation. Moorehead may be right in saying, " For aught told us to the contrary, they were slain by the order of these riders." The comment of Torrance here is excellent: "After the terrible calamities the powers of the world have brought upon themselves, they try to disown the fact that they are the cause of all the evil and commotion, and so they turn upon God's people and vent their rage upon them as scapegoats" *(op. cit.*, p. 46).

12-17. Events transpiring at the opening of the sixth seal must be placed at the end of this age. This is perhaps the place to consider the question of celestial phenomena, so frequently referred to in the OT and NT Scriptures in passages relating to the end of the age. With the advent of Sputnik, a number of articles were published on this subject, some of which contain some very foolish statements. The subject of celestial disturbances is introduced first by Joel, in texts that clearly point to "the day of the Lord" (1:15; 2:1-11,30,31). One passage in Joel (2:28-32 a) is quoted by Peter in his great Pentecost sermon (Acts 2:16-21). There were no celestial disturbances at that time, so far as we know. These predictions were reiterated by Isaiah, also, in relation to "the day of the Lord" (13:6-10; 24:21-23). Our Lord placed much emphasis upon this particular aspect of eschatology in the Olivet Discourse (Mt 24:29,31; Mk 13:24-26; Lk 21:11,25). All of these statements refer to the period "after the tribulation"

## CHAPTER 7

AND after these things I saw four angels standing on the four corners of the earth, holding the four winds of the earth, that the wind should not blow on the earth, nor on the sea, nor on any tree.

2. And I saw another angel ascending from the east, having the seal of the living God: and he cried with a loud voice to the four angels, to whom it was given to hurt the earth and the sea,

3. Saying, Hurt not the earth, neither the sea, nor the trees, till we have sealed the servants of our God in their foreheads.

4. And I heard the number of them which were sealed: *and there were* sealed a hundred *and* forty *and* four thousand of all the tribes of the children of Israel.

5. Of the tribe of Juda *were* sealed twelve thousand. Of the tribe of Reuben *were* sealed twelve thousand. Of the tribe of Gad *were* sealed twelve thousand.

6. Of the tribe of Aser *were* sealed twelve thousand. Of the tribe of Nephthalim *were* sealed twelve thousand. Of the tribe of Manasses *were* sealed twelve thousand.

7. Of the tribe of Simeon *were* sealed twelve thousand. Of the tribe of Levi *were* sealed twelve thousand. Of the tribe of Issachar *were* sealed twelve thousand.

8. Of the tribe of Zabulon *were* sealed twelve thousand. Of the tribe of Joseph *were* sealed twelve thousand. Of the tribe of Benjamin *were* sealed twelve thousand.

(Mt 24:29), with the exception of Lk 21:11, which implies that there will be some celestial disturbances even before the Tribulation itself sets in. It is principally in the Revelation, however, that these disturbances are recorded as taking place. The first is set forth in the passage before us, at the time of the opening of the sixth seal. But this type of phenomenon occurs four times during the trumpet judgments, at the first, third, fourth, and fifth (8:8—9:2). During the pouring out of the fourth vial, the sun seems to be affected (16:8), and during the pouring out of the seventh vial, great stones fall down from heaven on men (16:17-21).

A careful study of these passages seems to reveal that we are not to consider any unusual celestial aberrations before the Tribulation period as having prophetic significance. This is especially true of these devices made by man, important as they are; for the celestial manifestations referred to in the prophetic Scriptures are the result of a direct interference of God himself. On two occasions in the past, men experienced divine judgment in the form of great darkness: at the time of the ninth plague upon Egypt (Ex 10:21-23); and during the last three hours in which our Lord hung upon the cross (Mt 27:45 and parallels).

### III. The Judgments of the Seven Trumpets. 7:1—9:21.

7:1-8. The second series of judgments is far more severe and extensive than those introduced by the opening of the seals. Before any of the seven angels sound these seven trumpets, two great multitudes are introduced, one on earth (7:1-8) and the other certainly in heaven, **standing before the throne and before the Lamb** (7:9-17). The first group is identified as 144,000 **sealed out of every tribe of the children of Israel** (v. 4). They are not said to be martyrs. The seal implies that this particular group will be divinely protected in the tribulations about to fall upon the earth.

There has been much disagreement as to who these people are, resulting in four major interpretations of the passage. One is that they should be looked upon in a general way as "representing a continuous process of preservation under the trials and afflictions of all times down to the end." There seems to be nothing in the text to justify such an indefinite designation of these tribal groups. Another

9. After this I beheld, and, lo, a great multitude, which no man could number, of all nations, and kindreds, and people, and tongues, stood before the throne, and before the Lamb, clothed with white robes, and palms in their hands;

10. And cried with a loud voice, saying, Salvation to our God which sitteth upon the throne, and unto the Lamb.

11. And all the angels stood round about the throne, and *about* the elders and the four beasts, and fell before the throne on their faces, and worshipped God,

12. Saying, Amen: Blessing, and glory, and wisdom, and thanksgiving, and honor, and power, and might, *be* unto our God for ever and ever. Amen.

13. And one of the elders answered, saying unto me, What are these which are arrayed in white robes? and whence came they?

14. And I said unto him, Sir, thou knowest. And he said to me, These are they which came out of great tribulation, and have washed their robes, and made them white in the blood of the Lamb.

15. Therefore are they before the throne of God, and serve him day and night in his temple: and he that sitteth on the throne shall dwell among them.

16. They shall hunger no more, neither thirst any more; neither shall the sun light on them, nor any heat.

17. For the Lamb which is in the midst of the throne shall feed them, and shall lead them unto living fountains of waters: and God shall wipe away all tears from their eyes.

view, somewhat similar, identifies these as Christians, the Church — and here many names speak with authority, as Bengel, Alford, Lenski, David Brown, Milligan, etc. Among minor interpretations is the ridiculous one of Albert Barnes that this refers to the ten divisions of the Christian Church. Some sects have claimed identity with these groups, such as the Jezreelites of a former generation.

Finally, there is the literal interpretation, that this is a prophecy concerning the children of Israel at the end of the age. The great prophetic scholar of the nineteenth century, J. H. Todd, summarizes this view in saying: "In strict accordance with the fact revealed in many prophecies, this tells us that at the period referred to in the vision, the Jewish people shall be in existence as a nation, and the majority of them will be still in their unbelief." This is the view held by Godet, Fausset, Nathaniel West, and Weidner.

Fausset adds: "Out of these tribes a believing remnant will be preserved from the judgments that shall destroy all the anti-Christian Confederacy" (JFB). It is significant that the tribe of Dan is here omitted — for which omission many reasons have been suggested—and **Levi** is included. "Since the Levitical ceremonies have been abandoned, Levi is again found on an equal footing with his brethren" (Albert Bengel, *Introduction to the Exposition of the Apocalypse, in loco*). Instead of Ephraim, the name Joseph is used. This I consider the second passage of unusual difficulty in the Apocalypse.

**9-17.** The other multitude is of a universal nature—certainly not confined to Israel, but from all tribes and peoples now in glory—singing the great hymn to God and the Lamb, together with the angels, the elders, and the four living creatures. These, John is told, are they that have come out of **great tribulation, and have washed their robes, and made them white in the blood of the Lamb** (v. 14). The **great tribulation** can be none other than that referred to in the Olivet Discourse (Mt 24:9,21,29). The entire scene is a heavenly one: The Lamb is presented as their shepherd or ruler; the promise is made that he shall guide them to fountains of waters of life; and, anticipating the detailed later description of the Holy City, they are told that God shall wipe away every tear from

## CHAPTER 8

AND when he had opened the seventh seal, there was silence in heaven about the space of half an hour.

2. And I saw the seven angels which stood before God; and to them were given seven trumpets.

3. And another angel came and stood at the altar, having a golden censer; and there was given unto him much incense, that he should offer *it* with the prayers of all saints upon the golden altar which was before the throne.

4. And the smoke of the incense, *which came* with the prayers of the saints, ascended up before God out of the angel's hand.

5. And the angel took the censer, and filled it with fire of the altar, and cast *it* into the earth: and there were voices, and thunderings, and lightnings, and an earthquake.

6. And the seven angels which had the seven trumpets prepared themselves to sound.

7. The first angel sounded, and there followed hail and fire mingled with blood, and they were cast upon the earth: and the third part of trees was burnt up, and all green grass was burnt up.

8. And the second angel sounded, and as it were a great mountain burning with fire was cast into the sea: and the third part of the sea became blood;

9. And the third part of the creatures which were in the sea, and had life, died; and the third part of the ships were destroyed.

10. And the third angel sounded, and there fell a great star from heaven, burning as it were a lamp, and it fell upon the third part of the rivers, and upon the fountains of waters;

11. And the name of the star is called Wormwood: and the third part of the waters became wormwood; and many men died of the waters, because they were made bitter.

12. And the fourth angel sounded, and the third part of the sun was smitten, and the third part of the moon, and the third part of the stars; so as the third part of them was darkened, and the day shone not for a third part of it, and the night likewise.

13. And I beheld, and heard an angel flying through the midst of heaven, saying with a loud voice, Woe, woe, woe, to the inhabiters of the earth by reason of the other voices of the trumpet of the three angels, which are yet to sound!

their eyes (Rev 21:4).

**8:1-6.** The trumpet judgments are unfolded in chapters 8 and 9, and, as with the seven seals, the first four belong together. Before any trumpet is blown by one of the angels, we have statements regarding the prayers of the saints (vv. 3,4). Perhaps Todd is right in thinking we can infer from this "that the judgments foretold in this prophecy will be the consequence, in some remarkable manner, of the prayers of saints crying to God to accomplish speedily the number of His elect and to hasten His kingdom" (*op. cit.*, p. 131). There is no reference here to the Roman Catholic doctrine of intercession by angels or saints. The thunder, voices, lightnings, and earthquakes are the symbolic precursors of the divine judgments about to fall upon the earth.

Before considering the judgments themselves, we do well to recall the significance of trumpets in the Holy Scriptures. All these phenomena (except the earthquake) are found in the account of God's descending at Mount Sinai to meet Moses, where we have the first reference to *trumpet* in the Bible (Ex 19:16). The blowing of trumpets called the Israelites together for instruction (Num 10:3,4) or for marching (Num 10:3-7); it summoned them to assemble for war (Jer 4:19; 42:14, etc.), and to return from dispersion (Isa 27:13); it announced release in the year of jubilee (Lev 25:8-10), and here it announces judgment. The trumpet judgments are quite similar to the plagues which God sent upon Egypt at the time of the deliverance of Israel, though they do not occur in the same order.

**7-13.** The result of the blowing of the first trumpet is the burning up of a third part of the flora of the earth. At the sound of the second trumpet, a third part of the sea becomes blood, a third of the creatures in the sea die, and a third part of the ships are destroyed (cf. the first plague, Ex 7:20-24). With the blowing of the third trumpet, a great star, burning as a torch, falls upon the rivers and waters of the earth, turning them to wormwood and causing wide-spread death. The first two judgments affect nature, and man only indirectly, but the third brings about the death of many. The blowing of the fourth trumpet brings about celestial disturbances, so that a third part of the sun, moon, and stars are smitten, and their light diminished

## CHAPTER 9

AND the fifth angel sounded, and I saw a star fall from heaven unto the earth: and to him was given the key of the bottomless pit.

2. And he opened the bottomless pit; and there arose a smoke out of the pit, as the smoke of a great furnace; and the sun and the air were darkened by reason of the smoke of the pit.

3. And there came out of the smoke locusts upon the earth: and unto them was given power, as the scorpions of the earth have power.

4. And it was commanded them that they should not hurt the grass of the earth, neither any green thing, neither any tree; but only those men which have not the seal of God in their foreheads.

5. And to them it was given that they should not kill them, but that they should be tormented five months: and their torment *was* as the torment of a scorpion, when he striketh a man.

6. And in those days shall men seek death, and shall not find it; and shall desire to die, and death shall flee from them.

7. And the shapes of the locusts *were* like unto horses prepared unto battle; and on their heads *were* as it were crowns like gold, and their faces *were* as the faces of men.

8. And they had hair as the hair of women, and their teeth were as *the teeth* of lions.

9. And they had breastplates, as it were breastplates of iron; and the sound of their wings *was* as the sound of chariots of many horses running to battle.

10. And they had tails like unto scorpions, and there were stings in their tails: and their power *was* to hurt men five months.

(cf. the ninth plague, Ex 10:21-23). This miraculous eclipse of the sun, moon, and stars is predicted by Amos as a sign of the coming day of judgment (Amos 8:9; see also Joel 2:2, 10). Note that all four of these judgments relate to some disaster falling upon the world of nature. (Weidner, *op. cit.*, has an excellent summary of the various fanciful interpretations of these four trumpet judgments, pp. 343-345). Before the judgments of the next two trumpets, an eagle flying in mid-heaven is heard to cry, Woe, woe, woe, for them that dwell on the earth. This is the first time the word translated woe appears in the Apocalypse.

9:1,2. To the judgment of the fifth trumpet, which is called the first Woe (v. 12), John devotes more space than to all the preceding judgments combined. It is probable that, apart from the exact identification of Babylon in chapters 17 and 18, the meaning of the two judgments in this chapter presents the most difficult major problem in the Revelation. Probably the star falling from heaven, to whom was given the key of the pit of the abyss, is, as Weidner says, "an evil angel, the instrument of carrying out God's purpose with reference to the ungodly world" (p. 114; so also Alford, and others). The abyss is not hell, but the present abode of the devil and his angels, including Hades, where are the souls of the ungodly dead awaiting the last judgment. So dense is the smoke rising from the pit that it darkens the sun and the air (see 6:12; 8:12).

3-10. Also from the abyss come creatures described as locusts (v. 3) having great power, who are allowed to torment men (though not to kill them) for a period of five months (v. 5). So intense will be men's suffering that they will seek death, in vain (v. 6). Locusts are used in the famous prophecy of the book of Joel as symbols of invading armies. Men are likened to locusts in Jud 6:5; Jer 46:23; etc.; and in the prophetic Scriptures they are symbols of divine judgment (Deut 28:38,42; Nah 3:15,17; Amos 7:1-3, etc.). It is not possible here to examine each descriptive phrase, but we must come to some conclusion as to what these creatures represent. I personally have not felt I could be more specific than was Milligan, who said—and surely all would agree with this—that the judgment refers to "a great outburst of spiritual evil which shall aggravate the sorrows of the world, make

11. And they had a king over them, *which is* the angel of the bottomless pit, whose name in the Hebrew tongue *is* Abaddon, but in the Greek tongue hath *his* name Apollyon.

12. One woe is past; *and,* behold, there come two woes more hereafter.

13. And the sixth angel sounded, and I heard a voice from the four horns of the golden altar which is before God,

14. Saying to the sixth angel which had the trumpet, Loose the four angels which are bound in the great river Euphrates.

15. And the four angels were loosed, which were prepared for an hour, and a day, and a month, and a year, for to slay the third part of men.

16. And the number of the army of the horsemen *were* two hundred thousand thousand: and I heard the number of them.

17. And thus I saw the horses in the vision, and them that sat on them, having breastplates of fire, and of jacinth, and brimstone: and the heads of the horses *were* as the heads of lions; and out of their mouths issued fire and smoke and brimstone.

18. By these three was the third part of men killed, by the fire, and by the smoke, and by the brimstone, which issued out of their mouths.

19. For their power is in their mouth, and in their tails: for their tails *were* like unto serpents, and had heads, and with them they do hurt.

20. And the rest of the men which were not killed by these plagues yet repented not of the works of their hands, that they should not worship devils, and idols of gold, and silver, and brass, and stone, and of wood; which neither can see, nor hear, nor walk:

21. Neither repented they of their murders, nor of their sorceries, nor of their fornication, nor of their thefts.

## CHAPTER 10

AND I saw another mighty angel come down from heaven, clothed with a cloud: and a rainbow *was* upon his head, and his face *was* as it were the sun, and his feet as pillars of fire:

2. And he had in his hand a little book open: and he set his right foot upon the sea, and *his* left *foot* on the earth,

3. And cried with a loud voice, as *when* a lion roareth: and when he had cried, seven thunders uttered their voices.

4. And when the seven thunders had uttered their voices, I was about to write: and I heard a voice from heaven saying unto me, Seal up those things which the seven thunders uttered, and write them not.

it learn how bitter is the bondage of Satan, and teach it to feel even in the midst of enjoyment that it were better to die than to live."

11. The description concludes with the word that over these creatures is **the angel of the abyss,** called in Hebrew, *Abaddon,* and in the Greek, *Apollyon,* the latter meaning "destroyer." In the Septuagint the word carries this idea in Job 26:2; 28:22; Prov 15:11, etc.; another form is the word translated "destruction" in Mt 7:13 and "destroy" in II Thess 2:8.

13-21. The blowing of the sixth trumpet is identified with the **second Woe** (11:14). We are now taken to a known geographical area on this earth, to the river **Euphrates** (v. 14), which here probably should be taken literally. Four angels bound somewhere along this river are now loosed, *that they should kill the third part of men* (v. 15). This fearful destruction will be brought about by armies of horsemen. Surely we here have come to the days of the beginning of Antichrist. Todd has said, and Weidner and others agree, that "we are probably to look to this region as the scene of this great judgment, which is in exact comformity with the inferences to which we are led by the prophecies of Daniel, where those countries in the region of the Euphrates, once the stage of such mighty empires, are destined to become the scene of the last great struggle between the princes of the world and the people of God."

The result of all this is not a turning to God, or repentance, but a stubborn continuation in the sins that have brought about this judgment, the worship of demons, idolatry, murder, sorceries, fornication, and thefts. In fact, I cannot find any evidence in the Revelation that there will be any great turning to God during the time that these fearful judgments are falling upon men.

## IV. The Darkest Hour of World History. 10:1–13:18.

*The Angel with the Little Book. 10:1-11.*

The tenth chapter presents a pleasant interlude. **Another strong angel** comes down out of heaven with a small **book** in his hand, and as John is about to record what he has seen, he hears a voice from heaven saying, **Seal up those things which the seven thunders uttered, and write them not** (v. 4; cf. Dan 12:9).

5. And the angel which I saw stand upon the sea and upon the earth lifted up his hand to heaven,

6. And sware by him that liveth for ever and ever, who created heaven, and the things that therein are, and the earth, and the things that therein are, and the sea, and the things which are therein, that there should be time no longer:

7. But in the days of the voice of the seventh angel, when he shall begin to sound, the mystery of God should be finished, as he hath declared to his servants the prophets.

8. And the voice which I heard from heaven spake unto me again, and said, Go and take the little book which is open in the hand of the angel which standeth upon the sea and upon the earth.

9. And I went unto the angel, and said unto him, Give me the little book. And he said unto me, Take it, and eat it up; and it shall make thy belly bitter, but it shall be in thy mouth sweet as honey.

10. And I took the little book out of the angel's hand, and ate it up; and it was in my mouth sweet as honey: and as soon as I had eaten it, my belly was bitter.

11. And he said unto me, Thou must prophesy again before many peoples, and nations, and tongues, and kings.

## CHAPTER 11

AND there was given me a reed like unto a rod: and the angel stood, saying, Rise, and measure the temple of God, and the altar, and them that worship therein.

2. But the court which is without the temple leave out, and measure it not; for it is given unto the Gentiles: and the holy city shall they tread under foot forty and two months.

3. And I will give power unto my two witnesses, and they shall prophesy a thousand two hundred and threescore days, clothed in sackcloth.

Apparently he never did record them, and so we do not know what the thunders said. The angel utters a famous, and more or less enigmatical, statement—there shall be delay no longer (ASV); or, as the margin reads, there shall be time no longer. Swete translates this, There shall no more be any interval of time, any further delay. This declaration, coupled with the one immediately following, then is finished the mystery of God (v. 7), convince us that the purpose of this vision, and especially of these utterances, is to prepare us for the final pouring out of God's judgments, the close of the end of the age, and the destruction of the enemies of the Lamb. The little book (v. 8) which John is told to take and eat (cf. Ezk 3:1-3; Ps 19:10,11; Jer 15;16) is never opened, and hence its exact nature must be a matter of dispute. But Düsterdieck is quite right, I think, when he says that it "appears to be an inner instruction and interpretation given the seer concerning visions still impending, and which are to continue until the full end. The more important the subjects of the prophecies that now follow, the more natural appears the new special preparation of the prophet" (p. 308).

The Two Witnesses in Jerusalem. 11:1-12. The eleventh chapter of the Revelation has always been to me one of greatest interest. The scene is certainly laid in Jerusalem, which though spiritually called Sodom and Egypt (v. 8; cf. Isa 1:9,10) is specifically referred to as the place where also their Lord was crucified. The events recorded here have never yet taken place, but they will literally occur in "the holy city" at the end of the age.

1,2. John is told to take a reed and measure the temple of God, and the altar, and them that worship therein (v. 1), which certainly implies that there will be some kind of temple building in Jerusalem at this time. The statement is made that the holy city will be trodden under foot for forty and two months (v. 2), a time period found also in 13:5, and equal to the 1,260 days of 11:3, and 12:6. I take this to be the first half of the seven-year terminus of our age, during the last half of which the Great Tribulation will occur, when Antichrist will be exercising universal power.

3-12. Two witnesses now appear, sent of God to prophesy to this city, though what their message is, we are not told. They are likened to the two olive trees

4. These are the two olive trees, and the two candlesticks standing before the God of the earth.

5. And if any man will hurt them, fire proceedeth out of their mouth, and devoureth their enemies: and if any man will hurt them, he must in this manner be killed.

6. These have power to shut heaven, that it rain not in the days of their prophecy: and have power over waters to turn them to blood, and to smite the earth with all plagues, as often as they will.

7. And when they shall have finished their testimony, the beast that ascendeth out of the bottomless pit shall make war against them, and shall overcome them, and kill them.

8. And their dead bodies *shall lie* in the street of the great city, which spiritually is called Sodom and Egypt, where also our Lord was crucified.

9. And they of the people and kindreds and tongues and nations shall see their dead bodies three days and a half, and shall not suffer their dead bodies to be put in graves.

10. And they that dwell upon the earth shall rejoice over them, and make merry, and shall send gifts one to another; because these two prophets tormented them that dwelt on the earth.

and candlesticks (v. 4) portrayed in Zechariah 4. They are given supernatural power, such as Elijah and Moses had (I Kgs 17:1), to slay their enemies, to cause a drought, to turn water into blood, and to smite the earth with plagues at their will (vv. 5,6). When they have finished the work God has assigned to them, **the beast that cometh up out of the abyss shall make war with them, and overcome them, and kill them** (v. 7; ASV). The bodies of these two prophets are placed in the street of this city, and from all over the earth men look upon them for three days and a half day, and enter upon a time of rather universal rejoicing because these men who had tormented them are now, they think, destroyed (vv. 8-10). To the astonishment of their enemies, when three and a half days have expired, God raises them to their feet, calls them into glory, and they ascend into heaven in a cloud (vv. 11,12).

The question is, Who are these **two witnesses?** The answers have been many. The text cannot in any way, I definitely believe, be interpreted as referring to a movement, or, as Lange insists, to the Christian state and the Christian Church (for where is a Christian state today?), or to the OT and NT, or to the Word and the Spirit, or to faithful Christians, as Milligan and Swete believe. I think these witnesses must be regarded as individuals. Many assert that they are Moses and Elijah (Simcox, etc.), others that they are Enoch and Elijah (Seiss, Lang, Govett). But in regard to such views I agree with Moorehead's position: "It is extremely improbable that these saints, after centuries of bliss in heaven, should be dispatched to earth to bear witness to Jews and Gentiles" (*op. cit.*, p. 86). Frankly, I think we gain nothing by prolonged debate as to their identity. They are two witnesses sent by God, and endued by God with great power.

Though written as far back as 1864, Govett's comment upon the peoples, tribes, and nations looking upon these dead bodies (vv. 9,10) is still worth attention: "The word *blepō*, that is, *to look upon*, denotes not merely the nations seeing them but their directing their eyes to this great sight and gazing upon them. 'But how,' it is asked, 'is it conceivable that men all over the earth should be rejoicing in the news when only three days and a half intervene between their

11. And after three days and a half the Spirit of life from God entered into them, and they stood upon their feet; and great fear fell upon them which saw them.

12. And they heard a great voice from heaven saying unto them, Come up hither. And they ascended up to heaven in a cloud; and their enemies beheld them.

13. And the same hour was there a great earthquake, and the tenth part of the city fell, and in the earthquake were slain of men seven thousand: and the remnant were affrighted, and gave glory to the God of heaven.

14. The second woe is past; *and,* behold, the third woe cometh quickly.

15. And the seventh angel sounded; and there were great voices in heaven, saying, The kingdoms of this world are become *the kingdoms* of our Lord, and of his Christ; and he shall reign for ever and ever.

16. And the four and twenty elders, which sat before God on their seats, fell upon their faces, and worshipped God,

17. Saying, We give thee thanks, O Lord God Almighty, which art, and wast, and art to come; because thou hast taken to thee thy great power, and hast reigned.

18. And the nations were angry, and thy wrath is come, and the time of the dead, that they should be judged, and that thou shouldest give reward unto thy servants the prophets, and to the saints, and them that fear thy name, small and great; and shouldest destroy them which destroy the earth.

death and resurrection? . . .' Is it not perfectly conceivable if the electric telegraph shall then have extended itself at the rate it has done of late years?" *(op. cit.,* pp. 243, 246, 247) Now, with television available, we can understand this passage better.

Lenski's words regarding these enemies of God making merry over the death of the two prophets (v. 10) are especially thought-provoking: "The wicked world cannot let them alone and simply pass on in its obduracy. Even when it is finally and utterly silenced, the obdurate world cannot dismiss the divine testimony. It must talk about it, bring everybody to look at the voiceless lips. Those who spurn the Word *never* get rid of it. Their very rejoicing over its silencing keeps them busy with the Word" *(op. cit.,* p. 346).

13,14. At the ascension of the two witnesses, Jerusalem experiences a great earthquake, resulting in the death of seven thousand persons, and the rest were affrighted, and gave glory to the God of Heaven (v. 13). We detect no conviction of sin here, merely a sense of fear, which soon passes.

*The Seventh Trumpet and the Scene in Heaven. 11:15-18.* As with the opening of the seventh seal, when the seventh angel sounds the seventh trumpet, no events directly follow, and no immediate judgment is announced. Rather, with the sounding of this trumpet, we have a scene in heaven, and one of the grandest statements concerning Christ in all the Bible: "The kingdom of the world is become the kingdom of our Lord, and of his Christ: and he shall reign for ever and ever" (v. 15). Note the difference here between the AV translation, "the *kingdoms* of the world," and the more accurate ASV rendering of **kingdom,** singular, as in the Greek text. The whole world now appears under one powerful universal government.

This declaration is followed by a song of praise offered by the four and twenty elders to God the Almighty. This is the only time that the elders are described as prostrating themselves before God. With the announcement that the reign of God through Christ is near at hand, we are given a graphic summary (v. 18) of the events that are about to take place: (1) the nations are wroth; that is, there will be an

**19.** And the temple of God was opened in heaven, and there was seen in his temple the ark of his testament: and there were lightnings, and voices, and thunderings, and an earthquake, and great hail.

## CHAPTER 12

AND there appeared a great wonder in heaven; a woman clothed with the sun, and the moon under her feet, and upon her head a crown of twelve stars:

**2.** And she being with child cried, travailing in birth, and pained to be delivered.

**3.** And there appeared another wonder in heaven; and behold a great red dragon, having seven heads and ten horns, and seven crowns upon his heads.

**4.** And his tail drew the third part of the stars of heaven, and did cast them to the earth: and the dragon stood before the woman which was ready to be delivered, for to devour her child as soon as it was born.

**5.** And she brought forth a man child, who was to rule all nations with a rod of iron: and her child was caught up unto God, and *to* his throne.

attempted assault upon Christ and his own; (2) the wrath of God is about to descend; (3) the dead will be judged; (4) believers, here divided into three groups — the prophets, the saints, and those that fear His name, will be rewarded; and (5) the destroyers are now to be destroyed. From this, one may surely conclude that as the time nears for Christ to seize his kingly authority over this earth, the hatred of earthly nations for God's people will be intensified, and opposition to the Gospel will increase.

**11:19.** Most students will agree that 11:19 should be considered as the introduction to what is about to be revealed in chapter 12. Here again, as at the beginning of the passages on the seven seals (4:5) and the seven trumpets (8:5), there are lightnings, voices, thunders, and an earthquake. What John now sees in heaven—a temple of God and **the ark of his covenant** (ASV)—presents a problem in interpretation. This can scarcely be that actual ark of the covenant which was in the midst of Israel during her wilderness journeys (as some insist); for this did not exist even in the time of Christ. The word here translated **temple,** *naos,* means "sanctuary," the innermost part of the temple. When the Holy City descends from heaven, it is explicitly said that there will be no temple there (21:22).

*The Woman with the Man Child. 12:1-17.*

**1-5.** Chapter 12 presents another problem in identification—the **woman** seen **in heaven** who was **travailing . . . to be delivered** of a child (vv. 1,2). One thing seems certain—that this child "who is to rule all the nations with a rod of iron" (v. 5) must be the Lord Jesus Christ (see Ps 2:9; Isa 66:7; Rev 19:15). A number of identifications have been suggested for the **woman.** In the period of the Church Fathers, Victorinus said this is "the ancient church of fathers, and prophets, and saints, and apostles" (*Ante-Nicene Fathers,* VII, 355). Many writers say this is Israel, from whom Christ came; while some, as Auberlen, Lenski, etc., interpret it more comprehensively as the Israel of both Testaments. I think we can affirm that this is Israel. The Roman Catholic Church, of course, insists that this is the Virgin Mary, but the Roman Church also says that Mary gave birth to Christ without pain,

6. And the woman fled into the wilderness, where she hath a place prepared of God, that they should feed her there a thousand two hundred *and* threescore days.

7. And there was war in heaven: Michael and his angels fought against the dragon; and the dragon fought and his angels,

8. And prevailed not; neither was their place found any more in heaven.

9. And the great dragon was cast out, that old serpent, called the Devil, and Satan, which deceiveth the whole world: he was cast out into the earth, and his angels were cast out with him.

10. And I heard a loud voice saying in heaven, Now is come salvation, and strength, and the kingdom of our God, and the power of his Christ: for the accuser of our brethren is cast down, which accused them before our God day and night.

11. And they overcame him by the blood of the Lamb, and by the word of their testimony; and they loved not their lives unto the death.

12. Therefore rejoice, *ye* heavens, and ye that dwell in them. Woe to the inhabiters of the earth and of the sea! for the devil is come down unto you, having great wrath, because he knoweth that he hath but a short time.

13. And when the dragon saw that he was cast unto the earth, he persecuted the woman which brought forth the man *child.*

14. And to the woman were given two wings of a great eagle, that she might fly into the wilderness, into her place, where she is nourished for a time, and times, and half a time, from the face of the serpent.

15. And the serpent cast out of his mouth water as a flood after the woman, that he might cause her to be carried away of the flood.

16. And the earth helped the woman; and the earth opened her mouth, and swallowed up the flood which the dragon cast out of his mouth.

17. And the dragon was wroth with the woman, and went to make war with the remnant of her seed, which keep the commandments of God, and have the testimony of Jesus Christ.

which is contradicted by this verse (see Isa 66:7). There stands before this woman the great enemy of God, **the dragon** (Rev 12:4), who hopes to destroy Christ. But in this effort he will fail.

6. I personally believe, with Weidner, Walter Scott, and many others, that this verse is anticipatory, and points to Israel's time of tribulation at the end of the age. It is placed here to emphasize the fact that Satan, who hates Christ, and hence His people, will especially persecute Israel as the age draws to a close.

7-9. We are now introduced to what Swete rightly designates as "the supreme ·attempt on the part of the dragon to unseat the Woman's Son, and to re-establish himself in the presence of God." There are more terms for Satan in this paragraph (v. 9) than in any other single passage in the Word of God: **the great dragon, that old serpent . . . the Devil, and Satan,** and—one of the most dreadful phrases in Scripture—not something Satan boasts of, but something which heaven acknowledges—**the deceiver of the whole world** (see II Tim 3:13; II Jn 7). He is opposed here not by Christ, but by Michael and his angels (Rev 12:7; see Dan 10:13,21; Jude 9), who apparently is the leader of the angelic hierarchy. Satan is cast out of heaven. There may be a reference here to some words of our Lord regarding Satan's falling from heaven (Jn 12:31), though I am convinced that the scene unfolds at the end of this age. Note that Satan is not cast into the abyss, but **down to the earth** (ASV; Rev 12:9), just before Antichrist assumes his temporary and dreadful reign.

10-12. No detail is necessary here on the subsequent song of rejoicing. Emphasis is upon the power of God and the authority of Christ. The brethren **overcame** Satan **because of the blood of the Lamb,** and **the word of their testimony** (v. 11). It is because they have given a faithful testimony even unto death that they are victorious.

13-17. What was referred to in anticipation in verse 6 is stated in more detail here. The time period, **time, and times, and half a time** (v. 14), similar to the 1,260 days of verse 6, is the period of darkest tribulation. The earth's aiding the woman (v. 16) may represent, as Walter Scott says, the governments of the earth befriending the Jew "and providentially (how, we know not) frustrating the efforts of the serpent" *(Ex-*

## CHAPTER 13

AND I stood upon the sand of the sea, and saw a beast rise up out of the sea, having seven heads and ten horns, and upon his horns ten crowns, and upon his heads the name of blasphemy.

2. And the beast which I saw was like unto a leopard, and his feet were as *the feet* of a bear, and his mouth as the mouth of a lion: and the dragon gave him his power, and his seat, and great authority.

3. And I saw one of his heads as it were wounded to death; and his deadly wound was healed: and all the world wondered after the beast.

4. And they worshipped the dragon which gave power unto the beast: and they worshipped the beast, saying, Who *is* like unto the beast? who is able to make war with him?

5. And there was given unto him a mouth speaking great things and blasphemies; and power was given unto him to continue forty *and* two months.

6. And he opened his mouth in blasphemy against God, to blaspheme his name, and his tabernacle, and them that dwell in heaven.

7. And it was given unto him to make war with the saints, and to overcome them: and power was given him over all kindreds, and tongues, and nations.

8. And all that dwell upon the earth shall worship him, whose names are not written in the book of life of the Lamb slain from the foundation of the world.

9. If any man have an ear, let him hear.

10. He that leadeth into captivity shall go into captivity: he that killeth with the sword must be killed with the sword. Here is the patience and the faith of the saints.

11. And I beheld another beast coming up out of the earth; and he had two horns like a lamb, and he spake as a dragon.

12. And he exerciseth all the power of the first beast before him, and causeth the earth and them which dwell therein to worship the first beast, whose deadly wound was healed.

13. And he doeth great wonders, so that he maketh fire come down from heaven on the earth in the sight of men,

14. And deceiveth them that dwell on the earth by *the means of* those miracles which he had power to do in the sight of the beast; saying to them that dwell on the earth, that they should make an image to the beast, which had the wound by a sword, and did live.

position of the Revelation of Jesus Christ, *in loco*). The reference to the woman and **her seed** (v. 17) recalls the first Messianic prophecy (Gen 3:15).

*The Appearance of the Two Beasts. 13:1–18.*

**1-10.** Two dreadful rulers enter the scene in chapter 13, one coming up **out of the sea,** and the other coming up out of the earth. The **sea** here is undoubtedly "a symbol of the agitated surface of unregenerate humanity, and especially of the seething caldron of national and social life out of which the great historical movements of the world arise" (Swete). The first beast, whose horns and diadems represent power, is energized by Satan (v. 2). It is almost unbelievable that **the whole earth** will worship both **the dragon** and **the beast** (vv. 3, 4). There will be much religion on earth, but it will be godless and blasphemous. This first beast is against God (vv. 5, 6); he is satanically energized (v. 2); he is militarily supreme (v. 4); he possesses world-wide power (v. 7); and he persecutes the saints of God (v. 7). Who would deny that the stage of world history is rapidly being set by tendencies that will ultimately lead to the rule and adoration of such a monster? All who do not belong to the Lamb of God will worship the beast.

**11-15.** While the first beast is undoubtedly a political world power, the second beast (v. 11), as Lee has said, "is a spiritual world power, the power of learning and knowledge, of ideas, of intellectual cultivation. Both are from below, both are beasts, and therefore they are in close alliance. The worldly anti-Christian wisdom stands in the service of the worldly anti-Christian power" (p. 671). The second beast enforces the commands of the first beast, and accompanies his evil work with various forms of miraculous manifestations (vv. 12, 13). The period of the "times of the Gentiles" began with the forced worship of an image set up by a powerful ruler (by Nebuchadnezzar, in Daniel 3); and this period will close with a similar enforced worship, this time on a universal scale.

**16,17.** The chapter concludes with a prophecy of what might be called economic dictatorship. The text does not say that men will not be able to eat unless they have **the mark . . . of the beast,** but that they will not be able to

15. And he had power to give life unto the image of the beast, that the image of the beast should both speak, and cause that as many as would not worship the image of the beast should be killed.

16. And he causeth all, both small and great, rich and poor, free and bond, to receive a mark in their right hand, or in their foreheads:

17. And that no man might buy or sell, save he that had the mark, or the name of the beast, or the number of his name.

18. Here is wisdom. Let him that hath understanding count the number of the beast: for it is the number of a man; and his number *is* Six hundred three score *and* six.

carry on business without that mark.

18. The concluding verse of this chapter, in which **the number of the beast** is revealed as 666, has given rise to a multitude of interpretations, and to a vast literature. Whole books have been written on this one text. Luther erred in thinking that this is a chronological statement. Adding 666 to the year 1000 gave him A.D. 1666, a year when nothing of prophetic significance occurred. Many have tried to identify this person by discovering names the numerical sum of whose letters is 666. In our language, e.g., X equals 10, L equals 50, and C equals 100. There are similar equivalents for letters in the Hebrew, Greek, and Latin languages. Some have believed, then, that this number so translated refers to the first century Caesar, Nero; others interpret it as *Lateinos,* meaning, "the Latin One." I think we need go no further than to recognize that six is the number of fallen man and thus of incompleteness, and that 666 is the trinity of six. Even in this passage there is a demonic trinity—Satan, the beast **out of the earth** (Antichrist, v. 11), and the beast **out of the sea** (the false prophet, v. 1). (For a tabulation of various interpretations of these two beasts, see Charles Maitland: *The Apostles' School of Prophetic Interpretation* [London, 1849], p. 329.)

Torrance rightly asks: "Do we not see today that image being set up in nation after nation upon the earth by the power of propaganda and lies? . . . Have we not heard the raucous voice of that beast blaring and shouting over the radio, and read his boasts and threats on the pages of the world press? . . . All that can be done apart from Jesus Christ is to give a fresh disposition to unbelief, to give organic or subtle shape to human evil and pride and selfishness. . . . All the time the latent evil in the world is setting up its image and making its imprint upon the persons and minds and deeds of men" (*op. cit.,* pp. 86-89).

Note that these two world rulers are designated as *beasts.* The Russian philosopher, Nicholas Berdyaev, writing on the bestiality of modern man, says: "Movement toward super-humanity and the superman, toward super-human powers, all too often means nothing other than a bestialization of man. Modern antihumanism takes the form of bestialism. It uses the tragic and unfortunate Nietzsche as a superior sort of justification for dehumanization and bestialization.

## CHAPTER 14

AND I looked, and, lo, a Lamb stood on the mount Sion, and with him a hundred forty *and* four thousand, having his Father's name written in their foreheads.

2. And I heard a voice from heaven, as the voice of many waters, and as the voice of a great thunder: and I heard the voice of harpers harping with their harps:

3. And they sung as it were a new song before the throne, and before the four beasts, and the elders: and no man could learn that song but the hundred *and* forty *and* four thousand, which were redeemed from the earth.

4. These are they which were not defiled with women; for they are virgins. These are they which follow the Lamb whithersoever he goeth. These were redeemed from among men, *being* the firstfruits unto God and to the Lamb.

5. And in their mouth was found no guile: for they are without fault before the throne of God.

6. And I saw another angel fly in the midst of heaven, having the everlasting gospel to preach unto them that dwell on the earth, and to every nation, and kindred, and tongue, and people,

. . . A bestial cruelty toward man is characteristic of our age, and is more astonishing since it is displayed at the very peak of human refinement, where modern conceptions of sympathy, it would seem, have made impossible the old barbaric forms of cruelty. Bestialism is something quite different from the old, natural, healthy barbarism; it is barbarism within a refined civilization. Here the atavistic, barbaric instincts are filtered through the prism of civilization, and hence they have a pathological character. Bestialism is a phenomenon of the human world, but a world already civilized" *(The Fate of Man in the Modern World,* pp. 26-29. For a full discussion of this chapter, see my volume, *This Atomic Age and the Word of God,* pp. 193-221).

## V. The Judgments of the Seven Vials. 14:1—16:21.

As there are introductory chapters preceding the judgments introduced by the opening of the seven seals, and by the blowing of the seven trumpets, so here, preceding the last *series* of judgments, we have an introductory chapter.

**14:1-5.** The chapter opens with a scene on **the mount Zion,** which no doubt stands for heaven—the only reference to Zion in the Revelation. We are introduced to a large company of 144,000, having characteristics which set them apart as unusually dedicated: (1) on their foreheads are the names of the Lamb and of the Father—which shall be true of all the redeemed throughout eternity (22:4); (2) they alone are able to understand the new song sung before the throne by harpers; (3) they have not been defiled with women, for they are virgins—a statement considered later in this study; (4) they follow the Lamb wherever he goes; (5) they are the first fruits unto God; (6) they are without blemish. This is no doubt a select group of God's saints, of which we hear nothing more.

The only real problem here is in verse 4. Many have insisted that this must be taken literally, as Govett, who devotes five pages to the verse. Nowhere in the Scriptures is virginity as such, or celibacy, mentioned as a synonym for holiness, or as making one particularly fit for divine service. The family is a divine institution from the beginning of Scripture. Therefore, I think this must have symbolic significance, similar to Paul's

7. Saying with a loud voice, Fear God, and give glory to him; for the hour of his judgment is come: and worship him that made heaven, and earth, and the sea, and the fountains of waters.

8. And there followed another angel, saying, Babylon is fallen, is fallen, that great city, because she made all nations drink of the wine of the wrath of her fornication.

9. And the third angel followed them, saying with a loud voice, If any man worship the beast and his image, and receive *his* mark in his forehead, or in his hand,

10. The same shall drink of the wine of the wrath of God, which is poured out without mixture into the cup of his indignation; and he shall be tormented with fire and brimstone in the presence of the holy angels, and in the presence of the Lamb:

11. And the smoke of their torment ascendeth up for ever and ever: and they have no rest day nor night, who worship the beast and his image, and whosoever receiveth the mark of his name.

12. Here is the patience of the saints: here *are* they that keep the commandments of God, and the faith of Jesus.

13. And I heard a voice from heaven saying unto me, Write, Blessed *are* the dead which die in the Lord from henceforth: Yea, saith the Spirit, that they may rest from their labors; and their works do follow them.

14. And I looked, and behold a white cloud, and upon the cloud *one* sat like unto the Son of man, having on his head a golden crown, and in his hand a sharp sickle.

15. And another angel came out of the temple, crying with a loud voice to him that sat on the cloud, Thrust in thy sickle, and reap: for the time is come for thee to reap; for the harvest of the earth is ripe.

16. And he that sat on the cloud thrust in his sickle on the earth; and the earth was reaped.

17. And another angel came out of the temple which is in heaven, he also having a sharp sickle.

18. And another angel came out from the altar, which had power over fire; and cried with a loud cry to him that had the sharp sickle, saying, Thrust in thy sharp sickle, and gather the clusters of the vine of the earth; for her grapes are fully ripe.

19. And the angel thrust in his sickle into the earth, and gathered the vine of the earth, and cast *it* into the great winepress of the wrath of God.

20. And the winepress was trodden without the city, and blood came out of the winepress, even unto the horse bridles, by the space of a thousand *and* six hundred furlongs.

use of these terms in II Cor 11:2,3. Marriage is not defiling (Heb 13:4).

6,7. We now have a description of three successive messages of three different angels. The first has an eternal gospel, proclaimed to everyone on earth, consisting of the following admonition: Fear God, and give him glory; for the hour of his judgment is come: and worship him that made the heaven, etc. I wholly agree with Swete that this proclamation "contains no reference to the Christian hope; the basis of the appeal is pure theism. It is an appeal to the conscience of untaught heathenism, incapable as yet of comprehending any other." There is no indication here that this message is believed or that, through believing it, any are redeemed.

8-13. The second angel announces the fall of Babylon, which is described in detail in chapters 17 and 18. The third angel utters a judgment upon all those who have worshiped the beast and his image, with an anticipatory statement about the eternal punishment of those who bear the mark of the beast. A century ago the Seventh-Day Adventists seized upon these verses as being fulfilled in their particular convictions regarding the church. They regarded the early Millerite movement as a warning to the church that she is Babylon. Hence, believers should come out of organized Christendom—and the message of the third angel was immediately to follow. Adventists insist that this is a promise that in the last days only those will be acceptable to God who keep the commandments of God, and the faith of Jesus (v. 12), and that this is "a call to men to honor the true sabbath of God, the seventh-day sabbath of the Decalogue" (Francis D. Nichol: *The Midnight Cry*, p. 462). Why they particularize the commandment regarding the seventh day, not even hinted at here, and do not incorporate in this scheme the other nine Words of the Decalogue, I do not know.

14-20. The chapter concludes with two scenes that can occur only at the end of the age. The first (vv. 14-16) represents a harvest, a reaping of souls, and apparently a gathering in of the redeemed, to which our Lord refers in Mt 13:30,39; 24:30,31. There has been some dispute over these two scenes, but it seems to me that the second one, which is not a harvest but a vintage scene, must depict the gathering of the unbelieving

**CHAPTER 15**

AND I saw another sign in heaven, great and marvelous, seven angels having the seven last plagues; for in them is filled up the wrath of God.

2. And I saw as it were a sea of glass mingled with fire: and them that had gotten the victory over the beast, and over his image, and over his mark, *and* over the number of his name, stand on the sea of glass, having the harps of God.

3. And they sing the song of Moses the servant of God, and the song of the Lamb, saying, Great and marvelous *are* thy works, Lord God Almighty; just and true *are* thy ways, thou King of saints.

4. Who shall not fear thee, O Lord, and glorify thy name? for *thou* only *art* holy: for all nations shall come and worship before thee; for thy judgments are made manifest.

5. And after that I looked, and, behold, the temple of the tabernacle of the testimony in heaven was opened:

6. And the seven angels came out of the temple, having the seven plagues, clothed in pure and white linen, and having their breasts girded with golden girdles.

7. And one of the four beasts gave unto the seven angels seven golden vials full of the wrath of God, who liveth for ever and ever.

8. And the temple was filled with smoke from the glory of God, and from his power; and no man was able to enter into the temple, till the seven plagues of the seven angels were fulfilled.

**CHAPTER 16**

AND I heard a great voice out of the temple saying to the seven angels, Go your ways, and pour out the vials of the wrath of God upon the earth.

2. And the first went, and poured out his vial upon the earth; and there fell a noisome and grievous sore upon the men which had the mark of the beast, and *upon* them which worshipped his image.

3. And the second angel poured out his vial upon the sea; and it became as the blood of a dead *man:* and every living soul died in the sea.

and wicked ones of the earth. These are anticipatory paragraphs. Govett summarizes this passage correctly in saying, "The Woman's seed furnishes the Harvest, while the Dragon's seed furnishes the Vintage." See also Joel 3:13.

**15:1-4.** Chapter 15 is still occupied with introductory matters and a scene in heaven. It presents one of the great songs of the book, this time sung, apparently, by those who have triumphed over the evil forces of the last days, who have come off victorious from the beast, and from his image, and from the number of his name (ASV; v. 2). This is called the song of Moses the servant of God, and ... the Lamb (v. 3; on the former, see Ex 14:31; 15; Num 12:7; Deut 32). "The song in which Moses celebrated the deliverance from Egypt is now renewed and receives its perfect close when God's people are finally delivered by the Lamb" (Lee). The song is a mosaic of material from Exodus, from the Psalms (86:9; 111:2; 145:17), and from Isaiah (2:2-4; 66:23, etc.).

**5-8.** John says that he saw the sanctuary of the tabernacle of the testimony in heaven (v. 5). This is the last occurrence of the word translated sanctuary in this book (cf. 11:19). Out from this most holy place proceed five angels, with the seven plagues which are now to be poured out upon the earth, bowls full of the wrath of God (v. 7). Just before this series begins, we are told that the sanctuary was filled with smoke from the glory of God, and from his power (v. 8), which recalls to mind the unapproachableness of God at Sinai (Ex 19:21), and in Isaiah's vision (Isa 6:4,5). The great exegete of a former century, John Albert Bengel, remarked on this passage: "When God pours out His fury it is fitting that even those who stand well with Him should withdraw for a little, standing back in profound reverence till by and by the sky becomes clear again" (*Introduction to the Exposition of the Apocalypse, in loco*).

**16:1,2.** We are now ready to consider the seven bowls of the wrath of God. The first, comparable to the sixth plague of Egypt, resulted in men who had the mark of the beast being tormented by a noisome and grievous sore, not specifically identified. When the second bowl is poured out (cf. the first plague of Egypt), the sea takes on the appearance of blood as of a dead man, and all life within it dies (v. 3). Weidner directs

4. And the third angel poured out his vial upon the rivers and fountains of waters; and they became blood.

5. And I heard the angel of the waters say, Thou art righteous, O Lord, which art, and wast, and shalt be, because thou hast judged thus.

6. For they have shed the blood of saints and prophets, and thou hast given them blood to drink; for they are worthy.

7. And I heard another out of the altar say, Even so, Lord God Almighty, true and righteous *are* thy judgments.

8. And the fourth angel poured out his vial upon the sun; and power was given unto him to scorch men with fire.

9. And men were scorched with great heat, and blasphemed the name of God, which hath power over these plagues: and they repented not to give him glory.

10. And the fifth angel poured out his vial upon the seat of the beast; and his kingdom was full of darkness; and they gnawed their tongues for pain,

11. And blasphemed the God of heaven because of their pains and their sores, and repented not of their deeds.

12. And the sixth angel poured out his vial upon the great river Euphrates; and the water thereof was dried up, that the way of the kings of the east might be prepared.

attention to the similarity and the difference between this plague and that of the second trumpet (8:8,9): "The judgments of God grow more and more terrible as wickedness increases and the end approaches."

4-11. The third vial of wrath also affects the rivers and fountains of waters, bringing a response from **the angel of the waters** acknowledging the righteousness and holiness of God, and the justification of such terrible manifestations of divine judgment (vv. 5,6). The fourth vial, involving the sun, in some way increases the intensity of heat derived on earth from the sun; and men are scorched with it, as a result of which they blaspheme God (vv. 8,9). The fifth bowl of wrath is similar to the fourth trumpet judgment and the ninth plague of Egypt, in its manifestation of darkness, except that on this occasion it is the kingdom of the beast that is darkened (vv. 10,11). God is now beginning to strike at the very throne of his great enemy, who has been the vital cause for the deception of men, their awful crimes, and their hatred of God.

12-16. In the pouring out of the sixth vial upon the river Euphrates, basically John sees **the kings that come from the sunrising**, or, from the East, driven, as it were, by satanic power to march to **Armageddon** (v. 16) for **the war of the great day of God, the Almighty** (v. 14). This is the only place that **Armageddon** is mentioned by name in the book of Revelation. The battle itself is described in the last part of chapter 19. Moorehead wrote, even before World War I and the modern awakening of Asia, "The vast hordes of Asia will be involved in the decisive and overwhelming battle of the great day of God." The Far East has had deep significance for Western civilization only within the last century, and the same is true for the Near East since the close of the Crusades. What an enormous difference between the powerful China of today, in its communistic, atheistic regime, and the comparatively weak empire we knew at the beginning of this century! The drying up of the **Euphrates River** (v. 12), allowing for the approach of these armies from the East, may or may not be taken symbolically; but it most assuredly cannot refer to the weakening of the Ottoman empire, nor is this the Mississippi River, as some contend. Hengstenberg has accurately commented: "The Euphrates is

13. And I saw three unclean spirits like frogs *come* out of the mouth of the dragon, and out of the mouth of the beast, and out of the mouth of the false prophet.

14. For they are the spirits of devils, working miracles, *which* go forth unto the kings of the earth and of the whole world, to gather them to the battle of that great day of God Almighty.

15. Behold, I come as a thief. Blessed *is* he that watcheth, and keepeth his garments, lest he walk naked, and they see his shame.

16. And he gathered them together into a place called in the Hebrew tongue Armageddon.

17. And the seventh angel poured out his vial into the air; and there came a great voice out of the temple of heaven, from the throne, saying, It is done.

18. And there were voices, and thunders, and lightnings; and there was a great earthquake, such as was not since men were upon the earth, so mighty an earthquake, *and* so great.

19. And the great city was divided into three parts, and the cities of the nations fell: and great Babylon came in remembrance before God, to give unto her the cup of the wine of the fierceness of his wrath.

20. And every island fled away, and the mountains were not found.

21. And there fell upon men a great hail out of heaven, *every stone* about the weight of a talent: and men blasphemed God because of the plague of the hail; for the plague thereof was exceeding great.

mentioned here merely in respect to the hindrance it presented to the march of the ungodly power of the world into the Holy Land." These kings are not Jews coming to Palestine for blessing, but pagan kings coming to Megiddo for battle. This passage embraces one of the most dreadful statements in the Bible, i.e., that **unclean spirits** (v. 13), the spirits of demons working miracles, **go forth unto the kings of the whole world, to gather them together unto war** (v. 14). This can mean nothing else than that at the end of the age the rulers of the earth will be demonized. And we are almost compelled to believe, by the events of the last forty years, that already some rulers have been demon-possessed.

**17-21.** While the seventh seal did not immediately follow the opening of the sixth, and the blowing of the seventh trumpet was postponed for some time, in this chapter the pouring out of the seventh vial promptly follows the pouring out of the sixth. Here the wrath of God is directed toward **the air,** and the declaration of judgment is followed, as others previously have been, by **lightnings, voices, thunders,** and an **earthquake** (vv. 18,19). I cannot help thinking that **the air** here is to be given the same significance it has in Paul's phrase regarding "the prince of the power of the air" (Eph 2:2). (For a further discussion of this, see my volume, *This Atomic Age and the Word of God,* pp. 222-248.) The disturbances in the air culminate in the falling of great hailstones (Rev 16:21), weighing about a talent each (either fifty-seven or ninety-six pounds); and once again men blaspheme God. The statement that at this time **the cities of the nations fell** (v. 19), or, as some translate, *the cities of the Gentiles,* may be, as Weidner suggests, a reference to Mic 5:10-15. Two other cities are named here, **Babylon** and **the great city,** the latter being, according to Milligan, Simcox, Weidner, and many others, Jerusalem.

It has been claimed by some commentators that these three successive septenary series of three judgments are a recapitulation of the same events. That is, the trumpets review what the seals previously set forth, but with greater intensity; and the vials review the same events, characterizing them with even more severity. I have not been able to accept this view. For one reason, the sequence in each series is altogether different, and this alone, it seems, makes the concept of

CHAPTER 17

AND there came one of the seven angels which had the seven vials, and talked with me, saying unto me, Come hither; I will show unto thee the judgment of the great whore that sitteth upon many waters;

recapitulation impossible. In the following chart I have set forth the sequence of the series of judgments, using the judgment of the vials as a guide. Appearing below the line for the trumpets and seals are phenomena which do not appear in the vial judgments. No attempt has been made to place those below the line in any chronological order, or even to parallel the seals and the trumpets; rather, they have been placed opposite each other to save space.

| Nature of the Judgment | Vials ch. 16 | Trumpets chs. 8; 9 | Seals ch. 6 | Plagues of Egypt Ex. 7—10. 12:29-33. |
|---|---|---|---|---|
| Sores.................. | I.   2 | | | V, VI. 9:1-12 |
| Seas turned to blood..... | II.   3 | II. 8:8, 9 | | I. 7:20 - 24 |
| Waters turned to blood... | III.   4 - 7 | II. 8:8, 9 | | I. 7:20 - 24 |
| Great heat............. | IV.   8, 9 | I. 8:7 | | |
| Darkness: Pain......... | V.   10, 11 | IV. 8:12 | | IX. 10:21 - 23 |
| Kings demon-possessed... | VI. 12 - 16 | | | |
| Lightnings; Voices; Thunders; Earthquakes Great hail stones...... | VII. 17 - 21 | 1.  8:7 (hail) | VI.  12-17 | (hail) VII. 9:22 - 35 |
| False peace............ | | | 1.  1, 2 | |
| Locusts............... | | V.  9:1-12 | | VIII. 10:12-20 |
| War.................. | | VI.  9:13-21 | II.  3, 4 | |
| Scarcity of food........ | | | III. 5, 6 | |
| Death................ | | | IV. 7, 8 | X.  12:29-33 |
| Bitter waters.......... | | III.  8:10, 11 | | |
| Martyrs.............. | | | V.  9-11 | |

2. With whom the kings of the earth have committed fornication, and the inhabitants of the earth have been made drunk with the wine of her fornication.

3. So he carried me away in the spirit into the wilderness: and I saw a woman sit upon a scarlet-colored beast, full of names of blasphemy, having seven heads and ten horns.

4. And the woman was arrayed in purple and scarlet color, and decked with gold and precious stones and pearls, having a golden cup in her hand full of abominations and filthiness of her fornication:

5. And upon her forehead *was* a name written, MYSTERY, BABYLON THE GREAT, THE MOTHER OF HARLOTS AND ABOMINATIONS OF THE EARTH.

6. And I saw the woman drunken with the blood of the saints, and with the blood of the martyrs of Jesus: and when I saw her, I wondered with great admiration.

7. And the angel said unto me, Wherefore didst thou marvel? I will tell thee the mystery of the woman, and of the beast that carrieth her, which hath the seven heads and ten horns.

8. The beast that thou sawest was, and is not; and shall ascend out of the bottomless pit, and go into perdition: and they that dwell on the earth shall wonder, whose names were not written in the book of life from the foundation of the world, when they behold the beast that was, and is not, and yet is.

9. And here *is* the mind which hath wisdom. The seven heads are seven mountains, on which the woman sitteth.

10. And there are seven kings: five are fallen, and one is, *and* the other is not yet come; and when he cometh, he must continue a short space.

11. And the beast that was, and is not, even he is the eighth, and is of the seven, and goeth into perdition.

12. And the ten horns which thou sawest are ten kings, which have received no kingdom as yet; but receive power as kings one hour with the beast.

## VI. Babylon and Armageddon. 17:1—19:21.

*Judgment upon Babylon. 17:1—18:24.* One-eighth of the entire book of Revelation, some fifty verses, is devoted to the subject of judgment upon Babylon (14: 8-10; 16:17—19:5). Yet, the interpretation of **Babylon** in the Apocalypse has given rise to more differing opinions than any other major passage in this book. In the OT the name *Babylon* takes its origin from *Babel,* which of course has always symbolized revolt against God, and confusion (Gen 10:8-12; 11: 1-9). Babylon was the conqueror of the kingdom of Judah, the theocracy (II Kgs 24; 25, etc.). With Nebuchadnezzar, king of Babylon, began the "times of the Gentiles" (Jer 27:1-11; Dan 2:37,38). Babylon occupies a large place in the prophecies of the nations in the OT (Isa 13; 14; 47; Jer 50; 51).

**Babylon** is set before us in these two chapters under two different aspects. In chapter 17, she is identified with the great harlot, a woman who does not appear as such in chapter 18. The beast with seven heads and ten horns is confined to chapter 17, where alone we find the kings of the earth going out to make war on the Lamb. In chapter 18 Babylon seems to be some city along a great river, crowded with the ships of the merchants of the earth, details that are not present in chapter 17. We should perhaps first look at the text itself and then discuss interpretation.

**17:1-12.** There are three groups to be identified in this opening paragraph: the **beast,** who has seven heads and ten horns; the **harlot** herself who rides the beast; and those referred to by **many waters,** later said to be "peoples and multitudes, and nations, and tongues" (v. 15). The ten horns, we are later informed, are ten kings (v. 12), certainly contemporaneous; and the seven heads are seven moun-

13. These have one mind, and shall give their power and strength unto the beast.

14. These shall make war with the Lamb, and the Lamb shall overcome them: for he is Lord of lords, and King of kings: and they that are with him *are* called, and chosen, and faithful.

15. And he saith unto me, The waters which thou sawest, where the whore sitteth, are peoples, and multitudes, and nations, and tongues.

16. And the ten horns which thou sawest upon the beast, these shall hate the whore, and shall make her desolate and naked, and shall eat her flesh, and burn her with fire.

17. For God hath put in their hearts to fulfil his will, and to agree, and give their kingdom unto the beast, until the words of God shall be fulfilled.

18. And the woman which thou sawest is that great city, which reigneth over the kings of the earth.

## CHAPTER 18

AND after these things I saw another angel come down from heaven, having great power; and the earth was lightened with his glory.

2. And he cried mightily with a strong voice, saying, Babylon the great is fallen, is fallen, and is become the habitation of devils, and the hold of every foul spirit, and a cage of every unclean and hateful bird.

tains (vv. 9,10), which also represent kingdoms. We must never forget that every federation of kings in the OT, and here, is always opposed to God and the people of God (Gen 15:18-21; Dan 2:41,42; 7:7,20,24; Ps 2:1-3; 83:1-8; Rev 12:3; 13:1; 16:12-16). This woman, called THE MOTHER OF THE HARLOTS (17:5), commits fornication with the kings of the earth (v. 2), and for a while dominates them.

To whom or what does this woman refer? The majority of commentators, since the time of the Reformation, identify her with the papacy, as Luther, Tyndale, Knox, Calvin (*Institutes*, IV, 2.12), Alford, Elliott, Lange, and many others. The Roman Catholic Church itself identifies this woman with Rome—but of course pagan Rome, now past. She is definitely some vast spiritual system that persecutes the saints of God, betraying that to which she was called. She enters into relations with the governments of this earth, and for a while rules them. I think the closest we can come to an identification is to understand this harlot as symbolic of a vast spiritual power arising at the end of the age, which enters into a league with the world and compromises with worldly forces. Instead of being spiritually true, she is spiritually false, and thus exercises an evil influence in the name of religion.

13-18. The kings of the earth now, having one mind, federate, and give their authority unto this great enemy of God, the beast, and go out to make war against the Lamb (vv. 13,14). When this hour is come, the beast, with the power of the kingdoms of the earth, turns upon the harlot, this pseudo-spiritual force, and destroys her (v. 16). That is a very conforting statement in verse 17—"God did put in their hearts to do his mind, and to come to one mind . . . until the words of God should be accomplished."

Chapter 18 seems to have a geographical definiteness not present in chapter 17. Here we have the statement that Babylon has become a habitation of demons, and a hold of every unclean spirit (v. 2). Most of the chapter is occupied with a description of the wealth of the city, the merchandise which is brought here for sale, and the grief of the merchants, who have been made rich by this traffic, as they look upon the city now being made desolate by fire. In verses 4-8 judgment is announced; in verses 9-20 we have the lament of kings

3. For all nations have drunk of the wine of the wrath of her fornication, and the kings of the earth have committed fornication with her, and the merchants of the earth are waxed rich through the abundance of her delicacies.

4. And I heard another voice from heaven, saying, Come out of her, my people, that ye be not partakers of her sins, and that ye receive not of her plagues.

5. For her sins have reached unto heaven, and God hath remembered her iniquities.

6. Reward her even as she rewarded you, and double unto her double according to her works: in the cup which she hath filled, fill to her double.

7. How much she hath glorified herself, and lived deliciously, so much torment and sorrow give her: for she saith in her heart, I sit a queen, and am no widow, and shall see no sorrow.

8. Therefore shall her plagues come in one day, death, and mourning, and famine; and she shall be utterly burned with fire: for strong is the Lord God who judgeth her.

9. And the kings of the earth, who have committed fornication and lived deliciously with her, shall bewail her, and lament for her, when they shall see the smoke of her burning,

10. Standing afar off for the fear of her torment, saying, Alas, alas, that great city Babylon, that mighty city! for in one hour is thy judgment come.

11. And the merchants of the earth shall weep and mourn over her; for no man buyeth their merchandise any more:

12. The merchandise of gold, and silver, and precious stones, and of pearls, and fine linen, and purple, and silk, and scarlet, and all thyine wood, and all manner vessels of ivory, and all manner vessels of most precious wood, and of brass, and iron, and marble,

13. And cinnamon, and odors, and ointments, and frankincense, and wine, and oil, and fine flour, and wheat, and beasts, and sheep, and horses, and chariots, and slaves, and souls of men.

14. And the fruits that thy soul lusted after are departed from thee, and all things which were dainty and goodly are departed from thee, and thou shalt find them no more at all.

15. The merchants of these things, which were made rich by her, shall stand afar off for the fear of her torment, weeping and wailing,

16. And saying, Alas, alas, that great city, that was clothed in fine linen, and purple,

of the earth; and in 21-24 Babylon's final doom is reported.

We must now return to the problem of interpretation. Some insist upon a geographical identification here. Those who have adopted the historical scheme of interpretation make **Babylon** refer generally to pagan Rome. Some have asserted that **Babylon** here must mean Jerusalem, as Weidner, Kiddle, etc., but this seems utterly impossible. I have read books that defend the view that this city is London or Paris. Even Alford once said, though he admitted he felt this difficulty "unsolved," "Certainly the details of this mercantile lamentation far more nearly suit London, than Rome, at any assignable period of her history" (p. 718). One thing cannot be denied: the muddy Tiber River, flowing through Rome, could never carry the enormous maritime traffic portrayed in chapter 18; moreover, pagan Rome was never famous as a center of exchange and selling of merchandise. Some have contended that this prophecy can only be fulfilled when the city of Babylon is restored. The Scofield Bible specifically repudiates this, but many of its editors personally believed this to be true, as Gray and Moorehead; so also Seiss, Govett, Pember, G. H. Lang, and many others.

Those adopting the ecclesiastical interpretation, as we have noted, make **Babylon** stand for the papacy, and there is much here to support their view. However, I believe that there is more than the papacy implied here. This is apostate Christendom, a world religion that has betrayed Christianity, and is interlocked with the pagan, godless governments of the world. Many believe—and I would agree—that the day is coming when the Roman Church itself will, in some mysterious way, enter into a compromising relationship with atheistic Communism. (A searching treatment of this subject may be found in G. H. Pember, *The Antichrist, Babylon, and the Coming of the Kingdom* [1886].)

*The Battle of Armageddon. 19:1-21.*

19:1-8. While chapter 19 of this book is generally given the heading, "The Battle of Armageddon," actually the first half of the chapter is devoted to a scene in heaven, where we have the last three songs of the Apocalypse. First, a great multitude is heard singing, **Hallelujah; Salvation, and glory, and power,** because of the judgment upon the great harlot

and scarlet, and decked with gold, and precious stones, and pearls!

17. For in one hour so great riches is come to nought. And every shipmaster, and all the company in ships, and sailors, and as many as trade by sea, stood afar off,

18. And cried when they saw the smoke of her burning, saying, What *city is* like unto this great city!

19. And they cast dust on their heads, and cried, weeping and wailing, saying, Alas, alas, that great city, wherein were made rich all that had ships in the sea by reason of her costliness! for in one hour is she made desolate.

20. Rejoice over her, *thou* heaven, and *ye* holy apostles and prophets; for God hath avenged you on her.

21. And a mighty angel took up a stone like a great millstone, and cast *it* into the sea, saying, Thus with violence shall that great city Babylon be thrown down, and shall be found no more at all.

22. And the voice of harpers, and musicians, and of pipers, and trumpeters, shall be heard no more at all in thee; and no craftsman, of whatsoever craft *he be,* shall be found any more in thee; and the sound of a millstone shall be heard no more at all in thee;

23. And the light of a candle shall shine no more at all in thee; and the voice of the bridegroom and of the bride shall be heard no more at all in thee: for thy merchants were the great men of the earth; for by thy sorceries were all nations deceived.

24. And in her was found the blood of prophets, and of saints, and of all that were slain upon the earth.

## CHAPTER 19

AND after these things I heard a great voice of much people in heaven, saying, Alleluia; Salvation, and glory, and honor, and power, unto the Lord our God:

2. For true and righteous *are* his judgments; for he hath judged the great whore, which did corrupt the earth with her fornication, and hath avenged the blood of his servants at her hand.

3. And again they said, Alleluia. And her smoke rose up for ever and ever.

4. And the four and twenty elders and the four beasts fell down and worshipped God that sat on the throne, saying, Amen; Alleluia.

5. And a voice came out of the throne, saying, Praise our God, all ye his servants, and ye that fear him, both small and great.

6. And I heard as it were the voice of a great multitude, and as the voice of many waters, and as the voice of mighty thunderings, saying, Alleluia: for the Lord God omnipotent reigneth.

7. Let us be glad and rejoice, and give honor to him: for the marriage of the Lamb is come, and his wife hath made herself ready.

8. And to her was granted that she should be arrayed in fine linen, clean and white: for the fine linen is the righteousness of saints.

9. And he saith unto me, Write, Blessed *are* they which are called unto the marriage supper of the Lamb. And he saith unto me, These are the true sayings of God.

10. And I fell at his feet to worship him. And he said unto me, See *thou do it* not: I am thy fellow servant, and of thy brethren that have the testimony of Jesus: worship God: for the testimony of Jesus is the spirit of prophecy.

11. And I saw heaven opened, and behold a white horse; and he that sat upon him *was* called Faithful and True, and in righteousness he doth judge and make war.

12. His eyes *were* as a flame of fire, and on his head *were* many crowns; and he had a name written, that no man knew, but he himself.

that has now been completed (vv. 1,2). **Hallelujah** is taken directly from the Hebrew and is made up of two words *hallel,* meaning "praise," and *jah,* a basic word for God. Hallelujahs occur at the beginning of Psalms 111 and 112, at the beginning and end of Psalms 146 to 150, etc. This song is repeated a second time. Then the twenty-four elders and the four living creatures fall down before God, also crying out **Amen; Hallelujah** (v. 4).

Finally, John hears voices, which he does not specifically identify (v. 6), singing the last of the songs, beginning with **Hallelujah,** this time not because of the judgment on Babylon, but because **the marriage of the Lamb is come, and his wife hath made herself ready** (vv. 6-8). With this, John is commanded to write the last of the beatitudes of this book, in which is announced that the marriage supper of the Lamb has come (v. 7). The relationship of God and Christ to the redeemed as expressed by the terms of marriage is frequently found in both Testaments (Hos 2:19-21; Ezk 16:1ff.; Ps 45; Mk 2:19; I Cor 6:15-17; Eph 5:25-27). The bridal attire is noticeably different from the attire of the great harlot, for the holy bride wears only glistening white and pure **linen** (Rev 19:8), symbol of the righteous acts of the saints. All that the NT speaks of as relating to Christ the bridegroom and the Church the bride is now consummated.

**11-16.** This paragraph has always seemed to me almost too overwhelmingly glorious for exposition. Christ is now seen riding upon a white horse, coming down from heaven to "judge and make war." Here he takes the title, **Faithful and True,** which was assigned to him at the beginning of this book (1:5; 3:7,14). The phrase, **in righteousness,** is important. Judgment, throughout the Bible, is always identified with righteousness. This is exactly the phrase used by the Apostle Paul in Acts 17:31. In fact, this is the word used in the first reference to God as the judge of all the earth (Gen 18:25; see also Ps 9:4,8; 98:9; Isa 11:4; etc.). Righteousness, says the lexical authority, Cremer, is "that divine standard which shows itself in behavior conformable to God . . . which corresponds with the divine norm." Our Lord himself said, "My judgment is righteous; because I seek not mine own will, but the will of him that sent me" (Jn 5:30). The description of Christ here (Rev 19:12,13), with eyes **a flame of fire** and garments

13. And he *was* clothed with a vesture dipped in blood: and his name is called The Word of God.

14. And the armies *which were* in heaven followed him upon white horses, clothed in fine linen, white and clean.

15. And out of his mouth goeth a sharp sword, that with it he should smite the nations; and he shall rule them with a rod of iron: and he treadeth the winepress of the fierceness and wrath of Almighty God.

16. And he hath on *his* vesture and on his thigh a name written, KING OF KINGS, AND LORD OF LORDS.

17. And I saw an angel standing in the sun; and he cried with a loud voice, saying to all the fowls that fly in the midst of heaven, Come and gather yourselves together unto the supper of the great God;

18. That ye may eat the flesh of kings, and the flesh of captains, and the flesh of mighty men, and the flesh of horses, and of them that sit on them, and the flesh of all *men, both* free and bond, both small and great.

19. And I saw the beast, and the kings of the earth, and their armies, gathered together to make war against him that sat on the horse, and against his army.

sprinkled with blood (ASV), takes us back to the beginning of the book (1:14; 2:18). The phrase, sprinkled with blood, is from Isa 63:3.

Christ now is assigned the great title, The Word of God (Rev 19:13). As the Word of God, he made the worlds. It was by rejection of the Word that sin was brought into the world. By the Word of God, salvation is offered to men. Sin and anarchy, godlessness and rebellion, are in one way or another the repudiation of the Word of God. That Word, the Eternal, Omnipotent Word, now descends from heaven to fulfill prophecy, to destroy the enemies of God, to reveal to the universe, once and forever, the folly of resisting Christ and the indisputable pre-eminence of the King of Kings, and Lord of Lords (v. 16). We are now introduced to an earthly scene in which the kings of the earth take a prominent part. How strange, how tragic is this situation we now behold, in which it seems that the rulers of the whole world are united in one terrible effort to destroy the anointed of God. How contrary this is to the dreams of men, to the foolish statements of their false prophets, and to their unjustified belief that human society is ever progressing in the areas of peace, goodness, comradeship, and social welfare. We are now to see the fulfillment of Psalm 2.

17-21. I cannot help believing that this battle is to be taken literally, and hence it needs some careful, though brief, attention here. The plain of Megiddo, elsewhere called the plain of Jezreel, or Esdraelon, was famous in Israel's history, both for her defeats and for her victories. Here was the victory of Barak over the Canaanites, when the very stars fought in their courses against Sisera (Jud 4; 5); the victory of Gideon over the Midianites (Jud 7); and likewise the defeat and death of King Saul and his three sons, at the hands of the Philistines (1 Sam 4). Here occurred the tragedy of the defeat and death of King Josiah at the hands of the Egyptians, (II Kgs 23:29,30). Later in history the crusaders were defeated here, in the battle at the Horns of Hattin, A.D. 1187. Here General Allenby, in 1917, won a great victory against the Turks, for which he was honored, later, with the title, Lord Allenby of Megiddo. This great plain, about twelve miles wide, situated in the middle of Palestine, runs from the shores of the Mediterranean to the Jordan

20. And the beast was taken, and with him the false prophet that wrought miracles before him, with which he deceived them that had received the mark of the beast, and them that worshipped his image. These both were cast alive into a lake of fire burning with brimstone.

21. And the remnant were slain with the sword of him that sat upon the horse, which *sword* proceeded out of his mouth: and all the fowls were filled with their flesh.

Valley. On this plain, says a great authority, we have "the first battle in history in which we can in any measure study the disposition of troops, and thus, it forms the starting point for the history of military science." This was the battle in May, 1479 B.C., between the Syrian forces and the Egyptians under Thutmose III (see Harold H. Nelson, *The Battle of Megiddo,* pp. 1, 63).

Of this battlefield, George Adam Smith once wrote: "What a plain it is! Upon which not only the greatest empires, races, and faiths, east and west, have contended with each other, but each has come to judgment—on which from the first, with all its splendor of human battle, men have felt that there was fighting from heaven, the stars in their courses were fighting—on which panic has descended so mysteriously upon the best equipped and most successful armies, but the humble have been exalted to victory in the hour of their weakness—on which false faiths, equally with false defenders of the true faith, have been exposed and scattered—on which, from the time of Saul, wilfulness and superstition, though aided by every human excellence, have come to nought, and since Josiah's time the purest piety has not atoned for rash and mistaken zeal" (*Historical Geography of the Holy Land,* p. 409).

Prophecies that probably refer to this coming battle are found as early as 800 B.C. (Joel 3:9-15; see also Jer 51:27-36; Zeph 3:8; and Rev 14:14-20; 16:13-16; 17:14).

The battle is over almost as soon as it begins. Two great enemies of God are now seized, the beast and the false prophet (whose work was outlined in chapter 13), and are **cast alive into the lake of fire** and brimstone (v. 20). (For further treatment of this subject consult: George Adam Smith, *op. cit.,* pp. 379-410; William Miller, *The Least of All Lands,* 1888, pp. 152-212; and articles in various encyclopedias; as well as my own volume, *World Crises in the Light of Prophetic Scriptures,* pp. 96-119).

The word *Armageddon* is now a part of the English language, and is correctly defined by the *Oxford English Dictionary* as "the place of the last decisive battle." Swete, writing before World War I, rightly said, "Those who take note of the tendencies of modern civilization will not find it impossible to conceive that a time may come when throughout Christendom, the spirit of Anti-Christ will,

**CHAPTER 20**

AND I saw an angel come down from heaven, having the key of the bottomless pit and a great chain in his hand.

2. And he laid hold on the dragon, that old serpent, which is the Devil, and Satan, and bound him a thousand years,

with the support of the State, make a final stand against a Christianity which is loyal to the person and teaching of Christ."

**VII. The Millennium; the Last Judgment; the New Jerusalem and Eternity. 20:1—22:50.**

*The Millennium. 20:1-6.* We now approach one of the most debated passages in the Word of God. Throughout the ages this passage has been generally taken to set forth a Millennial period during which Christ will be reigning on this earth. All of us would agree with C. J. Vaughan when he says, "Never did we need more the help of God than in entering upon the interpretation of the chapter now before us." Only here in the Scriptures do we have the phrase, *"the* thousand years," which chronological factor is referred to six times in six verses. The word *millennium* is a Latin word composed of *mille,* "a thousand," and *annum,* "year"; thus, a thousand years, whatever this particular Scripture portion may mean. The passage begins by informing us that during this time Satan is cast into the bottomless pit, where he remains bound for **a thousand years.** This pit is not hell. Satan seems to have no power to resist this act of an angel in binding him. John now sees a great multitude who have not worshiped the beast, sitting upon thrones, and reigning with Christ for **a thousand years.** This is not the place to argue about the Millennium. It certainly seems clear, however, that the OT, over and over again, refers to a great and glorious time to come when peace will prevail on the earth, when the Messiah will reign in righteousness, and when nature will be restored to her original beauty (see, for example, Isa 9:6,7; 11:1; 30:15-33; also chs. 35; 44; and 49; 65:17—66:14, Jer 23:5,6, etc.).

There are four views regarding the Millennium. (1) Some say that this is just a spiritual condition of the redeemed, and must not be given any chronological interpretation, the idea of a thousand being symbolical of fullness and completeness. (2) Some have held the strange view that the Millennium has already taken place, many assigning the beginning of it to the conversion of Constantine. But if the period known as the Dark Ages is to be called the Millennium, then the prophecies in the Bible

3. And cast him into the bottomless pit, and shut him up, and set a seal upon him, that he should deceive the nations no more, till the thousand years should be fulfilled: and after that he must be loosed a little season.

4. And I saw thrones, and they sat upon them, and judgment was given unto them: and *I saw* the souls of them that were beheaded for the witness of Jesus, and for the word of God, and which had not worshipped the beast, neither his image, neither had received *his* mark upon their foreheads, or in their hands; and they lived and reigned with Christ a thousand years.

5. But the rest of the dead lived not again until the thousand years were finished. This *is* the first resurrection.

6. Blessed and holy *is* he that hath part in the first resurrection: on such the second death hath no power, but they shall be priests of God and of Christ, and shall reign with him a thousand years.

7. And when the thousand years are expired, Satan shall be loosed out of his prison,

referring to such a period will never be fulfilled. (3) Some have said that we are now in the Millennium, but once again we insist that if this war-ridden age of anarchy and atheistic communism is the Millennium, then the hopes created by the Word of God for this earth must be abandoned. (4) Finally, many believe that this is an actual prophecy of a thousand-year period, following Armageddon, when Christ will reign on this earth as King of kings. The early church was unanimous in holding this view. Charles *(op. cit.)* who does not accept the Millennium at all, nevertheless admits that "the prophecy of the millennium in chapter 20 must be taken literally."

There is a famous statement on this passage in Alford's *New Testament for English Readers* that has been quoted in many subsequent volumes, but I feel compelled to quote it once again: "It will have been long ago anticipated by the readers of this Commentary, that I cannot consent to distort words from their plain sense and chronological place in the prophecy, on account of any considerations of difficulty, or any risk of abuses which the doctrine of the millennium may bring with it. Those who lived next to the Apostles, and the whole Church for 300 years, understood them in the plain literal sense: and it is a strange sight in these days to see expositors who are among the first in reverence of antiquity, complacently casting aside the most cogent instance of consensus which primitive antiquity presents. As regards the text itself, no legitimate treatment of it will extort what is known as the spiritual interpretation now in fashion."

Much discussion has arisen about the brief phrase, **This is the first resurrection** (Rev 20:5). The theory that by the **first resurrection** conversion is meant, a passing from death unto life, i.e., a *spiritual* resurrection, seems wholly out of order in such a passage as this. The *second* resurrection, though it is not so designated, is certainly the one referred to in verses 11-15 of this same chapter. It is not necessary to limit those participating in the *first* resurrection to the groups enumerated in verse 4. The first resurrection may easily be considered as occurring in stages—the dead in Christ, then we who are alive, and then, after a brief period, these martyrs and faithful ones of the Tribulation period.

**7-10.** At the end of the Millennium,

8. And shall go out to deceive the nations which are in the four quarters of the earth, Gog and Magog, to gather them together to battle: the number of whom *is* as the sand of the sea.

9. And they went up on the breadth of the earth, and compassed the camp of the saints about, and the beloved city: and fire came down from God out of heaven, and devoured them.

10. And the devil that deceived them was cast into the lake of fire and brimstone, 'where the beast and the false prophet *are*, and shall be tormented day and night for ever and ever.

11. And I saw a great white throne, and him that sat on it, from whose face the earth and the heaven fled away; and there was found no place for them.

12. And I saw the dead, small and great, stand before God; and the books were opened: and another book was opened, which is *the book* of life: and the dead were judged out of those things which were written in the books, according to their works.

we have a strange episode inserted, the source of which could be nothing but divine inspiration, namely, that Satan will be loosed from his prison, and will go out once more to deceive the nations, assembling them to war (vv. 7,8), and leading them to an attack upon the camp of the saints . . . and the beloved city (v. 9). This probably refers to the earthly city of Jerusalem, though some have made it refer to the Holy City, which seems to be most irrational. Scott has a good point here when he says, "No mention is made of how Christ and His people regard this last mad attempt of Satan. All is silent in the camp and city. The apostate nations march into the jaws of death. Their judgment is sudden, swift, overwhelming, and final (*op. cit.*, p. 388). With the destruction of God's enemies, Satan is seized and cast into hell, where he will be forever. The beast and the false prophet have already been consigned to this place of awful doom. No doubt the plural pronoun they (v. 10) refers to this trinity of evil.

The question is often asked, How can one account for this last rebellion after the beneficent Millennial reign of Christ? For one thing, it reveals that a thousand years of imprisonment do not alter the evil character of the devil. Furthermore, unregenerate man does not change, and though the whole earth is under the rule of Christ, great multitudes obey him only from fear and not from love.

*The Last Judgment. 20:11-14.* One more great universe-embracing event must take place before there can be eternal peace and righteousness, namely, the judgment of the impenitent dead. This is set forth in the last paragraph of this epoch-crowded chapter. A day of judgment, sometimes called "The Last Day," is referred to more often by our Lord than by all of the apostles and their writings put together (see Mt 10:15; 11:22,24; 12:36; Jn 5:28,29; 6: 39-54; 11:24; Heb 9:27; 10:27). Christ is everywhere identified as the judge (see especially Acts 17:31; Jn 5:22-27; II Tim 4:1). Bishop Gore spoke for all the Church when he said, "It seems to me any believer in the God of the prophets, and of our Lord, must believe with them in a Day of God, as bringing the present age of human history to its climax" (*Belief in Christ*, p. 149).

From the judgment for crime exercised by the State, thousands escape every

13. And the sea gave up the dead which were in it; and death and hell delivered up the dead which were in them: and they were judged every man according to their works.

14. And death and hell were cast into the lake of fire. This is the second death.

15. And whosoever was not found written in the book of life was cast into the lake of fire.

year; in fact, many crimes are not even known to those in authority. But no one will be able to escape this judgment. The dead will be called forth from their graves, and from the sea, from Hades itself (v. 13); and those whose names are not found in the Book of Life will be cast into the lake of fire, which is the second death (v. 14). The records of every human life in this vast assembly will then be produced. Death itself, it seems, is not abolished until the Great White Throne is set up, and human destiny is forever settled. If we believe and embrace with joy the promises of eternal glory that are in this book, we must also believe with equal conviction that this terrible doom of the unrepentant dead is equally true. (For a discussion of the entire matter of judgment, see my book, *Therefore Stand,* the section called, "A Righteous Judgment to Come," pp. 438-466).

### The Holy City. 21:1—22:5.

We have now come to the final revelation given to us in Holy Scripture, a glorious climax to all that God has inspired men to write for the edification of his people throughout the ages. In this passage we move from time into eternity. Sin, death, and all the forces antagonistic to God are now forever put away. Most students of the Word are convinced that what we have in this last section (I am not here thinking of the epilogue) is a description of the eternal home of the redeemed in Christ. It is probably not to be identified with heaven, but it must certainly be that to which the Scriptures have previously pointed—the City of God, the New Jerusalem, the Zion that is above. One must not be dogmatic here as to what may be interpreted symbolically and what must be considered literally. Different scholars, with equal devotion to the divine authority of the Scriptures, have different views concerning the hermeneutics of this great passage. Even Lang, normally a literalist, insists upon a strong symbolism here and states that "the reason for the employment of symbols may be that there simply is no other way of creating in our minds any just conception of reality" (*op. cit.*, p. 369).

### The Origin and Nature of the City. 21:1-8.

1. This famous description, the equal of which cannot be found in any other

## CHAPTER 21

AND I saw a new heaven and a new earth: for the first heaven and the first earth were passed away; and there was no more sea.

2. And I John saw the holy city, new Jerusalem, coming down from God out of heaven, prepared as a bride adorned for her husband.

literature of the ancient world, begins with John's stating that he saw a new heaven and a new earth. There are two Greek words translated new in the NT, *neos* and the one used here, *kainos,* suggesting "fresh life rising from the decay and wreck of the old world" (Swete). Therefore, this passage does not teach that the heavens and earth are now brought into existence for the first time, but that they possess a new character. (See for other uses of the word, Mt 27:60; II Cor 5:17, etc., and some excellent remarks on these two Greek words in R. C. Trench: *Synonyms of the New Testament,* pp. 219-225.)

As to the statement that there will be no more sea, no one has more sensibly interpreted this affirmation than Swete himself, "The sea belonged to the order which has passed. It has disappeared because, in the mind of the writer, it is associated with ideas which are at variance with the character of the New Creation. For this element of unrest, this fruitful cause of destruction and death, this divider of nations and churches, there could be no place in a world of deathless life and unbroken peace."

2. John now beholds **the holy city . . . coming down out of heaven from God.** As the Jerusalem of old was called "the Holy City," so is the new Jerusalem so designated; only this time the word truly describes the actual character of the abode of the redeemed. Holiness, the great attribute of God, has been the divinely set goal for God's people from the beginning. It is significant that our eternal abode is called a **city,** even in the OT (Ps 48:1,8; Heb 11:16).

C. Anderson Scott, in a remarkable chapter on this aspect of the abode of the blest, has well said: "A city is first the ambition and then despair of man . . . Men are proud of a city; they name themselves by its name; they sun themselves in its power and splendor, and yet in the hands of men, the city has become a monster which devours its children. We can hardly dare to look at the spoil-heaps of *outworn* humanity out of which its wealth has been extracted, at the misery and vice on the top of which most of its comfort and splendor rest. All our effort, legislative, philanthropic, and religious, seems to fail piteously in the attempt to meet the evils inseparably connected with a great city. Yet God prepares for us a city. The instinct to

3. And I heard a great voice out of heaven saying, Behold, the tabernacle of God *is* with men, and he will dwell with them, and they shall be his people, and God himself shall be with them, *and be* their God.

4. And God shall wipe away all tears from their eyes; and there shall be no more death, neither sorrow, nor crying, neither shall there be any more pain: for the former things are passed away.

seek a common life, to form a complicated web of mutual sympathy and dependence, which is represented by a city, is after all a true one, and the opportunity for its exercise essential alike to man's true happiness and to the full development of his powers. 'It is not good for man to be alone'; neither is it good for a family to be alone, nor yet for a group of families; and this vision shows us 'the far-off Divine event' as realised in the corporate life of humanity, in a society so vast that none of God's children is left out of it, and yet so compact that it can best be described as the society of those who dwell in one city" *(The Book of Revelation,* pp. 308-310).

That the Holy City comes down **out of heaven** seems to imply that it is not identical with heaven. There is a phrase here that is too often passed over—**as a bride adorned for her husband.** One time in a woman's life she has a right to be extravagant, one time she prepares herself with the greatest care and dresses as elegantly and beautifully and attractively as she can—the time of her marriage. Even young women who have no particular beauty have had it said of them, as they walked down the aisle of a church to the altar for the wedding ceremony, "Isn't she beautiful!" As a bride adorns herself for her husband, so will God adorn and beautify this city for his loved ones. All the beautiful things in the world God has made—sunsets, mountains, lakes, roses, beautiful trees, snowflakes, clouds, waterfalls. What will a city be like made by the Divine Architect! (See also Jn 14:2.) A **holy** city will be one in which no lie will be uttered in one hundred million years, no evil word will ever be spoken, no shady business deal will ever even be discussed, no unclean picture will ever be seen, no corruption of life will *ever* be manifest. It will be **holy** because everyone in it will be holy.

3,4. As in so many other passages in the book of Revelation, we have in verse 3 the perfect consummation and conclusion of the great theme of God—*tabernacling* among men. The Greek word here for **tabernacle** is the same as in the Greek translation of the OT passages describing the Tabernacle, where also we are told that in the Holy of Holies, God would meet with his people (Lev 26:11 ff.). This is the word in its verbal form which is used in John's

5. And he that sat upon the throne said, Behold, I make all things new. And he said unto me, Write: for these words are true and faithful.

6. And he said unto me, It is done. I am Alpha and Omega, the beginning and the end. I will give unto him that is athirst of the fountain of the water of life freely.

7. He that overcometh shall inherit all things; and I will be his God, and he shall be my son.

8. But the fearful, and unbelieving, and the abominable, and murderers, and whoremongers, and sorcerers, and idolaters, and all liars, shall have their part in the lake which burneth with fire and brimstone: which is the second death.

9. And there came unto me one of the seven angels which had the seven vials full of the seven last plagues, and talked with me, saying, Come hither, I will show thee the bride, the Lamb's wife.

10. And he carried me away in the spirit to a great and high mountain, and showed me that great city, the holy Jerusalem, descending out of heaven from God,

11. Having the glory of God: and her light was like unto a stone most precious, even like a jasper stone, clear as crystal;

12. And had a wall great and high, and had twelve gates, and at the gates twelve angels, and names written thereon, which are the names of the twelve tribes of the children of Israel:

13. On the east three gates; on the north three gates; on the south three gates; and on the west three gates.

14. And the wall of the city had twelve foundations, and in them the names of the twelve apostles of the Lamb.

initial description of the Incarnation: "And the Word became flesh, and dwelt among us (and we beheld his glory, glory as of the only begotten from the Father), full of grace and truth" (Jn 1:14). This time the tabernacle abides; this time there will be no separation between God and his people, a fact that seems to be immediately introduced (Rev 21:3). Here, too, is the assurance of the elimination of five tragic aspects of human life: tears, death, mourning, crying, pain (v. 4). The Bible does not deny the reality of pain and death, but it does give us assurance that the day is coming, by the grace of God, when, for the believer, these will no longer exist.

5. It has been suggested by some that in this verse, for the first time in the Apocalypse, the speaker is God himself. There is certainly great significance in the fact that in this book above all others in the NT, the truth of what is here revealed is emphasized. "God authenticates His own magnificent declaration. He demands our attention, and claims our hearts and unqualified assent" (Walter Scott, op. cit., p. 404). **Faithful and true** characterizes not only the spoken (and written Word), but the Incarnate Word as well (19:9; 21:5).

6,7. Once more we have the title of Christ, **the Alpha and the Omega,** which are the first and last words of the Greek alphabet, indicating that Christ is before the universe which was created by him, and will be at the end of all time, for all things will be consummated in him.

8. We now come upon something that we really would not expect to find in this description of the Holy City, namely, an indication of the classes of sinners who will not be there but rather will be found in **the lake which burneth with fire and brimstone.** These are dreadful words. If we embrace with enthusiasm and thanksgiving the promises of this book, we must also believe its solemn warnings. Lang calls attention to the phrase, "their part," commenting that "the heart could wish that the vision closed on the radiant heights but instead it sinks to the lowest depths."

*A Description of the Holy City. 21:9-23.*

12-21. The City has **twelve gates,** on each of which is the name of one of the twelve tribes of Israel, and each gate is guarded by an angel. The wall rests upon **twelve foundations,** which ap-

15. And he that talked with me had a golden reed to measure the city, and the gates thereof, and the wall thereof.

16. And the city lieth foursquare, and the length is as large as the breadth: and he measured the city with the reed, twelve thousand furlongs. The length and the breadth and the height of it are equal.

17. And he measured the wall thereof, a hundred *and* forty *and* four cubits, *according to* the measure of a man, that is, of the angel.

18. And the building of the wall of it was *of* jasper: and the city *was* pure gold, like unto clear glass.

19. And the foundations of the wall of the city *were* garnished with all manner of precious stones. The first foundation *was* jasper; the second, sapphire; the third, a chalcedony; the fourth, an emerald;

20. The fifth, sardonyx; the sixth, sardius; the seventh, chrysolite; the eighth, beryl; the ninth, a topaz; the tenth, a chrysoprasus; the eleventh, a jacinth; the twelfth, an amethyst.

21. And the twelve gates *were* twelve pearls; every several gate was of one pearl: and the street of the city *was* pure gold, as it were transparent glass.

parently means twelve sections of the foundation, and on each of these is a name of one of the twelve apostles. The length, breadth, and height of the city is twelve thousand furlongs, or about 1,500 miles. This would seem, upon first reading, to be in the shape of a cube, but I certainly would follow Simcox, and many others, in believing that this is a pyramidal structure. The word translated street, *plateia*, means literally *a broad place;* from this word derives our word *plaza.* The wall is made of jasper, the city is of gold, the gates of pearl, and the foundations of twelve precious stones. (For a study of the possible population of a city this size, see a remarkable essay in F. W. Boreham's *Wisps of Wildfire,* pp. 202-212).

J. N. Darby rarely said that he did not know what a passage of Scripture might mean, but regarding these stones, he once wrote, "The difference of the stones contains details which are above my knowledge" (*Collected Writings,* Volume V, p. 154). "If we compare the colours of the foundation stones with those of the rainbow," says Govett (*op. cit., in loco*), "we shall find, I believe, a designed resemblance, though, from our ignorance in regard of the precious stones, we cannot come to any very close or satisfactory conclusion. The stones, then, with their colours, and the tints of the rainbow, are as follows:

|  |  |
|---|---|
|  | 1. Jasper, greenish? yellow? |
|  | 2. Sapphire, azure. |
|  | 3. Chalcedony, doubtful, green and blue. |
| The Rainbow: | 4. Emerald, green. |
| 1. Red | 5. Sardius, red. |
| 2. Orange | 6. Sardonyx, red and white. |
| 3. Yellow | 7. Chrysolite, yellow. |
| 4. Green | 8. Beryl, sea-green. |
| 5. Blue | 9. Topaz, yellow. |
| 6. Indigo | 10. Chrysoprasus, golden-green. |
| 7. Violet (lake) | 11. Jacinth, violet. |
|  | 12. Amethyst, rose-red." |

22,23. John proceeds to tell us that the city has no temple within, and that it is so brilliantly illuminated by the glory of God that it has no need of the light of the sun or moon, though they

22. And I saw no temple therein: for the Lord God Almighty and the Lamb are the temple of it.

23. And the city had no need of the sun, neither of the moon, to shine in it: for the glory of God did lighten it, and the Lamb is the light thereof.

24. And the nations of them which are saved shall walk in the light of it: and the kings of the earth do bring their glory and honor into it.

25. And the gates of it shall not be shut at all by day: for there shall be no night there.

26. And they shall bring the glory and honor of the nations into it.

will still be shining. "So long as men dwell here under the conditions of earthly life, they cannot do without these temples, the place, the time, the thoughts marked off for God, the place where we learn the secret of realising His presence in life, the time when we claim and proclaim His fellowship with Him, the thoughts, which, of set purpose, we direct toward the manifestation of His love in Christ, and of His will in duty. But there is no temple *there;* for the simple reason that none is needed. That which now has to be delimited from the world, and set apart for God—yes, and held with determination and force of will against invading hosts—has there expanded to cover the whole area of human experience and activity. God's presence has no longer to be sought; it is known; it is felt, universal and all-pervading as the light of day" (C. Anderson Scott, *op. cit., in loco.*). Our text does not say that there will not be any sun or moon in eternity, but that we will not *need* the light of the sun and moon, for the very glory of God will illuminate the city. As we need a candle in the night, but not at noon, when the sun is shining, so we do need the sun and moon in our present state of existence, but will need them no more when in the presence of God, who is light indeed.

*Those Who Enter the City. 21:24-27.*

24-26. The paragraph embracing these three verses is extremely difficult to interpret. Who are these nations that walk in the light of the Holy City, and who are the kings of the earth that bring their glory into it? Govett is probably right in saying: "By 'the kings of the earth' are meant the kings of the nations. As the nations are now transferred to the new world, so have they kings. Subordination of ranks is a part of God's abiding scheme for eternity. They are called 'kings of *the earth*,' to distinguish them from the kings of *the city.* For there are two classes of kings: those made kings and priests to God by Jesus' blood, who are risen from the dead and dwell with God; and those who are men in the flesh, and live among the nations outside the metropolis. For the citizens are *kings of kings,* and 'they shall reign for ever and ever' (22:5). The kings of the nations, then, sensible of their inferiority, and desirous to appear before God and His risen servants, bring presents."

27. And there shall in no wise enter into it any thing that defileth, neither *whatsoever* worketh abomination, or *maketh* a lie: but they which are written in the Lamb's book of life.

### CHAPTER 22

AND he showed me a pure river of water of life, clear as crystal, proceeding out of the throne of God and of the Lamb.

2. In the midst of the street of it, and on either side of the river, *was there* the tree of life, which bare twelve *manner of* fruits, *and* yielded her fruit every month: and the leaves of the tree *were* for the healing of the nations.

3. And there shall be no more curse: but the throne of God and of the Lamb shall be in it; and his servants shall serve him:

4. And they shall see his face; and his name *shall be* in their foreheads.

5. And there shall be no night there; and they need no candle, neither light of the sun; for the Lord God giveth them light: and they shall reign for ever and ever.

27. Here is one of the most reassuring, comforting, and hope-filled statements of all the Bible: those will enter the city whose names are **written in the Lamb's book of life.** Two terrible, inescapable factors keep any man from the Holy City—sin and death. It is the Lamb of God who takes away the sin of the world, and it is the Son of God who gives us life instead of death. To be in the Lamb's Book of Life is to be redeemed by the Lamb of God.

*The State of Blessedness Prevailing in the Holy City. 22:1-5.* It is strange that in chapter 21 there are no descriptive details pertaining to natural phenomena, trees, rivers, etc., such as we find in the description of the original paradise in Genesis 2. Such details are now introduced, reminding us not only of that early chapter but also of Ezk 47:1-12. "Sin drove man from one garden. Grace brings man to an eternal Paradise." Here we have beauty, life in full abundance, the sovereignty of God, health for the nations of the earth, the absence of all curse; **no curse** (v. 3), on man nor on the earth where he lives nor in the city of his habitation, nor on any relationships prevailing among men—Christ has removed the curse and all the consequences of it). Here also is a picture of service, the perfect vision, which is to behold the face of our Lord, and his name stamped upon our foreheads. Here are two more cancellations or final eliminations of things that have troubled and burdened man: the removal of all curse, and the elimination of night forever.

It is not, however, the negative aspects of this passage which most delight our heart, but its positive affirmations. Here the blessedness that God has desired through the ages and made provision for is brought to a climax of perfection: in heaven we shall be serving the Lord (v. 3b); we **shall see his face;** his name will be on our foreheads (v. 4); we shall reign with him forever and ever (v. 5). Here such promises as those found in Mt 5:8; I Jn 3:2; I Cor 15:49; etc., will become the eternal experience of believers. In other words, we shall bear the character of the Lord, we shall serve the Lord, reign with the Lord, and forever rejoice and forever be satisfied as we look upon his glorious face. (One of the most profound and satisfying treat-

6. And he said unto me, These sayings *are* faithful and true: and the Lord God of the holy prophets sent his angel to show unto his servants the things which must shortly be done.

7. Behold, I come quickly: blessed *is* he that keepeth the sayings of the prophecy of this book.

8. And I John saw these things, and heard *them*. And when I had heard and seen, I fell down to worship before the feet of the angel which showed me these things.

9. Then saith he unto me, See *thou do it* not: for I am thy fellow servant, and of thy brethren the prophets, and of them which keep the sayings of this book: worship God.

10. And he saith unto me, Seal not the sayings of the prophecy of this book: for the time is at hand.

11. He that is unjust, let him be unjust still: and he which is filthy, let him be filthy still: and he that is righteous, let him be righteous still: and he that is holy, let him be holy still.

ments of the Holy City will be found in the work of Govett, pp. 549-610.)

All the glorious purposes of God, ordained from the foundation of the world, have now been attained. The rebellion of angels and mankind is all and finally subdued, as the King of kings assumes his rightful sovereignty. Absolute and unchangeable holiness characterizes all within the universal Kingdom of God. The redeemed, made so by the blood of the Lamb, are in resurrection and eternal glory. Life is everywhere—and death will never intrude again. The earth and the heavens both are renewed. Light, beauty, holiness, joy, the presence of God, the worship of God, service to Christ, likeness to Christ —all are now abiding realities. The vocabulary of man, made for life here, is incapable of truly and adequately depicting what God has prepared for those that love Him.

*The Epilogue. 22:6-20.* For the closing verses of the Apocalypse, it is not necessary that we give an extended interpretation. Most of these statements here, like the latter part of nearly all the NT epistles, are hortatory.

6-10. The first statement is almost identical with the opening declaration of the Apocalypse (1:1,2), except that there one "servant" is mentioned, John, while here servants are mentioned. "The 'spirits of the prophets' are the natural faculties of the Prophets, raised and quickened by the Holy Spirit" (Swete). So likewise in verse 7 we are carried back to 1:3. This command to keep the words of the prophecy of this book (see 3:8,16; 14:12, 12:17) emphasizes a truth we are too prone to forget, namely, that the prophetic Scriptures have ethical implications. Prophecies and commandments are here bound together.

11-15. In verse 11 we have a solemn truth, sometimes referred to as "the permanence of character." I must once more at this point bring to my readers the concise and solemn lines of Swete. "It is not only true," he says, "that the troubles of the last days will tend to fix the character of each individual according to the habits which he has already formed, but there will come a time when change will be impossible—when no further opportunity will be given for repentance on the one hand or for apostasy on the other."

The coming of Christ is the pre-

12. And, behold, I come quickly; and my reward *is* with me, to give every man according as his work shall be.

13. I am Alpha and Omega, the beginning and the end, the first and the last.

14. Blessed *are* they that do his commandments, that they may have right to the tree of life, and may enter in through the gates into the city.

15. For without *are* dogs, and sorcerers, and whoremongers, and murderers, and idolaters, and whosoever loveth and maketh a lie.

16. I Jesus have sent mine angel to testify unto you these things in the churches. I am the root and the offspring of David, *and* the bright and morning star.

17. And the Spirit and the bride say, Come. And let him that heareth say, Come. And let him that is athirst come. And whosoever will, let him take the water of life freely.

18. For I testify unto every man that heareth the words of the prophecy of this book, If any man shall add unto these things, God shall add unto him the plagues that are written in this book:

19. And if any man shall take away from the words of the book of this prophecy, God shall take away his part out of the book of life, and out of the holy city, and *from* the things which are written in this book.

eminent theme of both the Prologue and the Epilogue (1:7; 22:7,12,20). By **quickly** (v. 12) is not meant that the Second Advent would occur soon after John completed the writing of this book. Rather, it means that the events of the Second Coming will occur so fast, one event quickly following another, that many will be taken completely by surprise. Verse 13 repeats the title of Christ (1:11; 21:6), which is also ascribed to God (1:8). The classes listed here of those debarred from entering the Holy City, each introduced by the article *the*, are substantially the same as those of 21:8. These verses surely cannot mean that there will still be groups of men *on earth* at this time indulging in these sins.

16. Christ himself now speaks, first simply stating that it is he who has originated the revelations John has recorded. This is the first time the word *church (ekklēsia)* has occurred since the letters to the seven churches. He then assigns a twofold title to himself: he is **the root and the offspring of David,** as was long ago foretold by the prophets (Isa 4:3; 11:1,2; 55:1-5; Amos 9:11,12); and he is **the bright, the morning star** (cf. Rev 2:28). The morning star precedes the full brightness of the sun's light.

17. The threefold invitation, so full of grace, is uttered by (1) the Spirit, (2) the Bride, and (3) those who have heard. This is followed by a specific dual designation of those to whom the invitation is particularly sent—those who are athirst (Jn 7:37), and those that will.

18,19. The book, except for a salutation, closes with one more solemn warning, against adding to or taking away from **the words of the book of this prophecy.** I know of no one who has commented on this more acceptably than Lang: "Revelation of truth is complete, for nothing can lie *beyond* the *eternal* state. While in the strict letter the threats of this terrible warning apply to the Revelation, yet inasmuch as this portion of the Book of God is rooted in, interwoven with, and is the completion of all the Word of God, it becomes impossible to tamper with this final book without maltreating what had been given of God before" *(op. cit.,* pp. 384, 385).

**20.** He which testifieth these things saith, Surely I come quickly: Amen. Even so, come, Lord Jesus.

**21.** The grace of our Lord Jesus Christ *be* with you all. Amen.

**THE END**

**20,21.** The three last words are those (1) of Christ: **Yea, I come quickly;** (2) of the Church: **Amen: come, Lord Jesus;** and (3) of John: **The grace of the Lord Jesus be with the saints** (ASV). While this parting formula is similar to what we often find at the conclusion of the NT epistles (Rom 16:20,24; I Cor 16:23; Eph 6:24; II Tim 4:22; Heb 13:25; I Pet 5:12; etc., in the exact form as found here it is used nowhere else. As this age draws to its end, and we behold taking place, in a preliminary way, some of the dreadful consequences of rejecting the Word of God, these three last words become increasingly precious and vital.

# BIBLIOGRAPHY

ALFORD, HENRY. *The New Testament for English Readers.* 2 vols. 5th ed. London: Rivington, 1872.

GOVETT, ROBERT. *The Apocalypse Expounded.* London: Charles J. Thynne and Jarvis, Ltd., 1929.

LANG, G. H. *The Revelation of Jesus Christ.* London: Paternoster Press, 1945.

LENSKI, R. C. H. *The Interpretation of St. John's Revelation.* Columbus: Wartburg Press, 1943.

OTTMAN, FORD C. *The Unfolding of the Ages.* New York: The Baker and Taylor Co., 1905.

SCOTT, WALTER. *Exposition of the Revelation of Jesus Christ.* London: Pickering and Inglis, n. d.

SEISS, JOSEPH A. *The Apocalypse.* 3 vols. 10th ed. New York: Charles C. Cook, 1909.

SWETE, HENRY BARCLAY. *The Apocalyse of St. John.* 3rd ed. London: Macmillan and Company, 1909.